WHO WAS WHO
IN EGYPTOLOGY

CHAMPOLLION LE JEUNE

painted by Léon Cogniet in 1831

WHO WAS WHO
IN EGYPTOLOGY

FIFTH REVISED EDITION

BY

MORRIS L. BIERBRIER

THE EGYPT EXPLORATION SOCIETY

3 DOUGHTY MEWS, LONDON WC1N 2PG

www.ees.ac.uk

2019

LONDON

Exclusive distribution outside of North America and Mexico by
Bloomsbury Publishing
www.bloomsbury.com

*A Biographical Index of Egyptologists; of Travellers,
Explorers, and Excavators in Egypt; of Collectors of
and Dealers in Egyptian Antiquities;
of Consuls, Officials, Authors, Benefactors, and
others whose names occur in the Literature of Egyptology,
from the year 1500 to the present day, but excluding
persons now living*

BRITISH LIBRARY CATALOGUING PUBLICATION DATA

A catalogue record for this book
is available from the British Library

ISBN 978 0 85698 242 2

Printed in Great Britain
Typeset by Jan Geisbusch

Printed by Hobbs the Printers Ltd
Brunel Road, Totton SO40 3WX, UK

The production of this fifth, revised and expanded edition of *Who Was Who in Egyptology* was generously supported by the following individuals and organisations:

David Redvers Armistead[†]
The Association for the Study of Travel in Egypt and the Near East - ASTENE
Martin Davies
Philip Feakin
Hazel Gray
Patrick Moore
Bruce Redwine
The Vanellus Trust

FOREWORD

Who Was Who in Egyptology remains the essential reference material for anyone studying the characters that have contributed to the history of Egyptology since 1500. It is only right, then, that it is published by the Egypt Exploration Society, itself a cornerstone in UK Egyptology since 1882 and to which many individuals in this, the fifth edition, owe their entry. The histories presented here can be both illustrious and controversial with many of the individuals included coming from a largely colonial past. It is therefore with great pleasure that I see characters such as Ali Suefi (*fl.* 1891-1925), someone whose contribution to the early regional history of Egypt has been largely overlooked, added in this edition.

It is also, however, with great sadness that I see entries for those who have passed more recently. Their contributions will not be forgotten and we are grateful to those nearest to them for providing biographical information vital for maintaining the accuracy of *Who Was Who in Egyptology*.

Since 1882, the Egypt Exploration Society has surveyed or excavated at over 150 locations across Egypt and Sudan, and published over 350 volumes reporting on this research and the work of others. The Society's ongoing mission of supporting and promoting Egypt's unique cultural heritage could not be enacted without the passion and dedication of its donors as well as its staff and representatives in the field. Many people in this volume have played important roles in this work, and I note here the recent and sudden passing of Dr Geoffrey Tassie (1959-2019) whose involvement in EES fieldwork and passion for knowledge-sharing cannot be overstated.

Reflecting on the foreword of the fourth edition by Dr Christopher Naunton (writing in 2012), it is with great pride to consider that the projects he discussed have come to fruition, with further glass-plate negative rehousing completed in summer 2019 by Stephanie Boonstra and Alix Robinson. Alongside this, online access has been provided to over 25,000 digitised images from the Society's earliest work and a catalogue of its entire holdings was uploaded in 2014. These projects have greatly aided the work of researchers, not least Dr Morris L. Bierbrier.

This will be the third edition of *Who Was Who in Egyptology* edited by Dr Bierbrier, who has been aided by submissions from colleagues around the world. The Society is extremely grateful to him for his hard work over the years. This edition includes his late predecessor, Dr Eric Uphill, who edited the second edition in 1969 but sadly passed away in 2018.

The commitment of Dr Bierbrier and his predecessors has made the history of Egyptology accessible and given new light to eminent as well as little-known characters that have contributed toward the subject. From excavators to secretaries, donors to collectors, the fifth edition updates *Who Was Who in Egyptology* to September 2019. In the future, it is hoped that these entries will become an online resource to which can be added many other individuals whose stories have not yet been told and who may inspire future scholars of Egyptology to build upon their work.

CARL GRAVES
Director of the Egypt Exploration Society

September 2019

PREFACE TO THE FIRST EDITION

Egyptology, as a science, dates from the time of Champollion, and as is the case with all the comparatively young branches of learning, its history is very much bound up with the lives of its personnel: we still speak of the discoveries of Mariette, Brugsch, Maspero, and Erman, for instance, by their personal names rather than by those of the discoveries themselves. For many years I have collected biographical notes of the scholars, excavators, travellers, and writers whose names are connected with research in Egypt or are associated with important collections, monuments, or papyri, and at the suggestion of my colleagues I have now extended what was originally merely note-book material for my own use into a general biographical index of all the names I have met with in the course of my studies concerning whom any facts of interest could be discovered.

In addition to Egyptologists in the strict sense, there are many names that have an association with Egypt. In the formation of the great museum collections of Europe and America, many travellers, both of pre- and post-Champollion date, have played an important part, and the consuls of the European Powers, as well as physicians, missionaries, and other officials or residents in Egypt, have played no less important a role. In the latter connection such names as Drovetti, Salt, Anastasi, Mimaut, and Sabatier are significant examples among consuls: Abbott, Clot Bey, and Grant Bey among physicians; Lieder, Lansing, and Murch among missionaries, and Maunier, Edwin Smith, and Insinger among independent residents. It is therefore hoped that this book will be a convenient source of reference not only to Egyptologists who take an interest in the subject, but also to librarians and museum officials, who may thus be assisted in tracing the history of some of their earlier acquisitions (received in the days when registers were not so carefully kept as they are now), by a record of the dates, activities, and movements of the persons whose names are associated with such specimens.

Of the 'lions' of Egyptology, there are usually adequate biographies or obituary notices in existence (although it is surprising that some, even of these, have disappeared without record), but of the lesser-known names it is often very difficult to collect data. It is upon the latter that I have mainly concentrated my efforts, and I have made use of every source of information available to me, both printed and manuscript. In some cases I have succeeded in getting into touch with descendants, relatives, or others who possess knowledge that is nowhere to be found in print. I have also had much verbal information from some of the Egyptologists whom I knew personally but who are no longer with us - Naville, Budge, Sayce, Griffith, Newberry, and others; I have had access to the correspondence of some of the earlier scholars and travellers in various collections, public and private, and have made copies of large numbers of letters, and I have consulted many diaries and note-books. In summarizing the results, I have aimed at the greatest brevity, but in nearly all cases references are given to sources where fuller information can be found; in the few instances where no references are quoted, I have obtained the information by direct inquiry and research.

The term Egyptology has until recently been understood to comprise not only the study of Pharaonic Egypt, but that of two branches that are tending to separate themselves from the parent stem and to take on an independent and specialized existence of their own, namely Coptic and Greek. Most of the earlier Egyptologists concerned themselves not only with ancient Egypt, but equally also with the Graeco-Roman and Christian periods. Of purely Coptic scholars, therefore, I have included only the pioneers such as Peyron and Tattam, and such of the later scholars as have been definitely connected with the Egypt Exploration Society, the Institut Français d'Archéologie Orientale or other bodies operating in Egypt, or who have themselves undertaken excavations or have visited Egypt in order to procure manuscripts. The same applies to students of Graeco-Roman Egypt whose main study is that of the numerous Greek papyri that have been found there. These scholars have labelled themselves 'papyrologists', a term which seems to me a usurpation, ignoring as it does the great mass of far more ancient papyri of Pharaonic times, and implying that the significance of papyri is confined to those that are written in Greek. Be this as it may, I have applied the same selection as in the case of Coptic scholars: thus, such names as Grenfell, Hunt, Jean Maspero, and Jouguet are included whilst many others are omitted, chiefly those of 'Savants de cabinet' not directly connected with work or institutions in Egypt.

In addition to the names set forth in this book, I have a considerable list of travellers, collectors, and others who ought to have taken their places with the rest, but concerning whom I have been unable to obtain any information. I shall be grateful for any additions or corrections sent to me at the office of the Society.

Whenever the present location of papers, drawings, or diaries of the earlier Egyptologists and travellers is known to me, I have stated the names of the museums or libraries that contain them together with their official registration numbers if ascertainable. I have also noted public sales of antiquities, some of which were anonymous but which I have identified. Sale catalogues are often a valuable aid in tracing the history and provenance of antiquities. Within my limits of space, it has been impossible to name publications except to a small extent, but references to bibliographies of the works of particular authors are given whenever they exist: most of the works of authors can be traced by the aid of two general bibliographies, neither of which, however, is absolutely complete. These are, for the older authors and publications up to 1887, *The Literature of Egypt and the Soudan* by Prince Ibrahim Hilmy, 2 vols, London 1886-7, and for later writers up to 1941, *Ancient Egypt: sources of information in the New York Public Library*, by Ida A Pratt, N.Y., 1925 and *Supplement*, 1925-41, N.Y., 1942.

It gives me great pleasure to record my sincere thanks to the many colleagues, friends, and even strangers, who have assisted me by answering queries, looking up references, and supplying a variety of information by correspondence. Many of these have put themselves to infinite trouble on my account. The names of my correspondents and helpers are too numerous to set out in this preface, but I trust I have adequately thanked each and all of them either personally or by letter. The work has been, not only to me, but to all who have participated in it, a labour of love and my deepest gratitude is due to an old and valued friend [Sir Alan Gardiner] who has defrayed the cost of printing and to the committee of the Egypt Exploration Society who have undertaken the publishing and distribution of the book. I trust that critics will not be too severe on this pioneer effort, carried out under difficult conditions, and indeed I can wish this little book no happier fate than to see it superseded by a better, undertaken by an author whose knowledge and facilities for research are greater than my own.

WARREN R.DAWSON

15 August 1951

PREFACE TO THE SECOND EDITION

The author of the first edition of this work suggested that Egyptology as a serious study began with Champollion; perhaps more correctly it began with Silvestre de Sacy, who not only read the first Demotic words but also paved the way for the decipherment both of the ancient Egyptian scripts and also of cuneiform. Nevertheless there were many precursors deserving mention, and it has been one of the aims of this revised edition to open up, albeit only partly, the subject of Egyptological studies from the beginning of the sixteenth century. Many early travellers and scholars such as Kircher have a more than academic interest today.

In another respect also Dawson's work needed considerable expansion and in some cases revision, namely in those entries dealing with the great figures and notables in Egyptology. Unfortunately many of these luminaries do not possess adequate biographies, as he suggested, and a work of this type and with such a title, cannot neglect giving them a special and full treatment in every particular. For this reason a considerable enlargement of biographical data and of bibliographical references has been undertaken. It is hoped that the latter will be of especial use both to the professional Egyptologist and to the ordinary reader with a more than casual interest who seeks to follow the fascinating story of this subject in further detail. A very considerable addition in material is also given by listing for the first time the major works of most of the principal figures. While Champollion remains of course the key figure, a standard system has been evolved in treating all names included, the only one to receive special treatment being Wilkinson owing to the fact that his life and work have never been adequately treated in print before.

Dawson's work remains, nevertheless, the core of this book, and his approach to the history of Egyptology the right one. To him is the honour of having first listed and made a statement of the achievements of previous generations who helped to wrest the story of ancient Egypt from oblivion and preserve its archaeological and epigraphical remains. The value of his contribution is that it deals with facts and figures, the basic source material for other works, not in opinions.

The eighteen years since the first slim volume appeared, in an era of restriction and post-war shortage, represent a period of great activity in the story of Egyptology. Every possible effort has been made to bring the work up to date in all respects, to include all who have died in the interim and who qualify for entry, and to introduce the names of some omitted from the first edition. Unfortunately a few suitably qualified subjects must inevitably have been overlooked, and it is hoped that readers will assist the editor by indicating omissions and corrections which can be incorporated into a later edition. A terminal date of December 1968 has been fixed for the present revision.

Abbreviated references have been brought into line with those employed in the *Annual Egyptological Bibliography* published in Holland. Wherever possible this work has been consulted.

In conclusion I should like to express my thanks to all who have been kind enough to help in the course of preparing this new edition, and especially M. J. Vandier and the Louvre for the photograph of Champollion that forms the frontispiece, Prof J. J. Clère for constant interest and help, Miss Helen Murray of the Griffith Institute, Oxford, Mrs C. Blankenburg, Miss Jadwiga Duda of Warsaw University, Prof R. A. Caminos of Brown University, Prof Silvio Curto, Turin Museum, Dr M. Heerma van Voss and the AEB, Leiden, Dr Steffen Wenig, Berlin Museum, Dr B. J. Peterson of Stockholm Museum for much information on Scandinavian figures, Mr J. D. Cooney of Cleveland Museum of Art, E. Iversen of Copenhagen. Prof W. B. Emery and Prof H. S. Smith have very kindly read parts of the rough draft and made helpful suggestions. I also owe a special debt to Mr T. G. H. James of the British Museum for his advice and encouragement during the whole of the revision. Without the help of all these colleagues and friends the work could not have been completed in the form it now is.

ERIC P. UPHILL

21 December 1969

PREFACE TO THE THIRD EDITION

The success of the second edition of this history of Egyptologists and travellers to Egypt can be judged by the many favourable reviews which appeared with suggestions for further additions and corrections. Much new material has become available on the early periods, and sadly many new entries have had to be written for those who have died since the last edition. I have tried whenever possible to standardize the format of the entries. It has been decided to avoid any personal comments on the merits of any individual and to present a concise biographical summary. The length of an entry does not necessarily indicate the importance of the subject to Egyptology. The older entries have not been changed except to correct factual errors or misconceptions, and to add new material. If no source is indicated, much new information derives from archival sources of births and deaths. The final entries were compiled in June 1994. For the first time the text has been computerized and I wish to express my thanks to the late Mrs Hannah Lawlor and Mrs J. A. Casey who successfully accomplished this process. The text is now stored on disk and changes for future editions will be much more easily accomplished. Naturally some errors in transmission and format may have crept in, and I would be grateful for any notice of these.

This new edition would not be possible without the wholehearted co-operation of the Egyptological community at large. I have received help, advice and information from almost every active Egyptologist at one time or another and from the families of these commemorated here. I would especially like to thank Mr Eric Uphill, the former editor, who kindly put at my disposal all the material that he collected and the drafts to several new entries, and Mr T. G. H. James, who has encouraged my work as editor, provided useful information, and checked the text prior to publication. Mrs C. Macmillan has unravelled many a difficult genealogical problem. I am indebted to the following for details on their nationals and additional bibliography: M. M. Azim, M. Jean-Pierre Codaccioni, Bibliothèque Muncipale de Marseille, M. M. Dewachter, Prof J. Leclant, and Prof O. Masson in France, Prof H. De Meulenaere in Belgium, Dr Heerma van Voss in The Netherlands, M. J. Kettel in Luxemburg, Prof S. Curto in Italy, Dr S. Wenig in Germany, Dr E. Staehelin and Mr T. Schneider in Switzerland, Prof J. Śliwa in Poland, Prof R. Holthoer in Finland, Dr A. Elanskaya in Russia and Dr S. Stadnikov in Estonia, Mr J. Larson in America, Dr Dia Abou-Ghazi in Egypt, and the late Mr D. Sakai in Japan. Mr N. Cooke, Revd S. Tillett, and Dr J. Thompson have provided useful information on early travellers. It has not always proved possible to use all the material provided, and I take full responsibility for all editorial decisions. Any corrections or additions would be welcome.

It has been decided for this edition to include photographs of some of the subjects for the first time. A small selection has been put together at short notice, and it is hoped in future editions to expand coverage. I would like to thank Birmingham Library Services for permission to reproduce the photograph of T. Davis; Mr J. Chester; Mr P. Clayton; Prof Silvio Curto; Dr C. Eyre, Miss P. Winker and The School of Archaeology, Classics and Oriental Studies, University of Liverpool; Dr I. Finkel; Madame Garnot; The Griffith Institute, Ashmolean Museum, Oxford; Ms Marsha Hill, Metropolitan Museum of Art, New York; Mr T. G. H. James; Mrs R. Janssen,The Petrie Museum, University College London; Prof J. Leclant, Dr C. Lee and Mrs M. Orr; Dr A. Mekhitarian, Fondation Égyptologique Reine Élisabeth, Brussels; Madame Anne Minault-Gout, Institut français d'archéologie orientale, Cairo; Dr D. O'Connor; Dr A. Onasch, the University of Leipzig; Dr M. Raven, Rijksmuseum van Oudheden, Leiden; the late Miss M. Rowlatt; Dr. S. Spurr, Eton College; Dr E. Staehelin; Revd S. Tillett together with Mr G. Hay (R. Hay) and a private collection (Birch and Bonomi); Dr. J. Taylor; Mrs D. Woolner (C. Firth), the Board of Trinity College Dublin (E. Hincks); The Museum of Fine Arts, Boston; the Département des Antiquités Égyptiennes, Musée du Louvre; the Department of Coins and Medals, the Department of Egyptian Antiquities, the Department of Prints and Drawings, and the Trustees of British Museum; the Egypt Exploration Society; and the President and Council of the Royal College of Surgeons of England (Sir E. Wilson) for supplying photographs with permission to publish.

MORRIS L. BIERBRIER

1995

PREFACE TO THE FOURTH EDITION

The last edition of *Who Was Who in Egyptology* was completed in 1994 and appeared in 1995. It was well received and has been out of print for several years. The Board of Trustees of the Egypt Exploration Society has now agreed to support this fourth edition. Much has changed since 1995 as the widespread use of email and the internet has enabled more rapid communication with colleagues and more immediate access to information and databases. It has been decided that the original time span, set by the first editor Warren Dawson, should be maintained so there are no entries for individuals before 1500. Similarly entries for scholars in the fields of Greek papyrology and Coptic studies have been restricted to those who worked actively in Egypt although some exceptions have been made. All previous entries have been examined and updated when necessary. However, I have no doubt that mistakes and omissions still remain and these will hopefully be corrected in future editions. The text closed for new entries at the end of September 2011.

I would like to thank Dr Chris Naunton, Director of the Egypt Exploration Society, who first proposed the fourth edition, scanned the majority of the images and set the volume to page. I also thank him for his patience in explaining to me the intricacies of the Windows personal computer. Special thanks are given to Dr Patricia Spencer, General Editor and former Director of the Society, for her constant support for this project over the years and, more especially, for proof-reading the text. Other members of staff contributed to the production with helpful advice, notably Roo Mitcheson. I would also like to thank Tom Hardwick who read through the entire text, suggesting many corrections and additional entries. Any faults that remain are entirely my responsibility.

This volume could not have been produced without the help of many Egyptological colleagues in various institutions around the world. Most are mentioned as sources at the end of the biographies to which they contributed. However, special thanks are due to Dr Beatrix Gessler-Löhr who not only corrected those entries in which she had an interest but put me in touch with many other colleagues in Germany who could add information to other biographies or contribute new ones. In much the same way Dr Dirk Huyge performed this task for the entries from Belgium and Dr Hélène Virenque for the entries from France. Their help has been invaluable in the preparation of this edition.

The inclusion of photographs proved very popular in the last edition and many more have been added to this edition. Only time for research and expense has limited the numbers so there will still be room for additions in any future edition. I would like to thank Prof W. Y. Adams (Thabit); Dr S. Gitin and the W. F. Albright Institute, Jerusalem; Mrs C. Aldred; the Annual Egyptological Bibliography (the late J. Janssen); the Ashmolean Museum, Oxford (A. Evans, J. Evans); M M. Azim; Dr J. von Beckerath (Barta); Dr I. Begg (Anti, Bagnani); Birmingham Library Services (T. Davis); Mr M. Borin (Dupuis); The British Institute for the Study of Iraq (Woolley); Bolton Museum and Dr C. Routledge; M. Borin (Dupuis); the Department of Coins and Medals, the Department of Ancient Egypt and the Sudan, the Department of Prints and Drawings, and the Trustees of British Museum; The Brooklyn Museum; Dr A. Cappel (von Halle); Mr J. Chester; Dr W. Clarysse (Quaegebeur, Vergote); Mr V. Chrysikopoulos (Dimitriou, Rostovitz); Mr P. Clayton; Miss L. Collins (Eady); Mr R. Cooper and Miss J. Schottlander (H. Price); Mr John Crowfoot; Prof Silvio Curto; Mr Roger Davies (Bosse-Griffiths, G. Griffiths); Mme F. Debono; Dr E. Delange and E. David and the Département des Antiquités Égyptiennes, Musée du Louvre; the Deutsche Archäologische Institut, Cairo and I. Lehnert; Dr A. Dodson; Alisa Douer (Zaloscher); Dumbarton Oaks, Washington, DC and S. White (Whittemore); Durham University Library and Ms J. Hogan; Mrs A. Eggebrecht; The Egypt Exploration Society; Dr K. Exell; Prof C. Eyre; Dr L. French (Wace); Dr I. Finkel; Dr L. Limme and Fondation Égyptologique Reine Élisabeth, Brussels; Dr R. Friedmann (Adams, Hoffman); Madame Garnot; Miss A. Garnett (Rankin); Dr. Beatrix Gessler-Löhr and the Institut für Ägyptologie, Rupprecht-Karls-Universität Heidelberg; Mrs M. Gilula; Prof M. Görg (Edel); The Griffith Institute, Oxford and Dr J. Malek; Dr K. Grzymski (Shinnie); W. Guglielmi (Brunner and Brunner-Traut); Dr Prof W. Habermann (Bilabel); T. Hardwick (Nahman); Dr W. Benson Harer (Caillaud) and Dr A. Bednarski; Mr M. G. Heinz (Ranke, C. Schmidt, Schweinfurth); Marsha Hill, Metropolitan Museum of New York; Prof D. Huyge; the late Mr T. G. H. James; Mrs R. Janssen (F. Grenfell); Mr A. Jeffreys; Dr D. Jeffreys; Prof P. Janosi; F. Kalloniatis (Colman); Jill Kamil; the late Mr Max Karkegi; Kelsey Museum and Mr S. Encina; Prof K. A. Kitchen (Childe); M. Kobusiewicz (Krzyżaniak); Kunsthistorisches Museum, Vienna and Dr. R. Hölzl and Dr E. Hassmann; the late Prof J. Leclant, Dr C. Lee and Mrs M. Orr (Mace); Dr C. Lilyquist; Prof U. Luft (Wessetzky); Mr and Mrs J. Mawas (Menasce); The Metropolitan Museum of New York; M C. Meurice and the Archives Mallet, Bouch (Clédat); Madame Anne Minault-Gout, Institut français d'archéologie orientale, Cairo; Mrs A. Morecroft (Donati); Musée de l'Archéologie nationale, Saint-Germain-en-Laye and Mme C. Lorre; The Museum of Fine Arts, Boston (Bissing, Crum, Dunham, S. Smith); Prof D. O'Connor; Mrs Y. Neville-Rolfe (Bonomi); Newnham College, Cambridge (Caton-Thompson); the late Mrs A. Nibbi; Prof W. Oerter; Dr A. Onasch, the University of Leipzig; The Palestine Exploration Fund and Miss F. Cobbing (Hogarth); Dr D. Patch (Romano); Mr S. Payne; Mr I. Pearce (W. Dixon); The Petrie Museum, University College London and Dr D. Challis and Miss K. Swientek; Prof P. Piacentini and the Università degli Studi di Milano; Dr L. Popko the Akademie Verlag, the publishers of *ZÄS* for permission to use photographs from their obituaries; Mrs J. Preston (Kirwan); Dr A. Stevenson and the Pitt Rivers Museum; Dr M. Raven, Rijksmuseum van Oudheden, Leiden; M J. Reinhold; G. Rosati (Bosticco); the late Miss M. Rowlatt

(A. Harris, S. Harris); the President and Council of the Royal College of Surgeons of England (Sir E. Wilson); Royal Museum of Art and History, Brussels and Mr C. Wouter; Mrs H. Sallam (Chaban, Hamza, Kamal); Dr B. Schlick (H. W. Muller); Dr B. Schmitz and the Roemer-und Pelizaeus Museum Hildesheim; Dr I. Shirin-Grumach (Lichtheim); The School of Archaeology, Classics and Oriental Studies, University of Liverpool and Miss P. Winker; The Society for the Study of Egyptian Antiquities and Ms L. Green (Millet); Dr S. Spurr, Eton College (Myers); Dr E. Staehlin; Dr J. Taylor; Dr Angela Thomas; Dr Jason Thompson; Revd S. Tillett together with Mr G. Hay (R. Hay); the Board of Trinity College Dublin (E. Hincks); Dr Y. Tristant (Arcelin, Hamy, Lenormant); Dr Lana Troy; Dr P. Usick; Prof M. Valloggia (Hari, Maystre); Dr G. Vörös; Dr U. Wallenstein and the Stiftung Schloss Friedenstein Gotha, Schlossmuseum (Seetzen); Dr E. Warembol (R. Tefnin); Prof K. Weeks; Wellcome Library and Dr M.-L. Collard; Dr D. Welsby and SARS; Dr D. Wildung (Bothmer and Settgast); and Mrs D. Woolner (C. Firth) for supplying photographs with permission to publish. I would also wish to thank any copyright holders who may have accidentally been omitted from the above list and apologize for their omission. I also apologize to any donors whose photographs have not been included for various technical reasons.

Finally, I would like to thank all the readers of the previous edition who have come forward with suggestions and additions. Your input is most welcome and hopefully will continue so that any future edition will build on those of the past.

MORRIS L. BIERBRIER

April 2012

PREFACE TO THE FIFTH EDITION

The fourth edition of *Who was Who in Egyptology* was published in 2012 and soon sold out. The Egypt Exploration Society has now agreed to publish a new edition with revisions to the previous entries and additions of new entries of former collectors and travellers which have come to my attention and biographies of recently deceased Egyptologists. The guidelines as set in the preface to the last edition still remain. The present text was completed at the end of April 2019.

Preparation of this volume has been greatly helped with the increasing volume of information on the internet in Wikipedia and other reference sites, the ability to find obscure article references, the availability of genealogical sites such as Ancestry and Geneanet, and the posting of civil registration indexes and documents such as those of the General Registry Office in England and Wales on FreeBMD and those from Paris on its archival website. All these sources and others have been used to improve earlier entries and complete new ones.

I would like to thank Dr Patricia Spencer, former Director of the Egypt Exploration Society, for her constant support and for keeping me abreast of the current state of the Egyptological world. This volume would be much poorer without her help and guidance. I would also thank Dr Carl Graves, Director of the Egypt Exploration Society, for his continued supply of information and practical support, notably on IT matters. Mr Neville Leslie, Financial Manager of the Egypt Exploration Society rendered timely assistance. Dr Aidan Dodson volunteered not only information and photographs but also much needed proof-reading skills. Most importantly, this volume could not have been completed without the assistance of Dr Jan Geisbusch, Publications Manager of the Egypt Exploration Society, who has seen it through the final stages of editing and prepared the text for publication.

Those who have provided information for previous volumes have already thanked in earlier prefaces. This volume benefited greatly from details supplied by Dr Francisco Bosch-Puche (Oxford), Mr Neil Cooke, Dr Marianne Eaton-Krauss (Germany), Dr Thomas Gertzen (Germany), Dr Ingelore Hafemann (Germany), Dr Rolf Krauss (Germany), Dr Luc Limme (Belgium), Dr Ed Meltzer (Canada), Dr. Jaromir Malek (Oxford), Dr Hana Navratilova (Czechia), Dr Maarten Raven (Leiden), Mr Tsubasa Sakamoto (Japan), and Dr Steffen Wenig (Germany). I would also like to thank those friends and relations who willingly gave information and photographs, notably Ernest Adams (William Adams), Helen Cockle (Walter Cockle) Dr. F. Förster (Rössler-Köhler), Jocelyn Gohary (Said Gohary), Ken Griffin (Vincent Donohue), Catherine Johns (Donald Bailey), Lyla Pinch-Brock (Ted Brock), Regine Schulz (Matthias Seidel), and Isabelle Therasse (Dirk Huyge). All their contributions have been acknowledged under the relevant entries.

Again, those who provided photographs for previous editions have already been acknowledged in earlier prefaces, but I would like to reiterate our thanks to the Boston Museum of Fine Arts, Durham University Library, and the Griffith Institute, Oxford. I would also thank Dr Nigel Fletcher-Jones of the American University in Cairo Press and Samir Simaika for use of the photograph of Marcus Simaika. We are most grateful to William Joy for supplying several photographs from his collection and Dr. Rosalind Janssen for that of Rambova. We also thank Dr. Gertzen, Richard Spiegelberg and the University of Strasbourg for the photograph of Spiegelberg, Dr. Gertzen, Dr. B. Nielsen and the Library of the Katz Center of Advanced Judaic Studies, Philadelphia for the photograph of Reich, and F. Förster for that of Wiedemann. I would like to apologize to any copyrightholders for whom thanks has accidentally been omitted or whose photographs we were unable to be used due to technical reasons.

MORRIS L. BIERBRIER

April 2019

ABBREVIATIONS

(Periodical Publications are marked by an asterisk.)

AAA *	*Annals of Archaeology and Anthropology*, Liverpool.
ADB	*Allgemeine Deutsche Biographie,* Leipzig.
AE *	*Ancient Egypt and the East*, London.
AEB	*Annual Egyptological Bibliography*, Leiden.
AfO *	*Archiv für Orientforschung*, Vienna.
AJA *	*American Journal of Archaeology*, New York.
Al. Cantab.	*Alumni Cantabrigienses*, edited by J. A. Venn. 10 vols. Cambridge, 1922-34.
A1. Oxon.	*Alumni Oxionienses 1500-1886*, edited by J. Foster, 4 vols. reprint New York, 1968.
Andrews Diary	Diary kept on board the *Bedawin*, the dahabiya of Theodore M. Davis during 17 trips to Egypt, 1889-1912 by Mrs Emma B. Andrews. MS copy in Metropolitan Museum, New York.
ASAE *	*Annales du Service des Antiquités*, Cairo.
Athanasi	*A brief account of the researches and discoveries in Upper Egypt made under the direction of Henry Salt Esq.* by Giovanni d'Athanasi. London 1836.
Barker	*Syria and Egypt under the last five Sultans of Turkey: being the experiences during Fifty years of Mr Consul-General Barker, chiefly from his letters and journals.* Edited by his son, Edward B. B. Barker. 2 vols. London, 1876.
BASOR *	*Bulletin of the American Schools of Oriental Research*, New Haven, Conn.
Belzoni	*Narrative of operations and recent discoveries in the Pyramids, Temples, Tombs, and Excavations in Egypt and Nubia.* By G. Belzoni. 3rd ed, London, 1822.
BES *	Bulletin of the Egyptological Seminar, New York.
BIBIB	*Biographical Index of deceased British and Irish Botanists.* By James Britten and George S. Boulger: 2nd ed, revised by A. B. Rendle. London, 1931. *Bibl. Ég.Bibliothèque Égyptologique, contenant les oeuvres des Égyptologues français* ... Publiée sous la direction de G Maspero. 40 vols. Paris, 1893-1915. (Those most frequently quoted are the volumes containing biographies of Mariette (vol 18), de Rougé (21), and Lefébure (34).
BIÉ *	*Bulletin de l'Institut d'Égypte*, Cairo.
BIFAO *	*Bulletin de l'Institut français d'archéologie orientale*, Cairo.
BiOr *	*Bibliotheca Orientalis*, Leiden.
BM	The British Museum.
BL	The British Library
BMMA *	*Bulletin Metropolitan Museum of Art*, New York.
BMRAH *	*Bulletin des Musées Royaux d'Art et d'Histoire,* Brussels.
BMQ *	*British Museum Quarterly*, London.
Boase	F. Boase, *Modern English Biography*, 1892-1921.
Bonomi Diary	The manuscript journal of Joseph Bonomi, for the years 1829-33. (W R D used his own abstract compiled from a copy in the Griffith Institute, Oxford).
BSAC *	*Bulletin de la Société d'archéologie Copte*, Cairo.
BSEG *	*Bulletin de la Société d'Égyptologie,* Geneva.
BSFÉ *	*Bulletin de la Société française d'égyptologie*, Paris.
Budge, *N & T*	*By Nile and Tigris: a narrative of journeys to Egypt and Mesopotamia on behalf of the British Museum between the years 1886 and 1913.* By Sir E. A. Wallis Budge. 2 vols. London, 1920.
Budge, *R & P*	*The Rise and Progress of Assyriology.* By Sir E. A. Wallis Budge. London, 1925.
Burton	*Personal Narrative of a Pilgrimage to Al-Medinah and Meccah.* Ed Stanley Lane-Poole. 2 vols. London 1913.
Carré	*Voyageurs et Écrivains français en Égypte.* By Jean-Marie Carré. 2 vols. Cairo, 1932; 2nd ed., 1956.
Chabas	*Notice Biographique de François Joseph Chabas.* By F. Chabas and Philippe Virey, Paris, 1898. (Also reprinted in *Bibl. Ég.* vol 9.)
Champollion	*Lettres et Journaux de Champollion.* Ed H. Hartleben. 2 vols. Paris, 1902. (*Bibl. Ég.,* vols 30, 31.)
CHÉ	*Cahiers d'histoire égyptienne*, Cairo.
Chron. d'Ég. *	*Chronique d'Égypte*, Brussels.
CRAIBL *	*Académie des Inscriptions et Belles-Lettres, Comptes Rendus*, Paris.
DAB	*Dictionary of American Biography*, 1928ff.
Dawson MSS	W R D's own manuscript collections bound in about 100 vols, now in the BL.
DBDI	*Dizionario Biografico degli Italiani*, Rome.
DBE	*Deutsche Biographische Enzyklopäde.* 2nd ed. 2005-8.

DBF	*Dictionnaire de Biographie Française*. Ed Balteau, Barroux, and Prévost. 1933 (in progress).
DNB	*Dictionary of National Biography*. London and Oxford, 1885ff.
EA*	*Egyptian Archaeology*, London.
EB	*Encyclopaedia Britannica*. 12th and subsequent eds.
EDAL	*Egyptian and Egyptological Documents, Archives, Libraries*. Milan.
EEF	Egypt Exploration Fund.
EEF *Arch. Rep.*	Egypt Exploration Fund, *Archaeological Reports*, London.
EES	Egypt Exploration Society.
Enc. It.	*Enciclopedia Italiana*, 36 vols. Rome, 1935-1939.
ERA	Egyptian Research Account.
Erman	*Mein Werden und mein Wirken*. By Adolf Erman, Leipzig, 1929.
Finati	*Life and Adventures of Giovanni Finati*. Dictated by himself, translated from the Italian and edited by W. J. Bankes. 2 vols. London, 1830.
FuF*	*Forschungen und Fortschritte*, Berlin.
GM*	*Gentleman's Magazine*. London, 1731-1868.
Goodwin	*Charles Wycliffe Goodwin, 1817-1878, a Pioneer in Egyptology*. By Warren R. Dawson. Oxford, 1934.
Gött. Misz.*	*Göttinger Miszellen*, Göttingen.
Griffith Corr.	The correspondence of F. Ll. Griffith, in the Griffith Institute, Oxford.
Hartleben	*Champollion: sein Leben und sein Werk*. by Hermine Hartleben. 2 vols. Berlin, 1906.
Hay Diary	The manuscript diary of Robert Hay, for the years 1824 to 1827. (W R D used his own copy made from BL Add MS 31054, supplemented by extracts from other Hay manuscripts, and a partial copy, fuller than the original, made by Bonomi.)
Henniker	*Notes during a visit to Egypt, Nubia ... and Jerusalem*. By Sir Frederick Henniker. 2nd ed. London, 1824.
Hill	*A Biographical Dictionary of the Anglo-Egyptian Sudan*. by Richard Hill. Oxford, 1951; 2nd ed., 1967.
Hilmy	*The Literature of Egypt and the Soudan: A Bibliography*. By Prince Ibrahim Hilmy. 2 vols. London, 1886-7.
Hincks	*Edward Hincks, a selection from his correspondence and a memoir*. by E. F. Davidson. Oxford, 1933.
Hincks Corr.	The correspondence of Edward Hincks in the Griffith Institute, Oxford. (595 documents, including many not published by Davidson).
IEJ*	*Israel Exploration Journal*, Jerusalem.
IFAO	Institut français d'archéologie orientale, Cairo.
ILN*	*Illustrated London News*, London.
Irby	*Travels in Egypt and Nubia, Syria and Asia Minor, during the years 1817 and 1818*. By the Hon. Charles Leonard Irby and James Mangles. 2nd ed London, 1844. (The 1st ed was privately printed, 1823.)
Iversen	*The Myth of Egypt and its Hieroglyphs in European tradition*. By Erik Iversen. Copenhagen, 1961.
JAI*	*Journal of the Anthropological Institute* (later *Royal*), London.
JAOS*	*Journal of the American Oriental Society*, Baltimore.
JARCE*	*Journal of the American Research Center in Egypt*, Princeton and New York.
JEA*	*Journal of Egyptian Archaeology*, London.
JHS*	*Journal of Hellenic Studies*, London.
JMEOS*	*Journal of the Manchester Egyptian and Oriental Society*, Manchester.
JNES*	*Journal of Near Eastern Studies*, Chicago.
JRAS*	*Journal of the Royal Asiatic Society*, London.
KMT*	*KMT. A Modern Journal of Ancient Egypt*, Sebastopol, CA.
Kürschner	*Kürschners Deutschen-Gelehrten-Kalender*. Berlin, various years.
Lamy	*L'Égyptologie avant Champollion*. By Florimond Lamy and Marie-Cécile Bruwier. 2005
Larousse	*Grand Dictionnaire Universel du XIXe Siècle*. 17 vols. Paris, 1866; and ditto, *XXe Siècle*. 6 vols, Paris, 1928.
Legh	*A Narrative of a journey in Egypt and the country beyond the Cataracts*. By Thomas Legh. London, 1816.
Lelorrain	*Notice sur le voyage de M Lelorrain en Égypt et observations sur le. Zodiaque Circulaire de Dendereh*. By P. Saulnier, Paris, 1822.
Lepsius	*Letters from Egypt, Ethiopia and the Peninsula of Sinai*. By Dr Richard Lepsius, trans by L. and J. B. Horner. London, 1853.
Lepsius (Life)	*Georg Ebers: Richard Lepsius: A Biography*, trans from the German by Zoe Dana Underhill. New York, 1887.

Light	*Travels in Egypt, Nubia and the Holy Land ... in the year 1814*. By Henry Light. London, 1818.
Linant Diary	Manuscript Journal of Linant de Bellefonds of his journey from Cairo to Meroe and back 15 June 1821 to 23 June 1822. In the Griffith Institute.
Lindsay	*Letters on Egypt, Edom and the Holy Land*. by Lord Lindsay. 4th ed. London, 1847.
Lugt	F. Lugt, *Répertoire des catalogues de ventes publiques intéressant l'art ou la curiosité 1600-1925*. 4 vols. The Hague, 1938-1987.
Madox	*Excursions in the Holy Land, Egypt, Syria*, etc. By John Madox. 2 vols. London, 1834.
MDAIK*	*Mitteilungen des Deutschen Archäologischen Instituts Abteilung Kairo*, Wiesbaden.
Minutoli	*Recollections of Egypt*. By Baroness von Minutoli, 1827.
MMA	Metropolitan Museum of Art, New York.
Moorehead	*The Blue Nile*, London. 1962.
Myers Diary	Manuscript Diary of Major William Joseph Myers, from 1879 to 1898. In 36 vols of which nos 11-14 and 24 are missing. At Eton College.
NARCE*	Newsletter of the American Research Center in Egypt, New York.
NBG	*Nouvelle Biographie Générale*. By H. Hoeffer. 46 vols. Paris, 1855-66.
NDB	*Neue Deutsche Biographie*, Berlin.
Newberry Corr	The Correspondence of Prof P. E. Newberry, in the Griffith Institute, Oxford.
NNBW	*Nieuw Nederlandsch Biografisch Woordenboek*. 10 vols. Leiden.
ÖBL	*Österreichisches Biographisches Lexikon*, 1815-1950. Vienna.
OFRS*	*Obituary Notices of Fellows of the Royal Society*. London
OLZ*	*Orientalistische Literaturzeitung*, Berlin and Leipzig.
Owen Diary	Diary of a Journey to Egypt by Prof (later Sir) Richard Owen, in 1869. MS in the Natural History Museum, London.
ODNB	*Oxford Dictionary of National Biography*, 2004.
PBA*	*Proceedings of the British Academy,* London.
PEFQS*	*Palestine Exploration Fund Quarterly Statements*, London.
PEQ*	*Palestine Exploration Quarterly,* London.
Petrie	*Seventy Years in Archaeology*. By Sir W. M. Flinders Petrie, London, 1931.
PSBA*	*Proceedings of the Society of Biblical Archaeology*, London.
QR*	*Quarterly Review*, London.
Rec Champ	*Recueil d'études égyptologiques dédiées à la mémoire de Jean-François Champollion*. Paris, 1922.
Rec Trav*	*Receuil de travaux relatifs à la Philologie et à l'Archéologie égyptiennes et assyriennes*. Paris.
Renouf Corr	Correspondence of Sir Peter le Page Renouf in the Griffith Institute, Oxford.
Rev. arch.*	*Revue archéologique,*Paris.
Rev. d'ég.	*Revue d'égyptologie*, Paris.
Rev. ég.	*Revue égyptologique*, Paris.
Richardson	*Travels along the Mediterranean and parts adjacent, in company with the Earl of Belmore, during the years 1816, 1817, and 1818*. By Robert Richardson. 2 vols. London, 1822.
Romer	*A Pilgrimage to the temples and tombs of Egypt, Nubia and Palestine*. By Mrs (Isabella Frances) Romer. 2 vols. London, 1846.
SAK*	*Studien zur Altägyptischen Kultur,* Hamburg.
Salt	*The Life and Correspondence of Henry Salt, Esq. late H. B. M. Consul-General in Egypt*. By J. J. Halls. 2 vols. London 1834.
Sayce	*Reminiscences*. By the Rev A. H. Sayce. London, 1923.
Sherer	*Scenes and Impressions of Egypt, India*, etc. By Moyle Sherer. 2nd ed. London, 1825. (1st ed pub anonymously, 1824.)
Tresson	*Le Voyage archéologique de M le Comte Louis de Saint-Ferriol en Égypte et en Nubie*. By P. Tresson. (*Bull. Acad. Delphinale* Grenoble, 1928).
TSBA*	*Transactions of the Society of Biblical Archaeology*, London.
Valentia	*Voyages and Travels in India ... Abyssinia and Egypt in the years 1802 to 1806*. By George (Annesley) Viscount Valentia. 3 vols. London 1809. (The 8vo ed of 1811 is here quoted.)
Vapereau	*Dictionnaire Universel des Contemporains*. Paris, 1878.
VDI*	*Vestnik Drevnel Istorii*, Moscow.
Vyse	*Operations carried on at the pyramids of Gizeh in 1837*. By Colonel (Richard William) Howard-Vyse. 3 vols. London, 1840-2.
Walpole	*Memoirs relating to European and Asiatic Turkey and other countries of the East, edited from Manuscript Journals*. by Robert Walpole. London, 1818.
Westcar Diary	The manuscript diary of a tour in Egypt and Nubia in 1823-4, by Henry Westcar. (The references are to the original MS formerly in the possession of Dr L. Keimer

but now in the library of the German Institute, Cairo. A transcript by W R D is in the BL, Add MS 52283.)

WW	*Who's Who*, London.
WWA	*Who's Who in America,* Chicago.
WWF	*Who's Who in France*, Paris.
WWW	*Who Was Who*, 5 vols. London, 1929-60. (vol I, 1897-1915; vol II, 1916-28; vol III, 1929-40; vol IV, 1941-50; vol V, 1951-60; vol VI, 1961-70, VII, 1971-80.
WWWA	*Who Was Who in America*, Chicago, covers 1897-1981.
Wilbour	*Travels in Egypt (Dec, 1880, to May, 1891), Letters of Charles Edwin Wilbour.* Ed by Jean Capart. Brooklyn, 1936.
Wilson	*Signs and Wonders upon Pharaoh.* By J. A. Wilson. Chicago, 1964.
*WZKM**	*Wiener Zeitschrift für die Kunde des Morgenlandes*, Vienna.
*ZÄS**	*Zeitschrift für ägyptische Sprache und Altertumskunde*, Leipzig and Berlin
*ZDMG**	*Zeitschrift der deutschen morgenländischen gesellschaft,* Leipzig and Wiesbaden.
ZPE	*Zeitschrift für Papyrologie and Epigraphik*, Bonn.

ABBATE, (*Pasha*) Onofrio (1824-1915)

Italian physician and writer on Egyptian archaeology; he was born in Palermo, 29 Feb. 1824; he graduated in medicine and after studying ophthalmology, he practiced as an oculist in Sicily; he emigrated to Egypt, 1845; he entered the service of the Khedival government, and during the cholera epidemic of 1848 worked as a doctor among the workmen constructing the Delta barrage; later he went to Sicily but returned to Egypt; Director of govt. hospital, Alexandria, and took part in Crimean war, 1855, as a doctor with the Egyptian fleet; he journeyed to the Sudan, again as doctor, 1856-7; harem doctor to Ismail and special consultant to Vicereine and Tewfik until 1887; Memb. Eg. Inst., 1859; VP 1881; Pres. 1890; during his later years he built and lived in a house near the Great Pyramid; he began his interest in ancient Egypt during the earlier part of his life and published, *Un basso-rilievo di Beni-Hassan. Interpretazioni medico-archeologiche*, 1843; articles on the Egyptian phoenix, the statue of Memnon etc, during the 1880s; also a volume *Egyptiaca* relating to medicine, geography and Egyptian archaeology, 1909; he died in Cairo, 11 Oct. 1915.

DBDI 1, 18-19; *Enc It* 1, 21.

ABBOTT, Henry William Charles (1807-1859)

British medical practitioner and collector; he was born 20 Aug. 1807 in Finchley, Middlesex, and baptized at St Mary's church in that parish 26 Sept. 1807; he was the eldest of three natural sons of Henry Robert Abbott (1776-1847) and Mary Ann White (1790-1852), who were subsequently married, 14 Dec. 1810, in St Clement Danes, London, she being still under age and called a minor in the licence; the family origins still remain obscure and it would seem that the father Henry Robert may have claimed descent from the family of the famous Archbishop George A. living in the reign of James I; equally mysterious are Abbott's early years; he is said to have begun his career as ship's surgeon in the Royal Navy and to have left his ship at Alexandria to join the fleet of Muhammad Ali; against this view is the fact that to date no records of his being a naval doctor have been found, while he certainly witnessed his grandmother's will at Hounslow in 1832; although he is often called MD he apparently held no British diploma; another story has it that he went to Egypt on a British official commission to look into the importation of drugs and other such commodities that reached England via the Nile Valley; all that can be said is that he signed himself "Henry Abbott, Surgeon", and that he later claimed to have been Chief Medical Officer of Muhammad Ali's fleet; he had left the Egyptian service and settled in Cairo in 1838 when David Roberts (q.v.) 'dined with Dr Abbott à la Turk'; in 1840 probably, he married at the Armenian church in Cairo an Armenian girl Nemza Kharkour (?), who died on 18 April 1865; in 1842 he founded jointly with Prisse d'Avennes (q.v.) the Egyptian Literary Association in Cairo, a rival to the Egyptian Society founded in 1836; both organizations served the same ends, to provide libraries and lectures, and to act as meeting places for those interested in Egyptian history and art; this new venture was short-lived but brought Abbott into touch with Wilkinson (q.v.) and Lepsius (q.v.) as well as other Egyptologists, and who had been elected to hon. membership; by this time he had acquired a considerable collection of antiquities and his 'museum' had become a show place, especially for British and American visitors, to whom he dispensed lavish hospitality; a catalogue of his collection of some five hundred items, was made by Bonomi (q.v.) in 1843, published in Cairo, 1846; by the 1850s this collection had grown to some twelve hundred pieces, and Abbott decided to try his luck in America, his parents and their family having emigrated to the United States in 1828, subsequently becoming American citizens; his sister Mary Ann had married Stewart Brown, member of a prominent American merchant family, and it was to his care that Abbott consigned his collection 1851-2; leaving his family in the care of his younger brother Dr George A., Vice-Consul in Cairo *c.*1856-9, he arrived in New York in the autumn of 1852; the collection was put on exhibition at Stuyvesant Hall in lower Broadway Jan. 1853, and an attempt made to raise $60,000 by public subscription, the sum he asked for it; interest in Egyptian antiquities was then lacking and the exhibition proved a financial failure, so that Abbott only succeeded in piling up debts; he returned to Egypt in 1854, leaving both his collection and debts behind him; the rest of his story is one of gradual decline; he apparently dabbled in trade, and having acquired from A. C. Harris (q.v.) the famous papyrus that bears his name, resold it to the British Museum through the mediation of Sir Gardner Wilkinson, 1857; Abbott remained a British subject even after going to the United States, unlike his brother who is described as 'physician' in his will made at Cairo 15 Nov. 1855, and to whom he bequeathed all his medical and surgical books and instruments; Wilkinson was a witness to it, and after Abbott's death vainly tried to interest the British Museum in this collection now grown to enormous proportions; after many ineffectual attempts had been made to sell the main collection, it was eventually acquired for America in 1860, being purchased by The New York Historical Society, which added $5,000 to the $29,581 already raised by public subscription, a bargain price; the Abbott collection was the first important collection of Egyptian antiquities owned by a public institution in the U.S.A., and in 1937 it was transferred on loan to The Brooklyn Museum, and purchased by it, 1948; Abbott died at his property near Benha, 30 March 1859.

Inf. Mrs E. Riefstahl; inf. Mr. P. J. Dyke; inf. Mr P. R. G. Jackson; inf. Brit. Consulate-General, Cairo; Michael Bird, *Samuel Shepheard of Cairo*, 1957; *Amer. Biogr. Notes*, Albany NY, 1875; C. Williams in *Bull. N.Y. Hist. Soc.* 4 (1920-1), 8-15; *Brooklyn Mus. Bull.* 10, no. 3 (Spring 1949), 17-23 (portr.); Romer i, 103, 368; ii, 113.

ABD EL-MEGID Hussein (*c*. 1850-1915)
Egyptian antiquities dealer; he was based in Luxor and married the sister of Muhammad Muhassib (q.v.); he owned land on the West Bank; he is mentioned by Maspero (q.v.) in 1884 and was arrested by Grébaut (q.v.) in 1888; he sold the el-hibeh papyri to Spiegelberg (q.v) in 1895; his business passed to his son Hassan (1889-1916) and his grandson Hussein.

F. Hagen and K. Ryholt, *The Antiquities Trade in Egpt 1880-1930*, 2017, 184-5.

ABDERRASUL family (*fl*. 1871-1926)
Egyptian family consisting of several brothers, sons of Ahmad Abderrasul and Fendia, living in Qurna, Abder-Rahman, Muhammad (who was in the service of Mustafa Agha (q.v.), Consular Agent at Luxor) and Soliman were dealers in antiquities, but have acquired almost legendary fame through their discovery about the year 1871 of the famous cache of Royal Mummies at Deir el-Bahri; this illicit find soon attracted attention, for they sold papyri and other small objects from it, whose appearance on the market aroused the suspicions of Maspero (q.v.); as a result of inquiries and official action, Muhammad A. disclosed the secret in 1881, and E. Brugsch (q.v.) went with the brothers to the hiding place and all the contents were removed to Cairo Museum; the same family also discovered another tomb, the contents of which were again exploited for some years before it was known; Muhammad A., who was then in the employment of the Antiquities Service, disclosed the secret to Grébaut (q.v.) in 1891, and about 105 coffins and mummies of Dyn. 21, with their funerary furniture, were taken to the Museum; Abderrasul, born *c*.1816, died about 1918 or 1919, and Muhammad, a very old man, about 1926; another brother Hussein worked for Howard Carter (q.v.).

Maspero, *Momies royales*, 511 ff.; *ASAE* 1 (1900), 141-5; 8 (1907), 3-38; Wilbour, 33, 74, and often (see Index); inf. Dr Hughes, Oriental Institute, University of Chicago; inf. Dr Rosalind Moss; *KMT* 3/3 (1992),87; F. Hagen and K. Ryholt, *The Antiquities Trade in Egypt, 1880-1930*, 2017, 185-7.

ABEKEN, Heinrich Johann Wilhelm Rudolf (1809-1872)
German diplomat and archaeologist; he was born Osnabrück, 19 Aug. 1809, son of Christian Wilhelm A., a merchant, and Benedicta Mayer; he studied theology at the University of Berlin, and became chaplain to the Prussian Embassy in Rome and later in London; he accompanied the expedition of Lepsius, in Egypt and Nubia, 1842-44, and acted as chaplain; he afterwards entered the diplomatic service; he was a life-long friend of Lepsius (q.v.), studying Egyptology under him; he published a report on the expedition, and produced other works; he died in Berlin, 8 August 1872.

Lepsius, 12 et passim, (see Index); Lepsius (*Life*), 141, 159, 228; Hill, 19; Hilmy, i, 7; H. Abeken, *Heinrich Abeken*, 1898; English trans. *Bismarck's Pen*, 1911; *NDB* 1, 8-9; F. Frischbier, *Heinrich Abeken*, 2008.

ABEL, Carl (1837-1906)
German philologist; he was born in Berlin, 25 Nov. 1837, son of Gerson Abel, a Jewish banker; he studied ancient Egyptian and Coptic and became an opponent of Erman's (q.v.) interpretation of ancient Egyptian philology; Erman prevented his appointment as Professor of Philology at Bonn; he also clashed with Renouf (q.v.); he became a bookseller and then entered the Prussian Foreign Service, resigning in 1862; he lectured at the University of Oxford on comparative lexicography; he served as a correspondent for *The Times* in Berlin, 1862-1879 and then *The Standard*; he founded the Anglo-German Association, 1874; he published *Koptische Untersuchungen*, 1876; *Zur ägyptischen Kritik*, 1878; *Linguistic Essays*, 1882; *Einleitung in ein ägyptisch-semitisch-indo-europäisches Wurzelwörterbuch*, 1886; *Gegen Herrn Professor Erman*, 1887; *Über Wechselbeziehungen der ägyptischen, indoeuropäischen und semitischen Etymologie*, 1889; *Offener Brief an Professor Dr. Gustav Meyer in Sachen der ägyptisch-indogermanischen Sprachverwandtschaft*, 1891; *L'Affinité étymologique des langues égyptienne et indo-européennes*, 1892; he died in Wiesbaden, 26 Nov. 1906.

The Times 18 Dec. 1906, 11 and 24 Dec. 1906, 9; *Biographisches Jahrbuch und Deutscher Nekrolog* 11 (1908), *6.

ABEL, Hans Bernhard Ambrosius (1883-1927)
German Egyptologist, expert in Old Nubian language, and school teacher; he was born at Leipzig, 20 Dec. 1883, son of a general agent; he studied Egyptology, classical and German philology, comparative linguistics in Marburg, Leipzig, Göttingen; PhD, 1909 (Göttingen); he was the assistant at the Deutsche Institut für ägyptische Altertumskunde in Cairo, 1908- 31 Dec. 1911 and participated in the excavations at the pyramid of Khafre and at Amarna; with Friedrich Bilabel (q.v.) and Karl Breith he took part in the German excavations at Qarara/el Hibeh in 1914; he was a school teacher in Wismar, 1913-15, Leipzig and Dresden after World War I; after his dissertation *Tonverschmelzung gewisser Wortgruppen im Altaegyptischen*, 1910, he published studies on Old Nubian language,

Eine Erzählung im Dialekt von Ermenne (Nubien), 1913; *Die Verbalformen des abhängigen Satzes (Subjunktiv und Infinitive) im Nubischen*, 1921; a Nubian Dictionary was left uncompleted; he died after a heart attack while on tour in the Reisengebirge, 1 Oct. 1927.

54.Jahresbericht des Staatsgymnasiums zu Dresden-Neustadt. Schuljahr Ostern 1927 bis Ostern 1928, 1928; G.Willgeroth, *Die Lehrer der Großen Stadtschule zu Wismar*, 1935; inf. W. Habermann (Univ. of Frankfurt a.M.).

ABEMAYOR, Michel (1912-1975)
Egyptian-American dealer; he was born in Cairo, 22 Dec. 1912, son of Elie Albert Abemayor and Violet Benghiat; his family had been dealing in antiquities for several generations; the family shop was founded in Cairo by his grandfather Michel Abemayor in 1888 and later run by his father Elie Albert Abemayor (1883-1941) at one time in association with his brother Joseph Abemayor (1894-1954); the shop was located in rue Kamel opposite Shepheard's Hotel; Michel Abemayor left Egypt for America where he was naturalized in 1946; he established himself in New York as a dealer in Egyptian and Graeco-Roman antiquities supplying museums and private collectors; antiquities from his collection were sold at Sotheby's (New York), 11 Dec 1976, 21 May 1977, and 16 May 1980; he died in New York, 8 Oct. 1975.

Inf. Mrs M. Abemayor; F. Hagen and K. Ryholt, *The Antiquities Trade in Egypt 1880-1930*, 2017, 189-90.

ABITZ, Friedrich (1924-1994)
German Egyptologist; he was born in Hamburg in 1924; he specialized in the study of the Valley of the Kings; he published *Die religiöse Bedeutung der sogenannten Grabräuberschächte in den ägyptischen Königsgräbern der 18. bis 20. Dynastie*, 1974; *Statuetten in Schreinen als Grabbeigaben in der ägyptischen Königsgräbern der 18. und 19. Dynastie*, 1979; *König und Gott*, 1984; *Ramses II. in den Gräbern seiner Söhne*, 1986; *Baugeschichte und Dekoration des Grabes Ramses' VI*, 1989; *Pharao als Gott in den Unterweltsbüchern des Neuen Reiches*, 1995; he died in Groenwohld, 6 June 1994.

Introduction to *Pharao als Gott*.

ABOU-GHAZI, Dia Mahmud (1924-2001)
Egyptian Egyptologist; she was born in Cairo 24 Jan. 1924, daughter of Mahmud Abou-Ghazi; she studied at Fuad I (later Cairo) University, 1946-9; she began her thesis in 1949 under Gabra (q.v.) but was unable to complete it until 1966; she was appointed Librarian at the Egyptian Museum, Sept. 1950 and greatly expanded its range; she became assistant curator and later director, 1977-8; she was appointed Director-General of the Museums Service, 1978; she revised and published Moret's *Tables d'offrandes et autels*, 1980 and published *Catalogue de la bibliothèque du Musée égyptien du Caire*, 1973; she died in Cairo, 10 April 2001.

DIE 54 (2002), 105-7 (portr.) (A. Nibbi).

ABOU-SEIF, Hakim (1889-1951)
Egyptian archaeologist; he was born 29 Oct. 1889; he joined the Egyptian Antiquities Service and worked in various areas as an inspector; he was inspector at Karnak from at least 1919 until Sept. 1923 where he carried out excavations near the Temple of Khonsu (*ASAE* 21 (1921), 214-21); inspector at Tanta 1923-25, during which time he excavated at Samannud two sarcophagi (*ASAE* 24 (1924), 91-6 and 146-50); he was inspector at Minya from Nov. 1925 carrying out work at Tihna (*ASAE* 26 (1926), 32-8) and Tuna el-Gebel (*ASAE* 28 (1928), 61-5); he later held posts at Saqqara and Giza when he cleared the Great Pyramid in 1940 (*ASAE* 46 (1947), 235-8); he was appointed a curator in the Coptic Museum 21 Sept. 1940 and then Librarian of the Egyptian Museum 17 March 1946 retiring on 29 Oct. 1946; he died on 7 April 1951.

D. Abou-Ghazi, *The Library of Egyptian Museum*, 1988, 19-20.

ABROYAN, Arakel (1832-1875)
Armenian official and traveller; he was a cousin of Nubar Pasha and son of Bedros Abroyan; he was educated in Paris; a man of enlightened views and literary taste he accompanied several distinguished visitors in journeys up the Nile; he went with Ferdinand de Lesseps (q.v.) to the White Nile, and on another trip to Upper Egypt, 1865, with the author Prévost-Paradol (q.v.); in 1868 he went with Edmond About; after serving in the Egyptian Foreign Office, he became private secretary to the Khedive Ismail; he was made Governor of Massawa, 1873; in the Abyssinian war he served with Arandrup's force; after the defeat at Gundet, he shot himself to avoid capture, 13 Nov. 1875; he is not to be confused with Arakel Bey Nubarian (1826-59).

Carré, ii, 270, 291; E. About, *Le Fellah*, 131; Lady Duff Gordon, *Letters*, 334; Hill, 58; R. Adalian, *The Armenian Review* 33 (1980), 133-4.

ABU BAKR, Abdel-Moneim Youssef (1907-1976)
Egyptian archaeologist; he was born in Cairo, 23 March 1907; he attended the El Hamiah School and the Faculty of Arts, Cairo University where he studied under Golenischeff (q.v.); BA, 1930; he continued his studies at the University of Berlin under Sethe (q.v.) and Grapow (q.v.), 1932-7 as well as under Ranke (q.v.) at Heidelberg, 1933; PhD, 1937; Assistant Professor at the University of Alexandria, 1939; Professor, 1948; Director of the Antiquities Section and Assistant Dean of the Faculty of Arts; Professor at Cairo University, 1954 and later Dean; he undertook excavations at Giza, 1949-50 and Hermopolis, 1949-50; from 1960-65 he was the Egyptian representative on the UNESCO campaign in Nubia and excavated at Aniba; his publications include *Untersuchungen über die ägyptischen Kronen* 1937; *Excavations at Giza 1949-50,* 1953 and preliminary reports of his excavations in various journals; he died in Cairo, 26 July 1976.

NARCE 88 (1974), 22; *NARCE* 99/100 (1977), 2 (S. Tawfik); *BSAC* 23 (1981), 307 (L. Habachi), *Gott. Misz.* 76 (1984), 84 (H. Attiatalla); E. Endesfelder, *Die Ägyptologie an der Berliner Universität-Zur Geschichte eines Fachgebietes,* 1988, 50.

ACERBI, Giuseppe (1773-1846)
Italian traveller and diplomat; he was born in Castelgoffredo, 3 May 1773, son of Giacomo A. and Marianna Riva; he studied law at Pavia and in 1798-9 undertook a journey to Scandinavia; he was nominated Austrian Consul-General in Lisbon in 1815 but did not take up the appointment; he stayed in Milan where he founded the literary review *Bibliotheca Italiana* in which later were published his letters from Egypt; he became Austrian Consul-General in Egypt 1826-1834; he travelled in both Upper and Lower Egypt and put together a small collection of Egyptian antiquities which is largely in the Egyptian Museum, Mantua with some pieces in Milan; his papers are in the Mantua Library; he was a friend and supporter of Champollion (q.v.); he died in Castelgoffredo, 25 Aug. 1846.

DBDI 1, 134-6; S. Curto, *Atti del Convegno la Lombardia e l'Oriente 11-15 giugno 1962,* Milan, 1963, 89-120; L. Donatelli, *La Raccolta di Guiseppe Acerbi,* Mantua, 1983, 13-27; Barker, ii, 192; Hilmy, i, 14; BL Add. MS 25663, ff. 42-107; Champollion, ii, 234, 244, 245; S. Pernigotti, *Egitto e Vicino Oriente* III (1985), 15-16 and n. 17-18; A. Calderini, *Studi Rosellini,* I, 1949, 62 and bibliogr.; E. Bresciani in N. Bonacasa and A. di Vita, *Alessandria e il Mondo ellenistico-romano,* 1984, 203-8; P. Gualtierotti, *Il Console Giuseppe Acerbi ed il viaggio nell'alto Egitto,* 1984; L. Donatelli in C. Morigi Govi, S. Curto, and S. Pernigotti, *L'Egitto fuori dell'Egitto,* 1991, 201-4; C. Gallico, *Mantova e l'antico Egitto da Giulio Romano a Giuseppe Acerbi,* 1994.

el-ACHIRIE, Hassan (1928-1994)
Egyptian architect; he was born at Heliopolis, Cairo, 1 May 1928; he was educated at the Faculty of Engineering, Cairo University, graduating in 1951, and then in the Institute of Archaeology, diploma, 1955; he joined the Center of Documentation as an architect until 1979; later chief architect and director of the Department of Technical Affairs; his survey work included the Nubian monuments, 1957-1964; the temple of Isis at Aswan, the temple of Kanayis in the Wadi Miyah, and tombs and temples of the Theban area, notably the Ramesseum and the Theban graffiti, 1964-1979; he later turned his attention to work in Saudi Arabia, retiring in 1988 but working there until 1990; he contributed to the following publications in the Collection Scientifique of the Centre of Documentation, *Le Temple d'Amada* I, 1967; *Abou Simbel. Le Petit Temple* (with C. Desroches-Noblecourt), 1968; *Le Speos d'el-Lessiya* (with M. Dewachter), 1960; *Graffiti démotiques de Dodescaschoene* (with E. Bresciani), 1969; *Graffiti de la montagne thébaine* III (with A. Sadek), 1-4, 1970-72; *Le Temple de Dandour* I, 1972; *Le Ramesseum* I (with J.-Cl. Goyon), 1973; *Le Ramesseum* VI (with J.-Cl. Goyon), 1974; *Grand Temple d'Abou Simbel* III (with S. Donadoni and C. Leblanc), 1975; *Le Ramesseum* X (with J.-Cl. Goyon)), 1976; *Garf Hussein I* (with J. Jacquet), 1978; *Le Temple de Derr* (with J. Jacquet), 1980; *Le Ramesseum* IX (with J.-Cl. Goyon), 1980; *Grande Temple d'Abou Simbel* I (with J. Jacquet), 1984; he died in Cairo, 12 April 1994.

A. F. Sadek, *Memnonia* IV (1993-1994), 17-21.

ACWORTH, Joseph John (1853-1927)
British collector of antiquities; he was born in Chatham, 9 Feb. 1853, son of Joseph John A. and Mary Johnson; PhD, FIC, FCS; he visited Egypt many times and formed a large collection of Egyptian antiquities by purchase in Egypt and at sales, in particular the Meux sale of 1911; he retired in 1919 and devoted all his time to the study of Egyptology and to making additions to his collection; he died in London, 3 Jan. 1927; in 1939 his widow Marion Whiteford Acworth presented the major part of his collection to the British Museum and the

remainder to the Museum of Archaeology and Ethnology, Cambridge; further items from his collection were bequeathed to the British Museum in 1965.

Inf. Mrs Acworth; *BMQ* 15 (1941-50), 55-57.

ADAM, Abdelrahman (1924-1954)
Sudanese Egyptologist and archaeologist; he was born at Gedaref, 1924, a son of Yuzbashi Adam Muhammad, and was educated at Gordon College, Khartoum; he was appointed an Antiquities Officer in 1948, and worked at Jebel Morra in Darfur; he surveyed the region from Karima to Wadi Halfa with Alexander (q.v.) in 1952; he toured the southern provinces and assisted on the excavations at Amara West and Soba; he published 'The excavations of a mound grave near Ushara', in *Kush* 1 (1953) with K. Marshall; his career was tragically ended by his accidental death in Cambridge, 24 Dec. 1954.

Kush 3 (1955), 112 (P. L. Shinnie).

ADAM, Muhammad Shehata (1917-1986)
Egyptian Egyptologist; he held several posts in the Antiquities Service; inspector of the Eastern Delta, 1950-54 where he carried out various excavations (*ASAE* 55 (1958), 301-324; *ASAE* 56 (1959), 207-226); in 1954 he was transferred to Luxor and was involved in clearance operations at the temples of Karnak and Luxor, 1954-1958 (*ASAE* 56 (1959), 35-52; *ASAE* 60 (1968), 230); he was later Chief of the Nubian Office in the Ministry of Culture; in 1972 he was appointed Director-General of the Center of Documentation until 1978; in July 1978 he succeeded Muhammad A. Muhammad (q.v.) as head of the Egyptian Antiquities Organization until June 1981; he died in the summer of 1986.

JEA 73 (1987), ix.

ADAMS, Andrew Leith (1827-1882)
British surgeon and naturalist; he was born Banchory-Ternan, Aberdeenshire, 21 March 1827, son of Francis A. and Elspeth Shaw; he served as an army surgeon, 1848-73; Prof. of Zoology, Dublin, 1873-8; Prof. of Nat. Hist., Cork, 1878-82; during his career he visited India, Egypt, and Canada and published accounts of his travels; he travelled in Egypt with Alex Henry Rhind.(q.v.) and published *Notes of a Naturalist in the Nile Valley*, 1870, a work which besides dealing with natural history also contains much information on the people he met, such as Edwin Smith (q.v.); he died in Queenstown, Ireland, 29 July 1882.

ODNB 1, 94; *DNB* i,222-3; Hilmy, i, 15.

ADAMS, Barbara Georgina (née BISHOP) (1945-2002)
British archaeologist; she was born in Hammersmith, London 19 Feb. 1945, daughter of Charles Bishop and Ellaline Cowdrey; she attended Godolphin and Latymer School, Hammersmith and completed her education at night schools and the Extramural Dept of the University of London; Extramural Diploma in Archaeology, 1968; she was appointed a scientific assistant in the Dept of Entomology, British Museum of Natural History 1964 and transferred to the Sub-Dept of Anthropology, 1965; she was then appointed museum assistant at the Petrie Museum of Egyptian Archaeology, University College London, 1965-75; assistant curator, 1975-84; curator, 1984-97; research curator, 1997-2002; she became a lecturer in the Institute of Archaeology, 1998-2002; she was awarded an Hon Fellowship from University College London, 2002; during her career at the Petrie Museum, she was instrumental in registering many of the objects in the collection notably from Hierakonpolis in which she developed a great interest and organizing the conservation of the collection, in particular the mummy portraits; she wrote up the unpublished excavation of Garstang (q.v.) at Hierakonpolis and she then excavated at Hierakonpolis under Fairservis (q.v.) and Hoffman (q.v.) from 1980-6 plus study seasons in 1988 and 1992; she became co-director of the excavations with Dr. R. Friedman, 1996-2001; she founded the Friends of the Petrie Museum in 1988 and was a member of its committee 1988-2002; she was a member of the Committee of the Egypt Exploration Society, 1995-98, the London Federation of Museums and Art Galleries, 1982-4, the Area Museums Service for South East England advisory panel for the care of collections, 1986-91, and a representative of the University of London on the London Museums Consultative Committee, 1983-99; she was named a Corresponding Member of the German Archaeological Institute, 2000; she initiated and edited the Shire Egyptology Series with over 25 titles; apart from numerous articles and reviews, her published works included *Ancient Hierakonpolis* and *Supplement*, 1974; *Guide Poche Marcus: Egypt*, with A. Thomas, 1976; *Guide to the Petrie Museum of Egyptian Archaeology*, 1977, rev 1981, 1988, 1990, 1994, 1999; *Egyptian Objects in the Victoria and Albert Museum*, 1978; *Universal Pocket Guide: Egypt*, with A. Thomas, 1981; *The Koptos Lions*, with R. Jaeschke, 1984; *Egyptian Mummies*, 1984, rev 1988, 1992;

Sculptured Pottery from Coptos, 1986; *The Fort Cemetery at Hierakonpolis*, 1987; *Predynastic Egypt*, 1988; *Ancient Nekhen*, 1995; *Protodynastic Egypt*, with K. Cialowicz, 1997; *Excavations in the Locality 6 Cemetery at Hierakonpolis 1979-1985*, 2000 and she also edited, with R. Friedman, *The Followers of Horus: Studies Dedicated to Michael Allen Hoffman 1944-1990*, 1992; a memorial volume of studies *Egypt at its Origins*, edited by S. Hendrickx, R. Friedman, et al, was published in 2004; she died in London 26 June 2002.

The Guardian 13 July 2002 (portr.) (H. Smith); *Friends of the Petrie Museum Newsletter* 25 (2002), 1-3 (portr.) (H. Smith); *Debrett's People of Today 2002*, 2001; *Nekhen News* 14 (2002), 3-5 (portr.) (R. Friedman), 6-7 (S. Hendrickx), 26 (W. Johnson); *Egypt at its Origins*, 2004, xv-xix (portr.), xxiii-xxx (bibl.); inf. R. Friedman; *ODNB 2001-4*, 2-3.

ADAMS, William Yewdale (1927-2019)
American anthropologist and Sudanologist; he was born in Los Angeles, 6 Aug. 1927, son of Willian Forbes A., an historian, and Lucy Mary Wilcox; he was educated at Stanford University, 1943-5, then he served in the US navy, 1945-6; he then studied at the University of California at Berkeley and the University of Arizona; |PhD, 1957; he became professor in the Dept. of Anthropology, Unniversity of Kentucky, 1966; he married in 1955 Nettie Alice Kessler who assisted in her husband's archaeological work; he took part in the Nubian rescue campaign, 1959-66, excavating at Faras, Meinarti, and Kulubnarti; he collaborated with the EES in the excavation of Qasr Ibrim, 1972-88; he was Hon. President of the Sudan Archaeological Research Society and hon. board member of the International Society for Nubian Studies; he was awarded the Order of the Two Niles by Sudan, 2005; his publications included *Meroitic North and South*, 1976; *Nubia: Corridor to Africa*, 1977; *Ceramic Industries of Medieval Nubia*, 1986; *Kulubnarti I: The Architectural Remains*, 1994; *Qasr Ibrim. The Late Medieval Period*, 1996; with N. Adams, *Kulubnarti II: The Artifactual Remains*, 1998; *Kulubnarti III: The Cemeteries*, 1999; *Meinarti I: The Late Meroitic, Ballana and Transitional Occupation*, 2000; *Meinarti II: The Early and Classic Christian Phases*, 2001; *Meinarti III: The Late and Terminal Christian Phases*, 2002; *Meinarti IV and V: The The Church and Cemetery*, 2003; with H-A. Nordström, T*he West Bank Survey from Faras to Gemai*, 2005; *The Road from Frijoles Canyon*, 2009; *Churches of Nobadia*, 2009; *Qasr Ibrim. The Earlier Medieval Period*, 2010; *Qasr Ibrim. The Ballana Phase*, 2013; with J. Alexander, *Qasr Ibrim. The Ottoman Period*, 2019; he died in Lexington, Kentucky, 22 Aug. 2019

Internet obit.

ADANSON, Jean-Baptiste Félix Hubert (1732-1803)
French diplomat; he was baptized Paris, 3 July 1732, son of Léger Adanson, an official of the Archbishop of Aix and Marthe Buisson; he was the brother of Michel Adanson, a noted scholar in natural history; he studied oriental languages in Paris at the École des jeunes de langues from 19 Sept. 1740-50 and at Constantinople 1750-54; he was posted as third interpreter at Aleppo, 1754 and later Salonika on 14 March 1758, Saïda *c.*1763 as second interpreter, and Tripoli *c.*1774 as first interpreter; he was appointed first French dragoman in Alexandria, *c.*1775-85; he met the travellers Sonnini (q.v.) and Volney (q.v.) in Egypt; he became first dragoman in Tunis from 1785; his name is mentioned in certain early books of Egyptian travel, which recount his sufferings and scientific work; during his period in Egypt he made up some portfolios of drawings and paintings and some notebooks, which for a long time were believed to have perished except for a few drawings preserved in the Bibliothèque Nationale; in 1958, however, a unique collection of 151 original compositions by him was sold in Paris; this contained a very varied selection of 30 paintings and 121 sketches and drawings, which fetched 3 million francs; these reproductions and notes may be said to rank Adanson (q.v.) with Sonnini (q.v.) and Denon (q.v.); they consist of views of monuments such as the pyramids and Sphinx, and of many well-known sites, including Alexandria, Cairo, and Bizerte in Tunisia; also included were copies of fragments of sculptured stone, various animals and birds seen, and, most important of all, hieroglyphic inscriptions on monuments that have sometimes since disappeared; with these illustrations there were three written accounts by the author, and a group of pages with hieroglyphic signs copied on them; 100 drawings were sold at Sotheby's on 2 Nov. 1964 (lot 169) and acquired on behalf of Mr Paul Mellon; four manuscript notebooks were sold in Paris in 1997; a collection of his works was acquired by Johns Hopkins University in 1998; other drawings and manuscripts are in the Pierpont Morgan Library, New York, and Musée Voltaire, Geneva, and a drawing is in the Searight collection in the Victoria and Albert Museum, London; Adanson died in Tunis, 5 Nov. 1803.

Inf. Prof. J. J. Clère; EEF *Arch. Rep.* 1899-1900, 38; E. Hamy, *CRAIBL*, 4e sér. 27 (1899), 738-46; *DBF* 1, 504; A. Chevalier, *Michel Adanson*, 1934; A. Gauthier and M. de Testa, 'Quelques Dynasties de Dragomans' *Revue d'Histoire diplomatique* 105 (1991), 41-44; *Le Tour du Monde*, catalogue 42 (1997), 1; J. Kimpton in C. Foster (ed.), *Travellers in the Near East*, 2004, 73-106; F. Jacob, *Orages* 6 (2007), 143-58; inf. J. Kimpton.

ADDISON, Frank (1885-1958)
British archaeologist; he was born in Bradford, 6 Sept. 1885, son of Joseph A., teacher, and Ann Elizabeth Stansfield; he was trained as an engineer in Leeds, apprenticeship, 1901-4; he was attached to the Engineering Department of the University of Leeds, 1905-7 and then the Gordon College workshops, Khartoum where he then became a mathematical lecturer in the Upper School and later Inspector of Schools; as he showed an interest in antiquities, he was appointed Acting Conservator of Antiquities in 1921, later Conservator until 1931; he was then charged with the preparation of the reports of the Wellcome (q.v.) expedition in 1911-4; Fellow of the Society of Antiquities, 1945; he published *A Short Guide to the Museum of Antiquities Gordon College, Khartoum*; *Gebel Moya*, 1949; *Abu Geili*, 1951, with O. Crawford; he died in Leeds, 18 March 1958.

Kush 1 (1953) 56-9; *Kush* 7 (1959), 231-2 (J.W. Crowfoot). Photograph reproduced by permission of Durham University Library.

ADRIANI, Achille (1905-1982)
Italian archaeologist; he was born in Naples, 23 April 1905, son of Luigi A. and Luisa Numeroso; he was educated at the University of Rome, BA 1927; he was attached to the Italian Institute in Athens, 1929-30; he was appointed inspector of antiquities at Naples, 1930-2; he held the position of Keeper of the Graeco-Roman Museum at Alexandria, 1932-40 in succession to Breccia (q.v.); assistant secretary of the Société d'Archéologie d'Alexandrie, 1933; later Secretary-general, 1934-40 and editor of its bulletin, 1933-39; he excavated at Antinoe, 1939; in Italian civil service during World War II, 1940-4; he then became inspector of antiquities at Rome, 1945-8; he was reappointed to the keepership at Alexandria, 1948-52; he was successively Professor of Archaeology and Graeco-Roman Art at the Universities of Palermo, 1948-66; Naples, 1966-71; and Rome, 1971-75; in Egypt he undertook excavations in Alexandria, Antinoe, and Abukir; he was a member of the Accademia Nazionale dei Lincei, the Accademia di Lettre ed Arti di Napoli, and the Accademia di Scienze Lettre ed Arti di Palermo, and corresponding member of the German Archaeological Institue and the Institut d'Égypte; his main publications were *Annuario del Museo Greco-Romano 1932-33*, 1934; *Annuaire du Musée Greco-Romain 1933-34 - 1934-5*, 1936; *Le goblet en argent des amours vendangeurs du Musée d'Alexandrie*, 1939; *Annuaire du Musée Gréco-Romain 1935-39*, 1940; *ibid.*, 1940-50; *Repertorio d'arte dell'Egitto greco-romano* Series A, vols. I-II, 1961 devoted to sculpture; ibid. Series C, vols. I-II, 1963-6 devoted to architecture; a *Festschrift* in three volumes dedicated to his memory was edited by N. Boncasa and A. di Vita, *Alessandria e il mondo ellenistico-romano*, 1983; he died in Rome, 14 Dec. 1982.

Bonacasa and Di Vita, *op. cit.*, xv-xix (E. Epifano) (portr.) (bibl.); R. Lackany, *La Société Archéologique d'Alexandrie à 80 ans,* 1973, 160.

AFFRE, Denis Auguste (1793-1848)
French bishop and scholar; he was born Saint-Rome-de-Tarn, 27 Sept. 1793, son of Jean Louis A. and Marie-Christine Boyer and was trained for the priesthood at St Sulpice; Archbishop of Paris, 1840; he studied Champollion's works but considered them insufficient to explain hieroglyphic writing; he published *Nouvel essai sur les hiéroglyphes égyptiens*, Paris, 1834, a scholarly though mistaken work; he was killed in Paris, 27 June 1848.

L. Alazard, *Denis-Auguste Affre, Archevêque de Paris*, Paris, 1905; Hilmy, i, 16l.

AGOUB, Joseph (1795-1832)
Copt of Armenian birth; Arabic scholar; he was born in Cairo, 18 March 1795, son of Elias A. and Marie Chebib; he was taken as a child to Marseilles by his father, 1801, and to Paris, 1820; Prof. of Arabic at the Collège Louis-le-Grand; he published translations of Arabic songs, *Discours sur l'Égypte*, 1823; *Littérature orientale et française*, posth., 1835; Agoub was a friend of Champollion (q.v.); he died in Marseilles, 3 Oct. 1832.

Champollion, i, 285; ii, 421; Hilmy, i, 21.

AHMED, Khidir Abdelkarim (1947-2012)
Sudanese archaeologist; he was born in Kosti, 28 Jan. 1947; he was educated at the University of Khartoum; BA in ancient history,1970; MA in archaeology, 1975; he then studied at Cambridge, 1977-83; PhD, 1983; he was appointed teaching assistant in the Department of Archaeology, University of Khartoum, 1975-77; lecturer, 1983-91; assistant professor, 1991-98 and head of the dept., 1987-90 and 1991-93; he then became associate professor in the Department of Archaeology, University of Shendi, 2003-4 and then professor at el-Nillain University, Khartoum, 2005-2012; he was visiting professor at Humboldt University, Berlin, Oct.-Dec. 1999 and 2002-3; he assisted in excavations at Mograt Island, 1970; Sarurab, 1971-2, 1975; Meroe, 1975, Dafur, 1976; he directed surveys at Meroe, 1979-80, Sarurab, 1986, Dinder, 1997, 2002, and co-directed excavations at Meroe, 1983-4, 1991-2; he published *Meroitic Settlement in the Central Sudan*, 1984; he died in Khartoum, 27 March 2012.

Sudan and Nubia 16 (2012), 159-60 (portr.). (I. Elzein)

AHMED KAMAL *see* **KAMAL**

AIMÉ-GIRON, Noël (1884-1941)
French orientalist; born Paris, 22 Aug. 1884, son of (Jean Antoine) Aimé Giron, editor of *Figaro*; from boyhood was much attracted by oriental languages and was encouraged by Revillout (q.v.) whose classes he attended; he studied at the École des Hautes Études and the Sorbonne; he was sent to the East where he studied Arabic, Persian, Turkish and Hebrew while in the consular service; during the First World War he returned to France; from 1929 he was Consul-General at Port Said frequently visiting Cairo to study inscriptions; he was awarded honorary decorations by the governments of Egypt, Syria, and Greece, and was made Chevalier de la Légion d'honneur; he published many texts and articles in *ASAE* and other journals; he died suddenly in 1941.

ASAE 41, (1942) 3-6 (portr.), 6-9 (bibl.) (Leibovitch)

AINSLIE, (*Sir*) Robert (*c*.1730-1812)
British diplomat and numismatist; he was born *c*.1730, son of George A. and Jane Anstruther; he was Ambassador at Constantinople, 1776-92; knighted, 1775; created Baronet, 1804; he formed a large collection of ancient Eastern and N. African coins, a selection of which were published by Sestini in 3 vols; he also made a collection of drawings of Egypt executed by Luigi Mayer (q.v.) of which 48 were published in colour in 1801-2 and a further series in 3 vols., 1804; he died in Bath, 21 July 1812.

ODNB 1, 499-500; *DNB* i, 189; Hilmy, ii, 26; B. Taylor in *Souvenirs and New Ideas*, ed. D. Fortenberry (ed.), 2013, 158-78.

ÅKERBLAD, Johan David (1763-1819)
Swedish diplomat and orientalist; he was born in Stockholm, 6 May 1763, son of Johan A. and Anna Magdelena Lenngren and was appointed to the Swedish embassy in Constantinople in 1783; he studied oriental languages and travelled in the Eastern Mediterranean countries in order to perfect his Arabic, visiting Egypt, Palestine and Asia Minor in 1786; and he was attached to the consulate in Paris where he studied under Silvestre de Sacy (q.v.), 1801-2; after studying Coptic MSS, he obtained a copy of the Rosetta Stone; soon after, under the patronage of the Duchess of Devonshire he settled in Rome to continue his studies, and published works on Runic Inscriptions (1801) and Phoenician (1802); he had considerable success in deciphering the Demotic text of the Rosetta decree; in two months he succeeded, by comparing the Greek and Demotic texts, in identifying all the proper names in the latter that occurred in the Greek; he recognized the alphabetically written words for 'temples' and 'Greeks' in their correct Coptic forms and the pronominal suffix for 'him'; these results mark an important step in the decipherment of the Demotic version and were communicated in the famous *Lettre à M. de Sacy* in 1802, in which Åkerblad also showed that he recognized the cardinal numbers in the hieroglyphic text; apart from some smaller notes in later years, Åkerblad did not continue his Egyptological researches; that he made little progress after this seems to have been due to his belief that as the words he deciphered were alphabetically written all Demotic writing was exclusively so, but he had identified sixteen names and words in all; he is known to have collected various antiquities including Egyptian, which were probably sold in Rome; he died suddenly in Rome, 8 Feb. 1819.

Budge, *Mummy*, 2nd ed., 139; C. Callmer, *Johan David Åkerblad. Ett bidrag till hans biografi*, Lychnos, 1952, Uppsala, 1952, 130 ff.; Gardiner, *Grammar*, 3rd ed. 12; Hartleben, i. 108, 125, 364-72; Hilmy, i, 26; B. J. Peterson, 'Swedish Travellers in Egypt during the period 1700-1850', *Opuscula Atheniensia* 7 (1967), 12-13; *Svenska Män och Kvinnor* 8, 494-5; Lamy, 303-6; È. Gran-Aymerich, *Dictionnaire biographique d'archéologie 1798-1945*, 2001, incorporated in *Les Chercheurs de passé 1798-1945*, 2007, 557-8; F. Thomasson, *The Life of J. D. Åkerblad: Egyptian Decipherment and Orientalism in Revolutionary Times*, 2013.

AKMAR (prev. ANDERSSON), Ernst Teodor (1877-1957)
Swedish Egyptologist; born at Atvideberg, 7 Sept. 1877, son of Alfred A. and Hilma Sofia Gustavusdotter, he was a student of K. Piehl (q.v.); he was lecturer at the University of Uppsala (1904-17, 1924-42; after Piehl's death in 1904 he was editor of the journal *Sphinx* for a number of years, and contributed articles and reviews to it under the names Andersson, and (from 1915) Akmar; among his principal published works should be mentioned *Ausgewählte Bemerkungen über den bohairischen Dialekt im Pentateuch Koptisch*, 1904, under Andersson; *Les bandelettes de momie du Musée Victoria à Upsala et Le Livre des morts*, 1932-9, under Akmar; he died in Uppsala, 10 Dec. 1955.

Inf. B. J. Peterson; *Sphinx* 19 (1915), 96; *Svensk Biografiskt Lexikon* 1, 344-5 (portr.).

ALBERT, Honoré Théodoric Paul Joseph d', Duc de Luynes (1802-1867)
French collector and archaeological patron; he was born Paris, 15 Dec. 1802, son of Charles Marie Paul André d'A. Duc de Luynes and Françoise Marie Felicité Ermessinde Raymond de Narbonne-Pelet; he formed a

collection at Château Dampierre, mainly consisting of Greek and Roman antiquities, but he bought a collection of Egyptian antiquities in 1863, some of which were forgeries; he visited Egypt and Palestine in 1863-4, and met de Rougé (q.v.) in Egypt; he employed Mariette (q.v.) to excavate the Sphinx to ascertain whether it was the tomb of Harmais as stated by Pliny; he was a generous patron of excavation, and his name is associated with the Papyrus Luynes, part of which he gave to the Louvre (3661) and part to the Bibliothèque Nationale (139-40); he died in Rome, 15 Dec. 1867.

Bibl. Ég. 18, pp. lviii, 125, 131; 21, p. lxxv; Lepsius, 53, 55, 98; *Rec. Trav.* i, 89; Tristram, *Land of Israel*, 506, 514; È. Gran-Aymerich, *Dictionnaire biographique d'archéologie 1798-1945*, 2001, incorporated in *Les Chercheurs de passé 1798-1945*, 2007, 956-8.

ALBERT D'AILLY, Louis Marie Joseph Romain, d', Duc de Picquigny et Chaulnes (1741-1792)
French nobleman and traveller; he was born 18/24 Nov. 1741, son of Michel Ferdinand d'A., Duc de P. et C. and Anne Josèphe Bonnier de la Mosson; after a disreputable youth, he embarked on a tour to Egypt in 1765 where he visited Saqqara and engaged the services of Davison (q.v.); they returned to Europe together and Davison later accused him of stealing various plans of Saqqara which he later published as his own; Fellow of the Royal Society of London; he acquired at least two Egyptian objects which were published by the Society of Dilettanti in *Specimens of Antient Sculpture* Vol. I (London, 1809), pls. I-III, now in the British Museum (EA 60093 and 97); he wrote a pamphlet *Mémoire sur la véritable entrée du Monument Égyptien*, 1777, reprinted 1783; he died at Château de Chaulnes, 23/4 Oct. 1792.

DBF 8, 850; C. Leventhal, *Ducs et Pairs et Duchés-Pairies Laïques à l'Époque Moderne (1519-1790)*, 518-9.

ALBRIGHT, William Foxwell (1891-1971)
American philologist, archaeologist and Semitic scholar; born in Coquimbo, Chile, 24 May 1891, son of Revd Wilbur Finley A., a Methodist minister and missionary in S. America, and Zephine Viola Foxwell his wife; as a child he had a hard struggle, being educationally further set back with the physical handicaps of bad eyesight and a crippled left hand, the former defect hampering his epigraphic work and preventing his becoming a full time Assyriologist as he would have liked; despite these disabilities he became a scholar of the highest distinction and the 'Doyen' of Palestinian Archaeology in his later years; AB Upper Iowa University, 1912; Principal of High School Menno, S. Dakota; PhD Oriental Seminary Johns Hopkins University, 1916, his dissertation on *The Assyrian Deluge Epic* remaining unpublished; he went to Jerusalem where he was Thayer Fellow at the American School of Oriental Research, 1919; Acting Director, 1920; Director, 1921-9; Professor of Semitic languages J. H. Univ. 1929-58; Professor Emeritus of Semitic languages J. H. Univ., 1958-71; editor of *BASOR* for 38 years, 1931-68; Vice-President and Trustee for over 30 years; it is impossible to list here all the achievements of a man whose activity embraced so many fields in addition to Egyptology, and who acquired an unparalleled series of hon. degrees and awards from Universities and learned societies throughout the world, readers are therefore referred to the references given below; among the 30 hon. degrees he held were hon. Litt. D. Yale, 1950-1, and Harvard, 1961-2; he married Ruth Norton, 1921, a fellow student at J. H. Univ., who took a doctorate in Sanskrit; the part played by Albright in the establishment of systematic archaeological work in Palestine was fundamental, and he conducted what are now historic excavations at Tell el-Ful, north of Jerusalem, Shiloh, Bethel, and especially Tell Beit Mirsim,, 1926-32, where he discovered in stratigraphical context a then rare but important pottery type, and whose other occupational phases became standard site terminology for nearly 30 years; his interests were very wide and he accompanied the Arabian expedition of Wendell Phillips as Chief Archaeologist, 1948-50; Jordan Lecturer Univ. of London,1965; he visited Israel as a state guest and was presented with a large *Festschrift*, 1969; his first article related to the Nile Valley and was on the Elephantine papyri, 1911, and all his working life he maintained a keen interest in ancient Egypt so that in his works on Egyptological subjects and references abound; his bibliography numbered over 12 books as well as others on which he collaborated, and in addition reached the total of more than 1,000 other items, including articles, critical notes, reviews, notices and essays; from this may be selected, *The Vocalization of the Egyptian Syllabic Orthography*, 1934, a standard work in which he had the advice of Gunn (q.v.), and which if not wholly accepted by Egyptologists was nevertheless an important contribution to a very difficult subject; *The Archaeology of Palestine*, 1949, a classic and the work for which he is probably best known; *The Proto-Sinaitic Inscriptions and their Decipherment*, another book in which he broke new ground; his last major work was *Yahweh and The Gods of Canaan; a Historical Analysis of Two Contrasting Faiths*, the Jordan Lectures, 1968; he also contributed articles to *JEA* and among numerous other journals a number relating to Egyptian subjects in *BASOR*; he died in Baltimore, Maryland, 19 Sept. 1971.

History, Archaeology and Christian Humanism, W. F. Albright, contains autobiographical sketch. *AfO* 24 (1973), 240-1 (portr.) (E. Weidner); *BASOR* No 205 (Feb. 1972), 3-13 (portr.) (D. N. Freedman); No. 200 (bibl.); *BSFE* No. 62 (Oct. 1972), 4-5 (anon.); *Journ. N. W. Semitic Languages* 2 (1972); *PEQ* 104 (1972), 75 (O. Tufnell); *WW*

(1971), 32; H. Orlinsky, *An indexed bibliography of W. F. Albright,,* 1941; D. N. Freedman, *The Published Works of William Foxwell Albright: a Comprehensive Bibliography,* 1975; *Biblical Archaeologist* 56 (1993), 1-45; È. Gran-Aymerich, *Dictionnaire biographique d'archéologie 1798-1945,* 2001, incorporated in *Les Chercheurs de passé 1798-1945,* 2007, 559-60.

ALDERSEY, Laurence (*fl.* 1546-1597)
English traveller and merchant of London; he was born at Aldersey Hall, Sporstow, Cheshire *c.*1546 son of Thomas A. of Chester and Cecily Garnet; he made two journeys to the Levant, his accounts being preserved in Hakluyt; he reached Egypt in 1586 and visited all the places of interest around Alexandria and Cairo; he died about 1597/8.

ODNB 1, 611-12; *DNB* i, 242.

ALDRED, Cyril (1914-1991)
British Egyptologist and art historian; he was born in London, 19 Feb. 1914, son of Frederick A., a civil servant in the Post Office, and Lilian Ethel Underwood; he studied at the Sloane School, London where his interest in art was fostered; after a year at King's College, London, studying English, he transferred to the Courtauld Institute of Art, University of London; BA, 1936; he was appointed Assistant Keeper in the Department of Art and Ethnography in the Royal Scottish Museum, Edinburgh in charge of the archaeological and ethnographical collections, 1937; he served in the Scottish Education Office and Royal Air Force (Signals) 1942-6; he spent a year as Associate Curator, Dept. of Egyptian Art, Metropolitan Museum of Art, New York, 1955-6; Keeper, Dept. of Art and Archaeology, Royal Scottish Museum, 1961-74; Member of the Committee of the Egypt Exploration Society, 1959-76; Fellow of the Royal Society of Edinburgh, 1978; he specialized in the study of Egyptian art and jewellery and was a leading authority on the reign of Akhenaten; he greatly added to the Egyptian collection of the Royal Scottish Museum; his publications included *Old Kingdom Art in Ancient Egypt,* 1949; *Middle Kingdom Art in Ancient Egypt,* 1950; *New Kingdom Art in Ancient Egypt during the Eighteenth Dynasty 1590-1315 B.C.,* 1951; all three reissued as *The Development of Ancient Egyptian Art,* 1952; *The Egyptians,* 1961, 2nd ed. 1984; *Egypt to the End of the Old Kingdom,* 1965; *Akhenaten, Pharaoh of Egypt - a New Study,* 1968; *Egypt: The Amarna Period and the End of the Eighteenth Dynasty,* 1971, later published in Vol. II, Part 2 of *The Cambridge Ancient History,* 1975; *Jewels of the Pharaohs,* 1971; *Tutankhamun's Egypt,* 1972; *Akhenaten and Nefertiti,* 1973; *The Temple of Dendur,* 1978; *Tutankhamun, Craftsmanship in Gold in the Reign of the King,* 1979; *Le Monde égyptien. Les Pharaons,* with J. Leclant et al, 3 vols., 1979-80; *Egyptian Art in the Days of the Pharaohs, 3100-320 B.C.,* 1980; and *Akhenaten: King of Egypt,* 1988; he died in Edinburgh, 23 June 1991.

Who's Who 1990; *The Times* 6 July 1991; *KMT* (Fall, 1991), 23-6, 66 (J. Ruffle and L. Green); *JEA* 78 (1992), 258-266 (portr.) (T.G.H. James); *ODNB* 1, 628-9.

ALESSANDRI, Giovanni Maria degli (1765-1828)
Italian scholar; he was born in Florence 8 Sept. 1765, son of Cosimo degli A., a Florentine patrician and Virginia Capponi; he was Viec-President of the Florentine Acad. of Fine Arts, 1796; President, 1814; in 1815 he visited Paris to recover stolen art treasures; he and his colleague Zannoni (q.v.) were friendly to Champollion (q.v.) and gave him facilities for studying the Egyptian Antiquities in the museum at Florence; he died in Florence, 20 Sept. 1828.

Bio Univ 1, 395; Garollo, *Diz. Biogr. Univ.*; Champollion, i, 234, 236, 238; F. Cardini, *I "Libro d'Oro" della Nobilità Fiorentina e Fiesolana,* 1993, 81 (no. 172).

ALEXANDER, George (1810-1885)
British traveller and architect; in Egypt and Nubia sometime between 1831 and 1837; he exhibited at the Royal Academy in 1837 a watercolour of *The Amphitheatre at Pola* and in 1839 a watercolour of *The Ruins of the Temple of Kadassah, Nubia, from a sketch taken on the spot*; on 27 April 1840 he read at the Institute of Architects (now RIBA) a paper on Egyptian Architecture, the chief object of which was to apportion the various temples remaining to their several periods, and to classify as far as possible the changes observable in the style, their copy of his talk is now lost as is the copy he gave to the Royal Society of Arts having given the same lecture there; in 1841 when G. B. Greenough presented *Illustrations of Cairo* by Robert Hay to the RIBA Library 'Mr Alexander remarked on the various styles of architecture which are to be found in that city – Moorish, Turkish and a relaxed Italian style', obviously he was speaking from first-hand knowledge; in 1842 Bonomi (q.v.) on his way to Egypt with Lepsius (q.v.) sent a letter to Alexander, because he 'has been in Egypt and is therefore a very proper person to conduct the whole affair', transferring to him 'the business of the Egyptian structure' of Marshall's or Temple Mill, Holbeck, a building based on the Temple of Horus at Edfu, and to work alongside the structural engineer

James Combe [Temple Mill was not designed by Joseph Bonomi (q.v.), Ignatius Bonomi, or David Roberts (q.v.)]; he married Elizabeth-Maria Hicks in 1845 and bought Westrop House, Highworth, Wiltshire where he retired from architecture to pursue his interest in archaeology; he exhibited at the Town Hall Swindon in August 1860 a collection of Nubian shields, dresses, purses, charms, spear heads, knives, etc., he must have collected during his travels; he died at Westrop House, Sept. 1885.

Inf. N. Cooke.

ALEXANDER, (*Sir*) James Edward (1803-1885)
British Army General; he was born in Powis, Clackmannanshire, 16 Oct. 1803, son of Edward A. and Catherine Glas; Honourable East India Company Army, 1820; British Army, 1825; he saw much active service, including the Russo-Turkish war, 1817, and Crimea, 1855-6; he retired, 1881; he was largely responsible for the preservation and transport to England of Cleopatra's Needle in 1877, on which he published a descriptive work in 1879; he died in Ryde, Isle of Wight, 2 April 1885.

ODNB 1, 679-80; *DNB Suppl.* i , 31; Hilmy, i, 24.

ALEXANDER, John Amyas (1922-2010)
British archaeologist; he was born in Preston, Brighton 27 Jan. 1922, son of Charles A., who died in 1922 and Lily Blackman, a school teacher; he was educated at Varndeur School, 1933-40 and Borough Road College, 1940-1; he joined the army in 1941 and then the Indian Army, 1942; Captain, 1944; Major, 1945; he then studied history at Pembroke College, Cambridge, 1946-8; he became a teacher in the Sudan Education Service, 1948-53; he visited the excavation of Amara West by Shinnie (q.v.) and helped to prepare a register of archaeological sites, surveying from Karima to Wadi Halfa; he taught archaeology at Hantub and Ahlia and wrote the first school textbook on Sudanese archaeology; on his return to England, he retrained as a prehistorian at the Institute of Archaeology, 1953-5 and Pembroke College, 1955-8; PhD, 1958; Hon PhD, University of Khartoum, 1999; he became a tutor in the Department of Extra-Mural Studies, University of Cambridge, 1958-68 and then at the University of London, 1968-76, before returning to Cambridge as a lecturer in archaeology, 1976-83; Visiting lecturer, University of Ghana, 1967, University of Ibadan, 1971; External Examiner, University of Khartoum, 1977-9; he took part in the excavations at Amara West, 1948; Wad Medan, 1949; and Debeira West with Shinnie, 1963; and was in charge of the work at Qasr Ibrim, 1980-6; he surveyed Qalat Sai, 1996; FSA, 1958; Fellow of St. John's College, 1976-2006; he founded and edited the Cambridge Monographs in African Archaeology, 1980; he helped to found the Sudan Archaeological Research Society; vice-chairman, 1991-2001; he also served on the executive committees of the Egypt Exploration Society and the British Council of Archaeology; vice-pres. of the latter, 1998; he was one of the directors of the journal *Antiquity*, 1977-82; a volume of studies in his honour was published in *Azania* 39 (2004); among his published works, with W. Y. Adams, was *Qasr Ibrim. The Ottoman Period*, 2019; he died in Cambridge, 17 Aug. 2010.

Azania 39 (2004), 3-6 (P. Shinnie), 7-10 (G. and S. Wahida), 33-41 (bibl.); *Times* obit, 3 Sept. 2010; *Azania* 45 (2010), 233-4 (T. Insoll); *Sudan & Nubia* 15 (2011), 146-7 (portr.) (P. Rose).

ALEXANDER, William (1767-1816)
British artist; he was born in Maidstone, 10 April 1767, son of Henry A., a coach builder, and his wife Elizabeth; he trained as a student at the RA; Keeper of Prints, British Museum, 1808-16; Prof. of Drawing at Marlow Military Academy; he made drawings of the Egyptian antiquities in the British Museum collected by Napoleon's Commission, which were engraved by Medland and published in 21 plates, 1805-7; he died in Maidstone, 23 July, 1816.

ODNB 1, 645-6; *DNB* i. 281; Hilmy, i, 24.

ALEXANIAN, Nicole (1965-2016)
German archaeologist; she was born 6 Jan. 1965; she was educated in Egyptology at the University of Heidelberg; PhD, 2001; she joined the DAI in Cairo and excavated at Dahshur from 1988; project director from 2005; apart from articles, she published *Dahschur* II, 1999; she died 28 April 2016.

Al-Ahram 8 Sept. 2016 (Z. Hawass) (portr.)

ALI ABD El-HAJ EL-GABRI (*c.* 1840-1932)
Egyptian antiquities dealer; he was based in Kafr el-Haram near Giza and until 1896 was in partnership with Farag Ismain; he sold manuscipts to Freer (q.v.) and Schubart (q.v.); his business remained in the family for

11

two further generations and his grandson had a shop in Cairo; his cousin Ali Gabri (c.1833-1904), who worked for Howard Vyse (q.v.), Smyth (q.v.) and Petrie (q.v.), was also an antiquities dealer as was his son Muhammad.

F. Hagen and K. Ryholt, *The Antiquities Trade in Egypt 1880-1930*, 2017, 192-6, 245-6.

ALLBERRY, Charles Robert Cecil Augustine (1911-1943)
British Coptologist; he was born Sydenham, 9 Nov. 1911, son of William Henry A., insurance administrator, and Hilda Gertrude Bonnet; educated Christ's College, Cambridge, MA and first Lady Budge Fellow, 1936-9; he edited and published the Chester Beatty Manichean MS, and other Coptic texts, winning for himself a high reputation as a Coptic scholar; he also published articles in *JEA* of which he became the editor in 1939; the outbreak of war interrupted a brilliant career and in 1940 he joined the Royal Air Force, attaining the rank of Flying Officer; he was killed in action near Nederwort, Holland, 3 April 1943.

BMQ 28 (1964), 60; *JEA* 25 (1939), 221; *The Times*, 11 May 1943; P. Lewis, *Charles Allberry, A Portrait*, 1984; *The Coptic Encyclopedia* 1, 104 (A. S. Atiya).

ALLEMANT, Eugene Desiré Philippe (1837-?)
French dealer in antiquities; he was born at Lodève, 19 March 1837, son of Antoine Eugène A. and Catherine Guillaume; he was dragoman to Sultan Abd-ul-Aziz until he was deposed in 1876; being frequently in Egypt between about 1872 and 1885, he carried out excavations and purchased antiquities; a collection of antiquities was bought from him by the Antwerp Museum in 1879, and further pieces by the Louvre in 1881-7; in 1878 he published *Collection d'Antiquités Égyptiennes: description historique et religieuse des monuments découverts sur les lieux par l'auteur*, in which 832 objects are described; the sale took place in London, 9-10 May 1878, although his business was carried on in Paris; a further sale took place in Paris, 3-4 Dec. 1883.

Revue de l'Art 43,170; Wilbour, 7, 253; Lugt, 38372 and 43394; M.-P. Vanlathem, 'Die Egyptische verzameling E. Allemant in het Vleeshuis te Antwerpen', *Museumleven Jaarboek*, 1983, 82-97 and in *Van Nijl tot Schelde, Stad Antwerpen Culturell Jaarboek*, 1991, 105-8; *Journal des Savants* (1992), 161.

ALLEN, (Thomas) George (1885-1969)
American Egyptologist; he was born in Rockford, Illinois, 11 Aug. 1885, son of Harry A. and Ella Caroline Powell; he was educated at Beloit College; BA, 1909 and then studied under Breasted (q.v.) at the University of Chicago; PhD, 1915; Secretary of the Haskell Oriental Museum, 1917; Secretary of the Oriental Institute, Chicago, 1919; Editorial Secretary, 1927-1950; Assistant Curator of the Field Museum; his field of study concentrated on Egyptian mortuary literature; his publications, apart from articles, consist of *A Handbook of the Egyptian Collection of the Art Institute of Chicago*, 1923; *Egyptian Stelae in the Field Museum of Natural History*, 1936; *Occurrences of Pyramid Texts with Cross Indexes of these and other Egyptian Mortuary Texts*, 1950; *The Egyptian Book of the Dead Documents in the Oriental Institute Museum*, 1960; *The Book of the Dead or Going Forth by Day*, 1974; he died in Bradenton, Florida, 21 March 1969.

The Oriental Institute Report for 1968/9, 4-5; inf. from L. Bell.

ALLIOT, Maurice Ferdinand (1903-1960)
French Egyptologist; born at Ivry-sur-Seine, 24 Sept. 1903, son of Antoine A. and Blanche Renée Cognon; he studied at the Lycée Charlemagne and the Lycée Louis-le-Grand, entering the École Normale Supérieure 1923, where he attended papyrology classes under P. Jouguet (q.v.); his diploma subject was on *La Syntaxe des papyrus de Zénon*, 1926; he then studied Egyptology under Moret (q.v.), Drioton (q.v.), and Sottas (q.v.), and grammar and philology with Lefebvre (q.v.); he became a 'pensionnaire' at the Institut français d'archéologie in Cairo in 1930, and was sent to assist with the work at Deir el-Medina and Abu Rawash, 1931; he excavated at Edfu, 1931-33, and dug the great *kom* beside the temple at its summit and base, finding below the Roman and Greek towns a late Egyptian settlement and also an Old Kingdom cemetery, including the tomb of the vizier Isi who had been deified shortly after his death; these important discoveries were the subject of a lengthy article in *BIFAO* 37 (1937-38), which included also the texts relating to this cult; Alliot gained his doctoral thesis with the subject which later became his great interest, the scenes and texts relating to the worship of Horus in the great temple at Edfu, 1945; this was published as a long work in two volumes, *Le Culte d'Horus à Edfou à l'époque des Ptolémées*, 1945-54, which won him the Maspero prize; in 1937 Alliot was made Professor of Egyptology and Ancient Oriental History at the University of Lyons; in 1953 a chair of Egyptology was created for him at the Faculté des Lettres in Paris; before his death he was preparing a number of large-scale studies and other works which he was unable to complete; he died in Sceaux, 22 Oct. 1960.

AfO 20 (1963), 309-10 (J. Leclant); *BIFAO* 61 (1962), 7-10 (F. Daumas); *Rev. Arch.* 1861, 50-2 (J. Sainte Fare Garnot); *Rev. d'Ég.* 13 (1961), 7-8 (J. Sainte Fare Garnot); È. Gran-Aymerich, *Dictionnaire biographique d'archéologie 1798-1945*, 2001, incorporated in *Les Chercheurs de passé 1798-1945*, 2007, 561.

ALMAGRO BASCH, Martin (1911-1984)
Spanish archaeologist and prehistorian; he was born in Tramacastilla, 17 April 1911, son of Doroteo A. and Josefa Basch; he was educated at the Universities of Valencia and Madrid; PhD, 1935 in Library Sciences, Archives, and Museology; he later studied prehistory at Vienna and Marburg; Director of the Museo Arqueológico de Barcelona, 1939; Professor of Prehistory at the University of Barcelona, 1940; Professor at the University of Madrid, 1955; Director of the Museo Nacional Arqueológico, Madrid, 1968-1981; he excavated extensively in Spain, Italy, North Africa, and the Middle East; he was the founder and director of the Spanish Mission in Egypt which undertook the excavation of Heracleopolis Magna; he was director of the Spanish Archaeological Mission during the Nubian campaign, 1960-66 and edited the eleven volumes of reports, 1963-70; four volumes of studies in his honour *Homenaje al Prof. Martin Almagro Basch* were published in 1983; apart from articles, his Egyptological publications included three Nubian archaeological reports *Las necrópolis de Masmás, Alto Egipto*, with others, 1964; *La Necrópolis meroítica de Nag Gamus*, 1965; *Estudios de Arte rupestre Nubio*, with others, 1968; *El templo de Debod, 1971*; and *La tumba de Nefertari*, with others, 1978; he died in Madrid, 28 Aug. 1984.

Homenaje al Prof. Martin Almagro Basch, I, 1983 17-20, 21-38 (bibl.); *Italica* 17 (1984); inf. Prof. Martin Almagro Gorbea; È. Gran-Aymerich, *Dictionnaire biographique d'archéologie 1798-1945*, 2001, incorporated in *Les Chercheurs de passé 1798-1945*, 2007, 562-3.

ALMÁSY, László Ede (1895-1951)
Hungarian explorer; he was born in Borostyánkö (now Bernstein, Austria), son of György A., an explorer, orientalist and ethnologist, and Ilona Pittoni; he was educated at Graz and Berrow School, Eastbourne; he served with the Austrio-Hungarian air force during World War I; he later was trained at the Eastbourne Technical Institute and joined the Eastbourne Flying Club; from 1921 he worked for the Austrian firm Steyr Automobile during which he visited Egypt and became interested in desert travel; in the period 1929-35 he organized and led seven expeditions to the uncharted central parts of the Libyan Desert; in 1932 he and L. di Capoiacco discovered the prehistoric paintings of Ain Dua at Jebel Uweinat; in 1933 he found the paintings of Wadi Sora (the Cave of the Swimmers) at Gilf Kebir; during World War II he served as an intelligence officer for the Germans; he was tried and acquitted in Hungary for collaboration after the war and then escaped to Egypt allegedly with British help; he was named director of the Desert Research Institute in 1950; he published *Az ismeretlen Szahara*, 1934; Fr. ed., 1936; German ed. *Unbekannte Sahara*, 1939; *Recentes Explorations dans le Desert Libyque*, 1936; he died in Salzburg, 22 March 1951.

S. Kelly, *The Hunt for Zarzura*, 2002; J. Bierman, *The Secret Life of Laszlo Almasy*, 2004; E. Sensenig-Dabbous in *Comparative Studies of South Asia, Africa and the Middle East* 24 (2004), 163-180; G. Vörös, *Egyptian Temple Architecture*, 2007, 31-41; inf. A. Zboray.

ALPINI, Prospero (1553-1616)
Italian physician and botanist; he was born at Marostica, Veneto, 23 Nov. 1553, son of Francesco A., a doctor, and Bartolomea Tarsia; he studied medicine at Padua qualifying in 1578; he accompanied the Venetian consul, Giorgio Emo to Egypt as medical adviser, and remained there for three years 1581-4; during this time he studied the flora and noted many details, his most important work in this field being his observations on the pollination of the date palm; his account of the coffee plant growing in Cairo is said to be the first that was published in Europe; he did not confine his account to botanical subjects but visited and climbed the Great Pyramid, which he estimated as 125 paces high and 150 square; he also stated that in 1584 Ibrahim Pasha, Viceroy of Egypt, thinking great treasures still existed within it, enlarged the small entrance and intended to blow up the whole structure by filling it with gunpowder, but was dissuaded by Signor Emo, who said it would endanger Cairo; he also described the entrance and ascending passage, the King's Chamber and sarcophagus, went down the well for 70 feet and claimed he saw two further passages; he thought the Sphinx was an oracle; his account appeared under the name Prosper Alpinus; he published among other works, *De Medicina Aegyptiorum Libri IV*, 1591; *De Plantis Aegypti Liber Accessit etiam liber de Balsamo*, 2 vols 1592; *Historia Aegyptiaca Naturalis*, 1735; all three have been published in a French translation by IFAO 1979-80; in 1594 he was made first Professor of Botany in Europe at the University of Padua and in 1603 Superintendent of the Botanical Gardens; here he cultivated many Egyptian plants in the University Garden; he died in Padua, 23 Nov. 1616.

EB i, 670; Hilmy, i. 32; Vyse, ii; *DBDI* 2, 529-31; A. Silotti, *Padua e Egitto*, 1987, 19-26; Lamy, 86-91.

ALT, Albrecht (1883-1956)
German orientalist and Biblical scholar; born Stübach, 20 Sept. 1883, son of Revd Friedrich A. and Caroline née Alt; he studied theology and oriental subjects at Erlangen and Leipzig together with Biblical archaeology at the German Evangelical Institute; at the end of the First World War he was teaching at Basel and was appointed Professor at Leipzig in 1922; he also became Director of the Palestine Institute; he wrote *Pharao Tuthmosis III in Palästina*, 1914; a dissertation *Israel und Ägypten* 1909; *Die Landnahme der Israeliten in Palästina*, 1925; *Die Staatenbildung der Israeliten in Palästina*, 1930; he was interested in the contacts between Egypt and Palestine and wrote many articles on this subject in *ZÄS* discussing among other things the Execration Text place-names; *Die älteste Schilderung Palästinas im Lichte neuer Funde* was a commentary on the Story of Sinuhe, 1941; he produced an important study *Der Herkunft der Hyksos in neuer Sicht*, 1954; he died in Leiden, 24 April 1956.

AfO 17 (1954-1956), 482-4 (portr.) (K. Elliger); *Bulletin of the Israel Exploration Soc.* 20 (1956), 60 (B. Mazar); *FuF* 30 (1956), 286-7 (L. Rost); *Journal of Biblical Literature* 75 (1956), 169-73 (W. F. Albright); *Die Welt des Orients* 10 (1957), 304-6 (M. Noth); *ZÄS* 81 (1956), i-iii (portr.) (S Morenz); *Zeitschrift des Deutschen Palästina-Vereins* 72 (1956), 1-8 (portr.) (M Noth); *Wer ist's* 1935.

ALTOUNIAN, Joseph Alexandre (1890-1954)
Armenian-French dealer in antiquities; he was born in Constantinople, 27 Dec. 1889, son of Pierre A. and Maria Sarian-Tchoadjian; his family fled to Egypt to escape anti-Armenian pogroms; he moved to Paris in 1908, where he was a friend of Picasso and Van Dongen, whom he took to Egypt, and was later sketched by Modigliani; he dealt initially in antiquities and modern art; he visited Egypt several times between 1910-13, collecting antiquities for the French sculptor Auguste Rodin (q. v.); he was a purchaser at the Amherst and MacGregor sales (q. q. v.); he married the dealer Henriette Lorbet (9 June 1893–12 April 1986) in 1924; they spent time in Cairo before setting up a gallery in Mâcon, France, 1937, which also dealt in Mediaeval art; he sold significant material to American clients, often in collaboration with Joseph Brummer (q. v.); the Altounian-Lourbet Gallery's photographic archives are in the Getty Museum; he died in a car accident at Mâcon, 25 Sept. 1954.

Family archival information, per Nicole Cruz-Rousset; *Les donateurs du Louvre*, 134; *Grove Dictionary of Art* X, 91; B. Garnier, *Rodin: Antiquity is my youth, a sculptor's collection*, 2002, 20; Amis de Max Jacob, *60e anniversaire de la mort de Max Jacob: exposition*, 2004, 25; B. Garnier, *Rodin, Freud, Collectionneurs: la passion à l'œuvre*, 2009, 70, 220; inf. T. Hardwick.

AMEILHON, (*Abbé*) **Hubert Pascal** (1730-1811)
French scholar and librarian; he was born in Paris, 6 April 1730, son of Pierre Pascal A., a master tailor and Marie Cécile Rigaud; he entered the Church but renounced his calling shortly after becoming an abbé; academically an interest in ancient Egypt was with him from the beginning and he won the Academy prize with a famous *Mémoire sur le commerce et la navigation des Égyptiens sous le règne des Ptolemées*, 1762, publ. 1766; he had a long and highly successful career as librarian in Paris; he played quite an important part in work on the Rosetta Stone, for when J. J. Marcel (q.v.) made some copies of it and casts of the inscription which were brought to France by General Dugua, the Institut National requested a translation of the Greek text as a preliminary to decipherment from Ameilhon; in so doing he was among the very first to work on that historic document, thus paving the way for all the later great discoveries; he published *Éclaircissements sur l'Inscription Grecque du Monument trouvé à Rosette, contenant un Décret des Prêtres de l'Egypte en l'honneur de Ptolemée Epiphane, le cinquième des rois Ptolemées*, 1803; he died in Paris, 13 Nov. 1811.

DBF 2, 580-3 (M. Barroux); Hilmy, i, 33; Iversen, 127; H. Dufresne, *Le bibliothécaire Hubert-Pascal Ameilhon*, 1962.

AMÉLINEAU, Émile Clément (1850-1915)
French Egyptologist and Coptologist; he was born at La Chaize-Giraud, Vendée, 28 Aug. 1850, son of Tranquile Clément A. and Euphrasie Henriette Aglae Michou, and was trained for the Church, being ordained in the Diocese of Rennes; he was attracted to Egyptology by Felix Robiou (q.v.) whose lectures he attended; he then studied Egyptian and Coptic in Paris under Maspero (q.v.) and Grébaut (q.v.), 1877-83; he studied Coptic documents in Oxford, London, and Leiden, 1881-2; in 1883 he joined Miss. Arch. in Cairo where he remained four years; he seceded from the Church, 1887; he excavated at Abydos, 1894-8, where he was the first person to clear the royal tombs; the results of this excavation were most important, but his methods were unscientific and provoked severe criticism from Maspero, and also Petrie (q.v.) who followed him on the site; the antiquities he collected were sold in Paris, 8-9 Feb. 1904, after being inadequately published; he was lecturer, 1887-1903, and later Professor of the History of Religions in the École des Hautes Études, 1903-1915; a considerable number of Egyptian antiquities from his own excavations and other sources were deposited in the Musée Municipal at Châteaudun; his best work was in the field of Coptic studies and he published *Pistis Sophia* and the Bruce Papyrus, as well as a great mass of

Coptic texts contributed to *Rec. Trav., ZÄS*, and other journals; his principal works were, *Essai sur le gnosticisme, ses développements et son origine égyptienne ...*, 1887, his doctoral thesis being on this subject; *Contes et romans de l'Égypte chrétienne*, 2 vols 1888; *Un évêque de Keft au VIIe siècle*, 1889; *Les moines égyptiens; vie de Schnoudi*, 1889; *Monuments pour servir à l'histoire de l'Égypte chrétienne au 4e siècle*, 3 Pts. 1889, 1894, 1895; *Les actes des martyrs de l'Église Copte: étude critique*, 1890; *La géographie de l'Égypte à l'époque copte*, 1893; *Essai sur l'évolution historique et philosophique des idées morales dans l'Égypte ancienne*, 1895; *Histoire de la sépulture et des funérailles dans l'ancienne Égypte*, 2 vols., 1896; *Mission Amélineau: les nouvelles fouilles d'Abydos*, 1895-1898, 1899-1905, 3 vols., in 4; *Le tombeau d'Osiris: monographie de la découverte faite en 1897-1898*, 1899; he died in Châteaudun, 12 Jan. 1915.

DBF 2, 590-2 (M Prevost); Lugt, 6897; *Rev. arch.* 24 (1914), 333-4 (S. Reinach); *JEA* 2 (1915) 188 (J.O.); *The Coptic Encyclopedia* 1, 112 (A. S. Atiya); *Archaéonil* 17 (2007), 27-38 (portr.); inf. R. S. Merrillees; É. Gran-Aymerich, *Dictionnaire biographique d'archéologie 1798-1945*, 2001, incorporated in *Les Chercheurs de passé 1798-1945*, 2007, 564.

AMER, Mustafa (1896-1973)
Egyptian geographer and archaeologist; he was born at Ismailia, 16 June 1896, son of Abdel Aziz Amer, clerk in the ministry of Waqfs; he was educated at the Higher Training College, Cairo, diploma in education, 1917; he then studied geography at the University of Liverpool, 1917-1923; BA, 1921; MA, 1923; he was appointed lecturer and later professor of geography at the University of Cairo; Vice-rector of the University of Alexandria 1942-6; professor at the University of Cairo, 1946; Dean of the Arts Faculty 1948; Vice-rector of the University of Cairo 1948; Rector of the University of Alexandria, 1950; Under-secretary of State in the Ministry of National Education 1950; President of the Société Archéologique d'Alexandrie, 1952-4; Director-General of the Egyptian Antiquities Service, 1953-6, being the first Egyptian to hold this post; first Director of the Documentation Centre in Cairo which was founded in May 1955; President of the Egyptian Geographic Society; later adviser to the University of Riyadh; he undertook excavations at the prehistoric sites of Maadi 1930-5, Heliopolis 1950, and Wadi Digla 1950-53; his publications include *Stone Age Finds from the Kharga Oasis* 1932 with O. Menghin; *Excavations of the Egyptian University on the Neolithic Site at Maadi* 1932-6 with O. Menghin; and reports of the Wadi Digla excavations in the *Bulletin of the Faculty of Arts Fouad I University* vol. xv; he died March 1973.

Gött. Misz. 76 (1984), 82 (H. Attiatalla); *Les Grands Découvertes Archéologiques de 1954* in *La Revue du Caire* 33 no. 175 (1955), xi-xii; inf. from the University of Liverpool; R. Lackany, *La Société Archéologique d'Alexandrie*, 1973, 154-6 (portr.); inf. G. Mokhtar.

AMHERST, *(Baroness)*, Mary Rothes Margaret Cecil (1857-1919)
British traveller; she was born at Didlington, Norfolk, 25 April 1857; eldest daughter of Lord Amherst (q,v,) and Margaret Susan Mitford; she married Lord William Cecil, 1885; she frequently visited Egypt and excavated at Aswan, 1903-4; many antiquities found or acquired by her were incorporated in her father's collection; she published excavation reports in *ASAE*; also *Bird Notes from the Nile*, 1904; she succeeded as Baroness Amherst on the death of her father in 1909; she died in London, 21 Dec. 1919; generally known as Lady William Cecil.

Newberry Corr; *WWW* ii, 20.

AMHERST *(Baron)*, William Amhurst Tyssen-Amherst, 1st Baron Amherst of Hackney (1835-1909)
British collector and patron of excavation in Egypt; he was born at Narford Hall, Norfolk, 25 April 1835, eldest son of William George Daniel Tyssen and Mary Fountaine; he was educated at Eton and at Christ Church, Oxford; MP 1880-5; he was created Baron, 1892; a keen collector, notably of incunabula and Egyptian antiquities, and his museum at Didlington Hall, Norfolk, was one of the most notable private collections; he purchased the entire collections of the Revd R. T. Lieder (q.v.) in 1861, and of Dr. John Lee (q.v.) in 1865; he also made frequent additions when in Egypt, and from the excavations he supported, including those of Petrie (q.v.) and Lady William Cecil (see above); Howard Carter (q.v.) began his career in archaeology through his help; numerous purchases were also made for him by P. E. Newberry (q.v.); he financed the publication of volumes on the Egyptian, Coptic, and Greek papyri and the Cuneiform tablets in his collection; the papyri were acquired by the Pierpont Morgan Library, New York, in 1913; the rest of the collection (965 lots) sold at Sotheby's, 13-17 June 1921, fetching £14,533; he died in 23 Queen's Gate Gardens, London, 16 Jan. 1909.

Norfolk Notabilities, 1893, 67-75 (portr); Newberry Corr.; *WWW* i, 14; Lugt 82350; *ODNB* 1, 951-2.

AMIOT, Jean Joseph Marie (1718-1793)
French Jesuit missionary in China; he was born in Toulon, 8 Feb. 1718, son of Louis A.; he went to China in 1750; he published a dictionary and valuable works on the history and culture of the Chinese and a Life of Confucius; he also wrote an elaborate work on symbolic writing with 39 plates in which he compared Egyptian with Chinese writing (Brussels, 1773); he died in Peking, 9 Oct. 1793.

BIFAO 5 (1906), 83; *Bibl. de la Cie. de Jésus*, i, 294-303; Hilmy, i. 35; Sven Hedin, *Jehol City of Emperors,* 1932, 63 et passim; *DBF* 2, 674-7; E. Davin, *Bulletin de l'Association Guillaume Budé*, 4e série, 1961, 380-95.

el-AMIR, Mustafa Muhammad (1914-1974)
Egyptian demotist; he was born at Edfu 22 Feb. 1914, son of Muhammad el-Amir Ali; he was educated at Edfu Primary School, 1923-7; Asyut Secondary School, 1927-33; and the University of Cairo, 1933-40; BA, 1937; Diploma of Egyptian Archaeology from the Institute of Archaeology, 1940; he joined the Egyptian Antiquities Service; Inspector at Saqqara where he took part in excavations at the Apis temple (*JEA* 34 (1948), 51-6); he excavated with Hamada (q.v.) at Kom el-Hisn, 1943; Inspector at Thebes, 1943-5 and then Inspector in the Cairo Museum; he studied at University College London and then Cambridge under Glanville (q.v.), 1946-1950; PhD, 1950; Assistant Professor at the University of Alexandria from 1952; then Professor of Egyptology at the University of Khartoum, 1961-5; and finally Professor at the University of Cairo from 1965; Dean of the Faculty of Archaeology, 1972; Visiting Professor at Mainz and Peking; he took part in the Nubian campaign excavating at Gebel Adda, 1959; his main work was *A Family Archive from Thebes*, 1959; he died 17 March 1974.

BSFE 70-71 (1974), 9; *Gött Misz.* 76 (1984), 88-9 (H. Attiatalla); inf. from the University Archives, Cambridge; R. Janssen, *The First Hundred Years*, 1992, 52; inf. G. Mokhtar.

AMPÈRE, Jean Jacques Antoine (1800-1864)
French scholar and writer; he was born in Lyons, 12 Aug. 1800, son of André Marie A., the great physicist, and Antoinette Carron ; he was Professor of History of French Literature, Collège de France, 1833-64; Member of the Académie des Inscriptions, 22 April 1847; Officier de la Légion d'Honneur, 1846; he visited Egypt and Nubia 1844-5; later he went to Canada, U.S.A. and the Antilles, 1851; among numerous works he published two that especially relate to Egypt, *Des castes et de la transmission héréditaire des professions dans l'ancienne Égypte*, in *Rev. Arch.*, 1848; *Voyage en Égypte et en Nubie*, 1867; he died in Pau, 27 March 1864.

Hilmy i, 35; *La Grande Enc.* 2, 817-8 (R. de Gourmont); *Larousse XIX-cent.* 1, 296; Vapereau, 33; *DBF* 2, 720-5; A. C. E. Franquet de Franqueville, *Le Premier Siècle de l'Institut de France*, 1895, I, 270.

ANASTASI, Giovanni (1780-1860)
Greek merchant settled in Alexandria; his original name was Anastasiou; he was born in 1780, the son of a Damascus merchant who went to Egypt about 1797; here the father carried on a large business as a purveyor to the French Army, but the defeat of Napoleon and the subsequent evacuation of the French troops ruined him and he died shortly after becoming bankrupt; by great efforts the son re-established himself and became one of the most considerable merchants in Egypt, serving as Swedish-Norwegian Consul-General in Egypt, 1828-57; in addition to his commercial activities he carried on a large trade in antiquities, employing agents to buy from the inhabitants of Saqqara and Thebes; he sold a large collection of 5600 pieces to the Dutch government in 1828 for 230,000 francs; another was sold in London to the British Museum in 1839, and a third (1,129 lots) at auction in Paris, 23-27 June 1857; he bequeathed a part of his fortune for Swedish charities, and a large granite sarcophagus to Stockholm Museum; Anastasi's name is chiefly associated with the numerous important papyri from his collections now in the British Museum, Leiden, and Paris; he died in Alexandria, 6 Aug. 1860; his daughter Marie married Benedetti (q.v.) and his sister's daughter was the wife of Zizinia (q.v.).

JEA 35 (1949), 158-60; Champollion, i, 94, 210, 326; ii. 25; Lepsius, 39, 43, Minutoli, 20; Lugt 23712; inf. J. Settgast; H. Schneider; H. Schneider, *Atti del Convegno Internazionale Bologna 26-29 Marzo 1990*, 399-400; H. Schneider, *De Laudibus Aegyptologiae,* 1985, 117-20; C. Morigi Govi, S. Curto, and S. Pernigotti, *L'Egitto fuori dell'Egitto*, 1991, 400; E. Gran-Aymerich, *Dictionnaire biographique d'archéologie 1798-1945*, 2001, incorporated in *Les Chercheurs de passé 1798-1945*, 2007, 565

ANCESSI, (*Abbé*) **Victor** (1844-1878)
French priest; he was born at St. Affrique 14 Aug. 1844, son of Albert Antoine Louis A. and Marianne Eugénie Nathalie Bee; he studied under Maspero (q.v.) at the École des Hautes Études, 1869-73; he made a special study of the relations of Egypt to Biblical History, and published several works thereon, 1872-7; he was a correspondent of Chabas (q.v.); he died in St. Affrique, 12 Dec. 1878.

Maspero, *L'Égyptologie* (1915), 7; Chabas, 118; Hilmy, i, 36; *DBF* 2, 800-1.

ANDERSON, Henry James (1799–1875)
American doctor, traveller, and collector; he was born in New York, 6 Feb. 1799, son of Elbert A. and Sarah Banks; he graduated from Columbia College, 1818; he studied at the College of Physicians and Surgeons, AM, 1821; MD, 1824; he was Professor of Mathematics and Astronomy at Columbia College, 1825-43; in 1831 he married Fanny, youngest daughter of the librettist and poet Lorenzo Da Ponte; after leaving Columbia, he travelled in Europe where his wife died Jan. 1 1844; he remained abroad, and visited Egypt, Nubia and Abyssinia, 1847-8; he joined the US Expedition to the Dead Sea, 1848, and contributed the geological section of the official report (1853); he formed a collection of antiquities in Egypt; in 1864 he donated a sarcophagus, a coffin, and a mummy, which he unwrapped in public, and other pieces to the New-York Historical Society; the remainder of his collection was donated to the N-YHS by his son in 1877, and all pieces are now in Brooklyn; returning from studying a transit of Venus in Australia, he was taken ill and died in Lahore, 19 Oct. 1875.

Inf. Columbia University and New York Historical Society; *The Catholic Encyclopedia* I, 1913, 466; C. R. Williams, 'The Place of the N-YHS in the growth of American interest in Egyptology', *N-YHS Quarterly Bulletin* 4 (1920), 8; A Dodson and W. Raver, 'Dr Anderson's Mummy', *KMT* 14/3 (2003), 39-43; inf. T. Hardwick.

ANDERSON, John (1833-1900)
British anatomist and naturalist; he was born in Edinburgh, 4 Oct. 1833, son of Thomas A. and Jane Cleghorn; he studied medicine at Edinburgh University; MD;LLD; FRS; he was Superintendent of Calcutta Museum and Prof. of Anatomy, Calcutta, 1864-86; he made two scientific expeditions to China and to Arabia and Egypt, afterwards publishing *Reptiles and Batrachia*, 1898 (*Zool. of Egypt*, pt. i), a work of great value to Egyptologists in view of the importance of snakes, etc., in Egyptian texts and on monuments; he died in London, 15 Aug. 1900.

WWW i, 15; *ODNB* 2, 50-1.

ANDERSON, Robert David (1927-2015)
British Egyptologist and musicologist; he was born at Shillong, Assam, India, 20 Aug. 1927, son of Robert David A., chemist and scientific officer at at a tea plantation in Assam and Gladys Clayton (widow of Cyril Saunders); he was educated at Harrow, 1941-6, and Gonville and Caius College, Cambridge, 1948-54, studying classics and then Egyptology under Granville (q.v.); BA, 1952; MA, 1957; Hon. DMus., City Univ., 1985; Hon. Doc. in History, Russian State Univ. for Humanities, Moscow, 2000; Hon. Professor in History, Southern Federal University, Rostov-on-Don, 2002; he was an extra-mural lecturer, 1966-77, visiting lecturer, City University, 1983-92; Hon. Sec. Egypt Exploration Sciety, 1971-82; Fellow of the Society of Antiquaries of London, 1983; Freeman of the City of London; he excavated at Saqqara, 1953 and Qasr Ibrim,1976 and 1978; he was director of music at Gordonstoun School, 1958-62; he was also music critic for *The Times*, 1967-72; and associate editor of *The Musical Times*, 1967-85; he founded the Robert Anderson Research Charitable Trust which provides scholarships for postgraduate students, many of them, Egyptologists; apart from works on music, he published *Catalogue of Egyptian Antiquities in the British Museum* III: *Musical Instruments*, 1976; and with Ibrahim Fawzy, *Egypt in 1801*(alternative title *Egypt Revealed*), 1987; he died in London, 24 Nov. 2015.

International Who's Who of Authors and Writers, 2004, 16-17; D. Cummings, *Who's Who in Music*, 2000, 14; *Egyptian Archaeology* 48 (2016), 48 (portr.) (C. Naunton); inf. Howard Davies and L. Gray.

ANDERSSON, Ernst Teodor (1877-1955) **see AKMAR.**

ANDRAOS, Yassa (*Pasha*) (1882-1970)
Egyptian collector; son of Andraos Bishara, a trademan and landowner, originally from Qus who settled in Luxor; he inherited his father's estate and developed an interest in Egyptology; he entertained many of the Egyptologists who passed through Luxor and formed a large collection of antiquities which was later confiscated; with others, he helped to pay for doors to the Theban tombs in 1907; he died in 1970.

Egyptian Archaeology 44 (2014), 26-9 (S.Weens).

ANDREWS, Edward James (*c.* 1808-1841)
British artist; he was born in London *c.*1808, son of Thomas Robert Andrews, of Upper Bedford Place, London, and his wife Ann; he executed in 1837-8 the drawings, plans, and sections of the pyramids and Campbell's tomb for Col. Howard-Vyse (q.v.) and J. S. Perring (q.v.) which were used for the illustrations in their respective books; he brought back from Egypt a collection of antiquities which was sold by auction at Christie's 10 July 1848; he died in London, 6 Aug. 1841; his mother donated some antiquities to the British Museum in 1846.

Vyse, i, Pref. xvi, 236; ii, *passim*; Lugt 19097.

ANDREWS, Emma (1837-1922)
American diarist; she was born in Worthington, Ohio, 13 June 1837, daughter of Joel Buttles, newspaperman and landowner, and Lauretta Barnes; married 16 Dec. 1859 Abner Lord Andrews (d.1897); she became acquainted with Theodore Davis (q.v.) in 1860 through his wife, her cousin Annie Buttles Davis, and lived with Davis as his mistress from 1887 until his death in 1915; she visited Egypt with Davis seventeen times between 1887 and 1914, and from 1889 to 1914 wrote *A Journal of the Bedawin, 1889-1913*, an unpublished 1,000 page diary (now in the Metropolitan Museum of Art) which provides otherwise unavailable information about Davis's excavations and vivid descriptions of the lives of wealthy travellers in Egypt; she sponsored Newberry (q.v.) in his excavations at Thebes and in his publication of scarabs; she gave Egyptian objects to the Museum of Fine Arts, Boston, and the Metropolitan Museum; she also left a $25,000 bequest to the Metropolitan Museum; she died in Washington, DC, 19 Jan. 1922.

Inf. J. Adams and T. Hardwick; *Andrews Diary*; V. McCormick, *Scioto Company Descendants*, 1995.

ANDRZEJEWSKI, Tadeusz (1923-1961)
Polish Egyptologist; he was born at Lódz, 11 Dec. 1923, son of Szcepan A. and Antonina Radziewicz; after leaving school he joined the staff of the National Museum in Warsaw in the 1940s, and was appointed to a post in Warsaw University, 1951; he became secretary of the Polish Archaeological Mission in Cairo, 1959; he studied hieroglyphs and hieratic afterwards going abroad twice in order to learn Demotic, to Lexa (q.v.) at Prague and to Volten (q.v.), Erichsen (q.v.), and Sander-Hansen (q.v.) in Copenhagen; he had a great gift for languages and knew English, German, Italian, French, and Russian as well as Latin and Greek; he assisted Michalowski (q.v.) at the excavations at Mirmeki or Krym, 1956, next spending four years at Tell Atrib, 1957-61 in the Egyptian Delta; during his last year there he made an independent survey of many of the archaeological sites of the Delta and prepared a report on them; during the reconstruction work carried out by the Polish Arch. Institute at the temple of Hatshepsut at Deir el-Bahri he was responsible for the epigraphic work; the Eg. Antiquities Service also had chosen him to publish the tomb of Ramesses III, all the notes for this being almost completed at his death; he took part in the Polish expedition to Nubia, 1959, and made the documentation survey of Faras; he published 2 books in French, 23 articles, a *History of Ancient Egypt*, a book on Egyptian poetry, and a new commentary on *Faraon* by Prus, a 19th cent. Polish writer; his knowledge of palaeography is shown in *Księga Umarłych piastunki Kai*, 1951; he gained his doctorate in 1960 with a work on a mythological papyrus already published, *Le papyrus mythologique de Te-hem-en-mout*, 1958; he died in Warsaw, 28 June 1961.

Przegląd Orientalistyczny, Warszawa Nr. 4 (40) (1961), 511-14 (portr.) (K. Michałowski)

ANGELELLI, Guiseppe (1803-1844)
Italian artist and draughtsman; he was born in Coimbra, Portugal, 7 Dec. 1803, son of Pietro Angelelli of Rome and Carolina Grifoni; with his parents he went to Brazil, 1807, Peru, 1816, France, and England; he afterwards settled in Florence, 1818, and studied at the Accademia school of design; he accompanied Rosellini (q.v.) to Egypt, 1828-9, as a draughtsman; for his work see *Monumenti dell'Egitto*; he died in Florence, 4 Nov. 1844.

DBDI 3, 191; R. Paribeni (Mario Salmi editor); *Scritti dedicati alla memoria di Ippolito Rosellini nel primo centenario della morte* (1945), 47-53, pls. *b* and *c*; G. Gabrieli, *Ippolito Rosellini e il suo giornale della spedizione letteraria toscana* (1925), 3 n. 3 (correct 1893 to 1803); E. Saltini, *Giuseppe Angelelli, pittore toscano. Ricordo biographico*, 1866.

ANGELIN, Justin Pascal (1795-1859)
French naval surgeon; he was born in Marseilles, 17 May 1795; he accompanied as surgeon the expedition that went in the vessel Louqsor, led by J. B. A. Lebas (q.v.), to remove and transport to Paris the obelisk now in the Place de la Concorde; he published an account of the expedition, with plates, Paris, 1833; he also published reports on cholera in Egypt (*Annales maritimes* 46, Paris, 1831, and a separate thesis, Paris, 1834); he afterwards went to the W Indies and wrote a report on yellow fever in Guadeloupe (Toulon, 1839); he died on 8 Dec. 1859.

Wernich-Hirsch, *Allgemeines Lexicon der Aertze*, i, 148 (1884); Hilmy, i, 37.

ANIS, Samir (1948-2008)
Egyptian archaeologist; he was born at Dairut, 2 Aug, 1948, son of Anis Salib, an agronomist, and Nagafa Malak Girgis; he studied in the Dept. of Archaeology, University of Cairo; BA, 1970 with honors; he entered the Egyptian Antiquities Service, 1972; Inspector of Upper Egypt at Luxor 1972-3; he moved to Middle Egypt 1973 where for the rest of his career he played a leading role in administering the Middle Egypt Sector for the SCA; he also spent nine months training in restoration in Poland, 1976 on a scholarship from The Egyptian Antiquities Organisation; he worked at various sites and occupied various positions ranging from Inspector,

Director of the Mallawi Museum, Chief inspector; Deputy Director of Middle Egypt, 2002-04; he was promoted to the post of Director of Middle Egypt Antiquities Sector 2004-7 and later to the position of Middle Egypt Under Secretary of State 2007-8; he increased the ownership of and for the antiquities organization in Tuna el-Gebel, Hatnub, Deir el-Bersha, Amarna, and other sites; he also organized the restoration work at Beni Hassan and Deir el-Bersha and maintenance projects to improve magazines and site supervision at Ashmunein, Bahnasa, Beni Mazar, Meir, and Dakhla; discoveries from his excavations are displayed at the Mallawi Museum; he lectured in Minia University and participated in local, and international workshops, conferences and seminars in the UK, France, Belgium and Italy; he died in Minia, 23 April, 2008.

Inf. Samiha Anis Salib (sister); *Egyptian Archaeology* 33 (2008), 44 (B. Kemp)

ANNESLEY, Arthur Lyttelton (1802-1882)
British benefactor; he was born at Ealing 28 Nov. 1802, the son of Major-General Norman Macleod and Hester Annabella, daughter of Arthur Annesley, Visct. Valentia and 1st Earl of Mountnorris; he assumed the name of Annesley in lieu of Macleod by royal licence in 1844, and inherited Arley Castle, Staffs.; in 1854 he presented sixteen stelae and reliefs to the British Museum formerly in Lord Mountnorris's collection sold in 1852; (BM, EA 810-825); he died at Bournemouth, 24 Oct. 1882.

Burke's Peerage.

ANNESLEY, George, Viscount Valentia and 2nd Earl of Mountnorris (1770-1844)
British collector; he was born at Arley Castle 4 Dec. 1770, son of Arthur A., 1st Earl and Lucy Lyttleton; succeeded as 2nd Earl, 1816; he travelled in the East with Henry Salt (q.v.) acting as his secretary and draughtsman, 1802-6; FRS, 1796; he formed a large natural history collection and a collection of Egyptian antiquities at Arley Castle, Staffs, the latter mostly obtained for him by Salt in 1817-20; this was mainly sold 6-12 Dec. 1852, the majority being bought by Joseph Mayer (q.v.) of Liverpool, but some objects were presented to the British Museum in 1854 by his kinsman Arthur Lyttelton A. (q.v.) he published *Voyages and Travels to India, Ceylon, the Red Sea, Abyssinia and Egypt in the years 1802-6*, 1809; his son George Arthur having predeceased him in 1841, the earldom became extinct on his death, in Arley Castle, 23 July 1844.

BIBIB 8; BL Add. MS 19348; Salt, i, passim; Lugt 21070; D. Manley in P Starkey and N. el Kholy (eds), *Egypt through the Eyes of Travellers*, 2002, 1-12.

ANTES, John (1740-1811)
American missionary and composer; he was was born in Frederick Township, Penn., 24 March 1740, son of Johann Heinrich A., a carpenter, and Christiana Elizabeth DeWees; he trained as a missionary for the Moravian Brethren in Germany, 1764-70; he was based in Cairo, 1770-81 where he met Bruce (q.v.) and Boyleston (q.v.); he published *Observations on the Manners and Customs of the Egyptians*, 1800; and his autobiography *Excerpts from the Narrative of the life of our late dear and venerable Brother John Antes*, 1815; he died in Bristol, 11 Dec. 1811.

C. Vivian, *Americans in Egypt 1770-1915*, 2012, 9-23.

ANTHES, Rudolf Richard Georg Philipp Gottfried (1896-1985)
German Egyptologist; he was born in Hamburg, 1 March 1896, son of (Richard Johann Philipp Cleophas George) Albrecht Wilhelm Friedrich Jacob A, a pastor, and Magdalena Sofie Herzog; he was educated from 1909 at the Gymnasium Schulpforta near Naumburg where he learnt Hebrew and Arabic; he intended to study theology attending Universities of Tübingen and Greifswald, but his education was interrupted by World War I in which he served and lost an eye; in 1919 he studied Egyptology under Erman (q.v.) being the last of his graduate students at the University of Berlin; PhD, 1923; he was from 1920 an assistant with the *Wörterbuch* project; 1927-29 he was an assistant at the German Archaeological Institute in Cairo; on 1 Oct. 1929 he was appointed an assistant at the Egyptian Museum, Berlin; he finished his habilitation in 1931 at the University of Halle; in 1932 he was named as acting director of the museum in the absence of Schäfer (q.v.); in 1931-2 and 1932-3 he took part in the excavations of Hölscher (q.v.) at Medinet Habu; from 1931-37 he also lectured at the University of Halle; he was dismissed from his post on 1 Nov. 1939 but allowed to work in the museum from 1941-3; he was restored to the post of director on 25 Sept. 1945 when he faced the task of restoring the museum after the devastation caused by World War II; he also taught at the reopened Humboldt University at Berlin from 1947, professor in the faculty of Philosophy 24 Nov. 1948, professor of Egyptology 28 Dec. 1949;

he left East Germany in 1950 to become professor of Egyptology in the Department of Oriental Studies, University of Pennsylvania and curator of the Egyptian Section of the University Museum until 1963; apart from his teaching, he undertook archaeological excavation at Memphis for two seasons 1955-6; apart from numerous articles, his published works include *Die Felseninschriften von Hatnub*, 1928; *Lebensregeln und Lebensweisheit der alten Ägypter*, 1933; *Aegyptische Plastik in Meisterwerken*, 1954; *Die Büste der Königin Nofret Ete*, 1954; *Die Maat des Echnaton von Amarna*, 1952; *Mit Rahineh 1955*, 1959; *Mit Rahineh 1956*, 1965; *Ägyptische Theologie im dritten Jahrtausend v. Chr.* in *Studia Aegyptiaca* IX, 1983; he died in West Berlin, 5 Jan. 1985.

ZÄS 113 (1986), I-III (S. Wenig); *Expedition* 27 (1985), 34-36 (D. O'Connor); *Wer ist Wer* 1969-70, 19; E. Endesfelder, *Die Ägyptologie an der Berliner Universität-Zur Geschichte eines Fachgebietes*, 1988, 27, 42-54; M. Eaton-Krauss, *Gött. Misz.* 253 (2017), 11-4.

ANTI, Carlo (1889-1961)
Italian archaeologist; he was born in Villafranca Veronese 28 April 1889, son of Giorgio A. and Anita Bacchi; he studied archaeology in Rome; he served as inspector at the Prehistoric and Ethnographical Museum in Rome, 1914-21; he became lecturer at the University of Padua, 1922, where he was appointed rector, 28 Oct. 1932-43; he excavated in Libya, 1924-28; he became head of the Italian mission in Egypt, 1928; he took over the concession for Tebtunis from Breccia (q.v.) where he carried out excavations, 1930-32 but left future seasons to Bagnani (q.v.); a volume of studies in his honour *Anthemon* was published in 1955 which list his bibl., ix-xii; apart from some preliminary reports on Tebtunis, his work concentrated on classical subjects; his papers are now in Padua; he died in Padua, 5 June 1961.

Chi è? 1957, 28; *Studi Etrusci* 29 (1961), 389-92 (L. Laurenzi).

ANTONIADIS, (*Sir*) John (1819-1895)
Greek merchant of Alexandria; he was born in Lemnos, 1819, but settled in Egypt in 1833 where he established himself at Alexandria; in 1857-8 as a *favori* of Said Pasha, he became a famous public character; he was knighted by Queen Victoria, 1865; he presented to the Municipality his palace and garden, and was also a great benefactor to the Museum of Alexandria, one of its galleries was named in his honour 'Salle Antoniadis'; he died in Alexandria, 27 July 1895.

Breccia, *Alexandrea* (1914 ed.), 172; inf. Dr. T. D. Mosconas and V. Chrysikopoulos.

ANTRAIGUES, Louis Emmanuel Henri Alexandre de Launay (*Comte d'*) (1753-1812)
French traveller and spy; he was born in Montpellier, 25 Dec. 1753, son of Jules Alexandre de L., Comte d'Antraigues, and Sophie de Saint-Priest; he became a disciple of Rousseau; on 11 June 1778 he sailed to the Levant with his maternal uncle, ambassador to Constantinople; he visited Turkey and then sailed for Egypt 18 Dec. 1778 he stayed there from 2 Jan.-Feb. 1779 and was accompanied by Adanson (q.v.) in Alexandria, Cairo, Rosetta, Wadi Natrun, Suez, and Middle Egypt before returning to Constantinople and then to Europe; he became an initial partisan of reform in France but emigrated after the Revolution and served as a royalist spy; he also worked for the Russians and the British; he came to England in 1806 and was murdered by his servant at Barnes, 22 July 1812; his papers concerning his Egyptian trip are in the library at Dijon.

Inf. J. Kimper; DBF 3, 76-80; C. Duckworth, The d'Antraigues Phenomenon, 186; A. Barny, Le Comte d'Antraigues, 1991; L. Pingaud, Un Agent Secret sous la Révolution et l'Empire, 1893.

APOSTOLIDES, Vasileios (1827-1910)
Greek doctor; he was born in Serres, Macedonia, 1827; he was appointed physician to Ismail Pasha in 1870; he became a corresponding member of Institut Égyptien 1889; he was a co-founder of the scientific association Athinaion in 1892 whose library and collection became the basis of the Graeco-Roman museum in Alexandria; he was also co-founder and President of the Hellenic Scientific Association, The Hellenion, in Cairo; he wrote several articles on Greeks in ancient Egypt; he died in Geneva, 1910.

Inf V. Chrysikopoulos

ARAGO, (Dominique) François Jean (1786-1853)
French physicist and astronomer; he was born at Estagel 26 Feb. 1786, son of François-Bonavanture A. and Marie Ruig; he was made secretary at the Paris Observatory, 1804, and took part with J. B. Biot in the measurement of the terrestrial meridian; at only 23 he was elected a member of Acad. of Sciences and appointed Professor of analytical geometry at the École Polytechnique; he discovered the chromatic

polarization of light in 1811, and with A. Fresnel, the phenomenon of rotary polarization in 1817 and the laws on the interference of polarized light in 1819; he also made an important contribution to the establishment of the wave theory of light, and with Ampère discovered the electromagnet at the same time as Sir Humphry Davy in 1820; in addition to these and other discoveries Arago followed an active political career and secured the abolition of corporal punishment in the French armed forces and the abolition of slavery; a man of genius and wide interests he also took part in the controversies that went on over the decipherment of hieroglyphs and published several memoirs in support of Thomas Young (q.v.), but later seems to have swung over to Champollion (q.v.) whose system he ultimately favoured; he died in Paris, 2 Oct. 1853.

Autobiography, trans. Revd Baden Powell, 1855; Champollion, ii. 214, 250; Hilmy, i. 41; A. Wood, Thomas Young Natural Philosopher, 1954, 243, 248; DBF 3, 199-203; M. Daumus, Arago, 1943.

ARAKEL see ABROYAN

ARBUTHNOT, (*Lady***), Ann** (d 1882)
British traveller; daughter of Field Marshal Sir John FitzGerald, GCB. and Charlotte Hazen; she married, 20 March 1828 Sir Robert Arbuthnot, 2nd Bt. (1801-73); she and her husband were staying in Cairo at the time when Howard Vyse (q.v.) was exploring the Pyramids, and he named one of the newly-discovered construction-chambers of the Great Pyramid 'Lady Arbuthnot's Chamber' in her honour; she died in Florence, 6 March 1882, and is buried with her husband in the Cemetery of the Allori.

Vyse, i, 239, 256, 259, 265; inf. W. FitzGerald Arbuthnot (grandson).

ARCELIN, (Godefroi Marie Victor) Adrien (1838-1904)
French prehistorian and archaeologist; he was born at Fuissé, 30 Nov. 1838, son of François Antoine Marie Godefroi A., an architect, and Jeanne Josephine Justine Buget; he studied at the École des Chartes, 1860-4 and later obtained a position as archivist at the Département de la Haute-Marne; he undertook excavations at the prehistoric site of Solutré from 1866; he was sent on a mission to Egypt in 1869 and examined prehistoric sites from Cairo to Aswan; he became curator of the archaeological and historical collections at Mâcon, 1876 and secrétaire perpétuel de l'Académie de Mâcon; Member of the Institut d'Égypte; apart from articles, his main publications on his Egyptian work were *Matériaux pour l'histoire naturelle et primitive de l'homme*, 1869; and *L'âge de pierre et la classification préhistorique d'après les sources égyptiennes* which appeared in *Annales de l'Académie de Mâcon* XI (1873), 205-51; he died at Saint-Sorlin, 21 Dec. 1904.

DBF 3, 323-4; *Archaéonil* 17 (2007), 5-26 (portr.); È. Gran-Aymerich, *Dictionnaire biographique d'archéologie 1798-1945*, 2001, incorporated in *Les Chercheurs de passé 1798-1945*, 2007, 568.

ARDEN, Joseph (1799-1879)
British barrister and traveller; he was born in London, 10 May 1799, son of Joseph Arden of Islington, and Temperance Lunt; he lived at 27 Cavendish Square, being Barrister-at-Law in Clifford's Inn and at Rickmansworth House, Herts.; he was greatly interested in archaeology; FSA, 1847; visited Egypt 1846-7; he purchased at Thebes the Hypereides papyrus published by Churchill Babington (q.v.) and also two mummies; one of these was unrolled at Worcester by Pettigrew (*J. Brit. Arch. Assn.* 4, 337) and the other by Birch (q.v.) in Lord Londesborough's house (*Arch. Journal* 7, 273); he died in Rickmansworth, 10 June 1879.

JEA 35 (1949), 162; Dawson MS 23, f. 142; *Burke's Landed Gentry* 1905, 31.

ARIF, Sobhi Joseph (1870-1905)
Egyptian Egyptologist, he was born in 1870 from a Coptic family; he was admitted to the Secretariat of Cairo Museum, Oct. 1892, and on permanent staff, 1897; he accompanied de Morgan (q.v.) and Loret (q.v.) in their trips through Egypt as secretary, and having gained experience of the sites was appointed to various posts in Upper and Middle Egypt; Inspector at Dendera, 1899, Fayum, 1901, Minya, 1903; he published four articles in *ASAE* and died, 28 Sept. 1905.

ASAE 7 (1906), 113-4 (A. Aclimandos).

ARKELL, (*Revd*) **Anthony John** (1898-1980)
British archaeologist; he was born at Hinxhill Rectory, Kent, 29 July 1898, son of Revd John Norris A. and Eleanor Jessy Bunting; he was educated at Bradfield College and The Queen's College Oxford; his education was interrupted by World War I during which he served in the Royal Flying Corps, 1916-8 and was awarded MC, 1918; he continued in the RAF, 1918-9 and in 1920 joined the Sudan Political Service in which he held various political posts culminating in Acting Deputy-Gov. of Darfur, 1932-7; he was appointed first Commissioner for Archaeology and Anthropology in 1939; he returned briefly to Oxford, 1938-9; B. Litt. 1939; he then took up his new Sudanese post which he held until 1949 with a break in 1940-4 when he was Chief Transport Officer; he undertook the organization of the Museums of Antiquities and Ethnography at Khartoum and the creation of the Sudan Antiquities Service; he was editor of *Sudan Notes and Records*, 1945-8; he was appointed lecturer in Egyptology at University College London, 1948, later reader, 1953-63 and Curator of the Flinders Petrie Collection, 1948-63; he undertook the onerous task of unpacking and cataloguing the collection which had been in store since World War II; he remained Archaeological Adviser to the Sudan Government, 1948-53; he excavated at Khartoum in 1944-5 and in 1949-50 at Shaheinab; FSA and member of its council, 1956-7; ordained in the Anglican church; assistant curate of Great Missenden, 1960-63; vicar of Cuddington with Dinton, 1963-71; his publications include *Early Khartoum,* 1949; *Shaheinab*, 1953; *A History of the Sudan from the Earliest Times to 1821*, 1955; *Wanyanga*, 1964; and *The Prehistory of the Nile Valley*, 1975; he died in Chelmsford, 26 Feb. 1980.

JEA 67 (1981), 143-48 (portr; bibl.) (H. S. Smith); *ZÄS* 108 (1981), v-vii (P. L. Shinnie); *AfO* 27, 332 (H. Brunner); *WWW* 7, 25; *Times* 5 March 1980, 19; R. Janssen, *The First Hundred Years*, 1992, 58-9; *Sudan and Nubia* 22 (2018), 179-87.

ARMITAGE, (*Revd*) **Elkanah** (1844-1929)
British congregationalist minister; he was born in Clarton-upon Medlock, Manchester, 16 Dec. 1844, son of William A., manufacturer and Mary Rigby; he was educated at Stuttgart, Owens College, Manchester, and Trinity College, Cambridge; MA; Theological tutor in Philosophy and Comparative Religion in the Independent Colleges of Rotherham and Bradford; he visited Egypt in 1881 and obtained two important papyri which he gave to Aquila Dodgson (q.v.) and which were published by Griffith (q.v.); he died in Rawson, Leeds, 23 Dec. 1929.

PSBA 31, 289; *WWW* iii, 33.

ARNETH, (*Ritter von*) **Joseph Calasanza** (1791-1863)
Austrian numismatist and antiquarian; born in Leopoldschlag, 12 Aug. 1791, son of John Nepomuk A. and Magdalena Wiesinger; Director of the Imperial Coin and Antiquity collections; he published articles on Egyptian sarcophagi etc., during the 1840s and 50s; he died in Karlsbad, 21 Oct. 1863.

Allgemeines Gelehrten Lex., 30; *NDB* 1, 365; Hilmy, i, 43.

ARTAUD, (**Antoine Marie**) **François** (1767-1838)
French archaeologist and collector he was born in Avignon, 17 April 1767 son of Joseph Antoine A., a cloth merchant, and Madeleine Ritay; he was Inspector-General, later Director, of the Conservatoire of Arts and Antiquities in Lyons, 1806-30 and Director of the Musée Calvet, Avignon from 1812-34; he also held the post of Inspector of the Monuments of the Rhône from 1823; he was a staunch friend of Champollion (q.v.) who visited his museum to inspect the Egyptian antiquities in 1824 and 1828; he introduced Champollion to F. Sallier (q.v.); his collection of antiquities was bought by the Lyons Museum in 1835; he died in Orange, 27 March 1838.

Champollion, i. pp. viii., 4, 416; ii. 7, 9; *DBF* 3, 1135-7; J. B. Dumas, *Éloge historique de A. F. M. Artaud*, 1840; M. P. Foissy-Aufrère, *Égypte et Provence*, 1986, 255-6; G. Gruyère, *Essai de bibliographie descriptive de François Artaud (1767-1838)*, 1986; G. Bruyère and H. Lavagne in A.-F. Laurens and K. Pomian, *L'Anticomanie*, 1988, 145-154.

ARTIN *see* **CHRAKIAN**

ARUNDALE, Francis (1807-1853)
British architect and painter; he was born in London, 9 Aug. 1807, son of George A.; he was a pupil of Augustus Pugin and accompanied him to Normandy where he assisted in the *Arch. Antiquities of Normandy*; he spent several years in Rome and afterwards published *The Edifices of Andrea Palladio*, 1832; he was recommended to Robert Hay (q.v.) by Lane (q.v.) and Scoles (q.v.) and joined him in Qurna in 1832 as draughtsmen and landscape artist; he also made detailed but fanciful reconstructions of temple façades; he accompanied Catherwood (q.v.) and Bonomi (q.v.) to Palestine, 1833; although it is stated in the DNB and in the first ed. of this work that he never

practised as an architect, he seems to have done so as there are letters of his in existence showing that he worked as partner in a firm Arundale and Heape of 48, Greek Street; he exhibited some large paintings made from his oriental drawings; he published *Jerusalem and Mount Sinai*, 1837; *Selections from the Gallery of Antiquities in the British Museum*, 1842, in collaboration with Bonomi and Birch; some of his correspondence is in the Griffith Institute; he died in Brighton, 9 Sept. 1853.

Inf. Miss H. Murray, Griffith Inst.; *ODNB* 2, 560-1; *DNB* 2. 136; Bonomi Diary; Hilmy, i. 43; J Vialla, *Les Pickersgill-Arundale*, 1983; S. Tillett, *Egypt Itself*, 1984, 49-53;BL Add MS 29846; inf. S.Tillett.

ASHBURNHAM, Bertram, Viscount St Asaph and 4th Earl Ashburnham (1797-1878)
British collector; he was born at Ashburnham, Sussex, 23 Nov. 1797, son of George, 3rd Earl Ashburnham and Charlotte Percy, and succeeded as 4th Earl of Ashburnham, 1830; he visited Egypt, 1824-5, and carried out excavations at Thebes under the direction of Bonomi (q.v.); he was a keen collector of ancient coins and engraved gems, a gold ring in his collection is now in the British Museum (EA 71492); he died in Ashburnham, 22 June 1878.

Hay Diary, 1824, 5 Dec.; 1825, 2 Jan., 22 Feb., 24 Feb.

ASLANIAN, Oxan (1887-1968)
Armenian forger and dealer in antiquities; he was born in Thessalonika, 5 Oct. 1887; by 1900 he was living in Egypt, working for members of a family named Kalebdijan who were dealers in antiquities; he moved to Switzerland around 1915, and was established as a dealer in Berlin by 1918, selling material to the Berlin Museum, the Louvre, and other museums and collectors; as well as dealing in antiquities, he also manufactured and distributed forgeries, usually in the style of Old Kingdom or Amarna Period sculpture; his 'hand' was recognised by Borchardt (q. v.), although he was never publicly named or charged; he is often referred to as the 'Berlin Master'; he died in Munich, 20 March 1968.

Munich state archives; D. Wildung and S. Schoske, *Falsche Faraonen*, 1983; J.-J. Fiechter, *Faux et faussaires en art égyptien*, 2005, 27-34; inf. T. Hardwick; F. Hagen and K. Ryholt, *The Antiquities Trade in Egypt 1880-1930*, 2017, 198-200.

ASSELBERGHS, (Jean Jacques Matthieu) Henri Marie (1887-1980)
Dutch museum official; he was born at Lottum, Limburg 19 Feb. 1887, son of Peter Jan Victor A. and Anna Catharina Antonietta Zanders; he was educated at Venlo and eventually became director of the Railway Museum at Utrecht; he was greatly interested in Egyptology and took courses from de Buck (q.v.); he played an active part in the Dutch society Ex Oriente Lux and wrote numerous articles; his chief publications were *Beeldende kunst in Oud-Egypte*, 1942 and *Chaos en Beheersing*, 1961 with an English summary, a survey of predynastic Egypt; he died in Utrecht, 21 April 1980.

Phoenix 25 (1979), 60-2 (Heerma van Voss); inf. from Prof. Heerma van Voss.

ASSELIN DE CHERVILLE, Jean Louis (1772-1822)
French diplomat; he was born at Cherbourg, 10 July 1772; he was appointed second dragoman of the French mission in Egypt, 1806; Vice-Consul in Egypt, 1814; he retired and opened a guest-house in Cairo; an accomplished linguist he often acted as an interpreter for Europeans in Egypt; he had a valuable collection of Arabic and other manuscripts which are now in the Bibliothèque Nationale, Paris; he died in Cairo, 25 June 1822; the Paul Asselin who left a graffito in 1842 at Abu Simbel is a different man.

DBF 3, 1292-3; Carré, i, 201, 205; A. de Forbin, *Travels in Egypt*, 1817-18, 1819, 59; J. Madox, *Excursions in the Holy Land, Egypt, Nubia, Syria etc.*, 1834, i, 107; Salt ii, 178;*Travels of Lady Hester Stanhope*, 1846, i, 162; U. Seetzen, *Reisen durch Syrien etc.*, 1854-9, iii, 164-5; M. L. de Marcellus, *Souvenirs de l'Orient*, 1839, 204-7; H. Dehérain, *Silvestre de Sacy*, 1938, 93-112; J. F. Hamel, *Dictionnaire des Personnages remarquables de la Manche* I, 2001, 16.

ATHANASI, Giovanni d' (1798-1854)
Greek excavator and collector; he was born as Demetrio Papandriopulos, son of Athanasios P, a merchant of Lemnos, who afterwards settled in Cairo; Athanasi joined him in Egypt in 1809 and while still a boy in 1813 entered the service of Colonel Ernest Missett (q.v.), British Consul-General, on whose retirement, in 1815, he became servant to Henry Salt (q.v.); he excavated at Thebes for Salt, 1817-27, helping him build up his collection, and afterwards on his own account and for Consul Barker (q.v.); he sold many important antiquities and brought to England a large collection (some of which were engraved by Visconti), which was sold at Sotheby's 5 March 1836 and 13-20 March 1837; Athanasi, or d'Athanasi (properly Ioannes Athanasiou), was well known to all travellers in Egypt as Yanni, and he is frequently mentioned in diaries and travel books between 1817 and 1835; he had a house at Qurna, just above tomb No. 52; the residue of his collection was sold at Sotheby's 17 July 1845;

he settled in London by the winter of 1849-50 in an attempt to set himself up as a picture-dealer; his speculations failed and left him in great financial distress and he wrote to many of his former colleagues for assistance; Wilkinson (q.v.) and particularly Robert Hay (q.v.) provided for his support; he died in a boarding house in London, 19 Dec. 1854.

Researches and Discoveries in Upper Egypt made under the direction of Henry Salt Esq., 1836, mainly autobiographical; Hilmy, i, 44; frequently mentioned under the name of Yanni in contemporary diaries and books; Lugt 14240 and 14611; J. Thompson, *Sir Gardner Wilkinson and his Circle*, 1992, 104-5,272-3 note 112; letters of Robert Hay to Joseph Bonomi 22 Jan. 11 and 22 March 1851 (private collection); Gardner Wilkinson to Samuel Birch (MS, Dept. of Egyptian Antiquities, British Museum); Wilkinson to Hood 15 June 1860 (Wilkinson MSS, Bodleian Library); Gardner Wilkinson to Hay 1862; inf. S. Tillett; E. Gran-Aymerich, *Dictionnaire biographique d'archéologie 1798-1945*, 2001, incorporated in Les Chercheurs de passé 1798-1945, 2007, 569-70; J. Thompson, *Edward William Lane 1801-1876*, 2010, 160-1, 487; R. de Keersmaecker, *ASTENE Bulletin* 70 (2016), 16-18.

AUAD (*c.1773-c.1868*)
Egyptian guide; a native of Qurna who acted as foreman of Champollion's (q.v.) excavations in West Thebes in 1829 and as guide and attendant to Lepsius (q.v.) at Thebes in 1844-5, and who was severely wounded in consequence of a family feud; he was a faithful servant and had great knowledge of the district and of the antiquities; Brugsch (q.v.) met him at Thebes in 1853, he being then about 80 years of age.

Lepsius, 217, 321; Brugsch, *Mein Leben*, 183; L. Keimer *CHE* 7 (1955), 300; M. Dewachter, *BSFE* 111 (1958), 57-60; *Qurna History Project News* (2004) 1, 6 (portr.).

AURÈS, (Louis) Auguste (1806-1894)
French engineer and metrologist; born in Montpellier, 21 Dec. 1806, son of Joseph Felix A. and Marie Victoire Estève; he had a distinguished career in Gard; Officier de la Légion d'Honneur; Corr. Soc. of Antiquaries (French); he was very interested in ancient metrology, Assyrian, Egyptian etc., and wrote extensively on the subject, see especially, *Métrologie égyptienne; Détermination géométrique des mesures de capacité dont les anciens se sont servis en Égypte, précédée d'explications relatives aux mesures de capacité Grecques et Romaines*, 1880; he died in Nîmes, 17 Jan. 1894.

Vapereau Suppl., 4-5; Hilmy, i, 33; *DBF* 4, 668.

AVDIEV, Vsevolod Igorevitch (1898-1978)
Russian orientalist; he was born in Moscow 4/16 Oct. 1898; he graduated in 1922 from the faculty of Social Sciences of Moscow University; he was head of the Department of the Ancient East in the Pushkin Museum, Moscow 1924-41; he joined Moscow University in 1942, doctor of historical sciences, 1943; Professor 1944; Professor of ancient history 1951-1973; his chief work *Istoriia Drevnego Vostoka* (History of the Ancient East), 1948 was published in several editions and translated in Eastern Europe; his other works in Russian were *Ancient Egyptian Reformation*, 1924; *History of War in Ancient Egypt*, 2 vols., 1948, 1959; he was the editor for the Russian translation of A. Lucas, *Ancient Egyptian Materials and Industries*, Moscow, 1958; he died on 9 May 1978.

VDI 4 (146), 1978, 208; see also *Drevniy Vostok i Anticnyi Mir*, Moscow 1972, with his full bibl. for the years 1923-1972, pp. 244-252; S.D.Miliband, *Bibliograficeskiy slovar' sovetskikh vostokovego*, 1975, 14; inf. J. Sliwa and A. Elanskaya.

AVELING, (*Revd*) Thomas William Baxter (1815-1884)
British congregationalist minister; he was born in Castletown, Isle of Man 11 May 1815, son of Thomas A. and Bridget Kennan; he was trained in theology at Highbury; he travelled in Europe and the East, and published *Voices of Many Waters: Travels in the Lands of the Tibur, Jordan and Nile*, 1855, new ed. 1856; he died in Reedham near Croydon, Surrey, 3 July 1884.

ODNB 2, 1020; DNB 2, 274; Hilmy, i, 46.

AYER, Edward Everett (1841-1927)
American businessman and collector; he was born at Kenosha, Wisconsin, 16 Nov. 1841, son of Eldridge Gerry A. and Mary Titcomb; he became a lumbermill owner and supplier of timber to the railway through the Ayer and Lord Tie Company; he was a principal founder of the Field Museum, Chicago, President 1893-8 and Trustee to 1927; he purchased Egyptian antiquities for the Museum in 1896 and 1898; he died in Pasadena, 3 May 1927.

WWWA 1, 39; *DAB* 1, 448-9.

AYRTON, Edward Russell (1882-1914)
British Egyptologist and archaeologist; he was born at Wuhu, China, 17 Dec. 1882, son of William Scrope A. of the China Consular Service, and Ellen Louisa McClatchie his wife; he was educated at St. Paul's School; he first excavated with Petrie (q.v.) at Abydos, 1902-4, for the EEF; his first independent work being the excavation of the Shunet ez-Zebib, see *Abydos* III; he also worked near Ghurab in collaboration with W. L. S. Loat (q.v.); he then joined Naville (q.v.) and Hall (q.v.) at Deir el-Bahri, 1904-5, where he excavated and recorded the graves found; these are described in *The XIth Dynasty Temple at Deir el-Bahari*, i, chapter 3, which gives his account of the tombs of the princesses buried in Mentuhotep's temple; he also worked for Theodore Davis (q.v.) in the Biban el-Muluk, 1905-8, when the tombs of Siptah, Horemheb, and other kings were found, and he published short accounts of these discoveries in *PSBA* 28-30 (1906-8); with Loat he excavated the Sixth Dynasty tombs at Abydos and the predynastic cemetery at el-Mahasna, 1908-9; they published *The Pre-Dynastic Cemetery at El Mahasna*, 1911; he accepted an appointment in the Arch. Survey of Ceylon, where he went in 1911; he died in Ceylon, having been accidentally drowned while on a shooting expedition in the Tissa Tank, 18 May 1914.

JEA 2 (1915), 20-3 (portr.) (H. R. Hall).

AYZAC, C. L. d' (*fl.* 1807-1822)
French magistrate and chronologer; the facts of his life seem to be extremely obscure, but he was an Advocat in the Provence parlement and, becoming interested in ancient dating and astronomy, published two papers at the time when the Dendera zodiac was causing widespread interest; *Le rectificateur des faits et des dates erronées qui ont obscurci et dénaturé l'histoire sacrée et profane depuis l'origine du genre humain jusqu'à nos jours ...*, 1821; *Démonstration de la seule époque à laquelle dut être tracé le zodiaque de Tentyris (Denderah), déposé au Musée royal, à Paris ...*, 1822.

DBF 4, 970 (R. d'Amat).

AZIM, Michel (1942-2013)
French architect and archaeologist of Iranian origin; he was born in 1942; he was attached to CNRS, Feb. 1974-Dec. 1984 and took part in excavations in the Sudan at Mirgissa,1967 and Sai, 1970-3; he became director of the Centre d'étude franco-égyptien at Karnak, Dec. 1984; he was then attached to the Centre de recherches archaeologiques de Valbonne-Sophia Antipolis and then Histoire et Sources des mondes Antiques at Lyons; he had a particular interest in the history of the site of Karnak and early European travellers to Egypt; he published, with others, Le Temple de Deir Chelouit, 1992; Karnak et sa topographie, 2 vols., 1998-2012; Inventaire de la collection M. Pillet, 1999; with G. Reveillac, Karnak dans l'objectif de Georges Legrain, 2 vols., 2004; with others, Trésors d'Égypte, 2004; with others, Karnak avant la XVIIIe dynastie, 2012; his archives were donated to the Bibliothèque de la Maison de l'Orient et de la Mediterranée, Lyons; he died in Lyons, 7 July 2013.

ASTENE Bulletin 57 (2013), 4; *Sudan and Nubi*a 17 (2013), 154 (B. Gratien).

AZIZ, Youssef (*fl.* 1808-1820)
Egyptian interpreter to the British Consulate in Egypt where he served under the Consuls-General Missett (q.v.) and Salt (q.v.).

Legh, ii, 124, 132; Valentia, iii, 332 ff, 355, 356, 358, 362, 363, 386; Athanasi, 16; Richardson, ii, 174.

BABINGTON, (*Revd*) Churchill (1821-1889)
British scholar and naturalist; he was born in Roecliffe, Leicestershire, 11 March 1821, son of Mathew Drake B., Rector of Thringstone, and Hannah Fleetwood Churchill; a private pupil of Charles Wycliffe Goodwin (q.v.); educated at St. John's College, Cambridge, 1839; BA, 1843; MA, 1846; DD, 1879; elected Fellow and ordained, 1846; Vicar of Horningsea, 1848-61; Rector of Cockfield, Suffolk, 1861-89; Disney Professor of Archaeology, Cambridge, 1865-80; he published *editio princeps* of the Hypereides papyri of Joseph Arden (q.v.), A. C. Harris (q.v.), and Henry Stobart (q.v.), 1850-8; he was a man of many interests which included archaeology and natural history and wrote many works in these subjects; he died in Cockfield, 12 Jan. 1889.

ODNB 3, 82-3; *DNB Suppl.* i, 92-3; *BIBIB* 12; *Proc. Linn. Soc.* 1888-90, 46; Goodwin, 22, 61; *Journ. Bot.* 1889, 110.

BACK DE SURÁNY, Philipp (1862-1958)
Hungarian merchant, banker and businessman in Vienna and Cairo; he was born in Budapest, 31 Oct. 1862, son of Moric B. and Antonia Schnabel, sister of the company-director Adolf Schnabel later Orosdi; he was educated at the Universities of Budapest and Berlin as a mathematician; he joined the family firm now the Orosdi-Back World Trading Company and later became a director of the company in Paris, 1897 and then Cairo, 1898-1910; he initiated and sponsored the Austro-Hungarian excavations in agreement with G. Maspero (q.v.) in Sharuna and Gamhud, 1907-09, which were conducted by Smolenski (q.v.) and Ahmad Kamal (q.v.); he donated objects to the museums in Vienna, Cracow, and Budapest while some remained in the family; he was decorated by the Viennese Court with Franz-Joseph's Order, 30 Nov. 1904 and raised to the Hungarian nobility in 1909; he also served as Persian consul in Cairo; he left Egypt in 1910 and eventually settled in France in 1912; he died in Noisy-Le-Grand, 22 March 1958.

Bull. du Musée Hongrois des Beaux-Arts 30 (1967), 3-6 (V. Wessetzky); inf. J. Śliwa; R. Agstner, *Die Österreichisch-ungarische Kolonie in Kairo vor dem ersten Weltkrieg*, 1994, 123, 302; G. Vörös, *Egyptian Temple Architecture*, 2007, 20-30; G. Vörös, *Sharuna-Gamhud*, 2008.

BADAWI, Ahmad Muhammad (1905-1980)
Egyptian Egyptologist; he was born at Abu Girg near Beni Mazar in Middle Egypt, 13 March 1905, son of Muhammad Ahmad B., a farmer; from 1917 he studied at the Muslim Benevolent Society School at Minya and from 1921-6 at the Fuad I School in Cairo and later at the University of Cairo where he obtained his BA, 1930; after a year in the Antiquities Service both in museum and field work, he was sent to the University of Berlin to study Egyptology; after learning German, 1931-2, he undertook courses under Grapow (q.v.) and Sethe (q.v.) from 1932-7; DPhil., 1937; he continued his studies at the University of Göttingen under Kees (q.v.), 1937-8; D. Phil. habil., 1938; on his return to Egypt, he took up teaching positions in the University of Cairo, 1938-50 and later Ain Shams University, 1950; rector, 1956-61, Rector of Cairo University, 1961-64; from 1940 he undertook excavations at Saqqara and Memphis where in 1942 he discovered tombs of the high priests of Ptah of Dynasty 22 (*ASAE* 40 (1941), 495-506, 573-80, 607-14, 971-4; *ASAE* 42 (1943), 1-23; *ASAE* 44 (1944), 181-224; *ASAE* 54 (1956), 153-77); Member of the Institut d'Égypte 1959-80 and the Academy of Arabic Language, 1959-80; he succeeded Amer (q.v.) on 23 May 1956 as Director of the Documentation Center in Cairo until 1968; he published his two dissertations *Der Gott Chnum*, 1937; *Memphis als Zweite Landeshauptstadt im Neuen Reich*, 1948; and with H. Kees, *Handwoerterbuch der aegyptischen Sprache*, 1958; he died in Riyadh, Saudi Arabia, 12 May 1980.

Gött. Misz. 76, 83-4; inf. Univ. of Göttingen; D. Abou-Ghazi, *Vies et Travaux* IV, *Ahmad M. Badawi*, 1984, 20-4 (bibl.) (portr.); E. Endesfelder, *Die Ägyptologie an der Berliner Universität-Zur Geschichte eines Fachgebietes*, 1988, 50.

BADAWY, Alexander Mikhail (1913-1986)
Egyptian architect and archaeologist; he was born in Cairo, 29 Nov. 1913, son of Rizkalla Mikhail B. and Mathilde Grünberg; he was educated at the University of Cairo; BA Engineering in Architecture, 1936; Diploma of the Institute of Archaeology, 1939; PhD, 1942; he took part in the excavations at Tuna el-Gebel, 1937, 1939-41, 1949 and Qasr Qarun, 1950; he taught at the Universities of Cairo and Alexandria, 1941-55; he was appointed professor of the History of Architecture at the University of Kansas, 1957-61 and professor of Art Design and Art History at the University of California, Los Angeles, 1961-81; he was also Fulbright Professor at the University of Chicago; he took part in the Nubian campaign excavating the fortress at Askut, 1962-4 and recorded tombs at Giza, 1973-4 and Saqqara, 1974; his principal works were *Le Dessin architectural chez les Anciens Egyptiens*, 1948; *L'Art Copte*, 1949; *A History of Egyptian Architecture*, 3 vols., 1954-1968; *Ancient Egyptian Architectural Design*,

1965; *The Tombs of Iteti, Sekhem'ankh-Ptah, and Kaemnofret at Giza,* 1976; *The Tomb of Nyhetep-Ptah at Giza and the Tomb of 'Ankhm'ahor at Saqqara,* 1978; and *Coptic Art and Archaeology,* 1978; he died in Alexandria, 28 May 1986.

Inf. E. Badawy.

BADIA Y LEBLICH, Domingo (1766-1818)
Spanish adventurer; he was born in Barcelona 1 April 1766, son of Pedro Badia, a government official, and Caterina Leblich; he entered government administration becoming an official in the tobacco office in Cordova; he conceived the idea of exploring Africa and the Middle East and perhaps establishing a Spanish colony; after visiting France and England and learning Arabic, he set off for Morocco in 1803 passing himself off as the son of a Syrian exiled in Spain named Ali Bey; he set off on a pilgrimage to Mecca staying in Egypt in 1806 in Alexandria and Cairo where he formed a collection of antiquities which he sold to Drovetti (q.v.) before his departure for Mecca at the end of the year; after his pilgrimage he returned to Europe in 1808 by way of Jerusalem and Turkey; in Spain he became an official of Joseph Bonaparte, and, on his fall, went into exile in Paris where he published his memoirs *Travels of Ali Bey,* 1814 (English ed. 1816); he returned to the Middle East in 1818 and died en route to Mecca at Kalaat el-Blaka in Syria, 30 Aug. 1818.

J. Mercader, *Domenec Badia Ali Bey* , 1960; R. Hallett, *The Penetration of Africa to 1815,* 1965, 310-20; U. J. Seetzen, *Reisen durch Syrien...,* 1854-9, iii, 166, 373-4; E. G. de Herreros, *Quatre Voyageurs Espagnols à Alexandrie d'Égypte,* 1923, 60-162.

BAER, Klaus (1930-1987)
American Egyptologist; he was born in Halle, Germany, 22 June 1930, son of Reinhold B., a mathematician, and Marianne Kirstein; in 1933 his family emigrated to the United States where his father eventually became a professor at the University of Illinois in Champaign-Urbana; he was educated at the local high school and then at the University of Illinois where he majored in ancient Greek; BA, 1948; his interest in Egyptology had been aroused by visits to the museums in Chicago, and he taught himself ancient Egyptian; in 1948 he began graduate studies in Egyptology at the Oriental Institute, University of Chicago; from 1952-4 he held a Fulbright fellowship for research in Egypt under Ahmed Fakhry taking part in excavations at Saqqara and Giza; he returned to Chicago in 1954 and was awarded his doctorate in 1958 for a thesis on rank and title in the Old Kingdom; in 1959 he was appointed lecturer and later professor of Near Eastern languages at the University of California, Berkeley; in 1965 he returned to Chicago as associate professor and full professor from 1970; he served as chairman of the Dept. of Near Eastern Languages and Civilizations, 1972-5; he was also president of ARCE, 1981-4 and editor of *JARCE* IX; he took part in excavations at Hieraconpolis as epigrapher; his strength lay in his teaching abilities to which he devoted much of his energies; his main publication was his thesis *Rank and Title in the Old Kingdom,* 1960, but he also left manuscripts on Coptic Grammar and Egyptian chronology; he died in Chicago, 14 May 1987; his library was left to the Dept. of Near Eastern Languages, University of California, Berkeley, but his papers remain at the Oriental Institute, Chicago.

The Oriental Institute News and Notes 110, 2-3 (portr.) (E. Wente); *Varia Aegyptiaca,* 3 (1987), 101-2 (bibl.) (C. van Siclen); inf. from Mrs. K. Baer and J. Larson; D. Silverman, *For his Ka,* 1994, xviii-xix, 285-323.

BAGNANI, Gilbert Forrest (1900-1985)
Canadian-Italian archaeologist and classicist; he was born in Rome, 26 April 1900, son of Brig. Gen.Ugo B., sometime military attaché at the Italian embassy in London, and Florence Dewar from a distinguished Canadian family; he was educated in Rome and London and then studied at the University of Rome; BA, 1921; he then attended the Royal Italian School of Archaeology in Greece, 1921-3; he became Inspector of Antiquities for Campana, 1925-9; he went to Egypt in 1931 to assist Anti (q.v.) briefly at Tebtunis where he became nominal director, 1932-6; he settled in Port Hope, Ontario, Canada in 1937; he became lecturer in classics at University College, University of Toronto, 1945-65 and then lecturer at Trent University, Peterborough, 1965-75; Hon LLD. from Trent University, 1971; Fellow of the Royal Society of Canada, 1959; Vice-Pres of the American Institute of Archaeology, 1951-54; a study in his honour, *The Mediterranean World,* was published in 1975; his papers are preserved at Trent University; he died in Cobourg, Ontario, 10 Feb. 1985.

C. Brown (ed.), *Leonard E. Woodbury Collected Writings*, 1991, 613-9; I. Begg, *Echos du Monde Classique* 42 (1998), 385-405; I. Begg, *ibid.* 44 (2000), 225-254; I. Begg, *SSEA Newletter* (Spring 2019), 1-4.

BAGNOLD, Arthur Henry (1854-1943)
British Colonel, R. Engineers; he was born in London 18 March 1854, son of Captain Michael Edward B. and Eliza Larkins Walker; he was educated at Cheltenham and Woolwich Acad.; Lieut., 1873; Capt., 1884; Major, 1887; Lieut.-Col., 1899; Col., 1903; he retired, 1911; CB 1907; CMG., 1918 (for voluntary war-service); he served in Egypt, 1884-7, and undertook the removal of the colossus of Ramesses II at Mit Rahina, a difficult operation described in detail in *PSBA* 10 (1888), 452; in 1887 he presented some antiquities to the British Museum; he died in London, 9 Dec. 1943.

R. Eng. Journ. 58. 131 (portr.); Budge, *N & T* i, 103-4; *BIÉ* 37, 6-8.

BAGNOLD, Ralph Alger (1896-1990)
British soldier, explorer and scientist; he was born in Stoke, Devonport 3 April 1896, son of Arthur H. B. (q.v.) and Ethel Alger; he was educated at Malvern. 1909-14 and the Royal Military College, Woolwich, 1914-5 after which he joined the Royal Engineers and served in World War I; he then studied at Gonville and Caius College, Cambridge, 1919-21; BA, 1921; MA, 1925; he joined the Royal Corps of Signals serving in Egypt from 1926 when he explored the Eastern Desert and Sinai and later in India, 1928; he organized and led expeditions to the unknown parts of the Libyan Desert, notably in 1929, 1930, 1932 with Sandford (q.v.), during which numerous archaeological finds were made; in 1938 he was co-leader of the Sir Robert Mond (q.v.) expedition to the Gilf Kcbir and Jebel Uweinat, during which Winkler (q.v) collected material for the first systematic publication of the prehistoric rock art of the area; he was awarded the Royal Geographical Society's Founder's Medal, 1934; he later served in the Western Desert in World War II where he organized and initially commanded the Long Range Desert Group, one of the most successful Allied special units; he devoted the rest of his life to scientific research in sand movement, for which he received numerous distinctions; OBE 1941; FRS, 1944; he published *Libyan Sands*, 1935*; The Physics of Blown Sand and Desert Dunes*, 1941; and his autobiography *Sand, Wind and War*, 1990 apart from numerous other scientific works; his archives are preserved in the Churchill Archives Centre, Cambridge; he died in London, 28 May 1990.

ODNB 3, 235-6; F. Trayes (ed.), *Biographical History of Gonville and Caius College* V, 1948, 201; inf. C. Coleman and A. Zbory.

BAIKIE, (*Revd*) James (1866-1931)
British Free Church minister and author; born Bonnyrigg, Lasswade, Midlothian, 25 Nov. 1866, youngest son of Hugh Baikie, teacher, and Margaret McAndrew; he was educated at George Watson's College, Edinburgh, the University of Edinburgh, and New College, Edinburgh; he gained the Earl of Zetland's Scholarship, Edinburgh and an Open Scholarship at New College; FRAS, 1892; DD Edinburgh, 1928; he married 1903, Constance daughterof E Turner Smith; Baikie was Minister of Ancrum, Roxburghshire 1892; Minister of Wordie United Free Church, Edinburgh, 1912-22, and of St John's, Torphichen, 1922-31; he was Extension Lecturer on Egyptology for the University of Oxford; he wrote many popular books on astronomy and archaeology, and was one of the best authors in the field of popular books on Egyptology, due to his association with many of the leading figures of his day, like Petrie (q.v.); he published among other works, *The Story of the Pharaohs*, 1908; *The Sea-Kings of Crete*, 1910; *Peeps at Ancient Egypt*, a daily-life book for children, 1912; *Lands and Peoples of the Bible*, 1914; *Life of the Ancient East*, 1923; *A Century of Excavations*, 1923; *Egyptian Papyri*, 1925; *The Amarna Age*, 1926; *Glamour of Near East Excavation*, 1927; *A History of Egypt*, 2 vols. 1929; *Egyptian Antiquities in the Nile Valley*, 1932; the last a very serviceable and compact book for the tourist and an astonishing production in view of the fact that the author never went to Egypt himself; Baikie also contributed articles to the *Encyclopedia of Religion and Ethics* and the *National Geographic Magazine*, USA; he died in Broomieknowe, Lasswade, Midlothian, 3 Feb. 1931.

WWW iii, 50.

BAILEY, Donald Michael (1931-2014)
British archaeologist; he was born in London, 6 June 1931, son of Sydney A. B. and Dorothy Neal; he was evacuated during World War II and on his return attended the William Ellis School; he undertook national service in Egypt and Cyprus, 1951-3; he was appointed museum assistant in the Department of Greek and Roman Antiquities, British Museum, 1955 and later became research assistant until 1996; D. Litt. 1992; he was renown expert in lamps of the Greco-Roman period; he took part in excavations in Italy, Greece, Libya and at Ashmunein, 1980-90 and Mons Porphyrites, 1994-8; he was later part of the Faiyum survey; he was editor of *Libyan Studies*, 1990-7; *Image, Craft and the Classical World*, a volume of studies for him and Catherine Johns, was published in 2005; apart from articles and non-Egyptological works, he published *Greek and Roman Pottery Lamps*, 1963, rev. 1972; *A Catalogue of Lamps in the British Museum*, I-IV, 1975-96; with others, *British Museum Expedition to Middle Egypt Ashmunein (1980-5)*, 1982-86; with S.

Snape, *The Great Portico at Hermopolis Magna: Present State and Past Prospects*, 1988; *Hermopolis Magna: Buildings of the Roman Period*, 1991; *Excavations at El-Ashmunein* IV-V, 1991-1998; with others, *Marsa Matruh* II, 2002; with others, *The Roman Imperial Quarries* II, 2007; *A Catalogue of Terracottas in the British Museum* IV, 2008; and *The Fayoum Survey Project. The Themistou Meris* (vol. B): *The Ceromological Survey*, 2019; he died in London, 15 Aug. 2014.

Inf. C. Johns; *The Guardian* 15 Sept 2014 (C. Johns); *Libyan Studies* 45 (2014), 5 (portr.).

BAILEY, James (1791-1864)
British classical scholar; he was born in Otley,Yorks., 14 Oct. 1791, son of Reverend James B., vicar of Otley and master of Otley Grammar School, and his wife Agnes; he was educated at Trinity College, Cambridge; BA, 1814; Member's Prizeman, 1815 and 1816; MA, 1823; 1826-30 he was master of the Perse School, Cambridge, 1825-33; he moved to Peckham in London in 1841; he delivered an oration in Latin dealing with Egyptian hieroglyphs, using the texts of the Flaminian Obelisk and the Rosetta Stone, published as 'Origin and Nature of Hieroglyphics and the Greek Inscription on the Rosetta Stone', in *Classical Journal*, 16 (Cambridge, 1816), 313; he died in Peckham, London, 13 Feb. 1864.

GM 1864, 535-6; *DNB* 2, 407; *ODNB* 3, 262-3; *BIFAO* 5, 85; Hilmy, i, 48; *Al. Cantab.*

BAILLET, Auguste Théophile (1834-1923)
French Egyptologist and archaeologist; he was born in Fouilloy-près-Corbie, 27 Nov. 1834, son of Auguste Gabriel B. and Sidonie Langevin; he was engaged in commercial life, but in his leisure he made many contributions to the study of French medieval antiquities; he studied Egyptology under de Rougé (q.v.), and wrote many articles which were later collected by Maspero (q.v.) and published in *Bibl. Ég.*, vols 15, 16 (1905), with biographical notice written by his son; he died in Orléans, 6 Aug. 1923.

Bibl. Ég. 15, ut supra; *JEA* 9 (1923), 223; *DBF* 4, 1269.

BAILLET, Jules Auguste Constant (1864-1953)
French Egyptologist; he was born at Pussay 5 June 1864, son of the above Auguste T. B. and Julie Marie Pauline Dujoncquoy; he studied under his father and Maspero (q.v.); he wrote descriptions of the Egyptian collections at Sens and Vannes and contributed a number of papers to *Rec. Trav.* and other journals; he was attached to the French Institute in Cairo; his most important work was the publication of the Greek graffiti in the Royal Tombs at Thebes (*Mémoires*, 42, 1920); a paper on the same subject also in *Rec. Champollion*, 103 (1922); Baillet published a huge study on royal power and social conditions in ancient Egypt, *Le régime pharaonique dans ses rapports avec l'évolution de la morale en Égypte*, 2 vols. 1912-13; also *Le papyrus mathématique d'Akhmim*, 1892-3; *Introduction à l'étude des idées morales dans l'Égypte antique*, 1912; he died at Orléans 16 Jan. 1953.

Inf. M. Azim.

BAILLIE, David (1786-1861)
British traveller; he was born in Esslemont, 4 Sept 1786, son of James B., landowner, and Catherine Gordon; he was educated at Eton and and Trinity College, Cambridge, 1805-1810; BA 1810; Middle Temple, 1803; he was on tour in Italy in 1817; in Greece and Turkey, 1818; and in Egypt, 1818-9 with Barry (q.v.) and others where he met Salt (q.v.), Bankes (q.v.), and Beechey (q.v.); Fellow of Society of Dilettani, 1835; FRS 1836; he died in London, 17 June 1861.

R. Morkot, *ASTENE Bulletin* 78 (2019), 13-16.

BAKIR, Abel el-Mohsen Osman (1908-1992)
Egyptian Egyptologist; he was born at Alexandria, 13 Feb. 1908; he obtained his diploma from the Higher Training College, 1930 and studied at the Institute of Egyptology, University of Cairo under Vikentiev (q.v.) and Junker (q.v.); diploma, 1936; he assisted Hassan (q.v.) in his excavations at Giza, 1935-7; he then studied at Berlin under Grapow (q.v.), 1937-8 and at the University of Oxford under Gunn (q.v.) and Černý (q.v.), 1938-46; BLitt., 1941; DPhil., 1946; he specialized in Egyptian grammar and the hieratic script; he obtained a post in the Cairo Museum and then became lecturer, 1949 and assistant professor, 1952 at the University of Alexandria; Professor of Egyptian Philology at Cairo University, 1954-68; he held research posts at Göttingen, 1958; Oxford, 1971-2; and Cambridge, 1972-3 and was a guest lecturer at Cambridge from 1979; his monographs were *Slavery in Pharaonic Egypt*, 1952; *Grammar of ancient Egypt in its Golden Age* (Arabic), 1954; *The Cairo Calendar no. 86637*, 1966; *Egyptian Epistolography*, 1970; *Notes on Middle Egyptian Grammar*, 1983; *Notes on Late Egyptian Grammar*, 1984; he died in Cairo, 24 Jan. 1992.

Gött. Misz. 76 (1989), 86-7 (H. Attiatalla); *JEA* 78 (1992), x; *The Independent* 7 Feb. 1992. (J. Gwyn Griffiths); inf. Christ's College, Cambridge.

BALCZ, Heinrich (1898-1944)
Austrian Egyptologist; he was born in Vienna, 17 June 1898; after service in World War I, he studied Egyptology at the University of Vienna under Junker (q.v.); PhD, 1925; librarian at the Institut für Ägyptologie, 1923-7; he then worked on the publication of material from the excavations of the Wiener Akademie in the Kunsthistorischen Museum, 1925-30; he joined the teaching staff of the Institut, 1928; lecturer, Oct. 1939; Professor, May 1940; he completed his habilitation 24 Oct. 1934 entitled *Die Gefässdarstellungen des Alten Reiches* published in *MDAIK* 3 (1932), 50-87, 89-114; 4 (1933), 18-36, 206-226; 5 (1934), 45-94; he took part in the Austrian excavations at Giza, 1928; at the work at Merimda Beni Salama, 1929-30, 1932, at Hermopolis, 1932, and on the Theban west bank; he was assistant at the German Archaeological Institue in Cairo in succession to Schott (q.v.), 1 Oct 1931-30 Sep. 1932; he also published several articles and was part author of the preliminary report on the Hermopolis excavation of 1932; he edited *Archiv für ägyptische Archäologie* with Komorzynski (q.v.). He joined the army in 1942 and was killed in Yugoslavia in 1944.

Inf. Dr. J. Holaubek; G. Thausing, *Tarudet*, 1989, *passim*, especially 51-2; S. Voss, *Die Geschichte der Abteilung Kairo des DAI im Spanungsfeld deutscher politischer Interessen* II, *1929-1966*, 2017, 120-3.

BALDWIN, Edward Thomas (1846-1937)
British lawyer; he was born in Dalton-in-Furness, 31 May 1846, son of Revd John B. and Elizabeth Atkinson; he was educated at Trinity College, Oxford, 1864-8; BA, 1868; MA, 1871; he studied at the Inner Temple from 5 June 1867; barrister 30 April 1870; he became a member of the Northern Circuit; he visited Egypt about 1881-2 and bought a papyrus at Asyut which he presented to the British Museum in Jan. 1882, now known as the Papyrus Baldwin (EA 10061); the second half of this papyrus was given to the Musée d'Amiens also in 1882; he died in London, 24 Feb. 1937.

Al. Oxon I, 53; J. Foster, *Men-at-the-Bar*, 1885; D. Lynch, *Northern Circuit Directory 1876-2004*, 2005, 183; J. Janssen, *Grain Transport in the Ramesside Period*, 2004, 2.

BALDWIN, George (1744-1826)
British merchant and writer; he was born in The Borough near London May 1744, son of William B., hop-merchant, and Margaret Icard; he travelled extensively in the Near East and in Egypt in 1773, and he settled in Cairo from 1775-9 to promote trade between England and India via Egypt; he served as British Consul-General in Egypt, 1786-96 although the post was abolished in 1793; he left Egypt in 1798 but returned to Egypt briefly in 1801; he published reminiscences of conditions in Egypt and of the slave-trade and prevalent corruption; his collection was sold in London 8-9 May 1828; his wife Jane Maltass was the aunt of the wife of Thomas Burgon (q.v.); he died in Earl's Court, Brompton, 19 Feb. 1826.

FO Records; *ODNB* 3, 450-1 (portr.); *DNB* 3,35; *GM* 96, 283; Hilmy, i, 50; R. S. Zahlan in P. and J. Starkey (eds), *Travellers in Egypt*, 1998, 24-38.

BALFOUR, Henry (1863-1939)
British museum curator and anthropologist; he was born in Croydon, 11 April 1863, son of Lewis Balfour, a silk broker, and Sarah Walker Comber; he was educated at Charterhouse School, 1877-80 and Trinity College, Oxford, 1881-85; BA, 1885; after working with the material in the 1880s, he became the first curator of the Pitt Rivers Museum of the University of Oxford, 1891-1939; he also taught technology and prehistoric archaeology for the Oxford course on anthropology; professor, 1935; he was Pres. Of the Royal Anthropological Institute, 1902-4, of the Folklore Society, 1923-4, and of the Royal Geographical Society, 1936-8; FRS, 1924; FSA; Fellow of Exeter College, 1904; he was a member of the BSAE Committee and contributed studies of Egyptian lithics to *El Amrah and Abydos,* 1902; he died at his home in Oxford, 9 Feb. 1939.

ODNB 3, 529-31 (portr.); inf. A. Stevenson.

BALL, (*Revd*) **Charles James** (1851-1924)
British Hebraist and archaeologist; he was born in Guildford, 28 Jan. 1851, eldest son of Charles B. and Sarah Prior; he was educated at The Queen's College, Oxford; BA 1873; MA, 1876; Litt.D.; Classical Master and lecturer on Hebrew at Merchant Taylors' School; Chaplain of King's College, London; Rector of Bletchingdon, from 1899; he was an eminent Hebrew scholar and biblical critic and contributed to *PSBA* and other journals on the origin of Phoenician and Hittite scripts and their relation to Egyptian; he published *Light from the East*, a general introduction to biblical archaeology; he died in Bletchingdon, 7 Feb. 1924.

Al. Oxon.; Budge, *R & P*, 188.

BALL, John (1872-1941)
British geologist, geographer, and mining engineer; he was born at Derby, 15 Feb. 1872, son of Ebenezer B. and Louisa née Ball; he was apprenticed to the Pheonix Foundry Co. and was later engaged on the construction of

Battersea Bridge and the Liverpool Overhead Railway; he went to London and won a scholarship at the Royal School of Mines, 1891; silver medal and first prize in mechanical engineering City and Guilds College, London; first class Diploma and De la Beche medal of Royal School of Mines, 1894; he did mining work in the Isle of Man, Germany, and Spain, 1895-6, studied at the Royal Acad of Mines, Freiberg, and became PhD University of Zurich, 1897; he joined the Geological Survey of Egypt under Sir Henry Lyons, 1897; his first work was the survey of the Western Oases; next Nubia was surveyed and South-Eastern Egypt; as Resident Engineer at Aswan he carried out the underpinning of Philae Temple on the building of the first Aswan dam, 1901-2; Ball's last great geological survey was in West-Central Sinai, in 1919 he became Director of Desert Surveys, and by 1923 had completed the first comprehensive 1/500,000 map of Egypt; between 1923 and 1926 he accompanied Prince Kamal el-Din on expeditions to the Western Desert, finding much additional geological information; in 1932 he was appointed Technical Counsellor to the Survey Dept.; he was a member of the Institut d'Égypte, 1909; decorated with the Mejidie; OBE, 1918; Royal Geog. Soc. Victoria gold Medal, 1926; DSc university of London; Fellow of the Geological Soc.; FRGS.; he published *Kharga Oasis: its Topography and Geology*, 1900; *A Description of the First or Aswan Cataract of the Nile*, 1907; *The Geography and Geology of South-Eastern Egypt*, 1912; *The Geography and Geology of West Central Sinai*, 1916; *Contributions to the Geography of Egypt*, which contains a very thorough survey of the Faiyum and Lake Moeris as described by the classical authors, 1939; *Egypt in the Classical Geographers*; with H. J. L. Beadnell he also wrote *Baharia Oasis, Its Topography and Geology*, 1903; he died in Port Said, 11 July 1941.

BIÉ 24 (1942), 69-80 (Bibl.) (O. H. Little); *Sudan Notes & Records* 24 (1941), 209-12 (D. Newbold), 213-17 (G. Andrew).

BALLARD, Montague (1850-1936)
British brewer and excavator; he was born in Abingdon, 2 Sept. 1850, son of William Ballard, ale merchant, and Ann Griffin Jackson; he became the owner of the Royal Brewery, Brentford, 1880; he travelled widely and visited South Africa and Egypt; he excavated at Giza, 1901-2; his work was disorganized and undocumented, being subsequently described as a 'serdab hunt'; as a result the concession for the Giza plateau was subseqently divided among Reisner (q.v.), Schiaparelli (q.v.), and Steindorff (q.v.); Ballard's finds were dispersed after their discovery; the most notable piece, the 4th Dynasty slab stela of Nefret-iabet, is now in the Louvre; in Egyptological literature he is usually, but erroneously, referred to as an MP; in 1923 he retired to Èze-sur-Mer, France, and regularly overwintered in Khartoum; he died in Cairo, 20 March 1936.

Middlesex Independent, 28 March 1936 (obit.); *EEF Archaeological Report* 1901-2, 8; H. G. Fischer in *Mitteilungen des Instituts für Orientforschung* 7 (1959-60), 311; P. der Manuelian in *Egyptian Art in the Age of the Pyramids*,1999, 142.

BALLERINI, Francesco (1877-1910)
Italian Egyptologist; he was born in Como in 1877; he studied at the Accademia Scientifico-Letteraria of Milan from 1899 and then joined the staff of the Egyptian Museum, Turin 1902-10; he assisted Schiaparelli (q.v.) in his excavations at Giza, Heliopolis, the Valley of the Queens, Deir el-Medina, and Qau el-Kebir; he wrote several articles in *Bessarione*; he died at Como, 5 May 1910.

Rivista archaeologica dell' antica Provincia e Diocesi di Como 135 (1953), 35-51 (S. Curto) (portr.) (bibl.); S. Curto, *Storia del Museo Egizio di Torino*, 1976, 40, 86-7; P. del Vesco et al., *Missione Egitto 1903-1920*, 2017, 245-9.

BALODIS, Franz Alexander (1882-1947)
Russian Egyptologist; he was born in Wolmar, Lithuania, 26 July/7 Aug. 1882, son of Woldemar David B., a teacher, and Olga Mathilde Jakobson; he was first educated in Riga and later attended the University of Dorpat (Tartu) from 1902 where he studied theology and history and the University of Moscow and the Moscow Archaeological Institute where he studied archaeology; he studied Egyptology under von Bissing (q.v.) at Munich, 1910-2; DPhil, 1912 with the thesis *Prolegomena zur Geschichte der zwerghaften Götter in Ägypten* at Riga; Mag. Hist. in Moscow, 1914; he was appointed lecturer in Egyptology at the Moscow Archaeological Institute, 1914-8, Professor of Art History at Saratov, 1918-24, and Professor of ancient Near Eastern philology at the University of Riga, 1924-40; Pro-Rector of the University, 1932-40; Vice-Director of the Historical Institute, 1936-40; Doctor of Historical Sciences, 1926 with a thesis on the capitals of the Golden Horde which he excavated in 1919-21; president of the Latvian Philological Society, 1927-31; from 1932 head of the Latvian Office for the Protection of Monuments in which capacity he undertook excavations of medieval monuments; founder and editor of the quarterly *Senatne un Maksla* (Antiquities and Art); his works on Egyptian subjects apart from articles include *Drevnii Egipet*, 1913; *Kunstreform Echnatons*, 1923; he emigrated to Sweden in 1940 and died in Stockholm, 8 Aug. 1947.

Chron. d'Ég. 24 (1949), 94; inf. S. Wenig, J. Śliwa, and S. Stadnikov; *Z Otchłani Wieków* XIII (1938), 75-7 (portr.), (J. Kostrzewski).

BANCROFT, Edward Nathaniel (1772-1842)
British physician; he was born in London, 1772, son of Edward B., FRS and Penelope Fellows; after attending school under Dr. Charles Burney and Dr. Parr he entered St. John's College, Cambridge; MB, 1794; MD, 1804; he served as physician to the Forces in various localities; FRCP, 1806; he went with Abercromby's expedition to Egypt, 1801; while in Egypt he collected antiquities, 1803, and in 1807 he presented to the BM a pillar found at Abu Qir inscribed in Greek to Sarapis (BM, EA 99); he died in Kingston, Jamaica, 18 Sept. 1842.

ODNB 3, 637-8*; DNB* 3 106-7; Munk, *Roy. Coll. Phys.* iii. 31.

BANIER, (*Abbé*) **Antoine** (1673-1741)
French priest and scholar; he was born in Dallet (Puy-de-Dôme), 2 Nov. 1673, son of Gilbert B.; he was trained at the Jesuit College, Clermont, 1681, afterwards becoming a Member of the Académie for whom he published a number of communications on the mythology and cults of the Egyptians; see his *Mythologie et Fables*, 1st ed., 3 vols. 1738-40, 2nd ed., 8 vols., which was translated into English and published in 4 vols., 1740; he also edited Paul Lucas's *Troisième Voyage*, 1719 and later editions; he died 19 Nov. 1741.

DBF 5, 69-70; Carré, i, 45; Hilmy, i, 51, 394.

BANKES, William John (1786-1855)
British traveller, collector, and antiquarian; he was born 11 Dec. 1786, the second but eldest surviving son of Henry Bankes, MP of Kingston Lacy and Corfe Castle, Dorset, and Frances Woodward; he was educated at Trinity College, Cambridge; BA, 1808; MA, 1811; he had a political career and represented Truro in Parliament, 1810-12, Cambridge University, 1821-5, Marlborough, 1829-31, and Dorset, 1833-5; he first inherited Soughton Hall, Flints., from his great uncle, and then the Kingston estates in 1835; he was a friend of Byron and Rogers and other prominent figures of the day, and during the Peninsular War he visited Spain and for a time attached himself informally to the camp of the Duke of Wellington; he travelled extensively in the Near East and visited Egypt, Nubia, and Syria, 1815-9 with Giovanni Finati (q.v.) whose memoir he translated; he was very hostile to Champollion (q.v.), but was very interested in the decipherment of ancient Egyptian hieroglyphs and with the key provided by Young (q.v.) was able to read the name in the cartouche of a monument; he journeyed up the Nile as far as Abu Simbel where he made drawings of the temples, and his name is associated with the obelisk from Philae, discovered in 1815, which with the help of Belzoni (q.v.) he brought back to England and erected in his park at Kingston Lacy, Wimborne, with the table of kings discovered in 1819 in the temple of Ramesses II at Abydos which afterwards passed into the Mimaut (q.v.) collection and then to the British Museum; he assembled a large collection of works of art, which also included a considerable number of Egyptian antiquities now kept at Kingston Lacy; he published *Geometrical elevation of an Obelisk ... from the Island of Philae, together with the pedestal ... first discovered there by W. J. B.*, fol., 1821 and the memoirs of Finati (q.v.); Kingston Lacy and his collection there are now the property of the National Trust while other papers are in the British Museum; he died in Venice, 15 April 1855.

ODNB 3, 681-3 (portr.); *DNB* 3, 124; Burke's *Landed Gentry*, 18th ed., 38; *Official Guide to Kingston Lacy*, 4; J. Černý, *Egyptian Stelae in the Bankes Collection*, 1958; Athanasi, 41-5; Belzoni, passim; Champollion, i, 91, 251, 373, 422; ii. 78, 244, 278, 402; Hilmy., i, 51, 232; *Life and Adventures of Giovanni Finati*, ii, passim; Salt, i, 488; ii, 52, 118, 133, 139; T. G. H. James in E. Staehelin and B. Jaeger (eds.), *Ägypten-Bilder*, 1997, 301-12; P. Usick in P. and J. Starkey, *Travellers in Egypt*, 1998, 51-60; P. Usick, *Adventures in Egypt and Nubia*, 2002; *KMT* 14/2 (2003), 64-69 (P. Usick); A. Sebba, *The Exiled Collector*, 2004; D. Boyer, in N. Cooke and V. Daubney, *Every Traveller Needs a Compass*, 2015, 33-52; D. U. Seyler, *The Obelisk and the Englisman: The Pioneering Discoveries of Egyptologist William Bankes*, 2015; D. Boyer, in N. Cooke and V. Daubney (eds.), *Lost and Now Found*, 2017, 183-204.

BANVILLE, (*Vicomte*) **Aymar Athanase de** (1837-1917)
French nobleman and photographer; he was born in Vire, 19 Mar. 1837, a member of an ancient Norman family, son of Joseph Antoine B. and Marie Elisabeth Paulmier des Brosses; on his marriage in 1864 he settled in the Château de Rosel in Fresnes (Orne); Conseiller Général de l'Orne and Maire de Fresnes; he accompanied de Rougé (q.v.) to Egypt, 1863-4, and took the photographs for the *Album photographique* issued in 1865, which has considerable historical interest today as it shows the state of many buildings which have since changed through destruction or excavation and restoration; as his services in this expedition were gratuitous, they were recognized by the award of the Croix de la Légion d'Honneur; he died in the Château de Rosel, 2 Feb. in 1917.

Bibl. Ég. 21, pp. lxv. cxvi-cxvii; Hilmy, i, 177; inf. H. de Banville (grandson).

BARACCO, Giovanni (1801-1858)
Italian archaeologist; he was born in Turin in 1801; he entered the priesthood; he developed an interest in archaeology and ancient history and from 1833-58 was in charge of the Egyptian section of the Turin Museum; in 1828 he founded the Accademia di Sacra Eloquenza to encourage oratory; he died in Turin, 22 May 1858.

DBDI 5, 771-2.

BARAIZE, Alexandre Victor Noble *dit* **Émile** (1874-1952)
French architect and archaeologist; he was born in Cairo 27 Aug. 1874, son of Claude Alexandre Baraize, engineer, and Marie-Antoinette Noble; and was trained at the national school of Arts et Métiers, Aix-en-Provence; he then became a technical draughtsman for the Egyptian railways; shortly afterwards he attracted the attention of de Morgan; he became assistant to Barsanti (q.v.) and succeeded him as Director of Works of the Egyptian Antiquities Service; in this capacity he was to work on the restoration and reconstruction of many buildings over the next fifty years, except for a short break during the First World War when he served in Salonika; from 1897 he was involved in the restoration of the Coptic monasteries of Saint Menas and Bawit in Lower Egypt; at Giza in the clearance and repair of the Sphinx, and also work at Saqqara and Maidum; he also worked in Middle Egypt at Abydos and Ashmunein, protecting the reliefs in the temple of Sety I and in the Osireion; he carried out restorations on the temple of Darius at Kharga Oasis and other work at Dendera; he worked with Loret in the Valley of Kings, and at the Ramesseum with Quibell (q.v.), also helping at Deir el-Medina on the Ptolemaic temple; his greatest restoration works were those on the Hatshepsut temple where he was constantly employed for many years; while working here he discovered the burials of a priestly family of the Bubastite period; Baraize also cleared parts of the temple of Luxor, and was involved in the work of saving the Nubian temples; for his services to archaeology he was made Chevalier de la Légion d'Honneur; he published a number of articles in *ASAE* on his works; he died in Cairo, 15 April 1952.

AfO 16, I. (1952), 171 (anon.); *ASAE* 54 (1957), 5-10 (portr.) (B Bruyère); *Chron. d'Ég.* 27 (1952), 392 (anon.) ; É. Gran-Aymerich, *Dictionnaire biographique d'archéologie 1798-1945*, 2001, incorporated in *Les Chercheurs de passé 1798-1945*, 2007, 578-9.

BARAKAT, Abou al-Youn (1939-2002)
Egyptian archaeologist; he was born in 1939; he studied Egyptology and, joining the Egyptian Antiquities Service, he was appointed inspector at West Thebes in the 1960s; he then obtained his PhD in Warsaw, 1975; he became Director-General of the West Bank at Thebes, Dean of Sadat City University, Professor of Egyptology at the Universities of Sohag, Tanta, Cairo, and Alexandria, and visiting Professor at the Universities in Sanaa, Yemen and in Saudi Arabia, 1980-90; he was appointed a member of the Supreme Council of Antiquities in Egypt; he was awarded the Polish Order of Merit, 2000; he died 28 Sept. 2002.

PAM 13 (2001), 15-26 (portr.), (M Witkowski)

BARGUET, Paul (1915-2012)
French Egyptologist; he was born in Montbéliard, 8 Sept. 1915, son of Charles B. and Jeanne Marie Lucy Fischer; he studied at the Sorbonne and the École du Louvre under Desroches-Noblecourt (q.v.), 1946-7and was educated at the École pratique des Hautes Études under Lefebvre (q.v.), Garnot (q.v.), Posener (q.v.), Clère (q.v.), and Malinine (q.v.); PhD at the Sorbonne, 1963; he taught as a schoolteacher, 1945-6 andthen became an assistant to Vandier (q.v.); he was attached to IFAO, 1947-52 when he excavated at Karnak and western Thebes with Robichon (qv) and Leclant (q.v.); he was attached to CNRS, 1954-9; he then joined the Department of Egyptian antiquities at the Louvre, 1959-66, and was Professor of Epigraphy at the École du Louvre, 1956-79; he was appointed director of the Institut of Egyptology at Lyons, 1966-1981 and scientific director of the Centre franco-égyptien at Karnak, 1976-1978 in succession to Sauneron (q.v.); he excavated at Karnak Nord, 1949-51 and then conducted further studies there; he took part in the Nubian rescue campaign at Amada, 1966; a volume was published in his memory, *Un savant au pays du fleuve-dieu*, edited by L. Gabolde, 2015; apart from a number of articles, he published *La Stèle de la famine de Séhel*, 1953; with Leclant, *Karnak-Nord* IV, 1954; *Le Temple d'Amon-Rê à Karnak*, 1962; new ed., 2006; *Le Papyrus N. 3176 du Musée du Louvre*, 1962; *Le Livre des morts des anciens égyptiens*, 1967; with others, *Le Temple d'Amada*, 1967; *Les Textes des Sarcophages du Moyen-Empire*, 1986; *Aspects de la pensée religieuse de l'Égypte anciennne*, 2001; he died at Saint-Paul-lès-Dax, 1 Feb 2012.

BSFE 182 (2012), 3; *BIFAO* 112 (2012), 7-9 (D. Valbelle); L. Gabolde (ed.), *Un savant au pays du fleuve-dieu*, 2015, 8-12 (J.-C. Goyon) (portr.),13-16 (bibl.).

BARING, (*Sir*) Evelyn, 1st Earl of Cromer (1841-1917)
British statesman and diplomat; he was born in Cromer Hall, Norfolk, 26 Feb. 1841 son of Henry B., MP, and Anne Windham; educated at the Ordnance School, Carshalton, and Woolwich Academy; he was commissioned in the Royal Artillery, 1858; after various military appointments he became Secretary to the Viceroy of India, 1872; he was sent to Egypt as Commissioner of the Public Debt, 1877-9; after further Indian service he returned to Egypt as British Consul-General, 1883-1907; created Baron, 1892; Viscount, 1898; Earl, 1901; GCB; PC; OM; GCMG; KCSI; CIE; FRS; Hon. LL.D. Oxford and Cambridge; Hon. FBA; while in Egypt, Lord Cromer was one of the most influential and active administrators of his time; although not an archaeologist himself, his long association with Egypt brought him into constant touch with Egyptologists, particularly in connection with the Arch. Survey of Nubia, which he did much to promote; his book, *Modern Egypt*, 2 vols. 1908, gives a vivid picture of the social, political, and economic conditions of the country; after his retirement he continued his interest in Egyptological matters and was elected President of the EEF, 1906-17; he died in London, 29 Jan. 1917.

WWW ii, 246-7; *ODNB* 3, 821-27 (portr.); *DNB* 1912-21, 20-8; *JEA* 4 (1917), 58-60 (H. G. Lyons); R. Owen, *Lord Cromer*, 2004.

BARKER, John (1771-1849)
British diplomat; he was born in Smyrna, 9 March 1771, son of William B., merchant, and Flora Robin; after being educated in England he became private secretary to John Spencer Smith, Ambassador to the Porte, 1797; he was Pro-Consul at Aleppo, 1799, and Consul for the Levant, 1803; he had to flee from Aleppo owing to the rupture between Britain and the Porte, 1807, and remained in hiding rendering great service to the East India Co.; he returned to Aleppo after the peace of 1809 and remained there until 1825, when he was appointed British Consul in Alexandria, where he arrived in Oct. 1826, and Consul-General in Egypt in 1829, which office he had virtually held after the death of Salt in 1827; he retired in 1833 and resided in Syria; he visited England when on leave in 1818 and 1844; while in Egypt, Barker made an important collection of antiquities which was sent to England and sold (anonymously) at Sotheby's, 15 and 16 March 1833 (258 lots); the British Museum acquired many papyri, stelae, etc at this sale; he died in Betias, Syria, 5 Oct. 1849.

Biography by his son B. B. Barker, 2 vols. London, 1876 (portr.); *ODNB* 3, 8834; BL Add. MS 25659, ff. 19, 24, 25, 46; Lugt 13237.

BARLOW, Annie Elizabeth Finney (1863-1941)
British benefactor and collector; she was born in Edgworth, Bolton, 21 Dec. 1863, daughter of James Barlow, a wealthy cotton spinner, and Mayor of Bolton, and Alice Barnes; she studied at Bedford College and University College London, 1880-83; she became a member of the Egypt Exploration Fund in 1887, becoming honorary secretary for Bolton and raising considerable funds for excavations; she also gave money towards Petrie's work at Illahun; objects given to her in return for her subscriptions are now in the Bolton Museum; she formed a collection of Coptic textiles, now also in Bolton Museum; she published an account of a journey in the Delta in the EEF *AGM Report* (1888); she gave widely to charitable and humanitarian concerns; she died in Edgworth, 26 June 1941.

Correspondence, Bolton Museum; *Bolton Evening News* 26 June 1941; A. P. Thomas, 'Annie Barlow: Local Honorary Secretary of the Egypt Exploration Fund and Society,' *Discussions in Egyptology* 1 (1985), 51-57; A. P. Thomas in T. Schneider and K. Szpakowska, *Egyptian Stories*, 2007, 425-6; inf. C. Mitchell and T. Hardwick.

BARNETT, Charles John (1790-1856)
British Lieut-Colonel; he was born 13 Feb. 1790, bapt. London 12 March, son of Benjamin B. and Avice Wheate; he served with the 3rd Regt. of Foot, Captain, 1812; Lieut.-Col., 1821; retired, 1830; he fought at Waterloo; British Consul-General in Egypt, May 1841 to 1846; he died in Engelfield Green, 2 Aug. 1856.

FO Records; *GM* 1856, ii, 394; Romer, i, 87.

BARNS, *(Revd)* **John Wintour Baldwin** (1912-1974)
British Egyptologist and papyrologist; he was born in Bristol, 12 May 1912, son of William Henry Barns and Helen Maria Baldwin; he was educated at the University of Bristol, BA, 1932 and at Oxford, BA, 1937; MA, 1942; DPhil, 1947; there he studied under C. H. Roberts and B. Gunn (q.v.); he served as a code-breaker at Bletchley Park during World War II; he was Lady Wallis Budge Research Fellow in Egyptology, University College, Oxford 1945-53, Lecturer in Papyrology, Oxford 1953-65; Professor of Egyptology, Oxford 1965-74; he was ordained in 1956; although he published comparatively little in the field of Coptic studies, his strength lay in his teaching of the language and literature; apart from his papyrological studies and articles, his works include *The Ashmolean Ostracon of Sinuhe,* 1952; *Five Ramesseum Papyri,* 1956; *Four Martyrdoms from the Pierpont Morgan Coptic Codices: Greek and Coptic Papryi from the cartonnage of the covers,* 1981 with G. M. Browne and J. C. Skelton; he died in Oxford, 23 Jan. 1974.

JEA 60 (1974), 3 (Hugh Lloyd-Jones), 243-6 (portr.) (W. V. Davies); *JEA* 61 (1975), 227-30 (Gruen) (bibl.); *BSAC* 21 (1971-3), 219-22 (bibl.) (E. Maher); *BSFE* 69 (1974), 4.

BAROCAS, Claudio (1940-1989)
Italian Egyptologist; he was born in Alexandria in 1940, but his family later moved to Italy; he studied Egyptology under Donadoni at the Faculty of Letters and Philiosophy, University La Sapienza in Rome; he served as voluntary assistant of the Chair of Egyptology in Rome; he was appointed instructor of Coptic Language and Literature at the Istituto Universitario Orientale in Naples, 1969 and then in addition instructor of Egyptology, 1971; Professor of Egyptology, 1981; Director of the Seminario di Studi Africani (later in 1984 Dipartimento di Studi e Ricerche su Africa e Paesi Arabi), 1982-6; he excavated at Antinoe, Gebel Barkal, 1972-6 and at Naqada, 1977-86; he collaborated with the Archaeological Superintendency of Naples to reorganize the display in the Naples Museum and contributed to the catalogue *La Collezione egiziana del Museo Archeologico di Napoli,* 1989; apart from articles and reviews, he also published *Egitto,* 1970; English version, 1972; German version, 1974; *L'antico Egitto,* 1978; *Tebe,* 1982; he died 29 March 1989.

R. Pirelli, *Egyptological Studies for Claudio Barocas,* 1999, 9-10 (R. Fattovich), 16-18 (bibl.); inf. R. Gozzoli.

BARRACCO, *(Baron)* **Giovanni** (1829-1914)
Italian collector; he was born at Isola di Capo Rizzuto, 28 April 1829, son of Luigi B. and Chiara Lucifero; MP, 1861-86, Senator from 1886; he was the founder of the Museo Barracco, Rome, which mainly consists of Greek and Roman art, but also contains Egyptian antiquities, opened in 1905; he died in Rome, 14 Jan. 1914.

Wilbour, 256; *DBDI* 6, 515-7; G. Careddu, *Museo Barracco di scultura antica. La Collezione Egizia,* Rome, 1985, IX-X.

BARRY, *(Sir)* **Charles** (1795-1860)
British architect; he was born in Westminster, 23 May 1795, the son of Walter Edward B., a stationer, and Frances Maybank; RA; in 1817 he visited Greece and Turkey with Sir C. Eastlake and was about to return to England when he met Mr D. Baillie who admired his drawings and suggested that he go with him to Egypt and Palestine, 1818-19; his name, with the date 1819, is carved on the Abusir Rock at the Second Cataract for he went up the Nile beyond Philae before going on to Jerusalem and Syria; while in Egypt he executed a fine series of plans, sections, and drawings of temples, tombs, etc, and also of monuments in Nubia which are now in the Griffith Institute, Oxford; Barry afterwards designed many famous buildings in London, the most famous being the Houses of Parliament; he was also extremely successful in garden design and had a number of distinguished pupils, one of the most famous being Somers Clarke (q.v.); he was the first English architect to visit Egypt and leave a record of his journey; some of his papers are in the Griffith Institute; an Art Union of London portrait medal was issued in 1862; he died in Clapham, 12 May 1860, and was buried in Westminster Abbey.

ODNB 4, 111-20 (portr.); *DNB* 3, 310-13; Griff. Inst. *List of Records* (1947), 3; A. Barry, *Memoir of the Life and Works of the late Charles Barry,* 1870; *GM* 57 (1982), 73; P. Usick in D. Fortenberry (ed.), *Who Travels Sees More,* 2007, 87-100; D. Boyer in N. Cooke and V. Daubney (eds.), *Every Traveller Needs a Compass,* 2015, 33-52; R. Keersmaecker, *ASTENE Bulletin* 77 (2018), 15-17.

BARSANTI, Alexandre (1858-1917)
Italian technician and excavator; he was born in Alexandria, 28 Aug. 1858; after his education at the Institute of Fine Arts, Florence, he returned to Egypt and was engaged by Maspero (q.v.) to succeed Floris (q.v.) in Cairo Museum as restorer, technician, and artist; in 1891 he was given the title of Conservateur-Restaurateur; he was most skilled in the work of repairing, restoring, and mounting damaged objects, and also in the consolidation of buildings; in 1892 he went with de Morgan (q.v.) to Upper Egypt, and in 1894-5 assisted Daressy (q.v.) in the clearance of the Temple of Medinet Habu; in 1895-6 he was in Nubia to superintend the consolidation and

restoration of the temples and other buildings affected by the Aswan barrage; from 1899 to 1904, he worked in the pyramid-field at Saqqara, where he restored and repaired many mastabas and later tombs; at this period he conducted a number of excavations, particularly around the pyramid of Unas where the remains of the funerary temple were discovered, and also at Zawyet el-Aryan where he cleared the substructures of the so-called Layer Pyramid and the great incomplete shaft and burial chamber of the north pyramid; these discoveries were described in *ASAE* as were his other works; in addition he excavated the site of the Maru-Aten at Amarna, finding some fine fragments of painted pavements now in Cairo Museum, but this dig was never properly published; in 1907 he became Director of Works; in 1911-13 he worked on the Theban temples; he died in Cairo, 24 Oct. 1917.

ASAE 17 (1917), 245-57 (bibl. 258-60) (G. Daressy); J. P. Lauer, *Le Problème des Pyramides d'Égypte* (1952), 73-7; T. E. Peet and C. L. Woolley, *The City of Akhenaten* I, v; É. Gran-Aymerich, *Dictionnaire biographique d'archéologie 1798-1945*, 2001, incorporated in *Les Chercheurs de passé 1798-1945*, 2007, 581.

BARSKY, Vasily Grigorevitch (1701-1747)
Russian traveller; he was born in Litky, near Kiev, 1/12 Jan. 1701, son of Grigor B., a merchant; he became a monk in 1723 and began his travels in the East; he was in Egypt in 1727-8 and 1730; he was the author of *Pilgrimage to the Holy Places in the East from 1723 to 1747* (Russ.), St. Petersburg,1778 which gives short descriptions of Rosetta, Cairo, Siwa, and Alexandria where he described the obelisk of Thutmose III, now in New York, complete with a good drawing of legible hieroglyphs; he died in Kiev, 7/18 Oct. 1747.

O. Volkoff, *Voyageurs Russes en Égypte*, Cairo, 1972, 75-100; B. M. Dantsig, *Blizhny vostok v russkoy nauke i literature,* Moscow,1973, 63-66; inf. J. Śliwa.

BARTA, Winfried (1928-1992)
German Egyptologist; he was born in Dresden, 20 Aug. 1928; he was educated at the Philosophical and Theological Academy at Paderborn and from 1957 at the University of Munich under H. W. Müller (q.v.), PhD 1962; he obtained a post in the Egyptian Museum in Munich, 1 March 1962-30 Sept. 1963; he was then attached to the German Archaeological Institute visiting Egypt and the Sudan; he returned to a post at the museum, 1 May 1964-31 Jan. 1965; he was appointed as assistant at the Institut für Ägyptologie of the Ludwig-Maximilian University of Munich; he presented his habilitation in 1967; he was successively lecturer from 1 Jan. 1968, Professor from 1 April 1971, and full Professor from 27 Aug. 1974 in succession to Müller (q.v.); he was twice Dean of the Philosophical Faculty, 3 March 1975 - 30 Sept. 1977; 1 Oct. 1985 - 30 Sept. 1987; he was a member of the Senate of the University of Munich, 1976-8; member of the Academia Scientarium et Artum Europaea in Salzburg, 1991; his interests lay in the fields of religion, grammar, and chronology; he published over 150 articles and lexicon entries; he was editor of *Münchner Ägyptologische Studien*, with Müller, 1982-8 and *Münchener Ägyptologische Untersuchungen*, with D. Kessler, 1990-2; his main publications were his thesis *Die altägyptische Opferliste von der Frühzeit bis zur griechisch-römischen Epoche*, 1963; his habilitation *Aufbau und Bedeutung der altägyptischen Opferformel*, 1968; *Das Gespräch eines Mannes mit seinem Ba (Papyrus Berlin 3024)*, 1969; *Das Selbstzeugnis eines altägyptischen Künstlers*, 1970; *Untersuchungen zum Götterkreis der Neunheit*, 1973; *Untersuchungen zur Göttlichkeit des regierenden Königs*, 1975; *Die Bedeutung der Pyramidentexte für den verstorbenen König*, 1981; *Die Bedeutung der Jenseitsbücher für den verstorbenen König*, 1985; and *Komparative Untersuchungen zu vier Unterweltsbüchern*, 1990; a volume of essays was published in his memory, D. Kessler and R. Schulz, *Gedenkschrift für Winfried Barta*, 1995; he died at Ebersberg near Munich, 27 Oct. 1992.

Gött. Misz. 131 (1992), 5 (D. Kessler and R. Schulz); *ZÄS* 120 (1993), XII-XV (portr.) (J. von Beckerath); inf. R. Schulz; D. Kessler and R. Schulz, *Gedenkschrift für Winfried Barta*, 1995, VII, 1-15 (bibl.) (C. Beinlich-Seeber).

BARTH, Heinrich (1821-1865)
German explorer; born Hamburg, 16 Feb. 1821, son of Johann Christoph Heinrich B. and Charlotte Karoline Zadow; he was educated at the University of Berlin, graduated 1844; he studied Arabic in London, and from 1845 travelled throughout N. Africa from Tangier, visiting Egypt and Nubia as far as Wadi Halfa, crossing the desert to Berenice; he went through the Sinai Peninsula to Syria, Palestine, Asia Minor, Turkey and Greece, returning to Berlin in 1847; he published an account of his journey in *Wanderungen durch die Küstenländer des Mittelmeers*, 1849; in 1850 he made a second journey to Africa for the British Govt. to open up communications with the central and western Sudan, accompanied by James Richardson (who died in March 1851) and the German astronomer Adolf Overweg (who died in Sept. 1852); from the Sudan he reached Timbuktu and returned to Europe in 1855; he published *Travels and Discoveries in North and Central Africa*, 5 vols. 1857-8; decorated CB; Professor of Geography at the University of Berlin; he died in Berlin, 25 Nov. 1865.

Schubert, *Heinrich Barth*, Berlin 1897; Hilmy, i, 53; *Trans. R. Soc. Lit.* Ser. 2 iv, 181,200; *NDB* 1, 60 2-3.

BARTHÉLEMY, (*Abbé*) **Jean Jacques** (1716-1795)
French antiquarian, numismatist, and scholar; born at Cassis, 20 Jan. 1716, son of Joseph B. and Madeleine Rastis; he was educated in Marseilles; in 1744 he settled in Paris; in 1745 he became assistant in the cabinet of medals and in 1753 succeeded Gros de Boze as Keeper of the royal cabinet of medals, 1760; he was elected a member of the Académie des Inscriptions and he made many contributions to its *Mémoires*, several of them on Egyptian subjects; in a paper published in 1761 he made the fundamental observation that the 'ovals' or cartouche rings in the hieroglyphic inscriptions, enclosed royal names, thus antedating de Guignes (q.v.) and Zoëga to whom this discovery is usually attributed; in 1793 he was offered the Librarianship of the Bibliothèque Nationale, but declined it and continued as Keeper of Medals; many years after his death his works were collected and republished in 4 vols.; bronze portrait medals were issued in 1795 and 1824; he died in Paris, 30 April 1795.

Biogr. Memoir in *Oeuvres Complètes*, 1 (1821); *EB* 3, 448; Hilmy, i, 54; Madeleine V. David, *CRAIBL* (1961), 30-42; Maurice Badolle, *L'abbé Jean-Jacques Barthélemy (1716-1795) et l'hellénisme en France dans la seconde moitié du XVIIIᵉ siècle, Paris,* 1927; Lamy, 292-5; T. Sarmant, *Le Cabinet des Médailles de la Bibliothèque Nationale 1661-1848*, 127-57, 200-8, 214-8; É. Gran-Aymerich, *Dictionnaire biographique d'archéologie 1798-1945*, 2001, incorporated in *Les Chercheurs de passé 1798-1945*, 2007, 582-3.

BARTHOLDY, Jacob Ludwig Salomon (1779-1825)
Prussian diplomat; he was born in Berlin, 13 May 1779, son of Yehuda Levin Salomon and Bella Itzig; after his education at Königsberg he toured Greece with the artist Gropius; in 1805 he renounced the Jewish faith at Dresden and was baptized; in 1809 he joined the army as a volunteer and was later wounded at the Battle of Ebersperg; he served as Consul-General at Rome from 1816 until his death; Bartholdy had a fine collection of Egyptian antiquities which was inspected by Champollion in 1825 and afterwards acquired by the Berlin Museum; he died in Rome, 26 July 1825.

Champollion, i, 189, 218, 407; *NDB* 1, 609.

BARTHOW, François (*fl.* 1805-1832)
French-American guide and dealer; he was born in Santo Domingo or alternatively Bellville, New York and was or became an American citizen; he settled in Egypt for business reasons; he is mentioned by Valentia (q.v.) in 1805 and acted as the guide for Legh (q.v.) in 1812-3 and Bankes (q.v.) in 1815; he formed a collection of antiquities, some from excavations at Thebes, which was eventually acquired in part by de Lescluze (q.v.) and Mayer (q.v.); he offered his services as an excavator to the National Museum of Antiquities, Leiden in 1828; he also acted as an agent for Anastasi (q.v.) and Mendes Cohen (q.v.) in the acquisition of antiquities.

B. van de Walle, *Annales de la Société d'Émulation de Bruges* 97 (1960), 199-204; *Chron. d'Ég.* 79 (1965), 102-3; M. Dewachter, *BIFAO* 69 (1971), 139-41; H. Schneider in C. Morigi Govi, S. Curto, and S. Pernigotti, *L'Egitto fuori dell'Egitto*, 394; C. Vivian, *Americans in Egypt 1770-1915*, 2012, 56-72; A. Oliver, *American Travellers on the Nile*, 2016, 42-3.

BARTLETT, William Henry (1809-1854)
British topographical artist; born Kentish Town, London, 26 March 1809, son of William B. and his wife Anne; he was articled to John Britton the architect and antiquary, 1823, and employed to illustrate his works; he later travelled in Europe, America, and the Near East, producing his most famous work, *The Beauties of the Bosphorus*, with Julia Pardoe, 1839, after a visit to Turkey; in 1845 he went to Egypt of which he wrote a descriptive work, *The Nile Boat*, 1850, which ran to five editions; he also wrote a book on his journey from Cairo to Sinai, *Forty Days in the Desert, on the track of the Israelites; or, a Journey from Cairo ... to Mount Sinai and Petra*, 1848; another similar work was *Scripture Sites and Scenes ... in Egypt, Arabia, and Palestine, etc*; Bartlett had an astonishing power of conveying realism in his engravings and his work is of considerable historic interest as he recorded places which have greatly changed since his day; his correspondence is in the Griffith Institute; he died on a ship between Malta and Marseilles and was buried at sea, 13 Sept. 1854.

Beattie, William M. D., *Brief Memoir of the late W H Bartlett*, (portr.) 1855; Britton, John, *A Brief Memoir of W. H. Bartlett*, 1855; *ODNB* 4, 185; *DNB* 3, 335; Hilmy, i, 55.

BARUCQ, (*Père*) **André Albert** (1905-1986)
French Egyptologist; he was born in Paris, 5 April 1905, son of Marie Neoline Barucq; he was educated in schools of the Salesian order in Tournai and Château d'Aix in the Loire Valley; he entered the Salesian order in 1922, taking his first vows in 1923; he taught successively at schools at Marseilles 1924-5, Romans 1925-6 and Montpellier 1926-9 where he studied for a degree in Arts; following military service, he studied theology and was attracted to Old

Testament studies; he was ordained in 1933, he studied at the Institut Biblique in Rome 1933-5 and then took up a post teaching the Old Testament at the theological college of Fontanières near Lyons 1935-1970; in 1948 he was appointed professor of Hebrew and the Old Testament at the Institut Catholique in Lyons; in 1956 he obtained his doctorate in theology; from 1960 he substituted for three years for Daumas (q.v.) as professor of Egyptology at the University of Lyons; apart from articles, he published his thesis *L'Expression de la louange divine et de la prière dans la Bible et en Egypte*, 1962 and with Daumas, *Hymnes et prières de l'Égypte Ancienne*, 1980; he died in Lyons, 16 May 1986.

Inf. D. Sturtwegen.

BASTIS, Christos G. (1904–1999)
Greek-American restaurateur and collector; he was born in Trikala, Greece, 10 Jan. 1904, son of George Bastis; he moved to the United States in 1922, founding a small chain of seafood restaurants in New York; he collected Classical and Egyptian antiquities; many of the latter were loaned, and some thereafter donated, to the Brooklyn Museum, of which he served as Trustee; a special exhibition of his collections was held at the Metropolitan Museum in 1987, the Egyptian material being published by B. V. Bothmer (q. v.); a posthumous sale of his collections was held at Sotheby's (New York), 9 Dec. 1999, totaling $9,248,745; he died in Palm Beach, Florida, 21 May 1999.

Personal information; *New York Times* May 23, 1999; B. V. Bothmer in *Antiquities From the Collection of Christos G. Bastis* (Mainz, 1987); J. Theodorou, 'The Eye of Christos Bastis', in *The Greek American*, 23 May 1992; C. Picón in Sotheby sale catalogue, 9 Dec. 1999; inf. T. Hardwick.

BATAILLE, André (1908-1965)
French papyrologist; he was born in Paris, 22 March 1908; he studied classics at the Sorbonne and École Pratique des Hautes Études; he joined IFAO in 1935 and undertook epigraphic work at Deir el-Medina and Deir el-Bahri; he was a prisoner of war, 1940-42; after a post as a schoolteacher, he was appointed to the Sorbonne in 1946; he then completed his doctorate in 1948; he succeeded as Professor in 1946 and Director of the Institute of Papyrology; apart from his papyrological work and articles, he published *Les inscriptions grecques du temple de Hatshepsout à Deir el-Bahri*, 1951; *Memnonia*, 1952, and *Recherches de papyrologie et d'épigraphie grecques sur la nécropole de la Thèbes d'Égypte*, 1952; he was accidentally killed in Paris, 22 June 1965.

Chron d'Ég 40 (1965), 535-41 (H. Cadell); *Recherches de Papyrologie* 4 (1967), 5-10 (bibl.) (J. Scherer); M. Capasso (ed.), *Hermae*, 2007, 309-14 (portr.).

BATES, Oric (1883-1918)
American archaeologist; he was born in Boston, Mass., 5 Dec. 1883, son of Arlo B. and Harriet Leonora Vose; he studied at Harvard and in 1906 was appointed to a post in the Egyptian Dept. of the Boston Museum of Fine Arts; he afterwards studied in Berlin and took part in two Nubian expeditions 1908-9, those of the Khedival Government, and Harvard-Boston; in 1909 he conducted an expedition in Tripoli, and in 1910 he was again exploring in Nubia and the Sudan; he published his famous work *The Eastern Libyans* in 1913; in 1914 he was appointed Curator of African Archaeology in the Peabody Museum, Harvard; he inaugurated the series of volumes *Harvard African Studies* in 1917; he was taken ill when training for military service, and died at Camp Zachary Taylor, Louisburg, Kentucky, 8 Oct. 1918.

Memoir prefixed to *Harvard African Studies*, ii; *JEA* 6 (1920), 293; private inf.

BATISSIER, (Yves) Louis Joseph (1783-1882)
French diplomat and author; he was born Bourbon l'Archambault, 1783, son of Denis Joseph B. and Marie Angelique Lefort; he was French Consul at Suez, and wrote on ancient art, 1843-60; he presented papyri to the Louvre (nos. 3174, 3176, 3177, etc); he died in Enghien, 8 June 1882.

Vapereau, 123; *Rev. Arch.* 8, 467; Hilmy, i, 56.

el-BATRAWI, Ahmed Mahmud (1902-1964)
Egyptian anatomist and anthropologist; he was born at Kesna, Menufiya province, Lower Egypt, 12 July 1902, son of Mahmud el-Batrawi, the local schoolmaster; he was educated in his village and later at Alexandria and Cairo; he studied medicine at the Medical Faculty, Cairo University, graduating in 1926; in 1928 he was appointed assistant at the Anatomical Institute of Cairo University under Derry (q.v.); he took part in Emery's Nubian excavations as assistant anthropologist and doctor 1929-34 and published the human remains; from 1935 undertook post-graduate work in London, BSc in human anatomy and morphology, 1938; PhD in anthropology, 1940; he rejoined the Anatomical Institute and examined human remains from the excavations at Saqqara (*ASAE* 47 (1947), 97-111; *ASAE* 48 (1948), 487-497; *ASAE* 50 (1950), 477-494) and Dahshur (*ASAE* 48 (1948), 585-598; *ASAE* 51 (1951), 435-440); he was appointed professor of anatomy at the Medical Faculty 1949; he organized the Arabian-Polish anthropological expedition to the oases in the Western Desert

1958-59 and to the Fayum and Western Delta 1962; he was made an Hon. member of the Polish Anthropological Society 1962 and other foreign societies; his published works include *Report on the human remains. Mission Archéologique de Nubie*, 1935, 'The Racial History of Egypt and Nubia' in *Journal of the Royal Anthropological Institute of Great Britain and Ireland*, 75, 18-101 and 76, 131-156; and an Arabic translation of Gray's *Anatomy*; he died in Cairo 28 (or 25) Nov. 1964.

Anthropologie IV (1966), 77-8, 93-4 (E. Strouhal) (portr.); *Anthropologie* I (1963), 78 (bibl.); J. Buikstra and C. Roberts (eds.), *The Global History of Palaeopathology. Pioneers and Prospects*, 2012, 220-1 (B. Baker and M. Judd).

BAUD, Marcelle Gabrielle (1890-1987)
French Egyptologist and artist; she was born in Paris 28 Nov. 1890, daughter of Antoine B., an artist and Marthe Morel; she studied at the École des Beaux Arts and the Académie Julian, 1910-2 and the at the École du Louvre when she became interested in Egyptology; she was attached to IFAO in Cairo from 1921 and worked at various sites throughout Egypt as a copyist; she illustrated *Les Pleureuses*, 1938 by Werbrouck (q.v.) and Capart's (q.v.) work on the tomb of Nakht; she published, with others, *Les Dessins Ébauchés*, 1935; *Guide Bleu*, 1956; and *Le Caractère du Dessin en Égypte Ancienne*, 1978; she died at Mailhat, 13 Feb. 1987.

Internet bio.

BAUD, Michel (1963-2012)
French Egyptologist and Sudanologist; he was born in 11 Nov. 1963; he studied at the Sorbonne, 1982-94 under Nicholas Grimal and the École pratique des haues études; he was attached to IFAO in Cairo, 1994-8; on his reurn to France, he taught courses at the Collège de France and the Institut d'Égyptologie Keops; he was head of the Nubian section of the Department of Egyptian Antiquities, Louvre Museum, 2006-12; he was appointed assistant professor at the Sorbonne, 2012; he organized an exhibition on Meroe; he excavated at Balat-Ayn Asil 1995-2000, Abu Rawash 1995-2008, and Muweis in the Sudan from 2007; he published his doctoral thesis *Famille royale et pouvoir sous l'Ancien Empire*, 1999, 2nd ed. 2005; *Djéser et la IIIe dynastie*, 2002; and *Meroe, un empire sur le Nil*, 2010; he died in Paris, 13 Sept. 2012.

Sudan and Nubia 16 (2012), 155-6 (V. Rondot), (portr.); *BSFE* 184 (2002), 2 (portr.) (P. Tallet); *BIFAO* 112 (2012), 11-13 (P. Tallet), (portr.), 14-17 (bibl.).

BAUMGARTEL, Elise Jenny (*née* Goldschmidt) (1892-1975)
German-British prehistorian; she was born at Berlin, 5 Oct. 1892, daughter of Rudolph G., an architect, and Rose G. Hoeninger; she was educated at the University of Berlin where she studied medicine and later Egyptology under Erman (q.v.) and Sethe (q.v.); she married Hubert Baumgartel, an art historian in 1914; she obtained her doctorate at Königsberg in 1927 under Wreszinski (q.v.) specializing in the Neolithic period of North Africa; she later had a scholarship to study in Paris and Toulouse and took part in the excavations at Hermopolis; because of the Nazi regime, she left Germany in 1934 for Paris, where she studied flints, and then London; in Britain she held the post of Assistant Keeper of Egyptology at the Manchester Museum and was a voluntary worker at University College London from 1936, Honorary Research Assistant 1937-9, being subsidized by Robert Mond (q.v.), Temporary Assistant 1940-1; she later settled in Oxford to work on her history of predynastic Egypt; she lived in America 1957-64 but returned to Oxford to complete her work on Petrie's Naqada excavations; her principal publications were *Dolmen und Mastaba*, 1926; *The Cultures of Prehistoric Egypt* Vol. I, 1947, rev. 1955; Vol. II, 1960; the chapter *Predynastic Egypt,* 1965 in the *Cambridge Ancient History* third ed. I, 1970; *Petrie's Naqada Excavation. A Supplement*, 1970; she died in Oxford, 28 Oct. 1975.

JEA 62 (1976), 3-4 (J. Crowfoot Payne); *JEA* 63 (1977), 48-51 (bibl.) (V. A. Donohue); inf. C. Giepen (daughter); R. Janssen, *The First Hundred Years,* 34, 39, 42-5, 52.

BAYOUMI, Abbas (1904-1983)
Egyptian Egyptologist; he was born in Asyut, 25 July 1904; he studied Egyptology in Paris from 1924-31 at the École des Hautes Études where he wrote a thesis on the Fields of Iaru; on his return he entered the Antiquities Service being Chief Inspector of Upper Egypt in 1936; he then transferred to the Museum branch and became a curator in the Cairo Museum; he succeeded Hamza (q.v.) as Director of the Cairo Museum, 1950-6 and was briefly acting Director General of Antiquities following the revolution in 1952; he followed Amer (q.v.) as Director-General in 1956 but resigned in 1957; he published *Autour du Champ des Souchets et du Champ des Offrandes,* 1940 and aided Gauthier (q.v.) to complete Maspero's Cairo catalogue of Late period and Ptolemaic sarcophagi; he also translated Drioton and Vandier's *L'Égypte* into Arabic; he died in Cairo in 1983 and was buried in Asyut.

Inf. D. Abou-Ghazi, A. M. Bakir, and Dr. P. Vernus; *Bulletin of the Egyptian Museum* 1 (2004), 7.

BEADNELL, Hugh John Llewellyn (1874-1944)
English explorer and cartographer; he was born in Kildare, Ireland, 14 Oct. 1874, second son of Maj. Charles Edward Beadnell, RA, and Fanny Louisa Marsh; he was educated at King's College, London, and the Royal School of Mines; FGS; FRGS; he married May Grace Thomson, 1904, she died 1942; he entered the army, Major (re-employed, 1940-3); his connection with Egypt began with the Geological Survey of Egypt, 1896-1906, during which period he mapped large areas of the Nile Valley and Libyan Desert; he discovered new extinct fauna in the Fayum desert, including the ancestors of two species of modern elephants; also reclaimed extensive areas of desert in the Kharga depression by sinking artesian wells, 1906-10; he subsequently went ranching in Canada, 1912-15, but was on war service again in the Near East, 1916-19, with the rank of acting Lt. Col.; Order of the Nile; he surveyed the Red Sea Coast and Central Sinai, 1921-5; further work carried out in the Libyan desert, 1927-32; Beadnell was one of the major contributors to present day knowledge of the geography of both ancient and modern Egypt and the surrounding desert, and with Ball (q.v.) his studies are essential for the student; he received awards from the Geological and Royal Geographical Socs. for his survey work; his principal publications were: *Dakhla Oasis: its topography and geology*, in *Eg. Geol. Survey Report*, 1899, Pt. 4, 1901; *Farafra Oasis: its topography and geology*, Ibid, 1899, Pt. 3, 1901; *Bahariya Oasis: its topography and geology*, Ibid, with J. Ball, 1903; *The Topography and Geology of the Fayum Province of Egypt*, 1905; *An Egyptian Oasis: an account of the oasis of Kharga in the Libyan desert, with special reference to its history, physical geography and water-supply*, 1909; *The Wilderness of Sinai: a record of two years' recent exploration: with a foreword by D. G. Hogarth*, 1927; also two articles 'On some recent geological discoveries in the Nile Valley and Libyan desert', and 'Neolithic flint implements from the northern desert of the Fayum, Egypt' in *Geolog. Mag.* 1901-03; he died London 2 Jan. 1944.

WWW iv, 74-6.

BEAMONT, William John (1828-1868)
British traveller; he was born at Warrington, 16 Jan. 1828, son of William B., solicitor and mayor of Warrington, and Ann Gaskell; he was educated at Eton 1842-6 and Trinity College, Cambridge 1846-50, BA, 1850; MA, 1853; ordained 1854; he then toured the Levant in 1854-5 and again in 1860 visiting Sinai where he described the archaeological sites in detail; on his return he was vicar of St. John's, Drury Lane 1855-8 and of St. Michael's, Cambridge, 1858-68; he published *A Diary of a Journey to the East*, 1856 and *Cairo to Sinai*, 1860; he died in Cambridge, 6 Aug. 1868.

ODNB 4, 531; *DNB* 4, 11.

BÉATO, Antonio (*c.*1825-1905)
Italian professional photographer; he was born near Venice *c.*1825; brother of the photographer Felice Béato; he was resident in Calcutta in 1859; Cairo *c.*1860 and Luxor from 1862 until his death; he took a large series of excellent photographs of the principal temples and monuments in Egypt in the 1860s to 1880s, many of which constitute extremely valuable records of the contemporary state of monuments that have since been defaced or destroyed; sets of these photographs were sold to tourists and many were used as illustrations for books on Egypt; in 1906-7 Maspero (q.v.) bought from his widow his negatives and stock of prints for the records of Cairo Museum; he died in 1905.

Maspero, *Rapports sur la marche du Serv. des Ant. 1899-1910*, Cairo, 1912, pp. xli, 250; Wilbour, 217, 236, 272, 463, 509; Budge, *N & T*, ii. 326; N. Perez, *Focus East*, 1988; C. Osman, *History of Photography* April-June 1990, 101-111; I. Zannier, *Il Nilo della memorie. Fotografie di Antonio Beato in Egitto 1860/1900*, 1995; A. Ferri, *Il Fotografo dei Faraoni. Antonio Beato in Egitto 1860-1905*, 2008; G. Réveillac, *Trésors photographiques d'Égypte*, 2017.

BEATTY, (*Sir*) Alfred Chester (1875-1968)
American-British mining engineer, multi-millionaire industrialist, art and book collector, and philanthropist; he was born in New York, 7 Feb. 1875, son of John Cuming B. and Hetty Bull; naturalized Englishman, 1933; he married 1. Grace Madeline Rickard, 1900, 2. Edith Dunn, 1918; he was educated at Westminster School, Dobbs Ferry, New York; Columbia School of Mines; Princeton University; FSA; Hon. LLD. Dublin, Birmingham; Hon. DSc Columbia, 1928; Chairman of the Selection Trust etc; first hon. citizen of the Irish Republic, 1957; a friend of Cecil Rhodes he acquired and developed many of the Guggenheim mines, and was involved with gold, silver, and copper mines in Europe, Asia, and America, at one time in control of companies with £140 million capital; Chester Beatty collected 9,000 rare books; paintings; stamps etc.; he left 14,000 rare oriental MSS valued at £6 million to the Republic of Ireland; with his wife he presented a valuable collection of Egyptian papyri to the British Museum, subsequently published by Gardiner, *Hieratic Papyri in the British Museum*, 3rd Series, *The Chester Beatty Gift*, 2 vols. 1935; a further papyrus containing the story of the Contendings of Horus and Seth was retained by Beatty for his own collection and is now in the Chester Beatty Library, Dublin; it too was published by Gardiner, *The Library of A. Chester Beatty. Description of a Hieratic Papyrus with a mythological Story, Love-Songs, and other miscellaneous texts*, 1931; he died in Monaco, 19 Jan. 1968.

WWW vi, 74-5; *The Times*, 22 Jan. 1968; *The Daily Telegraph*, 22 Jan. 1968; *ODNB* 4, 572-3; *DNB* 1961-70,823; A. J. Wilson, *The Life and Times of Sir Alfred Chester Beatty*, 1985.

BECK, Horace Courthope (1873-1941)
British scholar of jewellery and collector; he was born in London, 13 Nov. 1873, son of Joseph B. and Emma Elizabeth Allen; he worked for the family firm of optical instrumental makers before retiring in 1924 to pursue his research; he became known as an expert on beads, and published beads from excavations including those of Brunton (q.v.) at Qau and Badari; he wrote also on on early glass and glazed stone, and a fundamental article on faience beads in Bronze Age Britain; FSA 1924; he formed a large collection of ancient beads and jewellery, purchasing at the MacGregor (q. v.) and other sales, and lending objects to the 1922 Burlington Fine Arts Club exhibition of Egyptian art and EES displays; some objects were sold at Sotheby's, 31 July-1 Aug. 1939; his bead collection and notes were given to the Cambridge University Museum of Archaeology and Anthropology after his death, and the Bead Study Trust was endowed to further his work in 1983; he died in Chichester, 7 Feb. 1941.

Inf. The Bead Study Trust, H. Hughes-Brock and T. Hardwick; F. Westlake, 'Horace C. Beck. "The Bead Man" 1873-1941', *The Bead Journal* 2/4 (Spring 1976), 30-31.

BECKERATH, Jürgen Rudolf Friedrich von (1920-2016)
German Egyptologist; he was born in Hanover,19 Feb. 1920, son of Dr. Gerhard v. B. and Therese Baroness von Eller-Eberstein; he was educated at the University of Munich; PhD, 1948; Habilitation, 1963; he worked at the Deutschen Forschungsgemeinschaft, 1955 and later as assistant at the Agyptisches Museum, Munich; he became lecturer in Egyptology at Munich, 1958; he was associate Professor at Columbia University, 1966-7; he succeeded Wolf (q.v.) as Professor of Egyptology at Münster, 1970-85; he was a specialist in the chronology and history of ancient Egypt;a volume of studies in his honour was edited by B. Schmitz and A. Eggebrecht, *Festschrift Jürgen von Beckerath*. Hildesheimer Ägyptologische Beiträge 30, 1990; apart from numerous articles, his published works included *Tanis und Theben*, 1951; *Untersuchungen zur politischen Geschichte der Zweiten Zwischenzeit in Ägypten*, 1965; *Abriss der Geschichte des Alten Ägypten*, 1971; *Handbuch der ägyptischen Königsnamen*, 1984; 2nd ed., 1999; *Chronologie des ägyptischen Neuen Reiches*, 1994; *Chronologie des pharaonischen Ägypten*, 1997; he died in Schlehdorf, Bavaria, 26 Jun. 2016.

Inf. A. Lohwasser; *Festschrift Jürgen von Beckerath*. Hildesheimer Ägyptologische Beiträge 30, 1990, ed. B. Schmitz and A. Eggebrecht, xi-xxvii.

BEDAIR or BEDAYR, John, also known as Mohammed Ashgar Bedr (1815-1874)
Egyptian servant and guide; he was born in Cairo the son of Selim Bedr, a potter; he accompanied Burton (q.v.) during the latter period of his travels in Egypt and then through France to look after a menagerie of animals until he was attacked and had his arm badly injured by the hyena, which was afterwards shot dead and the remaining animals sold to the Jardin des Plantes, Paris; he arrived with Burton in London at Christmas 1834; he married Martha Ford in St George's Church Hanover Square in July 1844; he set up as a china and glass dealer in Kilburn before working as a foreign courier, servant and guide for travellers to Egypt and the Near East; he is named by Wilkinson (q.v.) in Murray's *Handbook for Modern Egypt and Thebes* 1843 as an experienced guide to hire; he is recoreded many times in ships passenger lists accompanying families and individual tourists; with a wife and four surviving children to support and giving his religion as Protestant, he became a naturalised British citizen in 1860; because he could read, write and speak English and Arabic coupled with the extensive knowledge of Ancient Egypt he picked up while travelling with Burton, Wilkinson and others during the 1830s and subsequent decades, he was employed by the archaeologist Rhind (q.v.) to accompany him to Egypt over the winters of 1855-56 and 1856-57; he died at Alexandria on 16 June 1874 and is probably buried there.

Neil Cooke, in N. Cooke and V. Daubney (eds.), *Every Traveller Needs A Compass*, 64-86, 2015.

BEECHEY, Henry William (*c.*1789-1862)
British artist and traveller; he was the son of the portrait-painter Sir William Beechey, RA, and Anne Phyllis Jessop; he became secretary to Henry Salt (q.v.), British Consul-General in Egypt, 1815; he resigned in 1820 and returned to England; he was sent by Salt to supervise the operations of Belzoni (q.v.) and Athanasi (q.v.), 1817-18, and made drawings of the newly opened temple of Abu Simbel; in 1821-2; with his brother Frederick William, RN, a geographer, he explored and surveyed the N. African coast from Tripoli to Derna, the results being published in 1828; FSA, 1825; he was a biographer of Sir Joshua Reynolds, 1835; he emigrated to New Zealand in 1851, where he died at Governor's Bay, Lyttelton, near Christchurch, 4 Aug. 1862.

ODNB 4, 803-4; *DNB* 4, 122-3; frequently mentioned in Salt, Belzoni, Athanasi, Irby; Hilmy, i, 58; Mayes, *The Great Belzoni*, 1959, passim; inf. Mrs. P. Rée; P. Usick in P. Starkey and N. El Kholy (eds), *Egypt through the Eyes of Travellers*, 2002, 13-24; R. De Keersmaecker, *ASTENE Bulletin* 72 (2017), 21-2.

BÉHAGUE, (*Comtesse*) Martine Marie Octavie de (1870-1939)
French collector; she was born in Paris, 13 March 1870, daughter of Comte Octave de Béhague and Laure de Haber; she married Comte René de Béarn in 1890, but the marriage soon ended in divorce; she was a patron of arts and music and travelled widely; she visited Egypt on several occasions; she formed a large collection of

paintings, objets d'art and antiquities including Egyptian antiquities which were displayed in her two homes in Paris, her château near Fontainebleau, and her villa at St. Hyères, published by R. Froehner, *Collection de la comtesse R. de Béarn*, 3 vols, 1905-09; a statue base from the collection was sold to Leiden Museum in 1950 (A. Klasens, *Oudheidkundige Mededelingen uit het Rijksmuseum van Oudheden* 33 (1952)), while the rest of the collection was sold by Sotheby's at Monte Carlo, 5 Dec. 1987; her heirs presented a silver-gilt figure of a Ramesside pharaoh to the Louvre, 1988; she died in Paris, 26 Jan. 1939.

Inf. Sotheby's and T. Hardwick; *BCH* 112 (1988), 53; G. Schlumberger, *Mes souvenirs*, 1934, 2, 25-6; 337; *Journal des Savants* 1992, 159-60; foreword to Sotheby's sale catalogue; *Les Donateurs du Louvre* 145, 212; L. Stasi, 'Le mécénat de Martine de Béhague, comtesse de Béarn (1870-1939): du symbolisme au théâtre d'avant garde' *Bulletin de la Société de l'Histoire de l'Art français* (1999), 337-366.

BELGRADO, Iacopo (1704-1789)
Italian writer; he was born in Udine, 16 Nov. 1704; he studied Greek and Latin at Padua and entered the Jesuit order, 16 Nov. 1723; he later studied philosophy and mathematics at Bologna and theology at Parma; he taught at Jesuit colleges in Venice and from 1738 at Parma; he was transferred to Bologna in 1768; on the suppression of the Jesuit order, he retired to Udine; among his writings was a volume on Egyptian architecture, *Dell'architectura egiziana*, 1786; he died at Udine, 26 March 1789.

EI 6, 540; *DBDI* 7, 574-8.

BELL, Edward (1844-1926)
British publisher and writer on architecture; born Stockwell, 18 Oct. 1844, eldest son of George B., publisher and Hannah Simpson; he was educated at St. Paul's School and Trinity College, Cambridge; MA; FSA; he married Alice van Rees Hoets (d.1917), 1873; Chairman of G. Bell & Sons Ltd. publishers; President of Publishers Assoc., 1906-9; among his publications are works on Prehellenic architecture in the Aegean, Hellenic architecture and the Architecture of Western Asia; see especially *The Architecture of Ancient Egypt: a historical outline*, 1915, in the *Origins of Architecture series*; this contains an appendix with a translation of Lepsius' paper 'On some forms of Egyptian Art and their evolution'; he died in London, 8 Nov. 1926.

WWW ii, 77; Al. Cant.; *ODNB* 4, 896; M. Capasso (ed.), Hermae II, 2010, 31-35 (portr.) (P. Pinto).

BELL, (*Sir*) Harold Idris (1879-1967)
British papyrologist and classicist; born in Epworth, Lincs., 2 Oct. 1879, son of Charles Christopher Bell, who with an uncle owned a chemist's shop, and Rachel Hughes; he won a scholarship in Classics to Oriel College, Oxford, 1897, after being educated at Nottingham High School, and subsequently the Fraser Scholarship, 1901; he later studied at the Universities of Berlin and Halle; appointed Assistant in the Dept. of MSS in the British Museum, 1903; Deputy-Keeper of MSS, 1927, Keeper of the MSS and Edgerton Librarian, British Museum, 1929-44; Hon. Reader in Papyrology, Oxford, 1935-50; knighted, 1946; C.B., 1936; OBE, 1920; FBA; MA (Oxon); Hon. LL.D. (Liverpool); Hon. DLitt. (Wales, Michigan, Brussels); he married 1911, Mabel Winifred (d.1967) daughterof Ernest Ayling; seconded to War Office Intelligence Dept., 1915; member of Committee of the Egypt Exploration Society, 1922-59; Hon. Sec. of same, 1923-27, and Vice President, 1945-67; corr. member of the Bavarian (1928), Bologna (1934), Belgian (1945), and Norwegain (1946), Acads. and of FÉRE, Brussels (1939); Member of Arch. Institut des Deutschen Reiches (1934); Associate Institut d'Egypte (1940); Foreign member of the American Philosophical Soc. (1941); corr. member Acad. des Inscriptions et Belles-Lettres, 1947; Soc. Royale d'Arch. d'Alexandrie, 1950; Österreichische Akad. der Wiss., 1955; Instituto Sudamericano de Asuntos Legales, 1957; Pres. Hon. Soc. of Cymmrodorion, 1947-53; Vice-Pres., 1953-67; Pres. Soc. for Promotion of Roman Studies, 1937-45; Vice Pres. 1945-67; Vice Pres. Soc. for Promotion of Hellenic Studies, 1930-67; Vice. Pres. Int. Council for Philosophy and Humanistic Studies, 1949-52; Pres. of Internat. Assoc. of Papyrologists, 1947-55; Hon. Pres., 1955-67; Hon. Fellow of Oriel College, Oxford, 1936-67; Pres. of Brit. Acad., 1946-50; awarded Cymmrodorion Medal for services to Welsh literature, 1946; Hon. member, as Druid, of Welsh Gorsedd from 1949; during his keepership of MSS at the British Museum the Codex Sinaiticus and Luttrell Psalter were acquired, and despite official duties Bell found time to produce many works on his own special field, i.e. the Graeco-Roman papyri of Egypt; he was responsible with F. W. Kelsey of Michigan for organizing the Papyrus Syndicate, 1921, designed to buy and redistribute among its members specimens that came on the market; he retired to Aberystwyth in 1946 and he later gave his papyrological library to the National Library of Wales; his bibliography lists over 100 items, 19 separate publications, about 93 articles etc. and 9 obituaries; from this very varied output the following are selected as being among the most important, vols. III (with Sir F. Kenyon), IV and V of *The Catalogue of Greek Papyri in the British Museum*, 1907, 1910, 1917; *Wadi Sarga* (with W. E. Crum and introduction by R. Campbell Thompson), 1922; *Jews and Christians in Egypt*, 1924;

Pt. XVI of The Oxyrhynchus Papyri (with B. P. Grenfell and A. S. Hunt), 1924; Pt. XIX ibid (with E. Lobel, E. P. Wegener, and C. H. Roberts), 1948; *Juden und Griechen im römischen Alexandreia*, 1926; *Fragments of an unknown gospel and other Early Christian Papyri* (with T. C. Skeat), 1935; *New Gospel Fragments*, 1935; *Recent discoveries of Biblical Papyri*, an inaugural lecture delivered before the University of Oxford, 18 Nov. 1936, 1937; *A Descriptive Catalogue of the Greek Papyri in the Collection of Wilfred Merton, F.S.A.* (with C. H. Roberts), vol. I, 1948; vol. II (with B. R. Rees and others), 1958; *Egypt from Alexander the Great to the Arab Conquest*, 1948; *Cults and Creeds in Graeco-Roman Egypt*, 1953; *The Abinnaeus Archive*, (with V. Martin, E. G. Turner, and D. van Berchem), 1962; he edited the EES Graeco-Roman memoirs and also contributed to the 9th edition of Liddell and Scott's *Greek Lexicon*, and produced the large and very comprehensive bibliographies on Graeco-Roman Egypt (Papyri) in *JEA* 1914-25; his contributions to the *Cambridge Ancient History* appear in vols. X and XI; he died in Aberystwyth, 22 Jan. 1967.

ILN vol. 250 (28 Jan. 1967) 12 (portr.) (anon); *JEA* 40 (1954), 3-6, *Festschrift* (bibl. complete to 1953) (portr. frontispiece); 53 (1967), 131-4 (portr.) (E. G. Turner), 134-39 (bibl. additions and corrections) (T. C. Skeat and J. D. Thomas); *JRS* 58 (1968), 1-2 (portr.) (E.G.T.); 53 (1967) 1968, 409-22 (portr. pl xxxi) (C. H. Roberts); *WWW* vi, 82; *ODNB* 4, 941-3 (portr.).

BELL, Lanny David (1941-2019)
American Egyptologist; he was born at Fort Dodge, Iowa, 30 Apr. 1941, son of Gerald Eugene B. and Marjorie Ann Carlson; he studied at the University of Chicago 1959-63; BA, 1963, and at the University of Pennsylvania; PhD, 1976; National Merit Scholar, 1959-63; Woodrow Wilson Fellow, 1963-4; he taught at the University of Chicago from 1965; he became field director for the Pennsylvania University Museum Theban Tomb Project at Dra Abu el-Naga, 1967-77; unfortunately, the results of this work were never properly published; he married Martha Hope Rhoads (q.v.) 22 Sep. 1968; field director, University of Chicago Epigraphic Survey, Chicago House, 1977-89; Professor of Egyptology, Oriental Institute, University of Chicago, 1989-96; married Jill Baker 1994 (div. 2006); President of the Chicago Society of the Archaeological Institute of America, 1992-6, leading numerous tours for the AIA; he was Visiting Researcher in Egyptology, Brown University, from 1996; apart from over sixty articles in various periodicals and edited volumes including *Aspects of the Cult of the Deified Tutankhamun*, 1985; *Luxor Temple and the Cult of the Royal Ka*, 1985; *The Epigraphic Survey: The Philosophy of Egyptian Epigraphy after Sixty Years' Practical Experience*, 1987; *The Epigraphic Survey and the Rescue of the Monuments of Ancient Egypt*, 1990; *The Ancient Egyptian 'Books of Breathing', the Mormon 'Book of Abraham', and the Development of Egyptology in America*, 2008; with Daphna Ben-Tor, *A Collection of Egyptian Bronzes*, 2011; and with Daphna Ben-Tor, *Clay Sealings from the Moat Deposit*, 2016; he died in Old Saybrook, Ct, 26 Aug. 2019.

BELL, Martha Hope (*née* **Rhoads**) (1941-1991)
American archaeologist and Egyptologist; she was born in Philadelphia, 27 April 1941 daughter of Dr. Donald Ziegler Rhoads and Elsie Teetsel; she was educated at Cedar Crest College, Allentown, Penn. 1959-61 and Barnard College, New York 1961-3, BA 1963 in history; she undertook graduate studies at the Department of Classical Archaeology, University of Pennsylvania 1963-8 including work at the American School of Classical Studies at Athens 1966-7; PhD 1991 with her dissertation *The Tutankhamun Burnt Group from Gurob, Egypt: Bases for the Absolute Chronology of LH III A and B;* she married 22 Sept. 1968 Lanny Bell and assisted her husband during his excavations at Dra Abu en-Naga, Thebes 1970, 1972, 1974 and during his tenure as field director of the Epigraphic Survey of the Oriental Institute, Chicago at Luxor 1977-89; she specialized in the links between Egypt and the Aegean world; her principal articles were 'Preliminary Report on the Mycenaean Pottery from Deir el-Medina (1979-1980)', *ASAE* 68 (1982), 142-63; 'Egyptian Imitations of Aegean Vases: Some Additional Notes', *Gött. Misz.* 63 (1983), 13-24; 'Gurob Tomb 605 and Mycenaean Chronology', *Mélanges Gamal Eddin Mokhtar 1*, 1985, 61-86; 'A Hittite Pendant from Amarna', *American Journal of Archaeology* 90 (1986), 145-51; 'Regional Variation in Polychrome Pottery of the 19th Dynasty', *Cahiers de la Céramique Égyptienne* 1, 1987, 49-76; 'An Armchair Excavation of KV 55', *JARCE* 27 (1990), 97-137; and 'Notes on the Exterior Construction Signs from Tutankhamun's Shrines', *JEA* 76 (1990), 107-24; she died in an automobile accident near Hillside, New Jersey, 12 Nov. 1991.

Inf. L. D. Bell; *JEA* 78 (1992), x-xi; *The Oriental Institute Annual Report 1991-1992,* 6-9 (L. Bell).

BELLERMANN, Johann Joachim (1754-1842)
German antiquary and theologian; he was born at Erfurt, 24 Sept. 1754, son of Johann Martin B. and Kunigunde Elisabeth Nonne; he was particularly interested in antique gems and their symbols; he published works on Abraxas-gems (1817-18) and on scarabs and their inscriptions; he attempted to decipher hieroglyphic writing; he died in Berlin, 25 Oct. 1842.

BIFAO 5 (1905), 84; Hilmy, i, 60; *ADB* 2, 307-11.

BELMORE, Earl of *see* **LOWRY-CORRY**

BELON, Pierre (*c*.1517-1565)
French naturalist and traveller; he was born at La Soultière, Sarthe, *c*.1517, son of Giles B. and Anne Baignol and became an apothecary; in 1546 he made a journey to the East, visiting many places starting with Constantinople; he arrived in Egypt in 1547, where he visited the Pyramids and other places of interest, then went on to Cyrenaica, Palestine, and Syria; he later published an account, *Les Observations de plusieurs singularitez et choses mémorables trouvées en Grèce, Judée, Égypte, Arabie et autres pays étranges, redigées en trois livres*, 1553-8; he was found assassinated by thieves in the Bois de Boulogne, April 1565.

DBF 5, 1382-3; *La Grande Enc.* 6. 102-3; *Le Voyage en Égypte de Pierre Belon du Mans 1547* ed. Serge Sauneron, 1970; P. Delauny, *L'aventureuse existence de Pierre Belon du Mans*, 1936; Lamy, 74-85.

BELZONI, Giovanni Battista (1778-1823)
Italian excavator, explorer, and adventurer; he was born in Padua, 5 Nov. 1778, son of Giacomo B., a poor barber, and Teresa Pivato; two statues of Sakhmet which he later presented to his birthplace, still remain in Padua; at sixteen he went to Rome to seek his fortune, and is said to have studied hydraulics at this time and also to have been preparing to join the Capuchin order when the French entered Rome, 1798; he had grown to be a giant man said to have been six feet seven inches tall; after travels in Europe he worked for Charles Dibdin Jnr. as a Strong Man at Sadler's Wells theatre, credited with lifting an iron frame with up to twelve people on it; this period of his life is obscure but he married his wife Sarah (q.v.) then, and she was his faithful companion until his death; he visited Portugal and Spain, 1812-13, and the following year while in Malta met an agent of Muhammed Ali who suggested he might find a use for his knowledge of hydraulics in Egypt; here in 1815 he met Burckhardt (q.v.) and Drovetti (q.v.); as his water-wheel, although a success, had not received court backing, in 1816 Burckhardt recommended him to Henry Salt (q.v.), the British Consul-General in Egypt, to remove for them the upper part of a great statue of Ramesses II at Thebes, now BM, EA 19, and to collect for Salt antiquities destined for the British Museum; after successfully completing his first task, the remains of the vast granite sarcophagus of Ramesses III and its magnificent lid were next removed, the former now in the Louvre and the latter in the Fitzwilliam Museum, Cambridge; Belzoni visited Aswan and Nubia, intending to open the entrance to the temple of Abu Simbel, but although employing 40 men failed on this attempt to do so; he next excavated at Karnak finding over twenty Sakhmet statues in the Temple of Mut, and discovered the tomb of King Ay on the west bank; Henry William Beechey (q.v.) acted as his assistant in copying the reliefs and inscriptions found, Athanasi (q.v.) later joined him here; it was at this time that he entered the tombs of Qurna seeking funerary papyri, and described the damage that he did in the process, which later made him the subject of much criticism from archaeologists; his interests were very wide and he made a wax model of the portico of the Isis temple at Philae, before he continued work on opening up Abu Simbel; here he displayed much more archaeological sense, and Mangles (q.v.) drew a scale plan of the temple and marked out the positions of pieces of statuary found, while Beechey and Belzoni copied as many of the scenes and inscriptions as they could; in all he discovered six royal tombs at Thebes, his greatest find being that of Sety I which contained the alabaster sarcophagus now in the Soane Museum, London; he took wax impressions of the reliefs and hieroglyphs and noted the colours in order to be able to erect a facsimile in any part of Europe; in 1818 he opened the Chephren pyramid, showing much more care than Vyse later used on that of Mycerinus; Belzoni also discovered the site of the Ptolemaic Red Sea port of Berenice, and went on an expedition to the oases, visiting Bahariya and the Faiyum, but did not reach Siwa as intended; on his return to England in 1819 he held an exhibition at the Egyptian Hall, Piccadilly, 1821, displaying two full-scale reproductions of chambers from Sety's tomb, and an enormous model of the whole over 50 feet long, together with many other antiquities, sold at auction in the Egyptian Hall, 8 June 1822; this with the publication of his *Narrative* marked the culmination of his varied career; he cannot be judged by the standards of later excavators such as Petrie (q.v.), or even Mariette (q.v.), but must be seen in the context of the period before decipherment; at the start of his career he was neither better nor worse than other contemporaries in the field, but he later evolved techniques for his work and acquired knowledge that raised him above the general level; his published works were, *Narrative of the Operations and Recent Discoveries within the Pyramids, Temples, Tombs, and Excavations, in Egypt and Nubia; and of a Journey to the Coast of the Red Sea, in search of the ancient Berenice; and another to the Oasis of Jupiter Ammon*, 1820; *Forty-four Plates illustrative of the Researches and Operations of Belzoni in Egypt and Nubia*, 1820; *Six new plates*, 1822; reprinted several times, notably an edition by A. Silotti, *Belzoni's Travels*, 2001; *Hieroglyphics found in the Tomb of Psammis discovered by G. Belzoni... Copied from the originals in the said tomb and presented by the author to his Royal Highness Augustus Frederick Duke of Sussex*, 1822; a bronze portrait medal was issued in 1822; his collection of antiquities was sold in London at Sotheby's 5-6 April 1826; unable to gain adequate support for further work in Egypt, Belzoni set out on an expedition to try to trace the source of the Niger, and en route for Timbuktu died of dysentery in Gwato, Benin, 3 Dec. 1823.

Athanasi, *passim*; John Britton, *Autobiogr.* (1850) i, 112-15; *BIE* 6, 27-42; Champollion, ii, 277 (portr.); Hilmy, i, 61; Salt, *passim*; Lugt 10241 and 11167; *DNB* 4, 205; *ODNB* 5 47-9 (portr.); *DBDI* 8, 97-100; Colin Clair, *Strong Man Egyptologist*, 1957; M. Willson Disher, *Pharaoh's Fool*, 1957; Stanley Mayes, *The Great Belzoni*, 1959 (with extensive bibl.); L. Gaudenzio, *Giovan Battista Belzoni all' luce di nuovi documenti*, 1936; G. Danielli, *Gli esploratori ital. in Africa*, 1960; A. Silotti, *Padova e l'Egitto antico*, 1987, 33-92; C. N. Reeves in *JEA* 75 (1989), 235-7; P. Clayton in P. and J. Starkey, *Travellers in Egypt*, 1998, 41-50; A Lohwasser, *Antike Sudan* 11 (2001), 80-7; P. Wilson in P. Starkey and N. El Kholy (eds.), *Egypt through the Eyes of Travellers*, 2002, 45-56; S. Sobhi Abdel-Hakim in P. Starkey and N. El Kholy (eds.), *Egypt through the Eyes of Travellers*, 2002, 128-130; È. Gran-Aymerich, *Dictionnaire biographique d'archéologie 1798-1945*, 2001, incorporated in *Les Chercheurs de passé 1798-1945*, 2007, 589-90; I. Hume, *Belzoni: The Giant Archaeologists Love to Hate*, 2011; J. Taylor, Minerva (Dec. 2017), 14-20; A. Baghiani and J. Taylor, *ASTENE Bulletin* 75 (2018), 13-4; R. Morkot, *ASTENE Bulletin* 78 (2019), 17.

BELZONI, Sarah (*née* Parker Brown) (1783-1870)
British wife of Giovanni B. Belzoni; she was born in Bristol Jan. 1783; they married in 1804; she accompanied him on his travels to Egypt and Nubia, and went alone to Palestine; she contributed a chapter to the *Narrative*; after her husband's death she opened an exhibition in London showing his drawings and models of the Tomb of Sety I, but it was a failure and was closed in May 1825; in 1828 she proposed to publish a series of lithographic plates and issued a prospectus, but this scheme also proved abortive; see above; from 1833 she lived in Brussels; she died in Jersey, 12 Jan. 1870.

The Times, 7 May 1825; *Sunday Times*, 20 Jan. 1828; Belzoni's *Narrative*, passim; Champollion, i, 70; Finati, ii, 211, 220, 222; Richardson, ii, 235; *ODNB* 5, 49; M. Price in S. Searight (ed.), *Women Travellers in the Near East*, 2005, 41-4; A. Baghiani and J. Taylor, *ASTENE Bulletin* 75 (2018), 13-14.

BENEDETTI, (*Vicomte*) Vincent (1817-1900)
Corsican diplomat; he was born in Bastia, 29 April 1817, son of François B. and Pauline Morelli; he studied law in Paris and was afterwards made French Consul in Alexandria, 1840; he was Consul in Cairo, 1845, leaving Egypt to become Consul-General in Palermo etc, 1848; he married Marie d'Anastasi daughter of Giovanni d'A. (q.v.); he retired to Corsica but died in Paris, 28 March 1900.

French FO Records; Carré, i, 289, 314; ii, 28; *DBF* 5, 1404-5.

BÉNÉDITE, Georges Aaron (1857-1926)
French Egyptologist; he was born in Nîmes, 10 Aug. 1857, son of Samuel B. and Sara Isabelle Lisbonne; he studied Semitic languages at the Lycée St Louis, Paris, 1871, and then architecture, art, and drawing at the École des Beaux Arts and in private studios, 1878-80; he accompanied Chipiez (q.v.) to Egypt, 1880; he studied Egyptology at the École des Hautes Études under Maspero (q.v.) 1881-6; he joined the Mission Arch., 1887-8, and was mainly engaged in copying Theban tombs; he was appointed to the staff of the Louvre, 1888; Conservateur-Adjoint Eg. Dept., 1895; he succeeded Pierret (q.v.) as Conservateur, 1907, and also succeeded Maspero at the Coll. de France, 1899-1914; Member of the Acad., 15 Feb. 1924; he visited Egypt 19 times and in 1925 explored Abyssinia; he contributed articles to many journals, his principal publications being, *Le tombeau de la reine Thiti ... Le Tombeau de Neferhotpou*, 1893-4; *Le Temple de Philae*, 2 pts, 1893, 1895; *Guide d'Égypte*, 1900; *Miroirs*, Cairo Cat, 1907; *Objets de toilette; I part. peignes etc.*, Cairo Cat., 1911; *Le Couteau de Gebel el-Arak ...*, 1916; *L'Art égyptien dans ses lignes générales*, 1923; *Corpus Inscriptionum semiticarum*, on the Nabatean inscriptions in the Sinai peninsula; he died in Luxor, 23 March 1926.

Beaux-arts 4 (1926), 100 (P. Vitry); *CRAIBL* 1926, 63-6 (J. B. Chabot); *JEA* 12 (1926), 304 (F. Ll. Griffith); *Rev. arch.* 1926, sér. 5, tome 24, 73-5 (P. Jamot); *Rev. de l'Ég. anc.* i. (1927) 250-78 (bibl. and portr.) ; H. Danesi, *Institut de France. Le Second Siècle 1895-1995*, 1999-2001, I, 103; È. Gran-Aymerich, *Dictionnaire biographique d'archéologie 1798-1945*, 2001, incorporated in *Les Chercheurs de passé 1798-1945*, 2007, 590-1.

BENNETT, (Cyril) John Cole (1908-1977)
British epigrapher and schoolteacher; he was born in London, 10 June 1908, son of John Fletcher B., an inspector in the Board of Agriculture, and Hilda Margaret Summerley; he studied at University College London under Margaret Murray (q.v.); recommended by Glanville (q.v.), he served as epigrapher on the Amarna excavation under Pendlebury (q.v.), 1930-1 but did not get on well with him; he continued his studies at University College London under Glanville; he became a schoolteacher at Colchester, 1940-73; he contributed several articles to *JEA*; he died in Chichester, 8 Oct. 1977.

Family inf.; R. Janssen, *The First Hundred Years*, 1992.

BENSON, Margaret (1865-1916)
British excavator; she was born at Wellington College, 16 June 1865, daughter of Edward White Benson, Archbishop of Canterbury, and Mary Sidgwick; educated at Lady Margaret Hall, Oxford; she visited Egypt a number of times, 1894, 1895, 1896, and 1900; with P. E. Newberry (q.v.) as consultant she excavated the Temple of Mut at Thebes, with her friend Janet Gourlay (q.v.) in 1895-7; the results were published in *The Temple of Mut in Asher*, 1899; objects from her collection and excavations were sold at Christie's, 12 July 1972, and 5 Dec. 1972; she died in Wimbledon, 13 May 1916.

ODNB 5, 190*; Life and Letters of Maggie Benson*, by her brother, A. C. Benson, 1917 (portr.); Newberry Corr.; D. Williams, *Genesis and Exodus*, 1979, *passim*; M. Price in S. Searight, *Women Travellers in the Near East*, 2005, 46-8; M. Vicinus, *Intimate Friends*, 2005, 97, 134-141; R. Bolt, *As Good as God, as Clever as the Devil*, 2011;

BEREND, William Berman Sedgwick (1855-1884)
American banker; he was born in New York, 1855, son of Berman B. and Elizabeth Sedgwick; he took up the study of Egyptology and became a pupil of Maspero (q.v.); he published an account of the Egyptian stelae and sculptures in Florence, *Principaux Monuments du Musée Égyptien de Florence. Prem. Partie. Stèles, bas-reliefs et fresques*, 1882, pt. 2, 1884; also a French translation of Lepsius's memoir on Egyptian metals, 1879; he was sec. of the Congress of Orientalists at Lyons, 1878; he left a large fortune at his early death in Sweden, 1884.

Hilmy, i, 63; Maspero, *L'Égyptologie* (1915), 8, 9; Wilbour, 71, 309.

BERENS, (*Revd***) Randolph Humphrey** (1844-1922)
British clergyman and collector; formerly McLaughlin, he was born at Buraston, Shropshire, 11 Jan., 1844, son of Revd Hubert McLaughlin and Hon. Frederica Crafton; he assumed the surname Berens on his marriage in 1877 with Eleanor Frances, daughter of Henry Hulse Berens, JP; he studied at Trinity College, Cambridge; BA, 1866; MA, 1869; he was ordained, 1867, and made Vicar of Sidcup, Kent, 1877-81; becoming wealthy on his marriage, he retired from clerical duty, travelled in Egypt and collected coins and antiquities; his collection of Egyptian antiquities (155 lots) was sold at Sotheby's 18-9 June 1923; a further collection of antiquities belonging to his wife (who died in 1924) was sold in London 31 July 1923 (114 lots) and 28 Feb. 1924, 19-20 May 1924, and 7-8 July 1924; he died in London, 22 Dec. 1922.

Inf. P. E. Newberry; *Burke's Landed Gentry; Clergy Lists*; Lugt 85518, 85690, 86442, 86902 and 87207.

BERENSON, Bernard (1865-1959)
American art historian and critic; born in Butrimants, Lithuania, 26 June, 1865, eldest son of Alter Valvrojenski and Eudice Michliszanski; he was educated at Harvard University and became a leading authority on Italian Renaissance art; he married Mary daughter of R. Pearsall Smith, and later lived in Italy; author of many works on art, he was much interested in Egyptian art; he was a member of the EES 1922-59; he died in Florence, 6 Oct. 1959.

EES *Report*, 1959, 5; *WWW* v, 94-5; E. Samuels, *Bernard Berenson*, 1979; M. Secrest, *Being Bernard Berenson*, 1980

BERGMAN, Jan (1933-1999)
Swedish Egyptologist and religious historian; he was born in Motala, 2 June 1933, son of Sven B. and Ruth Stöberg; he was educated at Uppsala University, MA in Classics, 1955; he also attended the University of Strasbourg; he then studied theology, obtaining his degree in 1959 and his licentiate in 1963; he was ordained as a minister in the Swedish church in 1959; pastor of Linköping, 1968; he obtained his PhD in Egyptology in 1971; he was appointed Professor of Religion at Uppsala University 1974-98; he was director of the Institute of Religious Studies at Linköping, 1969-87; he published his theses *Ich bin Isis*, 1968 and *Isis-Seele und Osiris-ei*, 1970; he died at Linköping, 1999.

IAE internet obituary (L. Troy); *Who's Who in Scandinavia 1981*, 115; *Vem ar det* 1995, 109.

BERGMANN, (*Ritter von***) Ernst (1844-1892)**
Austrian Egyptologist; he was born in Vienna, 4 Feb. 1844, son of Josef B. and Luise Freiin von Pratobevera-Wiesborn; he studied at Göttingen under Brugsch (q.v.) and Ewald and was also taught by Reinisch (q.v.); he became a private lecturer, 1865 and later followed the Emperor Maximilan to Mexico; he was afterwards appointed Keeper of Egyptian Antiquities in the Imperial Museum of Vienna; he visited Egypt 1877-8; Bergmann published many texts and monuments, chiefly those in the Vienna collection, in *Rec. Trav.*, *ZÄS*, and other journals; his

principal works were, *Hieroglyphische Inschriften gesammelt während einer im Winter 1877-78 unternommenen Reise in Aegypten*, 1879; *Hieratische und hieratisch-demotische Texte der Sammlung aegyptischer Alterthümer des Allerhöchsten Kaiserhauses*, 1886; *Übersicht der Sammlung aegyptischer Alterthümer des Allerhöchsten Kaiserhauses im unteren K. K. Belvedere*, 1886; he died in Vienna, 26 April 1892.

ZÄS 30 (1892), 126; Biogr. by Dedekind, *Des Aegyptologen Ernst von Bergmanns Leben und Wirken*, 2nd ed., 1906; inf. G. Hamernik.

BERLEV, Oleg Dmitrievitch (1933 -2000)
Russian Egyptologist; he was born in Pyatigorsk, 18 Feb. 1993, son of Dmitri Berlev; he studied at the Historical Faculty of the Leningrad State University, graduating 1957; he worked in the Leningrad Department of the Institute of History of Sciences, 1956-9, and then in the Leningrad Department of the Institute of Oriental Studies; Doctor of Historical Sciences, 1965; Professor 1972; Dr-Professor, 1978; his publications included *The Working Population of Egypt in the Middle Kingdom*, 1972 (in Russian); *Social Relations in Middle Kingdom Egypt*, 1978 (in Russian); *The Egyptian Reliefs and Stelae in the Pushkin Museum of Fine Arts*, 1982, with S. Hodjash; *Ancient Egyptian Monuments in the Museums of the USSR* (in Russian with English summary), 1991, with S. Hodjash and *Catalogue of the Monuments of Ancient Egypt from the Museums of the Russian Federation, Ukraine, Bielorussia, Caucasus, Middle Asia and the Baltic States*, 1998, with S. Hodjash; he died 7 July 2000; a volume of studies *Discovering Egypt from the Neva* was published in his honour in 2003.

IAE obit (S. Hodjash); S. Quirke (ed.), *Discovering Egypt from the Neva*, 2003, ix-xv, (portr.) (bibl.).

BERNARD, Étienne (1923-2013)
French classical scholar; he was born in Molenbeek-Saint-Jean, Belgium, 11 July 1923, son of Alexandre B. and Gabrielle Linck; he was educated at the Lycées Buffon and Louis-le-Grand and then studied classics at the École Normale Superieur; he became a professor at Ain Shams University, 1950-56 and then was attached to CNRS, 1956-64; he was appointed lecturer and later professor at the Université de Franche-Comté at Besançon, 1965-91; professor emeritus, 1992; he was a member of IFAO, 1953-54; he published, with his brother André, *Les Inscriptions grecques et latines du Colosse de Memnon*, 1960; *Inscriptions métriques de l'Égypte gréco-romaines*, 1969; *Les inscriptions grecques de Philae*, 2 vols., 1969; *Receuil des inscriptions grecques du Fayoum*, 3 vols., 197-81; *Inscriptions grecques d'Égypte et de Nubie*, 1983; *Inscriptions grecques et latines d'Akoris*, 1988; *Inscriptions grecques d'Égypte et de Nubie au musée du Louvre*, 1992; with others, *Alexandrie, les quartiers rouyaux submergés*, 1999; *Inscriptions grecques d'Hermoupolis Magna et de sa nécropole*, 1999; *Inscriptions grecques d'Alexandrie ptolémaïques*, 2001; he died in Paris, 17 Feb. 2013; his twin brother André B (1923-2016), also a classicist and professor, collaborated with him and published *Alexandrie le Grand*, 1966, new eds. 1998, 2004; *De Koptos à Kosseir*, 1972; *Le Paneion d'El-Kanaïs*, 1972; *Alexandrie des Ptolémées*, 1995; *Alexandrie, les quartiers submergés*, with F. Goddio, 1998; *L'Égypte Engloutie*, with F. Goddio, 2002; he died on the same day as his brother.

WWWF 2013, 263; *BSFE* 185 (2013), 4.

BERTHELOT, (Pierre Eugène) Marcellin (1827-1907)
French chemist, member of Institute, senator and minister; he was born in Paris, 25 Oct. 1827, son of Jacques Martin B., a doctor, and Ernestine Sophie Claudine Biard; he was educated Coll. Henri IV, history prize, 1843; Doctor of Science, 1854; he was attached to Coll. de France, 1851; Professor of Organic Chemistry at the École Supérieure de Pharmacie, 1859; a chair in the same subject was specially created for him at the Coll. de France, 1865; Berthelot had the patronage of the princess Mathilde Bonaparte and Napoleon her brother, and visited Egypt for the inauguration of the Suez canal; he was named President of the Scientific Defence Committee, 1870, at a time of national crisis, and was involved in the manufacture of cannon and explosives during the siege of Paris; Inspecteur Général of Scientific Education, 1876; Senator, 1881; Minister of Public Instruction, 11 Dec. 1886-31 May 1887; Minister of Foreign Affairs, 3 Nov. 1895-28 March 1897; Member of the Académie de Médecine, 1867; Académie des Sciences, 1873, of which he became secrétaire perpétuel, and Académie française; Légion d'Honneur, 1900; a great ceremony was held at the Sorbonne to celebrate his fiftieth anniversary in science, before the President of the Republic, his friends and pupils, 1901; it is not possible to list the many achievements in chemistry and physics that he accomplished and the references below should be consulted for further reading; his list of works is gigantic, and these were used to make known his discoveries in no fewer than 500-600 works published between 1850 and 1888 alone; from this immense output must be cited his works relating to an interest in ancient as well as medieval science, see espec. *Introduction à l'étude de la Chimie des Anciens et du Moyen Age*, 1889; *Archéologie et Histoire des Sciences: avec publication nouvelle du papyrus Grec chimique de Leyde et impression originale du livre de septuaginta de Geber*, 1906; he also contributed articles on metals to excavation reports and journals after

the manner of Lucas later; see his long and detailed study 'Étude sur les métaux qui composent les objects de cuivre, de bronze, d'étain, d'or et d'argent, découverts par M. de Morgan dans les fouilles de Dahchour, ou provenant du Musée de Gizèh', in *Fouilles à Dahchour Mars-Juin 1894*, pp. 131-51, and *Ann. de Chimie et de Physique*, 1895; also 'Sur les métaux Égyptiens: étude sur un étui métallique et ses inscriptions', *Mon. et Mem. AIBL* 1900; 'Sur l'or Égyptien', in *ASAE* 2; he died in Paris, 18 March 1907.

DBF 6, 197-9 (E. Franceschini); *La Grande Enc.* 6, 441-4 (H. Marion); Vapereau, 145-6; I. Havelange, F. Huguet, and B. Lebedeff, *Les Inspecteurs Généraux de l'Instruction Publique*, 1986, 111-13.

BERTIN, Albert Henry (1802-1831)
French artist; born 1802, he was a pupil of Baron Gros; he accompanied Champollion (q.v.) to Egypt and Nubia, 1828-9; died 1831.

Carré, i, 236, 242; Champollion, ii, vi, 9, 142, 200, 238, 400, 417, 450; *DBF* 6, 242.

BERTIN, Édouard François (1797-1871)
French artist; he was born in Paris, 7 Oct. 1797, son of Louis François B., founder of the *Journal des Débats*; he studied art under Ingres; he visited Egypt and made drawings of various sites; he should not be confused with Albert Henry Bertin (q.v.); on the death of his brother in 1854, he took over the editorship of the *Journal des Débats*; he died in Paris, 13 Sept. 1871.

DBF 6, 242.

BETHELL, (*Hon*) **Richard** (1883-1929)
British collector; he was born in Brighton, 26 April 1883, only son of Richard B. 3rd Baron Westbury and Agatha Manners; he was educated at Eton and Magdalen College, Oxford; Capt. in the Scots Guards; he married Evelyn Lucia Millicent Hutton, 1911; he made a collection of small antiquities illustrating Egyptian art, of which the manuscript catalogue is in the Wilbour Library of Egyptology at the Brooklyn Museum, and was on the Committee of the EES, 1920-6; he assisted Howard Carter (q.v.) in the Tomb of Tutankhamun; his collection was sold at Sotheby's, 15-17 Dec. 1924; he died in London, 15 Nov. 1929.

WWW iii, 106; EES *Annual Rep.* 1929, 8; Newberry Corr. Lugt 87791

BETHMANN, Ludwig Konrad (1812-1867)
German scholar; he was born in Helmstadt, 23 June 1812, son of Ludwig Konrad B. and Anne Maria Dorothea Bockelberg; he was educated at the University of Göttingen and Jena; PhD, 1838; he was a contributor to *Monumenta Germaniae Historica*, 1837-54; he met Lepsius (q.v.) while in Egypt and travelled with him to Palestine; he was later Librarian at Wolfenbüttel, 1854-67; he died at Wolfenbüttel 5 Dec. 1867.

ADB 2, 573-4; Lepsius, *Life*, 163; H.-R. Jarck and G. Scheel, *Braunschweigisches Biographisches Lexikon*, 1996, 61 (portr.).

BEUGNOT, (*Vicomte*) **Auguste Arthur** (1797-1865)
French historian and scholar; he was born at Bar-sur-Aube. 18 March 1797, son of Jacques Claude B. and Marguerite Morel; a collector of antiquities which were sold in Paris, 5-13 May 1840; the sale catalogue, which includes many Egyptian items, was drawn up by J. de Witte (q.v.); he died in Paris, 15 March 1865.

DBF 6, 360-1; Lugt 15803.

BIANCHI, Alberto (1920-2003)
Uruguayan Egyptologist; he was born in Montevideo, Uruguay, 6 Sept. 1920, son of Angel B. and Nora Barzerque; he studied veterinary medicine at the University of the Repulic in Montevideo; he was a medical veterinarian by profession , becoming chief veterinarian of the Zoologico Municipal de Montevideo; he was sub-director of the Uruguayan Institute of Egyptology from 1984, founder and secretary of Sociedad Uruguaya de Egiptologia from 1980; he received the diploma of the Uruguayan Institute of Egyptology, 1997; his main interest was in Egyptian religion and language; he published a numbers of articles and monographs notably *El libro de los Muertos (Papiro de Ani),* 1991, reprinted 1998; *Contribución al estudio de las divinidades llamadas Mert(i0 y Merut(i),* 1991; *Estudios complementarios sobre la momia egipcia en el Museo Nacional de Historia Natural*, 1993; *Glosario de términos egiptológicos*, 1999; he died in Montevideo, 13 Feb. 2003.

Internet obituary (J. J. Castillos); inf. J. J. Castillos.

BIDOLI, Dino (1934-1973)
Italian Egyptologist; he was born in Cairo, 11 July 1934; studied Egyptology at Göttingen, 1958, and afterwards at Ain Shams University Cairo; prepared a dissertation under Siegfried Schott *Die Sprüche der Fangnetze in den altägyptischen Sargtexten*, published through the German Institute in Cairo; from the summer of 1966 until autumn 1970 he was in the Egyptian Museum Berlin - Charlottenburg, where he worked on hieratic papyri; Associate of the Egyptian Museum Berlin; he also took part in the German excavations at Qurna and Elephantine where the new papyrus finds were entrusted to him; Bidoli knew and studied many modern languages including Italian, French, German, English, Persian and Arabic; he died from an illness in Berlin, 10 Feb. 1973.

Informationsblatt der Deutschsprachigen Ägyptologie 5 (Jan. 1973) (anon).

BIEŃKOWSKI, Peter Ignatius Lada (1865-1925)
Polish classical scholar, archaeologist; he was born at Romanowce, 28 April 1865; he studied classical philology and history at the University of Lvov until 1886; for the next two years he studied at the University of Berlin under Th. Mommsen; PhD in Lvov, 1888; he continued his studies in Vienna, Rome and Athens, habilitation at the University of Cracow, 1893; Professor in 1897; he created at Cracow the first chair of classical archaeology at a Polish university; eminent specialist in the field of Greek and Roman sculpture with important studies on the representations of barbarians in classical art 1900, 1908, 1928; in the season of 1910-11 as a representative of the Cracow Academy, he took part in Austrian excavations conducted by Junker (q.v.) in el-Kubania heading the fieldwork at the Coptic monastery at a site called Mound of Isis; he died in Chylinie, 10 Aug. 1925.

J. Śliwa, *Egyptian and Nubian Pottery in the Cracow Collections,* Cracow 1982, 14; *Biograms of Polish Scholars* I, 1, Wroclaw 1983, 112-114; *Polski Słownik Biograficzny* 2, 73-4.

BILABEL, Friedrich Nikolas (1888-1945)
German papyrologist and ancient historian, he was born at Friedberg, 27 July 1888, son of Alexander B. and Katherina von Ruef; he studied classical and oriental philology including and Egyptian, Demotic, Coptic, and Arabic; PhD from the University of Munich, 1912; he succeeded Ranke (q.v.) as joint director, with Hans Abel and Karl Breith, of the German excavations at el-Hibeh/Qarara financed by the Heidelberg Academy of Sciences and Humanity and the Academic Society of Freiburg, 1914; he joined the staff of the University of Heidelberg, 1927 teaching ancient and oriental history and later in 1934 Greek and Roman history; professor, 1934; Supernumerary Professor, 1940; he published many articles on a wide variety of subjects relating to Demotic and Coptic ostraca, for which see esp. *Aegyptus* 2 (1921), 586-8 and 13 (1933), 555-62; he also published *Geschichte Vorderasiens und Aegyptens vom 16-11. Jahrhundert v. Chr.* (1927); he edited nearly 150 papyri; towards the end of World War II, he retired to the Bavarian village of Wallerstein where, during the American advance, he was found shot in the head, 22 April, 1945.

Chron. d'Ég. 23 (1948), 247-50 (C. Préaux); *Wer Ist's* 1935; B. Ottnad, *Badische Biographien,* I (1982), 54-6 (R. Seider); unpublished material; inf. W. Habermann, Univ. of Frankfurt a. M.

BINGEN, Jean François Henri Emmanuel (1920-2012)
Belgian papyrologist; he was born at Antwerp, 26 March 1920, son of Jean François B. and Marie Henriette Dierckx; he studied at the Université libre in Brussels; MA in classical philology, 1941; PhD, 1945; member of the Belgian resistance, 1944-5; he was appointed lecturer at the Université libre in Brussels. 1950, Professor 1957-1990, Assistant Rector 1967-8; also Professor at the Vrije Universiteit, 1957-85; Director of the Fondation égyptologique Reine Élisabeth, 1963-2002, part of the time with de Meulenaere (q.v); Director of the Centre de papyrologie et d'épigraphie grecque at the Université libre, 1972-90; Director of the Fondation archéologique at the Université libre, 1993-2012; Treasurer, 1986-92 and then Secretary-General of the International Council of Philosophy and the Humanities, UNESCO, 1996-8; Secretary of the International Association of Papyrologists, 1961-92, Hon Pres, 1992-2012; Vice-President of the Committee for Belgian excavations in Egypt, 1965-88, President,1988-2012; Director of the international programme for the excavation at Mons Claudianus, 1987-1993; he was chief editor of *Chronique d'Égypte*, 1986-2003 and editor of the Graeco-Roman section, 1986-89 and Christian section, 1991-2012; Hon Fellow, Society of Antiquaries, 1988; Corespondent of the Académie Royale de Belgique, 1984; Member, 1993; Correspondent and Associate Foreign Member of the Académie des Inscriptions et Belles-Lettres, Paris; a volume in his honour *Papyri in honorem Johannis Bingen octogenarii (P. Bingen)*, ed. H. Melaerts, was published in 2000; he published *Papyrus Revenue Laws*, 1952; *Menander. Dyscolos*, 1960, 1964; *Choix de papyrus grecs*, 1968; *Au temps où on lisait le grec en Égypte*,1977; *Le papyrus Revenue Laws*, 1978; *Fouilles d'Elkab* III. *Les ostraca grecs*, 1989; *Pages d'épigraphie*

grecque. Attique-Égypte (1952-1982), 1991; *Mons Claudianus. Ostraca graeca et latina*, I, with others, 1992; II, with others, 1997; *Pages d'épigraphie grecque* II. *Égypte (1983-2002)*, 2005; and *Hellenistic Egypt: Monarchy, Society, Economy, Culture*, 2007; he died at Woluwé-Saint-Pierre, 6 Feb. 2012.

Papyri in honorem Johannis Bingen octogenarii (P. Bingen), ed. H. Melaerts, 2000 (portr.) (bibl.); *Chron. d'Ég.* 87 (2012), (portr.), 5-8 (L. Limme and A. Martin), 11-14 (additional bibl.) (H. Melaerts); *Revue belge de Numismatique* 158 (2012), 391-2 (F, de Callatay); *Diogène* 241 (2013), 3-6 (A. Martin); inf. L. Limme and A. Martin.

BINION, Samuel Augustus (*c.*1837-1914)
Polish-American scholar and translator; he was born in Suwalki, Poland, 27 Apr. 1837, son of Joshua B. and Sarah Marshak; he was educated at Wilna and the Universities of Breslau and Padua and at King's College London; medical physcian; he was superintendant of schools at Seville, 1872-7; translator into English of the works of the Polish author Sienkiewicz; he later emigrated to America and studied at the Preabody Museum and John Hopkins University in Baltimore; he was much interested in Egyptology and published *Ancient Egypt or Mizraim*, 1887-1895; he died in New York, 8 Jan. 1914.

Inf. G. Mound

BIOT, Jean Baptiste (1774-1862)
French mathematician, physicist, and astronomer; he was born in Paris, 21 April 1774, son of Joseph B. who was employed in the Treasury; he was appointed Professor of Mathematics at Beauvais and in 1800 Professor of Physics at the Coll. de France; Member of the Acad. des Sciences, 11 April 1803; Chevalier de la Légion d'Honneur, 1804, Commander, 1849; FMRS, 1815; Rumford Medallist, 1840; a prolific writer, his works covered a wide field of physical science; he was particularly interested in the astronomy of ancient Egypt and China and published several memoirs thereon; he died in Paris, 3 Feb. 1862.

DBF 6, 506; *EB; Bibl. Ég.* 18, p. lxxiv; Hilmy, i, 70; A. C. E. Franquet de Franqueville, *Le Premier Siècle de l'Institut de France*, 1895, I, 147.

BIRCH, Samuel (1813-1885)
British Egyptologist and Sinologist; born London, 3 Nov. 1813, son of the Revd Samuel B. and Margaret Browning; he was educated at Merchant Taylors' School, 1826-31, then studied Chinese 1831-4, also the works of Young and Champollion on hieroglyphs; he entered the service of Commrs. of Public Records, 1834; was made assistant in the British Museum, 1836; became Assistant Keeper, Dept. of Antiquities 1844-61; Keeper of the Oriental, British, and Medieval Antiquities, 1861-6; Keeper of Oriental Antiquities, 1866-85, on the separation of this dept.; LL.D., Aberdeen University, 1862; LL.D., University of Cambridge, 1875; DCL, University of Oxford, 1876; FRSL; FSA; Corresponding Member of the Arch. Institute at Rome, 1839; of the Acad. of Berlin, 1851; of Herculaneum, 1852; of the Acad. des Inscriptions et Belles Lettres of the French Institute, 1861; Hon. Fellow of The Queen's College, Oxford, 1875; he established Champollion's system in England, at a time when many scholars were still uncertain of the relative merits of rival systems; as a museum official Birch was an excellent recorder and cataloguer of the rapidly growing collections in his care, being one of the very first people to put this work on a systematic basis; he not only made a register of every object acquired by the museum when it first arrived, but also recorded so many objects with descriptions and in some cases translations of inscriptions on them, that the slips thus made filled 104 vols. at the time of his death; an active publisher of texts, he first sorted out many of the papyrus fragments acquired from Salt (q.v.), Wilkinson (q.v.), and others; outside the Museum Birch was one of the first lecturers on Egyptological subjects in England; he was also the founder and first President of the Soc. of Biblical Archaeology, 1870; he was constantly consulted by scholars for half a century; he was sent to Italy to report on the Anastasi collection, 1846; the quantity of his published work like that of his unpublished work was immense, in all his bibl. lists 305 items and covers Near and Far East as well as British and Classical archaeology; his first Egyptological work was *Explanation of the Hieroglyphics on the Coffin of Mycerinus*, 1838; the same year he published a sketch for a hieroglyphic dictionary, already using the slip or *zettel* method employed on the great Berlin dictionary later; *Select Papyri in the Hieratic Character from the Collections of the British Museum*, pt. I, 1841, pt. II, 1842; *Gallery of Antiquities*, with Arundale and Bonomi, a handbook to the principal exhibits in the Eg. Coll., 1842; *Introduction to the Study of Egyptian Hieroglyphics*, 1857; *Select Papyri in the Hieratic Character*, 1860; *Egyptian Grammar and Egyptian Dictionary*, 1867, for vol. v of Bunsen's *Egypt's Place in Universal History*; this was his most famous work, the latter being the first complete dictionary ever published, an excellent concise work that listed 9,270 words and had *c.*30,000 refs.; *Ancient History from the Monuments*, a short work for SPCK,1875; he edited 12 vols. of *Records of the Past; Facsimile of an Egyptian Hieratic papyrus of the Reign of Ramesses III*, Pap. Harris I with trans., 1876; *Catalogue of the Collection of Egyptian Antiquities at Alnwick Castle*, 1880; he also contributed translations and notes to Vyse's vols., and revised Wilkinson's *Manners and*

Customs. 1878; in addition he wrote articles in the *EB, Times, Athenaeum*, and other journals; he died in Camden Town, London, 27 Dec. 1885; buried Highgate Cemetery.

TSBA 9. 1-43 (bibl. and portr.) (E. A. Budge, R. K. Douglas); *ODNB* 5, 798-9; *DNB Supp.* 1, 199 (E. A. W. Budge); *Rev. Ég.* 4. 187-92; Hilmy, i, 70; ii. 378; Budge, *Mummy*, 298; Budge, *N & T* and *R & P* has much interesting information and anecdotes; È. Gran-Aymerich, *Dictionnaire biographique d'archéologie 1798-1945*, 2001, incorporated in *Les Chercheurs de passé 1798-1945*, 2007, 606-7.

BIRCHER, André (1839-1926)

Swiss merchant in Cairo; he was born in Küttigen, Switzerland in 1839, son of André Bircher, a silk ribbon manufacturer; he came to Egypt in 1861 and began business as a general merchant dealing in imports and exports; he soon opened factories dealing in the preparation of gum and senna leaves and the manufacture of plaster; he was a founder of the Khedivial Geographical Society and a judge on the Commercial Tribunal and later the Mixed Tribunal; he also dealt in antiquities and formed a large and good collection, which he began to dispose of when he was old; Breasted purchased a considerable quantity for the Chicago collection; some of the scarabs and other antiquities were published by Newberry.

Inf. P. E. Newberry and L. Keimer; A. Wright, *Twentieth Century Impressions of Egypt,* 1909, 322; S. Sigerist, *Schweizer in Ägypten* , 2007, 28-32; F. Hagen and K. Ryholt, *The Antiquities Trade in Egypt 1880-1930*, 2017, 201-5.

BISSING, (*Freiherr von*) Friedrich Wilhelm (1873-1956)

German Egyptologist; he was born in Potsdam, 22 April 1873, son of Moritz Ferdinand von B. and Myrrha Wesendonck; he studied Classical Philology and Archaeology, then Egyptology and Art History at the University of Bonn 1892-6; later he was under Adolf Erman (q.v.) in Berlin; he visited Egypt in 1897 and worked on the *Cairo Catalogue* for Maspero, producing the volumes on metal, faience, and stone vases; with Ludwig Borchardt (q.v.) he excavated the remains of the sun temple of Nyuserre at Abu Gurob, 1898-1901; during World War I he published propaganda material for the German Empire in occupied Belgium and was engaged in efforts to convert the University of Ghent into a Flemish-speaking alma mater; he was appointed Professor of Egyptology in the University of Munich, 1906-22 and later at the University of Utrecht, 1922-26; he joined the Nazi party in 1925 which he was forced to leave due to his criticism of Hitler's policy towards the Protestant churches; he was, among others, a member of the Bavarian Academy of Science and the Göttingen Learned Society, the German and Austrian Archaeological Institutes; he received an Hon. Doctorate of the University of Riga; his output was immense extending over a period of 61 years and numbering 621 items, from this there may be selected *Die statistische Tafel von Karnak*, 1897; *Ein thebanischer Grabfund aus dem Anfang des Neuen Reiches*, 1900; *Die Mastaba des Gem-ni-kai*, 2 pts, 1905-11; *Das Re-Heiligtum des Königs Ne-woser-re (Rathures)*, 3 pts, 1905-28; *Tine: eine hellenistisch-romanische Festung in Mittelägypten*, 1928; *Ägyptische Kunstgeschichte*, 3 pts. 1934; *Zeit und Herkunft der in Cerveteri gefundenen Gefässe aus ägyptischer Fayence und glasiertem Ton*, 1941; *Die Baugeschichte des südlichen Tempels von Buhen, bei Wadi Halfa.*, 1942; his scarab collection was sold in 1954 and his library was auctioned in 1956; he died in Niederaudorf am Inn, 12 Jan. 1956.

AfO 17 (1954-6), 484-5 (portr.) (H. Brunner); *Bayerische Akad. der Wissenschaften. Jahrbuch* 1956, Munich, 190-202 (portr.) (F. Babinger); *Chron. d'Eg.* 31 (1956), 222 (anon.); EES *Ann. Report* 1956, 4-5 (J. Černý); *Studi Etruschi*, Florence, xxv (Serie ii), 1957). 671 (G. Botti); *ZÄS* 81 (1956), iv-vi (H.W. Müller); 84 (1959), 1-16 (bibl.) (I. Wallert) ; *Wer Ist's*, 1928; W. Dolderer in A.-F. Reginald de Schryver et al. (eds.), *Nieuwe Encyclopdie van de Vlaamse Beweging*, 1998, 498-9; È. Gran-Aymerich, *Dictionnaire biographique d'archéologie 1798-1945*, 2001, incorporated in *Les Chercheurs de passé 1798-1945*, 2007, 607-8; T. Beckh in E. Kraus (ed.), *Die Universität München im Dritten Reich. Aufsätze* I, 2006, 249-253, 283; T. Gertzen, *Gott. Misz.* 221 (2009), 109-118 and 222 (2009), 95-104; A. Grimm – S. Schoske (eds.), *Friedrich Wilhelm Freiherr von Bissing. Ägyptologe, Mäzen, Sammler, R.A.M.S.E.S.* 5 (2010); P. Raulwing and T. Gertzen, *Journal of Egyptian History* 5 (2012) (portr.). Photograph © 2011 Museum of Fine Arts, Boston.

BISSON DE LA ROQUE, Fernand (1885-1958)

French Egyptologist and archaeologist; he was born in Bourseville, Somme, 30 June 1885, son of Louis Augustin B. de la R. and Mathilde Félicité Henriette Desmoutier; after classical studies at the Coll. Saint-Stanislas, d'Abbeville, he went to the École des Langues Orientales, and entered Egyptology through courses at the École du Louvre, the École des Hautes Études, and the Sorbonne, where his teachers were Bénédite (q.v.), Guieysse (q.v.), and Moret; he assisted R. Weill (q.v.) in his excavations at Ophel Hill, Jerusalem, 1913, and also Zawyet el-Maiyitin in Egypt; during the First World War he served in France and, afterwards having met G. Jéquier (q.v.) in Switzerland, he became an assistant at the French Institute in Cairo; he became

director of excavations for the Louvre and dug successively a group of mastabas of the time of King Radjedef at Abu Rawash, 1922-4, at Thebes, and at Edfu; his most important work was, however, the excavation and publication of the temples of Montu at Medamud and Tod near Luxor, 1925-50, sites at which he found many important artistic and historical objects of the Middle Kingdom; see *Rapport sur les fouilles d'Abou-Roasch, 1922-1923*, 2 vols. 1924; *Rapport sur les fouilles de Médamoud*, var. vols. years 1926-33; *Tôd, 1934 à 1936*, 1937; *Le Trésor de Tod*, 1953; he died in Paris, 1 May 1958.

AfO 18 (1957-8), 490 (E. Weidner); *BIFAO* 58 (1959), 175-80 (portr.) (J. Sainte Fare Garnot) 181-4 (E. Drioton); *BSFE* 27 (Nov. 1958), 53-4 (E. Drioton); *Chron. d'Eg.* 33 (1958), 234 (H. de Morant) ; E. Gran-Aymerich, *Dictionnaire biographique d'archéologie 1798-1945*, 2001, incorporated in *Les Chercheurs de passé 1798-1945*, 2007, 685-6.

BLACAS D'AULPS, (*Duc de*) **Pierre Louis Jean Casimir** (1771-1839)
French nobleman and collector; he was born in the Château de Verignon (Var), 10 Jan. 1771, son of Alexandre Pierre Joseph B. and Marie Louise des Rollands, and was descended from the famous troubador Blacas; he was Captain of dragoons, 1789; a loyal royalist he left France after the Revolution and had an adventurous career in Italy and E. Europe from 1793; he married in London in 1814, and afterwards became Premier Gentilhomme de la Chambre du Roi to Louis XVIII and Charles X; he married 1814 Henriette Marie du Bouchet de Sourches de Montsoreau; he was created a duke in 1821; after the exile of the latter he again left France and lived in various European countries for the rest of his life; he was important in the history of Egyptology for two things: firstly as a staunch friend to Champollion (q.v.) using his influence to send him on his mission to Italy; Champollion's records in fact took the form of *Lettres à M. le Duc de Blacas*; secondly as a collector of coins, antique gems, and other antiquities; he formed a collection which was greatly increased by his eldest son; he (the son), Louis Charles Pierre Casimir was born in London on 15 April 1815 and died in Venice on 20 Feb. 1868; by a special Treasury Grant of £48,000 the whole of the huge and valuable Blacas collections were purchased by the British Museum in 1866; amongst the Egyptian items were two papyri (EA 9947-8); he died in Prague, 17 Nov. 1839.

DBF 6, 548-50; Champollion, i, *passim*; *Rec. Champ.* 1-20; C. W. King, *Handbook of Engraved Gems*, 2nd ed. (1885) 164; Edwards, *Lives of the Founders of the B.M.*, 689; E. Gran-Aymerich, *Dictionnaire biographique d'archéologie 1798-1945*, 2001, incorporated in *Les Chercheurs de passé 1798-1945*, 2007, 610-11.

BLACKDEN, Marcus Worsley (1864-1934)
British artist; he was born at Great Malvern, 25 Aug. 1864, son of Marcus Sefton B. and Fanny Franklyn; a volunteer member of the staff of the Archaeological Survey under Newberry (q.v.) at Beni Hasan, 1890-1 and Beni Hasan and El-Bersha, 1891-2; he made coloured drawings of the wall-paintings, but his work was brought to an end by a dispute with Newberry over the discovery of the alabaster quarries at Hatnub (see further below); many of Blackden's drawings were reproduced in colour in *Beni Hasan* I, III and IV and *El Bersheh* I; with G. Willoughby Fraser he published the hieratic graffiti at Hatnub; he later became a mystic and a member of the Societas Rosicruciana in Anglia, for which body he published *The Ritual of the Mystery of the Judgement of the Soul*, 1915, based on the Papyrus of Ani; he died in Blackfield, Hampshire, 21 Sept. 1934.

Beni Hasan, i, pref.; *JEA* 2 (1915), 52; Newberry Corr.; T. G. H. James, 'The Discovery and identification of the alabaster Quarries of Hatnub' *CRIPEL* 13 (1991), 79-84; inf. C. Naunton.

BLACKMAN, Aylward Manley (1883-1956)
British Egyptologist; he was born in Dawlish, S. Devon, 30 Jan. 1883, son of the Revd James Henry Blackman and Anne Mary Jacob; he was educated at St. Paul's School and The Queen's College, Oxford, where he read Arabic, and Egyptian and Coptic under Griffith (q.v.); he graduated in Oriental Studies, 1906; he spent the next few years working in Nubia, and acted as one of Reisner's assistants on the Archaeological Survey of Nubia, 1907-8; he was a member of the excavation team and published the inscriptions for the University of Pennsylvania expedition at Buhen, Wadi Halfa, 1909-10; he now performed the enormous task of completely recording the temples of Biga, Dendur, and Derr, 1911-15, and also began work on a fourth, Gerf Hussein, but had to desist owing to an attack of typhoid; he was elected Oxford Nubian Research Fellow and joined Griffith's staff at Faras; in 1912 he was elected Laycock Fellow of Egyptology at Worcester College, Oxford; MA, DLitt., FBA; after 1918 he assisted Griffith in teaching Egyptian at Oxford; he was appointed Brunner Professor of Egyptology at the University of Liverpool, 1934-48; Emeritus Professor at Liverpool, 1948-56; he was also special Lecturer in Egyptology in the University of Manchester, 1936-48; he was a member of the EES Committee for many years, and a member of the council of the Royal Asiatic Soc., 1922-35; joint editor of the *Annals of Archaeology and*

Anthropology; for the EES Blackman recorded the complete series of tombs at Meir in Middle Egypt, producing six vols., working at this site 1912-14, 1921, and 1949-50; in 1936 he visited Berlin in order to collate the Middle Egyptian papyri intended for his *Middle Egyptian Stories*; at this period he also directed the EES excavations at Sesebi, 1936-7, and was invited to act as tutor to the Crown Prince of Ethiopia, 1937-9; he combined the ability of a field worker and a great archaeological interest with a remarkable philological insight which was particularly apparent in his work on Ptolemaic texts; but his speciality was Egyptian Religion, a subject on which he wrote many studies and articles; his list of works is a long one; the following may be cited, *The Temple of Dendûr*, 1911; *The Temple of Derr*, 1913; *The Temple of Bigeh*, 1915; *The Rock Tombs of Meir*, 6 vols. 1914-53; *Luxor and its Temples*, 1923; *The Psalms in the Light of Egyptian Research*, in *The Psalmists*, 1926; *Middle-Egyptian Stories, pt. I of Bibl. Aeg.* 1932; *Egyptian Myth and Ritual*, 1932; *The Value of Egyptology in the Modern World*, 1935; he also contributed important studies to Hastings, *Encyclopaedia of Religion and Ethics*, and articles to *JEA* and other journals; his letters from Egypt are preserved in the archives of the University of Liverpool; he died in Abergele, N. Wales, 9 March 1956.

AfO 17 (1954-6), 492-3 (H. Brunner); *Chron. d'Ég.* 31 (1956), 309 (C. de Wit); *JEA* 42 (1956), 102-4 (portr.) (H. W. Fairman); *Nature*, London, vol. 177, no. 4512 (Apr. 21 1956), 731-2 (H. W. Fairman); *WWW* v, 108.

BLACKMAN, Winifred Susan (1872-1950)

British anthropologist; she was born at Preston Richards, Westmorland, 14 Aug. 1872, eldest daughter of the Revd James Henry Blackman and sister of Prof. Aylward M Blackman (q.v.); she studied anthropology at the Pitt Rivers Museum, Oxford, 1912-5 and worked as a volunteer there cataloguing the collections, 1913-20; she visited Egypt many times and from 1920 was engaged in anthropological research on the modern Egyptians, with special reference to survivals from Pharaonic times; she took part in the Percy Sladen Expedition, 1922-6; Wellcome Museum expedition, 1927; she published *The Fellahin of Upper Egypt*, 1927; and numerous articles in *JEA* and other journals; she died in Denbigh, 12 Dec. 1950; her anthropological collection is now largely in the Pitt Rivers Museum with some objects in the Science Museum and the British Musuem; her papers are preserved at the University of Liverpool.

The Times, 14 Dec. 1950; inf. A. Stevenson.

BLACKWOOD, (*Sir*) Frederick Temple Hamilton-Temple, 1st Marquis of Dufferin and Ava (1826-1902)

Irish statesman and diplomat; he was born at Florence, 21 June 1826, son of Price 4th Baron Dufferin and Helen Selina Sheridan; he succeeded as 5th Baron, 1841; created Earl, 1871; Marquis, 1888; PC; GCB; Hon. D.C.L.; LL.D.; FRS; Governor-General of Canada, 1872; Viceroy of India, 1884-8; he visited Egypt as a young man, 1858, and excavated at Deir el-Bahri Mar.-Apr. 1859; the work was largely left in charge of Cyril C. Graham (q.v.); despite the partial demolition of the wall in the Temple depicting the so-called "Queen of Punt" immediately after its discovery by Mariette (q.v.) in 1858 (the representation was afterwards recovered and is now in Cairo Museum), a portion of the Mentuhotep temple was excavated and carefully planned and recorded; a considerable number of antiquities and blocks were shipped back to the United Kingdom; most of the sculptures are at his home Clandeboye in Ireland, but the smaller antiquities from the collection were sold at Christie's, 31 May 1937 (Eg. lots 15-42); he was later special commissioner in Egypt, 1882-3; he died at Clandeboye, 12 Feb. 1902.

MS Journal describing his voyage up the Nile as far as the Second Cataract in 1859, now in Public Record Office of N. Ireland at Belfast (V./13A); Sir Alfred Lyall, *The Life of the Marquis of Dufferin and Ava*, 1905; *Bibl. Ég.* 18, p. xcvii; *JEA* 51 (1965), 16-28 (I. E. S. Edwards); *WWW* i. 212; *ODNB* 6, 42-6 (portr.).

BLANC, (Auguste Alexandre Philippe) Charles (1813-1882)

French art critic; he was born in Castres, 15 Nov. 1813, son of Jean Charles B., an official of the Empire, and Estelle Pozzo di Borgo and the brother of Louis B.; he contributed to many periodicals and published a work on the French Painters of the 19th cent., and an encyclopaedic history of painting in 14 vols.; he visited Egypt in 1869 and published an account *Voyage dans la Haute Égypte*, Paris, 1876; he was the first to describe the bas-reliefs in the Temple of Abydos explored by Mariette in 1864; he died in Paris, 17 Jan. 1882.

Carré, ii, 319-326; Hilmy, i, 76; *DBF* 6, 578-9.

BLANCHARD, Ralph Huntington (1875-1936)

American antiquities dealer in Cairo; he was born at Fulton, N.Y., 25 June 1875. son of Seymour Bailey B. and Anna Louise Franklin; he came to Egypt in 1905 and was in the American Consular Service until 1910; he then became a dealer in antiquities; his well-known shop was next to an entrance of the old Shepheard's Hotel; in addition to his stock, he had a large private collection of scarabs, some of which were published by Newberry; he published a *Handbook of Egyptian Gods and Mummy-amulets*, Cairo, 1909; his collection was dispersed after his death; his scarabs were acquired by Matouk (q.v.) and Michailides (q.v.); he died in Cairo, 22 July 1936.

Inf. P. E. Newberry; *Chron. d'Ég.* 12 (1937), 229; J. D. Cooney, *The Bulletin of the Cleveland Museum of Art*, 62 (1975), 11-14; F. Hagen and K. Ryholt, *The Antiquities Trade in Egypt 1880-1930*, 2017, 205-6.

BLANKENBERG-VAN DELDEN, Catharina (1906-1994)
Dutch Egyptologist; she studied with Jozef Janssen (q.v.) who encouraged her to research the commemorative scarabs of Amenhotep III; apart from articles on early New Kingdom queens, she published *The Large Commemorative Scarabs of Amenhotep III*, 1969, with supplements in *OMRO* 42 (1961), 7-12; *JEA* 62 (1976), 74-80; and *JEA* 63 (1977), 83-7; she died in 1994.

Inf. M. Raven.

BLAYDS, John (1753-1827)
British banker of Leeds; he was born 9 June 1753, son of John Calverley, Mayor of Leeds and Mary Walker; he took the name Blayds on 23 Feb. 1807 on inheriting the Blayds estate; he became senior partner in the house of Blayds, Beckett & Co. of Leeds (the firm as Beckett & Co. continued until 1920, when it was absorbed by the Westminster Bank); DL; he was twice Mayor of Leeds; a public benefactor he presented to the Leeds Philosophical Society a mummy of Dyn. 20 date which was examined and described by William Osburn (q.v.) in a special publication, 1828; this specimen is of importance in the history of the technique of mummification and is now in the Leeds Museum; Blayds died in Leeds, 21 Feb. 1827.

W. Osburn, *Account of an Egyptian Mummy*, Leeds, 1828; *GM* 1827, 285; 1828, 77; T. Whitaker, *Ducatus Leodensis*, 1816, 214.

BLEEKER, Claas Jouco (1898-1983)
Dutch Egyptologist; he was born at Beneden Knijpe, Friesland, 12 Sept. 1898, son of Johannes Jacob B. and Jantje Zuur; he was educated at Leiden University studying theology under Kristensen (q.v.) and Egyptology under Boeser (q.v.); Dr. Theol., 1929; he also studied at Berlin under Sethe (q.v.) and Grapow (q.v.); 1925-1946 he was a teacher at Apeldoorn, Gulemborg, and Enschede; in 1946 he was appointed Professor of History and Phenomenology of Religion, University of Amsterdam 1946-69; his main interest was the study of the ancient Egyptian religion; he was secretary-general of the International Association for the History of Religions and editor of *Numen*; he was awarded a doctorate by the University of Strasbourg; his principal works were *Die Beteekenis van de Egyptische godin Ma-a-t*, 1929; *De Overwinning op den dood naar oud-Egyptisch geloof*, 1942; *Die Geburt eines Gottes*, 1956; *Egyptian festivals*, 1967; *Hathor and Thoth*, 1973; *Het oord van stilte*, 1979; he died in Amsterdam, 5 May 1983.

Phoenix 30 (1984), 3 (H. van Voss); H. van Voss et al, *Studies in Egyptian Religion* (1982), 18-20; *Wie is dat*, 1948, 47; *Nederlands Theologisch Tijdschrift* 38 (1984), 67-9 (J. H. Kamstra); *The Encyclopedia of Religion*, 1987; *Numen* 30 (1983), 129-30 (portr.) (R. Werblowsky); inf. M. Raven.

BLOK, Henri Peter (1894-1968)
Dutch Egyptologist; he was born at Rotterdam, 28 Mar. 1894, son of Dirk Peter B. and Petronella Catharina Sara de Balbian; he studied at the Rotterdam Gymnasium and the University of Leiden 1913-4, 1918-25; PhD 1925, being a curator at The Hague Museum 1915-8; he was a lecturer in Egyptology at Leiden 1925-8 and curator at the University Library 1929-39; he worked at the Museum Scheurleer in The Hague 1922-31; in 1927 he joined the staff of the University of Utrecht becoming Professor in the History of Ancient Civilizations, 1928-50; he later became interested in African history; apart from articles, his major work was his thesis *Die beide volksverhalen van Pap. Härris 500 Verso*, 1925; he died in Oegstgeest, 25 Aug. 1968.

Wie is dat, 1948, 48-9; inf. Prof. Heerma van Voss; *Jaarboek der Leidse Universiteit* 1968-9, 268-9; inf. M. Raven.

BLUMENBACH, Johann Friedrich (1752-1840)
German anthropologist; he was born in Gotha, 11 May 1752, son of Heinrich B. and Charlotte Eleonore Hedwig Buddeus; he was educated at the Universities of Jena and Göttingen; MD 1775; he was appointed Prof. of Medicine, Göttingen, in 1775; one of his pupils was Seetzen (q.v.); FMRS; one of the founders of comparative anatomy and physical anthropology; he examined mummies in London in 1792 and arranged the gift of one from the Duke of Gotha to Göttingen in 1810; he wrote an account of Egyptian mummies in *Göttingisches Magazin der Wissenschaften und der Litteratur* 1 (1780), 109-39; *Phil. Trans.* 84 (1794), 177 and in *Beyträge zur Naturgeschichte*, ii (1811), 45-144; he died in Göttingen, 22 Jan. 1840.

EB; Haddon, *Hist. Anthropology*, 13; *Mem. Inst. Ég.* 13.8; Hilmy, i, 77; *NDB* 2, 328-30; F. W. Dougherty, *The Correspendence of Johann Friederich Blumenbach*, I, 2006; D. Graepler in D. Graepler and J. Migl (eds.), *Das Studium des schönen Altertums*, 52-6, 70; C. Di Biase-Dyson and B. Grosskopf in J. Arp-Neuman and T. Gertzen (eds.), *Steininschrift und Bibelwort*, 2019, 93-8.

BOCK *see* **BOK**

BOECKH, August (1785-1867)
German classical scholar; born at Karlsruhe, 24 Nov. 1785, son of Matthäus B. and Maria Salome Hörner; he became Professor of Classical Literature in the University of Berlin, 1813-67; he was a member and for many years secretary of the Berlin Academy; he was the author of numerous works and was editor of Pindar; on the Egyptological side he published a study on the chronology of Manetho and the Sothic Cycle, and he edited an important Greek papyrus with a facsimile produced by Champollion-Figeac (q.v.); he also edited vols. 1 and 2 of the *Corpus Inscr. Graecarum*; he died in Berlin, 3 Aug. 1867.

M. Hoffmann, *Aug. Böckh*, 1901; EB 4, 106; Hilmy, i, 78; Lepsius, (*Life*), 174; *NDB* 2, 366; È. Gran-Aymerich, *Dictionnaire biographique d'archéologie 1798-1945*, 2001, incorporated in *Les Chercheurs de passé 1798-1945*, 2007, 616-7.

BOESER, Pieter Adriaan Aart (1858-1935)
Dutch Egyptologist; he was born at Schellinkhout, 27 July 1858, son of Adriaan Johannes B. and Joanna Stoutjesdijk; he studied Egyptology in Berlin under Erman (q.v.) and at Leipzig under Steindorff (q.v.); Doctor, University of Leiden, 1889; Lecturer in Egyptology, Leiden, 1902-28; he succeeded Pleyte (q.v.) as Keeper of the Egyptian collections, Leiden Museum, 1892-1924; he worked with Pleyte on the Catalogue of Coptic MSS in Leiden Museum, 1897, and made a special study of Demotic, afterwards publishing many Coptic texts and antiquities in the Leiden collection; *Manuscrits Coptes du Musée d'Antiquités des Pays-Bas à Leide*, with W. Pleyte, 1897; *Catalogus ... Egyptische Afdeeling*, 1907; *Beschreibung der Aegyptischen Sammlung des Niederländischen Reichsmuseums der Altertümer in Leiden*, fol. 13 pts., 1909-26; *Transkription und Übersetzung des Papyrus Insinger*, 1922; he died at Leiden, 25 Feb. 1935.

Chron. d'Ég. 10 (1925), 317-18; *Netherlands Genealogieonline Trees*; inf. M. Raven.

BOESSNECK, Joachim (1925-1991)
German archaeozoologist; he was born in Glauchau, Saxony 26 Feb. 1925; following service in World War II, he studied veterinary medicine and zoology in Munich and Kiel; his dissertation on domesticated animals of ancient Egypt was awarded a *summa cum laude* by the Faculty of Veterinary Medecine, University of Munich, 1951; he was a member and later Director of the Institute of Animal Anatomy in Munich 1953-65; he became Director and Chairman of the Institute of Palaeoanatomy, Study of Domestication, and History of Veterinary Medicine, University of Munich 1965-91; he was a member of the German Archaeological Institute and the Bavarian Academy of Sciences and a foreign member of the Royal Swedish Academy of Letters, History, and Antiquities; he conducted research on faunal remains from archaeological sites in Europe, North Africa, and the Middle East but was particularly involved in work on remains from Egypt; his monographs in this field were his thesis *Die Haustiere in Altägypten*, 1953; *Tell el-Dab'a III. Die Tierknochenfunde 1966-1969*, 1976; with A. von den Driesch, *Studien an subfossilen Tierknochen aus Agypten*, 1982; with A. von den Driesch, *Die Tierknochenfunde aus der neolithischen Siedlung von Merimde-Benisalame am westlichen Nildelta*, 1985; *Tuna el-Gebel : Die Müncher Ochsenmumie*, 1987; *Die Tierwelt des Alten Ägypten*, 1988; with A. von den Driesch, *Tell el-Dab'a VII*, 1992; he died in Munich, 1 March 1991.

Zooarchaeological Research News 10 no. 2 (1991), 1-3 (A. von den Driesch and R. H. Meadow); *Archaeolozoologia* 4 (1991), 131-43 (bibl.); *International Journal of Osteoarchaeology* 2 (1992), 365 (D. Brothwell).

BOGHOS *see* **YUSUFIAN**

BOGOSLOVSKY, Evgeni Stepanovitch (1941-1990)
Russian Egyptologist; he was born in Novokuznetska, 21 Aug. 1941, son of Stepan B.; he studied under Matthieu (q.v.) and graduated in ancient history from the University of Perm in 1964; he was then attached to the Hermitage under Matthieu and Piotrovsky (q.v.); in 1968 he moved to the Leningrad branch of the Oriental Institute of the Academy of Sciences, USSR under Perepelkin (q.v.); he obtained his doctorate in 1986; his main interest centred on the workmen's community at Deir el-Medina and he wrote several articles in Russian academic journals often with English summaries, notably a survey of Deir el-Medina monuments in the USSR in *VDI* 119-125 (1972-3) and in English a survey of draughtsmen in *ZÄS* 107 (1980) 89-116; his monographs in Russian were *"Servants"*

of Pharaohs, Gods, and Private Persons, 1979 and *Ancient Egyptian Craftsmen*, 1983; he died in Leningrad, 21 July 1990.

VDI 1 (1991), 234-236.

BOK, Vladimir Georgevich von (1850-1899)
Russian art historian and archaeologist, pioneer of Coptic studies in Russia; he was born in Saratov province in Aug. 1850 and educated at the Natural Sciences department of St. Petersburg University; he was from 1886 curator of Mediaeval and Renaissance Art at the Hermitage, St. Petersburg and founder of its Coptic collection; from 1891, parallel to his post in the Hermitage, he was also curator of the Museum of the Russian Archaeological Society; in order to acquire Christian objects for the Hermitage, he was sent to Egypt in 1888-89 and 1897-98; in 1898 he organized a special exhibition of Coptic art in the Hermitage; during his second stay in Egypt he excavated monasteries near Sohag and a Coptic cemetery near Asyut; his posthumous notes and documentation on Christian churches and cemeteries seen by him in Egypt were issued in a bilingual Russian-French edition *Matériaux pour servir à l'archéologie de l'Égypte chrétienne*, St. Petersbourg 1901 with a complete list of his publications; he died on 16 May 1899.

Byzantinische Zeitschrift X (1900), 619-620 (J. Strzygowski); *VDI* 1 (151), 1980, 229-230 (A. Kakovkin); *Gött. Misz.* 131 (1992), 61-76 (portr.) (A. Kakovin); inf J. Sliwa.

BOKTY, Joseph (*fl.* 1799-1845)
Swedish Consul-General in Egypt before Anastasi (q.v.); he came from a Syrian family and had studied in France and Rome; he had acted as dragoman for the French forces in Egypt; his daughter was murdered in 1816 in Cairo; he resided in Salt's house in 1820; he was afterwards Prussian Consul in Egypt.

Athanasi, 17; Belzoni, i. 14, 33; Forbin, 60; Lepsius, 47; Minutoli, 20-1; Salt, ii. 155; T. Philipp, *The Syrians in Egypt 1725-1915*, 1985, 65; O. Volkoff, *Voyageurs russes en Égypte*, 1972, 145-6.

BOLLACHER, Alfred Wilhelm (1877-1968)
German artist; he was born in Strasbourg, 10 Aug. 1877, son of Franz Reihold B., a railway manager and Bertha Maria Schmid; he studied art at Muncih and Rome; he was employed by Borchardt (q.v.) at Abusir, 1907-8 where he produced drawings notably of the temple-complex of Sahure; he also illustrated some of the Giza publications of Junker (q.v.) and *Die ägyptische Religion*, 1905 by Erman (q.v.) under the direction of Schäfer (q.v.); he worked as an epigraphist for the Oriental Institute of Chicago at Medinet Habu, 1924-37; he died in Bonn, 2 Feb. 1968

M. Eaton-Krauss and W. El-Sadik, *JARCE* 47 (2011), 192-97.

BOMFORD, (Herbert) James Powell (1896-1979)
British collector and benefactor; he was born in Sutton, Surrey, 7 Jan. 1896, son of Revd Woodburn James B. and Katharine Johnson; he was educated Epsom College; in the First World War he served in the Artists' Rifles and Royal Flying Corps; he became a stockbroker and farmer in Wiltshire; with his second wife (Brenda) Jane (née Smith, 1912-1976) he formed collections of British furniture, Impressionist, post-Impressionist and modern British paintings, particularly the work of Francis Bacon; he donated paintings to Swindon Art Gallery in 1944; from the 1950s onwards the Bomfords became significant collectors of antiquities, buying and selling at auctions in London; a group of 'Luristan' bronzes was given to the Ashmolean Museum, 1965; other antiquities from their collection were exhibited at and thereafter advantageously sold and given to the Ashmolean; he established a purchase fund for antiquities at the Ashmolean; his collection of ancient glass was lent to and then sold to the Bristol Museum; he died in London, 26 March 1979.

Family inf. Nicholas Bomford and inf. T. Hardwick; *Daily Telegraph*, 30 March 1979 (by Desmond Morris); Ashmolean Museum, *Exhibition of Ancient Persian Bronzes Presented to the Department of Antiquities by James Bomford, Esquire*, 1966; Ashmolean Museum, *Ancient Glass, Jewellery and Terracottas: From the collection of Mr and Mrs James Bomford*, 1971; Bristol Museum, *Ancient Glass: the Bomford collection of pre-Roman and Roman glass*, 1976.

BONNEFOY, Marius François Joseph (*d.*1859)
French excavator, he was born at Boulogne-sur-Mer; he was assistant to Mariette (q.v.) in his Serapeum excavations, and afterwards his assistant in the museum of Bulaq; he directed excavations at Dra Abu'l Naga, 1858; he was a very loyal assistant to Mariette and active in suppressing illicit digging; nothing is yet known of his earlier history; he was presumably a relation of the painter Henri Arthur Bonnefoy, born in Boulogne-sur-Mer, 4 April 1839, died 1917; he died in Thebes, Aug. 1859.

Rec. Trav. 12, 215; Mariette, *Oeuvres diverses* 1 in *Bibl. Ég.* 18, xci, c; *Serapeum*, 42; French F.O. records; E. David, *Mariette Pacha 1821-1881*, 1994, 110.

BONNER, Campbell (1876-1954)
American papyrologist; born at Nashville, Tennessee, 30 Jan. 1876, son of Jesse Willis B. and Frances Campbell; he was educated at Vanderbilt and Harvard Universities becoming junior Professor of Greek at the University of Michigan in 1907; he was appointed Professor there, 1912-46; he acquired many papyri and was also concerned with excavation in Egypt; he published among other things *Studies in Magical Amulets*, 1950; he died in Ann Arbor, Michigan, 11 July 1954.

Chron. d'Ég. 31 (1956), 199-200 (A. E. R. Boak); *WWWA* 5, 73; *Gnomon* 27 (1955), 301-2 (H. Youtie).

BONNET, Hans (1887-1972)
German Egyptologist; he was born at Hirschberg, Silesia, 22 Feb. 1887, son of Fritz B. and Anna Stenzel; he studied classical philology at Breslau in 1906 and then from 1907 archaeology and Egyptology at the University of Leipzig obtaining his Dr. Phil. in 1916; from 1910 he was an assistant of Steindorff (q.v.) at the Institute of Egyptology in Leipzig; he acquired his habilitation from the University of Halle in 1922; lecturer at the University of Halle 1922-8; on 1 April 1928 he succeeded Wiedemann (q.v.) as Professor of Egyptology at the University of Bonn retiring in 1955; his particular interests were Egyptian archaeology and religion; his chief works were *Die ägyptische Tracht bis zum Ende des Neuen Reiches,* 1917; *Ägyptisches Schrifttum,* 1919; *Die ägyptische Religion,* 1924; *Die Waffen der Völker im Alten Orient,* 1926; *Ein Frühgeschichtliches Gräberfeld bei Abusir,* 1928; and his important *Reallexikon der ägyptischen Religionsgeschichte,* 1952; he died in Bonn, 27 Oct. 1972.

ZÄS 100 (1974), VI (E. Edel); E. Blumenthal, *Altes Ägypten in Leipzig,* 1981 29; *JEA* 60 (1974), 3; *Wer ist Wer* 1969-70, 117.

BONOMI, Joseph (1796-1878)
British sculptor, draughtsman, and traveller of Italian origin; he was born in London, 9 Oct. 1796, son of J. B. the elder (1739-1808), architect, and Rosa Florini; a cousin of the painter Angelica Kauffman; he studied at the RA schools under Nollekens and won the silver medal for drawing in the antique style; he continued his studies in Rome, 1823; he went from there to Egypt to assist Robert Hay (q.v.) in 1824, remaining there for no less than 9 years although estranged from Hay 1826-32; he also worked with Burton (q.v.), Lane (q.v.),Wilkinson (q.v.), and Rosellini (q.v.); in 1828 he assisted Burton with his *Excerpta Hieroglyphica*, and in 1829 ascended the Nile as far as Dongola, and in 1831 he accompanied Linant Bey (q.v.) in his expedition to the Gold Mines; he rejoined Hay at Qurna in Aug. 1832; he went with Arundale (q.v.) and Catherwood (q.v.) in a journey through Sinai, Palestine, and Syria, 1833-4; he was much used by Wilkinson and Birch (q.v.) for the production of their works because of his knowledge and excellence as a draughtsman; he returned to Rome to study the obelisks, 1838, and worked at the British Museum, 1839; at this time he prepared the illustrations for Wilkinson's *Manners and Customs*; he supervised the making of Hay's plaster casts of Egyptian sculpture and their entry into the British Museum; he was partly responsible for the design and decoration of the Egyptian-style Marshall's Mill at Holbeck, Leeds in 1842; he next went to Egypt with Lepsius's expedition, 1842-4; he returned to England and married Jessie daughterof the painter John Martin, 1845; Bonomi set up the Egyptian court at the Crystal Palace, 1853, and made the first hieroglyphic fount in England for Birch's *Dictionary*, pub. 1867; he catalogued and illustrated many Egyptian collections, and lithographed the sarcophagus of Sety I and other monuments; he was appointed Curator of Sir John Soane's Museum, 1861, and was still in office at his death; he was instrumental in the sale of much of Hay's collection to the British Museum in 1868 and Hay's MSS to the Museum (now in the British Library) in 1875; in 1876 he corresponded with Amelia Edwards (q.v.) as she prepared her account of her trip to Egypt; his principal publications were, *Gallery of antiquities selected from the British Museum*, by F. Arundale and J. Bonomi, with descriptions by S. Birch, 1842-1843; *Catalogue of the Egyptian antiquities in the Museum of Hartwell House*, 1858; *Egypt, Nubia and Ethiopia ...,* 1862; he also published articles, but these form but a fraction of his work; both Birch and Budge praise his abilities, the former considering him to have greater knowledge and experience of Egypt than anyone else of the period save Wilkinson; the number of works and projects he contributed to after 1830 was enormous and exceeded that of any other artist, so that although not an Egyptologist he yet made greater contributions than most; he died in Wimbledon, 3 March 1878 and is buried in Brompton cemetery beneath a slate Anubis.

ODNB 6, 569-71; *DNB* 5, 364; Diary (transcript at Griffith Institute); *TSBA* 6 (1879) 560-73; *BIE* 32. 51; Budge, *N & T* note on p. 14; Hay Diary; Hilmy, i, 81; BL Add. MS 35057 f. 121 (portr.); *ILN* 1878,245 (portr.); S. Tillett, *Egypt Itself,* 1984; inf. S. Tillett; È. Gran-Aymerich, *Dictionnaire biographique d'archéologie 1798-1945,* 2001, incorporated in *Les Chercheurs de passé 1798-1945,* 2007, 620-1.

BORCHARDT, Ludwig (1863-1938)
German Egyptologist and architect; he was born in Berlin, 5 Oct. 1863, son of Herman B. and Bertha Levin; his younger brother was the famous writer Georg Hermann B.; he trained as an architect at the Technische

Hochschule in Berlin, 1883-7 and studied Egyptology under Erman (q.v.) at the same time; he assisted in the Egyptian section of Berlin Museum, 1887-8; he became Königlicher Regierungsbauführer, 1888 and Königlicher Regierungsbaumeister für das Hochbaufach, 1892; between 1888 and 1891 he was in charge of building works at Königsberg; he worked worked for the Städtische Bau-Dezentation in Berlin, 1892-5 and prepared Gustav Erbkam's plans of the Lepsius (q.v.) expedition at the Berlin Museum for printing; he was sent by the German government to Egypt as a member of the international Philae project, 1895; PhD *hon. c.* Berlin, 1897; he was in charge of de Morgan's (q.v.) great project to catalogue the standing monuments of Egypt by the Egyptian Antiquities Service, 1896-99; he inaugurated a less grandiose scheme in conjunction with Maspero (q.v.) for the great *Catalogue Général* of Cairo Museum; he became scientific attaché to the German Consulate in Cairo, 1899; Prof., 1906; Borchardt founded and directed the Kaiserlich Deutsches Institut für Ägyptische Altertumskunde in Kairo, 1907-29 which became the Egyptian section of the German Institute of Archaeology (DAI, Abteilung Kairo) after his retirement; he then founded his own institute which later became the Swiss Institute; he also contributed a great many texts and much useful information to the Berlin Dictionary; using methods partly derived from Dörpfeld he excavated the sun temple of King Nyuserre at Abu Gurab, 1898-1901, and the pyramids of Abusir, 1902-4, 1907-8; he also excavated and established reconstructions of Amarna houses, 1911-14; Borchardt was the first person to make an intensive study of Egyptian architecture as a subject on its own; he also discovered the workshop of the sculptor Thutmose at Amarna and enriched the Berlin Museum with many fine objects from this excavation; another interest of his was chronology; he was a member of the German Arch. Institute, 1898, and a bibliography of his writings, 214 nos., was issued in 1933 to celebrate his 70th birthday; Doctor Ing *hon. c.* Danzig, 1931;he published, *Die aegyptischen Pflanzensäule,* 1897; *Denkmäler des Alten Reiches (ausser den Statuen) im Museum von Kairo,* pt. I, *Cat. Gén.,* 1901; *Das Re-Heiligtum des Königs Ne-woser-re (Rathures),* pt. I, *Der Bau,* 1905; *Zur Baugeschichte des Amonstempels von Karnak,* 1905; *Nilmesser und Nilstandsmarken,* 1906; *Das Grabdenkmal des Königs Ne-user-re ,*1907; *Works of Art from the Egyptian Museum at Cairo. With explanations by L. Borchardt,* 1908; *Das Grabdenkmal des Königs Nefer-ir-ke33-re,* 1909; *Das Grabdenkmal des Königs S'a3hu-re,* 3pts, 1910, 1913; *Statuen und Statuetten von Königen und Privatleuten im Museum von Kairo, Cat. Gén.,* 1911-36; *Die Annalen und die zeitliche Festlegung des Alten Reiches der ägyptischen Geschichte,* 1917; *Quellen und Forschungen zur Zeitbestimmung der Ägyptischen Geschichte,* 3pts. 1917, 1935, 1938; *Die Altägyptische Zeitmessung* 1920; *altägyptische Festungen an der zweiten Nilschnelle,* 1923; *Porträts der Königin Nofret-ete aus den Grabungen 1912/13 in Tell el-Amarna,* 1923; *Ägypten. Landschaft, Volksleben, Baukunst,* with H Ricke, 1930; *Allerhand Kleinigkeiten ... zu seinem 70. Geburtstage am 3. Oktober 1933,* 1933; *Beiträge zur ägyptischen Bauforschung und Altertumskunde,* with H Ricke, 1937; *Die Entstehung des Generalkatalogs und seine Entwicklung in den Jahren 1897-1899,* 1937; *Ägyptische Tempel mit Umgang,* 1938; the photographic archive of his excavations is preserved in the Egyptian Antiquities Service; he died in Paris, 12 Aug. 1938, and was buried in Cairo.

ASAE 39 (1939), 43-7 (portr.) (J. Leibovitch); *Chron. d'Ég.* 14 (1939), 141-3 (J. Capart) *JEA* 24 (1938), 248 (G. Steindorff); *NDB* 2, 455 (H. Ricke); E. Endesfelder, *Die Ägyptologie an der Berliner Universität-Zur Geschichte eines Fachgebietes,* 27 *KMT* 12/4 (2001/2), 78-80; È. Gran-Aymerich, *Dictionnaire biographique d'archéologie 1798-1945,* 2001, incorporated in *Les Chercheurs de passé 1798-1945,* 2007, 623-5; T. El Awady in *EDAL* 1 (2009), 49-52; Susanne Voß und Cornelius von Pilgrim, 'Ludwig Borchardt und die deutschen Interessen am Nil' in Charlotte Trümpler (ed.), *Das große Spiel – Archäologie und Politik zur Zeit des Kolonialismus (1860-1940),* 2008, 294-305; R. Krauss in *Égypte Afrique & Orient* 52 (2008-9), 47-54; Susanne Voß, 'Das DAI Kairo 1907-1979 im Spannungsfeld deutscher politischer Interessen' in *Menschen, Kulturen, Traditionen. Die Forschungscluster des Deutschen Archäologischen Instituts,* 2009, 110-11; Susanne Voss, '"Draussen im Zeltlager..." Ludwig Borchardts Grabungsalltag in Abusir' in Vinzenz Brinkmann (ed.), *Sahure. Tod und Leben eines grossen Pharao,* 2010, 109-21. inf. Susanne Voß; R. Krauss, *EDAL* III (2012), 121-62.

BORELLI, *(Bey)* **(Philippe) Octave** (1849-1911)
French lawyer of Italian extraction; he was born at Marseilles, 28 March 1849, son of Jerome B., merchant, and Marie Flavie Maxine de Roux; after service in the Franco-Prussian war, he went into government service; in 1878 he left for Egypt and in 1879 was attached as a lawyer to the Ministry of Finance and later other departments; he helped to reorganize the adminstration of justice and draw up a constitution; he founded the newspaper *Le Bosphore Égyptien* to oppose British influence although he later modified his views; he was elected to the Inst. Ég., 1884, and made several communications, resigning in 1900 when he finally left Egypt; he had a fine collection of Egyptian, Greek, and Roman antiquities which he disposed of to an unknown buyer; the collection was resold at Hôtel Drouot, Paris, 11-13 June 1913, and was described in the catalogue as 'provenant de l'ancienne collection Borelli-Bey appartenant à M. X'; he died in Paris, 25 July 1911.

J. Borelli, *Marseille* 92 (1973), 49-51; 93, 57-8; F. Garcin, *Revue de l'Occident Musulman et de la Mediterranée* 30 (1980), 71-99;*Inst. Ég. Records*; Myers Diary, 2 March, 1894; *DBF* 6, 1100; Lugt 72925.

BOREUX, Charles (1874-1944)
French Egyptologist; he was born in Caen, 3 Nov. 1874, son of Leon Claude Frédéric B. and Marie Mathilde Peltereau; he was educated at the Lycée of Caen and the Lycée Louis-le-Grand, Paris; he studied Egyptology under Revillout (q.v.), and entered the Louvre, 1903; he first visited Egypt in 1907; he worked under Bénédite (q.v.), attaché, 1913; arranged and catalogued the Louvre Egyptian collections, which grew considerably in size during his time; in 1939 he supervised the removal of the collection to places of safety during the war; he retired in 1940; he made a speciality of Egyptian ships and nautical matters; his bibl. lists about 40 items the most important being, *Études de nautique égyptienne. L'art de la navigation en Égypte jusqu'à la fin de l'Ancien Empire*, 1925; *L'Art égyptien*, 1926; *Musée national du Louvre. Dépt. des ant. ég. Guide-Catalogue sommaire*, 2 vols. 1932; *La Sculpture égyptienne au Musée du Louvre*, no date; he died in Paris, 3 April 1944.

Chron. d'Ég. 19 (1944), 259; *Rev. d'Ég.* 5 (1946), 1-9 (portr. and bibl.) (J. Vandier).

BORGHOUTS Joris Frans (1939-2018)
Dutch Egyptologist; he was born in Ginneken, 17 June 1939, son of Abrahaam Nicolaas B., a theoretical physicist and W. D. C. van Bosch; he studied Egyptian language and literature at the University of Leiden; PhD, 1971; he became a lecturer at the University of Amsterdam, 1969-76; he was appointed lecturer at the University of Leiden, 1976-85 and professor in succession to Janssen (q.v.), 1985-2004; he then became a research fellow at the Netherlands Institute for the Near East, Leiden; he published *The Magical Texts of Papyrus Leiden* I 348, 1971; *Egyptishe sagen en verhalen*, 1974; *Selected pieces: Allard Pierson Museum, archaeological collection of the University of Amsterdam*, 1976; *Gifts to Mark the Re-opening: Allard Pierson Museum, Amsterdam, Archaeological Collection of the University of Amsterdam*, 1976; *Ancient Egyptian Magical Texts*, 1978; 'Duizend goden van Chatti en duizend goden van Egypte': die relaties tussen Egypte en de Hettieten*, 1986; *Egyptisch: een inleding in schrift en taal van her Middenrijk*, 1993; with D. van der Plas, *Coffin Texts Word Index*, 1998; *Book of the Dead [39]: from Shouting to Structure*, 2007 and *Egyptian: An Introduction to the Writing and Language of the Middle Kingdom*, 2010; he died in Leiden, 15 Sept. 2018.

Inf. Nederlands Instituut voor het Nabije Ooosten and M. Raven.

BORGIA, (*Cardinal*) Stefano (1731-1804)
Italian prelate; he was born at Velletri, 3 Dec. 1731, son of Camillo B. and Maddalena Gagliardi, and became Prefect of the Congregation of the Propaganda Fide; he made a collection of Egyptian antiquities and Coptic codices which became the foundation of the Egyptian collection of the Naples Museum; his Greek papyri were published by Schow (q.v.); he died in Lyons, while escorting Pope Pius VII to France, 23 Nov. 1804.

DBDI 12, 739-42.

BOROZDINA-KOZMINA, Tamara Nikolaevna (1889-1959)
Russian Egyptologist; she was born in Kostroma, 1889; after studying at St. Petersburg University under Turaeff (q.v.) in 1916, she was associated with the State Museum of Fine Arts in Moscow at first as assistant and later curator; from 1920-31 head of its Department of Ancient Near East and Egypt; she was especially interested in problems of Egyptian art, preparing publications of objects from the Golenischeff collection *Egyptian sculptor's models,* 1917; *Archaic Pottery*, 1926; *Hellenistic objects from Egypt*, 1930; she was also an author of a study on Egyptian dance, 1919; she died on 4 Jan. 1959.

VDI 4 (70), 1959, 159-60; inf. J. Śliwa.

BORRER, Dawson (1817-1895)
British traveller; he was baptized Henfield, Sussex, March 30, 1817, son of William B. of Pakyns Manor and Barrow Hill, Henfield, Sussex, JP, FRS, and Elizabeth Hall; he travelled through Italy, Greece, Egypt, and the Sinai Peninsular as far as Jerusalem; while in Egypt he visited the Fayum; he published a narrative of his journey, 1845, which included a translation of the *Mémoire sur le Lac Moëris*, of Linant de Bellefonds (q.v.), 1842; he died at Altamont, Co. Carlow, Ireland 11 Oct. 1895.

Burke, *LG*; Hilmy, i, 83.

BOSSE-GRIFFITHS, Käthe (Kate) (1910-1998)
German/British Egyptologist; she was born in Wittenberg-an-der-Elbe, 16 July 1910, daughter of Dr. Paul B., a gynaecologist and Käte Gertrud Levin; she studied Classics and Egyptology at the Universities of Berlin, Bonn, and Munich under Scharff (q.v.); PhD, 1935; she was employed briefly by the Berlin State Museums, but was

dismissed under Nazi regulations as her mother was Jewish; she emigrated to Great Britain in 1936; she then obtained a grant to study in the Department of Egyptology, University College under Glanville (q.v.) where she taught and assisted in the Petrie Museum, registering objects, July 1937-July 1938; she was attached to the staff of the Ashmolean Museum and a member of Somerville College from 1938; in 1939 she married J. Gwyn Griffiths (q.v.) and moved to Wales where she became a prominent figure in the Welsh nationalist movement; on her husband's appointment to the Classics Department at Swansea, she became Hon. Curator of Archaeology at the Royal Institution of South Wales (now Swansea Museum) where she arranged the display of Egyptian antiquities; Hon. Curator of the Wellcome collection at the University of Wales, Swansea from 1971-95; her promotion of the latter collection led to the decision to construct the Egypt Centre at the University to house the collection; apart from novels in Welsh and numerous articles on objects in the collections under her charge, her principal Egyptological publications were her thesis *Die menschliche Figur in der Rundplastik der ägyptischen Spätzeit*, 1936, reprint 1978; a translation of E. Otto's *Osiris und Amun* as *Egyptian Art and the Cults of Osiris and Amon*, 1968; *Beadwork*, 1978; *A Musician Meets her Gods*, 1982; and *Five Ways of Writing between 2000 B.C. and A.D. 200*, 1994; her collected articles were published by her husband as *Amarna Studies and other Selected Papers*, 2001; she died in Swansea, 4 April 1998.

JEA 84 (1998), 191-3 (portr.) (A. B. Lloyd); IAE internet obituary (H. Middleton-Jones); inf. J. G. Griffiths; *The Times* 1 May 1998 (portr.); J. Gwyn Griffiths (ed), *Amarna Studies and other Selected Papers*, 2001, 7-14 (portr.); *The Guardian* 6 May 1998 (V. A. Donohue). Photograph courtesy of Roger Davies.

BOSTICCO, Sergio (1920-2007)

Italian Egyptologist; he was born in Turin, 19 Oct. 1920, son of Giuseppe B. and Maria Rogliatti; he studied Egyptology under Farina (q.v.), graduating in 1947 after war service; he was appointed assistant at the Museo Gregorio Egizio, 1950-55; he then became inspector at the Museo Archeologico in Florence, 1955-69; he was lecturer of Egyptology at the University of Florence, 1963-69 and professor, 1969-96; he excavated in Nubia at Ikhmindi, Tamit, Maharraqa, Kuban and Farreq during the rescue campaign and also helped run the Archaeological Department of the Italian Cultural Institute in Cairo, 1961-64; he later took part in excavations at Kiman Fares, 1964-5, Antinoopolis, 1965-2006, tomb 27 at Thebes, 1971-2000, Sonqi, 1966-70, and Gebel Barkal, 1973-1999; apart from many articles and four translations of other Egyptological works, he published *Musei Capitolini. I monumenti egizi ed egittizzanti*, 1952; *L'Oriente Antico*, with S. Moscati, 1952; *Le Stele Egiziane. Museo Archeologico di Firenze*. 3 vols, 1959-67; *Storia Universale* I, with others, 1959; *Ramessese II*, 1966; *Tamit (1964)*, with others, 1967; he died in Florence, 21 Oct. 2007.

Inf. G. Rosati; *Aegyptus* 87 (2007), 9-12 (M. Manfredi).

BOTHMER, Bernard Wilhelm V(on) (1912-1993)

American Egyptologist and art historian; he was born in Charlottenburg, Berlin, 13 Oct. 1912, son of Wilhelm Friederich Franz Karl von B., of a Hanoverian noble family, and Marie Julie Auguste Karoline Baroness von und zu Egloffstein; he studied Egyptology at the University of Berlin under Sethe (q.v.) but was unable to finish his dissertation on Egyptian art due to his professor's death; he was appointed as an assistant to Schäfer (q.v.) in the Egyptian Department, Berlin Museum, 1932-8 when his post lapsed; because of his opposition to the Nazi government, he fled to France in 1938 and to Switzerland in 1939 where he found temporary employment; he emigrated to the United States in Oct. 1941 where he worked for the Office of War Information and the War Department and later was in army intelligence in Europe until 1946; he was appointed assistant curator in the Department of Ancient Art, Museum of Fine Arts, Boston, 1 Aug. 1946-54; Director of the American Research Center in Egypt, 1954-6; Fulbright resident fellow in Cairo, 1954-6, 1963-4; he became associate curator in the Dept. of Ancient Art, The Brooklyn Museum, 1956-63; curator in succession to Cooney (q.v.), 1963-82; he lectured at the Institute of Fine Arts, New York University, 1960-78; professor, 1979; Lila Acheson Wallace Professor of Ancient Egyptian Art, 1982-93; Bothmer was a leading specialist in ancient Egyptian sculpture particularly of the Late Period and formed as a research tool the Corpus of Late Egyptian Sculpture, a photographic and bibliographic resource, now in The Brooklyn Museum; he was project director for the New York University's Mendes expedition and the also the Apis House project at Memphis, 1981-6; he organized an exhibition of sculpture of the Late Period Art in The Brooklyn Museum, 1960-1 and produced with E. Riefstahl (q.v.) the authoritative catalogue *Egyptian Sculpture of the Late Period*, 1960; he was also responsible for two other important exhibitions with significant catalogues *Akhenaten and Nefertiti*, 1971 and *Africa in Antiquity*, 1978 which was instrumental in encouraging the study of

Nubian and Meroitic Art; a *Festschrift* in his honour *Artibus Aegypti*, edited by H. De Meulenaere and L. Limme, was published in 1983; he wrote a large number of articles on Egyptian art and sculpture notably a series Membra Dispersa on fragments of sculpture in different locations; he wrote *Brief Guide to the Department of Ancient Art, The Brooklyn Museum*, with J. Keith, 1970 and edited the *Catalogue of the Luxor Museum of Ancient Egyptian Art,* 1979, and posthumously a travel diary *Egypt 1950: My First Visit*, ed. Emma Swan Hall, 2003; and *Egyptian Art: selected writings of B. V. Bothmer*, 2004, ed. by M. E. Cody; his catalogue of Late Period sculpture in the Cairo Museum remained unfinished at his death; his archives were acquired by the Egyptological Archives of the Università degli Studi di Milano in 2008; he died in New York, 24 Nov. 1993.

Directory of American Scholars, 1982, I, 74; *The Times* 3 Dec. 1993; *The New York Times* 29 Nov. 1993; *AJA* 98 (1994), 345-6 (portr.) (J. A. Josephson); *JEA* 80 (1994) xi-xii; *KMT* 5/1 (1994), 39 (D. Guzman); *In Memoriam Bernard V. Bothmer 1912-1993*, Institute of Fine Arts, New York University, 1994; *JARCE* 32 (1995), i-iii (R. Fazzini); *Antike Welt* (1994), 94 (D. Wildung); *BES* 12 (1996), 6-14 (portr.) (J. Romano), 15-24 (bibl.) (D. Bergman); *ZÄS* 122 (1995), I-III (portr.) (D. Wildung); inf. D. von Bothmer; P. Piacentini, *Egypt and the Pharaohs from the Sand to the Library*, 2010, 100-11; M. Eaton-Krauss, *MDAIK* 70/1 (2014/15), 11-120; M. Eaton-Krauss, *Bernard V. Bothmer Egyptologist in the Making*, 2019.

BOTTA, Paul Émile (1802-1870)

French naturalist and excavator of Italian origin; he was born in Turin, 6 Dec. 1802, the son of Carlo B., the historian who died in Paris in 1838, and Antoinette Vierville; he adopted French nationality; although mainly known as an Assyriologist, he went to Egypt in 1831 and visited Saqqara with Bonomi (q.v.) and Linant (q.v.); he was French Vice-consul at Mosul, 1842; Botta carried out excavations at Kuyunjik and Khorsabad until 1845 when he brought back the fine Assyrian sculptures now in the Louvre; he died in Achères, 29 March 1870.

Bonomi Diary, 16 Jan. 1831; Budge, *R & P*, 67; R. Campbell Thompson, *A century of Exploration at Nineveh*, 23 ff.; Glyn E. Daniel, *A Hundred Years of Archaeology*, 70, 71-3; È. Gran-Aymerich, *Dictionnaire biographique d'archéologie 1798-1945*, 2001, incorporated in *Les Chercheurs de passé 1798-1945*, 2007, 630-1.

BOTTI, Giuseppe (1853-1903)

Italian archaeologist; he was born at Modena, 3 Aug. 1853, son of Tommasso B. and Barbara Manzini; he went to Alexandria in 1884 as head of the Italian School; he carried out excavations and was the founder and first Director of the Graeco-Egyptian Museum; the project for the Alexandria Museum was set on foot in 1891, and the buildings erected in 1895, additional galleries being subsequently provided in 1896, 1899, and 1904; he died in Alexandria, 16 Oct. 1903; his papers are in the Egyptological Archives of the Università degli Studi di Milano.

Breccia, *Alexandrea ad Aegyptum*, 2nd ed. (1914), 143-5; Sayce, 274; EEF *Arch. Report*, 1894-5, I; *DBDI* 13, 443-4; S. Curto, *Studi di egittologia e di antichità puniche*, 13 (1994), 71-80 (portr.) (bibl.); P. Piacentini, *Egypt and the Pharaohs from the Sand to the Library*, 2010, 112-4; P. Piacentini (ed.), *Gli archivi egittologici dell'Università degli Studi di Milano. 2. Il fondo Giuseppe Botti "Primo"* (*Il Filarete*), 2011.

BOTTI, Giuseppe (1889-1968)

Italian Egyptologist and Demotist; he was born in Vanzone di S. Carlo, Novara, 3 Nov. 1889, son of Bartolomeo B., a trader, and Maria Gorini his wife; he was educated in the University of Turin obtaining 'laureato' in Classical Philology, 1913; he then studied Christian Literature, 1914-16; between 1916-32 he taught Latin, Greek, and Italian in various schools in Turin and several cities in Piedmont, and it was at this time that he took up the study of Egyptology, receiving lessons in Egyptian from Schiaparelli (q.v.), and also worked in the Egyptian collections at Turin, classifying and collecting hieratic papyri texts some of which he published; he now began his collaboration with Gardiner (q.v.), Peet (q.v.), Černý (q.v.), and Volten (q.v.); during the years 1932-56 he was exempted from teaching by the Ministry of Public Instruction and attached to the Department for Etruscan antiquities in Florence where he rearranged the Egyptian section of the Archaeological Museum; in 1932-3, 1934, 1939 he was sent by the Ministry to attend Demotic courses given by Lexa (q.v.) at the Karl IV University in Prague, in order to be able to work on the Demotic papyri found by the Italian Archaeological Mission under Anti at Tebtunis, 1931; he taught Egyptology in the University of Florence, 1942-56, and was appointed Ordinarius of Egyptology in the University of Rome, 1956-60; his principal publications were, *Il Giornale della necropoli di Tebe,* i.e. hieratic papyri of the Turin Museum, with T. E. Peet, 1928; *Testi demotici,* 1941*; Le sculture del Museo Gregoriano Egizio,* with P. Romanelli and others, 1851; *Le antichità egiziane del Museo di Cortona,* 1955; *Le casse di mummie e i sarcofagi da El Hibeh nel Museo Egizio di Firenze.* 1958; *La glorificazione di Sobk e del Fayum in un papiro ieratico da Tebtynis,* 1959; a collection of his articles was published as *Omaggio a Giuseppe Botti,* 1984; he died in Florence, 27 Dec. 1968.

Inf. Prof. S. Curto, Egyptian Museum, Turin; *Studi in onore G. Botti,* (bibl); *WW Italy,* 1958, 152; *DBDI* 13, 444-6; *ZÄS* 96 (1970), VI-VIII (portr.) (S. Curto); *Chron. d'Eg.* 44 (1969), 298-9 (B. van de Walle); *Aegyptus* 47 (1967) 246-52 (portr.) (S. Curto) *Rivista degli studi orientali* 43 (1960), 379-82 (S. Donadoni); *Oriens Antiquus* 6 (1967), 3-7 (bibl.); M. Botti, *Dal Monte Rosa alla Terra dei Faraoni,* 2011.

BOUCHARD, Pierre François Xavier (1772-1822)
French officer in the Engineers; he was born at Orgelet in Jura, 29 April 1772, son of Pierre B., a master carpenter and later merchant, and Pierrette Jeanette de Cressia; after studying at Besançon, he joined the French army; from 1796-8 he attended the École polytechnique and then joined the expedition to Egypt; while serving at Fort Julien; he was the real discoverer of the Rosetta Stone; when it was found Bouchard noted that it had inscriptions carved on it and that they might be of historical importance; he therefore reported the find to his superior, General Menou; some confusion has arisen, however, because of the likeness of his name to another officer serving in Egypt at the time whose name was Boussard; Bouchard then arranged the transport of the stone to Cairo; he later served at el-Arish where he was captured in 1799 and after his release, again at Fort Julien where he was captured by the British in 1801; he returned to France in July 1801 and later took part in the expedition to Santa Domingo and the Napoleonic wars in Spain and Portugal, being taken prisoner again in 1812 when he was brought to England; he was named chief engineer at Givet sur la Meuse 1821; he died at Givet sur la Meuse, 5 Aug. 1822.

JEA 43 (1957, 117 (W. R. Dawson) gives wrong officer; *JEA* 44 (1958), 123 (W. R. Dawson) gives correct one; R. Solé and D. Valbelle, *La pierre de Rosette,* 1999, 10-14, 16, 18, 21, 46-7; J. Leclant in *BSFE* 146 (1999), 6-24; È. Gran-Aymerich, *Dictionnaire biographique d'archéologie 1798-1945,* 2001, incorporated in *Les Chercheurs de passé 1798-1945,* 2007, 631-2.

BOUGHTON, (*Sir*) William Edward Rouse (1788-1856)
British traveller and antiquary; he was born in London, 14 Sept. 1788, son of Charles William B. 9th Bart. and Catherine Pearce, and succeeded as 10th Bart. of Lawford and 2nd Bart. of Rouse Lench, 1821; FRC, 1814; FSA; he visited Egypt with Dr John Lee (q.v.), 1810; he was a friend of Thomas Young (q.v.) and while at Luxor purchased a papyrus, 1814, which was damaged in transit and given to Young to study with important consequences as it aroused the latter's interest in hieroglyphic decipherment; Boughton published a *Letter respecting Egyptian Antiquities,* and 'Some remarks on Egyptian Papryi and the Inscription of Rosetta' in *Archaeologia* 18 (1815), 59; he died in London, 22 May 1856.

A. Wood, *Thomas Young,* 208; Hartleben, i, 369; Hartwell Museum, *Cat. Eg. Antiquities* (1858), 48; Pettigrew, *Hist. Eg. Mummies,* 139.

BOULOS, Tewfik (*fl.* 1902-1947)
Egyptian archaeologist; he was educated at the American Training College at Asyut; he became secretary to Carter, 1902-5; he was appointed 15 March 1905 inspector at Sohag but transferred to Minya later in 1905 to replace Arif (q.v.); inspector at Thebes, 1914-6; he then replaced Chaban (q.v.) as inspector at Giza, Dec. 1916; chief inspector at Thebes from 1923; he was present at the unwrapping of the mummy of Tutankhamun in 1925; he published several articles in *ASAE.*

Rapports sur la Marche du Service des Antiquités de 1899 à 1910, 1912, 92, 171; T G. H. James, *Howard Carter,* 1992, 346.

BOURGUET, (*Père*) Pierre Marie d'Audibert Caille du (1910-1988)
French Egyptologist and Coptologist; he was born at Ajaccio, Corsica, 21 Jan. 1910, son of Joseph Henri d'A. C. du B., an army doctor, and Marie Madeleine de Montgrand de Marzac; he early exhibited a religious vocation and joined the Jesuits in 1927, becoming a priest in 1943; he studied at the Sorbonne, 1929-31 and at Jersey, 1931-34; he became a teacher at various Jesuit colleges at Dole, Veirut, and finally Faggala in Cairo where he was attracted to Egyptology; he then studied Egyptology at Lyons, 1940-4, the École Pratique des Hautes Études under Lefebvre (q.v.), 1944-6 and at Oxford under Gunn (q.v.), 1947-8; from 1953-7 he was attached to the Institut français d'archéologie orientale in Cairo; in 1957 he became professor of Egyptology at the Institut Catholique in Paris, lecturer and

professor at the École du Louvre, Keeper of Coptic antiquities at the Louvre, 1957-78; he specialized in the study of Coptic art; his principal publications were *L'Art Copte au Petit Palais*, 1964; *Catalogue des Étoffes Coptes, Musée National du Louvre*, 1964; *La Peinture paléochretienne*, 1965; *L'Art Copte*, 1968; *L'Art paléochretien*, 1971; *Grammaire Égyptienne, Moyen Empire Pharaonique*, 1971; *Musée du Louvre L'Art Copte*, 1975 2nd ed. 1980; *Grammaire Fonctionelle et Progressive de l'Égyptien Démotique*, 1976; *Tissus Coptes*, 1977; *Les Coptes*, 1988; contributions to the *Coptic Encyclopedia*; and posthumously *Le Temple de Deir al-Médina*, edited by L. Gabolde, 2002; he died in Paris, 30 Dec. 1988.

BSFE 114 (1989), 6, 12-16 (C. Desroches-Noblecourt); *BSAC* 21 (1975), 1-12 (portr.) (bibl.) (M. B. Ghali); *BSAC* 28 (1986-1989), 1-4 (portr.) (add. bibl.) (R. Coquin); *the Coptic Encyclopedia* 2, 414 (M.-H. Rutschowskaya); *Journal of Coptic Studies* 2 (1992), 1-2 (M.-H. Rutschowscaya), 3-27 (bibl.) (D. Bénazeth and J.-L. Bovot); *Compagnie* 233 (1989), 211-2 (F. Graffin); *Le Monde Copte* 16 (1989), 100-1 (A. Guillaumont).

BOURGUIGNON D'ANVILLE, Jean Baptiste (1697-1782)

French cartographer; he was born at Paris, 11 July 1697, son of Hubert B. and Charlotte Vaugon; he published 211 maps, including one of Egypt (1766) in which he used the results of the journeys of Sicard (q.v.) in 1722; this map was used in the works of Sonnini (q.v.), Pococke (q.v.), and Norden (q.v.); Membre de l'Acad.; he was also secretary to the Duke of Orleans; he published *Mémoire sur l'Égypte ancienne et moderne*, 1766; he died in Paris, 28 Jan. 1782.

Carré, i, 74-5; Hilmy, i, 84; *DBF* 3, 85-6; Lamy, 208.

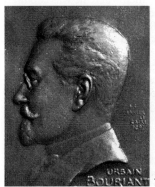

BOURIANT, Urbain (1849-1903)

French Egyptologist; he was born in Nevers, 11 April 1849, son of Pierre B. and Elizabeth Meissonnier; he at first led a varied life; he fought with MacMahon's army, 1870, and then became secretary to the governor of Martinique; he returned home to France in 1877, and, his interest in Egypt having originated in a visit to the Louvre, in 1876, he immediately joined Maspero's classes where he remained until the end of 1880; he was an original member of the French Archaeological Institute in Cairo, Jan. 1881-June 1883; was appointed assistant conservator of the Bulaq Museum, 1883-6; Director of IFAO, 1886-98, when his health failed and he returned to Europe; many of his publications relate to Theban tombs or to Coptic and Arabic texts; he contributed to *Mém. Miss. Arch., Rec. Trav.*, and other journals; his bibl. lists over 30 items; his chief works were , *Deux Jours de fouilles à Tell el Amarna*, with others 1884; *Le Livre des rois*, with E. Brugsch, 1887; *Monuments pour servir à l'étude du culte d'Atonou en Égypte, Tom. I. Les Tombes de Khouitatonou*, with G. Legrain etc., 1903; he died of apoplexy at Vannes, 19 June 1903.

BIFAO 3 (1903), 213-14 (É. Chassinat); *DBF* 6, 1509-1510 (F. Marouis); Hilmy, i, 85; *Le Grande Enc.* 7. 801; *Rec. Trav.* 26 (1904), 29-32 (bibl.) (P. Bouriant).

BOURVILLE *see* WATTIER DE BOURVILLE

BOUTIN, Vincent Yves (1772-1815)

Colonel in the French army; he was born at Louroux-Battereau, 1 Jan. 1772, son of Yves B., a farrier and local mayor, and Perrine Guillet; he was sent to Constantinople in 1807 and in 1808 to Algeria to report on the possibility of a landing there by the French army; in 1811 he visited Egypt on what was a secret political mission; he went up the Nile as far as Aswan, and was accompanied as far as Thebes by Drovetti (q.v.) who thereupon applied for a *firman* to excavate and thus began his long career of collecting antiquities; Boutin also crossed the Eastern desert and visited Quseir; he afterwards visited the Monastery of St. Catharine in Sinai, and crossed the Western desert reaching the Oasis of Siwa; while in Egypt, he made a small collection of antiquities including a papyrus now in Toulouse; upon leaving Egypt he travelled in Syria, where he was murdered by bandits near Nahe el-Kelb, April 1815;

Carré, i, 195-6; Stanhope, iii, 254, 284, 308, 333, 342; Hoskins, *Oasis*, 191, 219; Irby, 68; *DBF* 7, 61-2; P. Balagny, *Monsieur Boutin*, 1948; L. Berjaud, *Boutin*, 1950; F. Meyer, *Boutin Vincent-Yves, Colonel d'Empire*, 1991; J. Marchioni, *Boutin*, 2007.

BOVIER-LAPIERRE, Paul Henri Hippolyte (1873-1950)

French archaeologist and priest; he was born in Grenoble, 18 Nov. 1873, son of Claude Jean Baptiste B.-L., an administrative officer, and Marie Gabrielle Landre; he was educated Lyons and later in England and Holland; he studied theology and natural science and then entered the priesthood; he visited Egypt for the first time in 1905 and taught science in Cairo under Teilhard de Chardin; in 1906-7 he was in Beirut and then returned 1908 to the Institut Pasteur in Paris; in 1914 he returned to Egypt and after an accident to his eyes which prevented his using a microscope he gave up his scientific work and concentrated on the study of Egyptian prehistory; in 1917 he was associated with archaeological work at Elephantine on a predynastic site; the prehistoric environs of Cairo had remained practically unexplored since the time of de Morgan (q.v.) *c.*1896, and Bovier-Lapierre now made important discoveries at Abbassiya relating to the Chellean, Acheulean, and Levalloisian periods; he revealed more than eleven stations in all among which were Gebel Ahmar, the Petrified-Forest, Helwan, and Ma'adi, ranging in time from the Palaeolithic and Mesolithic well into later predynastic, to these may also be added his *Une Nouvelle Station néolithique (el Omari), au nord d'Hélouan*; he received many academic distinctions and was a corresponding member of a number of institutions; he left Egypt in 1942 for the Lebanon; he died in Beirut, 26 May 1950.

BIÉ 33 (1952), 473-82, (bibl.) (H. Fleisch); *Papyrus* 40 (1951), 157-60 (portr.); *Anthropologie* 58 (1954), 345; *Archaéonil* 17 (2007), 69-88 (portr.); È. Gran-Aymerich, *Dictionnaire biographique d'archéologie 1798-1945*, 2001, incorporated in *Les Chercheurs de passé 1798-1945*, 2007, 634.

BOYLSTON (*né* Howell), Ward Nicholas (1747-1828)
American traveller; he was born in Boston , 22 Nov. 1747, son of Benjamin Howell, Commissionier of Customs, and Mary Boylston; he travelled abroad in 1773, visiting Smyrna, Cyprus, and Jerusalem; he arrived in Egypt in Nov. 1774,visiting Giza and the Nilometer and met Antes (q.v.); he settled in London, 1775-1800 where he befriended William Browne (q.v.); he returned to America in 1800; he left a mummified head to the Harvard Medical School; he died in Princeton, 1828.

A. Oliver, *American Travellers on the Nile*, 2016, 5-18, 25-27.

BOWER, Denys Eyre (1905-1977)
British collector; he was born at Crich, Derbyshire, 2 July 1905, son of John Henry B. and Annie Saxton; he began collecting oriental art and Stuart memorabilia at an early age and was attracted to Egyptian antiquities in 1922 after the discovery of the tomb of Tutankhamun; he held a position in a bank 1922-42 and was sometime Secretary of the Derbyshire Archaeological Society; in 1942 he became an antiquities dealer in London and took the opportunity to increase his private collection; in 1955 he purchased Chiddingstone Castle, Kent to display his collections and opened it to the public in 1956; he died in Chiddingstone, 15 Aug. 1977.

Ancient June/July 1989, 4-6; inf. R. Eldridge; M. Eldridge, *Beyond Belief*, 1996.

BRACCI, Pietro (1700-1773)
Italian sculptor; he was born in Rome, 16 June 1700, son of Bartolomeo Cesare B. and Anna Francesca Lorenzoni; he worked in Rome notably on papal tombs and also the Neptune fountain at Trevi; he became interested in hierogylphs and wrote an unpublished treatise on the subject *I Geroglifici ed Obelischi Eggizzi* in 1767 based on Kircher (q.v.); the manuscript is now in the Griffith Institute, Oxford; he died in Rome, 13 Feb. 1773.

DBDI 13, 620-3; inf. Griffith Institute.

BRACK, Artur (1907-1993)
Swiss chemist; he was born at Rotmonten, St. Gallen, 19 July 1907 and worked as a chemist in the pharmaceutical industry in Basel; he and his wife Annelies Brack-Hug (born Winterthur, 5 July 1912, died Riehen near Basel, 23 Feb. 1980) developed an interest in Egyptology from 1953 following a visit to Egypt; he collaborated with Walther Wolf (q.v.) supplying photographs for his book *Kunst Aegyptens*, 1957; from 1967 he and his wife studied Egyptology at Basel and took part in the work of the Swiss Institute in Egypt at the mortuary temple of Merenptah and in the Theban tombs of Tjanuni and Haremheb, 1973-5, 1977; he also photographed the objects for the Basel scarab catalogue; following the death of his wife, he taught courses on ancient Egypt at the Basel Volkshochschule; he published with his wife *Das Grab des Tjanuni. Theben Nr. 74*, 1977 and *Das Grab des Haremheb. Theben Nr. 78*, 1980; he died in Riehen near Basel, 19 April 1993.

Gött. Misz. 135 (1993), 7-8 (E. Staehelin).

BRADBURY, Kate *see* GRIFFITH, K.

BRADISH, Luther (1783-1863)
American lawyer, diplomat, and statesman; he was born in Cummington, Mass., 15 Sept. 1783, son of John B and Hannah Warner; after having been admitted to the Bar, 1804, he was sent to Europe on a special mission to the Turkish Govt. concerning American trade; after leaving Constantinople he travelled in Egypt, Palestine, and Syria and in various European countries until 1826; while in Egypt in 1821 he happened to visit Dendera at the time when Lelorrain (q.v.) was removing the Circular Zodiac; he carried the news to Cairo and thereby caused many difficulties and obstacles, which were, however, eventually overcome; he died in Newport, R.I., 30 Aug. 1863.

DAB 2, 567-8; Henniker, 329; Lelorrain, 44, 48; Wilson, *WWWA* 4, 70; R. De Keersmaecker, *ASTENE Bulletin* 61 (2014), 15-16; A. Oliver, *American Travellers on the Nile*, 2016, 78-81.

BRAMSEN, Jens Andr (*fl.* 1814-1818)
Prussian traveller and author; born in Berlin he travelled extensively in Europe, Africa, and the Near East; he visited Egypt 1814-15; he afterwards published his travels in German, translated into French and English as, *Travels in Egypt etc.*, London, 1818.

Hilmy, i, 86.

BRANICKI, (*Count*) **Alexander** (1821-1877)
Polish collector, traveller, lover of natural history, entomology, botany; he was born in 1821, son of Wladyslaw Gregory B. and Rosa Potocki; he was one of the first Poles engaged in photography from about 1850; he took part in two private expeditions to Upper Egypt 1863-64 together with his brother Constantine (q.v.), and with Anthony Waga, zoologist, and 1872-73 up to Nubia together with H. Dziedzicki; specimens from these expeditions were offered then to the Zoological Cabinet of the Warsaw University; he also founded an interesting private family collection in Sucha near Zywiec as well as a library and museum; Branicki died suddenly in Nice, 19 Sept. 1877.

Polski Słownik Biograficzny 2, 197-398 (A. Maciesza); inf. J. Śliwa.

BRANICKI, (*Count*) **Constantine Gregory** (1824-1884)
Polish collector, traveller and huntsman, ornithologist; he was born 1824, son of Wladyslaw Gregory B. and Rosa Potocki; he was a patron of sciences and organizer of zoological expeditions, specimens from which were later given to the Zoological Cabinet of the Warsaw University and the Branicki Zoological Museum in Warsaw 1887-1919, later incorporated to the State Science Museum; in 1863-64 with his brother Alexander (q.v.) he took part in an expedition to Upper Egypt; apart from zoological specimens Branicki also acquired a wooden coffin with a mummy of a woman inside, which was presented to the Vilna University; Branicki died in Paris, 1884.

Polski Słownik Biograficzny 2, 407; W. Holubowicz, *Egyptian Mummies* at *Vilna,* Wilno 1933, 8; inf. J. Śliwa.

BRAUNEK, Florian Anthony (1797-1871)
Polish soldier; he was born at Grudno, 3 Feb. 1797, son of Jozef Wojciech B. and Brygida Malgorzata Borezewski; he took part in engagements on many fronts almost all over the world in Egypt, Sudan, Ethiopia, Palestine, Greece, Mexico, North America and was a participant in the 1830-31 Polish insurrection; he stayed in Egypt as an instructor in Muhammad Ali's army, 1825-30; during three years serving in punitive expeditions against rebel tribes; he gathered a large collection of antiquities, which was lost in a shipping disaster on the Black Sea 1830; among the few objects which were rescued and then taken to Poland was a scarab belonging later to Prof. H. Swiecicki and published by him in 1881; according to Wiedemann (q.v.) this scarab bore the names of Thutmose III and Amenhotep II, but this interpretation now is unreliable; this interesting scarab is lost; during the years 1845-60 Braunek was in America; in his last years he lived in Poland and died at Pegrzybowo near Poznan, 11 Feb. 1871.

J. Śliwa, *Skarabeusz xielnicki* (Polish), *Meander* 45, 1990 (in print); *Polski Słownik Biograficzny* 2, 420.

BREASTED, James Henry (1865-1935)
American Egyptologist and orientalist; born Rockford, Ill., 27 Aug. 1865, the son of Charles B. and Harriet N. Garrison; he was educated at North-Western College, Naperville, Ill., and then served as a clerk in local drug-stores for some years, entering Chicago College of Pharmacy 1882; he graduated 1886; he then returned to work on prescriptions and acquired much knowledge about drugs which was to prove useful in later life when dealing with medical texts; he studied Hebrew at the Congregational Institute, Chicago, and then entered Yale University 1890-1; took AM degree 1892; wishing to study Egyptology in detail he went to Berlin and was taught by Erman (q.v.); PhD, 1894; he married 1. Frances Hart, 1894, 2. Imogen (Hart) Richmond sister of (1) 1935; after a honeymoon spent in Egypt Breasted became assistant in Egyptology and assistant director of Haskell Oriental Museum, University of Chicago, 1895-1901; Director of Haskell, 1901-35; made instructor in Egyptology and Semitic languages, 1896; Professor of Egyptology and Oriental History, 1905, the first chair in this subject in America; he also helped with the work on the great Berlin dictionary at this time, 1900-4, and the Academies of Berlin, Leipzig, Munich, and Göttingen asked him to copy and arrange hieroglyphic inscriptions in various European Museums; he now resolved to publish a corpus of historical inscriptions in English for the benefit of historians in general, and gathered many texts in Egypt, including unpublished ones, 1899-1904; the accumulated 10,000 manuscript pages formed the basis of *Ancient Records*; Director of the University of Chicago Egyptian Expedition, 1905-7; from 1919 to 1924 he received a modest grant yearly from J. D. Rockefeller, Jnr., (q.v.) with which he founded the Oriental Institute at Chicago, and which with the great gifts given later by Rockefeller became the leading Egyptological institution in North America; Breasted saw to it that three fields of research were to be carried on by it, archaeological field work and excavation, salvage and recording of standing monuments, and the study of recovered records in a central research

centre; during his life he acquired many distinctions academic and otherwise, Hon. BD 1898; Corr. Member, Prussian Royal Acad. of Sciences, 1907; Pres. American Oriental Soc., 1918; LLD. University of California, 1918; Vice-Pres. American Philosophical Soc., 1919; Hon. Fellow Soc. of Antiquaries, London, 1919; DLitt. hon. c. Oxford, 1922; Hon. life member Royal Asiatic Soc., 1923; Pres. Hist. of Science Soc., 1926; Pres. American Hist. Assoc., 1928; LL.D. Princeton University, 1929; Foreign member Acad. des Inscriptions et Belles Lettres, 1930, Hon. member Arch. Institut des Deutschen Reiches, 1931, and of Bavarian Acad., 1931; Corresponding FBA, 1934; Member Danish Royal Acad., 1035; Breasted was the real founder of Egyptology in North America and with Reisner (q.v.), the leading American Egyptologist of his day; he published *De hymnis in solem sub rege Amenophide IV conceptis*, doctoral dissertation, 1894; *A New Chapter in the Life of Thutmose III*, 1900; *The Battle of Kadesh*, 1903; *A History of Egypt*, his popular masterpiece and probably the best general history of Pharaonic Egypt ever published, 1905; *Ancient Records of Egypt*, 5 vols., 1906-7; *The Temples of Lower Nubia*, 1906; *A History of the Ancient Egyptians*, 1908; *The Monuments of Sudanese Nubia*, 1908; *Development of Religion and Thought in Ancient Egypt*, 1912; *Short Ancient History*, 1914; *Ancient Times, A History of the Early World*, 1916, rev. 1935; *The Oriental Institute*, 1922; *The Edwin Smith Surgical Papyrus*, 2 vols. 1930; *The Dawn of Conscience*, 1933; he also contributed chapters in the *Cambridge Ancient History* and wrote many articles in journals; he translated Erman's *Egyptian Grammar* into English, 1894; his correspondence with Caroline Ransom Williams (q.v.) was edited by K. L. Sheppard, *My dear Miss Ransom*, 2018; he died in New York, 2 Dec. 1935.

Pioneer to the Past, biog. (good for family details), Charles Breasted, 1945; *DAB Suppl.* (E. W. Ware); *WWW* i, 133; *WWW* iii, 155; *AfO* 11 (1936), 99-100; *AE*, U (1935), 124 (W. M. F. Petrie?); *BASOR* No. 61 (1936), 1-4 (portr.) (W. F. Albright); Bayerische Akad. der Wissenschafter, *Jahrbuch*, 1936 (1935/6), 41-6 (A. Scharff); *Bull. F. Rylands Library*, Manchester 20 (1936), 188-9; *Chron. d'Ég.* 11 (1936), 458-9; *JAOS* 56 (1936) 113-20 (L. S. Bull, E. A. Speiser, A. T. E. Olmstead); *JEA* 21 (1935), 249-50; *JRAS* 1936, 179-84 (W. R. Dawson); *Rev. Arch.*, 8 (1936), 95 (R. Lantier); *Syria* 17 (1936), 204 (R. Dussaud); *ZÄS* 72 (1936), iii-iv (G. Steindorff); *National Academy of Sciences of the United States of America Biographical Memoirs* 35 1045 (1937), 93-121 (J. Wilson); *Dictionary of Literary Biography* 47 (1986) 53-64 (W. Murnane); *KMT* 14/4 (2003), 72-79; È. Gran-Aymerich, *Dictionnaire biographique d'archéologie 1798-1945*, 2001, incorporated in *Les Chercheurs de passé 1798-1945*, 2007, 638-9; E. Evans in D. Fortenberry (ed.), *Who Travels Sees More*, 2007, 163-178; P. Nicholson in D. Magee, J. Bourriau and S. Quirke (eds.), *Sitting Beside Lepsius*, 2009, 381-422; G. Emberling, *Pioneers to the Past: American Archaeologists in the Middle East, 1919-1920*, 2010; J. Abt, *American Egyptologist. The Life of James Henry Breasted and the Creation of His Oriental Institute*, 2011; T. Gertzen *EDAL* II (2010/1), 147-70.

BRECCIA, (Annibale) Evaristo (1876-1967)
Italian archaeologist; he was born at Offagna, Ancona 18 July 1876, son of Cesare B. and Angela Gatti; he studied ancient history at the University of Rome, 1900-03; in 1903 he went to Egypt with Vitelli (q.v.); he excavated at Giza, Feb.-March 1903 and joined Schiaparelli (q.v.) at his excavations at Ashmunein (Hermopolis Magna), March-April 1903; he later undertook work at Ashmunein, Feb.-May 1904; on 1 April 1904 he succeeded Botti (q.v.) as Director of the Graeco-Roman Museum in Alexandria until 29 Oct. 1931; he carried out excavations in the Alexandria area as well as at Oxyrhynchus, Dec. 1927- March 1928, 1929-34, Tebtunis, Dec. 1928-March 1929, el-Hibeh, 1933-4, Antinoe, 1936-7; in 1931 he occupied the chair of classical antiquity at the University of Pisa and in 1935 that of Greek and Roman history; he excavated at el-Hibeh in 1934 and at Antinoe in 1935-6; Rector of the University of Pisa, 1939-41 and later professor emeritus; his publications include *Guide de la ville et du Musée d'Alexandrie*, 1907; *Iscrizioni greche e latine.* Catalogue Général des Antiquités du Musée d'Alexandrie, 1911; *La necropoli di Sciatbi*, 1912; *Le musée gréco-romain*, 1925; *Le rovine e i monumenti di Canopo*, 1926; *Terrecotte figurate greche e greco-egizie del Museo di Alessandria*, 1930; *Egitto greco e romano*, 1937; *Faraoni senza pace*, 1939; he committed suicide in Rome, 28 July 1967.

DBDI 14, 91-93; *Aegyptus* 46 (1966), 293-6 (A. Calderini); *Atti del convegno "Ippolito Rosellini"* , 33-8; G. Bastianini and A. Casanova, *100 Anni di Istituzioni Fiorentine per la Papirologia*, 2009, vii; M. Marvulli in *EDAL* 1 (2009), 83-93; M. Capasso (ed.), *Hermae* IV, 2015, 25-37 (portr.) (M. Marvulli).

BREMNER, David (1822-1873)
British customs officer; he was born in Wick, Caithness, 1 July 1822, son of David B. and Janet Rhind; he was the trustee and executor of his cousin A. H. Rhind (q.v.), whose Egyptian collections were bequeathed to the National Museum of Antiquities, Edinburgh (now in the National Museum of Scotland); for some reason three of the papyri were not deposited with the main collection, and Bremner sold them to the British Museum in 1865; these were the Mathematical Papyrus (EA 10057-8), the Mathematical leather roll (EA 10250), and the magico-mythological text (EA 10188); to the last the name of Bremner has been quite unjustifiably attached; it was published by Faulkner in *Bibl. Aeg.* iii, and in *JEA* 22 (1936), 121-40; 23 (1937), 10-16, 166-85; 24 (1938), 41-53; Bremner joined the customs service being promoted to Examining Officer 1 Sept. 1861 but resigned on 26 Feb. 1864; he was living in Aberdeen from at least 1861 to 1865; between 1865-71 he moved to Great Totham, Essex in England; he died at Great Totham, 12 April 1873.

Inf. C. Aldred; R. O. Faulkner, *The Papyrus Bremner-Rhind* (Bibliotheca Aegyptiaca III), iii.

BRIGGS, Samuel (1767-1853)
British merchant and banker of Alexandria; he was born at Grantham, 11 Oct. 1767 and baptized there, 9 Nov. 1767, son of Samuel B and Mary Millner; he was partner in the house of Briggs, Schutz, and Walmas; he acted as pro-Consul in Egypt and agent of the Levant Company at Alexandria, 1803-10 and was very helpful to travellers in Egypt; he joined with Salt (q.v.) in financing Caviglia's (q.v.) explorations at the Pyramids; Belzoni's last letter, dated Benin, 2 Dec. 1822, was addressed to him; he died in Littlehampton, 3 Nov. 1853.

Belzoni, i, 211, 213, 216, 401; ii. 18, 142; Salt, ii, 111, 114, 115, 120; Westcar Diary; *Letters and Dispatches of Nelson*, vi. 336-7, 341; Vyse, i, 197; Richardson, i, 52, 130; W. R. Wilson, *Travels in Egypt*, 19, 245; F. S. Rodkey, *The Journal of Modern History* 5 (1933), 324-51; inf. Mrs. P. Rée.

BRINE, Charles (*d.*1821)
British manufacturer in the service of Muhammad Ali; a native of Devon he introduced the manufacture of sugar into Egypt; he went to Raramun in 1817 where he superintended the equipment of a factory on the model of those in the West Indies; it came into production in 1818; Brine was helpful to travellers in Egypt and received Belzoni (q.v.) at his house in 1817 and 1818, and Irby (q.v.) and Mangles (q.v.) in 1818; the discovery of the famous 'Tomb of the Colossus' at El Bersha, is probably due to him, as Irby (q.v.) and Mangles (q.v.), who first recorded it, were on a visit to him at the time; he collected antiquities for Salt (q.v.); Brine met his death in mysterious circumstances and was apparently murdered by his Sicilian servant in Cairo, 1821.

Belzoni, i, 224; ii. 1; Irby, 48, 52; Henniker, 198-9; Madox, i, 262; Bonomi Diary, 1831, June 23; Waddington and Hanbury, *Journal of a visit to Ethiopia*, pref. iv, 154; Sherer, 135; Wilkinson, *Modern Eg. and Thebes*, ii, 63; Richardson, i, 178; ii, 130; Baroness Minutoli, *Recollections of Eg.*, 98-9.

BROCCHI, Giovanni Battista (1772-1826)
Italian traveller and geologist; he was born in Bassano del Grappa, 18 Feb. 1772, son of Cornelio B., a notary, and Lucrezia Verci; he was educated at Padua in law and in 1808 became inspector of mines based in Milan until 1818; he developed an early interest in Egyptian geology and published *Ricerche sopra la scultura presse gli Egiziani*, 1792; in 1822 he went to Egypt and conducted several geological expeditions for Muhammad Ali visiting Upper Egypt, Syria, and finally Nubia and the Sudan; he died at Khartoum, 23 Sept. 1826; his diaries were published posthumously *Giornale delle osservazioni fatte ne' viaggi in Egitto, nella Siria e nelle Nubia*, 1841-3.

DBDI 14, 396-9; Hill, 87; S. Pernigotti, 'L'opera scientifica di Giambattista Brochi (1772-1826)' in *Atti del Convego, Bassano 9-10 novembre 1985*, 1987; S. Pernigotti, *Studi di Egittologia e di Antichità Puniche* 1 (1987), 47-62; G. Berti, *Un naturalista dall'Ancien Régime alla Restaurazione, Giambattista Brocchi (1772-1826)*, 1988; S. Pernigotti in N. Bonacasa et al. (ed.), *Alessandria e il mondo ellenistico-romano*, 1995, 220-226; S. Pernigotti in C. Morigi Govi, S. Curto, S. Pernigotti, *L'Egitto fuori dell'Egitto*, 1991, 311-330; P. Branca in J. Starkey and O. El Daly (eds.), *Desert Travellers*, 2000, 143-152.

BROCK, Edwin (Ted) Colville (1946-2015)
American Egyptologist; he was born in Syracuse, New York, 20 April 1946 as Robert George Simmons and adopted by John Brock, farmer, and Florence Helen Colville; he studied history and Egyptology at the State Univ. of New York at Binghampton under Gerald Kadish, 1964-9 and 1971-8; BA, 1969; MA, 1978; he served in the Viet Nam war, 1969-71; he was then educated at the University of Toronto, 1980-3; MA, 1982; he did not complete his PhD thesis; he worked on the Akhenaten temple project, 1979-80 and was a research assistant at the Royal Ontario Museum, 1980-3; he served as Director of the Canadian Institute in Egypt, Aug 1983-April 1994; he then worked for ARCE, 1994-8; he took part in excavations at Tell el-Masquta, 1981-5; at East Karnak, 1982, 1984, 1986; at Memphis, 1986, 1995-6; at Dakhla Oasis, 1984-94; and at Lahun, 1992-4; he served with the Theban mapping project, 1997-2004; he was co-director of the excavation in the Valley of the Kings of the tombs of Merenptah, 1987-8 and of Amenmesse, 1993-2004 and worked on Tomb 55, 1993-4; he acted as consultant at work in the Sinai, 1994; he was involved with further work in the Valley of the Kings, 1995-6, 2000, 2002 and directed the restoration project of the sarcophagi of Ramesses VI, 200-3 and Merenptah, 2011-5; he also undertook work at Tel el Borg, Sinai, 2002-4 and Luxor, 2005-7; he was especially interested in the study of the royal sarcophagi of the New Kingdom; apart from articles, he published *Guide to the Temples of Aydos*, 2002; *The Temple of Abu Simbel. An Illustrated Guide. The Houses of Ramesses and Nefertary*, 2006; he died in Heliopolis, Cairo, 22 Sept 2015.

Inf. Lyla Pinch-Brock; *ARCE Bulletin* 207 (2015/16), 57 (portr.) (M. Jones).

BROCKLEHURST, Marianne (1832-1898)
British collector; of Bagstone Grange, Swythamley, Staffs, daughter of John B. and Mary Coare; she visited Egypt 1873, 1882-3, 1890-1, and 1895-6; she made a considerable collection of antiquities some of which went to Macclesfield Museum at her death; this museum was founded by her and two papyri are called by her name, (1) the hieratic funerary papyrus of Djedptahefankh, from the royal cache, (2) a Book of the Dead used by Naville (*Todtb.* Ax); the latter was formerly in Sudeley Castle, Winchcombe and is now in Hanover; she died in London, 21 Oct. 1898.

Edwards, *Thousand Miles*, passim (where she is referred to as 'M. B.'); Wilbour, 235, 586; *JEA* 33 (1947), 75; *Miss Brocklehurst on the Nile: diary of a Victorian traveller in Egypt*, 2004.

BRODRICK, Mary (May) (1858-1933)
British writer and archaeologist; she was born in London, 5 April 1858, daughter of Thomas B., solicitor, and Mary Smith Haviside; she was a friend of Amelia Edwards (q.v.) and first seems to have visited Egypt in 1888; she studied Egyptology at the Sorbonne and the Coll. de France under Maspero (q.v.), Pierrat (q.v.), and Revillout (q.v.), 1888, being the first woman to do so, also Hebrew and Semitic archaeology with Renan; she later studied in England under R. S. Poole (q.v.) and Renouf (q.v.); she was a student at University College London, 1888-1906; PhD Kansas, 1893; she was Hon. Secretary to the American branch of the Egypt Exploration Society; she worked in Egypt under Maspero for some years, 1897-1908, and lectured in Cairo, England, Scotland, and Italy; she translated Mariette's *Aperçu* as *Outlines of Ancient Egyptian History*, 1890; revised the edition of Brugsch's *Egypt under the Pharaohs*, 1891; edited Murray's *Handbook for Egypt*, 1895, enlarged ed. 1900; published Murray's *Handbook for Travellers in Syria and Palestine*, 1903 and *The Trial and Crucifixion of Jesus Christ of Nazareth*, 1908, and collaborated with Alice A. Morton (q.v.) in an original work, *A Concise Dictionary of Egyptian Archaeology*, 1902; she was made Hon. FRGS, 1916; Dame of Grace of St. John of Jerusalem; Life member of the Comité de la Société archéologique d'Egypte; Hon. Fellow of the American Geographical Society, 1925; Member of the Geographical Society of America, 1927; in 1924 she founded the Mary Brodrick Prize for Geography at University Coll.; she bequeathed part of her library to College Hall, i.e. the hostel for women students at University Coll.; the Egyptological books are now on loan to the Edwards Library, University College London; she died in Hindhead, Surrey, 13 July 1933.

ODNB 7, 791-3; *May Brodrick, Papers and Lectures*, ed. Eversley Robinson, 1937, vii-xv (portr.); *JEA* 33 (1947), 86; *UCL Records*; Wilbour, 564; inf. D. Gill.

BROMFIELD, William Arnold (1801-1851)
British traveller; he was born at Boldre and baptized 8 Aug. 1801, son of Revd John Arnold B. and Anne Gott; he was educated at the University of Glasgow; MD, 1823; he visited the Levant in 1850-1, travelling in Egypt and as far south as Khartoum; he left descriptions of the principal sites in his posthumous volume *Letters from Egypt and Syria*, 1856; he died in Damascus, 9 Oct. 1851.

ODNB 7, 817; *DNB* 6, 398-9; Boase 1, 412.

BROMHEAD, Thomas Ayre (1793-1825)
British traveller; he was born at Lincoln or Reepham 2 Aug. 1793, only son of the Revd Edward B. of Repham, Lincs. and Catherine Ayre; educated at Christ's College, Cambridge, MA; while in the East he visited Egypt 1821, where he met Westcar (q.v.) and Madden (q.v.), and accompanied Joseph Cook (q.v.); from Egypt he went to Persia where he died in Kurkh, Carmania, 9 Sept. 1825.

Westcar Diary, 280; Madden, 2, 7; *GM* 96 (1826), 186.

BROOME, Myrtle Florence (1888-1978)
British artist; she was born in London, 22 Feb. 1888, daughter of Washington Herbert B., a publisher of music books, and Eleanor Slater; between 1911-3 she studied at University College London for the Certificate in Egyptology where she was a pupil of Margaret Murray (q.v.) and Flinders Petrie (q.v.); like most well educated ladies of the period, she also was trained as an artist; in 1927 she worked at Qau under the auspices of the British School of Archaeology copying tomb inscriptions; between 1929-37 she worked at Abydos as the assistant of Amice Calverley (q.v.); she retired from Egyptology in 1937 due to her father's illness; she died in Bushey, 27 Jan. 1978; her papers are in the Griffith Institute, Oxford.

JEA 64 (1978), 4; inf. K. Slater; K. L. Sheppard in W. Carruthers (ed.), *Histories of Egyptology*, 2015, 122.

BROSSES, Charles de (1709-1777)
French jurist; he was born in Dijon, 17 Feb. 1709, son of Charles de B., a counsellor of the local parlement, and Pierette Fevret; he was named counsellor to the parlement of Burgundy, 13 Feb. 1730; president, 1741; first president, 1775; he visited Italy, 1739-40 and later wrote on the ruins of Herculeaneum; he corresponded with notable intellectuals of the period such as Voltaire and David Hume; he also wrote *Du culte des dieux fétiches ou Parallèle de l'ancienne religion de l'Egypte avec la religion actuelle de la Nigritie*, 1760 which linked ancient Egyptian religious belief with that of the Sudan of his time; his *Lettres familières sur un voyage en Italie* was published in 1799; he died in Paris, 7/17 May 1777.

DBF, 7, 435-5; *Numen* 24 (1977), 81-94; J. C. Garreta (ed.), *Charles de Brosses 1777-1977*, 1981; S. Leoni (ed.), *Charles de Brosses et le Voyage lettré au XVIIIe siècle*, 2004 .

BROWN, (*Sir*) Robert Hanbury (1849-1926)
British irrigation engineer; he was born in Brixton, 13 Jan. 1849, son of Robert Brown, surgeon, and Sarah Few; after his training at the Royal Military Acad., Woolwich, he entered the RE, 1870; he served in the Afghan War, 1879-80; he was in the Irrigation Dept., Bengal, 1873; Egyptian Irrigation Dept., 1884-1903; KCMG, 1902; he retired as Major, 1903; he wrote technical works on irrigation and was also interested in the history of Lake Moeris and the Exodus; he published, *The Fayum and Lake Moeris*, 1892, and *The Land of Goshen and the Exodus*, 2nd ed. 1912; he died in Crawley, Sussex, 4 May 1926.

WWW ii, 134.

BROWNE, Alexander Henry (1845-1898)
British army officer; he was born at Peterstone Court, Llanhamllech, Brecknock, 10 May 1845, son of Alexander B. and Helena Gwynifred Forman, and of Callaly Castle, Northumberland, educated at Harrow and Cambridge; Major in Northb. Light Infantry; he was the nephew and heir of William Henry Forman (q.v.) whose property he inherited, including a large collection of antiquities; the antiquities were sold after Browne's death at Sotheby's, 19-22 June 1899, and the Forman Library, 3 July 1899; a privately printed Catalogue of the Forman Collection was issued by Browne in 1892; he died in Callaly Castle, 11 April 1898.

Private inf.; Lugt 57376 and 57417.

BROWNE, William George (1768-1813)
British oriental traveller; he was born in London, 25 July 1768, son of George B, a merchant, and Elizabeth Mills; BA, Oxford University, 1789; Browne went to Egypt in 1792, and to Darfur, 1793-6; he returned to England in 1798 and published an account of his travels *Travels in Africa, Egypt and Syria from the year 1792 to 1798*, 1799 which was translated into French and German; he afterwards visited Turkey and the Levant, 1800-2; he set out for Samarkand in 1812, but was murdered on his way in Persia at the Kirzk Uzan river near Ogan in early August 1813; his MS journal, 7191-8, is in the British Library (Add. MS 6132).

ODNB 7, 230; *DNB* 7, 76; Hilmy, i, 91; Lamy, 204-7; E. Wyatt, *In the Paths of Dangerous Fame: The Life and Travels of the Explorer W. G. Browne*, 2016.

BRUCE, (*Sir*) Frederick William Adolphus (1814-1867)
British diplomat; he was born Broomhall, Fifeshire, 14 April 1814, son of Thomas B., 7th Earl of Elgin, who collected the Parthenon marbles, and Elizabeth Oswald; he was attached to the Mission at Washington, 1842; Colonial Secretary at Hong Kong, 1844; Lieut.-Governor of Newfoundland, 1846; Chargé d'Affaires, Bolivia, 1848, and Uruguay, 1851; Consul-General in Egypt, 8 Aug. 1853-7; in embassy in China, 1857-62; envoy to Washington, 1865; KCB, 1862; he died in Boston, USA, 19 Sept. 1867.

FO Records; *ODNB* 8, 295-6; *DNB* 7, 97; Rhind, *Thebes, its Tombs, etc.* 79 n.

BRUCE, James (1730-1794)
British traveller; he was born in Kinnaird, 14 Dec. 1730, son of David B. and Marion Graham; after being educated at Harrow he entered a wine merchant's office in Portugal 1753, but abandoned commerce after his wife's early death and took to travelling; he studied oriental languages and travelled extensively in N. Africa, where in spite of many difficulties he carried out archaeological and geographical researches; he arrived in Egypt in July 1768; he visited Luxor and Karnak and cleared the tomb of Ramesses III at Biban el-Moluk, which is still called 'Bruce's Tomb'; he proceeded to explore Abyssinia, where he made a prolonged stay; he returned to Aswan in Nov. 1772 and reached Britain again in 1773; he published his *Travels* in 1790 (and later editions); his name is associated with the Bruce Papyrus, a Gnostic text in Coptic, now in the Bodleian Library (Bruce MS 96); he died in Kinnaird, 27 April 1794.

ODNB 7, 303-6 (portr.); *DNB* 7, 98; Hilmy, i, 9; Maj F. B. Head, *The life of Bruce, the African Traveller*, 1830 (portr.); J. M. Reid, *Traveller Extraordinary*, 1968; M. Bredin, *The Pale Abyssinian*, 1968; C Thompson in J. Starkey and O. El Daly (eds.), *Desert Travellers*, 2000, 85-110; Lamy, 198-203; J. Speake (ed.), *Literature of Travel and Exploration*, 2003, 1, 130-2.

BRUGSCH, (*Pasha*) Émile Charles Adalbert (1842-1930)

German Egyptologist; he was born in Berlin, 24 Feb. 1842, younger brother of Heinrich B. (q.v.); his early life and career was adventurous in many fields; he went to Egypt in 1870 as assistant to his brother when the latter was conducting his short-lived school of Egyptology in Cairo; afterwards he became assistant to Mariette (q.v.), 23 Apr. 1872, and then assistant curator in the Bulaq and Cairo Museums under Maspero (q.v.), 1881, Keeper 1883, remaining in this office until his resignation after 43 years on 1 Jan. 1914; he was a skilful lithographer, and made the plates for Mariette's *Papyrus de Boulaq*, being also an excellent photographer who made many of the plates for the *Cat. Gén.* of the Cairo Museum; he was the first European to enter the tomb of the Royal Mummies at Deir el-Bahri in 1881 in the absence of Maspero; he was made successively Bey and Pasha by the Khedive; he published *Le Livre des rois, contenant la liste chronologique des rois, reines, princes, princesses et personnages importants de l'Égypte depuis Ménès jusqu'à Nectanebo II*, with U. Bouriant, 1887, the standard work in this field until Gauthier's great study appeared; he retired to Nice, where he died 14 Jan. 1930; his private collection was sold in Paris 30 Sept.-1 Oct. 1996 and 29-30 Sept. 1997.

H. Brugsch, *Mein Leben*, 225, 331;*CHE* 3, pt. I, 35 (portr.); Erman, 213; *JEA* 33 (1947), 70; Petrie, index; H. Nehls, *Berlinische Monatsschrift* 7 (1998), 45-51; È. Gran-Aymerich, *Dictionnaire biographique d'archéologie 1798-1945*, 2001, incorporated in *Les Chercheurs de passé 1798-1945,* 2007, 645-6. Photograph courtesy of Università degli studi di Milano; H. Schmidt in J. Arp-Neuman and T. Gertzen (eds.), *Steininschrift und Bibelwort*, 2019, 19-24; H. Schmidt. N. Cooke (ed.), *Journeys Erased By Time*, 2009, 81-100.

BRUGSCH, (*Pasha*) Heinrich Ferdinand Karl (1827-1894)

German Egyptologist; he was born in Berlin, 18 Feb. 1827, son of Ernst Wilhelm B., who was in the army, and Dorothea Schramm; he became interested in Egyptology at an early age and visited the Berlin Museum, whose director Passalacqua (q.v.) and von Humboldt encouraged his Egyptological interests; evincing a precocious knowledge of Demotic he sketched out a grammar at sixteen years of age; when he was only twenty he published *Scriptura Aegyptiorum demotica ex papyris et inscriptionibus explanata*, 1848; in 1848 he began his studies at the University of Berlin where he obtained his doctorate; he also studied in Paris, where he met the leading Egyptologists of the day and visited many of the leading European museums; he married firstly in 1851, Pauline Harcke, and secondly in 1868, Antonie Verstädnig; he was sent to Egypt by the Prussian government, 1853; here he formed a close and lasting friendship with Mariette (q.v.), and worked with him at Saqqara, helping with the Serapeum inscriptions, 1853-7; he was sent to Persia on a special diplomatic mission under Baron von Minutoli, son of the Egyptian traveller, 1860, and after M.'s death was acting ambassador; Prussian Consul in Cairo, 1864; after being offered a post at the Collège de France in Paris, he was appointed Professor of Egyptology in the University of Göttingen, 1867; in 1870 he was made Bey by the Khedive and directed the School of Egyptology in Cairo founded by the Khedive until its closure in 1879; made Pasha, 1881; during the latter part of his life he remained chiefly in Germany, but he visited N. America in 1875, and still paid occasional visits to Egypt; Brugsch's contributions to Egyptology were enormous and his knowledge of all branches of Egyptian philology unrivalled in later life; an extremely versatile scholar with a wide range of interests he was also a pioneer in Demotic studies and Egyptian language in general; for the first time since the decipherment the Semitic side of Egyptian grammar was being noted, and the whole study of hieroglyphs put on a far more comprehensive and systematic basis; in his obituary of Brugsch, Erman (q.v.) classed him with Champollion, Lepsius, Birch, de Rougé, Goodwin, and Chabas (qq.v.), as one of the great formative figures in the development of Egyptology; Brugsch founded the *ZÄS* in 1863, the oldest surviving exclusively Egyptological journal, and contributed no less than 115 articles and items to it during the following thirty years; his most important works were, *Grammaire démotique*, 1855, the first work of its kind since the early pioneers; *Reiseberichte aus Aegypten ... in den Jahren 1853 und 1854*, 1855; *Geographische Inschriften altägyptischer Denkmäler*, 3 pts. 1857-60; *Histoire d'Égypte*, 1859; *Recueil de monuments égyptiens*, 6pts. 1862-85, with Duemichen, a quarto collection of over 500 plates illustrating important texts; *Matériaux pour servir à la reconstruction du calendrier des anciens Égyptiens*, 1864; *A. Henry Rhind's zwei bilingue Papyri, hieratisch und demotisch*, 1865; *Dictionnaire hiéroglyphique et démotique*, 7 vols. 1867-82, lithographed like many of his major work and a tremendous feat for one man to have produced; *Thesaurus Inscriptionum aegyptiacarum. Altaegyptische Inschriften*, 6 pts. 1883-91, another great corpus of material reaching 1,578 pages, and containing texts relating to astronomy, the calendar, geography, mythology, historical biography, and buildings; *Die ägyptische Gräberwelt*, 1868; *Hieroglyphische Grammatik*, 1872; *Index des hiéroglyphes phonétiques*, 1872; *Der Bau des Tempels Salomo's nach koptischen Bibelversion*, 1877; *Reise nach der grossen Oase El Khargeh*, 1878; *Dictionnaire géographique de l'ancienne Égypte*, 2 vols. 1879, another fundamental work of reference of 1,420 pages; *A history of Egypt under the Pharaohs*, 2 vols. trans. H. D. Seymour, 1879; *Religion und Morphologie der alten Aegypter*, 1888, a great religious study reaching 758 pages; *Die biblischen sieben Jahre der Hungersnoth nach dem Wortlaut einer altägyptischen Felsen-Inschrift*, 1891; the Università degli Studi in Milan holds a number of letters written to him by various scholars including Mariette; he died in Charlottenburg, 9 Sept. 1894.

Autobiogr. *Mein Leben und mein Wandern*, 1893; *NDB*; Hilmy, i, 93-100; ii, 383; *Actes du dix. Congrès international des orientalistes*, 1894, (Brill, 1897) pt. 4, sect. 4, 93-102 (Sir G. C. C. Maspero); *AFA* 10 (1895), 47-50 (W. Max Müller); *ZÄS* 32 (1895), 69-73 (portr.) (A. Erman); 89 (1962), 6-8 (bibl. of articles in journal); T. Brugsch, *Arzt seit fünf Jahrzehnten*, 1957, 11-87; H. Nehls, *Berlinische Monatsschrift* 7 (1998), 45-51; E. Endesfelder, *Berlinische Monatsschrift* 9 (1998), 58-64; È. Gran-Aymerich, *Dictionnaire biographique d'archéologie 1798-1945*, 2001, incorporated in *Les Chercheurs de passé 1798-1945*, 2007, 646-7; P. Piacentini, *Egypt and the Pharaohs from the Sand to the Library*, 2010, 90-96; H. Schmidt in J. Arp-Neuman and T. Gertzen (eds.), *Steininschrift und Bibelwort*, 2019, 19-24.

BRUMMER, Joseph (1883-1947)
Hungarian-American art dealer; he was born in Zombor in Hungary (now part of Serbia), 24 Nov. 1883; he moved to Paris in 1906, working in the atelier of the sculptor Rodin, and setting up an art gallery with his younger brothers Imre (3 July 1889, died New York, 19 June 1928) and Ernest (born 9 July 1891, died New York 21 Feb. 1964); Joseph and Imre moved to the United States in 1914, Ernest staying in Europe where he ran the Paris branch and purchased objects for Joseph; the Brummers specialised in antiquities, mediaeval sculpture, and also modern art, holding some of the first American exhibitions of work by Modigliani and Brancusi, Joseph being awarded the Legion d'Honneur for his services to art in France; he sold to numerous American museums and collectors, notably William Randolph Hearst (q.v.), Alastair Bradley Martin (q.v.), and the Metropolitan Museum; Joseph died in New York, 14 April 1947, selected objects from his private collection were sold to the Metropolitan Museum, before the rest of the collection and gallery stock were dispersed at three sales at Parke-Bernet, April-June 1949; ; a portrait of Joseph by Henri 'Douanier' Rousseau is in the National Gallery, London; Ernest continued to operate in Paris and New York until his death in 1964; his collection and stock were sold at Sotheby's, 16-17 Nov. 1964 (Egyptian and Near Eastern objects only, 205 lots) and Gallerie Koller Zurich, 16-19 Oct. 1979.

Inf. T. Hardwick; *The New York Times* 15 April 1947 and 23 Feb 1964 (obituaries); W. H. Forsyth, 'Acquisitions from the Brummer Gallery,' in P. Hunter (ed.), *The Grand Gallery* (New York, 1974), 1-5; The Joseph and Ernest Brummer Records, The Cloisters Library and Archives, Metropolitan Museum.

BRUNE, Emmanuel Jules (1836-1886)
French architect; he was born in Paris, 3 Oct. 1836, son of Christian B. and his wife Aimée; he studied at the École Polytechnique, 1855-7 and the École des Beaux-Arts, 1857-63; he then embarked on a tour of the Levant, visiting Egypt in 1866; in Luxor he stayed with Lady Duff Gordon (q.v.); he made detailed plans of Egyptian temples which were exhibited in Paris in 1867 and used by Perrot (q.v.) and Chipiez (q. v.), Rochemonteix (q.v.), and Mariette (q.v.); professor at the École des Beaux-Arts, 1871; he died in Paris, 4 June 1886.

DBF 7, 522; J.-L. Pascal, *Bulletin mensuel de la Société Centrale des Architectes*, 6e série, 3 (1886), 218-230; inf. M. Azim.

BRUNET DE PRESLE, Charles Marie Wladimir (1809-1875)
French antiquary; he was born at Paris, 10 Nov. 1809, son of Charles François Claude Quentin B. and Charlotte Louise Pres de Saigle de Presle; he wrote on various archaeological and historical subjects relating to Egyptology, the succession of dynasties, Mariette's discovery of the Serapeum, hieroglyphic writing, and on Greek papyri; he died in Parouzeau, 12 Sept. 1875.

Bibl. Ég. 18. 106; Hilmy, i, 102; *DBF* 7, 549-550.

BRUNNER, Helmut (1913-1997)
German Egyptologist; he was born in Frankfurt am Main/Höchst, 11 May 1913, son of Dr. Arnold B., a chemist, and Sophie Wimpff; he studied Egyptology at Berlin, University College London under Glanville (q.v.) and Margaret Murray (q.v.), Oct. 1933-March 1934, and Munich under Scharff (q.v.); PhD, 1936; he then worked in Egypt with Roeder (q.v.) at Hermopolis; he married the Egyptologist Emma Traut; Habilitation, 1942; he became at lecturer at the University of Tübingen, 1950; apl. professor, 1956; ao professor, 1960; full professor, 1964-78; and then professor emeritus; Hon. doctorate in theology from the University of Kiel, 1983; he was

in charge of the Egyptian collection of Tübingen University which he and his wife published; he organized an exhibition of ancient Egyptian objects from Tübingen and other German museums which was held in Stuttgart and Hanover in 1984; he was an initiator of the Tübingen Atlas of Near and Middle East; a volume of studies in his honour *Fontes atque Pontes* was published in 1983; and a further dedication was appeared in *Die Welt des Orients* 14 (1983) and 15(1984); he had a wide interest in all aspects of Egyptology but notably in grammar, literature, and religion; his principal publications were his doctorate *Die Anlagen der ägyptische Felsgräber*, 1936; *Die Texte aus den Gräbern der Herakleopitenzeit von Siut*, 1937; his habilitation *Die Lehre des Cheti, Sohnes des Duauf*, 1944; *Altägyptische Erziehung*, 1957; 2nd ed., 1991; *Ägyptische Schrift und Sprache*, 1959; *Hieroglyphische Chrestomathie*, 1964; 2nd ed., 1992; *Die Geburt des Göttkonigs*, 1964; 2nd ed., 1986; *Grundzüge einer Geschichte der altägyptischen Literatur*, 1966; 4th ed., 1986; *Abriss der mittelägyptischen Grammatik*, 1960; 2nd ed., 1967; English translation by B. Ockinga, *An Outline of Middle Egyptian Grammar*, 1979; with others, *Handbuch der Orientalisk. Literatur*, 1970; *Die südlichen Raume des Tempels von Luxor*, 1977; with E. Brunner-Traut, *Die ägyptische Sammlung der Universität Tübingen*, 1981; *Grundzüge der altagyptischen Religion*, 1983; *Osiris, Kreuz und Halbmond*, 1984; *Alatägyptische Weisheit*, 1988; a selection of his articles in *Das Hörende Herz*, 1988; and *Die Weisheitbücher der Ägypter*, 1991; he died in Tübingen, 18 Feb. 1997.

Inf. W. Guglielmi; Kürschner 16th ed., 1992; 428; Kürschner, 17th ed., 1996; *ZÄS* 124 (1997), I-III (portr.) (E. Blumenthal and E. Hornung); *Die Welt des Orients* 14 (1983), 6-21 (bibl.) (A. Schira); *BSFE* 138 (1997), 3; IAE Internet obituary (I. Gamer-Wallert); *AfO* 44/45 (1997/8), 578-9 (E. Winter).

BRUNNER, (*Sir*) John Tomlinson (1842-1919)
British chemist; he was born in Everton, Liverpool, 8 Feb. 1842, son of John B. and Margaret Catherine Curphey; with Dr Ludwig Mond, FRS, he founded the firm of Brunner, Mond & co. Ltd. and the great chemical works at Northwich, which were later incorporated in Imperial Chemical Co.; DL; PC, 1906; a benefactor of Liverpool University, in which he endowed three chairs, one of them being the Brunner Professorship of Egyptology, the first holder of which was P. E. Newberry (q.v.), appointed 1906; he also founded several public libraries and other institutions; Hon. LLD; he was created a Baronet, 1895; he died in Silverlands, Chertsey, 1 July 1919.

WWW ii, 140; S. E. Ross, *Sir John Brunner*, 1970.

BRUNNER-TRAUT, Emma (1911-2008)
German Egyptologist; she was born in Frankfurt am Main/Neiden, 25 Dec. 1911, daughter of Adam T. and Katharina Mechnig; she studied at Munich under Scharff (q.v.); Dr. Phil., 1937; she married the Egyptologist Hellmut Brunner (q.v.), 1937; she was attached to the Egyptological Institute in Tübingen and was awarded the title of Professor in 1972; she was a member of the Deutschen Archäologischen Instituts and International Society for Folk Narrative Research; a volume of studies *Gegengabe. Festschrift für Emma Brunner-Traut*, ed. by I. Gamer-Wallert and W. Helck, was dedicated to her in 1992; her publications included her thesis *Die Tanz im Alten Ägypten*, 1938, 3rd ed. 1992; *Die altägyptischen Scherbenbilder (Bildostraka) der deutschen Museen und Sammlungen*, 1956; *Altägyptische Tiergeschichte und Fabel*, 1959, 8th ed. 1988; *Ägypten: Kunst- und Reiseführer*, with V. Hell, 1962; 6th ed., 1988; *Altägyptische Märchen*, 1963, 11th ed. 1997; *Die Alten Ägypter Verbogenes Leben unter Pharaonen*, 1974; 4th ed., 1984; *Die altägyptische Grabkammer Seschemnofers III aus Gisa*, 1977; 2nd ed., 1982; *Egyptian Artists' Sketches*, 1979; *Gelebte Mythen*, 1981, 3rd ed., 1988; *Die Ägyptische Sammlung der Universität Tübingen*, with her husband, 1981; *Kleine Ägyptenkunde*, 1982, 9th ed., 1991; *Die Kopten*, 1982, 4th ed., 1993; *Osiris Kreuz und Halbmond*, with her husband, 1984; *Hieroglyphenschrift und Totenbuch: Die Papyri der ägyptische Sammlung der Universität Tübingen*, with her husband, 1985; *Lebensweisheit der Alter Ägyper*, 1985, 2nd ed., 1991; *Frühformen des Erkennens*, 1990, 3rd ed. 1995; *Die Grossen Religionen des Alten Orients und der Antike*, with others, 1992; *Feiere einen schonen Tag:Altägyptische Dichtung*, with E.-B. Korber, 1996; *Alltag unter den Pharaonen*, 1998; *Die Kopten-Leben und Lehre der frühen Christen in Ägypten*, 2000; she contributed the study *Aspektive* in H. Schäfer, *Von ägyptische Kunst*, 4th ed., 1963; she died at Tübingen, 18 Jan. 2008.

Inf. W. Guglielmi; Kurschner, 19th ed., 2003, 406; *ZÄS* 136 (2009), III-IV (I. Gamer-Wallert); K. Ranke, *Enzyklopädie des Märchens* 2 (1979), 954-6 (J. Gwyn Griffiths); *FABULA. Zeitschrift für Erzählforschung* 49 (2008), 350-2 (W. Röllig).

BRUNTON, Guy (1878-1948)

British Egyptologist and archaeologist; he was born in Beckenham, 18 July 1878, son of Spencer B., a stockbroker, and Janet Swift, and as a boy became interested in Egypt through reading Amelia Edwards' book; he afterwards read and studied books in the Edwards Library at Univ. Coll. London; at the age of 18 he went to S. Africa for several years, where he later married at Prynnsberg, Clocolan, 28 April 1906 Miss Winifred Newberry (see next entry) who became his collaborator in Egypt; he returned to London in 1911 where he studied for two years under Petrie (q.v.) and Miss Murray (q.v.); he then dug with the former at Lahun, 1912-14, where he discovered the famous royal jewellery of the 12th Dynasty and most carefully assembled it after weeks of work; after military service, 1914-18, he had another season at Lahun, 1919-21, after which he worked with Miss Caton Thompson (q.v.) at Qau and Badari; three important discoveries were made here, fossil bones, a Coptic Gospel of St. John, and espec. Badarian rippled pottery; this last led to the discovery of the oldest known cultures of predynastic Upper Egypt, which began a new epoch in the story of early Egypt; Brunton afterwards excavated at Der Tasa and found an earlier phase still; he was appointed assistant Keeper, Cairo Museum, 1931, and did a considerable amount of arranging in the galleries; Brunton was a careful excavator and one of Petrie's most distinguished followers, often improving on and refining his master's techniques; he published, *Lahun I. The Treasure*, 1920; *Sedment*, 2 vols., with Petrie, 1924; *Gurob*, with R. Engelbach, 1927; *Qau and Badari,* with Petrie and Gardiner, 3 vols., 1927-30; *The Badarian Civilisation and Predynastic remains near Badari*, with G. Caton Thompson, 1928; *Mostagedda and the Tasian Culture*, with G. M. Morant, 1937; *Matmar*, 1948; he also contributed many articles to *ASAE* and other journals and was working on button seals at the time of his death; he retired in March 1948 and went to S. Africa, where he died in White River, Transvaal, 17 Oct. 1948. His library is housed in the Library of the University of Witwatersrand, Johannesburg, as a separate collection and some of his papers are in the Griffith Institute.

ASAE 49 (1949), 95-8 (M. A. Murray); *Chron. d'Ég.* 49 (1950), 85; EES *Ann. Rep.* 1948, 6-7 (A. J. Arkell); Petrie, 232, 240, 242, 250, 254; inf. J. W. Perry, University Librarian, Witwatersrand; E. Gran-Aymerich, *Dictionnaire biographique d'archéologie 1798-1945*, 2001, incorporated in *Les Chercheurs de passé 1798-1945*, 2007, 648; K. L. Sheppard in W. Carruthers (ed.), *Histories of Egyptology*, 2015, 121-2.

BRUNTON, Winifred Mabel (*née* Newberry) (1880-1959)
British artist; she was born in London, 6 May 1880, daughter of Charles Newberry and his wife Elisabeth Mary; she married Guy Brunton (q.v.) and studied with her husband at University College London; she painted water colour illustrations of Egyptian works of art through his influence, using objects such as those found in Tutankhamun's tomb; she made a series of illustrations for two popular books with chapters written by various authors, *Kings and Queens of Ancient Egypt*, 1926, and *Great Ones of Ancient Egypt*, 1929; she also drew many of the plates illustrating objects discovered by her husband in his reports of excavations; some of her watercolours are in the Griffith Institute; she died in Clocolan, Orange Free State, South Africa, 29 Jan. 1959.

AfO 19 (1959-60), 269; inf. C. R. Newberry; R. Janssen, *The First Hundred Years,* 1992, 14; *KMT* 15/1 (2004), 69-80.

BRUYÈRE, Bernard Charles Marie Joseph (1879-1971)

French Egyptologist; he was born at Besançon, 10 Nov. 1879, son of Saint Martin Louis B., a military officer, and Marie Véronique Tournier; he was originally destined for a military career, but his interest in history led him to take courses at the École du Louvre under Bénédite (q.v.); he first visited Egypt in 1910; he served with distinction in World War I when he was wounded and taken prisoner; he joined the Institut Français at Cairo in 1921 and in that year began his excavations at Deir el-Medina which he undertook until he left Egypt in 1952 with a break during World War II; each year he published preliminary reports of his fieldwork in great detail; in 1928 he was named director of excavations at the Institut; apart from Deir el-Medina he also undertook work at Déversoir in 1928 and at Clysma-Qulzum 1930-2 at the request of the Suez Canal Authority; as well as at Tell Edfu with the Poles in 1937; in 1930 he married Françoise Demartres niece of Jouguet (q.v.); his publications include 17 volumes on his work at Deir el-Medina, *Rapport sur les fouilles de Deir el-Medineh*, 1924-53 as well as more detailed monographs: *La tombe de Nakht-Min et la tombe d'Ari-nefer*, with C. Kuentz, 1926; *Meret Seger à Deir el-Médineh*, 1930; *Tombes thébaines de Deir el-Médineh à decoration monochrome,* 1952; *La tombe no. 1 de Sen-nedjem à Deir el-Médineh*, 1959; and on other sites, *Tell Edfou 1937* with K. Michalowski and others, 1937; and *Fouilles de Clysma-Qolzoum (Suez)*, 1966; he died in Saint-Germain-en-Laye, 4 Dec. 1971, buried in Chatou.

BSFE 63 (1972), 5; *BSFE* 92 (1981), 7-8 (J. Leclant); È. Gran-Aymerich, *Dictionnaire biographique d'archéologie 1798-1945*, 2001, incorporated in *Les Chercheurs de passé 1798-1945*, 2007, 648.

BRUYN (BRUIJN), Cornelius de (*c.*1652-1727)
Dutch traveller; he was born in The Hague *c.*1652; he trained as an artist and visited the Levant, 1678-84; he was in Egypt in 1681 visiting Alexandria and Cairo; he returned to The Hague in 1693; he later travelled to Russia, Persia and the East, 1701-8; he published *Reizen van Cornelis de Bruyn door de vermaardste Deelen van Klein Asia*, 1698 with the first published drawing of the interior of the Great Pyramid; French ed. 1700, English ed. 1702; and *Reizen over Moskoviem door Persie en Indie*, 1711; he died in Zydebaelen, *c.*1727.

NNBW 2, 269-70; A. Kampman, *Ex Oriente Lux* 11-13 (1949-54), 154-60; J. Speake, *Literature of Travel and Exploration*, 2003, 1, 132-4.

BRYCE, William Moir (1842-1919)
British archivist; he was born in Edinburgh, 1842, son of William Miller B. and Eliza Hood Calder; on the staff of Register House, Edinburgh, he joined a firm of professional record-searchers; being interested in Scottish history he wrote on local antiquities; he went to Egypt with Sayce (q.v.), 1902-3, and made a small collection of Egyptian antiquities which was sold at Sotheby's after his death, 21-23 July 1920; LLD Edinburgh; a hieratic tablet from his collection was published by Griffith in *PSBA* 30 (1908), 272; he died in Edinburgh, 2 Aug. 1919.

Sayce, 316, 461; Lugt 80955; inf. C. Aldred.

BUCHANAN, Janet May (1866-1912)
British Egyptologist; she was born in Glasgow in 1866, the daughter of Rev. Prof. George B.; she was educated at a private school in Cheltenham; on the death of her father, she moved with her mother and sisters to Edinburgh; her inheritance (equivalent of £2m) allowed her to pursue her interests in archaeology; she was acquainted with Flinders Petrie (q.v.) and Hilda Petrie (q.v.), as well as Amelia Edwards (q.v.); she established the Egyptian Research Students Association (ERSA), with branches in Edinburgh and Glasgow, *c.*1906; she organised Glasgow's first major exhibition of Egyptian antiquities in 1912 in the Kelvingrove Museum & Art Gallery, with over one thousand objects on loan from Flinders Petrie (q.v.), Paisley Museum, D. Y. Cameron, Miss Amy Urlin (Petrie's sister-in-law), the Misses Blackie, and others; she died in a road traffic accident in Glasgow in December 1912; following her death, the two branches of the ERSA combined to fund the purchase of Egyptian objects for Glasgow Museums; many of the exhibition objects, whose actual ownership seems to have been lost sight of in the wake of Buchanan's death, also now form part of the Glasgow collection; she was unmarried, and was buried in Glasgow's Western Necropolis.

Inf. M. Wilson; B. Weightman; C. Gilmour.

BUCHER, (*Abbé*) Paul (1887-1966)
French Egyptologist he was born at Guebwiller, 16 May 1887, son of Paul Émile B. and Anne Marie Martz; he studied Egyptology at the University of Strasbourg under Spiegelberg (q.v.), through him developing a special interest in Demotic; the library there having a considerable collection of Demotic works he was able to gain his doctorate with a thesis on two papyri, 1917, which he later published in vols. 1 and 3 of *Kêmi* (1928, 1930) as, 'Les Hymnes à Sobk Ra seigneur de Smenou des papyrus 2 et 17 de la Bibliothèque nationale de Strasbourg'; he helped in the IFAO excavations at Deir el-Medina at which time he also copied and published the funerary texts in two royal tombs, *Les Textes des Tombes de Thoutmosis III et Aménophis II*, 1932; Bucher was always extremely interested in archaeology and field-work, and he later worked with Montet (q.v.) at Tanis being present at the opening of the tomb of Psusennes in 1940; he was actively associated with the teaching at Strasbourg and also helped in the reorganization of the University collection, publishing a long descriptive notice; he died in Rouffach, 22 May 1966.

Bull. de la Faculté des Lettres de Strasbourg 45 (1966), 229-31 (portr.) (J. Leclant); *Chron. d'Ég.* 42 (1967), 123-4 (P. Derchain); Univ. de Strasbourg, *Bull. d'information* 7 (1966), 4-12 (portr.) (P. Derchain).

BUCK, Adriaan de (1892-1959)
Dutch Egyptologist; born Oostkapelle, 22 Sept. 1892, son of Pieter de B., a clergyman, and Johanna Catharina Agatha Vermaas; he studied theology, religious history, and Egyptology in Leiden from 1911 and Egyptology at Göttingen under Sethe (q.v.), 1917-21, and at Berlin under A. Erman (q.v.) and Möller (q.v.); he gained a theological doctorate at the University of Leiden, 1922, for which he wrote a thesis on the Primeval Hill as a concept in Egyptian religion, a work which has exercised a profound influence on all later studies on the Heliopolitan theology; at this time from 1921 to 1925 he was the pastor of the reformed church as Ursum near Alkmaar; Gardiner (q.v.) and Breasted (q.v.) now asked him to act as editor for an exhaustive and fully comprehensive edition of the Coffin Texts to be published by the Oriental Institute of Chicago, 1925-9; this work involved him in much travel and

intensive study in Egypt and the Museums of Europe and America; at the time of his death six great volumes of texts had appeared and the manuscript of the seventh and last was ready; in addition a part of the other great work of translating and commenting on them had also been completed; de Buck was appointed Reader in Egyptology, 1928 and took up his post in 1929, and then Professor in the University of Leiden 1939 and 1949-59; Dean of the Faculty; he was a member of the Koninklijke Nederlandse Akad., 1941; first President of the International Association of Egyptologists; Chairman of the Dutch Oriental Society; Director of the Netherlands Institute of the Near East; Adviser of *Ex Oriente Lux* and editor of *Bibliotheca Orientalis*; his publications included, *De Egyptische voorstellingen betreffende den oerheuvel*, 1922; *Egyptische verhalen; wit het Oud-Egyptisch vertaald door A. De Buck*, 1928; *Traduction des contes égyptiens*, 1928; *De egepraal van het licht: voorstellingen en symbolen uit den oud-egyptischen zonnedienst*, 1930; *Egyptische grammatica*, 1944, (French ed. *Grammaire élémentaire du Moyen Égyptien*, 1952); *Egyptian reading book*, 1944; *The Egyptian Coffin Texts: texts of spells*, 7 vols., 1935-61; also various articles in journals; he died in Leiden, 28 Oct. 1959.

AfO 19 (1959-60), 267-8 (portr.) (H. Brunner); *Alseengoet Instrument. Leven en werken van Prof. A. de Buck*, Leiden 1960 (B. A. van Proosdij-J. M. A. Janssen); *BiOr* 16 (1959), i-iv (portr.) (A. A. Kampman); *Chron. d'Ég.* 35 (1960), 191-3 (J. M. A. Janssen); *EES Report*, 1959, 4 (J. Černý); *Jaarboek der Koninklijke Nederlandse Akad. van wetneschappen* 1959-60 (Amsterdam, 1960 366-72 (portr.) B. A. van Groningen); *Leidse Studentenalmanak* (Leiden) 2nd year (1960), 87-8, (portr.) (B. A. van Groningen); *Leids Universiteitsblad*, Leiden 25, no. 7 (6th Nov. 1959), 2 (portr.) (K. A. H. Hidding); *La Nouvelle Clio* 10 (1958-1959-1960), 173-7 (C. de Wit); *Phoenix*, 5 (1959), 118 (portr.) (B. a. van Proosdij); *ZÄS* 85 (1960), 1-11 (portr.) (S. Morenz); H. Willems, *The World of the Coffin Texts*, 1996, 41-4 (M. Heerma van Voss); D. Nauta (ed.), *Biografisch Lexikon voor de Geschiedenis van het nedelanse protestantisme*, 6, 57-8.

BUCKINGHAM, James Silk (1786-1855)
British author and traveller; he was born at Flushing, 25 Aug. 1786, son of Christopher B., a shipwright and later farmer, and Thomasine Hambly; he visited India, America, Syria, Palestine and Egypt in 1813-14 and 1815; he was involved in a legal dispute with Bankes (q.v.) over the use of material collected by Bankes; he was MP for Sheffield, 1832-7; he was one of the founders of the Syro-Egyptian Society (1844), and contributed articles to its publications; he also gave public lectures on Egyptian archaeology; he published an account of his travels in the east, 1825, and another on *A visit to the ruins of the ancient city of Naucratis, and the site of Sais*, 1844 and his *Autobiography*, 1855; he died in London, 30 June 1855.

ODNB 7, 510-1 (portr.); *DNB* 7, 202; Hilmy, i, 103; P. Rée in P. and J. Starkey, *Unfolding the Orient*, 2001, 169-78; R. de Keersmaecker, *ASTENE Bulletin* 71 (2017), 22-5; D. Boyer in N. Cooke and V. Daubney (eds.), *Lost and Now Found: Explorers, Diplomats and Artists in Egypt and the Near East*, 2017, 183-204; N. B. Wilson in *Genealogists' Magazine* 32 (20218), 439-445.

BUCKMAN, Percy Warner James (1865-1948)
British artist; he was born in Bradford Abbas, Dorset 31 Oct. 1865, son of James B., Professor of Geology and Botany, and Julia Sophia Savory, who died shortly thereafter; he studied art at the Royal Academy schools and exhibited there from 1886-1937; he was known as a landscape and portrait painter; he was elected to RMS 1920; during 1892-3 he joined Newberry (q.v.) and Carter (q,v.) as an artists at Beni Hasan and other sites; he was employed as an art master at the Goldsmiths Institute which from 1904 became Goldsmiths College of the University of London until Dec. 1930; his work was published in *Beni Hasan* IV, 1900 and several of his watercolours are preserved in the Egypt Exploration Society; his manuscript diary of the 1892-3 season is in the possession of his descendants with a copy in the EES archives; he died at Tonbridge, Kent 4 June 1948; inf. C. Naunton.

BUDGE, (*Sir*) Ernest Alfred Thompson Wallis (1857-1934)
British Egyptologist and orientalist; he was born at Bodmin, 27 July 1857, son of Mary Ann B. possibly by a Mr. Vyvyan, and became interested in Egyptian and oriental history at an early age, often visiting the British Museum as a boy; at fifteen he studied in his spare time while employed by W. H. Smith & Son, 1870-8, and was at this time encouraged and helped by Gladstone who took a personal interest in him, and Birch (q.v.) who taught him Egyptian and allowed him the use of the library in the Oriental Dept. of the British Museum; he later studied at Christ's Coll., Cambridge, 1879-82; Assyrian Scholar, Hebrew Prizeman, Tyrwhitt Hebrew Scholar; BA 1882; MA 1885; LittD; DLitt; DLit; FSA; assistant Keeper 1883-92, acting Keeper from 27 Jan. 1892, Keeper of Egyptian and Assyrian Antiquities, British Museum, 1894-1924; Corr. Member of the Acad. of Science, Lisbon;

Member of the American Historical Soc.; Knight, 1920; married 1883, Dora Helen (d.1926), daughter of the Revd Titus Emerson; Budge went to Egypt, the Sudan, and Mesopotamia many times to obtain antiquities for the British Museum; he excavated at Aswan in Egypt; at Gebel Barkal, the Island of Meroe, Semna, and other sites in Nubia and the Sudan; and at Nineveh and Der in Iraq; Order of the Star of Ethiopia, 3rd class; Dongola medals, 1898; he had great success in his dealings with the local inhabitants and in overcoming official obstruction, and obtained for the British Museum many thousands of cuneiform tablets and other Assyrian and Babylonian antiquities, as well as Egyptian sculptures, papyri, and other objects; he also procured large numbers of Coptic, Syriac, Arabic, Ethiopic, and other oriental MSS, plus many important Greek papyri; his output of published works is the largest of any single orientalist, the list of his works in *Who Was Who* being the longest recorded and numbering over 140 separate books and editions, some being works running into several vols., while in the field of articles in journals he published 20 in *PSBA* alone; he edited texts in Cuneiform, Hieroglyphic, Coptic, Syriac, and Ethiopic; he produced many official publications of papyri and monuments, and a great number of popular or semi-popular works in all these fields; in his text editions, Budge was too prolific for careful work, and many of them are inaccurate by modern standards; he persisted in the use of an old system of transcription, and did not utilize many of the grammatical discoveries of the Berlin School; nevertheless without his phenomenal energy and devotion, many hieratic, Coptic, and other texts of fundamental importance would not have become known and been made available until a very much later date; his general works have been of value to students and helped to arouse much popular interest; the following is a list of his major Egyptological books: *Coptic History of Isaac of Tiphre*, 1884; *Notes on the Egyptian Stelae*, 1884; *Dwellers on the Nile*, 1885; *The Sarcophagus of Ankhnesrâneferab*, 1885; *The Book of the Bee*, 1886; *Coptic History of Elijah the Tishbite*, 1886; *Catalogue of Egyptian Antiquities (Harrow School Museum)*, 1887; *Sepulchral Stele from Akhmîm*. 1887; *Cotpic Martyrdom of George of Cappadocia*, 1888; *Account of Excavations at Aswân*, 1888; *On Cuneiform Despatches from Tushratta (Tell el-Amarna Tablets)*, 1888; *The Nile, Notes for Travellers*, 1890; many eds.; *Festival Songs of Isis and Nephthys, The Litanies of Seker, and The Book of Over-throwing Apepi*, 1891; *Tell el-Amarna Tablets in the British Museum*, with C. Bezold, 1892; *Catalogue of the Egyptian Antiquities in the Fitzwilliam Museum*, 1893; *The Mummy*, 1894, several eds.; *St. Michael the Archangel*, 1894; *Book of the Dead (Papyrus of Ani)*, 1895; *First Steps in Egyptian*, 1895; *An Egyptian Reading Book for Beginners*, 1896; *The Lady Meux Collection of Egyptian antiquities*, 1896; *Bible Illustrations*, 1896; *The Chapters of Coming Forth by Day (Book of the Dead)*, 1897; *The oldest known Coptic Psalter*, 1897; *The Rhind Mathematical Papyrus*, 1898; *A guide to the First and Second Egyptian Rooms, British Museum*, 1898; *A Guide to the Third and Fourth Egyptian Rooms*, 1905; *Facsimiles of the Papyri of Hunefer, Anhai, Kerasher, Nu, Texts etc.*, 1899; *Egyptian Ideas of the Future Life*, 1899; *Egyptian Magic*, 1899; *Easy Lessons in Egyptian Hieroglyphics*, 1899, several eds.; *On the Orientation of the Pyramids in the Sudan*, 1899; *The Book of the Dead*, 1901; *A History of Egypt from the end of the Predynastic Period to the death of Cleopatra VII*, 8 vols., 1902; *The Gods of Egypt, or Studies in Egyptian Mythology*, 1903; *The Rosetta Stone, and Decree of Canopus*, 1904; *Cook's Handbook of Egypt and the Sudân*, 3rd ed. 1911; *Egyptian Books of Heaven and Hell; The Book Am-tuat; The Book of Pylons; Egyptian Texts and Translations*, 1905, 1925; *The Egyptian Sudân, 2 vols.*, 1907; *The Sarcophagus of Seti I (Soane Museum)*, 1908; *The Book of the Kings of Egypt, 2 vols.*, 1908; *Guide to the Egyptian Galleries in the British Museum (Sculpture)*, 1909; *Texts relating to St. Minas etc., in a Nubian Dialect*, 1909; *Liturgy of Funeral Offerings, and Book of Opening the Mouth*, 1909; *Coptic Homilies in the Dialect of Upper Egypt*, 1910; *Book of the Dead*, 1910; *Hieratic Papyri in the British Museum*, 1911; *Osiris and the Egyptian Resurrection*, 1911; *Legends of the Gods, and Annals of Nubian Kings*, 1911; *Coptic Biblical Texts in the dialect of Upper Egypt*, 1912; *The Papyrus of Nesi-ta-nebt-Ashru*, 1912; *Coptic Apocrypha*, 1913; *Papyrus of Ani*, 1913; *Coptic Martyrdoms*, 1914; *Short History of the Egyptian People*, 1914; *Literature of the Ancient Egyptians*, 1914; *Egyptian Wall-painting*, 1914; *Egyptian Sculptures*, 1914; *Miscellaneous Coptic Texts in the dialect of Upper Egypt*, 1915; *By Nile and Tigris, 2 vols.*, 1920; *An Egyptian Hieroglyphic Dictionary*, his largest work, 1920; *British Museum Monographs, Book of the Dead*, 1920; *Guide to the 4th, 5th, and 6th Egyptian Rooms*, 1922; *Egyptian Hieratic Papyri, 2nd Series*, 1923; *Tutankhamen*, 1923; *Guide to 1st, 2nd, and 3rd Egyptian Rooms*, 1924; *The Teaching of Amenemapt*, 1924; *Egypt* in Home Univ. Lib., 1925; *Cleopatra's Needles*, 1927; *Egyptian Tales and Romances*, 1931; *Wit and Wisdom of the Christian Fathers of Egypt*, 1934; *From Fetish to God in Ancient Egypt*, 1934; Budge founded in memory of his wife two Egyptological studentships at Christ's Coll., Cambridge, and University Coll., Oxford, and left his library to the former college; he died in London, 23 Nov. 1934 and was buried in Nunhead cemetery in south London.

ODNB 8, 556-8; *DNB* 1931-40, 121 (S. Smith); *By Nile and Tigris*, 2 vols., 1920; mainly autobiographical; *JEA* 21 (1935), 68 (portr.) (Campbell Thompson); *WWW* iii, 185-6 (bibl. of princ. works); *Bull. John Rylands Library*, Manchester, 19 (1935), 5-8; *JRAS* 1935, 436-8 (A. W. Shorter); *Nature* 135 (1935), 172-3 (S. R. K. Glanville); R. Morrell, *"Budgie...."*. *The Life of Sir E. A. T. Wallis Budge*, 2002; E. Gran-Aymerich, *Dictionnaire biographique d'archéologie 1798-1945*, 2001, incorporated in *Les Chercheurs de passé 1798-1945*, 2007, 650; M. Ismail, *Wallis Budge. Magic and Mummies in London and Cairo*, 2011.

BUHL, Marie-Louise (1918-2006)
Danish Egyptologist; she was born in Randers, 2 March 1918, daughter of Otto Richard B. and Martha Henrietta Frederiksen; she studied at the Univesity of Copenhagen; MA, PhD; she joined the Danish National Museum in 1946, Keeper of Antiquities, 1961; she was also lecturer in Near Eastern archaeology at the University of Copenhagen, 1966; she published *The Late Egyptian Anthropoid Stone Sarcophagi*, 1959; *A Hundred Masterpieces from the Ancient Near East in the Danish National Museum and the History of its Ancient Near Eastern Collections*, 1974, *The Danish Naval Officer Frederik Ludvig Norden*, 1986; and *Les dessins archéologiques et topographiques de l'Egypte ancienne par F. L. Norden 1737-1738*, 1993; she died in Nov. 2006.

Who's Who in Scandinavia, 1981, 186.

BULL, Ludlow Seguine (1886-1954)
American Egyptologist; born New York, 10 Jan. 1886, son of Charles Stedman B. and Mary Eunice Kingsbury; he was educated at Yale University and was for many years Hon. Curator of the Egyptian Collection of Yale Museum; he practiced as an attorney-at-law from 1910 to 1915 after having studied law at Harvard; he became PhD of Chicago 1922 and visited Egypt for the first in 1923 after changing to Egyptology; he was a lecturer at Yale 1925-36 and then Professor; with A. B. Chace and H. P. Manning he published the *Rhind (Mathematical) Papyrus*, vol. ii, 1929; he wrote a number of articles in the *M.M.A. Bulletin and the Metropolitan Museum Studies*, and was a member of the editorial board of the latter; he was also an Associate Curator in the Metropolitan Museum, New York; he wrote the appendix on the inscriptions at Deir el-Hagar in H. E. Winlock's *Ed Dakhleh Oasis*, 1936 and with Lindsley F. Hall edited part iii of the *Temple of Hibis in El Khargeh Oasis*, 1953; he was Recording Secretary of the American Oriental Society 1925-36, Vice Pres. 1938, Pres. 1939; he died in Litchfield, Conn., 1 July 1954.

BASOR No. 135 (Oct. 1954), 2-3 (portr.) (Ch. K. Wilkinson); *Orientalia* 23 (1954), 448 (A. Pohl); *WWA* 3, 120-1.

BULTÉ, Jeanne (1930-2013)
French Egyptologist; she specialized in the study of faience; she took part in the excavations at Tanis by Yoyotte (q.v.); she helped to produce the catalogue *Faïences de l'Antiquité, d l'Égypte à l'Iran*, 2005; apart from articles, she published *Iniation à la faïence*, 1980; *Catalogue des collections égyptiens du Musée Céramique à Sèvres*, 1981; *Talismans égyptiens d'heureuse maternité*, 1991; she died in Paris, 31 Jan. 2013.

BSFE 185 (2013), 3 (portr.).

BUNSEN, (*Baron von*) Christian Karl Josias (1791-1860)
Prussian scholar and diplomatist; he was born in Korbach, 25 Aug. 1791, son of Heinrich Christian B. and Johanettta Eleonore Brocken; after his education at the Universities of Marburg, 1808 and Göttingen from 1809; he studied Hebrew and Arabic at Munich and also attended universities in Leiden, Paris, and Copenhagen; he then travelled to Rome in 1816 where he was attached to the Prussian embassy, 1818; he married in Rome, 1 July 1817 Frances, daughter of Benjamin Waddington; he was appointed Prussian Ambassador to the Vatican, 1823-38, to Switzerland, 1839-41 and in London, 1842-54; DCL, Oxford, 1839; he was created a baron, 1857; Corresponding Member of the Académie des Inscriptions in Paris, 23 Dec. 1859; he wrote a considerable amount on philosophy and biblical subjects, provoking much controversy, but his name is remembered in Egyptology through his great encyclopaedic work *Aegyptens Stelle in der Weltgeschichte*, 6 vols. 1844-57, trans. into English as *Egypt's Place in Universal History*, 5 vols. 1844-57; the last volume was almost entirely written by Samuel Birch, and contains both his Egyptian Grammar and Dictionary; he died in Bonn, 28 Nov. 1860; his son Ernest Christian Ludwig was born in Rome, 11 Aug. 1811; he served as a Prussian army officer, 1837-42 and then became secretary to his father, 1841-8; he was appointed chamberlain to Wilhelm I, 1871; he retired to England in 1849; he was interested in biblical research and was a supporter of Amelia Edwards (q.v.) as evidenced by *Morning Post* of 29 March 1880; he wrote *Biblical Chronology*, 1874; he died in London, 13 May 1903.

ODNB 8, 689-92; *NDB* 3, 17-18; Brugsch, *Mein Leben*, 46; Hilmy, i, 105; *Lepsius (Life)*, passim); *Bentley's Miscellany*, vol. 50 (Sept. 1861), 284-92; W. H. Rule, *London Quarterly Review*, vol. 53 (Jan. 1880), 265-310; F. Bunsen, *Memoirs of Baron Bunsen*, 1868, 2nd ed. 1869; A. C. E. Franquet de Franqueville, *Le Premier Siècle de l'Institut de France*, 1895, II, 259; E. Geldbach, *Der gelehrte Diplomat*, 1980; È. Gran-Aymerich, *Dictionnaire biographique d'archéologie 1798-1945*, 2001, incorporated in *Les Chercheurs de passé 1798-1945*, 2007, 652-3.

BURATTINI, Tito Livio (1617-1681)
Italian traveller, inventor, draughtsman, amateur Egyptologist, and architect: he was born in Agordo, 8 March 1617; Burattini was in Egypt in the years 1637-41; he worked there on a new map of Egypt; in 1639 he co-

operated with Greaves (q.v.) on his research at the Giza pyramids, he also executed measurements, plans and drawings of other Egyptian subjects; his drawings were included by Greaves in his *Pyramidographia*, 1646; his materials were also used by A. Kircher (q.v.) in the descriptions of pyramids and of the Sphinx in *Oedipus Aegyptiacus*, Vol. 2, Rome 1653, 303-304 and by Stefano della Bella; in 1641 he settled in Poland; he had a great mind with versatile interests in physics, astronomy (installing an observatory near Warsaw), and astrology and constructed irrigation machines and a flying apparatus as well as microscopes and telescopes; he acted also as a diplomatic agent; Burattini was the author of a treatise *Niloscopio* written when still in Egypt, later changed to *Nuova dimonstrazione dell'inondazione del Nilo*, and of a printed treatise entitled *Misura universale,* Vilna 1675; he proposed a new measure called by him a metre; he tried to introduce some Egyptianizing elements into Polish architecture inspiring Tylman van Gameren when working on the project of the Warsaw Morstineum, the original design using the shape of a pyramid, is now in the Graphic Cabinet of the Warsaw University (no. 821); he died 28 Sept. 1681.

A. Favaro, *Intorno alla vita ed ai lavori di Tito Livio Burattini fisico Agordino del secolo XVII*, Venice 1896; A. Hnilko, *Wlosi w Polsce, I. Tytus Liwiusz Boratyni*, Cracow 1923; *Polski Slownik Biograficzny* 3, 133-6; *Funmkcja dziela sztuki,* Warsaw 1972, 225-41 (S. Mossakowski); *DBDI* 15, 394-8; *Belluno e L'Egitto,* 1986; inf. J. Śliwa.

BURCHARDT, Max (1885-1914)
German Egyptologist; he was born in Berlin, 6 March 1885, and studied Egyptology and Semitic languages in Berlin under Erman (q.v.) and Leipzig; PhD at Berlin, 1908; he wrote a doctoral thesis on *Die syllabische Schreibung im Ägyptischen*; he entered the Egyptian Department of the Berlin Museum in 1904 as an assistant, also helping with the work on the Wörterbuch from 1905; he published two books, *Die altkanaanäischen Fremdworte und Eigennamen im Aegyptischen*, 2 pts. 1909-10; *Handbuch der aegyptischen Königsnamen*, with Max Pieper, 1912; in addition he wrote 13 articles in *ZÄS*; Burchardt was killed while serving as an officer in the German army at Saint-Souplet in France, 7 Sept. 1914.

ZÄS 53 (1917), 149 (A. Erman?); E. Endesfelder, *Die Ägyptologie an der Berliner Universität-Zur Geschichte eines Fachgebietes*, 27.

BURCHART, Johannes (1776-1838)
Estonian doctor and collector; he was born in Reval (now Tallin, Estonia), 11 March 1776, son of Johannes B., a doctor and Dorothea Schumacher; he was educated there and at Halle 1792-4 and Jena 1794-8; he worked as a doctor in St. Petersburg and with a family in southern Russia before returning to Reval in 1802; in 1808 he took over his father's pharmaceutical practice; he formed a collection of Egyptian antiquities, now in Tallin, some of which he acquired from Butenev (q.v.) from the Anastasi collection (q.v.); he died in Reval, 6 March 1838.

Inf. S. Stadnikov; G. Hansen, *Die Sammlungen inländischer Alterthümer und anderer auf die baltischen Provinzen bezüglichen Gegenstände des Estlandischen Provincial-Museums,* 1875; S. Stadnikov, *Gött. Misz.* 135 (1993), 97-100; I. Brennsohn, Die Aetrze Estlands, 1922, 151-2..

BURCKHARDT, Johann Ludwig (1784-1817)
Swiss traveller and benefactor; he was born in Lausanne, 25 Nov. 1784, son of Rudolf B. and Sara Rohner; after attending the universities of Leipzig and Göttingen, he came to England in 1806 and studied Arabic at Cambridge; Burckhardt travelled extensively in the East, using the name Sheikh Ibrahim, and was in Egypt, 1812-17 where he was the first European to see Abu Simbel; full accounts of his travels have been published, see *Travels in Nubia*, published by the Association for promoting the discovery of the interior parts of Africa, 1819; under his will 800 vols. of oriental MSS were bequeathed to Cambridge University; he died in Cairo, 15 Oct. 1817.

DNB 2, 138-9; *EB*; BL Add. MSS 30239, 30240A; Cailliaud, ed. Jomard, *Travels in the Oasis of Thebes*, 36; Hilmy, i. 105; Moorehead, see index; Richardson, i. 53, 161, 428; Salt, i. 489; ii. 3, 39, 141; Sherer, 105, 175; K. Sim, *Desert Traveller*, 1956; *Journal of Semitic Studies* 18 (1973), 259-266; *Bibliothèque Universelle des Sciences, Belles-Lettres et Arts*, XIIIe a., XXXVIII (Genève-Paris, mai 1828), 28-41; T. Wollmann, *Scheich Ibrahim* 1984; Scheik Ibrahim, *Briefe an seine Eltern und Geschwister*. Edited by Carl Burckhardt-Sarasin and Hansrudolf Schwabe-Burckhardt, 1956; C. E. Bosworth,, *Bulletin of the John Rylands Library* 55 (1972-1973), 33-59; R. Stucky in *Antike Welt* 24 (1993), 90-100; È. Gran-Aymerich, *Dictionnaire biographique d'archéologie 1798-1945*, 2001, incorporated in *Les Chercheurs de passé 1798-1945*, 2007, 653; J. Speake (ed.), *Literature of Travel and Exploration*, 2003, 1, 143-4.

BURFORD, Robert (1791-1861)
British artist; he was born in 1791, son of John B., panorama painter; he exhibited panoramas in Leicester Square, London from 1827 to 1856; one of these displays was called the Temple of Karnak, 1833, painted from drawings made by F. Catherwood (q.v.) of which a description was published; Ruskin wrote of Burford's establishment, that it was 'an educational institution of the highest and purest value, and ought to have been supported by the Government as one of the most beautiful school instruments in London'; he died in London, 30 Jan. 1861.

ODNB 7, 747; *DNB* 7, 300; Hilmy, i, 106; Ruskin, *Praeterita,* i, 137.

BURGON, Thomas (1787-1858)
British merchant in Smyrna; he was born in Middlesex, 1 Aug. 1787, son of John B. and his wife Mary; his son, John William, who afterwards was Dean of Chichester, was his clerk; he acquired much of his Egyptian material in 1827; he failed in business about 1841, after which, being an able numismatist, he sought employment in the British Museum, but his application was opposed by the Archbishop of Canterbury; eventually, however, through the advocacy of Samuel Rogers and Lord Lyndhurst, he was made a supernumerary assistant in the Dept. of Antiquities (which then included Coins and Medals); his collection of antiquities was acquired by the British Museum in 1842; he died in London, 28 Aug. 1858, and his library was sold at Sotheby's, 22 Dec. of that year; a hieratic papyrus was acquired by the British Museum (EA 10045); his watercolours of his collection are now in the Ashmolean Museum.

ODNB 7, 805-5; P. W. Clayden, *Samuel Rogers and his Contemporaries*, ii, 240; Pettigrew, *Hist. Eg. Mummies,* 111; E. M. Goulburn, *John William Burgon*, 1842, I, 8-15; Lugt 24559.

BURNEY, Ethel Wordsworth (1891-1984)
British bibliographer; she was born at Oxford, 20 Jan. 1891, daughter of Falconer Madan, librarian at the Bodleian, and Frances Jane Hayter; she married in 1913 Charles Fox Burney, Professor of Interpretation of Holy Scripture at Oxford (d. 1925); in 1928 she began her collaboration with Dr. R. Moss (q.v.) in the production of Porter and Moss, *Topographical Bibliography* accompanying her on study trips throughout Europe, America, Egypt, and the Sudan; she retired with Miss Moss in 1970 and lived with her in Wales and Surrey; she died in Ewell near Epsom, 5 July 1984.

PM VII, xxviii; *PM* II^2, xv; F. Madan, *The Madan Family*, 1933.

BURNEY, Sydney Bernard (1876-1951)
British dealer in antiquities and modern art; he was born in 1876; he served as a Captain in World War I, CBE 1918; he set up as an art dealer in London in the mid-1920s, specialising in ethnographic art, modern sculpture and ancient and oriental art; he was an early patron of Henry Moore and Barbara Hepworth, and his gallery exhibitions, such as *Sculpture Considered Apart from Time and Place*, 1932, stressed the aesthetic continuity between different traditions and cultures; he sold a colossal head of a New Kingdom pharaoh to the Barber Institute, Birmingham, and other Egyptian objects to the British Museum; he was president of the British Antique Dealers' Association, 1932-33; he died in London, 3 Jan. 1951.

Who Was Who 1951-1960, 161; *The Times*, 4 Jan. 1951; D. Coke, *The Modern Model Art Gallery* (Chichester, 1997), 4; J. Wood, 'Gods, graves and sculptors: *Gudea*, Sumerian sculpture and the avant-garde, *c*.1930-1935', *Sculpture Journal* 10 (2003), 67-82; T. Hardwick, 'The Iconography of the Blue Crown in the New Kingdom,' *JEA* 89 (2003), 126; inf. T. Hardwick.

BURRELL, (*Sir*) William (1861-1958)
British shipowner and collector; he was born in Glasgow, 9 July 1861, son of William B., shipowner and Isabella Duncan Guthrie; he entered the family business, Burrell and Son, which salvaged Cleopatra's Needle from the Bay of Biscay in 1877; he sold most of the fleet in 1917 and devoted himself to the collection of art and antiquities of which he amassed a large number, mainly in French paintings and medieval art; he was knighted in 1927 for services to art; in 1944 he gave his entire collection to the City of Glasgow together with funds to house them; he continued to add to this gift and acquired groups of Egyptian and other ancient material to round out the collection; the Burrell Collection was opened in 1983; he died in Hatton Castle, 29 March 1958.

ODNB 8, 1004-5; *DNB* 1951-60, 161-3 (W. Wells); *WWW* 5, 162; R. Marks, *Burrell: portrait of a collector*, 1983, 168; J. K. Thomson 'The Burrell Collection: Egyptian and Mesopotamian Antiquities', *Arts of Asia* 20/3 (May/June 1990), 108-115; F. Herrmann, *The English as Collectors: A documentary sourcebook*, 1999, 413-417.

BURTON, Harry (1879-1940)
British archaeologist and photographer; he was born at Stamford 13 Sept. 1879, son of William Burton, carpenter, and Anne Hufton; he became secretary and companion to the art historian Robert Cust in Florence where he began his career as a photographer; in 1910 he was engaged as an excavator by Theodore Davis (q.v.) at Thebes and later succeeded his principal excavator Harold Jones (q.v.) in 1911 until 1913-4; in 1914 he joined the Egyptian Expedition of the Metropolitan Museum of Art, New York as a photographer, a position that he held for the rest of his career apart from some war work in Egypt 1916-19; he made photographic records of the excavations and also many of the private and royal tombs at Thebes; from 1922-33 his services were lent to Lord Carnarvon (q.v.) and Howard Carter (q.v.), and he took all the very numerous photographs of the tomb of Tutankhamun and its contents; executor of Carter's estate in April 1940, he was taken ill while working at Luxor and died in the American Hospital at Asyut, 27 June 1940 and was buried in the American cemetery there; his legacy consisted of 7,500 excavation negatives, 1,400 Tutankhamun negatives, 3,345 Theban negatives and 600 negatives of monuments in Cairo and Italy, now kept in the Griffith Institute, University of Oxford.

BMMA Jan. 1916, 13; May 1916, 102; Aug. 1940, 165; *Chron. d'Eg.* 21(1946), 207; Newberry Corr.; inf. M. Hill; R. T. Ridley, *JEA* 99 (2013), 117-29.

BURTON, James (1788-1862)
British Egyptologist and traveller; he was born in London, 22 Sept. 1788, son of James Haliburton, who had changed his name by licence to Burton,and Elizabeth Westley; for a short period he worked in the office of Sir John Soane the architect, 1805; he was educated at Trinity College, Cambridge; BA, 1810; MA, 1815; from 1819 to 1822, accompanied by his secretary Charles Humphreys (q.v.), he travelled in Italy where he met Wilkinson (q.v.) and Lane (q.v.) and fell under the influence of Sir William Gell (q.v.); he obtained a position as a mineralogist with Muhammad Ali, arriving in Egypt with Humphreys, 8 April 1822; he then took part in the search for coal as part of the Geological Survey of Egypt during which he decided the position of Myos Hormos or Aphrodite and located the ancient source of porphyry (see BL Add. MS 25624); in 1824 he travelled with Wilkinson in the Eastern Desert; it was not until 1825, after leaving Egyptian Service, that he took a greater interest in the monuments of ancient Egypt and went up the Nile with Lane stopping for many months in the area of Luxor where he cleared sand from Medinet Habu, Karnak, and from several tombs in the Valley of the Kings; although more traveller and copyist he yet deserves the distinction of being one of the first Egyptologists; assisted by Lord Prudhoe (q.v.), Capt. Orlando Felix (q.v.), Bonomi (q.v.), and Humphreys, he published *Excerpta Hieroglyphica,* 64 plates without letter-press, 1825-8; after several years in Cairo, the Delta, and the Eastern Desert, he left Egypt at the end of 1834 with his slaves, servants, and a collection of live animals and returned to England via Italy and France arriving home on Christmas Day 1835; within a few years his family had virtually disowned him; in 1838, after a chance meeting with Thomas Chandler Haliburton,the author and son of a long lost uncle who had emigrated to North America, he resumed the name of Haliburton, and devoted much time to genealogical research into his own family to prove a relationship to Sir Walter Scott and to a share in his estate; while in Egypt, Burton and Humphreys made an immense number of valuable drawings and plans of monuments; a very large collection of these together with copies of inscriptions and explanatory notes, was presented to the British Museum, now British Library, after his death, by his younger brother the celebrated architect Decimus Burton; these are bound up in 63 volumes (Add. MSS 25613-75) and constitute a most important record, for like those of Hay (q.v.) and Wilkinson they contain details of many monuments since damaged or destroyed; they are also of a high order of artistic skill and accuracy in detail; although as yet unpublished a complete list of contents may be found in Hilmy who gives the range of subjects and material covered; in addition many of his drawings and maps are to be found in the Hay collection; the mummy and coffin which he sent to England are now in Liverpool Museum; the Trilingual Stone that he found in Cairo may now be in the Louvre; Burton also made a large collection of Egyptian antiquities which sold at Sotheby's, 25-7 July 1836, a catalogue being issued describing the 420 lots; many lots were bought by the British Museum, including the well-known Papyrus of Nebseni (EA 9900), the basis-text in Naville's *Todtenbuch*; Burton died in Edinburgh, 22 Feb. 1862, and was buried in West Dean Cemetery, Edinburgh, with the epitaph: 'a zealous investigator in Egypt of its language and antiquities'; he was survived by his Greek wife Andriana Garofalaki (*c.*1813-1883) who had been bought as a slave during his first years in Egypt.

ODNB 24, 572-3 (portr.); DNB 24, 43; Bonomi Diary; Sir A. H. Gardiner, *Egypt of the Pharaohs*, 15; Hay Diary; Hilmy, i, 108-11; *Proc. R. Geogr. Soc.* 4, 102; Lugt 14440; J. M. Baines, *Burton St. Leonards*, 1956; R. Davies, *The Letters of Thomas Chandler Haliburton*, 1988; N. Cooke, *James Haliburton-the Forgotten Egyptologist* (forthcoming); J. Thompson, *Sir Gardner Wilkinson and his Circle*, 1992; N. Cooke in P. and J. Starkey, *Travellers in Egypt*, 1998, 85-94; N. Cooke in P. and J. Starkey, *Unfolding the Orient*, 2001, 209-18; inf. Neil Cooke; N. Cooke, *ASTENE Bulletin* 57 (2013), 16-21.

BURZYŃSKI (*Revd*) **Adam Prosper** (1755-1830)
Polish member of the Order of the Reformati; he received a medical and philological education at Rome; as a missionary, he stayed in Egypt, 1795-1815, where he was known as an accomplished physician; during Napoleon's expedition to Egypt he co-operated with the French army as a chaplain, physician, translator and an expert on local conditions; he returned to Poland in 1815; from 1819 he served as Bishop of Sandomierz; he died 9 Sept. 1830.

Polski Słownik Biograficzny 3, 140-41 (M. Godlewski); inf. J. Śliwa.

BUTENEV, Ivan Petrovitch (1801-1836)
Russian naval captain, collector of Egyptian objects; he was born in the Tula governorate, 30 April 1801, son of Peter Semenovitch B. and Alexandra Spaferiev; in the navy from 1815, Lieutenant from 1826; he visited Egypt twice in 1832-3 and formed a collection including two Middle Kingdom stelae, an alabaster canopic jar of the Late Period, some bronze figurines and shabtis, and a mummy of a crocodile, some of which he obtained from Anastasi (q.v.); also in his collection was a well preserved hieratic papyrus from the time of the Twenty-First or Twenty-Second Dynasties, a Book of the Dead belonging to Amenmose, head of craftsmen in the temple of Amun, which, after some years in the Reval Provincial Museum, is housed in the St. Petersburg Branch of the Oriental Institute of the Russian Academy of Sciences (Inv. No. 11-1-1952); he sent some of his objects to Burchart (q.v.); he died in St. Petersburg, 5 March 1836.

Palestinskiy Sbornik 4 (67), 1959, 172-181 + 1 pl. (N. S. Petrovsky) S. Stadnikov, *Gött. Misz.* 135 (1993), 100; inf. J. Śliwa.

BUTLER, (*Very Revd*) **George** (1774-1853)
British schoolmaster, mathematical scholar, and antiquary; he was born in Pimlico, London, 5 July 1774, son of Weedon B. and Anne Giberne; after being educated at his father's school in Cheyne Walk, Chelsea, he took his degree at Sidney Sussex College, Cambridge; BA, 1794; MA 1797; DD, 1805; he became headmaster of Harrow School, 1805-29; while there he married Sarah Maria Gray, 1818; appointed Chancellor, 1836, and Dean, 1842, of Peterborough; a friend of Thomas Young under whom he studied hieroglyphs and interested some of his pupils at Harrow, among whom was (Sir) J. Gardner Wilkinson (q.v.); he died in Peterborough, 30 April 1853.

ODNB 9, 137; DNB 8, 49; Dawson MS 18, f. 132; Nichols, *Lit. Anecd.* ix, 223.

BUTLER, (*Rt. Revd*) **Samuel** (1774-1839)
British schoolmaster and Bishop; he was born in Kenilworth, 30 Jan. 1774, son of William B., draper, and Lucy Brosell; after his education at Rugby he entered St. John's College, Cambridge; BA, 1796; Fellow, 1797; DD, 1811; he was appointed headmaster of Shrewsbury School, 1798-1836; Bishop of Lichfield, 1836-9; he had a fine library and collection of Greek, Latin, Hebrew, and other oriental MSS; the printed books were sold in two parts 23 March and 1 June 1840, but the MSS were withdrawn and sold *en bloc* to the British Museum (now BL Add. MSS 11828-12117); among the MSS were four papyri acquired at the Salt sale of 1835, the best known of which is the Butler Papyrus, containing the beginning of the Story of the Eloquent Peasant (BM, EA 10274), the others being two Books of the Dead (EA9987, 9988), one Demotic document (EA 10230), plus five other papyri from other sources (EA 10333, 10400, 10367, 10271); Butler died in Eccleshall Castle, 4 Dec. 1849, and was buried in St. Mary's Church, Shrewsbury.

ODNB 9, 212-3; DNB 8, 76; S. de Ricci, *English Collectors of Books and Manuscripts*, 114.

BUTTLES, Janet or Jeanette Ridgeway (1856-1947)
American writer; she was born in Columbus. Ohio, 20 July 1856, daughter of Albert Barnes Buttles of Columbus, Ohio and Mary Elizabeth Ridgeway (she gives 1859 as her birth date in passport applications but was described as 3 in the 1860 census); she was a relative of Theodore Davis (q.v.) through his wife Annie Buttles and a niece of his mistress Emma Andrews; she visited Egypt with Davis many times between 1898 and 1912; she published *The Queens of Egypt*, 1908, illustrated with good photographs from the monuments and coloured plates by Howard Carter (q.v.), the introduction being written by Maspero (q.v.).; she died in Florence, 1947

Andrews Diary, passim; inf. J. Larson., J. Adams, T. Hardwick; V. E. McCormick, *Scioto Company Descendants*, Worthington, Ohio, 1995; D. Gordon, *The Robber Baron Archaeologist*, 2007, 22-3.

BUTZER, Karl Wilhelm (1934-2016)

German-American environmental archaeologist; he was born in Mülheim, Germany, 19 Aug. 1934, son of Paul Anton B., a machinist in a steel mill and Wilhelmine Hansen; his family emigrated to England in 1937 as Catholics opposed to Nazism; they were interned in 1939 and transferred to Montreasl, Canada in 1941; he was educated at McGill University, 1950-55; BSc In Mathematics, 1954; MSc in Meterology and Geography, 1955; he later studied at the University of Bonn; DSc in Physical History and Ancient History, 1957; Hon. Doctorate, University of Stirling, Scotland, 2011; he became a research assistant at the German Academy of Sciences and Literature, 1957-9; he was appointed Assistant Professor at the University of Wisconsin-Madison, 1959-62, later Associate Professor, 1963-66 and Professor of Anthropology and Geography at the University of Chicago, 1966-80 and then Henry Schultz Professor of Environmental Archaeology at the same university, 1980-84; he also served as Professor of Human Geography at the ETH (Swiss Federal Institute of Technology), 1980-81; he was appointed Dickson Centennial Professor of Libertal arts in the Dept. of Geography and the Environment at The University of Texas, Austin, 1984-2016; he was also Visiting Professor at the University of British Columbia, 1995; apart from work in other areas, he undertook fieldwork in Egypt and Nubia for his dissertation, 1956; an archaeological survey for the German Archaeological Institute, 1958; Quaternary studies and geoarchaeology for Yale University, 1962-3; and geoarchaeology for 'Lost City of the Pyramids', 2001-2; his published works included *Environment and Archaeology*, 1964; with C. Hansen, *Desert and River in Nubia*, 1968; *Early Hydraulic Civilization in Egypt*, 1976; *Archaeology as Human Ecology*, 1982; he died in Austin, Texas, 4 May 2016.

Journal of Historical Geography, internet ed. (K. Mathewson) (bibl.); *Wikipedia* Biography.

BYSTRZOŃOWSKI, Louis Tadeusz (1797-1878)

Polish soldier, active politician in exile, diplomat in Turkish service; he was born in Cracow, 24 Aug. 1797, son of Kazimierz B. and Anna Russocka; a participant in Polish (1830-31) and in Hungarian (1848-49) insurrections, he obtained the rank of a general; representing the circles of Polish émigrés living in France, he followed General Dembinski to Egypt in 1833 in order to negotiate with Muhammad Ali the possibility of employing Polish officers in the programme of reorganizing and instructing the Egyptian army, but on rejection of this went back to Paris in 1834; a wooden coffin of the Twenty-first or Twenty-second Dynasty with a mummy inside, purchased by him during his stay in Egypt was dispatched directly to Cracow as a gift to the Jagellonian University 17 May 1834; the coffin belongs now to the Department of Mediterranean Archaeology (Inv. No. 10.628); a planchette once attached to the mummy, not retrieved after an exhibition is still in the Archaeological Museum, Cracow (Inv. No. MAK/AS/2442); it was one of the earliest relics of this kind, if not the first one, in Polish collections; from 1857-72 Bystrzonowski was in Turkish service, as a military attaché in Paris, at that time known also as Arslan Pasha; he died in Paris, 27 Aug. 1878.

Polski Słownik Biograficzny 3, 174-7 (M. Handelsman); in *Mel. Michałowski,* Warsaw 1966, 89-95 (C. Gałczyńska); Niwinski in *BIFAO* 86, 1986, 257-66; inf. J. Sliwa.

CADALVÈNE, Edmond Pierre Marie de (1799-1852)
French traveller; he was born in Carcassonne, 24 Aug. 1799, son of Louis Marie C. and Pauline Jacquette Thoron; he was appointed director of the French postal service at Alexandria in 1829 and arrived in Jan. 1830; in the spring he embarked on a journey up the Nile as far as Gebel Barkal leaving a graffito at Soleb in April; he later visited Sinai; he held further posts in Smyrna and Constantinople; he published *L'Egypte et la Nubie*, 1836 and *Deux années de l'histoire d'Orient*, 1840; he died in Paris, 13 Dec.1852.

DBF 7, 784.

CADET, Jean Marcel (1751-1835)
French collector; he was born in Metz, 4 Sept. 1751, hence he is usually called Cadet de Metz, son of Toussaint C. and Françoise Pereau; he was Délégué Général and Inspector of Mines in Corsica; his name is attached to the Papyrus Cadet which he owned and published: *Copie figurée d'un Rouleau de Papyrus trouvé à Thèbes dans un Tombeau des Rois, accompagnée d'une notice descriptive*, Paris, 1805; an essay on this papyrus was published by Alexandre Lenoir (q.v.): it is not from a royal tomb, but is a Ptolemaic Book of the Dead - the first to be published and is now in the Bibliothèque Nationale (Cartons 1-19); he died in Strasbourg, 23 Oct. 1835.

DBF 7. 792.

CAILLIAUD, Frédéric (1787-1869)
French traveller and mineralogist; he was born in Nantes, 10 June 1787, son of Jean C. and Marie Rosalie Monnier; he studied mineralogy in Paris, 1809; after visiting Holland, Italy, Sicily, Greece, and Asia Minor, he left Constantinople for Egypt, arriving May 12, 1815; he visited Upper Egypt and Nubia as far as Wadi Halfa with Drovetti (q.v.) in Jan.-Aug. 1816; he was then employed by Muhammed Ali to find the emerald-mines described by the Arabic historians; in the course of this work, he explored Upper Egypt, the routes to the Red Sea, discovering quarries and the ruins in the Eastern Desert, 1816-7 and the Kharga Oasis, 1818; after returning to Paris, he revisited Egypt in 1819 and explored Siwa Oasis, and in 1821 ascended the Nile as far as Meroë; he returned to France in 1822 with a collection of more than 500 objects, and was awarded the Cross of the Légion d'honneur in 1824; he was appointed an assistant curator at the Museum of Natural History in Nantes, 1826; he published detailed accounts of his expeditions at the expense of the French Govt. and with the assistance of Jomard (q.v.), *Voyage à l'oasis de Thèbes et dans les déserts situés à l'occident de la Thébaïde fait pendant les années 1815, 1816, 1817 et 1818*, 2 vols., 1821-62; *Voyage à Méroé, au fleuve Blanc au delà de Fazoql, dans le midi du royaume de Sennar, à Syouah et dans cinq autres oasis fait dans les années 1819, 1820, 1821, 1822, et 1826*, 1826; a huge work in 4 vols. text and 3 folio vols. plates.; *Recherches sur les arts et métiers, les usages de la vie civile et domestique des anciens peuples de l'Égypte, de la Nubie et de l'Éthiopie, suivies de détails sur les moeurs des peuples modernes de ces contrées*, fol. 1831-7; *The Lost Manuscript of Frédéric Cailliaud*, ed. A. Bednarski, 2014; part of his collection, notably the papyri, was acquired by the Bibliothèque National in 1824; he left the rest of his collections to the Museum of Natural History and the Archaeological Museum in Nantes; some of his papers are in the Museum of Natural History; he died in Nantes, 1 May 1869.

DBF 7, 863-4; Athanasi, 28-9, 33, 105-7 (there called 'Calliot'); Belzoni, i, 173, 385; ii, 7, 20-33, and often; Budge, *Eg. Sudan*, i. 38-54; Carré, i, 225-8; Hilmy, i, 113; Irby, 5, 41; *Journal des Savants*, 1935, 176; M. Chauvet, *Frédéric Cailliaud*, 1988; È. Gran-Aymerich, *Dictionnaire biographique d'archéologie 1798-1945*, 2001, incorporated in *Les Chercheurs de passé 1798-1945*, 2007, 660; P. Mainterot, *Aux Origines de l'Égyptologie. Voyages et Collections de Frédéric Caillaud 1787-1869*, 2011; P. Mainterot in *The Lost Manuscript of Frédéric Cailliaud*, ed. A. Bednarski, 2014, 3-29; A. Bednarski in W. Carruthers (ed.), *Histories of Egyptology*, 2015, 80-95.

CAIRD, (*Sir*) James Key Bt. (1837-1916)
British industrialist and collector; he was born in Dundee, 7 Jan. 1837, son of Edward C. and Mary Key; he was educated at Dundee and London Universities; LLD St. Andrew's 1903; he was a successful jute manufacturer and was created a baronet 8 Feb. 1913; he formed a small collection of Egyptian antiquities which he left to the Dundee City Museum; he died at Belmont Castle, 9 March 1916.

Burke's *Peerage* 1915; *WWW* 2, 162; *ODNB* 9, 458-9; *JEA* 49 (1963), 39.

CALICE, (*Graf von*) Franz von Assisi Alfred Heinrich Josef (1875-1935)
Austrian Egyptologist and diplomat; he was born in Vienna, 20 Aug. 1875, son of Heinrich Joseph Aloys, 1st Graf von Calice, Austrian diplomat and Maria Louisa Castelain of Liverpool; D. Jur. Vienna; he held various diplomatic appointments and at the time of his retirement was Ambassador at Budapest; all his life Egyptology had been his

principal interest and in his retirement at Vienna he studied Egyptian philology; before he could complete his thesis, he was killed in a motor accident, but one large work was published the following year, *Grundlagen der ägyptisch-semitischen Wortvergleichung ....*, 1936; he also contributed articles, mainly grammatical, to *ZÄS* and *WZKM*; he died in Vienna, 1 Jan. 1935.

Inf. Dr. E. Komorzynski.

CALLENDER, Arthur Robert (1875-1936)
British architect and engineer; he was born at Mount Bridge, Skirbeck, near Boston, Lincs., 13 Dec. 1875, son of Robert C., engineer, and Matilda Pepper; he married in Alexandria 14Aug. 1901 Eliza Clara Reynolds; he was manager of the Egyptian branch railways from which he retired in about 1920, when he built a house at Armant; he was a personal friend of Howard Carter (q.v.) whom he assisted in the excavation of the tomb of Tutankhamun; Callender was responsible for the successful dismantling of the shrines and many other objects; he also helped Emery (q.v.) and Mond (q.v.) during their excavations in the work of reconstructing the tomb of Ramose; in 1924 he supervised the construction of the old Chicago House on the West Bank at Luxor and was involved in the negotiations with local landowners in subsequent years; he conducted excavations for the landowner Victor Adda (1885-1965) on his property in the Delta; he sold objects to the Metropolitan Museum of Art, New York and the Oriental Institute, Chicago; he died in Alexandria, 12 Dec. 1936.

Inf. Prof. W. B. Emery; Carter, *The Tomb of Tut.ankh.Amen*, i, 91, 92, 93, 101, 107, 130, 180; ii, 39, 51.

CALLENDER, John Bryan (1940-1987)
American Egyptologist; he was born at Port Arthur, Texas, 11 June 1940, son of William Bryan C. and Ellen Muriel Goldsmith; he was educated at the University of Texas obtaining his BA and at the Oriental Institute, University of Chicago, PhD 1970; he specialized in the study of the Egyptian and Coptic language; in 1968 he took up a teaching appointment at the University of California, Los Angeles, professor of Egyptian and Coptic, 1985; in 1986 he began a two-year period as Study Center Director at the American University in Cairo but was obliged to cut short his stay due to ill health; his chief publications were *Middle Egyptian*, 1975 and *Studies in the Nominal Sentence in Egyptian and Coptic*, 1984; he died at Van Nuys, Calif., 20 Sept. 1987.

NARCE 138 (1987), 32 (A. Loprieno); *BSFE* 111 (1988), 5-6 (L. Pala); *Varia Aegyptiaca* 3 (1987), 187; California Vital Statistics.

CALLOT, (*Freiherr von*) **Eduard Ferdinand** (1793-1862)
Austrian army officer and traveller; he was born 1 Jan. 1793, son of Johann v. C. and Marie Magdalene Wagmuth; he served in the Napoleonic wars, 1809-15, and afterwards visited Egypt, 1831; he travelled as far south as Khartoum, visiting Meroë and other sites en route; discovered the remains of a Coptic church on the island of Tuki; he explored the Blue Nile and returned to Egypt by way of the Red Sea; an account of his travels *Der Orient und Europa* was published in Leipzig in 1855; he died at Vienna, 1 May 1862.

Hill, 94; *Gött. Misz.* 83 (1984), 137-9; M. Zach, *Die Österreicher im Sudan von 1820 bis 1914* Vienna, 1984, 13 ff.

CALVERLEY, Amice Mary (1896-1959)
British artist and musician; she was born at Chelsea, London, 9 April 1896, daughter of Edmond Leveson Calverley and Sybil Salvin; after being brought up in Canada she studied music; in 1922 she gained a scholarship to the Royal College of Music; in 1926 while in Oxford she was encouraged to take up archaeological drawing by Sir Leonard Woolley (q.v.); her association with the EES began in 1927 and in 1928, under the direction of Gardiner (q.v.) she began the work of copying the scenes in the temple of Sety I at Abydos; she produced for the EES and the Oriental Institute, Chicago, a set of four magnificent folio volumes with many colour plates, 1933-59; she died in Toronto, 10 April 1959.

JEA 45 (1959), 85-7 (portr.) (A. H. Gardiner and J. Leveson Gower); Royal Ontario Museum, *The Amice Calverley Memorial Exhibition* (Toronto, 1960)

CALVERT, Henry Hunter (1817-1882)
British diplomat; he was born at Valletta, Malta 26 Oct. 1817, son of James C. and Louisa Anne Campbell; he first served in the navy and then joined the consular service holding posts at Erzerum,Trebizond, Constantinople, Bulgaria, and Wallachia; Vice-Consul at Alexandria, 1856-82; he was a member of the Inst. Égyptien; he donated some objects to the British Museum in 1870; he was a brother of Frank C., the first excavator of Troy; he died at the Dardanelles, 29 July 1882.

Lord Cromer, *Modern Egypt*, i, 142; *BIÉ* 2nd Ser. iii, 77 (1882).

CALVET, Esprit Claude Joseph (1728-1810)
French collector; he was born at Avignon 24 Nov. 1728, son of Claude Joseph C. and Marguerite d'Hughes; he was educated by the Jesuits and then studied medicine at Avignon graduating in 1749; he early showed a keen interest in antiquities and in Paris in 1751-2 he frequented antiquarians such as Barthélemy (q.v.) and sale-rooms; he settled in Avignon as a doctor in 1753, occupied the chair of medicine at the University 1756-72, and was later doctor at various hospitals; he avidly collected Egyptian and other antiquities corresponding and exchanging objects with Caylus (q.v.); he was briefly arrested and his collection pillaged during the French Revolution; on his death he left his library and collection to the city of Avignon, thus founding the Musée Calvet; he died at Avignon, 25 July 1810.

H. Labande, *E. Calvet,* 1892; *DBF* 7, 931-2 (R. d'Amat); M.-P. Foissy-Aufrère, *Égypte et Provence*, 1985, 235-54; M.-P. Foissy-Aufrère in A.-F. Laurens and K. Pomian, *L'Anticomanie*, 1988, 135-44; È. Gran-Aymerich, *Dictionnaire biographique d'archéologie 1798-1945*, 2001, incorporated in *Les Chercheurs de passé 1798-1945*, 2007, 662-3.

CAMINOS, Ricardo Augusto (1915-1992)
Argentinian-American Egyptologist; he was born in Buenos Aires, 11 July 1915, son of Carlos Norberto C., a lawyer, and Maria Etelvina Crottogini; he was educated at the Instituto Nacional del Profesorado Secundario and the University of Buenos Aires; BA, 1932; MA, 1938; he worked briefly for the Railway Pension Fund but decided to pursue a career in Egyptology in which he was largely self-taught; he then studied at the Oriental Institute Chicago, research assistant 1 March 1944-30 June 1944, research fellow 17 Oct. 1946-30 June 1947; PhD, 1947; and at The Queen's College, Oxford with Gunn (q.v.), 1945-6; he was a member of the Epigraphic Survey of the Oriental Institute Chicago at Luxor, 1 Aug. 1947- 30 June 1950; he then returned to Oxford to work with Sir Alan Gardiner (q.v.); DPhil, 1952; he was appointed Assistant Professor at Brown University, Providence, Rhode Island, 1952, Associate Professor, 1957, Professor, 1964, and Wilbour Professor, 1972-9; Visiting Professor at the University of Leningrad and the USSR Academy of Sciences, Moscow, 1973-4; his chosen fields of specialization were hieratic palaeography and epigraphy; he undertook the copying of the texts and scenes at Gebel es-Silsila in 1955 and 1959-60, but his work was interrupted by the needs of the Nubian Rescue campaign; he worked at Qasr Ibrim, Buhen, and Semna-Kumma 1960-65; he returned to Gebel es-Silsila, 1975-6, 1978-82 and then copied the inscriptions at Wadi el-Shatt el-Rigal, 1983, all on behalf of the Egypt Exploration Society in London where he settled on his retirement; apart from articles and reviews, he published *Late-Egyptian Miscellanies*, 1954; *Literary Fragments in the Hieratic Script*, 1956; *The Chronicle of Prince Osorkon*, 1958; *Gebel es-Silsilah* I. *The Shrines,* 1963 with T.G.H. James; *The Shrines and Rock-Inscriptions of Ibrim*, 1968; *The New Kingdom Temples of Buhen,* 1974; and with H.G. Fischer, *Ancient Egyptian Epigraphy and Palaeography,* 1976; *A Tale of Woe,* 1977; his work at Semna-Kumma was in press at his death and his copies of Gebel es-Silsilah and Wadi el-Shatt el-Rigal were being prepared for publication; he died in London, 26 May 1992 and his ashes were buried in Holywell cemetery, Oxford; his house was purchased by the Egypt Exploration Society and now houses the Ricardo A. Caminos Memorial Library.

The Independent 30 May 1992 (A.F. Shore); *The Times* 1 June 1992 (T.G.H. James); *The Guardian* 15 June 1992 (Mark Smith); *JEA* 78 (1992), x; 79 (1993), 226-35 (T.G.H. James) (portr.); *ZÄS* 121 (1994), III-V (J. Osing).

CAMPBELL, (*Sir*) **Archibald Campbell (afterwards 1st Baron Blythswood)** (1835-1908)
British army officer and astronomer; he was born in Florence, 22 Feb. 1835, son of Archibald C. formerly Douglas and Caroline Agnes Dick; he entered the army and attained the rank of Colonel, Scots Guards; he served in the Crimea and was wounded; created Baronet, 1880; Baron Blythswood, 1892; FRS; FRAS; LLD; MP, 1873-4, 1885-92; he was very interested in political and military questions, but was also a physicist and astronomer; he visited Egypt in 1869-70 and 1874 in order to observe the transit of Venus and recorded his results in the *Monthly Notes* of the RAS; while in Egypt he bought the funerary papyrus of Pinodjem II, from the royal cache, for £400; this fine papyrus was presented to the British Museum in 1960 (EA 10793); Campbell died at his seat at Blythswood, in Renfrewshire, 8 July 1908.

WWW i, 72; *ODNB* 9, 739-40 (portr.); Chabas, 147; Maspero, *Momies Royales*, 512.

CAMPBELL, (*Revd*) **Colin** (1848-1931)
British minister and collector; he was born in Campbelltown, Argyllshire, 1848, son of Archibald C. and Ann Maclean; he studied at the University of Glasgow; MA; DD; he married 1. Penelope Anne Mackay, 1879, (d.1910); 2. Jessie Taylor; Campbell was minister of Dundee from 1882, and chaplain to Queen Victoria; he visited Egypt

several times, and also formed a collection of Egyptian antiquities, including many cones and ostraca, which are now in the Hunterian Museum, Glasgow, the Royal Museum of Scotland, Edinburgh, the Oriental Museum, Durham and the Dundee Museum; he published works on the Gospels and also translated Naville's lectures on Egyptian religion; he also wrote a number of semi-popular books on Theban tombs and related subjects, *Sennofer's Tomb at Thebes*, 1908; *Two Theban Queens, Nefert-Ari and Ty-ti and their tombs*, 1909; *Sarcophagus of Pa-ba-sa (c. 650 B.C.) in Hamilton Palace, Scotland*, 1909, (this coffin, once belonging to the Duke of Hamilton, being now in the Kelvingrove Museum, Glasgow); *Two Theban Princes, Kha-em-Uast and Amen-khepeshf* etc., 1910; *The Miraculous Birth of King Amon-hotep III and other Egyptian Studies*, 1912; he died at Lorachan, Callander, 20 June 1931.

WWW iii, 212-13.

CAMPBELL, Patrick (1779-1857)

British army officer and diplomat; he was born in Duntroon, 17 Dec. 1779, son of Neil C. and Jean Campbell; he entered the Army and attained the rank of Lieut.-Col., Royal Artillery, 1815; appointed Secretary to the British Legation in Colombia, 1825-30; Consul-General in Egypt in succession to John Barker (q.v.), 1833; he retired in 1840; he was associated with Col. Howard Vyse (q.v.) in the exploration of the Pyramids, 1837; his name is attached to Campbell's tomb, a large hypogeum of Dyn. 26 at Giza, discovered by Howard-Vyse (q.v.), and with one of the construction-chambers of the Great Pyramid; he died at Southampton, 29 Aug. 1857.

FO Records; Lindsay, 22, 23, 39; Vyse, passim; *The Genealogist* 28 (1912), 32-3.

CAPART, Jean (1877-1947)

Belgian Egyptologist; he was born at Brussels, 21 Feb. 1877, son of Alphonse C. and Alida Carbonelle; he was educated at the University of Brussels; he later studied Egyptology under Wiedemann (q.v.) at Bonn; he was appointed assistant Conservator in the Egyptian collections at the Musées Royaux du Cinquantenaire, Brussels, 1900, became Chief Conservator, 1925 and Director; under his regime the organisation of the museum was greatly improved and many important acquisitions made; he visited Egypt frequently and conducted excavations at Elkab, 1927-9, 1945, publishing reports in *ASAE*; in addition to his scientific works he contributed freely to the popular press and gave many public lectures which did much to stimulate and arouse interest in Egyptology not only in Belgium, but in many other countries he visited, notably England and USA; his speciality was Egyptian art on which subject he wrote many important books; in 1923 he conducted the Queen of the Belgians on a visit to Egypt and visited the Tomb of Tutankhamun while excavations were in progress, this so stimulated her interest that the Fondation Égyptologique Reine Élisabeth was established under his direction, 1923; with its fine library it has since become an important centre of research, and under its auspices many important publications have appeared including the journal, *Chronique d'Égypte,* which Capart managed to continue to publish even during the German occupation of Belgium; he also established *Bibl. Aegyptiaca*, 1932, and was in addition Professor at the University of Liège until 1929 and a Vice-Pres. of the EES whose Bibl. in *JEA* he edited for a time in the 1930s; from 1932 he was part-time Honorary Curator of Egyptology in The Brooklyn Museum, and from 1938 until his death Honorary Advisory Curator; his principal works were, *Recueil de monuments égyptiens*, 4⁰, 2 pts. 1902-5; *Les Débuts de l'art en Égypte*, 1904; *Primitive Art in Egypt*, trans. by A. S. Griffith, 1905; *Musées roy. du Cinq., Les Antiquités Ég. guide descriptif*, 1905; *Bulletin critique des religions de l'Égypte*, 1905-1913; *Une Rue de tombeaux à Saqqarah*, 2 vols., 4⁰, 1907; *L'art égyptien*, 2 vols. 1909-1911; *Donation d'antiquités égyptiennes aux Musées roy. de Bruxelles*, 1911; *Abydos: le temple de Séti Iᵉʳ, étude générale*, 1912; *Les Monuments dits Hycsos*, 1914; *Un Roman vécu il y a 25 siècles: histoire des relations d'une famille sacerdotale ég. avec les prêtres du Temple de Teuzoi ... par Pétéisis fils d'Essemteu*, 1914, *Leçons sur l'art égyptien*, 1920;*Lectures on Egyptian Art*, 1923; *L'Art égyptien: études et histoire*, 3 vols. 1924-48; *Egyptian Art: Introductory Studies*, trans. W. R. Dawson, 1923; *The Tomb of Tutankhamen* trans. W. R. Dawson, 1923; *Thebes: the glory of a great past*, with M. Werbrouck 4⁰, 1926; *L'Art égyptien. 1. L'Architecture*, 1922; *Documents pour servir à l'étude de l'art égyptien*, 2 vols. 1927-32; *Memphis à l'ombre des pyramides*, with M. Werbrouck 4⁰, 1930; *Propos sur l'art égyptienne*, 1931; *Makit: une histoire de souris au temps des Pharaons*, 1936; *La Beauté égyptienne - anthologie*, 1942; *Tout-ankh-amoun*, with others, 1943; *Le Message de la vieille Égypte*, 1944; *Fouilles en Égypte. El Kab*, 1946; *Pour faire aimer l'art égyptien*, 1949; he also edited the Wilbour letters 1936; he died in Brussels, 16 June 1947.

AfO 14 (1945-51) 188, (A. Scharff); *Aegyptus*, 26 (1946), 211; *Brief Guide to the Department of Ancient Art, Brooklyn Museum* (1970), 4 f.; *Chron. d'Ég.* 44 (1947), 181-90 (portr.) (B. van de Walle), 190-2 (P. Gilbert), 192-6 (M. Werbrouck), 196-8 (M. Honbert), 198-9 (J. Vergote), 199-202 (E. Bille-de-Mot), 202-6 (A. Mekhitarian), 206-9 (C. Préaux), 209-10 (E. de Keyser), 211 (J. M. Taupin), 212-15 (M. Paul); *JEA* 37 (1947), 2; *Rev. belge de philologie et d'histoire* 25 (1946-7); *BMRAH* 4e serie 19 (1947) 101-4 (Lavachery); *Liber memorialis de l'Université de Liège 1330-1966,* II, 39-57 (van de Walle); A. M. and A. Brasseur-Capart, *J. Capart* Brussels, 1974; È. Gran-Aymerich,

Dictionnaire biographique d'archéologie 1798-1945, 2001, incorporated in *Les Chercheurs de passé 1798-1945*, 2007, 667; Jean-Michel Bruffaerts, 'Jean Capart', in *Femmes d'Europe. Bulletin de l'Association Femmes d'Europe*, 1999; Jean-Michel Bruffaerts, 'Destins égyptologiques croisés: Alexandre Moret et Jean Capart', in M.-C. Bruwier (dir.), *Livres et archives de l'égyptologue Alexandre Moret (1868-1938) à Mariemont*. Catalogue de l'exposition organisée au Musée royal de Mariemont du 24 mars au 2 juin 2000, 2000, 11-17; Jean-Michel Bruffaerts, 'Un mastaba égyptien pour Bruxelles', *Bulletin des Musées Royaux d'Art et d'Histoire (Bruxelles)*, 76 (2005), 5-36; Jean-Michel Bruffaerts, 'Les coulisses d'un voyage royal. Le roi Albert et la reine Elisabeth en Egypte avec Jean Capart (1930)', *Museum Dynasticum*, XVIII (2006), 28-49; Jean-Michel Bruffaerts, 'Capart-Warocqué : une amitié manquée', in C. Derriks et L. Delvaux (éds.), *Antiquités égyptiennes au Musée royal de Mariemont, Morlanwelz, Musée royal de Mariemont*, 2009, 39-48 ; Jean-Michel Bruffaerts, 'Les fouilles archéologiques belges à Héliopolis. La campagne de 1907 (Jean Capart)', in A. Van Loo et M.-C. Bruwier (éd.), *Héliopolis*, 2010, 35-38.

CAPPELLARI, Bartolomeo Alberto (Pope Gregory XVI) (1765-1846)
Italian Pope; he was born at Belluno, 18 Sept. 1765, son of Giovanni Battista C. and Giulia Cesa-Pagani; he was elected 2 Feb. 1831, and took an interest in art and archaeology, improving the collections acquired by the Papacy; he founded the Egyptian Museum in the Vatican galleries in 1839, which was arranged by Ungarelli (q.v.); he died in Rome, 1 June 1846.

EB 10, 911-12; L. R. Muirhead, *Rome and Central Italy*, Blue Guides 1956, 287-8.

CAPPER, James (1743-1825)
British meteorologist and traveller; he was born in London, 15 Dec. 1743, son of Francis C. and Mary Bennett; he became a Colonel in the Honourable East India Company Service, and made a journey from Egypt to India, 1779, he published an account of this, *Observations on the Passage to India through Egypt* etc., 1784, which was trans. into French and German; he died in Ditchingham Lodge, Norfolk, 6 Sept. 1825.

ODNB 10, 2-3; *DNB* 9, 25; Hilmy, i, 119; Valentia, iii, 275; J. Starkey in N. Cooke and V. Daubney, *Lost and Now Found*, 2017, 127-40.

CARAMAN, (*Comte de*) Adolphe Marie Joseph Frédéric Victor de Riquet (1800-1876)
French traveller; he was born in Berlin, 8 Sept. 1800, son of Victor Louis Charles 1st Duc de Caraman and Josephine Leopoldine Ghislaine de Mérode; he visited Italy, the Ionian Islands, Asia Minor, Turkey, and Greece, 1828-9, and later Egypt and Nubia, as far as Abu Simbel, 1832-3; he was again in Syria and Palestine, 1837-8; the MS journals of these travels are in the British Library (Add. MSS 34197-9), 34198 being devoted to Egypt and Nubia; it contains a number of plans of temples, etc., e.g. Kom Ombo (f. 41), Elkab (f. 44), and the Palace at Karnak (f. 49); he died in Paris, 6 Feb. 1876.

Bull. Soc. Géogr. Paris, Ser. 2, 13. 321; 15. 5; *Cat. Add. MSS B. M.*, 1888-93, 233; *DBF* 7, 1100.

CARDOSO, Ciro Flamarion (1942-2013)
Brazilian historian; he was born at Goiânia, 20 Aug. 1942; he studied history at the Rio de Janeiro Federal University; PhD, 1965; he also attended Université de Paris-Nanterre, 1971 and took courses on Egyptology from Desroches-Noblecourt (q.v.); he became a professor at Fluminense Federal University, 1980 where he taught history and Egyptology; he wrote numerous books and article, notably *Historia da Antiguidade*, 1967; *O Egito Antigo*, 1982; *Sociedades de Antigo Oriente Proximo*, 1985; *Antiguidade oriental: politica e religiao*, 1990; and *Deuses, mumias e ziggurats*, 1999; he died at Niteroi, 29 June 2013.

Inf. Dr Moacir Santos; Wikipedia entry.

CARMICHAEL, (*Sir*) Thomas David Gibson (afterwards 1st Baron Carmichael) (1859-1926)
British politician and collector; he was born in Edinburgh, 18 March 1859, son of William Henry C. 13th Bt. and Eleanora Anne Anderson; he succeeded as 14th Bart., 1891; educated St. John's College, Cambridge; MA; DL; KCMG; created Baron Carmichael of Skirling, 1912; he formed a collection of antiquities sold at Sotheby's, 8-10 June 1926, Eg. ant. lots 179-294, many of which came from the Hilton Price (q.v.) Collection; he died in London, 16 Jan. 1926.

WWW ii, 174; Newberry Corr.; *ODNB* 10, 179-80 (portr.).

CARNARVON, Earl of see HERBERT

CARNE, (*Revd*) John (1789-1844)
British traveller and author; he was prob. born in Truro, 18 June 1789, son of William C., banker and businessman, and Anne Cock; after studying at Queens' College, Cambridge, he was ordained 1826; he visited Greece, Turkey, Egypt, and Palestine in 1821, and was captured by Bedouin on returning from St. Catherine's monastery Mount

Sinai, but was released after a few days and returned safely; he married Ellen Lane, 1824; Carne published two works on his eastern travels, *Letters from the East*, 2 vols. 1826; *Recollections of Travels in the East*, 2 vols. 1830; he died in Penzance, 19 April 1844.

ODNB 10, 187; *DNB* 9, 135-6; Hilmy, i. 120.

CARTARI, Vincenzo (*c*.1531-1569)
Italian humanist; he was born in Reggio Emilia *c*.1531, son of Cesare C.; he served as a courtier in the ducal court at Ferrara; he wrote several works including a translation of Ovid and *Le Immagini colla sposizione degli Dei degli Antiche*, 1556, a manual of mythology which for the first time featured Egyptian deities; he possibly died 10 Sept. 1569.

DBDI 20, 793-6.

CARTER, Howard (1874-1939)
British Egyptologist, and artist; he was born in Kensington, London, 9 May 1874, son of Samuel John C. artist, and Martha Joyce Sands; owing to delicate health Carter was educated privately and later taught to draw and paint by his father who was an animal painter; on the recommendation of Lady Amherst, he joined the staff of the Arch. Survey under P. E. Newberry in 1891 when he was seventeen, and thus began his career in Egyptology; he was trained under Petrie (q.v.), Griffith (q.v.), Naville (q.v.); after some preliminary training for the EEF in England, he did drawings for the Survey at Beni Hasan and El Bersheh, 1892-3; in 1892 Carter joined Petrie (q.v.) in excavating at Amarna where he worked for Lord Amherst (q.v.) under Petrie's supervision; he was then made draughtsman to the Deir el-Bahri expedition under Naville where he worked for six years, 1893-9, his pencil drawings being reproduced in collotype in the six published vols.; this gigantic task, undertaken with the help of other artists, involved the copying of all the scenes and inscriptions then visible on the temple for the folios, and showed him to be the equal of the greatest copyists; in 1899 he was appointed Chief Inspector of Antiquities of Upper Egypt in the Antiquities Service of the Egyptian Government, and he reorganized the antiquities administration for Upper Egypt under Sir William Garstin and Maspero (q.v.); in this capacity he installed electric light for the first time in the Tombs of the Kings and at Abu Simbel; from 1902 he supervised the excavations of Theodore Davis (q.v.) in the Valley of Kings; in 1904 Carter was given the inspectorate of Lower Egypt; he was at Saqqara in Jan. 1905 when a dispute with some French tourists led to his transfer to new headquarters at Tanta; his dissatisfaction with his treatment in this matter led to his resignation from the Service in Nov. 1905; he spent the next four years as a water-colour painter and guide, returning to work in the Theban necropolis for Lord Carnarvon (q.v.), 1909; in all at different times he discovered no less than six royal tombs, including his most famous find, that of Tutankhamun; the first in chronological order was the dummy tomb of Neb-hepet-re Mentuhotep, Queen Hatshepsut's later tomb, the tomb of Thutmose IV, a tomb identified as that of Amenhotep I, and that of Hatshepsut when consort, and the valley temple of Hatshepsut; after the war Carter spent the winters from 1917 to 1922 searching the Valley of Kings but found little until the dramatic discovery of Tutankhamun in Nov. 1922, the greatest archaeological discovery ever made in Egypt; the clearance of the tomb, the packing and removal of its contents to Cairo Museum, took Carter and a staff of experts a full ten years to complete, the extensive records, a body of material, much of which yet remains unpublished, and together with Carter's diaries and papers is preserved in the Griffith Institute, Oxford, to which they were given by his niece Miss Phyllis Walker; Carter was unable to bring out a definitive report on his discovery and only published a popular but detailed account of it; during his last years he suffered much ill-health, and did no further archaeological work; he published a number of articles in journals, particularly *ASAE* and the following books; *The Tomb of Thoutmôsis IV*, with Newberry, 1904; *The Tomb of Hâtshopsîtû*, with Theodore M. Davis and others, 1906; *The Tomb of Iouiya and Touiyou*, with Maspero and Newberry, 1906; *Five Years' Explorations at Thebes; a record of work done, 1907-1911 ...*, with Lord Carnarvon, 1912; *The Tomb of Tut.ankh.Amen*, 3 vols., with A. C. Mace, 1923-33, and his privately circulated statement *Tut.ankh. amen. The Politics of Discovery*, 1998; Carter died in Kensington, London, 2 March 1939 and was buried in Putney Vale cemetery, London.

General Register Office Records; *WWW* iii, 228; *ODNB* 10, 352-3 (portr.); *DNB* 1931-40, 151 (P. Newberry); Newberry Corr.; *ASAE* 39 (1939), 49-53 (G. Brunton) (portr.); *Chron. d'Ég.* 14 (1939), 323-4 (J. Capart); *JEA* 25 (1939), 67-9 (P. E. Newberry); *Rev. arch.* 13 (1939), 260 (C. Picard); H.V.F. Winstone, *Howard Carter and the Discovery of the Tomb of Tutankhamun*, 1991; T.G.H. James, *Howard Carter. The Path to Tutankhamun*, 1992; N. Reeves and J.H. Taylor, *Howard Carter before Tutankhamun*, 1992; *KMT* 14/4 (2003), 80-83; È. Gran-Aymerich, *Dictionnaire biographique d'archéologie 1798-1945*, 2001, incorporated in *Les Chercheurs de passé 1798-1945*, 2007, 674; D. Forbes in *KMT* 22/1, 54-68.

CARTER, Owen Browne (1803-1859)
British architect; he was born in London and baptized 9 June 1806, son of James C. and his wife Elizabeth; he practised at Winchester; he visited Egypt 1829-1, when he was employed by Robert Hay (q.v.) to make drawings, plans, and sections of Egyptian temples; he worked up several of his own and Hay's drawings for Hay's *Illustrations of Cairo,*1840, but was prevented from taking a larger part in the publication by the opinions of Hay's other collaborators; he published a small number of articles on the architecture of Wiltshire and Hampshire churches, 1844-5; he also exhibited architectural drawings in the Royal Academy, 1847-9; he was secretary of the Wiltshire Archaeological Institute; he died in Salisbury, 25 March 1859.

ODNB 10, 364-5; *DNB* 9, 205; Bonomi Diary, 17 Aug. 1831; inf. S. Tillett.

CASSAS, Louis François (1756-1827)
French artist; he was born at Azay-le-Ferron, 27 Dec. 1756; he was trained as an artist in Tours and Paris; he visited Rome, 1779-83; he joined the suite of Choiseul-Gouffier (q.v.), the French ambassador in Constantinople, in 1784 and travelled through Syria, Palestine, and Egypt in 1785; he left Constantinople in late 1786, possibly stopping in Greece and was back in Italy in Feb. 1787; he returned to Paris in 1791 but was unable to publish a proposed volume of his travels; in 1806 he opened an architectural musuem; in 1816 he was named to a post in the Gobelins Factory; Chevalier de la Légion d'honneur, 1825; he died at Versailles, 2 Nov. 1827; his drawings were sold in 1878; many are preserved in the Musée des Beaux-Arts, Tours and the Wallraf-Richartz-Museum, Cologne.

DBF 7, 1320; A. Gilet and U. Westfehling, *Louis-François Cassas*, 1994; È. Gran-Aymerich, *Dictionnaire biographique d'archéologie 1798-1945*, 2001, incorporated in *Les Chercheurs de passé 1798-1945*, 2007, 676-7; *ASTENE Bulletin* 65 (2015), 23.

CASSIRER, Manfred (1920-2003)
German-British Egyptologist, dealer in antiquities, and parapsychologist; he was born in Berlin, 12 July 1920, son of Erich C., a Jewish dealer in Oriental and ancient art, and Erika Michael; he and his father left Germany for Britain in 1937, being interned as enemy aliens for part of the Second World War; he obtained a BA in Theology and an MLitt in Hebrew and Egyptology at St Peter's Hall Oxford, 1942-51; he inherited his father's London gallery after his death in 1963; in the 1950s he published a number of articles on Egyptian objects and topics; he sold and donated objects to the British Museum and the Ashmolean Museum; he later became interested in parapsychology, publishing on the topic and serving on the committee of the Society of Psychical Research; he died in London, Dec. 18-19 2003.

B. Falk, *Caught in a snare: Hitler's refugee academics*, 1933-1949, 1988, 73; *Journal of the Society of Psychical Research* 68/3 (July 2004), 188-192; inf. T. Hardwick

CASTELLARI, Andrea (1798-1847)
Italian dealer in antiquities; he was born in Bologna, 1798, son of Antonio C. and Francesca Fato; he was resident in England from 1837 where he married in London, 30 May 1840 Emily Foreman (born Briston, Surrey, 17 Aug. 1819; died London, 29 Dec. 1878), his children being born between 1837 and 1841; he was a well-known figure in Luxor, 1845-9, where he dwelt in a hut on the roof of the temple; he had great power over the local diggers, many of whose finds he appropriated and sold to tourists; many important objects passed through his hands, including the Hypereides Papyri which he sold to A. C. Harris (q.v.) and Jospeh Arden (q.v.) and the coffin of Princess Ahmose-Henutempet; he died in Cairo, 1847.

JEA 35 (1949), 162-3; *LD Text*, i, 222; Romer, i, 148, 280; Internet genealogy; A*STENE Bulletin* 30 (2006-7); F. Hagen and K. Ryholt, *The Antiquities Trade in Egypt 1880-1930*, 2017, 206.

CASTIGLIONI, Alfredo (1937-2016)
Italian explorer and anthropologist; he was born in Milan, 18 March 1937; he was educated at the Caholic University of the Scared Heart, Milan; together with his twin brother Angelo, they undertook ethnological research in North and West Africa, 1959-69; they discovered prehistoric graffiti in the Libyan desert at Berguig, 1982; they undertook research at the emerald mines at Jebel Sikeit and Jebel Zabareth, 1985 and identified the site of Berenice Panchrysos, 1989; prehistoric tombs were discovered at Wadi Elei, 1993; further exploration took place in the Nubian and Libyan desert, 1989-94 and the Eastern desert in Egypt, 1997 when bodies that were discovered were alleged to be the remains of the army of Cambyses; the Nubian desert was explored in 2001 when hieroglyphic inscriptions were discovered and from 2004-8 when they worked with Charles Bonnet on Kerma culture, 2005-6 and discovered prehistoric graffiti, 2007 and a gold mine, 2008; they later involved in work in Eritrea from 2011; apart from works on African ethnology, they published *L'Eldorado dei Faraoni*, 1995; *La Città Fantasma*, 2002; *Nubia. Magica terra millenaria*, 2006; Alfredo C. died at Gallerate, 15 Feb. 2016.

Internet biography; *Sudan and Nubia* 20 (2016), 180 (A. Roccati).

CASTIGLIONI, Francesco (*fl.*1811-30)
Italian collector; he was born in Milan and served in the Austrian army; he lived for many years in Cairo and Alexandria; his Egyptian collection of 1,200 objects was acquired by the Russian Acad. of Sciences in 1825, apart from 246 scarabs bought separately by Czar Alexander I; through the intervention of Golenischeff (q.v.), the collection was transferred to the Hermitage Museum, Saint Petersburg in 1862; he was in Leghorn from 1827 where he acted as the agent in the sale of the Anastasi (q.v.) collection to Leiden in 1828 including making the drawings for the sale catalogue; he also became an independent dealer seling the Horemheb reliefs to Leiden in 1830; ; he met Rossellini (q.v.) who came to view his collection; he sold a papyrus and other objects to the museum in Parma in 1830 and 1832; he moved back to Milan in 1835; he has been wrongly identified with Carlo Ottavio Castiglioni (1785-1849), a numismatist and expert in Arabic coinage from the same Milan family who is not known to have gone to Egypt.

Golenischeff, *Coll. Ég. Erm.* p. v.; inf. Dr. V. Kalpakcian.

CATHERWOOD, Frederic (1799-1854)
British artist and traveller; he was born London, 27 Feb. 1799, son of John James C., Receiver of General Corn Returns and Accountant General of Excise, and Anne his wife; he trained as an artist in London and in Rome where he met Bonomi (q.v.), Parke (q.v.), and Scoles (q.v.), 1822; he visited Egypt with Parke, Scoles,and Henry Westcar (q.v.), 1823-4; he was introduced by Bonomi to Robert Hay (q.v.) on his return; he later joined Hay's party at Qurna in Sept. 1832 and went to the Kharga Oasis with Hay and Hoskins (q.v.), 1832-3; he remained with Hay until early 1833, making a complete survey and excavation of the Colossi of Memnon and a large-scale plan of all the sites of Thebes; he later visited Syria and Palestine with Bonomi, 1833-4; he made many drawings and notes, some which are in the Hay MSS, and also drawings of the Temple of Karnak from which a panorama was painted for Burford's circular viewing room in Leicester Square, London in 1833; Burford (q.v.) published a description of the site to accompany the exhibition, but Catherwood quarrelled with Hay over plans to issue a smaller version for sale to visitors; he took the panorama to the United States, and while there became involved in railway engineering projects; these took him to Central America which he explored with John L. Stephens (q.v.); he made illustrations of Central American antiquities and published two volumes of these; his library was sold at Puttick and Simpson's, 1 Dec. 1856; he died in the sinking of SS *Arctic* off Cape Race, Newfoundland, 27 Sept. 1854.

ODNB internet ed.; BL, Add. MSS 29831; 38094, ff. 75-91, 95, 107, 184-6; Bonomi Diary; Hoskins, *Oasis*, 22; Madox, ii, 28, 34; Westcar Diary; V. W. von Hagen, *F. Catherwood, Architect*, New York, 1950; new ed. 1967 (reliable on later life but misleading on career before and with Hay); H. E. Rollins, *The Keats Circle*,1948; S. Tillett, *Egypt Itself*, 1984, 52-59,67-70; inf. S. Tillett; J. and A. Thompson in P. and J. Starkey (eds.), *Travellers in Egypt*, 1998, 130-9; J. Thompson and A. Thompson in *Minerva* 8 (1997), 17-25, repr. *The Codex* 6 (1998), 17-25; inf. N. Cooke.

CATON-THOMPSON, Gertrude (1888-1985)
British archaeologist; she was born in London, 1 Feb. 1888, daughter of William Caton-Thompson, a solicitor, and Ethel Gertrude Page; she was educated in private schools in Eastbourne and Paris and visited Egypt in 1911 with her mother; she worked as a civil servant during World War I and then from 1921-6 was a student of Petrie (q.v.) at University College London; she took part in Petrie's excavations at Abydos and Oxyrhynchus 1921-2; her interest was in the prehistoric period in which she became a specialist; she excavated in Malta in 1921 and 1924; she joined Petrie and Brunton (q.v.) at Qau 1923-5 where she discovered the predynastic village at Hemmamiya; she inaugurated the first archaeological and geological survey of the Northern Fayum where she uncovered two neolithic cultures 1924-8 under the auspices of the British School of Archaeology and then the Royal Anthropological Institute; in 1929 she carried out excavations in Rhodesia at Zimbabwe and other sites; she undertook further excavations at Kharga Oasis 1930-2 and in southern Arabia in 1937-8; she served on the council of the Royal Anthropological Institute, the Royal Geographical Society, and the British Institute of History and Archaeology in East Africa; she was awarded the Cuthbert Peek award of the Royal Geographical Society, 1932; Rivers medallist of the Royal Anthropological Institute, 1934; Huxley medallist, 1946; Burton Medal of the Royal Asiatic Society, 1954; Fellow of Newnham College, Cambridge, Hon. Fellow, 1981; FBA, 1944; Hon. Litt. D. Cambridge, 1954; she served as Governor of Bedford College for Women and the School of Oriental and African Studies, University of London; her chief Egyptological publications were *The Badarian Civilisation*, with G. Brunton, 1928; *The Desert Fayum*, 1934, *Kharga Oasis in Prehistory*, 1952; and her reminiscenses *Mixed Memoirs*, 1983; she died at Court Farm, Broadway, Worcestershire, 18 April 1985.

ODNB 54, 436-7; *WWW* viii, 127; *The Times* 26 April 1985; *PBA*71 (1985), 523-31 (portr.) (bibl.) (G. Clark); M. Drower in G. Cohen and M. Joukowsky, *Breaking Ground*, 2004, 351-79; *Archaéonil* 17 (2007), 89-106 (portr.); È. Gran-Aymerich, *Dictionnaire biographique d'archéologie 1798-1945*, 2001, incorporated in *Les Chercheurs de passé 1798-1945*, 2007, 677-8.

CATTANEO, Carlo (1801-1869)
Italian antiquarian and economist; he was born Milan, 15 June 1801, son of Melchior C. and Maria Antonia Songiorgi; he was a pupil of Romagnosci; in 1839 he founded in Milan the scientific journal *Il Politecnico*, in later life he became an economist and an important figure in public life; at the time of Champollion's visit to Italy he was keeper of the collection in the Palace of Brera which he placed at Champollion's disposal, and also introduced him to the Marquis Malaspina (q.v.); he died at Castagnola di Lugano 5 Feb. 1869 and a statue of him was erected at Milan in 1901.

Garollo, *Diz. Biogr. Univ.; Enc. It.*; Champollion, i, 116, 181, 182, 409; *DBDI* 22, 422-39.

CATTAUI, (*Bey*) **Adolphe** (1865-1925)
Egyptian administrator and geographer; he was born in Cairo, 1 Jan. 1865, son of Aslan C. and Grazia Benrubi; he was educated in France, Lycée Condorcet, Paris, and the École des Hautes Études; he studied Egyptology under Revillout (q.v.), and was sent on a mission to Egypt, 1886; he settled permanently in Egypt, 1888, where he became an official in the financial administration; he reorganized the Soc. Roy. de Géographie d'Egypte of which he was the secretary, 1918-25; he sold material to the Louvre; he published some Egyptological articles; three important papyri bear his name: (1) a long funerary text, now in the Louvre; (2) a Greek judicial papyrus ed. by Botti (q.v.) and by Grenfell and Hunt (qq.v.), now in the Museum of Alexandria; (3) a surgical text in Greek; he died in Cairo, 11 June 1925.

Bull. Soc. Roy. Géogr. d'Ég. 13 (1925) (portr).

CAULFIELD, Algernon St. George Thomas (1869-1933)
British prospector and excavator; he was born in London, 31 July 1869, son of St. George Francis Robert C. and Louisa Anne Crampton; he was educated at Eton and the University of Cambridge; he prospected in Mashonaland, 1890-3, being afterwards employed by the Board of Agriculture, 1894; he succeeded to his paternal estate in Donomon, Ireland, 1896; JP; High Sheriff of Roscommon, 1900; DL; he went to Egypt, 1901-2, and worked for Petrie on the Temple of Sety I at Abydos; he published the report on it, *The Temple of the Kings at Abydos (Sety I)*, for the Eg. Research Account; he died in London, 4 July 1933.

WWW iii, 231; Petrie, 180.

CAVIGLIA, Giovanni Battista (1770-1845)
Genoese mariner; he was born in 1770 and was the owner and master of a trading vessel in the Mediterranean; his usual home-port being Malta, he regarded himself as a British subject; he was employed by Salt (q.v.) and others to excavate the Great Sphinx, 1817; he also explored the Pyramids and neighbouring necropolis; on subsequent visits to Egypt he made further explorations of the pyramids and worked for a time for Col. Howard Vyse (q.v.), but the arrangement terminated at the end of 1836; Caviglia was a man endowed with energy and enterprise and an ingenious excavator; he elicited new information concerning the interior of the Great Pyramid, discovered the steps ascending the Sphinx and the pavement between its paws; he also discovered the colossus of Ramesses II at Mit Rahina; Salt sent him to Italy when Champollion (q.v.) was there to beg him to come to Egypt; he was a deeply religious man, well versed in the Bible, which he constantly read and quoted; he was also interested in occultism and mysticism; he presented a number of Egyptian antiquities to the British Museum, 1818; he retired to Paris early in 1837, and lived there as a protégé of Lord Elgin; he died in the Faubourg St. Germain, Paris, 7 Sept. 1845.

Baedeker, *Egypt*, 1914 ed., p. 144; Belzoni, i, 213-17, 396; Champollion, i, 393; ii. 98, 101, 105, 114, 122; Lauer. *Le Probléme des pyramides d'Égypte*, 1952, 50-8, 60; Lindsay, 40-6, 52; *QR* 19. 395; Salt, passim (*see* index); Selim Hassan, *The Sphinx*, Cairo, 1949, 10-13; Vyse, i. passim; ii. 152-76, 288-94; Wilkinson, *Modern Egypt and Thebes*, 1843, i, 352; also frequently mentioned in contemporary diaries and travel books; *Tait's Edinburgh Magazine*, vol. 8, o.s. = vol. 4, n.s., Nov. (1837), 706-9; E. Gran-Aymerich, *Dictionnaire biographique d'archéologie 1798-1945*, 2001, incorporated in *Les Chercheurs de passé 1798-1945*, 2007, 679; . P. Usick and D. Manley, *The Sphinx revealed: a forgotten record of pioneering excavations*, 2007; J. Thompson, *Edward William Lane 1801-1876*, 2010, 32-3.

CAYLUS, (*Comte de*) **Anne Claude Philippe de Tubières de Grimoard de Pestels de Lévis** (1692-1765)
French antiquarian and collector of antiquities; he was born in Paris, 31 Oct. 1692, son of Jean Anne de T. and Marthe Marguerite Hippolyte Le Valois; besides being a patron of art and a prominent figure in the social life of Paris, he travelled extensively in Italy, Greece, and the Near East; he formed a great collection of antiquities which was housed in large galleries in his mansion, and published in 7 vols., Paris, 1752-60, *Recueil d'antiquités égyptiennes, étrusques, grecques et romaines*; most of his Egyptian antiquities are now in the Bibl. Nat. (Cabinet des Médailles), where there is a MS catalogue by Georges Legrain (q.v.); Caylus was a Member of the Academy, to which he made many contributions; he died in Paris, 5 Sept. 1765.

EB; Mém. Inst. Ég. 13. 12; Misard, *Correspondance du comte de Caylus*, 1877; B. Jaeger, in, *Gött. Misz.* 92 (1986), 41-62; D. Syndram, *Ägypten-Fazination*, 1990, 29-47.

CAZEMIER, Lukas Jan (1899-1975)
Dutch clergyman; he was born at Zwartluis, 1 Sept. 1899, son of Gerrit C. and Foktje Knottnerus; he was educated at the University of Groningen, 1918-24 studying Egyptian religion under van der Leeuw (q.v.); in 1922-3 he studied one semester at Berlin under Erman (q.v.); Dr. Theol. 1924; he then became a minister in the Dutch Reformed Church but continued to write articles mainly on religion; his chief work was his final thesis in 1930 on ancient Egyptian notions of the soul, *Oud-Egyptiese voorstellingen aangaande de ziel*, 1930; he died in Voorschoten, 12 July 1975.

Phoenix 21 (19750, 3-4 (Heerma van Voss); inf. Prof. Heerma van Voss.

CECIL, Lady William *see* **AMHERST, Baroness.**

CENIVAL, Jean-Louis Hellouin de (1927-2003)
French Egyptologist; he was born 9 Dec. 1927; he studied at the École du Louvre under Vandier (q.v.) and École Pratique des Hautes Études under Posener (q.v.); Diploma, 1962; he briefly attended IFAO in Cairo and took part in the excavations in Nubia, 1961; he joined the Dept. of Egyptian Antiquities at the Louvre as assistant curator, 1964; Keeper, 1982-92; he began the programme to document fully and computerize the objects in the collection; he also taught epigraphy at the École du Louvre, 1968-89; he published, *Égypte Époque pharaonique*, 1964; Eng ed., *Living Architecture*, 1964, repr, 1980; *Hieratic Papyri in the British Museum. 5th series. The Abu Sir Papyri*, 1968, with Posener-Kriéger (q.v.)*; L'Égypte avant les Pyramides*, 1973; *Le Livre pour sortir le jour: Le Livre des morts des anciens Égyptiens*, 1992; he died in an accident at Bad Honneff, near Bonn, 6 Feb. 2003.

Rev. d'Ég. 54 (2003), vii-xiii (portr.) (bibl.) (B. Letellier); inf. E. Delange.

ČERNÝ, Jaroslav (1898-1970)
Czech Egyptologist; he was born at Pilsen, 22 Aug. 1898, the son of Anthony Č., who held a civil service post as a revenue inspector, and Anna Navrátilova; he was educated at Pilsen Grammar School and became interested in Egyptology while a schoolboy; he studied in Charles University, Prague with Lexa (q.v.), Alois Musil, the Arabian geographer, 1915, and the founder of Hittitology, Bedrich Hrozny, 1917; he completed his studies under Erman (q.v.) in Berlin; as there were then no posts in Egyptology available in Czechoslovakia, he earned his living at the Zivnostenka Banka from 1919 while reading for his doctorate; this he gained with a thesis on Deir el-Medina village, a subject that remained a dominant interest with him until the end of his life; he spent his summer holidays in Turin working on this material, meeting Ludlow Bull (q.v.) and Breasted (q.v.) who recommended him to Gardiner (q.v.); he visited London and worked on hieratic papyri in the British Museum, 1925; in this year also began the important association with B. Bruyère (q.v.) at Deir el-Medina under the auspices of the French Institute in Cairo; he was granted leave of absence from his bank in 1925 and 1926 to work in Egypt; in 1927 he was awarded a two year scholarship to study the hieratic ostraca in the Cairo Museum; he was lecturer in Egyptology at Charles University, Prague, 1929-46; his main work was on the immense number of ostraca that had been found by the French expedition, and in addition Gardiner engaged him for a period of three months annually to assist him in the preparation of his private collection of ostraca, 1933; this work lasted until the war, 1939, and he also worked with Gardiner on papyri; at this time he visited Sinai and later used his own copies of inscriptions when revising the Gardiner-Peet volume, 1935; on the outbreak of war, he went to Egypt from France and was on the Deir el-Medina excavations, 1939-40; he stayed on in Egypt and eventually was attached to the Czechoslovak Legation, Cairo, and the Czechoslovak Ministry of Foreign Affairs, then in London, 1942-45; he now copied Old Kingdom texts at Saqqara and began to assemble cards forming a corpus of Early Dynastic inscriptions, also turning to Coptic lexicographical studies; he suffered a nervous breakdown and was in a nursing home at Helwan for 18 months; on recovering he began to collect material for a Late Egyptian Grammar; he moved to England, 1943; through Gardiner's recommendation he was appointed Edwards Professor of Egyptology, University College London, 1946-51; following another nervous breakdown in 1950, his health improved after his appointment as Professor of Egyptology University of Oxford, 1951-65; Fellow of The Queen's College, Oxford; at this time he married Mrs Marie Sargant née Hlouskova, 1951 (d.1991); MA, PhD, Prague; FBA, 1953; after his retirement, Professor Emeritus of Egyptology, University of Oxford, Emeritus Fellow of The Queen's College, Oxford, 1965-70; he was visiting Professor Brown University, Providence, 1954-5;

also at University of Pennsylvania, 1965-9; University of Tübingen, 1967; he gave a course of lectures at the Collège de France, 1968; Order of the Nile Egypt; he served on the committee of the EES, 1947-70; Corr. member Fondation Égyptologique Reine Élisabeth, Brussels; American Oriental Soc.; German Archaeological Institute; Assoc. Member Inst. d'Eg.; he helped with UNESCO work on the epigraphical record of the Nubia temples, going regularly to Nubia to copy texts at the temple of Amada, Gebel el-Shems, and Abu Simbel; he also helped prepare the publication of rock-graffiti at El-Lessiya, also working some months each year at the Centre of Documentation, Cairo, on the publication of the Theban necropolis graffiti; he spent four seasons assisting in the preparation of a map showing the location of hieratic graffiti; a *Festschrift* was published to mark the occasion of his seventieth birthday, 1967; Černý also assisted the *Topographical Bibliography* with advice; due to his close association with Deir el-Medina the French government donated a valuable collection of objects from that site to the National Museum in Prague, now kept in the Náprstek Museum; undoubtedly his most important work and contributions lay in the field of palaeography, but he also found time to write on Egyptian religion and maintained an interest in history especially of the Ramesside period; his speciality was in the difficult Late New Kingdom hieratic script to which studies he made major contributions, as also in connection with Late Egyptian grammar; new ground was also broken in Coptic with the dictionary again published only after his death; his bibliography numbers about 110 items, books, articles, reviews etc., the principal works being, *Ostraca hiératiques*, 4 pts., 1930-35; *Catalogue des Ostraca hiératiques non Littéraires de Deir el Médineh*, 5 vols., *1935*-51; *Late Ramesside Letters*, 1939; *Répertoire Onomastique de Deir el-Médineh.* 1949; *Ancient Egyptian Religion*, 1952; *Paper and Books in Ancient Egypt*, 1952; *The Inscriptions of Sinai*, 1952-55; *Graffiti hiéroglyphiques et hiératiques de la Nécropole Thébaine*, 1956; *Hieratic Ostraca, Vol. I.* with Sir A. H. Gardiner, 1957; *Egyptian Stelae in the Bankes Collection*, 1958; *Egypt from the death of Ramesses III to the end of the Twenty-first Dynasty* in *The Cambridge Ancient History* rev. ed. of Vol. II, 1965; *Hieratic Inscriptions from the Tomb of Tutankhamun*, 1965; *Abou Simbel. Chapelle de Rê-Herakhty. Textes Hiéroglyphiques*, with A. A. Youssef, n.d.; *Gebel el-Shems. Textes Hiéroglyphiques*, with E. Edel, n.d.; *Le Temple d'Amada*, 1967; *Graffiti de la Montaigne Thébaine*, 1969-1970, *IV,* 1st and 2nd fasc., 1971; in Czech he wrote a *History of Egypt* in the *History of Mankind* ed. by Josef Susta, in vol. 1, 1940; his posthumous works were A *Community of Workmen at Thebes in the Ramesside Period*, 1973; *The Valley of the Kings*, 1973; *A Late Egyptian Grammar*, 1975 with S. I. Groll; *Coptic Etymological Dictionary*, 1976; *Papyrus hiératiques de Deir el-Medineh*, 1978 completed by G. Posener; he completely revised *The Inscriptions of Sinai*, see above, Pt. 1, 1952, Pt. II, 1955, adding new material and completing it; with H. W. Fairman he contributed the long and important section on *Hieratic Inscriptions* in *The City of Akhenaten III,* chapter 10, 1951; other shorter works include 9 articles in the *EB*, 1961, and subsequent annual eds.; and *Language and Writing* in *The Legacy of Egypt*, 2nd ed.; his papers are now in the Griffith Institute, Oxford, while his library was left to Charles University, Prague; he died in Oxford, 29 May 1970.

ODNB 10, 823; *AfO* 24 (1973), 251-2 (portr.) (H. Brunner); *Archív Orientální* 39 (1971), 385-8 (Z. Zába; *Expedition* 12 No. 4 (1970), (D. O'Connor); *International W.W.* 31st ed. (1967-8), 224; *JEA* 54 (1968), 9-10 (portr.) (B. Bruyère); 3-8 (bibl. incomplete) (C. H. S. Spaull); 57 (1971; 185-9 (portr.) (T. G. H. James); *Novy Orient* 26 (1971), 20-23 (Z. Zába); *PBA* 58 (1972), 367-77 (portr.) (I. E. S. Edwards); *The Times* May 30 1970 (portr.) (I. E. S. Edwards); *WWW* vi, 192; R. Janssen, *The First Hundred Years*, 1992, 54-63; *The Coptic Encyclopedia* 2, 511 (M. L. Bierbrier); J. Malek, *Archív Orientální* 66 (1998), 27-30; J. Růžová, *Pisar Mistra pravdy:Život egyptologa Jaroslava Černého*, 2010; J. Malek in P. Bukovec (ed.), *Christlicher Orient im Porträt-Wissenschaftsgeschichte des Christlichen Orients. Religionen im Vorderen Orient* 3, 2014, 795-802

CHABAN (var. SHABAN), Muhammad (*Bey*) (1866-1930)
Egyptian archaeologist; he studied at the Bulaq school run by Maspero (q.v.) in the 1880's; he was a nephew of Ahmad Kamal (q.v.); he was the local inspector at Rodah in Middle Egypt from at least 1897 until 1903; inspector in the Fayum, 1903-4; inspector at Zagazig with responsibilty for Sharkiyeh and Dakahlieh from 1904-1912; he assisted Edgar (q.v.) with his excavations at Tukh el-Karamus and the recovery of the Zagazig treasure; inspector at Giza from May 1912-Dec. 1916; later assistant curator at the Cairo Museum; he published several articles in *ASAE* on his work; he was present at the unwrapping of the mummy of Tutankhamun in 1925; he died in 1930.

Rapports sur la Marche du Service des Antiquités de 1899 à 1910, 1912, xxv, 96, 171, 204; H. Sallam in C. Eyre (ed.), *Proceedings of the Seventh Congress of Egyptologists*, 1998, 1018-9; T. G. H. James, *Howard Carter*, 1992, 346.

CHABAS, François Joseph (1817-1882)
French Egyptologist; he was born in Réguignier, Hautes-Alpes 2 Jan. 1817, son of Vincent C. and Marie Ferrus; he attended primary school at Chalon-sur-Saône; at this period during the 1830s he studied Latin and Greek and became interested in hieroglyphs; he married in 1841 and was a wine-merchant by profession, spending all his life at Chalon-sur-Saône engaged in his business, but devoting his leisure to study and taking an interest in archaeology; he only took up the study of Egyptology seriously in 1852 under the guidance of de Rougé (q.v.) and

made rapid progress; he corresponded regularly with Birch, Hincks, Goodwin, Mariette, Lepsius, Brugsch (qq.v.), and other leading Egyptologists of the day, and although working in a provincial town far from museums and libraries, was kept well supplied with material by his colleagues; thanks to their help he made many discoveries in the field of texts, which were of great value in their day and published them regularly; he was offered but declined to accept de Rougé's chair on the death of the latter; he visited the museums of Italy, but never went to Egypt; Chabas was President of the Chamber of Commerce at Chalon, and a monument was erected to his memory there in 1899; he wrote many books and articles, and Maspero (q.v.) later collected all his smaller works in 4 vols. in the *Bibl. Ég.* 9-12; see espec., *Mélanges égyptologiques*, 4 vols. 1862-73; *Le Papyrus magique Harris*, 1861; *Les Papyrus hiératiques de Berlin, récits d'il y a quatre mille ans*, etc., 1863; *Recherches sur le nom égyptien de Thèbes, avec quelques observations sur l'alphabet sémitico-égyptien et sur les singularités orthographiques*, 1863; *Revue rétrospective à propos de la publication de la liste royale d'Abydos*, 2 pts. 1865; *Voyage d'un Égyptien en Syrie, en Phénicie, en Palestine, etc. au XIVe siècle avant notre ére.* *Traduction analytique d'un papyrus du Musée Britannique, comprenant le fac-simile du texte hiératique et sa transcription complète en hiéroglyphes et en lettres coptes*, with C. Wycliffe Goodwin, 1866; *L'inscription hiéroglyphes de Rosette analysée et comparée à la version grecque*, 1867; *Les Pasteurs en Égypte*, 1868; *Réponse à la critique du 'Voyage d'un Égyptien' de M. Brugsch*, 1868; *Études sur l'antiquité historique d'après les sources égyptiennes et les monuments réputés préhistoriques*, 1st ed. 1872, 2nd 1873; *Recherches pour servir à l'histoire de la 19me dynastie et spécialement à celle des temps de l'Exode*, 1873; *Les Études préhistoriques et la libre-pensée devant la science, réponse à G. de Mortillet*, 1875; *Choix de textes égyptien: traductions inédites ...*, 1883; *Le Calendrier des jours fastes et néfastes de l'année égyptienne: traduction complète du papyrus Sallier IV*, 1890; *Oeuvres diverses*, 5 vols. 1899-1909; his valuable scientific correspondence is in the library of the Institut de France; he also made the translations in W. R. Cooper's book on obelisks; he died in Versailles, 17 May 1882.

F. Chabas and P. Virey, *Notice biogr. de François Joseph Chabas, Oeuvres div. I Bibl. Ég.* 9, 1899 (also pub. separately, 1898) (portr.); *JRAS* 15 (1883), 3 and *Annual Rep.*, pp. xxiv-xxvi; *DBF* 8, 110 (P. Hamon); *C. R. Congrès provincial des orientalistes français*, session I, t. 2 (1878), 9-68 (Textor de Ravisi); *La Grande Enc.* 10. 181-2 (E. Amélineau); *Rev. ég.* 9 (1900), 78-81, 'Le monument de Chabas' (E. Revillout); *Les Collections égyptiennes dans les musées de Saône-et-Loire*, 1988, 18-21; È. Gran-Aymerich, *Dictionnaire biographique d'archéologie 1798-1945*, 2001, incorporated in *Les Chercheurs de passé 1798-1945*, 2007, 685-6.

CHACE, Arnold Buffum (1845-1932)
American manufacturer and mathematician; he was born in Valley Falls, Rhode Island, 10 Nov. 1845, son of Samuel C., cotton manufacturer, and Elizabeth Buffum; he was educated at Brown University; BA, 1866 and Harvard; MA, 1869; Hon. DSc, 1892; he took over his family business and later became a Trustee of Brown University, 1876-1907; treasurer, 1882-1900; and Chancellor until his death; his interest in mathematics was combined with Egyptology following a visit to Egypt in 1910; he published *The Rhind Mathematical Papyrus*, 1927-9, reprint 1979; he died in Providence, Rhode Island, 28 Feb. 1932.

WWA 1, 205; *American Mathematical Monthly* 40 (1933), 139-42; *The Rhind Mathematical Papyrus*, reprint 1979, x.

CHAÎNE, (Abbé) Marius Jean Joseph (1873-1960)
French Coptologist; born at Tarascon, Bouches-du-Rhône, 10 Aug. 1873, son of Claude C. and Maria Arnoux; he was trained for the priesthood and later became an Abbé; Jesuit, 1897-1922; Chaîne studied under Joseph Halévy at the École Pratique des Hautes Études; he published a *Grammaire éthiopienne* in 1907, which remains the standard work on this subject in French; he now became interested in Coptic literature and published in Rome a *Compendium morphologiae copticae*; he later produced at Paris *Éléments de grammaire dialectale copte*, 1933, using a new teaching technique in this work, instead of using a single dialect as Steindorff had done with Sahidic or Mallon (q.v.) with Bohairic, he gave a simultaneous account of the four principal Coptic dialects, Bohairic, Sahidic, Akhmimic, and Fayumic; this work again led him to the study of hieroglyphic Egyptian and he shortly afterwards produced *Notions de langue égyptienne*: vol. i *Langue du Moyen Empire*, vol. ii *Langue du Nouvel Empire, le néo-égyptien, ses rapports avec le moyen-égyptien et les dialectes coptes*, 1938 and 1942; in this study he formulated the idea that the various Coptic dialects were not the successors of the official written hieroglyphic language of the scribe, but the popular spoken language, which changed in the different parts of Egypt, an idea that had not been much discussed in Egyptian philological studies; he also wrote *Les dialectes coptes assioutiques*, 1932; *La Préposition nominale dans les dialectes coptes*, 1955; *Le Manuscript de la version copte en dialecte sahidique des 'Apophthegmata Patrum'*, 1960; he also catalogued Ethiopic and other MSS. in public and private collections; see also his monumental *Chronologie des temps chrétiens de l'Éthiopie*, 1925; he died in the Cistercian Abbey of Sainte-Marie-du-Désert, Haute-Garonne, 19 Jan. 1960.

BIFAO 61 (1962), 11-13 (A. Guillaumont); *The Coptic Encyclopedia* 2, 511-2 (A. S. Atiya).

CHAMPOLLION, Jean François (1790-1832)

The Founder and 'Father' of Egyptology and the decipherer of hieroglyphs; commonly called 'le Jeune' to distinguish him from his brother; he was born at Figeac (Lot), 23 Dec. 1790, son of Jacques C. (1744-1821), a bookseller, and Jeanne Françoise Gualieu his wife (1747-1807); he was educated at Figeac by his brother and then 1801-7 at the Lyceum, Grenoble; at the age of sixteen he read a paper before the Grenoble Acad. maintaining that Coptic was the ancient language of Egypt; he studied under Silvestre de Sacy (q.v.) and Louis Mathieu Langlès at the Coll. de France and the École spéciale des langues orientales vivantes in Paris, 1807-9, at this time completing the first part of his *Egypt under the Pharaohs* and also the *Religion and History of Egypt and the Geography of Egypt*; he was appointed to a teaching post in History and Politics at Grenoble, 1809-16; Docteur-ès-Lettres, 1810; assistant in the library, 1812; secretary of the Faculty of Grenoble; he now married Rose (Rosine) Blanc, born 1794, by whom he had a daughter Zoraïde later Chéronnet-Champollion (1824-89); it was from his grand-daughter the Comtesse d'Autroche as well as from his nephew and niece Aimé C. (q.v.) and Zoë Falathieu that Hartleben gained much of her information for her biography; Member of the Acad. of Grenoble and appointed to a chair in History and Geog. at the Royal College, Grenoble 1818-21; it was from now on that Champollion was able to concentrate more and more on Egyptian language and archaeology; although he has been described as a 'friend of the people' with republican ideas, he secured the patronage of Louis XVIII and Charles X; he visited various collections abroad and was sent on a mission to work in the museums of Turin, Leghorn, Rome, Naples, and Florence, 1824; on his return he was appointed Conservator of the Egyptian collections at the Louvre., 1826, which were opened 15 Dec. 1827; he visited Egypt with a team of helpers including Rosellini (q.v.), 1828-9, conducting the first systematic survey of the monuments, history, and ancient geography of the country; Member of the Acad. des Inscriptions, 1830, and in 1831 the first chair in Egyptian history and archaeology was created for him at the Collège de France; his interest in hieroglyphs was first aroused as a boy when on a visit to Fourier (q.v.) he learnt about the Rosetta stone and the problem of reading the Egyptian versions; the popular and oft-quoted idea that he had a sudden inspiration and, after seeing how the cartouche name of Ramesses was to be translated, then worked out and published a complete system in the famous letter to M. Dacier, is really a complete misconception; in order to decipher hieroglyphs and understand ancient Egyptian texts he prepared himself in every possible way; as a boy he already learnt or attempted Hebrew, Arabic, Syriac, Chaldean, and Chinese, later he added Coptic an essential tool, Ethiopic, Sanskrit, Zend, Pahlevi, Parsee, and Persian, his writings even have references to Mexican scripts; his progress was nevertheless slow at first and necessitated the making of many mistakes and the overcoming of many obstacles, not least the opposition of rivals; he took his first step in 1808 when he equated 15 Demotic signs with Coptic alphabetic signs or letters, correctly recognizing *f* and other signs; by 1818 he had obtained phenomenal success with the translation of the hieroglyphic version of the Rosetta decree, explainable in relation to other texts by the fact that there was a Greek version for help, but the meaning of many signs was clear, words were defined, and a key established; in this year he also showed knowledge far in advance of anyone else but had not yet published his partial results; the *Lettre à M. Dacier*, 1822, marks a turning-point in decipherment; but his work was still embryonic, the table of phonetic signs for Greek and Roman names being treated there as an alphabet of 26 letters with many syllabic signs included although he understood the use of determinatives; of the true Egyptian alphabet 10 signs were correctly identified, 2 partly, 6 were wrong, and 4 missing; the *Précis* of 1824 expanded these results and is also interesting as it shows that he looked to Silvestre de Sacy (q.v.) and Åkerblad (q.v.) as providing the germ or source of all later discoveries while correcting some of Young's (q.v.) results; but it was not until his grammar and dictionary and larger later works were published that his fully evolved ideas were apparent; Champollion was no library grammarian but had an interest in all branches of Egyptology, and his great vols. of notes on the monuments show an acute archaeological observation, like Wilkinson far ahead of his time; his principal works were, *Introduction à l'Égypte sous les Pharaons*, 1811; *L'Égypte sous les Pharaons ou Recherches sur la géographie, la religion, la langue, les écritures et l'histoire de l'Ég. avant l'invasion de Cambyse. Descript. géograph.*, 2 vols. 1814; *De l'écriture hiératique des anciens Égyptiens*, 1821; *Lettre à M. Dacier, relative à l'alphabet des hiéroglyphes phonétiques, employés par les Égyptiens pour inscrire sur leurs monuments les titres, les noms et les surnoms des souverains grecs et romains*, 1822; *Panthéon égyptien. Collection des personnages mythologiques de l'ancienne Égypte*, 1823; *Précis du système hiéroglyphique des anciens Égyptiens ou Recherches sur les éléments premiers de cette écriture sacrée, sur leurs diverses combinaisons et sur les rapports de ce système avec les autres méthodes graphiques ég. avec un volume de planches*, 1824, listed 450 words or hieroglyphic groups; *Catalogo dei papiri egiziani della Biblioteca Vaticana*, 1825; *Notice descriptive des monuments ég. du Musée Charles X*, 1827; *Lettres écrites d'Égypte et de Nubie en 1828 et 1829*, 1833; *Prospectus for the Monuments*, 1831; Posthumous works, *Monuments de l'Égypte et de la Nubie d'après les dessins exécutés sur les lieux, sous la direction de Champollion le jeune ...*, 4 vols. fol. 446 pls., 1835-47; *Notices descriptives conformes aux notices autographes rédirées sur les lieux par Champ. le jeune*, 2 vols. 4°, 1,641 pages, 1844-89, 2nd vol. autographed by G. Maspero; *Grammaire égypt., ou Principes généraux de l'écrit. sacrée égypte. appliquée à la représentation de la langue parlée. Publiée sur le ms. autographe*, 3 pts. 1836-41, ed. Champollion-Figeac; *Dictionnaire égypt. en écrit. hiéroglyph., publié par Champollion-Figeac d'après les mss. autographes; dessiné et écrit par Jules Feuquières*, 1841-4; while preparing the results of his expedition for publication he was struck down by a stroke, and died in Paris, 4 March 1832 and was buried in Père Lachaise cemetery; some of his papers were acquired by Salvolini (q.v.) and are now in the Biblioteca Comunale di Faenza; the centenary of the publication of the *Lettre à M. Dacier* was marked by a celebration by the Univ. of Grenoble which was attended by Egyptologists from all countries, and a volume of studies with 45 contributors, was issued in 1922 to commemorate the event; his statue was placed in the vestibule of the College de France after his death. The rival claims of Young and his supporters have given rise to a vast amount of literature which need not be noted here. Biographical notices of Champollion, of varying merit, are legion and the following list is a short selection of the most essential.

H. Hartleben, *Champollion, sein Leben und sein Werk*, 2 vols. 1906, is the definitive account, French ed., 1983; H. Hartleben ed., *Lettres de Champollion*, 2 vols. Paris, 1909 (*Bibl. Ég.* t. 21, 22), new ed., 1986; English version of diaries *Egyptian Diaries*, 2001; A. Champollion-Figeac, *Les Deux Champollion*, 1887; L. de la Brière, *Champollion inconnu*, 1897; M. Pourpoint, *Champollion et l'énigme égyptienne*, 1963; E. Iversen, *The Myth of Egypt and its Hieroglyphs*, 1961, 137-45; *DBF* 8, 350-1; Seymour de Ricci, in *Rec. Champollion*, 763-84, has very complete bibl.; Erman, 'Die Entzifferung der Hieroglyphen', *in Sitzungsb. Berlin Akad.*, 1922; F. Ll. Griffith, 'The Decipherment of the Hieroglyphs', in *JEA* 37. 38-46; J. Capart, 'Le centenaire du déchiffrement des hiéroglyphes par Champollion', in *Bull. Acad. roy. de Belgique*, no. 5, 1922; Renouf, 'Young and Champollion', *PSBA* 19, 188-209; E. Bresciani (ed.), *Jean-François Champollion. Lettres à Zelmire*, 1978; P. Vaillant (ed.), *Jean-François Champollion. Lettres à son frère 1804-1818*, 1984; J. Lacouture, *Champollion*, 1988; C. Ziegler and H. Champollion, *L'Égypte de Jean-François Champollion*, 1989; J. Kettel, *Jean-François Champollion le jeune. Répertoire de bibliographie analytique 1806-1989*, 1990; M. Dewachter, *Champollion, un scribe pour l'Égypte*, 1990; M. Dewachter and A. Fouchard, *L'Égyptologie et les Champollions*, 1994; Lamy, 312-20; È. Gran-Aymerich, *Dictionnaire biographique d'archéologie 1798-1945*, 2001, incorporated in *Les Chercheurs de passé 1798-1945*, 2007, 688-91; A. Faure, *Champollion. Le Savant Déchiffré*, 2004; P. Clayton (ed.), *The Code-Breaker's Secret Diaries*, 2009; J.-L. Bovot in *Égypte Afrique & Orient* 58 (2010), 47-64; F. Merlatti, *Manfrediana* 43/44 (2011), 11-36. A. Robinson, *Cracking the Egyptian Code. The Revolutionary Life of Jean-Francois Champollion* (2012); S. Guichard in M. Betrò and G. Miniaci (eds.), *Talking along the Nile*, 2013, 125-30; M. Maitland in N. Cooke and V. Daubney (eds.), *Every Traveller Needs a Compass*, 2015, 113-30.

CHAMPOLLION-FIGEAC, (Louis) Aimé (1812-1894)
French writer; he was born Grenoble, 15 Dec. 1812, son of J. J. Champollion-Figeac and Agathe Zoe Berriat;, and was assistant to his father at the Bibliothèque Nationale; he was the author of historical works, and compiled a biographical and bibliographical study of his family in *Les Deux Champollion*, Grenoble, 1887, a work containing transcripts of many letters relating to his father and uncle; he died in Vif, 20 March 1894.

DBF 8. 351.

CHAMPOLLION-FIGEAC, Jacques Joseph (1778-1867)
French archaeologist and historian - the elder brother of Jean François C.; he was born in Figeac (Lot), 5 Oct. 1778, the eldest son among five children; his education was interrupted by the Revolution and he had to cease his classical studies; at first he was employed in the municipal administration but in 1798 he asked to go with the expedition to Egypt; although this request was, unfortunately for him, refused, it is of great significance in the story of the birth of Egyptology as it shows his interest in the subject long before his brother began his studies; the influence he had on his brother in this respect has never been adequately explained, but it seems certain that here was the main origin of Champollion's extraordinarily early interest in the decipherment of Egyptian and other archaeological problems, rather than through occasional meetings with Fourier (q.v.) and other scholars; instead of going abroad Jacques Joseph was given the task of collecting and conserving the ancient inscriptions of Dauphiné by Fourier, which he did while living at Grenoble; he was made Assistant Librarian of Grenoble Library, 1808 and Chief Librarian, 1812; he also continued with his classical studies and was appointed Professor of Greek Literature, 1809, but lost this position on the restoration of the monarchy in 1814; at this period he also looked after his brother's interests and acted as his mentor and guardian; he married in 1807 and had several children; he became interested in Egyptian chronology, 1820-7, and published a *Résumé complet de chronologie*; he was made Keeper of MSS at the Bibliothèque Nat., Paris, 1828, and Professor of Palaeography, 1830; he again filled this position with distinction until deprived of both posts in the revolution of 1848; he was finally appointed Keeper of the Library of the Palace of Fontainebleau, 1849; it is extremely difficult to decide how much his great brother owed to him, for he was constantly assisting him in every way so that even his family were not sure; he appears to have been a very modest man who never tried to take any credit from his brother, but who had a brilliant career in spite of the sacrifices he made at times; what is certain is that the younger Champollion could never have achieved his great work without his brother; equally that most of the immense results would never have been published; while the actual decipherment was the work of Jean François, there is so much of the brother's work in the results

that the achievements of the two can only be taken together; Jacques Joseph did in fact prepare and often edited his brother's works, helped him with the classical authors' references to Egypt and translated their texts when needed, and also worked on the chronology, which was not J. F.'s strong point; his life is so bound up with that of his brother, that to a great extent the life of one is the life of the other and the reader is referred to the biographical works of Hartleben etc.; in addition to many important studies on French history, language etc., Jacques Joseph wrote the following on Egyptian subjects, *Lettre à M. Fourier sur l'inscription grecque du temple de Denderah en Égypte*, 1806; *Annales des Lagides, ou Chronologie des rois grecs d'Égypte successeurs d'Alexandre le Grand*, 2 vols. 1819; *Explication de la date égyptienne d'une inscription grecque tracée sur le colosse de Memnon à Thèbes d'Égypte*, 1819; *Observations sur les coudées égyptiennes découvertes dans les ruines de Memphis*, 2 pts, 1824; *Notice sur les manuscrits autographes de Champollion le jeune, perdus en l'année 1832 et retrouvés en 1840*, 1842; *Fourier et Napoléon, l'Égypte et les cent jours. Mémoires et documents inédits*, 1844; *Des Dynasties égyptiennes, à l'occasion des ouvrages de MM. Baruchi et Bunsen*, extract from *Nouvelle Revue enc.*, 1847; *L'Obélisque de Louqsor, transporté à Paris. Notice historique, descriptive et archéologique sur ce monument ... Avec la figure de l'obélisque et l'interprétation de ses inscriptions hiéroglyphiques d'après les dessins et des notes manuscrits de Champollion le jeune*, 1833; *Histoire des peuples anciens et modernes*, 1857; *Égypte ancienne*, 1858, a large history; he died at Fontainebleau, 9 May 1867.

A. Champollion-Figeac, *Les Deux Champollion*, 1887 (portr.); *DBF* 8, 349 (P. Hamon); Charles-Olivier Carbonell, *L'autre Champollion*, 1984; È. Gran-Aymerich, *Dictionnaire biographique d'archéologie 1798-1945*, 2001, incorporated in *Les Chercheurs de passé 1798-1945*, 2007, 691-2.

CHANDLER, Michael H. (*c.*1797-1866)
American dealer; he was born in Ireland *c.*1797; he married Francis F. Ludlow and they had four children prior to emigrating to the United States *c.*1829-30; he was living in Philadelphia in 1833 when he obtained eleven Egyptian mummies that had been exhumed between 1817-20 from the west bank of the Nile, opposite Thebes, by Antonio Lebolo (q.v.); the eleven mummies had been shipped from Trieste to a shipping company in New York City at Lebolo's request to be sold for the highest price; how Chandler learned of their existence is unknown; Chandler claimed that he was Lebolo's nephew, and that the mummies were willed to him, but Lebolo's will does not substantiate this; Chandler sold seven of the mummies in Philadelphia and other eastern cities "to gentlemen for private museums"; the last four mummies and some accompanying papyri were sold to the Mormon prophet Joseph Smith in Kirtland, Ohio, in July 1835 for $2,400; Joseph Smith announced to his followers that the papyri contained the writings of the ancient patriarchs Abraham and Joseph; a partial translation of the writings of Abraham is published by the Church of Jesus Christ of Latter-day Saints in a sacred text known as the *Pearl of Great Price*; Chandler purchased land in Parkman, Ohio, in 1836 where he farmed until his death on Oct. 21 1866.

Inf. H. Donl. Peterson; S. J. Wolfe, *Mummies in nineteenth century America*, 2009, 96-131.

CHARMES, (François Anne Marie) Xavier (1849-1919)
French administrator; he was born in Aurillac 23 Nov. 1849, son of Pierre François Julien Ildefonse Archange Ludjer C., notary, and his wife Marie Aglae; he entered the Ministry of Education, 1872 and became chef de cabinet, 1877, head of the division of arts and sciences finally and Director of the Secretariat, 1881; he prepared the report which led to the creation of the French Institute in Cairo and was instrumental in the appointment of heads of French missions abroad such as de Morgan (q.v.) at the head of the Antiquities Service in Egypt; he was a member of the Académie des sciences morales et politiques, 1887; he retired in 1897; he died in Paris 4 April 1919. His brother (Marie Adolphe François) Gabriel C. was born in Aurillac, 7 Nov. 1840 and became a journalist, writer and traveller in the Near East; he went to Egypt for his health in 1878 and remained in the Levant; among other works, he wrote *Cinq Mois au Caire et sans la Basse Égypte*, 1880, translated into English 1883 and *L'Égypte*, 1891; he died 19 April 1886.

DBF 8, 601-2; È. Gran-Aymerich, *Dictionnaire biographique d'archéologie 1798-1945*, 2001, incorporated in *Les Chercheurs de passé 1798-1945*, 2007, 697.

CHASSINAT, Émile Gaston (1868-1948)
French Egyptologist; he was born in Paris, 5 May 1868, son of Desiré Camille C., an engraver, and Charlotte Athanaïs Guinet; he left school at 14 and worked in the printing business for some years; he had a hard struggle at this time but began to study Egyptology in 1888, while working as a compositor at the Imprimerie Nationale, as a student of Maspero (q.v.) at the École des Hautes Études, and of Revillout (q.v.) and Pierret (q.v.) at the Louvre; he was made secretary for the production of the *Revue de l'histoire des religions*, 1892-5; also attached to the Egyptian Dept. of the Louvre, 1894; he went to Cairo in 1895 as a member of the IFAO; he worked under the Marquis de Rochemonteix (q.v.) whose great work on the Temple of Edfu he continued and completed; he was appointed a member of the Cairo Cat. Commission, 1897, and for this worked on the coffins of the high priests of Amun found at Deir el-Bahri; he succeeded Bouriant (q.v.) as Director of the IFAO, 1898 holding the post for 13 years; this was a highly successful period during which the activities of the Institute were enormously expanded, the printing press being inaugurated in 1989, the *Bulletin* in 1900-1, and the *Bibl. d'Étude*, 1908; under his direction large-scale

excavations were also undertaken, and he dug at Meir with Munier (q.v.), cleared a small temple of Isis at Dendera, worked on the necropolis at Abu Rawash finding the head of a statue of Radjedef now in the Louvre, and at the Coptic monastery of Bawit; he also discovered 30 untouched tombs at Asyut and worked at Qatta and the Valley of Kings; he was a Member of the Egyptian Inst. 1900, and made Chevalier de la Légion d'Honneur, 1909; he returned to France after 1912 where he mainly worked on the completion of his own vast temple publications at Le Vésinet; he also began a complete index to the Pyramid Texts, directed *Rec. Trav.* after Maspero's death until it lapsed in 1923, and was secretary for the production of *Rev. de l'Égypte Ancienne* and *Rev. ég.*; his most important publication was the great series of Edfu Texts, the whole of which after the first vol. was largely his work; in Coptic studies his most important work was his edition of the Medical Papyrus of Mashaykh; he wrote nearly 70 articles for journals and no less than 26 vols. in 4º; *Le Temple d'Edfou*, with de Rochemonteix, 14 vols., with over 3,000 pages and plates, 1892-1934; *Fouilles de Qattah*, with H. Gauthier, 1906; *La Seconde Trouvaille de Deir el-Bahari: sarcophages*, 1909; *Le Mammisi d'Edfou*, 2 pts. 1910-39; *Une Campagne de Fouilles dans la Nécropole d'Assiout*, with C. Palanque, 1911; *Fouilles à Baouît*, tom. i, 1911; *Le Quatrième Livre des entretiens et épîtres de Shenouti*, 1911; *Un Papyrus médical copte*, 1921; *Le Temple de Dendara*, 8 vols. 1934-78, with F Daumas; *Le Manuscrit Magique Copte*, 1955; and *Le Mystère d'Osiris au mois de Khoiak*, 2 vols., 1966-8; he died in Saint-Germain-en-Laye, 26 May 1948.

ASAE 51 (1951), 537-48 (portr.) (F. Daumas); *Chron. d'Ég.* 24 (1949), 95; *BSAC* 13, 197-203 (bibl.); *Mél. Maspero*, xxiii; É. Gran-Aymerich, *Dictionnaire biographique d'archéologie 1798-1945*, 2001, incorporated in *Les Chercheurs de passé 1798-1945*, 2007, 698.

CHATWIN, (Charles) Bruce (1940-1989)
British traveller, writer, and art dealer; he was born in Sheffield, 13 May 1940, son of Charles C. and Margharita Turnell; he was educated at Marlborough; he joined Sotheby's in 1958 as a porter, rising quickly to become a director, responsible for antiquities and Impressionist paintings in a booming art market; he catalogued the 1964 sale of the Egyptian and Near Eastern material from the collection of Ernest Brummer (q. v.), and bought and sold on his own account; he was involved with the dispersal of the private museum of A. H. Pitt Rivers (q. v.); he resigned from Sotheby's in 1966, studying archaeology at Edinburgh 1966-68; he subsequently worked as a journalist, travel writer, and novelist; he retained his interest in archaeology and the art world throughout his life, most visible in *The Songlines* (1987) and *Utz* (1988); he died in Nice, 18 Jan. 1989.

ODNB 11, 245-6; N. Shakespeare, *Bruce Chatwin* (1999); inf. T. Hardwick.

CHAULNES see ALBERT d'AILLY.

CHAZELLES, Jean Mathieu de (1657-1710)
French scientist and geographer; he was born in Lyons, 24 July 1657, his family being engaged in commerce; he studied under the Jesuits and went to Paris in 1675; after a varied career he visited the Levant and Egypt in 1693, where he determined the meridian of Alexandria, but found his results different from those of Tycho Brahe; he went to the pyramids at the same time as de Careri and was the first to orient them; he also measured the Great Pyramid and used the dimensions to calculate the volume, but his figures as recorded were not very accurate; on his return to France he was nominated Astronomer Associate of the Acad. of Sciences; he died in Paris, 16 Jan. 1710.

DBF 8, 199-6; Rollin, *The Ancient History of the Egyptians etc.* 15th ed. 1823, i, 140-1; Vyse, 2, 229-30 for de Careri.

CHERUBINI, Salvatore (1797-1869)
Italian artist; he was born 1797, son of the famous composer Luigi C. and Cecilie Tourette; he accompanied Rosellini (q.v.) and Champollion (q.v.) to Egypt, 1828; he was naturalized French, and was the brother-in-law of Rosellini who in 1827 married his sister Zenobia; on his return from Egypt, he was appointed Inspecteur des Beaux-Arts; he made donations of Egyptian antiquities to the Musée National de Céramique in Sèvres, 1842, 1851, and 1854; he died 1869.

Bellasis, *Cherubini, Memorials Illustrative of His Life*, 1874; Champollion, ii, pp. vi, 10; *BSFE* 111 (1988), 50-7; J. Bulté, *Catalogue des collections égyptiennes du Musée National de Céramiques à Sèvres*, 1981, 14; N. Cherpion in *EDAL* 1 (2009), 47-8.

CHESTER, (Revd) Greville John (1830-1892)
British clergyman, collector and author of archaeological articles; he was born in Denton, Norfolk, 25 Oct. 1830, youngest son of the rector the Revd William C, and his wife Elizabeth Wilson, a sister of Lord Berners; he

was educated privately and then took his degree at Balliol College, Oxford; after being ordained he served as curate at Crayke, Yorks., and Diss, followed by the family living of Farndish, near Wellingborough; he next became incumbent of St. Jude's, Moorfields, Sheffield, a poor parish that had become run down but which he quickly revived into a flourishing one; a man of very wide interests he founded the Sheffield Naturalists' Society; overwork brought on ill-health and caused him to retire from the parish of Iwade, Kent, in 1865, and thereafter he held no permanent post; he performed clerical duties in a number of capacities, acting as locum tenens for the Archdeacon of Barbados and assisting at the Victoria Docks; Chester now wintered abroad for many years, Petrie (q.v.) who saw him in Egypt in 1881 said that this was his 38th visit; he also visited Syria and Palestine frequently and assisted Sir Walter Besant and the PEF in many ways, constituting himself unofficial curator of their collections, and arranging their museum; he also contributed many notes and articles to their journal; he was no study archaeologist, but explored the Phoenician island of Aradus (mod. Ruad), 1875, and the area around lake Sirbonis in the E. Delta, making the difficult journey from Sân to El Arish, 1880; it is, however, as a collector that Chester is best remembered today; in the days when Birch and the British Museum relied on unofficial or rather semi-official collectors to supplement the growing collections he was one of the most active helpers, often purchasing objects abroad for the museum and also presenting others; he collected many antiquities, including Coptic MSS and Greek and Egyptian papyri, most of which were bought by the British Museum and the Bodleian Library; he also caused others to present objects; one of the most important items acquired in this way was the magnificent collection of glazed tiles and rosettes from the palace of Ramesses III at Tell el-Yahudiya (BM, EA 12305 and many more through to 26795), a unique group only comparable with those in Cairo Museum and the Qantir tiles in New York; had Chester not visited the site these would all have perished or become scattered throughout many collections by dealers; he did not confine his collecting to Egyptian objects but presented a Babylonian weight to the museum (WAA 91005); he fulfilled a similar function for many other museums, especially the South Kensington (now Victoria and Albert), the Ashmolean, and Fitzwilliam Museums; there is also a Hittite collection formed by him at Oxford, and coins and fragments of papyri in the Bodleian Library; in 1865 he presented an altar inscribed with Meroitic to the British Museum (EA 901) and in 1880 a fine stela of the Old Kingdom (EA 1011); he was a skilful buyer of antiquities and was held in great respect by native dealers; he also obtained many finger-rings and gems for Sir Woolaston Franks, and a large series of Arabic glass weights for the British Museum; he wrote a volume of poetry and an account of his travels in the USA; he published articles in the *Archaeological Journal* on the Old Churches of Cairo, the Coptic Monasteries of Wadi Natrun, and the rock drawings near Gebel es-Silsila; further articles relating to Egyptology appeared in the *Academy*, but his most important published work was a *Catalogue of the Egyptian Antiquities in the Ashmolean Museum*, 1881; Petrie was a friend of his and in memory of the help and encouragement he had received made a special shelf of books as a memorial to him in the Edwards Library, University College London; Greville Chester died of angina pectoris in London, 23 May 1892, and was buried in Kensal Green Cemetery.

Obituary Notices, pub. by Watlington, 1892; *PEQ* 1892, 179 (Walter Besant); Budge, *N & T* i. 84; Budge, *Guide to the Babylonian and Assyrian Antiquities-British Museum*, 1922, 138; Budge, *Guide to the Fourth, Fifth and Sixth Egyptian Rooms, and the Coptic Room - British Museum*, 1922, 236, 274, 330; Petrie, 22, 53, 77; *TSBA* vii (1881), 177; Wilbour, 215; G. Seidmann, 'The Rev. Greville John Chester and 'The Ashmolean Museum as a Home for Archaeology in Oxford', *Bulletin of the History of Archaeology* 16/1 (2006), 27–33.

CHEVRIER, Henri Charles Louis (1897-1974)
French architect; he was born at Moulins, 15 July 1897, son of Louis Georges C. and Félicie Marguerite Brunau; he served with distinction in World War I, Chevalier de la Légion d'honneur; he then studied at the École des Beaux-Arts, receiving his architect's diploma in 1925; in 1926 he succeeded Pillet (q.v.) as Director of Works for the Egyptian Antiquities Services at Karnak where he worked until 1954 apart from a break in World War II; among his many discoveries were the colossal statues of Akhenaten, the *talatat* blocks of Akhenaten found in the restoration of the second pylon, and the chapels of Senusret I and Hatshepsut found in the third pylon; apart from his numerous reports in *ASAE*, he also published *Le Temple Reposoir de Ramses III à Karnak*, 1933; *Le Temple Reposoir de Séti II*, 1940; *Une Chapelle de Sesostris Iᵉʳ à Karnak*, with P. Lacau, 1956, 1969; *Une Chapelle d'Hatshepsut à Karnak*, 1977; he died in Paris, 26 July 1974.

BSFE 70-1 (1974), 7-8; C. Traunecker and J.-C. Golvin, *Karnak*, 1984, 184-200.

CHILDE, Alberto (*né* Dmitri Vonizin or Vanitzin) (1870-1950)
Brazilian Egyptologist; he was born in St. Petersburg, 5 Sept. 1870, son of Sergei V., the Chief of Police of that city; he was educated at the University of Kazan and then joined the Cossack Regiment of the Imperial Russian Guard; he left Russia on the death of his parents and visited Egypt where he became interested in Egyptian antiquities and began to study hieroglyphs; he settled in Paris and then emigrated to Brazil *c.*1900; he first worked as a Preparer at the Museum of Pathological Anatomy of the Faculty of Medicine of Rio de Janeiro; he

was appointed Keeper of Classical and Oriental Antiquities at the National Museum of Rio de Janeiro 2 Jan. 1912 until Nov. 1937 when his post was restructured under the Ministry of Education; he retired in Oct. 1938; he helped to popularize archaeology in Brazil and wrote 77 articles and monographs including *A dama Takushit do Museu Nacional do Rio de Janeiro*, 1915; *Guia das colleccoes de Archaeologia Clasica, Museu Nacional do Rio de Janeiro*, 1919; *Como foram decifrados os hieroglifos egipciacos*, 1939; and numerous articles in his museum's journal in which he published parts of its Egyptian collection; he died in Petropolis, Rio de Janeiro, 1 July 1950.

L. de Castro Faria, *Alberto Childe*, 1970 (bibl.) inf. Dr. K. A. Kitchen; K. A. Kitchen, *Catalogue of the Egyptian Collection in the National Museum, Rio de Janeiro*, 1990, xx-xxi (portr.).

CHIPIEZ, (Jérôme) Charles (1835-1901)
French architect and archaeologist; he was born Ecully, 11 Jan. 1835, son of Jérôme André C., architect, and Marie Anne Blanc; he studied architecture at Lyons and Paris; Professor at the École spéciale d'Architecture, 1867-86; he collaborated with Georges Perrot (q.v.) in the *Histoire de l'art dans l'antiquité*, the first volume of which, on Egypt, was published in 1881; he died in Paris, 9 Nov. 1901.

DBF 8, 1165-6; inf. M. Azim; È. Gran-Aymerich, *Dictionnaire biographique d'archéologie 1798-1945*, 2001, incorporated in *Les Chercheurs de passé 1798-1945*, 2007, 703.

CHOISEUL-GOUFFIER, Marie Gabriel Florent Auguste (1752-1817)
French diplomat and scholar; he was born in Paris, 27 Sept. 1752, son of Marie Gabriel Florent Choiseul-Beaupré and Marie Françoise Lallemant de Betz; he was Ambassador at Constantinople, and travelled widely in Greece, publishing *Voyages dans la Grèce*; he formed a large collection of antiquities and made many communications to the Acad. des Inscriptions; some of his MSS are in the Bibliothèque Nationale (MSS Fr. 7558); his large collection of antiquities, which contained many Egyptian objects, was sold in Paris, 17 July 1818, the catalogue being drawn up by L. J. J. Dubois (q.v.); he retired on account of ill-health to Aix-les-Bains, where he died 20 June 1817.

Dacier, *Mém. Acad.* 1819; Lugt 9422.

CHOISY, (François) Auguste (1841-1909)
French architect; he was born at Vitay-le-François, 7 Feb. 1841, son of Jean François C. and Marie Adèle Pothier; he was Professor at the École Polytechnique and the École des Ponts et Chaussées; in addition to technical works he wrote a general history of architecture and also *L'Art de bâtir chez les Égyptiens*, Paris, 1904; he died 18 Sept. 1909.

DBF 8, 122-6.

CHRAKIAN (*Pasha*) **Artin** (1804-1859)
Armenian by origin, and an Egyptian official; he was born in Constantinople in 1804, son of Sukias C., who emigrated to Egypt in 1812; Muhammad Ali sent him to be educated in Paris where he studied civil administration; on his return he worked in the War Ministry and then was involved in the reorganization of education in Egypt; in 1836 he was appointed a member of the School Council later to become the Ministry of Education; in 1839 he became First Secretary and in 1844 succeeded Boghos Bey Yusufian (q.v.) as Minister of Commerce and Foreign Affairs; being a Christian, he was dismissed by Abbas with all other officials of that faith who had served under Muhammad Ali and Ibrahim in 1850; he married Katarine, sister of Joseph Bey Hekekyan (q.v.); he died in 1859.

R. Adalian, *The Armenian Review* 33 (1980), 129; Carré, i, 288; ii, 85; Pückler-Muskau, i, 94; Lepsius, 189; A. Melly, *Lettres*, 5, 10.36; G. Melly, *Khartoum*, 88.

CHRISTIE, Alexander Turnbull (*d.* 1833)
British physician; son of Alexander C. of Montrose and Jean Turnbull; MD Edinburgh, 1828; he published *Observations on Cholera*, 1828 and *Treatise on Cholera*, 1833, in preparation for which he visited Egypt to study the effects of epidemic diseases; while he was there he made a collection of zoological specimens and antiquities; these, which included the mummy, BM, EA 6692, were presented after his death to the British Museum; he died while on a visit to the West Indies, July 1833.

GM 1833; Edin. Univ. Records; *Burke's Landed Gentry;* J. E. Gray, *List of Mammalia in the B.M.* (1843), 197.

CHRISTOPHE, Louis Antoine Régis (1912-1996)
French Egyptologist; he was born in Villeurbanne, 2 April 1912, son of Louis Antoine C. and Jeanne Marie Tizieux; he studied Egyptology at Lyons under Alliot (q.v.); he was a pensionnaire at the Institut français in

Cairo, 1945-9 and took part in excavations at Karnak; he then stayed in Egypt; he was appointed UNESCO representative for Nubian affairs and coordinator for the archaeological work in Egyptian Nubia, 1960-7 and so played a major role in the Nubian rescue campaign; his principal publications were *Karnak Nord III (1945-1949)*, with C. Robichon, 1951; *Temple d'Amon à Karnak. Les divinités des colonnes de la grand salle hypostyle et leurs épithètes*, 1955; *Abou-Simbel et l'épopée de sa découverte*, 1965; and *Campagne internationale de l'UNESCO pour la sauvegarde des sites et monuments de Nubie*, 1977; he died at Malesherbes, 7 May 1996.

BSFE 136 (1996), 2-3; inf. R. de Keersmaecker.

CHRISTY, Henry (1810-1865)
British ethnologist; he was born 26 July 1810, son of William Miller C., banker, and Anne Fell; he joined the family firm and succeeded his father as director of the London Joint Stock Bank in 1858; he showed a keen interest in ethnology, travelling throughout the world from 1850 and building up a collection of objects, including Egyptian antiquities, which he left to the British Museum; FGS, 1858; he financed archaeological excavations in France; he died in La Palisse, Allier, France, 4 May 1865.

ODNB 11, 562-3; *DNB* 10, 295-6 Boase, I, 618; È. Gran-Aymerich, *Dictionnaire biographique d'archéologie 1798-1945*, 2001, incorporated in *Les Chercheurs de passé 1798-1945*, 2007, 705-6.

CHUBB, Mary Alford (1903-2003)
British archaeologist; she was born in London 22 March 1903, daughter of John Burland Chubb, surveyor, and Bertha Isabel Neile; while studying sculpture at the Central School of Art, she became assistant secretary at the Egypt Exploration Society, 1929-32 and excavated at Amarna for two seasons with Pendlebury (q.v.), 1930-2; she then joined the excavations of the University of Chicago in Iraq; she went to Chicago in 1938 to help write up the excavations; she returned to England in 1939 and was seriously injured in an accident, losing a leg; she then became a broadcaster and writer; her sister married Glanville (q.v.); she wrote an account of the Amarna excavations *Nefertiti Lived Here*, 1954; new ed 1998; and of the Iraq excavations *City in the Sand*, 1957, new ed 1999; *An Alphabet of Ancient Egypt*, 1966; *An Alphabet of Ancient Greece. Book One-Early Days*, 1967; *An Alphabet of Ancient Greece. Book Two-The Golden Years*, 1968; *An Alphabet of Assyria and Babylonia*, 1969; *An Alphabet of Ancient Rome*, 1971; *An Alphabet of the Holy Land*, 1973, as well as other popular works; she died in Salisbury, 22 Jan. 2003.

The Times Feb 2003.

CIASCA, (*Cardinal*) **(Pasquale Raffaele) Agostino** (1835-1902)
Italian Coptologist and orientalist; born at Polignano a Mare, near Bari, 7 May 1835, son of Leonardo C. and Olimpia Montanari; he became Prefect of the Vatican Archives, and was created a cardinal in 1899; Professor of Hebrew in the College of Propaganda, 1866-76; he visited Egypt in 1879 and acquired manuscripts for the Borgiano Museum; he edited *I papiri copti del Museo Borgiano*, 1881 and *Sacrorum bibliorum fragmenta copto-sahidica Musei Borgiani*, 1885-9; he died in Rome, 6 Feb. 1902.

Garollo, *Diz. Biogr. Univ.; Enc. It; DBDI* 25, 223-4;*The Coptic Encyclopedia* 2, 560 (A. S. Atiya)

CIBRARIO, (*Conte*) **Luigi** (1802-1870)
Italian statesman, historian, and antiquary; he was born Turin, 23 Feb. 1802, son of Giambattista C. and Maddelena Boggio; his collections were sold in his lifetime (1859) and scattered throughout many museums; some Egyptian antiquities went to the Hermitage; he died in Trebiolo, 1 Oct. 1870.

EB; Golenischeff, *Coll. Ég. Erm.*, p. vi; *DBDI* 25, 278-84.

CIMBA, Maria (*fl.* 1820-1826)
Italian wife of Dr. Cimba, the Italian physician; he came from Leghorn and settled in Cairo where he practised and was also the medical attendant to Henry Salt (q.v.); he and all his family, except for his wife, died of plague in Cairo in 1824; she recovered and returned to Leghorn in 1825, taking with her a magnificent collection of Egyptian antiquities which was sold in 1827; some of these were bought by the Leiden Museum for 5,000 guilders, including the magical papyrus I. 345 of which another portion came to Leiden in 1828 with the Anastasi Collection (I. 343).

Rijksmuseum van oudheden te Leiden, *Gids voor de verzameling van Egyptische beeldhouwwerken*, 25-8; Salt, ii. 231; H. Schneider in C. Morigi Govi, S. Curto, and S. Pernigotti, *L'Egitto fuori dell'Egitto*, 1991, 398.

CLACKSON (née **Quinn), Sarah Joanne** (1965-2003)
British Coptologist; she was born at Leicester 11 Dec. 1965, daughter of Peter Quinn and Audrey Wilberforce; she studied Classics and Egyptology at St John's College, Cambridge deciding to specialize in Coptic, 1985-89;

she then took a part-time PhD at University College London under W. J. Tait in 1992, completed in 1996; she acted as Project Officer for the Manichaean Documentation Centre, 1993-96; she held the Eugenie Strong Fellowship in Arts at Girton, 1996-98 and the Lady Wallis Budge Fellowship in Egyptology at Christ's College, Cambridge, 1998-2003; she served on the Committee of the Egypt Exploration Society Dec. 1998-Dec. 2001, Dec. 2002-July 2003; her publications include, with others, *The Elephantine Papyri in English*, 1996; *The Dictionary of Manichaen Texts* I, 1998; *Checklist of editions of Greek, Latin, demotic and Coptic papyri, ostraca, and tablets*, 2001; and as sole author *Coptic and Greek Texts Relating to the Hermopolite Monastery of Apa Apollo*, 2000; her papers are now in the Griffith Institute, Oxford; she died in Cambridge, 10 Aug. 2003; a commemorative volume of papers was edited by Anne Boud'hours and others, *Monastic Estates of Late Antique and Early Islamic Egypt*, 2009;

The Independent 18 Aug. 2003 (D. Thompson); *Egyptian Archaeology* 23 (2003), 44; *The Journal of Juristic Papyrology* 33 (2003), 7-14 (bibl.) (portr.) (P. M. Sijpesteijn).

CLARK, Robert Thomas Rundle (1909-1970)

British historian and Egyptologist; he was born at Devonport, 2 Oct. 1909, son of Robert Richard Rundle Clark, schoolmaster, and Edith Robinson; he was educated at Plymouth College, and St. John's College, Oxford 1928-31, BA in Modern History, 1931, MA, 1940; he had been interested in Egyptology since the age of ten and had taught himself to read ancient Egyptian but was unable to study Egyptology at Oxford for financial reasons; he joined the Department of Extramural Studies, University of Brimingham in 1941 as tutor; senior tutor 1945; senior lecturer 1953 and Deputy Director 1964; he initiated a course in hieroglyphs for extramural students and also taught Egyptology for the Department of Ancient History; his main interest was the study of Egyptian religion on which he published several articles and *Myth and Symbol in Ancient Egypt*, 1959; his papers are preserved in the Griffith Institute, Oxford; he died in Edgbaston, Birmingham, 14 Jan. 1970.

University of Birmingham Gazette Vol. 22 no. 4 (1970), 94-5; *JEA* 56 (1970), 3; inf. from Mrs. A. Wilcox (daughter).

CLARKE, (*Revd*) Edward Daniel (1769-1822)

British traveller; he was born at Willingdon, Sussex, 5 June 1769, son of Edward C., Vicar of Willingdon, and Anne Grenfield; he was educated at Jesus College, Cambridge, BA, 1790; MA, 1794; he then embarked on a tour of Russia, Sweden, Turkey, Syria, Palestine, Egypt and Greece; he visited Egypt briefly in April-May 1800, and June 1800, but his main stay was from 1 Aug. until 16Sept., 1800; he visited Cairo, Heliopolis, Giza and Saqqara where he collected some antiquities; he also visited sites in the Delta and arrived in Alexandria to be a member of the official party to which the Rosetta stone was surrendered by the French; he was subsequently Rector of Harlton 1805 and Yeldham 1810-1822, Professor of Mineralogy at Cambridge 1808, and Librarian at the University 1817; he was the author of *The Tomb of Alexander*, 1805; *The Tomb of Alexander reviewed*, 1806; *A Letter addressed to the Gentlemen of the British Museum*, 1807; *Travels in various Countries of Europe, Asia, and Africa*, 1810-23; his collection went to the Fitzwilliam Museum and MSS to the Bodleian Library, Oxford; he died in London, 9 March 1822.

ODNB 11, 863-5 (portr.); *DNB* 10, 421-4; *Al. Cantab* 2/2, 48; P. Rée, *Edward Daniel Clarke-A Civilian in Egypt*, 2003; J. Speake (ed.), *Literature of Travel and Exploration*, 2003, 1, 256-7.

CLARKE, Somers (1841-1926)

English architect and archaeologist; he was born in Brighton, 22 July 1841, son of Somers C., a solicitor, and Sarah Blaker; he was educated privately and later entered the office of Sir Gilbert Scott being mainly engaged in the restoration of churches; he was made Surveyor of the Fabric, St. Paul's Cathedral, 1897, and appointed Architect to the Dean and Chapter of Chichester Cathedral, 1900, retiring in 1922; FSA, 1881; he retired from general practice, 1902, afterwards making Egypt his home; he frequently had visited Egypt, and in 1893 joined J. J. Tylor (q.v.) in explorations at Elkab, afterwards assisting Quibell (q.v.) and Green (q.v.) during the excavations at Hierakonpolis; he later superintended the restoration of several temples and other buildings in Egypt; he also visited Nubia and the Sudan with Sayce (q.v.), 1909-10, before writing his book on Christian churches; he brought a new standard to the study of buildings and their remains in the 1890s before Reisner (q.v.) and Borchardt (q.v.) had started their work and his plan and section of the temple of Hierakonpolis showed for the first time in Egyptian archaeology an understanding of stratification although soon outmoded by later work in the Near East; he also made the plans and elevations for the tomb of Sobeknakht at Elkab, 1896, and that of Renni, 1900, and for the temple of Amenhotep III, 1898; he lived at the end of his life at Heliopolis and at Elkab, where he built himself a large mud brick house at Mehamid; he published articles in the *Journal of the Soc. of Ant.*, *JEA*, etc.; his important works were, *Report on certain excavations made at El-Kab ... I. Excavations 1901*, see A. H. Sayce, 1905; the architectural descriptions in Naville's *XIth Dynasty Temple at Deir el Bahari*, pt. 2, 1910; *Christian Antiquities in the Nile Valley*, 1912; *Les Temples Immergés de la Nubia*, 4°, with G. B. Mileham, 1920; *Ancient Egyptian Masonry: The Building Craft*, with R. Engelbach, 1930; his note-books are now and other papers are in the Griffith Institute; his negatives of Elkab are in the Dept. of Ancient Egypt and Sudan, British Museum; he died in Mehamid, 31 Aug. 1926.

JEA 13 (1927), 80; *WWW* ii, 202.

CLAYTON, (*Rt. Revd*) **Robert** (1695-1758)
Irish Bishop; he was born in probably at Fulwood, near Preston, Lancs. in 1695, son of John C., Dean of Kildare, and Eleanor Atherton; he was educated Trinity College, Dublin; BA, 1714; MA, 1717; LLB, 1718; LLD, 1722; DD, 1729; Bishop of Kiollala and Achonry, 1730; of Cork and Ross, 1735; of Clogher, 1745; he travelled in the east, and published an account of his journey from Cairo to Sinai, with remarks on hieroglyphics and mythology, *A Journal from Grand Cairo to Mount Sinai*, London, 1753; this was translated into German, 1754 and French, 1759; he died in Dublin, 26 Feb. 1758.

ODNB 11, 993-4; *DNB* 11, 19; Hilmy, i, 137; *Dictionary of Irish Biography*, 2009, 2, 564-5.

CLÉDAT, Jean (1871-1943)
French Egyptologist; he was born at Périgueux, 7 May 1871, son of Gabriel C. and Marie Gaillard; he was educated locally and then entered the École des Beaux-Arts in Paris at seventeen to study drawing but changed to Egyptology studying under Revillout (q.v.) at the École du Louvre until 1897 and at the École Pratique and the Collège de France; in 1899 he was made a lecturer at the École d'Anthropologie de Paris; in 1900 he was attached to the French Institute in Cairo and carried out a number of successful excavations for the Antiquities Service, the French Institute, the Comité de l'Art Arabe, and the Suez Canal Company; he worked at Meir, 1899-1901 and then at Coptic sites, at Bawit, 1901-5; Deir Abu Hennis, 1901; the monastery of Saint Simeon at Aswan, 1903 (*RT* 37 (1915), 41-57); Asyut and Akhmim, 1903 (*ASAE* 9 (1908), 213-230); and the monasteries at Sohag, 1903, 1905-6; he became involved in work in the Suez area: Tell Herr, 1905; Tell el Maskhuta, 1906-8 (*ASAE* 9 (1908), 210-1; *RT* 32 (1910), 40-2); Mahemdia, 1910; Qasr Gheit, 1911 (*ASAE* 12 (1915) 15-48); Khirbet el-Flusiya, 1914 (*ASAE* 16 (1916), 6-32); Tell Farama, 1904, 1909-11 (*ASAE* 13 (1914), 79-85); and Qantara, 1904, 1910-11, 1914 (*RT* 38 (1916), 21-31); he also took part in the excavations at Elephantine, 1906-8 with Clermont-Ganneau (q.v.) and 1910-11; in 1911 he organized a museum at Ismailia in his house; his work was cut short by World War I and a severe illness; his major publications were *Le monastère et la nécropole de Baouît*, 1904-16 and topographical notes on the Suez area in *ASAE* 10 (1910), 209-37 and *BIFAO* 16 (1918), 201-228, 17 (1919), 103-119, 18 (1920), 167-197, 21 (1922), 55-106, 145-187, 22 (1923), 135-189, 23 (1924), 27-84; he died in Bouch, Terrasson, 29 July 1943; antiquities from his excavations are in the Louvre, the Musée du Périgord, and the Musée Champollion, Figeac; his notebooks were given to the Louvre.

Revue du Louvre 3 (1988), 195-202; *L'Égypte en Périgord*, 1991, 1-17 (portr.); *Cahiers du Musée Champollion* 2 (1993), 13-15; inf. E. Gaillard and C. Meurice. Photograph ©Archives Mallet, Bouch, France; C. Meurice, *Jean Clédat en Égypte et en Nubie (1900-1914)*, 2014; K. Vogt, *ZÄS* 144 (2017),139-48.

CLEPHAN, Robert Coltman (1839-1922)
British collector; he was born in Gateshead, Durham, 8 Nov. 1839, son of Joseph C. and Mary Coltman; in addition to becoming a specialist on arms and armour, he made a considerable collection of Egyptian and other ancient material at his home in Tynemouth; the Egyptian section alone numbered 692 items, and contained among other objects, shabti figures, scarabs, and pieces of relief; he dedicated the catalogue to his wife who helped him collect them; his antiquities were sold at Sotheby's, 20-25 June 1918; FSA London; FSA Scotland, 1903-22; Vice-President of the Society of Antiquaries and of the National History Society of Newcastle-upon-Tyne; Pfleger für England des Vereins für Historische Waffenkunde, Germany; Corresponding Member of the Dresdener Waffengeschichte Seminar; he published *A Catalogue of Egyptian and other Antiquities at Marine House, Tynemouth, together with a study of Egyptology and other branches of Archaeology, as illustrated by the Collection*, 1907; *The Medieval Tournament*, 1917, reprint, 1995; he died at Marine House, Tynemouth, 23 March 1922.

Biog. inf. in the introduction to *The Medieval Tournament*, 1995; inf. E. Uphill; Lugt 77983.

CLÈRE, Jacques Jean (1906-1989)
French Egyptologist; he was born in Paris, 7 Sept. 1906, son of Georges Jacques C., fabricator of anatomical figures, and Celina Ernestine Robert; he was a cousin of Pierre Clère (q.v.); he was trained as an artist at the École Bernard Palissy and the École des Arts Decoratifs; he was attracted to Egyptology when drawing in the Louvre; in 1924 he began to attend the weekly class of Sottas (q.v.) at the École Pratique des Hautes Études and in 1925 he became a student at the École du Louvre; in 1926 he joined Bruyère (q.v.) at Deir el-Medina as a draughtsman; in 1927-8 he was with Bisson de la Roque (q.v.) at Medamud and in 1929 again at Deir el-Medina; he decided to specialize in the study of the Egyptian language under Moret (q.v.), Weill (q.v.), Lefebvre (q.v.), and Lacau (q.v.); in 1930 he studied in Berlin under Sethe (q.v.) and Grapow (q.v.); he also obtained qualifications in the history of religion, phonetics, Latin, Hebrew, Arabic, and Berber; he declined a post at the Louvre in 1930 to concentrate on his language studies but in 1931 gave a course at the École du Louvre and in 1934 and 1937 at the École Pratique; in 1949 he succeeded Lefebvre (q.v.) as Director d'Études at the École Pratique des Hautes Études; he was visiting Professor in Egyptology at Brown University 1951-2 and 1960-1 and Wilbour Fellow at The Brooklyn Museum in 1967; he published over eighty articles mainly on philological subjects; his monographs were *Rapport sur les fouilles de Médamoud (1927)* and *(1928)*, 1928 and 1929 with Bisson de la Roque; *Textes de la Première Période Intermédiaire et de la XIe Dynastie*, 1948 with Vandier; *Répertoire onomastique de Deir el-Médineh*,1949 with Černý and Bruyère;and *Le papyrus de Nesmin*, 1987; his papers were donated by his widow to the Griffith Institute, Oxford; he died in Paris, 5 June 1989.

Rev. d'Eg. 40 (1989), I-II (J. Vercoutter), III-IX (bibl.) (J. L. de Cénival); *CRIPEL* 13 (1991) 13-16 (I. E. S. Edwards).

CLÈRE, Pierre (1914-1962)
French draughtsman; born Paris, 1 April 1914 son of Lucien C. and Marguerite Nonnenmacher; he became interested in Egyptology and often visited the Louvre, taking courses under Moret (q.v.) and Lefebvre (q.v.) at the École Pratique des Hautes Études, 1933-5; before becoming draughtsman for the IFAO he worked for Dunand at Byblos where the drew objects indicating Egyptian and Asiatic contacts; he worked in Egypt, 1935-9, and drew among other things the scenes on the chariot ot Tuthmosis IV, which still remain unpublished; he taught Latin for a time at the Lycée Franco-Égyptien at Heliopolis, and worked again for the Lebanese government, 1942-6; between 1948 and 1953 he drew the scenes and hieroglyphic inscriptions on the gate of Euergetes at Karnak, which were incorporated with the work of Kuentz (q.v.) in a folio publication; his last work was the drawings for the first vol. of Sauneron's Esna hieroglyphic texts; he died in Paris, 5 Nov, 1962.

BIFAO 62 (1964), 237-8 (F. Daumas).

CLERMONT-GANNEAU, Charles Simon (1846-1923)
French orientalist; he was born in Paris, 19 Feb. 1846, son of Simon Ganneau, a sculptor, and Antoinette Clermont; he studied at the Institut national des langues et civilisations orientales and then entered the diplomatic service, working at Jerusalem, 1867-71 and Constantinople, 1871-4; he was involved with the discovery of the Moabite Stone of Mesha and undertook archaeological work in Palestine and Syria; after serving as vice-consul in Jaffa, 1880-2, he returned to Paris where he later became director of the École des Langues Orientales, 1889 and professor at the Collège de France, 1891; he undertook excavations at Elephantine, 1906-8 with Clédat (q.v.); chevalier of the Légion d'honneur, 1875; member of the Académie des Inscriptions et Belles-Lettres, 1889; he died in Paris, 15 Feb. 1923.

DBF 8, 1504-6; *Syria* 4 (1923), 83-4 (E. Pottier); *Rev. arch.* 17 (1923), 242-5 (portr.), 18 (1923), 139-58 (bibl.), (H. Ingolt); E. Delange in *EDAL* 1 (2009), 61-9.

CLOT, *(Bey)* **Antoine Barthélemy** (1793-1868)
French surgeon; he was born in Grenoble, 5 Nov. 1793, son of Louis C. and Marie Bérard; he studied medicine at the Hospice de la Charité, Marseilles, and Montpellier, then practised as a surgeon in Marseilles until 22 Dec. 1824, when he was appointed Surgeon-in-chief in Egypt by Muhammad Ali and took up his position on 11 Feb. 1825; although he then knew no Arabic, Clot accepted the appointment and with great energy and efficiency created a public health service and a centre of medical education, in spite of much local opposition; he overcame all difficulties, and with the help of a European staff trained many army surgeons for the Viceroy; he was awarded the dignity of Bey during the cholera epidemic on account of his exertions in 1831; in 1832 he returned to France, bringing with him some of his most promising pupils to complete their medical education; he visited England in Jan.-Feb. 1833 and was entertained by Pettigrew (q.v.), and also presented six Arabic MSS to the British Museum (now British Library) (Add. MSS 11558-63); he was soon recalled to Egypt, and in 1840 published his excellent *Aperçu général sur l'Égypte*, 2 vols.; he left Egypt in 1849 but was recalled by Said Pasha in 1856; in 1860 he

finally retired and settled in Marseilles; Clot Bey formed a large collection of Egyptian antiquities, two large batches of objects being acquired by the Louvre in 1852 and 1853, and in 1852 the British Museum purchased two papyri (EA 9901, used by Naville (*Todtb. Ag.*), and EA 9995, a Book of Breathings); the rest of his collection he sold for a nominal sum to the Municipality of Marseilles, and Maspero (q.v.) published a catalogue of it in 1889; a street between the railway Station and Ezbekiya in Cairo was named after him; he died in Marseilles, 28 Aug. 1868.

Brugsch, *Mein Leben*, 159; Carré, i, 286-90; *CHÉ* special number, 1949, 169-70; Dawson MS 63, ff. 106-7; Hilmy, i, 139; Pückler-Muskau, *Travels and Adventures in Egypt*, London 1847, i, 128, 159, 162, 223, 231-3; F. C. Madden, *The Surgery of Egypt*, 211-13; *Rev. de l'Art* 43, 167; H. Thiers, *Le Docteur Clot-Bey*, 1869; *Mémoires de A.-B. Clot-Bey*, ed. J. Tagher, 1949; *DBF* 9, 29-30; R.S. Merrillees and J. Evans, *Berytus* 28 (1980), 18-21; N. de Palatinat-Trillou, *Origine et répartition dans le sud-est de la France de la collection d'antiquités Egyptiennes du Docteur A. B. Clot-Bey*, 1975; J. Bulté, *Catalogue des collections égyptiennes du Musée National de Céramique à Sèvres*, 1981, 17; *Égyptes* 3 (1993), 6-9; *Les Savants en Égypte*, 1998, 119; *Pascal Coste. Toutes les Égypte*, 1998, 235-44.

COATES, Thomas (1774-1828)
British traveller; he became assistant surgeon in Bombay, India, 27 Nov. 1799, a deputy surgeon, 1 March 1807; he officially retired 29 Nov. 1822; he returned to England by the overland route in 1820, visiting Egypt in company with Walter Davidson; at Qurna he bought a mummy which he presented in Sept. 1821 to the Newcastle Literary Soc.; this is now in the Hancock Museum in Newcastle; he was later of Lipwood House, Haydon Bridge, Northumberland; he died 13 Jan. 1828.

Granville, 24-5; W. Lee, *Hist. Notes of Haydon Bridge*, 1876, 30-1; inf. W. G. R. Weeks; D. G. Crawford, *Roll of the Indian Medical Service* 1615-1930, 1930, 419.

COCHELET, Adrien Louis (1788-1858)
French diplomat; he was born in Charleville, 29 April 1788, son of Adrien Pierre Barthlémy C, a parliamentary deputy, and Marie Charlote Victoire Matis; he served as auditor in the ministry of Finances, 1809-13, intendant of Goritz and Bialystock, prefect of La Meuse, 1815; consular agent in Riga; and consul in Brazil, Mexico, and Wallachia; he was French Consul-General in Egypt, 1839-41; he then became state counsellor, 1841-8 and senator, 1857; he died in Paris, 7 March 1858.

French FO Records; Carré, ii, 28; *DBF* 9, 65-6; M. Robert, *Dictionnaire des parlementaires français*, 1891, 2, 142.

COCKLE, Walter Eric Harold (1939-2018)
British papyrologist; he was born in Harrow-on-the Hill, Middlesex, 2 Dec. 1939, son of Walter Ponsonby Shaw C., a civil engineer, and Geertruda Van Der Steen; he was educated at the University of St Andrews in Classics, 1958-62; MA 1962; PhD from Birkbeck College, University of London, 1974; he became Departmental Assistant in the Dept. of Greek, University College London, 1964 and Research Fellow, 1992-2002; he helped to organize the conservation of papyri in the Cairo Musem; he took part in the excavations at Mons Claudianus, 1987-93; FSA, 1987 apart from other papyrological publications, he edited seven volumes of the Oxyrhynchus Papyri series, 1991-2018; he died in Chorleywood, Herts., 6 Dec. 2018.

EA 54 (2019), 46 (D. Thompson) (portr.); inf. H. Cockle.

COHEN, Mendes Israel (1796-1879)
Jewish American collector of German origin; he was born at Richmond, Virginia 25 May 1796, son of Israel C. and Judith Solomon; he settled in Baltimore as a child and took part in the American War of 1812; in 1829 he went to Europe; in 1832 he made a voyage up the Nile, and reached the Second Cataract, as his name, with the date, is carved on the Rock of Abu Sir; he made many purchases from Egyptian antiquities dealers and took nearly 700 objects back to America, to which additions were made at the Salt sale, 1835; he was given the title of Colonel in 1836; Cohen generously placed his collection at the disposal of George R. Gliddon (q.v.) in 1845 to illustrate his lectures; he died in Baltimore, 7 May 1879; after his death, the collection passed to his nephews by whom it was sold in 1884 to Johns Hopkins University for a nominal sum.

Johns Hopkins Univ. Circulars iv, no. 35, 21-3 (1884); *N. Y. Hist. Soc. Quarterly Bull.* iv, 5 (1920); *Maryland Historical Magazine* 18 (1923), 371-76; A. Oliver, *American Travellers on the Nile*, 2016, 134-5.

COLMAN, Jeremiah James (1830-1898)
MP and food manufacturer; he was born in Stoke Holy Cross near Norwich, Norfolk, 14 June 1830, son of James C. and Mary Burlingham; MP for Norwich for 24 years; his family established, and Colman later headed, the firm which produced Colman's Mustard; he visited Egypt in the winter of 1896-97 to see his invalid son, Alan Cozens-Hardy Colman, who had travelled there for his health and who died in Luxor soon after his father's arrival; in Egypt he travelled from Cairo to Luxor, where he bought antiquities under the guidance of his son's physician, a Mr Worthington; the collection was later catalogued by J. E. Quibell (q.v.), who names several Luxor dealers including Mohammed Mohassib (q.v.), from whom Colman bought an exceptionally fine model granary ('A Painted Pottery Model of a Granary: In the Collection of the Late Jeremiah James Colman, Esq., of Carrow House, Norwich' by A. M. Blackman, *JEA* 6 (1920), 206-8); Quibell also mentions one other Luxor dealer, Abdul Medjid, whom he describes as 'a thorough scamp'; the collection was bequeathed to two of Colman's daughters, Ethel Mary and Helen Caroline, who made it available for study and publication; in 1921 they donated it to Norwich Castle Museum; he died at The Cliffe, Corton, Norfolk, 18 Sept. 1898.

ODNB 12, 757-9 (portr.); inf. F. Kalloniatis; F. Kalloniatis, 'The shroud of Ipu at Norwich Castle Museum' *Egyptian Archaeology* 39 (2011), 15-17; F. Kalloniatis in D. Fortenberry (ed.), *Souvenirs and New Ideas*, 2013, 68-79.

COLQUHOUN, (*Sir***) Robert Gilmour** (1804-1870)
British diplomat; he was born in 1804, son of Robert C. of Camstradden, RN, and Harriet Farrer; he was British Consul-General in Egypt, appointed 13 Dec. 1858; he resigned in 1865 and was succeeded by Sir Edward Stanton, KCB (q.v.); he died in Allian, Dulls Perthshire, 10 Nov. 1970.

FO Records; Duff Gordon, 373; *Khedives and Pashas*, 167, 213-14, 218.

COMPTON, Spencer Joshua Alwyne, 2nd Marquess of Northampton (1790-1851)
British collector; he was born at Erlestoke Park, Wilts. 2 Jan. 1790, son of Charles C. 1st Marquess and Mary Smith; he was educated at Trinity Coll. Cambridge MA 1810; MP for Northampton 1812-20; he succeeded his father in 1828; Fellow of the Royal Soc. 1830; LLD Cambridge 1835; Fellow of the Society of Antiquaries 1836; DCL Oxford 1850; he was President of the Royal Society 1838-48, President of the Royal Archaeological Institute 1845-51, and a Trustee of the BM 1849-51; he visited Egypt in 1849-50 with his son-in-law and daughter Lord and Lady Alford and acquired a number of Egyptian objects some of which he presented to the BM in 1850 (EA 38271 and 38282 which were published in the *Archaeological Journal* viii, 396-7), while others were given by his heir in 1852; other objects are in the Museum at Northampton; a small sphinx, given to Lady Alford by John Larking (q.v.) of Alexandria passed to the Brownlow family and was acquired by the Royal Scottish Museum Edinburgh in 1984; he died in Castle Ashby, 17 Jan. 1851.

Complete Peerage 9, 687; *GM* 35 (1850), 425-9; *JEA* 49 (1963), 5.

COMPTON, (*Sir***) William George Spencer Scott, 5th Marquess of Northampton** (1851-1913)
British nobleman; he was born at Castle Ashby, 23 April 1851, 2nd son of William C. 4th Marquess and Eliza Elliot; he was educated Eton and Trinity College, Cambridge; he succeeded to the title, 1897; he was in the diplomatic service and travelled in Egypt, 1898-9, becoming interested in Egyptian excavation; he accordingly financed the excavations in the Theban necropolis directed by Newberry (q.v.) and Wilhelm Spiegelberg (q.v.), the results of which were published in a memoir in 1908; he died in Acqui, Piedmont, 15 June 1913.

WWW i, 530; Newberry Corr; P. Whelan in M. Betrò and G. Miniaci (eds.), *Talking along the Nile*, 2013, 229-54.

COOK, (*Sir***) Francis, 1st Visconde de Monserrate** (1817-1901)
British merchant and art collector; he was born in Clapham, 3 Jan. 1817, son of William C., founder of the trading company Cook & Son, and Mary Ann Lainson; as a young man he travelled in Egypt and Portugal; he joined his father's company in 1833, partner 1843, and succeeded his father as its head in 1869; he thus became one of the richest men in England; he was created Portuguese Visconde de Monserrate, 1864, FSA 1873, and Bart., 1886; he formed a notable collection of paintings and other works of art, including Classical and Egyptian antiquities, housed at Doughty House, Richmond, Surrey, and the Palace of Monserrate in Cintra, Portugal; after his death his

collection was divided between his sons Frederick (born London 21 Nov. 1844, died Richmond, 21 May 1920) and Wyndham Francis (born 21 Aug. 1860, died 7 May 1905); Wyndham's share, which included some Egyptian bronzes, was sold at Christie's, 14-16 July 1925; Frederick inherited the paintings and most of the Egyptian material, which descended to his son Herbert (1868-1939); the collection was largely dispersed by Herbert's son Francis (1907-1978), most of the antiquities being sold to the Ashmolean and Manchester Museums after World War II; Francis Cook died at Doughty House, Richmond, 17 Feb. 1901.

ODNB 13, 97-8; *AE* 1917, 62; C. H. Smith, *Catalogue of the Antiquities in the Collection of the late Wyndham Francis Cook*, 1908; H. W. Mengedoht, *Catalogue of the Egyptian antiquities in the collection of Sir Herbert Cook, Bt., at Doughty House, Richmond*, 1924; E. Danziger, 'The Cook Collection, its Founder and its Inheritors' *The Burlington Magazine*, 146/1216 (Jul., 2004), 444-458; Lugt 88931.

COOK, (*Revd*) **Frederick Charles** (1804-1889)
English clergyman, archaeologist, and philologist; he was born at Millbrook near Southampton, 1 Dec. 1804, son of William C. and his wife Elizabeth; he was educated at St. John's College, Cambridge, 1824; BA, 1831; MA, 1844; he studied oriental languages at Bonn, and was ordained 1839; Inspector of Church Schools; Chaplain-in-ord. to the Queen, 1857, and Preacher at Lincoln's Inn, 1860-80; Canon Residentiary of Exeter Cathedral, 1864; Precentor, 1872; a scholar of widely ranging interests he was general editor of *The Speaker's Commentary*, 1871-81; he published *Origins of Religion and Language*, 1884; he took up Egyptology at the suggestion of Renouf (q.v.) and translated the Hymn to the Nile and the Piankhi Stela in *Records of the Past*; he is said to have known 52 languages and he bequeathed his library to Exeter Cathedral; he died in Exeter, 22 June 1889.

DNB Suppl. 2, 54; *ODNB* 13, 98- 9(portr.); Hilmy, i, 143; *Letters to Renouf*, Dawson MS 18, ff. 26-39.

COOK, (*Revd*) **Joseph** (1791-1825)
British clergyman and traveller; he was born in Alnwick 19 May 1791, son of Joseph C. and Sarah Brown; Fellow of Christ's College, Cambridge; MA, 1816; he visited Arabia and Egypt, 1824-5, and reached the Second Cataract of the Nile; his name and the date, 1824, are carved on the rock of Abu Sir; he died suddenly while riding a camel on his way to Sinai at Wadi Hebrim, 3 March 1825.

Al. Cantab.; *GM* 95 (1825), 90; Hay Diary, 1825, 24 Jan., 25 June; Westcar Diary, 280.

COONEY, **John Ducey** (1905-1982)
American Egyptologist; he was born at Boston, 23 Aug. 1905; he worked firstly as an interior decorator; he was later awarded a scholarship to Harvard College (AB, 1932) and then attended graduate school at Harvard, 1932-3 and the University of Pennsylvania, Department of Semitic Languages, 1933-37; he became registrar at The Brooklyn Museum, 1933; he then held the post of assistant curator, Department of Ancient Art, The Brooklyn Museum, 1937-9 and then curator of Ancient Art, 1940-63; from 1963-74 he was Curator of Ancient Art at the Cleveland Museum of Art and then research curator there, 1974-7; he was briefly director of the American Research Center in Cairo, 1952-3; he concentrated on acquiring objects of artistic merit for his museums and was an adviser to collectors such as Albert Gallatin (q.v.) and Norbert Schimmel (q.v.); he was a specialist in ancient Egyptian glass; his publications include *Pagan and Christian Egypt*, with E. Riefstahl, 1941; *Introduction to the Egyptian Art in the Brooklyn Museum*, 1952; *Amarna Reliefs from Hermopolis in American Collections*, 1965; the Egyptian sections of *The Beauty of Ancient Art: Catalogue of the Norbert Schimmel Collection*, 1964 and O., Muscarella (ed.), *The Norbert Schimmel Collection*, 1974; *Catalogue of Egyptian Antiquities in the British Museum*, IV *Glass*, 1976; he died in Sherman, Connecticut, 26 Nov. 1982.

NARCE 121 (1983), 3; *BES* 5 (1983), 4-6 (portr.) (N. Schimmel), 135-141 (bibl.) (D. Guzman); *New York Times* 30 Nov. 1982; inf. A. Kozloff; *Journal of Glass Studies* 25 (1983) 279; L. Berman, *The Cleveland Museum of Art. Catalogue of Egyptian Art*, 1999, 26-9.

COOPER, (*Revd*) **Basil Henry** (1819-1891)
British orientalist and Congregationalist minister; he was born at Cookham, Berkshire 29 June 1819, son of Basil Henry C., a solicitor, and his wife Harriet; he was educated at Highbury College, 1840-3 and the University of London,BA; he served as a minister in West Bromwich, 1843-52, London, 1853-64, Paris, 1865, and Torquay, 1867-8; he was a Foundation member of the Soc. of Biblical Archaeology; FRSL, 1878; he was very interested in Egyptology and a correspondent of Edward Hincks (q.v.); he published articles on the Exodus, the antiquity of metal-working in Egypt and on Mariette's discoveries; he acted as reporter for *The Times* at the Congress of Orientalists in 1874; he died at Cane Hill Asylum, Purley, Surrey, 5 May 1891.

Budge, *N & T* i, 10; Budge, *R & P*, 271; Hincks (see index).

COOPER, Edward Joshua (1798-1863)
Irish astronomer; he was born in Dublin, May 1798, son of Edward Synge C. and Anne Verelest; educated at Eton and Christ Church, Oxford; FRS, 1853; MP, 1830-41, 1857-9; he visited Egypt, 1820-1, mainly to study the Zodiacs of Dendera and Esna, but he also copied many inscriptions which were included in a volume *Views in Egypt and Nubia*, privately printed, 1824-7; he built an observatory on his estate at Markree, Sligo, and published astronomical works; he died in Markree Castle, Sligo, 23 April 1863.

ODNB 13, 245-6; *DNB* 12, 142; Hilmy, i, 143; *Proceedings of the Royal Society* 13; R. De Keersmaecker, *ASTENE Bulletin* 75 (2018), 28.

COOPER, William Ricketts (1843-1878)
British author, originally a carpet-designer; he was born London 12 March 1843, son of Daniel C., farmer, and Anne Pernell Brooks; after being introduced to Egyptology and Assyriology by Bonomi (q.v.), he played an active part in founding and organizing the Society of Biblical Archaeology, and was its Secretary from 1872 to 1878; he originated the 'Archaic Classes' conducted by Sayce (q.v.) and Renouf (q.v.), and the publication of *Records of the Past* and the *Archaic Classics*; he published, *The serpent myths of ancient Egypt: being a comparative history of these myths compiled from the Ritual of the Dead, Egyptian inscriptions, papyri, etc.*, 1873; *The Horus myth in its relation to Christianity*, 1877; *A short history of the Egyptian obelisks: with translations of many of the hieroglyphic inscriptions, chiefly by François Chabas*, 2nd ed., 1878; he died in Ventnor, 15 Nov. 1878.

ODNB 13, 292-3; *DNB* 12, 115; Budge, *N & T* i, 7, 11; Budge, *R & P*, 262; Hilmy, i, 143; Boase 1, 711.

CORBAUX, Marie Françoise Catherine Doetter (1812-1883)
English painter and biblical critic; commonly known as Fanny Corbaux, she was born in Paris in 1812, the daughter of Francis C., FSA, a mathematician who resided much in France; she studied at the National Gallery and British Institution, and in 1830 was elected Hon. Member of the Soc. of British Artists; she painted and drew portraits, landscapes, and book-illustrations; she was also interested in Biblical archaeology and wrote a long series of articles entitled 'Letters on the Physical Geography of the Exodus' in the *Athenaeum*, and another on the Rephaim in the Bible for the *Journal of Sacred Literature* (e.g. on Papyrus Anastasi I, Jan. 1852); she also wrote the introduction to Dunbar Heath's *Exodus Papyri*, 1855; she subsequently suffered ill health after having for many years supported her family by her artistic and literary work, and was granted a small Civil List pension, 1871; she died in East Hove near Brighton after a long illness, 1 Feb. 1883.

DNB 12, 195; ODNB 13, 381-2; Hilmy, i, 145.

CORDERO DI SAN QUINTINO, Giulio dei Conti (1778-1857)
Italian Egyptologist; he was born in Mondovi, 30 June 1778, son of Giovanni Antonio C. di San Quintino and Maria Caterina Botta; he graduated from the Collegio della Provincie, 1795; he studied ancient history and numismatics, and was later Keeper of the Egyptian Collections, Turin Museum 1824-31; he published a number of works on Egyptian subjects; he received Champollion (q.v.) when he was studying in Turin Museum; he died in Turin, 19 Sept. 1857.

Champollion, i, 48, 67, 109, 168, 210, 412, 422, and often; Hilmy, ii, 148; *DBDI* 28, 799-803.

CORY, Isaac Preston (1801-1842)
British writer; he was born in Great Yarmouth, 26 April 1801, son of Robert C., FSA, Mayor of Great Yarmouth, and Anne Preston; he became a Fellow of Caius College, Cambridge, MA, 1827; he published a work on the ancient nations of the Near East, 1832, and also wrote *Chronological Inquiry into the Ancient History of Egypt*, 1837; he died in Blundeston, Suffolk, 1 April 1842.

DNB 12, 258; *ODNB* 13, 56; Hilmy, i, 146; C. J. Palmer, *The Perlustration of Great Yarmouth*, 1874, II, 31-3.

COSTAZ, (*Baron*) Louis (1767-1842)
French savant and mathematician; he was born at Champagne, 17 March 1767, son of Claude C. and Claudine Goujon; he was a member of Napoleon's Commission; Membre de l'Inst. de France and of the Inst. Égyptien; he led the expedition to Upper Egypt, and contributed to the *Description de l'Égypte* accounts of the Valley of the Kings and of Elkab; he died in Fontainebleau, 15 Feb. 1842.

Carré, i, 148; Hilmy, i, 146; *DBF* 9, 794-5.

COSTE, Pascal Xavier (1787-1879)
French architect from Marseilles; he was born at Marseilles, 26 Nov. 1787, son of Bernard C., a textile manufacturer, and his wife née Tauffret; he was in the service of Muhammad Ali between 1818 and 1827, and

designed many public buildings, arsenals, and factories for him, including the Pasha's pavilion at Alexandria; he made many drawings of ancient buildings and was a pioneer in the study of Arab art in Egypt, publishing a monumental work on this subject, 1839; he later produced a similar work on the buildings of Persia; he travelled throughout all Egypt as well as in Europe and much of Asia; a friend of Champollion (q.v.) and Clot Bey (q.v.), he also accompanied the Comte de Forbin (q.v.) in his travels in Egypt ; he designed many buildings in France, notably the Bourse of Marseilles; his *Mémoires d'un Artiste*, 1878, contains much interesting information about Egypt; he died in Marseilles, 7 Feb. 1879.

Belzoni, i, 411; Champollion, i, 175; Carré, i, 287; Hilmy, i, 146; Montulé, 63, 67; Wilkinson, *Mod. Eg. and Thebes*, i, 281; *DBF* 9, 805; *Pascal Coste. Toutes les Égypte*, 1998; È. Gran-Aymerich, *Dictionnaire biographique d'archéologie 1798-1945*, 2001, incorporated in *Les Chercheurs de passé 1798-1945*, 2007, 723-4; C. Williams in D. Fortenberry and D. Manley (eds.), *Saddling the Dogs*, 2009, 53-80.

COSTER, Robert (Reuben) (1795-1864)
Dutch agent; he was born in Maarssen near Utrecht, 24 Jan. 1795 as Reuben, son of Elias C. and his wife Rijntje of Jewish origin; he was converted to Christianity in Edinburgh; he journeyed to the Levant in 1823 where he met Revd. Joseph Wolff, a Jewish-Christian missionary, who recommended him to John Barker (q.v.) as his secretary; he apparently followed Barker to Egypt and also served as secretary and translator to Consul Patrick Campbell (q.v.), 1833-9; he later worked as a clerk for the P and O Co; between 1833 and 1847 he obtained many Egyptian antiquities for Dr. Lee's (q.v.) Museum at Hartwell House; he was in England 1838-40 and visited Hartwell in Aug. 1839 and made coloured drawings of some of the objects; he died in Alexandria, 22 March 1864.

FO Records; Barker, ii, 68; Bonomi Diary, 1831, 16 June and 15 Nov.; *Hartwell Museum Registers* (MS); *Letter to Lee*, Dawson MS 18, f. 143; inf. Mrs. Herbert and P. Thomas.

COTTON, James Sutherland (1847-1918)
British barrister and archaeologist; he was born in Coonour, Madras, 17 July 1847, son of Joseph John C. and Susan Jessie Minchin; he was a scholar of Trinity College, Oxford, 1867-70, and a Fellow and Lecturer of The Queen's College, Oxford, 1871-4; after being called to the Bar, 1874, he became editor of the *Academy*; he also catalogued the European MSS relating to India in the India Office; he was an early member of the Committee of the EEF; Hon. Sec. 1896-1912; Assistant Editor, *JEA*, 1914-18; he died in Teffont near Salisbury, 9 July 1918.

JEA 5 (1918), 140; *WWW* ii.,232.

COTTRELL, Leonard Eric (1913-1974)
British author; he was born at Tettenhall near Wolverhampton, 21 May 1913, son of William Arthur C. and Beatrice Martha Tootell; he was educated at King Edward's Grammar School, Birmingham; he became a journalist and then joined the BBC as a writer-producer, 1942-59, after which he worked freelance; he wrote a large number of popular works on Egyptology and archaeology, notably *The Lost Pharaohs*, 1950; *The Mountains of Pharaoh*, 1956; *Concise Encyclopedia of Archaeology*, 1960; *Guide to Egypt*, 1964; *Queens of the Pharaohs*, 1966; *The Warrior Pharaohs*, 1968; *In Search of the Pharaohs*, 1973; he also wrote *The Buried Pyramid*, 1956 for Goneim (q.v.); he died in Solihull, Birmingham, 6 Oct. 1974.

WWW vii, 175; *Contemporary Authors*, New Revision, 4, 162-3.

COUSINÉRY, Baltzar (1747-1833)
French antiquary and numismatist; he was born in Marseilles, 8 June 1747, son of Barthélemy C. and Louise Duval; he contributed four letters to the *Mag. Encyclopédique* on the subject of the Rosetta Stone, 1807-8, reprinted separately, Paris, 1810; he collected coins and antiquities; the important stele Louvre C.14 formerly belonged to him; he acquired it through Rollin (q.v.) at the Thédenat-Duvent (q.v.) sale in 1822; his rich collection of Roman coins was acquired by the Vienna Museum; he died 17 Jan. 1833.

BIFAO 5 (1905), 84; Champollion, i, 47, 170; *TSBA* 5, 555; Hilmy, i, 149; *DBF* 9, 1078-9.

COUTELLE, Jean Marie Joseph (1748-1835)
French physicist; he was born at Le Mans, 3 Jan. 1748; he trained as a physicist and went to Paris in 1772; because of his speciality in gas, he became head of the ballooning corps and accompanied the Napoleonic expedition to Egypt; he directed excavations at Memphis and later at Giza in 1801; he visited Sinai and proposed the removal

of an obelisk to Paris; he also prepared a study on the cladding of the Great Pyramid; he took part in the wars in Germany and Spain; he was then appointed inspector of schools in Versailles and from 1814 Paris; Légion d'honneur, 1805; he retired in 1816; he died in Auteuil, 20 March 1835.

DBF 9, 1109-10; *Biographie Universelle* 9, 400-1.

COVENTRY, Henry (*c.*1708-1752)
British scholar and author; he was born at Twickenham, *c.*1708, son of Hon Henry C. and Anne Coles; he was educated at Eton and Magdalene College, Cambridge; MA, 1773; he published a theological work *Philemon to Hydaspes*, 1736-44, in which he discussed Egyptian hieroglyphs and was accused of plagiarizing Bishop Warburton's (q.v.) results, for which he afterwards published an *Apologetical Letter*, 1741; he died 29 Dec. 1752.

ODNB 13, 731-2; *DNB* 12, 358; Nichols, *Lit. Anecd.* v, 564.

COVINGTON (*né* Croninger), Lorenzo Dow (1862-1935)
American excavator; he was born at Covington, Kentucky, 16. Feb. 1862, son of Lorenzo Dow C., a printer, and Sarah Angeline Hoyt; he worked as a printer, undertook a world tour, 1880-3, and trained as an actor in New York where he changed his name in 1888; he later went to Europe where he claimed to have studied Egyptology at London, Berlin, and Paris; he went to Egypt in 1902,1903, and 1905-11 and undertook excavations at the Pyramids and in the neighbouring mastabas of Giza, 1902-10; he also explored Wadi el-Kattar, 1907 and Coptos, 1909; he also explored the Western Desert in 1909; he was assisted in his work by J. E. Quibell (q.v.); he published reports of his discoveries in *ASAE* 6, 9, and 10; elected FRGS, 1911 but never qualified; he gave some antiquities to the Eden Park Museum, Cincinnati, 1909; he later became an independent lecturer on Egyptian topics; he died when struck down by an automobile in New York, 2 June 1935.

Maspero, *Rapports sur la Marche du Serv. des Ant.* 101, 208, 234, 262, 292, 393; Petrie, *Gizeh and Rifeh*, 1907, 7; inf. J. Larson and D. M. Shoemaker.

COWPER, Henry Swainson (1865-1941)
British antiquary and collector; he was born at Harrow, 17 June 1865, son of Thomas Christopher C. and Catherine Anne Hall; educated at Harrow; JP, Lancs.; FSA, 1889, he had a choice collection of Egyptian antiquities which was presented to the British Museum in 1943; he died in Bowness-on-Windermere, 7 April 1941.

AE 1917, 146; *Ant. Journ.* 21, 261.

COXE, Eckley Brinton Jnr. (1872-1916)
American philanthropist; he was born in Philadelphia, May 1872, son of Charles B. C., who died in Egypt when his son was less than a year old, and Elizabeth Allen Sinkler; he visited Egypt and the Sudan many times and in 1895 became a prominent member of the American branch of the EEF, of which he was Hon. Sec., 1913-16; he gave substantial financial help to excavations in Egypt and Nubia; in 1907 an expedition to Nubia was led by Randall-MacIver (q.v.); in 1912, he discovered a large Predynastic settlement at Abydos, and in 1915 sent an expedition to excavate the palace of Merenptah at Memphis; he was President of the Penn. Museum, 1910-16; he died in Drifton, Pennsylvania, 20 Sept. 1916.

JEA 4 (1917), 61; *Penn. Museum Journal*, 7 (1916), no. 3, 139-44 (portr.); *Expedition* 21 (1979), 44 (portr.).

CRADOCK (CARADOC), (*Hon.*) John Hobart, 2nd Baron Howden (1799-1873)
British army officer; he was born in Dublin, 16 Oct. 1799, the only son of John Francis H. 1st Baron Howden and Theodosia Meade; he was sent to Egypt on a secret mission, 1827-8; he afterwards served in the Diplomatic service in S. America and Spain; he succeeded as 2nd Baron Howden, 1839; GCB; he died in St. Étienne, Bayonne, 9 Oct. 1873.

ODNB 10, 9; *DNB* 9, 29; Barker, ii, 73 ff.; BL Add. MS 25659, f. 21; *JEA* 35 (1949), 161; R. de Keersmaecker, *ASTENE* Bulletin 63 (2015), 21-2.

CRAWFORD, Osbert Guy Stanhope (1886-1957)
British archaeologist; born Bombay, 28 Oct. 1886, son of Charles Edward Gordon C., a High Court Judge, and Alice Luscombe; he was educated at Marlborough and Keble College, Oxford; becoming interested in archaeology he first wrote a paper on Early Bronze Age distributions and then joined the Wellcome Sudan excavations as an assistant, 1913-14; after war service he undertook field work in Britain and was appointed Archaeology Officer to the Ordnance Survey in 1920; he founded the archaeological journal *Antiquity*; he published *Wessex from the Air*, 1928, and *Archaeology in the Field*, 1953, two books which became standard works and which showed the use of new techniques; he visited Russia, Iraq, and N. Africa and also the Sudan again in 1950-1, producing the *History of the Fung Kingdom of Sennar*; he was awarded the Victoria Medal

of the RGS and Hon. DCL by the Universities of Cambridge and Southampton; CBE; FBA; he also wrote *Abu Geili* (with F. Addison), 1951; *Castles and churches in the Middle Nile Region*, 1961; some of his papers are in the Griffith Institute; he died in Southampton, 28 Nov. 1957.

Said and done (autobiog.), 1955; *AfO* 18 (1957-8), 490; *PEQ* 90 (1958), 79-83 (C.W. Phillips); *ODNB* 14, 76-8.

CROMER, Earl of *see* **Baring**

CROMPTON, Winifred Mary (1870-1932)
British museum curator; she was born in Stretford, Manchester, 10 July 1870, daughter of John C., manufacturing chemist and Victoria Becker; she studied at the University of Manchester; MA; she was appointed Assistant Keeper, Manchester Museum, 1912; for 20 years she was in charge of this important Egyptian collection and also did much to promote interest in Egyptology in Manchester; she took a prominent part in the Manchester Egyptian and Oriental Society, and contributed to *JEA* and other journals; she died in Manchester, 8 Oct. 1932.

JEA 18 (1932), 190; *JMEOS* 18 (1932), 33-5.

CRONSTRAND, Baltzar (1794-1876)
Swedish army officer and traveller; he was born in Törneby, 15 May 1794, son of Lars C. and Johanna Katarina Beckerström; Cronstrand visited various continental countries in order to study the art of fortification; he arrived in Egypt in Jan. 1836 and remained there until May 1838; during his stay he visited most of the accessible ancient sites, from Alexandria as far as the Second Cataract; he spent most of his time at Karnak working daily in the temple; Cronstrand was a very skilled draughtsman and was determined to copy the ancient monuments in a way that was superior to anything done by his predecessors; he was never able to publish his drawings, but this valuable collection of some 200 items is kept today in the National Museum of Stockholm; among this material there are about 100 drawings executed from various parts of Karnak temples, many being of an amazing exactness and also reproducing hieroglyphic inscriptions; there are also interesting drawings from Beni Hasan, Medinet Habu, the Ramesseum, Philae, and Beit el Wali; some of his notes on Egyptian art and diaries and drawings relating the travels were published posthumously; Cronstrand died in Stockholm, 26 Jan. 1876.

P. A. Siljeström, *Skrifter af Baltzar Cronstrand for forfattarens vanner samlade och utgifna*, Stockholm, 1877; B. J. Peterson, 'Swedish Travellers in Egypt during the period 1700-1850', *Opuscula Atheniensia* vii (Lund 1967), 17-18; B. George and B. Peterson, *Die Karnak-zeichnungen von Baltzar Cronstrand 1836-1837*, 1979; B. George and B. Peterson, *Baltzar Cronstrand i Egypten 1836-1837,* 1980; Svenskt Biografiskt Lexikon 9, 338-45 (portr.).

CROWFOOT, Elisabeth Grace (1914-2005)
British textile expert; she was born in Cairo, 12 Jan. 1914, third daughter of John C. (q.v.) and Grace May Hood C. (q.v.); she followed a career as an actress, stage manager and wardrobe mistress until 1952, after which she helped her parents with their publications and became a noted textile expert and consultant; she catalogued the textile material from the EES excavations at Qasr Ibrim in the 1960s and took part in the excavations, 1976-84; she died at Waveney, Suffolk, 31 Aug. 2005; her work was posthumously published, *Qasr Ibrim: The Textiles from the Cathedral Cemetery*, 2011.

Inf. J. Crowfoot (son).

CROWFOOT, Grace Mary (Molly) (*née* **Hood**) (1878-1957)
British archaeologist and craft expert; she was born at Nettleham Hall, Lincs., 3 Nov. 1878, daughter of Sinclair Frankland Hood and Grace Elinor Swan and was a granddaughter of William F Hood (q.v); she was interested in Natural History and published *Some Desert Flowers*, 1930, written in Egypt, and *Flora of the Sudan*, which formed an illustrated section of the official handbook; she took a keen interest in the women of the Sudan and played a considerable part in starting the government maternity service and a campaign against female genital mutilation; from the Sudanese women of Omdurman she learned to weave and this led to the subject for which she became noted, the study of ancient textiles; for this she learnt the techniques of primitive weaving from the Bedu in the Sudan; she wrote many articles on this subject in *JEA, Sudan Notes and Records, AAA,* and other journals; her monographs included *Models of Egyptian Looms*, 1921, with H. L. Roth; *Methods of hand spinning in Egypt and the Sudan*; 1931; *Coptic Textiles in Two-Faced Weave with Pattern in Reverse*, 1939; *The Tunic of Tut'ankhamun*, 1941; 1931; she wrote the section 'Textiles, Basketry and Mats' in the *Oxford History of Technology*, 1954; some unpublished manuscripts consisting of lectures on weaving belong to the library of

the Institute of Archaeology, London; she died in Geldeston, Norfolk, 20 March 1957; the eldest of her four daughters was the chemist Dorothy Hodgkin, the second was Joan Crowfoot Payne (q.v.) and her third daughter Elisabeth Grace Crowfoot (q.v.).

Archaeology 10 (1957), 281 (anon.); *PEQ* 89 (1957), 153-4 (T. L. H. and K. M. Kenyon); *ICON News* (Jan. 2006), 22-3; inf. J. Crowfoot.

CROWFOOT, John Winter (1873-1959)
British archaeologist and educationalist; born at Wigginton, 28 July 1873, son of John Henchman Crowfoot and Mary Elizabeth daughter of Robert Bayly; he married Grace Mary Hood (see above) 20 July 1909 at Nettleham; he was educated at Marlborough and Brasenose College Oxford, Senior Hume Exhibitioner; Hon. D.Litt., Oxon, 1958; he worked as an assistant master for the Ministry of Educ. Cairo, 1901-3; appointed Assistant Director of Educ., Cairo, 1908-14; Director of Educ., Sudan Government, and Principal of Gordon College, Khartoum, 1914-26, with responsibility for antiquities, during which time he drafted a model law to prevent looting and export; he was a Member of the Governor-General's Council, Sudan, 1917-26; Director of the British School of Archaeology at Jerusalem, 1927-35; Schweich Lecturer, 1937; Vice-President of the Soc. of Antiquaries, 1941-4; Chairman of the Palestine Exploration Fund, 1945-50; he published a number of archaeological reports including, *The Island of Meroe,* 1911 for the EEF; he died in Geldeston, Norfolk, 6 Dec. 1959.

PEQ 92 (1960), 161-3 (K. M. Kenyon); *WWW* 5, 263; inf. J. Crowfoot (grandson). Photograph reproduced by permission of Durham University Library.

CRUM, Walter Ewing (1865-1944)
British Coptologist; he was born in Capelrig, Renfrewshire, 22 July 1865, eldest son of Alexander C., merchant, and Margaret Stewart Ewing; he was educated at Eton, 1879, and Balliol College, Oxford; BA, 1888; becoming interested in Egyptology while an undergraduate; on leaving Oxford he studied first under Groff (q.v.) in Paris, and afterwards under Erman (q.v.) at Berlin, 1889-90; Hon. PhD Berlin; Crum shares with Steindorff (q.v.) the premier place among Coptic scholars of modern times; although generally grounded in hieroglyphs and ancient Egyptian, he decided while at Berlin to confine himself to Coptic, soon becoming the foremost scholar of his generation; from 1892 he began an intensive study of all the available materials, visiting British and foreign museums and libraries; he found the dictionaries of Parthey (q.v.), Tattam (q.v.), and Peyron (q.v.) inadequate for the modern student's needs, and as the Berlin scheme for a new work had been abandoned on account of the 1914-18 war, he set about collecting materials for a great *Coptic Dictionary*; in this task he worked with his companion Madge Hart-Davis (1876-1953) and devoted a large part of the rest of his life to it; the dictionary when ready for the printer was vast, based on some 240,000 slips; it was produced by the Oxford University Press in 6 pts, the first appearing in 1929 and the last in 1939, making a stout quarto volume of nearly 1,000 pages, closely printed in double columns; in honour of this great achievement, Crum was elected FBA, 1931, and awarded D.Litt., Oxford, 1937; his other publications are very numerous, the most important being, *Coptic Manuscripts brought from the Fayum by W. M. Flinders Petrie, together with a papyrus in the Bodleian Library*, 1893; *Coptic ostraca from the collections of the Egypt Exploration Fund, the Cairo Museum and others*, with a contrib. by F. E. Brightman, 1902; *Coptic Monuments*, Cairo Cat., 1902; *Catalogue of the Coptic Manuscripts in the British Museum,* 1905; *Catalogue of the Coptic Manuscripts in the Collection of the John Rylands Library, Manchester,* 1909; *Koptische Rechtsurkunden des achten Jahrhunderts aus Djême, Theben,* with G. Steindorff, 1912; *Theological texts from Coptic papyri, edited with an appendix upon the Arabic and Coptic versions of the life of Pachomius,* 1913; *Der Papyruscodex saec. VI - VII der Phillipsbibliothek in Cheltenham, koptische theologische Schriften,* 1915; *Short texts from Coptic ostraca and papyri,* 1921;*Wadi Sarga: Coptic and Greek texts from the excavations undertaken by the Byzantine Research Account, with an introduction by R. Campbell Thompson,* with Sir H. I Bell, 1922; *Jews and Christians in Egypt,* with Sir H. I Bell, 1924; *Varia Coptica,* 1939; his bibl. lists in addition *c.*20 bibliographies, 76 articles, 48 reviews, and 4 obits.; the 2nd part of *JEA* 25 was dedicated to him to celebrate the completion of the dictionary, and a further tribute in the form of a volume of studies was published by the Byzantine Institute of Boston after his death with contributions from 36 scholars; Crum's correspondence is in the British Library (Add. MSS, 45681-90) and his notebooks and papers in the Griffith Institute; he died in Bath, 18 May 1944.

ODNB 14, 534-5; *Coptic Studies in Honor of Walter Ewing Crum,* Boston Mass., 1950, contains complete bibl.; *BMQ* 28. 59-67; *AfO* 15 (1045-51), 191; *JEA* 25 (1939), 134-8 (portr. and bibl.); 30 (1944), 65-6 (Add. bibl.) (H. I. Bell); *Chron. d'Ég.* 20 (1945), 147-51 (J. Vergote); *The Coptic Encyclopedia* 3, 663 (M. Krause); R.

Hart-Davis, *The Arms of Time*, 1979, 147-8; E. Endesfelder, *Die Ägyptologie an der Berliner Universität-Zur Geschichte eines Fachgebietes*, 1988, 27; M. Capasso (ed.), *Hermae*, 2007, 107-13 (portr.). Photograph © 2011 Museum of Fine Arts, Boston.

CRUZ-URIBE, Eugene (1952-2018)
American Egyptologist; he was born in Green Bay, Wisconsin, 22 Dec. 1952, son of Antonio C.-U. and Lillian Mae Hasseler; he studied at the Oriental Institute, University of Chicago, 1971-83 under Nims (q.v.); BA, 1975; MA, 1977; PhD, 1983; he served as Assistant Professor of Egyptology, Brown University, 1983-88; Assisant and Asscoiate Dean, College of Social and Behavioral Sciences, Northern Arizona University, 1989-1998, Professor Emeritus 2007-18; Professor of Global History and World Civilizations, California State University, Monterey, 2011-3; and finally Professor of History, Indiana University East, July 2013-May 2017; he was editor of the *Journal of the Society for the Study of Egyptian Antquities*, 1998-2007, and the *Journal of the American Research Center in Egypt*, 2008-18; he was a board member of the Wayne County Historical Museum from 2014, Chairman, 2017-8; apart from articles, he published *Hibis Temple Project* III, 2008; with J. Dijkstra, *Syene* I, 2012; and *The Demotic Graffiti from the Temple of Isis on Philae Island*, 2016; he died as a result of a bicycle accident, at Indianapolis, 12 March 2018.

Website of Indiana University East; SSES Newsletter Summer 2018, 1-2 (portr.) (R. Leprohon).

CULLIMORE, Isaac (1791-1852)
Irish antiquary; he was born 1791; he took a great interest in the progress of hieroglyphic decipherment, and devoted his whole life to the study of Egyptian antiquities, being one of the first orientalists to use astronomical data for historical research; he published articles on Egyptian chronology, king lists, etc., most of his academic output being in *Proceedings of the Royal Society of Literature*; for the Syro-Egyptian Soc., he published *Pharaoh and his Princes*, 1845; in 1842 he began to issue plates illustrating oriental cylinders and seals in the British Museum; he was a friend of Dr. John Lee (q.v.), and a frequent visitor at Hartwell; he died in Clapham, 8 April 1852.

DNB 13, 282; *ODNB* 14, 569; Hilmy, i, 151; Hincks Corr. no. 151; *GM* 38 (1852), 208; *Dictionary of Irish Biography*, 2009, 2, 1078.

CUMING, Henry Syer (1817-1902)
British archaeologist and collector; he was born in Newington, 15 Jan. 1817 and baptized at St. Mary, Newington 24 Aug., son of Richard C. and Ann Warner; FRGS; member of the Brit. Arch. Association, from 1844 and for many years VP; FSA Scot., 1867; Member of the Society of Bibl. Arch. 1875; he contributed many papers to the *Journal Brit. Arch. Assn.*; he owned an Egyptian papyrus which was used by Naville in his great study (*Todtb.* Ay), and which formed part of his huge collection of antiquities, historical relics, etc.; this varied collection was started by his father Richard C. on his 5th birthday in 1782; the father died aged 92 and the son continued to add to it until it comprised 15,000 objects, including Egyptian and Babylonian antiquities; it contains such objects as ushabti figures of King Sety I etc.; he bequeathed the whole of it to the Borough of Southwark, and it was opened to the public as the Cuming Museum, Walworth Road, in 1906, where it is at present housed together with the Faraday Library; Cuming died in Kennington Park Road, London, 7 Oct. 1902.

Inf. Mr. Maitland Muller; Arthur Mee, *London-The King's England*, 1953, 698-9.

CUNY, (*Dr.*) **Charles** (1811-1858)
French physician and traveller; he was born at Gouin, 30 June 1811, son of Nicolas C. and Marie Charlotte Bade; he trained as a military doctor and served in Algeria 1831-7; he entered Egyptian service in 1837; chief medical officer in Middle Egypt 1841; he was stationed first at Minia and later in 1847 Qena and in 1848 Asyut; he was visited by Flaubert (q.v.) in 1850 when he already had a statue of Khaemwese in his possession; he was dismissed from his post in 1850; he married in Cairo in 1844 Émelie Elisabeth Zahra, daughter of Linant de Bellefonds (q.v.); he was reappointed to his medical post in 1854 but again dismissed in 1857; he then undertook a journey to Darfur during which he was killed in El-Fasher *c.* 25 June 1858; his statue was acquired by E. A. Diamandidi who later sold it to Sharpe (q.v.) who in turn presented it to the British Museum (EA 947) in 1866.

H. Roy. *La Vie héroique et romantique du Docteur Charles Cuny,* 1930; F. Teynard, *Égypte et Nubie* 1858I, 7; *Journal de Voyage du Dr. Ch. Cuny de Siout à El-Obeid,* 1862.

CURETON, Harry Osborn (1785-1858)
British dealer in coins and antiquities; he was baptized at St. James, Garlickhithe, London, 10 June 1785, son of John C. and Felicia Ann Osborn; he ran his business at 81 Aldersgate, Barbican, London, and had an excellent

reputation; he supplied many objects to the British Museum and other large museums, as well as to private collectors such as Dr John Lee (q.v.); he bought many Egyptian antiquities at the sales of Barker, Burton, Lavoratori, Salt, and Athanasi (qq.v.), and many coins and antiquities at the Strawberry Hill sale; a Demotic papyrus in the British Museum (EA 10413) is named after him; antiquities from his collection were sold at Sotheby's 17-25 Feb. 1851, and posthumously at Sotheby's 10-11 Jan. 1859; he died in London, 23 Aug. 1858.

Private inf.; Lugt 20190, 24584.

CURRELLY, Charles Trick (1876-1957)
Canadian Egyptologist; he was born at Exeter, Ontario 11 Jan. 1876, son of John C. and Mary Treble; he was educated at Victoria College, University of Toronto; BA, 1898; MA, 1902; in 1902 he joined the staff of the Egypt Exploration Fund and excavated under Petrie (q.v.) at Abydos, 1902-3, at Ehnasya, 1903-4 and in the Sinai, 1904-5 and under Naville (q.v.) at Deir el-Bahri, 1905-6 and 1906-7; he also took part in excavations in Crete, Asia Minor, and Palestine; from 1902-9 he formed a collection of objects for the Royal Ontario Museum of Archaeology, Toronto of which he was appointed first curator in 1907 and Director, 1914-46; he held the post of Professor of the History of Industrial Art at the University of Toronto; apart from contributing to excavation reports, he was the author of *Stone Implements*, 1913 and his autobiography *I Brought the Ages Home*, 1956; he died in Baltimore, 17 April 1957.

Encyclopedia Canadiana 3, 174; C. Currelly, *I Brought the Ages Home*, 1956.

CURTIS, George William (1824-1892)
American author; he was born in Providence, RI, 24 Feb. 1824, son of George C. and Mary Burrill; he spent some years in Europe and then established himself in New York in 1850 as a journalist and author; he contributed to many newspapers and periodicals; his trip to Egypt in 1850 was described in an account which he published in 1851, *Nile Notes of a Howadji*, a German ed. appearing in 1857; he died in Staten Island, New York, 31 Aug. 1892.

Life, by Edward Cary, 1894; Hilmy, i, 151; *WWWA* H, 131; *DAB* 4, 614-6.

CURTO, Silvio (1919-2015)
Italian Egyptologist; he was born at Bra, 20 Aug. 1919, son of ... Curto from Trieste and Margherita Siccardi from Bra; he was appointed an inspector in the Ministry of Culture, 1946-64, director of the Museo Egizio, Turin, 1964-84 and superintendant in the Ministry of Culture, 1971-84; he was lecturer in Egyptology at the University of Turin, 1964-9 and the Turin Polytechnic, 1964-84; he took part in the Nubian recuse campaign, 1961-5 with Rinaldi (q.v.) and Maragiolio (q.v.), working at Dehmit, 1961-2; Kalabsha, 1962, the area between Korosko and Qasr Ibrim, 1964; and Ellesiya, 1965; he was involved in the redesign of the Museo Egizio in Bologna, 1961 and the creation of the Museo Egizia in Milan, 1972 and Mantua, 1982; he published *Gli Scavi Italiani a el-Ghiza*, 1963; with others, *Kalabsha*, 1965; *Il tempio di Ellesija*, 1970; *The Military Art of the Ancient Egyptians*, 1971; *Medecina e medici nell'antico Egitto*, 1972; with others, *Dehmit*, 1973; *Museo Egizio di Torino 1824-La scoperta dell'arte egizia*, 1975; *L'antico Egitto*, 1981; *Tesori dei Faraoni*; 1984, English ed.*Treasures of the Pharaohs*, 1984; *L'Egitto antico*, 1985; *Le sculture egizie ed egittizzanti nelle villa Torlonia in Roma*, 1985; with L. Donatelli, *Bernardino Drovetti Epistolario*, 1985; with others, *Korosko Kasr Ibrim. Incisioni Rupestri Nubiane*, 1987; *La scrittura nella storia dell'uomo*, 1989; *Storia del Museo Egizio di Torino*, 1990; *Catalogo delle chiese dell'Egitto*, 1998; *La riscoperta dell'Egitto Cristiano*, 1999; *L'antico Egitto-Realtà e fantasia*, 2001; and *Umorismo e satira nell'Egitta antico*, 2006, and his memoirs, with R. Manzini, *Silvio Curto: una vita tra i faraoni*, 2010; he died at Turin, 24 Sept. 2015.

Internet obit; *Sudan and Nubia* 20 (2016), 180 (A. Roccati); R. Manzini, *Silvio Curto: una vita tra I Faraoni*, 2010.

CURZON, Robert, 14th Baron Zouche (1810-1873)
British scholar and traveller; he was born in Welbeck Street, London, 16 March 1810, son of Roger C. and Harriet Ann Bishopp, 13th Baroness Zouche; educated at Charterhouse and Christ Church, Oxford; he visited Egypt and then Syria, and Palestine on a research tour in June 1833 to Dec. 1834 looking for manuscripts among monastic libraries, and again toured Turkey, Greece, and Egypt from June 1837 to Sept. 1838; he amassed a fine collection; he also collected Egyptian antiquities; his travels are described in his *Monasteries of the Levant;* a privately-printed catalogue of the collection, limited to 50 copies, was issued in 1849, *Catalogue of Materials for Writing: Early Writings on Tablets and Stones, Rolled and other Manuscripts and Oriental Manuscript Books, in the Library of the Hon. Robert Curzon at Parham in the County of Sussex*; his own copy of this cat. with

many notes and letters from Birch and others inserted, is in the Dept. of MSS, BL; a large part of his collection of antiquities and oriental MSS was presented to the British Museum by his daughter in 1917; other Egyptian antiquities remained in the family until they were sold at Sotheby's 2 Nov. 1922, lots 327-56; he died in Parham Park, Sussex, 2 Aug. 1873.

DNB 13, 354-5; *ODNB* 14, 805-6 (portr.); 'Guide to Parham Park', *Country Life* - Christopher Hussey, passim; Hilmy, i, 151; Lugt 84159; I. Fraser, *The Heir of Parham*, 1986; J. Speake (ed.), *Literature of Travel and Exploration*, 2003, 1, 298-9; B. Muhs and T. Vorderstrasse in *JEA* 94 (2008), 223-45; B. Muhs, *JEA* 98 (2012), 285-7.

CZARTORYSKI, (*Prince*) **August Francis Maria Anna Joseph Cajetan** (1858-1893)
Polish collector; he was born in Paris, 2 Aug. 1858, son of Prince Wladyslaw C. (q.v.) and Maria Amparo Princess de Vista Allegre, daughter of Queen Maria Cristina of Spain; due to ill-health he spent the early years of his life in many resorts, including in Egypt; for some years he attended the Collège Charlemagne in Paris; during a visit to Egypt in 1882 he purchased for the Czartoryski collection in Cracow some Egyptian objects, including some interesting bronze figurines; he became a priest, 1882; he spent his last years in Italy, taking in 1888 the habit of the Salesian Order; he died in the Salesian monastery in Alassio, 8 April 1893 and was beatified by the Catholic Church in 2004.

Correspondence and archive material, Czartoryski Library, Cracow; G. Lardone, *Il servo di Dio, Principe Aug. Czartoryski*, 1930; J. Slósarcyk, *August Czartoryski, ksiaze Salexjanin*, 1932; *Polski Slownik Biograficzny* 4, 275-6; inf. J. Śliwa.

CZARTORYSKI, (*Prince*) **Marceli Adam Konstantin Michael Felix** (1841-1909)
Polish nobleman, owner of a large collection of art works and great library in Cracow at the palace in Wola Justowska; he was born at Weinhaus, 30 May 1841, son of Alexander Romvald C. and Marcelline Radziwill (1817-94); he was widely travelled; part of the contributions to his collection came probably from his mother, a talented pianist and pupil of Chopin in Paris; social activist and patron of music; some of the Egyptian amulets, scarabs, shabtis and bronze figurines which belonged once to him are now in the possession of the Dept. of Mediterranean Archaeology of the Cracow University, donated 1872 and 1913; he died in Lausanne, 25 Nov. 1909.

J. Śliwa, *Scarabs,* Cracow 1985, 14.

CZARTORYSKI, (*Prince*) **Wladyslaw** (1828-1894)
Polish nobleman and collector; a political activist in exile; he was born in Warsaw, 3 July 1828, son of Prince Adam George C. (1770-1861) and Anna, Princess Saphiela-Kodenska; he was educated in France, Collège Bourbon, Collège Charlemagne, Collège Rollin, Polish Military School; after the death of his parents he inherited the collections gathered at Hôtel Lambert, Paris, together with his younger sister Izabela Dzialynska (q.v.); he transferred his part of antiquities, paintings and library to Cracow, where in 1876 he opened an important museum (from Dec. 1950 a department of the Cracow National Museum); among the antiquities which are only a part of this rich collection of objets d'art and of artistic craftmanship from various epochs, the most important is a magnificent group of Greek vases, but some Egyptian objects are very important, such as the stela of Merer; he also donated many interesting objects to the Cracow University, 1872; the closing years of his life were devoted to setting up and expanding the family collection in Cracow; he was greatly interested in Egyptian art, making his purchases at sales in Paris and directly in Egypt where Makarios Shenuda (q.v.), Stephan Marusienski (q.v.) and Marius P. Tanos (q.v.) worked as his agents; the letters which have survived indicate that he corresponded with some scholars, among others Urbain Bouriant (q.v.); in winter 1889/90 he made a trip to Egypt in order to settle his affairs connected with the purchases for his collection; Wilbour (q.v.) (*Travels*, p. 546) made a note about their meeting at Medinet Habu, 22 Jan. 1890; he died in Boulogne-sur-Seine, 23 June 1894.

Polski Slownik Biograficzny 4, 300-2; Correspondence of Cz. from the years 1880-86, Czartoryski Library in Cracow, Inv. No. Ew 2113; B. Zaleski, *Life of Adam Czartoryski*, Paris 1881; K. Moczulska and J. Śliwa, *Prince Archeologiczne* 14, Cracow 1972, 85-114; Muzeum Narodowe w Krakowie; *Zbiory czaretoyrskich Historia i wybòr zabytkòw*, Warsaw 1979; J. Śliwa, *Scarabs,* Cracow 1985, 9-10.

CZERMAK, Johann Nepomuk (1828-1873)
Austrian physiologist; he was born in Prague, 17 June 1828, son of Conrad C., a doctor, and his wife Josefine; he studied medicine in Vienna, and was the perfector of the laryngoscope; he made anatomical and microscopical researches on mummies, *Sitzungsb. Akad. Wien,* 9 (1852), 427-67; he died in Leipzig, 16 Sept. 1873.

NDB 3, 458-9; *ÖBL* 1, 161.

CZERMAK, Wilhelm (1889-1953)

Austrian philologist; he was born in Vienna, 10 Sept. 1889, son of Wilhelm C., Professor of Ophtalmology, and Josefine Pfaff and great nephew of the above; he studied Semitics, Egyptology, and African languages in Vienna under Junker (q.v.); PhD, 111; Habilitation, 1919; he joined the staff of the University of Vienna as Associate Professor, 1923; Professor, 1931; he was guest prof. in the Geographical Soc. in Cairo; much interested in linguistics he wrote the specialist studies *Der Rhythmus der koptischen Sprache und seine Bedeutung in der Sprachgestaltung*, 1931, *Die Laute der ägyptischen Sprache; eine phonetische Untersuchung*, 1931-4, *Akten in Keilschrift und das auswärtige Amt des Pharao;* he died in Vienna, 13 March 1953.

Almanach der Österreichischen Akd. der Wissenschaften 103 (1953), 295-303 (portr., bibl.) (H. Junker); *AEB* 1953, 999; *AfO* 16 (1953), 399-400 (M. Höfner); G. Thausing, *Tarudet*, 1989, *passim.*, especially 16-; inf. T. Schneider.

DACIER, (*Baron*) **Bon Joseph** (1742-1833)
French savant; he was born in Valognes, 1 April 1742, son of Pierre D. and Marguerite Duchet; destined for a church career he entered academic life instead, refusing the offer of a finance post under Louis XVI in 1790; he was elected to the Acad. Fr., 1823; Secrétaire perpétuel de l'Acad. des Inscr., 1820, in which capacity he proved a firm friend to Champollion (q.v.) whose famous *Lettre* of 1822 was addressed to him; he was created a baron 1830; he died in Paris, 4 Feb. 1833.

DBF 9, 464-5; A. Robinet and J. Le Chaplain, *Dictionnaire historique et biographique de la Révolution et de l'Empire*, 1899, I 522-3; Hartleben, passim; È. Gran-Aymerich, *Dictionnaire biographique d'archéologie 1798-1945*, 2001, incorporated in *Les Chercheurs de passé 1798-1945*, 2007, 733.

DAKIN, Alec Naylor (1912-2003)
British Egyptologist; he was born in Mytholmroyd, Yorkshire, 3 April 1912, son of Bertram Alexander D., a sawmaker, and Annie Louise Naylor; he was educated at Heath School, Halifax, and read Literae Humaniores at The Queen's College, Oxford; BA, 1935; he was encouraged to study Egyptian by Gunn (q. v.), and was the first Lady Wallis Budge Fellow at University College, Oxford 1936-42; he published a number of articles in pre-War *JEA*s, including contributions to the Bibliography of Pharaonic Egypt, and an index of Egyptian words cited in volumes 1-25 of the *JEA*; with Barns (q.v.) and Smither (q.v.) he was recruited to 'Station X', the code-breaking station at Bletchley Park, where he translated German naval signals; after the War he became a schoolmaster in Bath; upon retiring he taught Egyptological classes at the North Bristol Institute; he presented papers on literary topics at the International Congresses of Egyptologists, 1991 and 1995, published in their proceedings; he died in Bristol, 14 June 2003.

JEA 63 (1977), 134; 'The Z Watch in Hut 4, Part I', in F. Hinsley and A Stripp (eds.), *Code Breakers: the inside story of Bletchley Park*, 1993, 50-56 (autobiog. sketch); *JEA* 89 (2003), viii-ix (portr.) (J. Malek); *The Times* 10 July 2003; *Daily Telegraph* 26 July 2003; inf. T. Hardwick.

DALTON, Richard (*c.*1715-1791)
British librarian, draughtsman, and engraver; he was born in Whitehaven, Cumberland, and baptized 29 Jan. 1715, younger son of Revd John D, of Darlington.; he studied in Rome; he joined the tour party headed by James Caulfield, Viscount Charlemont, visiting Greece, Turkey. and Egypt, 1749; he married Esther Deheulle, 1764; FSA; an original member of the Royal Academy; Dalton published *Views and Engravings in Greece and Egypt*, 52 plates, and another collection with 79 plates, 1790-1; also other works; he was librarian to the king and died in St. James's Palace, London, 7 Feb. 1791.

ODNB 14, 1025-6; *DNB* Suppl. ii, 108-9; Hilmy, i, 154.

DALZIEL (*Sir*) **Davison Alexander, 1st Baron Dalziel of Wooler** (1852-1928)
British businessman and collector; he was born London, 17 Oct. 1852, son of Davison Octavian D. and Helen Gaultier; he owned the *Evening Standard* newspaper, and later purchased the travel agency Thomas Cook; he was Conservative MP for Brixton, 1910-23 and 1924-7; he was created Bart., 1919 and Baron, 1927; his collection of antiquities was sold at Sotheby's, 31 July 1939 (Eg. ant. lots 17-25); he died in London, 18 April 1928.

The Complete Peerage 13, 355.

DANICOURT, Charles Alfred (1837-1887)
French collector; born Péronne, Saumur, 11 Dec. 1837, son of Charles August D. and Laure Constance Rossignol; he travelled in Egypt and made a good collection of antiquities which he bequeathed to his native town; the Musée Danicourt was destroyed by enemy action in 1914-18; he died in Péronne, 6 July 1887.

G. Legrain, *Description ... de Musée Danicourt*, 1890; inf. Olivier Masson.

DANINOS, (*Pasha*) **(Abraham) Albert** (*c.*1840/5-1925)
French Egyptologist of Algerian origin; he was an assistant in the Louvre under Longpérier (q.v.) and Devéria (q.v.); he studied hieroglyphs and went to Egypt in 1869 as assistant to Mariette (q.v.) in place of Gabet (q.v.); he took part in Mariette's excavations at Maidum in 1871, and in the absence of his chief discovered the famous statues of Rahotep and Nefert; he excavated at Fashn, Hiba, Heliopolis, the Fayum, and Abukir; he retired in 1897 and returned to Paris; he published *Les Monuments funéraires*, Paris, 1899, with a preface by Maspero (q.v.); also a *Catalogue of the Tigrane Pasha Collection* with 64 plates, 1911; he dealt in antiquities and also had a collection of antiquities which was sold at Hotel Drouot, Paris, 7 May 1926; two stelae from this collection were published by Maspero, *Rec. Trav.* 15. 84; he died in Egypt, 1925.

Maspero, ut supra; *JEA* 14 (1928), 175; *Rec. Trav.* 8, 69; *BIE* 8 (1926), 348; M.-C. Bruwier, *L'Égypte dans la bibliothèque de Raoul Warocqué*, 1992, 28-9; *Les Donateurs du Louvre*, 1989, 182; E. David, *Mariette Pacha*

1821-1881, 1994, 190-1, 211, 213.

DANSON, Francis Chatillon (1855-1926)
British businessman and collector; he was born in Barnston, Cheshire, 24 Nov. 1855, son of John Towne D., barrister and marine insurer, and Ann Eleanor Lockett; he founded the firm of F. C. Danson and Co. in 1879 which became Liverpool's leading firm of Average Adjusters; JP, President of the Liverpool Chamber of Commerce 1896-99; member of Liverpool University Court and Council from 1903, Deputy Treasurer 1903-14; member of the Committee of the Liverpool School of Tropical Medicine from 1902, Chairman 1913-26; because of ill health, he went on a trip to Egypt in 1898 and began to collect Egyptian and Classical antiquities; he supported the excavations of Garstang (q.v.) who dedicated his *Burial Customs* to him; FSA; his collection is now in the Merseyside County Museum, Liverpool and his papers are in the Merseyside County Archives; he died in Birkenhead, 3 July 1926.

WWW 2, 262; *The University of Liverpool Recorder* 82 (1980), 202-5.

D'ARC, Gauthier (*d.* 1844)
French Consul-General in Egypt, 1842-3; from 1830 he had resided in Spain, and on his resignation from Egypt he returned there, and died of tuberculosis in 1844.

Carré, i, 359; ii, 28; French FO Records; Tresson, 31.

DARESSY, Georges Émile Jules (1864-1938)
French Egyptologist; he was born at Sourdon, Somme, 19 March 1864, son of Henri Alphonse Jules D., master of arms, and Marie Euphrasie Arthémise Pieurd; he became interested in Egyptology as a boy, and later studied at the École des Hautes Études, 1881-5; he went to Egypt as a member of the Mission Arch. Française, 1886; made assistant keeper, Bulaq Museum, 1887; he carried out excavations under Maspero (q.v.) and Grébaut (q.v.), when he cleared the great cache of XXIst Dynasty mummies in 1891; he also excavated and helped with the restorations at the sites of the Malkata palace of Amenhotep III, Medinet Habu, Karnak, and Luxor, Abydos temples, etc.; he arranged the Egyptian collections after the removal of the museum to Giza in 1891 and on its return to Cairo in 1902; Member of the Institut d'Ég., 1894; Secretary General, 1913; Chevalier de la Légion d'honneur; Commander of the Order of the Nile; an extremely prolific contributor to journals he wrote over 500 articles and about 8 reviews; his principal works were, *Notice explicative des ruines de Médinet Habu*, 1897; *Le Mastaba de Mera*, 1898; *Ostraca*, 1901; *Les Cercueils des prêtres d'Ammon,* 1891; *Fouilles de la Vallée des Rois,* 1898-99; 1902; *Notes sur la momie de Toutmosis IV; Textes et Dessins magiques*, 1903; *La Faune mommifiée de l'antique Égypte,* 1905; *Statues de divinités*, 2 vols. 1905-06; *Cercueils des cachettes royales*, 1909; *La Pierre de Palerme et la chronologie de l'Ancien Empire*, 1916; *A brief description of the principal monuments exhibited in the Egyptian Museum*, Cairo, 3rd ed. 1925; *Les Branches du Nil sous la XVIIIᵉ dynastie*, 1933; he also edited the manuscripts of the French mineralogist Dolomieu, 1922; his notebooks are in the Collège de France; he died in Sourdon, where he lived after he retired in 1923, 28 Feb. 1938.

ASAE 39 (1939), 11-17, (bibl. 18-41) (J. Leibovitch); *BIÉ* 20, 259; *Chron. d'Ég.* 27 (1939), 139 (anon.); *DBF* 10, 181 (R. d'Amat); *KMT* 26 (2015-6), 72-4 (portr.).

DATTARI, Giovanni (*d.*1923)
Italian collector of coins and antiquities; he resided in Cairo, being originally in the service of Thos. Cook & Son and afterwards a purveyor to the British Army in Egypt; he had a fine collection of antiquities, particularly of XVIIIth Dynasty glass; some of these were published by Newberry, *PSBA* 1901, 220; he was well known as a numismatist; his glass collection was sold to Charles Freer (q.v.) in1909 and the rest at Hotel Drouot, Paris 17-19 June 1912, while his coin collection was sold to the University of Michigan; FRNS, 1900; he published *Num. Augg. Alexandrini*, 1901; he died in 1923.

Inf. P. E. Newberry; Newberry Corr. nos. 11/17-20; Lugt 71470.

DAUMAS, François Félix Eugène (1915-1984)
French Egyptologist; he was born at Castelnau-le-Lez 3 Jan. 1915, son of François Marius D., a draughtsman at the French Institute in Cairo who was killed in action in 1914, and Jeanne Marie Louise Castan; he was educated at Montpellier and inspired by his father's drawings and antiquities to follow a career in Egyptology; he began a correspondence course with Lefèbvre (q.v.) in 1941 and in 1944 was able to go to Paris to study with him at the École Pratique and with Lacau (q.v.) at the Collège de France; he was awarded his diploma in 1946 and became a pensionnaire at the French Institute in Cairo 1946-50; he was chosen by Chassinat to continue the publication of the temple of Dendera which became his life's work; from 1950-53 he was attached to CNRS and 1953-59 he taught Egyptology at the University of Lyons becoming Honorary Professor; he obtained his doctorate in 1956; from 1959-69 he was director of the French Institute in Cairo; he took part in the Nubian rescue campaign recording the temples of Kalabsha and Debod and excavating at Wadi es-Sebua; he supervised the excavation

at Kellia in 1964-5; from 1969-84 he was Professor of Egyptology at the Université Paul Valéry of Montpellier; member of the Institut d'Égypte 1959, vice-president 1967-9; member of the German Archaeological Institute, 1961; corresponding member of the Académie des Inscriptions et Belles Lettres, 1972; honorary member of Charles University, Prague and honorary doctorate from the University of Louvain; apart from numerous articles, his monographs were *Les moyens d'expression du grec et de l'égyptien comparés dans les décrets de Canope et de Memphis*, 1952; editor, *Mélanges Maspero I. Orient ancien*. 3e fasc., 1955; *Le mammisi de Nectanébo,* 1955; *Les mammisis des temples égyptiens*, 1958; *Les mammisis de Dendara*, 1959; *Kalabcha, Textes du sanctuaire (A)*, 1959 with P. Derchain and H. De Meulenaere; *Debod. Textes hiéroglyphiques et description archéologique*, 1963; *La civilisation de l'Égypte pharaonique*, 1965; *Les dieux de l'Égypte,* 1965; with E. Chassinat, *Le temple de Dendara* VI, 1965; *La vie dans l'Égypte ancienne*, 1968; *Dendara et le temple d'Hathor. Notice sommaire*, 1969; with A. Guillaumont, *Kellia* I, 1969; *Dendara*, 1970; *La ouabet de Kalabsha*, 1970; with Chassinat, *Le temple de Dendara* VIII, 1972; *Le temple de Dendara* VIII, 1978; with C. Aldred, Ch. Desroches-Noblecourt and J. Leclant, *L'Égypte du crepuscule,* 1979; with A. Barucq, *Hymnes et prières de l'Égypte ancienne*, 1980; with G. Castel and J. C. Golvin, *Les fontaines de la porte Nord*, 1984; *Le temple de Dendara* IX, 1987; and *Valeurs ptolémaiques des signes hiéroglyphiques d'époque gréco-romaine*, 1988; he died in Castelnau-le-Lez, 6 Oct. 1984.

Hommages à François Daumas, 1986 Vol I (portr.), I-VII (A. Guillaumont), IX-XXV (bibl.); *BIFAO* 85 (1985), v-viii (portr.) (A. Gutbub), ix-xxiii (bibl.) (S. Aufrère); *BSFE* 101 (1984), 9-14 (S. Aufrère).

DAUZATS, Adrien (1804-1868)
French artist; he was born at Bordeaux in July 1804, son of Jean Bernard D. and Marie Todeau; he accompanied Baron Taylor (q.v.) to Egypt in 1830 and executed many drawings which are engraved in the plates of Taylor's publication of his voyage; some of his works, of high merit, are in the picture-galleries of the Louvre; his diary of the voyage was utilized by Alexandre Dumas in his *Quinze Jours au Sinaï*, 1839; he died in Paris, 18 Feb. 1868.

Carré, i, 213; A. Dumas, *Portraits comtemporaires,* 1874; *DBF* 10, 319-21; M. Taymanova in P. and J. Starkey, *Travellers in Egypt*, 1998, 181-8.

DAVIDSON, John (1797-1836)
British physician and traveller; he was born in Cork St., London, 23 Dec. 1797, son of a tailor from Kelso; he studied medicine at Edinburgh and St. George's Hospital, London; in early life his health failed and he had to give up medical practice; FRS, 1832; he resided in Naples and travelled extensively in Africa and the Near East, visiting Egypt in 1829; he took up Egyptology under the influence of Pettigrew (q.v.), and studied the history of mummification; he unrolled and lectured upon two mummies at the Royal Institution, London, 13 July 1833, publishing a valuable account of them, *An Address on Embalming generally,* London, 1833; he was murdered in Swekeza while on an expedition to explore the interior of Africa, 18 Dec. 1836; his drawings are in the Society of Antiquaries, while his travel diary remained with the family.

ODNB 15, 309-10; *DNB* 14, 127-8; *JEA* 20 (1934), 171; *Mem. Inst. Ég.* 13, 13.

DAVIES, Anna (Nina) Macpherson (*née* **Cummings**) (1881-1965)
British artist and copyist; born Salonika, 6 Jan. 1881, daughter of Cecil J. Cummings and Sarah Tannoch; she was trained at the Slade School of Art and the Royal College of Art under Walter Crane; her interest in Egypt was aroused when she visited Alexandria in 1906, and she married Norman de G. Davies (see below) the following year, with whom she was to record a great many Theban tombs; an excellent artist she went to great pains to reproduce colours as exactly as possible, and achieved remarkable results in the days before colour photography; she used egg tempera when making copies of scenes instead of merely water colours; in all she worked at Thebes for over thirty years, 1908-39; three of the five vols. of *The Theban Tombs Series* were entirely her work, the others had drawings by her husband as well, while Gardiner (q.v.) edited the series; Nina Davies also copied at Amarna, 1925-6, and at Beni Hasan, 1931-2; in 1923 Gardiner exhibited a collection of her copies at the Victoria and Albert Museum, and this was followed by the publication of two folio vols. of *Ancient Egyptian Paintings*, 1936; in 1954 a miniature Penguin edition of some of these was illustrated with small reproductions and had a text by the artist; in 1958 she published a series of paintings from originals in the British Museum and the Bankes Collection; she, with her husband, also helped Gardiner in selecting and making drawings of good representative hieroglyphs of the XVIIIth Dynasty to use in his hieroglyphic fount, and published *Picture Writing in Ancient Egypt*, 1958; she contributed a number of articles to the *JEA* and left two of her copies to the Egyptian Department of the British Museum and other copies together with a shabti figure to the Ashmolean Museum; her Egyptological books were bequeathed to the Griffith Institute and to the Pitt Rivers Museum, Oxford; she died in Hinksey Hill, Berkshire, 21 April 1965.

JEA 51 (1965), 196-9 (portr.) (C. Aldred); Porter and Moss, *Top. Bibl.* i, 2nd ed., pt. i, Appendix B; È. Gran-

Aymerich, *Dictionnaire biographique d'archéologie 1798-1945*, 2001, incorporated in *Les Chercheurs de passé 1798-1945*, 2007, 735; N. Strudwick in *JEA* 90 (2004), 193-210.

DAVIES, Norman de Garis (1865-1941)

British Egyptologist; he was born Broughton, Lancashire 14 Sept. 1865, son of Revd James Dickerson Davies and Emma Mary de Garis; he entered Glasgow University, 1884, with a scholarship from Dr. Williams' Library, London; MA, 1889; BD, 1891; later postgraduate at Marburg Univ.; Hon. member of German Arch. Inst., 1928; Hon. MA, Oxon; he was Congregational Minister at Ashton-under-Lyne where he became acquainted with Miss Kate Bradbury (afterwards Mrs. F. Ll. Griffith) (q.v.) who interested him in Egyptology, which he began to study; he next went to Australia as a Unitarian Minister in Melbourne until 1898, when he joined Petrie at Dendera; during the following years he copied an enormous number of tombs for the Arch. Survey of the EEF: Sheikh Said, 1901, Der el-Gebrawi, 1902, and Amarna, 1903-8; these, together with five more tombs at Thebes were published in 10 vols. of the Arch. Survey memoirs, both text and plates being executed by Davies; the merit of this work was recognized by the award of the Leibniz medal of the Prussian Acad.; he also accompanied Breasted in his expedition to Nubia, and assisted Reisner at the pyramids; he married in 1907, Miss A. M. Cummings (see above), herself an accomplished artist and a trained copyist; he then settled at Thebes and worked for many seasons copying tombs for the MMA, which were published in a series of sumptuous volumes; in addition to these larger works he made many contributions to *JEA* and other journals; he published, *The Mastaba of Ptahhetep and Akhethetep at Saqqarah, 2 vols.* 1900-1; *The Rock Tombs of Sheikh Said*, 1901; *The Rock Tombs of Deir el Gebrawi, 2 vols.* 1902; *The Rock Tombs of El Amarna*, 6 vols. 1903-8; *The Tomb of Nakht at Thebes*, 1907; *Five Theban Tombs, being those of Mentuherkhepeshef, User, Daga, Nehemaway and Tati*, 1913; *The Tomb of Antefoker, Vizier of Sesostris I, and of his wife Senet, No. 60*, with chap. by A. H. Gardiner, 1920; *The Tomb of Puyemrê at Thebes, 2 vols.* 1922-3; *The Tombs of Two Officials of Tuthmosis the Fourth, Nos. 75 & 90*, 1923; *The Tomb of Two Sculptors at Thebes*, 1925; *Two Ramesside Tombs at Thebes*, 1927; *The Tomb of Ken-Amun at Thebes, 2 vols.*, with G. R. Hopgood and Nina M. Davies, 1930; *The Tomb of Nefer-hotep at Thebes, 2 vols.*, 1933; *The Tombs of Menkheperrasonb, Amenmose, and another. Nos. 86, 112, 42, 226*, with Nina M. Davies, 1933; *Paintings from the Tomb of Rekh-mi-Re at Thebes*, 1935; *The Tomb of the Vizier Ramose*, based upon prelim. work by T. E. Peet and with H. Burton, Nina M. Davies, W. B. Emery, and G. S. Mileham. 1941; *The Tomb of Rekh-mi-Re at Thebes, 2 vols.* 1943; *Seven Private Tombs at Kurnah*, ed. A. H. Gardiner, 1948; *The Temple of Hibis in El Khargeh Oasis*, pt. 3, ed. Ludlow Bull and Lindsley F. Hall, 1953; *A Corpus of Inscribed Egyptian Funerary Cones*, ed. M. F. Laming Macadam, pt. I, 1957; his notebooks are in the Griffith Institute, Oxford, and a number of illustrated ostraca, small antiquities, and his large collection of funerary cones are in the Ashmolean Museum; he died at The Copse, Hinksey Hill, Berkshire, 5 Nov. 1941.

Erman, 220; *JEA* 28 (1942), 59-60 (portr.) (A. H. Gardiner); Newberry Corr; L. Pinch-Brock, *JSSEA* 26 (1996), 81-92; E. Gran-Aymerich, *Dictionnaire biographique d'archéologie 1798-1945*, 2001, incorporated in *Les Chercheurs de passé 1798-1945*, 2007, 735; D. Pétro in *Égypte, Afrique & Orient* 52 (208-9), 39-46.

DAVIS, Theodore Montgomery (Monroe) (1838-1915)

American lawyer, investor, businessman, and benefactor; he was born in Springfield, New York, 7 May 1838, son of Revd Richard Montgomery Davis and Catherine Hubbell; he settled in Iowa City where he studied law and was admitted to the Bar in 1857; he married in Iowa City, Iowa, 21 Aug. 1860 Annie F. Buttles (*b.*1836, *d.*7 March 1916), daughter of Joel Benoni Buttles; he later moved to Washington, DC and finally lived and worked in New York City and Newport, RI where he settled permanently in 1883; he amassed a fortune through dubious legal practices; he first visited Egypt in 1887-8 and later made seventeen trips from 1889 until 1914, all recorded through 1913 in the unpublished diary of his mistress and companion Mrs. Emma Andrews (q.v.); he was introduced by Sayce (q.v.) to Newberry (q.v.), who interested him in Egyptology; being a wealthy man he was able to finance excavations carried out by Newberry and others, and from 1903 to 1912 had a permit to explore the Valley of the Kings under the supervision of the Antiquities Service; Davis bore the cost of the work, and also of the seven sumptuous volumes in which the important results were recorded; the tombs discovered were those of Queen Hatshepsut, Thutmose IV, Siptah, Horemheb, Yuia and Tuiu and the so-called 'Tomb of Queen Tiye' (KV 55), as well as some minor ones; most of the objects discovered went to the Egyptian Museum, Cairo where they are exhibited in a special gallery known as Salle Theodore Davis, but some objects from the tomb of Thutmose IV were presented by Davis to the Metropolitan Museum, New York, and to the Boston Museum which also received the sarcophagus of

Thutmose I from the tomb of Hatshepsut; his private collection is also now in the Metropolitan Museum; he died in Miami Florida, 23 Feb. 1915.

Inf. from Museum of Fine Arts, Boston and John M. Adams; Andrews Diary; *JEA* 2 (1915), 251; Newberry Corr.; Sayce, 307, 322; *KMT* 11/2 (2000), 82-84; D. Gordon, *The Robber Baron Archaeologist. An Essay about the Life of Theodore M. Davis*, 2007; C. Vivian, *Americans in Egypt 1770-1915*, 2012, 221-34; J. M. Adams, *The Millionaire and the Mummies*, 2013.

DAVISON, Nathaniel (1737-1809)
British diplomat and traveller; he was born in 1737, son of George Davison of Bowsdon and Newton, Northumberland and Mary Brown; he accompanied Edward Wortley Montagu (q.v.) on his travels in the East in 1763; he supervised Montagu's excavation at Saqqara until his departure in 1764; he visited Giza, 9 July 1765, with Cousinéry (q.v.), Consul at Rosetta, and Meynard, a French merchant, to explore the Great Pyramid; he discovered the first of the construction-chambers over the 'King's Chamber,' which is called by his name; he accompanied the Duc de Chaulnes (q.v.) to Saqqara and back to Europe; he was afterwards British Consul-General at Algiers, 1780-3; he died in Alnwick, Northumberland in 23 Feb. 1809; his journals and observations on the Pyramids and the Catacombs at Alexandria were published in 1812 by Walpole (q.v.).

FO Records; Lauer, *Le Problème des pyramides*, 40, 48, 56, 67, 128; Lindsay, 42, 155; Nichols, *Lit. Anecd.* iv, 637; Vyse, ii, 255; Walpole, 350-87; *Quarterly Review* 19 (1818), 391-96.

DAWSON, Warren Royal (1888-1968)
British broker at Lloyds and historian; he was born at Ealing, 13 Oct. 1888, youngest son of Charles Royal-Dawson and Edith Rosalie Smith; he was educated at St. Paul's School, afterwards going into business; OBE, 1959; FRSE.; FRSL; FSA; Hon. Fellow: Imperial College of Science; Medical Society of London; Linnean Society; Hon. Member EES; he married Alys Helen Wood, 1912; his interest in Egyptology dated from before the First World War and he learned hieroglyphs in order to further his research into early medicine, in particular that of Egypt; he was one of the people on whom Gardiner's Grammar was first tried out; he served as Treasurer of the EES for five years from 1917-18; Dawson's interests were very varied and he published many hundreds of articles on a wide variety of subjects ranging from the history of Lloyds to natural history; in addition to articles, reviews, bibliographical, and shorter works on Egyptian subjects, he published the following books, *Egyptian Mummies,* with Sir G. Elliot Smith, 1924; *Magician and Leech. A study in the beginnings of medicine, with special reference to Ancient Egypt, etc.,* 1929; *A Bibliography of Works relating to Mummification in Egypt,* 1929; *The Bridle of Pegasus. Studies in magic, mythology and folklore,* 1930; *The Life of T. J. Pettigrew,* 1931; *The Life of Charles Wycliffe Goodwin, 1817-1878. A pioneer in Egyptology,* 1934; *Life of Sir Grafton Elliot Smith,* 1938; *Who Was Who in Egyptology,* 1st ed. 1951; *The Banks Letters,* 1958, with supplements, 1962, 1965; with P. H. K. Gray, *Catalogue of Egyptian Ant. in the British Museum. I. Mummies and Human Remains,* 1968; he also edited the Frazer lectures 1922-32; Trans. Capart's Egyptian Art, 1923, and *Toutankhamon,* 1923; he contributed three articles to *EB*; he died in his home Simpson House, Bletchley, Bucks., 5 May 1968.

WWW 6, 288; *JEA* 55 (1969), 211-14 (portr.) (T. G. H. James).

DAWSON-DAMER, (*Rt. Hon.*) **George Lionel** (1788-1856)
British traveller; born 28 Oct. 1788, 3rd son of John, 1st Earl of Portarlington, and Caroline Stuart; Lieut.-Col. 69th Regt.; CB; PC; he visited Egypt in 1829 with his wife (q.v.) and in 1856 with the 3rd Earl; his name and the date 1856 is carved on the Temple of Abu Simbel; he died in London, 14 April 1856.

Burke's Peerage; Army Lists.

DAWSON-DAMER, Henry John Reuben, 3rd Earl of Portarlington (1822-1889)
British traveller; he was born in London, 5 Sept. 1822, son of Henry D. and Eliza Moriarty and nephew of the 2nd Earl; he succeeded in 1845, and in 1856 he made a journey through Egypt as far as Wadi Halfa; he was accompanied by his relative George Lionel D. (q.v.), and his name and the date are also inscribed on the Temple of Abu Simbel; he died in Nice, 1 March 1889.

Burke's Peerage.

DAWSON-DAMER, Mary Georgiana Emma (1798-1848)
British traveller; she was born at Brompton, 23 Nov. 1798, daughter of Lord Hugh Seymour (5th son of 1st Marquess of Hertford) and Lady Anne Horatia Waldegrave, wife of George Lionel D. (q.v.); she travelled with her

husband in Greece, Turkey, Egypt, and Palestine in 1839, and published a descriptive diary of her travels, *Dairy of a Tour in Greece, Turkey, Egypt, and the Holy Land*, 1841, containing many interesting observations on Egypt ancient and modern; she died in St. Leonard, Sussex, 30 Oct. 1848.

Burke's Peerage; Hilmy, i, 154.

DEBONO, Fernand (1914-1997)
Egyptian prehistorian; he was born in Cairo, 11 Oct. 1914, son of Paul Debono, of British nationality, and Madeleine Romanelli; although he initially intended to become a lawyer, after two years of study in Cairo, he decided to become an archaeologist specializing in the prehistoric period with the encouragement of Bovier-Lapierre (q.v.), and Drioton (q.v.); he undertook a series of excavations at prehistoric sites for the Antiquities Service; he surveyed el-Omari in 1936, and the worked briefly in the Sudan with Arkell (q.v.); he returned to El-Omari and excavated there 1943-4, 1948, 1951; he also excavated at Heliopolis in 1950; he worked in the Western Desert in 1949, and then at Wadi Hammamat with Goyon (q.v.); he worked in the Sudan with Vercoutter (q.v.) 1954-55; he became an expert from UNESCO attached to the Centre of Documentation 1971-73 and took part in the Nubian Rescue campaign at Wadi es-Seboua and Amada; he also worked at Maadi, Saqqara, Esna, Karnak, and the Theban west bank where he was part of the graffiti project; he later undertook excavations at the Monastery of St. Pachomius at Nag Hammadi; he was awarded a doctorate by the German Institute at Berlin; he edited *Cahiers d'Histoire Égyptienne* from 1956; he was a member of the German Archaeological Institute, the Institut d'Égypte and the Société d'archéologie copte; apart from his preliminary reports mostly in *ASAE*, he published, with B. Mortensen, *The Predynastic Cemetery at Heliopolis*, 1988 and *El-Omari*, 1990 and contributed to *Nubie*, 1966; *Le Temps des Pyramides*, 1978, and UNESCO's *General History of Africa* I, 1981; he died in Cairo, 6 Aug. 1997.

Inf Mme J. Debono-Ayrout; *BSFE* 140 (1997), 6 (Mme J. Debono); *Memnonia* IX (1998), 29-30 (portr.) (bibl) (Mme Debono); *Archaéonil* 17 (2007), 115-130 (portr.).

DE BUCK *see* **BUCK**

DEDEKIND, Alexander Eduard Wilhelm (1856-1940)
Austrian Egyptologist; he was born in Wolfenbüttel, 5 April 1856, son of Franz Carl Ludwig D., a notary, and Augusta Henrietta Juliana Seeliger; he studied law at Gottingen and Vienna, 1875-9 and then Egyptology from 1885-8; PhD, 1888; he held a post in the Austrian Museums' service, 1887 and was appointed Keeper of the Egyptian collection in the Kunsthistorisches Museum, Vienna, 1892, in succession to E. von Bergmann (q.v.), of whom he published a biography (2nd ed. 1906); he contributed to various journals and published, *Ägyptologische Untersuchungen*, 1902; *Geschichte der Kaiserlichen Sammlung altägyptischer Objekte in Wien*, 1907; he died in Vienna, 8 Nov. 1940.

H.-R. Jarck and G. Scheel, *Braunschweigisches Biographisches Lexikon*, 1996, 135.

DEFRÉMERY, Charles François (1822-1883)
French orientalist; he was born in Cambrai, 8 Dec. 1822, son of Pierre Joseph François Xavier D. and Adèle Guislaine Thérèse Cacheux; he studied Arabic and Persian, being a pupil of the Arabist Caussin de Perceval; in 1869 he was appointed by the Académie to edit with de Slane, in succession to Laborde, the works of the Arabic historians of the Crusades; in 1868 he succeeded Caussin de Perseval, to whom he had long been assistant, at the Collège de France, but soon had to retire through ill-health; with B. R. Sanguinette he edited *Voyages d'Ibn Batoutah*, 4 vols., Paris, 1853-9; the vacancy in the Acad. caused by his death was filled by Maspero; he died in Saint-Valéry-en-Caux, 18 Aug. 1883.

Journ. Asiatique, Ser. 8. 4, 26-9; *JEA* 33 (1947), 77; Hilmy, i, 8; *DBF* 10, 536-7

DE GUIGNES *see* **GUIGNES**

DELAPORTE, Pacifique Henri (1815-1877)
French diplomat; he was born in Tripoli, North Africa, 25 Sept. 1815, son of Jacques Denis D. and Ange Thérèse Antoine Regini; French Consul in Cairo *c*. 1850-5; he made a collection of Egyptian antiquities which was acquired by the Louvre in 1864; he died in Paris, 12 Oct. 1877.

French FO Records; *Bibl. Ég.* 18, pp. xxxix, lii; *Rev. de l'Art,* 43, 168; *Les Donateurs du Louvre*, 1989, 186.

DE LESCLUZE *see* **LESCLUZE**

DELGEUR, Louis Henri (1819-1888)
Belgian educationalist; he was born in Rotterdam, 31 May 1831; he received his PhD in Brussels, 1838; he was a teacher at Charleroi, 1840-1, and Malines, 1841-51 and then private tutor and librarian; he developed an interest in hieroglyphic writing and was commissioned to design the hieroglyphs at the zoo in Antwerp, 1856-61; he visited Egypt, 1873-4 where he discovered a fragmentary colossus at Zawiyet el-Mayetin; he also purchased antiquities from Mustapha Aga (q.v.); he designed another Egyptian room at the château of Chevalier de Schoutheete de Tervarent, 1877; he examined the Allemant (q.v.) collection prior to its purchase by the city of Antwerp. 1879 and contributed to the publication of the Antwerp collection, *Catalogue de la Collection d'Antiquités Égyptiennes*, 1881 by P. Genard; Secretary of the Académie Archéologique de Belgique, 1879-84; Pres., 1886-7; apart from articles, he published *Schets eener geschiedenis der oostersche taalstudien in Belge*, 1847; he died in Antwerp, 11 Sept. 1888.

E. Warmenbol in *Scriba* 4 (1995), 207-224; inf. E. Warmenbol.

DELLA FOSSE, Giovanni Pietro (*c.*1477-1558)
Italian author; also known as Valeriano Bolzani; he was born in Bolzani, *c.*1477, son of Lorenzo della F. and Domenica Ballerini; he was educated in Belluno; he became an apostolic pronotary under Pope Leo X and later attached himself to Cardinal Ippolito de Medici; he settled in Florence in 1524; he published a study *Hieroglyphica*, 1556, largely based on Horapollo; he died in Padua, 20 June 1558.

DBDI 32, 84-8; Lamy, 262-5.

DEL ROSSO, Giuseppe (1760-1831)
Italian architect; he was born in Rome, 16 May 1760, son of Zanobi Del R. of Florence, an architect, and Francesca Straditti; he was educated in Florence and trained as an architect by his father; he later undertook major construction works in Florence; he published a volume *Ricerche sull'architecttura egiziana* in Italian, 1787 and German in 1801; he died in Florence, 22 Dec. 1831.

DBDI 38, 272-6.

DE MAILLET *see* **MAILLET**

DEMBIŃSKI, Henry (1791-1864)
Polish soldier, active politician in exile, art collector; he was born in Strzalków near Stopnica, 16 Jan. 1791; after completing the Technical Academy in Vienna 1809, he participated in the Napoleonic wars; as a general he took part in the Polish insurrection of 1830-31 and was one of the commanders of the revolutionary Hungarian army, 1848-49; in the name of Polish émigrés in France he travelled in 1833 to Egypt to offer the use of Polish officers in a programme of reorganisation then under way for an Egyptian army; at the beginning he was warmly received by Muhammad Ali and obtained the high position of an "army organizer"; but after the failure of the whole operation in Feb. 1834, he was dismissed from the service and decided to go back to Paris; as an art collector Dembinski was also interested in Egyptian objects; in 1839 his family donated to Cracow University "a mummy of ibis" now in the Department of Mediterranean Archaeology, Inv. No. 10.558 (formerly Inv. No. 22/476); part of his collection was placed later in Borkowice near Konskie and another group of his curiosities gathered in the East was transmitted to Prince Adam Czartoryski; he died in Paris, 13 July 1864.

Polski Słownik Biograficzny 4, 65-71; E. Chwalewik, *Zbiory Polskie I*, Warsaw 1926, 29-30; J. S. Bystron, *Polacy w Ziemi Sw., Syrii i Egipcie 1147-1914*, Cracow 1930, 120-34; M. Brandys, *Oficer największych nadziei*, Warsaw 3, 1966, 259-266; inf. J. Śliwa.

DEMEL von ELSWEHR (*Ritter*)**, Hans** (1886-1951)
Austrian Egyptologist; he was born in Teschen, 14 April 1886, son of Johann D. von E. and his wife née Friedrich; he studied at the University of Vienna, Dr. Jur. 1911; he began to study Egyptology and gained Dr. phil. 1913; he joined the museum service in 1913 and in 1922 he was appointed director of the Ägyptisch-Orientalische Sammlung and in 1951 director of the Kunsthistorischen Museum in Vienna; H/Professor, 1945; Hofrat, 1947; he made a speciality of Demotic and Art History; in 1926 he was assistant to Junker (q.v.) in the excavations of the Giza necropolis and he wrote a chapter in the latter's *Ermenne*; he also published *Die Reliefs der Grabkammer des Kaninsut; Der Totenpapyrus des Chonsu-Mes*, 1944, and *Ägyptischer Kunst*, 1947; he died in Vienna, 28 Dec. 1951.

AfO 16, I (1952), 171 (E. Komorzynski); *Chron. d'Ég.* 27 (1952), 147 (anon.); *Who's Who in Central Europe 1935/6*, 250.

DE MORGAN *see* **MORGAN**

DENNIS, James Teackle (1865-1918)
American attorney and Egyptologist; born Baltimore, 6 Oct. 1865, son of James Upshur D. and Mary Wilson Teackle; he was educated at Lafayette College and Johns Hopkins University 1896-1903; he travelled in Egypt 1895-6 and again 1905-6 and 1907 when he acted as a volunteer assistant to Naville (q.v.) at Deir el-Bahri; he journeyed from Cairo to Uganda in 1907; he published *On the Shores of an Inland Sea,* 1908; *From Cataract to Equator,* 1910; *The Burden of Isis,* 1910, and various articles in journals; he died in Woodbrook, Md., 1 April 1918; his antiquities are in The Johns Hopkins University and the Malden Museum, Missouri and some of his papers in the Griffith Institute.

WWWA i, 315; Andrews Diary; B. Needle, *The Dennis Collection of Egyptian Antiquities.*

DENON, *(Baron)* **Dominique Vivant** (1747-1825)
French antiquary, artist, author, and scholar; he was born in Givry, near Chalon-sur-Saône, 4 Jan. 1747, son of Vivant D. and Nicole Marie Boisserand; he at first studied Law in Paris, but abandoned it for art and letters; he was a favourite of Louis XV, who entrusted him with the arrangement of a collection of gems and medals for Madame de Pompadour; Denon was also a great success with the ladies and his pleasing disposition and winning ways brought him advancement at each stage of his career; at this time he wrote a comedy *Julie, ou le Bon Père,* 1769, which was produced in Paris, and also studied drawing under Halle; a diplomatic career now interrupted his academic work, and he was attached to the French Embassy at St. Petersburg, 1772, afterwards leaving Russia and being transferred to Sweden; in 1775 he was sent on a special mission to Switzerland and in 1776 as chargé d'affaires at Naples remaining until 1787; he was in Venice at the time of the Revolution until 1792; whilst in Italy in 1793 he heard that his property had been confiscated by the revolutionaries and his name proscribed; with great courage he returned to Paris and his life was spared; under the Directory he frequented the salon of Joséphine de Beauharnais where he met Napoleon and later joined the Commission in Egypt; he not only visited the Delta but travelled throughout Upper Egypt making a great collection of drawings and antiquities; he carried out his task of recording the Egyptian monuments very well, and also wrote an account of his journey *Voyage dans la Basse et la Haute Égypte*, 1802, new ed., 1989; the main collection of drawings consisting of 150 plates was published by Jomard in the *Description de l'Égypte,* 1809-22; the *Voyage* was issued in 2 large fol. vols. and had a profound effect on European scholarship running to several editions and being translated into English and German; in his return he was appointed Director of the Central Museum of Arts, 1802, and in 1804 Director-General of Museums, a post he held until 1815; he was also a member of the Académie des Beaux-Arts 28 Jan. 1803 and reconfirmed 21 March 1816; at this time he played a very important part in creating the Louvre collections; by going along with the French army he was able to choose objects and works of art from all over Europe, with the result that Paris became temporarily the artistic capital of the Western World; a bronze portrait medal was issued in 1822; his own extensive collections were sold in Paris on 15 Jan. 1827, a considerable part of them being acquired by provincial museums, especially that of Boulogne; one of his papyri acquired from Hamelin (q,v,) is now in the Museum Meermanno-Westreenianum, The Hague, while a second, discovered by Denon at Medinet Habu, is untraced; his art collection was sold in Paris, 1826, the sale catalogue entitled *Descriptions des objets d'art qui composent le cabinet de feu M. Le Baron V. Denon...*; he died in Paris, 28 April 1825 and was buried in Père Lachaise cemetery.

DBF 10, 1066-8; *BIÉ* 5 (1923), 163-93; Carré, i, 119-43; Hilmy, i, 172;Lugt 11328; A. C. E. Franquet de Franqueville, *Le Premier Siècle de l'Institut de France*, 1895, I, 145; I. Ghali, *Vivant Denon,* Cairo, 1986; Jean Chatelain, *Dominique Vivant Denon et le Louvre de Napoléon.*, Paris, 1973; Pierre Lelièvre, 'Dominique Vivant Denon: Égyptologue et directeur de la Monnaie des Médailles', *L'Institut et la Monnaie. Deux palais sur un quai,* 1990, 153-7; Norbert Miller, 'Vivant Denons Reisen ins Unheimliche oder die Entdeckung des Fremden im Eigenen', *Daidalos. Berlin Architectural Journal* 19, (1986), 39-52; C. Sollmann, *De Ibis* N.S. 9 (1984), 11-24; H. De Meulenaere, *Chron. d'Ég.* 64 (1989), 58-63; M. Dewachter, *Aegyptus Museis Rediviva,* 1993, 77-89; P. Lelièvre, *Vivant Denon. Hommes des Lumières "ministre des arts" de Napoléon,* 1993; *Les Savants en Égypte,* 1998, 57; O. Bonnerot in M Bertaud, *Architectes et architecture dan la littérature française,* 1999, 7-6; E. Gran-Aymerich, *Dictionnaire biographique d'archéologie 1798-1945,* 2001, incorporated in *Les Chercheurs de passé 1798-1945,* 2007, 744-6; D. Brahimi in C. Grell, *L'Égypte imaginaire,* 2001, 163-171; F. Saragoza in *Égypte, Afrique & Orient* 58 (2010), 37-46.

DE RICCI *see* **RICCI.**

DE ROUGÉ *see* **ROUGÉ**

DERCHAIN, Philippe (1926-2012)
Belgian Egyptologist; he was born in Verviers, Belgium, 24 July 1926; he studied classical philology and Egyptology at the University of Liege under van der Walle (q.v.) and also attended courses in Paris under Posener (q.v.); PhD at Liege; he lectured at Brussels and Strasbourg and was appointed professor at Cologne, 1 April 1968; his publications include with F. Daumas, *Le Temple de Kalabscha*, 1959; with others, *Le pouvoir et le sacré*, 1962; *Le sacrifice de l'oryx*, 1962; with F. Daumas, *Debod*, 1963; with A. Delatte, *Les intailles magiques gréco-égyptiennes*, 1964; *Le Papyrus Salt 825 (B.M. 10051)*, 1965; *Le Tableau d'Osymandyas et la Maison de la vie à Thèbes*, 1965; with S. Sauneron, *Annuaire de l'Égyptologie*, 1971; *Hathor Quadrifons*, 1972; *El Kab* I, 1971; with U. Verhoeven, *Le voyage de la déesse libyque*, 1985; *Le dernier obélisque*, 1987; *Les impondérables d'hellénisme*, 2000; and *La création*, 2004, with D. von Recklinghausen; two volume of studies in his honour were published, E. Graefe and U. Verhoeven, *Religion und Philosophie im alten Ägypten*, 1991 and M. Broze and P. Talon, *L'atelier de l'orfèvre*, 1992; he died in Liege, 3 Oct. 2012.

Inf. F. Labrique.

DERRY, Douglas Erith (1874-1961)
British anatomist and anthropologist; he was born in Edmonton, Middlesex, 1 Nov. 1874, son of David D., a banker, and Mary Elizabeth Erith; he studied medicine at Edinburgh University; ChB, 1903; in 1905 he was Assistant Professor of Anatomy at the Government School of Medicine Cairo; in 1909 he became anthropologist to the Archaeological Survey of Nubia and he took part in the Wellcome expedition to Jebel Moya, 1911-2; from 1910 he joined the Anatomy Dept. of University College London and later served in World War I; in 1919 he was appointed Professor of Anatomy at the School of Medicine, Cairo, later the Faculty of Medicine of the Egyptian University; in 1923 he carried out the first examination of the mummy of Tutankhamun although his report was only published much later by F. Leek, *The Human Remains from the Tomb of Tutankhamun*, 1972; he carried out many anatomical examinations notably on the so-called body of Akhenaten and the remains discovered by Brunton (q.v.) at Saqqara, Emery (q.v.) at Saqqara, and Arkell (q.v.) at Khartoum; he greatly increased the anatomical collection at the School of Medicine from which he retired in 1952; FRCS, 1949; apart from his reports, he was also the author of an article on the dynastic race in *JEA* 42 (1956), 80-5; he died at Radwinter near Saffron Walden, 20 Feb. 1961.

V. Plarr, *Lives of the Fellows of the Royal College of Surgeons,* 101-2; *The Times* 27 Feb. 1961, 14; *J. Anat.* 95 (1961), 441 (U. Fielding); J. Buikstra and C. Roberts (eds.), *The Global History of Palaeopathogy. Pioneers and Prospects*, 2012, 217-20 (B. Baker and M. Judd).

DESPIRRO, Antonio (*fl.*1828-9)
Italian antiquities dealer; he lived in Cairo and carried out excavations in Egypt; Champollion had dealings with him.

Champollion, ii, 411.

DESROCHES NOBLECOURT, Christiane (1913-2011)
French Egyptologist; she was born in Paris, 17 Nov. 1913, daughter of Louis D., a lawyer, and Madeleine Girod; she studied Egyptology at the École du Louvre under Drioton (q.v.) and Boreaux (q.v.); Diploma in archaeology, 1935; she also attended the École Pratique des Hautes études of the Sorbonne under Lefebvre (q.v.), Moret (q.v.), and Weill (q.v.); PhD in philology, 1937; she then joined the staff of the Dept. of Egyptian Antiquities at the Louvre, 1934; assistant, 1942; she was the first woman attached to IFAO in Cairo, 1938-40 and took part in its excavations at Edfu; during World War II, she served in the Resistance and helped to safeguard the Louvre's collection; she married André Noblecourt, 1942; she succeeded Vandier (q.v.) as Keeper of Egyptian Antiquities, 1974-81; she was also Professor at the École du Louvre, 1937-82, and Inspector-General of Museums, 1981; from 1954 she was involved in organizing the Nubian Rescue campaign as a counsellor of UNESCO and helped to found the Centre of Documentation in Cairo, 1955 and the Centre Franco-Égyptien in Karnak; she organized two major loan exhibitions in Paris, on Tutankhamun in 1967 and Ramesses II in 1976; Hon PhD, Institut Catholique; Légion d'honneur, Grand Cross, 2008; Medal of the Resistance; Gold Medal of the CNRS, 1975; *Acta Orientalia Belgica* XV (2001) was dedicated to her; her numerous publications included, with K. Michalowski, *Tell-Edfou 1939*; *Le style égyptien*, 1946; *Ancient Egypt. The New Kingdom and the Amarna Period*, 1960; *L'art égyptien*, 1962; *Temples de Nubie*, 1961; *Peintures des tombeaux et des temples égyptiens*, 1962; English ed. *Egyptian wall-Paintings from Tombs and Temples*, 1962; *Toutânkhamon, vie et mort d'un pharaon*, 1963, new ed. 1976; English ed., *Tutankhamen: Life and Death of a*

Pharaoh, 1963; *Toutankhamon et son temps*, 1967; with C. Kuentz, *Le petit temple d'Abou Simbel*, 2 vols., 1968; with others, *Le Speos d'el-Lessiya*, 1968; with S. Donadoni, *Grand temple d'Abou Simbel*, 1971; with others, *Ramesseum* X, 1976; with C. Aldred (q.v.), J-P. Lauer (q.v.), J.Leclant and J.Vercoutter (q.v.), *Le temps des pyramides*, 1978; with C.Aldred, P.Barguet, J.Leclant and H.W.Müller (q.v.), *L'empire des conquérants*, 1979; with C.Aldred, F.Daumas (q.v.), and J.Leclant, *L'Égypte du crépuscule*, 1980; with J. Vercoutter, *Un siècle de fouilles françaises en Égypte 1880-1980*, 1981; with L. Balout et C. Roubet, *La momie de Ramsès* II, 1985; *Le grand Pharaon Ramsès II et son temps*, 1985; English ed. *Ramses II. The Great Pharaoh and His Time*, 1985; *La femme au temps des pharaons*, 1986, new ed., 2001; with others, *Sen-nefer*, 1986; *La grande Nubiade ou le parcours d'une égyptologue*, 1992; *Amours et fureurs de La Lointaine*, 1995; *Ramsès II, la véritable histoire*, 1997; English ed. *Ramses II*, 2007; *Philae, la domaine d'Isis*, 1997; *Dictionnaire de l'Égypte ancienne*, 1998; *L'Égypte vue en haut*, 1998; *Toutânkhamon*, 1999; *Le secret des temples de la Nubie*, 1999; *La reine mystérieuse: Hatshepsout*, 2002; *Sous le regard des dieux*, 2003; *Lorsque la nature parlait aux Égyptiens*, 2003; *Symboles de l'Égypte*, 2004; *Le fabuleux héritage de l'Égypte*, 2004; English ed. *The Fabulous Heritage of Egypt*, 2005; *Le secret des découvertes*, 2006; she died at Epernay, 23 June 2011.

WWF 2005, 673; *Acta Orientalia Belgica* XV (2001), xvii-xxi (C. Vandersleyen), xxii ff. (bibl.) (I. Franco); *Le Monde* 26/7 June 2011, 24; *The Daily Telegraph* 2 July 2011, 29; *BIFAO* 111 (2011), 1-12 (portr.) (bibl.) (G. Andreu-Lanoë); inf. E. David; *Memnonia* 22 (2011), 57-74 (C. Leblanc) (portr.) (bibl.), 75-82 (M. Kurtz).

D'ESTOURMEL *see* ESTOURMEL

DÉVAUD, Eugène Victor (1878-1929)
Swiss Egyptologist; he was born in Fuyens (now Villaz-Saint Pierre) 11 Jan., 1878, son of François Joseph Théophile D. and Marie Séraphine Deillon; he studied under Loret (q.v.) at Lyons, and afterwards at Berlin; he was appointed lecturer at Freibourg University 1923, Professor 1927; his first important work was a study of Papyrus Prisse and its variants, his later work being mainly concerned with Coptic; he made important contributions on Coptic etymology in various journals; in addition to Egyptian, Dévaud studied other oriental languages, including Assyrian and Chinese; his manuscripts are now in the Griffith Inst. Oxford; he wrote, *Les Maximes de Ptahhotep d'après le papyrus Prisse, les papyrus 10371/10435 et 10509 du British Museum et la tablette Carnarvon*, 1916; *Études d'etymologie copte*, 1922; *Psalterii Versio Memphitica e Recognitione Pauli dé Largarde: réedition, avec le texte copte en caractères coptes*, with O. Burmester, 1925; *Les Proverbes de Salomon. ... Texte bohaïrique*, etc., with O. Burmester, 1930; some of his papers are in the Griffith Institute; he died in Freiburg, 18 July 1929.

Griffith Inst. List of Records, 1947, 5; *JEA* 5, (1929), 273; *Kêmi* 3 (1930), 20-2 (bibl.) (P. Montet); *Voyages en Égypte de l'Antiquité au début du XXe siècle*, 2003, 314-5; *Historisches Lexikon der Schweiz* 3, 691.

DEVERELL, Robert (1760-1841)
British politician and author; formerly Pedley; he was baptized in Bristol, 24 June 1760, son of Simon P. and Ann, daughter of Robert Deverell, whose name he later adopted; after school in Bristol he entered St. John's College, Cambridge, 22 June 1777; BA (7th Wrangler), 1781; MA, and Fellow of St. John's 1784; a brilliant scholar he appears to have been somewhat unbalanced and published a number of most eccentric works, also advocating the slave trade; he wrote *A Supplement to notes on the ancient method of treating Fever of Andalusia, deduced from an explanation of the Hieroglyphics painted on the Cambridge Mummy*, 1805; *Discoveries in Hieroglyphic and other Antiquities: In treating of which many favourite pieces of Butler, Shakespeare and other great writers are put in a light entirely new*, 6 vols., London, 1813; in this work he tried to show that all the phrases, characters, and incidents in Shakespeare's plays are allusions to the appearances of the moon; this work he suppressed after the 2nd ed., 1816, and it is very rare, but there is a copy in the British Library; he died in New Norfolk St., London, 29 Nov. 1841.

ODNB 15, 943-4; *DNB* 14, 424; *BIFAO* 5 (1906), 85.

DEVÉRIA, (Charles) Théodule (1831-1871)
French Egyptologist; he was born in Paris, 11 July 1831, son of Achille Jacques D. (*d.*1857), the painter, and Céleste Ursule Marie Motte; he first became interested in Egyptology under the influence of Prisse d'Avennes (q.v.) who was a friend of the family; a visit to the Leiden Museum in 1846 intensified his interest; he studied Coptic under Charles Lenormant (q.v.) and Arabic at the Écoles des Langues Orientales; he was employed at the Bibliothèque Nat. 1851; in 1854 he published his first contribution to Egyptology; on the recommendation of de Rougé (q.v.), he was appointed to a position in the Egyptian Dept. of the Louvre in 1855, where the collections were being much enlarged by the discoveries of Mariette; in 1858 he accompanied Mariette to Egypt as copyist, making 4 visits in all; he was made Assistant Keeper in 1860; he contributed an entry on ancient Egyptian

musical instruments for the History of Music by Fétis, 1860; the last ten years of his life were mainly devoted to examining and cataloguing the Eg. papyri in the Louvre, but he did not live to see his catalogue published; Devéria was a brilliant scholar but had time to publish little of his great mass of notes and manuscripts of which he left 40 vols. as well as 16 boxes of slips; these are all in the Louvre and consist of the following: 11 vols. of monuments in European museums, 7 of reproductions of historical monuments, 1 of funerary docs., 1 of moral docs., 3 of docs. of the Book of the Dead, 1 of Serapeum docs., 3 of docs. relating to the Egyptian Pantheon, 1 on Demotic writing, 1 on modern Egyptian, 1 on Egyptian natural history, 3 of views of monuments classified geographically, and an Egyptian Dictionary in MSS in 6 vols.; other papers are preserved in the Collège de France; his published works were, *Catalogue des Manuscrits Égyptiens, etc.,* 1874, 1881; *Le Papyrus judiciaire de Turin et les papyrus Lee et Rollin* 1897; his health was always frail and was affected by the climate of Egypt so that he died early in Paris, 25 Jan. 1871.

Théodule Devéria, Mémoires et Fragments. 2 vols., pub. by G. Maspero. Paris 1896-7. Vol. i. has a biogr. notice by his brother G. Devéria, pp. i-xlviii (portr.), *Bibl. Ég.* 4; E. David, *Mariette Pacha 1821-1881,* 1994, 110, 211; È. Gran-Aymerich, *Dictionnaire biographique d'archéologie 1798-1945,* 2001, incorporated in *Les Chercheurs de passé 1798-1945,* 2007, 751-2.

DEVILLIERS *see* **VILLIERS**

DE WITTE *see* **WITTE**

DIAMOND, Hugh Welch (1809-1886)
British physician and photographer; he was born 1809, son of William Batchelor D., a surgeon in the E. India Co. service, and Jane Welch; he was educated at Norwich Grammar School and afterwards studied medicine at St. Bartholomew's Hospital where he became assistant to Abernethy; he practised in Soho, and greatly distinguished himself in the cholera outbreak of 1832; he specialized in mental disease and founded a home at Twickenham, 1858, in which he lived as resident physician until his death; one of the pioneers of scientific photography; FSA; he published an account of a mummy purchased by him in 1843 (*Archaeologia,* 31, 408); this mummy at one time in Maidstone Museum was afterwards sent to the Royal College of Surgeons where it was destroyed by enemy action in 1941, but some of its linen was given to Dr. Lee's Museum; he died in Twickenham, 21 June 1886.

ODNB 16, 13-14; *DNB* 15, 1; Hilmy, i, 187; *Mem. Inst. Ég.* 13.15.

DIDOT, Ambroise Firmin (1790-1876)
French publisher; born in Paris, 21 Dec. 1790, son of Firmin D. and Elisabeth Catherine Denise Magimel; he was a member of the famous family of publishers established in Paris in 1713 by François Didot; after a classical education in Paris, he spent three years in Greece and in the East; with his brother Hyacinthe he succeeded to the direction of the business in 1827 and inaugurated the series of Greek and Latin texts for which the house of Didot became celebrated; he visited Egypt in 1816, but confined his tour to the Delta not visiting Upper Egypt; ten years later he published *Notes d'un voyage fait dans le Levant, 1816 et 1817;* in Cairo he met Salt (q.v.) for whom he had great admiration; he died in Paris, 22 Feb. 1876.

EB viii, 207; Carré, i, 197; Hilmy, i, 188; È. Gran-Aymerich, *Dictionnaire biographique d'archéologie 1798-1945,* 2001, incorporated in *Les Chercheurs de passé 1798-1945,* 2007, 753.

DIMITRIOU, Ioannis (*c.*1826-1892)
Greek collector; he was born at Pesperago in Lemnos and settled in Alexandria where he became a cotton merchant and financier; he put together a collection of 3,406 Egyptian antiquities including ten mummies from Akhmim and 3,625 coins which he donated to the National Museum at Athens from 1880-87; many of his antiquities were supplied by Marius Panayiotis Tano (q.v.); he died in Alexandria, 21 Dec. 1892.

Inf V. Chrysikopoulos; *RecTrav* 18 (1896), 1-15; O. Tzachou-Alexandri, ed., *The World of Egypt in the National Archaeological Museum,* 1995, 21; R. Merrillees, *The Tano family and Gifts from the Nile to Cyprus,* 2003, 6; O. Tzachou-Alexandri (ed.), *The World of Egypt in the National Archaeological Museum,* 1995, 21.

DINGLI, Alexander (*fl.* 1887-1904)
Egyptian antiquities dealer of Greek or Maltese extraction; he orinally delat in ostrich feathers, but turned to trading in antiquities because of the war in the Sudan; he sold a statue of Niuserre to the Cairo Museum in 1888, to Valdemar Schmidt (q,v,) in 1894-5 and donated objects to the Graeco-Roman Museum in Alexandria; he also helped Budge (q.v.) in shipping objects from Egypt; he retired to Larnaca about 1904; his son Paul Dingli (fl. 1910-30) also dealt in antiquities but trained as a restorer in the Cairo Museum and later became a noted forger of antiquities.

F. Hagen and K. Ryholt, *The Antiquities Trade in Egypt 1880-1930*, 2017, 207-10.

DINIACOPOULOS, Vincent (1886-1967)
Greek-Canadian dealer and collector; he was born in Constantinople, 11 Sept. 1886, son of Nicolas D. and Marie Lotos; he initially worked as a dealer in antiquities in Constantinople but with his wife Hélène (1906-2000) he established shops in Paris and Egypt by 1922; he also worked as a restorer, and was suspected by Borchardt (q. v.) and others of being a forger; he emigrated to Canada, 1951, opening the Ars Classica Gallery in Montréal; a large collection of Classical antiquities formed by him is now in the Musée des Beaux-Arts, Québec; Egyptian objects from his estate were sold at Sotheby's New York, 10 Dec. 1999 ('Property from a Canadian private collection'), and by the American dealers 'Fragments of Time', 1 June 2001; others are in the Royal Ontario Museum and other collections; he died in Montreal, 9 Jan. 1967

Inf. Concordia University; J.-J. Fiechter, *Faux et faissaires en art égyptien*, 2005, 48-9; C. Epstein in J. Fossey and J. Francis, *The Diniacopoulos collection in Québec*, 2004, 17-26; J. Francis and G.W.M. Harrison, *Life and Death in Ancient Egypt: The Diniacopoulos Collection*, 2010; inf. T. Hardwick.

DIXON, David Marshall (1930-2005)
British Egyptologist; he was born at Conway (Gyffin Conwy), Wales 30 Dec. 1930, son of William Francis D. and Ellen Williams; he was educated at the Royal Grammar School, High Wycombe and at University College London from 1950, obtaining his BA and PhD; he took part in Emery's (q.v.) excavations at Saqqara in 1956 and 1968-70 and Buhen 1957-9; he was appointed Research Fellow at the Wellcome Institute to classify the Egyptian collection in 1960 and arranged its transfer to the Petrie Museum in 1964; he then became Hon. Research Associate at the Department of Egyptology, University College London and later lecturer 1967-95; he was Hon. Curator of the Petrie Museum 1967-1978; he served as Hon. Secretary of the Egypt Exploration Society 1983-92; his principal interests were in fauna and flora and trade in ancient Egypt and latterly on the British in Egypt in the 19th century on which subjects he wrote a number of articles; he died at High Wycombe, 1 Nov. 2005.

JEA 92 (2006), 241-3 (bibl.), (portr.), (G. T. Martin); *Egyptian Archaeology* 28 (2006), 44; inf J. Picton; *ASTENE Newsletter* 26 (2006), 4 (J. Picton).

DIXON, James Alfred (1891-1915)
British Egyptologist; he was born at Stoke Damarel, 28 March 1891, son of Jesse D., RN, and Elizabeth Marianne Secretan, and educated at St. Paul's School; a good draughtsman and copyist he was sent out at a very early age to assist Blackman (q.v.) in copying the Temple of Dendur, 1908; in 1909-10 he worked for the EEF, with Naville, Peet, and Legge (qq. v.) at Abydos, and again 1910-11; in 1912 he joined the Wellcome Sudan Expedition near Sennar as excavator and draughtsman; in addition to Egyptology, Dixon was interested in medieval history and heraldry; he might well have been successor to Ayrton (q.v.) as head of the Archaeological Department in Ceylon but was commissioned in the Forces in 1914, as 2nd Lieut., in the 6th Battalion, Border Regt., and was killed in action in Suvla Bay, Gallipoli, 9 Aug. 1915.

JEA 3 (1916), 48-9 (portr.)

DIXON, Waynman (1844-1930)
British civil engineer and ship-builder; he was born Newcastle-upon-Tyne, 17 March 1844, son of Jeremiah D. and Mary Frank; Assoc. Member Inst. Civil Engineers, 1878; Member, 1882; resigned, 1909; he associated with his brother John Dixon and Mr (later Sir) Benjamin Baker in the removal of Cleopatra's Needle to London; Dixon designed an iron cylinder, supervised its assembly around the obelisk in Alexandria, and accompanied it on the towing ship; see his account published as a letter in the Newcastle Daily Chronicle, 'Cleopatra's Needle. Intimate story of its transport to London', 1925; while in Egypt he also made investigations at the Pyramids and discovered the air-passages from the 'Queen's Chamber', 1873; objects which were found in the Great Pyramid were acquired by the British Museum in 1972; he was the heir of Selima Harris (q.v.); his personal papers

including many photographs and paintings, were sold at auction on 30 Jan. 2008 and again on 13 Nov. 2008 and are now in the possession of Bob Brier; he died in Great Ayton, Yorks., 24 Jan. 1930.

Engineering, 31 Jan. 1930; *Proc. Inst. Civil Eng.* 61. 233; Edwards, *The Pyramids of Egypt* (1947), 92; R. Morkot in *Bulletin of ASTENE* 35 (2008), 9-10; I. Pearce in *Souvenirs and New Ideas,* ed. D. Fortenberry (ed.), 2013, 129-41; I. Pearce, *ASTENE* Bulletin 60, 9-14, 61 (2014), 13-5.

DOBROVITS, Aladár (1909-1970)
Hungarian Egyptologist; he was born in Budapest, 15 Oct. 1909; he studied at the Lycée Toldi Ferenc and at the University of Budapest 1928-32; from 1931 he worked as a voluntary assistant at the National Museum and from 1934 was on the staff of the Musée des Beaux-Arts becoming Keeper of the Dept. of Antiquities 1945-51; from 1937-8 he also worked at the Louvre in Paris; he taught at the University of Budapest from 1946 and was presidential counsellor of the Musée National Hongrois 1946-9; he became chief curator of the Musée des Arts Décoratifs 1949-61 and Professor of the History of the Ancient Orient at the University Eötvös Lorand 1958-70; he wrote a number of articles mainly on religion in the Graeco-Roman period in Egypt, notably on Harpocrates, in *Emlekhönyv Dr. Nahler Ede*, 1937, 72-122; he died in Budapest, 4 April 1970.

Acta Archaeologica Academiae Scientiarum Hungaricae 23 (1971), 259-62 (portr.) (bibl.) (L. Kákosy); *Bulletin du Musée Hongrois des Beaux-Arts* 36 (1971), 115-16 (V. Wessetzky); *Acta Antiqua Academiae Scientiarum Hungaricae* 18 (1970), 421-2 (V. Wessetzky).

DOBRZAŃSKI, Lucas (1864-1909)
Polish photographer and excavator in Egypt; he was born in Warsaw, 23 Jan. 1864, son of Joseph D.; studied medicine at the Jagellonian University, Cracow, but shortly before completing his studies, his poor health led him to go to Egypt; between 1893-95 he spent the winter seasons on the Nile and engaged in artistic photography, constantly improving his skill and successfully participating in many international exhibitions e.g. Alexandria, Paris, Hamburg; he also published his photographs in Polish and foreign magazines, for example, *Warsaw Photographer, Weekly Illustrated, Photographische Mitteilungen, Strand Magazine;* all his artistic output was destroyed in Warsaw during World War II; the only trace of Dobrzanski's activities in the field of archaeology is an object, a small kohl container made of alabaster, now in the Kunsthistorisches Museum in Vienna sold by him to the Museum in 1896; as indicated in the Museum's inventory this came from excavations undertaken by Dobrzanski together with some workers near Koptos in 1895; unfortunately, it has proved impossible to obtain more information about his field activity in Egypt, Dobrzanski spent his last years in Warsaw; he died in Cracow, 6 Sept. 1909.

Inventory of the Kunsthistorisches Museum, Vienna, p. 214, No. 6296; E. Komorzynski, *Das Erbe des Alten Ägypten*, Vienna 1965, 46, n. 1 and 70, n. 41; J. Śliwa, 'Lusasz Dobrzanski and his "excavations" in Egypt, 1895', *Schriften zur Geschichte und Kultur des Alten Orients,* 13 (1977), 397-400; *Polski Słownik Biograficzny* 5, 267.

DODGSON, Aquila (1829-1919)
British congregational minister; he was born in Elland, Yorkshire, 9 Sept. 1829 and baptized in Halifax, 6 Dec. 1829, son of Joshua D., a dyer and Hannah Lightowler; he became a minister in Hull, but resigned in 1870 owing to the failure of his voice, becoming a cotton-spinner at Ashton-under-Lyne; he was very interested in Egyptology and arranged lectures by Amelia Edwards (q.v.) and Petrie (q.v.), and raised funds for the promotion of Egyptology in Manchester; he retired in 1891, and in the winter 1891-2 visited Egypt, spending some time with Petrie at Amarna; he later lived in Leeds and arranged the coins in the museum there; he was also interested in astronomy and built an observatory in his garden; Dodgson's name is associated with an important Demotic papyrus obtained in Egypt in 1881 by the Revd Elkanah Armitage (q.v.) and published by Griffith, *PSBA* 31. 100, 289; it was presented by his family to the Ashmolean Museum in 1932; another Dodgson papyrus is in Melbourne; his Egyptological collection was acquired by the Leeds City Museum; his correspondence is in the Griffith Institute, Oxford; he died in Headingley, Leeds, 10 Aug. 1919.

Inf. Mrs. R. A. Talbot (daughter); *JEA* 19 (1933), 97; *PSBA*, ut supra.

DODWELL, Edward (1767-1832)
British traveller, antiquarian, and collector; he was born 1767, son of Edward D. and Frances Jennings; he was educated Trinity College, Cambridge, BA, 1800; he collected coins and vases, chiefly Greek and Roman; he settled in Rome, 1806; FSA; his collection of Egyptian, Greek, Roman, and Etruscan antiquities was acquired after his death by the Munich Museum; the glass chalice of the time of Thutmose III now in that museum was published by Newberry, *JEA* 6. 154; his drawings and papers are in the British Library, contained in 4 vols., the first of which in entirely devoted to Egyptian antiquities (Add. MSS 33958-61); he died in Rome, 13 May 1832.

ODNB 16, 442-4; *DNB* 15, 178-9; Champollion, i, 189, 204, 208.

DOLZANI, Claudia (1911-1997)
Italian Egyptologist; she was born in Trieste, 28 April 1911; she was educated in Trieste and Florence, graduating in 1935; she taught Italian and Classics in schools in Fiume and Trieste; she developed an interest in Egyptology from 1950 and studied under Botti (q.v.); she obtained a teaching licence in 1964 and obtained a post at Trieste University, 1967-81; apart from articles, her publications included *Il dio Sobk*, 1961; *La collezione egiziana del Museo dell'Accademia dei Concordi in Rovigo,* 1969; and *Catalogo del Museo Egizio di Torino: Vasi canopi,* 1982; she died in Trieste, 6 Jan. 1997.

Aegyptus 76 (1996), 179-183 (S. Curto); IAE Internet obituary (S. Curto); inf. S. Curto.

DONADONI, (Fabrizio) Sergio (1914-2015)
Italian Egyptologist; he was born in Palermo, 13 Oct. 1914, son of Prof. Eugenio D., a literary historian, and Melina Pastorelli; he studied at University of Pisa, graduating 1934, and at Paris, 1934-6 under Lefevre (q.v), Moret (q.v.), and Drioton (q.v.) and then at the University of Copenhagen, 1948; he excavated in Egypt under Breccia (q.v.), 1935-40 at Antinoe and at Medinet Maadi under Vogliano (q.v.), 1939-40; he taught at the Universities of Pisa from 1950, Milan from 1959, and Rome (La Sapienza) to 1989; he was appointed to the advisory board of the UNESCO Nubian Rescue Campaign, 1955; he served as an epigraphist at Abu Simbel and Ellesiya and directed the mission of the University of Rome in Nubia from 1958-68 at Ikhmindi, Farriq, Kuban, Maharraq, Tamit, 1964, Sabagura, Sonqi Tino, 1967-8; he also excavated at Antinoe, 1965-8, at Theban tomb 27 in Egypt and Gebel Barkal in the Sudan, 1972-88; he was awarded the Feltrinelli prize for archaeology, 1975; apart from articles and preliminary excavation reports, he published *La civiltà egiziana,* 1940; *L'Arte Egizia,* 1955; *La religione dell'Egitto antico,* 1957; *Storia della letteratura egiziana antica,* 1957; *Appunti di grammatica egiziana,* 1963; *Tamit (1964),* 1967; *Le spéos d'Ellisiya,* 1968; *Antinoe (1965-8),* 1974; *Cultura dell'antico Egitto,* 1986; *La pitture murali della Chiesa Sonki Tino nel Sudan,* 1968; *Cairo, Museo Egizio,* 1969; *Grand Temple of Abu Simbel* III, 1975; *L'Egitto,* 1981; with others, *L'Egitto dal mito all'egittologia,* 1990, English ed. *Egypt from Myth to Egyptology,* 1990; with others, *L'Uomo Egiziano,* 1990 (French ed. *L'Homme Egyptien*), 1992; *The Egyptians,* 1997; he died in Rome, 31 Oct. 2015.

Internet obit; *Sudan and Nubia* 29 (2016), 179-80 (A. Roccati)

DONALDSON, Thomas Leverton (1795-1885)
British architect and author; he was born in Bloomsbury Square, London, 19 Oct. 1795, son of James D., an architect, and Jane Leverton; he was appointed Professor of Architecture, University College London, 1841-64; President of the Institute of Architects, 1864; Member of the Inst. de France; he travelled in the East and wrote books on the history of architecture, and on pyramids, obelisks, Mariette's excavations etc.; he died in Upper Bedford Place, London, 1 Aug. 1885.

ODNB 16, 516-7; *DNB* 15, 214-15; H. H. Bellot, *Univ. Coll. London* (1929), 265-6; Hilmy, i, 190.

DONATI, Vitaliano (1717-1762)
Italian naturalist and traveller; he was born at Padua, 8 Sept. 1717, son of Angelo D. and Elisabetta Vicentini; he studied medicine and philosophy at the University of Padua, obtaining his doctorate, 10 June 1739; he was appointed Professor of Natural History and Botany at the Royal University of Turin, 6 Oct. 1750; he undertook travels in Italy, Istria, Dalmatia, Bosnia and Albania, combining scientific research with his interest in antiquities; he gained an international reputation with his major discovery that coral was not a plant or mineral but of animal nature, published in 1750; he became a member of the Academies of Stockholm, Florence, and Montpellier and the Royal Society of London and had two plants named after him; under the auspices of King Carlo Emanuele III of Sardinia, he led a scientific-commercial expedition to Egypt and the East Indies to collect scientific samples, study commerce, find new trade routes, and purchase antiquities; he left Venice on 20 June 1759 and landed at Alexandria on 18 July 1759 where he was delayed for seven months; he visited Rosetta, Damietta and Cairo, and from Feb. 1760 went up the Nile into Nubia; returning to Cairo, he travelled through the Sinai Peninsula to Palestine and Damascus, Baghdad, Basra, Sohar, and Muscat; while he was in Egypt he sent home on 20 Feb. 1761 over 1,000 scientific specimens including 600 Egyptian objects for the Royal Museum of Antiquities in Turin; he died 26 Feb. 1762, in the Persian Gulf en route from Basra to India.

DBDI 41, 61-4; G. G. Bonino, *Biografia Medica Piemontese,* 1825, II, 145-176; G. Vedova, *Biografia degli Scrittori Padovani,* 1832, 330-5; P. Revelli in G. Cora, *Cosmos,* serie II, XII (1894-6), 273-354; G. B. de Toni, in a. Mieli, *Gli scienziati italiani,* vol. i, pt. 2, (1923), 452-5; P. Barocelli, *Atti della R. Accadamia di Torino,* 47 (1912), 3-17,

411-25; 48 (1913), 471-96; A. Silotti, *Viaggiatori Veneti alla scoperta dell'Egitto*, 1985, 69-70; E. D'Amicone in C. Morigi Govi, S. Curto, *L'Egitto fuori dell'Egitto*, 1991, 101-6; A. Scattolin Morecroft, 'The Vitaliano Donati collection at the Turin Egyptian Museum', *JEA* 92 (2006), 278-82; A. Scattolin Morecroft, *Vitaliano Donati and the search for his collection at the Museo Egizio di Torino*, PhD Thesis, Cambridge, 2008; inf. A. Scattolin Morecroft.

DONOHUE, (Vincent) Anthony (1944-2016)
British Egyptologist; he was born at Prestbury, 26 Nov. 1944, son of Vincent D. and Marjorie Jones; he studied Egyptology at the University of Oxford; BA; and at Durham; he worked with the Egyptian collection at Bolton Museum, notably the shabtis, and also with the Egypt Centre in Swansea; he wrote a number of articles in various journals and the guidebook *The Egyptian Collection, Bolton Museum and Art Gallery*, 1967; he died in Oxford, 6 June 2016.

Inf. K. Griffin.

D'ORBINEY, Elizabeth (née Fearnley) (c.1804-1893)
British collector; she was born c.1804, daughter of Henry F. and Elizabeth Circuit; she adopted the style d'Orbiney while resident in France; she purchased the famous papyrus that bears her name while in Italy; this contains the Story of the Two Brothers; when she was in Paris during the winter of 1851-2, she confided the papyrus to de Rougé (q.v.) who perceived its nature, and published an account of it in the *Athenaeum français*, 30 Oct. 1852, followed by a translation in the *Rev. Arch.* ix. 385; in 1857 she sold the papyrus to the British Museum (EA 10183) and a facsimile of it was published in *Select Papyri*, 2nd ser., 1860; she died in New York, Jan. 1893.

Maspero, *Popular Stories* (London, 1915); BM *Select Papyri*, ii, p. 7, inf. S. B. Rudge; ; P. Usick, 'Mysterious Madame d'Orbiney,' *BM Magazine* 61 (Autumn 2008), 48.

DORIA, Niccolo Maria, so-called *Marchese di Spineto* (1773/4-1849)
Italian teacher and Egyptologist; he was apparently born to a Neapolitan noble family, although his claim to the title of Marquis is doubtful; he held a commission in a cavalry regiment, and fought against Napoleon at the Battle of Marengo, 1800; he subsequently fled Italy for Britain; he settled in Cambridge, and was appointed Ensifer to the University, 1807; Deputy to the Professor of Modern History by 1828; Teacher of Italian, 1829; he lectured on European literature, and wrote occasional verse for the University; he served as translator for the Government at the 'trial' of George IV's wife Queen Caroline, 1820; in 1828 he delivered a course of 13 lectures on Egyptian language, history, and chronology, being a synthesis of the work of Young (q.v.), Champollion (q,v,), and other early scholars; this course was repeated at the Royal Institution in London, and published, dedicated to George IV, as *Lectures on the Elements of Hieroglyphics and Egyptian Antiquities*, 1829; he also wrote a short article on the identity of the 'bee' hieroglyph in the royal titulary; he died in Cambridge, 26 Aug. 1849.

Hilmy, i, 183; *Notes and Queries* 27 June 1914, 510; 15 Aug. 1914, 137; C. P. Brand et al. (ed.), *Italian Studies Presented to E. R. Vincent*, 1962, 18-23; inf. T. Hardwick.

DOUCE, Francis (1757-1834)
British antiquary and collector; he was born in London, 13 July 1757, son of Francis D., attorney, and Ellen Tapley; he worked as an attorney before joining the Department of Manuscripts at the British Museum, 1807, Keeper, 1807, resigning 1811; FSA, 1779; inheritances from his parents and the sculptor Joseph Nollekens enabled him to form important collections of books, manuscripts, works of art, and antiquities, including a large number of small Egyptian objects; his notebooks and annotated books and auction catalogues, now in the Bodleian Library, contain information on contemporary sales and collections of antiquities, including those of Belzoni (q.v.) and Thomas Hope (q.v.); he attended Pettigrew's (q.v.) mummy unwrappings, and Pettigrew studied a crocodile mummy in his possession; he bequeathed his antiquities to Samuel Rush Meyrick (q.v.), and his books, manuscripts, and drawings, including a collection of papyri, to the Bodleian Library; he died in London, 30 March 1834.

ODNB 16, 594-5; Pettigrew, *History of Egyptian Mummies*, 1834, xvi, xvii, 214; S. G. Gillam (ed.), *The Douce legacy: an exhibition to commemorate the 150th anniversary of the bequest of Francis Douce, 1757–1834*, 1984; C. Wakefield, *Bodleian Library Record* 14 (1991), 94-7; M. Coenen, *JEA* 86 (2000), 81-98; inf. T. Hardwick.

DRACH, Solomon Moses (1815-1879)
British astronomer, mathematician, and antiquarian; he was born London, 15 Nov. 1815, son of Josiah (Shimmy) ben David and Zipporah Levy; he worked as commission-agent in the firm of his aunt's husband Lipman Drach who died in 1840 when he adopted his surname; he retired from business in 1847 on the death of his aunt to

devote his time to research; FRAS, 1841; FRGS; he was an active member of the Soc. of Bibl. Arch. to whose *Transactions* he contributed many articles, including two on the Great Pyramid; he also wrote on the Temple of Jerusalem, and a great deal on statistics, magic squares, etc. he contributed to *Records of the Past* and to the publications of the Royal Asiatic Society; he died London, 8 Feb. 1879.

Royal Asiatic Society records; Hilmy, i. 192; *Monthly Notices of Royal Astronomical Society* 40 (1880), 191-2.

DREXEL, Anthony Joseph II (1864-1934)
American financier and collector; he was born in Philadelphia, 9 Sept. 1864, son of Anthony Joseph D., the financier, and Ellen Bicking Rozet; he was a nephew of Joseph William Drexel (q. v.), and a cousin of Saint Katharine Drexel; he was educated in France, Britain and America; he entered the family business aged 16, and retired after his father's death in 1893; in 1895 he commissioned E. Brugsch (q. v.) to form a collection of Egyptian objects; this he gave to the Drexel Institute of Art, Science and Industry in Philadelphia, founded by his father; the collection was sold *en bloc* to the Minneapolis Institute of Arts, 1916; numerous objects were dispersed from this in the 1950s, many passing into the Harer collection; some items are now in the Rosicrucian Egyptian Museum, San Jose, California; he died in New York, 14 Dec. 1934.

Drexel University archives; M. C. Harrison, *Prominent and progressive Americans* I, 1902, 99-101; G. D. Scott, *Temple Tomb and Dwelling: Egyptian Antiquities from the Harer Family Trust Collection*, 1992; W. B. Harer, 'The Dexel Collection: from Egypt to the Diaspora,' in S. d'Auria (ed.), *Servant of Mut: Studies in Honor of Richard Fazzini*, 2008, 111-119; inf. T. Hardwick.

DREXEL, Joseph William (1833–1888)
American banker, collector, and philanthropist; he was born in Philadelphia, 24 Jan. 1833, son of Francis Martin Drexel and Catharine Hookey; he was associated with the family bank of Drexel Morgan & Co.; he travelled in Egypt and acquired objects there; he was president of the Metropolitan Opera and was involved with New York charities; he was a trustee of the Metropolitan Museum, 1881-88; he donated casts of Egyptian sculpture to the Metropolitan Museum, 1879-80, effectively founding the Museum's Egyptian holdings, and subsequently donated and loaned other objects; his wife Lucy Wharton Drexel (13 May 1841- 25 Jan. 1912) gave the remainder of his Egyptian collections to the Metropolitan Museum after his death; upon her death she bequeathed money to the University of Pennsylvania Museum; she had earlier endowed the Lucy Wharton Drexel Medal, awarded by the University of Pennsylvania Museum for outstanding archaeological work in the English language; he died in New York, 25 March 1888.

New York Times March 26 1888 and Jan. 25 1912 (obits); *New York Times* March 10 1912; J. W. Jordan, *Colonial and Revolutionary Families of Pennsylvania* I, 1911, 535; J. N. Ingham, *Biographical Dictionary of American business leaders* I, 1983, 302-3; *Bulletin of the Metropolitan Museum of Art* 6/11 (Nov. 1911), 203; inf. T. Hardwick.

DREYER, Günter (1943-2019)
German Egyptologist; he was born in Schwichteler, 5 Oct. 1943; he studied Egyptology, Assyriology and Near Eastern Archaeology at the University of Hamburg and the Free University of Berlin, 1969-78; PhD, 1978; Habilitation, 1997; he joined the German Archaeological Institute in Cairo, 1978-87; he was appointed lecturer at the Free University of Berlin, 1987-88; he became deputy Director of the German Archaeological Institute in Cairo, 1989-98; Director, 1998-2008; he undertook excavations at the Temple of Seti I at Qurna, Elephantine, Wadi Garawi, Abydos from 1980 with Kaiser (q.v.) and as director from 1985, Sinki, Giza, 2002-3, and Saqqara from 2002; he published *Der Tempel der Satet* I, 1986; *Umm el-Qaab* I, 1998; with D. Polz, *Begegnung mit der Vergangenheit. 100 Jahre in Ägypten*, 2007; he died 12 March 2019.

Internet obit. on DAIK website 18 March 2019 (D. Polz and S. Seidlmayer).

DRIOTON, (*Chanoine***) Étienne Marie-Félix** (1889-1961)
French Egyptologist; born at Nancy, 21 Nov. 1889, son of Étienne D. and Félicie Maria Moitrier; he was educated at the École Saint-Sigisbert, and in 1905 went on to the Séminaire at Nancy to be trained as a priest; he later became a Canon of the Church; he went to Rome in 1912, becoming a Doctor of Philosophy at the St. Thomas Academy and in 1913 received a Doctorate in Theology at the Gregorian University; at this period he was mainly interested in Hebrew and Bible studies; he became a Lic. in Biblical Sciences of the Pontifical Commission; his interest now turned to oriental studies and in 1918 he gained the Diploma of the École Libre des Langues

orientales at the Catholic Institute of Paris, taking Egyptian and Coptic as his subjects; he had been interested in ancient Egypt from the age of eleven and he took Egyptian grammar lessons by correspondence with Bénédite (q.v.); in 1919 he was appointed Professor of Egyptian philology and Coptic language at the Catholic Institute in succession to Virey (q.v.); for his students he now produced a handy *Cours de Grammaire égyptienne*, a work praised by F. Ll. Griffith (q.v.) in *JEA* 9, and the first teaching grammar other than translations of Erman's *Äg. Grammatik* that had been written in France for many years; Drioton worked as Assistant Keeper with Boreux (q.v.) at the Louvre from 1926, and from 1925 he undertook the epigraphic survey at the Medamud excavations of the Institut Français directed by Bisson de la Roque (q.v.), publishing afterwards two volumes of inscriptions; he now showed his interest in the reading of Ptolemaic texts; he also at this period worked on cryptographic writings and published several articles on this subject which were to become classics; in 1936 he was appointed Director of the Egyptian Antiquities Service succeeding Lacau (q.v.), and filled this position for sixteen years; this was also an immensely productive period of his life as he published scores of articles and reviews; he also found time to give courses at the Institute of Egyptology of the University of Cairo and helped to train many young Egyptians in Egyptology; he was appointed Director, 1952, at the Centre National de la Recherche Scientifique and Professor at the Collège de France, 1957; he gained many awards and decorations from different countries including Egypt and Iran, and was an Officer of the Légion d'Honneur; his specialities were religious subjects, Egyptian monotheism, and maxims and morals written on scarabs; *Essai sur la cryptographie privée de la fin de la XVIIIe dynastie*, 1933 and *Recueil de cryptographie monumentale*, 1940, were among his most important works in this field exhibiting notable insight into the ancient Egyptian mind; besides these subjects religious mystery plays also interested him and he showed the existence in ancient Egypt of a profane as well as sacred theatre, whose subjects like those of the Greeks were derived from mythology although not liturgical; painting of the Coptic period also fascinated him, as well as the 'Teaching of Amenemope' and its relationship with the Biblical book of Proverbs; on his return to France Drioton was made a member of the Conseil Artistique for Museums; he had a easy and fluent style which made his books and articles very readable; his bibliography up to 1955 numbered 287 items in all; his monographs included *Introduction à l'étude des hiéroglyphes*, with H. Sottas; with Marcelle Baud he produced two vols. on the Theban tombs, *Le Tombeau de Röy*, 1928, *Le Tombeau de Panehesy*, 1932; also *Le Drame sacré dans l'antique Égypte*, 1929; *Une Scène des mystères d'Horus*, 1929; *Ce que l'on sait du théâtre égyptien*; *Le Théâtre égyptien*, 1942; *Procédé acrophonique et principe consonantal, 1943*; *An explanation of the enigmatical inscriptions on the Serapeum plaques of Ptolemy IV*, 1946; *L'Égypte*, with J. Vandier, 1946; *La Religion égyptienne*, 1955; *Maximes morales sur des scarabées égyptiens*, 1957; *Sur la sagesse d'Aménémopé*, 1957; *Le Livre des proverbes et la sagesse d'Aménémopé*, 1959; *Égypte pharaonique*, 1959; *Boiseries coptes de style pharaonique*, 1960; he died in Montgeron, 17 Jan. 1961.

AfO 20 (1963), 308-9 (portr.) (J. Leclant); *L'Ami du clergé*, Langres 71 (1961), 295-6 (L. Christiani); *BIFAO* 61 (1962), 1-6 (portr.) (F. Daumas); *BSAC* 16 (1961-2), 335-7 (Sami Gabra), 337-42 (P. du Bourguet); *BSFE* 32 (Dec. 1961), 31-4 (J. Sainte Fare Garnot); *Bulletin de la Faculté des Lettres de Strasbourg*, 40th year, no. 2 (Nov. 1961), 163-7 (portr.) (J. Leclant); *Chron. d'Ég.* 36 (1961), 175-8 (B. van de Walle) ibid. no 73 (1962), 5-7 (P. Gilbert); *CRAIBL* 1961, 24-5 (P. Chantraine), 106-7 (C. Schaeffer); *La Croix*, Paris, 27 Jan. 1961 (P. du Bourguet); *Ecclesia*, Paris, no. 145 (Apr. 1961), 123-30 (5 illus.) (M. Colinon); *Enciclopedia Pomba*, Turin, vol. ii (1962), 353 (F. Jesi); *Études*, Paris, 94th year, vol. 309 (Apr. 1961), 73-84 (P. du Bourguet)); *JEA* 47 (1961), 4 (J. Cerny); *Journal de Genève*, 20 Jan. 1961, 2 (C. Maystre); *Le Monde*, Paris, 1 Feb. 1961 (no. 4988), 8 (G. Wiet); *Nouvelles de l'Institut Catholique de Paris*, 12, no. 3 (Feb-Mar. 1961), 17-22 (2 illus.) (P. du Bourguet); *Rev. Arch.* 1961, ii. 83-5 (J. Sainte Fare Garnot); ibid. 1962, i. 97 (Ch. Picard); *La Revue du Caire*, vol. xlvi, no. 246 (Feb. 1961), 173-4 (A. Papadopoulo); *Rev. d'ég.* 13 (1961), 9-18 (portr.) (J. Vandier); *ZÄS* 87 (1962), pp. i-ii (portr.) (J. Vandier); *BIFAO* 56 (1957), 1-18 (bibl.) (J. Jacquiot); *BSFE* 116 (1989) 5-7 (J. Vercoutter); E. Gran-Aymerich, *Dictionnaire biographique d'archéologie 1798-1945*, 2001, incorporated in *Les Chercheurs de passé 1798-1945*, 2007, 760-1.

DROHOJOWSKI, (*Revd*) **Joseph** (1739-1811)
Polish member of the Order of Reformati; he was born 1739, son of Joseph D.; he made a pilgrimage to the Holy Land and stayed longer as a missionary in the Near East 1788-91; on his return to Europe, he wrote an account, which was printed in Cracow in 1812, after his death; he arrived at Alexandria by ship and gave quite a detailed description of the town, Pompey's pillar, other objects and hieroglyphs; he visited Rosetta and Damietta; in Cairo he listed Catholic monasteries and made an excursion to the Pyramids giving also some information on this group of monuments; he wrote about the Nile and its importance for the whole of Egypt; some passages in his account are concerned with nature and with the inhabitants of the country.

J. Bystron, *Polacy w Ziemi Swietej, Syrii i Egipcie 1147-1914*, Cracow 1930, 64-73; *Polski Słownik Biograficzny* 5, 386-387; inf. J. Śliwa.

DROVETTI, Bernardino Michele Maria (1776-1852)
Italian diplomat, politician, and antiquities collector; he was born in Barbania, Piedmont, 4 Jan. 1776, son of Giorgio Francesco D., a notary, and Anna Vittoria Vacca; he graduated from school on 13 Aug. 1791; he then trained in law at the Collegio della Provincie at Turin, graduating 1 April 1795; he later enlisted in the French army in Italy, June 1796 where he became acquainted with Murat; Commissioner for Turin, 1799; on the General Staff of the Reserve Army, 1800; he then served in the Ministry of War in Piedmont, 1800; Chief of Staff of the Piedmontese Division, 19 March 1801; Judge of the Criminal Tribunal in Turin, Oct. 1801; he was named as French Vice-Consul at Alexandria on 20 Oct. 1802, arriving in Alexandria, 29 May 1803; acting Consul-General from 1804; general Vice-Consul and thus chief French representative in Egypt, 22 March 1806; French Consul-General in Egypt, 1811-14; he was replaced 25 Sept. 1814 but remained acting in post until the arrival of the new vice-consul Thédénat-Duvent (q.v.) on 14 Nov. 1815 in advance of his successor Roussel (q.v.); he was reappointed to his position, 20 June 1821-20 June 1829; he visited Upper Egypt for the first time in 1811 with Boutin (q.v.) when he began his collection of antiquities; Drovetti is best remembered today as an ardent collector of Egyptian antiquities and for his acquisition of the Turin Canon of Kings; the carelessness with which his assistants handled it is also supposed to have been responsible for its fragmentation and the disastrous condition in which it arrived in Italy; he employed many agents to excavate and buy from native diggers, particularly at Thebes; his first great collection, offered to and rejected by France, was bought by the King of Sardinia in 1824 for 400,000 lire, and forms the principal part of the great Egyptian collection at Turin; his second great collection was bought by France in 1827 by order of Charles X, fetching 150,000 francs, and is now in the Louvre; a third collection was acquired for the Berlin Museum by Lepsius (q.v.) in 1836 for 30,000 francs; Drovetti thus played a major part in the formation of no less than three of the principal European Egyptian collections; he made several journeys to Upper Egypt in 1811, 1816 with Rifaud (q.v.) and Cailliaud (q.v.), 1817 and 1819 and to the Kharga and Dakhla Oases in 1819 and to Siwa in March-April 1820 with Linant (q.v.), Ricci (q.v.), and Frediani (q.v.); his notes and geographical observations were embodied in Jomard's (q.v.) works of 1821 and 1823; he had great influence with Muhammad Ali and suggested many administrative reforms; he was made Chevalier of the Légion d'honneur, 1819, Officier, 1825; his papers are in Turin's Academy of Sciences and National archives, while others were purchased by the French Ministry of Culture; his correspondence has been published by S. Curto and L. Donatelli, (ed.), *Bernardino Drovetti, Epistolario*, 1985; S. Guichard, *Lettres de Bernardino Drovetti, Consul de France à Alexandrie (1803-1830)*, 2008, and L. Donatelli, *Lettere e Documenti di Bernardino Drovetti*, 2011; he died in Turin, 9 March 1852.

References to Drovetti, esp. in contemporary accounts, are too numerous to specify here: he is constantly mentioned in Athanasi, Belzoni, Carré, Champollion, Hartleben, Salt, and many others; see also, Minutoli, 14-16; *Enc. It.* 13.223 (G. Farina); Guide to *Museo egizio de Torino*, 4; Gardiner, *Egypt of the Pharaohs* (1964 ed.), 15, 47; Marro, 'Louis Alexis Jumel e Bernardino Drovetti', *BIÉ* 31 (1948-9), 278-95; *DBF* 11, 836-7; *DBDI* 41, 712-6; J.-J. Fiechter, *La moisson des dieux*, 1994, *passim*; S. Zavatti, *Oriente moderno* 45 (1965), 879-88; S. Curto in C. Morigi Govi, S. Curto, *L'Egitto fuori dell'Egitto*, 1991, 97-100; R. T. Ridley, *Napoleon's Proconsul in Egypt. The Life and Times of Bernardino Drovetti*, 1998; E. Gran-Aymerich, *Dictionnaire biographique d'archéologie 1798-1945*, 2001, incorporated in *Les Chercheurs de passé 1798-1945*, 2007, 761-3; L. Donatelli in M. Betrò and G. Miniaci, *Talking along the Nile*, 2013, 93-9.

DROWER, Margaret (Peggy) Stefana (1911-2012)
British Egyptologist; she was born in Southampton, 8 Dec 1911, daughter of Sir Edwin Mortimer D., a lawyer who served as an adviser in Iraq, and Ethel Stefana Stevens, an anthropologist and noted expert on Mandaeans; she was educated at Cheltenham Ladies College, 1926-30 and University College London, 1930-5 under Petrie (q.v.), Margaret Murray (q.v.) and Glanville (q.v.); BA, 1935; she excavated at Armant with Myers (q.v.), 1935-7 and Amarna with Pendlebury (q.v.), 1936; she was appointed assistant lecturer in the History Department at UCL, 1937, later becoming lecturer, 1940 and reader in Ancient History, 1966-79; Hon Research Fellow, 1986; she was also appointed visiting professor at the Institute of Archaeology, 1997-2012; she served on the executive committee of the Egypt Exploration Society from 1937, later Hon. Secretary, 1956-70, Chairman, 1978-82 and Vice-President, 1983-2012; FSA, 1978; MBE, 1946; she married Campell Hackforth-Jones in 1947; she contributed to the Cambridge Ancient History and published *Flinders Petrie: A Life in Archaeology*, 1985 and *Letters from the Desert. The Correspondence of Flinders and Hilda Petrie*, 2004; she died in London, 12 Nov 2012.

The Times 20 Dec. 2012; *Egyptian Archaeology* 42 (2013), 2 (portr.) (D. Jeffreys).

DRUMMOND, (*Sir*) William (*c*.1770-1828)
British scholar and diplomat; he was born *c*.1770, son of John D. of Logiealmond and Lady Catherine Murray; he may be identified with William, son of John D. of Perth, who matriculated at Christ Church, Oxford, 24 Jan. 1788; FRS, 1799; DCL Oxford, 1810; PC, 1801; he was Minister Plenipotentiary at Naples, 1801 and 1806; Ambassador to the Porte, 1803-6; Drummond became interested in oriental history and archaeology, and published works on the Old Testament in which he explained many of the episodes as astronomical allegories; he published *Memoir on the Antiquity of the Zodiacs of Esna and Dendera*, 1821; he died in Rome, 29 March 1828.

ODNB 16, 993; *DNB* 16, 51; Champollion, i, 194; Hilmy, i, 193.

DUAN, Fang *see* **TUAN-FANG**

DUANE, Matthew (1707-1785)
British lawyer, numismatist, and antiquary; he was born in 1707, and had rooms in Lincoln's Inn; FRS, 1763; FSA; Trustee of the British Museum, 1765-85, of which he was a considerable benefactor, 1764-77; he had a large collection of coins, chiefly purchased from well-known cabinets; he had also a large collection of Greek, Roman, and other antiquities and was one of the first people in England to collect Egyptian antiquities; several of these were included in the sale of his coins and other collections, 3 May 1785; his library was sold in 1838; he died in Bedford Row, London, 6 Feb. 1785, and was buried in St. Nicholas, Newcastle-upon-Tyne.

ODNB 17, 8-9 (portr.); *DNB* 16, 76; Nichols, *Lit. Anecd.* iii, 497; Lugt 3875; R. Welford, *Men of Mark 'Twixt Tyne and Tweed*, 1895, 2, 122-6 (portr.).

DUBOIS, Léon Jean Joseph (1780-1846)
French draughtsman and lithographer; he was born in Paris, 1780; in 1807 he became acquainted with Champollion (q.v.) and remained a staunch friend of his; he was made draughtsman of Egyptian antiquities at the Louvre, 1817; he executed the drawings for the illustrations of Champollion's *Panthéon*, 1823, and for other works; he also made the drawings for the first fount of hieroglyphic type for the Imprimerie Nationale, 1840; he was Conservator of the Egyptian collections of the Louvre, 1832-46; he had some strange notions, one of his methods being to cut out from the papyri the coloured vignettes of the gods in order to frame them and place them with the statues of divinities, regarding the texts themselves as indecipherable and therefore useless; he drew up the sale-catalogues of many important collections of antiquities, including those of Choiseul-Gouffier (q.v.), 1818; Léon Dufourney (q.v.), 1819; Grivaud de la Vincelle (q.v.), 1820; Thédenat-Duvent (q.v.), 1822; Mimaut (q.v.), 1837, and Pourtalès (q.v.), 1841; he died in Paris, 2 Dec. 1846.

Bibl. Ég. 21, p. xviii; Hartleben, *passim*; Hilmy, i, 194; *Rev. Arch.* 3 (1846), 691; *Rev. de l'Art,* 43, 166; J. Bulté, *Catalogue des collections égyptiennes du Musée National de Céramiques à Sèvres*, 1981, 16.

DUBOIS-AYMÉ, Jean Marie Joseph Aimé (1779-1846)
French engineer; he was born in Pont-de-Beauvoisin, 22 Dec. 1779, son of Joseph Martin Dubois, customs officer, and Marie Thérèse de Romand; he joined the army and was trained at the École Polytechnique; he took part in the expedition to southern Egypt in 1799 with Jollois (q.v.) and de Villiers (q.v.) but quarrelled with his superior and was sent to Quseir; he also helped in the Survey concerning the proposed Sinai canal; he later contributed to the *Description*; customs official in Italy, 1811; director-general of customs in Tuscany, 1812; MP, 1831-4; he died in Meylan, 15 March 1846.

DBF 3, 975; J. E. Goby, *Un compagnon du Bonaparte en Égypte*, 1952.

DU CAMP, Maxime (1822-1894)
French traveller and photographer; born Paris, 8 Feb. 1822, son of Theodore Joseph du C. and Alexandrie Cleronnet; a man of letters he travelled extensively with Gustave Flaubert in Europe and the East, 1849-52; one of the earliest amateur photographers the account of his journey, *Égypte, Nubie, Palestine et Syrie*, 1852, being illustrated by 125 photographic plates, many of a very high standard and of historical interest as they show the contemporary state of buildings and monuments either still in existence or destroyed since; in his *Souvenirs littéraires*, 1882, he made many bitter and grossly false statements about his contemporaries, especially Prisse d'Avennes (q.v.) and Mariette (q.v.); he was elected a member of the Académie Française 20 Feb. 1880; he died in Baden-Baden, 8 Feb. 1894.

EB 8, 627; Carré, ii, 77-128; Hilmy, i, 194; *DBF* 11, 1131-5; A. C. E. Franquet de Franqueville, *Le Premier Siècle de l'Institut de France*, 1895, I, 383-4; M. Dewachter and D. Oster, *Un voyageur en Égypte vers 1850*, 1987; V. Magri-Mourges in P. Starkey and N. El Kholy (eds.), *Egypt through the Eyes of Travellers*, 2002, 149-165; È. Gran-Aymerich, *Dictionnaire biographique d'archéologie 1798-1945*, 2001, incorporated in *Les Chercheurs de passé 1798-1945*, 2007, 763.

DUCHESNE, Alexandre St. Romain (1802-1869)
French painter and traveller; born in Paris 1802, he was the son of Jean D. (1779-1855); he joined the Franco-Tuscan expedition to Egypt, 1828-9; Marc Lang has collected the letters written to his family and 22 drawings made during his travels in Egypt; he died in Paris, 2 July 1869.

Champollion, ii. 9, 47, 142, 186, 238, 400, 420; inf. Marc Lang; M. Dewachter, *Cahiers du Musée Champollion*, I, (1988), 50.

DUELL, Prentice (1894-1960)
American archaeologist; he was born in New Albany, Indiana 17 Aug. 1894, son of Martin H. D. and Mary Hannah Gray; BA from Univ. of California, 1916, MA from Univ. of Arizona, 1917, M. Arch. from Harvard, 1924; he held posts at the Univ. of Cinncinnati, 1925-6 and Bryn Mawr, 1927-9; Prof. of Mediterranean Art at the Univ. of Chicago, 1931-6 and Field Director of the Chicago expedition at Saqqara, 1930-36; research fellow at the Fogg Art Museum, Harvard 1939-60; although primarily a classical archaeologist, he directed work at the tomb of Mereruka at Saqqara published as *The Mastaba of Mereruka*, 1938; he died in Boston, 16 April 1960.

WWWA 4, 267; *N.Y. Times*, 20 April 1960, 39.

DUEMICHEN, Johannes (1833-1894)
German Egyptologist; he was born in Weissholz, 15 Oct. 1833; he studied theology and philology at Berlin and Breslau; he then took up Egyptology and became a student of Lepsius (q.v.) and Brugsch (q.v.), 1859-62; he was appointed Professor of Egyptology in the University of Strasbourg (Strassburg), 1872-94; he first visited Egypt in 1865 and afterwards went there frequently to make copies of many important inscriptions and texts; his principal publications are both numerous and important, being mainly epigraphic; of these that devoted to the great Theban tomb of Pedamenope (No. 33) was left unfinished, only two of the projected seven parts having appeared, 1884-5; some additions were made by Spiegelberg in 1894; his bibl. lists about 40 nos., the main works being, *Bauurkunde der Tempelanlagen von Dendera,* 1865; *Geographische Inschriften altägyptischer Denkmäler,* 4 vols. 1865-85; *Altägyptische Kalenderinschriften,* 1866; *Historische Inschriften altägyptische Denkmäler,* 2 pts. 1866; *Altägyptische Tempelinschriften,* 2 pts. 1867; *Die Flotte einer ägyptischen Köningin,* 1868; *Der Felsentempel von Abu Simbel, etc.,* 1869; *Eine vor 3000 Jahren abgefasste Getreiderechnung,* 1870; *Resultate einer ... archaeologisch-photographischen Expedition,* 2 pts. 1869-71; *Über die Tempel und Gräber im alten Aegypten,* etc., 1872; *Die erste bis jetzt aufgefundene sichere Angabe über die Regierungszeit eines Aegyptischen Königs,* etc., 1874; *Baugeschichte des Dendera-Tempels, 1877; Die Oasen der libyschen Wüste,* 1877; *Geschichte des Alten Aegyptens,* 1879; *Die Kalendarischen Opferfestlisten im Tempel von Medinet-Habu,* 1881; *Der Grabpalast des Patuamenap,* 1884; *Zur Erinnerung an Richard Lepsius,* 1884; *Zur Geographie des Alten Ägypten; lose Blätter aus dem Nachlass von Johannes D.,* edit. by W. Spiegelberg, 1894; a large mass of copies, squeezes, and other material was bequeathed by him to Strasbourg University; he died in Strassburg (now Strasbourg), 7 Feb. 1894.

Rec. Trav. 16 (1894), 74-7 (bibl.) (W. Spiegelberg); *ZÄS* 32 (1894), 63 (H. Brugsch-A. Erman); Brugsch, *Mein Leben,* 262, 285; G. Ebers, *Richard Lepsius* (trans. Underhill), pp. i-v (1887); Hilmy, i, 194; *The Athenaeum* 17 Feb. 1894; *Biblia* 6 (1893), 41-2 (portr.); G. Ebers, *Aegyptische Studien und Verwandtes,* Stuttgart und Leipzig, 1900, 471-484; E. Endesfelder, *Die Ägyptologie an der Berliner Universität-Zur Geschichte eines Fachgebietes,* 1988, 14; inf. T. Getzen.

DUFFERIN, (*Marquis of***) see BLACKWOOD.**

DUFF GORDON, (*Lady***) Lucie (***née* **Austin)** (1821-1869)
British authoress; she was born in Westminster, 24 June 1821, the only child of the jurist John Austin (1790-1859) and Sarah Taylor; she married Sir Alexander Duff Gordon, Bt. (1811-72), 1840, and was a prominent figure in literary society; owing to ill-health, she resided at the Cape of Good Hope, 1860-3, and in Egypt, 1863-9, where she lived mainly at Luxor in the Maison de France vacated by Maunier (q.v.); apart from her literary works she wrote, *Letters from Egypt,* 1865; *Last Letters from Egypt,* 1875, a fuller edition of which with a preface by George Meredith, edited by her daughter, Mrs Janet Ross, appeared in 1902; an enlarged edition of *Letters from Egypt (1862-1869)* was published by her great-grandson Gordon Waterfield, 1969; she died in Cairo, 14 July 1869.

ODNB 22, 941-2; *DNB* 22, 220-1; Edwards, *Thousand Miles,* 2nd ed., 451-5; Hilmy, i.,197; memoir prefixed to *Last Letters* (2nd ed. 1876) by her daughter (portr.); G. Waterfield, *Lucie Duff Gordon*, 1937; K. Frank, *Lucie Duff Gordon: a Passage to Egypt*, 1994; J. Speake (ed.), *Literature of Travel and Exploration*, 2003, 1, 350-2; S. Searight in S. Searight (ed.), *Women Travellers in the Near East*, 2005, 52-60.

DUFOURNEY, Léon (1754-1818)
French architect; he was born in Paris, 5 March 1754; he travelled in Italy, 1782, and built the zoo buildings and observatory at Palermo, 1789-92; he became Professor at the École de l'Architecture, 1804-16; Member of the Académie des Beaux-Arts, 1 Aug. 1796; he collected works of art and antiquities, and the sale-catalogue of his Greek and Egyptian antiquities was drawn up by L. J. J. Dubois (q.v.), in Paris, 1819; he died in Paris, 16 Sept. 1818.

DBF 2, 1448-9; A. C. E. Franquet de Franqueville, *Le Premier Siècle de l'Institut de France*, 1895, I. 127; Lugt 9683.

DULAURIER, (Jean Paul Louis François) Édouard Leuge (1807-1881)
French orientalist; he was born in Toulouse, 29 Jan. 1807, son of Hugues Leuge D. and Jeanne Claire Josephine du Touzet; he was elected to the Acad. des Inscr., 1864; he published descriptions of the stelae in Toulouse Museum and various Coptic texts, 1833-5; he visited London in 1838 and copied the MS Pistis Sophia, with a view to complete publication of the text, but he only issued a general account of it in 1847; he also published an examination of the doctrines of Champollion (q.v.), 1847; Member of the Légion d'Honneur; he died in Meudon, near Paris, 21 Dec. 1881.

Hilmy, i, 198; *DBF* 12, 71-2.

DUNHAM, Dows (1890-1984)
American Egyptologist; he was born at Irvington-on-Hudson, New York, 1 June 1890, son of Dr. Carroll D. and Margaret Dows; he was educated at Hackley School, Tarrytown, N.Y. and Berkshire School, Sheffield, Mass.; before attending university he toured Europe and Egypt in 1908 and decided to specialise in art history; he studied at Harvard, 1909-13 with a year out to tour Europe with his parents; BA, 1913; he was taught by Reisner (q.v.) in 1913 who offered him a post on his excavations and he rapidly became one of Reisner's chief assistants; he excavated with Reisner at Giza, 1914 and 1915; assistant in the Department of Egyptian Art, Boston Museum, 1914-5; he undertook his own excavation at Gammai in 1915 and joined Reisner at Gebel Barkal in early 1916; he studied under Breasted (q.v.) at the Oriental Institute Chicago for three months in 1916; served as an ambulance driver in France and then army officer, 1916-19; from 1919-23 he excavated with the Harvard-Boston expedition in the Sudan and in 1923 at Nag-ed-Deir (and at Sheikh Farag); in 1923-5 he was seconded to the Egyptian Government assisting Firth (q.v.) at Saqqara and Jéquier (q.v.) at Dahshur; he rejoined Reisner at Giza in 1925-8; assistant curator at Boston, 1928, associate curator, and in 1942 curator in succession to Reisner; on his retirement in 1956 he devoted himself as curator emeritus to the publication of Reisner's excavations, a task which he accomplished with tenacity and diligence; founder member of ARCE and treasurer, 1955-64; FSA, 1952; recipient of the Boston Museum Award, 1973 and the gold Medal for Distinguished Archaeological Achievement from the Archaeological Institute of America, 1979; his major publications were *Two Royal Ladies of Meroe*, 1924; *Excavations at Gammai*, with O. Bates, 1927; *Fouilles à Saqqarah: Le Mastabat Faraoun*, with G. Jéquier, 1928; *Nag-ed-Deir Stelae of the First Intermediate Period*, 1937; *El Kurru*, 1950; *Decorated Chapels of the Meroitic Pyramids at Meroe and Barkal*, with S. E. Chapman,, 1952; *Nuri*, 1955; *Royal Tombs at Meroe and Barkal*, 1958; *The Egyptian Department and Its Excavations*, 1958; *Semma-Kumma*, with J. M. A. Janssen, 1960; *The West and South Cemeteries at Meroe*, 1963; editor of *The Predynastic Cemetery N7000 at Naga-ed-Deir*, by A. M. Lythgoe, 1965; *Uronarti, Shalfak, Mirgissa*, 1967; *The Barkal Temples*, 1970; *Recollections of an Egyptologist*, 1972; *The Mastaba of Queen Mersyankh III (G7530-7540)*, with W. K. Simpson, 1974; *Zawiyet el-Aryan*, 1978; *Excavations at Kerma IV*, 1981; he died in Boston, 10 Jan. 1984.

Recollections of an Egyptologist; Studies in Ancient Egypt, The Aegean, and the Sudan edited by W. K. Simpson and W. M. Davis (1981), (portr.), i, iv-viii (bibl.) *The Boston Globe* Jan. 11 1984, 36; *ARCE Newsletter* 125 (1984), 55 (anon.). Photograph ©2011 Museum of Fine Arts, Boston.

DUPUIS, Charles François (1742-1809)
French scientific writer and politician; he was born at Trie-Château, 26 Oct. 1742, son of a teacher and Clotilde Chauquet; professor at Lisieux; he studied law and became an advocate; Deputy to the Convention from 1792 and senator from 1802; Member of the Académie des Beaux-Arts, 20 Nov. 1795; being very interested in astronomy and the evolution of the calendar, he ascribed the origin of the Zodiac to Upper Egypt; he also wrote many works

on the origin of cults, etc., and on the Zodiac of Dendera; Légion d'honneur, 1809; he died at La Metairie du Fossé, near Échevannes, 29 Sept. 1809.

EB; Hilmy, i, 200; *DBF* 12, 557-8; *Dictionnaire historique et biographique de la Révolution et de l'Empire*, 1899, I, 714; A. C. E. Franquet de Franqueville, *Le Premier Siècle de l'Institut de France*, 1895, I, 85; inf. M. Borin.

DUPUY, A. (*fl.* 1830-34)
French artist, architect and lithographer; in 1829-30 he accompanied Bonomi (q,v.) and Linant (q.v.) up the Nile as far as Dongola, and to the Gold Mines in 1831; in 1832 with Bonomi he joined Robert Hay (q.v.) at Qurna and spent a year making coloured copies of tomb-scenes and a supposedly complete collection of coloured hieroglyphs; from December 1833 to the spring of 1834 he did similar work for Hay at Beni Hasan, his coloured copies are of more importance for an understanding of Hay's working methods than for any intrinsic reliability of their own, as Hay and Bonomi themselves acknowledged; by 1840 he had resumed work as an architect in Paris; he illustrated Begin's *Histoire de la Cathédrale de Metz* in 1842-3, and Merignac's *Histoire de l'Escrime* as late as 1883; he published some recollections of his own, *Voyages en Abyssinie et en Nubie* (8th edition, Tours 1865) under the pseudonym 'H. Lebrun'.

Hay Diary and correspondence; Add MSS 29813, 29823 et sim; S. Tillett, *Egypt Itself*, 1984, 57-65.

DUQUESNE (*né* **DEAKIN), Terence James** (1942-2014)
British Egyptologist and poet; he was born in Cambridge, 26 Dec. 1942; he studied at Dulwich and Oxford University but did not complete his degree; he later worked as a pharmacologist; he had a great interest in Egyptian religion especially the worship of Anubis; he founded Darengo Publications which produced his own works; he published *Anubis and the Spirits of the West*, 1990; *A Coptic Initiatory Invocation*, 1991; *Jackal at Shaman's Gate*, 1991; *At the Court of Osiris. Book of the Dead Spell 194 – A Rare Egyptian Judgement Text*, 1994; *Black and Gold God*, 1996; *The Jackal Divinities of Egypt* I. *From the Archaic Period to Dynasty X*, 2005; with others, *Anubis, Upwawet, and Other Deities. Personal Worship and Official Religion in Ancient Egypt*; *The Salakhana Trove: Votive Stelae and Other Objects from Asyut*, 2009; his papers are in the Griffith Institute, Oxford; he died in Croydon, 17 April 2014.

Internet obits (A. Baron and D. Jacobs).

DURAND, Édme Antoine (1768-1835)
French collector; he was born at Auxerre, 8 July 1768; son of a rich merchant, he went into business but retired in 1800 and built up a large art collection including Egyptian antiquities; he was in Italy 1824-6 when he acquired the Egyptian collection of the Bishop of Nola; in 1825 he sold a large part of his collection to the Louvre notably papyrus 3088; he died in Florence, 28 March 1835; the remainder of his antiquities were sold 25 April-27 May 1836, some of which went to the Musée National de Céramique at Sevres.

Champollion, i, 134, 245, 248, 249, 280, 295, 357; *DBF* 12, 652; Lugt 14322; J. Bulté, *Catalogue des collections égyptiennes du Musée National de Céramique à Sevres*, 1981, 15; I. Jenkins in A.-F. Laurens and K. Pomian, *L'Anticomanie*, 1988, 269-78; È. Gran-Aymerich, *Dictionnaire biographique d'archéologie 1798-1945*, 2001, incorporated in *Les Chercheurs de passé 1798-1945*, 2007, 767.

DURAND, (Emmanuel) Paul Hilaire (1806-1882)
French traveller and architect; he was born Paris, 1806, son of Camille Hilaire D. and Jeanne Rosalie Therresse; he made several voyages to Egypt in 1840's, notably with Ampère (q.v.) 1844-5 and in 1864-6; he made many drawings and copies of monuments most of which he gave to de Rougé (q.v.); some of his antiquities are now in the Louvre; his squeezes were sold in Paris 29 Nov. 1992; died in Paris, 27 Dec. 1882.

DBF 12, 678-9; M. Dewachter, *BiOr.* 37 (1980), 304; D. Berg, *JEA* 73 (1987), 213-6; inf. M. Azim.

DUSSAUD, (Elie Pierre) René (1868-1958)
French orientalist and archaeologist; born Neuilly-sur-Seine, 24 Dec. 1868, son of Joseph Louis D. and Angèle Bartle Venem; he was appointed Chief Conservateur of Oriental Antiquities in the Louvre, 1928; throughout a long career he had an especial interest in Syria and Palestine and was connected with the excavation of many sites in this area, Byblos, Ras Shamra, and Mari, the first two having many contacts with Egypt during the third and second millennia BC; he died in Neuilly, 17 March 1958.

AfO 18 (1957-8), 482-3 (portr.) (W. Baumgartner); *Journal des Savants*, Paris (1958), 37-8 (A. Merlin); *Rev. d'assyriologie* 52 (1958), 93-4 (E. Dhorme); *DBF* 12, 866-7.

DUTEIL, Camille (1808-1861)
French Egyptologist; he was born at Libourne, 8 Sept. 1808, son of Jean D. and Geneviève Cheveau; he was assistant in charge of Egyptian antiquities in the Louvre under Longpérier (q.v.); he wrote studies on the Dendera Zodiac and on ancient weights and measures; he also began to publish a *Dictionnaire des Hiéroglyphes* of which only one part appeared (1839); he was an opponent of Champollion (q.v.); he was appointed Keeper of Egyptian Antiquities in 1848 by the Revolutionary Government, but this was terminated in a few weeks; involved in an uprising in 1851, he fled to South America; he died in Buenos Aires, 19 Nov. 1861.

Bibl. Eg. 21, xviii-xix; Hartleben, ii, 556; Hilmy, i, 201; *DBF* 12, 882-3; *Nouvelle Revue de Paris*, 1, 19 ff.

DYROFF, Karl (1862-1938)
German Egyptologist; he was born at Aschaffenburg 25 Feb. 1862, son of Andreas D., merchant, and Margarethe Flach; he was educated at Munich and Berlin under Erman (q.v.); he obtained a post at the Munich Egyptian collection where he served for thirty years and also taught at Munich University, becoming Honorary Professor in Egyptian and Arabic; he published *Münchener Grab-und Denksteine*, 1904 with B. Poertner and the section on Egypt in H. F. von Helmolt *Weltgeschichte*, 1914; he died in Munich, 12 Nov. 1938.

ZÄS 77 (1941), 1-2 (A. Scharff); *Wer Ist's* 1922..

DZIAŁYŃSKA, (*Countess*) **Izabela (Elisabeth)** (1830-1899)
Polish art collector and social activist; she was born in Warsaw, 14 Dec. 1830, daughter of Prince Adam George Czartoryski and Princess Anna Sapieha and the sister of Prince Wladyslaw Czartoryski (q.v.); she spent her childhood and her early years in Paris where she obtained a splendid education, especially in the history of art; she herself was a talented painter and sculptor and travelled extensively abroad; in 1857 she married Count John Dzialynski and moved with him to Poznan and Goluchów; after the death of her parents she inherited together with her brother, the famous family house in Paris, Hôtel Lambert, where for some time she managed the Institute for daughters of Polish emigrants; in 1873 she took over from her husband Goluchów Castle while he resided in a palace in Kórnik near by; with great expenditure she reconstructed the castle 1875-82, establishing a park and finally transferred from Paris her part of family's collection and library; she founded in Goluchów one of the richest private museums, competing here with her own brother Wladyslaw Czartoryski (q.v.); her antiquities collection was well described by W. Froehner, *Collections du Château de Goluchów. L'orfèvrerie, Egypte*, 1-9, pls. I, II, IV, (Paris 1897) and *Collections du Château de Goluchów. Antiquités Egypte,* 1-69 (Paris 1899); the antiquities from her collection including the famous Greek vases are now in the National Museum in Warsaw; she died suddenly in Menton, 18 March 1899.

Polski Słownik Biograficzny 6, 75-77; Z. Karczewska-Markiewicz, *Panna Lodowata*, Poznan 1973; inf. J. Śliwa.

EADY, Dorothy Louise (1904-1981)
British eccentric; she was born in Blackheath, East Greenwich, London 16 Jan. 1904, daughter of Reuben Ernest E., a master tailor, and Caroline Mary Frost; following a serious accident at the age of three, she began to believe that she was the reincarnation of an Egyptian temple attendant from Abydos; she visited the British Museum frequently and claimed to have been taught hieroglyphs by Budge (q.v.); while working on a magazine in favour of Egyptian independence she met Iman Abdul Meguid and in 1933 journeyed to Egypt to marry, adopting the name Bulbul Abdul Meguid; after the birth of her son Sety she was more commonly known as Omm Sety; the marriage ended in divorce in 1936 and she became the personal assistant of Selim Hassan (q.v.) aiding him in his publications; in 1951 she joined the staff of Ahmed Fakhry (q.v.) at Dahshur; in 1956 at her insistence she was transferred by the Antiquities Service to Abydos; she retired from the Service in 1969 but continued to reside in Abydos where she was a familiar figure to tourists; apart from her contributions to the publications of Hassan and Fakhry, she also produced *Omm Sety's Abydos,* 1982 and *Abydos: Holy City of Ancient Egypt*, 1981 with H. el-Zeini; she died in Abydos, 21 April 1981.

Omm Sety's Abydos, 1-4; *Abydos*: Holy City, iii-vii; *The Times* 29 April 1981; *N.Y. Times* 17 April 1979; *Observer Magazine* 2 Dec. 1973; *NARCE* 116, 4-5 (L. Habachi); J. Cott, *The Search for Omm Sety,* 1987; G. Lenox-Smith, *Ancient Egypt* 16 (2016), 16-21.

EAGLE, William (1787-1854)
British barrister and collector of Lakenheath Hall, Suffolk; he was born in 1787 and baptized at Wangford, Suffolk 16 Aug. 1787, son of Robert E. of Wangford, Suffolk and Elizabeth King; he was educated at Charterhouse, afterwards Trinity College, Cambridge; BA, 1809; MA, 1812; called to the Bar, Middle Temple, 1817; Equity Draughtsman; he was a collector of antiquities and his Egyptian, Babylonian, and Etruscan gems were sold in London, 9 May 1859; he died at Mildenhall, 23 July 1854.

Al. Cantab. ii; inf. Vicar of Lakenheath, 1949; Lugt 24888.

EBBELL, Bendix (1865-1941)
Norwegian doctor; he was born in Oslo, 12 April 1865, son of Johan Peter E. and Petronelle Marie Hansen; he obtained a degree in theology from the University of Christiania (Oslo) in 1888 and a degree in medicine in 1892; he worked as a medical missionary in Madagascar from 1893-1903, 1905-12; his interest in ancient languages was encouraged by Lieblein (q.v.) under whom he studied 1903-5 while on leave in Norway; he practised as a medical doctor in Norway 1912-35; he was elected a member of the Norwegian Academy in 1937; he wrote several articles on medicine in ancient Egypt and on his retirement produced several major volumes, *The Papyrus Ebers*, 1937; *Alt-ägyptische Chirurgie,* 1939; *Beiträge zur Ältesten Geschichte einiger Infektionskrankheiten*, 1967; he died 9 June 1941.

Norske Videnskaps-Akademie Sitzung der Hist.-Filos. Klasse (1941), 61-73; (portr.) (W. Schenke); *Beiträge*, op. cit., 111-2 (L. Amundsen).

EBERS, Georg Moritz (1837-1898)
German Egyptologist and novelist; he was born in Berlin, 1 March 1837, son of Meier Moses Ephraim E., 1802-37, known as Moritz George from 1828, banker, and Franziska Martha Levysohn, (Fanny from 1828); he married Antonie daughter of Robert Beck, 1830-1913, at Riga, 1865; he studied law at the University of Göttingen, and, after an illness, he became interested in Egyptology through W. Grimm, and afterwards studied at Berlin under Lepsius (q.v.), 1859-62; PhD at Jena, 1862, Habil, 1865; he was made Professor at Jena, 1869, and Professor of Egyptology at Leipzig 1870, Ordinarius Professor 1875; Ebers was a successful teacher and numbered Erman (q.v.) among his students; he visited Egypt many times and is remembered for his huge descriptive work on Egypt, *Aegypten in Wort und Bild*, 2 vols. 1879-80, of small fol. size, which enjoyed great popularity in its day and was translated into French and English; it contained many pictures of historical interest today, but in some cases extremely ugly and much inferior to the more delicate illustrations of the earlier travel books on Egypt; Ebers also wrote many historical novels, his *Ägyptische Königstochter*, 1864, trans. as *An Egyptian Princess,* was very successful and had by 1928 reached 400,000 copies in 16 languages, doing much to arouse public interest in Egypt; in all he published over 200 books, articles, reviews, and novels between 1857 and 1899 among his serious works being, *Aegypten und die Bücher Mose's: sachlicher Commentar zu den aegyptischen Stellen in Genesis und Exodus*, 1868; he acquired from Edwin Smith at Luxor the famous medical papyrus which bears his name, of which he

published a facsimile with an introduction and a glossary by Ludwig Stern, *Papyros Ebers: das hermetische Buch über die Arzneimittel der Alten Ägypter in hieratischer Schrift ...*, 2 pts. fol. 1875; *Durch Gosen aus Sinai: aus dem Wanderbuche und der Bibliothek*, 1881; *Papyrus Ebers: Die Masse und das Kapitel über die Augenkrankheiten; von G.E.*, 1889; he was the main contributor to the first ed. of Baedeker's *Egypt*, which appeared at that time in 2 vols. on Upper and Lower Eg. from 1877, with over 900 pages and many maps and plans; his works were collected in 25 vols., *Gesammelte Werke*, Stuttgart, 1893-5, and a *Festschrift* in his honour was published in 1897 with contributions by seventeen Egyptologists; he retired 1889, and his library was purchased by Bissing (q.v.) in 1898 and presented to the German Archaeological Institute in Cairo; it was confiscated during World War II and the main part was acquired by the Centre of Documentation in Cairo; he died in Tutzing, Bavaria, 7 Aug. 1898.

Aeg. Studien,1900, has complete bibl. 511-17 (portr.); autobiogr. *Die Geschichte meines Lebens,* 1893; G. Gosche, *Georg Ebers*, 1887; *Academy* 51. 284; L. v. Kobell, 'Gespräche mit Georg Ebers. Zum 60. Geburtstag des Dichters und Gelehrten', *Deutsche Revue über das gesamte nationale Leben der Gegenwart* 22 (1897), 334-344; *Deutsche Rundschau*, 97 (1898), 132-7 (W. Boelsche); *ZÄS* 36 (1898), 140-2 (A. Erman); *Westermanns Illustrierte Deutsche Monatshefte. Ein Familienbuch für das gesamte geistige Leben der Gegenwart* 85 (Oct. 1898/ March 1899), 520-530 (E. Petzet); *Biographisches Jahrbuch und Deutscher Nekrolog* (1900), 86-99 E. Meyer); Hilmy, i. 205; *NDB* 4, 249-50; G. Poethke, 'Georg Ebers und Jena', *ZÄS* 107 (1980), 71-76; E. Blumenthal, *Altes Ägypten in Leipzig* (1981), 8-14; E. Endesfelder, *Die Ägyptologie an der Berliner Universität-Zur Geschichte eines Fachgebietes*, 1988, 14; H. Fischer, *Der Ägyptologe Georg Ebers*, 1994; È. Gran-Aymerich, *Dictionnaire biographique d'archéologie 1798-1945*, 2001, incorporated in *Les Chercheurs de passé 1798-1945*, 2007, 773; inf. I. Lehnert and T. Gertzen.

EDE, Charles Richard Montagu (1921-2002)
British publisher and dealer in antiquities; he was born in Sevenoaks, 22 Oct., 1921, son of Bertram E., colonel in Military Intelligence, and Alice Warde; he was educated at Imperial College Haileybury; he served in the Royal Tank Regiment in France and the Middle East during the Second World War; after demobilisation he studied at the London College of Printing; in 1947 he set up the Folio Society, offering 'poor man's fine editions' of literary classics to subscribers; Folio Fine Art, founded 1959, sold artworks and small antiquities by mail order; after selling the Folio Society in 1971 he established Charles Ede Ltd., which offered antiquities by catalogue; he wrote *Collecting Antiquities: an Introductory Guide*, 1976 (revised editions 1983, 1989); he published numerous catalogues devoted to Egyptian sculpture and inscribed objects; he retired as managing director in 1986, succeeded in the business by his son James; he died in Basingstoke, Hampshire, 29 May 2002.

Guardian June 6 2002; *Telegraph* June 6 2002; *Independent* June 7 2002 (N. Barker), inf. J. Ede and T. Hardwick.

EDEL, Elmar Armin (1914-1997)
German Egyptologist; he was born at Ludwigshafen 12 March 1914, son of Eduard E., a railway engineer; he studied Egyptology, Hittitology, and Assyriology at the Universities of Heidelberg under Ranke (q.v.), 1933 and Berlin under Sethe (q.v.) and Grapow (q.v.) from 1934 and became an assistant at the Wörterbuch project; PhD, 1941; after war service, he returned to Heidelberg where he produced his habilitation under Ranke (q.v.), 1947; he succeeded Bonnet (q.v.) as associate Professor at Bonn, May 1955; full Professor, Sept 1963-82; his particular interests were epigraphy in the Old and Middle Kingdom and Hittite-Egyptian relations; he took part in excavations of the private tombs at Aswan and undertook epigraphic work during the Nubian Rescue campaign; he was a corresponding member of the Akademie der Wissenschaften zu Göttingen, 1960, the Institut d'Égypte, 1977, and Österreichischen Akademie der Wissenschaften, 1979, and member of the Rhenisch-Westfälischen Akademie, 1970, and the Academia Mediterranea delle Scienze, Catania, 1982; Festschrift Elmar Edel edited by M. Görg and E. Pusch was published in his honour in 1979; apart from numerous articles, his principal Egyptological publications were his habilitation Altägyptische Grammar. 2 vols, 1955-67; with J. Černy, Gebel el-Shams, 1963; with Cerny, Abou-Odda, 1963; Die Ortsnamenlisten aus dem Totentempel Amenophis III, 1966; Die Felsengräber der Qubbet el Hawa bei Assuan. 5 vols, 1967-80; Das Akazienhaus und seine Rolle in der Bergräbnisriten, 1970; Beiträge zu den Inschriften des Mittleren Reiches in den Gräbern der Qubbet el Hawa, 1971; with C. Desroches-Noblecourt and S. Donadoni, Grand Temple d'Abou Simbel. La Bataille de Qadech, 1971; with S. Wenig, Die Jahreszeiten-reliefs aus dem Sonnenheiligtum des Königs Ne-usere, 1974; Ägyptische Artze und ägyptische Medezin am hethitischen Königshof, 1976; Hieroglyphische Inschriften des Alten Reiches, 1981; Beiträge zu den ägyptischen Sinaiinschriften, 1983; Die Inschriften der Grabfronten der Siut-Gräber in Mittelägypten aus der Herakleopolitenzeit, 1984; Der Vertrag zwischen Ramses II. von Ägypten und Hattusili III. von Hatti, 1997; and posthumously, with M. Görg, Die Ortsnamenlisten im nördlichen Säulenhof des Totentempels Amenophis' III., 2005; and, ed. by K.J. Seyfried and G. Vieler, Die Felsgräbernekropole der Qubbet el-Hawa bei Assuan, I, 2008; his library and archives were acquired by the Egyptological Archives of the Università degli Studi di Milano in 1999; he died 25 April 1997.

ZÄS 125 (1998), I-II (portr.) (M. Görg); IAE Internet obituary (M. Görg); *Festschrift Elmar Edel*, 1-12 (bibl. to 1979*); Almanach der Österreichischen Akademie der Wissenschaften* 147 (1996/7), 661-9 (portr.) (M. Bietak); P. Piacentini, *Gli archivi egittologici dell'Università degli Studi di Milano. 1. Il Fondo Elmar Edel*, 2006 (portr.), 67-82 (bibl.); P. Piacentini, *Egypt and the Pharaohs from the Sand to the Library*, 2010, 63-4.

EDGAR, Campbell Cowan (1870-1938)
British Egyptologist and Greek scholar; he was born in Tongland manse, 26 Dec. 1870, son of Andrew E., a minister, and Mary Sybil Cowan; educated at Ayr Acad. and at Oriel College, Oxford; Craven Fellow, 1895; he later studied in Munich; he joined the British School in Athens, 1896-1900; he went to Cairo and worked for the Catalogue Commission, 1900; appointed Chief Inspector of Antiquities in the Delta, 1905-20; Ass. Keeper, Cairo Museum, 1920; Keeper 1923 and Secretary-General, 1925; retired 1927; he published, *Greek Sculpture*, Cairo Cat., 1903; *Greek Moulds*, Cairo Cat., 1903; *Greek Bronzes,* Cairo Cat., 1904; *Graeco-Egyptian Coffins, Masks and Portraits,* Cairo Cat., 1905; *Graeco-Egyptian Glass,* Cairo Cat., 1905; *Sculptors' Studies and Unfinished Works,* Cairo Cat., 1906; *Greek Vases,* Cairo Cat., 1911; *Select Papyri,* vol. 2, Official Documents, with A. S. Hunt, 1934; he died in Berkhamsted, Herts, 10 May 1938.

ASAE 39 (1939), 3-10 (O. Guéraud); *JEA* 24 (1938), 133-4 (H. I. Bell); M. Capasso (ed.), *Hermae*, 2007, 181-6 (N. Pellé).

EDGERTON, William Franklin (1893-1970)
American Egyptologist; he was born at Binghampton, New York, 30 Sept. 1893, son of Charles Eugene E. and Annie Benedict White; he was educated at Cornell University; BA, 1915; and the University of Chicago; PhD,1922 under Breasted (q.v.); he also studied at the University of Pennsylvania, 1919, Columbia University, 1923-4, and the University of Munich, 1927; he was a fellow of the Dept. of Oriental Languages and Literatures, University of Chicago, 1915-18 and 1920-22 and took part in the first field expedition of the Oriental Institute, 1919-20; Assistant in the Oriental Institute, 1922-3; Assistant Professor of Ancient History, Louisville, Kentucky, 1924-5; Associate Professor of History, Vassar College, 1925-6; epigrapher at Luxor with the Oriental Institute, 1926-9; Associate Professor of Egyptology, Chicago, 1929-37, Professor, 1937-59; Visiting Professor at the University of California, 1965-7; Chairman of the Dept. of Oriental Languages and Literatures, Chicago, 1948-54; President of the American Oriental Society; his main interest lay in the study of the Egyptian language; his principal publications include *Medinet Habu* I, 1930 with H. H. Nelson and J. A. Wilson; *Notes on Egyptian marriage, chiefly in the Ptolemaic Period,* 1931; *The Thutmosid Succession,* 1933; *Historical Records of Ramses III*, 1936 with J. A. Wilson; *Medinet Habu* IV: *Graffiti Facsimiles*, 1937; his intention to produce a Demotic dictionary remained unfulfilled; he died in Bridgeview, Illinois, 20 March 1970.

The International Who's Who 1970-71, 449; *The Oriental Institute Report for 1969-70,* 5-6; *WWWA* V, 208.

EDMONSTONE, (*Sir*) **Archibald** (1795-1871)
British traveller and author; he was born at 32 Great Russell Street, London, 12 March 1795, eldest son of Sir Charles E. Bart. of Duntreath, Stirlingshire, and Emma Bootle; he was educated at Eton, 1808, and Christ Church, Oxford, 1812; BA, 1816; in 1819 he went to Egypt and explored two oases Kharga and Dakhla, publishing a detailed account of them with views, plans, etc., of temples and tombs, *A Journey to Two of the Oases of Upper Egypt,* 1822; he married his cousin Emma Wilbraham; he brought back some antiquities from Egypt including a mummy which he gave to A. B. Granville (q.v.), who published a very full account of it in *Phil. Trans.*, 1825, ii. 269; he died in Wilton Place, London, 13 March 1871.

ODNB 17, 752; *DNB* 6, 398-9; Hilmy, i, 213; A. J. Mills in J. Thompson (ed.), *Cairo Papers* 23/3 (2000), 43-9.

EDWARDS, Amelia Ann Blandford (1831-1892)
British author, Egyptologist, and founder of the Egypt Exploration Fund (later Society) and the Department of Egyptology at University College London; she was born in London, 7 June 1831, daughter of Thomas E., an army officer who had served under Wellington in the Peninsular War and later a bank employee, and Alicia Walpole; as a child she showed a precocious talent for writing and drawing, and a poem which she wrote at the age of 7 was published in a weekly journal; already ancient Egypt fascinated her, 'as a child' she later said '*Wilkinson's Manners and Customs of the Ancient Egyptians* shared my affections with the Arabian Nights'; possessing an excellent voice she might have become an opera singer, but decided to take up journalism as a profession and to write novels also; she contributed to *Chambers' Journal, Household Words, Sat. Review, Morning Post,* and *Academy*, and published 8 novels between 1855 and 1880; in addition she edited popular books on history and art; she visited Syria and Egypt, 1873-4, and thereafter Egyptology became her chief interest and she took lessons in hieroglyphs; she published her best-known book *A Thousand Miles up the Nile,* 1877, 2nd ed. 1889, 2nd rev. ed. 1891; she considered

scientific exploration and accurate recording of standing monuments the only remedy for the widespread destruction and appalling mutilation to sites and buildings that was prevalent at that time; with the help of Reginald Stuart Poole (q.v.) and Sir Erasmus Wilson (q.v.) she founded the Egypt Exploration Fund to carry out this work, 1882; she acted as Secretary and gave up all her other work, also doing much to publicize the work of its excavators Naville (q.v.) and Petrie (q.v.); in this capacity she wrote an immense number of popular articles, contributing over 100 to the *Academy* in 15 years alone, and many more for the *Bull. Amer. Geogr. Soc., Harper's Monthly,* and the EEF *Arch. Reports*; she was the first person to identify the Cypriote, Phoenician, and other signs on the potsherds found by Petrie in the Fayum from the letters that he wrote home to his mother; these letters formed an unofficial journal of the excavations and were passed to her so that she could write notices of his work for *The Times*; they are now at the Griffith Institute, Oxford; she visited USA, 1889-90, lecturing on Egypt and stimulating interest in the American section of the EEF; her lectures were published as *Pharaohs, Fellahs and Explorers*, 1891; she helped Sir E. Wilson (q.v.) with *The Egypt of the Past*; for her many services she was made LLD of Columbia University, 1887, LHD of Smith College and PhD of the College of the Sisters of Bethany, Topeka; she had decided to found the first chair in Egyptian Archaeology and Philology in England at University College London, and on her death by her will she left it her library and valuable collections of Egyptian antiquities together with £5,000, privately expressing a wish that Flinders Petrie should be appointed; he held the post for 40 years, retiring in 1933; never well off she achieved an immense amount with small resources, and at the end of her life a Civil List pension was conferred on her; although not an Egyptologist by training and having no academic advantages, her accomplishments in Egyptology were significant, the results of her two foundations being incalculable; she died in a nursing home in Royal Terrace (now Royal Grosvenor Hotel), Weston-super-Mare, 15 April 1892 and was buried in Henbury, Bristol; a marble bust of her, made in 1873, is in the collection of the National Portrait Gallery, London, and a copy together with portraits at University College London; a further portrait is kept at the Egypt Exploration Society.

ODNB 17, 907-9; *DNB* Suppl. ii, 176; Wm. Copley Winslow, *The Queen of Egyptology, Amelia B. Edwards,* [Chicago, 1892]; *Arena* (Boston), iv, no. 3, 299-310; Hilmy, i. 213; Warren R. Dawson, 'Letters from Maspero to Amelia Edwards', *JEA* 33 (1947), 66-89 (portr.); *New England Mag.* (Boston) N.S. 7, no. 5, 547-64; Newberry Corr; R. Janssen, *The First Hundred Years*, 1992, 1-3; J. Rees, *Amelia Edwards. Traveller, Novelist & Egyptologist,* 1998; J. Rees in P. Starkey and N. El Kholy (eds.), *Egypt through the Eyes of Travellers*, 2002, 39-44; J. Rees in *KMT* 13/4 (2003/3), 80-84; È. Gran-Aymerich, *Dictionnaire biographique d'archéologie 1798-1945*, 2001, incorporated in *Les Chercheurs de passé 1798-1945*, 2007, 773-4; P. O'Neill in P. and J. Starkey, *Interpreting the Orient*, 2001, 165-174; B. Moon in *ibid.*, 175-85; J. Speake (ed.), *Literature of Travel and Exploration*, 2003, 1, 378-9; M. Price in *Women Travellers in the Near East*, 2005, 45-6; B. Moon, *More Usefully Employed*, 2006; A. Dodson, *ASTENE Bulletin* 67 (2016), 20; A. Dodson, *KMT* 27 (2017), 20-1; 70-3 (D. Forbes).

EDWARDS, (Iorwerth) Eiddon Stephen (1909-1996)
British Egyptologist; he was born in London, 21 July 1909, son of Edward E., a Persian scholar in the Department of Oriental Manuscripts and Printed Books, British Museum, and Ellen Jane Higgs; he was educated at Merchant Taylors' school and Gonville and Caius College, Cambridge from 1928 when he studied oriental languages notably Hebrew and Arabic; BA, 1931; MA, 1935; he did postgraduate study in Semitic grammar and Arabic, 1931-3; he then joined the Inner Temple, 1933; he became Assistant Keeper in the Department of Egyptian and Assyrian Antiquities, British Museum, 6 Feb. 1934; he then studied ancient Egyptian under Glanville (q.v.) at University College London and taught there in 1936; he was seconded to the Foreign Office during World War II and served at the British embassies in Cairo and Baghdad and the Secretariat in Jerusalem, 1942-5; Deputy Keeper, 1950; he became Keeper of the new Department of Egyptian Antiquities, 1955-74; visiting professor at Brown University, 1953-4; he was the Egyptological organizer of the exhibition '5000 Years of Egyptian Art' at the Royal Academy, 1962; he organized the successful Tutankhamun exhibition at the British Museum, 1972; honorary treasurer of the Egypt Exploration Society, 1949-62; Vice-President, 1962-88; Chairman of the IAE Committee for the *Annual Egyptological Bibliography*; Glanville Memorial Lecturer, 1980; member of the UNESCO-Egyptian committee for saving the monuments of Philae, 1973-80 and on other UNESCO committees dealing with the Cairo Museum and the Giza plateau, 1981, 1985, 1990; FSA, 1942; FBA, 1962; LittD, 1963; he was awarded the CBE, 1968 and the CMG, 1973; he was a member of the German and Austrian Institutes and the Committee of Visitors of the Metropolitan Museum, New York; he published, with S. Smith, *Ancient Egyptian Sculpture lent by C. S. Gulbenkian, Esq.*, 1937; with A. Shorter, *A Handbook to the Egyptian Mummies and Coffins exhibited in the British Museum*, 1938; *Hieroglyphic Texts in the British Museum* 8,1939; *The Pyramids of Egypt*, 1947; revised, 1961, 1985, 1991, and 1993, which became the standard account of this subject for many years; *Hieratic Papyri in the British Museum, 4th series. Oracular Amuletic Decrees of the Late New Kingdom,*

1960; with A. F. Shore and R. Pinder-Wilson, *5000 Years of Egyptian Art*, 1962; with T. G. H. James and A. F. Shore, *A General Introductory Guide to the Egyptian Collections in the British Museum*, 1964; *Treasures of Tutankhamun*, 1972 for the British exhibition; *Treasures of Tutankhamun*, 1976 for the American exhibition; *Tutankhamun's Jewellery*, 1976; *Tutankhamun: his tomb and its treasures*, 1976; he was joint editor of vols I-III of the third edition of the *Cambridge Ancient History* and wrote the chapter on *The Early Dynastic Period in Egypt*, 1964; a volume of 36 papers in his honour entitled *Pyramid Studies and Other Essays* was published in 1988; his memoirs *From the Pyramids to Tutankhamun* were published posthumously in 2000; he died in London, 24 Sept. 1996.

ODNB 17, 921-2; *JEA* 84 (1998), 181-90 (portr.) (add. bibl.) (H. S. Smith); *BSFE* 137 (1996), 5 (J. Vercoutter); *PBA* 97 (1997), 273-90 (portr.) (T. G. H. James); *Who's Who*, 1995, 576; IAE Internet obituary (J. Malek); *AEB* 1994, vii (J. Malek); *Almanch der Österreichischen Akademie der Wissenschaften* 147 (1996/7), 661-9 (portr.) (M. Bietak); *Pyramid Studies*, 1-4 (bibl.) (A. Leahy); R. M. Janssen, *The First Hundred Years*, 1992, 34, 38; I. E. S. Edwards, *From the Pyramids to Tutankhamun*, 2000.

EGGEBRECHT, Arne (1935-2004)

German Egyptologist; he was born in Munich 12 March 1935, son of Dr Jürgen E. and Elfriede Stier; he studied Egyptology at Göttingen and Munich; PhD, 1955; he later worked in the Egyptian collection in Munich; he was appointed Keeper at the Roemer-Pelizaeus Museum in Hildesheim, 1974; Director, 1984-2000; during his tenure, he organized several major exhibitions notably Echnaton-Nofretete-Tutanchamun, 1976, Götter und Pharaonen, 1979, Nofret-die Schöne, 1985, and Ägyptens Aufstieg zur Weltmacht, 1987; with Gundlach (q.v.), he founded the International Committee of Egyptology, 1977, and was a leading force in the production of the Corpus Antiquitatum Aegyptiacarum; he excavated at Thebes with the German mission and supported excavations near Qantir from 1980; he was a long-term chairman of CIPEG, the Egyptological committee of ICOM; he was named Hon. Professor of Museology at Hildesheim University; he published *Schlachtungsbräuche im alten Ägypten und ihre Wiedergabe im Flachbilk zum Ende des Mittleren Reiches*, 1973; *Das Land am Nil*, 1979; *Corpus Antiquitatum Aegyptiacorum*, 1981; *Ägypten-faszination und abenteur*, 1982; *Pelizaeus-Museum Hildesheim, Das Alte Reich*, 1986, Fr trans. *L'Égypte ancienne*, 1986; *Ägyptens Aufstieg zur Weltmacht*, 1987; *Suche nach Unsterblichkeit*, 1990; *Antike Welt im Pelizaeus-Museum Hildesheim Die Ägyptische Sammlung*, 1993; he died 8 Feb. 2004.

Süddeutsche Zeitung 11 Feb. 2004 (W. Seipel); *Amun* 21 (2004), 35 (D. Wildung); *Die Antiken Sudan* 15 (2004), 194-5 (portr.) (S. Wenig); *ZÄS* 132 (2005) XI (portr.) (D. Wildung); *WW in Germany* 1996, I, 345.

EID, Albert (1886-1950)

Egyptian antiquities dealer and collector; he was born in Cairo in 1886, son of George Alphonse E., Belgian consul and Zoe Kher; his shop was located in the Khan Khalili area; among the objects which passed through his hands was the Jung Codex of the Nag Hammadi Codices; his collection was later nationalized by the Egyptian authorities and placed in the Cairo Museum; he died in Cairo, 29 Nov. 1950.

Inf. G. A. Eid; A. Wright, *Twentieth Century Impressions of Egypt*, 115-6; J. M. Robinson, *The Facsimile Edition of the Nag Hammadi Codices. Introduction* (Leiden, 1984), 7-8; F. Hagen and K. Ryholt, *The Antiquities Trade in Egypt 1880-1930*, 2017, 212-3.

EISENLOHR, August Adolf (1832-1902)

German Egyptologist; he was born at Mannheim, 6 Oct. 1832, son of Wilhelm E. 1786-1848, a doctor of medicine, and Auguste Catoir; he married, 1. Pauline André, 1840-60, in 1859, 2. Sofie Schreiber, 1847-1935, in 1880; he studied theology at the Universities of Heidelberg and Göttingen, 1850-3, then changed to natural science and chemistry, taking his doctorate in the latter, 1860; he founded a factory in Heidelberg, and then became interested in Chinese and Egyptian, being taught the latter by Chabas (q.v.) and Brugsch (q.v.); he joined the staff of Heidelberg Univ. in 1869, became Professor of Egyptology, 1872-85; retired and made Hon. Professor, 1885; Eisenlohr visited Egypt several times, and also London in 1872, when he studied the Great Harris Papyrus and published a translation of it in collaboration with Samuel Birch (q.v.); while in London he was given a copy of Birch's facsimile of the Rhind Mathematical Papyrus and published *Ein mathematisches Handbuch der Alten Aegypten: Papyrus Rhind des British Museum, übersetzt und erklärt von August E.*, 2 pts. 1877; and also *Corpus papyrorum aegypti*, with E. Revillout, 3 vols. 1885-92; he contributed articles to *ZÄS, PSBA*, and other journals; he died in Heidelberg, 24 Feb. 1902.

NDB 4, 417; *Sphinx* 6, 39-40 (portr.); Hilmy, i, 220; *JEA* 35 (1949), 164; *PSBA* 21 (1899), 49-50.

el-ACHIRIE *see* **ACHIRIE**

el-AMIR *see* **AMIR**

el-BATRAWI see BATRAWI

ELGOOD, (*Lt.-Col.*) **Perceival George** (1863-1941)
British army officer and administrator; he was born in London, 30 July 1863, son of George James E. auctioneer, and Susan Minshall Jones; he was educated at Marlborough and in 1883 entered the army in the Devonshire Regiment; Major, 1903; retired 1903; Lt.-Col., 1916; he held several posts in the Egyptian Government notably Financial Secretary, Egyptian army and Controller-General of Food Supplies; he was the author of several books including *The Ptolemies of Egypt,* 1938 and *The Later Dynasties of Egypt,* 1951; he died in Cairo, 20 Dec. 1941.

WWW 4, 353.

el-KERETI see KHERETI

el-KHOULI *see* **KHOULI**

ELNUR, Osama Abdel Rahman (1942-2007)
Sudanese archaeologist; he was born in Omdurman, 9 Jan. 142, son of Abdel Rahmin Elnur Ibrahim, a judge; he studied Egyptology at Leningrad University under Petrovsky (q.v.); BA, 1968; he then joined the Sudan Antiquities Service, 1969-72 but was dismissed for his leftist leanings; he then returned to Russia where he studied at Moscow University; PhD, 1975; he was appointed lecturer in the Department of History, College of Higher Education, University of Aden, 1976-9; assistant professor, 1979-81; he then became associate professor in the Department of History and Geography, College of Education, Fatih University, Tripoli, Libya, 1981-3; following a period in Spain when he established a publishing house *Oriental International*, he was employed as Professor of Anthropology, College of Social Sciences, Oran University, 1985-6; he rejoined the Sudan Antiquities Service in 1987 and succeeded Sherif (q.v.) as Commissioner for Archaeology; he organized an excavation service and was active in securing UNESCO support for salvage archaeology at the Fourth Cataract; he was removed from his post in 1991 and then went to Egypt and Libya where he became Professor of Archaeology at Fatih University, 1992-8 and later Professor of Archaeology and Anthropology, Department of Graduate Studies at the same university, 1998-2002; he then held the same post at the University of Sebha, 2002-7; he wrote a number of books and articles in Arabic, Russian, English and French notably, with others, *La prospection archéologique de la vallée du Nil au sud de la cataracte de Dal*, fasc. 2-3, 1975-6; he died in London, 12 May 2007.

Sudan and Nubia 12 (2008), 104-6 (J. Reinhold).

el-SAGHIR *see* **SAGHIR**

el-SAWI *see* **SAWI**

ELWOOD (*née* **Curteis), Anne Katherine** (1796-1873)
British traveller; she was born in 1796, daughter of Edward John Curteis, MP, of Windmill Hill near Battle, Sussex and Mary Barrrett; she married on 9 Jan. 1824 Major Charles Elwood (1782-1860) of the Hon. East India Company; in 1825 she set out with her husband for India via Egypt which they reached in April 1826; in Cairo she met Bonomi (q.v.) and Hay (q.v.); she crossed the Eastern Desert and crossed to Djeddah and thence by ship to Bombay; She published *Narrative of a Journey Overland from England to India*, 1830; she returned to England in 1828 with her husband and devoted herself to literary pursuits, publishing *Memoirs of the Literary Ladies of England from the Commencement of the Last Century*, 1841; she died at Clayton Priory, Sussex, 24 Feb. 1873.

ODNB 18, 374-5; inf. D. Manley

EMBER, Aaron (1878-1926)
American Egyptologist and Semiticist of Russian-Jewish extraction; born in Tulnas, Lithuania, 25 Dec. 1878, son of Mendel E. and Rebekah Quitz; he was taken to America as a small child; his family settled in Baltimore, where he studied Hebrew with Paul Haupt and later became interested in the Semitic side of the Egyptian

language; he went to study under Sethe (q.v.) at Göttingen, 1910, when the latter was working on the Pyramid Texts; he later returned to America and became Professor at the Johns Hopkins University in Baltimore; he died trying to save from his burning house a manuscript of a work on which he had been working for a number of years; Ember wrote four articles in *ZÄS*, his main work being published after his death, *Egypto-Semitic studies,* 1930; he died in Baltimore, 1 June 1926.

Chron. d'Eg. 1 (1925-6), 63; *The Times* 4 June 1926; *ZÄS* 62 (1927), 130-1 (K. Sethe). *WWWA* 1, 370.

EMERY, Walter Bryan (1903-1971)
British Egyptologist; he was born Liverpool, 2 July 1903, son of Walter Thomas E., a principal of a technical college, and Beatrice Mary Benbow; he was educated at St. Francis Xavier's College, Liverpool; while at school his interest in Egyptology was aroused at the age of 13 by reading novels of Rider Haggard and hearing public lectures given by Garstang (q.v.) on his discoveries in Egypt and the Sudan; after leaving college, he was apprenticed for a short time to a firm of marine engineers where he was trained in draughtsmanship and constructional drawing; he studied at the Institute of Archaeology, University of Liverpool under Newberry (q.v.) and Peet (q.v.) 1921-23; MA Liverpool (hon. causa) 1939; FSA, 1941; MBE, 1943; DLitt University of London, 1959; FBA, 1959; CBE, 1969; in 1923 his first article appeared in *AAA* and the same year he was sent out by the EES as assistant to help survey and plan the urban site at Amarna under Newton (q.v.) and Griffith (q.v.), 1923-24; he was chosen by Mond (q.v.) to be Director of the latter's excavations carried out on behalf of the University of Liverpool at Luxor and Armant, 1924-28; on the W. bank at Thebes he cleared and restored about 20 tombs in the Upper Enclosure, including Kenamun, published in *AAA* 1927, 1929; he also prepared facsimile drawings of the reliefs in the tomb of Ramose, 1928-29, later used for Davies's publication; he made a notable discovery of the Bucheum at Armant, an excavation undertaken against the advice of Carter (q.v.), 1925; he married Mary Magdalene (Molly) Emery (*d.*3 Dec 1973), 1928; his next work was for the Egyptian Government Antiquities Service as Director of the Archaeological Survey of Nubia, lasting for six years, 1929-35; assisted by L. P. Kirwan, thousands of graves and houses as well as settlements were excavated, and some work was also undertaken on the Nubian fortresses at Quban; here Emery first acquired the technique for analyzing mud brickwork in buildings; the great mounds of Ballana and Qustul were investigated and excavated, providing very rich finds of the Roman-Byzantine (X-Group) period, 1931-34 now in the Egyptian Museum, Cairo; he was made Director of Excavation at N. Saqqara in succession to Firth (q.v.), 1935-39; this work involved the almost complete excavation of the great First Dynasty cemetery and is certainly the work for which he will probably be remembered more than any other; the clearance of the great tomb of Hemaka in 1935 was followed by numerous others with many unique features, both before and after the war; he served in the British Army during the war, 1939-46, and was with the Eighth army in the Western Desert; mentioned in Dispatches, 1942; he left the army as Director of Military Intelligence with the hon. rank of Lt. Col.; as no Egyptological post was then available he became Attaché British Embassy Cairo, 1947-50, afterwards First Secretary, 1950-51; he was able to resume full time work in Egyptian archaeology on his appointment to the Edwards Professorship, University College London, 1951-70; Field Director EES excavations, 1952-71; he worked at Buhen in N. Sudan for seven seasons, 1957-63 and at Qasr Ibrim 1961, as part of the UNESCO campaign from 1960 onwards; he supervised the dismantling and transport of the temples at Buhen to Khartoum; he also had overall direction of surveying and other work in Nubia; he returned to Saqqara to work in 1964; among his subsequent discoveries was the Iseum or burial place of the 'Mothers of Apis', 1970; much material from his later finds went to the Cairo Museum, British Museum and Petrie collections as well as to other museums throughout the world; he was Norton Lecturer of the Archaeological Institute of America, 1954-55; also gave the first series of de Buck memorial lectures, 1961; Member of the German Arch. Institute, l'Institut d'Egypte etc.; his principal published works were, *The Excavations and Survey between Wadi es-Sebua and Adindan,* 1929-31, with L. P. Kirwan, 2 vols., 1935; *The Royal Tombs of Ballana and Qustul,* with chapters by L. P. Kirwan, 2 vols., 1938; *Excavations at Saqqâra. The Tomb of Hemaka,* with Zaki Yusef Saad, 1938; *Excavations at Saqqâra 1937-38. Hor Aha,* with Zaki Yusef Saad, 1939; *Nubian Treasure: an account of the discoveries at Ballana and Qustul,* 1948; *Excavations at Saqqâra. Great Tombs of the First Dynasty* I, 1949, vol. II, 1954, vol. III, 1958; *Saqqâra and the Dynastic Race* (inaugural lecture),1952; *Archaic Egypt,* 1961; *A Funerary Repast in an Egyptian tomb of the Archaic Period* (A. de Buck memorial lecture), 1962; *Egypt in Nubia,* 1965; and posthumously *The Fortress of Buhen: The Archaeological Report,* with H.S. Smith and A. Millard,1979; he collapsed suddenly on 7 March, had a second stroke and died in the Anglo-American hospital, Cairo, 11 March 1971; he was buried 12 March in the civil section of the British Cemetery, Cairo.

ODNB 8, 395-6; *DNB* 1971-80, 291-2; *Popski's Private Army,* Lt. Col. Vladimir Peniakoff, Reprint Soc., London, 1953, (portr.) 22-24, 28, 29, 30; *AfO* 27 (1973), 250-51 (H. Brunner); *BSFE* 61 (June 1971), 3-4 (anon.); *International WW* 31st ed. (1967-68), 380; *JEA* 57 (1971), 190-201 (portr.) (H. S. Smith); *JEA* 58 (1972), 296-99 (bibl. complete until death (E. P. Uphill); *Life* vol. 46 No. 3 (Feb. 17 1969), 'Ancient Egypt, Pt. VI', 21-8 (portrs.) (E. Kern); *Proc. Brit. Acad.* 58 (1972), (1973), 379-92 (portr.) (A. Klasens) (definitive); *Prism* vol. III (1971), 78-9 (portr.) (anon.); *The Daily Telegraph* March 13, 1971; *The Times* March 13, 1971 (I. E. S. Edwards); the *Sunday Telegraph* March 14, 1971 'A Life for Imhotep' (portr.) (J. Tunstall); *WWW* vii, 247; *Antiquity* 45 No. 178 (1971), 81-2 (editorial anon.); R. Janssen, *The First Hundred Years*, 1992, 70-85.

EMPAIN, *(Baron)* **Édouard Louis Joseph** (1852-1929)
Belgian engineer, financier, industrialist, and creator of the new Heliopolis; he was born at Beloeil, 20 Sept. 1852, son of François Julien E. and Catherine Solivier, and acquired an immense fortune; he helped in the colonial development schemes of Leopold II and in the creation of the Paris Metro; during the First World War he directed, with the rank of General, the armaments production for the Belgian army at Paris and Le Havre; in private life he was a benefactor of the Brussels Museum and of the Fondation Égyptologique Reine Élisabeth; in 1905 he assisted the Belgian government in the acquisition of an Old Kingdom mastaba for the museum in Brussels and in 1907 suggested to Capart (q.v.) that he excavate at Heliopolis, where he was directing great building schemes and where he constructed a truly astonishing residence, the Indian-style Qasr al-Baron; he was also interested in Belgian participation in Nubian excavation after the first heightening of the original Aswan dam, but the project had to be abandoned later; Empain made it possible for Capart to acquire some fine pieces for the museum, see *Une Donation d'antiquités égyptiennes aux Musées royaux de Bruxelles*, 1911; he died in Woluwe, Brussels, 22 July 1929.

Chron. d'Ég. 9 (1930), 29-30 (J. Capart); *Larousse* 4, 489; *Biographie Nationale de Belge* 34, 265-9.

ENDESFELDER (*née* **Thürmer**), **Erika** (1935-2015)
German Egyptologist; she was born in Berlin, 3 July 1935; she studied Egyptology under Hintze (q.v.) at the Humboldt University in Berlin, 1954-62 with a year in Moscow under Katznelson (q.v.) ; BA, 1958; PhD, 1962; Habilitation, 1980; she then joined the diplomatic service of East Germany and was posted to Egypt; she became a research assistant at the Institute for Egyptology and Meroitic Studies at Humboldt University in Berlin, 1972-81; Senior lecturer, 1981; Professor 1984-2001 in succession to Hintze; she took part in the Butana survey, 1957-8 and in the excavtions at Tell Basta; a volume of studies was dedicated to her and others edited by C.-B. Arnst and others, *Begegnungen – Antike Kulturen im Niltal*, 2001; apart from articles, she published, with others, *Ägypten und Kusch*, 1977; *Die Ägyptologie an der Berliner Universität*, 1988; with others, *Studia in honorem Fritz Hintze*, 1990; *Probleme der frühen Gesellschaftsentwicklung im Alten Ägypten*, 1991; *Von Berlin nach Meroe*, 2003; her habiliation *Beobachtungen zur Entstehung des altägyptischen Staates*, 2011 and her thesis *Die Arbeiter der thebanischen Nerkropole im Neuen Reich*, 2018 were posted on the internet; she died in Berlin, 28 Jan. 2015.

Inf. C. Loeben; C.-B. Arnst and others, *Begegnungen – Antike Kulturen im Niltal*, 2001, XIV (portr.), XV-XIX (bibl.) (C. Loeben and M. Roth); L. Mertens, *Das Lexikon der DDR-Historiker*, 2006, 199; inf. I. Hafemann.

ENEMAN, Michael (1676-1714)
Swedish orientalist; born Enköping 12 Jan. 1676, son of Olof E. and Anna Wingia; he was associated with the ecclesiastical staff of King Charles XII of Sweden; Eneman accompanied the Swedish army on the Continent and in Russia; he was sent to Turkey in 1709 and in 1711 he made a journey through the entire Near East; he visited Egypt between Feb. and May 1712, staying mainly in Cairo but also making a three-week tour to the monastery of Sinai; after his premature death Eneman left a voluminous manuscript containing not only a careful survey of contemporary life in Egypt, but also notes on ancient monuments around Cairo; the part describing his tour to Sinai is very detailed and contains several copies of Greek texts in the monastery; the main part of this manuscript was published in 1889; he died in Uppsala, 5 Oct. 1714.

M. Eneman, *Resa i Orienten, 1711-1712*. Utgifven av K. U. Nylander, i-ii, Uppsala, 1889; E. Gren. *Bidrag till Michael Enemans biografi*, in Donum Grapeanum, Uppsala, 1945; B. J. Peterson, 'Swedish Travellers in Egypt during the period 1700-1850',*Opuscula Atheniensia*, vii, Lund, 1967, pp. 5-9; *Svensk Biografiskt Lexikon* 13, 508-12.

ENGELBACH, Reginald (1888-1946)
British Egyptologist and engineer; he was born in Moretonhampstead, Devon, 9 July 1888, son of Frederick George E., surgeon, and Marianne Wrench; he was educated at Tonbridge School and afterwards trained as an engineer at the City and Guilds Institute, 1905-8, but his studies were interrupted by a long illness, and a visit to Egypt during convalescence in 1909-10 turned his attention to Egyptology; he studied Egyptian, Coptic, and Arabic at University College London, and in 1911 went as assistant to Petrie (q.v.), excavating at Heliopolis, Shurafa, Kafr Ammar, Riqqa, and Haraga; in 1914 he joined the Artists Rifles, and served in France and

Gallipoli and was then sent by Allenby to report on the ancient sites in Syria and Palestine; he married Nancy Lambert, 1915; after the war, he returned to help Petrie at Lahun and Gurob, 1919-20, and was appointed Chief Inspector in Upper Egypt for the Antiquities Service, 1920; Assistant Keeper, Cairo Museum, 1924; Chief Keeper, 1931; retired 1941; Hon. Member French Inst. 1935; Chevalier de la Légion d'Honneur, 1937; Hon. Fellow University Coll. London, 1946, but died before confirmed; Technical Adviser to Cairo Museum, 1941-6; Engelbach had an active career in the field and in museum work and arrangement, his greatest achievement being without doubt his great museum Register for Cairo, a vast index of 100,000 nos.; he contributed articles to *ASAE* and other journals regularly; his main publications were, *Riqqeh and Memphis* VI, with chaps. by M. A. Murray, H. Petrie, W. M. F. Petrie, 1915; *The Aswân Obelisk, with some remarks on ancient engineering*, 1922; *The Problem of the Obelisks, from a study of the unfinished Obelisk of Aswan*, 1923; *Harageh*, with B. G. Gunn, 1923; *A Supplement to the Topographical Catalogue of the Private Tombs of Thebes, nos. 253-334. With some notes on the Necropolis from 1913 to 1924*, 1924; *Gurob*, with G. Brunton, 1927; *Ancient Egyptian Masonry*, with Somers Clarke, 1930; *Index of Egyptian and Sudanese Sites from which the Cairo Museum contains Antiquities*, 1931; edited the *Introduction to Egyptian Archaeology. With special reference to the Egyptian Museum*, Cairo. 1946; some of his papers are in the Griffith Institute; others were sold at Bonhams, London, 23 June 2009, lot 110; he died in Cairo, 26 Feb. 1946.

ASAE 48 (1948), 1-7 (portr.) (bibl.) (G. Brunton); *BIÉ* 29 (1946-7), 329-44 (O. Guéraud); *JEA* 32 (1946), 97-9 (S. R. K. Glanville); R. Janssen, *The First Hundred Years*, 1992, 14; K. L. Sheppard in W. Carruthers (ed.), *Histories of Egyptology*, 2015, 121.

ENGLISH, George Bethune (1787-1828)

American artillery officer; he was born in Cambridge, Mass., 7 March 1787, son of Thomas E. and Penelope Bethune; he entered the service of the Egyptian army and accompanied the expedition of Ismail Pasha to Dongola and Sennar, 1820; he published *A Narrative of the Expedition to Dongola and Senaar*, London, 1822, Boston, Mass., 1823; he died in Washington, 20 Sept. 1828.

DAB 6, 165; Hilmy, i, 222; Westcar Diary, 12, 173, 179; D. Finnie, *Pioneers East*, 1967, 143-9; C. Vivian, *Americans in Egypt 1770-1915*, 2012, 73-94; A. Oliver, *American Travellers on the Nile*, 2016, 72-7.

EPSTEIN, (Sir) Jacob (1880-1959)

American-British sculptor and collector; he was born in New York, 10 Nov. 1880, son of Max E. and Mary Solomon; he studied in Paris, 1902-4, and moved to Britain, 1905; he was a prominent modernist sculptor, and acknowledged the influence of 'primitive' and ancient art on his work; he formed an important collection of ethnographic and Egyptian art, exhibited in London in 1960, sold at Christie's 15 Dec. 1961; some Egyptian objects were bequeathed by his wife to the New Art Gallery, Walsall; he was knighted in 1954, and died in London, 19 Aug. 1959.

ODNB 18, 477-81; Arts Council of Great Britain, *The Epstein Collection of Tribal and Exotic Sculpture*, 1960; E. Bassani and M. D. McLeod, *Jacob Epstein, Collector*, 1989, 182-198; inf. T. Hardwick.

ERICHSEN, Wolja (1890-1966)

Danish Egyptologist and Demotist; he was born in Copenhagen, 21 Nov. 1890, the son of a ship's captain Erich Anthop Jørgen Christian E. and Alfriede Eugenie Olsen-Andersen; he studied oriental languages under H. O. Lange (q.v.), took an MA in Coptic, Arabic, and ancient Egyptian, 1923; he next went to Berlin, where he remained 1925-44, to help Erman (q.v.) with his work on the great *Wörterbuch*; because of his excellent handwriting he in fact wrote out all 5 vols. as well as vol. ii of the *Belegstellen*; as writer and assistant author he also helped with the 4th ed. of Erman's *Grammar* (1928), the hieroglyphic transcription of the Edwin Smith Surgical Papyrus (1930), and the 2nd ed. of Erman's *Late Egyptian Grammar* (1933); under Sethe's guidance he began to specialize in Demotic which with Coptic became his main interest; he was Hon. Professor at Mainz, 1948-53; Lecturer in Coptic, 1953, and Professor of Egyptology in the University of Copenhagen, 1963; he was a Member of the Danish Akad.; Corr. Member of the Mainz Akad.; Member of the German Archaeological Institute; Leibniz-medal of Prussian Akad. Berlin, 1939; he published, *Papyrus Harris I,* hierog. transcript, 1933; *Fragmenta memphitischer Theologie in demotischer Schrift, Pap. demot. Berlin 13603*, with S. Schott, 1934; *Historisch-biographische Urkunden des Mittleren Reiches*, with Sethe, 1935; *Demotische Lesestücke*, i and ii, 1937-9, a fundamental work; *Eine ägyptische Schulübung in demotischer Schrift*, 1948; *Auswahl frühdemotischer Texte*,

1950, also fundamental; *Die Satzungen einer ägyptischen Kultgenossenschaft aus der Ptolemäerzeit ...*, 1959; *Demotisches Glossar*, a dictionary and his most important work, 1959; his archives were acquired by the University of Milan in 2006; he died in Frederiksberg, 25 April 1966.

EES *Report* 1965/66, 4-5 (H. S. Smith); *Festschrift zum 70. Geburtstag W. Erichsens: Acta Orientalia* 25. 3-4 (1960), 183 ff.; *JEA* 52 (1966), 1 (H. S. Smith); *ZÄS* 95 (1968), i-v (E. Lüddeckens); *AfO* 22 (1968-9) 1221; *Chron. d'Ég.* 41 (1960), 327-34 (bibl.) (E. Lillesø); P. Piacentini, *Egypt and the Pharaohs from the Sand to the Library*, 2010, 96-7. Photograph courtesy of Università degli Studi di Milano.

ERICKSON, Ernest (1893-1983)

American collector; he was born in Åland, Finland, 10 Oct. 1893; he emigrated to America, 1923, and became president of a wood pulp distributing company; he collected Egyptian, Oriental, Pre-Columbian, and native American art, placing many pieces on loan to the Brooklyn Museum, of which he was a governor, 1965-83; after his death the Ernest Erickson Foundation divided his collections among a number of museums, the Brooklyn Museum receiving most of the Egyptian collections; other Egyptian pieces are in Swedish museums; he died in New York, 29 Aug. 1983.

Inf. Brooklyn Museum and T. Hardwick; *The Collector's Eye: the Ernest Erickson Collections at the Brooklyn Museum*, 1987; *The Ernest Erickson collection in Swedish Museums*, 1989.

ERMAN, Jean Pierre Adolphe (Adolf) (1854-1937)

German Egyptologist; he was born in Berlin, 31 Oct. 1854, of Swiss Protestant descent, the family being orig. called Ermatinger or Ermendinger, his father being Adolf E. 1806-77, Professor of Physics at Berlin, and his mother Marie Bessel 1816-1902; he studied Egyptology at Leipzig under Ebers (q.v.), 1875-5 and in Berlin, 1875-8 where Lepsius (q.v.) helped him become an assistant in the library and museum; PhD, 1878; Habilitation, 1880; he began teaching in the University in 1881, his first pupils being U. Wilcken (q.v.) and G. Steindorff (q.v.); many others followed and achieved fame afterwards, including Crum (q.v.), Jéquier (q.v.), Turaev (q.v.) and Reisner (q.v.); on 13 Jan. 1885 he was made Director of the Egyptian (until 1914), and Assyrian (until 1899) departments in the Berlin Museum and Extraordinary Professor of Egyptology; Ordinary Professor 1892-1923; he promoted the foundation of the German Oriental Society, 1898; he was excluded from the Faculty of Philosophy in 1934 because of his Jewish ancestry; he married in 1884 Käthe (1862-1943), daughter of Charles d'Heureuse, who helped him write his last works when he was nearly blind; Erman's influence on Egyptology was formidable; he completely revolutionized the subject, especially in the approach to grammar and teaching of philology, his studies leading to a completely new conception of Egyptian, which his own numerous works, and those of his pupils and successors have established as the basis of all modern philological study; he was the first to recognize fully the early relationship between Egyptian and ancient Semitic languages, the first to divide the language into three periods - Old, Middle, and Late Egyptian, and the first to establish what can be termed scientific and accurate philology including Coptic; he headed the *Wörterbuch* commission from 1897 which also included supervision of the archaeological work of Borchardt (q.v.); from 1892 the influence of the 'Berlin School' made itself felt all over the world so that all students of Egyptian language today are in a sense his pupils; Erman was enormously fertile of ideas; his bibl. lists 284 nos. with 82 reviews as well, extending over 60 years, 1875-1936; in the field of pure grammar, *Die Pluralbildung des Aegyptischen*, 1878; *De Forma pluralis in lingua aegyptiaca*, his dissertation, 1878; *Die Sprache des Papyrus Westcar*, 1889; *Die Flexion des ägyptischen Verbums*, 1902; *Liste der wichtigsten hieratischen Zeichen*, 1890; *Neuägyptische Grammatik*, 1880, 2nd ed. 1933; *Aegyptische Grammatik*, 1894, and 3 later eds.; both of these fundamental works; *Die Hieroglyphen*, 1912, 2nd ed. 1917; his greatest work was the immense dictionary, *Wörterbuch der ägyptischen Sprache*, edited jointly with H. Grapow (q.v.) and based on material collected by many of the leading Egyptologists, 5 vols., Leipzig, 1926-31, with two further vols., 1957-63, and 5 vols. of Belegstellen (references), 1935-53; for students a shorter *Ägyptisches Handwörterbuch* 1921, was produced; also *Aeyptisches Glossar*, 1904; *Zur ägyptischen Wortforschung* 1907-28; in the field of Coptic, *Bruchstücke der oberägyptischen Übersetzung des Alten Testaments*, 1880; *Bruchstücke koptischer Volksliteratur*, 1897; *Koptische Urkunden*, Aeg. Urk. Berlin Museum Bd. I, 1904; in literature and texts, *Aegyptische Chrestomathie*, 1904; *Die Märchen des Papyrus Westcar*, 1890; *Gespräch eines Lebensmüden mit siener Seele*, 1896; *Hymnen an das Diadem der Pharaonen*, 1911; *Papyrus Lansing*, with H. O. Lange, 1925; *Ein Denkmal memphitischer Theologie*, 1911; *Zaubersprüche für Mutter und Kind*, 1901; *Römische Obelisken*, 1917; *Die Obeliskenübersetzung des Hermapion*, 1914; *Die Sphinxstele*, 1904; *Ein Fall abgekürzter Justiz in Aegypten*, 1913; *Reden, Rufe und Lieder auf Gräberbildern des Alten Reiches*, 1919; on daily life, *Ägypten und ägyptisches Leben im Altertum*, 1885 and later eds, translated into English as *Life in Ancient Egypt*, 1895; *Die Literatur der Ägypter*, 1923, trans. *Literature of the Ancient Egyptians*, 1927; on religion, *Die ägyptische Religion*, 1905, and later eds. Eng. trans. 1907; he published many museum reports, 1885-1901; *Ausführliches Verzeichnis der ägyptischen Altertümer und Gipsabgüsse*, 1894; his last work was *Die Welt am Nil*, 1936; he was a Member of the Berlin Akad., his correspondence in the Bremen University library was published by H. Kloft, *Der Nachlass Adolf Erman,* 1952; his academy articles were edited by A. Burkhardt and W. F. Reineke, *Akademieschriften(1880-1928),*1986; he died Berlin, 26 June 1937.

Autobiogr. *Mein Werden und mein Wirken,* 1929; *NDB* 4. 598-9; C. Breasted, *Pioneer to the Past,* passim, many anecdotes; *AfO* 12 (1937), 95-7 (A. Scharff); *Berliner Museen* 59 (1938), 19-21 (R. Anthes); *Chron. d'Ég.* 13 (1938), 131-2 (J. Capart); *Eg. Gazette,* July 2 1937, 6 (G. A. Reisner); *FuF* 13 (1937), 271 (H. Grapow); *JAOS* 58 (1938), 413-18 (L. S. Bull and W. F. Edgerton); *JEA* 23 (1937), 81-2 (W. E. Crum); 24 (1938), 231; *ZÄS* 71 (1935), 1-14 (bibl.) (H. Grapow); 73 (1937), v (G. Steindorff); *ZDMG* 91, 484 f. (H. O. Lange); H. Grapow, *Worte des Gedenkens an Adolf Erman anlässlich seines hundertsten Geburtstages am 31. Oktober 1954, Sitzungsberichte der Deutschen Akademie der Wissenschaften zu Berlin. Klasse für Sprachen , Literatur und Kunst,* (1954), Nr. 3; *NDB* 4, 598-9; E. Endesfelder, *Die Ägyptologie an der Berliner Universität-Zur Geschichte eines Fachgebietes,* 1988, 14, 18-32; C.-B. Arnst and W. Müller, *Adolf Erman ein großer Berliner Gelehrter 1854-1937. Gedenkausstellung des Ägyptischen Museums/Papyrussammlung anläßlich des 50. Todestages von Adolf Erman vom 24. Juni bis 31. Dezember 1987 im Bodemuseum, Berlin,* 1987; E. Endesfelder in *Ethnographisch-Archäologische Zeitschrift* 28, 1987, 405-418; H.-A. Koch in: B. Adams and H. K. Boehlke, *Aratro Corona Messiora. Beiträge zur europäischen Wissensüberlieferung Festgabe für Günther Pflug zum 20. April 1988,* Bonn, 1988, 47-72 Ch. Velder, *300 Jahre Französisches Gymnasium Berlin,* 1989, 331-335; H. G. Bartel in Dahlemer Archivgespräche 7 (2001), 138-140; È. Gran-Aymerich, *Dictionnaire biographique d'archéologie 1798-1945,* 2001, incorporated in *Les Chercheurs de passé 1798-1945,* 2007, 777-8; N. Kehrer, '100 Jahre am Nil. Die Geschichte des Deutschen Archäologischen Instituts in Kairo' in G. Dreyer and D. Polz (eds), *Begegnungen mit der Vergangenheit. 100 Jahre in Ägypten,* 2007, 4; B. U. Schipper (ed.), *Ägyptologie als Wissenschaft. Adolf Erman (1854-1937) in seiner Zeit,* 2006; T. Gertzen, *ZÄS* 136 (2009), 114-125; inf. T. Gertzen; T. Gertzen, *EDAL* II (2010/1), 147-70; T. Gertzen in W. Carruthers, J. Buikstra and C. Roberts (eds), *The Global History of Paleopathology: Pioneers and Prospects,* 2012; W. Carruthers (ed.), *Histories of Egyptology,* 2015, 34-49; T. Gertzen, *Jean Pierre Adolphe Erman,* 2015.

ESDAILE, James (1808-1859)
British surgeon and hypnotist; he was born in Montrose, 8 Feb. 1808, son of Revd James E. and Margaret Blair; MD, Edinb., 1830; Honourable East India Company Med. Service, Bengal Presidency; he visited Egypt and Europe while on furlough, 1836-8; returned to India, 1838, and in charge of Hoogly Hospital; he practised mesmerism as anaesthetic in surgical operations, for which he claimed high results, and a govt. report was published on it in Calcutta, 1846; he published *Letters from the Red Sea, Egypt and the Continent,* Calcutta, 1839; he died in Sydenham, 10 Jan. 1859.

ODNB 18, 595-7; *DNB* 18, 1; D. G. Crawford, *Hist. Indian Med. Service,* ii. 153-6; *Fasti Ecclesiae Scoticanae* 4, 232.

ESTOURMEL, (*Comte*) (François Marie) Joseph Louis d' (1783-1853)
French traveller; born 1783, son of Louis Marié Marqus d'E. and Philiberte de Galard de Brissac; he visited Egypt in 1833 and with two companions went as far as Aswan; eleven years later he published his *Journal d'un voyage en Orient,* 2 vols. with 156 illustrations from his own drawings; he died in Paris, 13 Dec. 1853.

Carré, i, 220; Hilmy, i, 183; *DBF* 13, 119.

EUMORFOPOULOS, George (1863-1939)
British collector of Greek origin; he was born in Liverpool, 18 April 1863, son of Aristides E., merchant, and Mariona Scaramanga; in business he was a Director of Ralli Bros. Ltd; MRAS, 1924; FSA; he married Julia Scaramanga, 1890; he collected antiquities, ceramics, and *objets d'art,* and was also a generous supporter of archaeological and other learned societies and bodies; he formed one of the finest collections of Chinese ceramics and bronzes ever made, which later went to the British Museum and the Victoria and Albert Museum, a sumptuous catalogue by R. L. Hobson being privately printed in 6 vols., 1925-8; he was a benefactor of the EES; he travelled extensively in China and other parts of the East; his Egyptian antiquities were sold at Sotheby's, 6 June 1940 (lots 146-60); he died in London, 19 Dec. 1939.

ODNB 18, 645*; WWW* iii, 420; Newberry Corr.

EVANS, (*Sir*) Arthur John (1851-1941)
British archaeologist, the discoverer of the Minoan civilization; he was born at Nash Mills, Herts., 8 July 1851, and was the eldest son of Sir John E. (see below) and Harriet Dickinson; he was educated at Harrow and then studied history at Brasenose College, Oxford; afterwards at Göttingen; as a boy Evans helped his father in gathering material for the study of European prehistory, but later became famous for his work in Crete which he first visited in 1893 with D. G. Hogarth (q.v.); subsequently discovering a new and completely unknown civilization; adequate accounts of this work can be found elsewhere; he married in 1878 Margaret (*d.*1893) daughter of Prof. E. A. Freeman; he was Keeper of the Ashmolean Museum, Oxford, 1884-1908, and superintended its reorganization, also presenting to it his collection of Cretan antiquities, the finest in existence

outside the island itself; he also presented Egyptian objects, including many acquired at the MacGregor (q.v.) sale; he acquired many distinctions, Kt. 1911; DLitt Oxford; Hon. LLD Edin.; Hon. DLitt Dublin; PhD Berlin, 1910; FRS; PSA, 1914-19; Fellow of Brasenose, Oxford; etc,; he was Frazer Lecturer, Cambridge, 1930-1; Petrie Medal, 1931; he wrote some interesting studies on the relationship and early contacts between ancient Egypt and prehistoric Crete, see 'Further Discoveries of Cretan and Aegean Script with Libyan and Proto-Egyptian Comparisons', *JHS.* 17, 1898; *The Early Nilotic, Libyan and Egyptian Relations with Minoan Crete;* his great corpus of the three Cretan systems of writing, *Scripta Minoa,* 3 pts. 1921, contains Cretan hieroglyphs which in some cases may have been derived from Egyptian signs; the monumental study *The Palace of Minos,* 5 vols. in 6 pts. 1921-35, is full of references to Egyptian antiquities found in Crete and the Aegean area, and has a great amount of discussion of contacts between the two areas; Evans's interest in Egyptology extended to excavation and he was a member of the EEF and EES for nearly fifty years from 1893, and served on the committee for 32 years until 1925/6; in recognition of his services to classical archaeology the Hellenic Soc. presented him with an honorary scroll on his 90th birthday; he died at his home Youlbury, nr. Oxford, 11 July 1941.

ODNB 663-6 (portr.); *DNB* 1941-50, 240-3; *EB; WWW* iv, 363-4; Joan Evans, *Time and Chance*, London, 1943; Glyn E. Daniel, *A Hundred Years of Archaeology*, 150-1, 190-5; *Concise Enc. of Archaeology*, London, 1960, 176-8 (portr.); E. Gran-Aymerich, *Dictionnaire biographique d'archéologie 1798-1945*, 2001, incorporated in *Les Chercheurs de passé 1798-1945*, 2007, 78-1. Photograph courtesy of the Ashmolean Museum, University of Oxford.

EVANS, (*Sir***) John** (1823-1908)

British geologist and archaeologist; he was born at Britwell Court, Burnham, Bucks., 17 Nov. 1823, son of Revd Athur Benoni E., DD, and Anne Dickinson; he was educated at Market Bosworth School; he married 1. Harriet Ann daughter of John Dickinson, FRS, 1850, 2. Frances Phelps, 1859, 3. Maria Millington Lathbury, 1892; during his career he made geological investigations, especially into problems of water-supply, and formed large collections of fossils, stone and bronze implements, medieval antiquities, and ancient British coins; many of these, including the bronze 'sword' of Kamose, were presented to the Ashmolean Museum by his son Arthur (q.v.); FSA, 1852; FRS, 1864 and Treas. 1878-98; President of many Societies: Brit. Assn., 1897-8; Geological Soc., 1874-6; R. Numismatic Soc., 1874-1908; Soc. of Antiquaries, 1885-92; anthrop. Inst., 1877-9; Inst. of Chemical Industry, 1892-3; KCB, 1892; DCL; LLD; Hon. Fellow of Brasenose Coll.; his books include the standard works on the Coins of Ancient Britain and on Stone and Bronze Implements; he was interested in ancient Egypt and was President of the EEF, 1899-1906; he died at Berkhamsted, 31 May 1908.

ODNB 18, 719-22 (portr.); *DNB* Suppl. ii, 634-7; *WWW* i, 232; A. MacGregor (ed.), *Sir John Evans 1823-1908: antiquity, commerce and natural science in the age of Darwin*, 2008; E. Gran-Aymerich, *Dictionnaire biographique d'archéologie 1798-1945*, 2001, incorporated in *Les Chercheurs de passé 1798-1945*, 2007, 779-80. Photograph courtesy of the Ashmolean Museum, University of Oxford.

EVANS, John (1828-1903)

British army officer; he was born at Derby, 14 June 1828, son of Samuel E., banker, and Caroline Wollaston; Cornet in Inniskilling Dragoons, 1854; Cornet, 9th Lancers, 1856, retired Colonel; he saw war service in the Crimea and Indian Mutiny; with his regiment in Egypt, 1858-62; he frequently visited Egypt and formed an important collection of antiquities; these were exhibited at Burlington Fine Arts Club, 1895; the collection was sold at Sotheby's, 30 June and 1 July 1924 (356 lots); a Demotic papyrus, not in the sale, was acquired by the British Museum (EA 10480); he retired 1889, and died at Merle, Slinfold, Sussex, 30 May 1903.

Royal United Service Institution Records; Lugt 87180.

EVELYN-WHITE, Hugh Gerard (1884-1924)

British classicist and archaeologist; born Ipswich, 18 June 1884, son of Revd Charles Harold Evelyn W. FSA, FRHS and Charlotte Mary Reid; he was educated at King's School, Ely, and became a Scholar of Wadham College, Oxford, taking his BA in classical archaeology, 1907; he was made assistant to Sir Aurel Stein for work on Central Asian antiquities in the British Museum, 1909, and the same year also joined the Metropolitan Museum expedition to Egypt as a classical specialist; he served in Egypt for a period during the First World War, and resumed work for the Metropolitan Museum afterwards, remaining with the expedition until 1921, when he became lecturer in classical archaeology and literature in the University of Leeds; in intervals between his work abroad he carried out excavations in Britain at Caerleon and other sites; he worked with Winlock at El-Bagawat, Kharga Oasis and then at W. Thebes until 1914; he also took part in the exploration of the Coptic Monastery of Epiphanius at Qurna; he was later given the great task of making an architectural and archaeological description of the monasteries of Wadi Natrun and a history of the colony; he completed two vols. on this subject before his death and also wrote reports in the *BMMA*; he subsequently learnt Coptic in order to produce another book of texts derived from manuscripts that he had helped to recover; he committed suicide in Leeds, 9 Sept. 1924.

JEA 10 (1924), 331-2 (W. E. Crum); *BMQ* 28, 63.

EVERS, Hans Gerhard (1900-1993)
German art historian; he was born in Lübeck, 19 March 1900; he studied art history and archaeology at the Universities of Göttingen and Heidelberg under Ranke (q.v.); PhD, 1929; Habilitation, *Staat aus dem Stein-zur Entwicklung der Plastik des Mittleren Reiches*, 1932 at Munich; he was appointed lecturer in Munich, 1932; Professor, 1943; he became Professor of Art History at the Technische Hochschule in Darmstadt, 1950-68; although his major works were on painting and modern art, he published *Bibliographie zu Kunstgeschichte des 19. Jahrhunderts*, 1968 and an article, with R. Romero, on the monasteries of Sohag in K. Wessel (ed.), *Christentum am Nil*, 1964; he died at Hofgeismar, 8 April 1993.

Inf. B. Gessler-Löhr from internet sources.

FABRETTI, (Giuseppe Goffredo) Ariodante (1816-1894)
Italian historian and archaeologist; he was born at Perugia, 1 Oct. 1816, son of Giuseppe F. and Assunta Corsi; he studied veterinary medicine at Bologna, 1839-40; he became deputy librarian at Perugia where he became interested in archaeology; he was fled to Turin after the failure of 1848 revolution on account of his political views; he published historical works and wrote on Etruscan inscriptions; he was Professor of Archaeology at Turin and Director of the Museum of Antiquities, 1871-94; Corresponding Member of the Académie des Inscriptions, 22 Dec. 1876; he partly catalogued the Egyptian collection there; he was a Deputy, 1876-80 and Senator from 1889; he died in Monteu da Po, Turin, 16 Sept. 1894.

DBDI 43, 731-6; Garollo, *Diz. Biogr. Univ.; Enc. It.*; A. C. E. Franquet de Franqueville, *Le Premier Siècle de l'Institut de France*, 1895, II, 299; È. Gran-Aymerich, *Dictionnaire biographique d'archéologie 1798-1945*, 2001, incorporated in *Les Chercheurs de passé 1798-1945*, 2007, 783-4.

FACKR, Basila (*c.*1767-1825)
Syrian merchant; he supported the French invasion forces in Egypt and left with them; he returned as Consular Agent for France and five other European Powers at Damietta from 1803; a wealthy man of wide culture, he founded an Academy at Damietta, and translated Volney's *Ruines*, 1790 into Arabic; he was noted for his lavish hospitality to distinguished travellers in Egypt; after his death in 1825 his affairs were found to be heavily in debt, leaving his widow in distress.

Minutoli, 175, 178-87, 210; Forbin, 3, 6, 7, 9; Carré, i, 197-98, 257; Bramsen, *Travels*, i, 235; H. Cornille, *Souvenirs d'Orient*, 1836, 364-5; French F. O. records.

FAIRHOLT, Frederick William (1813-1866)
British artist, wood-engraver, and antiquary; of German origin (Fahrholtz), he was born in London, 1813, baptized at Westminster, 18 July 1813, son of John Frederick F. and Sarah Dugwell; he acted as a drawing master and scene painter until 1835; FSA, 1844; he illustrated many antiquarian books for Charles Knight, Sir John Evans, Sir Frederic Madden, and others, and also produced many works of his own, including the catalogues of antiquities and works of art in Lord Londesborough's collection; he toured Egypt and went as far as Abu Simbel 1859-60, afterwards publishing *Up the Nile and Home Again*, 1862; he bequeathed his Shakespeariana to Stratford-on-Avon, some of his books to the Soc. of Antiquaries, his collection of prints and drawings to the BM; the rest of his library was sold at Sotheby's 23 July 1866; he died in London, 3 April 1866.

ODNB 18, 946; *DNB* 18, 151; *EB* 10, 133; Hilmy, i, 227.

FAIRMAN, Herbert Walter (1907-1982)
British Egyptologist; he was born at Clare, Suffolk 9 March 1907, son of Revd Walter Trotter F., a Baptist missionary in Egypt, and Mary Amelia Prior; he was educated at Bethany School, Goudhurst, Kent and from 1926 at the Institute of Archaeology, Liverpool studying under Peet (q.v.) and Garstang (q.v.); Certificate in Archaeology (Egyptology) 1929; he took part in the excavations at Armant, 1929-31; assistant field director under Pendlebury (q.v.) at Amarna, 1931-6; field director for the EES at Sesebi and Amara West, 1936-9, 1947-8; he drew several of the text plates for Peet's *Great Tomb Robberies* and the plates for Gardiner's editions of the Chester Beatty papyri and the Late Egyptian Miscellanies; he also collaborated with Blackman (q.v.) on the reading of Ptolemaic texts; during World War II he was attached to the British Embassy in Cairo, 1940-7; he was appointed Brunner Professor of Egyptology at the University of Liverpool, 1948-74 and Special Lecturer in Egyptology at the University of Manchester, 1948-69; Dean of the Faculty of Arts, 1956-8; Emeritus Professor, 1974-82; he devoted himself to teaching during his university career and hence his publications are few; apart from articles and chapters in the excavation reports of Armant and Amarna, he edited *The City of Akhenaten* III, 1950 and wrote *The Triumph of Horus*, 1974; he died in Liverpool, 16 Nov. 1982.

Inf. Mrs. Fairman; *JEA* 70 (1984), 123-7 (portr.) (A. F. Shore).

FAIRSERVIS, Walter Ashlin (1921-1994)
American Egyptologist; he was born in Brooklyn, New York, 17 Feb. 1921, son of Walter Ashlin F. and Edith Yeager; he was educated at Columbia University; BA, MA; and at Harvard University; MA, PhD; Assistant at the

American Museum of Natural History from 1941 apart from war service; he excavated in Afghanistan, 1949 and Pakistan, 1960; he was appointed head of the Department of Anthropology, Vassar College, Poughkeepsie, 1969; he excavated at Hierakonpolis, 1967-9, 1978-92; he published *The Ancient Kingdoms of the Nile and the Doomed Monuments of Nubia*, 1962; *The Hierakonpolis Project* 1-3, 1983, 1986; he died in Sharon, Conn., 12 July 1994.

NY Times 16 July 1994.

FAKHRY, Ahmed (1905-1973)
Egyptian archaeologist; he was born in the Fayum Oasis 21 May 1905, son of Ali F. and Galila Abbas; he studied at the University of Cairo; BA, 1928; from 1929-32 he studied at Berlin under Sethe (q.v.), at Brussels under Capart (q.v.), and at Liverpool under Peet (q.v.); he joined the Antiquities Service in 1932 serving first under Selim Hassan (q.v.) at Giza and then at Luxor; Chief Inspector for Middle Egypt and the Oases in 1936 and Chief Inspector for the Delta in 1938; he later served as curator in the Cairo Museum and Chief Inspector of Upper Egypt, Nov. 1942-Oct. 1944; from 1937 his attention was directed to work on sites in the desert oases and from 1944-50 he served as Director of Desert Researches; in 1947 he visited Yemen and conducted an archaeological survey; from 1950-55 he was Director of Pyramid Researches excavating at the Bent Pyramid of Sneferu at Dahshur and at Shawaf, Saqqara, 1951 (see *ASAE* 71 (1987), 187-93); in 1952 he became Professor of the History of Ancient Egypt at Cairo University retiring in 1965; he was Visiting Professor at Brown University,1953-4, at Pennsylvania in 1966, and also at Amman and California; in 1969 he excavated tombs in the oasis of Dakhla; his principal published works were *Sept Tombeaux à l'est de la grande pyramide de Guizeh*, 1935; *Recent Explorations in the Oases of the Western Desert*, 1942; *The Egyptian Deserts. Bahria Oasis* 2 vols. 1942, 1950; *The Egyptian Deserts. Siwa Oasis*, 1944; *The Oasis of Siwa*, 1950; *The Necropolis of El-Bagawat in Kharga Oasis*, 1951; *An Archaeological Journey to Yemen* 3 vols., 1951-2; *The Egyptian Deserts. The Amethyst Quarries at Wadi el Hudi*, 1952; *The Bent Pyramid of Dahshur*, 1954; *The Monuments of Snefru at Dahshur*, Vol. I, 1959; Vol. II 2 *parts* 1961; *The Pyramids*, 1961; *The Oases of Egypt* Vol I, 1973, Vol. II, 1974; the notes of his last excavation were posthumously edited in *Denkmäler der Oase Dachla*, 1982; he died in Paris, 7 June 1973.

Chron. d'Ég. 48 (1973), 309-10 (A. Mekhitarian); *BSFE* 68 (1973), 5-7 (portr.) (J. Leclant); *ARCE Newsletter* 86 (1973), 1-3 (D. O'Connor); *The Oases of Egypt*. Vol. II (1974), v-vi (J. Wilson); *Denkmäler der Oase Dachla*, 1982, 7 (portr.) (R. Stadelmann), 11-12 (bibl.) (M. Moursi); *Gött. Misz.* 76 (1984), 82-3 (H. Attiatalla), *JEA* 59 (1973), 3-5 (I. E. S. Edwards).

FARAG Ismain (*c.* 1830-1900+)
Egyptian antiquities dealer; he was born c. 1830 and lived at Kafr el-Haram near Giza; he is cited as a dealer from 1881, obtaining objects from local diggers; he also conducted authorized excavations in return for allotting a portion of the finds to the Egyptian Museum; he excavated at Hawara, 1888; Soknopaiu Nesos, 1890-1; Asyut, 1894; Deir el-Aizam, 1897; and Deir el-Bersha; he sold objects to Maspero (q.v) for the Egyptian Museum and to Lange (q.v.) and Schäfer (q.v.), 1899.

F. Hagen and K. Ryholt, *The Antiquities Trade in Egypt 1880-1930*, 2017, 214-5.

FARID, Shafik (1911-1983)
Egyptian archaeologist; he was born at Akhmim, 19 Jan. 1911, son of Farid Nazmy, a civil servant, and Ettra el-Komos Feltaous; he studied in the Dept. of History, University of Cairo; BA, 1934; and the High Institute of Archaeology; MA, 1937; he entered the Egyptian Antiquities Service, 1937 and assisted Selim Hassan (q.v.) at Giza, 1937-9; Inspector of Upper Egypt, 1940-3; Inspector of Lower Egypt where from 1943-52 he excavated at various sites in the Delta with A. Hamada (q.v.): Kom el-Hisn, 1943-9; Kom el-Kharaz, 1946-7; Kom Trough, 1948; Kom Firin, 1949-52; and El-Qatta, 1949-51; Chief Inspector of Lower Egypt from 1953 when he excavated at Mit-Yaish, 1953-5; Maamoura, 1954; and Bubastis, 1961-7; he participated in the rescue excavations in Nubia working at Ballana, 1958-9; Qustul, 1958; Tafa, 1960; Amada, Debod, Kalabsha and Wadi es-Sebua, 1963-4; he carried out excavations at Kom Abu Billo, 1969-70; he was promoted to the post of Chief of Inspectorates of the Service of Antiquities and later was Director of the Coptic Museum, 1967-71; following his retirement he lectured at the University of Cairo and other bodies; he was a member of the Permanent Committee for Egyptian Antiquities; apart from articles and preliminary reports of his excavations in *ASAE*, his publications include *The Mastabas of the Eighth Season and their Description,* (with S. Hassan), 1960; *Excavations at Ballana, 1958-9,* 1963; *The Coptic Museum and the Ancient Coptic Churches of Egypt,* 1967; *The Temple of Luxor,* 1982; *The Temple of Karnak,* 1982; *The Pyramids of Giza,* 1982; *The Temple of Queen Hatshepsut,* 1983; *The Temple of Abydos,* 1983; *Abu Simbel,* 1983; *The Temple of Edfu,* 1983; he died at Zagazig, 4 May 1983.

Family inf.; *Les grands découvertes de 1954*, 69; *Varia Aegyptiaca* 2 (1986), 3-5 (bibl.) (C. Van Siclen).

FARINA, Giulio (1889-1947)
Italian Egyptologist; born Frascati, 30 May 1889, son of Gioacchino F. and Maria Formilli; Farina became interested in Egyptology at the age of fifteen after reading Marucchi's book on the obelisks in Rome; he published his first article while still a student, *L'obelisco lateranese e la riforma religiosa di Chuenaten*, 1906; he undertook excavations at Oxyrhynchus, 1910-11; he gained a Doctorate of the University of Rome 1914 with a thesis on the function of the Pharaonic vizier during the XVIIIth Dynasty based on the inscriptions in the tomb of Rekhmire; after working for a period at Florence Museum he became an assistant at Turin Museum 1927-39, Director, 1939-43; and also appointed Professor in the University there; Farina published 52 books and articles and 45 reviews in all, including an Egyptian grammar, Milan, 1926, French edit. Paris, 1927; his most famous work was *Il papiro dei Re restaurato*, Rome, 1938, an examination of the Turin king-list; he excavated several sites in Egypt, notably Gebelein (El-Gherera), 1930, 1935, and 1937, discovering a considerable quantity of predynastic material; he died in Turin, 23 Dec. 1947.

Chron. d'Ég. 23 (1948), 106-8 (E. Scamuzzi); *Aegyptus* 27 (1947/48), 240-4 (bibl.); *Rivista degli Studi Orientali* 23 (1945), 109-12 (G. Botti); inf. Dr Valenti.

FATTOVICH, Rodolfo (1945-2018)
Italian archaeologist; he was born in Trieste, 17 Nov. 1945; he studied at the University of Trieste under Dolzani (q.v.); Diplomaa, 1969; and then at the University of Rome under Donadoni (q.v.); Diploma, 1972; he was appointed to the University of Naples, 1974-2014 where he taught Ethiopian Studies and from 1987 Egyptology; he was also visiting Professor of Archaeology at the University of Addis Ababa; he excavated at Hammamiya, 1976-8; Naqada with Barocas (q.v.), 1977-9, 1981-3; in the Delta at Tell el-Farkha, 1987-90; Butana, 1984; Mersa/Wadi Gawasis from 2001; in Ethiopia at Kassala from 1980; and at Axum from 1993; apart from articles, he published, all with K. Bard, *Harbor of the Pharaohs*, 2007; *Egyptian Seafaring Expeditions to Punt in the Middle Kingdom*, 2018; and *Egyptian Seafaring Expeditions and the Land of Punt*, 2018; he died in Rome, 23 March 2018.

Azania 53 (2018), 1-3; *Sudan and Nubia* 22 (2018), 198-9 (A. Manzo)

FAULKNER, Raymond Oliver (1894-1982)
British Egyptologist; he was born in Shoreham, Sussex, 26 Dec. 1894, son of Frederick Arthur F., a bank clerk, and Matilda Elizabeth Wheeler; he entered the Civil Service in 1912; he served briefly in World War I before being invalided out and rejoined the Civil Service in 1916; his interest in Egyptology led him in 1918 to study hieroglyphs in his spare time at University College London under Margaret Murray (q.v.); in 1926 he became a full-time assistant to (Sir) Alan Gardiner (q.v.); he collaborated with Gardiner on his major publications in the autography of the hieroglyphic texts, the commentaries, and the indexes notably for *The Wilbour Papyrus* and *Ancient Egyptian Onomastica*; he received his training in Egyptian philology from Gardiner who encouraged his independent publications; he became an assistant in language teaching at University College, London 1951; lecturer in Egyptian language 1954-67; FSA 1950; DLitt from London University 1960; editor of *JEA* 1946-59; his main area of interest was Egyptian philology in which he made major contributions with his Middle Egyptian dictionary and translations of many important texts; his numerous publications include *The Plural and Dual in Old Egyptian*, 1929; *The Papyrus Bremner-Rhind*, 1933; *A Concise Dictionary of Middle Egyptian*, 1962, 2nd ed. 1972; *Egypt: From the Inception of the Nineteenth Dynasty to the Death of Ramesses III*, 1966 for the *Cambridge Ancient History*; *The Ancient Egyptian Pyramid Texts*, 1969; *Catalogue of Egyptian Antiquities in the British Museum. II Wooden Model Boats*, 1972, with S. Glanville; *The Ancient Egyptian Coffin Texts*, 3 vols. 1972-8; *The Literature of Ancient Egypt*, 1973, with E. Wente, and W. K. Simpson; *The Book of the Dead*, 1972; he also wrote many articles and reviews; he died in Ipswich, Suffolk, 3 March 1982.

JEA 60 (1974), 5-14 (portr.) (bibl.) (H. S. Smith and C. Spaull); *JEA* 69 (1983), 141-4 (portr.), (bibl.) (H S. Smith and C. Spaull); R. Janssen, *The First Hundred Years,* 1992, 72.

FECHHEIMER, Hedwig Jenny (*née* **Brühl**) (1871-1942)
German art historian; she was born in Berlin, 1 June 1871, daughter of Israel Isdior B. and Bertha Norden; she studied art history and philosophy in Berlin, 1896-1908, attending lectures on Egyptology by Erman (q.v.) and Sethe (q.v.); she married firstly, 1903, Sigfried Fechheimer (died 17 Jan 1904) and secondly, 1918, Richard Simon after which she was known as Fechheimer-Simon; she first went to Egypt in 1910 at the invitation of the

wife of Ludwig Borchardt (q.v.) and again in 1928 on a research grant; she served on the consulting committee for acquisitions to the Berlin Egyptian Museum, 1921-33; she published *Die Plastik der Ägypter*, 1914, which was a great success; the fourth edition in 1920 included additional plates of the Amarna finds and was followed by further editions in 1922 and 1923; despite a disparaging review by von Bissing (q.v.), her book was widely read and appreciated by writers such as Rilke and Hesse and artists like Klee and Giacometti; her ample use of photographs, illustrating rather than describing sculptures, was considered modern; she stressed the importance of the newly discovered art of Amarna and sought to explain Egyptian art by analogy with modern art rather than in the context of historical development; she also published *Kleinplastik der Ägypter*, 1921 as well as reviews and articles about Egyptian art in *Kunst und Künstler*, an art magazine published by Bruno Cassirer in Berlin; as a Jew, she was denied access to the Berlin Museum reading room from 12 Nov. 1938; her attempt to emigrate was unsuccessful and she and her sister Margaret committed suicide in Berlin, 31 Aug. 1942.

R. Wedewer, *Ägyptische und moderne Skulptur*, 1986, 3-34; R. Krauss, *MDAIK* 50 (1994) 223-4; S. Peuckert, *Jahrbuch der deutschen Schillergesellschaft* 53 (2009), 234-275; inf. S. Peuckert; R. Krauss, *EDAL* III (2012), 154-5; S. Peukart, *Hedwig Fechheimer und die Ägyptische Kunst*, 2014.

FECHT, Gerhard (1922-2006)
German Egyptologist; he was born in Mannheim, 6 Feb. 1922; he obtained his habilitation at the University of Heidelberg; he was a Professor of Egyptology at the Free University of Berlin; he was a specialist in the study of metre in Egyptian literature and inscriptions; a Festschrift was published in his honour *Form und Mass*, edited by J. Osing and G. Dreyer, 1987; apart from numerous articles, he published *Das Habgierige und die Maat in der Lehre des Ptahhotep (5. und 19. Maxime)*, 1958; *Wortakzent und Silbenstrukur*, 1960; *Literarische Zeugnisse zur "Persönlichen Frömmigkeit" in Ägypten*, 1965; *Vom Wandel des Menschenbildes in der ägyptischen Rundplastik*, 1965; *Der Vorwurf an Gott in dem "Mahnworten des Ipu-wer"*, 1972; *Metrik des Hebräischen und des Phönizichen*, 1990; he died 11 Dec. 2006.

Form und Mass, xi-xv (bibl.); *Kürschner* 22 (2009), 4797.

FEDERN, Walter (1910-1967)
Austrian-American Egyptologist and philologist; he was born in Vienna, 1910, son of Dr. Paul F., a psychiatrist, whose family had long been of standing and wealth and Wilma Alexandra Bauer; he studied Egyptology at the Vienna Institute and gained his PhD there; he and his parents fled from Austria soon after it was occupied by Hitler and settled in New York, 1938-9; here Federn began working in the Wilbour Library in Brooklyn and in the Oriental Room of the New York Public Library, doing research and also teaching some students; he published very few articles and these small, his reputation thus resting on more slender grounds than almost any other Egyptologist, but these works were of a high order and of considerable philological interest, and appeared mainly in *JNES* and *JEA*; his greatest work was undoubtedly the huge bibliography that he compiled for *Orientalia* which listed everything published in Egyptology between the years 1939 and 1947, *Orientalia* 17. 467-89; 18. 73-99, 206-15, 325-35, 443-72; 19. 40-52, 175-86, 279-94; this comprised 317 books, 1,597 articles and obituaries, and 298 reviews; for the last ten years of his life Federn was engaged on medical research and helped a scholar in that field whose subsequent death greatly affected him; a pathologically shy man he gave up the will to live, refused to eat, and literally wasted away; he died in New York, 28 July 1967.

Inf J. D. Cooney; *AEB* i (1947), 11; *JEA* 53 (1967), 2; *JSSEA* 11 (1981), 69 (bibl.) (W. Needler).

FELIX, Orlando (1790-1860)
British army officer and traveller; he was born in Bristol, 1790, son of Dr. Matthias Felix, a naval surgeon, who served at Trafalgar, and Anne Davis; he was educated at Harrow; he served as 2nd Lt. Royal Marines, 14 Aug. 1810; Ensign 27th Foot (later Rifle Brigade), 26 Aug. 1813; Lt 14th Foot, 10 Nov 1813; Lt, 95th Foot 4 May 1815; he was present at Waterloo and was wounded at Quatre Bras; Waterloo Medal; Capt., 20 May 1824 and later Major, 31 Oct. 1826 on half-pay; he accompanied his colonel to Egypt on a political mission, visiting Upper Egypt and later joined Lord Prudhoe (q.v.) (afterwards Duke of Northumberland), in his travels to Egypt, Nubia, and Sinai; he met Champollion (q.v.) in Cairo in Sept. 1828 and again in Nubia in Jan. 1829, and made many drawings and notes, some of which are at Alnwick, others in the British Library (Add. MS 25663, ff. 42-107); in 1830 he published a brochure with lithographic plates, *Notes on Hieroglyphics*; he later served in India as Private Sec. to the Gov. of Bombay and Deputy Quartermaster-General 18 June 1846-23 Oct. 1855; he retired as Major-General, 26 Oct. 1858; his Waterloo medal was sold at Glendinings, 28 Jan. 1947 (lot 20) and is now in the Royal Green Jackets Museum, Winchester; he died at the Villa Colombier, Montbrillant, Geneva, 5 April 1860.

Add. MS 25658, ff. 79-84; 25672, f. 29; Champollion, ii. 207-8; Dalton, *Waterloo Roll Call*, 197; Hartleben, ii,

88, 207, 268, 275, 345; Hay Diary; Hilmy, i, 230;*The Athenaeum* April 21, 1860, 544-5; *GM* Jan-June 1860, 639; Boase, Suppl. II, 280; J. Ruffle in P. and J. Starkey, *Travellers in Egypt*, 1998, 75-84; J. Ruffle in J. Thompson, *Cairo Papers* 23/3 (2000), 80-9; inf. N. Cooke.

FERLINI, Giuseppe (1797-1870)
Italian physician; he was born in Bologna, 23 April 1797; he joined the service of the Egyptian army and was appointed Surgeon-Major, 1830; he served at Senaar and later at Khartoum; while there he excavated the pyramid-field of Meroe, the expedition starting 10 Aug. 1834; the work was carried out in partnership with Antonio Stefani, an Albanian merchant settled in Khartoum; Ferlini's finds were afterwards sold and acquired by the museums of Berlin and Munich; a somewhat misleading account of the excavations was published (in Italian), Bologna, 1837, and a French trans., Rome, 1838; both publications contain a catalogue of the objects found; he died in Bologna, 30 Dec. 1870.

Budge, *Eg. Sudan*, i, 285 (extracts from Ferlini's publication, trans. into English, 307 ff.-313 ff.); Hill, 126; Hilmy, i, 230; Lepsius, 151, 197; P. Ducati, *Rassegna Italiana*, (Aug-Sept. 1940), 515; a new edition Nell'interno dell'Africa 1829-35 was edited by W. Boldrini, 1981; S. Curto, *Oriens Antiquus* 22 (1983), 141-3; Y. Markowitz and P. Lacovara, *JARCE* 33 (1996), 1-9; gravestone inscription

FERNANDEZ, Solomon (*fl.*1830-1860)
Jewish antiquity-dealer in Cairo; he exploited the necropolis of Saqqara, and many important objects passed through his hands; according to Prisse (q.v.), the famous 'Scribe accroupi' of the Louvre was not found by Mariette (q.v.), but was bought by him from Fernandez for 120 francs; Wilkinson (q.v.) examined his collection in 1830, and Lepsius (q.v.) in 1842.

Bibl. Ég. 18, xxvii, xxx, xxvi, lii; W. Reil, *Aegypten als Winteraufenhalt*, 1859, 198; Prisse, *Petits mém. secrètes*, ed. Auriant, 1930, 40; Wilkinson MSS; Lepsius, *Denkmäler*, *Text*. i, 14, 16, 222.

FEUARDENT, Felix Bienaimé (1819-1907)
French dealer and numismatist; he was born at Cherbourg, 26 April 1819 son of Jacques François F., a baker, and Bonne Marie Françoise Adam; he originally worked as a bookseller and printer and edited the sale catalogue of the coin collection of N. de Gerville in 1854; he was from 1859 a partner in the firm Rollin and Feuardent; he became co-editor of the *Revue Numismatique*, 1859 and edited several sale catalogues and published *Collections Giovanni de Demetrio. Numismatique. Egypte ancienne. Monnaies des rois. Domination romaine*, 1869-73; after the death of the last Rollin in 1906, the firm continued as Feuardent Frères in 4 Rue Louvois, Paris, until 1935; he died in Paris 1907; his son (Louis) Gaston F. was born in Cherbourg, 20 Aug. 1841 by his wife Louise Antoinette Cassini; from 1868 he represented the firm in London; he emigrated to the United States in 1876 and established his own firm in New York; Member of the American Numismatic and Archaeological Society, 1877; he translated the Greek inscription and identified the coins associated with the New York obelisk for Gorringe (q.v.); he died in New York, 12 June 1893.

DBF 13, 1212; *New York Times* 13 June 1893; E. McFadden, *The Glitter and the Gold*, 1971, 271; inf. R. Merrillees.

FINATI, Giovanni (1787-1829+)
Italian traveller; he was born in Ferrara, 1787; after deserting the French army to the Turks in Dalasta he went as a young man to Alexandria in 1809 and enlisted in the service of Muhammad Ali; he took part in the capture of Mecca and Medina, and the Wahhabi and Arabian campaigns; afterwards acted as dragoman and interpreter to European travellers in the East; he accompanied W. J. Bankes (q.v.) to Upper Egypt, Nubia, Syria, and Palestine, 1815-16, and Linant de Bellefonds (q.v.) to Meroe 1821-22; he went to Abu Simbel with Belzoni (q.v.) in 1817; to Nubia with Straton (q.v.) in 1817, and rejoined Bankes in Palestine accompanying him to Abu Simbel in 1818; he accompanied Sir Frederick Henniker (q.v.) to Abu Simbel, 1819-20, and afterwards he visited England for two years 1826-28; he returned to Cairo with Lord Prudhoe (q.v.) and accompanied him in his travels in Egypt, Nubia, and Syria, returning to Cairo in 1829, and is believed to have established a hotel there; he dictated an account of his life and travels to Bankes, who translated and published it in 1830; not traced after 1829.

Life and Adventures of Giovanni Finati, ed. W. J. Bankes, 2 vols., London, 1830; Sir Richard F. Burton, App. VI to *Pilgrimage to Medinah and Meccah*; G. Guémard in *Bulletin de la Société royale d'archéologie d'Alexandrie*, 39-43; S. Bono, *Levante* 13 (1966), 3-20.

FIRTH, Cecil Mallaby (1878-1931)
British Egyptologist; he was born in Ashburton, Devon, 5 July 1878, son of Henry Mallaby F. and Frances Caunter; he trained for the Bar and went to Cyprus to take up judicial work there, but went on to Egypt and entered the Antiquities Service, in which he served for 30 years, except whilst on military service, 1914-18; he

was associated with Reisner (q.v.) in the Arch. Survey of Nubia, 1907-10, and undertook the preparation of a long series of reports on the excavations; he organized the Aswan Museum in 1912; he was appointed Inspector of Antiquities at Saqqara, 1913, where he carried out many important excavations, including the pyramid of King Zoser; he was about to clear the 1st Dynasty tombs when he returned to England on leave in 1931, but was taken ill with pneumonia a few days after his arrival; he married Winifred Hansard Firth (q.v.); he published, *Archaeological Survey of Nubia. Report 1908-1909*, 2 vols. 1912; *Reports 1909-11*, 1915, 1927; *Teti Pyramid Cemeteries*, with B. G. Gunn, 2 vols. 1926; *The Step Pyramid*, with J. E. Quibell, 2 vols. 1935; he died in a London nursing-home, 25 July 1931.

JEA 17 (1931), 255; È. Gran-Aymerich, *Dictionnaire biographique d'archéologie 1798-1945*, 2001, incorporated in *Les Chercheurs de passé 1798-1945*, 2007, 794-5.

FIRTH, Winifred (Freda) Nest (*née* Hansard) (1872-1937)
British artist and copyist; she was born in Bethnal Green, 21 March, 1872, youngest child of the Revd Septimus Hansard, Rector of Bethnal Green, London, and Edith Mary Greaves; her education was informal yet she was widely read; she studied art, excelled in drawing, and was accepted by the Royal Academy Schools in 1893; after passing out, she painted in oils and exhibited at the Royal Academy and elsewhere; already interested in Egypt she was introduced to Flinders Petrie (q.v.) by her aunt (Lady Smyth) and worked for him as a copyist for a number of years at Abydos, Saqqara, Giza and elsewhere; she worked for her keep only, being more interested in the work and the life than remuneration; some of her very extensive and skilled professional output appeared in publication under other names than hers; while on holiday in Cyprus she met Cecil Firth (q.v.) and after their marriage in 1906 accompanied him to Nubia; soon after the outbreak of war she returned to England to devote herself to the upbringing of their only child; she did, however, take a 'crash' course in machine drawing and became the first draughtswoman employed by Woolwich Arsenal; she later transferred to the Danger Buildings where she was appointed an overseer; when Firth at last took up his Egyptian Government post at Saqqara, after five years of war, his wife was able to rejoin him; and assist in his work, including the rethreading of elaborate beadwork, unacknowledged officially; her study of the blue tiles South Tomb of the Pyramid of Zoser forms the frontispiece to the posthumous publication of Firth's last excavation; Freda Firth died, after a long illness, at home in Newton Abbott, Devon 12 Oct. 1937 and is buried beside her husband at Islington.

Family inf.

FISCHER, Henry George (1923-2006)
American Egyptologist; he was born in Philadelphia, Pennsylavania 10 May 1923, son of Henry G. Fischer and Beatrice Agnes Hurdman; he was educated at Princeton University where he obtained his BA in English 1945; he then taught English at the American University of Beirut, 1945-48; he returned to the USA to study Egyptology at the University of Pennsylvania under Anthes (q.v.); PhD, 1955; he also held the post of assistant in the University Museum in Philadelphia until 1956; he undertook archaeological work in Egypt at Saqqara under Emery (q.v.), 1954 and at Memphis, 1955-56; he was appointed assistant Professor at Yale University; he joined the Metropolitan Museum in New York as assistant curator in 1958 and associate curator in 1963; he became head of the Department of Egyptian Antiquities 1964-70 and then took up the Lila Acheson Wallace research curatorship 1970-92; he also served as visiting professor at Columbia University 1960-61 and lecturer at the Institute of Fine Arts from 1962, later adjunct professor from 1966; he was the secretary and treasurer of the American Committee to Preserve Abu Simbel 1964-70 and helped to arrange the gift of the Temple of Dendur to the New York Museum; he was Visiting Professor at Columbia University 1960-61 and then taught at the Institute of Fine Arts, New York from 1962; he served as a trustee of the American Research Center in Egypt 1955-1966; he published extensively on a variety of subjects notably epigraphy; his works included *Inscriptions from the Coptite Nome, Dynasties VI-XI*, 1964; *Dendera in the Third Millennium B.C. down to the Theban Domination of Upper Egypt*, 1968; *Egyptian Studies* I. *Varia*, 1976; II, *The Orientation of Hieroglyphics*. Part I *Reversals*, 1977; III. *Varia Nova*, 1996; *Ancient Egyptian Epigraphy and Palaeography*, with R. Caminos, 1976; *Ancient Egyptian Calligraphy*, 1979, 2nd ed. 1983, 3rd ed. 1988; *Egyptian Women of the Old Kingdom and of the Heracleopolitan Period*, 1989; 2nd ed. 2000; Egyptian *Titles of the Middle Kingdom*, 1985; *L'écriture et l'art de l'Égypte ancienne*, 1986; *The Tomb of Ip at El Saff*, 1996; he died at Newton, Pennsylvania 11 Jan. 2006.

NY Times 18 Jan. 2006; bibl. privately printed, 2003 (M. Eaton-Krauss); *ZÄS* 134 (2007), III-VII (portr.) (M. Eaton-Krauss); inf. M. Eaton-Krauss.

FISHER, Clarence Stanley (1876-1941)
American archaeologist and architect; he was born Philadelphia, 17 Aug. 1876, son of Frederick Theodore F. and Emily Margaret Shewell, and graduated from the University of Pennsylvania as an architect, 1897; he became interested in archaeology which he then took up and was appointed Egyptian curator and field director with the University Museum, Philadelphia 1914-25 and took charge at the excavations undertaken in the Near East; Hon. ScD Pennsylvania, 1924; appointed Professor of Archaeology at the American School of Oriental Research, 1925, also acting Director later; Fisher was connected with many excavations throughout the Near East at Nippur, Tepe Gawra in Mesopotamia, Zawiyet el-Aryan, Girga, Giza, Dendera, Thebes and Memphis in Egypt, Antioch in Syria, Khirbet Tannur in Jordan, Samaria, Beth-shan, Megiddo, and Beth-shemesh in Palestine; at Samaria he was architect for the Harvard Expedition for three years under Reisner, 1908-10; at Memphis he discovered the palace of King Merenptah and published reports between 1914 and 1921; during the First World War he also worked in Egypt on behalf of Near East
Relief; he published the important *Corpus of Palestinian Pottery* in 3-4 vols.; he died in Jerusalem, 20 July 1941.

BASOR 83 (1941), 1-4 (portr.) (Nelson Glueck); *PEQ* 41, 140; 42. 3; *Penn. Museum Journal,* nos. vi, viii, xii; *JEA* 27 (1941), 164 (A. H. Gardiner); J. A. Wilson, *Signs and Wonders upon Pharaoh,* 1964, 220; *Expedition* 21 (1979), 23-6; *WWWA* i, 400; È. Gran-Aymerich, *Dictionnaire biographique d'archéologie 1798-1945,* 2001, incorporated in *Les Chercheurs de passé 1798-1945,* 2007, 7.

FISKE, Daniel Willard (1831-1904)
American collector; he was born in Ellisburg, New York, son of Daniel Haven F. and Caroline Willard; he was educated at Cazenovia Seminary and Hamilton College and then spent two years studying in Copenhagen and Uppsala; he then held a post at the Astor Library, 1852-9, became General Secretary of the American Geographical Society, 1859-60, and was attached to the American delegation at Vienna, 1861-2; he was on the staff of the *Syracuse Daily Journal* and from 1867 the *Hartford Courant*; he was appointed Librarian and Professor of North-European Languages at Cornell University, 1868-81; from 1883 he lived in Florence and undertook many trips to Egypt, 1867-8, 1880-1, 1888-9, 1891, 1896-7 and 1898; he had a large library which he left to Cornell and a small collection of Egyptian antiquities which he bequeathed to the National Museum, Reykjavik, Iceland; he died in Frankfurt, 17 Sept, 1904.

DAB 6, 417; inf. from Cornell University; G. J. Gudmundsson, 'Egypsku munirnir í dánargjöf Willards Fiske', *Arbók Fornleifafélagsins* 1995, 49-74 (portr.).

FITZCLARENCE, George Augustus Frederick, Earl of Munster (1794-1842)
British traveller; he was born in London, 29 Jan. 1794, illegitimate son of Prince William Duke of Clarence (later King William IV) and Dorothy Bland, an actress; he joined the army, retiring in 1822 with the rank of Lt.-Col.; he served in India, 1815-8 and he returned to Europe via Egypt, carrying dispatches to Salt (q.v.); he crossed the Eastern Desert to Qena and visited Dendera, Asyut, and Antinoe *en route* to Cairo; he met Salt and Belzoni (q.v.) in Cairo and was taken by them to Giza where he entered the First and Second Pyramids; he published an account *Journal of a Route across India through Egypt 1817-1818*,1819 in which he describes some of the antiquities in Salt's collection prior to their shipment to London; Major-General, 1841; Constable of Windsor Castle, 1833-42; President of the Royal Asiatic Society, 1841; he committed suicide in London, 20 March 1842.

ODNB 19, 777-8; *The Complete Peerage* 9, 429-30; J. Thompson, *Edward William Lane 1801-1876,* 2010, 442-3, 487-8.

FLAUBERT, Gustave (1821-1880)
French novelist; he was born at Rouen, 12 Dec. 1821, son of Achille F., a surgeon, and Caroline Fleuriot; he visited Egypt, Palestine, Syria, and Turkey between Nov. 1849 and April 1851 with his friend M. du Camp (q.v.) leaving an interesting account of what he saw in the form of letters to his mother and friends, see below; he died in Croisset, Seine Inf., 8 May 1880.

Chron. d'Ég. 9 (1930), 53-80 (M. Weynants-Ronday); *EB* 9, 425-7 (portr.); *DBF* 13, 1494-7; A. Y. Nauman, *Les Lettres d'Égypte de Gustave Flaubert*, Paris, 1965; F. Steegmuller, *Flaubert in Egypt*, 1972; J. Speake (ed.), *Literature of Travel and Exploration*, 2003,1, 438-40.

FLETCHER, (Revd) William Roby (1933-1894)
Australian minister and traveller; he was born in Manchester, 6 April 1833, son of Revd Richard F. and Jane Walkis; he was educated at University of London; BA, 1853, MA, 1856; he joined the Congregationalist church in 1847 and emigrated to Australia in 1856; he served as pastor at Bendigo, 1858-66, Richmond, 1866-76, and Adelaide, 1876-90; he was a member of the University of Adelaide Council, 1878-87; Vice-Chancellor, 1883-7; he was later Principal of the Congregational Training College and Chairman of the Australasian Congregational Union from 1892; he visited Egypt en route to England in 1890 with a commission to acquire antiquities for the South Australian Museum; he met Grenfell (q.v.) in Cairo and travelled with him to Luxor; he encountered Petrie (q.v.) in London, and, on his return to Cairo, obtained antiquities from his excavations and from the Cairo Museum including casts; he was appointed Hon. Curator of Archaeology to the Public Library, Museum, and Art Gallery, 1893 and gave lectures on archaeology; he wrote an account of his visit to Egypt *Egyptian Sketches*,1892; he died in Adelaide, 5 June 1894.

Australian Dictionary of Biography 4, 189-90; J. Halley, *A Short Biographical Sketch of the Rev. Wm. Roby Fletcher*, 1895; R. S. Merrillees, *Living with Egypt's Past in Australia*, 1999, 23-6 (portr.).

FLITTNER, Natalia Davidovna (1879-1957)
Russian Egyptologist; she was born in St. Petersburg 14/26 Sept. 1879, daughter of David F., a doctor; she was educated in history and philology at the Bestuzhev High School for women, graduating in 1904; she then studied at the University of St. Petersburg 1905-9 under Turaev (q.v.) being the first woman in Russia to study the ancient orient; she graduated in 1913; she also studied under Erman (q.v.), Meyer (q.v.), and Schäfer (q.v.) in Berlin 1909, 1912-4; she was appointed curator at the Hermitage Museum 1919-50; she taught at the I. E. Repin Institute of Painting, Sculpture, and Architecture 1919-56 and at the University of Leningrad from 1921; she became candidate of historical sciences in 1938 and Doctor of Historical Sciences and Professor at the University of Leningrad 1940; her studies were mostly devoted to the art and handicrafts of ancient Egypt; her publications included *The Art and Culture of Mesopotamia and Adjacent Countries*, 1958 (in Russian); she died in Leningrad, 16 July 1957.

S. D. Miliband, *Bibliograficeskiy slovar' sovetskikh vostokovego*, 1975, 575; *AfO* XXVII (1980), 333; *Greater Soviet Encyclopedia* 27, 265; *VDI* 1 (151), 1980, 227-8 (R. I. Rubinstein); *Sobschenya Gosudarstvennogo Ermitazha* 14 (1958),61 (portr.) (M. Matthieu).

FLORIS, Michel Ange (1809-1888)
Corsican craftsman; he was born in Ajaccio, 12 Aug. 1809; he was employed by Mariette (q.v.) from at least 1859 and made cases, pedestals, and mounts for the first Cairo Museum at Bulaq whose general upkeep he supervised; he also made restorations and casts; he termed himself chief engineer of the museum; nothing is known of his previous history; he died in Cairo, 21 Sept. 1888.

Maspero, *Bib. Ég.* 18, xcii; *Guide* (4th ed. 1915), pref. xiv; *Rapports sur la marche du Serv. des Antiquités*, 152; Devéria, *Mém. et Fragm.* in *Bibl. Ég* 4, 326; French F.O. records; E. David, *Mariette Pacha 1821-1881*, 1994, 110.

FOLKARD VON SCHERLING, Erik Edzard Floris (1907-1956)
Swedish antiquary and orientalist; born Rotterdam, 20 May 1907, son of the Swedish consul and was brought up in that city; he went to Leiden and after learning Latin and Arabic went to Egypt, where he toured the villages looking for Coptic manuscripts, papyri, and antiquities; on returning to Leiden he established an antique business in his apartment; he died in Leiden, 16 July 1956.

Chron. d'Ég. 32 (1957), 81 (J. M. A. Janssen).

FOL, Walther (1832-1890)
Swiss collector; he was born in Paris, 16 May 1832, son of Étienne Joseph F., a banker from Geneva, and Marianne Straub; he was educated at the University of Geneva and the École centrale in Paris; he worked as a civil engineer in Switzerland but spent much time in Italy where he retired in 1881; he visited the East in 1858, 1864 and 1867; he formed a collection of antiquities, part of which he gave to Geneva in 1871 where it was first housed in the Musée Fol until 1909 and then the Musée d'art et histoire; he died at Spoleto 2 March 1890.

Chronique d'Art 1890, 94; É. Maystre in *Geneva* 58 (2010), 33-46.

FORBIN, (Comte de) (Louis Nicolas Philippe) Auguste (1777-1841)
French painter, writer on art, and traveller; he was born at the Château of La Roque d'Antheron, Bouches-du-Rhône, 19 Aug. 1777, son of (François Anne) Gaspard Palamède F. and Françoise Marthe de Milani; became Gentilhomme of the Chambre du Roi, and Director-General of Museums; he extended the Louvre and founded the Luxembourg Museum; he visited the Near East going twice to Egypt in 1817-18 and 1828 to acquire antiquities for the Louvre; he visited Upper Egypt where he conducted excavations which were directed by J. J. Rifaud

(q.v.) and in doing so came into conflict with the agents of Drovetti (q.v.) and Salt (q.v.); he published an account *Voyage dans le Levant*, Paris, 1819; he was hostile to Champollion (q.v.); he died in Paris, 23 Feb. 1841; his daughter married Marcellus (q.v.).

La Grande Enc. 17, 777; Belzoni, i, 389, 392; Carré, i, 196-205; Champollion, i, passim; Hilmy, i, 163; *DBF* 14, 397-8; A. Dumaine, *Quelques oubliés de l'autre siècle*, 65-122; È. Gran-Aymerich, *Dictionnaire biographique d'archéologie 1798-1945*, 2001, incorporated in *Les Chercheurs de passé 1798-1945*, 2007, 796-7; P. Linant de Bellefonds in C. Foster, *Travellers in the Near East*, 2004, 107-34.

FORMAN, William Henry (1793-1869)
British collector; he was born in Doncaster, 13 Nov. 1793, son of William F., ironmaster, and Mary Seaton; educated at Charterhouse; he lived at Pipbrook House, Dorking, Surrey, and formed a large collection of antiquities and works of art, including many Egyptian items; this collection was begun by his elder brother, Thomas Seaton F. who had travelled in the east, and who died at Pisa, 1850, and it eventually passed together with his library and all his property to his nephew, Major Alexander Henry Browne (q.v.) by whose executors they were sold at Sotheby's - the antiquities, 19-22 June 1899, and the library, 3 July 1899; he died unmarried at Tunbridge Wells, 28 Aug. 1869.

ODNB 20, 367-8; inf. from the Browne family; Lugt 57376, 57417.

FORRER, Robert Édouard (1866-1947)
Swiss-French prehistorian; he was born in Meilen near Zurich, Switzerland, 9 Jan. 1866, son of Robert F., and Madeleine Ryhner; he studied at Strasbourg (Strassburg) and Berne where he obtained his doctorate; in 1894 he visited Egypt and undertook excavations at Akhmim on a largely Coptic site; he published these in *Mein Besuch in El-Achmim*, 1895 and *Ueber Steinzeit-Hockergraber zu Achmim, Naqada etc. in Oberägypten und über europaische Parallelfunde*, 1901; he was appointed director of the Prehistoric and Gallo-Roman Museum in Strasbourg, 1909; he died in Strasbourg, 9 April 1947.

Rev. arch. 6e serie 39 (1952), 95-98; inf. H. De Meulenaere; B. Schnitzler, *Robert Forrer (1866-1947) archéologue, écrivain et antiquaire*, 1999.

FORRER, (Fritz) Rudolph (1896-1974)
British dealer in antiquities; he was born in Chiselhurst, 14 Jan. 1896, son of the Swiss-British numismatist Leonard Forrer, who had been in charge of the London numismatic and antiquarian dealers Spink and Son's coin dept. since 1889, and Aline Hermance Rohrer; he was the younger brother of the numismatic dealer Leonard Steyning Forrer; he trained as an engineer in Switzerland before joining his father and brother in 1920 to work at Spink and Son; he was responsible for Spink's antiquities division from the 1920s until 1959, and was closely involved with American collectors such as J. P. Getty and Albert Gallatin (q. v.), as well as the Brooklyn Museum and other museums; he was general manager of Spink, 1959-61; he died in Sidcup, 10 June 1974.

Inf. Albany Park Baptist Church; *Times*, 12 June, 1974 (death notice); *Numismatic Circular* Sept. 1974, 340; *Numismatic Chronicle* 1974, ii.; *British Numismatic Journal* 2003, 192, 203; *Historisches Lexikon der Schweiz* 4, 615; inf. T. Hardwick.

FORSSKÅL, Pehr (1732-1763)
Swedish botanist; born in Helsingfors (Helsinki), 11 Jan. 1732, son of Johan F., a Lutheran vicar, and Margareta Kolbeck; his family moved to Sweden in 1741; he was educated at the University of Uppsala, studying Oriental languages from 1742 and botany with Linnaeus, and at Göttingen, 1753-6; PhD, 1756; he then obtained a post of private tutor but left Sweden in 1760 for political reasons; he joined the Danish expedition to Arabia with Niebuhr (q.v.) in 1761; on the way to Arabia, he stayed with the expedition in Egypt, mainly in Cairo, from 26 Sept. 1761 to 8 Oct. 1762; in his diary and other manuscripts which were preserved, he describes several interesting subjects seen in Egypt; especially those relating to botany and agriculture; his posthumously published *Flora Aegyptiaco-Arabica* is the first modern survey of the Egyptian and Arabian flora; died in Yerim, Yemen, 11 July 1763.

Resa till Lycklige Arabien. Petrus Forsskåls Dagbok 1761-1763, Uppsala, 1950; T. Hansen, *Arabia Felix*, London, 1964; B. J. Peterson, 'Swedish Travellers in Egypt during the period 1700-1850', *Opuscula Atheniensia* vii (Lund, 1967), 11-12; F. N. Hepper and I. Friis, *The Plants of Pehr Forsskål's 'Flora Aegyptiaco-Arabica'*, 1994, 1-25.

FOŘTOVÁ-ŠÁMALOVÁ (née KROPFOVÁ), Pavla (1886-1974)
Czechoslovak Egyptologist and artist; she was born in Prague, 23 June 1886, daughter of Jan E. Kropf and Pavla Antonie Karolina Kavalier; after travelling through the Near East and North Africa, she began her studies of Egyptology as an adult at Charles University in Prague under Lexa (q.v.), 1923; her specialization

was in the creative art of the ancient Egyptians; from 1925, she devoted her interest to that of ornaments, which she studied in several museums in Europe (Vienna, Berlin, Leiden and London); during her stay in Egypt in 1930, she copied ornaments directly from temples and cemeteries, especially from those in Thebes; she also worked in the Cairo Museum, where she received help from Jaroslav Černý (q.v.); in 1930, in the National Museum in Prague, she exhibited approximately 354 artifacts from prehistory to Roman times in 174 cases; the exhibition was repeated in 1948, and the catalogue was entitled *Exhibition of Egyptian ornament in color drawing* her other publication, with text by Milada Vilímková (q.v.) was *Egyptian Ornament*, 1963; she died in Prague, 4 March 1974.

Inf. J. Ruzová; J. Ruzová, *Gött. Misz.* 152 (1996), 97-8.

FOSTER, John Lawrence (1930-2011)
American Egyptologist; he was born in Chicago, 11 Nov. 1930, son of Robert E. F. and Dorothy R. Lockwood; he was educated at Kalamazoo College where he received his BA and then Harvard University; after army service, he studied at the University of Michigan; MA, PhD, 1961; he became Professor of American literature at Roosevelt University in Chicago, 1966-94 and also served as chairman of the English Dept.; he studied at the Oriental Institute of Chicago under Wilson (q.v.), Hughes (q.v.), Baer (q.v.), Wente, and Johnson and served as a research associate, 1996-2011; he also held the post of editor of *JARCE*; his special field of interest was ancient Egyptian literature and poetry; he published *Love Songs of the New Kingdom*, 1974; *Echoes of Egyptian Voices: an Anthology of ancient Egyptian Poetry*, 1992; *Thought Couplets in the Tale of Sinuhe*, 1993; with S. Hollis, *Hymns, Prayers and Songs: an Anthology of ancient Egyptian lyric Poetry*, 1995; with L. Pinch Brock, *The Shipwrecked Sailor*, 1998; *Ancient Egyptian Literature: an Anthology*, 2001; he died at Evanston, Ill., 25 Jan. 2011.

Internet obit (F. Scalf); inf. F. Scalf; R Leprohon, *Journal of American Archaeology* 47 (2011), 1-2 (portr.); *JSSEA* 42 (2015-6), xi-xvii (A. Foster), (portr.), xviii-xxiii (bibl.).

FOUCART, Georges (1865-1943)
French Egyptologist; he was born at Versailles, 11 Dec. 1865, son of Paul F., a classical scholar and the Director of the French School in Athens; he was trained by his father and later attended classes at the École des Hautes Études; he first visited Egypt with his father when his enthusiasm was at once aroused; he was appointed by de Morgan (q.v.) Inspector of Antiquities in Lower Egypt; from 1892 to 1894 he visited all the sites in his district; Professor of Ancient Hist., University of Bordeaux, 1897, and of the History of Religions at Aix-en-Provence, 1903; D.Ph., 1910; Director of IFAO, 1915-28; he published many important articles in journals, his speciality being the history of religions; *Histoire de l'ordre lotiforme*, 1897; *Histoire des religions et méthode comparative*, 1912; *Tombes thébaines: nécropole de Dirâ Abû-Naga, Le Tombeau d'Amonmos*, 1935; he also contributed to Hastings *Enc. of Religion and Ethics*; he died in Zamalek, 18 May 1943.

BIÉ 26 (1944), 21-30 (É. Drioton); *Chron. d'Ég.* 21 (1946), 81-7 (É. Drioton); *ASAE* 44 (1944) 2-13 (portr.) (bibl.) (J. Leibovitch); E. Gran-Aymerich, *Dictionnaire biographique d'archéologie 1798-1945*, 2001, incorporated in *Les Chercheurs de passé 1798-1945*, 2007, 7799-800.

FOULD, Achille (1800-1867)
French statesman and art-collector; he was born in Paris, 17 Nov. 1800, son of Baer Leon F. a Jewish banker, and Charlotte Brollen; elected to the Acad. des Beaux-Arts, 1857; Ministre des Finances, 1861-7; he collected antiquities and bought many lots at the Anastasi Sale of 1857; his Egyptian antiquities were acquired by the Louvre in 1860; he died in Tarbes, 5 Oct. 1867.

Rev. de l'Art, 43, 1168; *DBF* 14, 663-4.

FOUQUET, Daniel Marie (1850-1914)
French physician; he was born in Doue-la-Fontaine, Saumur, 16 March 1850, son of Daniel F. and Arsène Desirée Lieutand; he studied medicine in Paris; he made two journeys to S. America, then settled in Cairo, 1881, where he rendered important service in the cholera outbreak in 1883; Maspero (q.v.) enlisted his service to examine the royal mummies (*Momies royales*, 773-82); he published a memoir on embalming full of erroneous observations and inferences (*BIÉ* 1896, 89); he formed a fine collection of antiquities, particularly rich in bronzes which was sold in Paris, 12-14 and 19-20 June 1922 (608 lots); he died in Cairo, Aug. 1914.

BIÉ 5 ser. 8, 295; Daressy, *Les Antiquités de la Collection Fouquet*, 1922; Lugt 83858; J. Buikstra and C. Roberts (eds), *The Global History of Palaeopatholgy: Pioneers and Prospects*, 2012, 211 (B. Baker and M. Judd).

FOURIER, (*Baron*) **Jean Baptiste Joseph** (1768-1830)
French mathematician and physicist; he was born in Auxerre, 21 March 1768, son of Joseph F. and Edmée Germaine Lebègue; he came from a poor family and was left an orphan at eight, so that he was sent to the military school of the town by the Bishop of Auxerre; here he had a brilliant career but was unable to join the artillery as he had no family influence, so he became a novice at a monastery; political events again changed the course of his career after 1789, and he found public life opened to him; he became secretary to the Acad. des Sciences and a member of Napoleon's Commission; he was made perpetual secretary of the Cairo Institute on arrival in Egypt in Aug. 1798; just before Napoleon left Egypt Fourier was made head of the two expeditions sent to Upper Egypt; he returned to France, Sept. 1801, and Napoleon made him Prefect of Isère, 1802, where he undertook important public works; he also worked on assembling the huge mass of material for the great *Description de l'Égypte*, and wrote the historical introduction and the account of the astronomical monuments; on the restoration of the monarchy he went to Paris, 1816, where he died 16 May 1830 and was buried in Père Lachaise cemetery; the town of Auxerre erected a statue to him in 1849.

La Grande Enc. 17, 908-9; Carré, i, 120 etc.; Hilmy, i, 238; *DBF* 14, 778-9.

FOURMONT, Claude Louis (1703-1780)
French scholar and traveller; he was born in Cormeilles-en-Parisis, 1703; he accompanied his uncle Michel Fourmont on his travels, and also went to Egypt in 1746 with Lironcourt, the newly appointed French Consul in Cairo; he was interpreter to the Bibliothèque du Roi; he published *Description historique et géographique des plaines d'Héliopolis et de Memphis*, 1755; unable to obtain adequate funds for the publication of his work he spent the rest of his life in poverty; his MSS are in the Bibl. Nat.; he died 4 June 1780.

Carré, i, 64; Hilmy, i. 238 (confusion with Étienne F.); *Larousse XIX-cent.* 8. 680; *NBG* 18, 370; *DBF* 14, 785; Lamy, 194-7.

FOURMONT, Étienne (1683-1745)
French orientalist and Sinologist; he was born in Herblay, Saint-Denis, 23 June 1683; member of the Acad.; FRS, 1738; Professor of Arabic, Collège de France; he travelled in the East, and published *Réflexions critiques sur les histoires des anciens peuples, jusqu'au temps de Cyrus*, 1735; he was the elder brother of Michel F., Professor of Syriac, Coll. de France, and uncle of Claude Louis Fourmont.; his MSS are partly in the Bibl. Nat., Paris, and partly at Munich; he died in Paris, 18 Dec. 1745.

Carré, i, 63-4; Hilmy, i. 238; *NBG* 18, 354; *DBF* 14, 785-6.

FOWLER, (*Sir*) **John** (1817-1898)
British civil engineer; he was born at Wadsley Hall near Sheffield, 15 July 1817, son of John F., land surveyor, and Elizabeth Swann; appointed Engineer-in-Chief, Forth Bridge, 1882-90; created Bart., 1890; in 1869 he visited Egypt to advise the Khedive Ismail on railway development in which he had played a prominent part in England, and was chief engineering adviser in Egypt for 8 years from 1871; he projected railway and irrigation works in Egypt and the Sudan; President Inst. Civil Eng., 1865; KCMG, 1885; although not an archaeologist his association with Egypt aroused his interest in Egyptology and he was elected Pres. of the EEF in 1887, which office he held until his death, which occurred in Bournemouth, 20 Nov. 1898.

ODNB 20, 585-7; *DNB* Suppl. ii, 233; *EB; WWW* i, 256; L. T. Mackay, *Life of Sir John Fowler*, 1900.

FOX, Robert (1798-1843)
British surgeon and antiquary; he was born in Huntington, 22 March 1798, son of John F., a cabinet-maker, and Frances Maples; MRCS, 1819; he practised in Huntingdon and later at Godmanchester; he founded the Literary and Scientific Inst. of Huntingdon, 1841; he lectured principally on natural sciences and had an interest in history, antiquities, numismatics, and geology; FSA, 1831; he published a leaflet describing a ushabti figure with cartouches, drawn by Bonomi (q.v.); he was a friend of Dr. Lee (q.v.) of Hartwell; his collections were purchased by the Huntingdon Literary and Science Institute; he died in Godmanchester, 7 June 1843.

ODNB 20, 676; *DNB* 20, 132; *GM* n.s. 20 (1843), 99; inf. P. Saunders.

FRANKE, Detlef (1952-2007)
German Egyptologist; he was born in Lüneburg, 24 Nov. 1952; he studied at the University of Hamburg, 1972 -83; PhD, 1983; he then moved to the University of Heidelberg, 1987-91; Habilitation, 1991; he then lectured at the University of Heidelberg; he was a specialist in the history and prosopography of the Middle Kingdom; he published his thesis *Altägyptische Verwandtschaftbezeichnungen im Mittleren Reich*, 1983, *Personendaten*

aus dem Mittleren Reich (20.-16. Jahrhundert v. Chr.), 1984; his habilitation *Das Heiligtum des Heqaib auf Elephantine*, 1994 and contributed to D. Polz, *Die Pyramidenanlage des Königs Nub-cheper-re Intef in Dra Abu el Naga*, 2003; *Egyptian Stelae in the British Museum from the 13th-17th Dynasties* I, edited M. Marée, 2013; he died at Hofheim, 2 Sept. 2007.

JEA 93 (2007), ix; *ZÄS* 135 (2008), V-XI (portr. and bibl.) (H. W. Fischer-Elfert). *Journal of Egyptian History* 1 (2008), 207-8 (A. Gnirs).

FRANKFORT, Henri (1897-1954)
Dutch Egyptologist, archaeologist, and orientalist; he was born in Amsterdam 24 Feb. 1897, son of Benjamin Philippe F., a merchant in Near Eastern trade, and Mathilde Israels; he studied history at the University of Amsterdam from 1919-21; MA, 1921; he then transferred to University College London where he took an MA under Sir Flinders Petrie (q.v.), 1924; PhD University of Leiden, 1927; he married 1. 1923 (m. diss. 1952) Henriette Groenewegen, 2. Enriqueta Harris; he served in the Netherlands Army 1915-17; in 1922 he joined the staff of Petrie's expedition to Egypt at Qau el-Kebir and later travelled throughout the Near East; in 1924-5 he was a student at the British School of Archaeology in Athens and between 1925 and 1929 the director of excavations of the EES, mainly at El-Amarna, Abydos, and Armant; in 1929 he was invited by Breasted (q.v.) to be field director of the Oriental Institute Iraq expedition and held this position until 1937; in 1932 he was appointed Research Professor of Oriental Archaeology at the Oriental Institute of the Univ. of Chicago, also holding the position of Extraordinary Prof. in the History and Archaeology of the Ancient Near East in the Univ. of Amsterdam to 1938; he was also chairman of the Dept. of Oriental Languages and Literatures at Chicago; in 1949 he became director of the Warburg Institute and Prof. of the History of Preclassical Antiquity in the Univ. of London; he was a Correspondent of the Royal Netherlands Academy of Sciences, Fellow of the Royal Anthropological Institute of Great Britain and Ireland, FSA, FBA, Member of the American Oriental Soc., Member of the American Philosophical Soc. and of the EES; he published 15 books and monographs and contributed parts to about 20 more, and 73 articles for journals as well as many book reviews; see especially *Studies in Early Pottery of the Near East*, 2 vols. 1924-7; *Cylinder Seals*, 1939; *Ancient Egyptian Religion: An Interpretation*, 1948; *Kingship and the Gods*, 1948; *The Art and Architecture of the Ancient Orient*, 1954; the *Mural painting of El-'Amarneh*, 1929; the *Cenotaph of Seti I at Abydos*, with A. de Buck and B. Gunn, 2 vols. 1933; *The City of Akhenaten*, vol. ii, with J. D. S. Pendlebury, 1933; *Before Philosophy*, 1946; he died in London, 16 July 1954.

Burlington Magazine, London, 96, no. 620 (Nov. 1954), 353-4 (R. D. Barnett); *Chron. d'Ég.* 29 (1954), 276 (anon.); *Ex Oriente Lux* 13 (1953-4), 269-70 (J. M. A. Janssen); *JNES* 14 (1955), 1-3 Memorial Issue (Pinhas Delougaz and Thorkild Jacobsen) (portr.) (bibl.) pp. 4-13; *Nature*, vol. 174, no. 4425 (21 Aug. 1954), 337-8 (V. G. Childe); *Orientalia* 23 (1954), 448 (A. Pohl); ; *Revue d'Assyriologie* 48 (1954), 206 (M. Lambert); *BiOr* 12 (1955), 89-90 (portr.) (A. W. Byvank); *WWW; WWWA* 3, 298; M. van Loon, *"Hans" Frankfort's Earlier Years*, 1995; È. Gran-Aymerich, *Dictionnaire biographique d'archéologie 1798-1945*, 2001, incorporated in *Les Chercheurs de passé 1798-1945*, 2007, 804-6.

FRANKS, (*Sir*) **Augustus Wollaston** (1826-1897)
British curator and collector; he was born in Geneva, March 20 1826, son of Frederick F., a naval officer, and Frederica Sebright; he was educated at Eton and Trinity College Cambridge (BA, 1849); he was appointed to the Department of Antiquities at the British Museum, 1851, and served at the museum until his retirement in 1896; he was elected FSA, 1853, and its Director, Vice-President and President (1892-7); knighted, 1894; his energy and numerous donations of objects were largely responsible for the expansion of the museum's Oriental, Mediaeval, Ethnographic, and Prehistoric collections and departments; although it was not a major interest of his, he donated Egyptian material to the museum throughout his career, and at his death bequeathed his other collections, which included Egyptian jewellery and amulets, to the BM; he died in London, 21 May 1897.

ODNB 20, 809-11; M. Caygill and J. Cherry (eds), *A W Franks: Nineteenth-century collecting and the British Museum*, 1997.

FRANTSOV, Yuri Pavlovitch (1903-1969)
Russian philologist; he was born in Moscow, 18 Sept./10 Oct. 1903; he undertook philological studies at Leningrad University in linguistics and history of literature completed in 1924; lecturer at Leningrad University, 1931-45; director of the Institute of International Relations, 1945-9; from 1949 a high functionary in the Foreign Office and in the Communist Party; Corresponding Member of the Soviet Academy of Sciences 1958, member 1964; in the

early stage of his activity he published in Russian Egyptological studies, concerned with the theme of the Island of the snakes in ancient Egyptian fairy-tales, 1929; with the history of Egyptian autobiographic texts, 1930; and with Egyptian tales about High Priests, 1935; and later a work on religion *U istokv religii i svobodomysliya*, 1959; and posthumously *Religiya drevnego Egipta*, 1976; he died in Moscow, 18 April 1969.

Great Sov. Enc. 28, 383; M. Korostovtsev in H. Heinen, *Die Geshichte des Altertums im Spiegel der sowjetischen Forschung*, 1980, 33-5; inf. J. Śliwa.

FRANZ, *(Pasha)* **Julius** (1831-1915)
German engineer and architect; he was born in Springen, now in Hesse, 25 Aug. 1831; he studied mathematics in Karlsruhe, 1848-51 and later architecture in Vienna, 1851-4; he went to Egypt in 1855; he was engineer in the army and architect to the Khedives Said and Ismail; from 1879 he was in charge of construction at the Wakf Ministry; he founded the Museum of Arab Art in Cairo, 1883, and was Director until he left the Government service in 1887; he inaugurated the Comité de Conservation des Monuments de l'Art Arabe; also published works on the Islamic architecture of Egypt and Andalusia; he was made Bey in 1869 and Pasha in 1885; he died in Graz, 20 March 1915.

Erman, 209, 276; inf. by Dr. P. E. Kahle; M. Stern, 'Österreich-Ungarns Beitrag zur Architektur in Ägypten am Beispiel von drei Architekten' in *Österreich und Ägypten*, 1993, 54-56.

FRASER, George Willoughby (1866-1923)
British civil engineer; he was baptised at Mereworth, Kent 5 Aug. 1866, son of Major General Sir Thomas Fraser and Matilda Wildman; he assisted Petrie (q.v.) in his excavations in the Fayum, 1889, and was attached to the EEF Archaeological Survey under Newberry (q.v.), for which he drew plans etc. at Beni Hasan and El-Bersha; with M. W. Blackden (q.v.) he copied and privately printed the hieratic inscriptions at the quarries of Hatnub; in 1897 he presented a limestone door-socket dated to the 30th year of Amenemhat II to the British Museum (EA 1236); he published articles in *PSBA*; FSA, 1893-6, resigned, and re-elected 1904, resigned again, 1906; his scarab collection was acquired by von Bissing (q.v.); it was published as *A Catalogue of Scarabs belonging to George Fraser*, 1900; he died in Bath, 24 Nov. 1923; part of his archive was acquired by the University of Milan in 2004.

Newberry, *El Bersheh*, ii. 55; Newberry Corr.; Petrie, 106, 107.

FRAZER, Kenneth John (1914-2012)
New Zealand archaeologist; he was born in Auckland, New Zealand, 28 July 1914, son of Sir Francis Vernon Frazer, a judge and Nina Jessie Black; he was educated at Wellesley College, Wellington, NZ; her served in World War II, 1939-45 rising to the rank of Major; MC; he then joined the Colonial Service, eventually becoming a district officer in Palestine and Gambia; he retired from the service for a second career as administrator, surveyor, and draughtsman at excavations in Greece, Turkey at Sardis, and Egypt at Qasr Ibrim, 1963, 1966 and 1969, and at Saqqara, 1966-71, 1974-9, 1981-8, 1991, 1994-6; FSA; he contributed to *The Sacred Animal Necropolis at North Saqqara: The Main Temple Complex*, 2006 and a chapter on architecture in G. T. Martin, *The Tomb of Maya and Meryt* I, 2012 as well as plans in other EES final reports; he died at Te Puke, New Zealand, 23 Nov. 2012.

EES Newsletter 11 Dec 2012 (H. S. Smith); family information.

FREDIANI, Domenico Ermenegildo (1783-1823)
Italian soldier and traveller; he was born in Serravezza near Milan, 1783; after serving in the Neapolitan army, he visited Egypt in 1817, where he met Belzoni (q.v.) and also accompanied Lord Belmore's (q.v.) party from Aswan; he was present at the opening by Belzoni at the Second Pyramid at Giza in 1818; in early 1820 he went to Siwa with Drovetti (q.v.) and later Palestine with Belmore; then he joined Ismail Pasha's expedition to Sennar, acting as tutor and dragoman to the Pasha; while at Sennar his mind gave way, and he suffered from the delusion that he was a prince; he was sent back to Cairo where he died insane in 1823.

Belzoni, i, 414, 420, 425; Henniker, 38; Hill, 129; Linant Diary; Salt, ii, 205; *Bollettino della Societa Geografica Italiana* 1891, 90-125; 295-324, 397-406; Dewachler *BIFAO* 69 (1920) 143-6; *Soleb* I, 15 note 16.

FREEMAN, Geoffrey James Evelyn (1921-2001)
Canadian Egyptologist; he was born in London, 26 Sept. 1921, son of Geoffrey James F., of Irish extraction, and Rosina Warwick; he was educated at Trinity College, Dublin and later enlisted in the British Army serving in India; he emigrated to Toronto and had a successful career as insurance broker; he had long been interested in Egyptology and took courses at the University of Toronto under R. Williams (q.v.) and D. B. Redford; in 1970 he was instrumental in the founding of the Society for the Study of Egyptian Antiquities and in the beginning of Canadian archaeological activity in Egypt initially at Thebes which led to the

foundation of the Canadian Institute in Egypt; a volume of *JSSEA* 25 (1995) was dedicated to him; he was the editor of the *SSEA Newsletter* and later *Journal* and helped to pioneer lecture series and colloquia; he died at Toronto, 3 Dec. 2001.

SSEA Newsletter Jan 2002, 1-2 (portr.) (T. Miosi); *JSSEA* 25 (1995), v-vi (G. E. Kadish).

FREER, Charles Lang (1856-1919)
American manufacturer and art collector; he was born in Kingston, NY, 25 Feb. 1856, son of Jacob F. and Phoebe Jane Townsend; he was educated Ulster County, NY; Hon. MA Michigan University; he visited Egypt three time between 1906-09 and formed a large and valuable art collection which included Egyptian antiquities purchased from Kelekian (q.v.), Nahman (q.v.) and 1388 glass objects from Dattari (q.v.); he presented his collection to the Smithsonian Inst., Washington, together with $1,000,000 for a building; he is also remembered for the valuable collection of Coptic MSS which he formed, which was published by W. H. Worrell (q.v.), 1923; he died in New York, 25 Sept. 1919.

WWWA i, 425; Worell, *The Coptic MSS in the Freer Coll.*, N.Y., 1923; A. Gunter, *A Collector's Journey. Charles Lang Freer and Egypt*, 2002.

FRÉRET, Nicolas (1688-1749)
French scholar; he was born in Paris, 15 Feb. 1688, son of Charles Antoine F. and Anne Antoinette Améline; he attempted to decipher hieroglyphic writing, and published *Essai sur les hiéroglyphes scientifiques*, 1744, as a commentary on Warburton's (q.v.) work and other works dealing with ancient astronomy, weights and measures, etc.; he died in Paris, 8 March 1749.

BIFAO 5 (1905), 82; Hilmy, i, 248; *DBF* 14, 1219-70; M. V. David in *Journal des Savants* (1978), 241-56.

FREUD, Sigmund (1856-1939)
Austrian psychoanalyst and collector; he was born in Freiberg, Moravia, 6 May 1856, son of Jacob F. and Amalie Nathansohn; he worked in Vienna as a consultant in nervous complaints, and created the discipline of psychoanalysis; he formed a large collection of antiquities and had an abiding interest in archaeology, often using archaeological practice as a metaphor for the way psychoanalysis uncovered hidden layers and origins; in *Der Mann Moses und die monotheistische Religion*, 1939, he interpreted Judaism as deriving from Akhenaten's cult of the Aten; he fled Austria in 1938, taking his library and collection with him, and settled in London; his house and collections are now preserved as the Freud Museum; he died in Hampstead, 23 Sept. 1939.

ODNB 21, 3-11; J. Forrester, 'Freud and Collecting', in J. Elsner and R. Cardinal (eds.) *The Cultures of Collecting*, 1994, 224-51; D. Montserrat, *Akhenaten. History, Fantasy, and Ancient Egypt*, 2000, 95-108; J. Burke, *The Sphinx on the Table. Sigmund Freud's Art Collection and the Development of Psychoanalysis*, 2006; B. Garnier (ed.), *Rodin, Freud, collectionneurs: la passion à l'oeuvre*, 2008.

FREY, Johann Jakob (1813-1865)
Swiss painter and traveller; born in Basel, 27 Jan. 1813, son of Samuel F., painter and engraver, and Katharina Gysin; he was trained under his father and the historical painter Hieronymus Hess; he went to Paris and earned a living by restoring pictures for Paris art dealers and working at a lithographer's, in his spare time teaching himself by copying 17th century Dutch landscapes in the Louvre; he returned to Basel, 1834, but soon left for Munich and from there to Rome, 1838; here he was very successful and set up his studio in the Palazzo Venezia, living in the Via S. Isidoro; Lepsius (q.v.) became a frequent visitor to his studio and recommended his friend to the Prussian government as a suitable painter to undertake landscapes and views of the archaeological sites for the Prussian expedition to Egypt, 1842; Frey went to Egypt via Naples and Malta where he joined Lepsius and arrived at Alexandria in mid-Sept.; the hardships encountered with the heat and violent sandstorms which often stopped his painting, so undermined his health that it was felt necessary to send Frey home in Aug. 1843; Lepsius recounted how after an attack by hordes of Arabs Frey was buried under the main tent and most of his work stolen, while on another occasion in camp at Giza the tents collapsed and torrents of rain water ruined their equipment; despite these set-backs he produced some of the plates used in the *Denkmäler* depicting Abu Rawash, Giza panoramas, the Step Pyramid at Saqqara etc.; he also had great success with his Egyptian subjects on his return to Europe, notably among German royalty; Frey later travelled extensively in Spain, France, Greece, Switzerland and England, and was one of the founders of the Deutsche Künstler-Verein; he married a Roman lady in 1854; he died from an attack of typhoid in Frascati, 30 Sept. 1865, and was buried in the cemetery near the Cestius Pyramid, Rome.

Exhibition Catalogue Maltzahn Gallery, 3 Cork St. London, July 1974 (portr.) (C. Haenlein); Lepsius, *Denkmäler* I, 12, 13, 15, 16-18, 36, 37; *Schweizer Lexikon* III, 668; *Schweizerisches Künstler-Lexikon* 1, 491-3; *Historisches Lexikon der Schweiz*, 4, 812.

FRIIS, Jesper (1593-1643)
Danish traveller; he was born in Hesselager, 10 Aug. 1593, son of Niels F. and Vibeke Gyldenstierne; he studied at Padua and then went on a tour to Palestine and Egypt in 1618; he brought back a number of antiquities including two stone sarcophagi; the lids were rediscovered by Zoega (q.v.) and are now in the National Museum in Copenhagen; he died in Orbaeklunde, 15 April 1643.

Dansk Biografisk Leksikon 4, 635-6; M.-L. Buhl, *Les dessins archéologiques et topographiques de l'Egypte ancienne faits par F. L. Norden 1737-1738*, 1993, 30-1.

FULLER, John (1787-1837+)
British traveller; he was born in Chesham, 13 Jan. 1787, son of Revd. John F. and Mary Stratton; he travelled to the Levant in July 1822, touring Greece and Turkey and reaching Alexandria on 6 Jan. 1819; he went south to Cairo and then on to Upper Egypt and Nubia where he encountered Belzoni (q.v.), Bankes (q.v), Beechey (q.v.) and Hyde (q.v.); he left graffiti at Abu Simbel, Kalabsha, Maharraqa, Philae, Edfu, and Deir el-Medina; he was nominated as a member of the Travellers Club, 1823 but failed to be elected and became a member of the Society of Dilettanti, 1834; he published an account of his travels, *Narrative of a Tour Through Some Parts of the Turkish Empire*, 1830; he is presumably to be identified as John Fuller of Hyde Heath, Chesham, and to be distinguished from Robert Fitzherbert Fuller (q.v.), who was in Egypt, 1817-8.

R. Morkot, *ASTENE Bulletin* 65 (2015), 19-21; 69 (2016), 22; R. de Keersmaecker, *ASTENE Bulletin* 64 (2015), 21-4.

FULLER, (*Revd*) **Robert Fizherbert** (1794-1849)
British traveller; he was born in East Grinstead, 11 Aug. 1794, son of John Trayton F. of Ashdown House, Sussex, and Anne Eliott; he was educated at Oxford, BA, 1817; MA, 1819; he presented a mummy and its coffins and a royal head, all said to have been acquired in Thebes, to the Devon and Exeter Institution (now in the Royal Albert Memorial Museum, Exeter) in 1819; he is presumably to be identified with the Mr. Fuller who travelled with Straton (q.v) in 1817 and left a graffiti in Philae; he became curate at Lingfield and Crowhurst, 1819, and incumbent of Chalvington, 1836; he died at Leamington Spa, 22 Aug. 1849.

R. Morkot in C. Price et al., *Mummies, Magic and Medicine in Ancient Egypt,* 2016, 355-70.

GAÁL, Ernö (1941-2005)
Hungarian orientalist; he was born in Szombathely, 19 July 1941; he was educated at Eötvös Loraánd University, Budapest from 1961 where he studied Ancient Near Eastern history; he joined the staff of the Ancient Near Eastern History Dept. in 1970; in 2003 he succeeded Kákosy (q.v.) as head of the renamed Dept. of Egyptology; he also directed the Institute of Classical Studies at the university, 2002-5; he served on the faculty senate and as Vice-Dean of the Faculty; although primarily an Assyriologist, he took part in the Hungarian expedition in Egypt at the tomb of Djehutymose (TT32) from 1983 and directed his own research at several other tombs from 1996; a joint volume of studies dedicated to him and two others *A Tribute to Excellence* was published in 2002; apart from his Assyriological books and articles, he published *A sör as ókari Egyiptomban és Mezopotámiában (Beer in Ancient Egypt and Mesopotamia)*, 1988; *Az egyiptomi vallás (Egyptian religion)*, 1988; and *The Stamped Bricks in TT 32*, 1993; he died in Casablanca, Morocco, 8 Aug. 2005.

Acta Antiqua 46 (2006), 1-2 (T. Bács); T. Baács, *A Tribute to Excellence*, 2002, 13-18 (bibl.).

GABALLA, Gaballa Ali (1939-2012)
Egyptian Egyptologist; he was born at Kufour al-Raml, Menufiya in the Delta, 10 Feb 1939, son of Ali Gaballa, a farmer; he was studied Egyptology at the University of Cairo, 1957-61 under Fakhry (q.v.), Abu Bakr (q.v.), and Mattha (q.v.); BA, 1961; he worked briefly in the Centre of Documentation and then as an assistant in the Dept. of Egyptology, Cairo University; he continued his studies at the University of Liverpool, 1963-7 under Fairman (q.v.); PhD, 1967; on his return he became a curator in the Cairo Museum, 1967-9 and editor of the Annales du Service; he returned to the Dept. of Egyptology, Cairo University as a lecturer, 1969-74, associate professor, 1974-9 and full professor, 1979; he held the post of vice-dean in the Faculty of archaeology from 1981; he became Secretary-General of the Supreme Council of Antiquities, 1997-2002; he also lectured at the Universities of Rabat, Kuwait and West Florida; he took part in excavations at Giza and Memphis; apart from articles and works and translations in Arabic, he published his thesis *Narrative in Egyptian Art*, 1976; *The Memphite Tomb-Chapel of Mose*, 1977; with others, *Glimpses of Ancient Egypt*, 1979; *The History and Culture of Nubia*, 1997, *Le grand Temple d'Abou Simbel* I. *La Facade (A-E)*, 2001; *Nubia Museum*, 2003; a volume of studies was published in his honour, O. El-Aguizy and M. Sherif Ali, *Echoes of Eternity*, 2010; he died at Alexandria, 15 April 2012.

O. El-Aguizy and M. Sherif Ali, *Echoes of Eternity*, 2010, 9-10, 11-13 (bibl.).

GABET, Charles Edmond (1818-1869)
French Egyptologist; he was born in Lyons(?) in 1818, and became assistant to Mariette (q.v.); he acted as inspector and superintendent of excavations, and as assistant conservator in the Bulaq Museum; he was appointed about 1859, but nothing is yet known of his previous history; a long letter from him to Mariette and dated Qurna, 16 Dec. 1862, reporting on his work in the Theban necropolis and temples, was published in *Rec. Trav.* 12. 215-18; he died in 1869.

Bibl. Ég. 4, 326-7; 18, xci, cvi; E. David, *Mariette Pacha 1821-1881*, 1994, 110; *Des dieux, des tombeaux, un savant. En Égypte, sur les pas de Mariette Pacha*, 2004, 20.

GABRA, Sami (1892-1979)
Egyptian archaeologist; he was born at Abnoub near Asyut, 24 April 1892, son of Gayed G.; he was educated at the American Colleges of Asyut and Beirut and studied law at the University of Bordeaux, 1911-9; he taught law at Cairo University, but his interest in ancient Egypt led him to study under Ahmad Kamal (q.v.) at the École Normale in Cairo; he then continued these studies at the University of Liverpool, 1923-5 and the Sorbonne, 1925-8; he was appointed a curator at the Cairo Museum, 1928-30 and Professor of Ancient Egyptian History at Cairo University, 1930-52; he excavated at Deir Tassa, 1929 and Tura, 1931, but devoted the rest of his career to work at Tuna el-Gebel, 1931-52 interrupted only by World War II; he later dug in 1957 at Dahshur; he was a founder member of the Société d'Archéologie Copte in 1934 and founder and Director of the Institute of Coptic Studies, 1953-79; he was visiting professor at the Oriental Institute, Chicago, 1952-3; apart from articles on his excavations, he was the author of *Peintures à fresques et scènes peintes à Hermoupolis-Ouest (Touna el-Gebel)*, 1954 (with E. Drioton) and *Chez les derniers adorateurs du Trismegiste*, 1971; he died in Masr el-Gedida, Heliopolis, 19 May 1979.

BSAC 24 (1979-82), 128-30 (M. B. Ghali); *AfO* 27, 332 (H. Brunner); *Bolletino d'Informazione* 50 (1979), 20; *NARCE* 108 (1979), 7; D. Abou-Ghazi, *Vie et Travaux* II *Sami Gabra* (1984), 11-39 (portr. and bibl.); Liverpool University records.

GADDIS, Abdallah Attiya (1889-1972)
Egyptian photographer; he was born in Tod, Upper Egypt, to a Coptic family, 1889; as a young man he worked from 1897 as an assistant to a photographer in Luxor, apparently with A. Beato (q. v.), before setting up in his own right, *c*.1907; in 1912 he entered into partnership with another Copt, Georges Seif (died 1942); Gaddis and Seif took numerous photographs of Theban tombs and monuments; Gaddis and his descendents also owned shops, bookshops, and a hotel in Luxor; a collection of glass negatives by Gaddis and Seif are now in Chicago House, Luxor; others are still in family possession; he died in Luxor in 1972.

G. Réveillac in *Voyages en Égypte*, Geneva 2003, 279-285; G. Réveillac, *Cahiers de Karnak* 11 (2003), 515-34.

GADSBY, John (*c*.1809-1893)
British traveller and collector; he was born in Manchester, *c*.1809, son of William G., a Baptist minister in Manchester and Elizabeth Marvin; he became a printer and publisher in Manchester and later in Bouverie Street, London, 1846-90; he visited Egypt frequently for his health in 1847, 1850-1, 1852-3, 1855-6, and 1859-60 travelling as far south as Wadi Halfa on two occasions; his small collection of Egyptian antiquities was sold to the British Museum in 1861; he published *My Wanderings in the East* 2 vols., 1855 and 1860; he died in Brighton, 12 Oct. 1893.

Boase, V, 378.

GAILLARD, Claude Antoine (1861-1945)
French naturalist; he was born in Villeurbanne, Rhône, 13 Jan. 1861, son of Claude G. and Marie Lagrange; he began life in commerce, but through the introduction of the anthropologist F. Chantre of the Lyons Museum, he joined its staff as preparator; with Loret's (q.v.) encouragement he studied at the Faculté des Sciences, and accompanied Loret to Egypt; he made a special study of the ancient fauna of Egypt and collaborated with Lortet and Daressy in works on this subject in the *Cairo Cat. Gen.* series and the *Archives* of Lyons Museum; he succeeded Lortet (q.v.) as Director of the Museum and retired in 1939 after 53 years' service; he was President of the Soc. Linnéene de Lyon, 1918; he published *La Faune momifiée de l'antique Égypte, Cairo Cat.*, 1905; *La Faune momifiée de l'ancienne Égypte (et recherches anthropologiques)* 2 vols., Lyons, 1905-9; *Recherches sur les poissons représentés dans quelques tombeaux égyptiens de l'Ancien Empire,* etc., *Mém. IFAO* 51, 1923; also articles in journals such as *ASAE*; he died in Lyons, 3 Feb. 1945.

DBF 15, 78-9.

GALARZA Y PÉREZ CASTAÑEDA, Vicente de (1881?-1938)
Spanish excavator; dates given for birth include 1878, 1887 and 1881; he relocated to Egypt between 1903 and 1906 (allegedly for 'spiritual' reasons); he obtained concession to excavate at Giza between 1907 and 1909, with supervision by Kamal (q.v.) and Daressy (q.v.), including the clearance of the tomb of Queen Khamerernebti (the so-called 'Galarza Tomb'); he then worked as a lawyer until appointed lecturer in philosophy at the Egyptian University, Cairo in 1913 (also given as 1914 or 1915) to 1920; at Teachers' Training College 1920-32; he died in 1938.

J. Puig Montada, *Anales del Seminario de Historia de la Filosofía* 22 (2005), 271-3.

GALASSI, Giuseppe (1890-1957)
Italian journalist, archaeologist and prehistorian; born Argenta, Ferrara, 12 Jan. 1890, son of Pietro G. and Erminia Martini, and was the son-in-law of G. Foucart (q.v.) who encouraged his interest in Egyptian prehistory; he founded two newspapers and a periodical in Egypt; he published a study on the subject of the origins of Egyptian civilization, *Tehenu e le origini mediterranee della civiltà egizia*, 1942, in which he sought to trace these origins and the source of Egyptian culture to Libya; in a further work, *Preistoria e protostoria mediterranea*, 1955, based on the predynastic art and painting preserved in the Turin Museum, he advanced further evidence in support of his thesis; he died in Rome, 29 July 1957.

Chron. d'Ég. 32 (1957), 267 (anon.); *Chi è* 1948, 411-2.

GALLATIN, Albert (1881-1965)
American collector; he was born in New York, 8 Jan. 1880, son of Frederic G., a descendant of Albert G. of Geneva, banker and later Treasury Secretary of the United States, and Almy Goelet Gerry; he inherited money and speculated on the stock exchange; he visited Egypt as a child of ten and bought his first Egyptian antiquities there, later forming a large collection; he also collected Classical, Near Eastern, Peruvian, and Islamic material; he published his collection of Greek vases in the *Corpus Vasorum Antiquorum*, 1925, and published *Syracusan Dekadrachms of the Euainetos Type*, 1930; his autobiography contains accounts of the dealers active in the 1920s-1950s; he donated material to the Brooklyn and Metropolitan Museums; after his death his Egyptian collections were purchased by the Metropolitan Museum; his other collections were sold at auction in London (Sotheby's, June 13 and 27 1966); he is often confused with his cousin Albert Eugene Gallatin (1881–1952), painter and collector of modern art; he died in New York, 1Sept. 1965.

The Saint Nicholas Society of the City of New York; Brooklyn Museum Archives; A. Gallatin, *The pursuit of happiness; the abstract and brief chronicles of the time*, 1950; *NY Times*, Sept. 2 1965; J. D. Cooney *JNES* 12 (1953) 1-19; H. Fischer, *BMMA* xxv (1966-7), 253-63.

GALTIER, (Jean Mathieu) Émile (1864-1908)
French orientalist; he was born at Millau (Aveyron), 23 Aug. 1864, son of Mathieu Emilien G. and Marie Octave Carbasse; he studied at the École des Hautes Études, and was a member of the IFAO, Cairo; he succeeded Léon Barry as Librarian of the Cairo Museum; he died in Cairo, 2 April. 1908.

Maspero, *Rapports sur la marche du Serv. des Antiq.* (1912), 279; *BIFAO* 6 (1908), 192-3.

GANNAL, Jean Nicholas (1791-1852)
French surgeon, chemist, and industrialist; he was born in Sarrelouis, 28 July 1791, son of François G.; he served in the Medical Dept. of the French Army and afterwards took up chemical research, making many improvements in technical and medical chemistry; he devoted much attention to the preservation of tissues for anatomy and to the embalming of the dead, for which he invented a new system which was widely adopted; he published *Histoire des Embaumements*, 1838, 2nd ed., Paris, 1841, in which he dealt very fully with Egyptian mummification; he died in Paris, 13 Jan. 1852.

La Grande Enc. 18, 454; *Larousse, XIXe siècle* 8, 996; *Mém. IE* 13 (1929), 16; *DBF* 15, 347-8.

GARDINER, (Sir) Alan Henderson (1879-1963)
British Egyptologist; born in Eltham, 29 March 1879, younger son of Henry John G., a wealthy businessman, and Clara Honey his wife; his brother Henry Balfour G. was the composer; he became interested in Egyptology while at school and was encouraged in this by Sir E. Wallis Budge (q.v.), W. E. Crum (q.v.), Petrie (q.v.), and Griffith (q.v.), the last of whom taught him some Egyptian philology at University College London; he was educated at Charterhouse, and before going up to Oxford attended some of Maspero's courses at the École des Hautes Études and the Collège de France, 1895-6; he wrote his first article at the age of fifteen and had it published in *Biblia*, 1895, his last being written nearly seventy years later; he read Classics, Hebrew, and Arabic at The Queen's College, Oxford, 1897-1901, there being at that time no Egyptological course in the University; he married Hedwig Rosen from Vienna, 1901, and visited Egypt for the first time that year; being endowed with sufficient income from his father Gardiner was able to pursue his studies without having to seek academic posts and also to obtain the best academic education; he lived in Berlin between 1902 and 1912 and studied philology intensively under Erman (q.v.), where he helped in the work of *Verzettelung*, making the preparatory slips for the great Egyptian dictionary, but did not attend actual classes; he was a most painstaking and systematic worker throughout his life, and he stressed his own contributions to these *Zettel* in Berlin and also to the amount he wrote then; he was made sub-editor on this dictionary project 1906-8, and held the Laycock Studentship at Worcester College, Oxford at this time, 1906-12; he visited Egypt in 1908 to see the MacIver excavations in Nubia, and on returning in 1909, he joined Weigall (q.v.) in making the Catalogue of the private Theban tombs; with N. de G. Davies (q.v.) he edited 5 vols. in the *Theban Tomb* series, and he also edited a collection of 104 reproductions by Nina M. Davies (q.v.), *Ancient Egyptian Paintings*; 3 vols., 1936; in addition he edited the first 3 vols. of the *Temple of King Sethos I at Abydos* and those of the *Egyptian Coffin Texts*; he often paid for publications himself or helped finance others; from 1912 to 1914 he was Reader in Egyptology in the University of Manchester; Research Professor in Egyptology in the University of Chicago, 1924-34, but in general did not accept University posts as he liked to work on publications without interruption; he helped to found the *JEA* to which he contributed nearly one hundred articles as well as reviews, and he edited it for several periods, 1916-21, 1934, and 1941-6; he was Hon. Secretary of the EES, 1917-20; Vice President and finally President, 1959-63; he acquired many distinctions throughout his long career, DLitt University of Oxford, 1909; Hon. DLitt Universities of Durham, 1952, Cambridge, 1956; FBA, 1929; Hon. Fellow of The Queen's College, Oxford, 1930; Member of the Institut de France, 12 April 1946; Knight Bachelor, 1948; Hon. Member of the Royal Danish Acad. of Sciences, 1942; the Bavarian Acad., 1929; the Oriental Institute of Prague, 1930; the Prussian Acad., 1935; the Philosophical Soc. of America, 1943; the Soc. Asiatique, 1946; the Institut d'Égypte, 1947; the Netherlands Acad., 1950; the American Acad., 1957; the Austrian Acad., 1958; the list of his publications is very long, the bibl. published on his seventieth birthday listing 26 Egyptological books of which he was author or part author, and 221 articles, reviews, and obituaries; his first major article was *The Installation of a Vizier*, 1904; *The Inscription of Mes*, dealing with a lawsuit in the reign of Ramesses II, 1905; he thereafter specialized in hieratic texts on papyri and ostraca, working on texts in the British Museum, Leiden, and Turin; he published *Die Klagen des Bauern*, with Vogelsang, 1908; *The Admonitions of an Egyptian Sage*, 1909; *Die Erzählung des Sinuhe und die Hirtengeschichte*, 1909; *Egyptian Hieratic Texts*, 1911; *Theban Ostraca*, with H. Thompson and J. G. Milne, 1913; *The Tomb of Amenemhet (No 82)* with Nina de G. Davies, 1915; *Notes on the Story of Sinuhe*, 1916; *The Inscriptions of Sinai* with T. E. Peet,

pt I, 1917, Rev. ed. with J. Cerny, 1952; *The Tomb of Huy, Viceroy of Nubia in the Reign of Tut'ankhamun*, with Nina de G. Davies, 1926; *Egyptian Letters to the Dead, mainly from the Old and Middle Kingdoms*, with K. Sethe, 1928; Chester Beatty (q.v.) entrusted to him the publication of the papyri he had acquired in 1928, *Description of a Hieratic Papyrus with a Mythological Story, Love Songs and other Miscellaneous Texts*, 1931; *Late Egyptian Stories*, 1932; *Le Papyrus Léopold II et le Papyrus Amherst*, which he edited with J. Capart, 1933; Third Series of *the Hieratic Papyri in the British Museum*, 1935; *The Attitude of the Ancient Egyptians to Death and the Dead*, Frazer Lecture, 1935; *Late Egyptian Miscellanies*, 1937; *Ramesside Administrative Documents*, 1940; *The Wilbour Papyrus*, 3 vols. dealing with a XXth Dynasty taxation survey, 1941-8; *Ancient Egyptian Onomastica*, 3 vols. 1947; *The Ramesseum Papyri*, 1955; *The Royal Canon of Turin*, a new treatment of the king-list published for his eightieth birthday, 1959; *The Kadesh Inscriptions of Ramesses II*, 1960; *Egypt of the Pharaohs*, a student's history of Egypt, 1961; he was assisted in his great work by a number of collaborators such as B. G. Gunn (q.v.), R. O. Faulkner (q.v.), and H. W. Fairman (q.v.); his most famous work was his *Egyptian Grammar*, 1st ed. 1927, which has gone through two further editions and which put the teaching of Middle Egyptian on an entirely new basis; but his greatest discovery was undoubtedly the recognition of the Sinaitic script and its role as an alphabetic link between the Egyptian hieroglyphic and the Semitic alphabets; Gardiner also undertook the translation of the inscriptions in the tomb of Tutankhamun; he donated objects to the British Museum, and gave to the Ashmolean Museum his large collection of ostraca and painted copies of Theban tomb paintings by Nina de G. Davies; his notebooks, photographs, slip indexes, vocabularies, and correspondence are now deposited in the Griffith Institute, Oxford, and a considerable part of his library is now housed at the Institute of Archaeology, University College London, to which it was bequeathed; he died in Iffley, Oxford, 19 Dec. 1963.

My Working Years, autobiography, (but not complete), 1962; *My Early Years*, autobiography, (but not complete), ed. J. Gardiner, 1986; *The American Phil. Soc. Year Book*, 1965, Philadelphia, 1966, 156-66 (J. Cerny); *Archaeology* 17 (1964), 57 (anon.); *AfO* 21 (1966), 269-70 (H. Brunner); *Chron. d'Ég.* 39 (1964), 99-101 (B. van de Walle); *ILN*, no. 6492, vol. 244 (4 Jan. 1964), 27 (portr.) (anon.); *Jahrbuch der Bayerischen Akad. der Wissenschaften*, 1965, Munich, 8p. (portr.) (H. W. Müller); *Jaarboek der Koninklijke Nederlandse Akad. van Wetenschappen*, 1964-5, Amsterdam, 4p. (B. H. Stricker); *JEA* 35 (1949), 1-12 (bibl.) (R. O. Faulkner); 50 (1964), 170-2 (portr.) (R. O. Faulkner); *Man* 65 (1965), 188, no. 219 (M. A. Korostovtsev); *Orientalia* 33 (1964), 169 (anon.); *Proceedings of the British Academy*, 5 (1965), 263-7 (portr.) (J. Cerny), republished in E. Bosworth (ed.), *A Century of British Orientalists*, 2001, 140-51; *Rev. Arch.* 1964, 53-6 (portr.) (Ch. Picard); *Rev. d'Ég.* 16 (1964), 7-8 (portr.) (J. Vandier); *VDI*, 3 (89), 1964, 241-2 (M. A. Korostovtsev); *ZÄS* 91 (1964), v-viii (H. Grapow); *ODNB* 21, 407-9; *DNB* 1961-70, 418-20 (J. Cerny); H. Danesi, *Institut de France. La Second Siècle 1895-1995*, 1999-2001, I, 546-7; È. Gran-Aymerich, *Dictionnaire biographique d'archéologie 1798-1945*, 2001, incorporated in *Les Chercheurs de passé 1798-1945*, 2007, 7815-6; H. Navrátilová, *EDAL* II (2010/1), 171-86; T. Gertzen in W. Carruthers (ed.), *Histories of Egyptology*, 2015, 34-49.

GARDNER, Ernest Arthur (1862-1939)

British classicist and archaeologist; he was born in London 16 March 1862, son of Thomas G., stockbroker, and Ann Pearse; educated at the City of London School, and afterwards entered Gonville and Caius College, Cambridge; he was appointed Director of the British School of Archaeology, Athens, 1887-95; Yates Professor of Archaeology, University College London, 1896-1929; LittD, Cambridge; Hon LittD, Trinity College, Dublin; etc,; he assisted Petrie in the excavation of the city of Naucratis 1885-6, helping then and later to establish important connections between Saite Egypt and Greece, and contributing the chapter on the inscriptions to the report; he was of great help to Petrie in his work of cross-dating Egyptian and Aegean objects; he also contributed to *Art of Egypt through the Ages*, 1931; he died in Maidenhead, 27 Nov. 1939.

WWW iii, 493; *ODNB* 21, 454-5 (portr.); È. Gran-Aymerich, *Dictionnaire biographique d'archéologie 1798-1945*, 2001, incorporated in *Les Chercheurs de passé 1798-1945*, 2007, 816.

GARNOT, Jean Henri Marie André Michel Sainte Fare (1908-1963)

French Egyptologist; he was born Paris, 26 July 1908, son of Georges Sainte-Fare G., an artist, and Marie Renée Hurault; as a boy he became very interested in Egyptology and obtained advice from É. Drioton (q.v.) and P. Lacau (q.v.); after studying at the École Normale Supérieure, 1929-32 and the École Pratique des Hautes Études, 1932-5, he joined the Institut Français in Cairo, and worked at Deir el-Medina and with the Franco-Polish mission at Edfu; he returned to France in 1938 and succeeded his former teacher Moret (q.v.) as the instructor in Egyptian religion at the École Pratique; he directed the Institut Français in Cairo in the difficult period from 1953 to 1959; that it survived then was as much due to his efforts and to those of his helpers as to any other cause; he succeeded Alliot (q.v.) at the Sorbonne, 1959, and was President of the Société Française d'Égyptologie, 1961; he was a member of the Acad. des Inscriptions et Belles Lettres, 1957; Garnot's great interest was in Egyptian religion to which subject he contributed many books and lengthy articles, his first major publication being *L'Appel aux vivants dans les textes funéraires égyptiens*, 1938; this was a very deep study for a first essay and showed his mastery of the obscure Old Kingdom religious texts; his doctoral thesis was also devoted to this complex subject, 1946, published later as *L'Hommage aux Dieux dans l'Ancien Empire égyptien d'après les Textes des Pyramides*, 1954; a series of articles on Egyptian religion was published in one vol. entitled, *Religions égyptiennes antiques. Bibliographies analytiques 1939-1943*, 1952; in the Mythes et religions series he published, *La vie religieuse dans l'ancienne Égypte*, 1948, which was a close psychological analysis of Egyptian thought and beliefs; *Défis au destin*, 1960, dealt with the subject of beneficial names given to new-born children; Garnot was particularly interested in onomastica; *Signes et Symboles dans l'écriture hiéoglyphique*, 1960, dealt with symbolism applied to concrete forms in writing; he published many articles in *BIFAO* and other journals, a full list of which can be found in the bibl. below; he died in Paris, 20 June 1963.

AfO 21 (1966), 273-5 (J. Leclant); *Annales de l'Université de Paris*, Paris, 34 (1964), 227-32 (J. Leclant); *Annuaire École Pratique des Hautes Études V^e section* - Sciences religieuses, Paris, 72 (1964-5), 1964, 30-42 (J. Yoyotte); *Bibl. d'Égyptologues Français Membres ou Anciens membres de l'I.F.A.O. du Caire* (1938-59) by Sainte Fare Garnot, gives his bibl. 1937-60 (134 nos); *BIFAO* 63 (1965), 265-7 (S. Sauneron); *BSFE* 36 (June 1963), 5-12 (J. Leclant); *Orientalia* 33 (1964), 169 (anon.); *Rev. Arch.* 1963, ii, 198-204 (Ch. Picard); *Rev. d'ég.* 16 (1964), 9-10 (J. Vandier); *Syria* 41 (1964), 186-7 (J. Vandier); È. Gran-Aymerich, *Dictionnaire biographique d'archéologie 1798-1945*, 2001, incorporated in *Les Chercheurs de passé 1798-1945*, 2007, 1137.

GARSTANG, John (1876-1956)

British archaeologist; born Blackburn, Lancs., 5 May 1876, son of Dr. Walter G. and Matilda Mary Wardley; he was educated at Blackburn Grammar School and Jesus College, Oxford, where he was a Mathematical Scholar, 1895-99; he married, 1907, Marie L. Bergès *d.*1949; MA, DSc, BLitt (Oxon); Hon, LLD (Aberdeen); FSA; Chevalier de la Légion d'Honneur; Order of St. John of Jerusalem, 1926; King's Silver Jubilee Medal, 1935; Professor Emeritus, University of Liverpool from 1942; Corresp. Institut de France, 1947; Chairman Cttee. 1947-52; Hon. Dir., 1947-8 and President, 1949-56, British Institute of Archaeology at Ankara; Hon. Fellow, Jesus College, Oxford; Hon Reader in Egyptian Archaeology, University of Liverpool, 1902; founder of the Liverpool Institute of Archaeology 1904; Professor of Methods and Practice of Archaeology, 1907-41; after conducting excavations on Roman sites in Britain he worked in Nubia and Egypt as well as in the Near East from 1900 onwards, at Beni Hasan, 1902-4, Esna, Naqada, Hierakonpolis, Edfu, and in Nubia, 1905-6, Abydos, 1906-9, and at Meroë, 1909-14; he was Director of the Dept. of Antiquities in Palestine, 1920-6 and Director of the British School at Jerusalem; he published on Egyptian subjects the following works, *El Arábah,* 1901*; Mahâsna and Bêt Khallâf,* 1903*; Tombs of the Third Egyptian Dynasty,* 1904*; Burial Customs of Ancient Egypt,* 1907*; Meroë,* 1911; also reports on excavations at Abydos and Meroë in the *Liverpool Annals of Archaeology*; he died in Beirut, 12 Sept. 1956; his excavation records are in the University of Liverpool.

AfO 18 (1957), 228 (portr.) (E. W.); *Anatolian Studies* 6 (1956), 27-34 (portr.) (var. authors); *Bulletin of the American Schools of Oriental Research* no. 144. (Dec. 1956), 7-8 (W. F. Albright); *JEA* 43 (1957), vii-viii (R. O. Faulkner); *PEQ* 88 (1956), 65-6 (anon.); *WWW* v, 408-9; *ODNB* 21, 551-3 (portr.); W. T.Pike, *Liverpool and Birkenhead in the Twentieth Century*, 1911, 210; È. Gran-Aymerich, *Dictionnaire biographique d'archéologie 1798-1945*, 2001, incorporated in *Les Chercheurs de passé 1798-1945*, 2007, 819.

GĄSIOROWSKI, Stanisław Jan (1897-1962)

Polish classical archaeologist and art historian; born in Warsaw, 26 July 1897; he studied at the Cracow University under Bienkowski (q.v.) 1915-20; PhD 1925; habilitation 1927; Professor at the Cracow University, 1930-53; Director of the Czartoryski Museum, 1942-51; he wrote about Egypt in his general work *Ancient Art*, Lvov 1934, 6-56 and, as a specialist in late Hellenistic and early Christian textiles, he published the fragments of Coptic textiles in Polish collections, 1928; he died in Cracow, 13 Sept. 1962.

Biograms of Polish Scholars I, 1, Wroclaw 1983, 396-400; inf. J. Śliwa.

GAU, Franz Christian (1790-1853)

French architect of German origin; he was born in Cologne, 15 June 1790, but was subsequently naturalized French, 1826, changing his names to François Chrétien G.; he studied in Paris, and in 1818-19 went to Egypt where he made drawings of the monuments of Nubia between the First and Second Cataracts which were later published in parts, 1821-7; this work, *Antiquités de la Nubie, ou Monuments inédits des bords du Nil, entre la première et la deuxième cataracte*, a large folio, was intended as a supplement to the *Description de l'Égypte*, but Champollion criticized the accuracy of the drawings; he did, however, discover the Greek inscription of Silko the Ethiopian at Kalabsha; Gau was afterwards a well-known architect of public buildings in France; he died in Paris, 26 Dec. 1853.

Carré, i, 224, 236, 243; Champollion, ii, 176, 177, 211, 455; Edwards, 376; Hilmy, i, 254; *La Grande Enc.* 18, 600; *Larousse, XIXe siècle* 8, 1073; *DBF* 15, 67.

GAUTHIER, Henri Louis Marie Alexandre (1877-1950)
French Egyptologist; born in Lyons, 19 Sept. 1877, son of Louis Romain G. and Henriette Clothilde Chéron; he studied at the Faculté des Lettres at Lyons under V. Loret (q.v.), 1897-1900, and later under Erman (q.v.) in Berlin, together with Breasted (q.v.), Gardiner (q.v.), and Roeder (q.v.); he became a member of the Institut Français d'Archéologie Orientale, 1903; he engaged in excavations at Dra Abu en-Naga and El-Qatta, but after this he turned to historical and geographical questions and produced the monumental *Livre des rois*, thus replacing older works by Brugsch (q.v.) and others in this field; he was secretary and librarian of the Institut, 1913-18, and at this time also worked for the Service des Antiquités on the Museum Catalogue, 1907-10; for Maspero (q.v.) he undertook the copying of the inscriptions of no less than three Nubian temples, Kalabsha, Wadi es-Sebua, and Amada; Gauthier became Inspector-General of the Delta and then succeeded as Secretary-General 1927-37; he was a Member of the Institut Égyptien, 1915, and later the secretary; Docteur és Lettres, Paris, 1925; the Acad. des Inscriptions et Belles-Lettres awarded him the Maspero prize, 1922, and made him a member, 1925; in forty years of literary work he produced 140 books and articles, many of the latter being major works and of considerable importance, some even reaching the scale of books; his output in the field of large publications was huge, his work being characterized by its methodical approach; his major works were, *Fouilles de Qattah*, with E. Chassinat and H. Pieron, 1906; *Le Livre des rois d'Égypte*, 5 vols. 1907-17; *Rapport sur une campagne de fouilles à Drah Abou'l Neggah en 1906*, 1908; *Le Temple de Kalabchah*, 4 vols. 1911, 1914, 1927; *La Grande Inscription dédicatoire d'Abydos*, 1912; *Le temple de Ouadi Es-Seboua*, 2 vols. 1912; *Cercueils anthropoides des prêtres de Montou*, 2 vols. 1913, for the Cairo Cat.; *Le Temple d'Amada*, 2 vols. 1913, 1926; *2e Supplément au Catalogue des signes hiéroglyphiques de l'imprimerie de l'Institut français d'Archéologie orientale du Caire*, 1915; *Dictionnaire des noms géographiques contenus dans les Textes Hiéroglyphiques*, 7 vols. 1925-31; *Un Décret trilingue en l'honneur de Ptolémée IV*, 1925; *Les Fêtes du Dieu Min*, Doctoral thesis, 1931; *Le Personnel du Dieu Min*, 1931; *Précis d'histoire de l'Égypte*, 1932; *Les Nomes d'Égypte depuis Hérodote jusqu'à la conquête arabe*, 1935; *Sarcophages des époques persane et ptolémaïque*, with G. Maspero and Abbas Bayoumi, 2 vols. 1939; as his obituary by Montet stated, Gauthier produced two out of the ten or twelve basic books for the Egyptologist; in 1918 he also helped to found the Soc. de Géog. d'Égypte; he went to live in Monaco in 1938, and died there, 26 Jan. 1950.

AfO 16 (1952-3), 402; *ASAE* 51 (1951), 523-5 (portr. and bibl.) (P. Montet); 527-35 (bibl.) (L. A. Christophe).

GAUTIER, (Étienne Paul) Joseph (1861-1924)
French archaeologist; he was born at Oullins, 6 Sept. 1861, son of Louis François Privat G. and Marie Louise Neuvesel; he took part with Jéquier (q.v.) in excavations at Lisht 1895-6; he also excavated in Western Asia at Susa and Homs; in 1910-2 he undertook excavations at Elephantine, 1909; he died in Paris, 1924.

Rev. Arch. 5th ser. 22 (1925), 287-8; *Syria* 6 (1925), 100; *Larousse de XXe.* Photograph courtesy of Musée de l'Archéologie Nationale de Saint-Germain-en-Laye

GAYER-ANDERSON, (*Major* and *Pasha*) **Robert Grenville** (1881-1945)
British army surgeon, administrator, and collector; he was born at Listowel, Ireland, 29 July 1881, son of Henry G. -A. and Mary Morgan; he was educated at Tonbridge School and afterwards received his medical training at Guy's Hospital; MRCS; LRCP; he joined the RAMC, 1904, and served in Gallipoli and Egypt, 1914-18; he retired with the rank of Major, 1920; he was Senior Inspector Ministry of the Interior, Eg. Govt.; Oriental Secretary at the Residency, Cairo, 1922, retired 1924; he resided in Cairo until 1942, when he handed over to the Egyptian nation his home Bayt el-Kiridliya, a sixteenth-century Arab house beside the mosque of Ibn Tulun, to be opened as the Gayer-Anderson Pasha Museum of Oriental Arts and Crafts; he also made a considerable collection of Egyptian antiquities which he presented to the Fitzwilliam Museum, Cambridge, 1943 while some of his ostraca were acquired by the Medelshavmuseet, Stockholm; a bronze cat from his collection was acquired by the British Museum; he died at Little Hall, Lavenham, Suffolk, 16 June 1945.

Chron. d'Ég. 21, 88; *Lancet*, 1945, ii, 62; Newberry Corr.; *WWW* iv, 426; T. Gayer-Anderson in R. G. Gayer-Anderson, *Christeros and Other Poems*, 1948, 1-26; N. El Kholy in P. Starkey and N. El Kholy (eds.), *Egypt through the Eyes of Travellers*, 2002, 57-63; S. Ikram, 'R. G. Gayer-Anderson and his Pharaonic Collection in Cairo,' in S. d'Auria (ed.), *Offerings to the Discerning Eye*, 2010, 177-85; L. Foxcroft, *Gayer-Anderson*, 2016; R. Warner, *Collecting for Eternity*, 2016.

GAYET, Albert Jean Marie Philippe (1856-1916)
French Egyptologist; he was born Dijon, 17 Sept. 1856, son of Antoine G. and Claudine Emélie Flessière; he studied under Maspero (q.v.) in Paris; he went to Egypt with the French Archaeological Mission, 1881, and was

first employed in copying the reliefs of the temple of Luxor; he afterwards excavated for many years at the site of Antinoë and undertook publications for the Musée Guimet; *Musée du Louvre. Stèles de la 12ᵉ Dynastie*, 3 pts. 1886; *Les Monuments coptes du Musée de Boulaq*, 1889; *Le Temple de Louxor*. 1ᵉʳ fasc. *Constructions d'Aménophis III*, 1894; *L'Exploration des ruines d'Antinoë et la découverte d'un temple de Ramsès II. Enclos dans l'enceinte de la ville d'Hadrien*, 1897; *L'exploration des nécropoles gréco-byzantines d'Antinoë et les sarcophages de tombes pharaoniques de la ville antique*, 1902; *L'Exploration des nécropoles de la Montagne d'Antinoe: fouilles exécutées en 1901-1902*, 1903; *Coins d'Egypte ignorés*, 1905; he died May 1916; his collection was left to Dijon which ceded it to the Louvre.

Maspero, *L'Égyptologie* (1915), 10, 17, 29, 30; Wilbour, 357, 521, 525, 532, 547, 589 (portr. facing p. 240); Sayce, 268; N. Hoskins, *The Coptic Tapestry Albums and the archaeologist of Antinoé, Albert Gayet*, 2004.

GAZZERA, Costanzo (1779-1859)
Italian scholar and bibliographer; born in Bene Vagienna, 20 March 1779, son of Giovanni Bartolomeo G. and Eleanora Maria Costamagna; he worked in the library of the University of Turin, 1819-44; Corresponding Member of the Académie des Inscriptions in Paris, 26 Dec. 1851; he published a number of works on the monuments and Egyptian antiquities in the museum, as well as pioneering translations of hieroglyphic inscriptions in Italy based on Champollion's system of decipherment; see espec. *Descrizione dei monumenti egizi del Regio Museo a Torino, contenenti leggende reali*, 1824; *Applicazione delle dottrine del signor Champollion minore ad alcuni monumenti geroglifico del Regio Museo Egizio (Mem. Reale Accad. d. Scienze di Torino)*, 1825; *Monumenti Geroglifici del Regio Museo Egizio*, 1834; he died in Turin, 5 May 1859.

DBDI 52, 764-5; *Diz. Enc. Ital*. 5, 249; Hilmy, i, 297; A. C. E. Franquet de Franqueville, *Le Premier Siècle de l'Institut de France*, 1895, II, 242; A. Cassani, *Manfrediana* 22 (1987), 8-18.

GELL, (*Sir*) William (1777-1836)
British classical archaeologist and traveller; he was born in Hopton, Derbyshire, 1 April 1777, son of Philip G. and Dorothy Milnes; he studied at Jesus College, Cambridge, BA, 1798; MA, 1804; Fellow of Emmanuel College; he studied art at the Royal Academy Schools; he visited the Troad, 1801, and published *Topography of Troy*, 1804; from 1804 he travelled for some years in Greece, publishing a number of works on the topography and antiquities of the area; he was sent on an archaeological mission to Ionia by the Society of Dilettanti, 1811-3; he was knighted in 1814; he accompanied Princess (later Queen) Caroline to Italy, 1814, and was at the centre of the scandals involving the queen at this time; from 1820 until his death he lived in Rome and Naples; he was very interested in the progress of hieroglyphic decipherment and corresponded with Young (q.v.), Salt (q.v.),and Champollion (q.v.) on the subject and encouraged Wilkinson (q.v.) to take up the study of Egyptian antiquities; FRS; FSA; he died in Naples, 4 Feb. 1836; three of his note-books on hieroglyphs are in the Griffith Institute.

ODNB 21, 733-4 (portr.); *DNB* 21, 115-17; Champollion, i, 204; 208, 376, 382; ii, 401; Hartleben, passim; *JEA* 2 (1915), 76-87; *Al. Cantab*; W. F. Petrie, *Ancient Egypt*, (1917), 162-6; E. Clay, *Sir William Gell in Italy*, 1976; inf. Jason Thompson; È. Gran-Aymerich, *Dictionnaire biographique d'archéologie 1798-1945*, 2001, incorporated in *Les Chercheurs de passé 1798-1945*, 2007, 822-3; C. Ploviez in S. Searight, *Travellers in the Levant*, 2001, 42-56; J. Thompson in D. Jeffreys (ed.), *Views of Egypt since Napoleon Bonaparte: Imperialism, Colonialism and Modern Appropriations*, 2003, 77-85.

GENSLER, Friedrich W. C. (*fl.* 1864-1872)
German mathematician; he studied the star-tables in the tombs of Ramesses VI and IX, from which evidence he inferred their date as being 1262-1261 BC; cf. Lepsius, *Denkm*. iii, 227-8 and Renouf, *op. cit.*, iii, 85-117, who inferred the date as about 1450 BC, Gensler's being thus much more accurate for the period in which he wrote; he published a treatise on the subject in 1872 and also made contributions to *ZÄS* 2, 8,10.

Hilmy, i, 256.

GEUS, Francis (1941-2005)
French archaeologist; he was born in Hazebroucq, 30 Jan. 1941; he studied at the University of Lille under Vercoutter (q.v.); he took part in the excavations at Mirgissa, 1964 and Sai, 1972-81; from 1967-72 he organized the French unit of the Sudan Antiquities Service from 1967; he then was appointed assistant at the University of Lille 1973-5; he became head of the French Unit in the Sudan 1975-84; he returned to the University of Lille as assistant lecturer and lecturer 1984-1999; PhD, 1999; in 2000 he went back to the Sudan as head of the French Unit until 2004; he undertook excavations at Ukma, Firka, Abudiya and the Neolithic site of el-Kadada and was director of the excavations at Sai from 1993; he edited the journal *Archéologie du Nil Moyen* from 1986; two volume of studies were dedicated to him in *CRIPEL* 26 (2006-2007) and *Archéo-Nil* 16 (2006); he died 12 Jan. 2005.

Sudan and Nubia 9 (2005), 85 (portr.) (Y. Lecointe); *Der Antike Sudan* 16 (2005), 177-8 (portr.) (D. Valbelle); *Archéo-Nil* 15 (2005), 7 (A. Minault-Gout); *Azania* 40 (2005), 159 (John Alexander).

GHALIOUNGUI, Paul Elias (1908-1987)
Egyptian doctor; he was born at Mansura, 18 Sept. 1908, son of Elias G. and Marie Deeb; he was educated at the College of the Christian Brothers, Cairo and the Faculty of Medicine, Cairo University; he also studied at Vienna, Paris, and London; MD; BCh; FRCP London; he was Professor, Faculty of Medicine and Chairman of the Dept. of Internal Medicine, Ain Shams University until 1966 and adviser to the Kuwaiti Ministry of Health until 1972; he was greatly interested in pharaonic medicine and wrote several articles and monographs on this subject, notably *Magic and Medical Science in Ancient Egypt*, 1963, revised ed. 1973; *Health and Healing in Ancient Egypt*, with Z. Dawakhly, 1965; *Food. The Gift of Osiris*, with W. J. Darby and L. Grivetti, 1977; *The Physicians of Pharaonic Egypt*, 1983; he died in Cairo, 2 Jan. 1987.

Who's Who in the Arab World 1988-89.

GIERS, Nikolai Karlovitch de (1820-1895)
Russian statesman and collector; he was born in Radzivilov, 21 May 1820, son of Karl de G. and Anne Litke; he held many important posts in the Ministry of Foreign Affairs, particularly in the East; in private life he collected antiquities, the Egyptian part of his collection being acquired by the Hermitage Museum in 1867; he died at St. Petersburg, 26 Jan. 1895.

EB xii, 2-3; Golenischeff, *Erm.*, pp. vi-vii; *La Grande Enc.* 18. 924.

GILBERT, Pierre (1904-1986)
Belgian Egyptologist; he was born in Uccle, Brussels, 19 Sept. 1904, son of Maurice G. and Marguerite alias Louise Vanderborght; after studying the classics, he obtained his thesis in 1929 with a study of Imhotep; he then taught classics at Uccle; in 1947 he was appointed assistant director of the Fondation Égyptologique Reine Élisabeth, succeeding as director in 1958-73; in 1951 he was named professor of the history of Art in Egypt and the Near East at the Université Libre of Brussels; he took charge of the Egyptian Department in the Musées Royaux and from 1963-9 was director of the Musées; he was also in charge of the excavations at Elkab; he wrote a number of articles especially about Egyptian art which was his speciality; his publications included *Le classicisme de l'architecture égyptienne*, 1943; *Tout-Ankh-Amon*, with J. Capart and others, 1943; *La poésie égyptienne*, 1943, 2nd ed. 1949; *Esquisse d'une histoire de l'Égypte ancienne et de sa culture*, 1949; *Catalogue d'exposition des objects provenant des fouilles d'El-Kab*, 1952; *L'Art d'Abou-Simbel*, 1960; *Couleurs de l'Égypte ancienne*, 1962; *Vingt oeuvres de l'Égypte ancienne*, 1963; *Présentation de la collection égyptienne*, 1969; *Le règne du Soleil. Akhnaton et Nefertiti*, with others, 1975; he died in Brussels, 22 Aug. 1986.

Chron. d'Eg. 62 (1987), 6-10 (portr.) (J. Bingen), 11-20 (bibl.) (R. Tefnin and A. Vaneigem); *Encyclopedia Universalis, Universalia 1987*, 558-9 (R. Tefnin); inf. A. Mekhitarian.

GILULA, Mordechai (1936-2002)
Israeli Egyptologist; he was born at Afula, 29 Jan. 1936, son of Moshe G. and his wife Haya; he studied at the Hebrew University of Jerusalem under Polotsky (q.v.) and Sarah Isralit-Groll (q.v.); PhD, 1968; he later undertook postgraduate work at the University of Chicago; he was on the staff of the Dept of Archaeology, Tel Aviv University; Professor 1980-94; he was a specialist in the ancient Egyptian language, notably Middle Egyptian, on which he wrote over 30 articles; his thesis *Enclitic Particles in Middle Egyptian* was summarized in *Gott. Misz.* 2 (1972), 53-9; he died 10 Aug. 2002.

Lingua Aegyptia 11 (2003), vii (D. Sweeney); inf. Mrs D. Gilula.

GIORGINI, Michela Schiff (*née* **Beomonte**) (1923-1978)
Italian archaeologist; she was born in Padua, 30 Oct. 1923, daughter of Belisario B., an officer, and Gemma Lucchesi; she married the banker Giorgio Schiff Giorgini; she developed an interest in Egyptian archaeology after visiting Egypt several times; in 1957 she organized the excavation of Soleb in the Sudan under the patronage of the University of Pisa (members Clément Robichon, Jozef Janssen and since 1960 Jean Leclant); in 1963 the expedition began work at Sedeinga, terminating its work in the Sudan in 1977; she was awarded an honorary doctorate from the University of Pisa, 1972 and the University of Khartoum, 1977; she received the Gold Medal of the Sudanese Government; she published with Clément Robichon and Jean Leclant *Soleb* I, 1965; *Soleb* II, 1971; *Soleb* III, 2002; *Soleb* IV, 2003; *Soleb* V, 1998; her division of the finds from her excavations was presented to the Museo di Ateneo in Pisa; she died in Benisa, Spain 3 July 1978; after her death the Michela Schiff Giorgini Foundation was established in her memory to award annual prizes to promote Egyptology.

Oriens Antiquus 17 (1978), 299-300 (S. Donadoni); *Studi classici e orientali* 29 (1979), 13-14 (E. Bresciani); *BSFE* 83 (1978), 6 (J. Leclant); *Atti del Convegno Ippolito Rosellini*, 39-43.

GIPPS, (*Sir*) **George** (1791-1847)
British army officer and Colonial Governor; he was born in Ringwould, Kent, and baptized there 1 Feb. 1791, son of Revd George G. and his wife Susannah Bonella Vense; after his education at King's School, Canterbury, and at the Military Acad., Woolwich, he entered the Royal Engineers in 1809; during the Peninsular War he was wounded at Badajoz, 1812; promoted Capt., 1814; he visited Aswan and Nubia in March-April 1822 and mentions Salt's (q.v.) excavation of the Nilometer at Elephantine which had been recorded by P. S. Girard of Napoleon's Commission d'Égypte; afterwards in the W. Indies, 1824-9; Commissioner to Canada, 1835-7; Governor of New South Wales, 1838-46; he returned to England and died in Canterbury, 28 Feb. 1847, a monument to him being erected in the cathedral.

ODNB 22, 339-40; *DNB* 21, 387-9; *Australian Dictionary of Biography* 1:*1788-1850 A-H*, 446-453; Henniker, 147, 345.

GIRGIS, Victor Antoun (1905-1969)
Egyptian archaeologist; he was born 12 April 1905; he was educated in Egypt and in Italy where he studied under Breccia (q.v.) 1934-38; on his return to Egypt he was appointed assistant curator in the Egyptian Museum 9 Oct. 1938; he was transferred to the Graeco-Roman Museum of Alexandria on 12 Oct. 1941 and rose to become its director; on 12 July 1958 he returned to the Egyptian Museum Cairo as its first curator and succeeded as Director on 12 April 1960; he retired from the Service on 12 April 1965 and died in July 1969.

JEA 56 (1970), 4; inf. Dia Abou-Ghazi; *Bulletin of the Egyptian Museum* 1 (2004), 8.

GIVEON, Raphael (Grüneberg, Richard) (1916-1985)
Israeli Egyptologist; he was born at Wuppertal (Elberfeld), Germany, 8 Feb. 1916, son of Louis Grüneberg, merchant, and Sophie Mendel; he was educated at Hochschule für die Wissenschaft des Judentums in Berlin and worked for the Youth Aliyah in Berlin, 1933-39; he emigrated to Great Britain in 1939 and became a schoolteacher at Wem, 1942-5; in 1945 he settled at Kibbutz Nishmar Ha-emeq in Israel as teacher, 1945-54; he studied Egyptology under Polotsky (q.v.) at the Hebrew University, Jerusalem, 1947-8 and under Posener (q.v.) in Paris, 1959-61; Ph.D., 1961; from 1962-84 he was lecturer, and later Associate Professor of Egyptian Archaeology and head of the Egyptology section of the Department of Archaeology and Near Eastern Studies, University of Tel Aviv; he organized epigraphic work in Sinai from 1968 and was interested in Egyptian-Canaanite relations; apart from articles his published works include *Les Bedouins Shosou des Documents Égyptiens*, 1971; *The Impact of Egypt on Canaan*, 1978; *Egyptian Scarabs from Western Asia from the collection of the British Museum*, 1985; *Egyptian Scarabs and Seals from Acco*, 1986 with T. Kertesz; *Scarabs from recent Excavations in Israel*, 1988; he died in Afula, 8 Aug. 1985.

IEJ 35 (1985), 304; *Who's Who in World Jewry*, 1981; *Scarabs from recent Excavations in Israel*, 1-7 (portr.) (bibl.) (O. Keel).

GLADSTONE, John Hall (1827-1902)
British chemist and physicist; he was born in London, 7 March 1827, son of John G., draper, and Alison Hall; he was educated at University College London 1844-47 and the University of Giessen; PhD 1848.; Lecturer on chemistry at St Thomas's Hospital 1850-52; Professor of Chemistry at the Royal Institution 1874-77; Hon DSc Trinity College Dublin 1892; FRS 1853; he wrote articles on ancient metals from Egypt in *PSBA*, vols. 12-16, and in Petrie, *Dendereh*; he died in London, 6 Oct. 1902 and was buried at Kensal Green.

ODNB 22, 382-3 (portr.); A. Lucas, *Anc. Eg. Materials*, 4th ed., 195, 214, 227; *WWW* i, 277.

GLANVILLE, Stephen Ranulph Kingdon (1900-1956)
British Egyptologist; he was born Westminster, 26 April 1900, son of Stephen James G., deputy editor of the *Daily Telegraph*, and Elizabeth, daughter of Francis Kingdon; he was educated at Marlborough College and Lincoln College, Oxford where he was a Modern History Scholar, Lit. Hum. and BA, 1922; MA, 1926; he was later Laycock Student of Egyptology, Worcester College, Oxford, 1929-35; he first visited Egypt as an assistant master in the Egyptian Government Service, 1922, and his enthusiasm for Egyptology having been aroused he joined the EES expedition to Amarna, 1923; he also studied the language under Griffith (q.v.); he was appointed Assistant in the Dept. of Egyptian and Assyrian Antiquities, British Museum, 1924; he later became Reader in 1933-5 and then Edwards Professor of Egyptology at University College London; he was elected a Fellow of King's College, Cambridge, 1946-54; he excavated at Amarna, 1925, and Armant, 1928, for the EES, was its Hon. Secretary, 1928-31 and 1933-6, and its Chairman of Committee, 1951-6; he served in the RAF (Air Staff) in the Second World War;

Herbert Thompson Professor of Egyptology in the University of Cambridge, 1946-56; Hon. Fellow of Lincoln College, Oxford; Master of the Grocers' Company, 1953; Provost of King's College, Cambridge, 1954-6, the first non-Cambridge man to be so elected in 500 years; MA, FBA, FSA; he married 1925, Ethel Mary daughter of J. B. Chubb; he contributed to *The Mural Painting of El-Amarneh*, 1929; published *Daily Life in Ancient Egypt*, 1930; edited *Studies Presented to F.Ll. Griffith*, 1932; *The Egyptians* (for children), 1933; *Catalogue of Demotic Papyri in the British Museum*, i. 1939; ed. *The Legacy of Egypt*, 1942; *The Growth and Nature of Egyptology*, 1947; 'Notes on a demotic papyrus from Thebes (B.M. 10026)' in *Essays and Studies presented to S. A. Cook*, 1950; *Catalogue of Demotic Papyri in the British Museum* II; *The Instructions of 'Onchsheshonkhy*, pt. i, 1955; also articles in the *JEA, Br. Mus. Quarterly*, etc.; he died in Cambridge, 26 April 1956.

ODNB 22, 425-6; *AfO* 17 (1954-6), 493 (H. Brunner); *ASAE* 54 (1957), 289-94 (portr.) (bibl.) (Mustafa el-Amir); *Chron. d'Ég.* 31 (1956), 309-10 (C. de Wit); EES *Report*, 1956, 4; *JEA* 42 (1956), 99-101 (portr.) (I. E. S. Edwards); *Nature*, London, vol. 177, no. 4518 (2 June 1956), 1013-14 (H. S. Smith); *WWW* v, 425; *The Times*, April-May 1956, letters Glyn Daniel, A. J. Arberry, G. M. W., C. Winter, G. H. Stainforth; *Proc. of the Brit. Acad.* 43 (1958), 231-40 (I. E. S. Edwards); *JEA* 57 (1971), 181-4 (bibl.) (E. Uphill); R. Janssen, *The First Hundred Years*, 1992, 27-53.

GLEYRE, (Marc) Charles Gabriel (1806-1874)

Swiss artist; he was born at Chevilly, Vaud, 2 May 1806, son of Charles-Alexandre G., farmer, and Suzanne Huguenin; as an orphan, he was brought up by an uncle in Lyons; he studied art in Paris from 1825; in 1828 he went to Italy and stayed in Rome until 1834 when he was engaged by John Lowell (q.v.) to accompany him as artist on a tour of the Levant; he stayed with Lowell until Nov. 1835 in Khartoum when they parted unceremoniously; most of his sketches and water-colours are now preserved in the Dept. of Prints, Drawings, and Photographs, Museum of Fine Arts, Boston while there are some drawings in the Griffith Institute; he returned to Europe in 1837 and settled in Paris where he became a noted artist; he died in Paris, 5 May 1874.

Ch. Clement, *Gleyre*, 1878; R. Lugeon, *C. Gleyre*, 1929; N. Scott Whitehouse, *Charles Gleyre 1806-1874*, 1980; *BES* 6 (1984), 70-1; Thieme-Becker, *Kunstler-Lexikon* 14, 252-3; W. Hauptman, *Charles Gleyre, 1806-1874*, 1996; C. Williams in D. Fortenberry (ed.), *Who Travels Sees More*, 2007, 55-7; *Grove Dictionary of Art* 12, 808-10.

GLIDDON, George Robins (1809-1857)

American Egyptologist; he was born in Devon, 27 Nov. 1809, baptized Exeter, 19 Feb. 1810, son of John G. a merchant who became US Consul at Alexandria, and Eleanor née Gliddon; he was taken to Egypt at an early age and later became U.S. Vice-Consul in Egypt; in 1842 he went to America and lectured on Eg. archaeology at Boston, 1842-3, and at the Lowell Institute, 1843-4; during the following years he made lecture tours as far West as St. Louis; he published several works on Egypt, one of which had a very large sale for those days and established his reputation as the first writer on ancient Egypt in the USA; he made a contribution to the study of mummification in his *Otia Aegyptiaca*, 52-113, which, though discursive, made some good points; he wrote, *An Appeal to the Antiquaries of Europe on the Destruction of the Monuments of Egypt*, 1849, perhaps the first expression of archaeological conscience in print; *Ancient Egypt, her Monuments, Hieroglyphics, History and Archaeology, and other subjects connected with Hieroglyphical Literature*, fol. 1843, rev. 1847; *Otia Aegyptiaca: Discourses on Egyptian Archaeology and Hieroglyphical Discoveries*, 1849; he died in Panama, 16 Nov. 1857.

N.-Y. Hist. Soc. Q. Bull. iv, 1920, 6-8; *BMMA* 15, 1920, 88-9; *Mém. Inst. Ég.* 13, 1929; Hilmy, i, 263; Wilson, 41-3, 201, 220; C. Vivian, *Americans in Egypt 1770-1915*, 2012, 95-111.

GODARD, Jean Ernest (1826-1862)

French doctor and traveller; he was born at Cognac, 6 Jan. 1826, son of Jean Pierre G., a merchant at Bordeaux, and Marthe Suzanne Caroline Léonide Marquet from a medical family; he studied medicine at Paris, 1845-58; he was a member of the Société d'anthropologie de Paris, and his interest in anthropology led to journeys to Spain and Algeria; he visited Egypt from Alexandria to Wadi Halfa in Jan. to July 1861, undertaking medical research and collecting antiquities; he then left for Palestine where he died at Jaffa, 21 Sept. 1862; his collection of 722 objects was left to the Musée d'Aquitaine at Bordeaux, where it was used by Ollivier-Beauregard (q. v.) as the basis for his *Simples observations sur l'origine et le culte des divinités égyptiennes, à propos de la collection archéologique de feu le Docteur Ernest Godard*, 1863.

Revue Historique de Bordeaux 32 n. s. (1986-1987), 61-73 (C. Orgogozo).

GODRON, Gérard (1927-1999)

French Egyptologist; he was born at Montpellier in 1927, son of Victor Godron, a lawyer; he studied at the École du Louvre, Institut Catholique, the École Pratique des hautes études and the University of Lyons under Barguet and du Bourget (q.v); he lectured in Egyptology and Coptic at the University of Rhode Island, 1951-2 and the Institut

Catholique at Paris, 1953-7; he became a member of the Centre National de Recherche Scientifique in 1953; he worked at the French Institute in Cairo, 1960-2; he obtained his doctorate from Lyons in 1981; he was appointed Professor of Egyptology and Coptology at the Paul Valéry University of Montpellier in 1984 in succession to Daumas (q.v.) until 1994; apart from his articles and reviews, he published two works on Coptic Studies and his thesis *Études sur l'Horus Den et quelques problèmes de l'Égypte archaïque*, 1990; he died on 22 Sept. 1999.

IAE Internet obituary (Y. N. Youssef); *BSFE* 146 (1999), 3-4 (J Yoyotte); *BSAC* 39 (2000), 344-9 (bibl.) (Y. N. Youssef).

GOEDICKE, Hans Georg (1926-2015)
Austrian-American Egyptologist; he was born in Vienna, 7 Aug. 1926, son of Erich G., an engineer, and Alice von Schuller-Goetzburg; he served in the German army, 1942-5; he later studied at the University of Vienna, 1945-9 under Czermak (q.v.); PhD, 1949; he worked as an assistant at the Museum of Fine Arts, Vienna, 1949-51; he was research assistant at Brown University, 1952-7 and then was a technical assistant for UNESCO at the work at Abu Simbel, 1958; he was employed at the University of Göttingen, 1958-60; he joined the Department of Near Eastern Studies at Johns Hopkins University as a lecturer, 1960; he was promoted to assistant professor, 1962; associate professor, 1967; full professor, 1968-93; professor emeritus 1993-2015; acting chairman of the Dept., 1968-9; chairman, 1969-73, 1979-84; he was editor of the Near Eastern series for the Johns Hopkins University Press; he conducted an epigraphic survey in Aswan, Gharb Aswan, and Gebel Tingare, 1964 and 1967, excavated at Giza, 1972 and 1974, and directed a survey in the Wadi Tumilat, 1977-8 and 1981; he was known for his controversial dating of the Exodus to the reign of Queen Hatshepsut; a volume *Essays in Egyptology in Honor of Hans Goedicke*, edited by B. Bryan and D. Lorton, was published in 1994; apart from articles, he published *Die Stellung des Königs im Alten Reich*, 1960; with E. Wente, *Ostraca Michaelides*, 1965; *Die Laufbahn des Mtn*, 1966; *Königliche Dokumente aus dem Alten Reich*, 1967; *Die privaten Rechtsinschriften aus dem Alten Reich*, 1970; *The Report about the dispute of a man with his ba: Papyrus Berlin 3024*, 1970; with G. Thausing, *Nofretari*, 1971; *Re-used Blocks from the Pyramid of Amemenhet I at Lisht*, 1971; with J. Roberts, *Unity and Diversity*, 1975; *Records of the Ancient Near East*, 1972; *Die Geschichte des Schiffbrüchigen*, 1974; *The Report of Wenamun*, 1975; *The Protocol of Neferyt*, 1977; *Die Darstellung des Horus*, 1982; *Studies in the Hekanakhte Papers*, 1984; *The Quarrel of Apophis and Seqenenre*, 1986; *Studies in 'The Instructions of King Amenemhet I for his Son*, 1988; *Old Hieratic Paleography*, 1988; *Problems Concerning Amenophis III*, 1992; *Comments on the 'Famine Stela'*, 1996; *Pi(ankh) y in Egypt. A Study of the Pi(ankh)y Stela*, 1998; *The Battle of Megiddo*, 2000; *The Speos Artimidos Inscription of Hatshepsut and Related Discussions*, 2004; he edited *Near Eastern Studies in Honor of William Foxwell Albright*, 1971 and *Perspectives on the Battle of Kadesh*, 1985; he died in Towson, Maryland, 24 Feb. 2015.

The Baltimore Sun 7 March 2015; B. Bryan and D. Lorton, *Essays in Egyptology in Honor of Hans Goedicke*, vii-viii (port.)

GOFF, Robert (1801-1866)
British antiquary of Irish origin; he was born in Dublin 1801, youngest son of Joseph Fade Goff of Dublin and Sarah Clibborn; in 1847 he presented a small collection of Egyptian antiquities to the British Museum including the important stela (EA 504) and the libation-bowl (EA 1386); the rest of his collections were sold at Christie's, 7 June 1866; towards the end of his life he lived in London at Kensington Gore; he was an Assoc. Member of the Egyptian Society of Cairo, 1836; he died unmarried, in Rome, 27 March 1866.

Inf. W. R. Dawson; Lugt 29197.

GOHARY, Said (1944-2015)
Egyptian Egyptologist; he was born in Cairo, 9 April 1944, son of Gaber Gohary and Zeinab Youssef; he was educated at the University of Cairo, 1961-5; BA, 1965; and the University of Liverpool, 1973-8; PhD, 1978; he took part in the Amarna talatat project under Ray Smith (q.v), 1967-73; he later became a lecturer at the University of Cairo, 1979-86; Associate Professor, 1986-92; Professor, 1992-2015; he also served as Vice-Dean of the Faculty of Archaeology. 1997-2003, Head of Department, 2003-4, and Head of Committee overseeing all colleges of Cairo University, 1997-2003; he was Chief Administrator and Head Librarian, Institut d'Egypte, 1980-6, Dean,Chief Administrator, and Professor of Egyptology, Misr College for Hotels and Tourism, Heliopolis, 1992-6; and Dean and Chief Admistrator, Higher Institute for Languages, Heliopolis. 1995-7; he acted as consultant for many construction projects in Cairo, Aswan, and Abydos, notably for UNESCO on the Cairo ring road, 1998-2015 ande SEAM Environmental Management Organization, 2002-5; he was also a consutant

for Sixth October University, Cairo, 2009-15; he was involved with work at Tuna el-Gebel and Saqqara; apart from articles in English and Arabic, he published *The Twin Tomb Chapel of Nebnefer and His Son Mahu at Sakkara*, 2009; he died in Cairo, 12 March 2015.

Inf. J. Gohary.

GOLENISCHEFF, Vladimir Semionovitch (1856-1947)
Russian Egyptologist; he was born in St. Petersburg, 30 Jan. 1856, son of Semion Vasilievitch G., a merchant, and Sophia Gavrilovna; he visited Egypt no fewer than sixty times and brought back a rich collection of antiquities which he sold in 1909 to the Moscow Museum thereby much enlarging it; after the Revolution he never returned to Russia, but resided at Nice; he was for some time employed in cataloguing the hieratic papyri in the Cairo Museum; Professor of Egyptology at the University of Cairo 1924-29; he published his first article in 1874, and his first important work on the Metternich stela, 1877; in cuneiform studies he also published *Vingt-quatre tablettes cappadociennes*, 1891, in which he made important contributions to the study of these documents; Golenischeff's name is today associated with many important papyri: the literary papyri and the Story of the Shipwrecked Sailor, now in the Hermitage Museum, and the Mathematical Papyrus, the Hymns to the Diadem, the Story of Wenamun, and other texts in Moscow; he published articles and studies on Wenamun, The Teaching of King Merikare, the Prophecy of the Priest Nefer-rehu, etc; his Glossary (the Onomasticon) formed the basis for Gardiner's *Anc. Egyptian Onomastica*; his main works were, *Die Metternich-stele in der Originalgrösse zum ersten Male herausgegeben*, 1877; *Ermitage Imperial. Inventaire de la collection égyptienne*, 1891; *Le Conte du Naufragé*, 1912; *Les Papyrus Hiératiques, no. 1115, 1116A et 1116B de l'Ermitage Impérial ...*, 1913; some of his papers are in the Griffith Institute; he died in Nice, 5 Aug. 1947.

AfO 15 (1945-51), 193; EES *Report* 1947, 6-7; *JEA* 33 (1947), 2; Hilmy, i, 265; Sayce, 592, 415; *BIFAO* 58 (1959), 159-63 (portr.) (J. Sainte Fare Garnot); *Bull. Faculty of Arts*, Fouad I Univ., xiii, pt. I (May 1951) (bibl.) (V. Vikentiev); *Egyptes* 2 (1993), 8-12.

GONEIM, Muhammad Zakaria (1911-1959)
Egyptian Egyptologist; born in Gharbiya in the Delta, 1911; he took a diploma in Egyptology at the University of Cairo in 1934, studying archaeology under P. E. Newberry (q.v.), H. Junker (q.v.) and V. Vikentiev (q.v.); in 1937 he was appointed assistant to the excavations carried out by the Dept. of Antiquities at Saqqara, working under Selim Hassan (q.v.), clearing the mastaba field that lies east of the pyramid of Unas; in 1939 he was made Inspector at Aswan, then at Edfu, becoming Keeper of the Theban Necropolis in 1943, Chief Inspector of Upper Egypt 1946-51; he again cleared the tomb of Kheruef in the course of his work there, and in 1946 began the excavation of the avenue of sphinxes of King Nectanebo before the temple of Luxor; he also excavated the important tomb of Montuemhat (TT 34) and published in collaboration with P. Barguet and J. Leclant the offering tables discovered in the great court of this tomb; in 1951 he was made Keeper of the Saqqara necropolis, where he made his world-famous discovery of the unfinished pyramid of King Sekhemkhet of the Third Dynasty; he began its excavation 1952-56 and the clearance of the vast underground galleries, discovering jewellery in the passage leading to the burial chamber and the empty sarcophagus within the tomb; these discoveries aroused great public interest and Goneim visited both Europe and America, see *Life, The Geographic Magazine, The Times, New York Times, Paris-Match* etc.; he published *Horus Sekhem-khet. The unfinished step pyramid at Saqqara*. i, 1957, the official account; and *The Buried Pyramid*, 1956, a popular account of these discoveries prepared with the help of Leonard Cottrell (q.v.); in Nov. 1958 he was named Director of the Cairo Museum, a post which he did not take up; he was found dead in the Nile at Kasr el-Nil in mysterious circumstances, 12 Jan. 1959.

Rev. Arch., Paris 1959, ii. 89-95 (J. P. Lauer); *La Revue du Caire*, vol. xliii, no. 229 (Sept. 1959), 135-8 (A. Papadopoulo); *La Revue du Caire, Grandes découvertes archéologiques de 1954*, 18-31; Menant, Georges. *La Vengeance des pharaons, Paris Match*, no. 518 (14 March 1959), 50-65; *The Times*, Jan. 13, 1959; E. Gran-Aymerich, *Dictionnaire biographique d'archéologie 1798-1945*, 2001, incorporated in *Les Chercheurs de passé 1798-1945*, 2007, 837.

GONZALES, (*Père*) **Antonius** (1604-1683)
Belgian traveller; he was born at Mechelen (Malines) 1604, son of a Spaniard; he joined the Franciscan Recollect order on 8 Sept. 1626, priest 1629; he undertook a pilgrimage to the Holy Land from 1665-8; he was in Egypt from Sept. 1665 to Aug. 1666 when he acted as priest to the French community in Cairo; he visited the pyramids,

the Sphinx, Saqqara, Alexandria, and Suez; his account of his journey was published in Dutch in 1673 (French translation of the Egyptian section, 1977); he died in Venlo, 2 July 1683.

C. Libois (ed), *Voyage en Égypte du Père Antonius Gonzales 1665-1666*, 1977, x-xiii, xxix-xxxi; Lamy, 112-3.

GOODISON, Anne Jane (*née* **PADLEY**) (1845-1906)
British collector; she was born in Waterloo, Liverpool 5 Jan. 1845, daughter of … Padley and Isabella Nunn; she married George G., an engineer, in 1868; she visited Egypt in 1887 and 1887 and formed a collection of over 1000 pieces, some acquired on the advice of Chester (q.v.); she presented an object to Kendal Museum in 1889; she became a member of the Society of Biblical Archaeology, 1887; after her death, her collection was acquired by the Bootle Museum and later passed to the Atkinson Art Gallery, Southport; she died in Thornton-in-Lonsdale, 16 Nov. 1906.

GOODWIN, Charles Wycliffe (1817-1878)
British judge and Egyptologist; he was born in King's Lynn, Norfolk, 2 April 1817, son of Charles G. a lawyer, and Frances Catherine Sawyer his first wife; he was educated at High Wycombe and St. Catherine's Hall, Cambridge; MA; Fellow; he was called to the Bar, Lincoln's Inn, 1843, and then practised as a barrister in London; appointed assistant judge, China and Japan, 1865; judge, 1877; a fine Greek, Hebrew and Anglo-Saxon scholar, he became interested in Egyptology as a small child at the time of the decipherment of hieroglyphs; this interest, begun in school days, became his principal one throughout life; he was a brilliant decipherer of hieratic texts and made many philological discoveries, his essay *Hieratic Papyri* in Cambridge Essays, 1858, marking an epoch in the story of Egyptology; he married Augustine Anne Rudderforth, 1865, and in the same year visited Alexandria and Cairo on his way to the Far East; he died in Shanghai, 17 Jan. 1878; his Egyptological MSS are in the British Library (Add. MSS 31268-98).

W. R. Dawson, *Charles Wycliffe Goodwin*, Oxford, 1934 (portr. and bibl.); S. R. K. Glanville, *Growth and Nature of Egyptology*, 1947, 6-9; *ODNB* 22, 814-5; *DNB* 22, 142; Dawson MSS 9, ff. 86-126; 18, ff. 41-79; Hilmy, i, 267.

GOODYEAR, William Henry (1846-1923)
American archaeologist; he was born in New Haven, Conn., 21 April 1846, son of Charles G. and Clarissa Beecher; educated at Yale University, Heidelberg, and Berlin; he was Curator in the Metropolitan Museum of Art, New York, 1881-8; he visited Egypt, 1891-2; Curator, Brooklyn Inst. of Fine Arts, 1899-1923, where he expanded the Egyptian collections, notably by the acquisition of Wilbour's (q.v.) collection and extensive library; founder of the American Anthropological Assn., 1902; he wrote many works on ancient art, his most important contribution to that of Egypt being his *Grammar of the Lotus*, 1891; he died in Brooklyn, New York, 19 Feb. 1923.

WWW ii, 418; *WWWA* i, 469; Newberry Corr.

GORDON, Alexander (*c.*1692-1754)
British author and antiquarian; he was said to have been born in Aberdeen, about 1692; MA, University of Aberdeen; Secretary Soc. for Encouragement of Learning; FSA, Sec. 1736-41; member of Spalding Soc.; he published many antiquarian works, and two large pamphlets, with good plates, on Egyptian subjects; *An Essay towards explaining the Hieroglyphical Figures on the Coffin of the Ancient Mummy belonging to Capt. William Lethieullier*, with *The Egyptian Mummy in the Museum of Doctor Mead*, 2 pts., fol. 1737; *An Essay towards illustrating the History, Chronology, and Mythology of the Ancient Egyptians*, etc., 1741; he was married by then, but went to S. Carolina as sec. to Governor Glen, where he died in Charleston shortly after 22 Aug. 1754, the date of his will; his Egyptian MS is in the British Library Add MS 8834.

ODNB 22, 851-3; *DNB* 22, 164-6; *BIFAO* 5 (1905), 82; Hilmy, i, 268; *JEA* 23 (1937), 259; Nichols, *Lit. Anecd.* 5, 329-37; *Proc. Soc. Ant. Scot.* 10, 363; D. Wilson, *Alexander Gordon*, 1873.

GORDON, John (*c.*1776-1858)
British traveller; he was born in Aberdeenshire about 1776, son of Charles G. of Cluny and Joanna Trotter; he served in the Royal Aberdeenshire Light Infantry, Lt. 2 Dec. 1800; and the 7th Co. of 55th Aberdeen Milita, 25 April 1804; Major, 11 Aug 1808; Lt.-Col., 6 June 1820; Hon. Col., 1836; he toured the Levant with the Earl of Aberdeen and others, 1803-5; he visited Egypt without most of his companions and probably reached as far as Philae; he left graffiti at Dendera, Karnak, Luxor, Medinet Habu, the Ramesseum, Gurna, Edfu, Esna, Elkab, and Gebel es-Silisila; MP for Weymouth, 1826-30; he died in Edinburgh, 16 July 1858.

Bulletin of ASTENE 6 (1998), 13-5 (R. Keersmaecker).

GORDON, Robert James (1786-1823)
British naval officer and explorer; he was born Bantry, Yorks., 1786; Capt., RN; he set out to explore the interior of Africa for the African Association; he sailed from Malta to Egypt with John Madox (q.v.), Feb. 1822, where he climbed the Second Pyramid and copied the Arabic inscription on the apex; Salt (q.v.) provided him with letters to various potentates and a firman from the Pasha; he ascended the Nile as far as Upper Nubia and reached Wad Medani near Sennar, where he died 1 July 1823.

Geogr. Journ. 122, 247; Henniker, 213, 343; Madox, i, 98, 122, 263; Salt, ii, 205, 211.

GÓRECKI, Tomasz Eugeniusz (1951-2017)
Polish archaeologist and ceramologist; he was born in Warsaw, 17 Nov. 1951; he studied archaeology at the University of Warsaw, 1970-1 and the Academy of Catholic Theology; he worked in the National Museum in Warsaw from 1976 in the Dept. of Ancient Art Conservation and the Gallery of Ancient Art; curator of the collection of Early Christian Art, later Ancient and Early Christian Art, from 1996; he excavated at Alexandria from 1979, Tell Atrib, Naqlun 1988-2002, Chenchour, Deir el-Baramus, Dongala, Gaza, Abu Fano, Minshat Abu Omar, and Tell Buto and was the director of the Polish Archaeological Mission in Sheikh Abd el-Gurna, 2003-13; he died on 29 Sept. 2017.

Inf. J. Bailey; *The Journal of Juristic Papyrology* 47 (2017), XXXIII-XLI (T. Derda), (portr.)

GÖRG, Manfred (1938-2012)
German Egyptologist; he was born in Blankenfelde (Berlin), 8 Sept. 1938, son of Rudolf G. and Maria Schulte; he studied from 1957 for the priesthood at Bonn, Würzburg, and Paderborn; he obtained a PhD in Theology at Bonn, 1965; he then ministered at Paderborn, 1963-8; he became an assistant at Ruhr-Universität Bochum, 1968 while studying Egyptology at Bonn; he obtained his Habilitation at Bochum, 1972 and was promoted to university lecturer; PhD in Egyptology, 1974; Prof. at Bochum, 1974-5; Prof. at the University of Bamberg, 1975-84; Guest Prof. at the Free University Berlin, 1984; Prof. of Old Testament Theology at the Katholische Theologische Fakultät of the Ludwigs Maximilian University in Munich, 1985-2003; he founded the journal *Biblische Notizen* and the publication series *Ägypten und Altes Testament*; he published over 1300 books, articles, and reviews; his principal works were *Gott-König-Reden in Israel und Ägypten*, 1975; *Religion im Erbe Ägyptens*, 1988; *Studien zur biblisch-ägyptischen Religionsgeschichte*, 1992; *Die Barke der Sonne. Religion im alten Ägypten*, 2001; *Ägyptische Religion*, 2007; *Mythos und Mythologie*, 2010; he also edited *Festschrift Elmar Edel*, 1979, with E. Pusch, and studies in honour of Brunner (q.v) *Fontes Atque Pontes*, 1983; he died in Munich, 17 Sept 2012.

Wiki obit; G. Gafus, *Bibliographie Manfred Görg. Schriftverzeichnis 1960-2003*, 2003; 'Schriftverzeichnis Manfred Görg 2004-2008', *Blätter Abrahams* 7 (2008); *Wer ist Wer?* 51 (2013-4), 345.

GORRINGE, Henry Honeychurch (1841-1885)
American naval officer; he was born in Barbados, 11 Aug. 1841, son of an Oxford-trained Swedish missionary who was rector of the established church at Tobago; his family removed to the USA in his youth and he went to sea, entering the US Navy in 1862; he is remembered in Egyptology for his brilliant work in overseeing the removal of an obelisk from Alexandria and its subsequent erection in Central Park, New York, the cost of the project being financed by W. H. Vanderbilt; the obelisk, which has inscriptions of Thutmose III and Ramesses II, was presented to the American people by the Khedive Ismail in 1877; it was transported in 1880 and set up in 1881; Gorringe published a detailed account with many illustrations and much close analysis of these monuments, *Egyptian Obelisks*, NY, 1882; he also collected antiquities an account of which was published in *AE*, 1916, 49; he retired with the rank of Lieut.-Commander in 1883 and became a partner in the American Shipbuilding Company at Philadelphia; he fell from a train and was seriously injured, dying six months later in New York, 6 July 1885 and was buried in Rockland Cemetery, Nyack, New York.

DAB 7, 437-8; Hilmy, i, 270; *WWWA Hist. Vol.*, 211; *The Metropolitan Museum of Art Bulletin* Spring 1993.

GOUDSMIT, Samuel Abraham (1902-1978)
Dutch-American physicist and collector; he was born in The Hague, 11 July 1902, son of Isaac G. and Marianne Gompers; he studied Physics at Leiden, PhD 1927, and also attended lectures on Egyptian language given by

Boeser (q.v.); he worked in the Physics faculty at Ann Arbor, 1927-19; he served in military intelligence in World War Two, assessing German progress in nuclear research; he became chair of Physics at the Brookhaven National Laboratory, 1951-75; he formed a collection of Egyptian objects, and published some articles on objects in his possession; his collection was bequeathed to the Kelsey Museum, Ann Arbor, by his wife; he died in Reno, Nevada, 4 Dec. 1978.

B. Bederson, *Samuel Abraham Goudsmit*, National Academy of Sciences Biographical Memoir, 2008; M. C. Root, *The Samuel A. Goudsmit collection of Egyptian Antiquities*, 1982; inf. T. Hardwick.

GOULIANOV, Ivan Alexandrovitch (1789-1841)
Russian Egyptologist; he was born in Moldavia, 1789; he served in the Russian Ministry of Foreign Affairs in a number of places; Member of the Russian Acad., 1821; he expressed great criticism against Champollion (q.v.) and his system; he published various Egyptological works including, *Discours sur l'étude fondamentale des langues*, 1822; *Opuscules archéologiques*, 1826; *Essai sur les hiéroglyphes d'Horapollon*, 1827; *Zamiechania o Diendierskom zodiakie* (Remarks on the Dendera Zodiac), Moscow, 1831; *Archéologie égyptienne*, Leipzig, 1839; he died in Nice, 1841.

Inf. Prof. J. Černý and J. Śliwa; Hilmy, i, 163; *Palestinskiy Sbornik* 5 (68), 1960, 121 (I. G. Lifschitz); I. Katznelson, *Ocherki pomistorii russkogo vostokovedeniya*, Vol. II, Moscow, 1956, 222-224; A. M. Koulikova, *Formirovaniye gumanisticheskoy traditsii otechestvennogo vostokovedeniya, do 1917 g.*, Moscow, 1984, 145-169.

GOURDIN, François Philippe (1739-1825)
French Benedictine monk; he was born at Noyon, 8 Nov 1739; he published a dissertation in *Mag. Encyclopédique* in which he attempted to prove the identity of Egyptian hieroglyphic and Chinese writing; he died in Bonsecours near Rouen, 11 July 1825.

BIFAO 5 (1905), 85; Hilmy, i, 271.

GOURLAY, Janetta Agnes (1863-1912)
British excavator, she was born at Dundee, 30 Jan. 1863, daughter of Henry G., engineer, and Agnes Christine Burrell; she was one of Petrie's (q.v.) first students at University College London, 1893; she met Miss Margaret Benson (q.v.) in Egypt in 1896 and joined her in the excavation of the Temple of Mut in Asher at Thebes for two seasons, and also in the publication of the results, *The Temple of Mut in Asher*, 1899, both being assisted by P. E. Newberry in this work; she spent several seasons in Egypt between 1895 and 1901; she died unmarried in Kempshot Park, Basingstoke, 3 March 1912.

A. C. Benson, *Life and Letters of Maggie Benson*, 152, 189, 420, and passim (portr. facing p. 376); Newberry Corr.

GOYON, Georges Emile (1905-1996)
French Egyptologist; he was born at Port Said, 5 Aug. 1905, son of Henri G., a French employee of the Suez Canal, and Ida Innino; he was brought up in Egypt; he was trained as an architect and engineer and initially worked for the Suez Canal Company in Ismailia; he later studied at the University of Strasbourg under Montet (q.v.); he worked with Montet on his excavation of Tanis, 1929-45, 1955 and was present during the discovery of the tombs of the kings of Dynasties 21-22; he also undertook epigraphical research in the Wadi Hammamat under the auspices of King Farouk; he was later attached to the Centre National de la Recherche Scientifique, 1956-72, working at Giza and Saqqara; he published *Les Graffiti et Inscriptions des voyageurs sur la Grande Pyramide*, 1957; *Nouvelles Inscriptions rupestres du Wadi Hammamat*, 1957; *Le secret des Bâtisseurs des Grandes Pyramides-Kéops*, 1977, new ed. 1982; German and Italian translations, 1979; *La découverte des trésors de Tanis*, 1987; he also edited the travels of Morison (q.v.), 1976; he died at Cassis, 12 Jan. 1996.

BSFE 135 (1996), 2-3.

GRAF, (*Ritter von*) Otto Theodor (1840-1903)
Austrian antiquities dealer; he was born at Engarda, 11 March 1840; he was in business in Cairo and Vienna, and many very important finds passed through his hands; he sold the great find of papyri from Arsinoë made in 1877-8 to the Archduke Rainer of Vienna, and 160 Amarna tablets to Berlin Museum, 1888; he acquired a collection of about 300 Romano-Egyptian portrait-panels in 1887, 90 of which formed a travelling exhibition prior to sale in Europe and America; the rest were sold after his death by his heirs; examples were acquired by many museum collections, notably Berlin; two were bequeathed by Ludwig Mond to the National Gallery (NG 3931-2) and others given and bequeathed to the British Museum by Robert Mond (q.v.) (EA 63394-7, 65343-6); he was made Ritter, 1884; he died in Rodaun, 25 Nov. 1903.

J. Karabacek, *Die Theodor Graf'schen Funde in Aegypten*, Vienna, 1883; Maspero, *Ét. de Myth*, vi. 288; Wilbour, 469; Hilmy, i, 369; Paul Buberl, *Die griechisch-ägyptischen Mumienbildnisse der Sammlung Th. Graf*, 1923;

Erman, 224-5; K. Parlasca, *Mumienporträts und Verwandte Denkmäler*, 1966, 23-9; F. Hagen and K. Ryholt, *The Antiquities Trade in Egypt 1880-1930*, 2017, 217.

GRAHAM, (*Sir*) **Cyril Clarke, Bt.** (1834-1895)
English traveller, excavator and diplomat; he was born 6 March 1834, son of Sir Sandford Graham, 2nd Bt. of Kirkstall (1788-1852) and Caroline Langston (1794-1850); he travelled to the upper Nile early in 1857 and then on to Syria and Palestine; during August of that year he explored the desert east of the Hauran plateau; in April 1859 he met Lord Dufferin (q.v.) in Cairo and was appointed to superintend the continuation of Dufferin's excavations at Deir el-Bahari during June-September 1859, and was also responsible for the packing and transport of the finds to Ireland; in the autumn he travelled to Syria as Dufferin's private secretary and was part of Dufferin's mission there during 1860-1; Foreign Secretary of the Royal Geographical Society 1866-71; during 1870-1, Graham undertook a mission to negotiate with the government of Canada on behalf of the Hudson's Bay Company; in 1873 he travelled extensively in Russia, and later published a paper on the Avar language of the north Caucasus; Lieutenant Governor of Grenada 1875-7; ultimately fluent in Arabic, Turkish, French, German and Italian, he succeeded his brother as 5th Bt. 1890; he died at Cannes, 9 May 1895.

Report of the Council to Seventy-sixth Annual General Meeting of the Royal Astronomical Society, February 1896, 199-200; *JEA* 51 (1965), 17-21 (I. E. S. Edwards); inf. A. Dodson.

GRANGER, (*prev.* **TOURTECHOT**), **N.** (*d.*1737)
French physician and traveller; he came from Dijon in Burgundy; he served as a doctor in Tunis 1723-8 where he befriended a French official later appointed consul in Egypt; he arrived in Cairo in 1730 in the suite of the new consul and from Jan. 1731 began an exploration of Middle and Upper Egypt, visiting the Fayum, Beni Hasan, Abydos, Thebes and Edfu; his account *Relation d'un voyage fait en Égypte en l'année 1730* was posthumously published in Paris in 1745, translations were made into German in 1751 and into English in 1773; Granger made a second visit to Egypt in Aug. 1734-Sept. 1735, whence he set out to Cyprus, Palestine, Syria and Persia; he died on his way back near Basra 15 Feb. 1737.

Carré, i, 53-55; Hilmy, ii. 292; inf. M. Azim; M. Martin, *Annales Islamologiques* 19 (1983). 51-8, 22 (1986), 175-80; C. Meurice, *Annales Islamologiques* 39 (2005), 328-334; Lamy, 180-4.

GRANT, (*Bey*) **James Andrew Sandilands** (1840-1896)
British physician and collector; he was born in Methlick, 14 Oct. 1840, son of William G., a banker, and Mary Clark; after his education at Aberdeen Grammar School he studied medicine at the University; MA, 1862; MD, 1864; LLD, 1882; he went to Egypt to deal with a violent outbreak of cholera, where he was so successful that he was awarded the Order of Medjidieh; he returned to Scotland as Superintendent of the Banff Asylum, but later settled in Cairo when he was given a government appointment, and was made Bey by the Khedive; he formed a good collection of Egyptian antiquities which he bequeathed to the Marischal Museum of Aberdeen University; he died in Bridge of Man, Logie, 28 July 1896.

Aberdeen Mus. Records; frequently mentioned in Petrie and Wilbour (see index).

GRANVILLE, Augustus Bozzi (1783-1872)
British physician of Italian origin; he was born in Milan, 7 Oct. 1783, son of Carlo B., postmaster-general of the city, and his wife Maria Antonietta Rapazzini; he studied medicine at Pavia under Spallanzani and Volta, but his studies were interrupted by political imprisonment; on his release he travelled in the East, and then settled in England assuming the name of Granville; MD, 1802; MRCS, 1813; LRCP, 1817; FRS, 1817; he practised in Savile Row, London, specializing in the diseases of women and children; he was very interested in Egyptology and published a valuable account of a mummy of the Persian period with uterine disease, 'An Essay on Egyptian Mummies, with observations on the Art of Embalming', *Phil. Trans.* 1825, 269-316; he left London in 1871 and settled in Dover, where he died, 3 March 1872.

ODNB 23, 355-7; *DNB* 22, 412-14; Hilmy, i, 272; *JEA* 11 (1925), 76-7; *Mem. I.E.* 13, 17 (1929); Munk, *Roll of the Royal Coll. of Physicians*, iii, 174-7 (bibl.); *DBDI* 13, 585-7; P. Cosmacini, *EDAL* II (2010/1), 193-214; J Buikstra and C. Roberts (eds), *The Global History of Paleopathology. Pioneers and Prospects*, 2012, 209-10 (B. Baker and M. Judd); G. Cosmacini and P. Cosmacini, *Il medico delle Mummie*, 2013.

GRAPOW, Hermann (1885-1967)
German Egyptologist; he was born in Rostock, 1 Sept. 1885; he studied Egyptian and Coptic under Erman (q.v.) and Steindorff (q.v.) at the University of Berlin, 1906-12, after having had his interest in Egypt aroused at the

age of 17 by reading Steindorff's *Blütezeit*; PhD, 1912; he was made Hon. Professor in Berlin University, 1928; Professor of Egyptology, 1938-45 when he was dismissed for supporting the Nazi government; Dean of the Philosophical Faculty, 1940-45; Rector of the University of Berlin, 1943-45; he later founded the Institut fur Orienforschung in the Berlin Academy of which he was director, 1956-62; Dr. Med. *hon. c.* Rostock University for his work on ancient Egyptian medicine and medical texts, 1955; Member of the Prussian Acad., 1938; Vice-Pres of the Academy of Arts and Sciences and Acting Pres 1943-5; Guest Professor at Cairo, 1960-1; it is as collaborator with Erman from 1907 in his great work on the *Wörterbuch* that Grapow is chiefly remembered, but he also wrote and helped to produce many other important works; for the dictionary he assisted in the preliminary task of gathering together the great mass of data, and played a major part in the sorting and arranging of the 1.5 million *Zettel* used in its production; he was responsible for the regular appearance of all the 11 subsequent vols., a truly gigantic editorial achievement; Grapow's other major interest was the study of medical texts, and with the help of two other writers he brought out no less than six vols. which were of fundamental importance, between 1954 and 1959; his bibl. published on his seventieth birthday lists 87 books and articles; his principal works were, *Das 17. Kapitel des ägyptischen Totenbuches und seine religionsgeschichtliche Bedeutung*, a dissertation, 1912; *Über die Wortbildungen mit einem Präfix-m-im Ägyptischen*, 1914; *Religiöse Urkunden: ausgewählte Texte des Totenbuches*, 3 pts. 1915-16; *Vergleiche und andere bildliche Ausdrücke im Ägyptischen*, 1920; *Die bildlichen Ausdrücke des Ägyptischen vom Denken und Dichten einer altorientalischen Sprache*, 1924; *Über die anatomischen Kenntnisse der altägyptischen Ärzte*, 1935; *Untersuchungen über die altägyptischen medizinischen Papyri*, 1936; *Sprachliche und schriftliche Formung ägyptischer Texte*, 1936; *Vom Hieroglyphisch-Demotischen zum Koptischen*, 1938; *Wie die alten Ägypter sich anredeten, wie sich grüssten und wie sie miteinander sprachen*, 4 pts. 1939-43, 2nd ed. 1960; *Studien zu den Annalen Thutmosis des dritten und zu ihnen verwandten historischen Berichten des Neuen Reiches*, 1949; *Die Begründung d. Oriental-Kommission v. 1912*, 1950; *Untersuchungen zur ägyptischen Stilistik I (Der Stilische Bau der Geschichte des Sinuhe)*, 1952; *Das Wörterbuch der ägyptischen Sprache*, 1953; *Die Erforschung der altägypt. Kultur im Rahmen d. Akademie*, 1954; *Worte des Gedenkens an Adolf Erman anlässlich seines hundertsten Geburtstages am 31 Okt. 1954*, 1954; *Grundriss der Medizin der alten Ägypter*, i-iii, v, 1954-8; *Meine Begegnung mit einigen Ägyptologen*, 1973; he also edited, *Der Benanbrief, Eine moderne Leben-Jesu-Falschung*, with C. Schmidt, 1921; *Wörterbuch der ägyptischen Sprache*, with A. Erman, 6 vols. 1931-55, and 5 of *Belegstellen*, 1935-55; *Grundriss der Medizin* etc., vol. iv with H. v. Deines and Westendorf, 1958, vol. vi *Wörterbuch der ägyptischen Drogennamen*, with H. v. Deines, 1959; on his seventieth birthday a *Festschrift* was pub. by his friends with 40 articles by colleagues; he died in Berlin, 24 Aug. 1967.

JEA 53 (1967), 2; *ZÄS* 95 (1969), vii-x (portr.) (W. Westendorf); Erman, 289; Kürschner 1966, 712; *AfO* 22 (1968-9), 217-8 (portr.) (H. Brunner); O. Firchow, *Ägyptische Studien* 1955, ix-xiv (bibl.); E. Endesfelder, *Die Ägyptologie an der Berliner Universität-Zur Geschichte eines Fachgebietes*, 1988, 27, 42-54; inf. T. Schneider and T. Gertzen; T. Gertzen, *Die Berliner Schule der Ägyptologie. Begegnung mit Hermann Grapow*, 2015.

GRAY, Peter Hugh Ker (1913-1984)

British radiologist; he was born in St. Germans, Cornwall, 17 Nov. 1913, son of Mark Ker G. of the Royal Marines and Marion Hypatia Aston; he was educated at Bradfield College, Berks. and Guy's Hospital obtaining the diplomas of LRCP Lond. and MRCS Eng., 1937; he entered the Royal Navy and became a specialist in radiology, obtaining the radiology diploma DMRD Eng. in 1948; on leaving the Navy, he obtained consultant appointments as radiologist at Haslemere and Milford; Fellow of the Royal Soc. of Medicine and member of the British Institute of Radiology; he had been interested in archaeology since his youth and with the help of Warren Dawson (q.v.) undertook the study of the Egyptian mummies at the British Museum; he later undertook X-ray investigations of mummies at Liverpool, Oxford, Cambridge, the Horniman Museum in London, the Louvre in Paris, Leiden, and Munich; apart from his publications in medical and Egyptological journals, he was the author of *Mummies and Human Remains. Catalogue of Egyptian Antiquities in the British Museum Vol. I* (with W. Dawson), 1968 and *Egyptian mummies in the City of Liverpool Museum*, 1968; his collection of X-rays is now in the Dept. of Egyptian Antiquities, British Museum; he died in Cosham, Hampshire, 19 Feb. 1984.

Inf. from Mrs P. Gray and Sir Thomas Lodge; J. Buikstra and C. Roberts (eds), *The Global History of Palaeopathology. Pioneers and Prospects*, 2012, 224 (B. Baker and M. Judd).

GRAY, Terence James Stannus (1895-1986)

British theatre producer; he was born in Felixstowe, 14 Sept. 1895, son of Sir Harold William Stannus G., MP, from an Irish gentry family, and Rowena Elizabeth Stannus; he was educated at Eton, 1909-11 and briefly at Magdalene College, Cambridge, 1914-5; he served in the Red Cross, 1915-7 and then the Royal Flying Corps, 1917-8; he developed an interest in Egyptology on a visit to Egypt and wrote several dramas based on Egyptian

themes; he became acquainted with Winifred Brunton (q.v.) who illustrated his works and took part in her husband's excavation at Badari, 1923; he was the first to copy the stela of Sety I at Nauri, 1924; he also was involved with the excavation at Armant, 1925 and the subsequent desert explorations with Winkler (q.v.); he became Director of the Festival Theatre, Cambridge, 1926-33; he retired to France and later wrote works of Taoist philosophy under the name of Wei Wu Wei; his published Egyptian dramas were *The Life of the King of the South and North Kamaria, Daughter of the Sun Hatshepsut*, 1920 and *And in the Tomb were Found*, 1923 and he contributed to W. Brunton's *Kings and Queen of Ancient Egypt*, 1924; he died in Monte Carlo, 5 Jan. 1986.

P. Cornwell, *Only by Failure*, 2004.

GRDSELOFF, Bernard (1915-1950)

Egyptian Egyptologist of Georgian nationality; he was born in Egypt, 1 July 1915; he began his Egyptological studies in Berlin Museum and became a pupil of Sethe (q.v.); he was afterwards attached to the Institut für Ägyptische Bauforschung und Altertumskunde in Cairo, 1937-46 and worked there under Borchardt (q.v.), who appointed him secretary; he was also editorial sec. of the Soc. des Études Juives en Égypte; a brilliant scholar, at his early death he left much unfinished work; during his last illness he prepared and dictated six articles which were published posthumously, *in memoriam*, in *ASAE*; his most important studies were on the purification rites and embalming of the king in the pyramid age, the beginnings of the cult of Reshef in Egypt, and the Sety I stela at Scythopolis; some of his papers are in the Griffith Institute; he died in Cairo, 8 Oct. 1950.

ASAE 51 (1951), 123-8 (portr. and bibl.) with 6 articles ut supra, 129-66, (Ibrahim Harari); *AfO* 15 (1945-51), 193; *Chron. d'Ég.* 26 (1951), 119; EES *Report*, 1950, 6 (H. W. Fairman); *Sefarad*, Madrid, 11 (1951), 437 (B. Celada); inf. R. Grdseloff.

GREAVES, John (1602-1652)

English mathematician, astronomer, and orientalist; born Colemore near Alresford, Hampshire, 1602, eldest son of Revd John G. and his wife Sarah; he entered Balliol College, Oxford, 1617; BA, 1621; he was elected to a fellowship Merton College, 1624; MA, 1628; in addition to studying natural philosophy and mathematics Greaves studied a number of oriental languages in order to read the ancient Greek, Arabian, and Persian writers on astronomy; he was appointed Professor of Geometry at Gresham College, London, 1630, and was introduced to Archbishop Laud to whose patronage he later owed his trip to Egypt; he travelled extensively in France, Holland, and Italy during the 1630s, reaching Constantinople in 1638; from there he went on to Egypt via Rhodes, and after staying four months at Alexandria went to Cairo equipped with mathematical instruments, in order to measure the pyramids; after having collected Greek, Arabic, and Persian MSS he returned to England, 1640; he was now chosen Savilian Professor of Astronomy at Oxford, but lost his Gresham professorship due to his absence; in 1645 he drew up a scheme for reforming the calendar, but it was not adopted; he published his famous *Pyramidographia, or a Discourse of the Pyramids in Aegypt*, 1646, a work which although criticized at the time, is of great interest today; it consists of a very thorough survey of the Giza pyramids and used every means available to a scholar of the period; Greaves quoted the descriptions of the pyramids given by classical authors and used what is an early critical approach in trying to decide how what he himself saw approximated to ancient traditions; he identified them correctly as burial places, tried to establish when they were built, included a discussion of embalming, and gave estimates of their dimensions which were more accurate than those of other early travellers although at times inaccurate; he climbed the Great Pyramid and measured the size of the stones, and explored the interior; the section through the Great Pyramid is astonishingly accurate for the period, as regards everything drawn above ground level; Greaves also noted the 'dwellings' discussed by Petrie at the back of the Second Pyramid, and the basalt foundations of a building before the Great Pyramid which he identified with great perception as the funerary temple; he also published *Demonstratio Ortus Sini Heliaci pro parallelo inferioris Aegypti*, 1648, which dealt with the vexed question of the rising of the dog-star Sirius; Greaves was ejected from his professorship during the Civil War, and also lost a large part of his books and MSS although some were recovered later; he returned to London and married, continuing to publish works on oriental astronomy and mathematics; he was in a sense an Egyptologist before his time, his being the first scientific and systematic survey of the Giza pyramids undertaken; he died in London, 8 Oct. 1652, and was buried in St. Benet Sherehog, London (destroyed in the Great Fire, 1666).

ODNB 23, 486-7 (portr.); *DNB* 23, 38-9; J. P. Lauer, *Le Problème des pyramides d'Égypte*, 1952, pp. 15, 27-9, 35, 38, 41, 119; Vyse, ii.

GRÉBAUT, Eugène (1846-1915)

French Egyptologist; he was born in Paris, 1 June 1846, son of Eugène G., a notary, and Jeanne Françoise Martine Sauvageot; he was educated at the École des Hautes Études and studied Arabic under Guyard and Egyptology under Maspero (q.v.); he published *The Hymn to Amun in Cairo Museum*, 1872-5, a work that showed great promise; he lectured at the École, 1876-8, and continued to study there until 1883; he was appointed to succeed Lefébure (q.v.) as Director of the French Arch. Mission at Cairo, 6 Oct. 1883-6; he then succeeded Maspero as Director of the Antiquities Service, June 1886-92; this appointment was unfortunate as he was by nature unsuited to this work and it caused much ill feeling both with Egyptologists and local Egyptians; he resigned in 1892 and returned to Paris, becoming lecturer in Ancient History at the Sorbonne until his death; he wrote, *Hymne à Amon-Ra des papyrus égyptiens du Musée de Boulaq*, 1874; *Recueil de monuments et de notices sur les fouilles d'Égypte*, 3 vols., Cairo Museum, 1890-1915; he died in Romainville, 8 Jan. 1915.

Maspero, *L'Égyptologie* (1915), 8, 13, 16; *Rev. Arch.* 4th Ser. 24 (1914), 332-3 (G. Maspero); numerous references to Grébaut will be found in the indexes of the following: Budge, *N & T*, Petrie, Sayce, Wilbour; *JEA* 33 (1947), 80; Hilmy, i, 276.

GREEN, Frederick William (1869-1949)

British Egyptologist and excavator; he was born in London, 21 March 1869, son of Frederick G., solicitor, and Sophia Rose; he studied at Jesus College, Cambridge; BA, 1898; MA, 1901; he became interested in Egyptology at an early age and studied it under Sethe (q.v.) at Göttingen and later at Strasbourg; he excavated sites in Egypt with Clarke (q.v.), Petrie (q.v.), and Reisner (q.v.), and in 1897-9 while working with Quibell (q.v.) on the predynastic site of Hierakonpolis for the Egyptian Research Account, he discovered the famous decorated tomb; he also worked for the Egyptian Govt. Geological Survey, 1897-1900, and prepared maps for other surveys, 1905-14; he was in charge of the Mond excavations at Armant, 1929-30; he was Hon. Keeper of Antiquities, Fitzwilliam Museum, Cambridge, 1908-49 to which institution he donated numerous objects; his notebooks are now in the Department of Egyptian Antiquities, British Museum and the Faculty of Oriental Studies, Cambridge; he died in Great Shelford, Cambs., 20 Aug. 1949.

Inf. Mrs. Green; *Chron d'Ég.* 25(1950), 273-4 (A. Mekhitarian); J. E. Quibell, *Hierakonpolis*; J. C. Green in *Nekhen News* 10 (1998), 15-6.

GREENE, John Baker Stafford (*c.*1832-1888)

British surgeon, barrister, and author; he was born in Dublin in 1832, son of John Alfred G., barrister, and Maria Baker; BA, MB Trinity Coll, Dublin, 1857; MD and LSA, 1853; MCS, 1853; Assistant Surgeon, 1st Royal Scots in the Crimean War; Barrister-at-Law, Middle Temple, 1858; LL.B. London, 1859; member of council, R. Hist. Soc., 1880-86; he also published *The Hebrew Migration from Egypt*, 1882, 2nd ed. 1883, contributions to *PEFQS* (1884, 230-7; 1885, 67) and other works; he died in London, 22 June 1888.

Hilmy, i, 276; ii. 418; *Med. Directory*, 1885; *Times* 26 June 1888; J. Foster, *Men-At-The Bar*, 1885, 187.

GREENE, John Beasley (1832-1856)

Franco-American archaeologist and photographer; he was born in Le Havre, 20 June 1832, son of John Bulkeley G., banker, and Marie Reine Dejoye; he studied Egyptology under de Rougé (q.v.); in 1853-4 he visited Egypt and took over 200 photographs of Egyptian views and antiquities, published in *Le Nil-Monuments-Paysages-Explorations Photographiques*, Lille, 1855; he excavated at Thebes 1854-5 and published his results in a large folio vol. *Fouilles exécutées à Thèbes*, Paris 1855; he died in Cairo, 28 Nov. 1856.

Chabas, 14, 18; *History of Photography* 5 (1981), 305-24; N. Perez, *Focus East*, 1988, 173.

GREENER, (Herbert) Leslie Standerwick (1900-1974)

British artist and writer; he was born at Constantia, Capetown, South Africa 13 Feb. 1900, son of Herbert G., a military officer, and Helen Bennett; he was educated at Felsted School 1914-7 and then Sandhurst, joining the Indian Army 1919-24; he then studied art at the Christchurch School of Art, New Zealand and the Académie Julien in Paris 1927-8 and became a teacher of art and French at Victoria College, Alexandria 1928-31; he joined the University of Chicago epigraphic mission in Luxor 1931-6 working at Medinet Habu and Karnak; he worked as a journalist in Australia 1937-41 when he joined the army and was taken prisoner at Singapore; he returned to journalism 1945-9 and then became Director of Adult Education in Tasmania 1949-54; he rejoined the Chicago House mission 1958-67 working in Luxor and Nubia and later participated in the Akhenaten temple project; he donated some Egyptian antiquities to the Tasmanian Museum and Art Gallery, Hobart; his home in Longley, Tasmania, and its contents were destroyed in a bushfire in 1967; his published works include *High Dam over Nubia*, 1962; *The Discovery of Egypt*, 1966; and *Discovering Egypt*, 1976; he died in Hobart, Tasmania, 8 Dec. 1974.

Contemporary Authors Permanent Series 2, 229; Felsted School Reg.; inf. Mr. and Mrs. R. Hood, Tasmania; R. S. Merrillees, *Living with Egypt's Past in Australia*, 1990, 46-8, 50, 57; *Australian Dictionary of Biography* 14, 322.

GREENFIELD, Edith Mary (*née* Bridges) (1868-1935)
British benefactress; she was born in Milton Mills, Enniscorthy, Ireland, 14 Dec. 1868, daughter of Edward B. and Anne Gifford; she was the widow of Herbert Bunce Greenfield of Derby, a contractor who carried out harbour works at Alexandria in 1880; while in Egypt he bought the fine funerary papyrus of Princess Estanebasher (Nesitanebtashru), from the cache of royal mummies, the longest funerary papyrus known; this papyrus was presented to the British Museum in May 1910 by Mrs. Greenfield (EA 10554), and it was at once published by the Trustees under the name, *The Greenfield Papyrus*, 1912, ed. Budge; Mrs. G. died in Morley Manor, Derby, 13 May 1935.

Cromer, *Modern Eg.* i, 171; *The Times*, 15 May 1935.

GREENHILL, Thomas (1681-1740)
British physician and surgeon; he was born posthumously, probably at Abbot's Langley, Herts., 1681, the thirty-ninth living child of William G., a counsellor-at-law and secretary to General Monck, and Elizabeth Jones, who married at 16 in 1631; in commemoration of this record number of births an augmentation was granted to the family arms dated 1 Sept. 1698; he practised in King Street, Bloomsbury, and had a distinguished clientele and a high reputation; he was not FRS, but he made two communications to *Phil. Trans.*; he published *NEKPOKHΔEIA, or the Art of Embalming*, London, 1705, in which Egyptian mummification figures largely; he died in 1740.

ODNB 23, 601-2; *DNB* 23, 80; Hilmy, i, 277; *Mem. I. E* 13 (1929), 18-20.

GREG, (*Sir*) Robert Hyde (1876-1953)
British diplomat and collector; born Styal, Cheshire, 24 Dec. 1876, son of Edward Hyde G. and Margaret Broadbent; he married 1914 Julia Schreiner of New York (*d.* 1953); in 1911 he was appointed Second Secretary at the British Agency in Egypt; from 1917-21 he was in charge of the Ministry of Foreign Affairs; he later returned to Cairo in 1929 as British Commissioner for the Egyptian Debt and continued to live there after his retirement in 1940 until his death; President of the EES, 1949-53; throughout his career he was interested in Egyptian art and bequeathed his private collection of Egyptian antiquities, together with an endowment, to the Fitzwilliam Museum, Cambridge; he was a member of the Committees of Egyptian, Coptic, and Moslem monuments and a member of the advisory panel set up in 1943 to make recommendations on the conservation of the Theban tombs; he died in Giza, 3 Dec. 1953.

EES *Report* 1953, 5 (W. B. Emery); *JEA* 40 (1954), 1-2 (I. E. S. Edwards); *WWW* v, 543.

GRENFELL, Alice (*née* Pyne) (1842-1917)
British collector and scarab specialist; she was born in London, 21 Oct. 1842, daughter of Henry P., barrister, and Harriet James; she married 1869 John Granville G., Master of Clifton College and was the mother of Bernard Pyne G. (see below); she contributed many learned articles to *Rec. Trav.* and other journals on the symbols etc. used on scarabs; she described the collection in The Queen's College, Oxford in *JEA* 2 (1915), 217; she died in Oxford, 8 Aug. 1917.

JEA 4 (1917), 280.

GRENFELL, Bernard Pyne (1869-1926)
British papyrologist; he was born in Birmingham, 16 Dec. 1869, son of John Granville G., Master of King Edward's School and later Clifton College, and Alice Pyne;he was educated at Clifton College, and studied at The Queen's College, Oxford; Fellow, 1894; MA; DLitt; FBA; Hon. member of many foreign academies; Professor of Papyrology, Oxford, 1916; he went to Egypt in 1894 for training in excavation technique under Petrie (q.v.), and in 1895 and succeeding years explored the Fayum sites for papyri for the EEF; on the formation of the Graeco-Roman Branch of the Fund he edited with Hunt (q.v.) many volumes of the *Oxyrhynchus Papyri* and other publications of that Branch, though his work was often interrupted by ill health; he also collaborated with Hunt in the catalogues of the Amherst, John Rylands, and Cairo collections; his first independent work was the *Revenue Laws of Ptolemy Philadelphus*, 1896, based on the important papyrus obtained by Petrie in 1894; he died in Eley, Perth, 17 March 1926.

Aegyptus 8, 114; *JEA* 12 (1926), 285-6 (J. G. Milne); *Rev. Arch.* Ser. 5 24. 76; *WWW* ii, 436; *ODNB* 23, 706-7; M. Capasso (ed.), *Hermae*, 2007, 115-41 (portr.).

GRENFELL, (*Rt. Hon.*) **Francis Algernon Wallace, 1st Baron Grenfell** (1841-1925)
British soldier and excavator; he was born in London, 29 April 1841, fourth son of Pascoe St. L. Grenfell JP, and Catherine Ann Dupré; he entered the Army, 1859; Colonel, 1882; General, 1904; Field Marshal, 1908; GCB; PC; GCMG; LL.D.; FSA; created Baron Grenfell of Kilvey, Glamorganshire, 1902; President of the Egypt Exploration Society 1916-9; married 1. Evelyn Wood, 1887 (*d.*1899), 2. Hon. Aline Majendie, 1903 (*d.*1911); he served in Egypt and the Sudan, 1882-9; Commander-in-Chief, Egyptian Army; he carried out excavations at Aswan 1886 and also formed a collection of antiquities the scarabs of which were described in *AE* 1916, 22; he presented a mummy to Swansea Museum and other objects to the Museum in Valletta, Malta; he was a good friend to archaeologists working in Egypt; his collections were sold at Sotheby's, 12-14 Nov. 1917 (479 lots); his papers are now in the Centre for Middle Eastern Studies, St. Anthony's College, Oxford; he died in Windlesham, Surrey, 27 Jan. 1925.

Budge, *N & T* I. 74, 81, 88; Petrie, 122, 135; *PSBA* x, 4-40; Sayce, 239; *ODNB* 23, 709-10 (portr.); *DNB* 1922-30, 362-4; *WWW* ii, 436; *Apollo* cxx No. 270 (1984), 122-77; *Memoirs of Field-Marshal Lord Grenfell*, 1925 (autobiography); Lugt 77232; inf. A. B. Lloyd; T. Baber in N. Cooke and V. Daubney (eds), *Lost and Now Found*, 2017, 28-9.

GRENIER, Jean-Claude (1943-2016)
French Egyptologist; he was born at Agen, 10 Sept. 1943, son of Etienne G. and Lucie Jeanne Simone Pinthon; he was educated in Roman history at the University of Bordeaux; Diploma, 1967; he later studied Egyptology at the Université Paris IV under Leclant (q.v.); Doctorat de IIIe cycle, 1972; Doctorat d'État ès lettres, 1985; he became an assistant at the Institut d'Art et Archéologie, Université Paris IV, 1969-73; he served as archivist at IFAO in Cairo, 1973-9, and was seconded to the Egyptian Antiquities Service where he edited ASAE, 1980-5; he was appointed Keeper of Egyptian Antiquities at the Museo Gregorio Egizio at the Vatican, 1985-9 and consultant thereafter; he then served as lecturer at the Université Paul Valéry at Montpellier, 1989-92; Professor, 1992-2012, and then emeritus; he also worked as as a director of studies at the École Pratique des Hautes Études, 1990-2012, and as a team director at CNRS, 2003-7; while in Egypt, he undertook epigraphy at Tod and took part in the excavations at Douch, 1976; he later excavated at Atfih, 2007-8; he founded the series *Aegyptiaca Gregoriana*, 1989; 4 volumes of studies in his honour were edited by A. Gasse, F. Servajean, and C. Thiers, *Et in Aegypto et ad Aegyptum*, 2012; apart from numerous articles, he published *Anubis alexandrine et romain*, 1978; *L'autel funéraire isiaque de Fabia Stratonice*, 1978; *Temples ptolémaïques et romains*, 1979; *Tôd. Les inscriptions du temple ptolémaïque et romain*, 1981; with S. Cauville and D. Devauchelle, *Catalogue de la fonte hiéroglyphique de l'Imprimerie de l'Institut Français d'Archéologie Orientale*, 1983; with A. el-Hafeez and G. Wagner, *Stèles funéraires de Kom Abou Billo*, 1985; *Les titulaires des Empereurs romains dans les documents de langue égyptienne*, 1989; *La décoration statuaire du Serapeum du Canope de la Villa Adriana*, 1990; *Museo Gregoriano Egizio, Musei Vaticani, Guide Cataloghi*, 1993; *Les statuettes funéraires du Museo Gregoriano Egizio*, 1996; *Les bronzes du Museo Gregoriano Egizio*, 2002; *L'Osiris Antinoos*, 2008; he died at Montferrier sur Lez, 22 July 2016.

A. Gasse, F. Servajean, and C. Thiers, *Et in Aegypto et ad Aegyptum*, 2010, I, i-iii, v-x (bibl.); *BIFAO* 116 (2016), 1-9 (A. Gasse and C. Thiers) (portr.) (bibl.).

GRENVILLE, George Nugent, 2nd Baron Nugent (1788-1850)
British administrator and collector; he was born in Kilmainham, Dublin, 30 Dec. 1788, younger son of George Grenville, the 1st Marquess of Buckingham and Mary 1st Baroness Nugent; he married Anne Lucy Poulett, 1813; he succeeded to his mother's Irish peerage, 1833; a Lord of the Treasury, 1830-2; High Commissioner of the Ionian Islands, 1832-5; he visited Egypt in 1844 and published an account *Lands, classical and sacred*, 1846; he made a collection of antiquities, which descended to Lady Boileau (née Lucy Henrietta Nugent) of Ketteringham Park, Norfolk; the collection of Lord Vernon, sold at Sotheby's, 16-17 Dec. 1926, was mistakenly linked to Grenville in the sales catalogue and in earlier editions of this work; he died in his home in Lillies, Bucks., 26 Nov. 1850.

DNB 23, 119-20; *ODNB* 23, 730-2 (portr.); A. Blackman in *JEA* 4 (1917), 39-43.

GREY, (*Revd*) **George Francis** (1792-1854)
British traveller and antiquarian; he was born 16/17 Dec. 1792 and baptized at Earsdon 13 Feb. 1793, son of Ralph William G. of Backworth, Northumberland and Elizabeth Brandling; educated at University College, Oxford; BA, 1814; MA, 1822; Fellow, 1814-53; he visited Egypt in 1820 and accompanied Sir Frederick Henniker to Upper Egypt; while there he bought some papyri at Thebes which he submitted to Thomas Young; he published 'Inscriptions from the Wady el-Makketeb copied in 1820', *Trans. R.S.L.* ii. 147 (1834); he died in Lausanne, 6 Oct. 1854.

Al. Oxon.; Champollion, i, 91, 92; Henniker, 75; Hilmy, i, 277; Pettigrew, *Hist. Eg. Mummies*, 150; *Syro-Eg. Soc. Inscr.* 1852; Young, *Discoveries*, 38, 55, 145.

GRIFFITH, Agnes Sophia *see* **JOHNS**

GRIFFITH, Francis Llewellyn (1862-1934)
British Egyptologist; he was born in Brighton, 27 May 1862, youngest son of the Revd John G., LLD, headmaster of Brighton College and a mathematician, and Sarah Foster his wife; educated at Brighton Coll., Sedbergh, and Highgate School; he gained a scholarship to The Queen's College, Oxford 1879, but while there refused to read for final hons. and studied on his own; in 1882 he was articled to his brother, a solicitor in Brighton; graduated 1884; MA; DLitt; Hon. LLD Aberdeen; FBA; FSA; his interest in Egyptology was first awakened by reading Belzoni (q.v.) as a child, later at school he became more involved with it and by 1884 had not only acquired a good knowledge of classics but had taught himself Egyptian; he asked Petrie (q.v.) for help and spent four seasons with Petrie and Naville (q.v.) excavating in Egypt, 1884-8, at the sites of Naucratis, Tanis, Tell el-Yahudiya, and Gumaiyema in the Delta; he also gained valuable experience 1886 when he accompanied Petrie on a trip through Upper Egypt from Minia to Aswan, and at this period made a trip across N. Sinai to Wady el-Arish to copy and publish an inscription found by Sayce (q.v.);
although by now one of the best qualified young Egyptologists in the world there was no position for him at the time and he worked as an assistant in the Dept. of British and Mediaeval Antiquities and Ethnography in the British Museum, 1888-96, but continued his Egyptian research in his spare time; he was also Assistant to the Professor of Egyptology, University College London, 1892-1901; Hon. Lecturer in Egyptology at Manchester University, 1896-1908; appointed Reader in Egyptology, University of Oxford, 1901; Professor, 1924; Deputy Professor, 1932; Professor Emeritus, 1933; Hon. Fellow of The Queen's Coll., Oxford; he undertook excavations at Faras and Sanam in Nubia 1910-3; he married 1. Kate daughter of Charles Timothy Bradbury of Ashton-under-Lyne, 1896, who had studied under Petrie, died 1902; 2. Nora C. C. daughter of Surgeon-Major James Macdonald, died 1937 (for both, see below); Griffith was the foremost philologist in the whole range of Egyptian texts in Britain, and in the field of hieratic studies broke new ground; with his transcriptions, translations, and interpretations of the Kahun and Gurob Papyri he dealt with extremely difficult cursive texts most accurately; he next turned to Demotic and his *Stories of the High Priests* raised him straight away to be the leading Demotist of his day; he also did valuable research in Old Coptic and the Nubian language, but his greatest achievement was the decipherment of Meroitic script; this with H. Schäfer's (q.v.) similar feat in Christian Nubian was the first pioneer work of its kind since Champollion (q.v.) and brought him world-wide recognition; he was a Corresp. member of, among others, Berlin and Vienna Acads.; a Member of the Royal Danish Acad.; Fellow of the Imperial German Arch. Instit.; Foreign Assoc. of the Soc. Asiatique; Corresp. of the Acad. des Inscriptions et Belles-Lettres; Hon. Member of the American Oriental Soc. and Hon. Dr. Phil. of the University of Leipzig; Griffith's bibl. lists over 260 books and articles without including all the reviews; his principal works were, *Tanis*, 1888, a chapter in Petrie's Pt. ii; *Naukratis*, Pt. ii, 1888; *The City of Onias and the Mound of the Jew*, 1890, ed. Naville; *Two Hieroglyphic Papyri from Tanis*, 1889; *Inscriptions of Siût and Der Rifeh*, 1889; *Beni Hasan*, pts. iii and iv, 1896, 1900; *Hieratic Papyri from Kahun and Gurob*, 2 vols. 1897, 1898; *Hieroglyphs from the Collections of the Egypt Exploration Fund*, 1898; *Stories of the High Priests of Memphis*, 1900; *Demotic Magical Papyrus of London and Leyden*, 3 vols. 1904-9, with Sir Herbert Thompson; *Catalogue of the Demotic Papyri in the Rylands Library at Manchester*, 3 vols. 1909; *The Meroitic Inscriptions of Shablûl and Karanôg*, 1911; *Meroitic Inscriptions*, 2 pts. 1911, 1912; *The Nubian Texts of the Christian Period*, 1913; 'Oxford Excavations in Nubia', in *Liverpool Annals of Arch. & Anth.*, 1921-8; *Christian Documents from Nubia*, 1928; after his death his wife also completed two of his works, *Catalogue of the Demotic Graffiti of the Dodecaschoenus*, 1935, 1937; *The Adler Papyri*, 1939; he wrote articles in *EB* (9-10 eds); Hastings' *Dictionary of the Bible*, etc.; in all Griffith wrote or contributed to 19 EEF reports and memoirs, and edited no fewer than 25 vols. of the Archaeological Survey of which he wrote 5; he was by far the greatest literary contributor to the work of the EES, writing many articles and reviews in *JEA* and editing the Annual Reports for twenty years; he wrote bibls. for 34 years from 1892 on; in later life he was again excavating at Amarna and Kawa in the Sudan; by his will he bequeathed his magnificent Egyptological library, the finest one in existence, and papers, together with a large financial endowment to build and maintain an Institute of Near-Eastern Archaeology at Oxford; this took effect on the death of his wife in 1937, and the Griffith Institute, attached to the Ashmolean Museum, was built and formally opened, 21 Jan. 1939, his portrait being kept there; on his 70th birthday, a fine volume of *Studies* by 72 of his colleagues, pupils and friends was presented to him; he died in Boar's Hill, Oxford, 14 March 1934.

Studies, ed. S. R. K. Glanville, portr. 485-94 (bibl.); *WWW* iii, 559; *ODNB* 23, 959-61; *DNB* 1931-40, 375-7 (B . Gunn); *JEA* 20 (1934), 71-7 (portr.) (A. H. Gardiner); *Proc. Br. Acad.* 20 (1934), 309-22 (W. E. Crum); *AE* 62-3 (Sir W. M. F. Petrie) is good for early years; *Bull. John Rylands Lib.*, 18 (1934), 260-3 (anon.); *Eg. Relig.* 2 (1934), 118-21 (A. M. Blackman); *Mizraim* 3 (1936), 7-8 (Sir F. G. Kenyon); *Rev. d'ég.* 2 125; *ZÄS* 70 (1934), 135 (anon.); Newberry Corr; R. Janssen, *The First Hundred Years*, 1992, 10-11; R. Janssen, *DE* 35 (1996), 49-59; M. Serpico in D. Magee, J. Bourriau and S. Quirke, *Sitting Beside Lepsius*, 2009, 491-514; E. Bosworth (ed.), *A Century of British Orientalists*, 2001 (J. Ray) (portr.), 186-99.

GRIFFITH, Kate (*née* **Bradbury**) (1854-1902)
British archaeologist; she was born at Ashton-under-Lyne, 26 Aug. 1854, daughter of Charles Timothy Bradbury, a wealthy businessman, and Elizabeth Ann Tomlins; she was a friend of Amelia Edwards (q.v.), whom she accompanied to America in 1890; she assisted in the early work of the EEF, rendering great assistance and serving for many years on the committee; she married in 1896 F.Ll. Griffith (q.v.); a settlement made by her father enabled her husband to devote the whole of his time to Egyptology and provided the basis of the endowment which he later bequeathed to the University of Oxford; she translated two of Wiedemann's books on Egyptian religion into English (1896-7) and took an active part in her husband's scientific works and publications; she died in Silverdale near Carnforth, Lancs, 2 March 1902.

EEF Arch. Report, 1901-2, 37; Newberry Corr.; R. Janssen, *The First Hundred Years*,1992, 3-4,7,9,11.

GRIFFITH, Nora Christina Cobban (*née* **Macdonald**) (1870-1937)
British second wife of F. Ll. Griffith; she was born in Aberdeen, 7 Dec. 1870, daughter of Surgeon-Major James M. of Aberdeen and Margaret Helen Leslie Collie; she visited Egypt in 1906 and becoming interested in Egyptology, she studied it under Griffith at Oxford, and married him in 1909; she assisted him in his studies and in excavations in Egypt and Nubia, 1910-13, 1923, 1929, 1930; after his death she maintained his library, destined for Oxford University, and also prepared his unfinished works for publication; by her will she added her fortune to that of her husband for the building and endowment of the Griffith Institute at Oxford; she died in Oxford, 21 Oct. 1937.

JEA 23 (1937), 262-3.

GRIFFITHS, John Gwynedd (Gwyn) (1911-2004)
British classicist and Egyptologist; he was born at Porth, Glamorgan, 7 Dec. 1911, son of Robert G., Baptist minister, and Jemima Davies; he studied classics at the Universities of Cardiff, Liverpool, and Oxford; he was appointed Assistant Lecturer in Classics, University College of Swansea 1946-47, Lecturer 1947-59, Senior Lecturer 1959-65, Reader 1965-73, Professor of Classics and Egyptology 1973-79 and then Emeritus; visiting Professor at Cairo Univ 1968; he married 1939 Käthe Bosse (q.v.); he was also active in the Welsh nationalist movement; a festschrift in his honour *Studies in Pharaonic Religions and Society*, ed. by A. B. Lloyd, was published in 1992; his principal interest was Ancient Egyptian religion and the Greek sources for it; he published *The Conflict of Horus and Seth*, 1960, translations of Plutarch's *De Iside et Osiride*, 1970, and Apuleius' *The Isis-book*, 1975; *The Origins of Osiris and his Cult*, 1980, *The Divine Verdict*, 1991; *Atlantis and Egypt*, 1991; and *Triads and Trinity*, 1996; he died at Swansea, 15 June 2004.

The Independent 18 June 2004 (portr.) (M. Stephens); A. B. Lloyd, *Studies in Pharaonic Religion and Society*, 1992, (portr.), 1-13 (bibl. to 1991). Photograph courtesy of Roger Davies.

GRINSELL, Leslie Valentine (1907-1995)
British archaeologist and prehistorian; he was born in London, 14 Feb. 1907, son of Arthur John Grinsell, silversmiths' manager, and Janet Christine Tabor; he was educated in schools in London and Hurstpierpoint and Pitman's College; he joined Barclay's Bank in 1925 until 1949; he had long had an interest in British archaeology which he pursued; during World War II he was attached to air photographic intelligence in Egypt, 1941-5 where, in his spare time he studied Egyptian monuments and was taught hieroglyphs by Fairman (q.v,); he joined the staff of the Victoria County History of Wiltshire, 1949 and was appointed curator of archaeology at Bristol City Museum, 1952-72; Hon. Treasurer of the British School of Archaeology in Egypt, 1948; Hon. MA from Bristol University; OBE,

1972; he endowed and inaugurated the Amelia Edwards Lecture in Egyptology at Bristol University, 1993; his Egyptological works were *Egyptian Pyramids,* 1947; *Guide Catalogue to the Collections from Ancient Egypt. Bristol City Museum*, 1972; *An Archaeological Autobiography*, 1989; he died Bristol, 28 Feb. 1995.

L. V. Grinsell, *An Archaeological Autobiography*, 1989 (portr.) (bibl.); *JEA* 81 (1995), vi (V. A. Donahue).

GRIVAUD DE LA VINCELLE, Claude Madeleine (1762-1819)
French collector; he was born in Châlon-sur-Saône, 5 Sept. 1762; his name was originally Grivaud, but he added de la Vincelle after his marriage to the illegitimate daughter of the Prince of Monaco; he was a pioneer of archaeology in France; he had a fine collection of Greek and Egyptian antiquities which was sold in Paris 21 June 1820, the catalogue being drawn up by L. J. J. Dubois; he published *Recueil des Monuments antiques*, 1817; he died in Paris, 4 Dec. 1819.

DBF 16, 1280; Lugt 9776; È. Gran-Aymerich, *Dictionnaire biographique d'archéologie 1798-1945*, 2001, incorporated in *Les Chercheurs de passé 1798-1945*, 2007, 844-5.

GROFF, William Nessly (1857-1901)
American Egyptologist; he was born in Cincinnati, Ohio, 4 May, 1857, son of William Tarbot. G., a physician, and his wife Sarah Elizabeth Talbot; he studied Egyptology in Paris under Maspero (q.v.) and Renan (q.v.); he lived in Cairo, where he worked as a translator, 1891-9 and Athens, 1899; his special interest was the relation of Egypt to Old Testament history; he published many articles in *BIÉ* and other journals; his works were collected and edited by Maspero, with a biographical notice by his sister, Florence Groff; he died in Athens, 4 Dec. 1901.

Bibl. Ég., Oeuvres de W. N. Groff, 1908, pp. i-iv (portr.)

GROPPI, Achille (1890-1949)
Swiss patissier and collector; he was born in Alexandria, 28 April 1890, son of Giacomo and Eugenie Groppi; he worked for the family business of J. Groppi, which owned a chain of fashionable cafés in Cairo; in the inter-war period he formed a collection of Egyptian antiquities, with particularly notable holdings of glass and faience; part of this was dispersed in three sales at Christie's (London, 9 Dec. 1992; 7 July and 8 Dec. 1993); part kept by his descendants was exhibited in Hanover and Basel, 2008-9; he died in Switzerland, 22 Nov. 1949.

Family inf. per A. Wiese; papers in family possession; C. Loeben and A. Weise (eds) *Köstlichkeiten aus Kairo!*, 2008; inf. T. Hardwick.

GRUEBER, Herbert Appold (1846-1927)
British numismatist and antiquary; he was born in Curry Rivell, Somerset, 14 Nov. 1846, son of the Revd Charles Stephen G. and Catherine Appold; he entered the British Museum, 1866; Assistant Keeper of Coins and Medals, 1893-12; he married Alice Emily Hewitt (*d.*1926); he was Treasurer of EEF 1887-1912; he published many numismatic works; his library was sold at Sotheby's, 14 Nov. 1912 (lots 99-148); he died in Bembridge, Isle of Wight, 21 Nov. 1927.

WWW ii, 442; Newberry Corr.

GRUNERT, Stefan (1946-2016)
German Egyptologist; he was born in Berlin, 14 Oct. 1946; he studied at the University of Leipzig under Morenz (q.v.) and Blumenthal, 1966-70; Diploma, 1971; PhD, 1977; he worked on the *Wörterbuch* project from 1971; he specialised in demotic studies; his contribution to the electronic corpus of Egyptain texts focused on the inssriptions in the tombs of the Old Kingdom, 1992-2011; he undertook excavations at Tell Basta, 1979-90; a volume edited by F. Feder, L. Morenz, and G. Vittmann, *Von Theben nach Giza* was published in his honour, 2011; apart from articles, he published *Demotische Papyri aus den Staalichen Museen zu Berlin* II, *Thebanische Kaufverträge des 3. und 2. Jahrhunderts v. u. Z.*, 1981; *Der Codex Hermpolis und ausgewählte private Rechtsurkunden aus dem ptolemäischen Ägypten*, 1982; with others, *Eine Reise durch Ägypten*, 1984; with J. Frösen, *Papyri Helsingiense* I. *Ptolemäische Urkunden (P. Hels. I)*, 1987; with M. Bakir, *Tell Basta* I, 1992; and edited, with I. Hafemann, *Textcorpus und Wörterbuch*, 1999; he died in Berlin, 10 March 2016.

Inf. I. Hafemann and S. Wenig.

GRYPHIUS, (Greif) Andreas (1616-1664)
German poet and dramatist; he was born on 2 Oct. 1616 in Glogau, Silesia, son of Paul G. and Anna Erhard; in 1662 Gryphius published an interesting pamphlet in Latin entitled *Mumiae Vratislavienses* (Wroclaw/Breslau, at Vitus Jacobus Drescher) in which he describes a dissection of two mummies which took place at Wroclaw on 7

Dec. 1658; this booklet contains interesting and comprehensive descriptions of the Wroclaw mummies and some information concerning the European commerce with mummies from Egypt; an important discussion on ancient sources about mummies and mummification is included; he died at Glogau, 16 July 1664.

Études Germaniques 19 (1964), 451-62; *NDB* 7, 242-6.

GUÉRAUD, (Edgard) Octave (1901-1987)
French papyrologist; he was born at La Tronche, 30 Jan. 1901, son of Marcel G., a teacher, and Marie Mathilde Godard; he was educated at the École Normale Supérieure, 1920-3; he worked with Jouget (q.v.) at the Sorbonne, 1920-24; after a short time as a teacher, he joined IFAO in Cairo in Jan. 1927 to 30 Nov. 1931; he briefly directed the excavations at Edfu in 1928; he was appointed Assistant Keeper at the Cairo Museum in charge of the Graeco-Roman section from 1 Dec. 1931-1947; he then became secretary-librarian at IFAO, 1947-67; apart from numerous articles on papyrology, he published *Rapport sur les Fouilles de Tell Edfou*, 1928; Ἐντευξεις. *Requêtes et plaintes adressées au roi d'Égypte au IIIe siècle avant J.-C.*, 1931; *Un livre d'écolier du IIIe avant J.-C.*, 1938; *Le Papyrus Fouad I*, 1939; and *Ostraca grecs et latins de l'wadi Fawakhir*, 1942; he returned to France and died at Bourg d'Oisans, 22 Sept. 1987.

Aegyptus 68 (1988) 199-204 (J. Scherer); *CRAIBL* 131 (1987), 669-70; M. Capasso (ed.), *Hermae*, 2007, 273-80 (N. Pellé).

GUÉRIN, Victor Honoré (1821-1891)
French archaeologist and traveller; he was born Paris, 15 Sept. 1821; he visited Egypt and Nubia in 1858 with the Comte de Maupas, and published an account of the journey in the *Bulletin* of the Soc. Géographique of Paris, and a larger illustrated volume of his travels in Egypt, Sinai, Syria, and Palestine (Paris, 1884); he died in Paris, 21 Sept. 1891.

Bull. Soc. Géogr. Sér. 4, 16 (1858), 404; Hill, 144; Hilmy, i, 279; *DBF* 16, 1505.

GUGLIELMI, Waltraud (*née* Strobel) (1938-2018)
German Egyptologist; she was born at Stuttgart, 23 Dec. 1938; she studied at the University of Tübingen under Brunner (q.v.), 1962-70; PhD, 1970; Habilitation 1978; she was appointed assistant at Tübingen, 1970 and extraordinary professor, 1991; she never held a permanent chair but acted as substitute professor at Hamburg, Berlin, Trier, Tübingen, Vienna ,and Marburg, 1997-2000; a volume in her honour was published K. Zibelius-Chen and H. W. Fischer-Elfert, *Von reichlich ägyptischem Verstande*, 2006; apart from articles she published *Die Feldgöttin Sh.t*, 1974; and *Die Göttin Mr.t*, 1991; she died 15 Jan. 2018.

K. Zibelius-Chen and H. W. Fischer-Elfert, *Von reichlich ägyptischem Verstande*, 2006, 7-8, 9-13 (bibl.).

GUIEYSSE, (Pierre) Paul (1841-1914)
French Egyptologist; he was born in Lorient, 11 May 1841, son of Pierre Eugène G. and Hermine Marie Suzanne Vaneau; he studied Egyptology under de Rougé (q.v.) and Maspero (q.v.); he published a study of the *Book of the Dead*, Chap. LXIV, 1876, and some minor works; he taught at the Sorbonne before virtually abandoning Egyptology for politics; he died in Paris, 19 May 1914.

Bull. Soc. d'Ethnogr. N.S. 4. 73; Hilmy, i, 279; Maspero, *L'Égyptologie* (1915), 6, 7; *DBF* 17, 76-77.

GUIGNES, Joseph de (1721-1800)
French orientalist and Sinologist; he was born at Pontoise, 19 Oct. 1721, son of Jean Louis de G. and Françoise Vaillant; Professor of Syriac at the Collège de France; he attempted to prove the unity of Egyptian hieroglyphs with Chinese characters considering that one derived from the other, being under the illusion that China was an Egyptian colony; he made several contributions to the Mémoires of the Académie des Inscriptions on the decipherment of hieroglyphs; like all scholars of the period he was not successful in this, but he is the first scholar known to have recognized the fact that cartouche rings contained royal names; in his own field he was also a scholar of considerable merit; he died in Paris, March 1800.

EB 12, 690; *DBF* 17, 91-2; *BIFAO* 5 (1906), 83; Gardiner, *Egyptian Grammar*, 2nd ed., 13; Hilmy i, 164 where his works are erroneously attributed to his son Christian Louis Joseph de G.; D. Syndram, *Ägypten-Faszination*, 1990, 64-7.

GUIMET, Émile Étienne (1836-1918)
French industrialist and founder of the Musée Guimet; he was born in Lyons, 2 June 1836, son of Jean Baptiste G., industrial chemist (1795-1871) and Marguerite Rosalie Bidault; he succeeded his father in the direction of the

factory at Fleurien-sur-Saône; he visited Egypt in 1865-6, publishing an account of his visit, *Croquis égyptiens*, 1867; he founded the archaeological and anthropological museum at Lyon, 1879; it contained a fine collection of antiquities from the Far East as well as Greek, Roman and Egyptian antiquities; it was handed over to the French Government and transferred to Paris, 1885; he funded the excavations of Gayet (q.v.) at Antinoe, and received a proportion of the finds, writing *Les portraits d'Antinoe au musée Guimet*, 1912; the *Annales du Musée Guimet* contain numerous articles on Egyptian topics; the Egyptian collections were transferred to the Louvre in the late 1940s, and the Musée Guimet now houses the French national holdings of Asian art; he died in Fleurieu, 12 Oct. 1918.

EB (11 ed.) xii. 696; Hilmy, i, 280; *La Grande Enc.* 19. 594; Musée Guimet Records; Vapereau, 740; *Rev. Arch.* 1918, ii. 341; *DBF* 17, 283.

GULBENKIAN, Calouste Sarkis (1869-1955)
Armenian oil magnate, collector, and philanthropist; he was born at Scutari, Istanbul, Turkey, 29 March 1869, son of Sarkis G. and Dirouhi née Gulbenkian; he received a varied education in Istanbul, Marseilles, and London; Fellow of King's College, University of London; he married Nevarte Essayan, 1892, becoming a British subject later but settling in Portugal during the last years of his life; by business acumen and astute diplomacy he amassed an enormous fortune in Near Eastern oil holdings, the income of which after his death has been variously estimated at from £5,000,000 to £10,000,000 p.a.; during his lifetime Gulbenkian also acquired one of the largest and most valuable private art collections ever assembled; the Egyptian sculpture and other objects of Pharaonic date constituted a special loan exhibition at the British Museum for eighteen months, and a Catalogue was published at the time, *Ancient Egyptian Sculpture lent by C. S. Gulbenkian, Esq.* 1937; this included the famous obsidian head of Amenemhat III from the MacGregor (q.v.) collection; this was subsequently exhibited with a similar catalogue at the National Gallery of Art, Washington DC, 1949-60; at his death he left almost the whole of his fortune to the Calouste Gulbenkian Foundation for educational and charitable work under the direction of three trustees; one of the beneficiaries under this scheme has been the Oriental Department in the University of Durham; the whole of the art collection was left to the Foundation with headquarters in Lisbon; he died in Lisbon, 20 July 1955.

Ralph Hewins, *Mr Five per Cent*, 1957; John Lodwick, *Gulbenkian*, 1958; *WWW* v, 462; L. M. de Araújo, *Egyptian Art: Calouste Gulbenkian Collection*, 2006; *ODNB* 24, 220-223 (portr.); J. Conlin, *Mr Five Per Cent*, 2019.

GUNDLACH, Rolf (1931-2016)
German Egyptologist; he was born in Heldenbergen, 29 Aug. 1931; he studied Egyptology at the Universities of Hamburg and Heidelberg; PhD, 1959; Habilitation, 1981; he lectured at institutes in Darmstadt, 1966-77; he was a lecturer at the Universities of Heidelberg, 1977-81; Mainz, 1980-2 and Saarbrücken, 1981; he became a lecturer in Egyptology at the University of Heidelberg, 1981-3 and the Johannes Gutenberg University of Mainz, 1982-3 and then professor, 1983-97 and examiner, 1997-2009; with Eggebrecht (q.v.), he founded the International Committee of Egyptology, 1977; secretary, 1983 and later member of the Executive Board; two volumes were published in his honour, M. Schade-Busch, *Wege öffnen*, 1996, and D. Bröckelmann and A. Klug, *In Pharaos Staat*, 2006; apart from many articles, he published or edited *Historische Wissenschaften und elektronische Datenverarbeitung*, 1976; with H. Weber, *Legitimation und Funktion des Herrschers*, 1992; *Die Zwangsumsiedlung auswärtiger Bevölkerung als Mittel ägypischer Politik bis zum Ende des Mittleren Reiches*, 1994; *Der Sudan in Vergangenheit und Gegenwart*, 1995; *Selbstverständnis und Realität*, 1997; *Der Pharao und seine Stadt*, 1998; with M. Rochholz, *Ägyptologische Tempeltagung* 4, 1998; with A. Klug, *Das ägyptische Königtum im Spannungsfeld zwischen Innen- und Außenpolitik im 2. Jahrtausend v. Chr.*, 2004; with U. Rössler-Kohler, *Das Königtum der Ramessidenzeit*, 2003; with A. Klug, *Der ägyptische Hof des Neuen Reiches*, 2006; *Die Königsideologie Sesostris' I anhand seiner Titulatur*, 2008; with J. Taylor, *Egyptian Royal Residences*, 2009; with C. Vogel, *Militärgeschichte des pharaonischen Ägypten*, 2009; with K. Spence, *Palace and Temple. Architecture - Decoration - Ritual*, 2011; he died in Darmstadt, 1 Feb. 2016.

Internet obit; M. Schade-Busch, *Wege öffnen*, 1996, vi-xvi (bibl.).

GUNN, Battiscombe George (1883-1950)
British Egyptologist; he was born in London, 30 June 1883, son of George G., a member of the Stock Exchange, and Julia Alice Philp; he was educated at Westminster and Bedale's Schools, and became interested in Egypt while still at school; he entered a City bank but found the work distasteful, and lived in Paris for some years working as a journalist; he was sub-editor of the Paris edition of the *Daily Mail*; he was private secretary to Sir Arthur Pinero, 1908-11; he was a good linguist and learnt Greek, Latin, Hebrew, and Arabic, also starting

hieroglyphs under M. Murray (q.v.) as a part-time student at University College London; he also received encouragement from Sir Alan Gardiner (q.v.); he excavated with Engelbach (q.v.) at Haraga, 1913-14; he served in the army 1914-5 when he was invalided out; he then became assistant to Gardiner and helped in the lexicographical work of *Onomastica*; he married 1. Lilian Florence, daughter of Charles Meecham and widow of Herbert Hughes, 2. Constance Anna Rogers; he was a member of the Amarna excavations for the EES, 1921-2; the Saqqara excavations for the Egyptian Antiquities Service, 1924-7; he was appointed Assistant Curator, Cairo Museum, 1928-31; Curator of Eg. antiquities, Philadelphia University Museum, 1931-4; Professor of Egyptology, Oxford, 1934-50; he edited the *JEA*, 1934-40; Gunn was a most exacting critic and maintained an extraordinarily high standard for his own publications so that his published work constituted but a small part of his total labour; his chief works in an output of 72 books, articles, and reviews, were *The Instruction of Ptah-hotep*, 1906, an early work which he afterwards repudiated; *Harageh*, ch. ix, with R. Engelbach, 1923; *The City of Akhenaten*, pt. i, ch. viii, with T. E. Peet and C. L. Wooley, 1923; *Studies in Egyptian Syntax*, 1924, his most important work compressing an immense amount of material into a compact form and breaking new ground in the study of the verb; *The Teti Pyramid Cemeteries*, with C. M. Firth, 1926; he also worked for many years on the *Hekanakhte Papers*, later published by T. G. H. James, 1962; his library went to the University of Durham and his papers and notebooks to the Griffith Institute, Oxford; he died in Oxford, 27 Feb. 1950.

AfO 15, 193; *ASAE* 50 (1950), 421-5 (portr.) (bibl.) (Abd El-Mohsen Bakir); *ODNB* 24, 237-8; *DNB* 1941-50, 234-5 (J. W. B. Barns); *JEA* 36 (1950), 104-5, (portr.) (J. W. B. Barns); *Proc. Br. Acad.* 36 (1950), 229-39 (portr.) (bibl. complete) (W. R. Dawson); *Nature* 165, 549; *WWW* iv, 480; S. Vinson and J. Gunn in W. Carruthers (ed.), *Histories of Egyptology*, 2015, 96-112.

GURA, Lucy Deborah Lloyd (1963-2006)
British freelance graphic artist and benefactor of the Egypt Exploration Society; born in London, 24 Sept. 1963, daughter of (Henry) Alan G., and his wife, Patricia Lloyd; after attending Mary Datchelor Girls' School, Camberwell, 1975-80, and Coopers School, Bromley, 1980-2, she studied French at the College of St. Hild and St. Bede, the University of Durham, and graduated in 1987; she was a member of the EES and cultivated a particular interest in the language, art and mythology of ancient Egypt: she died from cancer, 27 Feb. 2006; subsequently, her parents made a donation from her estate which enabled the EES to digitize over 14,000 images; in appreciation, the EES renamed the Society's Archive in her memory.

Egyptian Archaeology 30 (spring 2007), 44; inf. A. and P. Gura.

GUTBUB, Adolphe Gustave (1915-1987)
French Egyptologist; he was born at Strasbourg (Straßburg), 14 Jan. 1915, son of Philippe Jacques G. and Caroline Merkling; he was educated locally, baccalaureat 1933, diploma 1937; he then studied under Montet (q.v.) at the Faculté des Lettres showing a preference for the study of language notably Egyptian of the Ptolemaic period; during World War II he taught languages at Saverne and Zillesheim until forcibly conscripted into the German army; he escaped on the Polish front and ended up in a Russian prisoner of war camp until his release in 1945; from 1945-51 he taught classics at a school in Strasbourg and acted as a substitute lecturer for Montet (q.v.) while he was in Egypt; 1951-60 he was a pensionnaire at the French Institute in Cairo where he was assigned the publication of the texts from the Temple of Kom Ombo; from 1960-78 he was attached to CNRS; Professor at the University of Lille, 1978-82; he undertook several seasons at Kom Ombo to copy the texts and wrote on theological topics; he was offered a Festschrif *Mélanges Adolphe Gutbub* in 1984; apart from unpublished studies, his main publication was *Textes fondamentaux de la théologie de Kom Ombo*, 1973; he died Strasbourg 9 Sept. 1987.

BSFE 110 (1987), 18-23 (Portr.) (D. Inconnu-Bocquillon), 24-6 (J. C. Goyon); *Mélanges Adolphe Gutbub*, iii-v (bibl.).

GWILT, George (1775-1856)
British architect and antiquarian; he was born at Southwark, 8 Feb. 1775, son of George G., architect, and Hannah Trusted; he entered his father's office and became a well known architect and formed his own collection which included Egyptian antiquities purchased from Belzoni's sale in 1822; FSA, 1815; his collection was sold at Sotheby's 20 May 1875; he died in Southwark, 27 June 1856; his brother Joseph G., who was born at Southwark, 11 Jan. 1784, was also an architect and antiquarian; FSA 1815; he donated a shabti-box from the Belzoni sale to the British Museum (EA 8524); he died in Henley-on-Thames, 14 Sept. 1863.

H. Colvin, *Biographical Dictionary of British Architects 1600-1840*, 1978, 370-2; *DNB* 23, 397-0 (G. W. Burnett); *ODNB* 24, 344; Lugt 35684

HABACHI, Labib (1906-1984)
Egyptian Egyptologist; he was born in Salamun near Mansura, 18 April 1906, son of Habachi Ibrahim, a merchant, and his wife Mauna; he was educated at the Coptic School in Mansura and later at the Maronite School in Cairo; in 1924 he began the study of mathematics at Fuad I (later Cairo) University but transferred in 1925 to the Egyptology Section, BA, 1928; in 1930 he was appointed as an inspector in the Egyptian Antiquities Service; he held posts throughout the country at Aswan, 1930-2, Luxor, Cairo, Edfu, Fayum, Abydos, Sohag, Zagazig and Tanta; in 1944 he was appointed Chief Inspector of Upper Egypt until 1946, was at Saqqara, 1950-1, and was reassigned to Upper Egypt, 1951-58; in 1958 he was promoted to sub-director of field work which post he held until his resignation from the Service in Aug. 1960; he was then appointed archaeological consultant of the Nubian expedition of the Oriental Institute of Chicago, Dec. 1960-63; Labib Habachi was the leading Egyptian archaeologist of his generation and undertook excavations throughout Egypt notably at the Heqaib complex at Aswan, at Karnak where he discovered the Kamose stela, and at Bubastis and Qantir in the Delta; he travelled abroad extensively to visit collections in other museums and to deliver lectures which served to popularize Egyptology; he was chosen a member of the German Archaeological Institute, Berlin 1953, a member of the Institut d'Égypte in 1964, an honorary member of the Egyptological Institute of Charles University, Prague in 1965, and of the Société Française d'Égyptologie in 1983; he was awarded the State Prize of Egypt and the decoration First Class for Arts and Sciences in 1959, the Italian Order of Merit in 1973, the French Légion d'honneur 1979, and the Austrian Order of Merit 1980; on 1 May 1966 the honorary degree of doctor was conferred upon him by New York University; he was elected permanent Honorary President of the International Association for Coptic Studies, 1978; he married in 1961 Attiya Hanim Kamil Ayad (*d.*1987); on his 75th birthday a Festschrift with articles by 70 Egyptologists was prepared in *MDAIK* 37; he himself wrote over 170 articles, books, and notes on Egyptological subjects; the most notable were *Tell Basta*, 1957; *Features of the Deification of Ramesses II*, 1969; *The Second Kamose Stela and his Struggle against the Hyksos Ruler and his Capital*, 1972; *The Obelisks of Egypt*, 1977 later translated into several languages; *Tavole d'Offerta Are e Bacili da Libagione*, 1977; *Le Tombeau de Nay à Gournet Murei* (with P. Anus), 1977; *Sixteen Studies on Lower Nubia*, 1981; ed. *Actes du IIe Symposium International sur la Nubie*, 1981; *Untersuchungen im Totentempel Amenophis' III*, with H. Ricke and G. Haeny, 1981; and *Elephantine* IV, *The Sanctuary of Heqaib*. 1985; *Studies on the Middle Kingdom. Studia Aegyptiaca* X, 1987; he died in Cairo, 18 Feb. 1984 and was buried at Deir el-Moharreb near Luxor.

J. Kamil, *Labib Habachi: The Life and Legacy of an Egyptologist*, 2007; *ASAE* 70 (1984-5), 433-5 (portr.) (G. Mokhtar), 437-446 (bibl.) (M. Trad); *NARCE* 126 (1984), 3-13 (portrs.) (L. Bell); *BSFE* 99 (1984), 5 (J. Vercoutter); *Universalia* (1985), 571 (J. Leclant); *The Times* 1 March 1984 (T. G. H. James); *Oriental Institute News and Notes* 94 (1984), 4-5 (portr.) (G. R. Hughes); *Studia Aegyptiaca* X (1987), vii-ix (L. Kákosy); *Kemet* 3 no. 1 (1994), 30 (portr.); priv. inf; *KMT* 22/1 (2011), 76-80.

HADLEY, John (1731-1764)
British physician and chemist; he was born London, 1731, son of Henry H. and Anne Hofman; he was educated Cambridge; BA, 1753; MA, 1756; MD, 1763; FRS; he was Professor of Chemistry at Cambridge, 1756, and Physician to the Charterhouse the same year; FRCP, 1756; he published a scientific description of a mummy then belonging to the Royal Society, see *Phil. Trans.* 54 (1765), 1-14; he died in London, 5 Nov. 1764.

Munk, ii, 259; *Mem. Inst. Eg.* 13. 23; *Al Cantab.*; *ODNB* 24, 429-30.

HAENY, Gerhard (1924-2010)
Swiss architect and Egyptologist; he was born at Kölliken, 4 Feb. 1924, son of Edwin H., a merchant, and Ida Hägel; he was educated at the Polytechnical Federal University in Zurich 1943-1949 as an architect, he studied Egyptology at the University of Heidelberg under Otto (q.v.), 1955 and at the University of Munich under H. W. Müller (q.v.), 1958-9; he participated 1950-3 as field architect in the French Archaeological Mission in Iran; in 1953 he became assistant to the Director, H. Ricke (q.v.) at the Swiss Institute in Cairo whom he followed as Director from 1971-87; he wrote his dissertation on temple architecture of the New Kingdom, 1968 at the Institute of Architectural History at the Technical University in Karlsruhe; he undertook excavations at Kellia, 1965, 1968; at the mortuary temple of Amenhotep III in Thebes, 1964, 1970; at the mortuary temple of Merenptah in Thebes, 1971, 1972, 1978; at Philae, 1974-7; at Elephantine, 1969-95; his main publications were *Basilikale Anlagen in der ägyptischen Baukunst des Neuen Reiches*, 1970; *Architektur des Neuen Reiches*, 1975; *Untersuchungen im Totentempel Amenophis' III*, 1981; *A Short Architectural History of Philae*, 1985; he died in Egg b. Zurich, 25 Nov. 2010.

Inf. C. von Pilgrim; *Historisches Lexikon der Schweiz* (internet); *Jahresschrift der Vereinigung fur Heimatkunde Suhrental* 61 (2011), 7.

HAGEMANS, Gustav (1830-1908)
Belgian collector; he was born in Brussels, 27 May 1830, illegitimate son of Josse H., son of a banker, and Mary Gladstanes, a dancer; he adopted his father's name in 1851; he studied at the faculty of law at the University of Liège; he inherited his grandfather's wealth which enabled him to collect antiquities, including Egyptian pieces; Member of the Belgian Parliament, 1866-78; Corresponding member and then full member of the Institut Archéologique Liègeois and Keeper of its collections, 11 May 1855; Corresponding member of Académie d'Archéologie d'Anvers, 1853-4; Vice-President, 1864-66, 1875 and Pres. 1867, 1871, 1876; he visited Egypt in 1862; he sold his antiquities to the Musées Royaux Brussels in 1857 and 1861; he became bankrupt in 1875 and spent the rest of his life in penury; apart from several articles, he published *Lexique hiéroglyphique-français et français-hiéroglyphique*, 1896; he died at Waterloo, 15 Jan. 1908.

E. Warmenbol in A. Tsingarida and A. Verbanck-Piérard (eds.), *L'Antiquité au service de la Modernité?*, 2006, 223-258; E. Warmenbol, *La Caravane du Caire*, 2006, 121-41; E. Warmenbol *in Annales d'Histoire de l'Art et d'Archéologie* 28 (2006), 57-85; inf. E. Warmenbol.

HAGGARD, (*Sir*) Henry Rider (1856-1925)
British administrator and novelist; he was born at W. Bradenham Hall, Norfolk, 22 June 1856, son of William Meybohm R. H. and Ella Doveton; he married Mariana Louisa Margitson, 1880; he held many important official appointments in S. Africa, and on his retirement settled at Ditchingham Hall, Norfolk; KBE, 1919; JP; he did much to promote agriculture; his novels were extremely popular, several of them being based on ancient Egyptian themes; he had a small but choice collection of Egyptian antiquities, described by Blackman, some of which are now in the Norwich Castle Museum and the Liverpool Museum; he died in London, 14 May 1925.

The Days of My Life, autobiogr., 2 vols. 1926; A. Blackman in *JEA* 4 (1917), 43-6; *WWW* ii, 449-50; S. M. Addy, *Rider Haggard and Egyptology*, 1998; *ODNB* 24, 443-6 (portr.).

HAIGH, Daniel Henry (1819-1879)
British priest and antiquary; he was born in Brinscall Hall near Chorley, Lancs., 7 Aug. 1819, son of George H., calico printer; after some time spent in commerce in Leeds, he attached himself to St. Saviour's Church there, but in 1847 he joined the Roman Catholic Church and entered St. Mary's College, Oscott; he endowed St. Augustine's Church, Birmingham and resided there until 1876, when he returned to Oscott; he was very interested in Anglo-Saxon, Assyrian, Egyptian, and biblical archaeology generally, and was the chief authority in England on Runic inscriptions; he published many works and contributed to many archaeological journals, writing articles on Egyptian and Assyrian chronology, etc., in *ZÄS*; he died in Oscott, 10 May 1879.

BL Egerton MS 2856, ff. 373, 379; *ODNB* 24, 466-7; *DNB* 23, 440; Hilmy, i, 283.

HAKEM, Ahmed Mohammed Ali (1938-1996)
Sudanese archaeologist; he was born in Atbara 1938; he studied in the Department of History at the University of Khartoum, 1957-63 and then at Cambridge University, MA 1964; lecturer at the University of Khartoum, 1964-6; he studied at Cambridge, 1966-71; PhD, 1971; Professor of Archaeology at Khartoum, 1971-81; he took part in excavations at Meroe, 1966, 1971-83 and near Omdurman, 1973-95; Undersecretary for Antiquities and National Museums and editor of *Kush*, 1990-4; apart from works in Arabic, he published *Meroitic Architecture*, 1988; he died in Feb. 1996.

Kush 17 (1997), 379; *Sudan and Nubia* 1 (1997), 44 (portr.) (A. M. Khabir).

HALKEDIS, Theodore (1932-2001)
American collector; he was born in Philadelphia, 24 June 1932, son of John Halkedis and Simela Vasiliades; he worked in the international shipping industry, forming his own company, Thalassic Shipping, of which he was president; from the 1980s he collected Egyptian antiquities, Egyptological rare books and Egyptomanic objects; many of these were exhibited and published in 2001; he also hosted gatherings of Egyptologists at his house in New York; after his death his collection was sold *en bloc* to a private collector in the Middle East; he died in New York, 21 Aug. 2001.

Inf. T. Hardwick and B. Brier; P. Lacovara and B. Trope (eds.), *The Collector's Eye: masterpieces of Egyptian art from the Thalassic Collection Ltd.*, 2001.

HALL, Henry Reginald Holland (1873-1930)

British Egyptologist and historian; he was born in London, 30 Sept. 1873, son of Sydney H., MA, MVO, a well-known portrait painter and artist to the *Graphic*, and Hannah Holland; he was educated at Merchant Taylors' School, and at this time showed an interest in ancient history and Egypt; at the age of 11 he had compiled a History of Persia and at 16 had acquired some knowledge of Egyptian; his classical studies at St. John's College, Oxford, were supplemented by Egyptian language and history which he did under Griffith's (q.v.) guidance; BA, 1895; MA, 1897; DLitt, 1920; he entered the British Museum as an assistant to Budge, 1896; Assistant Keeper, Dept. of Eg. and Assyr. Ant., 1919; Keeper, 1924-30; he assisted Naville (q.v.) in the excavations at Deir el-Bahri, 1903-7, and dug for the EES at Abydos, 1909-10, 1925; during the war he served in the Military Section of the Press Bureau and after 1916 in Intelligence; mentioned in dispatches, MBE; at the end of the war he directed the British Museum excavations in Mesopotamia on the ancient Sumerian sites of Ur and Tell Obeid, 1919; FSA, 1911; FBA, 1926; Member of the German Arch. Inst.; his activities were very wide and he served as Chairman of the PEF; Vice Pres. of the Soc. of Antiquaries, 1929; Hon. Sec. of the EES and editor of the *JEA*; on the Council of RAS and the Hellenic Soc.; his interests were more comprehensive than many Egyptologists of his time, even extending to Chinese antiquities, and in general embraced the whole of the ancient Near East and the Aegean world; he travelled in Greece and W. Asia as well as Egypt, and published a number of works on the archaeology and history of these areas; he also contributed extensively to the EEF memoirs and official publications of the British Museum; Hall was with Breasted (q.v.) and Meyer (q.v.) the best and most authoritative historian of his day, and his *Ancient History of the Near East* went through no less than seven eds. in his lifetime; his encyclopaedic knowledge of historical facts and his forceful style accounted for much of his success in presenting new discoveries to the public; he was a master of the short article and brief communication of which he contributed over 100 to *JEA, BMQ*, and other journals; his main works were, *The Oldest Civilization of Greece*, 1901; *Coptic and Greek Texts of the Christian Period in the British Museum*, 1905; *Murray's Handbook for Egypt and the Sudan*, 11th ed. 1907; *Egypt and W. Asia in the light of Recent Discoveries*, with L. W. King, 1907; *The Eleventh Dynasty Temple at Deir el Bahari*, 3 vols., with E. Naville and others, 1907-13; *Hieroglyphic Texts in the British Museum*, vols. ii-vii, 1912-25, his largest project; *Catalogue of Scarabs in the British Museum*, i., 1913; *Ancient History of the near East from the earliest Times to the Battle of Salamis*, 1913; and many later eds.; *Cemeteries of Abydos*, I, with E. Naville and T. E. Peet, 1914; *The Civilization of Greece in the Bronze Age*, Rhind lectures 1923, 1928; *Aegean Archaeology*, 1915; *Al-'Ubaid*, with C. L. Woolley and others, 1927; *Ur Excavations*, with C. L. Woolley; *A Season's Work at Ur*, 1930; *A General Introductory Guide to the Egyptian Collections in the British Museum*, 1930; also a chapter in *How to Observe in Archaeology*, 1921, and chapters in the *Cambridge Anc. Hist.* as well as articles in *Enc. Brit.*; he attended the Semaine Égyptologique in Brussels, caught cold on returning, and died in London, 13 Oct. 1930.

Antiquaries Journal II (1931), 73-4 (C. J. Gadd); *BMQ* 5 (1930-1), 102; *Chron. d'Ég.* 6 (1931), 23-6 (extract from *The Times*, 14 Oct. 1930); *JEA* 17 (1931), 111-16 (portr.) (H. Last); *JRAS* 1931, 723-5 (R. Campbell Thompson); *Nature* 128 (1931), 131-2, 'Unofficial Moments of a Great Archaeologist', (S. R. K. Glanville); *Proc. Br. Acad.* 16 (1930), 475-85 (R. Campbell Thompson); *PEQ* 1931, 1, 9-11 (portr.); *WWW* iii. 579; *DNB* 1922-30, 387-8 (T. E. Peet); *JEA* 59 (1973), 205-17 (bibl.) (E. Uphill); È. Gran-Aymerich, *Dictionnaire biographique d'archéologie 1798-1945*, 2001, incorporated in *Les Chercheurs de passé 1798-1945*, 2007, 853.

HALL, Lindsley Foote (1883-1969)

American draughtsman; he was born in Portland, Oregon, 21 Dec. 1883, son of Robert F. H. and Aletta T. Lindsley; he studied architecture at the Massachusetts Institute of Technology and in 1913 joined the Metropolitan Museum of Art's Egyptian expedition as a draughtsman; he worked for the Museum until 1949 taking part in Winlock's major excavations; in 1922 he was loaned to the excavation at the tomb of Tutankhamun to draw plans of the main chamber; his films of the work on the tomb are now preserved in the School of Architecture, University of Oregon and his papers are in the Oregon Historical Society, Portland; he died in Portland, 3 Feb. 1969.

Inf. E. Uphill.

HALLE, Henriette (Henni) von (*née von Mossner*) (1878-1964)

German Egyptologist; she was born in Berlin 1 Jan. 1878, eldest daughter of Walther von M., Prussian general of cavalry and Meta Giebert; she married Ernst von Halle, Professor of Political Economy in Berlin; having taught herself hieroglyphs, she attended university seminars at Berlin, Strasbourg, and Heidelberg; in 1915 A. Erman (q.v.) asked her to work on his *Wörterbuch der ägyptischen Sprache*, which she continued to do until 1933; Erman dedicated his *Handwörterbuch* to her and Caroline Williams (q.v.); she also copied Theban graffiti for W. Spiegelberg (q.v.) in Strasbourg and assisted H. Ranke (q.v.) in writing *Die ägyptischen Personennamen*; although she never published anything on ancient Egypt on her own, Erman and Ranke underlined her contributions to their work in the respective prefaces; she died in Nussloch near Heidelberg, 2 Jan. 1964.

G. Jonker in T. Wobbe (ed.), *Frauen in Akademie und Wissenschaft* (2002), 136-8; A. Cappel, 'Ihre dankbar ergebene Henni von Halle', in C. Weiss, E. Simon (ed.), *Folia in memoriam Ruth Lindner collecta* (2010), 228-38; inf. Dr A. Cappel.

HAMADA, Abdel Hadi (*d.*1957)
Egyptian archaeologist; he was educated at the École Pratique des Hautes Études in Paris and then joined the Antiquities Service in Egypt,serving in various posts in the Service; sometime Chief of Inspectorates and Secretary-General; he excavated at Fustat, 1936-7 (*ASAE* 37 (1937), 58-70,135-142; 38 (1938), 479-492); with el-Amir (q.v.) and Farid (q.v.) at Kom el-Hisn, 1943, 1945-7 (*ASAE* 46 (1947), 101-111, 195-205; 48 (1948), 299-308; 50 (1950), 367-379), at Kom el-Kharaz (*ASAE* 48 (1948), 327-332, and at Kom Trouga; he died in 1957.

ASAE 55 (1955), 354

HAMADA, Kosaku (1881-1938)
Japanese archaeologist; he was born at Kishiwada, Osaka Prefecture, 22 Feb. 1881, son of Genjuro H.; he studied at the University of Tokyo specialising in the history of Western Art and was a pupil of Tsuboi (q.v.); he was appointed assistant professor at the University of Kyoto in 1909; he studied archaeology in England from 1913-6 under Petrie (q.v.) and lived for a time with Sayce (q.v.); he was responsible for pls. 30-1 in Petrie's *Stone and Metal Vases*, 1937; he returned to Japan in March 1916 and in Sept. 1916 was named the first Professor of Archaeology at the University of Kyoto; Member of the Japanese Imperial Academy 1931; President of the University of Kyoto 1937; from 1911 he arranged for his university to finance the excavations of the EEF and later the BSAE in return for antiquities which now form the Hamada collection of the University of Kyoto; and published *General Concept of Archaeology*, 1922 in Japanese; he was the founder of scientific archaeology in Japan; he died in Kyoto, 25 July 1938.

M. Suzuki, 'La Collection Égyptienne de l'Université de Kyoto', *Chichukai-Gakkai* 3 (1980), 61-2; T. Saitoh, *Dictionary of the Archaeological History of Japan* (1984) in Jap.; Petrie, 230; Sayce, 375, 404, 406, 409, 413, 415, 436, 439, 443.

HAMELIN, Antoine Marie Romain (1770-1855)
French traveller; he was born in Paris, 9 Oct. 1770, son of Monsieur H. and Marie Jeanne Puissant; his wife was a friend of Josephine Bonaparte through whose influence he was put in charge of provisions for Napoleon's army in Italy; he joined Napoleon in Egypt in 1799 and was put in charge of finances in Upper Egypt; he undertook excavations at Dendera, Thebes, and possibly Saqqara; at Thebes he excavated several Sakhmet statues from the Temple of Mut which were later acquired by the British Museum; he visited Nubia going as far as Ibrim; he acquired three funerary papyri while at Thebes; he left Egypt in 1800 and reached France in 1801 after being captured by the British; the largest of his papyri was appropriated by Napoleon for the Institut de France, but was later taken by Denon (q.v.) and sold by his heir to Baron van Westreen van Tiellandt (q.v.), now in the Museum Meermanno-Westreenianum; the other two were sold to the Emperor of Russia and are now in the M. E. Saltykov-Schedrin Library, St. Petersburg, Inv. SPL 1-2; his later years were unsettled as he parted from his wife and went bankrupt in 1810; he later took a post in Algeria; he died in Paris, 26 Sept. 1855.

DBF 17, 547; *Chron. d'Ég.* 64 (1989), 58-63; *La Revue de Paris* 33 (Nov.-Dec. 1926), 34 (Jan.-Feb. 1927).

HAMILTON, William Richard (1777-1859)
British antiquary and diplomat; he was born in London, 9 Jan. 1777, son of Anthony H., Archdeacon of Colchester, and Anne Terrick; educated at Harrow and the Universities of Oxford and Cambridge; he entered the Diplomatic Service and was appointed Secretary to Lord Elgin, Ambassador to Constantinople, 1799; he was sent by Lord Elgin on a mission to Egypt, 1801, on the evacuation of the French; he discovered that the Rosetta Stone had been secretly shipped by the French, and with a military escort, he recovered possession of it; he also superintended the shipment of the Elgin Marbles and the recovery of those lost at sea; he was Under-Secretary for Foreign Affairs, 1809-22; British Minister in Naples, 1822-5; Trustee of the British Museum, 1838-58; in 1809 he published *Aegyptiaca*, which contains much valuable information together with a transcript and translation of the Greek text of the Rosetta Stone; he presented Egyptian antiquities to the British Museum in 1840; he died in London, 11 July 1859.

ODNB 24, 933-41 (portr.); *DNB* 24, 234; Hilmy, i, 285; Legh, 34, 47.

HAMILTON, DOUGLAS-, Alexander 10th Duke of Hamilton (1767-1852)
British nobleman; he was born in London 3 Oct. 1767, son of Archibald 9th Duke of Hamilton and Lady Harriet Stewart; he was educated at Harrow and Christ Church, Oxford; MA 1789; he was MP 1802-6; FRS 1802; FSA 1802; Ambassador to St. Petersburg 1806-7 and Trustee of the British Museum 1834-52; in the last capacity he initiated in 1836 negotiations with a French dealer for the purchase of what the other trustees believed to be the Ankhnesneferibre sarcophagus; when it transpired that the sarcophagus was that of a private individual, the Museum declined the purchase and it was acquired by the Duke himself; he built a new mausoleum for his family at his estate at Motherwell in Scotland and arranged to be embalmed and buried in the sarcophagus; he died in London, 18 Aug. 1852; in 1922 the sarcophagus was reburied in a local cemetery; a second sarcophagus, of Pabasa, now in Glasgow Museum (22.86), was formerly in the Hamilton collection.

ODNB 24, 761-2; *DNB* 5, 464; *JEA* 20 (1934), 181; A. Hare, *The Years with Mother* (London, 1952), 188; BM Papers; A. Dodson, 'Legends of a sarcophagus' in T. Schneider and K. Szpakowska, *Egyptian Stories*, 2007, 47-54; A. Dodson, *Archiv Orientální* 70 (2002), 329-36.

HAMMER-PURGSTALL, (*Freiherr von*) **Josef** (1774-1856)
Austrian orientalist, poet, and historian; he was born in Graz, 9 June 1774, son of Josef v. H. and Maria Anna Schabel; after being educated in Vienna he entered the diplomatic service, 1796; he was attached to the Austrian embassy at Constantinople, 1799-1807; he visited Egypt in 1801 when he acquired a stone stela now in the Vienna Museum N.188; he inherited the Purgstall estates in Styria, Austria, 1835; President, Vienna Acad., 1847; he published numerous texts and translations of Arabic, Persian, and Turkish MSS; also a work on Egyptian hieroglyphs from an Arabic MS (1806), and an Egyptian papyrus *Copie figurée d'un rouleau de papyrus*, 1822, and a memoir on the Mysteries of Isis, 1815; his library was sold in Vienna, 1857; he died in Vienna, 23 Nov. 1856.

Biogr. by Schlottmann, Zürich, 1857; *NDB* 7. 593-4; Champollion, i, 9, 137, 241; Hilmy, i, 285.

HAMY, Théodore Jules Ernest (1842-1908)
French anthropologist; he was born in Boulogne-sur-Mer, 22 June 1842, son of Théodore Auguste H. and Marie Louise Julie Isaac; he studied medicine in Paris; doctor 1868; he visited Egypt in 1869 with F. Lenormant (q.v.) and collected prehistoric flints from the Theban area; he obtained a post at the Muséum d'histoire naturelle, 1872; he founded the Musée d'Ethnographie, 1880 and became Professor of Anthropology, 1892; Hamy wrote studies on the Stone Age in Egypt and on the races of man depicted on the monuments; he collaborated with Quatrefages, Longpérier (q.v.), and F. Lenormant in craniological and historical works; he died in Paris, 18 Nov. 1908.

Haddon, *Hist. Anthropology*, 24; Hilmy, i, 41, 286; *La Grande Enc.* 19, 811; *DBF* 17, 569-70; *Archéo-Nil* 17 (2007), 17, 5-26 (portr.).

HAMZA, Mahmud Ali (1890-1976)
Egyptian Egyptologist; he was born in Cairo, 1890; he studied Egyptology under Ahmad Kamal (q.v.) at the Higher Teacher's Training College in Cairo graduating in 1912 and subsequently married Kamal's daughter Nimet in 1919; he was sent to Europe on a government scholarship studying at the Institute of Archaeology Liverpool, 1923-5, and at the École Pratique des Hautes Études, Paris, 1925-7; he then entered the Antiquities Service becoming a curator at the Cairo Museum; in 1928 he undertook excavations at Qantir, published in *ASAE* 30 (1930), 31-68, and also excavated at el-Omari, unpublished; he became Director of the Cairo Museum 1941-50; he retired in 1950 and died in Cairo in 1976.

Inf. D. Abou-Ghazi and G. Mokhtar; University Archives, Liverpool; P. Vernus; H. Sallam; H. Sallam in C. Eyre (ed.), *Proceedings of the Seventh Congress of Egyptologists*, 1998, 1018-9; *Bulletin of the Egyptian Museum* 1 (2004), 7.

HANAFI MAHMUD, Ammar Hassan (1960-2013)
Egyptian archaeologist; he was born at Qus, 1960; he studied archaeology at the University of Cairo and joined the Antiquities Service; he became director of the Avenue of Sphinxes and the Temple of Mut; he was a member of the Muslim Brotherhood from 1978 and was killed in the disturbances in Cairo, 8 July 2013.

Internet notice.

HANBURY, (*Revd*) **Barnard** (1793-1833)
British clergyman and traveller; he was born in Halstead, Essex, 12 March 1793, son of Charles H. of Sloe Farm, Halstead and Priscilla Bland; he was educated at Hertford School and Jesus College, Cambridge; BA, 1816; MA, 1822; admitted to Trinity College, Cambridge, 1822; ordained 1817; Vicar of Bures, Suffolk, 1824-8; Rector of Chignall, Essex, 1832-3; Chaplain to the Duke of Sussex; he visited Egypt and Nubia with Revd George Waddington (q.v.) in 1821; he died in London, 26 Jan. 1833.

Al. Cantab.; Hilmy, ii, 314 (under Waddington).

HANKE, Rainer (1929-2001)
German Egyptologist; he was born in Lünen, 4 April 1929, son of Herbert H., a doctor, and his wife Thea; he studied Classical Archaeology and Egyptology at the University of Münster under Wolf (q.v.); PhD, 1960 with his dissertation *Untersuchungen zur Komposition des ägyptischen Flachbildes*; he became Wolf's assistant until 1964; he then became an assistant to Roeder (q.v.) and assisted in his publication of the Amarna reliefs from Hermopolis; he also arranged an Amarna exhibition in Hamburg in 1965; he taught Egyptology at the Volkshochschule in Munster, 1980-7; he inherited Roeder's archive which later was passed to the State Archive in Hildesheim; he published *Amarna-Reliefs aus Hermopolis*, 1978; he died in Leer, 23 May 2001.

Inf. R. Krauss; R. Krauss, *Gött. Misz.* 225 (2010), 107-9.

HANSARD *see* **FIRTH.**

HARANT, Kryštof (1564-1621)
Bohemian traveller; he was born in Klenová Castle near Klatovy, 1564, he succeeded his father as Lord of Polzice and Bezdinzice; last president of the Assembly of Nobles of Bohemia; as a young man he was much at the court of the Emperor Rudolf II; he married Eva Czernin of Chudenice, 1588, and by her had two children, one of his sons being later killed in a duel provoked by a slighting remark by his father; he fought against the Turks for six years in Hungary from 1591; after the death of his wife he set out on his oriental journey on 2 April 1598; he reached Egypt from Palestine via Gaza; chapter two of a second part of his account begins the section on Egypt; in this he describes a journey to Sinai, the Virgin's tree at Mataria, the pyramids with classical authors cited and with recent visitors' accounts, in fact his extensive bibliography lists 600 titles in all; a very inaccurate engraving of the pyramids is included, and he describes the ascent and interior briefly, wrongly calling the granite black marble; the Sphinx is included and its dimensions given, then following the usual tourist route of those days he went to Zaccara (Saqqara) to see the mummies, and cites Belon (q.v.) here; he left Egypt via Rosetta and Alexandria; although not one of the most important accounts from an Egyptological point of view, Harant's is interesting and in line with the general historical and antiquarian views of the time; the 2 vols. of his *Voyage* appeared after ten years' work, being published in Prague in 1608 in Czech; German ed. 1678; they were illustrated by wood engravings done under his direction, several of the originals being preserved in the National Museum, Prague; he was executed in Prague, 20 June 1621 for opposition to the Emperor Ferdinand II.

Voyage en Égypte, de Christophe Harant 1564-1621. IFAO no. 442 (5th vol. of series), 1972, with introduction and notes by Claire and Antoine Brejnik, (portr.).

HARARI, Ibram (1919-1989)
Egyptian lawyer; he was born in Cairo, 10 July 1919, son of Ernest H., a lawyer, and Pauline Najar; he was educated in Cairo and at the University of Paris where he obtained a doctorate in international law; he returned to Egypt in 1940 to pursue a career as a lawyer and journalist; his interest in Egyptology was encouraged by Grdseloff (q.v.) and he specialised in ancient Egyptian law; he left Egypt in 1963 and settled in France where he continued his legal career; in 1967 at the Sorbonne he formed a small group interested in Egyptian law; an attempt to found a formal group at Brussels in 1974 failed, but in 1984 the Association Internationale pour l'étude du Droit de l'Égypte Ancienne was formed in Paris with Harari as its first president; he was the author of *Contribution à l'étude de la procédure judiciaire dans l'Ancien Empire égyptien*, 1950 and articles in *ASAE* 51 (1951), 273-97; *ASAE* 54 (1957), 317-44; *ASAE* 56 (1959), 139-201; *CRIPEL* 2 (1974), 125-54; *L'Égyptologie en 1979* 2, 134-40; *Serapis* 6 (1980), 57-61; *Serapis* 7 (1981-2), 23-59; and *Revue internationale des droits de l'Antiquité* 30 (1983), 41-54; he died in Paris, 28 July 1989.

BSFE 116 (1989), 8-9 (B. Menu); *Revue historique de droit français et étranger* 68 (1990), 139-140 (J. Leclant); family inf.

HARI, Robert (1922-1988)

Swiss Egyptologist and educationalist; he was born at Nyon, 4 Oct. 1922, son of Adolf Joseph H, a merchant; he studied at the University of Geneva graduating in 1950 and became a foreign correspondent for a local newspaper; his interest in archaeology was aroused when he took part in an American excavation in Guatemala; on his return to Switzerland he became a pupil of Charles Maystre (q.v.) and completed his thesis on the end of the Amarna Period in 1964; the Amarna Period was to remain his principal area of academic interest; he was director-general of the Cycle d'Orientation in charge of 16 centres of education, 1962-77; he succeeded Maystre as Professor of Egyptology at the University of Geneva, 1977-87; he founded the series Aegyptiaca Helvetica and was editor of Classiques de l'Égyptologie which republished the folio works of Champollion and other early Egyptologists in a smaller format; he created the 'Fonds de l'Égyptologie' which from 1984 sent Swiss students to work in Egypt at Karnak and the Speos Artemidos; he was the founder and first president (1978-87) of the Société d'Égyptologie de Genève; apart from his articles, his principal publications were his thesis *Horemheb et la Reine Moutnedjemet*, 1964; *Répertoire onomastique amarnien*, 1976; *La tombe thébaine du père divin Neferhotep (TT 50)*, 1985; *New Kingdom: Amarna Period* in *Iconography of Religions*, 1985; he died in Geneva, 2 Jan. 1988.

BSEG 12 (1988), 4-7 (portr.), 13 (1989), 4-7 (portr.) (bibl.); *BSFE* 111 (1988), 5 (M. Patané); *CO Informations* June 1988, 91-112 (bibl.) (R. Farquet); *Historisches Lexikon der Schweiz* 6, 110; *Schweizer Lexikon* (J. L. Chappaz); *Voyages en Égypte de l'Antiquité au début du XXe siècle*, 2003, 229-31 (P. Germond); inf. J. L. Chappaz;.

HARKAVY, Albert otherwise Abraham (1839-1919)

Russian orientalist and historian; he was born at Novogrodek, 27 Oct. 1839 son of Jacob H., a merchant and Talmudic scholar, and Dvora Weisbren; he studied oriental languages at the University of St. Petersburg from 1863; Master of History 1868; he was especially interested in Arab, Hebrew and Egyptian and was student of Lepsius (q.v.) and Duemichen (q.v.) in Berlin and Oppert (q.v.) in Paris 1868-70; as historian he studied Arab sources concerning the history of Eastern Europe, 1870; for his interesting remarks on Hebrew-Egyptian etymologies see his 'Ägyptisch-semitisches I-II', *ZÄS* 7 (1869) 132 and 'Les mots égyptiens de la Bible I-XVI', *Journal Asiatique* (1870), 161-86; he obtained his PhD for a dissertation *On the original seats of Semites, Indo-europeans and Chamites,* 1872; from 1877-1903 he was the head of the Hebrew Department in the St. Petersburg Public Library; he died in Petrograd, May 1919.

Palestinskiy Sbornik 5/68, (1960), 122 (I. G. Lifschitz); *Sovetskaia Istoriceskaia Enciklopedia* 4 (1963), 110-11; for a list of his works see *Iubileiny Sbornik v cest A.Y.H.* (collected Papers in Honour of A.Y.H.), St. Petersburg, 1907; *The Jewish Encyclopedia* 6, 235-6; inf. J. Śliwa.

HARKNESS, Edward Stephen (1874-1940)

American philanthropist and collector; he was born in Cleveland, Ohio, 22 Jan. 1874, son of Stephen Vanderburg H.and Anna Richardson; he was educated at Yale; he inherited a large share of Standard Oil from his father and embarked upon a career of charitable giving; in addition to numerous donations to American institutions, he gave $10,000,000 to found the British Pilgrim Trust; in 1903 he married Mary Emma Stillman (4 July 1874 – 6 June 1950), a friend of Albert Lythgoe (q.v.); they honeymooned in Egypt; he was appointed trustee of the Metropolitan Museum in 1912, and chairman of the Museum's Egyptian Committee in 1914; he made many gifts to the Egyptian Department, funding its expeditions and purchasing objects; notable among these are the mastaba of Per-neb from Saqqara and the collection of Lord Carnarvon (q.v.); his collection of paintings and sculpture was given to the Metropolitan Museum after his wife's death; he died in New York City, 29 Jan. 1940.

ODNB 25, 294-5; W. Craven, *Gilded mansions: grand architecture and high society*, 2009, 326-33; *Bulletin of the Metropolitan Museum* 10/2 (Oct. 1951) dedicated to the Harkness gifts.

HARLÉ, Auguste (1806-1876)

French Hebrew scholar and orientalist; he attended de Rougé's (q.v.) Egyptian classes at the Collège de France, but did not take up the study seriously and published no Egyptological works; he had, however, a valuable Egyptological library, a catalogue of which was printed in 1872 and to which Devéria (q.v.) was much indebted in his early studies; Harlé's name is associated with the valuable stela, Louvre C. 201, which he presented to the museum in 1872.

Devéria, *Mém. et Fragm.* I. 287; *Revue de l'art* 43. 169.

HARRIS, Anthony Charles (1790-1869)
British merchant and commissariat official in Alexandria; he was born in London, 1790, and traded with his brother as Harris & Co. not being Consul as usually stated; he was a collector of, and dealer in, Egyptian antiquities, and formed an important and valuable collection, including many classic papyri - the Great Harris papyrus of Ramesses III (the largest surviving papyrus), the Harris Magical, Harris Homer, the Tomb-Robbery Papyri, etc.; the collection, which prior to his death he gave to his daughter (see below), was acquired from her by the British Museum in 1872; he published his Hypereides Papyrus, 1848 and *Hieroglyphical standards representing places in Egypt supposed to be its nomes and toparchies*, 1852; President of the Egyptian Soc. of Cairo, 1836; he died in Alexandria, 23 Nov. 1869; his papers and notebooks are preserved in the Graeco-Roman Museum in Alexandria.

Brugsch, *Mein Leben*, 121, 136; Hilmy, i, 289; Hincks Corr. 202-4; *JEA* 35 (1949), 161-6; Lane Corr, 31-4; *Rev. arch.* 15 (1859), 752; G. Hamernik in *JEA* 96 (2010), 236-42; M. Capasso (ed.), *Hermae* II, 2010, 16-19 (portr.) (A. Capone).

HARRIS, Selima (*c.*1827-1899)
British collector; the natural daughter of A. C. Harris (q.v.) by an African lady; she was educated in England, and was her father's constant companion; on his death she inherited his rich collection of antiquities which she brought to England in 1871 and sold to the British Museum; Lady member of the Soc. Bibl. Arch., 1872; she died in Ramla, Alexandria, 18 March 1899; she left her property to Waynman Dixon (q.v.).

Brugsch, *Mein Leben*, 122; *JEA* 35 (1949), 164; Newberry Corr.; Wilbour, 6, 7; E. Chennells, *Recollections of an Egyptian Princess*, 1893, II, 138-43; *Chron. d'Ég.* 58 (1983), 69-72.

HARRISON, Ronald George (1921-1983)
British anatomist; he was born at Ulverston, 5 April 1921, son of James H. and Alice Hannah Edmondson; he was educated at Ulverston Grammar School and Magdalen College, Oxford 1939-44; BA, 1942; BM, B.Ch., 1944; MA 1946; DM, 1949; he was appointed Demonstrator and Lecturer in Human Anatomy, Oxford, 1945-50 and Derby Professor of Anatomy at the University of Liverpool, 1950-83; his interest in Egyptology led him to examine the bodies of 'Smenkhkare' in 1963 and Tutankhamun in 1968 and a foetus from the tomb of Tutankhamun; he was Visiting Professor of Egyptology at the University of Cairo, 1972; his anatomical results were published in a series of articles *JEA* 52 (1966), 95-119; *Nature* 224 (1969), 325-6; *Antiquity* 46 (1972), 8-14; *JEA* 62 (1976), 184-6; *Antiquity* 53 (1979), 19-21; he died in Wallasey, near Liverpool, 31 Dec. 1982; his papers are deposited in the University of Liverpool Archives.

WWW viii; *The Times* 10 Jan. 1983; *Journal of Anatomy* 137 (1983), 209-11 (E. Macmillan); *University of Liverpool Recorder* 92 (1983), 125; J. Buikstra and C. Roberts, *The Global History of Palaeopathogy. Pioneers and Prospects*, 2012, 223 (B. Baker and M. Judd).

HARTLEBEN, Hermine Ida Augusta (1846-1918)
German biographer of Champollion (q.v.); she was born in Gemkenthal, Harz Mts., 2 June 1846, daughter of Johann Heinrich Friedrich H., a forester; she was related to the poet Otto Erich Hartleben; she became a private governess; she later studied for a teacher's diploma at Hanover, 1869-71; she taught in Paris, and lived for some years in Constantinople where she held a scholastic appointment at the School for Girls; she also spent about six years in Egypt as a teacher, after a later visit there in 1891, she became interested in Champollion, and in 1893 began systematic investigations into his life and career; to do this she visited Paris and Grenoble in order to inspect documents in public collections and in the hands of C.'s family; in 1906 she published *Champollion, sein Leben und sein Werk*, 2 vols., the definitive account, and in 1909, *Lettres et Journaux de Champollion*, 2 vols.; these two works constitute one of the most important contributions to the history of Egyptology; she retired to Templin, Brandenburg, where she died 18 July 1918.

JEA 8 (1922), 285-6; A. Wellner, *Unser Harz* 54 (2006), 203-16.

HARTMANN, Robert (1831-1893)
German zoologist and anatomist; he was born in Blakenburg am Hertz, 8 Oct. 1831, son of Carl H. and Eulalia Holzapfel; Professor and Prosector of Anatomy, Berlin, 1868; he visited Africa, 1859-60; he published zoological and anatomical works, and studied the animals of ancient Egypt (*ZÄS* 2 (1864), 7-12, 19-28); he died in 1893.

Hilmy, i, 290.

HARVEY, Julia Carol (1962-2019)

British-Dutch Egyptologist; she was born in Bristol, 22 June 1962, daughter of William H. H. and Elizabeth M. Gillespie, and grew up in Celbridge, near Dublin; she studied Egyptology at Durham,1979-82 and Heidelberg, 1982-4, and then earned her PhD at University College London, 1994; in 2001 she joined the staff of the Language Centre at Groningen University, becoming head of their Translation and Correction Service; she also taught Egyptology courses for the Senioren Academie ('University of the Third Age') in Groningen; she participated in fieldwork in Egypt, joining missions of the EES at Memphis, the EES-Leiden Museum in the New Kingdom Necropolis at Saqqara, and the Brooklyn Museum in the Temple of Mut, South Karnak; she married Dr. Jacobus van Dijk; apart from articles on Egyptian wooden statues, mainly of the Old Kingdom and First Intermediate Period, she published her thesis *A Typological Study of Egyptian Wooden Statues of the Old Kingdom*, 2001 she died on 8 Aug, 2019.

Inf. J. van Dijk

HASANEIN MOHAMMED, Fathy (1935-2013)

Egyptian Egyptologist; he was born in Cairo, 7 Feb. 1935; he was educated at the University of Cairo under Fakhry (q.v.), Mattha (q.v.), Bakir (q.v.), Abubakr (q.v.) and Saleh, 1954-8 and later at the University of Lyons under Barguet (q.v.), 1975-8; PhD, 1978; he joined the Antiquities Service in 1959 where he served at Giza, Helwan and Tura where he directed excavations until 1961; he was transferred to the Centre of Documentation where he took part in the Nubian rescue campaign as an epigraphist at Debod, Abu Simbel, Wadi es-Sebua, and Gerf Hussein and was also involved in the rescue of Philae; he later took part in epigraphic campaigns at the Valley of the Queens with Desroches-Noblecourt (q.v.) and the Ramesseum with Christian Leblanc; he became director of the Centre, 1982-9; his publications, with others, were *La tombe du prince Amon-(her)-khepchef [VdR no 55]*, 1976; *Le Ramesseum* X, 1976; *Le temple de Gerf-Hussein* IV, 1978; *La tombe aux vignes*, 1985, new ed. 1992; *Sen-nefer. Die Grabkammer des Bürgermeisters von Theben*, 1986; *La tombe du prince Khaemouaset [VdR no 44]*, 1997; he died 2 Feb. 2013.

BSFE 185 (2013), 3 (portr.); *ASAE* 85 (2011), 14-16 (C. Leblanc) (portr.), 17-19 (bibl.); *Memnonia* 24 (2013), 65-9 (C. Leblanc), (portr.) (bibl.).

HASSAN, Selim (1886-1961)

Egyptian Egyptologist; born Mit-Nagi, 15 April 1886, he studied at the Higher Teacher's College, Cairo under Kamal (q.v.); in 1912 he became a teacher and in 1921 obtained a post in the Egyptian Museum as assistant keeper; he studied in Paris 1923-7 at the École Pratique des Hautes Études; he was the first Egyptian to be appointed as a Professor of Egyptology in the University of Cairo, 1928-36; he was later made Deputy Director of the Egyptian Antiquities Service responsible for the care of all monuments in the Nile valley, 1936-9; PhD Vienna University, 1935; stimulated by the archaeological work of P. E. Newberry (q.v.) and Junker (q.v.) he began an active career in excavations with the clearance of some of the Giza mastabas in 1929; the excavations carried on by him in this necropolis continued until 1939 by which time a great deal of digging had been achieved, published in 10 parts; he also cleared the Sphinx and its temple, for the first time completely digging out the great amphitheatre around it and ensuring that it would not be buried by sand again so easily; he wrote a study on this work and on the temple of Amenhotep II here; in addition the so-called Fourth Pyramid or the palace-façade tomb of Queen Khent-kawes of the Fourth Dynasty was investigated and also the funerary town of the priests associated with it; he later worked on the Unas causeway at Saqqara and at the valley temple of this king, discovering some of the mastabas in this area and two great subterranean tombs dated to the Second Dynasty; his final excavations at Giza were carried out on the east and south faces of the Great Pyramid and at the mortuary temple of King Khufu, 1938-9; he also took part in the campaign to save the monuments of Nubia, and wrote a report on this subject; his papers are preserved at the Center for Documentation of Cultural and National Heritage (CULTNAT) at the Library of Alexandria; he published about 53 books and articles on Egyptological subjects in English, French, and Arabic, *Hymnes religieux du Moyen Empire*, 1928; *Le Poème dit de Pentaour et le rapport officiel sur la bataille de Qadesh*, 1929; *Excavations at Giza*, 10 pts., 1929-60; *The Sphinx. Its History in the Light of Recent Excavations*, 1949; *Report on the Monuments of Nubia*, 1955; *Excavations at Saqqara 1937-8*, 3 vols., 1975; in Arabic *Literature of Ancient Egypt*, 2 vols.; *Ancient Egypt from Prehistoric Times to the Age of Rameses II*, 6 vols.; he died in Giza, 30 Sept. 1961.

AfO 20 (1963), 310 (H. Brunner); *Archaeology* 14, no. 4 (1961, 293; *ASAE* 58 (1964), 61-84 (bibl.) (Dia Abou-Ghazi); *Orientalia* 31 (1962), 271; *Gött. Misz.* 76 (1984), 78-80; Reid, *JAOS* 105 (1985), 237, 241-4; È. Gran-Aymerich, *Dictionnaire biographique d'archéologie 1798-1945*, 2001, incorporated in *Les Chercheurs de passé 1798-1945*, 2007, 859-60; S. Quirke, *Hidden Hands*, 2010, 296-7.

HASSELQUIST, Fredrik (1722-1752)
Swedish scientist; born Törnevella, 3 Jan. 1722, son of Magnus H. and Helena Maria Pontin; he was a pupil of Carolus Linnaeus in Uppsala; Hasselquist travelled in the near East in order to study natural history and to collect specimens; he visited Egypt between May 1750 and March 1751, staying mostly in Cairo; his observations on Egypt are contained in his *Iter Palaestinum* which was published posthumously; they mostly relate to Natural History but there are also interesting and entertaining pages on his visits to ancient monuments and on folklore; he died in Bagda near Smyrna, 9 Feb. 1752.

F. Hasselquist, *Iter Palaestinum eller Resa til Helige Landet*, Stockholm, 1757 (English edition: *Voyages and travels in the Levant etc.*, London, 1766. There are also French and German eds.); B. J. Peterson, 'Swedish Travellers in Egypt during the period 1700-1850', *Opuscula Atheniensia*, vii (Lund, 1967), 10-11; *Svenskt Biografiskt Lexikon* 18, 327-8; *Svenska Män och Kvinnor* 3, 323.

HAUSER, Walter (1893-1959)
American archaeologist and architect; he was born at Middlefield, Mass., USA, 22 May 1893, son of Henry Lewis H. and Ann Elizabeth Smart, and trained as an architect at the Massachusetts Institute of Technology, where he later taught mathematics and drawing from 1914-19; he joined the staff of the Metropolitan Museum's Egyptian Expedition, working mainly on the excavations of the dynastic period at Deir el-Bahri and of the early Coptic period at Kharga Oasis; he prepared as part of this work the master plan of the Malkata Palace of Amenhotep III at W. Thebes, a formidable task involving the integration of many large architectural elements dug out over a number of years and covering in all an area of upwards of eighty acres; he later worked in Iraq and Iran; in 1946 he was appointed Curator of the Metropolitan Museum Library; from 1954 to 1958 he was Research Curator of Near Eastern Archaeology, being a member of the MMA staff for nearly forty years in all; he was a Life Member of the Archaeological Institute of America, a FRAS, Fellow of the American Oriental Soc.; Member of the Medieval Academy and of the EES; he contributed several articles to the *BMMA*; he died in New York, 13 July 1959.

AfO 19 (1959-60), 270; *AJA* 64 (1960), 85 (C. K. Wilkinson); *WWWA* 4, 418.

HAWKINS, Edward (1780-1867)
British curator and numismatist; he was born in Macclesfield, 5 May 1780, son of Edward H., banker, and Ellen Hodgson; he was educated at Macclesfield Grammar School, and worked with his father; he was elected FRS, 1821, FSA 1826; he was appointed Assistant Keeper in the Department of Antiquities at the British Museum, 1825, Keeper 1826-60; this period saw the consolidation of the museum's Egyptian holdings, with the acquisition of material from the third Salt collection, and from the Anastasi, d'Athanasi, Belmore, Burton, Sams and Wilkinson collections (q. q. v.) among other sources, for which Hawkins as well as Birch (q.v.), appointed as Assistant in 1836, deserves credit; Hawkins' only Egyptological publications are his forwards to volumes of *Select Papyri*, but he was a respected numismatist; his *Medallic Illustrations of the History of Great Britain and Ireland*, 1885, remains a standard work; he died in London, 23 May 1867.

Hilmy, i, 292; *DNB* 25, 207; *ODNB* 25, 909-10; S. Moser, *Wondrous Curiosities*, 2006.

HAWORTH, Jesse (1835-1920)
British manufacturer; he was born in Bolton, Lancashire, 4 Aug. 1835, son of Smalshaw H., a manager in the textile industry, and Mary Anne Jones; his interest in Egyptian archaeology was awakened by a tour in Egypt about 1880, and he became acquainted with Amelia Edwards (q.v.) who stimulated his interest; in 1887 he provided funds for Petrie (q.v.) to excavate and continued to do so for many years; he also supported the Egypt Exploration Fund; in 1912 he gave a large donation to be used for the extension of Manchester Museum, and presented to it all the antiquities he had received from Petrie's excavations; he made a further gift of £10,000 to the Museum in 1919, and £30,000 under his will; he was also a generous donor to the British Museum, Ashmolean, and other museums; Hon. LLD Manchester, 1913; he was first president of the Manchester Egyptian and Oriental Society; he died in Bowdon, 23 Oct. 1920.

JEA 7 (1921), 109; *JMEOS* 4, 49 (portr.); Petrie, 22, 79, 157; *Bulletin of ASTENE* 24 (2005), 11-12 (C. Riggs).

HAY, Robert (1799-1863)

British traveller, antiquarian, and collector; he was born in Duns Castle, Berwickshire, 6 Jan. 1799, 4th son of Robert H. of Drumelzier and Whittingehame and Janet Erskine; he inherited the estate of Linplum from his brother James in 1819 after having started life in the Navy as a midshipman; during his service, he visited Alexandria in 1818; he was drawn back to Egypt by the publications of Belzoni (q.v.); in 1824 he embarked on a tour to the Middle East, stopping in Rome where he employed Bonomi (q.v.) as his artist; at Malta he met Catherwood (q.v.) and Parke (q.v.) who had recently returned from Egypt, having journeyed up the Nile with Westcar (q.v.) and Scholes (q.v.); in Nov. 1824 he landed at Alexandria visiting the country 1824-8, 1829-34; in May 1828 at Malta he married Kalitza Psaraki, daughter of the chief magistrate of Apodhulo, Crete, whom he had previously rescued from the slave market in Alexandria; he was variously accompanied at different times by a number of artists and scholars, Arundale (q.v.), Bonomi, O. B. Carter (q.v.), Catherwood, Dupuy (q.v.), Hoskins (q.v.), Lane (q.v.), and Laver (q.v.); he was diffident but authoritarian and quarrelled with most of them; he published *Illustrations of Cairo*, 1840, lithographed from his own drawings and those of Carter and others; the publication sold badly and his huge financial loss turned him from similar speculations with his archaeological drawings and from Egyptology itself; he made a large collections of drawings, plans, copies of inscriptions, etc., of great value today in view of subsequent damage to the monuments; his papers and drawings are preserved in 49 vol. in the British Library (Add. MSS 29812-60; diary, 31054; letters 38510); many of his plaster casts were acquired by the British Museum; he was a meticulous copyist and a good draughtsman; he formed a large collection of antiquities, part being sold in 1868, to the British Museum which acquired most of the papyri and smaller objects, and the remainder to C. Granville Way whose son presented them to the Boston Museum of Fine Arts in 1872, founding its Egyptian collection; he died in Amisfield House, East Lothian, 4 Nov. 1863.

ODNB 25, 1030-1; *DNB* 25. 275; Bonomi Diary, passim; Hilmy, i. 292; Hoskins, *Ethiopia*, 2; *Oasis*, 16, 22, 183, etc.; S. Tillett, *Egypt Itself*, 1984; inf. S. Tillett.

HAYCOCK, Bryan George (1937-1973)

British Sudanologist; he was born in Maidstone, 4 May 1937, son of Henry Reginald H., a police officer, and Winifred Eileen Benjafield; from 1956 he studied at the University of Durham under Macadam; BA in Ancient Egyptian and Nubian Studies, 1959; PhD, 1963; M. Litt., 1966; after a short period as a schoolteacher, he was appointed lecturer in Ancient History at the University of Khartoum in 1963; he specialized in the field of Meroitic studies and wrote several articles in *Sudan Notes and Records*, *JEA*, and other journals; he died in Khartoum, 5 Aug. 1973 as a result of a traffic accident.

Meroitic Newsletter 14 (1974), 2-3 (bibl.) (P, Shinnie); *JEA* 60 (1974), 3; *BSFE* 69 (1974).

HAYES, Charles (1780-1803)

British soldier and surveyor; he was born 1780; he was educated Woolwich Academy, 1794; he served in the W. Indies, 1796, and in Holland, 1799; he went to Egypt under Abercrombie, 1800, where he surveyed the Delta and inspected Upper Egypt; Captain, Royal Engineers; he was retained in Egypt to assist Col. Missett (q.v.) the Consul-General, to supervise British interests; he made the drawings used for the plates for Hamilton's *Aegyptiaca*, published 1809; he died of disease in Egypt, 26 July 1803.

Hamilton, pref. vi-x; Hilmy, i, 285, 294; Light, 113.

HAYES, William Christopher (1903-1963)

American Egyptologist; born Hempstead, Long Island, 21 March 1903, son of William Christopher H. from England and Helen Hawthorne Maule from Philadelphia; he was educated at St. George's School, Newport, where he won a medal for classics; he graduated at Princeton University, 1924, MA, 1926; he won a Carnegie scholarship for the study of medieval and Byzantine art; one of his earliest published articles was on an engraved glass bowl in the Vatican collections; he joined the Metropolitan Museum's Expedition to Deir el-Bahri, 1927, in all serving for nine years in Egypt on expeditions sent out by this museum; he now began the study of hieroglyphs and Egyptian grammar on his own, but also received personal instruction from Alan Gardiner (q.v.) during the summer periods between his trips to and from Egypt, and in this way acquired a very strong philological background; he believed in the highest standards of work and in the most exacting research, which he combined with a most polished style; his first book *Royal Sarcophagi of the XVIII Dynasty*, 1935, was a good example of these qualities, gaining him his PhD and being in all ways a remarkable first work, combining archaeological observation and philological knowledge to establish the sequence of these sarcophagi for the first time; *Glazed Tiles from a Palace of Ramesses II at Kantir*, 1937, was perhaps an even more remarkable work in which Hayes traced the origin of many fragments and broken faience pieces to their original home in a Delta royal residence; *Ostraka and Name Stones from the Tomb of Sen-Mut (No. 71) at Thebes*, 1942, was the result of the clearance of one of the two tombs constructed by this courtier at Thebes, in which Hayes from what seemed the most unpromising material was able to show the origins of some of the wall scenes in the preliminary ostraca sketches and also to contribute valuable lexicographical work on words relating to the building craft; at this period he also helped in the reconstruction of the great broken statues of Queen Hatshepsut that Winlock had found in a quarry beside her temple at Deir el-Bahri; when the museum expedition went to work at the XIIth Dynasty pyramid site of Lisht, Hayes produced *The Texts in the Mastabeh of Sen-Wosret-jankh at Lisht*, 1937, Middle Kingdom copies of Pyramid Texts including one of which was previously unknown; he became Assistant Curator of Egyptian Art in the Metropolitan Museum, 1936, Curator in 1952; he served for four years in the US Navy during the Second World War and was awarded the bronze star; in the field of popular writing he contributed a most successful article entitled *Daily Life in Ancient Egypt*, to the National Geographic Magazine, illustrated by 32 unique paintings done by H. M. Herget under his guidance; *The Scepter of Egypt, a Background for the Study of the Egyptian Antiquities in the Metropolitan Museum of Art*, part i 1953, part ii 1959, was perhaps his most influential work; originally intended to be, as the name implied, a guide book to the collections but designed on a very large scale, it became in fact almost a history of ancient Egypt from earliest times to the end of the New Kingdom as told through the objects in the New York collections and is without parallel in this field; on the specialist side he produced *Papyrus of the Late Middle Kingdom in the Brooklyn Museum*, 1955 a restoration and translation of the hundreds of unsorted fragments of a papyrus acquired by Wilbour (q.v.), and a study of fundamental importance in the fields of administration and Asiatic infiltration into Egypt during the Second Intermediate Period; he contributed four important chapters to the revised *Cambridge Ancient History*, 1961-2, which with his other major works show his importance as an historian, undoubtedly the best of his generation; he was working on what was to be a vast History of Egypt intended to fill four vols. when he died; he only lived to complete the first three chapters together with a fragment of the fourth, which encompassed not even the whole predynastic section published as *Most Ancient Egypt*, 1965; this fragment demonstrates the quality of his scholarship and the loss suffered by Egyptology through its not being completed; in 1959 he was appointed American representative on the International Committee for the Preservation of the Nubian Monuments; in all Hayes wrote about 80 books, articles, and reviews, many of major importance like his three articles on 'Inscriptions from the Palace of Amenhotep III', in *JNES* 10 (1951); he died in New York, 10 July 1963.

Most Ancient Egypt, 1965, introduction cii-xii, (bibl.) xiii-xvii (Keith C. Seele); *Archaeology* 16 (1963), 204 (anon.); *AfO* 21 (1966), 276 (H. Brunner); *BMMA* 22 (1963-4), 47 (anon.); *JARCE* 2 (1963), 7-8 (Dows Dunham and H. G. Fischer); *Nature* vol. 200, no. 4911 (14 Dec. 1963), 1048-9 (C. Aldred).

HAYS, (Harold) Martin (1965-2013)
American Egyptologist; he was born at Decatur, Ill., 22 Dec. 1965, son of William B. H. and his wife Virginia L.; he was educated at the Military Academy at West Point and served in the army as an airborne ranger until his retirement with the rank of captain; he later studied Near Eastern Languages and Civilizations and Egyptology at the University of Chicago, specializing in Pyramid Texts; MA, 1999; PhD, 2006; he worked as an epigrapher in Luxor for the Chicago Epigraphic Survey, 2000-5; he was appointed lecturer at the University of Leiden, 2006-13; he also taught at the University of Groningen, 2010; he took part as joint field director in the Leiden excavations at Saqqara, 2008-10; he published *The Organization of the Pyramid Texts: Typology and Disposition*, 2012; and with other, *Interpretations of Sinuhe*, 2014; he died in Leiden, 20 Nov. 2012.

Internet obit. (O. Kaper and M. Van Crevel); herald-review.com 15 Dec, 2013.

HAYTER, Angelo George Kirby (1863-1927)
British schoolmaster and excavator; he was born London, 31 May 1863, son of Angelo H., clerk in the Inland Revenue, and Augusta Penelope Kirby; educated Highgate School and Queens College, Cambridge; MA; FSA, 1916; schoolmaster by profession he became interested in ancient Egypt and attended classes in Egyptology at University College London, 1901; he assisted in Petrie's (q.v.) excavations at Hawara and Memphis, 1910-11; those of Quibell (q.v.) at Saqqara, 1912-14, the EES at Amarna, 1921-2, and Michigan University in the Fayum, 1925-6; he published with Quibell *Teti Pyramid, north side*, 1927; he died in London, 15 Oct. 1927.

JEA 14 (1928), 323-4 (T.E. Peet); Petrie, 221.

HEARST, Phoebe Apperson (1842-1919)
American philanthropist and patron of archaeology; she was born Franklin Co., Missouri, 3 Dec. 1842, daughter of Randolph Walker A. and Druella Whitmire; she married in 1862 George H., a mine-owner and senator, and for many years financed the scientific expeditions of the University of California in Peru, N. America, and

Egypt; she bore the cost of the publications of the Hearst Expedition in Egypt under G. A. Reisner (q.v.); the Hearst Medical Papyrus, obtained by Reisner in 1901 and published by him, was named in her honour; she died in Pleasanton, California, 13 April 1919; her collection is now in the Lowie Museum of Anthropology, Berkeley.

Inf. Dr. Dows Dunham; *WWWA* i, 543; *DAB* 8, 488-9.

HEARST, William Randolph (1863-1951)

American newspaper proprietor, publisher, editor, and collector; he was born in San Francisco, 29 April 1863, only son of George H., a US Senator and mine-owner, and Phoebe Apperson (q.v.); he studied at Harvard University 1882-5; LLD Oglethorpe, 1927; he married Millicent Wilson, 1903; after inheriting millions of dollars invested in mines and real-estate, Hearst increased this tenfold by building up a huge publishing empire of newspapers, magazines, journals, and radio-stations which spanned the continent; a collector of antiquities and works of art of megalomaniac proportions, he built and purchased many great houses in America and Wales, which he filled with his collections; these at length grew to such proportions that it was impossible to assess properly what was in them, as they exceeded anything owned by any other individual of modern times; while he had a rather eccentric approach to collecting and did not have a single field of interest, Hearst nevertheless inherited from his mother a genuine interest and appreciation of Egyptian antiquities, and visited Egypt where he acquired objects; although most of his Egyptian antiquities were acquired in Europe, many coming from the Hilton Price (q.v.), Meux (q.v.), and MacGregor (q.v.) collections; in the 1930s Hearst overstretched his commercial empire and in the process of saving it much of his collections had to be sold through department stores in the USA, many objects fetching far less than their purchase prices; a large collection of Egyptian, Babylonian, Greek, Roman, and other antiquities were sold at Sotheby's, 11-12 July 1939 (403 lots; Eg. 11-189; other choice pieces were sold to Brummer (q.v.); recovering his financial equilibrium he resumed collecting in the mid-1940s; he donated Egyptian objects to the Los Angeles County Museum of Art; he died in Beverly Hills, California, 14 Aug. 1951.

WWWA iii, 385; W. A. Swanberg, *Citizen Hearst*, 1963; Mrs Fremont Older, *William Randolph Hearst, American*, 1936; F. Lundberg, *Imperial Hearst*, 1936; *EB* II. 219-20; M. Levkoff, *Hearst the Collector*, 2008.

HEATH, (*Revd*) Dunbar Isidore (1816-1888)

British scholar and clergyman; he was born London, 3 March 1816, son of George H., sergeant-at-law, and Anne Raymond Dunbar; he was educated Trinity College, Cambridge, BA, 1838; MA, 1841; Fellow; vicar of Brading, Isle of Wight; in 1859 he preached, and published 1860, a sermon considered heterodox, for which action against him was taken in the Court of Arches; his sentence was deprivation of his benefice, which took place in 1862, and was upheld on appeal; he then lived in retirement at Esher, Surrey, for the rest of his life; Heath was a man of wide interests, he had been 5th Wrangler, and he now took up the study of Egyptology, especially that of hieratic papyri; he was a good transliterator, but his 'translations' were fantastic; his copy of *Select Papyri* , full of valuable notes, was formerly in the possession of Sir Alan Gardiner; he wrote a number of works, *The Exodus Papyri*, 1855, in which he believed that he had found references to biblical history in the Sallier and Anastasi Papyri; *A Record of the Patriarchal Age or the Proverbs of Aphobis, B.C. 1900, now translated from the Egyptian*, 1858, which was based on the Prisse Papyrus; *Phoenician Inscriptions*, 1873; he died in Esher, 27 May 1888.

Al. Cantab.; ODNB 26, 169; *DNB* 25, 341-2; BL Add. MS 31295, f. 52; Goodwin, 58, 67, 75; Hilmy, i, 295.

HEATHCOTE, Reginald St. Alban (1888-1951)

British pharmacologist; he was born in West Deeping, Lincs., 17 June 1888, son of Revd. Gilbert Vyvyan H. and Mary Henrietta Perceval; he was educated at Winchester, 1902-7 and New College, Oxford, 1907-11; BA, 1911; MA, 1914; he then trained at University College Hospital; BM BCh, 1914; he served in the Royal Army Medical Corps and Royal Naval Volunteer Reserve in World War I; he then joined the Dept. of Pharmacology at Oxford; DM, 1920; BSc, 1922; he became Professor of Pharmacology at the University of Cairo. 1922-33 and then lecturer and professor at the Welsh National School of Medicine, Cardiff; MRCP, 1932; FRCP, 1937; Comm, Order of the Nile, 1933; while in Egypt, he joined Griffith (q.v.) on his expeditions to Philae and Kawa; his photographic collection of 2,500 negatives is in the Griffith Institute, Oxford; he died in London, 19 May 1951.

Inf. Griffith Institue and M. Azim; *WWW* v, 505.

HEBERER, Michael (*c.*1550-1623)

German traveller; he was born in Bretten *c.*1550, son of Johann H and Catherina Schwarzerdt, niece of the religious reformer Melanchton; he studied at the Universities of Wittenberg, Leipzig, 1578-9, and Heidelberg 1579-80; he travelled to Malta and was then made prisoner and enslaved by the Turks; he served as a galley slave in Egypt from May/June 1587-Dec 1587, during which time he was taken to Alexandria, Cairo where he saw the Sphinx and the Pyramids, Rosetta, and Damietta as well as Syria, Cyprus, and Turkey; on his release in

Constantinople, he returned to Germany and settled in Heidelberg; he obtained an administrative appointment in 1593; he made official trips to Sweden, Poland, and Bohemia; he published an account of his adventures *Aegyptiaca Servitus*, 1610; he died in Heidelberg, *c.*1623.

NDB 8, 170; O. Volkoff, *Voyages en Egypte* 18, 1976.

HECKER, Howard Michael (1935-2002)
American archaeozoologist; he was born in Brooklyn, New York, 15 Jan. 1935, son of Irving H. and his wife Ray Eiseman; he originally trained as a motor mechanic but became interested in archaeology following a stay in Israel; he then studied at Hunter College, New York, 1962-66; BA, 1966; he then obtained his PhD in 1975 from Columbia University; he taught at New York University, Potsdam Univ, Univ of New Hampshire and became Associate Professor of Anthropology at Franklin Pierce College, New Hampshire, 1988-2000; he took part in the excavations at Amarna from 1982 and also at Wadi Digla, 1982, Memphis, 1984-86; and Giza, 1988; his reports were published in *Amarna Reports* I, 1984 and III, 1988; he died Newmarket, New Hampshire, 26 May 2002.

JARCE 40 (2003), 1-3 (P. Nicholson) (portr.).

HEERMA VAN VOSS, Matthieu Sybrand Huibert Gerard (1923-2015)
Dutch Egyptologist; he was born in Leeuwarden 25 Sept. 1923, son of Dr. Alexander Lodewijk H. van V., state archivist of Friesland, and Elisabeth Clasina Maria van Rijsbergen; he was educated at the University of Groningen under van Leeuw (q.v.) and, after World War II, at Leiden under de Buck (q.v), Janssen (q.v), Kristensen (q.v.) and Klasens (q.v.); PhD, 1963; he lectured at Leiden as assistant lecturer, assistant professor and associate professor, 1962-70; he also taught Hebrew at the Rijnlands Lyceum; he was appointed Professor of the History of Ancient Religions, University of Amsterdam, 1969-88 in succession to Bleeker (q.v.); Dean of the Theological Faculty, 1974-7; he specialized in the study of the Coffin Texts and Book of the Dead; he edited the *Annual Egyptological Bibliography* 1962-6, and served on the editorial board 1963-70 as well as serving on the editorial board of the journals *Ex Oriente Lux*, 1974-2015, *Nisaba*, 1970-88, *Numen*, 1977-90 and *Phoenix*; he was chairman of the Ex Oriente Lux society, 1974-94, the Netherlands Oriental Society, 1974-6, and of the Dutch section of the International association for the History of Religions, 1980-6, and served of the council of the International Association of Egyptologists, 1984-8; a volume of essays was published in his honour *Funerary Symbols and Religion*, ed. J. Kamstra and others, 1988; he published *De Oudste Versie van Dodenboek 17a, Coffin Texts spreuk 335a*, 1963; *Kunst voor de eeuwigheid*, French ed., *Illustrations pour l'éternité*, 1966; *Ein mysteriekist ontsluierd*, 1969; *Zwervers van gene zijde*, 1970; *Zwischen Grab und Paradies*, 1971; *De spreuk om de kisten te kennen*, 1971; *Van beitel tot penseel*, 1973; *Een bezwering van het hart*, 1974; *30mjaar en 24 uur*, 1976; *Anoebis en de demonen*, 1978; *Ägypten, Die 21. Dynastie*, 1982; *Vijf dekaden-demonen da capo*, 1983; *Oud Egypte in het Princessehof*, 1987; *Een man en zijn boekrol*, 1988; he died at Voorschoten, 8 Jan. 2015

J. Kamstra et al., *Funerary Symbols and Religion*, 1988, vii-viii, 1-11 (bibl.); *Wie is Wie in Nederland 1984-1988*, 1984, 473; *Bibliotheca Orientalis* 72 (2015), 275-82 (H. Milde) (portr.), (bibl.).

HEICHELHEIM, Fritz Moritz (1901-1968)
German historian; he was born at Giessen, 6 May 1901 son of Albert H, a banker, and Bella Simonsfeld; he studied at the Universities of Munich and Giessen; Teacher's Diploma, 1919; PhD, 1925 with an important thesis, *Die Auswärtige Bevölkerung im Ptolemäerreich*, 1925; habilitation, 1929; he worked as an assessor and later as a lecturer in Giessen, 1929-33; he emigrated to Cambridge, England, 1933 where he wrote his major work, *An Ancient Economic History*, 2 vols., 1938 and edited *The Adler Papyri*, 1939; he later worked at the University of Nottingham, 1942-8 and then joined the Dept. of Classics, University College, Toronto, 1948; Lecturer, 1948; Assistant Professor, 1953; Associate Professor, 1959; Professor, 1962, and taught there; he died in Toronto, 22 April 1968.

IEJ 18, no. 2 (1968), 134; M. Strauss and W. Röder, *International Biographical Dictionary of Central European Emigrés 1933-1945*, 2, part 1, 1983, 474 (bibl.).

HEKEKYAN, (*Bey*) **Joseph** (1807-1875)
Armenian civil engineer and technician; born in Constantinople, 1807, son of Michirdiz H., an interpreter in the service of Muhammad Ali, of a Roman Catholic Armenian family; he was sent in 1817 under the care of Samuel Briggs (q.v.) to be educated in England; after a course of general study at Stonyhurst College, he was placed as a pupil in various technical trades, among them the construction of steam engines, cotton-spinning machinery, etc.; he was then articled to a civil engineer to study hydraulics and the construction of canals; he returned to Egypt in 1830, and in 1834 was appointed to act as Director of the Polytechnic School in Cairo, a position that he held until 1837, when he became technical adviser to the Government on many undertakings, such as the construction of roads, bridges, and canals; in 1850 he retired into private life having been dismissed from office by the Viceroy Abbas,

who discharged all officials who were Christians; in 1854 he supervised the geological investigations of Leonard Horner (q.v.) at Memphis and Heliopolis, in the course of which important archaeological discoveries were made and antiquities found; he was of great service to many distinguished visitors to Egypt; he wrote *A Treatise on the Chronology of Siriadic Monuments,* 1863; his journals, drawings, and correspondence are in the British Library, Add. MSS 37448-71, while other documents are in the archives of the Dept. of Ancient Egypt and the Sudan, British Museum; he died in Cairo, 14 Jan. 1875.

Inf. D. Jeffreys; *Phil. Trans. Royal Soc.* 148 (1858); *Trans. R. Soc. Lit.*, 2nd ser., 9, 197; Nicholson, *Aegyptiaca*, 117; *Mem. Inst. Eg.* 54. 153; *JEA* 14 (1928) 8; A. Melly, *Lettres*, 5, 10, 34, 36; G. Melly, *Khartoum*, i. 141-3; ii, 263; R. S. Owen, *Life of Richard Owen*, ii, 196, 207; Lady Duff Gordon, *Letters from Egypt*, 5 et passim; Hilmy, i, 296; Registers of the Armenian Catholic Patriarchate, Cairo; D. Jeffreys in *Studies on Ancient Egypt in Honour of H. S. Smith*, 1999, 157-68; D. Jeffreys, *The Survey of Memphis* VII. *The Hekekyan Papers and other sources for the Survey of Memphis*, 2010; D. Jeffreys in *EA* 37 (2010), 7-8; A. Bednarski in W. Carruthers (ed.), *Histories of Egyptology*, 2015, 88-9.

HELCK, (Hans) Wolfgang (1914-1993)
German Egyptologist; he was born in Dresden, 16 Sept. 1914, son of Prof. Dr. Hans H., a classical philologist and school director, and his wife Gertrud; he was educated at Leipzig under Steindorff (q.v.) and Göttingen under Kees (q.v.), Ph.D., 1939; he served in World War II and was a prisoner of war from 1943; he returned to Göttingen in 1947; Habilitation, 1951; he was appointed lecturer at Göttingen, 1951, and later became lecturer at the University of Hamburg, 1956; apl. Professor, 1957; o. Professor, 1963-79; he was a member of the German Archaeological Institute and a corresponding member of the Akademie der Wissenschaften, Göttingen; he was a prolific author and produced a number of indispensable reference works in Egyptology, mainly concerned with the New Kingdom; his greatest achievement was as editor of the *Lexikon der Ägyptologie*, 1975-92, with Otto (q.v.) and Westendorf (q.v.); he was also editor of *Ägyptische Abhandlungen* with Otto from 1960 and edited the Festschriften for Schott (q.v.), 1968 and Brunner-Traut (q.v.), with Gamer-Wallert, 1992; *SAK* 11 (1984) was dedicated to him and a further volume in his honour *Miscellanea Aegyptologica* was edited by H. Altenmüller and R. Germer; he published nearly 200 articles apart from reviews and lexicon entries; his principal works were his thesis *Der Einfluss der Militärführer in der 18. ägyptischen Dynastie*, 1939, reprint 1964; *Untersuchungen zu den Beamtentiteln des ägyptischen Alten Reiches,* 1954; *Kleines Wörterbuch der Ägyptologie*, with Otto, 1956, 4th ed., 1995 with the title of *Kleines Lexikon...*, ed. by R. Drenkhahn; *Untersuchungen zu Manetho und den ägyptischen Königslisten,* 1956; *Urkunden der 18. Dynastie,* Heft 19-22, 1956-8; *Zur Verwaltung des Mittleren und Neuen Reiches,* 1958; *Materialen zu Wirtschaftsgeschichte des Neuen Reiches,* 1961-9; *Urkunden der 18. Dynastie. Übersetzung zu den Heften 17-22,* 1961; *Die Beziehungen Ägyptens zu Vorderasien im 3. und 2. Jahrtausend v. Chr.,* 1962, 2nd ed. 1971; *Geschichte des Alten Ägypten,* 1968; 2nd ed., 1981; *Jagd und Wild im alten Vorderasien,* 1968; *Die Ritualszenen auf der Umfassungsmauer Ramses' II in Karnak,* 1968; *Ägyptologie an deutschen Universitäten,* 1968; *Der Text der "Lehre Amenemhets I. für seinem Sohn",* 1969; *Die Lehre des Dw3-Htjj,* 1970; *Die Prophezeiung des Nfr.tj,* 1970; *Betrachtungen zur Grossen Göttin und den Ihr verbundenen Gottheiten,* 1971; *Das Bier im Alten Ägypten,* 1971; *Die Ritualdarstellungen des Ramesseums,* 1972; *Der Text des "Nilhymnus",* 1972; *Altägyptische Aktenkunde des 3. und 2. Jahrtausends v Chr.,* 1974; *Die altägyptischen Gaue,* 1974; *Historisch-biographische Texte der 2. Zwischenzeit und neue Texte der 18. Dynastie,* 1975; *Wirtschaftsgeschichte des Alten Ägypten im 3. und 2. Jahrtausend v. Chr.,* 2 vols.,1975-95; *Die Lehre für König Merikare,* 1977; *Die Beziehungen Ägyptens und Vorderasiens zur Ägäis bis ins 7. Jahrhundert v. Chr.,* 1979; *Lehre des Hordjedef und Lehre eines Vaters an seinen Sohn,* 1984; *Politische Gegensätze im alten Ägypten,* 1986; *Untersuchungen zur Thinitenzeit,* 1987; *Tempel und Kult,* 1987; *Thinitische Topfmarken,* 1990, and posthumously, *Das Grab Nr 55 im Königsgräbertal,* 2002; *Die datierten und datierbaren Ostraka, Papyri, und Graffiti von Deir el-Medineh,* 2002; he died in Hamburg, 27 Aug. 1993.

Kürschner 16 ed., 1992, 1342; *JEA* 79 (1993), ix-x; *ZÄS* 121 (1994), VII-IX (portr.); *BSFE* 128 (1993), 5; *Antike Welt* 24 (1993), 363 (portr.) (D. Wildung); *SAK* 20 (1993), IX-X (L. Schmithausen); inf. Dr. B. Schmitz.

HENDERSON, Benjamin Clifton (1788-1881)
British surgeon in Hon. East India Co.'s service; he was born 14 Aug. 1788 and baptized at St. Mary's Newington, 13 Sept. 1788, son of William H. and his wife Mary; MRCS, 1810; Assistant Surgeon, Bombay Establishment, 1811; he was transferred to Prince of Wales Island Estab., 1818; Surgeon, 1825; he retired, 1830, remaining some years in India, then living in Southampton and finally Paris; he visited Egypt in 1820, and brought from Thebes two mummies, both of which are historic; they were sold in 1831 by D. Harwood, a dealer of Houndsditch: one bought by John Davidson (q.v.) was unrolled at the Royal Institution, the other, bought by the Royal Coll. of Surgeons, was unrolled by Pettigrew (q.v.); the latter was destroyed by enemy action in 1940; Henderson died in Paris, 1881.

India Office Med. Records; *JEA* 20 (1934), 171-4; Pettigrew, *Hist. Eg. Mummies*, p. xviii; RCS Records; Salt, ii, 158.

HENGSTENBERG, (Ernst) Wilhelm Theodor Herrmann (1802-1869)
German theologian; born in Fröndenburg, 20 Oct. 1802 son of Karl H., a clergyman, and Wilhelmine Bergh; he studied classical and oriental philology at Bonn; habilitation 1825; he published *Dei Bücher Mosis und Aegypten, nebst einer Beilage: Manetho und die Hyksos*, a work which had considerable influence at the time, trans. as *Egypt and the books of Moses, or, The Books of Moses illustrated by the monuments of Egypt: with an appendix*, by R. D. C. Robbins with additional notes by W. C. Taylor, 1841, 1843, 1845; he died in Berlin, 28 May 1869.

Hilmy, i, 297; Vapereau, 779; *NDB* 8, 522-3.

HENNIKER, (*Sir*) Frederick (1793-1825)
British traveller; he was born 1 Nov. 1793, son of Sir Brydges Trecothick H. of Newton Hall, Essex, and Mary Press; he was educated at Eton and St. John's College, Cambridge; BA, 1815; he succeeded his father as 2nd Bart. 1816; he visited Egypt and Palestine, 1820, and accompanied George Francis Grey to Upper Egypt; Henniker was the first known European to climb to the apex of the Second Pyramid, a difficult task owing to the smooth casing-stones being still in situ near the summit; he published an account of his travels, *Notes during a visit to Egypt, Nubia, the Oasis, Mount Sinai and Jerusalem*, 1823; he acquired the coffin of Soter in 1821, which he gave to Salt (q.v.) from whom the British Museum acquired it (EA 6705); he died, unmarried, in London, 6 Aug. 1825.

ODNB 26, 387-8; *DNB* 25, 425; Hilmy, i, 298; Salt, ii, 164; Westcar Diary, 12, 246.

HENRY, Dominique Marie Joseph (1798-1856)
French writer; born in Entrevaux (Basses-Alpes), 15 June 1798, son of Gaspard dit Bienvenu H., a soldier, and Francoise Bareti; he became interested in ancient Egypt and published *Lettre à M. Champollion*, 1828; later he produced a much more substantial work, *L'Égypte pharaonique: ou, Histoire des institutions des Égyptiens sous leurs rois nationaux*, 2 vols., 1846; he died in Toulon, 3 Oct. 1856.

Hilmy, i, 298; Vapereau, 781; *DBF* 17, 981.

HEPPER (Frank) Nigel (1929-2013)
British botanist; he was born in Leeds, 13 March 1929, son of Edward Raymond H. and Ada C. Heasman; he was educated at Leeds Grammar School and King's College Newcastle; B.Sc. in Botany; he joined the staff at the Herbarium at the Royal Botanic Gardens at Kew 1950-90, becoming Principal Scientific Officer and Assistant Keeper; he took part in several scientific expeditions and developed an interest in the plants of the ancient Near East and studied the plants from the tomb of Tutankhamun; Fellow of the Linnean Society; Fellow of the Society of Biology; Hon. Sec. of Kew Guild, 1967-75, Vice-Pres., 1983-4; Pres., 1991-2; he authored numerous publications on botany; his published works on Near Eastern flora were *Plants of the Yemen*, 1976; *Bible Plants at Kew*, 1980; *Baker Encyclopedia of Bible Plants*, 1993; *Planting a Bible Garden*, 1998; *Pharaoh's Flowers: the Botanical Treasures of Tutankhamun*, 1990; and with I. Friis, *Pehr Forsskal's Flora Aegyptiaco-Arabica*, 2000; he died in Kingston, 16 May 2013.

The Independent 3 June 2013; *PEQ* 145 (2013), 183-4 (portr.), (D, Jacobson).

HERBERT, George Edward Stanhope Molyneux. 5th Earl of Carnarvon (1866-1923)
British excavator and collector; he was born in Highclere Castle, Hants, 26 June 1866, only son of Henry Howard Molyneux H. 4th Earl, and his first wife Lady Evelyn Stanhope; he was educated at Eton and Trinity College, Cambridge; he succeeded to the title, 1890; married Almina Wombwell; after a serious motoring accident in 1901, he wintered in Egypt regularly from 1903, and from 1906 he excavated at Thebes, where with the aid of Howard Carter (q.v.) he made many important discoveries; these culminated in the finding of the Tomb of Tutankhamun in Nov. 1922; his previous excavations were published in a sumptuous volume, *Five Years' Explorations at Thebes*, 1912; he formed a very choice and valuable collection of Egyptian antiquities which was subsequently purchased by the Metropolitan Museum of Art, NY, in 1926; he did not live to see the clearance of the tomb of Tutankhamun completed, the story of his death thus giving rise to the notion that a curse was the cause; he was in fact bitten by a mosquito while in the Valley of the Kings in March 1923, the bite became infected and he left for Cairo where erysipelas and blood-poisoning set in, followed by pneumonia; after several rallies he died there 5 April 1923; his body was brought back to Highclere and buried on Beacon Hill on the estate.

Memoir by his sister prefixed to vol. i of Howard Carter's *Tomb of Tut.ankh.amen*, 1-40 (portr.); *JEA* 9 (1923), 114-15 (J. G. Maxwell); Newberry Corr.; *WWW* ii, 175; *KMT* 11/3 (2000), 82-83; *ODNB* 26, 686-7 (portr.); É. Gran-Aymerich, *Dictionnaire biographique d'archéologie 1798-1945*, 2001, incorporated in *Les Chercheurs de passé 1798-1945*, 2007, 671-2.

HERMANN, Alfred (1904-1967)
German Egyptologist; he was born in Leipzig, 11 May 1904; he was educated in Leipzig, Munich, and Marburg; PhD, 1928 in literary history; he then studied Egyptology under Schäfer (q.v.) in Berlin 1928-32; he worked as an assistant in the Berlin Museum, 1931-2, 1935-41; he joined the German Institute in Cairo 1932-5 when he took part in excavations at Hermopolis and in the Western Delta; he was editor of the Institutes *Mitteilungen*, 1937-9; he served in World War II, 1941-5; in 1949 he was employed by the Hamburgische Museum für Volkerkunde und Vorgeschichte and in 1953 obtained a position at the Franz-Dolger Institut, Bonn University; he completed his habilitation at the University of Cologne 1958; he was appointed to a post there 1961; Ausserordentlich Professor 1963; Professor 1965; he was the author of a number of highly specialized studies dealing with human emotions and literary forms in Egypt; he published, *Führer durch das Museum der ägyptischen Altertümer zu Kairo*, 1935; *Die ägyptische Königsnovelle*, 1938; *Die Stelen der thebanischen Felsgräber der 18. Dynastie*, 1940; *Altägyptische Liebesdichtung*, 1959, an analysis of love poetry; he died in Cologne, 4 Feb. 1967.

Chron. d'Ég. 42 (1967), 354 (B. van de Walle); *ZÄS* 95 (1968), xi-xvi (bibl.) (W. Wolf); *AfO* 22 (1968-9), 220-1 (H. Brunner); inf. T.Schneider; S. Voss, *Die Geschichte der Abteilung Kairo des DAI im Spannungsfeld deutscher politicher Interessen* (Band 2), *1929-1966*, 2017, 123-8.

HERTZ, Bram (1794-1865+)
European jeweller and dealer in antiquities and *objets d'art*; he was born in Hanover, 1794; he came to London in 1837; he is listed as a dealer in curiosities, antiquities and pictures at 11 Great Marlborough St. from at least 1845 to 1850 and in 1851 was at 32 Argyle St.; his pictures and articles of virtu were sold in a four days' sale in 1843; he had a valuable collection of engraved gems and in 1839 bought many from the famous Poniatowski Collection (q.v.) he had an extensive collection of antiquities; catalogue published 1851; *The Collection of Assyrian, Babylonian, Egyptian, Greek, Roman, Indian and Mexican Antiquities formed by B. Hertz*; the collection was sold in 1856 and was bought by Joseph Mayer (q.v.) of Liverpool, who resold the bulk to defray expenses at Phillips 24-26 March 1857 (excluding antiquities) and Sotheby's 7-24 Feb. 1859; many gems were sold at Mayer's death, Sotheby's 23-26 May 1887 and are now in the British Museum, the Liverpool Museum, and the Fitzwilliam Museum; he emigrated to Frankfurt-am-Main after 1857.

Inf. Liverpool Museum, Hilmy, i, 300; C. W. King, *Handb. of Engraved Gems*, 1885; Lugt 23471, 24633, 46620; M. Gibson and S. M. Wright (eds.) *Joseph Mayer of Liverpool 1803-1886*, 1988, 11, 94-7.

HERZ, (*Pasha*) **Max** (1856-1919)
Hungarian-Jewish Museum Director; he was born at Otlaka, 19 May 1856, son of Ignác H. and Róza Sonnenfeld; he studied architecture in Budapest and Vienna; he went to Egypt in 1882 and worked under Julius Franz (q.v.) in the service for the preservation of Arab monuments; he succeeded Franz as Director of the Museum of Arab Art, Cairo, 1888, where he remained until June 1914, when with all the Germans, Austrians, etc., he left Egypt; he settled in Switzerland where he died in Zurich, 5 May 1919; Member of the Inst. Ég.; he published many works on Arab art and architecture.

Al-Hilah 27 (1919), 921-8 (memoir and bibl. in Arabic, by Tewfik Askaros); M. Stern, 'Österreich-Ungarns Beitrag zur Architektur in Ägypten am Beispiel von drei Architekten', *Österreich und Ägypten*, 1993, 57-60; I. Ormos in Jill Edwards, *Historians in Cairo*, 2002, 123-154; I. Ormos, *Max Herz Pasha 1856-1919. His Life and Career*. 2 vols, 2009.

HESS, Jean-Jacques (1866-1949)
Swiss Egyptologist; he was born in Freiburg, 11 Jan. 1866, son of Casimir Balthasar Jacob H. and Maria Josefina Rudolf; he was educated at the Humboldt University Berlin, studying Egyptology under Brugsch (q.v.) and at the University of Strassburg where he received his doctorate; he was appointed Professor at Freiburg, 1889-1908; he travelled in Egypt, 1896-1900 and in Egypt and NW Arabia, 1908-13; Professor Extraordinary of Oriental Languages, Zürich, 1918; he retired in 1936 with the title of Hon. Professor; he published an edition of the London-Leiden Demotic papyrus, and the Demotic stories of Khaemwese, but in his later years he concentrated on Arabic; *Der demotische Roman von Stne Ha-m-us: Text, Uebersetzung, Commentar und Glossar, etc.*, 1888; *Die gnostische Papyrus von London: Einleitung, Text und Demotisch-Deutsches Glossar*, 1892; *Der demotische Teil der dreisprachigen Inschrift von Rosette*, 1902; his notebooks and papers are in the Griffith Institute, Oxford; he died in Zurich, 29 April 1949.

Kürschner, 1931; *Univ. Zürich Jahresbericht*, 1948-9; inf. Mrs. V. Weaver (great-granddaughter).

HESSEMER, (August Wilhelm) Friedrich Maximilian (1800-1860)
German traveller and architect; he was born in Darmstadt, 24 Feb. 1800, son of Johann Friedrich Bernhard H., building commissioner of Hesse, and Sophie Elisabeth Margrethe Flor; he studied briefly at the University of

Giessen and later trained as an architect in Darmstadt; he embarked in 1827 on a tour of Italy, Malta, and Egypt; he reached Alexandria in Sept. 1829 and travelled to Cairo and then to Philae; he returned to Germany in 1830 to take up a post at the Städelschule in Frankfurt where he became Professor of Architecture; he wrote *Briefe seiner Reise nach Italien, Malta und Ägypten, 1827-1830*; 2002-3; his drawings are preserved at the Johns Hopkins University; he died in Frankfurt, 1 Dec. 1860.

R. de Keersmaecker, *ASTENE Bulletin* 75 (2018), 14-17; K. Bott, J. Eichenauer, and M. Bommas, *Friedrich Maximilian Hessemer (1800-1860): ein Frankfurter Baumeister in Ägypten*, 2001.

HEUSER, Gustav (1892-1937)
German Coptologist; he was born at Remscheid, 6 Jan. 1892, and studied theology at Heidelberg; he afterwards made a speciality of Coptic subjects and published two important studies, *Die Personennamen der Kopten*, 1929; *Prosopographie von Ägypten*, 1939; he died 4 March 1937.

ZÄS 74 (1938), 72 (H. Ranke).

HEWETT, (Kenneth) John (1919-1994)
British dealer in antiquities and ethnographica; he was born in London, 7 July 1919, son of Henry J. H. and Emily Thorn; he left school aged 14, and worked as a gardener; he served in the Scots Guards during World War II; he set up as a dealer in London after the war; he sold to numerous museums, and advised and sold to many collectors, including Robert and Lisa Sainsbury and George Ortiz; he became an adviser on antiquities to the auction house Sotheby's in the 1950s, and was involved with the dispersal of the private museum of A. H. Pitt-Rivers (q. v.); he donated a Late Period jasper inlay to the Royal Scottish Museum to commemorate the retirement of Cyril Aldred (q.v.); he died in Ashford, Kent, 15 July 1994.

N. Shakespeare, *Bruce Chatwin*, London, 1999, 93; H. Waterfield, *Provenance: Twelve Collectors of Ethnographic Art in England* 1760-1990, 2006, 153-166.

HEYNE, Christian Gottlob (1729-1812)
German classical philologist; he was born at Chemnitz, 25 Sept. 1729, son of Georg H. and Elisabeth Schreyer; he studied at Leipzig, 1748-52 and then worked in the Dresden library, 1753-7; he became Professor of Poetry at the University of Göttingen, 1763-1809 as well as Director of the Philological Seminar and Librarian and also taught at Copenhagen where one of his pupils was Schow (q.v.); he became Secretary of the Göttingen Academy, 1770; he became interested in mummification in 1780 and in 1781 examined a mummy in the Göttingen collection given by the King of Denmark and published several articles on the subject; he died at Göttingen, 14 July 1812.

NDB 9, 93-5; *DBE* 4, 829; D. Graepler in D. Graepler and J. Migl (eds), *Das Studium des schönen Altertums*, 52-6, 70.

HICKMANN, Hans Robert (1908-1968)
German musicologist, producer, conductor, and specialist in oriental music; he was born at Rosslau, Anhalt, 19 May 1908, son of Paul H. and Frieda Krönert; he was educated at the University of Halle, then Berlin; he lived for 25 years in Egypt where he was the musical director of Musica Viva, Cairo, and also worked as a producer for the Egyptian State Broadcasting Service; while there he made a special study of both ancient and modern music and musical instruments in the Near East; organist at the Swiss church; PhD; appointed Professor at the University of Hamburg, 1957, and made head of Archiv Production Section of Deutsche Grammophon Gesellschaft, 1958; Hickmann published many books and articles on Egyptian music, *Catalogue général des antiquités égyptiennes du Musée du Caire - Instruments de musique*, 1949; *La Trompette dans l'Égypte ancienne*, 1946, *ASAE. Supp. Cah. I*; *Dieux et Déesses de la musique*, 1954 his articles in *ASAE* were collected and edited by D. Abou-Ghazi, *Vies et Travaux* I *Hans Hickmann*, 1980; he was a Member of the Instit. d'Ég., and a Corr. Member of the German Arch. Institute; he died suddenly while engaged in making an organ record in the parish church at Blandford Forum, Dorset, 4 Sept. 1968.

WW Germany;The Times, 13 Sept. 1968; D. Abou-Ghazi, *Vies et Travaux* I, 1980 (portr.) (bibl.).

HILMY, (*Prince*) Ibrahim (1860-1927)
Egyptian bibliographer; he was born in Cairo, 18 Oct. 1860, son of the Khedive Ismail and Djenanyar; he was educated by English tutors and then attended the Royal Military Academy, Woolwich, returning to Egypt in 1875; following the deposition of his father in 1879, he spent many years in exile abroad; his chief work was *The Literature of Egypt and the Soudan from earliest times to the year 1885 inclusive*, 1886-7; his library passed to the Egyptian University; he died in Nice, 15 March 1927.

Inf. M. L. Bierbrier.

HILZHEIMER, Max (1877-1946)

German zoologist; he was born in Kehnert, Kreis Wolmirstedt, Saxony, 15 Nov. 1877, son of Alfred H. and Johanna Pringsheim; Privatdozent at the Tieraerztliche Hochschule, Stuttgart, 1907-14, and at Berlin, 1928; Director of the Natural Science Dept. of the Märkisches Museum, Berlin; he published many works, chiefly on the history and evolution of domestic animals; he contributed a chapter to Borchardt's *Das Grabdenkmal des Königs Sahure*, 1910; he died in Berlin, 10 Jan. 1946.

Kürschner, 1931 and 1950; *NDB* 9, 168.

HINCKS, (*Revd*) Edward (1792-1866)

Irish Egyptologist, Assyriologist, and clergyman; he was born in Cork, 19 Aug. 1792, son of Thomas Dix Hincks, LLD, Professor of Hebrew and other Oriental languages in the Belfast Academical Institution, and Anne Boult; he was educated at Trinity College, Dublin, where he received a thorough grounding in Hebrew and where his interest in Egypt was first aroused by the papyri kept in the library; BA, 1812; Jnr. Fellow, 1813; MA, 1817; BD, 1823; DD, 1829; he was Rector of Ardtrea, 1819-25, and married Jane Boyd, 1823; Rector of Killyleagh, Co. Down, 1825-66; Hincks is unique in the story of ancient languages in that he made major discoveries in the decipherment of both Egyptian hieroglyphs and Babylonian cuneiform; Brugsch (q.v.) called him the first person to use the correct system of transliteration in Egyptian and thus achieve the first proper method of decipherment, and also stated that he was the first to recognize fully the Semitic character of Egyptian grammar; Sayce (q.v.) called him the founder of Assyrian grammar and remarked on his divinatory power as a decipherer in cuneiform; such praise was no more than his due for he made many important discoveries about both languages and corresponded or worked with most of the major figures of his day; he published a Hebrew grammar, and wrote an article on Demotic, 1833, which Tattam (q.v.) disagreed with, after which his next Egyptological paper did not appear until 1843; from then onwards he was an active producer of articles and papers espec. in *Trans. R.I. Acad.* and *Trans. R.S.L.*; Hincks has always suffered from a lack of real recognition except by scholars; he worked for the British Museum for a year in order to decipher some of their cuneiform inscriptions, but they only covered his expenses and did not publish his results despite the fact that he appears to have had priority over Rawlinson in some of his discoveries; he was interested in astronomical calculations and eclipses, and noted the erasure of the name of Amun at Karnak and its restoration in the post-Amarna period; he wrote the following important works, *Catalogue of the Egyptian Manuscripts in the Library of Trinity College*, 1843; *An attempt to ascertain the number, names, and powers of the letters of the hieroglyphs, or ancient Egyptian alphabet, etc.*, 1846; *The Egyptian dynasties of Manetho*, 2 pts., 1863-4; his correspondence is in the Griffith Inst., Oxford, also his original portrait in oils; another portrait is in Trinity College Library, Dublin; he died in Killyleagh, 3 Dec. 1866.

DNB 9, 889-90; *ODNB* 27, 258; E. F. Davidson, *Edward Hincks*, Oxford, 1933 (portr.); Budge, *R & P* see index (portr.); Dawson MS 18, ff. 80-90; Hilmy, i, 304; H. Thirlwall, Bishop of St. David's, *Annual Report of the Royal Society of Literature* 1867, 16-50 (bibl.); K. J. Cathcart and P. Donlon, *Orientalia* 52 (1983), 325-56 (bibl.); J. Ray in J. Cathcart (ed.), *The Edward Hincks Bicentenary Lectures*, 1994, 58-74; È. Gran-Aymerich, *Dictionnaire biographique d'archéologie 1798-1945*, 2001, incorporated in *Les Chercheurs de passé 1798-1945*, 2007, 872; K. J. Cathcart (ed.), *The Correspondence of Edward Hincks* I *1818-1849*, 2007; *Dictionary of Irish Biography*, 2009, 4, 708-9.

HINKEL, Friedrich Wilhelm (1925-2007)

German architect; he was born 28 Dec. 1925; he was trained as an architect; PhD, 1980 (Berlin Academy of Sciences); he became a state architect; he joined the expedition of Humboldt University at Musawwarat es-Sufra, 1960-4 and also took part in the Nubian rescue campaign, working for UNESCO; he salvaged the temples of Aksha in 1962, Semna and Kumma in 1964, Buhen, a tomb at Debeira East, and many rock inscriptions; he was appointed architect of the Sudan Antiquities Service, 1965-88; he designed the National Museum in Khartoum and restored the pyramids and temples at Meroe; after some years of absence, he resumed his work in the Sudan, 1994-2004, working at Naga, 1994-8 and at Meroe; he was awarded the Sudan Medal of Merit, 1973, German Order of Merit, 1992 and the The Order of the Two Niles; he founded the publishing firm *Monumenta Sudanica*, 1996; as well as articles, he published *Tempel Ziehenum*, 1966; *Auszug aus Nubien*, 1978; its English version *Exodus from Nubia*, 1983 and edited *The Archaeological Map of the Sudan* from 1977; he died at Weissensee, 12 June 2007.

Sudan and Nubia 11 (2007), 127-8 (portr.), (J. Yellin and W. Y. Adams); *Die Antiken Sudan* 18 (2007), 215-6 (portr.) (E. Freier).

HINTZE, Fritz (1915-1993)
German Egyptologist and Nubiologist; he was born in Berlin, 18 April 1915 son of Friederich H., a local boatman, and Elsbeth Albrecht; he was educated at Potsdam and from 1934-40 he studied at the Friedrich-Wilhelms-Universität in Berlin under Grapow (q.v.); he was attached to the *Wörterbuch* project in 1936; PhD, 1944; following war service, he rejoined the *Wörterbuch* section; Habilitation, 1947 on Late Egyptian grammar; he was appointed lecturer, 1947; Associate Professor, 1951; and then Professor, 1956-80 at the Humboldt-University at Berlin; dean of the Philosophischen Fakultät, 1954-6; in 1957 he founded the Institut für Ägyptologie, enlarged in 1968 to cover Sudanarchäologie and Meroitistik, director 1957-80; Director of the Akademie-Institut für Orientforschung, 1956-69 and member of the Akademie der Wissenschaften in East Germany, 1959-92; guest lecturer at the Universities of Heidelberg, Hamburg, Würzburg, Münster, and Coleraine; corresponding member of the German Archaeological Institute, 1957, member of the Société française d'Égyptologie, 1959; his principal interest lay in the study of the Meroitic civilization and the application of mathematical methods, seriation, and cluster analysis in archaeology; he undertook archaeological work in the Sudan in the Butana, 1957-8 and notably at Musawwarat es Sufra from 1960-70 and recorded rock inscriptions during the Nubian rescue campaign, 1961-63; editor of *Mitteilungen des Instituts für Orientforschung*, 1953-67; *ZÄS*, 1954-93; *Zeitschrift für Phonetik und allgemeine Sprachwissenschaft*, 1955-70; and *Orientalistische Literaturzeitung*, 1962-87; he founded and edited the journal *Meroitica,* 1973-90; founder of the series of Meroitic conferences from 1971; he married in 1948 Ursule Büttner (born in Neuruppin, 10 Nov. 1918, daughter of Otto B. and Else Lange, died in Berlin, 29 April 1989), a fellow student in African studies at Berlin, 1940-3, 1946-9, PhD, 1949, who supported her husband's work, acting as photographer during his expeditions and editing *Meroitica*, 1973-89; two volumes of studies were prepared in her honour, *Ägypten und Kusch*, edited by E. Endesfelder and others, 1977 and *Studia in honorem Fritz Hintze*, edited by D. Apelt, E. Endesfelder, and S. Wenig, 1990; his principal publications were his habilitation *Untersuchungen zu Stil und Sprache neuägyptischer Erzählungen*, 1950, 1952; *Die Stellung des Meroitischen*, 1955; *Studien zur Meroitischen Chronologie und zu den Opfertafeln aus den Pyramiden von Meroe*, 1959; *Die Inschriften des Löwentempels von Musawwarat es Sufra*, 1962; *Alte Kulturen im Sudan*, with U. Hintze, 1966; *Musawwarat es Sufra* 1, 2, 1971; *Beiträge zur meroitischen Grammatik*, 1979; and *Felsinschriften aus dem sudanesischen Nubien*, with W. Reinecke, 1989; and, with others, *Musawwarat es Sufra* 1,1, 1993; he also edited three volumes of seminar papers on Meroitic studies in *Meroitica* 1, 5, and 7; he died as a result of an accident in Berlin, 30 March 1993.

ZÄS 120 (1993), VIII-IX (portr.) (R. Krauspe, E. Hornung, E. Blumenthal); inf. S. Wenig; *JEA* 79 (1993), ix; *Informatique et Égyptologie* 8 (1993), III (J. Hallof); *OLZ* 88 (1993), 237-8; E. Endesfelder, *Die Ägyptologie an der Berliner Universität-Zur Geschichte eines Fachgebietes*, 1988, 51, 56-64; E. Endesfelder, *Von Berlin nach Meroe. Erinnerungen an den Ägyptologen Fritz Hintze (1915-1993)*, 2003, 95-108 (bibl.); for U. Hintze see *Ethnographisch-archäologische Zeitschrift* 30 (1989), 719-20 (E. Endesfelder); *Beiträge zur Sudanforschung* 4 (1989), 5-8 (S. Wenig); *Wer ist Wer in der DDR*, 2006, 554-5.

HIRSCH, Jacob (1874-1955)
German-Swiss dealer in numismatics and ancient art; he was born in Altenkunstadt, Bavaria, 17 June 1874; he studied at the German Archaeological Institute in Rome; he opened a numismatic dealership in Munich, followed by establishments in Geneva, Paris, and New York; he became a Swiss citizen in 1925, and moved to the United States in 1939; he catalogued the Dattari (q.v.) collection, buying material at the sale; property from his collection was sequestered during World War I and sold at auction in Paris (Drouot, 30 June– 2 July 1921; posthumous sales of his antiquities were held in Basel (30 June 1956; 29 Nov. 1958) and Lucerne (7 Dec. 1957; 2 May 1959); objects from his stock were sold after his death to raise money for charitable archaeological purposes; his executors gave a limestone Naucratic group and photographs of Egyptian material from his stock to the Brooklyn Museum; he died in Paris, 24 June 1955.

Schweizer Münzblätter 5 (1955) 105-107 (Leo Mildenberg); *New York Times* July 5 1955 (obit.) ; A. P. Kozloff in L. M. Berman, *The Cleveland Museum of Art: Catalogue of Egyptian Art*, 1999, 20-1. Lugt 82443

HIRT, Aloys (1759-1836)
German archaeologist and art historian; he was born at Behla, 27 June 1759, son of Franz H., a farmer, and Elisabeth Hofler; he was educated by the Benedictines and briefly became a monk; he later studied in Vienna; in 1782 he went to Italy where he stayed until 1796; in 1797 he became an associate of the Berlin Academy and in 1821 he was a member of the commission entrusted to make purchases for the new Berlin Museum; he helped to acquire the Minutoli collection of which he published a brief description, *Zur Würdigung der neuesten von dem General Freiherrn von Minutoli eingebrachten Sammlung Aegyptischer Alterthümer*, 1821; apart from his classical studies, his publications on Egyptian studies include *Versuch über den*

allmäligen Anbau und Wasserbau des alten Aegyptens, 1815; *Ueber die Bildung Aegyptischen Gotthieten*, 1821; *Die Geschichte der Baukunst bei den Alten.* Vol. I, 1821; *Ueber die Gegenstande der Kunst bei den Aegyptern. Die Gotter*, 1822 (in the *Abhandlungen der Preussische Akademie* 1820-21); he died in Berlin, 29 June 1836.

NDB 9, 234-5.

HOCH, James Eric (1954-2018)
Canadian Egyptologist; he was born in 1954, son of Revd Paul A. Hoch and Elsie Elizabeth Goettling; he studied Egyptology at the University of Toronto, 1980-92 under Williams (q.v.); BA, 1984; MA, 1985; PhD, 1992; he was an instructor at the University of Toronto, 1990-9 and taught religious studies at the University of Alberta, Edmonton, 2007-13; he was the editor of *JSSEA*, 1995 and 1999; he published *Semitic Words in Egyptian Texts of the New Kingdom and Third Intermediate Period*, 1994, last ed., 2016; *Middle Egyptian Grammar*,1996; he died at Edmonton, 19 Sept. 2018.

Internet notice.

HODGES, (*Sir*) George Lloyd (1790-1862)
British Consul and army officer; he was born in Old Abbey, Limerick, 1790, son of George Thomas H.; he entered 13th Regt. Light Dragoons, Lieut., 1808; he served at Waterloo; retired as Colonel, 1833; CB; KCB, 1860; British Consul-General in Egypt, 1833-41; afterwards Chargé d'Affaires, Hanse Towns; he died in Brighton, 14 Dec. 1862.

FO Records; *GM* 1863, i, 517.

HODJASH, Svetlana Adriana Guljef (1923-2008)
Russian Egyptologist; she was born in Eupatoria, Crimea 10 Nov. 1923, daughter of Samuil Moseivitch H. and his wife Tamara Bogdanovna; she studied at the Department of Art of the Moscow State University from 1941-5; PhD 1949; she joined the Pushkin State Museum of Fine Arts, Moscow, 1944; Head of the Department of the Ancient Orient, 1972; she was a frequent attender at international conferences usually as sole representative of the Soviet Union; apart from articles and works in Russian, she published *Les Antiquités Égyptiennes au Musée des Beaux-Arts Pouchkine*, 1971; with O. Berlev, *The Egyptian Reliefs and Stelae in the Pushkin Museum of Fine Art, Moscow*, 1982; *Ancient Egyptian Monuments in the Museums of USSR*, 1991, with O. Berlev; *Catalogue of the Monuments of Ancient Egypt from the Museum of the Russian Federation, Ukraine, Bielorussia, Caucasus, Middle Asia and the Baltic States*, 1998, with O. Berlev; *Ancient Egyptian Jewellery*, 2001; *Ancient Egyptian Vessels in the State Pushkin Museum of Fine Art, Moscow*, 2005; she died she died in Moscow 13 Aug. 2008.

Inf. M. L. Bierbrier.

HOFFMANN, Inge (1939-2016)
German Egyptologist and Sudanologist; she was born Essen, 9 Jan. 1939, daughter of Hermann H. and Hertha Werndel; she was educated at the Universities of Kiel, 1960-1, Freiburg im Breisgau. 1961-3, and Hamburg where she studied African Studies, Egyptology and Phonetics, 1963-7; PhD, 1967; Habilitation, 1973; she had a travel grant to the Sudan, 1970-1; she became a lecturer at Hamburg, 1971-5; she served as secretary at Vienna University, 1975 and taught courses there and at the Faculty of Catholic Theology; Associate Professor, 1983-99; Head of Dept., 1992-4; she co-edited the *Annual Egyptological Bibliography*, 1975-84; she specialized in Meoritic studies; she published *Die Kulturen des Niltals von Aswan bis Sennar vom Mesolithikum bis zum Ende der christlichen Epoche*, 1967; Indices zu W. Helck, *Materialien zur Wirtschaftgeschichte des Neuen Reiches*, 1970; *Studien zum meroitischen Königtum*, 1971; *Wege und Möglichkeiten eines indischen Einfluss auf die meroitische Kultur*, 1975; *Beiträge zur meroitischen Chronologie*, 1978; *Der Äthiopenlogos bei Herodot*, 1979; *Der Sudan als ägyptische Kolonie im Altertum*, 1979; *Material für eine meroiticshe Grammatik*, 1981; *Das nubische Wörterverzeichnis des Arcangelo Carradori (O. F. M.)*, 1983; *Einführung in den nubischen Kenzi-Dialekt*, 1983; with H. Tomandl and M. Zach, *Der antike Sudan heute*, 1985; *Nubisches Wörterverzeichnis*, 1986; with H. Tomandl, *Unbekanntes Meroe*, 1986; with H. Tomandl, *Die Bedeutung des Tieres in der meroitischen Kultur vor dem Hintergrund der Fauna und ihre Darstellung bis zur Napata-Zeit*, 1987; *Hase, Perlhuhn und Hyäne. Spuren meroitischer Oralliteratur*, 1988; *Stein für die Ewigkeit*, 1991; she died in Podersdorf, 15. Oct. 2016.

Beiträge zur Sudanforschung 12 (2017), 5-22 (M. Zach) (portr.) (bibl.)

HOFFMANN, Jean Henri (1823-1897)
French collector and antiquities dealer; he was born in Hamburg, 1823, son of Jean Conrad H. and Jeanne Marie Landvogel; he came to Paris at an early age to assist his father who was a mineralogist and conchologist; he took up the study of antiquities and visited the principal museums of Europe; he set up in business in Rue Benouville,

and from 1862 to 1864 edited *Le Numismate*; in 1894, G. Legrain (q.v.) published *Collection H. Hoffmann: Cat. des antiquités ég.*; the objects came from many well-known collections - Stier, Sabatier (q.v.), Castellani, Menasce (q.v.), Posno (q.v.), Fournier, etc.; part of the collection was acquired by the Louvre in 1886 and further objects in 1895; some objects from the Hoffmann Collection are in the Palais des Beaux-Arts, Paris; his fine collection of Roman coins was sold in Paris, 2-11 May 1898, and there was a further sale of antiquities, 15-19 May 1899; he died in Paris, 30 April 1897.

Rev. de Numismatique, 1897, 226; *Rev. de l'art*, 43, 171, 284; *Cat. Sommaire des Collections Dutuit*, Paris, 1925; also Legrain work quoted above; Lugt 56259, 57247.

HOFFMANN, Michael Allen (1944-1990)

American archaeologist and anthropologist; he was born in Washington DC, 14 Oct. 1944, son of Donald H. and his wife Mary; he was educated at the University of Kentucky; BA Anthropology, 1966 and the University of Wisconsin, MA Anthropology 1968; PhD Anthropology, 1971 with a thesis *Culture History and Cultural Ecology at Hierakonpolis from Palaeolithic Times to the Old Kingdom*; he was appointed Assistant Professor at the University of Virginia, firstly in the Department of Anthropology, 1972-77 and then the School of Architecture, 1977-79 and Director of the Archaeology Laboratory in the Earth Sciences and Resources Institute; he was later Associate Professor, Department of Sociology and Anthropology, Western Illinois University, 1980-82 and from 1982 Research Professor at the University of South Carolina; in 1969 he became a staff archaeologist on the Hierakonpolis Expedition and director of the Predynastic Research team in 1978 and later principal director of the Hierakonpolis project; he organized in 1988-90 a touring exhibition in the United States entitled *The First Egyptians*; apart from articles on his excavations and the prehistoric period, he published *Egypt before the Pharaohs*, 1979, reprint 1991; and *The Predynastic of Hierakonpolis*, 1982; he died in Washington, 23 April 1990.

Inf. B. Adams; *JARCE* 27 (1990), viii-iv (W. Fairservis); *Friends of the Petrie Museum Newsletter* 5 (1990-1), 6-7; *VA* 6 (1990); 107 (C. Van Siclen); *KMT* 2 (1991), 20-5, 65; R. Friedman and B. Adams, *The Followers of Horus*, 1992,

ix-xxvii (portr.)

HOGARTH, David George (1862-1927)

English classicist and excavator; born in Barton-on-Humber, Lincs., 23 May 1862, eldest son of the Revd George H., vicar of that parish, and Jane Elizabeth, daughter of John Uppleby of Scarborough; he was educated at Winchester College where he was commoner, 1876-81; afterwards read classics at Magdalen College, Oxford, 1881-5; MA; Tutor of Magdalen, 1886-93, and Fellow, 1886; FBA, 1905; DLitt Oxford, 1918; Hon. LittD Cambridge, 1924; in 1886 he was awarded the Craven travelling scholarship and thus started his career as an archaeological field worker and his interest in the Near East, for his career in these earlier stages see *Accidents of an Antiquary's Life*, 1910; he excavated at Paphos in Cyprus, 1888; this was followed by three seasons in Egypt working for the EEF at Deir el-Bahri, Alexandria and in the Fayum, 1894-6; this close association with Egypt and the Fund's work did not, it was said, make him particularly enthusiastic for Egyptian archaeology or field work as he was by training and vocation a classicist, nevertheless he was to continue his links and support for Egyptology for the rest of his life; at this time he married Laura Violet, dau. of Charles Uppleby of Barrow Hall, a distant relative of his mother, 1894; appointed Director of Brit. School of Arch. at Athens, 1897-1900; a season at Naukratis was in the nature of a follow up of Petrie's earlier work there, 1899; Hogarth now transferred his interest to Crete where in 1900 he joined (Sir) Arthur Evans (q.v.) in excavation at Knossos, particularly being engaged at the Diktaean Cave, and with a season at Zakro; he was again at Naukratis, 1903; he then worked for the British Museum in Asia Minor at Ephesus on the site of the Artemis temple, 1904-5; a final season in Egypt followed, when he was co-director of the British Museum expedition that dug the cliff tombs at Asyut, 1907; he was apparently dissatisfied with this work and never published the results, but discovered some interesting early Middle Kingdom coffins for the BM collections (a chapter on this work may be found in the above quoted book); he surveyed the sites of Carchemish and Tell Bashar, 1908, 1909, 1921; he was appointed Keeper of the Ashmolean Museum, Oxford, 1909-27; he started the excavations at Carchemish, 1911, the work for which he is perhaps best remembered, but which was continued by (Sir) C. L. Woolley (q.v.) and T. E. Lawrence (q.v.); during the first World War he served as Comdr. RNVR, 1915-19, and was made Director of the Arab Bureau in Cairo, 1916; CMG, 1918; also a member of the British delegation at the Peace Conference at Versailles; Gold Medal of Roy. Geogr. Soc., 1917; Pres. RGS, 1925; Vice Pres. Hellenic Soc.; Radcliffe Trustee; Order of Nile 3rd class, 1917, etc.; Committee of Brit. School of Arch.

in Egypt; member of Committee of EES for twenty years, 1907-27, and lectured to society; an excellent linguist with a first hand knowledge of the Near East Hogarth influenced both T. E. Lawrence and Gertrude Bell; his most important contact with Egyptology was undoubtedly through Petrie (q.v.); like Evans his term at the Ashmolean saw a great widening of interest in the material obtained for the collections, especially in regard to the Egyptian; among his published works the following books are the most relevant, *Devia Cypria*, 1889; *Fayum Towns and their Papyri* ed. for the EEF and with others, 1900; *The Nearest East,* 1902; *The Penetration of Arabia*, 1904, a country which he never visited until 1917; *The Ancient East,* 1914; *Carchemish* Pt. I, 1914; *Hittite Seals*, 1920; *Kings of the Hittites* (the Schweich lectures for 1924), 1926; he also contributed chapters to the *Cambridge Ancient History* relating to Hittite history and archaeology; his main articles on Egyptian subjects will be found in *EEF Arch. Reports, English Historical Review; JEA; JHS; BSA Annual* etc.; he died suddenly in his sleep in Oxford, 6 Nov. 1927.

AE N (1928), 31 (anon.); *DNB* 1922-30, 421-23 (F.G. Kenyon); *Fortnightly Review* Jan. 1928 (Mrs Courtney, Hogarth's sister); *Geographical Journal* April 1928); *JEA* 14 (1928), 128-30 (H. R. H. Hall); *PBA* 13 (1927), 379-83 (A. H. Sayce); *WWW* ii, 505; *ODNB* 27, 537-42 (portr.); È. Gran-Aymerich, *Dictionnaire biographique d'archéologie 1798-1945*, 2001, incorporated in *Les Chercheurs de passé 1798-1945*, 2007, 874.

HOGARTH, Joseph (1801-1879)
British print dealer and restorer of papyri and manuscripts; he was born in London, 31 Oct. 1801, son of Joseph H. and his wife Ann; he worked under his own name in London as a printseller (from 1868, Joseph Hogarth and Sons) and also carried out restoring, mounting, and framing of works of art; in the 1830s and 1840s he was employed by the British Museum to unroll, restore, and frame some of its papyri, including the satirical papyrus (EA 10016); his notes on some of his work for the British Museum between 1838-42 are preserved in the Museum; he also carried out work for Harris (q.v.) and Lee (q.v.) on the King (q.v.) papyri, now at Trinity College Dublin and on papyri from the collection of d'Athanasi (q.v.) in the possession of the auctioneer Sotheby's; died at Paxton House, West Drayton, 9 Oct. 1879.

Inf. National Portrait Gallery; S. Quirke, 'An early conservation register of work undertaken on Egyptian papyri of the British Museum, 1838-42', in M. Capasso, *Il Rotolo Librario*, 1994, 165-186.

HOGG, Edward (1783-1848)
British physician and traveller; he was born 1783; MD Glasgow, 1824; he practised in Hendon and later in Naples; he made an extensive visit to the Near East in 1832-3, and ascended the Nile as far as Wady Halfa, his name being carved on the rock of Abu Sir; some Egyptian objects from his collection are now in the British Museum; he published *Visit to Alexandria, Damascus and Jerusalem etc.* 2 vols. London, 1835; he died in Chester, 12 March 1848.

Med. Times, 8 April 1848; Hilmy, i, 306.

HOGG, John (1800-1869)
British scholar and naturalist; born at Norton, Durham, 21 March 1800, son of John H. and Prudentia Jones; he was educated at Peterhouse, Cambridge, BA, 1822; MA, 1827; Fellow, 1827; FRS, 1839; Foreign Secretary to Royal Soc. Lit., 1852; he published many papers on botanical subjects and on natural history, and also wrote on archaeological subjects, including Egypt, in *Trans. R. Soc. Lit.*; he supported Lepsius's identification of Mount Sinai with Mount Serbal; he died in his birthplace, 16 Sept. 1869.

ODNB 27, 569-70; *DNB* 27, 103; *BIBIB,* 151; E. W. Braybrook, *Hist. R. Soc. Lit.* 2nd ed. 1897, 54, 62, 84; Hilmy, i, 306.

HOLLADAY, John Scott (1930-2016)
American-Canadian archaeologist; he was born in Chiang Mai, Thailand, 15 Oct. 1930, son of John S. H., a missionary, and Gladys Marie Carder; he was educated at the University of Illinois; BSc, 1952; after service in the American air force, 1952-6, he studied for the ministry at McCormick Theological College, Chicago; BDiv, 1959.; and Harvard Divinity School under the Near Eastern archaeologist G. Ernest Wright; ThD, 1966; he worked at Princeton University as instructor, 1963-6, assistant professor, 1966-8 and then as associate professor at the Dept. of Near Eastern Studies, University of Toronto, 1968-97; he was visiting prof at the Lutheran Theological Seminar at Philadelphia, 1966-7; he excavated at Sechem, 1964; Tel Gezer, 1966-71; Khirbet al-Qom, 1971; Karnak, 1972; and Tell el-Maskhuta from 1977-85; he served on the Board of Governors of ARCE, 1986-91 and on the Board of Trustees of SSEA, to 2006; a volume of studies in his honour was edited by T. Harrison, E. Banning, and S. Klassen, *Walls of the Prince*, 2015; he published *Pottery from the 1971 and 1972 Excavations at the Temple of Osiris Heqa Djet at Karnak*, 1975; *Cities of the Delta* III: *Tell el-Maskhuta*, 1982; and *Gezer* IV, 1986; he died in Toronto, 23 Sept. 2016.

The Toronto Star 26 Sept. 2016; T. Harrison, E. Banning, and S. Klassen, *Walls of the Prince: Egyptian Interactions with Southwest Asia in Antiquity*, 2015, ix-xiii (T. Harrison) (portr.) (bibl.); *SSEA Newsletter* (winter 2016), 1-2.

HÖLSCHER, Uvo Adolf (1878-1963)

German archaeologist and architect; he was born at Norden, 30 Oct. 1878, son of Revd Wilhelm H., a noted theologian, and Sophie Steinhömer; he became interested in the history of architecture and the evolution of building art and technique, and worked in Egypt with L. Borchardt (q.v.) on the German excavations at Abu Sir in 1906; he then excavated and studied the causeway area of the pyramid of Chephren, publishing an architectural study of this building complex which is still the standard work, 1912; he was with the German Amarna excavations for the season 1910-11; in 1911 he was appointed lecturer at the Hanover Technical University (now University of Hanover), becoming assistant Professor there in 1921 and Professor in 1937-47; an Hon. chair was also awarded him by the Oriental Institute Chicago, for whom he directed the famous excavations at Medinet Habu, 1926-37; in all he carried out eleven years intensive work on this great building and its site, completely clearing all the late buildings in the area as well, in a campaign that was conducted on a far more intensive and thorough manner than anything known in Egyptian archaeology before; completely new standards were set in the recording of this great building, and superlative plans with an immense amount of detail were drawn for the monumental publication; Hölscher also made a special study of the palace buildings of Ramesses III using the most careful methods to reconstruct its inlays and decoration; in his eightieth year he undertook further field work at the Old and Middle Kingdom rock tombs at Aswan; he published many large architectural vols., *Das hohe Tor von Medinet Habu, eine baugeschichtliche Untersuchung*, 1910; *Das Grabdenkmal des Königs Chephren*, 1912, with L. Borchardt and G. Steindorff; *Medinet Habu, 1924-1928 . 2. The architectural survey of the great temple and palace of Medinet Habu*, 1929; *Medinet Habu studies, 1928/29*. I. *The architectural survey*, 1930; *Excavations at ancient Thebes, 1930/31*, 1932; *Work in Western Thebes, 1931-33*, with H. H. Nelson and S. Schott, 1934; *The Excavation of Medinet Habu*, vol. I. *General plans & views*, 1934; vol. 2. *The temples of the Eighteenth Dynasty*, 1939; vol. 3. *The Mortuary Temple of Ramses III*, pt. i. trans. by Mrs. K. C. Seele, 1941; vol. 4, pt. ii., 1951; vol. 5. *Post-Ramessid remains*, edit. and trans. E. B. Hauser, 1954; he died at Hanover, 21 Feb. 1963.

AfO 21 (1966), 270-1 (portr.) (H. Brunner); inf. T. Schneider.

HOLT, (*Revd*) Robert Fowler (1791-1870)

British traveller; he was born at Finmore, Oxfordshire, 29 June 1791, son of Revd Robert H., Rector of Finmore, and Sarah Fowler; educated Eton and Brasenose College, Oxford; BA, 1813; MA, 1816; Chaplain to the Earl of Belmore whom he accompanied in his travels in Egypt, Nubia, Syria, and Palestine, 1816-18; his name is carved on the rock of Abu Sir, 2nd Cataract; Chaplain to Slough Union, 1836-70; he died in Reading, 27 Jan. 1870.

Al. Oxon.; Richardson, i, 365; ii, 233.

HOLTHOER, Rostislav (1937-1997)

Finnish Egyptologist of Russian extraction; he was born in Helsinki, 29 July 1937; he was educated at the University of Helsinki, MA, 1968; he then studied Egyptology at the University of Uppsala under Säve-Söderbergh (q.v.); PhD,1977; he was appointed part-time lecturer in Egyptology at the Department of Asian and African Studies in Helsinki in 1968; senior lecturer, 1979; Professor of Egyptology at the University of Uppsala in succession to Säve-Söderbergh (q.v.), 1 July 1980-96; Visiting Professor at the Ludwig Maximilian University in Munich, 1994; he took part in the Scandinavian Joint Expedition during the Nubian rescue campaign, 1961-4 and the Finnish Nubia expedition, 1964-5; he also undertook work at Deir Abu Hennis, 1978 and Kom es- Sultan, 1978 and 1983; he founded the Finnish Egyptological Society in 1969 and was its chairman until his death; he organized several Egyptological exhibitions in Finland including at Tampere Art Museum, 1993-4 writing the catalogue *Muikainen Egypti-Hetki Ikuisuudesta*; he wrote several works in Finnish on Egyptian grammar, 1978; love songs *Mietelmiä Sykomorin Siimeksessä*, 1993; hieroglyphs *Muinasien egyptin kielioppi*, 1993; and history, 1994; he published *New Kingdom Pharaonic Sites. The Pottery*, 1977 in the reports of the Scandinavian Joint Expedition to Sudanese Nubia as well as contributing to the volumes *Late Nubian Cemeteries*, 1981; *Middle Nubian Sites*, 1989; he also wrote the section on pottery in A. El-Khouli, R. Holthoer, C. Hope, and O. Kaper, *Stone Vessels, Pottery and Sealings from the Tomb of Tut'ankhamun*, 1993; he died at Helsinki, 28 April 1997.

IAE Internet obituary (J. Toivari); E. Salmenkivi (ed.), *Täältä Ikuisuuteen*, 1997, 7-10, 11-8 (bibl.).

HOLYROYD. Arthur Todd (1806-1887)

British traveller; he was born in London, 1 Dec 1806, son of Stephen Todd H. and Elizabeth Lofthouse; he studied medicine at Winchester; University of Edinburgh MD, 1830; and Christ's College, Cambridge MB, 1832, and law at Lincoln's Inn, 1835; he became a Fellow of the Zoological Society of London, 1826; he travelled to Egypt and the Sudan, 1836-7, being the first European to cross the Bayuda desert; he became a barrister in 1841; he emigrated to New Zealand in 1843 and Australia in 1845; member of the Legislative Council 1851-6, and of the Assembly, 1856-7, 1861-4; he died at Sherwood Scrubs, NSW, 15 June 1887.

Dict of Australian Biography 1851-1890, iv, 312; inf R. Morkot; *ASTENE Bulletin* 62 (2014-5), 16-7 (R. Keersmaecher).

HOMMEL, Fritz (1854-1936)
German orientalist; he was born at Ansbach, Bavaria, 31 July 1854, son of Friedrich H. and Therese Liesching; although primarily an Assyriologist, Arabic and Old Testament scholar, being Professor at the Ludwig-Maximilian University, Munich, he was also interested in Egyptology; he published nearly thirty articles relating to Egyptian subjects which are listed in the obit. cited below; he died in Munich, 17 April 1936.

Egyptian Religion, 2 (1935), 161-8 (portr. and bibl.) (T. Dombart); *NDB* 9, 591-2.

HONEY, *(Revd)* **Charles Robertson** (1835-1918)
British clergyman and philologist; he was born in Kennington, Surrey, 1835, son of William H., stockbroker's clerk, and Sarah Waynman; he was educated at Magdalen Hall, Oxford, 1862-66; BA, 1866; MA, 1869; he became curate at Oakley, Beds., 1866-68, at St Paul Bedford, 1868-70, and at St. Lawrence Reading, 1870-6; he was then vicar at Earley, Berks., 1877-90 and curate at St. John the Evangelist, Clapham, 1893-4 and Stokesay, Salop, 1896-8; he published *The Egyptian Negative*, 1901; *The Egyptian Hieroglyph, its original function in the evolution of written language*, 4 eds., 1902-1916; *Three Egyptian Hieroglyphs*, 1910; The *Furca. An Egyptian Hieroglyph*, 1910; *Liberty: a Study in Comparative Philology*, 1911; *The Nile Mud*, 1911; and *Olympus: a Study in Comparative Philology*, 1912; he died in Broadstone, 13 Dec. 1918.

Crockford; *Al. Oxf 1715-1886* II, 684.

HOOD, *(Revd)* **William Frankland** (c.1825-1864)
British clergyman and collector; he was the son of John H. of Nettleham Hall near Lincoln and Anne Smith Robb; MA; he visited Egypt several times between 1851 and 1861 and made a valuable collection of antiquities; on one of these journeys he travelled with A. H. Rhind (q.v.); the Hood Papyrus (onomasticon) was sold to the British Museum in 1872 (EA 10202); the rest of the collection remained at Nettleham Hall until it was sold at Sotheby's, 11 Nov. 1924 (172 lots); he was grandfather to Grace Crowfoot (q.v.); he died in Nettleham, 21 March 1864.

Burke's Landed Gentry; Preface (by Newberry) to Sale Cat.; Rhind, *Thebes, its Tombs and their Tenants*, 166; *Al. Oxon*; Lugt 87492.

HOPE, Thomas (1769-1831)
British author and virtuoso; he was born Amsterdam, 30 Aug. 1769, eldest son of John H. of Amsterdam and Philippina Barbara van der Hoeven; he spent the years 1787-95 recording the architectural remains in Egypt, Syria, Turkey, etc.; he settled in England in 1795 on the occupation of Holland by the French; FRS; FSA; he was in Cairo in 1797; he amassed a large art collection, which included Egyptian sculpture, displayed in a room with Egyptian-style decoration and furniture; he died in Duchess St., London, 2 Feb. 1831; his youngest brother Henry Philip H., born Amsterdam, 8 June 1774, also travelled in Turkey and added to his brother's collection; this was very valuable and included Egyptian gems, being catalogued by Bram Hertz (q.v.); he died at Bedgebury Park, Cranbrook, Kent, 5 Dec. 1839; the Hope collection was moved to Deepdene, near Dorking, Surrey, before being sold by Christie's in 1917; the antiquities were sold 23 July 1917 (261 lots), many being acquired by Gulbenkian (q.v.), Lever (q.v.), and Wellcome (q.v.).

ODNB 28, 36-8; *DNB* 27. 327-9; Lugt 77060; D. Watkin, *Thomas Hope 1769-1831 and the Neo-classical Idea*, 1968; B. J. Kemp, *Orientalia* 37 (1968), 63-66; D. Watkin and P. Hewart-Jaboor, *Thomas Hope: Regency Designer*, 2008.

HOPFNER, Theodor (1886-1946)
German classicist and specialist in the field of history of religions in Late Ancient Egypt; he was born in Trutnov (Trautenau) in Northern Bohemia, 7 April 1886, son of Friedrich H., secondary school teacher, and his wife Anna, and brother of Friedrich Hopfner (1881-1949), Professor of Geodesy at Vienna Technical Highschool; he was educated in Prague where he attended German Primary school, 1891-1896, and German state gymnasium, 1897-1905; he then enrolled in Classics at Kaiserlich-königliche deutsche Karl-Ferdinands-Universität Prague, 1905, the German branch of the present Charles University; at the end of his studies he obtained the qualification to teach Latin, Greek, and German at Secondary schools, 1909; he worked then as a teacher at several Secondary schools in Prague, 1909-1919; Ph.D., 1911; with his study *Der Tierkult der alten Aegypter nach den griechisch-römischen Berichten und den wichtigeren Denkmälern*, 1913, he was appointed lecturer at Deutsche

Universität in Prague, 1919; he was appointed assistant Professor, 1923, and full Professor in Classics, 1928; in 1935 he became dean of the Faculty of Arts and subdean, 1936/37; he was a member of Deutsche Gesellschaft für Altertumskunde in Prague, 1916, of Prüfungskommission für das Lehramt an Mittelschulen at Prague, 1927, ordinary member of the then prestigious Oriental Institute of Prague, 1934; real member of the German Society for Humanities and Arts of the Czechoslovakian Republic, 1936; in 1938 he was elected corresponding fellow of the Institut d'Égypte au Caire; after the Deutsche Universität in Prag was taken over by Deutsches Reich administration in 1939, he was once again appointed full Professor by Nazi German authorities, 1941; he married Beatrix Beneš, daughter of a state railway inspector, 1921; he devoted himself to teaching during his university career, hence his bibliography lists only 55 items, above all monographs, but also studies, and numerous articles, notably in *Archiv Orientální*; his publications on religion and magic in Hellenistic and Roman Egypt were *Über die koptisch-sa'idischen Apophthegmata Patrum Aegyptiorum und verwandte griechische, lateinische, koptisch-bohairische und syrische Sammlungen,* 1918; *Über Form und Gebrauch der griechischen Lehnwörter in der koptisch-sa'idischen Apophthegmenversion,* 1918; *Griechisch-ägyptischer Offenbarungszauber mit einer eingehenden Darstellung des griechisch-synkretistischen Dämonenglaubens und der Voraussetzungen und Mittel des Zaubers überhaupt und der magischen Divination im besonderen,.* vol. 1, 1921 (updated edition 1974), vol. 2, 1924 (updated in two semi-volumes 1983 and 1990); *Fontes historiae religionis Aegyptiacae,* vols. 1-5, 1922-25; *Mystik in Aegypten,* 1921; a continuing standard work *Plutarch über Isis und Osiris,* 2 vols., 1940-1941 (repr. Hildesheim 1991); he died in Prague, in a prison camp for Czech citizens of German nationality, 9 Feb. 1946.

ÖLB 1815-1950 (1957), 415-16; H. Strum, *Biographisches Lexikon zur Geschichte der Böhmischen Länder,* 1 1979, 679; *Eikasmos* IV (1993), 203-16 (F. Brunhölzl); XIV (2003), 393-419 (M. Sicherl); *H. Harrauer and R. Pintaudi (eds.),* W. B. Oerter in *Gedenkschrift Ulrike Horak,* 2004, 305-10; Archives Charles University, Hopfner's Curriculum vitae; inf. W. B. Oerter; *Analecta Papyrologica* 21/2 (2009-10), 317-41 (W. Oerter) (bibl.); W. Oerter, *Die Ägyptologie an der Prager Universität 1882-1945,* 2010, 64-74.

HOPKIN MORRIS *see* MORRIS

HOREAU, Hector (1801-1872)
French architect; he was born in Versailles, 4 Oct. 1801, son of Yves Jean H. and Marie Charlotte Dubose; he was trained at the École des Beaux-Arts, 1819-22; he drew plates for Cailliaud's *Voyage à Meroé,* 1826-7; after visiting many countries in Europe he made a long journey to the east, especially Egypt and Nubia, 1839, making many fine and extremely accurate drawings; on his return he was appointed treasurer of the Soc. Asiatique, 1842; Horeau was responsible for a number of improvements in the different quarters of Paris, and made a speciality of cast-iron architecture; in 1850 he competed for the Crystal Palace design in London and won the first medal for the best design, although the project was carried out by Sir Joseph Paxton with another scheme; in 1856 he went to live in England; Horeau produced many designs for public and exhibition buildings; he published *Panorama d'Égypte et de Nubie,* fol. 1841; in 1967 the Griffith Institute in Oxford was bequeathed by T. Staines-Read a portfolio of 45 sheets mounted with the water-colour drawings and sketches made by Horeau on his visit to Egypt in 1838, many of which were subsequently engraved to illustrate the above publication; he died in Paris, 21 Aug. 1872.

Ashmolean Museum Report 1967; *Allgemeines Lex. der bildenden Künstler von der Antike bis zur Gegenwart,* U. Thieme and F. Becker, herausgegeben von Hans Vollmer, 17 Bd. (Leipzig, 1924); *DBF* 17, 1292-4.

HORNBLOWER, George Davis (1864-1951)
British civil servant; born London, 19 Sept. 1864, son of Jethro H., merchant, and Sarah Crothers; he was an official at one time in the Egyptian Ministry of the Interior where he became interested in Egyptology; OBE, FSA; he also had an interest in Anthropology which strongly influenced his work especially as this was concerned with Predynastic Egypt and Egyptian Religion; he wrote a number of articles on Predynastic subjects, see *JEA* 13 (1927), 222-46; 15, 29-47 and espec. 'Funerary Designs on Predynastic Jars' in *JEA* 16 (1930), 10-18; also articles on Osiris in *Man* between the years 1937 and 1946; see as well 'The Foundations of Ancient Egyptian Religion' in *Islamic Culture,* vols. vi and vii; he died in Penzance, 15 May 1951.

AfO 16 (1952), 172 (anon.); EES *Report* 1951, 6 (H.W. Fairman); *JEA* 37 (1951), 2; *Man* 52 (1952), 164-5 (portr.) (W. Fagg).

HORNER, (*Revd*) George William (1849-1930)
British Coptologist; he was born in London, 10 June 1849, son of John Stuart Hippsley H. and Sophia Gertrude Dickinson; he was educated at Eton and Balliol College, Oxford; Curate of Cirencester, 1874-5; Rector of Selwood Mells, 1875-91; in 1891 he withdrew from parochial work and devoted himself to Coptic, which he studied under Steindorff (q.v.) at Berlin, but he was mainly self-taught, as also in Arabic and Ethiopic; he published a critical text of the New Testament, Bohairic in 4 vols., and Sahidic in 7 vols., a task that occupied him for 26 years; he also published *Coptic Consecrations,* 1902; *Ethiopic Statutes of the Apostles,* 1904; and a trans. of *Pistis Sophia,* 1924; he died in Selwood Mells, 10 Aug. 1930.

JEA 16 (1930), 258; *The Coptic Encyclopedia* 4, 1257 (M. Krause).

HORNER, Leonard (1785-1864)
British geologist and educational reformer; he was born in Edinburgh, 17 Jan. 1785, son of John H. and Joanna Baillie; educated at the High School afterwards taking a degree in chemistry at Edinburgh University; FRS, 1813; Secretary of the Geological Soc., 1810-14, President, 1845-7 and again 1860-2; in 1854 he undertook the investigation of the depth and rate of increase of the alluvium deposited by the Nile, borings and excavations being made under the direction of Hekekyan (q.v.) at Mit Rahina (Memphis) and Mataria (Heliopolis temple) at both of which sites important archaeological finds were made; the most interesting results were published in the *Philosophical Transactions of the Royal Soc.* in 1855 and 1858; the objects and manuscripts from this excavations were presented to the British Museum in 1861; Horner died in London where he had lived for some years, 5 March 1864.

ODNB 28, 163-5 (portr.); *DNB* 23, 371; *Trans. R. S. Literature*, 2nd ser. 9. 197; *Mem. Inst. Eg.* 54. 153; J. Ball, *Contributions to the Geography of Egypt*, 1939, 174; H. B. Woodward, *Hist. Geol. Soc.* 34. 289, 291.

HORNIMAN, Frederick John (1835-1906)
British tea merchant and collector; he was born in Bridgewater, 8 Oct. 1835, son of John H. and Ann Smith; he was educated at Friend's College, Croydon; he married 1. Rebekah daughter of John Elmslie, 2. Minnie Louisa Bennet; his work as head of a business with world-wide connections, especially in the Far East, enabled him to form a vast collection of curios, natural history objects, antiquities, implements and weapons, etc., which far exceeded any other private collection in England; these are now housed in the Horniman Museum and Library, Forest Hill, London, built and endowed by him in 1897; the buildings consist of two great halls 260 by 60 feet, with an additional gallery added by his son as a memorial; there are also students' rooms and an aquarium; the collections contain Egyptian objects, in particular those illustrating burial customs and mummy cases; Horniman was MP for Falmouth and Penryn, 1895; he died in London 5 March 1906.

ODNB 28, 167-8; *DNB Suppl.* 2, 2/1, 304-5; *WWW* i, 352.

HORRACK, Philippe Jacques Ferdinand de (1820-1902)
French Egyptologist, of Austrian origin; he was born in Frankfurt, 7 Sept. 1820, son of Michael von H. and Catherine Herzog; he trained for a commercial career and in 1843 entered the banking-house of Greene & Cie, Paris; in 1851 he joined the firm of Tiffany & Co., of New York, London, and Paris, in which he remained till his death; he developed a taste for archaeology and in 1858 became a life-long correspondent and friend of Chabas (q.v.), under whose guidance he studied Egyptian; having begun his studies with the false doctrines of Seyffarth (q.v.) and Uhlemann (q.v.); after becoming acquainted with Chabas, he said, 'j'ai perdu presque une année dans des études stériles'; although he had little leisure for study, he worked methodically and accurately and became a good copyist of texts; the plates of his publications of the Lamentations of Isis and the Book of Breathings from papyri in the Louvre and Berlin, were beautifully lithographed by himself; he was acquainted with Devéria (q.v.), Birch (q.v.), and Lepsius (q.v.) and he studied in the Louvre and the British and Berlin Museums; his works were collected by Maspero (q.v.) in the *Bibl. Ég.*, 1907; his books and papers were presented by his widow to the Musée Guimet, Paris; he died in Villa Laurina, Maisons-Laffitte, 1902.

Virey, *Notice Biogr. (Bibl. Ég.* 17), 68 pp; EEF *Ann. Arch. Rep.* 1902-3, 37.

HOSKINS, George Alexander (1802-1863)
British traveller, antiquary and amateur artist; he was born 1802, 2nd son of George H. and Mary Alison; he visited Egypt and Nubia; 1832-3, and worked with Robert Hay (q.v.) at Qurna and on a journey to the Kharga Oasis; he published *Travels in Ethiopia*, London, 1835 and *Visit to the Great Oasis of the Libyan Desert*, London, 1837; the latter provides a vivid picture of the conduct of Hay's expeditions; three large volumes of drawings made on these journeys by himself and his companion Luchese Bandoni were acquired by Sir Alan Gardiner (q.v.) and deposited in the Griffith Institute, Oxford; he was Secretary and Treasurer of the White Nile Ass., 1839 he married Mary Thornton, 1843 (d.1858); in later life he became interested in the prison reform movement and wrote a number of books and pamphlets comparing the British and European prison systems; he revisited Egypt, 1860-1, and published *A Winter in Upper and Lower Egypt*, 1863; he died in Rome, 21 Nov. 1863.

Burke's Landed Gentry, 1894; Budge, *Eg. Sudan*, i, 56-61; BL Add.MS 25652, ff. 4, 8, 14; *GM* 1864, i, 130; Hilmy, i, 310; R. Morkot in *Souvenirs and New Ideas*, ed. D. Fortenberry, 2013, 98-118.

HOUGHTON, (*Revd*) **William** (1828-1895)
British naturalist and archaeologist; he was born in Liverpool and baptized there 8 Oct. 1828, son of Richard H. and Jane Ellen Jones; MA, Oxford, 1853; Headmaster of Solihull School, 1858; Rector of Preston, Wellington, Salop, 1860; the author of many popular books on natural history, he made a special study of the nat. hist. of the ancients, on which he published a general work in 1879, embodying the results of many special studies (e.g. *TSBA* 5, 33, 319; 6. 454; *PSBA* 12, 81, etc.); he died in Tenby, 3 Sept. 1895.

Proc. Linn. Soc. 1895-6, 37.

HOVING, Thomas Pearsall Field (1931-2009)
American museum director and author; he was born in New York City, 15 Jan. 1931, son of Walter H. and Mary Osgood Field; he studied art history at Princeton; PhD, 1959; he became an assistant curator of medieval art at the Metropolitan Museum in 1959; he was appointed Director of the Metropolitan Museum in 1967; he acquired the Temple of Dendur for the Museum in 1968; he also led negotiations for the American touring exhibition of objects from the tomb of Tutankhamun, 1976-79; he left the museum in 1977 and worked as an arts journalist and editor of *Connoisseur*; among other works, he wrote *The Search for Tutankhamun*, 1978 as a popular account of the tomb's discovery, and *Making the Mummies Dance*, 1993; he died in New York City, 10 Dec. 2009.

New York Times, Dec. 11 2009; *The Times*, Dec. 15 2009; T. Hoving, *Making the Mummies Dance*, 1993; inf. T. Hardwick.

HSIA (XIA), Nai (1910-1985)
Chinese archaeologist; he was born at Yungchia (Wen-chou), Chekiang province 7 Feb. 1910, son of Hsia Wen-pu; he studied at the National Tsinghua University in Peking (Beijing) graduating in 1934; he obtained a scholarship to study in England where in 1935-6 he worked at the Courtauld Institute; from 1936-9 he studied Egyptology at University College London under Glanville (q.v.); in 1939 he was awarded the Douglas Murray Scholarship and the Margaret Murray Scholarship both in Egyptology; MA, 1939; he obtained his PhD in 1946 with a thesis on ancient Egyptian beads; he took part in several archaeological excavations including Armant and Lachish and met Petrie (q.v.); in 1939, on his way back to China, he visited Egypt and studied objects in the Cairo Museum; he reached China in 1941 and held various posts in the National Central Museum; in 1949 he was named Professor at the University of Chekiang; in 1950 he was appointed Deputy Director of the Institute of Archaeology, Chinese Academy of Sciences and Director, 1958-82; Vice-President of the Chinese Academy of Social Sciences and Hon. Director of the Institute of Archaeology 1982-85; Corresponding Fellow of the British Academy, 1974 and the German Archaeological Institute, 1982; although his career was largely concerned with Chinese archaeology, he maintained a lively interest in the progress of Egyptology; he died in Beijing, 19 June 1985.

Inf. Professor R. Whitfield and Univ. College London; R. Janssen, *The First Hundred Years*, 1992, 37; Linghu Ruoming, *Journal of Ancient Civilizations* 16 (2001), 1-3.

HUBER, Christian Wilhelm von (1804-1871)
Austrian diplomat and numismatist; he was born in Vienna, 26 Feb. 1804; he studied at Vienna and Padua and then entered the Austrian diplomatic corps; he was Austrian Consul-General in Egypt 1850-8 in succession to Laurin (q.v.); he put together a collection of Egyptian antiquities some of which came from excavations at Saqqara; some objects were sent to Vienna in 1857, but the bulk of his collection was sold to the Boulaq (Cairo) Museum in 1859; from 1869 he was attached to the Numismatic Bureau in Vienna; he died in Vienna, 1 Dec. 1871.

ÖBL 2, 444; Dewachter, *Rev. d'Ég.* 36 (1985), 57-8; Dewachter, *BIFAO* 85 (1985), 122-3; *Numismatische Zeitschrift* 3 (1871); H. Brugsch, *Meine Leben und mein Wandern*, 1894, 155-8.

HUGHES, George Robert (1907-1992)
American Egyptologist; he was born in Wymore, Nebraska, 12 Jan. 1907, son of Evan H., a farmer, and Pyne Jones; he was educated locally and at the University of Nebraska; BA, 1929; he attended McCormick Theological Seminary, Chicago, 1929-1932; BD, 1932; he was awarded the Nettie F. McCormick Fellowship in Old Testament to continue his education; in 1931 he had taken a course with Edgerton (q.v.) at the Oriental Institute and was encouraged to study ancient Egyptian; in 1932 he began his studies at the University of Chicago; PhD, 1939; his field of special interest was Demotic language and literature; research assistant, Oriental Institute working on the Demotic dictionary project, 1934-42; he worked in the Intelligence Service in Washington, 1942-46; he joined the Epigraphic Survey in 1946 working on the Temple of Khonsu and the Bubastite Portal in Karnak; he became Field Director 1 Jan., 1949-1 Jan., 1964 when work concentrated on

the Temple of Medinet Habu; also acting Field Director in the Sudan 1961-62 at Serra East; he was assistant Professor at the Oriental Institute, 1948-55; associate Professor, 1955-61; Professor 1961-30 June, 1975; and Professor Emeritus; he was Director of the Oriental Institute, 1968-72; he was a member of the Board of Governors of the American Research Center in Egypt, 1952-68; Vice-President 1969-72; President of the Midwest Branch of the American Oriental Society, 1967-68; he was an honorary member of the Deutsches Archäologisches Institut and the Institut d'Égypte, Cairo; a volume of articles dedicated to him *Studies in Honor of George R. Hughes* was published in 1976; his published works, apart from articles, were his thesis *Saite Demotic Land Leases*, 1952; with the Epigraphic Survey, *Reliefs and Inscriptions at Karnak* III, 1954; *Medinet Habu* V, 1957; *Medinet Habu* VI, 1963; *Medinet Habu* VII, 1964; *Medinet Habu* VIII, 1970; *The Temple of Khonsu* I, 1979; *The Tomb of Kheruef*, 1980; with H. Ricke and E. Wente *The Beit el-Wali Temple of Ramesses II*, 1967; and posthumously *The Oriental Institute Hawara Papyri*, with R. Jasnow, 1997; *Catalogue of Demotic Texts in the Brooklyn Museum*, 2005; he died in Chicago, 21 Dec. 1992.

Inf. J. Larson; J. Johnson and F Wente, *Studies in Honor of George Hughes,* 1976, xv-xviii (portr.), 281-2 (bibl.); *NARCE* 160 (1993), 29; *The Oriental Institute 1991-1992 Annual Report*, 13-15 (J. Johnson); *JARCE* 30 (1993), xi-xiv (J. Johnson); *Enchoria* 19/20 (1992/3), 1-4 (portr.) (J. H. Johnson).

HUGHES-HUGHES, Walter Oldham (1847-1894)
British archaeologist; he was born in London, 17 May 1847, son of William H.-H., a barrister, and Ellen Oldham; he was educated at Tonbridge and Wadham College, Oxford, 1865-9; BA, 1869; MA, 1872; he became Senior Classical Master at Taunton College School, 1870-6, Headmaster at St. Leonards Preparatory School, 1876-80, Assistant Master at Tonbridge, 1880-8, and Assistant Master at Uppingham, 1888-9 when he retired through illness; he was engaged by Petrie (q.v.) to take part in the excavation of Gurob (q.v.), 1889-90 but proved unsatisfactory; he briefly returned to Tonbridge in 1891 and then became a breeder of St. Bernard dogs; he shot himself in London, 23 April 1894.

Inf. M. Vygus and R. Samways; J. Foster, *Men-at-the-Bar*, 1885, 230; H. D. Furley, *The Register of Tonbridge School from 1861 to 1945*, 1951, 27.

HULL, John Fowler (1800-1825)
British orientalist; he was born in Uxbridge, 28 May 1800, son of Samuel Hull, a banker and miller, and Anne Fowler; he was educated at Epping School where he exhibited a great aptitude for languages; he left school in 1816 to go into business but on inheriting substantial funds on his father's death, he devoted himself to the study of oriental languages; from 1818 he studied at the Oriental College in Hertford and from 1820 at Paris; in 1823 he set off for India, visiting Egypt on his way, Jan.-July 1824, when he explored Thebes with Madox (q.v.), buying a mummy and some papyri there; he died at Shiggaon near Dharwar, India 18 Dec. 1825; he owned a valuable collection of Indian, Chinese, Persian, and Arabic MSS, which he bequeathed to the British Museum; his Egyptian antiquities were apparently inherited by his brother Samuel Hull of Uxbridge (1799-1880) and sold by local auction in 1880, when some pieces were acquired by the British Museum, including the New Kingdom gilded cartonnage mask of the Lady Satdjehuty (EA 29770).

Athanasi, 62, 126; Madox, i, 417 ff.; ii, 378-9; Westcar Diary, 196, 201, 209, 241, 260; *The Classical Journal* 38 (1828), 259-267 (T. G.); J. H. Taylor, *Apollo* (July 1996), 33-8; no record of sale in Lugt.

HULST, (*Count*) Riamo d' (*fl.* 1870-1921)
German excavator; he is said to have been a German officer who deserted the army in 1870 and became a citizen of Luxembourg; he later went to Egypt where he excavated a Christian cemetery in Alexandria, 1887; he became an assistant to Naville (q.v.) in his excavations at Bubastis, 1888-9 and Ahnas, 1892; he was sharply criticized by Petrie (q.v.) and was not further employed by the EEF from 1893; he also excavated at Fustat near Cairo for Coptic and Arabic antiquities in 1889-90 when he found some Geniza documents and was employed by the Bodleian library to search for more in 1898; he later became an antiquities dealer in Cairo; he was interned in World War I, and his collections were sold at public auction 6 Nov. 1916; he was dead by 11 June 1921.

T. G. H. James, *Excavating in Egypt*, 1982, 30, 52, 54; Public Record Office, Kew, FO 141/4415; M. Drower, *Flinders Petrie*, 1985, 123, 150, 157, 163, 176, 179, 274, 280; R. Jefferson, *Journal of the History of Collections* 21 (2009), 125-142; no record of sale in Lugt.

HULTSCH, Friedrich (1833-1906)
German mathematician; he was born in Dresden, 22 July 1833, son of Traugott H. and Juliane Mäcke; he devoted special study to the mathematics of the ancients and published important papers on Egyptian metrology and mathematics in *Abh. Sächs. Ges. der Wiss.*, *Bibl. Mathematica*, *ZÄS*, and other journals; he died in Dresden, 6 April 1906.

Hilmy, i, 312; ii, 422; Peet, *Rhind Math. Pap.*, passim; *NDB* 10, 30-31.

HUMBERT (*Lt.-Col.*) **Jean Émile** (1771-1839)
Dutch engineer and agent; he was born in The Hague, 28 July 1771 son of Jean J., a portrait painter, and Antoinette Elisabeth Deel; he was educated as a military engineer; in 1796, 1806-18, and 1822-4 he was sent on missions to Tunis where he identified the site of Carthage and carried out excavations; he collected antiquities later sold to National Museum of Antiquities, Leiden; in 1826 he was sent to Italy where he successfully negotiated several purchases for Leiden including the acquisition of the Cimba (q.v.) collection in 1827 and the Anastasi (q.v.) collection in 1828; he also obtained the famous Horemheb reliefs; his papers are preserved in the archives of the National Museum of Antiquities, Leiden; he died in Leghorn, 20 Feb. 1839.

Inf. R. B. Halbertsma; H. Schneider, *De Laudibus Aegyptologiae*, 1985, 17-23; H. Schneider in C. Morigi Govi, S. Curto, and S. Pernigotti, *L'Egitto fuori dell'Egitto*, 398-401; R. B. Halbertsma, *Le solitaire des ruines*, 1995; R. B. Halbertsma, *Scholars, Travellers and Trade: The Pioneer years of the National Museum of Antiquities in Leiden, 1818-40*, 2003, 71-111.

HUMPHREYS, Charles (1800-1839)
English traveller, artist and private secretary to Burton (q.v.) during his travels 1819-35; he was born in the parish of St Giles Cripplegate, London, 11 Dec. 1800, son of Charles H., a silversmith, and Ann, a nurse who may have attended the birth of Burton's siblings; he made fair copies of Burton's notes and journals; alongside Bonomi (q.v.) he drew many plates in Burton's *Excerpta Hieroglyphica* 1825-8, the first lithographs produced in Egypt, and assisted in their printing and distribution; it is likely he produced many of the drawings and watercolours in Burton's *Collectanea Aegyptiaca* now in the British Library (Add.Mss.25613-75); he assisted Wilkinson (q.v.) with plates for his *Materia Hieroglyphica*, published in Malta 1828; in 1832 he prepared a coloured map of the Fayoum for Gliddon's (q.v.) *Otia Aegyptiaca*, although this was not published until 1849; he returned to London in 1835 and lived with Burton and his wife Andreana in Jermyn Street; he purchased a few items from the July 1836 sale at Sotheby's of Burton's collection but resold them in June 1837 at Philips auctioneers; he prepared the chromolithographs for Wilkinson's *Manners and Customs of the Ancient Egyptians*, 1837, which are among the earliest book illustrations of their kind used in England; he was secretary to the Geological Society from November 1836 to May 1839 when he resigned because of ill health; he died 6 June 1839, an Egyptianized headstone without inscription marking his grave in Kensal Green cemetery, paid for by Burton.

Inf. N. Cooke.

HUNT, Arthur Surridge (1871-1934)
British papyrologist; he was born in Romford, 1 March 1871, son of Alfred Henry H., a legal official, and Emily Pertwee; he was educated Cranbrook School, Eastbourne College, The Queen's College, Oxford; MA; DLitt; FBA; Hon. member of many foreign academies; Professor of Papyrology, Oxford, 1913-34; he frequently excavated in Egypt, 1895-1907, chiefly for papyri at Oxyrhynchus and sites in the Fayum; he edited singly or jointly with B. P. Grenfell (q.v.) many volumes of the *Oxyrhynchus Papyri*, and catalogues of many important collections, such as Amherst, John Rylands, and Cairo, and many separate editions of particular papyri or groups of papyri, including two volumes in the Loeb Classical Series; he died in Oxford, 18 June 1934.

ODNB 28, 835-6; *Aegyptus* 14 499; *Chron. d'Ég.* 9. 335; *JEA* 20 (1934), 204-5 (portr.) (J. G. Milne); *WWW* iii, 678; *DNB* 1931-40, 455 (H. I. Bell); M. Capasso (ed.), *Hermae*, 2007, 115-41 (portr.).

HUNT, Lucy Ellen (1880-1959)
The daughter of Sir Alexander Frederick Bradshaw, KCB who served in India, and Ellen Ewart; she married A. S. Hunt the papyrologist (q.v.) 1918; she was a member of the EES from 1934, and a benefactor of the Ashmolean Museum, Oxford; she died in Oxford, 6 March 1959.

EES *Report*, 1959, 5.

HUNTER, (*Revd*) **George Rivers** (1796-1872)
British traveller and collector; he was born in Burton Bradstock, Dorset and baptized there 4 Nov. 1796, son of Robert H., doctor, and his wife Marian; he was educated at Wadham College, Oxford 1815-9; BA, 1819; he held the post of rector of Okeford Fitzpaine, 1820-72; in 1826-7 he undertook a tour to Egypt in the course of which he built up a collection of scarabs; part of this collection was purchased by the British Museum in 1849; drawings of the scarabs are in the Griffith Institute; he died in London, 26 May 1872.

Al. Oxon. ser. 2 ,1/2, 717; BM corr.

HUNTINGTON, Robert (1637-1701)
British traveller and collector; he was born at Deerhurst, Gloucs., Feb. 1637, son of Revd Robert H., curate of Deerhurst and later vicar of Leigh; he was educated at Bristol and Merton College, Oxford; BA, 1658; MA, 1663, where he learnt oriental languages; chaplain to the Levant Company at Aleppo, 1670-81; he visited Egypt twice in 1678-9 and 1681 touring Cairo, Giza, Saqqara (where he acquired two inscriptions) and the Wadi Natrun; he also amassed a large collection of Coptic MSS; on his return, he gave his antiquities to the Ashmolean Museum in 1683 and sold his MSS to the Bodleian Library; DD, Oxford, 1683; provost of Trinity College, Dublin, 1683-92; rector of Great Hallingbury, 1692; bishop of Raphoe, 1701; his published works consist of his letters edited by Thomas Smith, 1704 and one article; he died in Dublin, 2 Sept. 1701.

ODNB 28, 938-40; *DNB* 28, 308-9 (W. Courtney); *Al. Oxon.* i, 773; *GM* Jan-March 1825, 11-15, 115-9, 218-21; *Oxford Magazine* (1969), 48; O. Volkoff ed., *Voyages en Égypte pendant les années 1678-1701* (Cairo, 1981), xiii-xvii, 161-99; *The Ashmolean* 4 (1983/4), 12-3; unpubl. MA, thesis by K. Pickavance at University of Liverpool, F26-62.

HUSSON, Hyacinthe (*fl.* 1868-1878)
French writer; he was a pupil of Maspero (q.v.) at the Coll. de France; author of 'Mythes et Monuments Comparés' in *Rev. Gén. de l'Architecture*, 1868; also *La chaîne traditionnelle: Contes et Légendes au point de vue mythique*, Paris, 1874.

Maspero, *L'Égyptologie* (1915), 7; Hilmy, i, 313.

HUYGE, Dirk Lucien (1957-2018)
Belgian archaeologist; he was born in Bornem, 18 April 1957, son of Alfons H. and Bertha Bosteels; he studied archaeology and art history at Louvain (Leuven) University under Pierre M. Vermeersch, 1975-80; MA, 1980; PhD, 1995; he became a research assistant at the Laboratory for Prehistory, 1980-3; he was editor of two journals at the University, 1990-1; he was secretary of the Master's programme Eastern Mediterranean Archaeology at Leuven University, 1993-5; he was a lecturer there, 1995-2007 and post-doctoral research fellow, 1996-8; he was appointed curator of Prehistoric and Early Dynastic Egypt at the Royal Museums of Art and History, Brussels, 1998-2018; field-director of the Belgian excavations at Elkab, 1978-80, 1982-8, and 1995-2000; Director, 2009-2018; he documented the rock art near Elkab, notably at Wadi Hellal, 1982-6, at el-Hosh, 1998, 2004-5, 2010; and at Qurta, 2007-9, 2011; he also excavated at Shenhur, 1996; was a member of the Belgian Middle Egypt Prehistoric Project, 1981, 1984, 1988; and the North Kharga Oasis Survey, 2007; he was honorary president (2013) and member of the Royal Academy for Overseas Sciences (Brussels), 2006-18; he was an active collaborator in the fourth edition of *Who Was Who in Egyptology*; he was a renowned specialist of Egyptian rock art and Pre- and Early Dynastic Egypt; apart from numerous articles on his research and excavations, he published with S. Hendrickx, *Elkab* IV/21989; he died in Duffel, 31 July 2018.

Archéo-Nil 28 (2018), 11-16; Inf. L. Limme and I. Therasse; internet obit, 28 Oct. 2018. Art and History Museum, Brussels, 1-4. (W. Claes and S. Hendrickx).

HUYOT, Jean Nicolas (1780-1840)
French architect; he was born in Paris, 27 Dec. 1780; a friend of Champollion (q.v.) who travelled in Egypt and the Near East, 1818-19, and brought back a large collection of drawings which he placed at the disposal of Champollion; these were of great service to him in correcting the errors in the plates of the *Description de l'Égypte*; he was architect of the Arc de Triomphe, Paris; he died in Paris, 2 Aug. 1840; his journal and drawings are in the Bibl. Nat., Paris, among those of Nestor L'Hôte (q.v.)

NBG 25, 682-3; *BSFE* 32 (1961), 35-42; Champollion, i, 175, 359; Forbin, 73, 74; Montulé, 19, 10; È. Gran-Aymerich, *Dictionnaire biographique d'archéologie 1798-1945*, 2001, incorporated in *Les Chercheurs de passé 1798-1945*, 2007, 885; *DBF* 18, 110-1.

HUYSHE, Wentworth (1847-1934)
British antiquary and journalist; he was born in Meerut, India 13 April 1847, son of General Alfred Huyshe and Julia Maria Hagar; he was a war correspondent in the Russo-Turkish War, 1877-8 and the Sudan campaign in 1885; he had a specialist interest in heraldry and medieval armour; he was a Member of the Kermoosers Club for the study of ancient armour, see BL Add. MS 40678, ff. 27, 38, 55, 65; member of the Society of Biblical

Archaeology 1879; he presented the British Museum with a stela (EA 962) in 1875; he died in Chipping Camden, 2 Dec. 1934.

The Times 4 Dec. 1934

HYDE, John (*c.*1780-1825)
British traveller; he was born in Manchester c.1780; he made a journey through Egypt as far as the Second Cataract and tried unsuccessfully to reach Dongola, 1818-19, travelling with Bankes (q.v.); he next travelled through Palestine, Syria, and Mesopotamia to India; his journals and notebooks recounting these expeditions are in the British Library, see Add. MSS 42102-8; Hyde's name is carved on the Rock of Abu Sir, with the date 22 Feb. 1819 and in various places in Nubia; he died in Murshidabad, 24 April 1825.

Finati, ii, 320-40; Henniker, 298; Athanasi, 41-6; Hoskins, *Oasis*, 94; *GM* 95, 478; *BIFAO* 70 (1971), 117 note 2; R. de Keersmaecker, *ASTENE Bulletin* 67 (2016), 15-18; P. Rée, *ASTENE Bulletin* 68 (2016), 12-16.

HYVERNAT, (*Abbé*) **(Eugène Xavier Louis) Henri** (1858-1941)
French orientalist; he was born in Saint-Julien-en-Jarret (Loire), 30 June 1858, son of Claude H. and (Marie Josephine) Léonide Meyrieux; educated at the Séminaire de Saint Jean, Lyons, and the University of Lyons; he then studied theology in Paris, 1882, and was appointed Doctor of Theology at the Pontifical University, Rome, 1882-5; acting Professor of Assyriology and Egyptology at Rome, 1885-9; he was sent by the French Govt. on a scientific mission to Armenia, 1888-9; Professor of Biblical Archaeology at the Catholic University of Washington, 1889; head Dept. of Semitic and Egyptian Languages and Literature 1895; Hon. Ph.D., Michigan, 1919; he published many works of which the most important were, *Acta Martyrum*, 1886, 1907-24, Coptic and Latin; *Album de Paléographie Copte*, 1888; he died in Washington, 20 May 1941.

Chron. d'Ég. 19 (1944), 153-7; *Catholic Univ. Bull.* 8 (1941) (portr.); *Cath. World*, 1941, 653-6; *WWWA* 1, 616; *DBF* 18, 122..

IBSCHER, Hugo (1874-1943)

German technician and restorer of manuscripts and papyri; he was born in Berlin, 28 Sept. 1874; he trained as a bookbinder, but entered the service of the Berlin Museum in 1891, where he was entrusted with the mounting and restoring of the papyri, in which task he displayed a quite remarkable ability and skill; he served at first under Ludwig Abel, but from 1894 was in sole charge; although on the staff of the museum, he was permitted to undertake work elsewhere and many important papyri have been restored and mounted by him in the collections of Turin, London, Oxford, Brussels, Paris, Prague, Copenhagen, Cairo, Rome, and many others; in this work he made a special study of the fibre patterns; for his work on the restoration of parchments and other MSS in the Vatican, he was awarded the Order of St. Gregory; he was Hon. Dr. of Strasbourg, and received the Leibnitz Medal of the Prussian Acad., and the medal of the Bavarian Acad.; he died in Berlin, 26 May 1943; his son, Rolf Ibscher (*d*.1967), carried on his work at Berlin.

FuF 24, 245 (bibl.); *Gnomon*, 1943, 286-7.

IDELER, Julius Ludwig (1809-1842)

German scholar; he was born Berlin, 3 Sept. 1809, son of Christian Ludwig I., the astronomer and chronologist and Professor at Berlin University (1766-1846), who taught on Egyptian chronology, and Friederike Burchardt; he studied at Berlin and Königsberg; habilitation, 1835 at Berlin; he taught at Berlin, 1835-42; he published *Hermapion sive Rudimenta Hieroglyphicae vetum Aegyptiorum Literaturae*, 2 parts. Leipzig, 1836-41, and many other works on Egypt; he died Berlin, 17 July 1892.

Brugsch, *Mein Leben*, 45; Hilmy, i, 318; *NDB* 10, 118; E. Endesfelder, D*ie Ägyptologie an der Berliner Universität-Zur Geschichte eines Fachgebietes*, 1988, 7, 9-10.

IDRIS, (Effendi) (*d*.1898)

Egyptian dealer in antiquities at Thebes; he built a house on the West Bank at Dra Abu en-Naga which Newberry (q.v.) rented and occupied while working there in 1895; he died 24 Nov. 1898.

Wilbour, 461, 479, 497; Budge, *N & T* i, 114; Newberry Diary, 1895, 1898; Myers Diary, 1897.

INSINGER, Jan Herman (1854-1918)

Dutch traveller, collector, and amateur Egyptologist; he was born Amsterdam, 12 May 1854, son of Herman I., member of the Dutch Parliament and private banker, and Johanna Jacoba Wilhelmena née Insinger; he was from 1879 resident in Luxor on account of his suffering from tuberculosis, first travelling on his dahabiya, and from 1889 living in his own house in Luxor with his family; he was closely associated with Maspero and other representatives of the Antiquities Service, and occasionally acted as official photographer for them; during his stay in Luxor, he becam a landowner and moneylender which allowed him to live in wealth and to start a collection of antiquities, notably the famous Demotic papyrus that bears his name which was obtained from the French Condular Agent at Akhmim in 1895 for 4,000 francs;most of his collection was sold at cost price to the Leiden Museum of Antiquities; the Museum also holds much correspondence and a set of his photographs; he does not seem to have sold antiquities to other parties; his memoir *In het land der Nijlcataracten*, 1883 was edited by M. Raven, 2004; he died in Cairo, 27 Oct. 1918.

ASAE 2 (1902), 148 (Maspero); Budge, *N & T* i. 364; *Dutch Consular Records*; Pleyte and Boeser, *Le Livre Royal: Le Papyrus Démotique Insinger*, 3; Sayce, 453, 457; Wilbour, passim (portr. facing p. 240); *Nederland's Patriciaat* 72 (1988) 273; M. Raaven, *OMRO* 71 (1991), 15-24; inf. T. Harding; M. Raven, *Insinger and Early Photography in Egypt*, 1991; F. Hagen and K. Ryholt, *The Antiquities Trade in Egypt 1880-1930*, 2017, 224-5; M. J. Raven, *The Most Prominent Dutchman in Egypt*, 2018; inf. M. Raven.

IRBY, (Hon.) Charles Leonard (1789-1845)

British naval officer and explorer; he was born at Boyland Hall, Norfolk, 9 Oct. 1789, youngest son of Frederick I. 2nd Lord Boston and Christiana Methuen; he entered the Navy, 1801, and saw much service, retiring through ill health with the rank of Captain, 1815; with Capt. James Mangles (q.v.) he ascended the Nile as far as the Second Cataract and also visited Palestine and Syria; they printed privately in 1823 *Travels in Egypt, Nubia, Syria and Asia Minor in 1817 and 1818*, a popular edition being published in 1844; he was the first to mention the 'Tomb of the Colossus' i.e. Djehuty-hotep at El-Bersha, but the discovery of it was probably due to Charles Brine (q.v.) as suggested; he and Mangles assisted Belzoni (q.v.) in the opening of Abu Simbel; Irby subsequently married Frances Mangles, 1825, and saw further service 1826-8; he was in Egypt again in Aug. 1827 and took Prudhoe (q.v.) and Felix (q.v.) to Smyrna; he died in Torquay, 3 Dec. 1845.

ODNB 29, 327; *DNB* 29, 28; Athanasi, ii, 25; Belzoni, i, 314-16, 332, 342; Hilmy, i, 325; O'Byrne, *Naval Biogr.* 545; Richardson, ii, 294; Salt, ii, 72.

IRWIN, Eyles (1751-1817)
British traveller; he was born in Calcutta, baptized there 23 Feb. 1751, younger son of Capt. James I. of the East India Company and Sarah Beale; he was educated in England and appointed to a post in Madras 21 Nov. 1766, returning to India in Feb. 1768; he was suspended from office in 1776 and set off for England to seek redress; he travelled via Egypt, landing at Quseir in 1777 and visiting Cairo, Alexandria, and Rosetta; on reaching England, he was reinstated in his post and returned to India in 1780 by the overland route through Aleppo to Basra; he was back in England in 1785 due to ill health and was sent to China 1792-4; he published his account of Egypt, A Series of Adventures in the course of a voyage up the Red Sea, on the coasts of Arabia and Egypt,1781, 2nd ed. 1784; he died in Clifton, Bristol, 12 Aug. 1817.

ODNB 29, 391; *DNB* 29, 57-8; J. Starkey in N. Cooke and V. Daubney, *Lost and Now Found*, 2017, 127-40.

ISKANDER Hanna, Zaki (1916-1979)
Egyptian chemist and conservator; he was born in Sherbeen, 16 Nov. 1916; he was educated at the Faculty of Science, Cairo University; BSc 1935; Diploma of the Institute of Egyptology 1942; MSc in Organic Chemistry 1945 and PhD 1953; he was appointed chemist in the laboratory of the Cairo Museum in 1936 where he trained under Lucas (q.v.); Director of the Research Archaeological Laboratory, Department of Antiquities 1953-66; Director General of Technical Affairs 1966-71; Director General, Department of Antiquities (later Organization of Egyptian Antiquities) 1971-2; Professor of Science and Technology in Ancient Egypt, American University of Cairo from 1970, Professor of Technology of Painting, Cairo and Alexandria Universities from 1969; honorary member of the American Research Center in Egypt, 1974; he undertook the cleaning and restoration of most major archaeological finds discovered during his career; apart from numerous articles, he was the author of A *Brief History of Egypt* with A. Badawy 1948 and subsequent editions, *The Cheops Boat* I, 1960 with M. Z. Nour, and *The Discovery of Neferwptah*, 1971 with N. Farag; he died in Cairo, 16 July 1979.

NARCE 88, 23; *NARCE* 109, 2 (L. Habachi).

ISRAELIT-GROLL, Sarah (1925-2007)
Israeli Egyptologist; she was born in Tel Aviv, 25 Dec. 1925, daughter of a doctor in Jerusalem; she first trained at the David Yellin Teachers' Seminary and also took history classes at the Hebrew University of Jerusalem and literature classes at the University of Basel; she married Menahem Groll, later a founder of Tel Aviv University; she then taught at the Kibbutz Ma'abarot High School; she returned to Jerusalem to study Biblical history and Egyptology under Polotsky (q.v.); BA, 1955; MA, 1957; PhD., 1964; she also studied under Černy (q.v.) at Oxford from 1960; she was appointed lecturer at the Hebrew University, 1964; senior lecturer 1968; associate Professor, 1971; on the creation of the Department of Egyptology in 1972, she became Professor and head of the department until 1994; she was visiting lecturer at Brandeis University 1969-70; she was a specialist in Egyptian philology; *Lingua Aegyptia* 9 (2001) was dedicated to her; apart from articles, she published *Non-verbal sentence patterns in Late Egyptian*, 1967; *The Negative Verbal System of Late Egyptian*, 1970; and with Černy, *A Late Egyptian Grammar*, 1975; she also edited *Pharaonic Egypt, the Bible and Christianity*, 1985; and *Studies in Egyptology Presented to Miriam Lichtheim*, 1990; she died in Jerusalem, 15 Dec. 2007.

Lingua Aegyptia 9 (2001), 1-4, 5-8 (bibl.) (D. Sweeney and O. Goldwasser); *Lingua Aegyptia* 15 (2007), vii-viii.

IVERSEN, Erik Frode Bülow (1909-2001)
Danish Egyptologist; he was born in Copenhagen, 11 Feb. 1909, son of Emil Frode I. and Kirsten Helen Jensen; he was educated at the University of Copenhagen under Lange (q.v.); Gold Medal 1936; he then studied at Berlin under Sethe (q.v.), 1930-1 and at Oxford under Gardiner (q.v.), 1935-6 and at University College London under Černy (q.v.), 1945-7; he took part in the excavation at Amara West, 1947-8; a volume T*he Heritage of Ancient Egypt*, edited by J. Osing and E. Kolding Nielsen was published in his honour in 1992; his published works included *The Myth of Egypt and its Hieroglyphs in European Tradition*, 1961; *Canon and Proportion in Egyptian Art*, 1955, rev. 1975; *Obelisks in Exile*, 2 vols.; he died 5 July 2001.

Dansk Biografishe Leksikon 7, 148-9; EES archives; *The Heritage of Ancient Egypt* (portr.) (bibl.) 121-3 (T. Holm-Rasmussen and P. Frandsen); R. Janssen, *The First Hundred Years*, 1992, 60-1.

JABLONSKI, Paul Ernst (1693-1757)
German theologian and orientalist of Polish origin; he was born in Berlin, 28 Dec. 1693, son of the theologian Daniel Ernst J. and Barbara Fergushill; became Professor of Theology and Philosophy in the University of Frankfurt-an-der-Oder; he spent much time collecting all that had been written by classical authors on the subjects of Egyptian religion, archaeology and hieroglyphs, and he criticized the extravagances of Athanasius Kircher (q.v.), but despite this arrived no nearer to the solution of decipherment; during his lifetime he published studies on the history of Nestorianism, 1724, and Egyptian religion, 3 vols. 1750-2; his memoirs on various Egyptian subjects were included in his collected works published in Leiden many years after his death, 4 vols. 1804-13; he died in Frankfurt-an-der-Oder, 13 Sept. 1757.

Polski Slownik Biograficzny 10, 255; *ADB* 13, 526-7; *La Grande Enc.* 20. 1153; Budge, *Mummy*, 3rd. ed., 138; Hilmy i, 328.

JACOBSEN, Carl Christian Hillman (1842-1914)
Danish brewer and collector; he was born in Copenhagen, 2 March 1842, son of Jacob Christian J., a brewer, and Laura Cathrine Holst; he worked in his father's Carlsberg brewery until he founded his own Ny Carlsberg brewery in 1882; he later became managing director of the merged breweries in 1906; in 1884 he began to collect Egyptian antiquities and purchased further objects at the Sabatier (q.v.) sale in 1890; he later used Valdemar Schmidt(q.v.) to purchase objects for him in Cairo and elsewhere and also from 1908 financed Petrie's (q.v.) excavations in return for objects; he founded the Ny Carlsberg Foundation in 1902 to promote art; he donated his entire art collection to the state and the antiquities were displayed in a wing of the Ny Carlsberg Glyptotek, which opened in 1906; he died in Frederiksberg, 11 Jan. 1914.

Dansk Biografisk Leksikon 7, 166-71; T. Bagh, *Finds from W. M. F. Petrie's Excavations in Egypt in the Ny Carlsberg Glyptotek*, 2011, 7-8 (portr.).

JACQUET-GORDON, Helen Katherine (1918-2013)
American Egyptologist; she was born in New York, 7 Feb. 1918, daughter of James Henry G., a cellist, and Nellie Meyer, an artist; she was educated at Barnard College, 1936-40; BA, 1940; she then studied at Columbia Univ, MA, 1942; she served in Army Intelligence during World War II; she then studied Egyptology under Leo Oppenheim, the Assyriologist, and Walter Federn (q.v.) at the Asia Institute in New York and the École Pratique des Hautes Études in Paris from 1949 under Posener (q.v.), Malinine (q.v.), Clère (q.v.), and Vandier (q.v.); she took part in excavations at Memphis, 1956, with her later husband, the architect Jean Jacquet (b. at Carouge, 5 March 1921, d. at Carouge 7 Jan. 2016) whom she married in 1959 and who worked with her, as architect for IFAO 1966-86, on her excavations including the Nubian rescue campaign, 1957-65, notably at Abdallah Nirqi, 1962-64; at Tabo in the Sudan, 1967-77; at Tyre, 1964-8; she also worked with her husband and Sauneron (q.v) in the desert at Esna and at Karnak Nord, 1968-77, 1989-92; she undertook epigraphic work at the Temple of Khonsu in Karnak, 1958-9, 1989-92; she specialized in ceramics but also worked as an epigraphist; she was editor of the *Bulletin de Liaison de la Céramique Égyptienne* 2-22 (1977-2004); the photographic archive assembled by her husband and herself was donated to Chicago House, Luxor; apart from articles, she published, with Piankoff, *Egyptian Religious Texts and Representations*, 1954; *Les noms des domaines funéraires sous l'ancien empire égyptien*, 1962; with Sauneron and her husband, *Les ermitages chrétiens du désert d'Esna*, 1972; *Karnak-Nord* VI, 1988; *Karnak-Nord* VIII, 1999; *The Graffiti on the Khonsu Temple Roof at Karnak*, 2003; *Karnak-Nord* X, 2012; her husband published *Karnak-Nord* V, 1983; *Karnak-Nord* VII, 1994; and *Karnak-Nord* IX, 2001; she died in Carouge, Switzerland, 26 April 2013.

Oriental Institute Chicago (R. Johnson); *JARCE* 49 (2013), 1-2 (R. Johnson) (portr.), 3-8 (bibl.) (A. Arnaudies).

JACOBY, Adolphe (1875-1943)
French-Luxemburg folklorist and Coptologist; he was born at Lauterbourg, 9 March 1875; he studied theology at Neuchâtel, Berlin, and Strasbourg, 1896-8 where his friendship with Spiegelberg (q.v.) led to his interest in Egyptology; he wrote several articles in *Sphinx* and *Recueil de Travaux* mainly on Coptic studies; in 1912 he was named pastor at Luxembourg and concentrated on the study of local folklore; he published *Ein neues Evangelienfragment*, 1900; *Ein bisher unbeachteter apokrypher Bericht über die Taufe Jesu*,1902; and *Papyri graecae magicae*, 1928-31; he died in Luxembourg, 10 Oct. 1943.

Annuaire. Institut Grand-Ducal, Section de Linguistique.de Folklore et de Toponymie (1947), 180-94 (bibl.); *Annuaire. Société de Amis des Musées du Grand-Duché de Luxembourg* (1949), 80-1.

JAMES, (*Sir*) Henry (1803-1877)
British soldier and surveyor; he was born in Rose-in-Vale, nr. St. Agnes, Cornwall, 1803, son of John J. of Truro and Jane Hoskin; Colonel, Royal Engineers; Director-General of the Ordnance Survey; entered RE, 1826; FRS,

1848; he published standards of length of various countries and a work on the measurements and standards of the Great Pyramid; see *Ordnance Survey of the Peninsula of Sinai*, 1869-71; he died in Southampton, 14 June 1877.

ODNB 29, 700-2; *DNB* 29, 210-13; Hilmy, i, 330.

JAMES, Thomas Garnet Henry (Harry) (1923-2009)
British Egyptologist; he was born in Neath, West Glamorgan, 8 May 1923, son of Thomas Garnet J. and Edith Griffiths; he was educated at Neath Grammar School and Exeter College, Oxford; after a year, his education was interrupted by war service in the Royal Artillery where he attained the rank of captain; he returned to Oxford and studied under Gunn (q.v.) and Gardiner (q.v.); BA in Classics, 1947; MA, 1948; BA in Egyptology, 1950; he became assistant keeper in the Dept. of Egyptian and Assyrian Antiquities, 1951; deputy keeper in the Dept. of Egyptian Antiquities, 1974 and Keeper, 1974-88; he served as Laycock Student of Egyptology, Worcester Coll., Oxford, 1954-60; Wilbour Fellow, Brooklyn Museum, 1964; Visiting Prof. College de France, 1983 and Memphis State Univ., 1990; Chairman, Egypt Exploration Society 1983-9; Vice-Pres. 1990-2009; Editor *JEA*, 1960-70 and EES publications, 1960-89; Chairman, Freud Museum Committee, 1986-2003; President of ASTENE; Member of the Management Board of the Griffith Institute; CBE, 1984; Hon Fellow Exeter Coll, Oxford 1998; FBA, 1976; he undertook epigraphic work at Saqqara in 1951and joined Emery's (q.v.) expedition there in 1953; he undertook further epigraphic work with Caminos (q.v.) at Gebel es-Silsilah in 1955; apart from articles, he published *The Mastaba of Khentika called Ikhekhi*, 1953; *Hieroglyphic Texts in the British Museum* I, 1961; *The Hekanakhte Papers and other Early Middle Kingdom Documents*, 1962; *Gebel es-Silsilah* I, 1963, with Caminos; with Edwards (q.v.) and Shore (q.v.), *A General Guide to the Egyptian Collections in the British Museum*, 1964; *Egyptian Sculptures*, 1966; *Myths and Legends of Ancient Egypt*, 1969; *Hieroglyphic Texts in the British Museum* 9, 1970; *Archaeology of Ancient Egypt*, 1972; *Corpus of Hieroglyphic Inscriptions in the Brooklyn Museum* I, 1974; *Egyptian Sculpture*, 1983, with W. V. Davies; *Pharaoh's People*, 1984 (repr. 2003); *Egyptian Painting and Drawing in the British Museum*, 1985; *Ancient Egypt: the land and legacy*, 1988; *The British Museum and Ancient Egypt*, 1989; *Howard Carter: the Path to Tutankhamun*, 1992 (repr. 2006); *Egypt: the living past*, 1992; *A Short History of Ancient Egypt*, 1996; *Egypt Revealed*, 1997; *Tutankhamun: the eternal splendours of the boy Pharaoh*, 2000; *Ramesses II*, 2002; *The British Museum Concise Introduction: Ancient Egypt*, 2005; he edited *An Introduction to Ancient Egypt*, 1979 and *Excavating in Egypt*, 1982 and contributed to W. B. Emery, *Great Tombs of the First Dynasty* II, 1954; T. J. Dunbabin, *Perachora* II, 1962; and *The Cambridge Ancient History*, 3rd ed. Vol. II, 1973, Vol. III, 1991; he died in London, 16 Dec. 2009.

WW 2010, 1186; *ASTENE Bulletin* 42 (2009/10), 1-2 (J. H. Taylor); *Egyptian Archaeology* 36 (2010), 2 (P. Spencer); *KMT* 21/1 (2010), 62-4 (D. Ryan and N. Reeves), 65-70; *JEA* 97 (2011), 195-200 (J. H. Taylor) (portr.).

JAMESON, William (*fl.* 1676-1720)
British theologian; he possibly attended the University of Glasgow from 1676; he was appointed a lecturer in civil and ecclesiastical history there in 1690; apart from his religious works, he published *Spicilegia Antiquatatum Aegypti*, 1720, a compendium of contemporary knowledge about Egypt from classical and Biblical knowledge.

ODNB 29, 765-6; inf. Dr. Geoffrey Raper.

JANSSEN, Jacobus (Jac) Johannes (1922-2011)
Dutch Egyptologist; he was born in Utrecht, 15 June 1922, son of Jacobus Johannaes J. and Theodora Elselina Battenberg; he initially studied history and geography at the University of Utrecht and became a grammar school teacher; his interest in Egyptology led him to continue his studies in a one-to-one capacity with de Buck (q.v.) at the University of Leiden; PhD, 1961; he became Lecturer at the University of Leiden, 1970-79, and then Professor of Egyptology, 1979-83; he was editor of the *Annual Egyptological Bibliography*, 1970-83; he took early retirement to continue in his research work in London where in 1989 he married the Egyptologist Rosalind Hall who collaborated in many of his publications; he was Hon. Research Fellow in the Dept. of Egyptology, UCL; he was an expert in the hieratic script and a specialist on the economy of the Ramesside period and the workers' community at Deir el-Medina; apart from numerous articles, he published *Two Ancient Egyptian Ship's Logs*, 1961; *Commodity Prices from the Ramessid Period*, 1975; with R. Janssen, *Egyptian Household Animals*, 1989; with R. Janssen, *Growing up in Ancient Egypt*, 1990; *Late Ramesside Letters and Communications*, 1991; with R. Janssen, *Getting Old in Ancient Egypt*, 1996; *Village Varia. Ten Studies on the History and Administration of Deir el-Medina*, 1997; with others, *Woodcutter,*

Potters and Doorkeepers: Service Personnel of the Deir el-Medina Workmen, 2003; *Grain Transport in the Ramesside Period*, 2004; *Donkeys at Deir el-Medina*, 2005; *Daily Dress at Deir el-Medina*, 2008; *Furniture at Deir el-Medina*, 2009; his papers are now in the Griffith Institute, Oxford; he died in London 23 Aug. 2011.

Inf. R. Janssen.

JANSSEN, Jozef Marie Antoon (1907-1963)
Dutch Egyptologist; born at Roermond, Dutch Limbourg, 10 Nov. 1907; after studying in his native town he entered a Catholic seminary and was ordained priest, 1932; his bishop allowed him to pursue his Egyptological bent at the University of Leiden, where he specialized in Egyptian philology, being taught by A. de Buck (q.v.); Janssen later gained a doctorate with a thesis on the subject of Egyptian autobiographies, *De traditioneele egyptische Autobiographie voor het Nieuwe Rijk*, 1946, 2 vols.; he was appointed lecturer 1940-62 and ultimately became Professor extraordinary in the University of Amsterdam, 1962-3; he was also lecturer at the University of Leiden, 1940-61; he visited Egypt many times acting as philologist on various expeditions, from 1947 to 1950 he was at Elkab, working on rock inscriptions mainly dating from the Middle Kingdom; in 1953 he went with the Griffith Institute expedition to record texts in the Theban necropolis, and in 1954 was invited to Boston by Dows Dunham (q.v.) to collate and prepare for publication Reisner's notes and records on the excavations of the forts at Semna and Kumma; between 1958 and 1960 he took part in three campaigns of the Schiff-Giorgini expedition to Soleb, and worked, often under very difficult conditions, on recording the inscriptions in the ruined temple of Amenhotep III; Janssen published a number of articles in journals and magazines, but his greatest work and the one which was to assume a unique character as well as to take up more and more of his time, was the *Annual Egyptological Bibliography*, a work of immense value and one of the Egyptologists' standard tools today; he first began this work in *Ex Oriente Lux* from 1936 onwards; German Egyptologists impressed by his labours in this direction, and having been cut off from outside publications during the war, asked him to prepare a special bibliography for them of all the works that had appeared outside Germany between 1939 and 1947; it ultimately appeared in the *Jahrbuch* of the Berlin Archaeological Institute for 1950 and contained 800 numbers; from these smaller beginnings sprang the *AEB* whose first fifteen vols. were entirely edited and mainly achieved by Janssen; with further work in the sixteenth issue this achievement had involved the summarizing of no less than approximately 9,000 books and articles in fifteen years; Janssen also published *Catalogue de la collection W. A. van Leer; Hiërogliefen. Over lezen en Schrijven in oud-Egypte*, 1952; he died in The Hague, 29 Aug. 1963.

AEB 1961, Leiden, 1963, vii-xiii (portr.) (B. van de Walle); *Aegyptus* 42 (1962), (publ. 1963), 297-8 (F. Jesi); *AfO* 21 (1966), 275 (H. Brunner); *Archaeology* 16 (1963), 286 (anon.); *Chron. d'Ég.* 37 (1963), 263 (M. Heerma van Voss); *EES Report 1963* (1965), 5 (A. Klasens); *Folia Civitatis*, Amsterdam, 17ᵉ Jaargang, nr. I (14 Sept. 1963), I (D. Cohen); *Ex Oriente Lux*, Leiden 16 (1959-62), 1964, i-ii (portr.) (B. van de Walle); *ZÄS* 91 (1964), ix-x (S. Morenz); inf. M. Raven.

JAYE, William Robert (1874-1949)
British business man and collector; he was born in London 1874, son of William J. and Isabella Crook; he was a merchant in London, who travelled widely and made a collection of antiquities which was sold at Sotheby's, 18 July 1949, lots 84-97, the most important piece being the quartzite head of a statue, said to be Ramesses II as Amun; he retired in 1920 to the Old House, Ryde, Isle of Wight, where he died 22 March 1949, and was buried at Binstead, near Ryde.

Private inf.

JELF, (Charles) Gordon (1886-1915)
British excavator; he was born in Rochester, 8 June 1886, son of George Edward J., Canon of Rochester and Master of Charterhouse, and Katherine Frances Dalton; he was educated at Marlborough School, 1900-5 and Exeter College, Oxford; BA, 1910; he undertook excavations for Sir Robert Mond (q.v.) in the private tombs on the West bank at Luxor, 1909-10; his excavation notebook is now in the Griffith Institute archive; he became assistant correspondent of *The Times* in Berlin; he joined the army as 2ⁿᵈ Lt. in the 6ᵗʰ Buffs, 1914 and was killed at Loos, 13 Oct. 1915.

Inf. J. Malek and A. Hobby; L. W. James, *Marlborough College Register 1843-1952*, 9ᵗʰ ed., 1952, 441.

JÉQUIER, Gustave Louis (1868-1946)
Swiss Egyptologist; he was born in Neuchâtel, 14 Aug. 1868, son of Jean J., an official, and Lina Bovet; he studied in Paris under Maspero (q.v.) and Guieysse (q.v.); he afterwards went to Berlin, 1895-7, and then joined the de Morgan expedition to Persia; he worked for the IFAO and conducted many important excavations in the

Egyptian necropolises, mainly at Saqqara but also at other sites; Jéquier was the most eminent Swiss Egyptologist after Naville (q.v.) and his work in the pyramid fields did much to reveal the history and architecture of the Old Kingdom; he studied the architectural history of Egyptian temples and published a series of monographs thereon; his speciality was architecture but he published works on philology and religion as well; he was a Corr. Member of the French Acad., and an Officer of the Légion d'Honneur; he wrote many articles of *ASAE*, his principle works being, *Le livre de ce qu'il y a dans l'Hadès ... Version abrégée, publiée d'après les papyrus de Berlin et de Leyde, avec variantes et traduction*, 1894; *Mémoire sur les fouilles de Licht*, with J. E. Gautier, 1902; *L'art décoratif dans l'antiquité. Décoration égyptienne. Plafonds et frises végétales du Nouvel Empire Thébain, 1400 à 1000 avant J. C.*, 1911; *Les frises d'objets des sarcophages du Moyen Empire*, 1921; *Matériaux pour servir à l'établissement d'un Dictionnaire d'Archéologie Égyptienne*, 1921; *L'architecture et la décoration dans l'ancienne Égypte* 1. *Les Temples Memphites et Thébains des origines à la XVIIIᵉ dynastie*; 2. *Les Temples Ramessides et Saïtes de la XIXᵉ à la XXXᵉ dynastie*; 3. *Les Temples Ptolémaïques et Romains*, 3 fol. vols. 1921-4; *Le Papyrus Prisse et ses variantes: papyrus de la Bibl. Nat. nos 183 à 194, papyrus 10371 et 10435 du British Museum, tablette Carnarvon au Musée du Caire, publiés en fac-simile*, 1911; *Histoire de la Civilisation Égyptienne, des origines à la conquête d'Alexandre*, 1923; *Manuel d'Archéologie Égyptienne* I. *Les éléments de l'architecture*, 1924; *Le Mastabat Faraoun*, with Dows Dunham, 1928; *La Pyramide d'Oudjebten*, 1928; *Tombeaux de particuliers contemporains de Pepi II*, 1929; *Deux Pyramides du Moyen Empire*, 1933; *Les Pyramides des Reines Neit et Apouit*, 1933; *La Pyramide d'Aba*, 1935; *Le Monument Funéraire de Pepi II*, 3 vols. 1936-40; *Douze Ans de fouilles dans la Nécropole Memphite, 1924-1936*, 1940; *Considérations sur les Religions Égyptiennes*, 1946; he also completed Naville's work on the temple of Abydos, 1930; some of his collections were acquired by the University of Basel, while others passed to his family and were sold at Christie's New York, 4 June 2008; his archives are in the Musée d'ethnographie de Neuchâtel; he died in Neuchâtel, 24 March 1946.

Chron. d'Ég. 21 (1946), 207-8 (J. Capart), 208-9 (P. Humbert); EES *Ann. Rep.* 1946, 4; G. Jéquier, *En Perse 1897-1902*, 1965 (bibl.); È. Gran-Aymerich, *Dictionnaire biographique d'archéologie 1798-1945*, 2001, incorporated in *Les Chercheurs de passé 1798-1945*, 2007, 892-3; *Historisches Lexikon der Schweiz* 6, 790; I. Rogger in *Edal* 1 (2009), 53-60.

JERNSTEDT, Petr Viktorovitch (1890-1966)

Russian linguist, papyrologist and Coptologist; he was born in Gatchina, 21 June 1890, son of Viktor K. J., eminent Hellenist and palaeographer, and founder of Russian papyrology; he studied at the University of St. Petersburg, 1908-13; later he was associated with the Asiatic Museum, 1918-50, transformed later into the Institute of Oriental Studies and Institute of Asian Peoples of the Soviet Academy of Sciences; from 1950-54 he was at the Linguistic Institute of the Academy; he was engaged in preparation and editing of the important Greek and Coptic texts, *Papyri russischer und georgischer Sammlungen*, Vol. 3-5, Tiflis 1927-35; he published works on Egyptian loan-words in Greek *Egipetskiye zaimstvovaniya v grecheskom yazyke*, 1953; *Koptyskiye teksty Gos. Museya izobrazitel 'nykh iskusstv imeni A. S. Pushkina*, 1959; and *Issledovaniya po grammatike koptskogo yazyka*, 1986; he died in Leningrad, 25 Dec. 1966.

VDI 3 (101), 1967, 168-9; *Journal of Juristic Papyrology* 16-17 (1971), 257-60 (I. Fikhman); *Wissenschaftliche Zeitschrift der Martin-Luther Universität; Halle-Wittenberg Gesellschafts-und Sprachwissenschaftliche Reihe* 26 (1977), 93-9 (bibl.) (A. Elanskaya); *The Coptic Encyclopedia* 4, 1323 (M. Krause); inf. J. Śliwa.

JOHNS, Agnes Sophia (née Griffith) (1859-1949)

British writer and translator; she was born in Brighton, 27 Dec. 1859, being the sister of Francis Llewellyn G. (q.v.); she kept house and looked after her brother after the death of his first wife; she married in Oxford, the Revd Claude Hermann Walter Johns (d.1920), 9 March 1910, the well-known Assyriologist and Master of St. Catharine's College, Cambridge; she published *Catalogue of Eg. Ant. Manchester Museum*, 1910; also translated into English works by Capart, Erman, Maspero, and Koldewey under the following titles: *Primitive Art in Egypt*, 1905; *Handbook of Eg. Religion*, 1907; *Egyptian Archaeology* (6th ed.), 1914; *Popular Stories of Ancient Egypt* (4th ed.), 1915; *The Excavations at Babylon*, 1914; she died in Brighton, Sussex, 18 Nov. 1949.

Inf. Griffith family; *JEA* 20 (1934), 74.

JOHNSON, John de Monins (1882-1956)

British papyrologist; he was born at Kirmington, Lincs., 17 May 1882, son of Revd John Henry J. and Anna Braithwaite Savory; he was educated at Magdalen College School and Exeter College, Oxford; he served in the Egyptian Civil Service, 1905-7; he returned to Oxford and studied under Hunt (q.v.), 1908-11; he excavated for the Graeco-Roman branch of the EES at Atfih, 1911 and Antinoe, 1913-4; he joined the Oxford University Press in 1915 and was appointed Printer to the University, 1925; he died in Oxford, 15 Sept. 1956.

ODNB 30, 280-2 (portr.); *DNB* 1951-60, 548-50.

JOHNSTONE, James L'Estrange (1865-1906)

British army officer; he was born at Alva House, Scotland, 8 Aug. 1865, son of James J. and Sarah Mary L'Estrange; he was educated at Eton, Royal Military Acad., Woolwich, and the School of Military Engineering, Chatham; Lieut., Royal Engineers, 1884; Asstistant Engineer, Works Dept. of India at Aden, 1888-9; Inspecting Engineer, RE, Malta, 1890-1; MVO, 1904; he was employed in the preservation of the Temple of Abu Simbel by the Egyptian Public Works Dept., 1892; Inspector of Structures and Railways, War Office, 1895-9; President of the Egyptian Railway Administration, 1899-1906; he died, a major, London, 27 Sept. 1906.

Maspero, *Ruines et Paysages*, 403; *WWW* i, 383.

JOHNSTONE, John *see* **JONSTON.**

JOLIFFE, (*Revd*) **Thomas Robert** (1780-1872)

British traveller; he was born at Charlton, Somerset, 12 Nov. 1780, son of Thomas Samuel J. and Anne Twyford; he was educated at Trinity College, Cambridge, BA, 1804; MA, 1807; he visited Palestine and Egypt in 1817 with Capt. Bennett who then joined Straton's (q.v.) expedition to Nubia; at Alexandria he witnessed the embarkation of 'the young Memnon' to England; vicar of Babington, Somerset 1810-72; chaplain to George IV; author of *Letters from Palestine ... to which are added Letters from Egypt*, 2nd ed. 1820; he died in Ammerdown Park near Bath, 15 June 1872.

Al. Cantab.; Boase 2, 121-2; P. Usick in P. and J. Starkey (ed.), *Unfolding the Orient*, 2001, 219-24.

JOLLOIS, (Jean Baptiste) Prosper (1776-1842)

French engineer; he was born at Briénon-l'Archêveque, 24 Jan. 1776; he was educated at the military school at Auxerre and the École Polytechnique; he took part in the Napoleonic expedition to Egypt; he worked in the Delta and Cairo; he was in March 1799 sent to Upper Egypt with Devilliers (q.v.) where he drew plans of many of the temples; he then worked in the Delta until his return to France; he became secretary of the Committee undertaking the publication of the *Description*, contributing 115 drawings and commentaries; he was later appointed chief engineer of Vosges and later Seine and conducted research into medieval archaeology; he was vice-president and from 1835 President of the Société des Antiquaires; he died at Paris, 24 June 1842.

Journal d'un ingénieur (*BIÉ* 6), 1904; *Les Savants en Égypte*, 1998, 63; *Biographie Universelle* 21, 114-5; *DBF* 24 June 1842; *DBF* 18, 723-3.

JOMARD, Edmé François (1777-1862)

French engineer, geographer, and antiquarian; he was born in Versailles, 17 Nov. 1777, son of Nicholas François J., a silk merchant, and Louise Marguerite Michel; he took a prominent part in the foundation of the École Polytechnique, Paris; he was a member of Napoleon's Commission in Egypt, and on leaving Egypt, he visited Greece and other European countries before returning to Paris in 1803; he took a large part in the editing of the *Description de l'Égypte* to which he made many contributions; he also edited the works of Gailliaud; elected to the Acad. des Inscr., 1818, and appointed conservateur of the Bibl. Nationale, 1828; he produced 6 vols. of commentaries for the *Description: Sur les Signes numériques des anciens Égyptiens*, 1816-19; *Étalon métrique trouvé à Memphis*, 1822; *Voyage à l'oasis de Syouah*, 1823; *Observations sur le voyage au Darfour*, 1845; also notes for Mengin's History of Egypt; Jomard was very hostile to Champollion (q.v.) and obstructed his advancement in every possible way; he wrote a great deal on education; Comm Légion d'honneur, 1862; his library and collections (Egyptian, lots 1-42) were sold in Paris in 1863; he died in Paris, 22 Sept. 1862.

BIÉ 8, 1864; Carré, passim, see index (portr.); Hartleben, passim; Hilmy, i, 333; Lugt 27630; *La Grande Enc.* 21, 184; *Larousse, XIXᵉ siécle* 9, 1008; *DBF* 18, 759-62; *Les Savants en Égypte*, 1998, 57; È. Gran-Aymerich, *Dictionnaire biographique d'archéologie 1798-1945*, 2001, incorporated in *Les Chercheurs de passé 1798-1945*, 2007, 895; Y. Laissus, *Jomard. Le Dernier Égyptien 1777-1862*, 2004.

JONAS, Mary Charlton (1874-1950)

Secretary of the Egypt Exploration Society, 1919-39; she was born at Ickleton, 15 Aug. 1874, daughter of George J., a farmer, and Jane Ellen Payne; formerly secretary to Prof. C. G. Seligman; on her retirement she was made Hon. Life Member; she died in Salisbury, 3 April 1950.

EES *Ann. Rep.* 1950, 4; *JEA* 37 (1951), 2; Newberry Corr.

JONCKHEERE, Frans (1903-1956)

Belgian medical practitioner; he was born in Brussels, 30 June 1903 son of Professor Tobie J.; he became a doctor in 1928; he was interested in the history of medicine and in particular that of ancient Egypt, visiting Egypt in 1939; he was encouraged by J. Capart (q.v.) to continue his researches in this field; in 1942 he was given access to the mummy of Butehamun, a scribe of the Theban necropolis during the XXIst Dynasty and made new types of observation on the process of mummification and the state of the limbs, published as *Autour de l'autopsie d'une momie*, 1942; he was a member of the Comité belge d'histoire des sciences, the Société française d'histoire de la médecine, and an hon. member of the Deutsche Vereinigung für Geschichte der Medizin; in all he wrote 30 articles on Egyptian subjects relating to medicine and science, *Une maladie égyptienne, l'Hématurie parasitaire*, 1944; *Le papyrus médical Chester Beatty*, 1947; *La Circoncision des anciens Égyptiens*, 1951; *Le Cadre professionnel et administratif des médicins égyptiens*, 1951; *L'Examen du malade dans la pratique médicale pharaonique*, 1952; *Prescriptions médicales sur Ostraca hiératiques*, 1954; *Les médecins de l'Égypte pharaonique: Essai de prosopographie*, 1958; he died in Brussels, 10 March 1956.

Archives Internationales d'Histoire des Sciences, Paris. 9th year, no. 35 (April-June 1956), 176-9, (bibl.) (E. Wickersheimer); *Chron. d'Ég.* 31 (1956), 303-8 (bibl.) (B. van de Walle); *Histoire de la Médecine*, Paris, 6th year, no. vii (July 1956), 73-9 (bibl.) (B. van de Walle); *Nachrichtenblatt der Deutschen Vereinigung für Geschichte der Medizin*, Naturwissenchaft und Technik E. V. Frankfurt, no. 7 (May 1956), 2-9 (P. Diepgen); *Wetenschappelijke Tijdingen*, Ghent, year 16, no. 5 (June 1956), 206-7 (L. Elant).

JONES, (Ernest) Harold (1877-1911)

British excavator and artist; he was born in Barnsley, 7 March 1877, son of William J., Headmaster of Barnsley School of Art and later Headmaster of Carmarthen School of Art, and Mary Anne Sprake; he was educated at Queen Elizabeth's Grammar School, Carmarthen and was a pupil teacher at Carmarthen School of Art, 1895-1902; he won a scholarship to the Royal College of Art in London but was unable to complete the course due to ill health; partly for this reason, he joined Garstang (q.v.) at Beni Hasan, 1903-4 and later worked for him at Hierakonpolis and Esna, 1905-6 and Abydos, 1906-7; in 1907 he joined the expedition of Theodore Davis (q.v.) in the Valley of the Kings; he made many water-colour drawings of antiquities for Davis, Lord Carnarvon (q.v.) and others, some of which have been reproduced as colour plates; he donated objects to the Carmarthen Museum, while other pieces from his collection are in Swansea Museum; his papers are in the National Library of Wales Aberystwyth and the Carmarthen Museum; he died in Luxor, 10 March 1911 while working at Biban el-Moluk and is buried at Luxor.

C. Delaney, *A Son to Luxor's Sand*, 1986; *The Mardunian* IV no. 6 (1911), 10-11; Andrews Diary; Newberry Corr.; K. Bosse-Griffiths, *JEA* 47 (1961), 66-70; L. Pinch-Brock in D. Fortenberry (ed.), *Who Travels Sees More*, 2007, 31-40; N. Evans, *Ancient Egypt* 14 No. 6 (2014), 26-33.

JONES, Owen (1809-1874)

British architect and designer; he was born in Thames St., London, 15 Feb. 1809, only son of Owen J., Welsh antiquary, and Hannah Jane *née* Jones; he was educated at Charterhouse and trained as an architect by L. Vulliamy; with the French architect Jules Goury (1801-34), he visited Egypt, Greece, and Turkey, 1832-3; he was superintendent of the Great Exhibition, 1851; he published with Bonomi (q.v.) and Sharpe (q.v.) a *Description of the Egyptian Court*, 1854; also *Scenery of the Nile*, 1840, and *Views on the Nile from Cairo to the Second Cataract*, with notes by Samuel Birch, 1843; he designed the frontispiece to Robert Hay's *Illustrations of Cairo*, 1840; his *Grammar of Ornament*, 1856, a landmark of chromolithographic printing, contained numerous colour depictions of Egyptian patterns and motifs, and played an important role in inspiring and sustaining the Egyptian style; he died in Argyll Place, London, 19 April 1874.

ODNB 596-8 (portr.); *DNB* 30, 150-1; Hilmy, i, 336; *ILN* 19 (1851) (portr.); S. Searight, *Alif* 26 (2006), 128-46; K. Ferry in D. Fortenberry (ed.), *Who Travels Sees More*, 2007, 100-118; S. Moser, *Designing Antiquity. Owen Jones, Ancient Egypt and the Crystal Palace*, 2012; T. Baber in N. Cooke and V. Daubney (eds.), *Lost and Now Found*, 2017, 26-7.

JONSTON (JOHNSTONE), John (1603-1675)

Polish-Scottish physician, naturalist, philosopher and antiquarian; he was born in Szamtuly near Poznań, 3 Sept. 1603, son of Simon J., from the Scottish family Johnstone of Craigieburn, and Anna Becker; author of many medical, philosophical, botanical and historical works; adherent of empiricism and scientific methodology; he attended from 1619 the grammar school in Torun matriculating as "Sametuliensis Polonus Scotus domo"; from 1623 he studied philosophy, theology and Hebrew at St. Andrews University; in 1625 in Leszno he wrote his *Thaumatographia naturalis*, published in Amsterdam 1632 and later 1661 and 1664 where he explained that the pottery found in the earth came from ancient cemeteries with cinerary urns and was not grown in the earth; he was acquainted with pottery urns from the collections in Torun, and from the Arundel collection in England, and later also from Italy; he attended lectures on medicine and botany in Cambridge, 1629 and medicine at Leiden, 1630; in Leiden he published his *Sceleton historiae universalis civilis et ecclesiasticae*, 1633; there also he obtained the title of doctor in medicine with a dissertation *De febribus*, 15 April 1634; in 1634, during his third stay in Britain he obtained also a doctorate of medicine from Cambridge University, in his work *De naturae constantia*, 1634, p. 65 English edition *A History of the Constancy of Nature*, London 1657, 78 he remarks on burials and tombs of the ancients, as in Egypt; in his *Thaumatographia naturalis*, 1632, 166-7, he wrote about bronze plates deposited on the dead in Egypt and about bronze blades in embalmed corpses; as a physician he noted the use of mummies as a medicine, p. 484; mummies used as a medicine are mentioned also in his *Notitia regni mineralis seu subterraneorum catalogue cum praecipuis differentis*, Lipsiae 1661, 28; his library contained many books on Egypt; by 1636 he was back in Poland at Leszno near Poznań where he acted as a doctor of the Leszczynski family and also as city physician and teacher in a grammar school there; he retired around 1655 to his estate in Leszno, Silesia, where he died 3 June 1675.

DNB 10, 968-9; *ONDB* 30, 405; T. Bilikiewicz, *Jan Johston 1603-1675. Zywot i dzialalnosc lekarska*, Warszawa 1931; *Polski Slownik Biograficzny 11*, 268-70 (T. Bilikiewicz); A. Abramowicz, *Urny i ceraunie*, Lódz 1970, 83-97; inf. J. Śliwa;

JORET, (Pierre Louis) Charles Richard (1829-1914)
French philologist and historian; he was born in Formigny, Calvados, 14 Oct. 1829, son of Thomas Richard J. and Angélique Adelaide Vernier; Hon. Professor of Foreign Literature at Aix; Member of Acad. des Inscr., 1902; he published *Les plantes dans l'antiquité et au Moyen Âge*, Paris, 1897, which called forth an important article by Maspero, *Journ. des Savants*, 1897, 477-86; he died in Paris, 29 Dec. 1914.

La Grande Enc. 21, 199.

JOUGUET, Pierre Félix Amédée (1869-1949)
French Hellenist and Egyptologist; he was born in Bessèges, 14 May 1869, son of Félix Marc Antoine J., a civil engineer, and Claire Bathilde Lentherie; after his education at the Lycée of Nîmes and the Lycée Henri IV in Paris he studied at the École Normale 1890-3 and was appointed to the French School in Athens in 1893; at the request of de Morgan (q.v.), he went to Egypt in 1894 to study Graeco-Roman sites and antiquities, especially papyri; he was appointed to the University of Lille in 1898; he went again to Egypt 1897-8 and in 1901 when he excavated in the Fayum and returned to Europe with a rich store of papyri which he took to the Inst. of Papyrology then founded at Lille; here he began a long series of publications of the papyri; he remained at Lille until 1919, having in 1914 explored the great Kom of Edfu; he lectured at the Sorbonne, Paris, 1919-28; he succeeded G. Foucart (q.v.) as Director of IFAO in Cairo, which brought him into active contact with all branches of Egyptology, 1928-40; Professor at the University of Cairo, 1937-49; he was Pres. of the Soc. de Papyrologie founded under the auspices of Fuad I, 1930-49; editor of *Revue Égyptologique* with Moret (q.v.); member of the Académie des Inscriptions et Belles Lettres, 1927; he also organized the Inst. of Hellenic Research, Alexandria, 1947; he wrote *La Vie Municipale dans l'Égypte Romaine*, 1911; *L'Égypte Gréco-Romaine de la conquête d'Alexandre à Dioclétien*, 1932, in Zaky el-Ibrachy's *Précis de l'Histoire d'Égypte*; the Ptolemaic part of *Histoire de la Nation Égyptienne*, ed. G. Hanotaux, 1933; he returned to France in 1949 and died in Paris, 9 July 1949.

BIÉ 32 (1949-50), 335-47 (O. Guéraud); *Bull. Soc. Roy. d'Arch. Alexandria* 38 (1949), 113-18 (portr.); *Chron. d'Ég.* 25 (1950), 365-81; *Journal of Juristic Papyrology*, Warsaw, 4 (1950), 9-18 (portr. and bibl.); *Rev. du Caire*, 13, no. 130 (May 1950) 'Hommage à P. Jouguet'; *Rev. d'Ég.* 7 (1950), i-iv (portr.) (G. Lefebvre) memorial vol; *BIFAO* 54 (1954), 165-72; (bibl.) (O. Guéraud); R. Lackany, *La Société Archéologique d'Alexandrie à 80 ans*, 1973, 37-41; È. Gran-Aymerich, *Dictionnaire biographique d'archéologie 1798-1945*, 2001, incorporated in *Les Chercheurs de passé 1798-1945*, 2007, 898-9; M. Capasso (ed.), *Hermae*, 2007, 143-52 (portr.); *DBF* 18, 841-2.

JOWETT, (Revd) William (1787-1855)
British missionary and traveller; he was born 1787, son of John J. of Newington, Surrey; he was educated St. John's College, Cambridge; MA, 1813, and Fellow; Missionary in Mediterranean countries and Palestine, 1815-24; in Egypt, 1818, when he visited Upper Egypt before returning to Cairo and going on to Syria, May 1819; he was again in Alexandria, April 1820; he published works on his travels and missionary labours, 1822 and 1825; Secretary Church Miss. Soc., 1832-40; Vicar of St. John's Church, Clapham, 1851; he died in Clapham, 20 Feb. 1855 and was buried in Lewisham churchyard..

ODNB 30, 765-6; *DNB* 30, 215-16; Salt, ii, 109, 110, 124, 154 n.

JUMEL, Louis Alexis (1785-1823)

French industrialist; he was born in Breuil-le-Sec (Oise), 14 Jan. 1785, son of Alexis J. and Cécile Bouclat; he became a cloth manufacturer; he went to Egypt in 1817; he entered the service of Muhammad Ali, and introduced and organized the cotton industry in Egypt, 1820; he was a friend of Linant de Bellefonds (q.v.), who was his executor, Drovetti (q.v.), and Piccinini (q.v.); he spent a lot of money in collecting antiquities and also undertook excavations, his most important find being the great tomb of Bakenrenef at Saqqara, which Champollion (q.v.) visited in 1828 and called 'le tombeau Jumel'; his collection was sold after his death; he died in Cairo, 17 June 1823.

DBF 18, 1023-4; *BIÉ* 22 (1939-1940), 49-97; Champollion, ii, 117; French F. O. records; P. Ghazabeh in D. Panzac and A. Raymond, *La France et l'Égypte à l'époque des vice-rois 1805-82*, 2002, 163-70.

JUNKER, Hermann Josef Bartholomäus (1877-1962)

German Egyptologist; he was born at Bendorf am Rhein, 29 Nov. 1877, son of Stefan J., a bookseller, and Katherina Friesenhahn; he at first intended to train for the Catholic priesthood and studied at Trier, 1900; he then changed his subjects and studied Egyptology at Berlin under Erman (q.v.); PhD, 1904; he joined the University of Vienna, becoming assistant Professor, 1907, and Professor, 1912-29; Dean of the Philosophy Faculty, 1921-2; he was also involved in the foundation of the important Institute of Egyptology and African Studies at Vienna University, 1923; Director of the German Archaeological Institute, Cairo, 1929-45 when he was dismissed as a supporter of the Nazi government; Professor of Egyptology, Cairo University, 1933-9; Hon. Professor, Vienna University, 1938; he was also a Corresponding Member of the Akademie der Wissenschaften Vienna, 1914, and a full member 1919; the Prussian Akad. der Wissenschaften, 1922; the Bavarian, 1932; also the Swedish; Dr. theol. *hon. c.* University of Würzburg, 1931; Hon. Doct. of the National University of Dublin, 1953; Hon. member of the Catholic Theological Faculty in Trier; he received the Großes Verdienstkreuz der Bundesrepublik Deutschland, and the title of a Prelate from the Pope; with an almost universal outlook and an immensely wide range of interests Junker was primarily an archaeologist, epigraphist, and 'field man'; he began his career with studies on the writing and grammar of the Dendera texts, then investigated the Osiris mysteries depicted in several Ptolemaic temples; he excavated at Tura, 1909, where he discovered a considerable Proto- and Early Dynastic cemetery, the first time such remains had been found on the east side of the river in the Memphite area; he next began a long series of excavations in Nubia for the Vienna Academy, digging at El-Kubaniya, Armenna and Toshka, 1910-12; he then transferred his field work to northern Egypt and the Delta; his greatest work was the systematic excavation clearance, and recording of a large part of the Giza mastaba field, a tremendous task that lasted fifteen years, except for the war period, 1912-29; with Reisner he may be justly said to have recovered the bulk of what is known today of the actual history of the Old Kingdom in the administrative, economic, and religious departments, through the recovery of so many titles and names of officials, the offices they held and the priestly duties they performed; family relationships and estates held by these families are among the many subjects to be found in the vast publication that resulted; the report came out in 12 parts between 1929-55; he excavated the Predynastic site at Merimda in the West Delta, 1929-38; after the war he edited the inscriptions on the first pylon at Philae; an active teacher he trained a number of Egyptologists in both Germany and Egypt; Junker published more than 100 works in all, covering the fields of archaeology, history, philology, religion, art, and cultural history, the following being his principal publications, *Über das Schriftsystem im Tempel der Hathor in Dendera,* 1903; *Grammatik der Denderatexte,* 1906; *Koptische Poesie des 10. Jahrhunderts,* 1908-11; *Die Stundenwachen in den Osirismysterien nach den Inschriften von Dendera, Edfu und Philae,* 1910; *Bericht über die Grabungen ... auf dem Friedhof in Turah, Winter 1909-1910,* 1912; *Das Götterdekret über das Abaton,* 1913; *Die Onurislegende,* 1917; *El Kubanieh-Süd, Winter 1910-1911,* 1919; *El Kubanieh-Nord, Winter 1910-1911,* 1920; *Der nubische Ursprung der sogenannten Tell el-Jahudiye-Vasen,* 1921; *Das Kloster am Isisberg, El-Kubanieh, Winter, 1910-1911,* 1922; *Ermenne,* 1925; *Bericht über die Grabungen ... auf dem Friedhof von Toschke, Nubien, im Winter 1911-1912,* 1926; *Dem Westdelta entsendete Expedition, 20 Dezember 1927 bis 25 Februar 1928,* 1928; *Grabungen auf dem Friedhof des Alten Reiches bei den Pyramiden von Gîza,* 12 pts. 1929-1955; *Vorläufiger Bericht über die Grabung ... auf der neolithischen Siedlung von Merimde-Benisalâme, 1929, 1930,* 1929-30; *Die Götterlehre von Memphis, Schabaka Inschrift,* 1940; *Die politische Lehre von Memphis,* 1941; *Der sehende und blinde Gott,* Mhntj-irtj *und* Mhntj-n-irtj, 1942; *Pyramidenzeit: Das Wesen der Altägyptischen Religion,* 1949; *Der große Pylon des Tempels der Isis in Philä,* 1958; *Die gesellschaftliche Stellung der ägyptischen Künstler im Alten Reich,* 1959; *Das Geburtshaus des Tempels der Isis in Philä,* with Erich Winter, 1965; he died in Vienna, 9 Jan. 1962.

Ärztliche Mitteilungen - Deutsches Ärzteblatt, Cologne 60 (1963), 2541-4 (portr.) (R. Watermann); *AfO* 20 (1963), 301-2 (portr.) (G. Thausing); *Almanach der Österreichischen Akad. der Wissenschaften,* Vienna 112 (1962), (publ. 1963), 329-56 (portr.) (A. Grohmann); *Arab Bulletin,* Vienna, pt. i (23 July 1962), 29-32 (Abdul Moneim Abu Bakr); *Bustan,* Vienna, pt. 1/2 (1962), 53 (G. Thausing); *Chron. d'Ég.* 36 (1962), 133-4 (P. Derchain); *FuF* 36 (1962), 283-5 (E. Winter); *Jahrbuch der Bayerischen Akad. der Wissenschaften 1963,* Munich, 1963, 1-8 (portr.)

(H. W. Müller); *JEA* 48 (1962), 4 (H. W. Fairman); *Kairos*, Salzburg 4 (1962), 47 (G. Thausing); *MDAIK* 18 (1962), xi-xii (portr.) (H. Stock); *Oriens Christianus* 46 (1962), 158 (anon.); *Österreichische Hochschulzeitung,* Vienna, 14 year, no. 3 (1 Feb. 1962), 5 (portr.) (G. Thausing); *ZÄS* 88 (1962), i-ii (G. Thausing); *NDB* 10, 692-3; *WZKM* 54 (1957), vii-xv; E. Endesfelder, *Die Ägyptologie an der Berliner Universität-Zur Geschichte eines Fachgebietes*, 1988, 27; G. Thausing, *Tarudet*, 1989, 13-6; R Teichl, *Österreichcher der Gegenwart*, 1951, 135-6; È. Gran-Aymerich, *Dictionnaire biographique d'archéologie 1798-1945*, 2001, incorporated in *Les Chercheurs de passé 1798-1945*, 2007, 901-2; inf. T. Schneider; S. Voss, *Die Geschichte der Abteilung Kairo des DAI im Spannungsfeld deutscher politischer Interessen, 1929-1966* (Bd. 2), 2017, 215-22; C. Gütl, *Hermann Junker*, 2017.

KADRY Mohamed Helmy, Ahmed (1931-1990)
Egyptian Egyptologist; he was born at Zagazig, 18 March 1931, son of Mohamed Helmy Ali, an employee in the Ministry of Finance, and Afaf Ibrahim Suleiman; he originally pursued a military career, BSc Military Sciences, Military Academy, 1950; BSc Air Force Sciences, Air Force Academy, 1956; he later obtained BSc Law, Cairo University, 1964, Higher Studies Diploma in Islamic Antiquities, 1976; PhD in Egyptology, Budapest, 1978; he was director of Public Relations in the Ministry of Culture, 1957-65; in 1965 he joined the Egyptian Antiquities Organization as head of the department for the salvage of Nubian monuments; Director-General and later Under-Secretary of State, Preservation of Nubian Antiquities Authority 1972 until March 1978; Chairman of the Egyptian Antiquities Organization 1981 until Feb. 1987; apart from articles, he published his thesis *Officers and Officials in the New Kingdom* in *Studia Aegyptiaca* VII (1982) and two works in Arabic *The Military Organization in the Era of the Empire,* 1984, and *Our National Heritage between Challenge and Response,* 1984; he died in Pittsburgh, USA, 4 Oct. 1990.

Inf. V. Teague, British Council, Cairo and Prof. L. Kákosy; *JEA* 77 (1991), xi; T. Säve-Söderbergh, *Temples and Tombs of Ancient Nubia,* 1992,170.

KAHLE, Paul Eric (1923-1955)
British Coptologist; born Bonn, 27 Oct. 1923, son of Paul Ernst K., Professor of Oriental Languages at Bonn, and Marie Gisevius; his family left Germany for Britain in 1939 in opposition to the Nazi Regime; he was Lady Wallis Budge Fellow at University College, Oxford, at the time of his death; MA, D.Phil.; he published a large collection of literary and documentary material from the monastery of Deir el-Balaizah, arriving at important conclusions regarding the distribution of Coptic dialects; see *Bala'izah. Coptic Texts from Bala'izah in Upper Egypt,* 2 vols. 1954; he died in Charlbury, Oxon., 30 April 1955.

AfO 17 (1954-6), 495 (anon.); *Chron. d'Ég.* 31 (1956), 222 (J. Vergote); EES *Report,* 1955, 4 (J. W. B. Barns); *JEA* 41 (1955), 2 (R. O. Faulkner); *ZÄS* 80 (1955), v-vi (S. Morenz); *The Coptic Encyclopedia* 5, 1389 (M. L. Bierbrier); inf. W. Kahle.

KAISER, Werner (1926-2013)
German Egyptologist; he was born in Munich, 7 May 1926, son of an army major; he served in World War II until wounded and taken prisoner; he studied Egyptology at the University of Munich under Scharff (q.v) and Stock (q.v.), 1946-50, 1951-5; PhD, 1955; he worked briefly at the Munich Museum, 1955 and then obtained a scholarship to visit European Egyptian collections in Vienna, London, Oxford, Cambridge, Paris, Brussels and Leiden, 1956; he was part of the excavation team at Abusir under Ricke (q.v.) and Stock, 1955-7, and undertook a survey of Middle and Upper Egypt, 1958; he became an assistant lecturer at the University of Heidelberg under Otto (q.v.), 1958-62; he was appointed Director of the Egyptian Museum in West Berlin, 1962-7 and oversaw the opening of the Egyptian collection in Schloss Charlottenburg; he became the first director of the German Archaeological Institute in Cairo, 1969-89; he specialized in the history of Prehistoric and Early Dynastic Egypt; he oversaw the excavations of the German Institute at Elephantine from 1969; *MDAIK* 47 (1991) was dedicated to him and *MDAIK* 70/71 (2014/15) was a memorial volume of studies; he published a number of articles, many in *MDAIK*; he died Munich, 11 Aug. 2013

BSFE 190 (2014), 2; *MDAIK* 47 (1991), v (portr.); xi-xv (bibl.); *MDAIK* 70/1 (2014/15), 1-11 (G. Dreyer) (portr.).

KÁKOSY, László (1932-2003)
Hungarian Egyptologist; he was born in Budapest, 15 Aug. 1932; he studied archaeology and ancient oriental history at the Eötvös Loránd University in Budapest under Dobrovits (q.v.) and Wessetzky (q.v.) from 1951-6; he was then attached to the Fine Arts Museum in Budapest for a year and then to the Hungarian Academy where he completed his thesis on Egyptian myths in 1961; he became lecturer under Dobrovits in 1960 and senior lecturer in 1972; PhD, 1974; he eventually succeeded Dobrovits as Professor of Ancient Near Eastern History at Eötvös Loránd University in Budapest, 1974-98; he established Egyptology as a separate discipline at the university in 1983; he took part in the Nubian rescue campaign from 1964 at Abdallah Nirqi and directed the Hungarian excavations at the tomb of Djehutimes at Thebes from 1983; Corresponding Member of the Heidelberg Academy from 1996 and Member of the Hungarian Academy of Sciences from 1998; apart from many articles and works in Hungarian, he published *La Magia in Egitto ai Tempi dei Faraoni,* 1985; German ed. *Zauberei im Alten Agypten,* 1989;

Dzsehutimesz Sírja Thébában, with an English summary, 1989; *Egyptian Healing Statues in Three Museums in Italy*, 1999, and posthumously *The Mortuary Monument of Djehutimes (TT 32)*, 2004; his selected papers were published in *Studia Aegyptiaca* VII (1981) and studies in his honour were published in *Studia Aegyptiaca* XIV (1992); he died in Budapest, 29 Jan. 2003.

Studia Aegyptiaca XIV (1992), 17-25 (bibl.) (M. Szücs); *ZÄS* 131 (2004), vii-viii (U. Luft); inf. G. Vörös.

KAMAL, Ahmed (*Pasha*) (1851-1923)
Egyptian Egyptologist; born in Cairo, 29 July 1851, son of Hassan Abdullah from Heraklion, Crete and his wife Ruksh; he was the first native Egyptian to become both an archaeologist and Egyptologist; he was a student of H. Brugsch (q.v.), and was attached to the then developing Antiquities Service, first as Secretary-Interpreter, and afterwards as Assistant Curator of the Museum from which post he retired in 1914 after 30 years service, when he was appointed Hon. Curator; he supported the classification of the Egyptian Collections in Cairo, and with their transference from Bulaq to Giza and then to Qasr el-Nil; he carried out numerous excavations throughout Egypt, at Deir el-Bersha, Gebel el-Teir, Tihna, Sharuna and Gamhud, 1908-9 for Back (q.v.), Atfih, Sheikh Said, and Asyut; he also wrote reports on other sites in the Delta and Upper Egypt; he published accounts of his work in *ASAE*; his literary works were numerous and included, *Stèles ptolémaiques et romaines,* 2 vols. 1904-5 and *Tables d'offrandes,* 2 vols. 1906-9, both for the *Cairo Cat.*; he spent many years on research into the relationship of Egyptian to Semitic languages and in particular Arabic, but died before publishing his work on it; he was also a member of the Inst. Eg., and a lecturer on Ancient Egyptian in Cairo University; having received the title of Bey from the Khedive, he was made Pasha shortly before his death, and was nominated Director of the School of Egyptology established on his suggestion by the Egyptian Government; Ahmed Kamal was the real pioneer of Egyptian studies in his own country; his daughter Nimet married in 1919 Muhammad Hamza (q.v.); his nephew was Muhammad Chaban (q.v.); he died in Cairo, 5 Aug. 1923.

BIÉ 6 (1924), 171-2 (V. M. Mosséri); *JEA* 9 (1923), 241; *ASAE* 64 (1981), 1-5 (portr.) (D. Abou-Ghazi); *Gött. Misz.* 76 (1984), 73-4; *JAOS* 105 (1985), 235-237; inf. H. Sallam; H. Sallam in C. Eyre (ed.), *Proceedings of the Seventh Congress of Egyptologists*, 1998, 1015-8; *KMT* 16/1 (2005), 82-4; È. Gran-Aymerich, *Dictionnaire biographique d'archéologie 1798-1945*, 2001, incorporated in *Les Chercheurs de passé 1798-1945*, 2007, 903; S. Quirke, *Hidden Hands*, 2010, 294-6.

KAMAL, Moharram (1908-1966)
Egyptian Egyptologist; he was born in 1908 and was educated at Cairo University, graduating in 1928; he studied abroad before joining the Antiquities Service first as a curator in the Cairo Museum and in the field becoming Chief Inspector in Middle Egypt; he was in charge of excavations at Asyut in 1931-2 (*ASAE* 34 (1934), 49-53, 125-6) and Amarna in 1934-5 (*ASAE* 35 (1935), 193-6); he resumed his post as Chief Inspector of Middle Egypt and carried out excavations at Ashmunein in 1942 (*ASAE* 46 (1947), 289-95); he then returned to the Cairo Museum where he succeeded Abbas Bayoumi (q.v.) as Director in 1956; he then followed as sub-Director General of Antiquities in 1957 but he was transferred to the Centre of Documentation in 1959 after the loss of one of the staves of Tutankhamun from the Cairo Museum; he retired in 1960; apart from his articles, he published an Arabic translation of Erman, *Life in Ancient Egypt*, with A. Abu-Bakr; he died in 1966.

Inf. Dr. D. Abou-Ghazi; *Bulletin of the Egyptian Museum* 1 (2004), 7-8.

KANTOR, Helene Juliet (1919-1993)
American archaeologist and art historian; she was born in Chicago, 19 July 1919, daughter of Prof. Dr. Jacob Robert K., a psychologist, and Helen Rich; she was educated at Indiana University; BA, 1938 and the Oriental Institute, University of Chicago from 1938; PhD, 1945 supervised by Frankfort (q.v.); she was appointed research assistant, Oriental Institute, 1945-8; instructor in Archaeology, Dept. of Oriental Languages and Literatures, University of Chicago, 1948-51; assistant Professor, in both the Institute and Dept., 1951-8, associate Professor, 1958-63; Professor of Near Eastern Art and Archaeology, 1963-30 Sept. 1989; Professor emeritus, 1989-93; she excavated at Khirbet al Kerak in Israel, 193-4 and Choga Mish in Iran from 1961, co-director from 1969, director from 1975; she visited Egypt in 1953-4; her principal publications relating to Egyptology were *The Aegean and the Orient in the Second Millennium B.C.*, 1947; 'The Chronology of Egypt and its Correlations with that of Other Parts of the Near East in the Periods before the Late Bronze Age' in R. Ehrich, *Relative Chronologies in Old World Archaeology*, 1st ed. 1954, 2nd ed. 1965, 3rd ed. 1992; 'Ägypten' in M. Mellink and J. Filip, *Frühe Stufe der Kunst*, 1974; she was awarded the Percia Schimmel Archaeological Prize, 1984 and a volume of studies was dedicated to her in 1989; she died in Chicago, 13 Jan. 1993.

A. Leonard and B. B. Williams, *Essays in Ancient Civilization presented to Helene J. Kantor*, 1989, vii-viii (J.

Johnson), xxxi-xxxix (bibl.) (C. Jones); *Annual Report, The Oriental Institute* 1989/90, 6-8 (W. Sumner); *The Oriental Institute 1991-1992 Annual Report,* 16-18 (A. Alizadeh); *JARCE* 30 (1993), ix-xi (B. Williams); inf. J. Larson.

KAPLONY, Peter Arpad (1933-2011)

Swiss Egyptologist; he was born in Budapest, 15 June 1933; his family left for Switzerland in 1944 and he obtained Swiss nationality in 1958; he studied ancient history and Egyptology at the Universities of Zurich and Basel; PhD in Zurich, 1959; Habilitation, 1964; he served as assistant professor for Egyptology at the University of Zurich, 1970-2000; his main area of interest was the epigraphy of the Early Dynastic Period and the Old Kingdom; his publications include *Die Inschriften der ägyptischen Frühzeit*, 4 vols, 1963-4; *Kleine Beiträge zu den Inschriften der ägyptischen Frühzeit*, 1966; *Steingefässe mit Inschriften der Frühzeit und des Alten Reichs*, 1968; *Studien zum Grab des Methethi*, 1976; *Die Rollsiegel des alten Reichs*, 2 vols, 1977-81; he died in Zurich, 11 Feb. 2011.

Inf. T. Schneider.

KASSER, Rodolphe (1927-2013)

Swiss Coptologist; he was born in Yverdon-les-Bains, 14 Jan. 1927, son of Georges K., pharmacist, and Dora von Fellenberg; he studied theology at Lausanne and Paris, 1946-50; Diploma, École Pratique des Hautes Études, 1964; he served as a pastor, 1953-9; he was appointed lecturer and then extraordinary professor of Coptic language and literature at the University of Geneva, 1963-76; professor, 1976-98; he directed the excavations at Kellia from 1965; he served on the committee of the International Association for Coptic Studies from 1876; President, 1984-8; apart from translations of Coptic religious texts, notably *The Gospel of Judas*, 2006, he published, with others, *Dictionnaire auxiliare, étymologique et complet de la langue Copte*, 1967; *Kellia* 1965, 1967; *EK 8184 I*, 1981; *Survey archéologique des Kellia (Basse-Égypte), rapport de la campagne 1981*, 1983; *Le site monastique des Kellia (Basse-Égypte). Recherches des annees 1981-1983*, 1984; *Kellia*, 2013; he died at Yverdon-les-Bains, 8 Oct. 2013.

Aegyptus 91 (2011), 303-8 (P. Luisier); *BSAC* 52 (2013), 8-10 (portr.) (W. Boutros-Ghali).

KATARY, Sally Louise (née Dolan) (1946-2016)

American-Canadian Egyptologist; she was born in New Rochelle, New York, 11 Oct. 1946. Daughter of William Henry D. and Alice Mary Collins; she was educated at the University of Pennsylvania, 1964-8 under Schulman (q.v.) and O'Connor; BA, 1968; she then studied at the University of Toronto, 1968-76 under Ronald Williams (q.v.) and Redford; MA, 1970; PhD, 1977; she held a post at State University of New York at Geneso and then became Affiliate Professor in Classical Studies at Thorneloe University at Laurentian University, Sudbury, Ontario where she introduced Egyptology to its Ancient Studies programme; she specialized in the social and economic history of Egypt; with Freeman (q.v.) and others, she was a co-founder of the Society for the Study of Egyptian Antiquities, 1969 and served as a Trustee of the Society and Associate editor of its journal and head of its Book Review Committee; she took part in the excavation of the Temple of Osiris Heqa-Djet at Karnak; apart from articles, she published *Land Tenure in the Ramesside Period*, 1989; she died in Sudbury, Ontario, 6 Aug. 2016.

SSEA Newsletter (Summer 2016), 1 (portr.); *JSSEA* 42 (2015-6), xxiii-xxvii (S. and N. Katary and E. Meltzer), (portr.); *JSSEA* 44 (2017-8), xi-xx (E. Meltzer) (portr.) (bibl.).

KATCHENOVSKY, Mikhail Trofimovitch (1775-1842)

Russian historian, literary critic and art connoisseur; he was born in Kharkov, 1 Nov. 1775; editor of an important journal *Vestnik Evropy (European Herald)*, 1805-30; Professor of fine arts and archaeology of the Moscow University, 1810; from 1837 its rector; in Russian historiography his name is connected with the so-called sceptic school; he was much interested in Egyptology; in 1819 he lectured on the arts of ancient peoples including Egyptian art, the text being printed in *Vestnik Evropy* 1819, no. 12, 249-274; P. Ulanov (q.v.) wrote under his supervision an interesting thesis on Egyptian art; he published a summary of the hieroglyphic system of J. F. Champollion (q.v.) in Russian also in *Vestnik Evropy* 1825, no. 4, 292 ff.; he was a member of the St. Petersburg Academy, 1841; he died in Moscow, 19 April 1842.

Sovetskaya Istoricheskaya Enciclopedia, vol. 7, 1965, 135-136; inf. J. Śliwa.

KATO, Ichiro (1921-2009)
Japanese Egyptologist; he was born 1921; he studied at Kyoto University and at Chicago as a Fulbright Scholar; he was lecturer and then professor of Egyptology at Kansai University; he died in 2009.

Y. Nishimura and S. Miyagwa, in C. Langer (ed.), *Global Egyptology*, 2017, 152.

KATZNELSON, Isidor Savvitch (1910-1981)
Russian Egyptologist and historian; he was born in Odessa, 5 Oct. 1910; he studied under V. V. Struve (q.v.) in Leningrad, obtaining his first degree in 1931; he worked in the Public Library of Leningrad until 1936, later lecturing at the Universities of Kiev, 1939-40, and Leningrad, 1940-41; during 1941-45 he entered the Red Army as a volunteer; at the end of the World War II he was a captain distinguished with many orders and battle distinctions; after obtaining his doctorate in 1947 with a thesis *Problems of the origin of the state in ancient Nubia,* he again lectured at the University of Leningrad; from 1956 he was at the Oriental Institute of the Academy of Sciences in Moscow where he founded a group working on the problems of Meroitic studies; he obtained his habilitation degree in history for a work on Meroe; he wrote in Russian *Fables and Tales of Ancient Egypt*, 1956; *Faraon Chufu i charodei*, 1958; *Lirika drevnego Egipta* (*Lyric Poetry of Ancient Egypt*), 1965 with Anna Akhmatova; *Fables of the Peoples of Sudan*, 1970; *Napata i Meroe*, 1970; he was also interested in the history of Egyptology in Russia; he was a member of Société française d'Égyptologie from 1957, of the Odessa Archaeological Society from 1959 and also a honorary member of the Egyptological Institute of the Charles University, Prague from 1966; he died in Moscow, 21 March 1981.

Meroe 4 (1989), 4-8 (9141-81); *BSFE* 91 (1981), 3; inf. obtained from R. I. Roubinstein.

KAVANAGH, (*Lady*) **Harriet Margaret** (*née* **Le Poer Trench**) (1799-1885)
Irish traveller, artist and antiquarian; she was born 13 Oct. 1799 to Richard, 2nd Earl of Clancarty (1767-1837), and his wife, Henrietta Margaret, daughter of the Rt. Hon. John Staples of Lissan, Co. Tyrone; she married Thomas Kavanagh, M.P., in 1825 after the death of his first wife; Thomas died in 1837, and shortly afterwards Harriet began travelling extensively around Europe; departed for Egypt and the Near East 1846, accompanied by three of her four children and their tutor, returning to Ireland in 1848; during her time in Egypt painted and kept daily diaries of her travels, recording her meetings with Alice Lieder (q.v.), Sophia Poole (q.v.), and Harriet Martineau (q.v.), who travelled with her from Cairo to Palestine; she collected over 300 artefacts, bequeathed to the Royal Society of Antiquaries of Ireland, and now in the National Museum of Ireland, and forming its single largest private donation of Egyptian antiquities; she died at her residence, Ballyragget Lodge, Co. Kilkenny, 14 Jul. 1885.

DIB 5, 7 (D. Murphy); R. Le Poer Trench, *Memoir of the Le Poer Trench Family*, 1874, 24; E. Jackson, in D. Fortenbury (ed.), *Travellers and Collectors*, 2013, 55-67; inf. E. Jackson.

KAWAMURA, Kiichi (1930-1978)
Japanese archaeologist; he was born at Nishigahara, Kitaku, Tokyo, 8 July 1930, son of Chujiro K., a silk dealer, and Shizu Usami; he was educated at Waseda University specializing in Near Eastern Studies; BA, 1953; MA, 1958; he took part in excavations in Japan; member of the Society of Japanese Archaeology, 1960; he was appointed lecturer at Waseda University 1966; assistant Professor 1969; Professor 1974; in 1977 he was appointed head of the newly-formed Dept. of Research on Ancient Egypt; in 1967, 1969 and early 1971 he led surveys in Egypt to choose a site for excavation; in Dec. 1971 he directed the first Japanese archaeological excavations in Egypt at Malkata near Luxor supervising seven seasons of work, 1971-77; he published preliminary reports of his work in the journal *Orient* and posthumously *Pharaoh's Staircase*, 1979; he died in Tokyo, 19 Dec. 1978.

Inf. D. Sakai.

KAYSER, Hans Richard (1911-1989)
German Egyptologist; he was born in Teutleben near Gotha, 18 Jan. 1911, son of Wilhelm K., a parson, and Hildegard Stolzenberg; he studied under Ranke (q.v.) in Heidelberg, 1930-35 (unpublished PhD 1935, on private temple statues), and worked there 1935-37 as university assistant, 1937-41; he belonged to the staff of Herzögliches Museum Gotha, at the same time cooperated on a project with Roeder (q.v.); in 1941 he was appointed museum's assistant of the Roemer-Museum Hildesheim; Director, 1943; during these war years he organized the evacuation of all the museum's holdings, including the Egyptian Collection of the Pelizaeus-Museum (together with Roeder); after returning from war service, he was appointed Director of the Roemer-Pelizaeus-Museum from which position he retired in 1974; in 1956 he succeeded in convincing the magistrate of Hildesheim to build a new museum on the location of the old buildings destroyed in the war; when it opened on 29 May 1959, it was the first Egyptian museum in Germany to re-open after World War II; he published catalogues and books on the Egyptian collection and on

Egyptian arts and crafts in general for a broader public, notably *Kleine Geschichte der Archäologie*, 1963; *Die Mastaba des Uhemka: Ein Grab in der Wüste*, 1964; *Hundert Tore hatte Theben. Historische Stätten am Nil*, 1965; *Das Pelizaeus-Museum in Hildesheim (Kulturgeschichtliche Museen in Deutschland, 11)*, 1966; *Ägyptisches Kunsthandwerk (Bibliothek für Kunst- und Antiquitätenfreunde, 16)*, 1969; *Die ägyptischen Altertümer im Roemer-Pelizaeus-Museum in Hildesheim (Wissenschaftliche Veröffentlichung des Pelizaeus-Museums 8)*, 1973; he died in Heidelberg, 9 Oct. 1989.

Inf. Dr. B. Schmitz.

KEES, Hermann Alexander Jakob (1886-1964)
German Egyptologist; he was born in Leipzig, 21 Dec. 1886, son of Paul K. and Thekla Schmidt; he was educated at the Thomas School, and studied classical archaeology at Innsbruck and the University of Göttingen; he afterwards turned to Egyptology which he studied at Munich under von Bissing (q.v.); PhD, 1911, writing as his thesis his first major work, *Der Opfertanz des ägyptischen Königs*, 1912; he thus showed his interest in religious thought in ancient Egypt at the beginning of his career; after serving in World War I, Kees studied under Sethe (q.v.) at Göttingen, and, together with de Buck (q.v.), produced *Göttinger Totenbuchstudien*, 1919, in which a new method of analysis was applied to the very abstruse funerary texts; from now on Kees concentrated on the history and development of Egyptian religion, and on the geography of the land in ancient times; he lectured at the Universities of Freiburg am Breisgau, where he obtained his habilitation in 1920, and Leipzig, 1921-4; he succeeded Sethe as Professor at Göttingen in 1924-45 when he was dismissed as a supporter of the Nazi government; he was later made Professor Emeritus, 1952-64; he served as president of the Humanities division of the Academy of Arts and Sciences, 1942-44; he was visiting Professor at the University of Ain Shams in Egypt for six years 1951-6; his output was a very considerable one in his chosen fields, his bibl. lists no less than 280 items, books, articles, and reviews; he employed an extremely compressed style, which made his books difficult to read, and a system of analysis which concentrated an immense amount of material in each volume; he wrote among other works, *Das Re-Heiligtum des Königs Ne-woser-re (Rathures)*, pt. ii, with von Bissing, 1932; pt. iii, 1928, a survey of all the remains of the scenes and inscriptions from the great sun temple; *Ägyptische Kunst*, 1926; *Totenglauben und Jenseitsvorstellungen der alten Ägypter*, 1926, rev. edit. 1956; *Der Götterglaube im Alten Ägypten*, 1941, rev. edit. 1956; considered to have been his greatest work and a great religious synthesis; *Das Priestertum im ägyptischen Staat vom Neuen Reich bis zur Spätzeit*, 1953; *Das Alte Ägypten. Eine kleine Landeskunde*, 1958 (trans. into English as *Ancient Egypt. A cultural Topography*, ed. T. G. H. James, 1961); *Handwörterbuch der ägyptischen Sprache unter Mitarbeit von Ahmed Badawi*, 1958; *Die Hohen-priester des Amun von Karnak von Herihor bis zum Ende der Äthiopenzeit*, 1964; he also wrote a great many of the Egyptian articles in Pauly-Wissowa *Real-Encyclopädie*; he died in Osterwald, 7 Feb. 1964.

AfO 21 (1966), 271-2 (portr.) (H. Brunner); *Chron. d'Ég.* 39 (1964), 97-8 (P. Derchain); *JEA* 50 (1964), I; *MDAIK* 14 (1956), Festschrift vol.; *OLZ* 59 (1964), 229 (S. Morenz); *ZÄS* 91 (1964), xvi-xx (E. Otto); *NDB* 11 389-90; *ZÄS* 92 (1966), 78-86 (bibl.) (C. Müller); inf. T. Schneider; O. Witthuhn in J. Arp-Neuman and T. Gertzen (eds.), '*Steininschrift und Bibelwort*', 2019, 65-72.

KEEVES, Winifred Adelaide (1897-1963)
Secretary of the Egypt Exploration Society; she was born in London, 29 Aug. 1897, daughter of Arthur Alfred K., tin plate worker, and Gertrude Annie Slade; she was educated at Skinners' School and at University College London; she graduated in English and filled a number of secretarial appointments before joining the Society; one employer was novelist George Moore whose last work only survived due to the fact that she made an extra copy against the advice of Moore himself; she became secretary of the Society in June 1939 a few months before the Second World War broke out; that the Society's administration and *Journal* survived at all during this very difficult period was in no small part due to her efforts; she died in London, 7 April 1963.

Inf. M. S. Drower; EES *Ann. Rep.* 1959, 5; *JEA* 49 (1963), I (I. E. S. Edwards).

KEIMER, Ludwig Joseph Gustav (1892-1957)
German Egyptologist; born Hellenthal, Germany, 23 Aug. 1892, son of Hubert K., a forester; he studied German Language and Literature, Ancient History and Classics at Münster, 1912-3 and then Archaeology at Berlin, 1913-17 where he took courses on Egyptology under Erman (q.v.) and Möller (q.v.); he also studied Law and National Economy; he took several doctorates at this time, PhD in the University of Münster, 1917; Doctor Juris utriusque at the University of Würzburg, 1920; Doctor rerum politicarum, Würzburg, 1922; he later obtained his habilitation from the German University in Prague, 20 Sept. 1930; influenced by G. Schweinfurth (q.v.) he became interested in the flora and fauna of Egypt, particularly in relation to those existing in the Pharaonic period, and he published his first important work in this field, *Die Gartenpflanzen im Alten Ägypten*, 1924, repr. 1967; he then went to work with V. Loret (q.v.) at Lyons and then settled

in Egypt in 1928, where he was made Professor at the School for Dragomans and Guides, 1929-31, and was also attached to the General Catalogue of the Museum, 1932; he directed the historical section of the Fuad I Agricultural Museum from 1931-36; he became Professor of Egyptian Archaeology in the University of Cairo, 1936; he was closely associated with the Institut d'Égypte to which he was elected in 1937, contributing many communications to its *Mémoires* and serving as secretary-general and vice-president; from 1930-40 he was appointed lecturer at the German University of Prague, 1938 and took Czechoslovak nationality; on his return to Egypt, he was arrested as a German spy, 1940-1 and later released thanks to Emery's (q.v.) intervention in 1951 he became an Egyptian national; he was a member of numerous scientific organizations, notably Société Royale de Géographie d'Égypte, 1929; Fondation égyptologique - Reine Elisabeth, Bruxelles, 1930; Société française d'Égypte, 1937; Association des amis de l'art copte, 1938; committee member of the Société Royale de Papyrologie d'Égypte, 1934;. in all his published output reached 200 items, including *Egyptian formal bouquets*, 1925; *Études d'Ég.* fasc. i-vii, 1940-5; *Histoires de serpents dans l'Égypte ancienne et moderne*, 1947; *Interprétation de quelques passages d'Horapollon*, 1947; *Remarques sur le tatouage dans l'Égypte ancienne*, 1948; *Notes prises chez les Bisarin et les Nubiens d'Assouan*, 1951-3; *Jardins zoologiques d'Égypte*, 1954; *À propos des 'ânes sauvages' abattus par Amenophis II près de Qadesh*, 1956; his library and archives were acquired by the German Archaeological Institute in Cairo; he died in Deir el-Chifa Hospital, Cairo, 16 Aug. 1957.

AfO 18 (1957-8), 488-9 (portr.) (J. Leclant); *BSAC* 14 (1950-7), 58, 252 (A. Piankoff); *Chron. d'Ég.* 33 (1958), 66-73 (portr.) (B. Van de Walle); 74-8 (bibl.), 235 (bibl. since 1940); *Études d'Égyptologie* i (1940) has his bibl. up to 1940; W. Oerter in *Gött. Misz.* 191 (2002), 71-5; W. B. Oerter in N. Kloth, K. Martin, and E. Pardey (eds.), *Es werde niedergelegt als Schriftstück. Festschrift für Hartwig Altenmüller zum 65. Gerburtstag*, 2003, 305-14; I. Lehnert in G. Dreyer and D. Polz, *Begegnung mit der Verganagheit-100 Jahre in Ägypten Deutsches Archäologisches Institut Kairo 1907-2007*, 2007, 16-24; I. Lehnert, *Antike Welt* 6 (2007), 60-2; inf. I. Lehnert and W. B. Oerter; W. Oerter, *Die Ägyptologie an der Prager Universitäten 1882-1945*, 2010, 20, 36-9, 47-63, 75-95, 123-6, 155-7; I. Lehnert in *Souvenirs and New Ideas*, ed. D. Fortenberry (ed.), 2013, 80-97.

KELEKIAN, Charles Dikran (1900-1983)
American art and antiquities dealer; he was born in Marseilles, France, 14 July1900, son of Dikran K. (q.v.) and Makrouhi (Marguerite) Gumchian; he joined his father's business in 1919, working with him until his death in 1951 and continuing it thereafter; the Cairo branch was nationalized in 1952, and he closed the Paris gallery in 1953, remaining active in New York until his death; he presented the Louvre with some Egyptian objects; many other Egyptian objects were given in his memory to the Metropolitan Museum NY and the Harvard Art Museums by his daughter, Nanette; a portrait of him as a child by Mary Cassatt is now in the Walters Art Gallery, Baltimore; he died in New York, 16 Jan 1982.

New York Times, obit,; inf. Nanette Kelekian and T. Hardwick; Kelekian archives, Metropolitan Museum; *Les Donateurs du Louvre*, 1989, 240.

KELEKIAN, Dikran Garabed (1868-1951)
Armenian art and antiquities dealer; he was born in Caesarea, Anatolia, 19 Jan. 1868, son of Garabed K., a banker, and his wife Mariam; he started as an antiques dealer in Istanbul in 1892; he visited the Chicago World's Fair in 1893, helping to arrange the Persian pavilion there, and later organized displays of Persian art at World's Fairs in Europe and the USA; he became a citizen of USA in 1898, and was appointed Persian consul in New York in 1902; he conducted business in Paris and New York; he purchased antiquities both in Egypt and at the great European sales such as those of the MacGregor (q.v.) and Fouquet (q.v.) collections; most of the Egyptian and oriental antiquities in the Walters Art Gallery in Baltimore were acquired by Henry Walters (q.v.) from him; many important antiquities were procured through him and his son Charles (q.v.), who joined the business in 1919, for the Metropolitan Museum, the Brooklyn Museum, the Freer Gallery in Washington, DC, the Victoria and Albert Museum, and other museums in America and Europe; his collection of Egyptian seals is in the Brooklyn Museum; he had great knowledge of his subject and business and enjoyed the highest reputation, playing a significant role in popularizing Middle Eastern art in the West; he maintained galleries in Paris, New York, and Cairo; he was awarded the title of Khan by the Shah of Persia for his services to Persian art and diplomacy, and was awarded the French Légion d'honneur; he formed a private collection of Impressionist and Post-Impressionist paintings, sold on 30 Dec.-1 Jan. 1922; he died in New York, 30 Jan. 1951.

New York Times, obit.; inf. P. E. Newberry; Newberry Corr. Nos. 27/40-58; Lugt 83081; M. Jenkins-Madina, 'Collecting the "Orient" at the Met: Early Tastemakers in America', *Ars Orientalis* 30 (2000), 69-89; M. S. Simpson, ' "A Gallant Era": Henry Walters, Islamic Art, and the Kelekian Connection', *Ars Orientalis* 30 (2000), 91-112; inf. Nanette Kelekian; Kelekian archives, Metropolitan Museum; L. Berman, *The Cleveland Museum of Art. Catalogue of Egyptian Art*, 1999, 12-3; inf. N. Kelekian and T. Hardwick; F. Hagen and K. Ryholt, *The Antiquities Trade in Egypt 1880-1930*, 2017, 226-7.

KELLER, Cathleen (Candy) Anne (1945-2008)
American Egyptologist; she was born in San Francisco, 7 Nov. 1945; she studied at the University of California Berkeley; BA, 1967; MA, 1971; PhD, 1978; she became curator of the Sutro Egyptian Collection at San Francisco State University as well as assistant Professor of Classical Archaeology, 1975-77; she was then appointed assistant and later associate curator at the Metropolitan Museum of Art New York, 1977-83; she became Associate Professor of Egyptology at Berkeley, 1983 and curator of the Phoebe Hearst Museum of Anthropology from 1987; she was a guest lecturer at Harvard University, 1990-1; she oversaw special exhibitions at the Berkeley Art Museum and the Hearst Museum and an exhibition on Queen Hatshepsut which toured the USA from 2005; she specialized in art history especially in the Valley of the Kings and Deir el-Medina where she sought to identify the individual hands of painters; apart from articles, she co-edited *Hatshepsut: From Queen to Pharaoh*, 2005; she left her books and papers to the Klaus Baer Library of Egyptology (now the Baer-Keller Library) at Berkeley; she died at Walnut Creek, Calif., 18 April 2008.

Internet obit; *The Daily Californian* 8 May 2008; *JARCE* 45 (2009), 1-2 (T. Logan).

KELSEY, Francis Willey (1858-1927)
American classicist; he was born in Ogden, New York, 23 May 1858, son of Henry K. and Olive Cornelia Trowbridge; he was educated at the University of Rochester graduating in 1880 and in Europe, 1883-5; Ph.D. from Rochester, 1886; he was appointed Professor of Latin at Lake Forest College, 1882-9 and Professor of the Latin Language and Literature at the University of Michigan, 1889-1927; he was awarded an honorary LLD from the University of Rochester, 1910; he was president of the American Philological Association, 1906-7 and of the Archaeological Institute of America, 1907-12; he was an active sponsor of archaeological excavations in the Near East and directed the excavations of the University of Michigan at Antioch in Pisidia, 1924; Carthage, 1925; and Karanis in Egypt from 1925; he was instrumental in the acquisition by the University Museum of much of the papyrus collection and the Dattari (q.v.) coin collection through his friend Charles Freer (q.v.); he published numerous works on classical subjects; he died in Ann Arbor, 14 May 1927; the University Museum was named the Kelsey Museum in his honour.

Inf. from the Kelsey Museum, Ann Arbor; *DAB* 10, 313-4; *WWWA* i, 664; J. G. Pedley, *The Life and Work of Francis Willey Kelsey*, 2011.

KENNARD, Henry Martyn (1833-1911)
English benefactor; he was born 17 Feb. 1833, son of Robert William K. and Mary Anne Challis; he lived at Falkirk and Crumlin Hall, Newport, Mon., and Lowndes Sq., London; DL; JP; he was a generous patron of archaeology, and, with Jesse Haworth (q.v.), supported the excavations of Petrie (q.v.) at Hawara, Amarna, Koptos, and Naqada; he excavated with Petrie at Hawara, 1888; he also supported the excavations of the EEF, and of Garstang (q.v.) and others; he presented most of his shares from Petrie's excavations to the Ashmolean, the foundations of its important collections of Predynastic and Amarna material; he presented antiquities to the British Museum, Manchester, and other museums, his own extensive collection of antiquities being sold at Sotheby's, 16-19 July, 1912 (743 lots) realizing £5,220; his portrait by W. W. Ouless was exhibited at the Royal Academy, 1891; his name is associated with an important Coptic papyrus which he presented to the British Museum (now BL Or. 7561); he died in London, 3 Aug. 1911.

Petrie, 79, 83, 89, 110, 137; private inf.; Lugt 71563.

el-KERETI, Abduh (1927-1978)
Egyptian workman and an experienced reis from a Qufti family; he was born on 6 March 1927; he started at the archaeological expedition in Abusir with Žába (q.v.) at the Ptahshepses mastaba in the early 1960s and led the team of workmen until his death in 1978; he cooperated with Czech(oslovak) expeditions during all seasons headed by Žába and Miroslav Verner (q.v.) in Nubia and Abusir; he also cooperated with the EES Mission headed by Walter B. Emery (q.v.) and the French team led by Jean Leclant (q.v.) and J. F. Lauer (q.v.); he died on 22 April 1978 and was succeeded by his sons Muhammad Abduh and Ahmad el-Kereti (q.v.).

Inf. Jiřina Růžová, Miroslav Verner, Ladislav Bareš.

el-KERETI, Ahmad (1959-2013)
Egyptian foreman of workmen at Czech(oslovak) archaeological excavations, he was born on 7 May 1959, son of Abduh el-Kereti (q.v.) and brother of Muhammad Abduh el-Kereti (q.v.); together with his brother, reis Muhammad Abduh el-Kereti (known as Tallal) cooperated with members of the Czechoslovak and later Czech Institute of Egyptology since 1978; his work began with the Pyramid Complex of Queen Khentkaus, followed by the Raneferef Pyramid Complex, and the intact shaft tomb of Iufaa and mastaba of Neferinpu; he was involved

largely with restoration and conservation of excavated finds; during his last years he led workmen in the Oasis el-Hez; he visited the Czech Republic in 2008; as was the case with his father and brother, his field expertise in Abusir contributed to excavation results, including published works in the Abusir series of the Czech(oslovak) Institute of Egyptology; he died on 22 March 2013.

Inf. Jiřina Růžová, Miroslav Verner, Ladislav Bareš.

el-KERETI, Muhammad Abduh otherwise Tallal (1952-2015)
Egyptain foreman of the team of workmen at the Czech(oslovak) concession at Abusir; he was born on 1 Sep. 1959, brother of Ahmad el-Kereti (q.v.) and son of Abduh el-Kereti (q.v.); known as reis 'Tallal', he worked with the Czech(oslovak) Egyptologists from 1977; he prolonged the family line of professional foremen started by his great-grandfather, his father Abduh (q.v.) and his uncle Mital el-Kereti; he – like his ancestors – was one of the most important foremen working for the Supreme Council of Antiquities, and was active also at excavations of other foreign expeditions in Egypt; in 2007 he visited Prague where he was awarded with the Silver Medal of Charles University, in acknowledgement of his service to Egyptology; he died unexpectedly on 20 March 2015.

Inf. Jiřina Růžová, Miroslav Verner, Ladislav Bareš.

KESTNER, (Georg Christian) August (1777-1853)
German collector; he was born in Hanover, 28 Nov. 1777, son of Johann Christian K., archivist and state counsellor, and Charlotte Buff; he studied law at Göttingen and then held various posts in Hanover; in 1816 he became secretary to the Hanoverian legation in Rome and from 1825-49 agent to the Vatican; he developed a keen interest in archaeology and was a friend of Bunsen (q.v.) and Lepsius (q.v.); he formed a large collection of antiquities which he left to his nephew Hermann Kestner (1820-1890) with the wish that he should try to organise a Kestner Museum; in 1884 the collection was given to the Government of Hanover which opened the Museum in 1889; he died in Rome, 5 March 1853.

I. Woldering, *Kestner Museum 1889-1964*, 1964, 5-10; M. Jorns, *August Kestner und seine Zeit*, 1964; *NDB* 11, 553-554; *KMT* 24 (2013), 54-58 (C. Loeben).

KEVORKIAN, Hagop (1872-1962)
Armenian benefactor, collector and dealer in ancient and Islamic art; he was born in Caesarea, Anatolia, 1872; he was educated at Roberts College, Istanbul; he organised 'excavations' in Iran; he came to the United States before World War I; he specialised in Islamic art, but also sold antiquities, and purchased Egyptian objects at the Hilton Price (q.v.) and other sales; he had a showroom in New York before World War II; in 1955 he gave money to Brooklyn Museum to purchase a group of Assyrian sculptures; his will endowed a foundation to support Near Eastern art and archaeology, funded in part through the sale of his collections through the 1960s and 1970s; notable groups of Egyptian objects were sold at Parke-Bernet, 14 Dec. 1962 (lots 50-60), and 4-5 Nov. 1967 (lots 197-244); he died in Paris, 10 Feb. 1962.

Les Donateurs du Louvre, 241; *Grove Dictionary of Art* XVIII, 4; H. Vartanian in *AGBU Magazine*, April 2002; M. Jenkins-Madina, 'Collecting the "Orient" at the Met: Early tastemakers in America', *Ars Orientalis* 30 (2000), 69-89; inf. Kevorkian Foundation and T. Hardwick.

KHASHABA, Sayed (*Pasha*) (*fl.* 1910-1950)
Egyptian landowner, merchant, and collector from Asyut; he financed excavations at Asyut, Meir, Deir el-Gabrawi, Tihna, and Soknopaiu Nesos, 1910-14, employing Kamal (q.v.); he also paid for restorations at Meir; he built a private museum at Asyut for his share of the finds; the objects were eventually sold off to, among others, the Metropolitan Museum of Art in New York, the Royal Scottish Museum, and the Berlin Museum, while the remainder are in the Mallawi Museum and the Salam Mosern School in Asyut.

F. Hagen and K. Ryholt, *The Antiquities Trade in Egypt 1880-1930*, 2017, 260-1.

KHAWAM, Joseph (1883-1964)
Egyptian dealer in antiquities; he was born in Cairo, 23 March 1883, son of Selim K., a Christian Syrian jeweller who had settled in Egypt in 1860 and founded an antiquities business in 1862, and Helene Hathoun; after working for his father selling antiquities, Joseph and his brothers Jean (*d.* 1918), Amin (1875-1944), and Faragallah (1884-1956) founded Khawam Brothers in Cairo in 1912; this became a successful dealership in Egyptian antiquities, Classical and Islamic antiquities, and coins, selling notable pieces to Western museums; the family business was located near Shepheard's Hotel and later moved to the Khan el-Khalil; he was a friend of Chassinat (q.v.); Joseph Khawam died in Paris, 17 July 1964; his son Roger (1922-22 April 2016) was educated at the Lycée Français du Caire and later at the École Pratique des Hautes Études in Paris and the Institut Catholique de Paris, where he

studied Egyptology, 1945-50; he joined the firm in 1952 and took over the family business in 1955 and supplied antiquities to tourists and many museums, including the Metropolitan Museum of Art in New York, the Louvre, and the Munich Museum; Khawam Brothers in Cairo closed in 1977 and opened in Paris the following year as R. Khawam et Cie / Khepri Gallery; Roger retired in 2005 and handed over to his sons; his remaining antiquities and libraray were sold in Paris 29-30 Nov. 2012.

Family inf. per Bertrand and Roger Khawam; inf. T. Hardwick; *The Times* 13 May 2016, 53; Wikipedia biog.; F. Hagen and K. Ryholt, *The Antiquities Trade in Egypt 1880-1930*, 2017, 228-9.

KHAYAT, Azeez (1875-1943)
Lebanese dealer in antiquities; he was born in Tyre, 1875, son of Habib K., a Christian shoemaker; he worked as a tailor before leaving for the United States, *c.*1892, where he established himself as a dealer in antiquities, specializing in ancient glass; he commissioned and loosely supervised excavations in the Levant, exporting his finds to the USA; he sold a large quantity of objects at auctions in New York, and more expensive pieces from a showroom on Fifth Avenue; his Egyptian pieces were mostly small objects and necklaces of uneven quality, but he was a significant supplier of ancient glass to J. P. Morgan (q.v.) and other collectors, including Albert Gallatin (q.v.); he was assisted by his son, Victor; in 1933 he settled permanently in Haifa (Jaffa), where he died 9 Oct. 1943.

A. Gallatin, *The Pursuit of Happiness*, 1950, 150-2; S. Bergman in *Carnegie Magazine* 46/6 (June 1974), 238-44; D. Grose, *Early Ancient Glass in the Toledo Museum of Art*, 1989, 20; Lugt lists 26 sales from 1905-1925; inf. T. Hardwick.

el-KHOULI, Ali Abdel-Rahman Hassanain (1934-2006)
Egyptian archaeologist; he was born in El-Siff, Giza, 27 Sept. 1934; he studied Egyptology at the University of Cairo; BA 1958; he subsequently studied at University College London, 1971-4; PhD, 1974; he joined the Egyptian Antiquities Organization in 1958 and served as inspector in the Fayum and Beni Suef, chief inspector in 1964 and later Director at Saqqara until 1973, general director of Upper Egypt, head of the technical office, general director of Middle Egypt, and finally Director General of the EAO; he also served as inspector at Qasr Ibrim during the Nubian Rescue campaign; he taught at the Universities of Cairo, Asyut, and Tanta; apart from articles on his excavations, he published *Egyptian Stone Vessels. Predynastic Period to Dynasty III: Typology and Analysis*, 1978; *Excavation in the Royal Necropolis at el-Amarna*, with G. T. Martin, 1987; *Excavation at Saqqara North west of Teti's Pyramid*, 1984-8, with A. Kanawati; *Saqqara Tombs* I-III, with W. V. Davies, A. B. Lloyd, and A. J. Spencer, 1984-2008; *Quseir el-Amarna*, 1989; *The Old Kingdom Tombs of el-Hammamiya*, 1990, both with A. Kanawati; *Meidum*, 1991; and *Stone Vessels, Pottery, and Sealings from the Tomb of Tutankhamun*, 1993, with others; he died in 2006.

Egyptian Archaeology 29 (2006), 44 (portr.); inf. G. T. Martin, P. Spencer, Wendy Butler, UCL Records Dept.

KIECHEL, Samuel (1563-1619)
German traveller; he was born at Ulm, 24 May 1563, son of Matthäus K., merchant and local official, and Apollonia Weihenmeyer; he set off in 1585 on a lengthy tour of Europe and the Levant; he was in Egypt for five months, 25 April to 16 Sept. 1588, visiting Alexandria, Cairo, and the Sinai; his account is longer than some of the period but adds nothing new as regards Egyptological antiquities; he returned to Ulm in 1589 and joined the family business; he died in Ulm, 30 Jan. 1619; his manuscript account of his travels was published in 1866 and a French translation of his Egyptian section was edited by Sauneron in 1972.

Voyages en Égypte pendant les années 1587-1588, trans. from the German by Ursula Castel, notes by S. Sauneron, 1972; *NDB* 11, 575-6.

KING, Edward, Viscount Kingsborough (1795-1837)
British peer, collector, and writer on antiquarian subjects; he was born 10 Nov. 1795, eldest son of George King, the 3rd Earl of Kingston and Helena Moore; educated Exeter College, Oxford; MP for Cork, 1818, 1820-6; he was interested in ancient writing and owned a large collection of MSS including Egyptian papyri, which he presented to Trinity College, Dublin, and of which a Catalogue was subsequently published by Hincks in 1843; at the suggestion of Sir Thomas Phillipps he studied Mexican picture-writing and spent a fortune in producing the *Antiquities of Mexico*, 9 vols. 1830-40, containing upwards of 1,000 plates; in this great work he tried to prove that the ancient Mexicans were the lost Tribes of Israel; his library and MSS were sold in Dublin in 1824; he died in Dublin, 27 Feb. 1837.

ODNB 31, 614; *DNB* 31, 1301; S. de Ricci, *Eng. Collectors of Books and MSS*, 1930, 123; A. N. L. Munby, *Phillipps Studies*, iv (1956), 11-13.

KINGLAKE, Alexander William (1809-1891)

British historian, writer, and traveller; he was born in Taunton, 5 Aug. 1809, son of William K. and Mary Woodforde; he was educated at Eton 1823-8 and Trinity College, Cambridge 1828-32, BA, 1832; he was a barrister by training and was called to the Bar, Lincoln's Inn, 1837; he visited the East, 1834-5, and described his journey in the famous account *Eothen*, 1844, which became an English classic; he visited the Crimea, 1854, and published a history of the campaign in 8 vols., 1863-87; he died in London, 2 Jan. 1891.

ODNB 31, 695-7 (portr.); *DNB* 31, 171-3; Hilmy, i, 342; G. de Gaury, *Travelling Gent*, 1972; Jan Morris (introd.), *Eothen*, 1982; J. Speake (ed.), *Literature of Travel and Exploration*, 2003, 2, 676-8; P. Starkey in N. Cooke and V. Daubney (eds.), *Lost and Now Found*, 2017, 273-82.

KIRCHER, Athanasius (1602-1680)

P. ATHANASIVS KIRCHERVS FVLDENSIS
è Societ: Iesu Anno ætatis LIII.

German priest and antiquarian; born at Geisa near Fulda, 2 May 1602, son of Johann K. and Anna Ganseck; he entered the Jesuit order in 1618 and was educated at Münster, Cologne, Coblenz, and Mainz; in 1630 he was appointed Professor of philosophy, mathematics, and oriental languages at Würzburg, but had to leave Germany the following year on account of the Thirty Years War; he went to Avignon 1633-5, and then to Rome, where he was made Professor of mathematics of the Roman College, 1635-43; Kircher now seems to have decided to dedicate the rest of his life to linguistic and archaeological research; he also wrote many works on scientific subjects, in which field he was an experimenter; a man of extraordinary intellect and very wide interests. Kircher has become, perhaps unfairly, the symbol of all that is absurd and fantastic in the story of the decipherment of Egyptian hieroglyphs, and has in consequence been branded as the supreme charlatan; in fact much of his work was important and not without significance; he was entrusted with the translation of a Coptic-Arabic vocabulary brought from Egypt by Pietro della Valle (q.v.), and his *Prodromus Coptus sive Aegyptiacus*, 1636, was the first of a long series of books on Coptic that provided a considerable quantity of knowledge which was needed by scholars when at last they had the key to hieroglyphic inscriptions; his *Lingua Aegyptiaca restituta*, 1643, marked the beginning of a new interest in Coptic, the latest phase of the ancient Egyptian language; Kircher's efforts to read the royal names and inscriptions on the obelisks in Rome were nullified by the mistaken belief, commonly held at that time, that the signs were purely symbolic; his largest work was *Oedipus aegyptiacus*, 4 vols. 1652-4; with these works he probably did more than anyone else to arouse interest in ancient Egypt before the French expedition; he also invented many instruments and machines, his collections being later formed into the Museum Kircherianum, a state institution in Rome after 1870; he died in Rome, 28 Nov. 1680.

Gardiner, *Egyptian Grammar*, 3rd ed., p. 11; *La Grande Enc.* 21; *NDB* 11, 641-5; R. Dieterle et al, *Universale Bildung im Barock*, 1981; J. Fletcher in *The Library* xxiii (1968), 108-117; J. Godwin, *Athanasius Kircher*, 1979; John Fletcher, ed., *Athanasius Kircher und seine Beziehungen zum gelehrten Europa seiner Zeit*, 1988; B. Merrill, *Athanasius Kircher* (1602-1680), 1989; Alberto Bartola, *L'Egitto di Athanasius Kircher*, in: *L'Egitto nei libri e nelle immagine della Biblioteca Reale di Torino*, 1991, 25-35 (supplementary bibl.); E. Leospo in C. Morigi Govi, S. Curto, S. Pernigotti, *L'Egitto fuori dell'Egitto*, 1991, 269-275; H. Beinlich et al, *Spurensuche. Wege zu Athanasius Kircher*, 2002; H. Beinlich et al, *Magie des Wissens. Athanasius Kircher 1602-1680*, 2002; P. Findlen, *Athanasius Kircher*, 2005; Lamy, 281-7; J. Godwin, *Athanasius Kircher's Theatre of the World*, 2009; H. Beinlich, *Gött. Misz.* 225 (2010), 15-20; D. Stolzenberg, *Egyptian Oedipus*, 2013.

KIRWAN, *Sir* (Archibald) Laurence Patrick (1907-1999)

British archaeologist; he was born in London, 13 May 1907, son of Patrick K. of Galway, Ireland and Mabel Norton; he was educated at Wimbledon College, Merton College, Oxford, and University College Lon don where he studied under Petrie (q.v.) from 1927-8; he took part in the excavations of Guy Brunton (q.v.) in Middle Egypt, Dec. 1928-April 1929; he then assisted Carter (q.v.) and Lucas (q.v.) in the assembly of the shrines of Tutakhamun at the Egyptian Museum; he was appointed to the post of assistant director under Emery (q.v.) on the Archaeological Survey of Nubia, 1929-34 during which he participated in the discovery of the tombs at Ballana and Qustul in 1931; he returned to Oxford to study under Griffith (q.v.); BLitt, 1935; he was then appointed Director of the Oxford University Excavations in the Sudan, 1934-7, excavating at Firka, 1934-5 and at Kawa with Macadam (q.v.), 1935-6; he held the Tweedie Fellowship in Archaeology and Anthropology from Edinburgh University, 1937-9; he served on the joint staffs at the Offices of the Cabinet and Ministry of Defence during World War II rising to the rank of Lt.-Col., 1943; he then became Director and Secretary of the Royal Geographic Society, 1945-75 and editor of the *Geographic Journal*, 1945-78; Hon. Vice-President from 1981; he became adviser to the Sudanese Government during the Nubian rescue campaign, 1958-61; he briefly surveyed Faras with W. Y. Adams and encouraged the Polish excavation of that and other sites; he founded the British Institute of History and Archaeology in Eastern Africa with Sir Mortimer Wheeler; President, 1961-81; Hon. Life President from 1981; Visiting Professor at Cairo University, 1976; Mortimer Wheeler Lecturer at the British Academy, 1977; Hon. President of the Sudan Archaeological Research Society from 1992; he was awarded the Royal Geographical Society's Founder's Gold Medal, 1975; CMG, 1958; KCMG, 1972; he published with W. Emery, *The Excavations and Survey between Wadi-es-Sebua and Adindan*, 1935; with Emery, *The Royal Tombs of Ballana and Qustul*, 1938; *The Oxford University Excavations at Firka*, 1939; and with Macadam, *The Temples of Kawa II*, 1955; his collected articles were edited by T Hägg, L. Török, and D. Welsby as *Studies on the History of Late Antique and Christian Nubia*, 2002; he died in London, 16 April 1999.

ODNB 31, 822-3; *Sudan and Nubia* 3 (1999), 88-90 (portr.) (H. S. Smith); *Who's Who* 1998, 119; *The Times* 22 April 1999; *The Daily Telegraph* 21 April 1999; *The Guardian* 21 April 1999.

KITCHENER (*Lord*), **Horatio Herbert, 1st Earl Kitchener** (1850-1916)
British army officer and collector; he was born in Crotter House, Ballylongford, Co. Kerry, 24 June 1850, son of Henry Horatio K. and Frances Chevallier; KG; PC; GCMG; Field Marshal; Sirdar of the Egyptian Army, 1890; created Baron, 1898; Viscount, 1902; Earl Kitchener of Khartoum, 1914; during his long connection with Egypt he did much to encourage archaeology; he collected antiquities and ceramics, and his collection was sold at Sotheby's, 16-17 Nov. 1938; he was lost at sea with HMS *Hampshire*, 5 June 1916.

Budge, *N & T* i, 110; ii, 152, 289, 356; Sayce, *passim*; *WWW* ii, 591; *ODNB* 31, 828-36 (portr.).

KLAPROTH, Heinrich Julius (1783-1835)
German orientalist and traveller; he was born in Berlin, 11 Oct. 1783, son of the chemist Martin Heinrich K. (1743-1817) and Christiane Sophie Lehmann; he studied Asiatic languages and held an appointment at the St. Petersburg Acad.; he was a member of Count Golovkin's embassy to China, 1805; he explored the Caucasus, 1807-8; he then moved to Berlin, 1812, afterwards settling in Paris, 1815; he obtained the title and salary of Professor of Asiatic Languages, Berlin, with leave to remain in Paris and publish his works; besides a number of works on his Asiatic travels and on languages he published an elaborate but worthless *Examen Critique des Travaux de feu M. Champollion sur les Hiéroglyphes*, Paris, 1832, which was in turn criticized by de Saulcy in *Rev. Arch.* 1846, i. 12, 65; in 1829 he published in Paris a collection of plates of Egyptian antiquities collected by Palin (q.v.) and Passalacqua (q.v.), with a criticism of Champollion (q.v.) prefixed; he died in Paris, 28 Aug. 1835.

Champollion, i, 127, 171; Hilmy, i, 344; *NDB* 11, 706-7.

KLASENS, Adolf (1917-1998)
Dutch Egyptologist; he was born in Hoogezand, 24 Feb. 1917, son of Johannes K. and Marchien Pathuis; he was educated in classics and Egyptology at Groningen University under van der Leeuw (q.v.); he then studied with de Buck (q.v.) at Leiden, 1945-52; DLitt, 1952; learnt Demotic from Glanville (q.v.) at Cambridge and trained as an archaeologist under Emery (q.v.) at Saqqara, 1953-8; he worked as a librarian and then research assistant at the Rijksmuseum van Ouheden in Leiden, 1946-54; Curator of the Egyptian Dept., 1954-9; Director, 1959-78 in succession to van Wijngaarden (q.v.); Professor of Egyptology, 1960-78 in succession to de Buck; he excavated archaic sites at Abu Roash, 1957-9; he took part as a field director in the Nubian Rescue campaign, excavating the Meroitic town site of Shokan and the central Church of Abdallah Nirqi near Abu Simbel, 1962-4; apart from many articles, he published his thesis *A Magical Statue Base (Socle Behague) in the Museum of Antiquities in Leiden*, 1952; *Egyptologie avant la lettre*, 1961; *Egyptische Kunst*, 1962; *Universiteit, universitaire collecties, musae*, 1970; and was a contributor to W. B. Emery, *Great Tombs of the First Dynasty* II, 1954; III, 1958; he died in Katwijk, 1 July 1998.

IAE Internet obituary (H. Schneider); *JEA* 84 (1998), ix; *Phoenix* 46 (2000), 3 (H. Schneider); inf. M. Heerma van Voss; inf. M. Raven.

KLEBS, Luise (*née* Sigwart) (1865-1931)
German Egyptologist; she was born in Tübingen, 13 June 1865, daughter of Christoph von Sigwart and Charlotte Georgii; she married Georg Klebs, Professor of Botany; she studied at Heidelberg University; she published *Reliefs des Alten Reiches*, 1914; *Reliefs und Malereien des Mittleren Reiches*, 1921; a similar work for the New Kingdom was in preparation but remained unfinished at the time of her death; one part *Szenen aus dem Leben des Volkes* was published posthumously in 1934; she died in Lugano, 24 May 1931.

JEA 17 (1931), 255-6; *ZÄS* 66 (1931), 75; *NDB* 11, 720-1.

KMINEK-SZEDLO, Jan (1828-1896)
Czech Egyptologist; he was born in Prague, 12 April 1828, son of Alois K.-S., a doctor, and Elisabetta Stampfova; his family moved to Pilsen where he studied in the local gymnasium 1841-6 and later attended the University of Prague; implicated in the 1848 rebellion, he was inducted into the Austrian army and stationed in Italy where he settled after leaving the army; he developed a keen interest in Egyptology, being the first of his nationality to study ancient Egyptian; he was a demonstrator in the Museo dell'Archiginnasio, Bologna in 1876; in 1878 he was appointed a lecturer in Egyptology at the University of Bologna until his death; from 1882 he also held the post of inspector of the Museo Civico, Bologna; he wrote his works mainly in English and Italian, notably *Il grande sarcophago del museo di Bologna*, 1876; *Saggio filologico per l'apprendimento della lingua egiziana*, 1877; *Museo Civico di Bologna. Catalogo di antichità Egizie*, 1895; he died in Bologna, 24 Nov. 1896.

Annuario dell'Università di Bologna 1897-1898, 239 ff.; *Asian and African Studies in Czechoslovakia*, Moscow, 1967 (F. Váhala, Z. Zába); S. Curto, *Atti del Convegno su la Lombardia e l'Oriente*. Instituto Lombardo. Accademia di Scienze e Lettre, 1963, 120-6; *Archív. Or.* 54 (1986), 89-91 (B. Vachala); *Novy Orient* 40 (1985), 246-8 (B. Vachala); *Studi di Egittologia e di Antichità Puniche* 2 (1987), 1ff. (S. Curto).

KNIGHT, Alfred Ernest (1861-1934)
British writer and antiquarian; he was born in Camberwell, 4 Sept. 1861, son of Willian Henry K, artist, and his wife Jane Sarah Pain; he was employed by the London numismatic dealers Spink and Sons in their antiquities department, for which he catalogued the collection of William MacGregor (q.v.), and wrote *Amentet: The gods, amulets, and scarabs of the ancient Egyptians*, 1915, dedicated to Acworth (q.v.); he wrote a number of popular works, including *Bible Plants and Animals*, 1889, *The Romance of Colonization*, 1897, *Crown and Empire*, 1902; he died in Beddington, Croydon, 24 Feb. 1934.

WWW 3, 763; *Books Abroad* 9/1 (Winter 1935), 22; inf. T. Hardwick.

KOCH, Johann Georg (*fl.*1780-1790)
Dutch theologian; he attempted to decipher hieroglyphic writing, publishing three works on the subject at St. Petersburg, 1788-9.

BIFAO 5 (1906), 83; Hilmy, i. 346; *Palestinskiy Sbornik* 5 (68), 1960, 119 (I. G. Lifschitz).

KOEFOED-PETERSEN, Otto (1901-1983)
Danish Egyptologist; he was born in Copenhagen, 31 Aug. 1901, son of Lorentz K.-P and Astrid Stiholm; he was educated at the University of Copenhagen, MA (history), 1925; he was attached to the Ethnographical Collection of The National Museum of Copenhagen 1922-5; he held a scholarship from The Rockefeller Foundation 1927-9; he studied Egyptology and Near Eastern History at the Universities in Paris and Berlin 1927-30; he was appointed Keeper of the Egyptian Department of the Ny Carlsberg Glyptotek 1933-71; he was visiting lecturer at the Universities of Greifswald, 1937, Frankfurt and Göttingen, 1958, and the École du Louvre, 1960; he was awarded a Bachelor of Laws, 1945 and was Assistant Chief Constable of Copenhagen 1946-8; he was responsible for the publication of many of the monuments in his charge; his principal publications were *Amenhetep IV og hans religise Revolution*, 1923; *Recueil des inscriptions hiéroglyphiques de la Glyptothèque Ny Carlsberg*, 1936; *Aegptisk Billedhugger-kunst i Ny Carlsberg Glyptotek*, 1938; *Det gamle Aegypten*, 1941; *Aegyptens Kaetterkonge og hans Kunst*, 1943; *Koptisk Kunst*, 1944; *Aegyptens Guder*, 1946; *Les stèles égyptiennes*, 1948; *Catalogue des statues et statuettes égyptiennes*, 1950; *Catalogues des sarcophages et cercueils égyptiens*, 1951; *Egyptian sculpture in The Ny Carlsberg Glyptothek*, 1951; *de gamle Aegyptere Laeste*, 1953; *Catalogue des bas-reliefs et peintures égyptiens*, 1956; he died in Copenhagen, 25 April 1983.

Inf. M. Jorgensen.

KOEHLER, Clemens (1840-1901)
Polish physician and archaeologist; he was born in Bydgoszcz, 9 July 1840, son of Gustav Adolf K., a surgeon-doctor, and Klementina Bronnessel; he studied medicine at Heidelberg, Paris and Vienna, being the first

Polish laryngologist; active member of the Archaeological Committee of the Poznan Society of the Friends of Sciences, 1875-91; its first secretary and later its president 1891-1901; he owned a considerable numismatic and archaeological collection including some Egyptian objects; on the session of 24 April 1893 of the above-mentioned Committee he presented a paper concerning some Egyptian scarabs belonging to the Poznan Society and from his own collection; he died in Poznan, 12 Jan. 1901.

J. Śliwa, 'Skarabeusz zielnick', *Meander* 45, 1990.

KOFLER, Ernst (1899-1989)
Swiss collector and dealer; he was born 21 June 1903; his family owned a department store in Lucerne; with his wife Marthe Truniger (8 Sept. 1918-11 March 1999) he purchased material in Egypt, often with the collaboration of the Egyptian dealer Maguid Sameda (*fl*.1945-1970), and selling objects in Europe and America; the Kofler-Trunigers amassed a large collection of Egyptian, Islamic, Mediaeval, and Indian art, exhibited in Zürich in 1964; the Egyptian material was published by H. W. Müller (q.v.), and contained significant groups of Early Dynastic objects and glass and faience inlays; their collections were sold off piecemeal from the 1970s onwards; the glass collection was sold privately to a Middle Eastern purchaser who retained the Islamic material and sold the Egyptian and Classical pieces at auction (Christie's, 5-6 March 1985); other Egyptian pieces were sold through Galerie l'Ibis, New York; he died 14 July 1990.

Family information; C. M. Kaufmann, 'The Kofler Collection: an important exhibition in Zürich' *The Connoisseur,* May 1964, 15-23; R. Wehrli (ed.), *Sammlung E. und M. Kofler-Truniger* (Zurich, 1964); H. W. Müller, *Ägyptische Kunstwerke, Kleinfunde und Glas in der Sammlung E. und M. Kofler-Truniger Luzern* (MÄS 5, 1964); *New York Times,* 22 Feb. 1985; Sale catalogue Christie's, March 5-6, 1985, with preface; *Antiques Trade Gazette* 13 Mar. 1985, 30; inf. T. Hardwick.

KOLLER, (*Baron*) **Franz von** (1767-1826)
Austrian general and collector; he was born in Munchengraetz, 27 Nov. 1767; after his retirement from the army he resided in Italy and formed a notable collection of Greek and Roman coins, and many other antiquities including Egyptian; his coins were sold in at Sotheby's, 27 May-7 June 1846 and 2 April 1854; the Egyptian antiquities were acquired by Berlin Museum and Zagreb Museum; most of his collections were obtained in Italy but he made purchases in Egypt in 1824; his name is attached to a papyrus (Berlin 3043) published by Gardiner in *Late Eg. Misc.*, 116; he died in Naples, 22 Aug. 1826.

Larousse, XIXe siècle 9, 1245; Lugt 18255, 21883.

KOMORZYNSKI-OSZCZYNSKI, Egon von (1910-1989)
Austrian Egyptologist; he was born in Vienna, 19 July 1910, son of Egon K., a Mozart scholar; he studied Egyptology at the University of Vienna under Czermak (q.v.), Junker (q.v.), and Till (q.v.), PhD 1936; he excavated at Giza with Junker, 1937; he undertook voluntary work in the Institut für Ägyptologie at the University, 1933-8, in the Egyptian Department of the Kunsthistorisches Museum, 1939 and the Papyrussammlung of the National Library, 1939; apart from active service, he worked with the railways during and after World War II, 1939-47; he joined the staff of the Egyptian Department of the Museum on 1 Nov. 1948 and succeeded Demel (q.v.) in charge of the Department on 28 Jan. 1952; he was given the title Director of the Ägyptisch-Orientalischen Sammlung on 1 Jan. 1964; he retired on 1 Jan. 1976; apart from over 80 articles, he published *Altägypten - Drei Jahrtausende Kunstschaffen am Nil*, 1952; *Altägyptische Denkmäler aus drei Jahrtausenden*, 1956; *5000 Jahre Aegyptische Kunst*, 1961; and *Das Erbe des Alten Ägypten*, 1965; he edited *Archiv für ägyptische Archäologie* with Balcz (q.v.); he died in Sandl, Upper Austria, 11 June 1989.

Inf. H. Satzinger; R. Teichl, *Österreichcher der Gegenwart*, 1951, 154-5.

KOROSTOVTSEV, Mikhail Alexandrovitch (1900-1980)
Russian Egyptologist and historian; he was born at Popvka in Dnepropetrovsk, 10/23 April 1900; he completed his secondary education in Tbilisi, 1919; during the years 1921-24 he served in the Red Army; from 1924 he was in the Navy rising from a common seaman to the post of a captain in 1935; in 1934 he completed a correspondence course from the Dept. of History at the University of Baku, and leaving the Navy in 1935, he began to work in Egyptology as a research worker at the Institute of History of the Soviet Academy of Sciences in Leningrad; senior research worker, 1943-65; he was the pupil of V. V. Struve (q.v.); he obtained his PhD in 1940 for a study *Slavery in Egypt during the 18 Dynasty*; he served as a volunteer in the Red Army during World War II, later transferred to an administrative post in the Moscow Academy of Sciences; on 16 Oct. 1943 he obtained his second degree, doctor of historical sciences with a study, *Language and script in ancient Egypt*; Professor, 29 Jan. 1944;

he was sent to Egypt 1943-7 as a correspondent of the TASS news agency, and until 1947 he was an official representative of the Academy of Sciences there; after a false accusation for political reasons, he spent eight years in a prison camp in Siberia, 1947-55; from 1965 head of the department of Ancient East at the Institute of Oriental Studies as successor to Struve; Hon. PhD Charles University, Prague, 1965; member of the Soviet Academy of Sciences, 1974; a Festschrift entitled *Drevnii Vostok* was dedicated to him by his colleagues and pupils in 1975 and a memorial volume *Ancient Egypt and Kush* was published in 1993; his most notable publications concerned the hieratic papyri from the Pushkin Museum in Moscow; *Puteshestvie Un-Amuna v Bibl.*, 1960; *Ieraticheskiy papirus No. 127*, 1961; he was also an author of *Egipetski iazyk*, 1961; *Pistsy Drevnei go Egipt*, 1962; *Vvediniye v egiptskuyu filologyu*, 1963; *Religia Drevnego Egipta*, 1976 and of *Grammaire du néo-égyptien*, 1973; he died in Moscow, 21. Oct. 1980

VDI 1 (55), 1981, 230; *Great Soviet Encyclopedia* 13, 419; *VDI* 1 (192), 1990, 238-9; Miliband, 1975, 273-4; *BSFE* 90 (1981), 4; inf. J. Śliwa.

KOSEGARTEN, (Johann) Gottfried Ludwig (1792-1860)
German orientalist; he was born at Altenkirchen, Rugen island, 10 Sept. 1792, son of Ludwig Theodul K., the poet, and Katharina Linde; he became Professor of Oriental Languages at the University of Jena, 1817, and later Greifswald, 1824; he published various Persian and Arabic literary works, and an Arabic Chrestomathy, 1828; at this period he became interested in Egyptian texts, and attempted to explain the significance of a funerary papyrus, i.e. a Book of the Dead, in the Minutoli collection, *Bemerkungen über den ägyptischen Text eines Papyrus aus der Minutolischen Sammlung*, 1824; he was also with Young (q.v.) and Champollion (q.v.) one of the first people to publish Egyptian texts, and the *Dictionary* of the former contains numerous pages with references extracted from Kosegarten; he died in Greifswald, 18 Aug. 1860.

Hilmy, i, 348; A. Wood, *Thomas Young*, 249; Young and Tattam, *Egyptian Dictionary*, passim; *ADB* 16, 742-5; Gustave Dugat, *Histoire des Orientalistes de l'Europe du XIIᵉ au XIXᵉ siècle* I, 1868, 3-7.

KOSMATCH, Albert Georg (1846-1872)
Austrian Egyptologist; he was born in Laibach (now Ljubljana, Slovenia) in 1846 son of Georg K., a librarian; he studied at the University of Vienna under Reinisch (q.v.), graduating 1868; in 1866 he copied the inscriptions on a coffin in the Museum at Laibach given by Laurin (q.v.); he obtained a position in the library of the University of Graz, 1872; he died in Laibach (Ljubljana), 7 Oct. 1872.

Inf. G. Hamernik.; *Slovenski Biografski Leksikon* I, 532

KOSSAKOWSKI, (*Comte*) Stanisław Fortunat Szczęsny (1795-1872)
Polish writer and collector, diplomat in Russian services; he was born Hamburg, 4 Jan. 1795, son of Józef Dominik K. and Łuduika Zofia Potocki; he spent his childhood in France and was educated there; from 1822-26 he acted as a secretary of the Russian embassy in the Vatican; during his stay in Italy he was in contact with the sculptor B. Thorvaldsen (q.v.) whose marble bust of K. is now in the Thorvaldsen Museum, Copenhagen and with J. F. Champollion (q.v.); Kossalowski was very interested in his discoveries and soon became his faithful adherent, propagating the hieroglyphic system established by him; for the use of the Russian ambassador in Vatican Kossakowski prepared a memorial in 1825-6 entitled *Compte rendu sur le système hiéroglyphique de Mr Champollion fait pour son excellence Mr d'Italinski par le comte Kossakowski (*manuscript, now in the Manuscript Branch of the Oriental Institute of the Russian Academy of Sciences); Kossakowski owned a gallery of valuable paintings in his Warsaw palace along with other art objects including some Egyptian antiquities (now lost), old armour, and a valuable library; his home was famous in Warsaw as an artistic-literary salon; he died in Warsaw, 26 May 1872.

Palestinskiy Sbornik 2 (64-5), 1956, 115-21 (I. G. Lifschitz); *ibid.* 3 (66), 1958, 151-70 (I. G. Lifschitz); *Przeglad Orientalistyczny* 1966, 139-41 (J. Reychman); *Polski Słownik Biograficzny* 14, 286-7; inf. J. Śliwa; *Ocherki po istorii rosskogo vostokovedeniya,* Vol. II, Moscow 1956, 224-31 (I. S. Katznelson).

KOUCHAKJI, Fahim Joseph (1886-1976)
Syrian-American dealer in antiquities; he was born to a family of Armenian origin in Aleppo, 17 March 1886, son of Georges K. and Emilienne Chargi; he studied business in Cairo, and joined the family firm of Kouchakji Frères, which had branches in Aleppo, Paris, and New York, moving with his father to Paris around 1910; his uncles Salim and Constantine managed the Aleppo branch, and his uncle Habib the New York branch; he moved to New York in 1924; the firm specialized in Islamic ceramics and ancient and Islamic glass, as well as ancient jewellery, selling from a gallery and also at auction; the best known piece to have passed through the firm's hands was the 'Antioch Chalice', an early Christian silver vessel popularly identified as the Holy Grail, in their possession

from around 1910 and sold to the Metropolitan Museum in 1950; after the liquidation of the firm around 1928, he traded from New York as Fahim Kouchakji; he assisted G. A. Eisen in writing *Glass: its origin, history, chronology...* (2 vols., 1927), illustrated with many pieces from his stock; Egyptian objects from his estate were sold at Sotheby's New York, 21 May 1977; he died in Shendaken, New York, 19 Aug. 1976.

Family information; *New York Times* 21 Nov. 1929; *New York Times* 21 Aug. 1976 (obit.); inf. T. Hardwick.

KRALL, Jakob (1857-1905)
Austrian Egyptologist; he was born in Volosca, Istria, 27 July 1857, son of Nicolaus K., an administrator; he was educated in Trieste, Athens, 1875-8, later at the University of Vienna, 1879-80; he then studied Egyptology at the Coll. de France and at the Louvre, 1880; he was appointed Professor Extraordinary in Vienna University, 1890, Ordinary, 1897, and full Professor, 1899; Corresp. Member, Vienna Acad., 1890; he made many important contributions to Egyptology, especially in the fields of chronology, Coptic Studies, and Demotic, notable amongst which is his edition of the Petubastis Story; *Studien zur Geschichte des alten Ägypten*, 1881-8; *Corpus papyrorum Raineri. Bd. 2. Koptische Texte*, 1895; *Demotische Lesestücke I. Der Demotische Theil der Inschrift von Rosette. Der Sethon-Roman. Der Leidener-Papyrus I 384. II. Das Dekret von Kanopos nach den Inschriften von Tanis und Kom el Hisn. Der Historische Roman aus der Zeit des Königs Petubastis*, fol. 1897-1903; *Grundriss der altorientalischen Geschichte*, 1899; his bibl. comprises about 70 nos.; he died in Vienna, 27 April 1905.

Rec. Trav. 28 (1906), 131-6 (bibl.) (K. A. Wiedemann); *WZKM* 19 (1905), 251-62 (D. H. Mueller); *ZÄS* 42 (1905), 86 (A. Erman); *ÖBL* 4, 202.

KRISTENSEN, William Brede (1867-1953)
Dutch orientalist and anthropologist of Norwegian origin; he was born at Kristianssand, Norway, 21 June 1867, son of Kristen K. and Karoline Emilie Björnson; he was educated at the Universities of Kristiana (Oslo) under Lieblein (q.v.) from 1885, Leiden, Paris, and London, 1887-1895; PhD at Oslo, 1896; reader in the History of Religion, Oslo, 1897; Professor for the History of Religion, Leiden, 1901-37; he made a special study of ancient religions and anthropology, including Egyptian beliefs; he wrote a number of articles relating to subjects such as the Osiris mysteries, the Egyptian Sphinx and the Cartouche ring, for which see bibl. listed below; his collected lectures were published as *The Meaning of Religion*, 1960; he died in Leiden, 25 Sept. 1953.

Chron. d'Ég. 29 (1954), 102 (anon.); *AEB* 1953, 999; *Ex Oriente Lux* 5 (1937-8), 284 (bibl.); II (1949-54), 265 (bibl.); *Wie is dat*, 1948, 290; H. Heerma van Voss, *Studies in Egyptian Religion*, 1982, 12-13; S.-A. Naguib in S. Hjelde, *Man, Meaning and Mystery*, 2000, 105-6.

KRUCHTEN, Jean-Marie (1944-2010)
Belgian Egyptologist; he was born in Uccle (Brussels), 23 Aug. 1944, son of Arthur K. and Louise Peters; he was educated at the Athénée d'Ixelles (Brussels), 1956-62 and then at the Université Libre of Brussels where he studied Law and Egyptology under Théodoridès (q.v.); MA in law, 1967 and in philology and oriental history, 1977; PhD, 1979; he was attached as a jurist to the Court of Audit of Belgium, 1967-2009 and succeeded Théodoridès as Professor of Egyptian Language at the Université Libre, 1981-2009; he was visiting Professor at the University of Copenhagen, 1994-5; he undertook epigraphic work at Elkab, 2005; he was particularly interested in the philology of the New Kingdom and the administration of the temples; apart from numerous articles, his principal works were *Le décret d'Horemheb*, 1981; *Etudes de syntaxe néo-égyptienne*, 1982; *Le grand texte oraculaire de Djéhoutymose, intendant du domaine d'Amon sous le pontificat de Pinedjem II*, 1986; *Les annales des prêtres de Karnak (21-23es dynasties) et autres textes contemporains relatifs à l'initiation des prêtres d'Amon*, 1989; and, with L. Delvaux, *Elkab VIII. La tombe de Sétaou*, 2010; he died in Brussels, 18 Aug. 2010 after a bicycle accident.

Inf. L. Limme; *Chron. d'Eg.* 86 (2011), 2-11 (portr.) (bibl.) (N. Braekman *et al*); *BSFE* 177-8 (2010), 2-3 (O. Perdu).

KRZYŻANIAK, Lech (1940-2004)
Polish archaeologist; he was born in Wilkowo, Szamotuly, 8 Feb. 1940, son of Leon K. and his wife Jadwiga; he was educated at Adam Mickiewicz University in Poznań, studying archaeology and prehistory; BA, 1962; PhD, 1968; Habilitation, 1975; he was appointed director of the Poznań Archaeological Museum from 1982 and taught at Poznań University; Professor 1992; he expanded the Poznań collection so that it became the second most important in Poland; he was also Vice-Director and later Chairman of the Research Council of Warsaw University Centre for Mediterranean Archaeology and a member of the UNESCO Executive committee for

Egyptian museums; he took part in excavations at Alexandria and in the Sudan at Old Dongola from 1966 and directed work at the Neolithic site of Kadero from 1975 ; he also took part in the German excavations at Minshat Abu Omar from 1977 and Naga from 1995; he undertook a survey of the Blue Nile area in 1985 and participated in the Fourth Nile Cataract archaeological rescue in Dec. 2003; in Egypt he acted as field director at Minshat Abu Omar from 1978 and was involved in the Dakhla Oasis Project researching African rock art, and the American excavations at Kom el-Hisn; he published *Early Farming Cultures on the lower Nile: the Predynastic Period in Egypt*, 1977; *Origin and Early Development of Food-Producing cultures in NE Africa*, 1984; and, with others, *Environmental Change and Human Culture in the Nile Basin and Northern Africa until the Second Millennium B.C.*, 1993; he died in Poznań, 10 July 2004.

Die Antiken Sudan 15 (2005), 196-7 (portr.) (M. Chiodnicki); internet obituary (R. Kolinski); *Sudan and Nubia* 9 (2005), 85-6 (portr.) (M. Kobusiewicz); *ZÄS* 132 (2005), XII (portr.) (D. Wildung); *Archeonil* 14 (2004), 5-9 (bibl.) (M. Chlodnicki).

KUENTZ, Charles (1895-1978)
French Egyptologist; he was born in New York, 18 June 1895, son of Joseph K. and Marie Styler; he studied at Lyons under Loret (q.v.) and the École Normale Supérieure, Paris, 1914-7; after teaching in various schools, notably at Dijon, he became a pensionnaire at the French Institute in Cairo, 1919-34; secretary and librarian, 1934-40 and finally director, 1940-53; he was also Professor in the Faculty of Law in Cairo University, 1923-8; he was named as Directeur de Recherches at CNRS in 1953 but remained in Cairo and was attached to the Centre of Documentation and took part in its work during the Nubian rescue campaign; he was a corresponding member of the Académie des Inscriptions et Belles Lettres from 1938, secretary-general of the Institut d'Égypte, and a member of the council of the Société d'Archéologie Copte; his principal works were *Recherches sur les poissons réprésentés dans quelques tombeaux égyptiens de l'Ancien Empire*, with C. Gaillard and V. Loret, 1923; *Deux stèles d'Amenophis II*, 1925; *La Tombe de Nakht-Min et la tombe d'Ari-Nefer*, with B. Bruyère, 1926; *La bataille de Qadech*, 1928-34; *Obélisques* in the *Catalogue General du Musée du Caire* series; *La porte d'Évergète à Karnak*, with P. Clère, 1961; *La face sud du massif est du pylone de Rameses II à Louxor, 1971; Le petit temple d'Abou Simbel,* with C. Desroches-Noblecourt, 1968; *Garf-Hussein*, II and III, with M. A. L. El-Tanbouli and A. A. Sadek, 1974 and 1975; he left several works in manuscript; he died in Cairo, 24 May 1978.

BIFAO 78 (1978), v (J. Vercoutter); 79 (1979), v-xvi (portr.) (bibl.) (M. Trad); *BSFE* 82 (1978), 4-5; *BSC* 24 (1978-82), 127 (M.B. Ghali); *Onoma* 23 (1979), 224-30 (bibl.) (G. Roquet); *BIÉ* 82 (1978), 4-5; *Annuaire. Association amicale des anciens élèves de l'École Normale Supérieure, Paris* 1979, 81-2 (J. Leclant).

KÜTHMANN, Carl (1885-1968)
German Egyptologist; he was born in Wendthöhe, 8 June 1885; he was educated at the Universities of Göttingen and Berlin under Meyer (q.v.) and Erman (q.v.); PhD, 1911; he was appointed research assistant at Kestner Museum, Hanover, 1911; assistant keeper, 1919 and director, 1920-38, 1945-51; he arranged the purchase of the von Bissing (q.v.) collection in 1935; he died in 1968.

C. Loeben in J. Arp-Neuman and T. Gertzen, '*Steininschrift und Bibelwort*', 2019, 59-64.

KYTICAS, Panayotis (*fl.* 1879-1824)
Cairo antiquities dealer of Greek origin; his shop was located opposite Shepheard's Hotel until 1896 when he moved just south of it; he supplied objects to Budge (q.v.) and to the Cairo Museum; he died in Cairo, 22/3 March 1924; his son Denis (*fl.* 1913-1930) took over his business.

Newberry Diary, 27 Sept. 1900; Myers Diary, 28 Feb. 1894, 4 and 28 March 1896; *RdE* 41 (1990), 32 and n. 8; F. Hagen and K. Ryholt, *The Antiquities Trade in Egypt 1880-1930*, 2017, 229-30

LABIB, Pahor Cladios (1905-1994)

Egyptian Coptologist; he was born at Ain Shams, Cairo 19 Sept. 1905, son of Prof. Cladios Labib, a Coptic scholar; he studied law and Egyptology at the University of Cairo, 1926-1930; BA, 1930; and at Berlin under Sethe (q.v.) and Grapow (q.v.) from 1932-7; PhD, 1937; lecturer at the University of Cairo from 1935; Professor of Ancient History at the University of Alexandria, 1941-2; a Keeper at the Cairo Museum from 1945; Director of Provincial Museums and Acting Director of the Coptic Museum, 1948; Director of the Coptic Museum in succession to Mina (q.v.), 1951-19 Sept. 1965; Acting-director of the Cairo Museum, 1964; he conducted excavations at Babylon in Cairo, 1949; Elephantine, 1951-2, and the shrine of St. Menas, 1961; Member of the High Council for antiquities; Member of the Institut d'Égypte, the German Archaeological Institute, and the Czech Archaeological Institute; Member of the Council of the Société d'Archéologie Copte from 1962; he was involved in the acquisition and later publication of the Nag Hammadi texts as a member of the committee for Facsimile Edition of the Nag Hammadi Codices; Hon. President of the International Association for Coptic Studies; apart from articles, publications in Arabic, and collaborative works with foreign scholars, his major publications were his thesis *Die Herrschaft der Hyksos in Ägypten und ihr Sturz*, 1936; *The Coptic Museum and the Fortress of Babylon of Old Cairo*, 1953 and subsequent eds; *The Coptic Gnostic Papyri in the Coptic Museum* Vol I, 1956; he died in Cairo, 7 May 1994.

M. Krause, *Essays on the Nag Hammadi Texts in Honour of Pahor Labib*, 1975, 1-3, 4-8 (bibl. by V. Girgis); E. Endesfelder, *Die Ägyptologie an der Berliner Universität-Zur Geschichte eines Fachgebietes*, 1988, 50; *Newsletter of the International Association for Coptic Studies* 34 (1994), 28; *Le Monde Copte* 24 (1994), 98; *Kemet* 3 no. 4 (1994), 27 (portr.); *BSAC* 34 (1995), 181-2 (W. Boutros-Ghali); *BSAC* 36 (1997), 1-4 (portr.) (bibl.) (V. Girgis).

LACAU, Pierre Lucien (1873-1963)

French Egyptologist; born at Brie-Comte-Robert, 25 Nov. 1873, son of Louis Clément L., an architect, and Lucie Adèle Belin; he at first entered the École Normale intending to take up geology and studied Natural Science at the Sorbonne; he then turned to philosophy taking his degree in this subject 1897, but studying oriental languages simultaneously; he learnt Hebrew and wrote an article on a text in this language in the *Revue d'Assyriologie* when he was only twenty-one; the influence of Maspero (q.v.) led him to study Coptic and Egyptian and he joined the Institut Français at his suggestion and began work for the Cairo general catalogue; he arrived in Egypt in 1899 and in 1901 published his first article on an Egyptian subject, *Textes de l'Ancien Testament en copte sahidique*, in the *Rec Trav*; his first volume for the *Catalogue Général* on the coffins in the museum in Cairo followed in 1906; in this work he not only revealed his philological knowledge in transcribing the texts, but also noted most carefully all the constructional details and provided useful diagrams as illustration; this work led him to become interested in religious texts and he published a series of articles on the Coffin Texts in *Rec Trav*, 26-37, which was of great importance before the appearance of the comprehensive work of de Buck (q.v.); he also wrote a number of articles on Egyptian grammar at this period; in 1912 Lacau was appointed Director of the IFAO in Cairo, 1912-34 and the following year was elected a member of the Institut Égyptien; on 7 Oct. 1914 he was appointed Director of the Antiquities Service, but delayed his departure to Egypt for war service until Sept. 1915 when he was sent back to Egypt so that he could arrange a proper administration for the Antiquities Service throughout the war period; this done he returned to France, 1916, after delegating his work to the Secretary-General G. Daressy (q.v.); he returned to Egypt in 1917 and resumed his duties; in 1919 he married Anne-Marie Bernard, daughter of the Geography Professor at the Sorbonne, and was made Director of the Institut Français; he was made a correspondant of the Acad. des Inscriptions et Belles-Lettres, 1923; in the period after the war Lacau issued directives for the partial uncovering of the funerary temples and their dependant buildings at Saqqara, and for the study of the Memphite tombs both architecturally and functionally, and for essential restoration and consolidation work to be carried out at Karnak; sondages were also to be made with a view to making possible the publication of all the completed parts; at the time of the discovery of the Tomb of Tutankhamun Lacau insisted on all the finds being retained in Egypt and secured the entire collection for the Egyptian Museum; he returned to France in 1936, and succeeded Moret (q.v.) in his chair in Paris, 1938-67; in 1939 he became a Member of the Acad. des Inscriptions et Belles-Lettres; after the war he paid three further visits to Egypt, 1950-4, and died in Paris, 27 March 1963; his principal works were, *Sarcophages antérieurs au Nouvel Empire*, 2 vols. 1904-6; *Fragments d'apocryphes coptes*, 1904; *Textes coptes en dialectes akhmimique et sahidique*, 1908; *Textes religieux égyptiens*, I pt. 1910; *Stèles du Nouvel Empire*, 2 vols. 1909, 1926, for *Cairo Cat.*; *Une stèle juridique de Karnak*, 1949; *Sur le système hiéroglyphique*, 1954; *Une chapelle de Sésostris Ier à Karnak*, with H. Chevrier, 1956; *La Pyramide à degrés*, tom. 4. *Inscriptions gravées sur les vases*, with J. P. Lauer,

2 pts., 1959, 1961; *Une chapelle d'Hatshepsout à Karnak*, with H. Chevrier, 2 vols., 1977, 1979; part of his archives are in the Centre W. Golénischeff in Paris while other papers have been loaned to Egyptological Archives of the Università degli Studi di Milano in 2009; he died in Paris, 27 March 1963.

ASAE 59 (1966), 33-52 (portr.) (J. P. Lauer); *Annuaire du Collège de France* 63 (1963), 39-41 (M. Bataillon); *AfO* 21 (1966), 272-3 (J. Leclant); *BIFAO* 62 (1964), 231-5 (F. Daumas); *Chron. d'Ég.* 38 (1966), 244-6 (B. van de Walle); *CRAIBL* 1963, 1964, 105-11 (P. Montet); *Rev. Arch.* 1963, ii, 55-8 (Ch. Picard); *Rev. d'Ég.* 15 (1963), 7-10 (portr.) (J. Sainte Fare Garnot); *Rev. de l'Histoire des Religions*, cxliv, no. 444 (1963), 128-31 (J. Sainte Fare Garnot); C. Charle and E. Telkes, *Les Professeurs du Collège de France, dictionnaire biographique 1910-39*, 1988, 117-8; P. Piacentini, *Egypt and the Pharaohs from the Sand to the Library*, 2010, 111-2; *DBF* 18, 1464

LACOUR, Pierre (1778-1859)

French painter and antiquarian; he was born at Bordeaux 16 March 1778, son of Pierre L., an artist, and Catherine Chauvet; he succeeded his father as director of the Musée des Beaux-Arts in Bordeaux; he became Professor at the École des peintures in Bordeaux and published *Essai sur les hiéroglyphes*, 1821, with 14 plates, followed by a larger work on the same subject; in these he attempted to prove the identity of Egyptian and Hebrew etymology; he died in Bordeaux, 17 April 1859.

BIFAO 5 (1906), 86; Hilmy, i, 352; *DBF* 19, 34-5.

LADISLAUS, (Padre) (1780-1828)

Italian missionary; he was born Rome, 8 Oct. 1780; he was educated at the Franciscan College 1798-1805; he went to Egypt in 1806; he was superior of the RC convent at Girga, one of the oldest in Egypt; he became interested in Egyptian antiquities and excavated at Abydos for Drovetti (q.v.); a gold sphinx, for which he paid 30 dollars, was confiscated by the local governor through the indiscretion of his servant; he entertained Linant de Bellefonds (q.v.) in 1821 and Robert Hay (q.v.) in 1826; he died in Girga, 30 June 1828; when Champollion (q.v.) visited the convent in late 1828, the superior was Padre Davielle di Procida, a Neapolitan.

Champollion, ii, 149; Linant Diary, 25 June 1821; Hay Diary, 7 May 1826; Minutoli, 111-3; G. Forni, *Viaggio nell Egitto e nell'alta Nubia*, 1859, i. 317; G. Golubovick, *Bibliotheca bio-bibliografica della Terra Santa e dell'Oriente Francescano*, Nuova Serie, 13, 363.

LAMACRAFT, Charles Tandy (1879-1945)

British restorer and mounter of manuscripts; he was born at Bromley, 23 May 1879, son of Charles L., cabinet maker, and Hannah Eliza Tandy; he was a skilful craftsman and was for many years attached to the Dept. of MSS, British Museum; but he also undertook much outside work; in addition to his work on vellum and paper MSS he unrolled and mounted many of the Egyptian, Coptic, and Greek papyri in the British Museum, and many papyri in other collections, such as those of Chester Beatty (q.v.) and Lord Amherst (q.v.); he died in Finchley, Middlesex, 3 March 1945.

Private inf.; Newberry Corr.

LAMBRUSCHINI, (Cardinal) (Emanuele Nicolo) Luigi (1776-1854)

Italian ecclesiastic; he was born at Sestri Levante, 16 May 1776, son of Bernardo L. and Pellegrina Raggi; he took his first vows, 1794 and became a priest, 1799; he taught theology at Bolgna, 1799-1800, Macerata, 1801, and Rome 1803; he became a member and later secretary of the Congregazione degli affari ecclesiastici straordinari, 1814-9; he served as archbishop of Genoa, 1819-30, and papal nuncio in Paris 1827-31; Cardinal 1831; secretary of State for Gregory XVI 1836-46; he was involved in the foundation of the Vatican Egyptian Museum and acquired antiquities for his own collection which was sold in Paris, 20-1 Nov. 1854; he died in Rome, 12 May 1854.

DBDI 63, 218-23; J. Leblanc, *Dictionnaire biographique des cardinaux du XIXe siècle*, 2007, 507-12 (bibl.); *Diz. It.* 20, 414; *New Catholic Ency.* 8, 346-7; B. van de Walle et al, *La Collection Égyptienne*, 1980, 13, 58; Lugt 22106.

LANCI, Michelangelo (1779-1867)

Italian orientalist; he was born at Palestrina, 22 Oct. 1779; he became a priest, 1800 and Professor of Arabic Language at La Sapienza University in Rome; he was an opponent of Champollion; he died in Rome, 30 Sept. 1867.

Enc. It.; Champollion, i, 223.

LANE, Edward William (1801-1876)

British Arabic scholar; he was born in Hereford, 17 Sept. 1801, son of Theophilus L., a military officer and prebendary of Hereford Cathedral, and Sophia Gardiner; after being educated at the Grammar Schools of Bath and Hereford, he joined his brother in London as an engraver, but abandoned that career owing to ill health; he learned Arabic and went to Egypt, 19 Sept. 1825-7 April 1828, where he spent most of his time in Cairo although making voyages up the Nile from 15 March-28 Oct. 1826 where he went as far as the Second Cataract, and 23 June-19 Dec. 1827 with Hay (q.v.) up to Abu Simbel; he left in MS a voluminous description and a large number of drawings (BL Add. MSS 34080-8: others in the Griffith Inst. Oxford); he returned to Egypt from 13 Dec. 1833-29 Aug. 1835; Lane spoke Arabic fluently and in 1836 published *Manners and Customs of the Modern Egyptians*, a companion work by Wilkinson (q.v.) which dealt with the Ancients being published later; he was in Egypt again, 19 July 1842-16 Oct, 1849, when he compiled his great Arabic dictionary, *An Arabic-English Lexicon*, for which funds were provided by Algernon Percy, the Duke of Northumberland (q.v.), which appeared in parts from 1863-93; Lane was the leading Arabic scholar of Europe, and although his works are primarily concerned with the modern Egyptians, they are of great value to Egyptologists as he was closely associated with Hay (q.v.) and Wilkinson (q.v.); he was elected a corresponding member of the Académie des Inscriptions et Belles Lettres, 16 Dec. 1864; his collection of antiquities was acquired by the British Museum in 1842; there is a MS collection of his letters in the Bodleian Library and the Griffith Institute, Oxford; he also translated *The Thousand and One Nights*, 1839-41; *Selections from the Kur-án, 1843; Forty-one Eastern Tales and Anecdotes*, 1854; posthumously *Cairo Fifty Years Ago*, 1896; his unpublished work, *Description of Egypt* was edited and published by J. Thompson, 2000; he died in Worthing, 10 Aug. 1876.

ODNB 32, 418-9 (portr.); S. Lane-Poole, 'Life of Edward William Lane' in pt. vi of the *Arabic-English Lexicon*, 1877; *ILN* 69 (1876), 213 (portr.); *DNB* 32, 71; Hilmy, i, 355; A. C. E. Franquet de Franqueville, *Le Premier Siècle de l'Institut de France*, 1895, II, 273; L. Ahmed, *Edward W. Lane*, 1978; J. Thompson, *Turkish Studies Association Bulletin* 17 (1993), 138-41; J. Thompson, *Gainsborough's House Review* (1993/4), 33-42; J. Thompson, *NARCE* 166 (1994-5), 1-5; J. Thompson, *Minerva* 6 Sept/Oct 1995, 12-7; J. Thompson, *JARCE* 34 (1997), 243-61; D. S. Richards, *Journal of the Royal Asiatic Society* 3rd ser. 9 (1999), 1-25; J. Rodenbeck in P. and J. Starkey, *Travellers in Egypt*, 1998, 233-243 and G. Roper, in *ibid.*, 244-54; J. Speake (ed.), *Literature of Travel and Exploration*, 2003, 2, 692-4; J. Thompson, *Edward William Lane, 1801-1876. The Life of the Pioneering Egyptologist and Orientalist*, 2010; A. Bednarski in W. Carruthers (ed.), *Histories of Egyptology*, 2015, 84-6.

LANGE, Hans Ostenfeldt (1863-1943)

Danish Egyptologist; he was born in Århus, 13 Oct. 1863, son of Hans L., merchant, and Catherine Marie Ostenfeldt; he studied Egyptology under Valdemar Schmidt (q.v.) at the University of Copenhagen, 1881-5; he was made Assistant Librarian in the Royal Library, 1 Oct. 1885; Chief Librarian, 1901; he studied with Erman (q.v.) at Berlin, 1886-7; he worked on the catalogue of the Cairo Museum, 1899-1900; in 1903 he first showed the importance of the Leiden papyrus of Ipuwer; he published the Middle Kingdom Stelae in the Cairo Cat. series, and with Erman edited the Lansing Papyrus; Lange did much to promote the study of Egyptology in Denmark, and in 1924 he founded and directed an Egyptological Institute in Copenhagen; he acquired antiquities for Danish museums during his trips to Egypt in 1899-1900 and 1929-30; he was also connected with the publications *Analecta Aegyptiaca consilio Instituti Aegyptologici Hofniensis edita*; besides assisting with the Berlin Dictionary he also contributed to *ZÄS* and other journals; he was made a member of the Order of the Dannebrog, 1906; his main works were, *Grab- und Denksteine des Mittleren Reichs*, 4 vols., Cairo Cat., with H. Schäfer, 1902-25; *Religiose Tekster fra det gamle Aegypten: i Dansk Oversaettelse ...* , 1921; *Das Weisheitsbuch des Amenemope*, 1925; *Papyrus Lansing, eine ägyptische Schulhandschrift der 20. Dynastie*, 1925; *Der Magische Papyrus Harris*, 1927; *Fra det gamle Aegyptens kultur og historie: historiske texter efter originalerne, med indledning og noter ...* , 1928; *Papyrus Carlsberg No. I, ein hieratisch-demotischer kosmologischer Text*, with O. Neugebauer, 1940; he died in Gentofte, 15 Jan. 1943.

Chron. d'Ég. 19 (1944), 259-61 (J. Capart); *Dansk Biografisk Leksikon* 8, 481-3; F. Hagen and K. Ryholt, *The Antiquities Trade in Egypt 1880-1930. The H. O. Lange Papers*, 2017, 296-9.

LANGE, Kurt Eberhard (1898-1959)

German art historian; he was born in Berlin, 25 Feb. 1898; he published a book dealing with the art of the Amarna age, *König Echnaton und die Amarna-Zeit. Die Geschichte eines Gottkünders*, 1951; also, with Max Hirmer, a general study of Egyptian art and monuments, *Aegypten*, 1955; he died in Oberstdorf-im-Allgau, 1959.

AfO 19 (1959-60), 270.

LANGTON, Henry Neville Scott (1874-1948)

British collector; born 8 Harley St., London, 30 May 1874, son of John, surgeon, and Sophie Scott; he was educated at Westminster and Trinity College, Cambridge; he was for many years prior to his retirement private secretary to Lord Knutsford; he took a keen interest in Egyptian archaeology but ill health prevented his working in Egypt; helped by his wife he formed a collection of figurines illustrating the cult of cats in ancient Egypt, which was exhibited in London (see references below) and is now in the Petrie Museum, University College London; he produced a book *The Cat in Ancient Egypt*, 1940; he was secretary of the London Hospital for some years; he died in Bassetts Storrington, Sussex, 30 June 1948.

Inf. Mrs. Langton; *Chron. d'Ég.* 25 (1950), 86; EES *Report*, 1948, 7-8; *JEA* 22 (1936), 115-20.

LANSING, Ambrose (1891-1959)

American Egyptologist and museum curator; he was born in Cairo, Egypt, 20 Sept. 1891, son of Joseph McCarrell L. and Isabella Strang; although a national by birth he went to the USA first in 1904; he studied at Washington Jefferson College; BA, 1911, later becoming a student at Leipzig University under G. Steindorff (q.v.) during the summers of 1912-14; Doctor of Humane Letters, Bowdoin College, 1948; he married Caroline Cox, 1923; he entered the Metropolitan Museum of Art in New York in 1911, becoming assistant curator of the Department of Egyptian Art, 1922-6; associate curator, 1926-39, and Curator, 1939; he was associated with the arrangement of its collections and with its excavations, and participated in field archaeology in Egypt between 1911 and 1922; he was especially connected with the work at the Malkata palace of Amenhotep III, and he contributed articles to the *BMMA*, also one to *JEA*; he died in Apache Junction, Arizona, 28 May 1959.

AFO 19 (1959-60), 270; *WWWA* iii, 499.

LANSING, (*Revd*) **Gulian** (1825-1892)

American missionary of Dutch origin; he was born in Lishaskill, Albany County, NY, 1 Feb. 1825, son of John L. and Elizabeth Groat; he graduated from Union College, 1847, and joined the Associated Reformed Church; he was ordained 1850 and went as missionary to the Jews at Damascus; in 1856 he went to Egypt where he remained for the greater part of the rest of his life; he was a good Hebrew and Arabic scholar; he published *Egypt's Princes: a Narrative of Missionary Labour in the Valley of the Nile*, NY, 1865; in 1886 his health failed and he spent much time in England and America, but returned to Cairo; Lansing's name is associated with a fine literary papyrus, acquired from him by the British Museum in 1886 (EA 9994); in the following year, on the recommendation of Renouf (q.v.), the British Museum purchased from him a large number of Coptic papyri (EA 10128-42); he died in Cairo, 12 Sept. 1892.

DAB 10, 607-8; Budge, *N & T*, i, 411; Sayce, 337; *WWWA hist. vol.*, 303.

LANZONE, Rodolfo Vittorio (1834-1907)

Italian Egyptologist and Arabist; he was born in Cairo, 1834, son of Luigi L., a doctor; he was appointed to the staff of the Turin Museum, 1872-95; he collected and sold antiquities, selling a collection to John Pitcairn (q.v.); a gold-inlaid bronze statuette of Osorkon I from his collection is now in the Brooklyn Museum (57.92); his principal publications were, *Dizionario di mitologia egizia*, 3 vols. autographed, 1881-6, re-edited by M. Tosi (q.v.) with a fourth volume, 1974-5; *Le Domicile des Esprits*, 1879; *Les papyrus du Lac Moeris*, 1896; he died Aug. 1907.

Enc. It. 20, 517 (G. Farina); M. Tosi (ed.), *Dizionario di mitologia egizia* 4,1975, vii-xii (portr.); S. Curto, *L'Egitto nei libri e nelle immagini della Biblioteca Reale di Torino*, 1991; È. Gran-Aymerich, *Dictionnaire biographique d'archéologie 1798-1945*, 2001, incorporated in *Les Chercheurs de passé 1798-1945*, 2007, 919; inf. T. Hardwick.

LANZONI, Giuseppe (1663-1730)

Italian physician and philosopher; he was born at Ferrara, 29 Oct. 1663 (or 29 Oct, 1665), and from 1696 until his death was Professor of Philosophy at the University there; he published a work on embalming at Geneva, *Tractatus de Balsamatione Cadaverum*, 1696, which dealt very fully with the art of mummification; he died at Ferrara, 1 Feb. 1730.

Mem. Inst. Ég. 13, 25; Hilmy, i, 357; Garollo, *Diz. Biogr. Univ.*

LARKING, John Wingfield (1802-1891)
British merchant and diplomat; he was born in East Malling, Kent, 20 March 1802, son of John L., Sheriff of Kent, and Dorothy Style; he became a merchant at Alexandria in association with Briggs (q.v.) who married his sister Camilla as his second wife in 1835; he was named British consul at Alexandria 1838-41 in succession to Thurburn (q.v.); he had a collection of Egyptian antiquities, one of which, a sphinx with the cartouche of Merenre, was seen by Wilkinson (q.v.); it was given in 1849 to Lady Alford daughter of the Marquess of Northampton (q.v.) and is now in the National Museum of Scotland, Edinburgh; the rest of the collection was sold at Sotheby's 21 Dec. 1891; he died in Lee, Kent, 18 May 1891.

Walford's *County Families* 1868, 652; Wilkinson, *Manners* iii, 310; Boase 2, 307; C. Aldred in *Studies I. E. S. Edwards*, 41-7; inf. Mrs. P. Rée.

LARREY, *(Baron)* **(Jean) Dominique** (1766-1842)
French surgeon; he was born in Baudéan near Bagnères de Bigorre, 8 July 1766, son of Jean L., a shoe manufacturer, and Philipinne Perès; he was surgeon-in-chief to the French army, and a member of Napoleon's Commission in Egypt; member Inst. Ég.; he contributed to the *Description de l'Égypte* and published medical works; his treatise on military surgery was translated into English by J. Waller, 1815; he brought back a collection of antiquities, some of which are in the Louvre; he died in Lyons, 25 July 1842.

DBF 19, 1086-9; *NBG* 29, 686-94; P. Triaire, *Napoléon et Larrey*, 1902; Carré, i, 145, 149; *Rev. de l'Art*, 43. 280; Hilmy, i, 358; A. Soubiran, *Le Baron Larrey*, 1966; *DBF* 19, 1086-7

LAUER, Jean-Philippe Charles (1902-2001)
French Egyptologist and architect; he was born in Paris, 7 May 1902, son of Philippe L., a keeper in the Dept. of MSS in the Bibliothèque nationale, and Marie Eclancler; he was educated at the Ecole nationale supérieure des Beaux-Arts, obtaining his diploma in architecture; he was appointed architect at Saqqara for the Egyptian Antiquities Service, July 1926 as assistant to Firth (q.v.); he became director of Works at the pyramid of Djoser at Saqqara, 1931-9, 1945-56 and thereafter adviser to the Antiquities Service at Saqqara to his death; Maître de recherche at CNRS, 1957; Directeur de recherche, 1964-73; Hon Directeur from 1973; Vice-President of the Institut d'Egypte and the Société française d'Egyptologie; Corresponding Fellow of the Académie des Inscriptions et Belles-Lettres 1956, the British Academy and the Fondation Reine Elisabeth in Brussels; Member of the German Archaeological Institute and the Czech Institute of Charles University; he was made a member of the Légion d'honneur and the order of the Republic of Egypt; he was awarded the medal of archaeology by Sociéte Centrale des architectes de France in 1929 and by the Académie d'architecture in 1989 and the Prix quinquennal Gaston Maspero in 1977; in 1929 he married Marguerite, daughter of Jouget (q.v.); he devoted his career to the necropolis at Saqqara especially the restoration of the step-pyramid of Djoser; apart from numerous articles, he published *La pyramide à degrés*, 5 vols, 1936-65; *Le problème des pyramides d'Égypte*, 1948; *Études complémentaires sur les monuments du roi Zoser à Saqqarah*, 1948; *Le temple haut du complexe funéraire de Teti,* with J. Leclant, 1972; *Sakkarah: les monuments de Zoser*, with E. Drioton, 1939; 5th ed. 1977; *Les statues ptolémaïques du Sarapieion de Memphis*, with C. Picard, 1955; *Observations sur les pyramides*, 1960; *Histoire monumentale des pyramides d'Égypte I*, 1962; *Le temple haut du complexe funéraire du roi Teti*, with J. Leclant, 1972; *Le Mystère des pyramides*, 1974; 2nd ed. 1988; *Saqqara. The Royal Cemetery of Memphis*, 1976; French ed. *Saqqareh. La nécropole royale de Memphis*, 1977; *Le temple haut du complexe funéraire du roi Ounas*, with J. Leclant and A. Labrousse, 1977; *Les complexes funéraires d'Ouserkaf et de Néferhétepès*, with A. Labrousse, 2000; *L'Architecture des pyramides à textes*, 2000; *Je suis né en Égypte il ya 4700 ans*, 2000; he died in Paris, 15 May 2001.

WWF 2000, 1037; *Le Monde* 18 May 2001, 33 (A. Buccianti); C. Le Tourneur d'Ison, *Une Passion égyptienne*, 1996; *BSFE* 151 (2001), 5-10; A. Zivie, *KMT* 12/3 (2001), 18-20; C. Le Tourneur d'Ison, *Lauer et Saqqara*, 2000.

LAUFFRAY, Jean Louis Raymond Marie (1909-2000)
French architect; he was born at Alençon 23 June 1909, son of Pierre L. and Jeanne Lahaye; he studied at the Institut d'art et d'archéologie de Paris, the École du Louvre, and the École supérieure des beaux arts, obtaining a diploma in architecture; he became site architect for the excavation at Mari, Syria in 1936; he became inspector of antiquities in Lebanon, 1941 and was attached to the Aleppo Museum from 1942; he was chief architect for the Syrian Antiquities Service, 1944-51 when he worked primarily at Byblos from 1947 and Sidon; he was also

Professor of architecture at the École normale des beaux arts at Beirut, 1950; he returned to France to become architect for the bâtiments de France at Pau, 1951-61; maître de recherche at CNRS, 1963; he was sent to Karnak in 1961 to head the team of French architects restoring the temple; Maître de Recherche at CNRS, 1963-73; Directeur de Recherche, from 1973; he became director of the Centre franco-égyptien d'Étude des Temples de Karnak on its foundation in 1967 to 1978; adviser to UNESCO on the restoration of Beirut; Maître de recherche honoraire at CNRS from 1980; he published in the field of Egyptology *Karnak d'Égypte. Domaine du divin*, 1979; and *La Chapelle d'Achôris à Karnak I*, 1995; he died at Calvados, 5 March 2000.

Le Monde 14 March 2000; *BSFE* 147 (2000), 4; WWF 2000, 1037-8; *Syria* 78 (2001), 221 (portr.) (H. de Contenson).

LAURIN, (*Ritter von*) **Anton Joseph** (1789-1869)
Austrian diplomat; he was born in Wippach (Vipava), 21 Jan. 1789, son of Bartholomaeus L. and Josefa Urschich; Consul-General in Egypt 1834-49, afterwards Consul at Bucharest; he was succeeded in Egypt by von Huber (q.v.); he presented two sarcophagi and other objects to the Egyptian Dept. of the Kunsthistorisches Museum, Vienna and buried his parents and son in two Old Kingdom sarcophagi at Vipava; he presented a mummy and coffin to the Museum at Ljubljana; part of his collection was acquired for the Miramar collection; he died in Milan, 12 June 1869.

Rec Trav 6, 131; Vyse, i, 148, 228; ii, 154; inf. G. Hamernik.

LAUTH, Franz Joseph (1822-1895)
German Egyptologist; he was born in Anzheim, 18 Feb. 1822, son of Franz Josef L., a farmer, and Barbara Siener; he studied at the University of Munich and was afterwards made a professor there, 1869; he was a member of the Munich Acad., 1866, but resigned 1882; he made many contributions to the literature of Egyptology, but although he was a brilliant scholar, he was too fond of forming hypotheses on insecure bases, and, although an acute and often enterprising writer, his work was unsound; it was, however, widely read during the nineteenth century and was of considerable importance in certain fields; his principal publications were, *Les Zodiaques de Denderah: mémoire où l'on établit que ce sont des calendriers commemoratifs de l'époque Gréco-Romaine*, 1865; *Catalogue raisonné der in München befindlichen Denkmäler des Ägyptischen Alterthums*, 1865; *Manetho und der Turiner Königs-Papyrus: unter sich mit den Denkmälern und andern Urkunden verglichen und kritisch geprüft ...* , 1865; *Papyrus Prisse*, 3 pts., 1869-70; *Die zweite älteste Landkarte nebst Gräberplänen*; 1871; *Die Pianchi-Stele*, 1871; *Altägyptische Lehrsprüche*, 1872; *Ueber die altägyptische Hochschule von Chennu*, 1872; *Ueber altägyptische Musik*, 1873; *Die Sothis oder Siriusperiode der alten Aegypter*, 1874; *Die Schaltage des Ptolemäus Euergetes I und des Augustus*, 1874; *König Nechepsos, Petosiris, und die Triakontäeteris*, 1875; *Ein neuer Kambyses-Text*, 1875; *Aegyptische Chronologie basiert auf die vollständige Reihe der Epochen seit Bytes-Menes bis Hadrian-Antonin, durch drei volle Sothis-perioden = 4380 Jahre*, 1877; *Augustus-Harmais*, 1877; *Die ägyptische Teträeteris*, 1878; *Sipthas und Amenmeses*, 1879; *Moses-Hosarsyphos Sali'Hus Levites-A'Haron frater, Ziphorah-Dabariah conjux, Miriam-Bellet soror, Elisheba-Elizabat fratria. Ex monumento inferioris Aegypti per ipsum Mosen ab hinc annos MMMCD. etc.*, 1879; *Aus Aegyptens Vorzeit: eine übersichtliche Darstellung der ägyptischen Geschichte und Cultur, von den ersten Anfängen bis auf Augustus*, 1881; *Die Phoenixperiode*, 1881; he died in Munich, 11 Feb. 1895.

Dawson MS 18, f. 91; Chabas, 49; Hilmy, i, 359; ii, 429; *NDB* 13, 741-2.

LAVALETTE, (*Marquis de*) **Charles Jean Marie Felix** (1806-1881)
French diplomat; he was born Senlis (Oise), 25 Nov. 1806, son of Jean Louis Achille de L. and Marie Eleanore Carteron de Moutiers; French Consul-General in Egypt in 1844; he was afterwards attached to the French Embassy in London, from which he was recalled in 1870; he died in Paris, 2 May 1881.

French FO Records; Carré, ii, 28; *DBF* 19, 1518

LAVER, Charles (*fl.* 1828-40)
British artist and engraver; he specialized in architectural subjects and published (with M. Dunnage) *Great Hall of the Royal Palace of Eltham*, 1828; he was recommended to Robert Hay (q.v.) by Edward Lane (q.v.) as a suitable artistic replacement for Joseph Bonomi (q.v.), and in his turn recommended Owen Carter (q.v.) as colleague; he worked with Hay in Cairo and along the Nile 1829-1832; he produced not only detailed architectural drawings and camera lucida sketches but all the expedition's hieroglyphic copies; when not ill, he quarrelled repeatedly with Hay over his salary and was ultimately dismissed; nevertheless the sketches produced by himself, Carter and Hay formed the basis of Hay's *Illustrations of Cairo*, 1840.

Hay Diary during dates above; letters, Lane to Hay of similar dates in Bodleian Library; S. Tillett, *Egypt Itself*, Chaps. 4 and 5; inf. S. Tillett.

LAVERS, Ralph Stephenson (1907-1969)
British architect and illustrator; he was born in Broken Hill, New South Wales, 7 Aug. 1907, son of Henry Lavers, later of Buckhurst Hill, Essex, and his wife Lillian E.; he studied at Architectural Association Schools, Sept. 1924-July 1929; he became an Associate of the Royal Institute of British Architects, Sept. 1930; he worked on the Amarna excavation under Pendlebury (q.v.), 1931-37; he also took part in excavations in Crete and at Alalakh under Woolley (q.v.); he designed the torch holder for London Olympics, 1948; he illustrated a mural for the Science Museum in London; he illustrated several books, notably *Nefertiti Lived Here*, by Mary Chubb (q.v.), 1954; he died at Hastings, 8 March 1969.

Archives of RIBA; *Building Magazine* 216, 28 March 1969, 13/71.

LAVISON, Prosper de (1791-1840+)
French diplomat; he was born in Marseilles, 1791, son of Jean Joseph Antoine de L. and Marie Anne Reboul; Chancellor and dragoman to the Russian Consulate in Egypt; acting Consul-General for Russia from Feb. 1831 to Sept. 1832; he received Champollion (q.v.) in Egypt in 1828; in 1840 he presented a papyrus to the Hermitage Museum (1113); Cattaui wrongly identifies him with his son Édouard de Lavison (1822-89), who also held the post of consul.

R. Cattaui, *Le Règne de Mohamed Aly*, passim; Champollion, ii, 25, 199; Geneanet pedigree which wrongly gives 1831 as his death date).

LAVORATORI, Maria (*d.*1832)
Italian wife of a merchant of Trieste; her husband was in Egypt 1818-22 and acted as deputy for Salt during his absence from Cairo; he formed a collection of antiquities, which, after his death in Cairo, were sent to Leghorn; this collection was owned by his wife in Florence, 1822-32, but on her death it was sent to London where it was sold at Sotheby's, 13-15 May 1833 (373 lots); some items were purchased by the British Museum (including the papyrus EA 9941) and many by Dr. Lee (q.v.); his copy of the sale catalogue is now in the Griffith Institute and contains a note on which the above is partly based.

Champollion, i, 245; Madox, i, 107; *sale cat.* ut supra; Lugt 13310.

LAWRENCE, Thomas Edward (1888-1935)
British traveller and archaeologist; also known as Shaw, Ross, and 'Lawrence of Arabia'; he was born in Tremadoc, N. Wales, 15 Aug. 1888, illegitimate son of Thomas Robert Chapman, who had assumed the name of Lawrence, and Sarah Junner; he was educated at Oxford High School and Jesus College, Oxford, BA, 1911; at this time he wrote a thesis later published as *Crusader Castles*, 1936; in 1911 he joined D. G. Hogarth (q.v.) and Sir Leonard Woolley (q.v.) at Carchemish, assisting on these excavations until 1914; in 1914 he took part in a mapping project in Sinai for the Palestine Exploration Fund; during this period he joined Petrie (q.v.) for most of the season 1911-12 at Kafr Ammar helping on the large cemetery site; for details of his later career see bibl. below; Lt.-Col., 1918; served on the British Delegation at the Peace Conference, 1919; Adviser on Arab Affairs, Middle East Division, Colonial Office, 1921-2; his experiences in Sinai led to the publication of *The Wilderness of Sin*, 1915; he later joined the RAF under the name of J. H. Ross, 1922, served on the NW frontier of India, was recalled, 1928, and served as an aircraftman until Feb. 1935; he died in Bovington Camp Hospital, 19 May 1935 after a motor-cycle accident.

Petrie, *Tarkhan* I *and Memphis* V; Petrie, *Heliopolis, Kafr Ammar and Shurafa*, I; *AE* vol. U., 72 (Petrie); *Seven Pillars of Wisdom*, 1935; *DNB* 1931-1940, 528-31 (R. Storrs); *WWW* iii, 1226; *ODNB* 32, 865-7; É. Gran-Aymerich, *Dictionnaire biographique d'archéologie 1798-1945*, 2001, incorporated in *Les Chercheurs de passé 1798-1945*, 2007, 926; A. Sattin, *Young Lawrence: A Portrait of the Legend as a Young Man*, 2014; N. Faulkner, *Lawrence of Arabia's War*, 2016.

LAYCOCK, Ruth Ann (*née* **Bates**) (1840-1898)
British benefactoress; she was born at Bradford, 20 June 1840, daughter of Joshua Bates, merchant, and Mary Jowett, she married 25 Aug. 1869 James Akenhead Laycock, who was born at Harewood 11 Oct. 1845, son of Joshua L., clergyman, and Eleanor Akenhead; he was educated at Worcester College, Oxford, matric. 1864; BA, 1869; MA, 1871; he died in Halifax 17 July 1890; his widow, by her will dated 22 Aug. 1890, founded an Egyptological Studentship at Worcester College in memory of her husband; this became effective in 1900, after her death at Scarborough 19 Oct. 1898, when the first Laycock student, D. Randall MacIver (q.v.), was appointed.

EEF *Arch. Rep.* 1900-1, 53; inf. Bursar of Worcester College.

LEAKE, William Martin (1777-1860)
British army officer and traveller; he was born in London 14 Jan. 1777, son of John Martin L., Chester Herald, and Mary Calvert; he was educated at the Royal Military Academy, Woolwich; Lt. in the artillery, 1794; Capt. 1799; Major; Lt.-Col., 1813; retired 1823; in 1799-1800 he was sent on a mission to Constantinople during which time he toured parts of Asia Minor; in 1801 he reached Egypt with the Turkish forces and in 1801-2 accompanied W. R. Hamilton (q.v.) on his tour of Egypt and Syria; Leake's papers were all lost in a shipwreck on his return to England in 1802; in 1805-10 he was stationed in Greece and Albania; Hon. DCL Oxford, 1816; fellow of the Royal Society, Royal Geographic Society and the Royal Society of Literature; member of the committee of the African Association; he edited Burckhardt's *Travels in Nubia*, 1819 and *Travels in Syria and the Holy Land*, 1822; he published an article on Egyptian antiquities in England with C. Yorke, (q.v.) and a map of Egypt, 1840; he died in Brighton, 6 Jan. 1860; his papers are now in the Hertford County Record Office, Hertford.

ODNB 32, 982-3; *DNB* 32, 323-4; Boase, 2, 342; *Anatolian Studies* 37 (1987), 23-28; M. Wagstaff in S. Searight, *Travellers in the Levant*, 2001, 3-16; H. Ferguson, *ibid.,* 17-34; D. Huxley, *ibid.*, 35-41; J. Speake (ed.), *Literature of Travel and Exploration*, 2003, 2, 704-6.

LEAR, Edward (1812-1888)
British artist and author; he was born Holloway, London, 12 May 1812, son of Jeremiah L., stockbroker, and Ann Clark Skerrett; although best known for his nonsense verses for children, Lear was also an accomplished artist and sketcher, and made drawings of Egypt and Nubia when he visited the Nile valley during 1849, 1853-4, and 1866-7; these, although not as widely known as his illustrations of Palestine, are nevertheless of considerable interest; he died in San Remo, 29 Jan. 1888.

ODNB 32, 994-1000 (portr.); *DNB* 32, 325-6; *EB* 13, 858-9; V. Noakes, *Edward Lear,* 1968; P. Levi, *Edward Lear*, 1995; G. Khatib in S. Searight (ed.), *Travellers in the Levant*, 2001, 197-214; J. Speake (ed.), *Literature of Travel and Exploration*, 2003, 2, 706-8.

LEBAS, Jean Baptist Apollinaire (1797-1873)
French engineer; he was born, Le Luc (Var), 13 Aug. 1797, son of Joseph Charles L. and Thérèse Christine Ferrier; he was educated at the École Polytechnique, Paris; he joined the Corps of Marine Engineers, 1818; he lowered the Luxor obelisk and transported it to Paris where it now stands in the Place de la Concorde, 1831; he published a detailed account of this operation illustrated by 15 plates, *L'Obélisque de Luxor: histoire de sa translation à Paris*, etc., Paris, 1839; he was Keeper of the Marine Museum of the Louvre, 1836-52; Member of the Légion d'honneur; he died in Paris, 1 Jan. 1873.

B. Dibner, *Moving the Obelisks* (1950), 56; Bonomi Diary, 1831; *DBF* 20, 285; Hilmy, i, 361; *NBG* 30, 69.

LEBOLO, (Giovanni Pietro) Antonio (1781-1830)
Italian excavator and adventurer; he was born Castellamonte, Piedmont, 27 Jan. 1781, son of Pietro L., grocer, and Marianna Meuta; he served as a police officer under the Bonapartist administration and on its overthrow went to Egypt where he excavated at Thebes for Drovetti (q.v.) and also on his own account; he found a number of mummies in a pit-tomb at Qurna; the best of these now in Turin went to Drovetti; Berlin 504, 505; two sent to Minutoli (q.v.) were of the Roman period but were lost at sea; one went to Cailliaud (q.v), another to Anastasi (q.v.), and one he kept for himself; several were acquired by Salt (q.v.), and then by the British Museum in 1823 (EA 6705-6, 6708, and 6950); further ones appear to have been received in America by the Mormon prophet Joseph Smith in 1835, from a Michael H. Chandler (q.v.); an account of these mummies was written by Quintino de San Giulio, *Lezioni archeologiche* (Turin, 1824), 25; the paper was read in the Acad. of Turin in the presence of Champollion (q.v.); Lebolo was very hostile to Belzoni (q.v.), who was working for Salt, and Belzoni claims that in company with Rosignani (q.v.), also employed by Drovetti, they made a violent assault upon him at Karnak with the intent of frightening him away or possibly even of murdering him; he afterwards endeavoured by a trick to secure some antiquities at Philae that belonged to Belzoni; he left Egypt about 1822 and died in Castellamonte, 18 Feb. 1830.

Inf. J. M. Todd and H. D. Peterson, Salt Lake City; Athanasi, 51; Belzoni, i, 235, 237, 239; ii, 107; *Oudheidkundige Mededeelingen*, Leiden, N.S. xxiii, 31; Salt, ii, 23.

LECLANT, Jean (1920-2011)
French Egyptologist; he was born in Paris, 8 Aug. 1920, son of René L., a merchant and Laurence Pannier; he studied at the École normale supérieure, 1940-5 and the École pratique des hautes études, 1953; Dr ès lettres, 1963; he was attached to CNRS, 1946-8 and served at IFAO, 1948-52; he directed a mission to Ethiopia, 1952; he became lecturer, 1953-5 and then professor, 1955-63 at the University of Strasbourg; he was appointed

Professor of Egyptology at the Sorbonne, 1963-79 and director of studies at the the École pratique des hautes études, 1964-90; he became Professor of Egyptology at the Collège de France, 1979-90; he excavated at Axum, 1952-6; Karnak, Saqqara from 1963-99; Soleb, 1960-78; and Sedeinga from 1979; he produced the annual 'Fouilles et travaux en Égypte et au Soudan' in the periodical *Orientalia,* 1948-2002; editor of the *Meroitic Newsletter* and *Annales d'Éthiopie,* 1955-72; Grand Officer of the Légion d'honneur; Member of the Académie des inscriptions et belles-lettres, 3 May 1974 and its secrétaire perpétuel, 24 June 1983; Vice-President of the Sociéte française d'égyptologie, 1965; President, 1970-9; he was head of the Advisory Committee on overseas excavations, 1973-88; Vice-President of the French section of UNESCO; his principal publications were *Enquêtes sur les sacerdoces et les sanctuaires égyptiens à l'époque dite Éthiopienne (XXVe dynastie),* 1954; with others, *Karnak-nord* IV, 1954; *In the Steps of the Pharaohs,* 1958; *Montouemhat, Quatrième Prophète d'Amon,* 1961; *Recherches sur les monuments thébains de la XXVe dynastie dite 'éthiopienne',* 1965; with others, *Soleb* I-II, 1965-71; with J.-P. Lauer, *Mission archéologique de Saqqarah I. Le temple haut du complexe funéraire du roi Téti,* 1972; with G. Clerc, *Inventaire bibliographique des Isiaca,* 1972-4; with others, *Mission archéologique de Saqqarah II. Le temple haut du complexe funéraire du roi Ounas,* 1977; with others, *Le temps des pyramides,* 1978; *Recherches dans la pyramide et au temple haut du Pharaon Pépi Ier à Saqqarah,* 1979; with R. Parker and J.-C. Goyon, *The Edifice of Taharqa by the Sacred Lake of Karnak,* 1979; with others, *l'Empire des conquérants,* 1979, with others, *L'Égypte du crépuscule,* 1980; *De l'égyptophilie à l'égyptologie,* 1985; with H. Fischer, *L'écriture et l'art de l'Égypte ancienne. Quatre leçons sur la palaéographie et l'épigraphie pharaoniques,* 1986; with A. Zivie, *Memphis et ses nécropoles au Nouvel Empire,* 1988; with J.-P. Lauer and A. Labrousse, *L'architecture des pyramides à textes I, Saqqara-Nord,* 1996; with M. Rassart-Debergh, *Textiles d'Antinoe,* 1997; with others, *L'expédition d'Egypte, postérités et prospectives,* 1998; with D. Valbelle, *Le décret de Memphis, bicentenaire de la découverte de la Pierre de Rosette,* 1999; *Répertoire d'épigraphie méroïtique: corpus des inscriptions publiées,* 2000; *Au fil du Nil, le parcours d'un égyptologue,* 2001; with others, *Les textes de la pyramide de Pépy Ier* I, 2001; *Dictionnaire de l'Antiquité,* 2005; he died in Paris, 16 Sept. 2011; his library was added to the Champollion Library at the Collège de France, Paris.

Sudan and Nubia 16 (2012), 160-2 (C. Berger-el Naggar) (portr.); *Der Antike Sudan* 12 (2011), 143-5 (C. Rilly) (portr.); *BIFAO* 112 (2012), 1-5 (N. Grimal) (portr.); *Archéo-Nil* 23 (2013), 5-7 (B. Midant-Reynes), 17-24 (C. Berger-el-Naggar), 25-32 (J. L. Le Quellec); *Bayerische Akademie der Wissenschaften Jahrbuch* (2012), 168-71 (E. Blumenthal).

LEDRAIN, (Fréjus) Eugène (1844-1910)
French Assyriologist; he was born in Sainte Suzanne (Mayenne), 22 June 1844, son of Guillaume L., a policeman, and Eugénie Couriot; he studied Egyptology under Maspero (q.v.) at the College de France; he later taught at the École du Louvre; he published *Les monuments égyptiens de la Bibliothèque Nationale, Cabinet des médailles et antiques,* 1879-81; he also contributed articles on Egyptological subjects to *Gazette archéologique, Le Contemporain,* and other journals; he published the Luynes Papyrus in *Rec. Trav.* i. 89; his most important work was probably a *Dictionnaire de la Langue de l'ancienne Chaldée,* which he compiled, 1908; he also contributed to *Rev. d'Assyriologie*; he died in Paris, 10 Feb. 1910.

Budge, *R & P,* 214; Hilmy, i, 362; *Rev. Arch.* 4th ser. 16, 152.

LEDYARD, John (1751-1789)
American traveller; he was born in Groton, Conn., Nov. 1751, son of John L., a sea captain, and Abigail Hempstead; he became a sailor in 1773 and joined the British navy in 1774; he accompanied Captain Cook in his last voyage, 1776-1780; he returned to America in 1782 and published an account of his voyage in 1783; he then left for Europe in 1784 with the intention of organizing an expedition across Siberia; he set off in 1786 but was expelled from Russia in 1788 after he reached Irkutsk; he went to London where he was employed by the African Association to undertake a journey up the Nile to Sennar; he reached Alexandria and then Cairo in Aug. 1788 but died in Cairo, 10 Jan. 1789 before he could set out for the south; his papers went to the African Association but some were published in the *Transactions of the African Association* 1790 and in his 1828 biography.

ODNB 33, 46-7; J. Sparks, *The Life of John Ledyard, the American Traveller,* 1828; S. Watrous, *John Ledyard's Journey through Russia and Siberia 1787-88,* 1966, 3-31; E. Gray, *The Making of John Ledyard,* 2007; C. Vivian, *Americans in Egypt 1770-1915,* 2012, 24-38; A. Oliver, *American Travellers on the Nile,* 2016, 19-22.

LEE, John (1783-1866)
British ecclesiastical lawyer, antiquarian, and patron of science; he was born at Totteridge, Herts., 28 April 1783, son of John Fiott and Harriet Lee; he graduated from St. John's College, Cambridge; MA, 1809; LLD, 1816; his name was Fiott, but he changed it by royal licence on inheriting from the Revd Sir George Lee, Bart., the estate of Hartwell, Bucks., and other estates elsewhere, 1815; he studied law and was admitted to the Coll. of Advocates, of which he was Librarian and Treasurer; he practised in the Ecclesiastical Courts and at the age of 80 was admitted Barrister, Gray's Inn, becoming Bencher and QC the following year; he married 1. Cecilia Rutter, 1833 (*d.*1854), 2. Louisa Catherine Heath, 1855; he took great interest in the promotion of science and archaeology all his life, and was a generous patron, forming an extensive library and museum at his seat at Hartwell; he had a rich collection of Egyptian antiquities, many of which he had bought at the Barker (q.v.), Lavoratori (q.v.), Burton (q.v.), and Athanasi (q.v.) sales; others he acquired during a visit to Egypt in 1807-10; a printed catalogue of the Egyptian collection, by Bonomi (q.v.), was issued in 1858; after his death, most of the Egyptian collection was bought by Lord Amherst (q.v.), his library and MSS were sold at Sotheby's, 1876, and collections of deeds, etc., 8 March 1939; some of the geological specimens and some minor Egyptian pieces are now in the Buckinghamshire County Museum, Aylesbury, while other geological specimens are in the Natural History Museum, London; the MS. registers of Lee's Museum in 4 vols. folio are also at Aylesbury; he was foundation member of the Royal Astron. Soc., 1820, President, 1862; FRS, 1831; FSA, 1828; scientific meetings were held at his house and out of these grew the Meteorological Soc., the Syro-Egyptian Soc., the Anglo-Biblical Soc., the Palestine Arch. Assn., and the Chronological Institute; the last four were dissolved in 1872 and merged in the Soc. of Biblical Arch.; Lee's name is associated with a judicial papyrus which passed into Lord Amherst's coll. and is now in the Pierpont Morgan Library, NY; some of his papers are in the Griffith Institute, Oxford; Lee died in Hartwell, 25 Feb. 1866.

ODNB 33, 84-6 (portr.); *DNB* 32, 362; W. H. Smythe, *Aedes Hartwellianae*, 1851.

LEE, Peter (*d.*1825)
British Consul at Alexandria; he was probably born in Smyrna, son of Richard Lee, merchant of Smyrna; he became a member of the firm headed by Briggs (q.v.); he was helpful to British travellers in Egypt; he died suddenly in Alexandria, 16 Sept. 1825. Married Mary Arbouin (*b.*3 Nov. 1775, *d.* in London, 7 July 1845) in London, 16 Sept. 1801.

Barker, ii, I; Henniker, 6, 115; Light, 4, II; Madox, i, 99, 101, 125, 127, 239, 241; ii, 50; Salt, ii, 226, 232, 234, 235; Sherer, 197, 203; Westcar Dairy, 6, 12, 13-18, 78.

LEEK, Frank Filce (1903-1985)
British dentist; he was born in London, 5 Feb. 1903, son of Frank John L. and Florence Rachel Filce; he studied dentistry at King's College Hospital Dental School in London, 1926-30; he then became a dental surgeon at Lincoln County Hospital and later at Hemel Hempstead until his retirement in 1971; his interest in archaeology led him to study Egyptology at the Institute of Archaeology, London under V. Seton-Williams (q.v.) finishing in 1963; he specialized in the dental history of the Ancient Egyptians and related questions of diet and environment; in 1968 he took part in the examination of the mummy of Tutankhamun and later edited Derry's report on the mummy; from 1975 he was a member of the team of the Manchester Mummy Project; he was elected a fellow of the Society of Antiquaries in 1966, and Honorary Member of the Swedish Academy of Medical Science in 1980, an Honorary member of the Dental Association of South Africa and of the Sociedad Peruana de Ortondoncia; he published numerous articles in Egyptological and scientific journals and notably *The Human Remains from the Tomb of Tutankhamun*, 1972; some of his papers are at the Griffith Institute, Oxford; he died in London, 26 Jan. 1985.

JEA 72 (1986), 175-8 (D. M. Dixon) (portr.) (bibl.); *ZÄS* 113 (1986), VII (E. Strouhal); *Palaeopathology Newsletter* 50 (1985), 4 (E. Tapp); inf. from Mrs Leek; J. Buikstra and C. Roberts (eds.), *The Global History of Palaeopathology. Pioneers and Prospects*, 2012, 222-3 (B. Baker and M. Judd).

LEEMANS, Conradus (1809-1893)
Dutch Egyptologist; he was born at Zalt-Bommel, 28 April 1809, son of Dr. Willem L. and Gonna Ganderheijen; he was a student of Theology at Leiden, 1826-8, at first intending to go into the Church, but on the advice of Reuvens (q.v.), he took up archaeology instead; he accompanied the latter to Paris where they met Champollion (q.v.) in 1829; after military service, 1830-1, he joined the staff of the Leiden Museum; he succeeded Reuvens as Conservator in 1835 and was appointed Director in 1839-91; he married Cornelia Maria de Virieu (1818-1904) in 1840; he was really the first Egyptologist to publish a systematic catalogue of all the contents of one of the major European Egyptological collections; he began the great official government publication of the monuments and papryi in the Leiden collection in 1839, which appeared in parts from then until 1882; Leemans also wrote articles on other branches of archaeology, both European and Far Eastern, as did Birch and other museum officials of the

period, and published an enormous quantity of studies and books during his very long career; in 1885 a *Festschrift* was published in his honour, see below; his main publications were, *Horapollinis Niloi hieroglyphica*, 1835, an academic dissertation; *Lettre à M. François Salvolini, sur les monuments égyptiens, portant des légendes royales, dans les Musées d'Antiquités de Leide, de Londres, et dans quelques collections particulières en Angleterre: avec des observations concernant l'histoire, la chronologie, et la langue hiéroglyphique des Égyptiens: et un Appendice sur les mesures de ce peuple*, 1838; *Papyrus égyptien démotique à transcriptions grecques du Musée d'Antiquités des Pays-Bas à Leide*, 1839; *Papyrus Égyptien Démotique à transcriptions Grecques du Musée d'Antiquités des Pays-Bas à Leide ...*, 1840; *Papyrus égyptien funéraire hiéroglyphique du Musée d'Antiquités des Pays-Bas à Leide: description raisonnée*, 1841-2; *Aegyptische Monumenten van het Nederlandsche Museum van Oud-heden te Leyden*, his largest work in 15 pts. issued in 3 groups, fol., 1842-82; *Papyri Graeci Musei Antiquarii Publici Lugduni-Batavi. Regis augustissimi jussu edidit, interpretationem Latinam, annotationem, indicem et tabulas addidit C.L.*, 2 vols. 1843-85; his bibl. reached 120 nos.; he died in Leiden, 14 Oct. 1893.

Études archéologiques, linguistiques et historiques, dedicated to him on the occasion of the 50th anniversary of his appointment as Director of the Leiden Museum, 1885. This contains an 'Egyptische Feestmarsch' by W. F. G. Nicolai, and has a bibl. on pp. 341-8; *Nieuw Nederlandsch Biogr. Woordenboek* 9 (1935), 584-7; Hilmy, i, 363; W. F. Leemans, *L'Égyptologue Conrade Leemans et sa correspondance. Contribution à l'histoire d'une science*, 1973; inf. M. Raven.

LEEUW, Gerardus van der (1890-1950)
Dutch Egyptologist; born at The Hague 18 March 1890, son of Gerardus v.d. L. and Elisabeth Antoinette Nelck; studied theology at Leiden University and later Egyptology with A. Erman (q.v.) and K. Sethe (q.v.) at Berlin and Göttingen; doctoral thesis in 1916 on the conception of divinity in the Pyramid Texts; Professor in the University of Groningen 1918-46, 1948-50; Minister of Education 1945-6; he published a number of books and articles relating to Egyptian religion, notably *De godedienst van het oude Aegypte*, 1944; *Egyptische eschatologie*, 1949; *Phaenomenologieder Religion*; he died in Utrecht, 18 Nov. 1950.

Chron. d'Ég. 27 (1952), 140-2 (bibl.) (M. S. H. G. Heerma van Voss); *Jaarboek der Koninklijke Nederlandse Akademie van Wetenschappen*, 1951-2, 232-44 (portr.) (A. de Buck); *AEB* 1952, 819; *Wie's dat*, 1948, 308; inf. M. Raven.

LEEUWBURG, Ludovic Gerard (1916-1999)
Dutch Egyptologist and classicist; he was born in Rotterdam, 3 Oct. 1916, son of Barend Dorus Constantijn L. and Berthe Susanne Vandenberghe; he studied in Leiden under de Buck (q.v.); he was a staff member in the Leiden Institute of Classical Archaeology, and a teacher of classics; apart from a number of articles, notably on Medinet Habu, he was the author of *Indexes on Bibleotheca Aegyptiaca VIII*, 1943, and *Echnaton*, 1946; he died in Leiden, 7 March 1999.

Phoenix 46 (2000), 4 (M. Heerma van Voss); inf. Prof. M. Heerma van Voss.

LEFÉBURE, (Jean-Baptiste Louis Joseph) Eugène (1838-1908)

French Egyptologist; he was born in Prunoy, Yonne, 11 Nov. 1838, son of Jean Baptiste L. and Louise Elisabeth Honorine Mouchon; he married young, and the early death of his wife caused him to take up Egyptology to engage his interest; he came under the notice of Chabas (q.v.) and studied under his direction; he was employed in the French Postal Service until 1879, when he was appointed lecturer in Egyptology at Lyons; in 1880 he joined the French Arch. Mission in Cairo, and became director of it the next year; his great work in Egypt was the publication of the Tombs of the Kings, those of Ramesses IV and Sety I being copied *in extenso*; he was not physically fitted for field-work, and the frequent leaves of absence for which he applied led to his recall in July 1883; he resumed his work at Lyons for a short time, and then succeeded Grébaut (q.v.) at the École des Hautes Études; he began work there in 1885, but was soon replaced by Guieysse (q.v.), and went to the École de Lettres at Algiers, where he remained until his death; Lefébure was an able man, and made valuable contributions to Egyptology, but he was by nature a poet and a mystic, and a tendency to mysticism is observable even in his Egyptological works; he was an intimate friend of the poet Stéphane Mallarmé; his shorter works were collected by Maspero (q.v.) and published in the *Bibl. Ég.*, vols. 34-6; *Traduction comparée des hymnes au soleil composant le 15e chapitre du rituel funéraire égyptien*, 1868; *Le Mythe Osirien*, 2 pts., 1874-5; *Le Puits de Deir el Bahari etc.*, 1882; *Les Hypogées royaux de Thèbes. Ire division. Le Tombeau de Séti Ier. 2me division. Notices des hypogées. 3me division. Tombeau de*

Ramsès IV, 2 vols. with É. Naville and E. Schiaparelli, 1885-9; *Rites égyptiens: construction et protection des édifices, Oeuvres Diverses*, 3 vols. 1910-15; he died in Algiers, 9 April 1908.

Notice biographique, by E. Lefébure and P. Virey, *Bibl. Ég.* 34, ii-xci; *BIFAO* 6 (1908), 194-5; *Sphinx* 12 (1909), 1-13 (E. Andersson); Hilmy, i, 364; *La Table Ronde*, no. 38 (1951), 68-95 (Corresp. with Mallarmé).

LEFEBVRE, Gustave Désiré Louis (1879-1957)
French Egyptologist; born 17 July 1879 at Bar-le-Duc (Meuse), Lorraine, son of Constantin Désiré Louis L. and Marie Longeaux; he studied at the Faculté des Lettres, Paris, 1879-1900, and was also a pupil at the École Pratique des Hautes Études, Paris, 1899-1901; he was a member of the French School at Athens, 1901-4; he worked in Egypt, 1902-4; he became Professor at the Lycée de Valenciennes, 1904; he was appointed Inspector for Middle Egypt in the Egyptian Antiquities Service, 1905-14; in war service 1915-19; Assistant Keeper, 1919 then Keeper, Cairo Museum, 1926-28; Director of Studies at the École Pratique des Hautes Études, Section IV, Chair of Egyptian Philology, 1928-48, Docteur-ès-lettres, Faculté des Lettres, Paris, 1929; Maspero Prize, 1942; member of the Acad. des Inscriptions et Belles-Lettres, 1942; Paul Pelliot Prize, 1956; an authority on Egyptian philology Lefebvre received a classical background to his education at the Sorbonne; with Pierre Jouguet (q.v.) he studied Greek papyri found in the Nile valley and assisted in excavations at Medinet Madi in the Fayum, 1902, at Medinet Nahas (Magdola), El Majabda (the burial place of mummified crocodiles), and at Tihna, 1903-4; he was invited by Gaston Maspero (q.v.) to join the Antiquities Service and after studying hieroglyphs, he began the publication of Egyptian texts from 1907; he was also an officer of the Order of the Nile and of the Légion d'honneur; his published work numbered 155 items, see espec. *Papyrus de Magdôla*, with P. Jouguet, 1902-3; *Inscriptions grecques de Tehneh*, 1903; *Une chapelle de Ramsès II à Abydos*, 1906; *Fragments d'un manuscrit de Ménandre*, 1907; *Recueil des inscriptions grecques chrétiennes d'Égypte*, 1907; *Les Graffites grecs du Memnonion d'Abydos*, 1919; *Le tombeau de Pétosiris*, 3 vols. 1923-4, following the clearance of this tomb at Tuna el-Gebel; *Histoire des grands prêtres d'Amon de Karnak*, 1929; *Inscriptions concernant les grands prêtres d'Amon Romé-Roÿ et Amenhotep*, 1929; *Grammaire de l'Égyptien classique*, 1940, for many years one of the three standard works used for teaching students, with those of Gardiner and de Buck; *Romans et contes égyptiens de l'époque pharaonique*, 1948; *Inscription dédicatoire de la chapelle funéraire de Ramsès I à Abydos*, 1951; *Tableau des parties du corps humain mentionnées par les Égyptiens*, 1952; *Essai sur la médecine égyptienne de l'époque pharaonique*, 1956; he died in Versailles, 1 Nov. 1957.

AfO 18, pt. ii (1958), 487-8 (portr.) (J. Leclant); *BIFAO* 58 (1959), xi-xxiii 131-48 (bibl.) (J. Leclant); *Bulletin de la Soc. Française d'ég.*, no. 25 (March 1958) 1-2 (É. Drioton); École Pratique des Hautes Études. *Extrait de l'annuaire* 1959-60 (J. J. Clère); *JEA* 44 (1958), viii (R. O. Faulkner); *Journal des Savants* 1957, 187-8 (A. Merlin-J. Longnon); *Rev. de l'Université de Bruxelles* II (1958-9), 114-16 (M. Stracmans); *La Revue du Caire* 39, 20th year, no. 208 (Dec. 1957), 473-80 (Mahmoud el-Nahas); *Rev. philosophique*, Paris 148 (1958), 137 (anon); *ZÄS* 83 (1958), I (G. Posener); *CRAIBL* 1957, 376-7 (C. Perrin); *Revue Archéologique* 1958, 84-6 (J. Sainte Fare Garnot); *Rev. d'Ég.* 13 (1961) 19-25 (portr.) (bibl.) (E. Drioton); *DBF* 20, 719-20.

LEFORT, (*Mgr.*) **Louis Théophile** (1879-1959)
Belgian Coptologist and orientalist; born at Orchimont, 31 July 1879, son of François Joseph L. and Marie Pauline Renault; he studied at the Jesuit College at Namur and the Petit Séminaire at Bastogne before going to the University of Louvain, 1901; Doctor of Philosophy and Letters 1905 with a thesis on the cult of Asclepius; then he studied under Alfred Wiedemann (q.v.) at Bonn; he became Professor and Hon. President of the Oriental Institute of the University of Louvain; he was also director of the journal *Le Muséon*; among his many publications were *S. Pachomii Vita. Bohairice Scripta,* 1925 and 1936; *S. Pachomii Vita. Sahidice Scriptae*, 1933; *Les vies coptes de Saint-Pachôme et de ses premiers successeurs*, 1943; *Correspondance du Nouveau Testament Sahidiques I. Mots d'origine grecque,* 1950; *Les Pères apostoliques en copte*, 1952; *S. Athanase. Lettres festales et pastorales,* 1955; *Oeuvres de S. Pachôme et de ses disciples*, 1956; he died in Louvain, 30 Sept. 1959.

BSAC 15 (1958-60), 193-4 (O. H. E. Khs-Burmester) 168-71 (bibl.) (Ant. Khater); *Chron. d'Ég.* 35 (1960), 325-30 (J. Vergote); *Le Flambeau* 42 (1959), 630-1 (H. Grégoire); *Muséon* 72 (1959), 247-76 (portr.) (bibl.) (E. Lamotte, R. Draguet, G. Garitte, J. Vergote); *Muséon* 59 (1946), 54-62 (bibl.); *Orbis* 7 (1958), 599-603 (bibl.); *The Coptic Encyclopedia* 5,1437 (A. S. Atiya).

LEGGE, George Francis (1853-1922)
British barrister and classical scholar; he was born at Lee, Kent, 17 July 1853, son of George L., architect, and Anne Hay; he became very interested in Egyptology, and especially in Gnosticism and magic; he began to contribute a long series of articles on Egyptological subjects from 1897 onwards, and published them in

PSBA, JRAS, and other journals; he seems to have been encouraged by Budge (q.v.); he was also a contributor to the *Athenaeum*; FSA, 1910; he went to Egypt 1908-10 to assist Naville (q.v.) at Abydos; he was also a good Greek scholar and published a translation of the *Philosophumena* of Hippolytus (2 vols. 1921), and a valuable introduction to Horner's translation of *Pistis Sophia,* 1924, which was published after his death, unfortunately without revision; his principal work was *Forerunners and Rivals of Christianity,* 2 vols. 1915; Legge was a very able and versatile man, and was Foreign Secretary, Society of Biblical Archaeology; during the First World War he was employed in the Censor's office; he died by his own hand, possibly due to financial worries, London, 31 Oct. 1922.

Inf. Dr. M. A. Murray; *JRAS* 1923, 151; Newberry Corr.

LEGH, Thomas (1793-1857)
British traveller and author; he was born about 1793, illegitimate son of Thomas Peter L. of Lyme Park; he was educated at Brasenose College, Oxford from 1810; DCL, 1817; he lived at Lyme Park, Cheshire; J.P.; LLD; MP, 1816-32; FRS, 1817; FSA; he visited Egypt and Nubia, 1812-3, and again in 1814, accompanied on the first occasion by the Revd Charles Smelt (1784-1831) afterwards Rector of Gedling, Notts., 1824-31; Legh published *Narrative of a Journey in Egypt and the Country beyond the Cataracts,* 1816; he obtained a batch of Coptic papyri, now in the British Library (Crum. *Cat.* Nos. 447-54); he died in Lymington, 8 May 1857.

Guide to Lyme Park, portr. in oriental dress on staircase; Budge, *Eg. Sudan,* i. 26; Henniker, 97; Hilmy, i, 364; Finati, ii, 79, 225, 231, 234; Irby, 5, 100, 101, 103, 109, 148, 150; Burckhardt, *Travels in Nubia,* 16-20; Moorehead, 142-4; *GM* 2 N.S., 742; W. Beamont, *A History of the House of Lyme,* 1876, 195-205; R. Morkot in N. Cooke and V. Daubney (eds.), *Lost and Now Found,* 2017, 205-28.

LE GOUZ DE LA BOULLAYE, François (1623-*c.*1669)
French traveller; he was born at the Château de Bordes near Baugé, Anjou, 22 July 1623, son of Gabriel le Gouz, seigneur de Bordes and Jeanne Le Bault de la Boullaye; he became seigneur de La Boullaye; he studied at La Flèche and then embarked on various travels; he went to England in 1643 and fought for Charles I, returning to France via Ireland, and northern Europe; he then journeyed through Italy, Greece, Turkey, Persia, India, Syria and Egypt before returning to Europe in 1650; while in Egypt in 1649 he visited Cairo, Giza and Saqqara and obtained a small number of antiquities; he published an account of his travels *Les Voyages et observations...* in 1653 including the earliest illustration of a hieroglyphic text on papyrus or linen; he was sent as a royal envoy to Persia in 1664 and died in Isfahan, *c.*1669.

NBG 30, 414-7; *Bio. Univ.* 17, 275; *DBF* 20, 1015-6; G. Moreau, *F. Le Gouz de la Boullaie, gentilhomme angevin,* 1955.

LEGRAIN, (Albert) Georges (1865-1917)
French Egyptologist; he was born in Paris, 4 Oct. 1865, son of Constant Germain L, a printer, and Armide Marie Grandhomme; at first he studied art and architecture in Paris under Gérôme and Choisy (q.v.), Heuzey and Pottier, and Egyptian archaeology and philology under Pierret (q.v.) and Revillout (q.v.) at the Louvre, and under Guieysse (q.v.) at the Sorbonne; he published his first article in 1887, and a work on a Demotic subject (*Rev. Arch.* 5 (1888), 89); he went to work for the IFAO in 1892; he copied graffiti around Aswan, the frescoes of the monastery of Saint Simeon, and the scenes in the tombs of Qubbet el-Hawa, 1892-3; he also did a great deal of recording in the area between Aswan and Kom Ombo where he began with Bouriant (q.v.) and others the complete copying of the temple; he was at El-Amarna, 1893-4, the results of his work being used in Bouriant's vol.; he also contributed water-colour illustrations to de Morgan's (q.v.) publication of the princesses' jewellery from Dahshur; he was appointed Inspecteur-Dessinateur, 1894; he made further copies at Kom Ombo and also discovered the archaic necropolis at Gebel es-Silsila, 1894-5; he was at Dahshur, 1895; the same year he was appointed by de Morgan to make systematic investigations of Karnak, and continued on this his main life's work until 1917; he visited Kharga Oasis and Sinai with de Morgan, 1896; Legrain also copied graffiti at Tura and Massara and explored the area between Cairo and Suez searching for prehistoric sites, 1907; he was made Chief Inspector of Luxor, where he also worked on the temple during the 1914-18 war; although he began as a copyist and produced a great deal of work in this branch, it is as the restorer and excavator of Karnak that he is remembered today; Legrain was the first Egyptologist to carry out such work on a vast scale and has in general been followed by all later architects and engineers similarly engaged; when appointed he devised an excellent programme but later found Maspero (q.v.) and other directors less sympathetic than de Morgan; despite incredible difficulties he accomplished an immense amount and not only cleared the great hypostyle hall and the area round it, but also restored and rebuilt much that was unsafe or that had fallen; during these years he made the famous find of the Karnak cachette of 17,000 statues and figures, 1903; he was very thorough and kept complete records of his work, but little was published unfortunately, except for many articles and preliminary reports in

ASAE; his list of works is a long one and his bibl. reached 141 nos., of these many being substantial quarto vols.; beside books on ancient Egypt he also wrote a popular work on the Christian and Muslim dwellers in modern Thebes; *Le Livre des transformations,* thesis, 1890; *Catalogue d'une collection d'antiquités égyptiennes, grecques et romaines* (R. Sabatier), 1890; *Description des peintures et antiquités égyptiennes du Musée de Péronne* (Musée Danicourt), 1890; *Collection de M. le baron de Menascé. Ant. Ég*, 1891; *Catalogue des antiquités égyptiennes de la collection H. Hoffmann,* 1894; *Catalogue des monuments et inscriptions de l'Égypte antique. I. De la frontière de Nubie à Kom Ombos. II. Kom Ombos,* 3 vols., with J. de Morgan and others, 1894-1909; *Fouilles à Dahchour,* 2 vols., with J. de Morgan, 1895-1903; *L'aile nord du pylône d'Aménophis III à Karnak,* with E. Naville, 1902; *Monuments pour servir à l'étude du culte d'Atonou en Égypte,* with U. Bouriant and others, 1903; *Statues et statuettes de rois et particuliers,* 3 vols., Cairo Cat., 1906, 1909, 1914; *Répertoire généalogique et onomastique du Musée Égyptien. I.,* 1908; *Inscriptions françaises de Haute-Égypte,* 1911; *Aux Pays de Napoléon: l'Égypte,* with J. de Metz, 1913; *Où vécurent les savants de Bonaparte en Égypte?,* 1913; *Louqsor sans les Pharaons. Légendes et chansons populaires de la Haute-Égypte,* 1914; posth. works, *Les Temples de Karnak. Fragment du dernier ouvrage de Georges Legrain,* edit. J. Capart, 1929; *Une Famille copte de Haute-Égypte,* 1945; he died of pneumonia in Luxor, 22 Aug. 1917; his archives can be found on the internet at http://www.mom.fr/.

AE E (1920), 18-19 (Somers Clarke), also D (1917), 142; *ASAE* 19 (1919), 105-18 (portr.) (P. Lacau), 118-26 (bibl.) (H. Munier); *BIE* sér. 5, 11 (1918), 425-6 (J. B. Piot); *JEA* 4 (1917), 278 (F. Ll. Griffith), 280; *Rev. Arch.* 6 (1917), 309-11 (A. Moret); C. Traunecker and J.-C. Golvin, *Karnak,* 1984, 153-76; M. Azim and G. Réveillac, *Karnak dans l'objectif de Georges Legrain,* 2004; È. Gran-Aymerich, *Dictionnaire biographique d'archéologie 1798-1945,* 2001, incorporated in *Les Chercheurs de passé 1798-1945,* 2007, 931-2; *DBF* 20, 1017-8; S. Pizzarotti in *Égypte Afrique & Orient* 44 (2006), 5-14; inf. Gérard Legrain; *DBF* 20, 1018.

LEHOUX, (Pierre) François (1803-1889)
French painter; he was born in Paris, 25 June 1803, son of Pierre Louis L. and Anne Victoire Raffard; a pupil of Baron Gros and Horace Vernet; he accompanied Champollion's expedition to Egypt and Nubia, 1828-9; when Champollion (q.v.) returned to France, Lehoux, Bertin (q.v.), and L'Hôte (q.v.) remained in Cairo to execute a large panorama of the town; he exhibited paintings of Egyptian and Oriental subjects at the Paris Salon, 1831-5; he died in Paris, 12 Oct. 1889.

Champollion, ii, vi, 142, 238, 400, 417, 450; Carré, i, 231, 236, 242; Hill, 210; E. Benezit, *Dictionnaire des Peintres…* 6, 550; *DBF* 20, 1219; Archives de Paris, état-civil; *DBF* 20, 1219.

LEIBOVITCH, Joseph (1898-1968)
Israeli archaeologist; he was born in Alexandria, 9 June 1898, son of Jacques L. and his wife Tonie; he studied at the Universities of Cairo and Vienna, and published his first study on the Sinai inscriptions found by Petrie, 1930; he made a speciality of the relationships between ancient Egypt and the Semitic field, also the history of the Semitic gods in Egypt such as Reshep, Horon, and Anath; another of his interests was the form of the Cherubim and the worship of Ptah among non-Egyptians; he was Borchardt's (q.v.) secretary for some years and was appointed Chief Librarian of the Dept. of Antiquities and Egyptian Museum, Cairo, 1937-49; a founding member of several Zionist organizations he later left Egypt and settled in Israel where he worked in the Dept. of Antiquities until 1963; he excavated at Dor, and also published several articles on scarabs, the Hyksos problem, and the Exodus; he died at Ramat Gan, 4 April 1968.

IEJ 18, no. 2 (1968), 133-4; *Chron. d'Ég.* 44 (1969), 299-300 (J. Schwartz); inf. D. Sweeney.

LEIPOLDT, Johannes (1880-1965)
German Coptologist; born Dresden, 20 Dec. 1880, son of Professor Gustav L., and Elise Martha Grosse; he began his career with the study of church history and became a lecturer at Leipzig, then Halle, 1906; he was made professor at Kiel, 1909, Münster, 1914, and Leipzig 1916-54; he published a considerable number of Coptic works, *Epiphanios von Salamis' 'Ancoratus' in saïdischer Übersetzung,* 1902; *Der Hirt des Hermas in saïdischer Übersetzung,* 1903; *Koptische Urkunden,* 1904/5; he also worked on a catalogue *Koptische Handschriften auf der Leipziger Universitätsbibliothek,* 1906; his great work on Shenouti, Abbot of Athribis, which took many years to complete, *Sinuthii Archimandritae vita et opera omnia … ,* 1906-36; *Heilige Schriften,* 1953; he died in Ahrenshoop, 22 Feb. 1965.

Gnomon 37 (1965), 743-4 (C. Schneider); *Oriens Christianus* 50 (1966), 139 (anon.); *Theologische Literaturzeitung* 86 (1961), 75 sqq., (bibl.); 91 (1966), 635-8, (bibl.); *ZÄS* 92 (1966), vii-viii (S. Morenz); *NDB* 14, 151-2; *The Coptic Encyclopedia* 5, 1439 (M. Krause).

LELORRAIN, Jean Baptiste (*fl.* 1820-1823)
French engineer; he was sent to Egypt in 1820-1 by Saulnier (q.v.) to remove the Circular Zodiac of Dendera and convey it to Paris; in order to disarm suspicions of his intentions, he first proceeded up the Nile as far as Aswan, and bought antiquities at Thebes, some of which were studied by Champollion (q.v.); on his return journey, he

detached with great skill the heavy blocks inscribed with the Zodiac and successfully embarked them, but his operations were discovered by Luther Bradish (q.v.) who carried the news to Cairo, where Lelorrain encountered great opposition from Salt (q.v.) and Drovetti (q.v.), but succeeded in finally carrying off his booty to France.

S. L. Saulnier, *Notice sur le voyage de M. Lelorrain en Égypte*, Paris, 1822; Champollion, i, 6, 38, 57; ii, 155.

LEMM, Oskar Eduardovitch von (1856-1918)
Russian Egyptologist; he was born in St. Petersburg, 5 Sept. 1856 son of Eduard v. L., army officer and lecturer, and Luise von Hirschheydt; educated at the Alexander Lyceum 1871-7; in 1877 he went to Germany to study at Leipzig and Berlin and obtained his PhD degree at Leipzig University, 1882; he was keeper of the Asiatic Museum of the Russian Imperial Academy of Sciences, 1883-1918; Member of the Imp. Acad., 1906; from 1887-91 he lectured in the Oriental Faculty of St. Petersburg on Egyptian, Coptic, and Semitic languages; his publications, mainly on Coptic subjects, included *Ein Ritualbuch des Ammondienstes*, 1882; *Aegyptische Lesestücke ... mit Schrifttafel und Glossar*, 1883; *Das Triadon*, 1903; *Der Alexanderroman bei den Kopten*, 1903 he died in St. Petersburg, 3 June 1918.

B. Turaev, in *Christianski Vostok*, 6, pt. 3 (1917-20), Leningrad, 1922, 325-33 (bibl.); *The Coptic Encyclopedia* 5, 1439-40 (A. S. Atiya); S. Stadnikow in M. Dietrich, *Religionen in einer sich ändernden Welt*, 1999, 113-35; inf. S. Stadnikov.

LEMOYNE, Arnaud Hilaire Auguste (1800-1891)
French diplomat; he was born in Paris, 10 May 1800, son of Hilaire L. and Barbe Sophie Nouet de l'Orme; French Consul-General in Egypt, 1849-52, when he left to become Minister Plenipotentiary at Lima, Peru; retired, 1862; he was very helpful to Mariette (q.v.) on his first arrival in Egypt; he died in St-Jean-Le-Blanc, 27 Jan. 1891; his collection was sold in Paris, 30 April-2 May 1891.

French FO Records; Carré, ii, 28; *Bibl. Ég.* 18, pp. xxvii, xlix; Lugt 49933; *DBF* 21, 215.

LENOBLE, Patrice Pierre Ghyslain (1942-2007)
French archaeologist; he was born in Saint-Cyr-sur-Loire, 6 Oct. 1942, son of Jean L., a schoolteacher, and Jeanne Ernotte; he trained as a teacher, graduating in 1963; after teaching for two years, he studied for a degree in archaeology at the Sorbonne and took part in numerous excavations in France and Switzerland; MA from the University of Besançon, 1978; PhD from the Sorbonne, 1994; Librarian at the Art History and Archaeology Institute at the Sorbonne, 1968-72; he was a member of the French Unit of the Sudan Antiquities Service, 1976-84, 1985-93 excavating at el-Kadada and el-Hobagi and surveying the Fourth Cataract region; archaeologist at the French Institute of Archaeology of the Near East excavating at Beirut, 1993-95; he later served as a research engineer for the Service of Regional Archaeology of the Pays de la Loire in Nantes, 1995-2002; he returned to excavate in the Sudan at Sedeinga and el-Hassa, 2000-05; he died at Saint Herblain, Nantes, 25 Feb. 2007

Sudan and Nubia 11 (2007), 128-9 (portr.) (J. Reinhold); *Syria* 84 (2007), 315-9 (portr.) (V. Rondot and F. Villeneuve); *Die Antiken Sudan* 18 (2007), 217-8 (portr.) (V. Rondot).

LENOIR, Marie-Alexandre (1761-1839)
French Egyptologist and antiquarian; he was born in Paris, 26 Dec. 1761, son of Alexandre L. and Louise Catherine Adam; he studied art and published many works of archaeological nature, including the following relating to Egypt: *Antiquités ég. apportées à Paris par M. Passalacqua*, 1821; *Essai sur le zodiaque de Denderah*, 1822; *Examen des nouvelles salles du Louvre contenant les antiquités égyptiennes*, 1833; he also wrote works on decipherment, on which he held erroneous views, *Nouvelle explication des hiéroglyphes*, 4 vols. 1809-10, and *Nouveaux essais sur les hiéroglyphes*, 1826; Egyptian objects from his collection were sold in Paris, 11-16 Dec. 1837; he died in Paris, 11 June 1839.

NBG 30, 671-5; *BIFAO* 5 (1906), 85; Hilmy, i, 368; *Larousse, XIXe siècle* 10, 362; Lugt 14877; Lamy, 296-8; È. Gran-Aymerich, *Dictionnaire biographique d'archéologie 1798-1945*, 2001, incorporated in *Les Chercheurs de passé 1798-1945*, 2007, 933-4; D. Poulot in C. Grell, *L'Égypte imaginaire*, 2001, 127-49; *DBF* 21, 321-2.

LENORMANT, Charles (1802-1859)
French Egyptologist and numismatist; he was born in Paris, 1 June 1802, son of Charles François L., a notary, and Agathe Celeste Beatrix Gravier; he accompanied Champollion (q.v.) to Egypt, 1828, and his journal of the journey through Egypt was posthumously published in 1861; Librarian to the Arsenal, 1830; editor of the *Correspondant*; he was appointed an assistant at the Cabinet des Medailles 14 Nov. 1832-37 when he went to the National Printing Press until 8 Aug. 1840; Keeper of Antiquities at Bibliothèque Nationale, 1841-59; Professor of Egyptian Archaeology, Collège de France, 1849-59; he was elected to the Académie des Inscriptions, 25 Jan. 1839; several of his many publications deal with Egyptology

and were of great value in their time, notably *Musée des antiquités égyptiennes*, with L'Hôte, 1842; it was at his suggestion that Mariette (q.v.) was first sent to Egypt; he died of fever in Athens while travelling with his son (see below) in Greece, 24 Nov. 1859.

CRAIBL ser. 4, 6 (1878), 263-310 (H. Wallon); Champollion, ii, *passim*; Carré, *passim*; Hilmy, i, 368; A. C. E. Franquet de Franqueville, *Le Premier Siècle de l'Institut de France*, 1895, I, 257; *Larousse, XIXᵉ siècle* 10, 363; J. Bulté, *Catalogue des collections égyptiennes du Musée National de Céramiques à Sèvres*, 1981, 14; T. Sarmant, *Le Cabinet des Médailles de la Bibliothèque Nationale 1661-1848*, 275-77; È. Gran-Aymerich, *Dictionnaire biographique d'archéologie 1798-1945*, 2001, incorporated in *Les Chercheurs de passé 1798-1945*, 2007, 934-6; *DBF* 21, 387.

LENORMANT, (Charles) François (1837-1883)
French orientalist; he was born in Paris, 17 Jan. 1837, son of Charles L. (see above) and Marie Josephine Cyvoet; he was a precocious child and began to learn Greek at the age of 6, and at 14 published a paper on Greek Inscriptions from Memphis in *Rev. Arch.*; he accompanied his father on a visit to Greece, 1859, when his father died, and revisited Greece and the Levant several times afterwards; he obtained the post of under-librarian at the Institut de France; he visited Egypt in 1869 with Hamy (q.v.) ; he served in the army, 1870, and was wounded at the siege of Paris; Deputy Librarian at the Institut de France, 1862; Professor of Archaeology at the Bibl. Nat., 1874; he founded *Gazette Archéologique*, 1875; he was elected to the Académie des Inscriptions, 6 May 1881; as early as 1867 he had studied cuneiform, and this, with Egyptian and other oriental languages, occupied him all his life; his knowledge was encyclopedic, and his published works very numerous, the most celebrated being *Les Premières civilisations*, 2 vols. Paris, 1874 (vol. i, Egypt; vol. ii, Assyria, Chaldea, and Phoenicia); he was injured in an accident whilst exploring Calabria, and returned to France where he died, after a long illness, in Paris, 9 Dec. 1883.

Academy, 1883, no. 599, 280; *Athenaeum*, no. 2929, 783; *Gaz. Arch.* 8, 361; Hilmy, i, 369; *Archaéonil* 17 (2007), 5-26 (portr.); A. C. E. Franquet de Franqueville, *Le Premier Siècle de l'Institut de France*, 1895, I, 388; È. Gran-Aymerich, *Dictionnaire biographique d'archéologie 1798-1945*, 2001, incorporated in *Les Chercheurs de passé 1798-1945*, 2007, 936-7; *DBF* 21, 386.

LEOSPO, Enrichetta (1947-2001)
Italian Egyptologist; she was born in Turin 4 Dec. 1947; she was educated at Turin University, graduating in 1971; she taught Latin and Greek literature at the Liceo di Stato in Oulx; she was appointed assistant to the lecturer in Egyptology at Turin University, 1975-82; she was a curator at the Museo Egizio, Turin from 1980; apart from articles and contributions to exhibition catalogues, she published *La Mensa Isiaca di Torino*, 1978; *Progetto di un Museo Egizio per le scuole*, with G. Rigotti, 1981; *Museo Archeologico di Asti: La Collezione Egizia*, 1986; *L'Antico Egitto di Ippolito Rossellini*, with E. Bresciani and others, 1993; *Gebelein*, with A.-M. Donadoni Roveri, 1994; *La Collezione Egizia del Civico Museo Archeologico di Como*, with M.-C. Guidotti, 1994; *Bilderwelten und Weltbilder der Pharaonen*, with E. Bresciani and others, 1995; *La donna nell'Antico egitto*, 1997; she died in Racconigi, 2 Feb. 2001.

Inf S. Curto

LE PÈRE, Jacques Marie (1763-1841)
French engineer; he was born in Paris, 25 April 1763, son of Jacques L. and Marie Monchain; he was trained at the École des Ponts et Chaussées in 1781 and was headmaster of a branch of the École Polytechnique in Belgium; he accompanied the Napoleonic expedition as civil engineer-in-chief; he undertook a survey of Lake Mazalah and explored the possibility of opening a canal from Suez; he contributed to the *Description*; on his return he published *Mémoire sur la communication de la mer des Indes à la Mediterranée par la Mer Rouge et l'Isthme de Soueys*, 1815; he died in Granville 15 Dec. 1841; his brother Gratien was born in Versailles, 2 June 1769 and also educated as an engineer; he joined his brother in the Egyptian expedition where he surveyed the Natron Lakes and the Sinai; he was later chief engineer at Cherbourg, 1808, La Spezia, and Vienne; he contributed to the *Description* and also wrote *Mémoire sur les pyramides d'Égypte et sur le système religieux de leur érection et de leur destination*, 1826; he died at Granville, 15 June 1841.

Biographie Universelle 24, 228-9; inf. C. Pernumian; *DBF* 21, 626-7.

LEPÈRE, Jean Baptiste (1761-1844)
French architect; he was born in Paris, 1 Dec. 1761 and trained as an architect; he visited Santo Domingo and then served as part of a French delegation to Constantinople, 1796-8; he joined the Napoleonic expedition to Egypt in 1798 and drew plans of many Egyptian monuments; Member of the Institut d'Égypte; he took part in the excavations at Giza in Feb. 1801; on his return to France he designed an Egyptianizing pedestal for the base of

the statue of General Desaix and became architect of Malmaison in 1803; he designed the architectural elements of the Sevres Egyptian tea service presented to Czar Alexander I in 1808; architect of Fontainebleau, 1824; he died in Paris, 16 July 1844.

Inf. C. Pernumian and P. Bret; .F. Labrique and U. Westfehling, *Mit Napoleon in Ägypten. Die Zeichnungen des Jean-Basptiste Lepère*, 2010; *DBF* 21, 627-8.

LEPSIUS, (Karl) Richard (1810-1884)

German Egyptologist; he was born at Naumburg an der Saale, 23 Dec. 1810, son of Carl Peter L., Saxon Procurator for the district of Thuringia, and Friederike Gläser; he was educated at Naumburg school, 1823-9; the Universities of Leipzig, 1829-30; Göttingen, 1830-2, where he attended lectures on archaeology and Greek Antiquities and also learnt Sanskrit; Berlin, 1832-3, where he was critical of the philological school under Boeckh (q.v.); PhD on the Eugubian Tablets, 1833; he went to Paris in 1833 to collect materials on ancient weapons for the Duc de Luynes and while there attended lectures given by Letronne (q.v.) on the history of Egypt, whose critical approach to the subject he afterwards praised; under the influence of Bunsen (q.v.) and Humboldt he studied Egyptology, but although well qualified in many ancient languages he would not learn Egyptian until Champollion's *Grammar* had appeared; in this he showed his orderly mind which was to be of great service to him later; he required to make comparisons of the different systems of decipherment then being discussed in order to establish the correct one at a time when scholars were still uncertain about them; his famous letter to Rosellini (q.v.) marked the turning-point in the study of hieroglyphs; in this he accepted the Champollion system and showed once and for all that it was the correct one, but also expanded and corrected it where necessary, showing the use and nature of syllabic signs for the first time and the relationship of certain features to Coptic; in his spare time Lepsius learnt engraving on copper and lithography which he rightly considered would be useful in his work later; he also wrote poetry and music as diversions from his studies; while in Paris Lepsius made many squeezes and tracings of inscriptions and then spent four years visiting the principal Egyptian collections in England, Holland, and Italy; in 1842-5 he led the Prussian Expedition to Egypt and Nubia after having prepared for it most thoroughly; this was the best-equipped expedition that had ever gone to Egypt with skilled draughtsmen among the members; intending mainly to survey the monuments and gather objects Lepsius also excavated the site of the Labyrinth in the Fayum and made a stratified drawing of sections across the site, using a method not normally used in the Near East again until the present century; at this time his interest in Nubian languages was aroused; he went as far south as Khartoum and Sennar and also to Sinai in the north-east; he visited Palestine and later published the Nahr el-Kelb inscription of Ramesses II; in all he sent home 15,000 Egyptian antiquities and plaster casts; he was appointed Professor at Berlin University, 1846; he married Elisabeth daughter of Bernard Klein, the composer and niece of Gustav Parthey (q.v.) 1846; Member of the Acad., 1850; Corresponding Member of the Académie des Inscriptions in Paris, 24 Dec. 1858; co-director of the Egyptian Museum, Berlin, 1855; on the death of Passalacqua (q.v.) in 1865, he was made Keeper of the Egyptian collections and in 1873, Keeper of the Royal Library; the epigraphic and other material collected on the expedition was published in 1859 in the 12 vast volumes of the *Denkmäler*, probably the largest Egyptological work ever produced; the work consists entirely of folio plates, 894 in all, extremely accurate compared with earlier works of this type; the text did not appear until after his death, when it was compiled from his papers by Naville (q.v.) and others, and published in 5 further vols., 1897-1913; the Egyptian museum in Berlin was largely built according to his specification; in his later works he showed an interest in chronology and mensuration; he visited Egypt with another expedition, 1866, exploring the Suez area and the east Delta; this resulted in the discovery of the decree of Canopus at Tanis, of tremendous importance, as this bilingual stone acted as a check to prove the results achieved by Egyptologists up to 1866 by using the Rosetta stone and Champollion's system; for many years from 1864 on he edited *ZÄS*; his last visit to Egypt was in 1869 when he was present at the opening of the Suez Canal; Knight of the Bavarian order of Maximilian, 1873; Privy Councillor, etc.; his bibl. lists 142 works the chief of which were *Über die Anordung und Verwandtschaft der semitischen, indischen, altägyptischen und äthiopischen Alphabete*, 1835; *Lettre à M. le Professeur H. Rosellini sur l'alphabet hiéroglyphique*, 1837; *Auswahl der wichtigsten Urkunden des ägyptischen Alterthums, theils zum ersten Male, theils nach dem Denkmälern berichtigt, ...*, 1842; *Das Todtenbuch der Aegypter ...*, 1842; *Reise von Theben nach Halbinsel des Sinaï vom 4 März bis 14 April, 1845*, 1845; *Lettre de M. le Dr. R. Lepsius à M. Letronne ...*, 1847; *Denkmäler aus Aegypten und Aethiopien*, 6 pts. in 12 vols., fol. max., 1849-59; *Die Chronologie der Aegypter*, pt. I, 1849; *Briefe aus Aegypten, Aethiopien und der Halbinsel des Sinaï, geschrieben, 1842-1845*, 1852; *Königliche Museen, Abtheilung der Aegyptischen Alterthümer. Die Wandgemälde*, 1855; *Verzeichnis der ägyptischen Alterthümer und Gipsabgusse von R. Lepsius*, 1871; *Königsbuch der alten Aegypter*, 2 pts. 1858; *Das bilingue Dekret von Kanopus in der Originalgrösse mit Übersetzung beider Texte*, 1886; *Älteste Texte des Todtenbuchs nach Sarcophagen des altägyptischen Reichs im Berliner Museum*, 1867; *Nubische Grammatik mit einer Einleitung über die Völker und Sprachen Afrikas*, 1880; his journals are in the Berlin Museum apart from one in the Griffith Institute; he died in Berlin, 10 July 1884.

Richard Lepsius: ein Lebensbild, by Georg Ebers, Leipzig, 1885, trans. by Z. D. Underhill, NY, 1887; *Das Haus Lepsius,* Bernhard Lepsius, Berlin, 1933; *Academy,* 26 (1884), 44-6 (F. M. Mueller); *Athenaeum,* July-Dec. 1884, 80-1; Brugsch, *Mein Leben,* 32, 46, 74, 91, 262, 270, 375; Hilmy, i, 375; ii, 431; *Lit.-Blatt für orientalische Philologie,* Bd. I (1883-4), 473-6 (A. Erman); *Rev. Hist. des Relig.* 10 (1884), 238-43 (Leblois); *ZÄS* 22 (1884), 45-8 (H. K. Brugsch); A. C. E. Franquet de Franqueville, *Le Premier Siècle de l'Institut de France,* 1895, II, 255; *NDB* 14, 308-9; E. Freier and W. Reinecke, (ed.) *Karl Richard Lepsius,* 1988; E. Endesfelder, *Die Ägyptologie an der Berliner Universität-Zur Geschichte eines Fachgebietes,* 1988, 11-18; B. Adams et al (eds.), *Aratro Corona Messoria,* 1988, 47-72; È. Gran-Aymerich, *Dictionnaire biographique d'archéologie 1798-1945,* 2001, incorporated in *Les Chercheurs de passé 1798-1945,* 2007, 937-8; C. Loeben in *Égypte Afrique & Orient* 52 (2008-9), 21-30; I. Hafemann (ed.), *Preussen in Ägypten. Ägypten in Preussen,* 2010; H. Mehlitz, *Richard Lepsius. Ägypten und die Ordnung der Wissenschaft,* 2011.

LESCLUZE, Jean Baptiste de (1780-1858)

Belgian shipowner and merchant; born at Bruges, 13 May 1780, son of Pierre Jean D. and Marie-Françoise Mallet; he came of a family of French origin long settled in Flanders; his ships traded in the Mediterranean and Black Sea ports; in addition to mercantile cargoes he also imported Greek antiquities; then after establishing a branch office at Alexandria, Egyptian antiquities as well; in 1824 a mummy imported by him was publicly exhibited in Bruges, Ghent, and Antwerp, drawing great crowds; in 1825 a large collection of antiquities including statues, stelae, mummies, papyri, amulets, ceramics, etc. was sold by auction at Antwerp after being imported, 5 July 1826, when most of the lots were bought by Reuvens (q.v.) for the Leiden Museum; he apparently ceded part of his collection to Charles Bogaert (1791-1875) from whom it passed via Sams (q.v.) to Mayer (q.v.); he died in Bruges, 11 March 1858.

B. van de Walle, *Ann. Soc. d'Émulation de Bruges* 96 (1959), 64-88; 97 (1960), 154-236 where copious refs. are given; *Biographie Nationale de Belgique* 32, 432-40; *Chron. d'Eg.* 51 (1976), 47-57; H. de Meulenaere in *BSFE* 127 (1993), 6-19.

LESQUIER, (Marie Adolphe) Jean (1879-1921)

French Egyptologist; he was born at Lisieux, 11 Oct. 1879, son of Charles Edouard L. and Madeleine Gabrielle Allain; he made a special study of Graeco-Roman Egypt and papyrology in which subjects he published many works; he worked with Jouguet, and also excavated at Tihna for the IFAO, 1908; he published an adaptation of Erman's Egyptian Grammar for the *Bibl. d'études* of the French Inst., 1914; also *Les Institutions militaires de l'Égypte sous les Lagides,* 1911; *L'armée romaine d'Égypte d'Auguste à Dioclétien;* he died in Neuilly-sur-Seine, 28 June 1921, buried in Lisieux.

Aegyptus 2 (1921), 339-43 (A. Calderini); *Bull. Soc. Arch. d'Alexandrie,* no. 18 (1921), 96-8 (E. Breccia); *JEA* 7 (1921, 218-20 (H. I. Bell).

LESSEPS, (*Vicomte*) Ferdinand Marie de (1805-1894)

French diplomat, the creator of the Suez canal; he was born in Versailles, 19 Nov. 1805, son of Matthieu Maximilie Prosper Comte de L., a diplomat, and Françoise de Grivegnée; he entered the diplomatic service, vice-consul in Tunis, 1828-32 under his father; he was appointed vice-consul in Alexandria, Egypt in 1832 and then consul in Cairo, 1833-8; he was stimulated by J. M. Lepère's (q.v.) memoir on a proposed Suez canal,; he was later invited back to Egypt by Said Pasha, 1854; he was given the concession for a canal which was constructed between 1859 and 1869; in 1857 he recommended to Said Pasha the appointment of Mariette (q.v.) as curator of monuments in Egypt; he facilitated the uncovering of the Darius inscriptions concerning a canal between the Mediterranean and Red Seas; although he is not known to have made a personal collection of Egyptian antiquities, he directed his staff to keep a careful record of all objects found during the construction of the Suez canal; he later failed to complete the Panama canal, 1879-89; he published many important works on the Suez area, espec. *Percement de l'isthme de Suez,* 5 vols. 1855-61; *Lettres, journal et documents pour servir à l'histoire du canal de Suez,* 5 vols. 1875-71; his autobiography also enjoyed considerable popularity, *Souvenirs de quarante ans,* 2 vols. 1887; he died in La Chenaie, Indre, 7 Dec. 1894 and was buried in Père Lachaise cemetery, Paris.; his brother Théodore Antoine Lopez de la Sainte Trinité de Lesseps (1802-1874) visited Egypt in 1822-3 with Count Peter von Medem (q.v.) and Baron Alexander von Üxküll (q.v.).

G. Edgar Bonnet, *Ferdinand de Lesseps,* 2 vols. 1951-9; *EB* 1968, 13, 991-2; *La Grande Enc.* 22, 96-8; R. Dussaund, *La nouvelle Académie des Inscriptions et Belles-Lettres* (1795-1914) I, 1946, 299, 528; D. Dewachter in *L'Égyptologie en 1979* I, 1982, 221-7; *DBF* 22, 42-4.

LESUEUR, Jean Baptiste Cicéron (1794-1883)

French architect; he was born in Claire-Fontaine, Rambouillet, 5 Oct. 1794; Légion d'Honneur, 1846, Comm., 1870; Professor of Beaux-Arts, 1853; he became interested in Egyptian art and chronology and published

Chronologie des rois d'Égypte, Paris, 1848-50; also a work on the origins of art with special reference to Egyptian architecture; he died in Paris, 25 Dec. 1883.

Chron. des Arts, 1883, 333; Hilmy, i, 380; *Larousse, XIXe siècle.*

LETHIEULLIER, William (1701-1756)

British traveller and collector; he was baptized at St. Botolph Bishopsgate, London, 17 Jan. 1701, son of Abraham L. and Protesay Pitt; he was a member of a very intellectual family of Huguenot extraction that included Charles L., LLD, FSA, Smart L. FSA and others of distinction; he visited Egypt in 1721 and brought back from Saqqara a fine mummy, which was engraved and published by Alexander Gordon (q.v.) in 1737, as well as other antiquities which he bequeathed to the British Museum (EA 6695-6); Captain, 1723; Lt.-Colonel, 1740, retiring from the army 1752; FSA, 1725; member of the Egyptian Society 1743; he also had in his possession the naos of Khaemwese and the pyramidion of Tia which he gave to his cousin Smart L. (born Aldersbrook 3 Nov. 1701, son of John L. and Elizabeth Smart, died Aldersbrook 27 Aug. 1760) and which were also published by Gordon; Smart L. was also a member of the Egyptian Society 1742-3 and had a small collection of Egyptian antiquities; William L. died in London, 12 Feb. 1756.

Edwards, *Lives of the Founders*, 347; Nichols, *Lit. Anecd.* v. 372; Bierbrier in J. Baines et al, *Pyramid Studies and other essays presented to I.E.S. Edwards*, 1988, 220-8.

LETORZEC, Pierre Constant (1798-1857)

French traveller; he was born in Rochefort, 24 Feb. 1798, son of Pierre L., a ship's captain, and Théophile Boiscourbeau; he served in the French merchant marine until 1819, when he accompanied Cailliaud (q.v.) on his expedition to Sennar; he made the entire journey in 1820-2, making observations with a sextant; on his return to France he became a Captain in the French merchant marine; he died in Nantes, 27 April 1857.

Cailliaud, xi; Hill, 213; Waddington and Hanbury, *Journal*, 257; M. Chauvet, *Frédéric Cailliaud*, 1989, 343-8; *ASTENE Bulletin* 74 (2017), 15-17 (R. de Keersmacker).

LETRONNE, Jean Antoine (1787-1848)

French archaeologist and classical scholar; he was born in Paris, 25 Jan. 1787, son of Jean Louis L., an engraver; he served as Director of the École des Chartes, 1817; Inspector-Gen. of Studies, 1819-32; Professor of History at the Collège de France, 1831-7, Director of the Cabinet des Médailles 14 Nov 1832-40, and Professor of Archaeology at the Collège de France, 1837-48; he also became Keeper of National Archives, 1840-48; he was elected to the Académie des Inscriptions 21 March 1816; he took a prominent interest in the decipherment of hieroglyphics by Champollion (q.v.) and Young (q.v.), and reviewed Egyptological books by Wilkinson and others; he also corresponded with Nestor L'Hôte (q.v.); among his many published archaeological works those relating to Egypt were, *Recherches ... l'histoire de l'Égypte pendant la domination des Grecs et Romains*, 1823; *L'histoire du Christianisme en Égypte*, 1832; *Inscriptions grecques et latines du Colosse de Memnon restituées et expliquées*, 1832; *Sur l'origine grecque des Zodiaques prétendus égyptiens*, 1837; *Recueil des inscriptions grecques et latines de l'Égypte étudiées dans leur rapport avec l'histoire politique ...*, 3 vols., 2 text and atlas, 1842-8, his most important work; posth. *Nouvelles recherches sur le calendrier des anciens Égyptiens, sa nature, son histoire et son origine*, 1863; many of his smaller works were gathered together and published as, *Œuvres choisies: assemblées, mises en ordre et augmentées d'un index par E. Fagnan*, 1 *Égypte ancienne*, 2 vols. 1881; he died in Paris, 14 Dec. 1848.

Oeuvres Choisies, i (1881), iii-vi (portr.) (M. Burnouf), vii-xvii (M. E. Egger); Hartleben, see index; Hilmy, i, 380; *Mem. AIBL* 18 (1855), 396-430 (C. A. Baron Walckenaer); *Rev. Arch.* 5 (1848), 637-49 (A. Maury); A. C. E. Franquet de Franqueville, *Le Premier Siècle d'Institut de France*, 1895, I, 185-6; T. Sarmant, *Le Cabinet des Médailles de la Bibliothèque Nationale 1661-1848*, 273-5; È. Gran-Aymerich, *Dictionnaire biographique d'archéologie 1798-1945*, 2001, incorporated in *Les Chercheurs de passé 1798-1945*, 2007, 942-3.

LEUCHTENBERG, (*Duc de*) Maximilien Eugène Joseph Napoléon de Beauharnais (1817-1852)

French collector; he was born in Munich, 2 Oct. 1817, and was the second son of Eugène de B., the stepson of Napoléon, on whose downfall the Beauharnais family settled at Munich and assumed the title of Duke (Herzog) von Leuchtenberg, and Princess Auguste of Bavaria; Maximilien married Marie daughter of Tsar Nicholas I, 1839, he had some important Egyptian antiquities, which passed to the Hermitage Museum; he died in St. Petersburg, 20 Oct. 1852.

Larousse, XIXe siècle 10, 432.

LEVER, William Hesketh, 1st Viscount Leverhulme (1851-1925)
British businessman and philanthropist; he was born in Bolton, 19 Sept. 1851, son of James L. and Eliza Hesketh; he founded the soap company Lever Brothers; MP for the Wirral, 1906-9; he was created Baronet 1911, Baron 1917, and Viscount 1922; he included Egyptian objects in his large art collections, purchasing at the 1917 sale of the collection of Thomas Hope (q.v.), and the 1924 John Evans sale (q. v.); he also received material through his support of Garstang's (q.v.) excavations at Abydos and Meroe; he gave Egyptian objects to the Lady Lever Art Gallery, of which some are now in Bolton Museum; others were sold in New York (Anderson Galleries, Feb. 25 1926, lots 199-236); the Leverhulme Trust, founded in his will, became a major funder of research; he died in London, 7 May 1925.

ODNB 33, 526-9; G. B. Waywell, *The Lever and Hope Sculptures*, 1984); A. P. Thomas, 'Lever as a Collector of Archaeology', *J. Hist. Colls.* 4/2 (1992), 267-271; inf. T. Hardwick.

LEVI, Simeone (1843-1913)
Italian lexicographer; he was born in Carmagnola, 30 Jan. 1843, son of Samuel Moise L., a jeweller, and Susanna Clava; he was educated at Moncalieri and Real Collegio Carlo Alberto in Turin, graduating 1861; he then studied mathematics at the Universities of Turin, 1861-4 and Pisa, 1864-5; he was briefly Professor of Mathematics at the Technical Institute of Tortona and then a private tutor; he obtained a post at the University of Turin, 1869; he had a great interest in Egyptology and attended classes given by Rossi (q.v.) from 1876; he briefly served on the staff of the Egyptian Museum, Turin; he published *Raccolta dei segni ieratici egizi nelle diverse epoche*, 1880; *Della antichità egiziane di Brera*, 1886; *Vocabolario geroglifico copto-ebraico*, 1887-94; he died in Turin, 17 March 1913.

G. A. Levi and E. Viterbo, *Simeone Levi. La storia sconosciuta di un noto egittologo*, 1999.

LEVY DE BENZION, Moise (1873-1943)
Egyptian Jewish businessman and collector; he was born in Alexandria 1873, son of Isaac L.; he was educated at Paris and at eighteen entered the family business founded in 1857; he eventually took over and transformed this into the 'Grands Magasins Benzion', one of the most important department stores in Cairo; he formed a collection of Egyptian antiquities; his collection of paintings and objects kept in France were looted during World War II; antiquities from his collection kept in the Villa Benzion, Zamalek, were sold in Cairo, 20 March 1947; an important silver statue of a hawk-headed deity, now in the Miho Museum, Japan, was sold in Paris, 26 Feb. 1953; while in Europe, he was arrested by the Germans and died in France, 26 Sept. 1943.

Annuaire des Juifs d'Égypte 1942; *BMMA* 11 (1952), 119.

LEWIS, (*Sir*) **George Cornewall,** 2nd Bt (1806-1863)
British writer, journalist and politician; born London, 21 April 1806, son of Sir Thomas Frankland L., MP, and Harriet Cornewall; he became the editor of the *Edinburgh Review*; he was educated at Christ Church Oxford, 1824-8; he became the editor of the *Edinburgh Review*, 1851-5; he succeeded his father as Liberal MP for Radnorshire, 1855-63; he served as Chancellor of the Exchequer, 1855-8; Home Secretary, 1859-61; War Secretary, 1861-3; he was a prolific writer and published *An Historical Survey of the Astronomy of the Ancients*, 1862, and *Suggestions for the Application of the Egyptological method to Modern History*, 1862, attacking Egyptology as it then was; this purported to show that the whole subject was bogus and was refuted by Renouf (q.v.); Lewis died at Harpton Court, Radnor, 13 April 1863.

ODNB 33, 611-5 (portr.)

LEXA, František (1876-1960)
Czech Egyptologist; born at Pardubice, 5 April 1876, son of Vilibald L., a lawyer, and Eleanora Strasserová; he graduated at Prague University, 1895; Lexa was at first a secondary-school teacher of mathematics and philosophy; he wrote a thesis on the history of writing for his doctorate, 1903, the subject being the psychology of script, and was attracted to the hieroglyphic writing of Egypt as a result; he later studied Egyptian philology under A. Erman (q.v.), 1907-8, and Demotic with Spiegelberg (q.v.), 1908-9, which marked a turning-point in his career; habilitation, 1919; he became a lecturer and afterwards in 1922 extra Professor and in 1927 full Professor at the Charles IV University in Prague, a chair being created for him in Egyptology, 1927; he was the real founder, although not the first figure in, Czech Egyptology and became the doyen of it before his death; in 1952 he received the national prize first class, the highest distinction available to men of science; he was also for many years a corresponding member of the Fondation Égyptologique Reine Élisabeth in Brussels; Director of the Czechoslovak Egyptian Institute, 1958; he published about 100 books and articles and about 50 book reviews in

all, see *On the relationship between the spirit, the soul and the body among the Egyptians of the Old Kingdom,* 1919; *Ancient Egyptian religious literature,* vols. i-ii, 1920-1; *Magic in Ancient Egypt,* vols. i-ii, 1924; *L'Origine vraisemblable de la forme verbale de l'égyptien ancien* sdm.f *et des formes qui s'y rattachent,* 1923/4; *La Magie dans l'Égypte antique de l'ancien empire jusqu'à l'époque copte,* vols. i-iii, 1925; *Les formes relatives dans la langue ancienne égyptienne,* 1937; *Le Développement de la langue égyptienne aux temps préhistoriques,* 1938; *Grammaire démotique,* in 7 vols., 1938-50, his most important work; as a teacher he numbered Botti (q.v.), Ort-Geuthner (q.v.), Malinine (q.v.), Černy (q.v.) and Zába (q.v.) among his students; he also wrote *Das demotische Totenbuch der Pariser Nationalbibliothek, Papyrus des Pamonthes,* with Spiegelberg, 1910; *Papyrus Insinger,* 2 vols. 1926; *Deux notes sur l'astronomie égyptienne,* 1950; *Public Life in Ancient Egypt,* 2 parts, 1955; he died in Prague, 13 Feb. 1960.

Asian and African Studies in Czechoslovakia, Moscow, 1967, Egyptology (F. Váhala, Z. Zába); *Archiv orientální* 20 (1952), 1-6 (portr.) (Z. Zába), 7-14 (bibl.); *Archiv Orientální* 28 (1960), 169-71 (Z. Zába); *Chron. d'Ég.* 35 (1960), 193-5 (B. van de Walle); *AEB* 1955, nos. 4,902-3; 1957, nos. 57, 336-7; W. B. Oerter in *Enchoria* 14 (1986), 71-8; *BSAK* 1 (1988) 77-83; M. Verner et al,, *František Lexa,* Prague, 1989 with bibliography; L. Suková in J. Holaubek and H. Navrátilová (eds.), *Egypt and Austria* I, 2005, 149-61; L. Bareš in J. Holaubek, H. Navrátilová, and W. B. Oerter (eds), *Egypt and Austria* III, 2007, 21-6; inf. W. B. Oerter; W. Oerter, *Die Ägyptologie an der Prager Universität 1882-1945,* 2010,6-35.

LEXOVÁ-ZÁMOSTNÁ, Irena (1908-?)
Czech Egyptologist; she was born in 1908, daughter of František Lexa (q.v.) and his wife Milada; the focus of her systematic study was dance, in which one of her teachers was Jacques Dallcrosse; she was a graduate of the Dance school of Rosalie Chládková; in 1928 she began her studies at the Faculty of Philosophy and Arts (Charles University) in Physical education, Egyptology and Psychology; her seminar work concerned dance in Ancient Egypt; her father reviewed this work and published it under the title: *O staroegyptském tanci. Skresbami podle reprodukcí staroegyptských originálů od Milady Lexové,* 1930; English ed. *Ancient Egyptian dances with drawings made from reproductions of Ancient Egyptian originals,* 1955.

Inf. J. Ruzová; J. Ruzová, *Gött. Misz.* 152 (1996), 98-9.

LHEUREUX, *(Baron)* Armilde (1872-1957)
Belgian benefactor and member of the administrative council of the Fondation Égyptologique Reine Élisabeth; he was born at Paturages, 28 Nov. 1872, son of Louis L. and Marie Rose Cauffrier; he presented a cuneiform tablet with a letter of Amenhotep III (E. 6753) and a wooden sarcophagus of Horkaui (E. 7042) to the museum in Brussels; he died in Antwerp, 24 April 1957.

Chron. d'Ég. 32 (1957), 267 (anon.).

L'HOTE, (Hippolyte Antoine) Nestor (1804-1842)
French draughtsman and archaeologist; he was born in Cologne, 24 Aug. 1804, son of François Isidore L., a Customs official, and Zoé Dequen; his parents returned to France in 1814 and the family lived at Charleville where he studied archaeology and drawing; his father arranged for him to have a job in the Customs office, 1822, and for several years he held various posts until his appointment to a position in Paris in 1827; here he met Champollion (q.v.) and having been interested in Egyptology since he was a child, he frequented his home and was invited by him to accompany him to Egypt as draughtsman, 1828; on this expedition he was so active that he produced an immense number of drawings, published in the *Monuments* of Champollion and in *I monumenti* of Rosellini (q.v.) which formed but a small part of the total drawings; during this journey he stated that he had up till then made 500 water colours and drawings and 300 to 400 pages of notes; the heat of summer and the strenuous conditions upset him and he nearly quarrelled with Champollion, but continued to work for him, in the end returning to France, 1830; he made a second trip to Egypt to complete his drawings, 1838-9, and a third and final one, 1840-1; he had frail health, and finally the climate of Egypt and the hardships of travel and camping may have helped to hasten his end; he published, *Notice historique sur les obélisques égyptiens et en particulier sur l'obélisque de Louqsor,* 1836; *Lettres écrites d'Égypte en 1838 et 1839,* sent to Letronne who added notes, 1840; *Lettres d'Égypte en 1840-41,* 1841; also in manuscript *Abrégé de la grammaire copte*; he published a few articles but the greater part of his work remains unpublished, and his manuscripts are in the Bibl. Nat., Nouv. acq. franc., 20377, 20395-20404, and his drawings and watercolours in the Louvre, E. 25423a and E. 25423b; he was a relation of Mariette (q.v.) and it was through going through his papers that the latter became interested in Egyptology; he died in Paris, 24 March 1842.

J. Vandier d'Abbadie, *Nestor L'Hôte (1804-1842). Choix de documents conservés à la Bibl. Nat. et aux archives du Musée du Louvre,* 1963 (portr. and bibl.); D. Harlé and J. Lefebvre, *Lettres, journaux et dessins inédits de Nestor L'Hôte,* Orléans-Caen, 1994; *Revue de Paris* 9 (1842), 108-21 (E. L'Hôte) *Revue de l'Orient* 1 (1843),

225-30 (H. Horeau); *BSFE* 32 (1941), 35 sqq.; Carré, passim (see index); Champollion, ii, passim; Hartleben, ii, 112 et passim; D. Harlé in *VI Congresso Internazionale di Egittologia Atti,* II, 1993, 167-175; D. Harlé and J. Lefebvre, *Nestor L'Hôte: sur le Nil avec Champollion,* 1993; D. Harlé in M. Dewachter and A. Fouchard, *L'Égyptologie et les Champollions,* 1994, 149-59; D. Harlé in P. and J. Starkey, *Travellers in Egypt,* 1998, 121-9; È. Gran-Aymerich, *Dictionnaire biographique d'archéologie 1798-1945,* 2001, incorporated in *Les Chercheurs de passé 1798-1945,* 2007, 944-5.

LICHTHEIM, Miriam (1914-2004)

American Egyptologist; she was born in Constantinople 3 May 1914, daughter of Richard Lichtheim and Irene Hefter; her family later returned to Berlin, and moved to London and later Jerusalem; she studied Semitic languages and Egyptology at Berlin, 1932-3 and, after she left Germany, at the Hebrew University, Jerusalem under Polotsky (q.v.) 1934-38; MA, 1939; and atThe Oriental Institute, University of Chicago, 1941-44; PhD, 1944; she was employed as a research assistant at Chicago, 1944-48, 1949-52; she then trained as a professional librarian at the University of Illinois at Urbana; M.Lib Sciences 1953; she was employed at Yale University, 1953-56 and the University of California, Los Angeles as Near Eastern bibliographer, 1956-74 and also lecturer in Ancient Egyptian history; after retirement she moved in 1982 to Israel and began her most productive period of publication; she was particularly interested in ancient Egyptian texts and literature; she published *Demotic Ostraca from Medinet Habu,* 1957; *Ancient Egyptian Literature,* 3 vols, 1973-76; *Late Egyptian Wisdom Literature in the International Context,* 1983; *Ancient Egyptian Autobiographies chiefly in the Middle Kingdom,* 1988; *Maat in Egyptian Autobiographies and related Studies,* 1992; *Moral Values in Ancient Egypt,* 1997; and her autobiography *Telling it Briefly,* 1999; she died at Ganel Omer, Israel, 27 March 2004.

M. Lichtheim, *Telling it Briefly,* 1999; *ZÄS* 132 (2005), I-IV (portr.) (I. Shirun-Grumach).

LIDDON, *(Canon)* Henry Parry (1829-1890)

British traveller and collector; he was born at North Stoneham, Hampshire, 20 Aug. 1829, son of Matthew L., RN, and Anne Bilke; he was educated at Christ Church, Oxford; BA, 1850; MA, 1853; DD 1870; he was a leading member of the Oxford Movement; Professor of exegesis of holy scripture 1870-82; canon of St. Paul's 1870; chancellor 1886; he visited Egypt in 1885-6 and his account was later published by his sister A. King, *Dr. Liddon's tour in Egypt and Palestine in 1886,* 1891; his collection of antiquities was left to Bristol City Museum by his widow in 1925; he died in Weston-super-Mare, 9 Sept. 1890.

ODNB 33, 737-40 (portr.); *Al. Oxf.* 2, 852; Wilbour, 356; Sayce, 34-5; L. Grinsell, *Guide Catalogue to the Collections from Ancient Egypt,* 1972, 11; *DNB* 33, 223-8 (H. Scott-Holland); Boase 2, 425-6.

LIDMAN, Sven Fredrik (1784-1845)

Swedish orientalist, traveller, and clergyman; he was born Norrköping, 11 Dec. 1784, son of Sven L. and Catherina Brigitta Landberg; he later became Dean of Linköping; after having been lecturer in Arabic at the University of Uppsala, Lidman was appointed chaplain to the Swedish Embassy in Constantinople, 1811; he travelled in the Near East with the Livonian O. F. von Richter (q.v.), 1815, and in the summer of that year sailed up the Nile from Cairo to Qasr Ibrim in Nubia; Lidman's observations in Nubia are carefully recorded in two notebooks, illustrated with drawings by Richter; there are elaborate descriptions of Ibrim, Derr, Es-Sebua, Maharraka, Dakka, Gerf Hussein, Dendur, Kalabsha, Taffa, Qertassi, and Debod; the descriptions of the temples are very careful, and there are also several copies of Greek inscriptions; Lidman took an interest in Egyptian art which he admired very much; in the history of the discovery of Egyptian art these impressions are thus of some importance; a large collection of antiquities, mainly Egyptian, which Lidman had brought back with him was destroyed by fire in Constantinople in 1818, some few specimens only could be saved; the notebooks, now owned by Lidman's descendants, are unpublished, but there is a microfilm of the books in the Victoria Museum of Egyptian Antiquities of Uppsala University; an extract of this account, including copies of Greek inscriptions, was published by the Swedish journal *Iduna,* Sjunde haftet, Stockholm, 1817, pp. 46-85; he died in Linköping, 9 March 1845.

B. J. Peterson, 'Swedish Travellers in Egypt during the period 1700-1850', *Opuscula Atheniensia,* vii (Lund, 1967), 14-16; *Svanska Män och Kvinnor* 4, 562-3; *Svenskt Biografiskt Lexikon* 22, 715.

LIEBLEIN, Jens Daniel Carolus (1827-1911)
Norwegian Egyptologist; he was born at Christiania, 23 Dec. 1827, son of Johan Martin L. and Anna Karine Hofgaard; he had a very hard life in his early years as he was left an orphan at 11; until his 20th year he worked as a labourer in a sawmill, and later as a clerk; when he was 28 he became a student at the University of Christiania, Oslo, and later studied Egyptology while visiting Berlin and many other European museums; at this time he met most of the principal Egyptologists of his day; he was associated with the University of Christiania in 1867, and made Professor of Egyptology there in 1876; he visited Egypt in 1869 with Ibsen as an official Norwegian representative at the opening of the Suez Canal; Lieblein's work was mainly in the fields of chronology, history, and religion; his bibl. lists about 148 books, articles and communications and one or two reviews; in his monumental *Dictionnaire de noms hiéroglyphiques*, 1871-92, he collected a great corpus of genealogical lists, still of great value for the study of prosopography and personal names in Egypt; Lieblein also published, *Die aegyptischen Denkmäler in St. Petersburg, Helsingfors, Upsala und Copenhagen ...*, 1873; *Index alphabétique de tous les mots contenus dans le Livre des Morts publié par R. Lepsius, d'après le papyrus de Turin*, 1875; *Egyptian Religion*, 1884; *Handel und Schiffahrt auf dem Rothen Meere in alten Zeiten, nach ägyptischen Quellen*, 1886; *Pistis Sophia*, a Coptic study in 2 pts., 1908-9; he died in Eidsvold, Norway, 13 Aug. 1911.

Inf. B. J. Peterson; *Rec. Trav.* 34 (1912), 114-16 (G. Maspero); *Sphinx* 15, 161-7 (E. Andersson) (portr.), 168-79 (bibl.); Hilmy, i, 385; *Norsk Biografisk Leksikon* 8, 357-61; S. Hjelde, *Man, Meaning and Mystery*, 2000, 103-5.

LIEDER, (*Revd*) **(Johann) Rudolph Theophilus** (1798-1865)
German missionary and collector; he was born in Erfurt, Prussia, 29 May 1798, son of Christian Wilhelm L. master shoemaker, and Anna Maria Bormann; he worked for many years in Cairo under the Church Missionary Society, 1825-62; he was ordained priest in the Church of England, 1842, and revised the New Testament in Coptic and Arabic for the SPCK; he translated into Arabic the Homilies of St. Chrysostom and other works; Member of the Egyptian Society of Cairo, 1836; he was hostile to Mariette (q.v.); he married 1838/9 Alice Holliday (*d.*Cairo, 1868) who made squeezes of many Egyptian monuments which are now in the Griffith Institute, Oxford and Grantham Museum; they collected Egyptian antiquities and in 1861 Lord Amherst (q.v.) purchased the collection of 186 items for £200, the inventory of which is now in the Eg. Dept. of the British Museum; in the preface to the Amherst Sale Catalogue (1921) he is wrongly called 'the Revd W. Leider'; he died of cholera in Cairo, 6 July 1865.

Inf. from Church Miss. Soc.; *Bibl. Ég.* 18, xxxvii; Lepsius, 36, 47, 74; Lindsay, 22, 33, 34, 37; Lane Corr. 49-63; Sophia Poole, *Englishwoman in Egypt*, ii, 183; iii, 33, 40, 41; J. Malek in *JEA* 72 (1986), 101-112; D. Magee and J. Malek in *JEA* 77 (1991), 195-7; J. Thompson, *Edward William Lane 1801-1876*, 2010, 530-1.

LIFSCHITZ, Isaac Grigorievitch (1896-1970)
Russian Egyptologist; he was born in Khovno (now Kaunas), Lithuania, 17 Oct. 1896; he was educated at Leningrad University under Struve (q.v.) and later worked in the Oriental Institute of the Soviet Academy of Sciences; he published in Russian studies on Russian Egyptology and Egyptian writing and literature, notably a translation of tales, published posthumously, 1979; he died 13 July1970.

Inf. J. Śliwa.

LIGHT, (*Sir*) **Henry** (1783-1870)
British army officer and traveller; he was born in Madras, India 7 Feb. 1783, son of William L. of the Madras civil service, and Lucretia Anstey; he was educated at Rugby and Woolwich; he entered the army, 1799; 2nd Lieut. Royal Artillery; he served with his regiment until 1824 when he retired, afterwards being made Lieut.-Governor of Antigua, 1836; Governor and Commander-in-Chief British Guiana, 1838-48; KCB, 1848; while serving with his regiment in Malta, he obtained leave to explore Egypt, Nubia, and Palestine, 1814; he went up the Nile as far as Derr; he published *Travels in Egypt, Nubia and the Holy Land*, 1818; he obtained a painted coffin at Thebes which he presented to Col. Misset (q.v.) from whom it probably passed to Salt; part of Light's notes were used by the Revd Robert Walpole in his works on eastern travel, 1817-20; he died in Falmouth, 3 March 1870.

Army Lists; Hilmy, i, 386; Legh, 79; Westcar Diary, 111; Boase 2, 428; G. Solly, *Rugby School Register 1*, 1938, 132.

LIGHT, William (1786-1839)
British army officer; he was born in Kuala Kedah, Malaya, 27 April 1786, son of Francis L., the founder of Penang, and Martinha Rozells; he served in the Royal Navy as midshipman, 1799-1802; he was interned in

France, 1803-4 and was in India, 1804-7; Ensign, 4th Dragoons from 1808; he retired from the army in 1822 with the rank of Major; Colonel in the Spanish Constitutional army, 1823; he toured the Mediterranean in his yacht, 1827-1830; he reached Egypt in Dec. 1830 and went up the Nile to the Second Cataract, Jan.-May 1831 where he met Hay (q.v.),Wilkinson (q.v.) and others; he returned to England to recruit seamen for Muhammad Ali's navy; in 1834 he commanded the paddle-steamer *Nile* out to Egypt and served on her until Nov. 1835; Surveyor-General, S. Australia, 1836-8; he founded the City of Adelaide, where he died 6 Oct. 1839.

ODNB 33, 750-1 (portr.); *DNB* 33, 228; Bonomi Diary, 1831, No. 23; *Australian Dictionary of Biography* 2, 116-8; G. Dutton and D. Elder, *Colonel William Light*, 1992.

LIKHATCHEV, Nikolai Petrovitch (1862-1936)
Russian nobleman, historian and art collector; a specialist in palaeography and numismatics and expert in the art of icons; he was born in Clistopol, 12/24 April 1862, son of Peter F. L. and Klaudia Andreev; he was educated at the University of Kuzan; MA, 1890; Ph.D. 1892; member of the Archaeographic Commission, 1894; Professor at the St. Petersburg Archaeological Institute; assistant director of St. Petersburg Public Library, 1902; he founded a private museum of palaeography, which contained examples of Egyptian writing such as stelae, papyri, seals and some Coptic objects; he also owned three autograph letters of J. F. Champollion (edited 1979 by I. S. Katznelson); from 1925 member of the Soviet Academy of Sciences; in 1925 he transferred his museum to the Academy, from where in 1938 Egyptian objects were given to the collection of the Hermitage Museum, Leningrad; he died in Leningrad, 14 April 1936.

Y. Y. Perepelkin, *Opisanie vystavki "Pismennost drevnego mira i rannego srednevekovya"*, Moscow-Leningrad 1936; *Sovetskaya Istoricheskaya Enciklopedia* 8 (1965), 742; *Great Soviet Encyclopedia* 14, 496-7; inf. J. Śliwa.

LINANT DE BELLEFONDS, (*Bey* and *Pasha*) **Louis Maurice Adolphe** (1799-1883)
French geographer, explorer, artist, and engineer; he was born in Lorient, 23 Nov. 1799, son of Antoine Marie L., a naval officer, and Perrine Jeanne Adelaide Touboulic; he was intended for a career at sea and passed his exam. in 1814, after which he was sent to do charting and surveying along the coast of Canada and USA, 1815; in 1817 he accompanied the Comte de Forbin (q.v.) on an expedition as a midshipman to various countries in the Near East, but was invited to proceed to Egypt to make drawings and maps to illustrate the works of various writers; he arrived in Egypt in 1817, and afterwards worked for a time in Cairo staying on in the service of Muhammad Ali; he then met W. Bankes (q.v.), 1818 and joined his party as draughtsman, going as far south as the second cataract; he visited Siwa in March-April 1820 with Drovetti (q.v.); he was in Sinai Sept.-Nov. 1820 with Ricci (q.v.) and also visited other parts of Egypt; he was asked by Bankes to go south again and to determine the site of Meroe, making drawings of the antiquities he saw *en route* which he accomplished from June 1821 to July 1822; he was thus the first European traveller to see the ancient sites and monuments at Musawwarat and Naga; he had a further expedition to explore the White Nile and the Sudan, from March 1826-Sept. 1827, under the auspices of the Assoc. for Promoting the Discovery of the Interior Parts of Africa, when he travelled as far as the Shilluk country; he journeyed to the Atbai looking for gold in the gold-mine district between the Nile and the Red Sea for Muhammad Ali, 1831-2; he executed many drawings of monuments and inscriptions at this time; he devoted himself in later life to irrigation projects and also played a considerable part in the planning of the Suez Canal; he also explored Darfur, and in 1847 directed with Bourdaloue the topographical studies of the Isthmus of Suez; another of his interests was the Fayum lake area; he was made Egyptian Minister of Public Works, 1869, Pasha, 1873; he kept a fine establishment in Cairo, where he and his family always wore Turkish dress; his first wife died of cholera in 1831; he was a brilliant draughtsman and artist, and his great collection of drawings and notes are extremely valuable today, as many of the monuments recorded have since been destroyed or damaged; he rendered much help to Champollion (q.v.) in 1828; the Louvre has one copy of his journal with drawings and other papers presented by his family; a typed version is in the Griffith Institute, Oxford; with it are 6 folders of drawings and a map of the route; he made and published many maps of Egypt, see *Carte hydrographique de la moyenne Égypte*, scale 1:250,000, 1854; *Carte de l'Elbaye. Carte hydrographique de la partie septentrionale de la Haute Égypte*, 1854; *Carte hydrographique de l'Égype (Nord et Moyenne)*, 1855; *Carte hydrographique de la Basse-Égypte et d'une partie de l'Isthme de Suez. En 2 feuilles*, 1856?; *General-Karte von Aegypten und der Sinaï Halbinsel, mit Benutzung der handschriftlichen hydrographischen Aufnahmen des Nilthales von L. de B. bearbeitet ... von H. Kiepert*, scale 1:1,500,000, Berlin, 1859; also published the following works, *Account of a Journey into the Oases of Upper Egypt*, London, 1822; *Mémoirs sur les principaux travaux d'utilité publique exécutés en Égypte depuis la plus haute antiquité jusqu'à nos jours. Accompagnés d'un Atlas renfermant neuf planches grand in-folio imprimées en couleur*, 1872-3; also *Mémoire sur le Lac de Moeris, présenté et lu à la Société Égyptienne le 5 juillet 1842*. Carte. 1843; *Journal d'un voyage à Méroé dans les années 1821 et 1822*, edited Margaret Shinnie, Khartoum, 1958; many more of his drawings are with those of Burton in the British Museum and also in Kingston Lacy House, Dorset; he died in Cairo, 19 July 1883.

Margaret Shinnie, *see above*, biogr. on ix-xii; Brugsch, *Mein Leben*, 159; Carré, ii, 24 etc.; Champollion, ii, 78 and often; Clot Bey, i, 41; ii, 479; Finati, 301, 320, 345, 354, 394, 427; Hilmy, ii, 387 (wrongly called *Ernest*); *Journ. RGS* 2, 171; *Larousse, XIXe siècle* 10, 531; *La Grande Enc.* 22. 270; *Proc. RGS* 6, 381; M. Kurz and P. Linant de Bellefonds in P. and J. Starkey (eds.), *Travellers in Egypt*, 1998, 61-9; M Kurz and P. Linant de Bellefonds in J. Starkey and O. el Daly (eds.), *Desert Travellers*, 2000, 153-182; È. Gran-Aymerich, *Dictionnaire biographique d'archéologie 1798-1945*, 2001, incorporated in *Les Chercheurs de passé 1798-1945*, 2007, 945-6; P. Linant de Bellefonds in P. and J. Starkey, *Unfolding the Orient*, 2001, 193-208.

LINCKE, Arthur Alexander (1853-1898)
German orientalist; he was born in Dresden, 13 Nov. 1853; he studied under Ebers (q.v.) and Delitzsch; he published the hieratic papyri of Bologna and other works on Egyptian epistolography, but afterwards forsook Egyptology for Assyriology; he died 2 June 1898.

Hilmy, i., 387; *OLZ* 1898, 224.

LINDSAY, (*Lord*) Alexander William Crawford (*afterwards* 25th Earl of Crawford and 8th Earl of Balcarres) (1812-1880)
British nobleman, traveller, and writer on art; he was born in Muncaster Castle, Cumberland, 16 Oct. 1812, eldest son of James, 24th Earl of C. and 7th of B. and Margaret Marian Frances Pennington; he was educated at Eton and Trinity College, Cambridge; MA, 1833; he travelled a great deal and collected books for the celebrated Lindsay Library; he visited Egypt and Palestine, 1836-7, and published *Letters from Egypt, Edom and the Holy Land*, 2 vols. 1838, 4th ed. 1847, which contains interesting particulars of Caviglia (q.v.); his best-known works were *Progression by Antagonism*, 1846, and *History of Christian Art*, 1847; he succeeded to the earldoms, 1869; he died in Florence, 13 Dec. 1880.

ODNB 33, 850-1 (portr.); *DNB* 33, 285-6; Hilmy, i, 149 (entered under *Crawford*).

LIPIŃSKA (*neé* Freyer), Jadwiga (1932-2009)
Polish Egyptologist; she was born in Warsaw, 29 Nov. 1932, daughter of Edward F. and Zofia Kodis; she studied at Warsaw University, graduating 1958; she joined the Ancient Art Gallery in the National Museum in Warsaw, 1958; gallery curator, 1991-2000; she was awarded the title of Professor in 1991; she worked with Michałowski (q.v.) at the Polish Centre of Mediterranean Archaeology and acted as his assistant in lecturing at Warsaw University; she excavated at Tell Atrib, 1960, 1963, 1965 and at Deir el-Bahri from 1961 where she discovered the temple of Thutmose III; field director at Deir el-Bahri from 1964 and then director of the work at the Thutmose III temple, 1978-96; she also excavated at Alexandria, 1963, Faras, 1962-3, and in Syria, 1965; a volume of essays was published in her honour in *Warsaw Egytpological Studies* I, 1997; apart from many articles in English and Polish, she published *Amulety egipskie*, 1964; *Polskie badania archeologiczne na Bliskim Wschodie I w basenie Morza Czarnego* (an exhibition catalogue), 1969; *500 zagadek z Egiptu Starozytnegom*, 1969; *Polskie badania archeologiczne w basenie Morza Srodziemnego i Czarnego*, 1970; *The Temple of Tuthmosis* III./ *Architecture. Deir el-Bahari* II, 1977; *Historia architektury starozytnego Egiptu*, 1977; *Historia rzezby reliefu i malarstwa starozytnego Egiptu*, 1978; *The Temple of Thutmosis III. Statuary and Votive Monuments. Deir el-Bahari* IV, 1984*; W cieniu pyramid*, 2003; *Sztuka starozytnego Egiptu*, 2008; she died in Warsaw, 4 Oct. 2009.

Internet obit; *Warsaw Egyptological Studies* I, 1997, iii-iv, v-x (bibl.).

LITHGOW, William (*c*.1582- *c*.1645)
Scottish traveller; he was born in Lanark, about 1582, the elder son of James L., a merchant, and Alison Grahame; he was educated at Lanark Grammar School he was, according to the rather doubtful authority of Sir Walter Scott, brought up to be a tailor; he got into a scrape over a Miss Lockhart whose four brothers cut off his ears, according to legend, however improbable, and was afterwards certainly known by this peculiarity; a great traveller he claimed to have journeyed 36,000 miles on foot; he set out from Paris for Palestine and Egypt, 1610, returning in 1612, and made many other expeditions in Europe, Asia and Africa; on his last journey to Spain, 1619-21, he was seized and tortured as a spy; Gondomar the Spanish ambassador in London promised redress but did nothing and so Lithgow assaulted him in the King's ante-chamber and was accordingly put in Marshalsea prison; his account of Egypt is longer than some written then and appeared as *Rare Adventures and Paineful Perigrinations* published incompletely, 1614, fully 1632; his later life and adventures are rather obscure but he is said to died in Lanark about 1645, and to have been buried in the churchyard of St. Kentigern.

Voyages en Égypte des années 1611 et 1612 trans. and annotated by Oleg V. Volkoff, 1973; *ODNB* 34, 11-4; *DNB* 11, 1238-40 (F. H. Groome); *Chamber's Biogr. Dict.* (1929), 595; R. A. Davenport, *Dict. of Biogr.* (1831), 392; J. Speake (ed.), *Literature of Travel and Exploration*, 2003, 2, 729-30; C. E. Bosworth, *An Intrepid Scot: William Lithgow of Lanark's Travels in the Ottoman Lands*, 2006.

LLOYD, George (1815-1843)
British botanist, excavator, and traveller; he was born, probably in India, 17 Oct. 1815, illegitimate son of Sir William L. of Brynestyn, Wales, soldier and pioneer mountaineer, and an Indian lady; he edited his father's journal *Narrative of a Journey from Caunpoor to the Boorendo Pass in the Himalaya Mountains, via India, Gwalior, Agra, Delhi and Sirhind*, 1840; member of the Cairo Literary Society; he excavated at Thebes with Prisse d'Avennes (q.v.), 1839-43; he died through the accidental discharge of his gun at Qurna, 31 Oct. 1843; his papers and botanical collections were given to the Botanic Garden of Montpellier.

Carré, i, 311; Prisse, *Oriental Album* (1851) (portr.); D. Leslie Davies, *Transactions. Denbigh Historical Society* 26 (1977), 7-12, 40; J. Thomson, *Edward William Lane 1816-1876*, 2010, 360-1.

LOAT, William Leonard Stevenson (1871-1932)
British naturalist and archaeologist; he was born at Norwood, Surrey, 15 Oct. 1871, son of William L. and Marianna Eliza Stevenson; he first visited Egypt in 1899 as assistant to G. A. Boulenger, FRS, in the ichthyological survey of the Nile; he excavated at Gurob for Petrie (q.v.), 1903, and at Abydos for the EEF, 1908-9 and 1912-13, where he found and published an account of the Ibis Cemetery; the war put a stop to his Egyptological work, and he afterwards married and settled at Mevagissy, Cornwall, taking up horticulture; FZS, 1895-1902; he visited the Andes in 1927; he presented some Egyptian objects to the Plymouth Museum in the 1920s; he published *Predynastic Cemetery at El Mahasna*, with E. R. Ayrton, 1911; *Gurob*, with M. A. Murray's *Saqqara Mastabas*, 1905; he died at Treclome, Mevagissey, Cornwall, 10 April 1932.

JEA 18 (1932), 190; Petrie, 190; inf. G. T. Martin.

LOFTIE, (*Revd*) **William John** (1839-1911)
British clergyman, archaeologist, and collector; he was born in Armagh, 25 July 1839, son of John Henry L., of Tanderagee, Co. Armagh, and Jane Crozier; he studied at Trinity College, Dublin; BA; FSA; he married Jeannie Burnett 1865; he published many works on the history and antiquities of London; he was Chaplain of the Queen's Chapel of the Savoy, 1871-95; he spent several years in Egypt and was closely associated with Sayce (q.v.), Budge (q.v.), and Petrie (q.v.); Loftie formed a small collection mainly consisting of scarabs, which he purchased at El-Amarna, Luxor, and many other sites throughout Egypt, which was eventually bought by the British Museum for £400; he published a general work, *A Ride in Egypt from Sioot to Luxor in 1879, with notes on the present state and ancient history of the Nile Valley, and some account of the various ways of making the voyage out and home*, 1879; *An Essay of Scarabs: together with the catalogue of a private collection of Ancient Egyptian Amulets of various kinds, bearing the names of kings*, 1884, only 125 copies of which were printed; this was one of the first studies on the subject and precedes Petrie's by five years; he also contributed articles to the *Arch. Journ.* on Maidum and the Pyramids; he died in London, 16 June 1911.

Inf. letter of L. in Edwards Lib. UCL; Budge, *N & T* i, 76, 82, 151; ii, 290; Petrie, 30; *WWW* i, 436; *ODNB* 34, 298-9.

LONG, George (1800-1879)
British classical scholar; he was born in born in Poulton-le-Fylde, Lancs., 4 Nov. 1800, eldest son of James L., a merchant, and Isabel Brodbelt; he was educated at Macclesfield Grammar School and entered Trinity College, Cambridge, 1818; here he had an outstandingly brilliant career, being bracketed Craven scholar with Lord Macaulay and Prof. Malden; BA, 1822; wrangler and senior chancellor's medallist, 1823, gaining a Fellowship over the two above mentioned; in 1824 he was appointed Prof. of Ancient Languages in the University of Virginia, where he became a friend of T. Jefferson; appointed Professor of Greek in the newly founded University College London, 1828; editor of the *Quarterly Journal of Education*, 1831; one of the founders of the Royal Geogr. Soc., 1830, and Hon. Sec., 1846-8; he prepared maps of Egypt and Persia for the Atlas of the Soc. for the Diffusion of Useful Knowledge; edited the *Penny Cyclopaedia*, 29 vols., for this soc. 1833-46, and other works also; Professor of Latin, University College London, 1842, resigned 1846, after which he lectured on jurisprudence and civil law in the Inner Temple; he was called to the bar, 1837; from 1849 to 1871 he was classical lecturer at Brighton College; he published a descriptive guide, *Antiquities in the British Museum*, 1832, 1836, two vols.; the first part is mainly a description of Egypt, the second dealing with the existing collections, Burton's drawings being used for illustration among others; he died in Portfield, Chichester, 10 Aug. 1879, and is buried there.

ODNB 34, 362-4 (portr.); *DNB* 34, 102-4.

LONGPÉRIER, (Henri) Adrien Prévost de (1816-1882)
French archaeologist and numismatist; he was born Paris, 21 Sept. 1816, son of Henri Simon P. de L., Mayor of Meaux, and Adrienne Martine Amélie L'Hoste; he joined the Cabinet des Médailles in 1836, Assistant

Keeper, 1842-7; from 1847 he was Director of Oriental Antiquities in the Louvre Museum, where he made great improvements in the arrangement of the Egyptian collections; he made numerous contributions to archaeological journals which were collected, with a biographical notice by G. Schlumberger, 7 vols., Paris, 1883; he died in Paris, 17 Jan. 1882; his son Henri (*fl.* 1860-70) also an archaeologist, was a student of de Rougé (q.v.) and Maspero (q.v.) at the Coll. of France, but did not follow Egyptology as a profession, writing on various archaeological subjects in scientific journals instead.

Oeuvres, ut supra; *Bibl. Ég.* 21, xvii, xviii; Hilmy. i, 169; Maspero, *L'Égyptologie* (1915), 7; T. Sarmant, *Le Cabinet des Médailles de la Bibliothèque Nationale 1661-1848*, 1994, 286-7; È. Gran-Aymerich, *Dictionnaire biographique d'archéologie 1798-1945*, 2001, incorporated in *Les Chercheurs de passé 1798-1945*, 2007, 952-3; N. Warner, *Collecting for Eternity*, 2016.

LOOS, Cornelius (1686-1738)
Swedish officer and military governor of Hamburg; born Stockholm, 4 Feb. 1686, son of Cornelius L. and Marie Nääf; he was the leader of an expedition to the Near East during his military career; in 1710 he was sent by King Charles XII of Sweden to obtain descriptions of ancient monuments and curiosities; he visited Egypt in May-July 1710 with two officer companions; they stayed in Alexandria, Rosetta, and Cairo and surveyed the neighbouring monuments, including the pyramids at Giza; they returned with many drawings, mostly executed by Loos, who was a clever draughtsman, and also with a number of antiquities, arriving at the royal Swedish camp at Bender in Turkey; unfortunately almost all this material was destroyed by fire in 1713; four preserved drawings of the Great Pyramid are in existence today in the National Museum of Stockholm, three of them showing the exterior while another is a profile; he died in Hamburg, 15 April 1738.

E. Wrangel, *Den första svenska orientexpeditionen och Cornelius Loos' techningar*, Karolinska förbundets Åårsbok 1931, 1932, 113 ff.; B. J. Peterson, 'Swedish Travellers in Egypt during the period 1700-1850', *Opuscula Atheniensia* vii, (Lund, 1967), 1-7; *Svenska Män och Kvinnor* 5, 72; *Svenskt Biografiskt Lexikon* 24, 101-3.

LÓPEZ, Jesús (1933-2002)
Spanish Egyptologist; he studied history at the University of Madrid and at the École Pratique des Hautes Études in Paris, 1960-65; he was later attached to CNRS; he took part in the Spanish expedition during the Nubian campaign and later was director of the excavations at Herakleopolis, 1966-69; he was particularly interested in texts and published the hieratic ostraca, mainly from Deir el-Medina, in the Turin Museum; apart from numerous articles, he published *Las inscripciones rupestres faraónicas entre Korosko y Kasr Ibrim*, 1966, and *Ostraca Ieratici*, 1978-84; he died in 2002.

Rev d'Eg 54 (2003), xiv-xvi. (J. Yoyotte); *Boletin de la Asociancion española de Egiptologia* 13 (2003), 7-10 (portr.) (J. M. Galán Allué); J. Cervelló Autuori and A. J. Quevedo Álvarez (eds.), *...ir a buscar leña. Estudios dedicados al Prof, Jesús López*, 2001; J. Cervelló Autuori and D. Rulli Ribó in J. Lopez (ed.), *Cuentos y fábulas del antiguo Egipto*, 2005, 9-13.

LORD, William Keast (1818-1872)
British naturalist and veterinary surgeon; he was born in Cornwall, 1818, and is said to be the son of Edward L.; he served as a vet. surgeon in the Crimean War, and was a man of many activities, being the first manager of the Brighton Aquarium, and naturalist to the Boundary Commission of British Columbia, 1858; he carried out archaeological and scientific researches in Egypt and wrote accounts of them in the popular press, his results being utilized by Chabas (q.v.) and Maspero (q.v.); he also published catalogues of his collections of Egyptian lepidoptera and hymenoptera, 1871; he died in Brighton, 9 Dec. 1872.

DNB 34, 136; Maspero, *Hist. Anc.* i, 356, n. I.

LORET, Victor, Clément Georges Philippe (1859-1946)
French Egyptologist, naturalist, and musician; he was born in Paris, 1 Sept. 1859, son of Clément L., an organist, and Philippine Colonius; his interest in Egyptology was aroused when as a child three leaves of Champollion's *Grammar* fell into his hands; he studied Egyptology under Maspero (q.v.) at the École des Hautes Études and the Coll. de France; he afterwards went with Maspero to Cairo as an original member of the French Institute of Arch., 1881; he at first worked with Lefébure (q.v.) on texts in the Valley of Kings, and copied and published many Theban tombs; he was made Director, 1886; appointed Reader in Egyptology at Lyons, 1886-1929; he also became Director General of the Antiquities Service, 1897-9, but was unfitted for an administrative post and antagonized both Europeans and Egyptians; nevertheless in his short time as Director a great amount of important work was carried out, systematic work went on in the Valley of Kings and the tombs of Thutmose III and Amenhotep II were cleared, the latter having the cache of 9 mummies of Pharaohs;

at Saqqara the 'Street of Tombs' was discovered and excavated; also during this period the *Annales du Service* was founded; Loret later founded a school of Egyptology at Lyons, and was one of the most successful teachers in France; his interests were very wide and covered Egyptian grammar, history, early and predynastic religion, botany, and zoology; he also was interested in popular Egyptian music of the villages; he received the Grand Prix Maspero of the Acad. des Inscr. and was made a Chevalier of the Légion d'honneur; at his death he left a number of posthumous works, the most important of these being a truly monumental *Dictionnaire hiéroglyphique*; he had begun this work in 1884 intending to produce a definitive one-man work, but had later abandoned it on the production of the Berlin Dictionary; for this work he went through all the known Ptolemaic texts and had completed two vols. numbering 1,636 and 543 words each, but constituting only a fraction of the whole scheme; instead he started to adapt it as a Thesaurus and had completed 21 notebooks with notes; he also left in MSS *Notes de grammaire*, completing the *Manuel de Langue Ég.*; Loret's list of publications numbered 139 items up to 1930, the chief works being, *Quelques documents relatifs à la littérature et à la musique populaires de la Haute-Égypte*, 1884; *La Tombe d'un ancien Égyptien*, 1886; *La Flore pharaonique, d'après les documents hiéroglyphiques et les spécimens découverts dans les tombes*, 1887, 2nd ed. 1892; *L'Égypte du temps des Pharaons, la vie, la science et l'art*, 1889; *Manuel de Langue égyptienne. Grammaire, tableau des hiéroglyphes, textes et glossaire*, 1889; *L'Égypte au temps du totémisme*, 1906; *Recherches sur les poissons représentés dans quelques tombeaux égyptiens de l'Ancien Empire*, with C. Gaillard and C. Kuentz, 1923; *La résine de térébinthe, sonter, chez les anciens Égyptiens*, 1949; his archives, which had passed to Varille (q.v.) were acquired by the Egyptological Archives of the Università degli Studi di Milano in 2002; he died in Lyons, 3 Feb. 1946.

ASAE 47 (1947), 7-13 (portr.) (A. Varille); *Mélanges Victor Loret, BIFAO* 30 (1931) (portr.), xi-xxiii (bibl. to 1930 - C. Kuentz); *Chron. d'É.* 21 (1946), 202-5; *Kêmi* 12 (1952), 5-23 (G. Lefebvre) 'Correspondence de Victor Loret', 13 (1954), 5-27 (G. Lefebvre), 17 (1964), 7-25, on dictionary (P. Montet); Budge, *N & T* ii, 365, 392; Petrie, 168, 173; Sayce, 306; *KMT* 14/3 (2003), 82-8; È. Gran-Aymerich, *Dictionnaire biographique d'archéologie 1798-1945*, 2001, incorporated in *Les Chercheurs de passé 1798-1945*, 2007, 953-4; P. Piacentini and C. Orsenigo, *La Valle dei re Riscoperta*, 2004; P. Piacentini and C. Orsenigo, *The Valley of Kings Rediscovered*, 2005; *Kyphi* 5 (2006); E. Seibel, P. Piacentini, et al, *Victor Loret in Egypt (1881-1899)*, 2008; P. Piacentini, *Egypt and the Pharaohs from the Sand to the Library*, 2010, 68-82. Photograph courtesy of Università degli Studi di Milano.

LORING, Edward Robbins (1937-2015)
American Egyptologist; he was born in Chicago, 25 Aug. 1937, son of Edward D'Arcy L. and China Robbins Logeman; he graduated from the Culver Military Academy, 1955; he developed an interest in Egyptology and later studied at the Universities of Graz, Athens, and Basel; he pioneered underwater archaeology in Greece, 1966; he then worked at MIT on imaging analysis and used his experience to create informations systems and databases for the Basel Museum of Cultures, the Berlin-Brandenburg Academy of Sciences, and the Russian Academy of Sciences; he was a research fellow at the Centre for Egyptological Sciences of the Russian Academy of Sciences from 1997 and began the Database of Eastern European Egyptology to catalogue Egyptian objects in the museums of this area; he had a special interest in the coffins of the Twenty-First Dynasty; he funded the German-Russian expedition to the Royal cache, 1998; he created websites to publish his research on the subject ofr royal mummies and coffins of this period; he died in Basel, 9 March 2015.

Internet obit. (S. Ivanov).

LORTET, Charles Louis (1836-1909)
French naturalist; he was born in Oullins (Rhône), 22 Aug. 1836, son of Pierre L. and Jeanne Muller; Doyen honoraire of the Faculty of Medicine, Lyons; appointed Professor of Natural History, Lyons, 1867; Director of the Museum of Natural Hist., Lyons, 1869-1909; he made a special study of the mummified animals of ancient Egypt and the zoological and archaeological data provided by them working in collaboration with his assistant Claude Gaillard (q.v.); he published articles thereon in *ASAE,* the Lyons *Annales du Musée*, and the Cairo *Cat. Gén.*; he died in Lyons, 26 Dec. 1909.

Private inf.

LORTON, David M. (1945-2011)
American Egyptologist; he was born 4 March 1945; he studied at Johns Hopkins University under Goedicke (q.v.); he published *The Juridical Terminology of International Relations in Egyptian Texts Through Dyn. XVIII*, 1974; he is best known as the translator of works by German and French Egyptologists, namely, G. Andreu, *Egypt in the Age of the Pyramids*, 1997; E. Hornung, *History of Ancient Egypt. An Introduction*, 1999; E. Hornung, *Akhenaten and the Religion of Light*, 1999; E. Hornung, *Ancient Egyptian Books of the Afterlife*, 1999; K Mysliwiec, *The Twilight of Ancient Egypt: First Millenium B.C.E.*, 2000; M. Chauveau, *Egypt in the Age of Cleopatra*, 2000; S. Sauneron, *The Priests of Ancient Egypt*, 2000; J. Assmann, *The Search for God in Ancient Egypt*, 2001; E. Hornung, *Secret Lore of Egypt*, 2001; C. Traunecker, *Gods of Egypt*, 2001; M. Chauveau, *Cleopatra*, 2002; C.

Zivie-Coche, *Sphinx*, 2002; P. Vernus and J. Yoyotte, *Book of the Pharaohs*, 2003; P. Vernus, *Affairs and Scandals in Ancient Egypt*, 2003; J. Assmann, *Death and Salvation in Ancient Egypt*, 2005; F. Dunand, *Gods and Men in Egypt*, 2006; F. Dunand and R. Lichtenberg, *Mummies and Death in Ancient Egypt*, 2007; F. Ebeling, *Secret History of Hermes Trismegistus*, 2007; A. Zivie and P. Chapius, *The Lost Tombs of Saqqara*, 2008; A. Schweizer and E. Hornung, *The Sungod's Journey through the Netherworld*, 2010; T. Schneider, *Ancient Egypt in 101 Questions and Answers*, 2013; he died in Baltimore, 22 Oct. 2011.

LOTTIN DE LAVAL, Pierre-Victorien (1810-1903)
French archaeologist and painter; he was born in Orbec, 19 Sep. 1810, son of Tranquille Victorien Constant L., a hatter, and Marie Victoire Delavel; he moved to Paris around 1820, where he became a protegé of François Guizot, later President of the Council of Ministers, and secretary to the Comte d'Avesnes; he also became involved in the artistic life of Paris, and in writing poetry and for the theatre; in 1834 he travelled to Italy and the Adriatic coast and became interested in archaeology; he began to develop a moulding process that would later be patented as lottinoplasty; he joined scientific expedition to Near East 1843-6; he travelled to Sinai and the Arabian Peninsula in 1850-51, making casts of the reliefs in the Wadi Maghara and at Serabit el-Khadim; he published *Voyage dans la péninsule arabique du Sinaï et l'Égypte moyenne: histoire, géographie, épigraphie*, 1855-9, with a folio volume of plates which included many hieroglyphic inscriptions; he moved to Menneval, near Bernay in 1852 and devoted his time to painting, based on sketches made during his Eastern travels, the study of Norman history, and the development of the Bernay Museum of Fine Arts; his squeezes are preserved in the Musée de Bernay and the Louvre; he died in Menneval, 23 February 1903.

Hilmy, i. 393; *BSFE* 80 (1977), 11-12; È. Gran-Aymerich, *Dictionnaire biographique d'archéologie 1798-1945*, 2001, incorporated in *Les Chercheurs de passé 1798-1945*, 2007, 954-5; N. Zapata-Aubé, *Lottin de Laval: archéologue et peintre orientaliste 1810-1903*, 1997; inf. A. Dodson.

LOUKIANOFF, Gregory Ivanovitch (1885-1945)
Russian Egyptologist and antiquities dealer; he studied Egyptology in Russia before the 1917 Revolution and in 1920 sought refuge in Egypt; he became an antiquities dealer acting as an agent and consultant for collectors and other dealers; he was also involved in exacavtions near Alexandria and other sites; he published a number of articles in various journals; he died in Cairo in 1945.

F. Hagen and K. Ryholt, *The Antiquities Trade in Egypt 1880-1930*, 2017, 230-4.

LOURIE, Izidore Mikhailovitch (1903-1958)
Russian Egyptologist; he was born 3 Dec. 1903, and studied at the University of Minsk, 1922, afterwards working in the library and at the University; he became interested in the history of ancient Egypt and moved to Leningrad, 1923, where he studied Egyptology at the University; he later became the first secretary of Leningrad Museum's scientific work; he was appointed to the Hermitage, 1927, his first task being to superintend the museum's register; he was later made head of the Eastern Dept. and an assistant to the General Scientific Director; Lourie was also the editor of a journal and for a long time directed the editorial section of the Hermitage; he was made a doctor of historic science, 1946; he published over 50 studies and articles, his main interests being research into the history of technique and the social-economic life of Egypt in which field he was a specialist; his work embraced the fields of jurisdiction, the court of justice in the New Kingdom and judicial oracles; he also taught students; he published *The History of Ancient Egyptian Technique*, 1940; *Outline of the history of Ancient Egyptian Law*, 1946-8, with which he gained his second degree; also *Elements of an animal epic in Ancient Egyptian representations*, a work on Egyptian stelae in the Hermitage and *Ocerki drevnegipetskogo prava XVI-X vekov do n.e.*, Leningrad, 1960 (German trans. *Studien zum altägyptischen Recht*, 1971); he died in Leningrad, 26 Jan. 1958.

VDI 3 (65) 1958, 233-6 (anon.); *Sobshchenia Gosudarstvennego Ermitazha* 14 (1958), 62-3 (portr.) (I. Diakonov and B. Piotrovski).

LOWE, (*Sir*) Hudson (1769-1844)
British army officer and traveller; he was born in Galway, 28 July 1769, son of Hudson L. and his wife née Morgan; he entered the army, 1787; Capt., 1795; he served in Toulon, Corsica, Elba, Portugal, and Egypt, 1805-12; Major-Gen., 1814; KCB, 1817; Governor of St. Helena during the confinement of Napoleon, 1815-21; governor of Antigua, 1823; on staff in Ceylon, 1825-30; Lieut.-Gen., 1830; he visited Egypt in 1826 and explored Thebes with Hay (q.v.) and Bonomi (q.v.); he died 10 Jan. 1844; his library was sold 1 May 1844.

ODNB 34, 567-70 (portr.); *DNB* 34, 189-93; Madden, *Travels*, i, 339; ii, 37; Hay Diary, 1826, May.

LOWELL, John (1799-1836)
American philanthropist, traveller, and collector; he was born in Boston, Mass. 11 May 1799, son of Francis Cabot L. and Hannah Jackson; he first travelled to India, 1816-17; in 1832 his health was seriously affected by the death of his wife and two children from fever, and he set out on a voyage around the world; he first visited Europe where he employed the artist Gleyre (q.v.) and later arrived in Egypt in Dec. 1834; at Thebes in the spring of 1835 following a serious illness at Asyut, he made his will there bequeathing the sum of £237,000 for the foundation of the Lowell Institute at Boston; in June he set out for Nubia, arriving at Meroë in Sept. and at Khartoum in Nov.; he then embarked at Massawa for the coast of Arabia, but was shipwrecked in the Red Sea and reached Mocha 1 Jan. 1836, from where he set out for India; he was again taken ill and died in Bombay, 4 March 1836; while in Thebes he made a collection of Egyptian antiquities which later passed to the Museum of Fine Arts, Boston, on the death of his younger brother in 1875; his diaries are on deposit in the Museum of Fine Arts.

Ed. Everett, *Memoirs of John Lowell*, Boston, 1840; *Bull. Mus. of Fine Arts*, Boston, June, 1952, 19-27; *WWWA* Hist., 323; *BES* 6 (1985), 69-77; C. Williams in D. Fortenberry (ed.), *Who Travels Sees More*, 2007, 55-7; R. de Keersmaecker, *ASTENE Bulletin* 69 (2016), 17-19; A. Oliver, *American Travelers on the Nile*, 2016, 188-92.

LOWRY-CORRY, Somerset, 2nd Earl of Belmore (1774-1841)
Irish administrator, traveller, and collector; he was born Dublin, 11 July 1774, son of Armar L.-C. 1st. Earl of Belmore and Margaret Hamilton and succeeded to the title, 1802; governor and Custos Rotulorum, co. Tyrone; sometime Governor of Jamaica; he visited Egypt, Syria, and Palestine, in 1816-18, and excavated in Western Thebes, also ascending the Nile as far as the Second Cataract; he brought back a number of antiquities, including a stone sarcophagus found by Belzoni (q.v.) (now in the BM, EA 39, presented 1820); also a considerable number of stelae, of wood and stone, and five papyri (EA 9906, 10000, 10030, 10043-4); he had lithographed plates of these objects prepared intending to issue them for private circulation; after his death, the latter were used in two official BM publications *Papyri from the Collection of the Earl of Belmore*, and *Tablets* ditto, 1843; the bulk of his collection was purchased by the British Museum in 1843, but remaining items were sold at Sotheby's 20 Nov. and 4 Dec. 1972; Lord Belmore also brought home on his yacht a considerable collection of antiquities for Henry Salt (q.v.); his party, besides his own family and several relatives, included a chaplain (Revd R. Holt), a physician, (Robert Richardson, q.v.), and many servants; he died in Leamington Spa, 18 April 1841.

R. Richardson, *Travels along the Mediterranean ... with the Earl of Belmore*, 2 vols. 1822; Athanasi, 15; Belmore (4th Earl), *Hist. of Two Ulster Manors,* 1881, 275-84; Belzoni, i, 386, 435; Cailliaud, *Oasis*, 51; Irby, 52, 72, 100, 101; Salt, i, 487; ii, 40-7; D. Manley in P. and J. Starkey, *Unfolding the Orient*, 2001, 179-92; B. Ockinga in N. Cooke (ed.), *Journeys Erased by Time*, 2019, 157-72.

LUBENAU, Reinhold (1556-1631)
German traveller and physician; he was born in Königsberg, E. Prussia, 1556; became a doctor and court apothecary; he joined an embassy sent by Rudolf II to Constantinople returning in 1589; his account of Egypt is short and has no original antiquarian material; he died 17 May 1631.

Voyages en Égypte pendant les années 1587-1588, trans. from the German by Ursula Castel, notes by S. Sauneron, 1972.

LUBBOCK, (*Sir*) **John, Lord Avebury** (1834-1913)
British peer, archaeologist and prehistorian; born in London, 30 April 1834, eldest son of John William L. third Baronet and Harriet Hotham his wife; afterwards fourth Bart. and first Baron Avebury; PC; DCL; LL.D.; FRS; DL; Commander of the Légion d'honneur, etc.; although a banker by profession, and head of Robarts Lubbock & Co., he maintained an active interest in pre-history and followed a second career in this subject; he married 1. Ellen Hordern. 2. Alice daughter of General A. A. L. Fox-Pitt-Rivers; educated Eton; full details of his important career can be found in the works listed below; in his earlier career he made important contributions to archaeological classification and typological definition that are now used throughout the world; he followed the French prehistorians in distinguishing two stone ages and invented the now standard terms for them, i.e. Palaeolithic and Neolithic in the classic work *Prehistoric Times*, 1865; in the field of Egyptology he published an article 'Notes on the discovery of stone implements in Egypt' in *JRAI* 1875; he died in Kingsgate Castle, 28 May 1913.

Glyn E. Daniel, *A Hundred Years of Archaeology*, 1950, 33, 42, 65, 79, 85-6, 90, 107, 112, 118, 154, 186,

273, 320; *ODNB* 34, 651-2 (portr.); *DNB* 1912-21, 345-7 (A. Smithells); *WWW* i, 29-30; È. Gran-Aymerich, *Dictionnaire biographique d'archéologie 1798-1945*, 2001, incorporated in *Les Chercheurs de passé 1798-1945*, 2007, 955-6.

LUCAS, Alfred (1867-1945)

British chemist; he was born Chorlton-upon-Medlock, Manchester, 27 Aug. 1867, son of Joshua Peter L., commercial traveller, and Sarah Thomas; he was educated at the School of Mines, London, and the Roy. Coll. of Science; he worked for eight years as an assistant chemist at the Government Laboratory in London, when lung trouble sent him to Egypt in 1897; here he became Chemist to the Govt. Salt Dept., 1898; he was in charge of the laboratories of the Survey Dept. and Assay Office, later Chemist to the Antiquities Service, 1923-32; from 1932 until 1945 he acted for it as Hon. Consulting Chemist; OBE; FIC; Membre Inst. Ég.; Lucas made a speciality of those fields for which his scientific training had prepared him, and made many analyses of materials and substances, as well as restoring and consolidating objects; in this field he played a very important part in the cleaning and restoration of the objects found in the tomb of Tutankhamun, and was lent to Carter (q.v.) by the Dept. of Antiquities, so that he could live and work with him on this material for 9 winters; he also dealt with the silver coffin of Sheshonq and its contents, found by Montet at Tanis, 1939; he was on the committee to investigate and report on the restorations and repairs being carried out in the Theban tombs; he was a forensic and ballistic expert and his evidence was used in law courts in this field; during the Second World War he helped in the work of safeguarding the objects in Cairo Museum, and wrote two popular booklets for the forces serving in Egypt, entitled, *Potted History of Egypt*; he wrote 65 works in all, many of which still remain fundamental; *Analyse de quelques spécimens de gris pris dans les colonnes de la Salle Hypostyle*. 1901; *The Blackened rocks of the Nile Cataracts and of the Egyptian Deserts*, 1905; *The Chemistry of the River Nile*, 1908; *Preservative materials used by the Ancient Egyptians in embalming*, 1911; *Antiques: Their restoration and preservation*, 1924; *Ancient Egyptian Materials and Industries*, 1926, 4th ed., rev. J. R. Harris, 1962; *The Route of the Exodus of the Israelites from Egypt*, 1938; he died while on a visit to Luxor, 9 Dec. 1945.

Ant. Journ. 26. 321; *ASAE* 47 (1947), 1-6 (portr.) (G. Brunton); *BIE* 28 (1945-6), (1947) 163-5 (H. E. Hurst); *Chron. d'Ég.* 21 (1946), 205-6 (P. Coremans); 22 (1947), 301-4 (bibl.) (P. Coremans); M. Gilberg, *Journal of the American Institute for Conservation* 36 (1997), 31-48.

LUCAS, Paul (1664-1737)

French antiquary and traveller; he was born in Quevilly, near Rousen, 31 Aug.1664, son of Centurion L., a printer, and Judith Mauclerc; he visited the Levant, 1696 and 1699, Greece and Asia Minor, and Egypt 1704, Palestine and Egypt, 1714-7; although he was not a scholar he was a careful observer of what he saw, and took an interest in coins, manuscripts, and antiquities; although unable to read their inscriptions, he collected some good specimens; he published accounts of all his voyages which became very popular and were translated into several languages; *Voyage dans la Turquie, l'Asie, Sourie, Haute et Basse-Égypte*, 3 vols. 1719; among other sites in Egypt he visited the pyramids and the underground ibis galleries at Saqqara; Lucas having no literary skill, his works were drawn up by Baudelot de Dairval, Étienne Fourmont (q.v.), and the Abbé Antoine Banier (q.v.); he died in Madrid, 12 May 1737.

Carré, i, 44-7, 75; Hilmy, i, 393; *La Grande Enc.* 22, 727; Lamy, 146-56.

LUCOVICH, Anton von (1815-1879)

Austrian architect; he was born in Prčany (Pezagno), Croatia in 1815 son of Vincento von L., later an official in the Austrian consulate in Alexandria and at Damietta; he studied at Padua and later worked as an architect in Alexandria and on various projects in Egypt including Suez; he arranged the donation of three granite columns to Vienna in 1869; he later moved to Venice, and died on a visit to Alexandria 16 Jan. 1879

Inf. G. Hamernik.

LÜDDECKENS, Erich Gottfried Leberecht (1913-2004)

German demotist; he was born at Hirschberg im Riesengebirge (now Jelenia Gora), 15 June 1913, son of Reverend Eugen L. and his wife Marie; he was educated at Berlin University under Grapow (q.v.); PhD, 1939; he became an assistant at the Berlin *Wörterbuch* project 1935-43 and then served in World War II, 1943-45; he also was briefly employed in the papyrus collection of the Berlin Museum; he then trained in theology and briefly served as a pastor; he studied Demotic at Mainz University under Erichsen (q.v.) from 1950; Habilitation, 1953; he was appointed Professor at Würzburg University 1959; ordin. Professor 1964; Emeritus, 1981; Dean 1976-77; he also taught at Mainz from 1963; he was a specialist in the Demotic script and Egyptian religion; he founded and edited the journal *Enchoria* from 1971 and *Ägyptische Handschriften*; a festschrift *Grammatica Demotica* was published in his honour in 1983; apart from numerous articles, he published his thesis *Untersuchungen über religiösen Gehalt, Sprache und Form des ägyptischen Totenklagen,* 1943 in *MDAIK* 11; *Ägyptische Eheverträge,* 1960; *Papyrus Wien D10151,* 1965; *Demotische und Koptische Texte,* Papyrologica Coloniensia II, 1968; *Demotisches Urkunden aus Hawara,* 1998; and edited with W. Brunsch, *Demotisches Namenbuch,* 1980; he died at Veitshöchheim, 1 July 2004.

Kürschner, 2003, 2032; H. J. Thissen and K.-T. Zauzich (eds.) *Grammatica Demotica,* ed., 1983, 283-87(bibl) (Hilde Lüddeckens.); *Enchoria* 29 (2004/5), vi (portr.), 1-3 (H. J. Thissen and K.-Th. Zauzich); P. Piacentini, *Egypt and the Pharaohs from the Sand to the Library,* 2010, 96; M. Capasso (ed.), *Hermae* II, 2010, 61 (portr.) (A. Jördens)

LUGN, Pehr Johann (1881-1934)
Swedish Egyptologist; born Undersaker, 9 Oct. 1881, son of Anders L. and Caroline Allmin, he was an assistant in the Victoria Museet of the University of Uppsala, and in 1928 was the founder and head of the Egyptian Museum in Stockholm, Egyptiska Museet; this is now the Egyptian Dept. of the Medelhavsmuseet; he also led the Swedish expedition that excavated at Abu Ghalib from 1932; in addition to popular works in Swedish and smaller contributions to scientific journals he published *Ausgewählte Denkmäler aus ägyptischen Sammlungen in Schweden,* 1922; he died in Stockholm, 13 March 1934.

Inf. B. J. Peterson; *Svenska Män och Kvinnor,* 5 83-4; *Svenskt Biografiskt Lexikon* 24, 162-4.

LUSHINGTON, Edmund Law (1811-1893)
British classical scholar; he was born Prestwich, 10 Jan. 1811, son of Edmund Henry L. and Sophia Phillips; educated at Charterhouse and Trinity College, Cambridge; Professor of Greek at Glasgow, 1838-75; Hon. LLD, Glasgow, 1875; Lord Rector, Glasgow University, 1884; he married Cecilia, sister of Lord Tennyson, 1842; he took up Egyptology late in life, and published articles in *TSBA* and contributions to *Records of the Past* (1st ser. vols. ii and xii); he died in Park House, Maidstone, 13 July 1893.

ODNB 34, 790; *DNB* Suppl. iii, 114; Hilmy, i, 396; Renouf Corr., nos. 111-16; *Alumni Cantab.*

LUTZ, Henry Ludwig Frederick (1886-1973)
American Egyptologist and Assyriologist; he was born in New York, 16 Feb. 1886, son of Heinrich L., photographer, and Alma Harnickel; he was educated at various schools in Germany 1892-1904 and then several theological seminaries; he was ordained a minister of the Lutheran Church 1908; BD, 1911 from the Chicago Lutheran Theological Seminary; he was a graduate student at Yale University, 1913-6, PhD in Semitics, 1916; he was appointed research fellow in Semitics at the University of Pennsylvania, 1916-19, and later instructor, 1919-21; he obtained the post of Assistant Professor of Assyriology and Egyptology at the University of California, Berkeley, 1921-4, then associate Professor, 1924-9, Professor, 1929-54, and Emeritus Professor, 1954-73; he was also Associate Curator of the Anthropological Museum, 1929-54; DD, 1922; apart from his articles, his chief publications were *Viticulture and Brewing in the Ancient Orient,* 1921; *Egyptian Tomb Steles and Offering Stones of the Museum of Anthropology and Ethnology of the University of California,* 1927; *Egyptian Statues and Statuettes in the Museum of Anthropology of the University of California,* 1930; he died in Berkeley, 17 Aug. 1973.

Inf. from Prof. L. Lesko; *NARCE* 87 (1973), 3-4 (L. Lesko); *JEA* 60 (1974), 3-4.

LUYNES (*Duc de*) *see* **Albert**

LYCKLAMA, (*Baron*) **Tinco Martinus François** (1837-1900)
Dutch traveller and collector; he was born at Beetsterzwaag, Holland, 9 July 1837, son of Jananne L. and Ypckjen Hillegonda Van Eysinga; he travelled throughout Europe and the Near East, 1866-8, and published a long account, *Voyage en Russie,* etc., 4 vols. Paris, 1872; he also made an extensive collection of antiquities which was bequeathed to the Museum of Cannes; the Egyptian objects were described in a pamphlet illustrated with 4 plates, by A. Duriage, Lyons, 1907; the Baron died at his home in Cannes, 7 Dec. 1900.

Sphinx 11, 232; J. Juillet, *Annales de la Société scientifique et littéraire de Cannes et de l'arrondissement de Grasse* 39 (1994). 135-46.

LYONS, (*Sir*) **Henry George** (1864-1944)
British army officer, geologist, meteorologist, and excavator; he was born in London, 11 Oct. 1864, son of Gen. Thomas Casey L. and Helen Young; he was educated at Wellington and Woolwich; he entered the Royal Engineers, 1884; colonel; he married Helen Julia Hardwick, 1896; his long association with Egyptology began

when he was posted to Egypt in 1890; he served for some years in Nubia from 1891, and cleared the temples of Buhen, 1892; he visited Dakhla Oasis, and surveyed the temples of Philae, 1895-6; he also organized and directed the Geological and Cadastral Surveys of Egypt, 1897-1909; he organized and directed the first Archaeological Survey of Nubia, 1907; retired from Egypt, 1909; he was appointed Assistant Director, Science Museum, London, 1911; Director, 1919-33; FRS, 1906; For. Sec. RS, 1928-9; Treas. RS, 1929-39; knighted, 1926; Hon. D.Sc., Oxon; Hon. Sc.D., Dublin; Treas. EES, 1925-30; Vice-Pres., 1931-40; while in Egypt, Lyons discovered many antiquities of importance; he published, *A report on the island and temples of Philae: with an introductory note by W. E. Garstin*, 1896; *The physiography of the river Nile and its basin*, 1906; *The cadastral survey of Egypt, 1892-1907*, sm. fol., 1908; he died in Great Missenden, Bucks., 10 Aug. 1944.

DNB 1941-50, 543-5 (Sir Henry H. Dale); *ODNB* 34, 928-9; *JEA* 31 (1945), 98-100 (portr.) (Sir Ernest M. Dowson); *OFRS* 4, 795-809 (portr. and bibl.); *WWW* iv, 711-12.

LYTHGOE, Albert Morton (1868-1934)
American Egyptologist; he was born Providence, RI, 15 March 1868, son of Joseph L and Mary Ellen Howarth; he was educated at Harvard University, 1892; A.M., 1897; he afterwards studied with Wiedemann (q.v.) at Bonn (q.v.); he assisted Reisner in the Hearst Expedition at Naga ed-Der, 1899-1904; first curator of Egyptian Art at the Museum of Fine Arts, Boston, 1902-6 and lecturer at Harvard University, 1898-1906; he entered the service of the Metropolitan Museum of Art, New York, 1906; Curator of Egyptian Art, 1906-29; Curator Emeritus, 1929-33; he conducted excavations for the MMA at Lisht, Thebes, and other sites, and also arranged the Egyptian collections in the museum; he published articles in *BMMA*; see *The Predynastic Cemetery, N7000: Naga-ed-Dêr*, pt. iv, ed. Dows Dunham; he died in Boston, 29 Jan. 1934.

BMMA 29 (1934), 42-3; *JEA* 20 (1934), 107.

MACADAM, Miles Frederick Laming (1909-1997)
British Egyptologist; he was born in Bridge of Weir, Scotland, 8 March 1909, son of Frederick John Ledger, merchant, and Elma Alexandra Laming; he was adopted by his step-father Chavely Macadam and assumed the name Laming Macadam; he was educated at Eastbourne College, 1923-8 and The Queen's College, Oxford, 1928-32, specializing in ancient Egyptian with Coptic under Gardiner (q.v.); BA, 1932; Senior Scholar, New College, Oxford, 1933-5; DPhil, 1935; Laycock student of Egyptology, Worcester College, Oxford, 1935-9, 1945-7; he took part in the excavations at Kawa in the Sudan, 1935-6; he served in the RAF and worked as a decoder at Bletchley Park during World War II; Research Fellow, University of Durham, 1947-8; Reader in Egyptology, University of Durham, 1949-69; FSA, 1951-68; Visiting Professor of Egyptology, Brown University, 1955-6; Hon. Keeper, Durham University Oriental Museum, 1950-60; Hon. Keeper of the Egyptian collection, The Gulbenkian Museum of Oriental Art, 1960-9; he catalogued the objects in the Durham collection received between 1880-1954 and set up the initial display in 1960; external examiner in history and archaeology, Khartoum University, 1965-9; he had a special interest in Nubian history and language; his principal publications were *The Temples of Kawa* I. *The Inscriptions*, 1949; II. *History and Archaeology of the Site*, 1955; and with N. de G. Davies, *A Corpus of Inscribed Egyptian Funerary Cones*, 1957; he died at Nutley, Sussex, 16 Nov. 1997.

Inf. from Eastbourne College and The Queen's College, Oxford; IAE Internet obituary (H. Kuhn and J. Ruffle).

MacCALLUM, Andrew (1822-1902)
British landscape painter; he was baptized in Nottingham, 15 Dec. 1822, son of Andrew M., an employee in the hosiery industry; he began life working in a factory, but later studied art in Nottingham, Manchester, and the RA schools; he settled in London, 1852, where he exhibited many works; he was especially well known for his forest scenes; he travelled in Europe and visited Egypt several times between 1870 and 1875 with Lord Alfred Paget; in 1874 he procured the hieratic tablet and canopic jars of Princess Eskhons (Neskhons) from the cache of royal mummies; these are associated with his name; the former is now in the British Museum (EA 16672) and the latter he disposed of to Dillwyn Parish (q.v.), and were afterwards to be sold at Sotheby's, 5 July 1928, but were withdrawn and presented to the British Museum (EA 59197-200); in 1874 he discovered a painted chamber on the S. side of the Temple of Abu Simbel; he died in Kensington, London, 22 Jan. 1902.

ODNB 35, 88-9; *DNB* Suppl. ii, 2/1, 503-4; Edwards, *Thousand Miles*, ed. 2, 325 ff., 493; Budge, *Greenfield Papyrus*, p. xv; Maspero, *Momies royales*, 594; *Rec. Trav.* 4, 81.

McCAULEY, Edward Yorke (1827-1894)
American naval officer and Egyptologist; he was born Philadelphia, Pa., 2 Nov. 1827, son of Daniel Smith M. and Sarah Yorke; he spent much of his boyhood in Tripoli, where his father was US consul, and by 1840 he could speak five languages; after a distinguished career in the US Navy he retired as a rear admiral, 1887; his early environment had given him an interest in the Orient and in later life he took up Egyptology; he was elected to the American Philosophical Soc., Philadelphia, 1881, and presented a contribution to its Proceedings, *A Manual for the Use of Students in Egyptology*, 1883; he also published a *Dictionary of the Egyptian language, Transactions of the Amer. Philosoph. Soc.*, N.S. Vol. 16, 1890; he died in his country home on Canonicut Island, Narragansett Bay, 14 Sept. 1894.

DAB 11, 573-4.

McCLURE, Mary Louisa Dora (née Herbert) (1857-1918)
British translator; she was born in London, 17 July 1857, daughter of Revd George William Herbert and Louisa Hopgood; she was the wife of Canon Edmund McClure (*d.* 18 Nov. 1922), Secretary, SPCK 1875-1915; she joined the EEF in 1888 and served on the Committee for many years; she translated Maspero's *Hist. Anc.* in 3 vols., entitled *The Dawn of Civilization, The Struggle of the Nations, The Passing of the Empires*; she died in London, 20 July 1918.

JEA 5 (1918), 140.

MacDONALD, (*Major*) Charles Kerr (*c.*1806-1867)
British army officer, traveller, and antiquarian he was born 1 Jan. *c.*1806, son of Capt. (later Lt.-Col.) Robert M. and Mary Douglas; he joined the army in 1823 rising to the rank of Major; retired 1847; he first visited Sinai in the 1840s; he went there to look for and to mine turquoise and Brugsch (q.v.) speaks of him in connection with the Lepsius expedition, which was there in April 1845; at this time he made a fairly complete survey of Sinai, then called Arabia, the notes attached to his finds now in the British Museum showing his route; he excavated chiefly at the temple of Hathor at Serabit, see Birch, *Cat. Alnwick Coll.*, p. 179, and presented his finds to the British Museum; these consisted of a considerable quantity of New Kingdom glass fragments, sculpture, stelae, and stone vessels; he appears to have returned to London by 1849 when he gave these objects, but his residue collection was sold at Sotheby's on 20-22 April 1857; it was eclectic and covered nearly all fields, fetching £778. 10*s*. 6*d*.; he probably used the money to finance his turquoise mine schemes; Brugsch described him as a man of

45 years old when he was there, who spoke English, French, and Arabic, and both he and Ebers (q.v.) call him a major in the English Cavalry; Palmer (q.v.) also refers to his finding pieces of faience and a beautifully executed female foot in black stone now in the British Museum; he returned to Sinai and settled with his wife there in the 1850s; Petrie (q.v.) refers to his being there 'about 1862' and says of the Naqb el-Budera pass, 'The present track, and the banking up of it with retaining walls, seems entirely modern, due to Major Macdonald in 1863'; he built a house on the east of the 'Fort' hill and many Bedouin worked for him, settled near and learnt from him how to build stone huts; he tried mining vainly until 1866, when he left and lived at Serabit for a year; he took many paper squeezes of inscriptions and looked for fresh ones, the British Museum collection of these being mainly due to him; he returned to Cairo and died in poverty in Alexandria, 17 Oct. 1867.

J. D. Cooney, *JEA* 58 (1972), 280-4; H. K. Brugsch, *Wanderung nach den Türkis-Minen und der Sinai-Halbinsel*, 1866 (1868 ed.), 66-9; G. Ebers, *Durch Gosen zum Sinai*, 1881, 142, 145, 147; E. H. Palmer, *The Desert of the Exodus, Journey on Foot in the Wilderness of the Forty Years' Wanderings. Undertaken in Connexion with the Ordnance Survey of Sinai and the P.E.F.* 1871, 201; W. M. F. Petrie, *Researches in Sinai*, 1906, 7, 20, 53; Lugt 23540; inf. P. Dyke.

McDONELL, Thomas (1785-1849?)
British naval officer; he entered the RN in 1804; Lieutenant, 1810; he served throughout the Napoleonic wars, and retired on half-pay, 1815; he visited Egypt in 1820, and was still alive in 1849.

Henniker, 209-12; Salt, ii, 164.

MACE, Arthur Cruttenden (1874-1928)
British Egyptologist; he was born Glenorchy, Hobart, Tasmania, 17 July 1874, son of Revd John Cruttenden M. and Mary Ellen Bromby; he was educated at St. Edward's School, Oxford, and Keble College, Oxford, BA, 1895; he joined Petrie (q.v.) at Dendera, 1897-8, Hu, 1898-9, and Abydos, 1899-1901; in 1901 he joined Reisner (q.v.) with whom he continued to work on the California University excavations at Giza and Naga ed-Der until 1906; in 1906 he began work for the Metropolitan Museum, NY at Lisht; he married Winifred Blyth in 1907; in 1909 he was appointed assistant Curator in New York where he helped Lythgoe (q.v.) in arranging the Egyptian Department of the Museum and from 1912-14 he worked on the Amenemhat pyramid and the tomb of Senebtisi at Lisht; during the First World War in 1915 he enlisted in the 2nd Battalion, 29th London Territorial Regiment known as the Artists' Rifles, but was later transferred to the Army Service Corps until 1919; he went back to New York, 1919-20, in order to work on the restoration of the jewel caskets of the Lahun princess; he was again at Lisht, 1920-2; he was made Assoc. Curator in the Department of Egyptian Art, MMA, 1922; plans for further work in Thebes and Lisht were postponed in order to assist Howard Carter (q.v.) in the gigantic task of clearing the tomb of Tutankhamun, 1922-24, but after serving two winters thus he had a breakdown in health and was unable to continue his Egyptological work; he spent the next four winters in England and the Riviera; Mace's achievement in Egyptian archaeology was considerable; he founded and directed the camp of the Metropolitan Museum's first expedition, and was also the real organiser of its field work; in addition to articles in the *JEA* and *BMMA* he was part-author of the following works, Petrie's *Diospolis Parva. The Cemeteries of Abadiyeh and Hu, 1898-9*, 1901; *El Amrah and Abydos, 1899-1901*, with D. R. MacIver, 1902; *The Early Dynastic Cemeteries of Naga-ed-Dêr* of Reisner, pt. 2 is by Mace, 1908-9; *The Tomb of Senebtisi at Lisht*, with H. E. Winlock, 1916; *The Tomb of Tut.Ankh.Amen*, with H. Carter, 1923-33, the first vol.; his MSS are in the Griffith Institute, Oxford and with his family; he died in Haywards Heath, Sussex, 6 April 1928.

JEA 15 (1929), 105-6; inf. R. Merrillees and Mrs. M. Orr (daughter); C. Lee, *...the grand piano came by camel*, 1992; R. S. Merrillees, *Living with Egypt's Past in Australia*, 1990, 11-12, 28.

MacGREGOR, (*Revd*) William (1848-1937)
British collector; he was born in Liverpool, 16 May 1848, son of Walter Fergus M. and Anne Jane Moon; he was educated Exeter College, Oxford; BA, 1871; MA, 1874; vicar of Tamworth, Staffs., 1878-87; he was a leading social reformer in Tamworth, and patron of many of the town's institutions; he served on the Committee of the EEF, 1888-1930; FSA, 1908; he formed one of the most remarkable collections of Egyptian antiquities ever made by a private individual, which was kept in his house, Bolehall Manor, Tamworth; the ceramic section was described by Henry Wallis (q.v.), *Egyptian Ceramic Art*, 1898; he subscribed funds for many excavations in Egypt and Nubia and was with Naville at Bubastis, 1889-91; his collection was sold over nine days at Sotheby's, 26 June-6 July 1922 (1800 lots, cat. with 53 plates); the sale fetched over £34,000, the top lot, an obsidian head of a king, being purchased for £10,000 by Gulbenkian (q.v.); Wellcome (q.v.) purchased nearly a quarter of the lots; MacGregor bequeathed some minor pieces to the Ashmolean Museum, and a stela remains built into the walls at Bolehall Manor; he died in Tamworth, 26 Feb. 1937.

ODNB 35, 446; *Chron. d'Ég.* 13, 132; *JEA* 4 (1917), 71; Sayce, 294, 307; T. Hardwick, *Journal of the History of Collections* 23/1 (2011), 179-92; T. Hardwick, *Discussions in Egyptology* 65 (2010); Lugt 83901.

MacIVER, David Randall (1873-1945)

British Egyptologist and archaeologist; he was born in London, 31 Oct. 1873, son of John M. (*d.*1875) and Eliza Mary Rutherford (who married secondly Richard Randall); he was educated at The Queen's College, Oxford; became Laycock Student of Egyptology, 1900; FSA, 1907; FBA, 1938; he excavated under Petrie (q.v.) at Dendera and Abydos, 1898-1901; he was curator of the Egyptian section of the University Museum of Pennsylvania 1906-11 and Director of the Eckley B. Coxe expedition to Egypt and the Sudan, and with C. L. Woolley (q.v.) excavated at the sites of Areika, Buhen, and Karanog, 1907-10; he was Librarian of the American Geographical Soc., but gave up this appointment to serve on Intelligence Staff in France during the First World War; he afterwards gave up this work and went to Italy where he did research and published works on Etruscan and Italian archaeology; he published articles in the Penn. Univ. Museum Journal; his principal works were, *The Earliest Inhabitants of Abydos: a craniological study*, 1901; *Libyan Notes*, with A. Wilkin, 1901; *El Amrah and Abydos, 1899-1901*, with A. C. Mace, 1902; *The Ancient Races of the Thebaid, etc.*, 1905; *Areika: with a chapter on Meroitic inscriptions by F. Ll. Griffith*, with C. L. Woolley, 1909; *Karanôg: the Romano-Nubian cemetery*, 1910; *Buhen*, 2 vols., with C. L. Woolley, 1911; he also edited G. S. Mileham's *Churches in Lower Nubia*, 1910; he died in New York, 30 April 1945.

Ant. Journ. 26 (1946), 231; *AJA* 49 (1945), 359-60; *ODNB* 35, 488-9; *DNB* 1941-50, 709-710; *Expedition* 21 (1979), 19-22; *PBA* 69 (1983), 559-77.

MacKAY, Ernest John Henry (1880-1943)

British archaeologist; he was born Bristol, 5 July 1880, son of Richard Cockrill M. and Mary Dermott Thomas; he was educated at Bristol Grammar School and the University of Bristol; MA; D.Litt.; FSA; he married Dorothy Mary Simmons, 1912; he assisted in excavations in Egypt, 1907-12, receiving training in field work under Petrie (q.v.) and contributing to the publications of the British School; he was engaged on excavations and the photographic survey of the Theban Tombs, 1913-16; in 1913 he loaned his collection of Egyptian antiquities to the Bristol City Museum, selling it to the museum in 1919; he served during the First World War as a Capt. in the RASC, 1916-19, in Egypt and Palestine; Member of the Army Commission for the Survey of Ancient Monuments in Palestine and Syria, 1919-20; he was then appointed Custodian of Antiquities by the Palestine Govt., 1919-22; he was Field Director of the Oxford University and Field Museum, Chicago, Archaeological Expedition to Mesopotamia, 1922-6; at this time he also directed the excavations at Bahrain on the Persian Gulf for the BSAE, 1925; he became Special Officer for Exploration for the Archaeological Survey of India, 1926-31; he then was appointed Director of the Expedition of the American School of Indic and Iranian Studies and the Boston Museum of Fine Arts to Chandhu-daro, India, 1935-6; Mackay began his archaeological work in Egypt, but he later moved into Palestine and Iraq where he made important discoveries on early Sumerian sites; it is, however, his work in India for which he is best known, for with Sir John Marshall he was one of the founders and initiators of work on the Indus valley civilization; in Egyptology he was part author of *Heliopolis, Kafr Ammar and Shurafa*, with W. M. F. Petrie, 1915; *City of Shepherd Kings and Ancient Gaza* V, with M. A. Murray, Petrie, and others, 1952; he also wrote, *The 'A' Cemetery at Kish*, 1925; *A Sumerian palace and the 'A' Cemetery at Kish*, 1926; *Excavations at Jemdet Nasr, Iraq*, 1930; *Mohenjodaro, and the Indus Civilization*, with Sir J. Marshall and others, 1931; *The Indus Civilization*, 1935; *Further Excavations at Mohenjo-daro (1927-31)*, 1938; *Chandu-daro Excavations*, 1941; in addition he published numerous articles in journals, such as *AE* to which he contributed reviews; he died in London, 2 Oct. 1943.

Ant. Journ. 1944, 179; *WWW* iv, 730-1; T. Hardwick in D. Magee, J. Bourriau and S. Quirke, *Sitting Beside Lepsius*, 2009.

MADDEN, Frank Cole (1873-1929)

Australian surgeon; he was born in Emerald Hill, Melbourne, 1873, son of Daniel Antony M., a councillor, and Clara Cole; he was educated at Melbourne University, MB and ChB, 1893; St. Mary's Hospital, London; MRCS and LRCP, 1896; FRCS, 1898; he held many surgical appointments in Egypt, and was Professor of Surgery, Cairo School of Medicine, Consulting Surgeon, Kasr el-Ainy Hospital, Cairo; his book, *The Surgery of Egypt*, Cairo 1919, with its lucid text and abundant illustrations, although dealing with modern Egypt, is of the utmost value in studying the Egyptian Medical Papyri; he died in Cairo, 20 April 1929.

BMJ 1929, i, 833.

MADDEN, Richard Robert (1798-1886)
Irish traveller, administrator, and writer; he was born in Dublin, 22 Aug. 1798, son of Edward M. and Elizabeth Ford; he studied medicine in Paris and London; MRCS, 1829; FRCS, 1855; he never practised as a surgeon, but travelled extensively and was a personal friend of Lady Blessington (whose biography he published), Byron, and D'Orsay; he visited Egypt, June 1825-7, attending Henry Salt in his last illness, and again in 1840; he held administrative appointments in the West Indies and Ireland and was Colonial Secretary of Western Australia, 1847-50; he published his *Travels*, 2 vols. 1829, in which there is much of interest to Egyptologists; he died in Booterstown, Ireland, 5 Feb. 1886.

ODNB 36, 72-3; *DNB* 35, 295-6; *BMJ* 1929, ii, 628; Hilmy, ii, 3; *Mem. Inst. Ég.* 13, 27; Salt, ii, 282, 286.

MADOX, John (1768-1837)
British traveller; he was born in Greenwich, Kent, 1 Sept 1768, son of Erasmus Madox, a brewer, and Anne Perry; he set off from Italy to the Levant in April 1821 and visited Egypt on several occasions; on his first visit in March-April 1822 he went as far as Cairo and Saqqara; he returned in Aug. 1823 and journeyed as far as the Second Cataract, viewing Abu Simbel and the Nubian temples; he undertook excavations in Karnak and on the West Bank at Luxor together with Athanasi (q.v.); he met Passalacqua (q.v.) and Hull (q.v.) at Luxor where he purchased the heart scarab belonging to a mummy which Hull acquired; he left Egypt in Aug. 1824 for Syria and Palestine; he was in Egypt again in 1827 and 1829; he published *Excursions in the Holy Land, Egypt, Syria etc.*, 1834; he died in London, 31 March 1837.

M. Dewachter, *BIFAO* 69 (1971), 151-4; BM corr.; inf. J. H. Taylor; E. Serdiuk in *Memnonia* 25 (2014), 169-184; R. de Keersmaecker, *ASTENE Bulletin* 66 (2015), 16-7; J. Taylor in *Souvenirs and New Ideas*, ed. D. Fortenberry (ed.), 2013, 179-92.

MAGARIOS *see* **Shenuda**

MAGEE, Diana Norma Elizabeth (*née* **Mayhew**) (1936-2017)
British Egyptologist; she was born in Isleworth, 2 Dec 1936, daughter of Stanley Constable Mayhew, solicitor's clerk, and Noreen R. Harvey; she studied archaeology in London and Egyptology in Oxford, 1978-82; BA, 1982; DPhil, 1989 with her thesis, *Asyut to the End of the Middle Kingdom: A Historical and Cultural Study*; she worked in the Griffith Institute on the Topographical Bibliography and the Archive, 1982-2004 and part-time thereafter, 2005-15;she surveyed at Asyut in the 1980s; she served on the committee of the EES, 1995-8; she helped to edit Vol. 8 of *The Topographical Bibliography of Ancient Egyptian Hieroglyphic Texts etc.*, 1999-2012 and the collection of studies in honour of Jaromir Malek, *Sitting Beside Lepsius*, 2009; she published *Asyut to the End of the Middle Kingdom*, 1988; she died in Bexhill-on-Sea, 11 Feb. 2017.

Inf. Dr. J. Malek; Mrs. J. Malkin (sister), and F. Bosch-Puche.

MAHAFFY, (*Sir*) **John Pentland** (1839-1919)
Irish classical scholar; he was born in Chapponaire near Vevey, Switzerland, 26 Feb. 1839, son of Reverend Nathaniel M. and Elizabeth Pentland; he studied at Trinity College, Dublin, scholar, graduate, fellow, 1899, and Provost, 1914; GBE; CVO; DD; DCL; LLD; MD; Fellow of The Queen's College, Oxford; hon. member of many foreign academies; he published many works on Greek history and literature; edited the Petrie Papyri, see *Cunningham Memoirs*, 8, 9, 11, published by the RIA, 1891-1905; he also wrote vol. iv of Petrie's *History of Egypt* dealing with the Ptolemaic Period; Pres. Royal Irish Academy, 1911-16; he died in Dublin, 30 April 1919.

ODNB 36, 151-3 (portr.); *Aegyptus* 1 (1920), 217-221 (A. S. Hunt); *Rev. Ég.* N.S. i. 259-60 (P. Jouget); Sayce, passim (see index); *WWW* ii, 693; M. Capasso (ed.), *Hermae* III, 2013, 11-19 (portr.) (F. Valerio).

MAHLER, Eduard (1857-1945)
Hungarian Egyptologist, astronomer, mathematician and chronologer; he was born Cziffer, Hungary, 28 Sept. 1857, son of Salamon M., Chief Rabbi of Pozsony; he was a relation of the composer Gustav Mahler; Doctor of Mathematics and Natural Science, 1880; he studied under Theodor Oppolzer in Vienna, 1882; assistant at the Vienna Observatory, 1882; assistant at the Institute of Weights and Measures, 1885; he began to study oriental languages under Reinsich (q.v.) and returned to Hungary where he worked at the Institute of Trigonometry in Budapest.; he was awarded a Ph.D. from the Royal Hungarian University in Budapest (later Loránd Eötvös University), 1890 and joined the teaching staff in 1898; he was an assistant on the staff of the Archaeological Dept. of the National Museum of Hungary, 1898; he was created extraordinary Professor of the Department of the Ancient History

of Oriental Nations, 10 Nov. 1910; full Professor, 1914-1 June 1928 although he continued to teach after his retirement; Member of the Hungarian Acad. of Sciences, 1909; a *Festschrift* was presented on his 80th birthday, 1937, which contains an account of his career and a bibl. of his works (275 items of which 37 are separate works); he wrote a great number of studies on the Egyptian calendar and chronology; he died in Ujpest, 29 June 1945.

Dissertationes in Honorem Eduardi Mahler, Budapest, 1937 (portr.); *ÖBL* 5, 411; J. Horvath in *Studia Aegyptiaca* 12 (1989), 142-51; *Encyclopedia Judaica* 11, 726; inf. G. Vörös.

MAHMOUD ABDELQADER, Adel (1953-2008)
Egyptian Egyptologist and curator; he was born in El Mehalla el Kobra, Gharbia, 16 March 1953; he studied Egyptology at Cairo University; BA, 1975, Diploma in Tourist Guidance, 1993; he studied for a year at Johns Hopkins University, 1998; he worked in the New Kingdom section of the Egyptian Museum, 1978-2003; he re-arranged and wrote labels for the museum displays, and wrote entries in numerous exhibition catalogues on the objects in his care; he had fellowships at the Metropolitan Museum New York, 1995 and 2000, where he studied material from the tomb of Sennedjem at Deir el-Medina, unpublished at the time of his death; he was Director of the Information Centre of the Museum Sector of the SCA, 2003-2008; he participated in the installation of new displays at the Luxor Museum, Imhotep Museum at Saqqara, and elsewhere; he died in Cairo, 15 Nov. 2008.

Inf. Mohamed Saleh.

MAI, (*Cardinal*) **Angelo** (1782-1854)
Italian Jesuit priest and scholar; he was born at Schilpario, Clusone, near Bergamo, 7 March 1782, son of Angelo M., a merchant, and Pietra Mai dei Battistei; he studied under the Jesuits and joined the order in 1804; he taught at Naples from 1804, Rome from 1806 and Milan from 1810, becoming librarian of the Bibliotheca Ambrosiana, Milan; he left the Jesuit order in 1819 when he became librarian of the Bibliotheca Apostolica at the Vatican to 1833; he was appointed head of the Congregation for the Propagation of Faith, 1833; he was made Cardinal, 1837; a loyal supporter of Champollion (q.v.), to whom he was very helpful at the time of the latter's visit; he published *Catalogo de' papiri egiziani della Bibliotheca Vaticana*, 1825; he died in Castel Gandolfo, 9 Sept. 1854.

DBDI 63, 218-223; J. Leblanc, *Dictionnaire biographique des cardinaux du XIXe siècle*, 2007, 560-4 (bibl.); Garollo, *Diz. Biogr. Univ.*; *Enc. It.*; Champollion, i, 188, 191, 212, 215, 226, 323, 370.

MAILLET, Benoît de (1656-1738)
French diplomat; he was born in Saint-Mihiel, Lorraine, 12 April 1656; he served as Consul-General for France in Egypt, 1692-1708; he travelled and observed many things in Egypt, and sent back to France a considerable number of antiquities which found their way into the cabinets of the King and of Counts Pontchartrain (q.v.), de Caylus (q.v.), and others; he also obtained many Coptic and Arabic MSS; he retired to Marseilles and compiled an elaborate *Description de l'Égypte*, which was edited and published in his lifetime by the Abbé Le Mascrier, 1735; he died in Marseilles, 30 June 1738.

Carré, i, 56-65; Hilmy, i, 170; Lamy, 185-94.

MAKRAMALLAH, Rizkallah Naguib (1903-1949)
Egyptian Egyptologist, born 1 July 1903; he came from a Coptic family; educated at the French School, Khronfish; he joined the Egyptology section later attached to Cairo University, 1923; graduated 1928; he was a member of the Nubian Survey expedition and served as assistant archaeologist under W. B. Emery (q.v.) and L. P. Kirwan, 1929; Assistant Director of Works, Saqqara, 1931-7; at this time he cleared and restored the tomb of Idut, and also examined an area near the Serapeum where he discovered an archaic cemetery; Chief Inspector, Upper Egypt at Luxor, 1937; Chevalier, Légion d'honneur; appointed Lecturer, University of Cairo, 1939; Lecturer, University of Alexandria, 1941; while there he formed a museum attached to the Archaeology section; he also cleared the basilica at Ashmunein with Henri Riad in 1945; subsequently transferred to the library of the Antiquities Dept. against his wishes; he published articles in *ASAE* and two major works, *Le Mastaba d'Idout*, 1935; *Un Cimetière archaïque de la classe moyenne du peuple à Saqqarah*, 1940; he had suffered from heart disease for some time before his premature death in Cairo, 11 Nov. 1949.

ASAE 54 (1957), 43-6 (portr.) (Labib Habachi).

MALAISE, Michel (1943-2016)
Belgian Egyptologist; he was born in Dinant, 30 Nov. 1943, son of Oscar M., a magistrate, and Françoise Loneux; he studied history and Oriental languages at the Université de Liège under van de Walle (q.v.); he became lecturer at the Université de Liège and then professor in the Faculty of Philosopy, 1979, and professor in succession to van de Walle, 1988-2004; he was visiting professor at the Université de Lille, 1982, and taught at the École Pratique des Hautes Études, 1993; he specialized in the study of Egyptian religion in the Greco-Roman world; a volume of *Acta Orientalia Belgica* 18 (2005) entitled *La Langue dans tous ses états* was dedicated to him as was a second volume, *Isis on the Nile*, ed. L. Bricault and M. Versluys, 2010,; apart from articles and reviews, he published *Antiquités égyptiennes et verres du Proche-Orient ancient des Musées Curtius et du Verre à Liège*, 1971; *Inventaire préliminaire des documents égyptiens découverts en Italie*, 1972; *Les Conditions de pénétration et de diffusion des cultes égyptiens en Italie*, 1972; *Les Scarabées de coeur dans l'Égypte ancienne*, 1978; with J. Winand, *Grammaire raisonnée de l'égyptien classique*, 1999; *Pour une terminologie et une analyse des cultes isiaques*, 2005; and *À la découverte d'Harpocarte à travers son historiographie*, 2011; he died in Liege 25 Jan. 2016.

Acta Orientalia Belgica 18 (2005), vii-xi (J. Winand) (portr.), xii-xxiv (bibl.).

MALAN, (*Revd*) **César Jean Solomon** (1812-1894)
Swiss orientalist and biblical scholar; he was born in Geneva, 23 April 1812, son of César M. and Georgette Jeanne Schönberger, but on coming to England as tutor in the family of the Marquess of Tweeddale, 1830, he changed his name to Solomon Caesar M.; he studied at St. Edmund Hall, Oxford, 1833-7; he was ordained in the Church of England, 1838; he married 1. Mary Mortlock, 1834, 2. Caroline Selina Mount, 1843; lecturer at Bishop's Coll., Calcutta, 1838-40; he left India and travelled in Egypt and Palestine, 1841-2; entered Balliol College, Oxford, MA, 1843; after holding various curacies he was made Vicar of Broadwindsor, Dorset, 1845-85; he again visited the East, 1849-50 where he assisted the excavations of A. H. Layard at Nineveh; he retired to Bournemouth where he remained for the rest of his life; Malan studied many oriental languages: Hebrew, Arabic, Syriac, Chinese, and various Indian dialects, and was much interested in Egyptology, corresponding with Birch (q.v.) and Chabas (q.v.) and publishing Coptic works; he died in Bournemouth, 25 Nov. 1894.

ODNB 36, 274-5; *DNB* Suppl. i, 3, 133-4; Chabas, 52, 146; Hilmy, ii, 9; *Memoirs of his Life and Writings*, by his son, Revd A. N. Malan, (Murray, 1897).

MALASPINA DI SANNAZRO, (*Marchese*) **Luigi** (1754-1835)
Italian nobleman, collector and author; he was born in Pavia, 19 Aug. 1754, son of Francesco M. and Caterina Beccaria; he became a chamberlain of the Austrian Emperor, 1816; he had a collection of antiquities, some of the Egyptian items of which came from Nizzoli (q.v.) and were subsequently inspected by Champollion (q.v.) in 1825; apart from works on art, architecture and the history of Pavia, he wrote *Cenni sulla Mitologia Egizia*, 1826; *Elenco di idoli egizi e di altri oggetti relativi*, 1832; he died in Milan, 28 March 1835; his collection is now in the Pinacoteca Malaspina in Pavia; (in previous editions the collector has been wrongly identified as Marchese Tomasso Malasapina (1749-1834), an architect and chamberlain to the Duke of Modena).

Champollion, i, 116, 181, 183; Garollo, *Diz. Biog. Univ.*; *Luigi Malaspina di Sannazarro 1754-1835*, 2000.

MALCOLM, (*Sir*) **John** (1769-1833)
British administrator and diplomatist; he was born in Burnfoot, Dumfriesshire, 2 May 1769, son of George M. and Margaret Pasley; he entered the service of the Hon. East India Co. as a boy, 1783, and rose to fill very important military and administrative posts in India and Persia; KCB, 1815; he returned to England in 1821, and occupied himself with literary work, but returned to India, 1827, as Governor of Bombay; he retired in 1830, and on his way home spent some time in Egypt, bringing back a collection of antiquities to England; these included a mummy presented to the Royal Asiatic Soc., and several papyri now in the British Museum (EA 9971-2, 10081, 10384, 10466); he died in London, 30 May 1833.

ODNB 36, 292-5; *DNB* 35, 404-12; Pettigrew, *Hist. Eg. Mummies*, Introd., i; R. Pasley, *Send Malcolm*, 1982.

MALET, (*Rt. Hon. Sir*) **Edward Baldwin** (1837-1908)
British diplomat; he was born at The Hague, 10 Oct. 1837, son of Alexander M. 3rd Bart. and Marianne Dora Spalding; 4th Bart.; GCB; PC; GCMG; educated Eton and Christ Church, Oxford; he held many important posts in the diplomatic service; Consul-General in Egypt, 1879-82; he died in Chorleywood, Herts., 29 June 1908.

ODNB 36, 309-11 (portr.); Hilmy, ii, 9; *Khedives and Pashas*, 75-7 and passim; *WWW* i, 469.

MALININE, Michel (1900-1977)

French Egyptologist; he was born in Moscow, 1 Aug. 1900, son of Vladimir M., Mayor of Moscow, and Ludmilla Lasarev; he was educated in Moscow and attended the University of Moscow 1918-9, but political events forced his family to leave Russia for Prague; he then studied the history of religions at Charles University, Prague until 1925 when he left for Paris; he took his degree at the Sorbonne in 1930 but was attracted to Egyptology and studied at the École du Louvre, diploma 1928, the Institut Catholique under Drioton (q.v.) and the École Pratique des Hautes Études under Sottas (q.v.) where he learned Demotic which was to become his speciality; in 1929 he went to Egypt and thereafter collaborated with Foucart (q.v.) on editing a geographical work of Prince Yusuf Kamal; he was attached to the French Institute 1932-5 and took part in excavations at Deir el-Medina; Professor of Coptic at the Institut Catholique 1936-48; temporary lecturer in Coptic at the École Pratique from 1938; member of CNRS 1939-52; he was awarded his diploma from the École Pratique in 1947 with a thesis on Abnormal Hieratic and Demotic texts; he was named Directeur d'Études at the École Pratique 1952-70; Visiting Professor at Brown University 1956-7; in various articles he published a large number of Hieratic, Demotic and Coptic texts; his monographs were his thesis *Choix de textes juridiques en hiératique "anormal" et en démotique XXVᵉ-XXVIIᵉ dynasties* I, 1953 II, 1983; a revision of Mallon's *Grammaire Copte*, 1956; *Evangelium Veritatis*, with H. Puech, 1956; Supplement, 1961; *De Resurrectione*, with H. Puech, 1963; *Epistula Iacobi apocrypha*, with H. Puech et al, 1968; *Catalogue des stèles du Sérapéum de Memphis* I, with G. Posener and J. Vercoutter, 1968; *Tractatus Tripartitus*, I-II, with R. Kasser et al, 1973-5; he died in Paris, 9 April 1977.

WWF; BIFAO 83, v-ix (portr.) (F. de Cenival and G. Posener); *Rev. d'Ég.* 30 (1978), 7-9 (bibl.) (F. le Corsu); *Le Monde Copte* 10 (1983), 57-8.

MALLET, (*Baron***) Alphonse** (1819-1906)

French amateur Egyptologist; he was born in Paris, 19 Feb. 1819, son of Baron Adolphe Jacques otherwise James M., banker and Regent of the Banque de France, and Laura Oberkampf; he also became a prominent banker and Regent of the Banque de France, 1860-1905; he attended the classes of de Rougé (q.v.) at the Coll. de France; he discovered the Papyrus Judiciaire de Turin in the reserves of the museum and made a tracing of it which he offered to de Rougé in exchange for a copy of the d'Orbiney Papyrus; the exchange did not take place so he handed his tracings to Devéria (q.v.) who edited the text; he also copied the long inscription of Bakenkhons at Munich which was also published by D.; Mallet's name is attached to the hieratic papyrus which he bought at the Anastasi sale of 1857 and afterwards presented to the Louvre; it was published by Maspero (q.v.) in 1870; he also owned a Book of the Dead which was used by Naville (*Todtb.* Ph.); whilst always ready to place material at the disposal of his colleagues, he apparently published nothing himself; he was elected an Associate Member of the Inst. Ég., 18 Oct. 1861; he died in Paris, 10 March 1906.

Bib. Ég. 21, iv; Devéria, *Mém. et Fragm.* i, 263, 276, 302; Hincks, 99; A. Plessis, *Régents et Gouverneurs de la Banque de France sous le Second Empire*, 1985, 420.

MALLON, (Marie) Alexis (1875-1934)

French Egyptologist, Coptologist, and archaeologist; he was born at La Chapelle-Bertrin, Haute-Loire, 8 May 1875, son of Jean M. and Marianne Langlade; he entered the Jesuit order in 1895; he became interested in Egyptian religion and published an article on this subject; from 1902 he taught Coptic at the Saint Joseph University at Beirut and from 1913 at the Pontifical Biblical Institute in Rome, although living at Jerusalem; he visited Egypt regularly and while at Beirut produced a *Grammaire copte avec bibliographie, chrestomathie et vocabulaire*, 1904, on the Bohairic dialect; he also wrote a study, *Les Hébreux en Égypte*, 1921; Mallon later turned to Palestinian archaeology and the last six years of his life were spent excavating the large prehistoric settlement at Teleilat Ghassul in Jordan; he died in Bethlehem, 7 April 1934.

Chron. d'Ég. 19 (1935), 78-9; *The Coptic Encyclopedia* 5, 1516-7 (A. S. Atiya).

MALLON, Paul (1884-1975)

French dealer in ancient art; he was born in Le Havre, 1 Aug. 1884, son of Gustave M., a shipping agent, and Eugenie de Poilly; he was established as a dealer in oriental art in Paris before the First World War; his collection was published in 2 fascicles, G. Migeon, *Collection Paul Mallon*, Paris *c.* 1919, including a number of Egyptian objects; in 1926 he married Marguerite Nadaud Girod (*b.*9 July 1900, *d.*30 May 1977); with her son Milton Girod-Mallon, the Mallons supplied American museums with major works of ancient and eastern art; they sold three statuettes of Pepi I and II to the Brooklyn Museum in 1939; the Cleveland Museum was a notable purchaser from the 1950s to the 1970s; material from their collection was sold in New York (Sotheby's, 12-13 Dec. 1991); he died in Paris, 16 Dec. 1975.

New York Times 18 Dec. 1975 (obit.); *Grove Dictionary of Art* X, 91; A. P. Kozloff in L. M. Berman, *The Cleveland*

Museum of Art: Catalogue of Egyptian Art (New York, 1999), 11-26 (incorrectly giving the wife's maiden name as Nabaud); inf. T. Hardwick.

MALMBERG, Vladimir Konstantinovitch (1860-1921)
Russian art historian and archaeologist; he was born in Moscow, 1/13 Dec. 1860, son of Konstantine M., a merchant; he studied at the University of Kazan, 1879-1884; from 1890 Professor at the University of Dorpat; from 1907 at the Moscow University; in 1913 named Director of the Museum of Fine Arts (later the Pushkin Museum); he wrote a study *An Old Prejudice. Concerning the Representation of Human Figure in Egyptian Relief* (Russ.), Moscow 1915; together with B. A. Turaev (q.v.), he was the co-author of *Description of Egyptian Collection. Statues and Statuettes in the Golenischeff Collection* (Russ.), Moscow 1917, in which he was concerned with the art, while Turaev dealt with the religious meaning of Egyptian statues; he died in Moscow, 9 Dec. 1921.

Great Soviet Encycl. 15, 383; inf. J. Śliwa.

MANFREDI, Manfredo (1925-2011)
Italian papyrologist; he was born in Aulla, 13 Dec. 1925; he was educated at the University of Genoa, graduating in 1948; he then studied at the University of Florence and the Istituto Papyrologico "G. Vitelli", 1949-52; he served there as a voluntary assistant, 1953-63 and ordinary assistant, 1963-7; he became assistant professor of Papyrology, 1967-81 and full professor, 1981-98; he was appointed director of the Istituto Papirologico, 1968-98; he excavated at Arsinoe (Medinet el-Fayum), 1964-5, at Antinoopolis (el-Sheikh Abada), 1965-2000, and at Tuna el-Gebel, 1986 and 1988; he also helped to conserve papyri in the Egyptian Museum, Cairo; he published numerous papyrological studies; he died at Florence, 4 Dec. 2011.

Aegyptus 90 (2010), 207-8 (G. Bastianini), 209-220 (bibl.); M. Capasso, *Hermae* IV, 77-81 (G. Menci) (portr.).

MANGLES, James (1786-1867)
British naval officer and explorer; he was probably born at Hurley, Berks., 1786, son of John M. and Harriet Camden; he entered the Navy, 1800, and saw much service until 1815 when he held the rank of Capt.; he visited Egypt, Nubia, Syria, and Palestine with the Hon. Charles Irby (q.v.), 1817-18; FRS, 1825; FRGS; he died in Fairfield, Exeter, 18 Nov. 1867.

ODNB 36, 413-4; *DNB* 36, 33-4; O'Byrne, *Naval Biogr*. 718; for other refs. see under Irby, C. L.; inf. R. Mangles.

MANN, Maurice (1814-1876)
Polish journalist and publicist; he was born 2 Oct. 1814, son of Ernest and Janna M.; author of an interesting account of his journey to Egypt and the Near East; together with Adam Potocki and a painter Francis Tepa, he sailed out from Trieste on 10 Dec. 1852; after visiting Egypt, Palestine, Syria, Lebanon and Greece he returned to Cracow in June 1853; his written impressions were published as *Travel to the East*, Vol. I-III, Cracow 1854-55; printed later also as *Egypt, Syria and Constantinople*, Cracow 1858; in the Egyptian part, there is a description of Alexandria and her monuments and of Cairo with an excursion to the Pyramids; in Upper Egypt he reached the Second Cataract; he died in Cracow, 15 Nov. 1876.

J. Bystron, *Polacy w Ziemi Swietej, Syrii i Egipcie 1147-1914*, Cracow 1930, 207-211; *Polski Slownik Biograficzny* 19, 483-5; inf. J. Śliwa.

MANSOOR, Mansur Abd al-Sayyid (1881-1968)
Egyptian dealer in antiquities; he was born in Cairo, Oct. 1881 from a Coptic family of Qena; he served in the Egypt State Railways and then opened a shop dealing in jewellery and antiquities in Shepheards' Hotel; he sold portions of his private collection in London, at Sotheby's 17 Dec., 1926 and 22 Oct., 1934 and in New York 15-16 Oct. 1947 and 30-31 Jan. 1952; he also owned a large collection of sculptures in the Amarna style of disputed authenticity; he died in Heliopolis, 16 June 1968.

Family inf.; E. R. Mansoor, *Je cherche un homme*, 1971; A. L. Becker-Colonna, *Ancient Egypt: Exhibit of sculptures and reliefs from the M. A. Mansoor Amarna Collection*, 1991; E. R. Mansoor, *The Truth is on the March*, 1993; F. Hagen and K. Ryholt, *The Antiquities Trade in Egypt 1880-1930*, 2017, 237-8.

MANTEUFFEL-SZOEGE, George Richard (1900-1954)
Polish classical scholar and papyrologist; he was born in Taunagi near Dyneburg (Daugavpils), 3 March 1900, son of Henry and Marion Zielinski; he studied classical philology at the Warsaw University 1918-25, supplemented later in the field of papyrology in Berlin with W. Schubart, and U. Wilcken (q.v.), Paris with P. Jouguet (q.v.), Oxford with A. S. Hunt (q.v.) and London with H. I. Bell (q.v.); habilitation 1929 at the University of Warsaw, *De opusculis Graecis Aegypti e papyris ostracis lapidibusque collectis*, 1930; he took part in Franco-Polish excavations at Tell Edfu, 1937-9; he was made Professor at the Lublin Catholic University 1936 and later at Lwów University 1937-9, next becoming Professor of the Ukrainian University in Lwów 1939-41, 1944-5; after World War II he transferred

to Wroclaw, then was appointed to the Warsaw University Chair of papyrology especially created for him, 1945; from 1949 co-editor of the *Journal of Juristic Papyrology* together with T. Taubenschlag; from 1946 member of the Comité International de Papyrologie Brussels; in 1932 he organized at the Warsaw University the first Polish collection of papyri and ostraca, to which were added the ostraca formerly collected by A. Deissman, purchased in 1934; author of *Papyri Varsovienses*, 1935, and many specialistic papers and also more popular texts concerning papyrology and the culture of Hellenistic and Roman Egypt; he died in Warsaw, 14 Jan. 1954.

Chron. d'Ég. 60 (1955), 421-3 (M. Giorgie); *Polski Slownik Biograficzny* 19, 494-5; *Biograms of Polish Scholars*, 1, 2, (Wroclaw 1984), 437-9; inf. J. Śliwa.

MARAGIOLIO, Vito Giuseppe (1915-1976)
Italian army officer; he was born in Gropparello 1915 of a Sicilian family; he served in the Italian army rising to the rank of colonel in the artillery; he retired due to ill health in 1945, and concentrated on the study of palaeography, on which he obtained a diploma, and Egyptology; he studied informally with Botti (q.v.); in 1946 he met Rinaldi (q.v.) who became his collaborator in a project to document the architecture of the pyramids in Memphite region; he also took part in the work of the Turin Museum during the Nubian rescue campaign 1961-5; his publications with Rinaldi were *Notizie sulle piramidi di Zedefra, Zedkara Isesi, Teti*, 1962; *L'Architettura della Piramidi Menfite*, ii-viii, 1963-1977; and with S. Curto and others, *Kalabsha*, 1965; *Dehmit*, 1973 and *Korosko-Kasr Ibrim. Incisioni ruperstri nubiane*, 1987; he died at Rapallo, 23 Feb. 1976.

BSFE 75 (1976), 4; *Aegyptus* 58 91028), 222-4 (S Curto); inf. S. Curto

MARCEL, Jean-Joseph (1776-1854)
French orientalist; he was born in Paris, 24 Nov. 1776, son of Joseph M. and Anne Giraud; he wrote works on Arabic and on Arab history, and was the author of a dictionary and many other works; he and Silvestre de Sacy (q.v.) did much to promote Arabic studies in France; Member of Napoleon's Commission in Egypt, of which he wrote a history; Marcel's name is associated with a papyrus in the Bibl. Nationale, Paris; he died in Paris, 11 March 1854; his library was acquired by Lee (q.v.).

Carré, i, 125, 149, 158, 164; ii, 36; Hilmy, ii, 14; *Journal Asiatique* 5e serie, 3, 553-62.

MARCELLUS, (*Comte de*) Marie Louis Jean Charles André de Martin du Tyrac (1795-1861)
French diplomat and historian; he was born at the Château de Marcellus (Lot), 19 Jan. 1795, son of Marie Louis August de M. du T. and Marie Madeleine Françoise Sophia de Piis; he was responsible for the acquisition of the Venus de Milo by the Louvre; he visited Egypt, 1820, and published *Souvenirs de l'Orient*, 1839, as well as other works; he died in Paris, 29 April 1861.

Carré, i, 205-11; A. Dumaine, *Quelques oubliés de l'autre siècle*, 1-64, 1931; È. Gran-Aymerich, *Dictionnaire biographique d'archéologie 1798-1945*, 2001, incorporated in *Les Chercheurs de passé 1798-1945*, 2007, 968-9.

MARCINIAK, Marek (1937-1996)
Polish Egyptologist; he was born in Piotrków Trybunalski, 25 April 1937, son of Leszek M. and his wife Janine; he studied Egyptology at the University of Warsaw under Andrzejewski (q.v.) and Černy (q.v.); MA, 1959; PhD, 1972; he was closely associated with Michałowski (q.v.); he took part in Polish excavations at Athribis, Alexandria, Palmyra and Deir el-Bahri and during the Nubian rescue campaign, 1961-4 at Faras and Dabod, where he was in charge of the work, 1960-1; he was Deputy Director of the Mediterranean Archaeology Department of the Polish Academy in Warsaw in the 1970s and Scientific Secretary of the Polish Centre of Mediterranean Archaeology in Cairo, 1981-4; in 1977-9 he undertook epigraphic work in the Tomb of Ramesses III, but the tomb remained unpublished; he published *Deir el-Bahari* I. *Les Inscriptions hiératiques du Temple de Thoutmosis III*, 1974 and, with J. Lipinska, *Mitologia starozytnego Egiptu*, 1977; he died in Berkeley, California 11 Oct. 1996.

Polish Archaeology in the Mediterranean 8 (1997), 9-10 (portr.) (K. Mysliwiec); IAE Internet obituary (Z. Kiss); *Memnonia VIII* (1997), 17-8; inf. J. Śliwa.

MARCKS, Dietrich (1882-1969)
German architect he was born in Berlin 1882, son of Hermann M., a merchant, and Marie Nordmann; he was educated in Berlin at the Technische Hochschule; he took part in the excavations at Amarna, Jan.-April, 1911 and Nov.-Dec. 1911, and at Aniba under Steindorff (q.v.), Jan.-April 1912; he later worked at Medinet Habu with the Oriental Institute of Chicago, 1932-3; he contributed a chapter in the publication of G. Steindorff, *Aniba* II, 1937; he died in 1969.

Inf. R. Krauss.

MARIETTE, (*Pasha*) **François Auguste Ferdinand** (1821-1881)

French Egyptologist and founder of the Egyptian Antiquities Service; he was born in Boulogne-sur-Mer, 11 Feb. 1821, son of François Paulin M., an official in the town hall, and Eugénie Sophie Mélanie Delobeau; as a child Mariette lived in the town hall where his father had lodgings; he was educated at the Coll. de Boulogne where he won various prizes; his father, a widower, remarried and had another family by his second wife, so that Mariette was unable to complete his education and was put into his father's office as a supernumerary, 1837-9; at eighteen he went to England to teach French and Drawing at a school, Shakespeare House Academy, Stratford, for a Mr. Parker, 1839-40; he then went to Coventry to earn his living by designing models for ribbon manufacturers, but as he did not make money he returned to Boulogne in 1841 to complete his studies; he gained his Bacc.-ès-Lettres at Douai in only six months with hon. mention, 1841; appointed Maître d'études at Coll. de Boulogne, 1841; Professor of French, 1843; editor of *L'Annotateur Boulonnais*, 1843-6; he kept up his artistic work which was to prove useful later and also wrote articles on topical subjects at this time; in 1842 the family received their relative Nestor l'Hôte's (q.v.) papers and young Mariette became fired with interest by going through them and learnt the Egyptian alphabet and decipherment, later filling the gaps in his knowledge when in Paris; he may also have been inspired by the Denon (q.v.) collection of Egyptian antiquities in Boulogne; for seven years he worked alone and unaided, often ignorant of the fact that hieroglyphic plates in the *Description* contained errors; he married Éléonore Millon, 1845; he learnt Coptic and had his first article published in the *Annotateur Boulonnais*, 'Catalogue analytique des monuments composant la Galerie ég. du Musée de Boulogne' in 1847; he also wrote a long paper on Tuthmosis III's Hall of Ancestors, 1849; in 1849 he obtained for a short time a minor post at the Louvre, but although now able to work full time on Egyptology he had a hard struggle in Paris; the first of his great feats of industry was to transcribe all the inscriptions then in the Louvre, many of these copies being later destroyed when his Cairo house was flooded, but they formed the basis for a general inventory of Egyptian monuments, July 1850; this was a period of intensive study and the production of articles for the *Rev. Arch.*; in 1850 he was sent to Egypt to acquire Coptic, Ethiopic, and Syriac MSS and made a Bibl. Copte now preserved with his papers at the Bibl. Nat.; he also began the excavation of the Serapeum at Memphis and its dromos, finding the Apis galleries and many famous antiquities and monuments; he succeeded in raising further funds and excavated for four years, 1850-4; the Serapeum was perhaps his greatest discovery and first made him famous; Mariette not only intended to publish the monuments in transcription but also to reproduce the principal ones, nearly 7,000 in all; he devised a special system for making a rapid analysis of each leaving the finer points of philology to others such as Brugsch (q.v.) who helped him at this time; only a small portion of this immense work was ever published; his notes, filling very many vols., are now in the Louvre; in 1853 he cleared the area near the Sphinx and discovered the Valley Temple of Chephren; he was attached to the Louvre 1 Jan. 1852; he was appointed assistant curator in the Egyptian department of the Louvre, 1855-61, hon. assistant from 1861; Mariette visited Berlin and Turin where he was made a Corr. of the Acad., 1856-7; he received many other honours, Corr. of the Rio de Janeiro Acad.; member of the Soc. of Antiquaries, 1856; Commander of the Légion d'honneur, 1877; Commander Order of Medjideh, etc.; he suggested fresh schemes for publishing monuments in museums but these were often so gigantic that they were impossible to realize; Mariette's three greatest achievements were, the creation of the first National Antiquities Service, the formation of the first National Museum in the Near East from his important discoveries, and the developing of a firstly Egyptian then world-wide conscience about the destruction, expropriation, and proper care and conservation of antiquities; backed by de Lesseps (q.v.) he made a successful plea to Said Pasha for an organization to deal with the standing Egyptian monuments which were being rapidly destroyed and for a Cairo Museum in an old house at Bulaq; Mariette started simultaneous excavations at numerous sites from Nubia to the Delta and dug at Saqqara and Giza with Brugsch, also at Thebes, Abydos, and Elephantine where he started workshops as well, 1857-8; many important discoveries were made such as the mastaba of Khufu-ankh; the Mastabat el-Farun was entered for the first time and at Thebes a necropolis of the 11th and 17th Dynasties excavated; the Khedive appointed him Director of Egyptian monuments, 1 June 1858; Mariette began a huge excavation programme with 'digs' at Qurna, Karnak, Tell el-Yahudiya, Menshiet-Ramleh, Abydos, Giza pyramids, Saqqara, Mit-Rahineh, Tuna, Esna, Medinet Habu, Deir el-Bahri, Edfu and Sais, and later at Mendes and Bubastis, employing over 7,280 workmen in all; no adequate site supervision could be achieved with such vast numbers but it should be remarked in Mariette's defence, against attacks by Petrie and later archaeologists, that his work was a great deal better than any undertaken in the Near East up to that time and that he again established workshops for dealing with antiquities at Edfu, Thebes, Abydos, and Memphis; whole temples as Luxor and Edfu were now freed from the sand and accumulated rubbish of ages and their innumerable texts revealed fully for the first time; other important discoveries were the burial and jewellery of Queen Aah-hotep and the famous statues and monuments excavated at Tanis (San) 1859-61; in 1863 he opened the Museum of Egyptian Antiquities at Bulaq; most of his papers were destroyed when his house at Bulaq was flooded in 1878; with C. du Locle Mariette composed the libretto of Verdi's 3-act opera Aïda, first performed in Cairo in 1871; member of the Académie des Inscriptions 1878; Pasha 1879; during his last years in spite of illness he found time to publish many works, although they included but a small part of what he had discovered, *Mémoire sur la mère d'apis*, which rather shocked the church, 1856; *Choix de monuments* et de dessins découverts ou exécutés pendant le déblaiement du sérapéum de Memphis, 1856; Le Sérapéum de Memphis, fol. 1857; Description des fouilles exécutées en Égypte, 1863, fol.; Aperçu de l'histoire d'Égypte, 1864; Notice des principaux monuments exposés dans les galeries provisoires du Musée ... à Boulak, 1864; Description du parc égyptien, for the popular exhibition of 1867 in Paris, also another for the 1878 exhibition; Abydos, 2 vols. 1869-80; Dendéreh, 5 vols. fol. 1870-5; Dendéreh, gen. description, 4°, 1875; Boulaq, fol. 1871; Monuments divers recueillis en Égypte et en Nubie, fol. 1881; Itinéraire de la Haute-Égypte, 1872; Listes géographiques des pylones de Karnak, fol. and 4°, 1875; Karnak. Étude topographique et archéologique, 4°, Atlas, fol., 1875; Deir el-Bahari, 2 pts. fol., 1877; Voyage de la Haute-Égypte, 2 vols. fol., 1878-80; Catalogue général des monuments d'Abydos découverts pendant les fouilles de cette ville, 1880; posth. works published by G. Maspero, Le Sérapéum de Memphis, 4°, 1882; Les Mastabas de l'Ancien-Empire, fol., 1883; some of his papers are in the Griffith Institute, Oxford; Mariette died in Bulaq, 18 Jan. 1881; his remains were interred in a sarcophagus later moved to the forecourt of Cairo Museum, surmounted by a bronze statue by Xavier Barthe unveiled 17 March 1904.

Édouard Mariette, Mariette Pacha, Paris, 1904; Maspero, Mariette (1821-1881). Notice biogr. in A. Mariette, Oeuvres diverses, Bibl. Ég. 18, 1904, tom. i, pp. i-ccxxiv (portr.); Rev. deux mondes 1881, 789-92 (E. de Vogüé); Rev. ég. 2, 317-20 (E. Revillout); Gazette des beaux-arts 24 (1881), 239-265; J. Sainte Fare Garnot, Mélanges Mariette. IFAO Bibl. d'études, tom. 32 1961 (portr.); La Grande Enc. 23. 114-16 (E. Chassinat); Larousse, 7 (1963), 89 (portr.); ASAE 5 (1904), 54-68, inaug. of monument; Chron. d'Ég. 14 (1939), 69-78, 'Lettres inédites de Mariette' (M. C. Weynants-Ronday); Brugsch, Mein Leben, 125, 137, 168, and often; Gaz. des Beaux-Arts, Sér. 2, 24, 239-65; Guide ... au Musée du Caire, 1915, vii-xxv (portr.) (G. Maspero); CRAIBL ser. 4. 11, 481-584; Hilmy, ii, 16; Maspero, Rapports sur la Marche de Serv. des Antiquités, 147-59; Glyn Daniel, A Hundred Years of Archaeology, 56, 69, 118, 135, 156, 160-4, 175; J. Cassar, BSFE 90 (1981), 12-28; J. Leclant, CRAIBL 1981, 487-96; R. T. Ridley, Abr-Nahrain 22 (1983-4), 118-58; M.-C. Bruwier, 'Autographes de Mariette à Mariemont. Quelques travaux de l'égyptologue français de 1868 à 1879', Les Cahiers de Mariemont 16, 1985, 6-40; E. David, Mariette Pacha. 1821-1881, 1994; G.Lambert, Auguste Mariette, 1997; KMT 9/4 (1999), 82-84; È. Gran-Aymerich, Dictionnaire biographique d'archéologie 1798-1945, 2001, incorporated in Les Chercheurs de passé 1798-1945, 2007, 969-71; Des dieux, des tombeaux, un savant. En Égypte, sur les pas de Mariette Pacha, 2004; C. Humber in Ancient Egypt 11/4 (2011), 16-9; P. Piacentini in D. Magee, J. Bourriau and S. Quirke, Sitting Beside Lepsius, 2009, 423-438; E. David, BSFE 186-7 (2013), 7-12.

MARILHAT, Prosper George Antoine (1811-1847)
French artist; born in Vertaizon, 26 March 1811, son of Pierre Luc M. and Jeanne Boudal Delapchier du Chasseint; he joined the expedition of Carl Alexander Freiherr von Hügel, the naturalist, as a draughtsman; they embarked for the East 1831, but he was left at Alexandria, the rest of the party proceeding to India; he remained two years in Egypt, returning to France in 1833, in the vessel which conveyed J. B. A. Lebas (q.v.) and the Luxor obelisk; two of his pictures of Egyptian subjects are in the Louvre, many more are reproduced in the plates of the first edition of Carré; he died in Paris, 14 Sept. 1847.

Carré, i, passim; A. Dumas, Portraits Contemporains, 234-64; inf. from Vertaizon.

MARKIEWICZ, Tomasz (1974-2009)
Polish demotist and papyrologist; he was born in Warsaw, 2 Dec. 1974; he studied at the Warsaw School of Economics, 1993-8 and Egyptology at the University of Warsaw, 1994-9 under Winnicki (q.v.); PhD, 2005 with a thesis Indebtedness in Abnormal Hieratic and Demotic Documents; he also studied at Cologne, 1999-2002 under Thissen; he was later employed in the Department of Papyrology at the University of Warsaw; he was Kosciuszko Foundation Fellow at the Department of Classics, Stanford University, 2008; he published several articles, mainly in The Journal of Juristic Papyrology; he died in Warsaw, 30 Sept. 2009.

The Journal of Juristic Papyrology 39 (2009), 15-21 (portr.) (T. Derda).

MARMONT, Auguste Frédéric Louis Viesse de, Duc de Raguse (1774-1852)
French Marshal and writer; he was born in Châtillon-sur-Seine, 20 July 1774, son of Nicolas Edmé M. and Clothilde Victoire Chapron; he became Napoleon's aide-de-camp, and fought with his army in Italy and Egypt and in subsequent campaigns; created Duc de Raguse, 1808; he fell into disgrace by concluding a secret convention in 1813, but was reinstated under the restoration of the Bourbons; he published Voyages en Hongrie ... Égypte et en Sicile, 5 vols., 1837 (2nd ed. 1839); he died in Venice, 22 March 1852.

Carré, i, 279-84; Hilmy, i, 170.

MARTIN, Alastair Bradley (1915-2010)
American collector, benefactor, and tennis player; he was born in New York, 11 March 1915, son of Bradley M., financier, and Helen Margaret Phipps, daughter of a Pittsburgh steel magnate; he was educated at Princeton, BA 1938; from the 1940s onwards he and his wife Edith (née Park, 1917-1989) formed a large and varied art

collection, with particular strengths in pre-Columbian and Egyptian material, most notably an ivory grasshopper of the New Kingdom; many pieces were purchased from Joseph Brummer (q.v.); for Egyptian material he was advised by J. D. Cooney (q.v.) of the Brooklyn Museum, where many of his Egyptian objects were displayed on loan or donated; objects from the 'Guennol' (Welsh for 'Martin') collection were also loaned and given to the Metropolitan Museum and the American Museum of Natural History; the collection was published in three vols, 1975-91, and was the subject of special exhibitions at the Metropolitan and Brooklyn Museums in 1969 and 2000; he was a trustee of the Brooklyn Museum 1948-2004, and its chairman 1984-89; he divided his collections among his family and some pieces were dispersed from the 1990s onwards; an early Mesopotamian statuette of a lion headed woman was sold for $57,161,000 (Sotheby's New York, 5 Dec 2007, lot 30), a record price for an antiquity or work of sculpture at auction; he was US national real tennis champion in the 1930s and 1940s, and president of the US Lawn Tennis Association, 1969-70; he died in Katonah, New York, 12 Jan. 2010.

Brooklyn Museum Library and archives; inf. T. Hardwick; D. Porter, *Biographical dictionary of American Sports: 1992-1995 supplement*, 1995, 646-647; *Wall Street Journal*, 20 Jan. 2010; *New York Times*, 20 Jan. 2010; A. B. Martin, *Guennol: reflections on collecting*, 1998; D. Fane and A. G. Poster, *The Guennol Collection: Cabinet of Wonders*, 2000; A. G. Poster, *Orientations* 41/3 (April 2010), 57.

MARUCCHI, Orazio (1852-1931)
Italian Egyptologist and archaeologist; he was born in Rome, 1 Feb. 1852, and became Director of the Egyptian Museum of the Vatican and the Christian Museum of the Lateran; he held the chairs in Christian Archaeology at the College of San Apollinare and Rome University, and edited the *Nuovo bolletino di archeologia cristiana*, continuing the work of G. B. de Rossi (d.1904) in this field; his principal Egyptological works were, *Monumenta papyracea aegyptica Bibliothecae Vaticanae ... recensuit et digessit Horatius Marucchi*, 1891; *Gli obelischi egiziani di Roma, illustrati con traduzione dei testi geroglifici: edizione riveduta*, 1898; *Il Museo Egizio Vaticano, descritto da Orazio Marucchi*, 1899; he died in Rome, 21 Jan. 1931.

Aegyptus 11 (1931), 190-4 (bibl.) (G. Farina); *Dict. of Catholic Biogr.* (1962), 764; Garollo, *Diz. Biogr. Univ.; Enc. It.*

MARUSIEŃSKI, Stephan (1856-?)
Polish journalist and publicist; he was born in the vicinity of Cracow, 1856; he left Poland in 1878 for London, where he began to work as merchant's agent; at first he was sent to Algiers, but later, about 1880, to Egypt where he stayed until 1888; he travelled all over the country; being very interested in Egypt's past, he visited many sites and monuments; he spoke Arabic fluently and probably knew some hieroglyphs; a large proportion of his letters to his family in Poland were published in the *Weekly of Fashions and Novels*, 1879-83; he contributed also systematically to the *Wanderer*, 1882-87, and to other Polish magazines giving details of political events in Egypt, describing geographical conditions, as well as customs and manners of the people; for the Polish press he provided direct news and information about Orabi's (1882) and the Mahdi's (1883-85) insurrections, giving distinctly his favourable opinion about the latter movement; he also wrote some tales based on Arab motifs; he stayed at Naqada in Upper Egypt from at least 1881 until 1886; from 1884 on behalf of Prince Wladyslaw Czartoryski (q.v.) he was concerned with purchases for his Cracow museum replacing Shenuda (q.v.) who for a long time was owed money sent for this purpose; he was soon very familiar with dealing in antiquities and he dispatched to Cracow three large shipments in 1884, 1885 and one, of later date, not so well documented, probably connected also with an offer by M. P. Tanos (q.v.); the exact list accompanying the two first shipments, completed with additional information, forms an important source for the provenance of many objects from the Cracow collection of the Czartoryski family.

K. Moczulska and J. Śliwa, *Prace Archeologiczne* 14 (1972), 85-104; H. Szymanska, 105-114; K. Moczulska, *Folia Orientalia* XIX (1978), 198; inf. J. Śliwa.

MASARRA, Youssef (c.1785-1842+)
Egyptian dragoman and dealer of Syrian origin; he was born in Cairo; he was a dragoman to the French Consulate in Cairo from 1807 to 1842; he appears to have been an agent for Drovetti (q.v.) in the Memphite area; with Segato (q.v.), he opened the Step Pyramid of Djoser at Saqqara in 1820-1 for Minutoli (q.v.); from 1828 he is attested as an antiquities dealer who exploited tombs at Giza and Saqqara; he is to be distinguished from his relation Hanna Masarra, born in Cairo of Syrian parents, who was appointed interpreter to the British Consulate in 1837 and to the Consul-General in 1852 and was still in office in 1862; Hanna also ran a shop in antiquities.

Bonomi Diary, 1830, July 12, 30; Champollion, ii, 73; *L.D., Text*, i, 14, 16; Nicholson, *Aegyptiaca*, 95; Pückler-Muskau, *Travels*, i. 243; Vyse, *Pyramids*, i, 187, 201, 256, 266; J. Málek, *Orientalia Lovaniensia Perodica* 17 (1986), 11-15; *Foreign Office Confidential Print* 768, 113; French F. O. records.

MASON, Robert (*Revd*) (1782-1841)
British clergyman, collector, and benefactor: he was baptized at Hurley, Berks, 5 July 1782, son of Robert and Catharine Mason; he matriculated from St Edmund Hall Oxford 1807, and studied at The Queen's College, BA, 1810; MA, 1813; BD, 1820; DD, 1823; he served as curate of Hurley 1812-24; he formed a collection of around 1,500 Egyptian objects, mainly amulets and shabti figures, and smaller collections of Greek vases and classical gems, some of the Egyptian objects coming from the Belzoni (q.v.), Salt (q.v.), and Burton collections (q.v.); he bequeathed his papyri and £40,000 to the Bodleian Library, and £30,000 and his other collections to The Queen's College; the Egyptian objects were deposited by the College on loan to the Ashmolean Museum in 1949; he died at Hurley, 7 Jan. 1841.

Alumni Oxonienses III, 924; J. R. Magrath, *The Queen's College* II, 1921, 172; The Queen's College, MSS 419; *Ashmolean Museum Annual Report* 2003-4, 11; inf. T. Hardwick.

MASPERO, (*Sir*) **Gaston Camille Charles** (1846-1916)
French Egyptologist, of Italian origin; he was born in Paris, 24 June 1846, illegitimate son of Camillo Marsuzi de Aguirre, a Neapolitan political refugee, and Miss Adèle Maspero, daughter of a Milanese printer (she later married Eugène Bazil); he was naturalized when very young and educated at the Lycée Louis-le-Grand, 1853-65, and the École Normale, Paris, 1865-7; he was made Professor of Egyptology, École des Hautes Études, 1869; he gained Doct.-ès-Lettres, 1873; appointed Professor of Egyptian Philology and Archaeology, Collège de France, 4 Feb. 1874; Maspero became interested in hieroglyphs at the age of 14 while still at school, and in 1867 met Mariette (q.v.), who gave him two newly discovered hieroglyphic texts to study, which he then translated in less than a fortnight; he published these the same year, but his career was temporarily interrupted when he went with a French family to Montevideo and worked on the Inca language Quichua; he returned to France and studied with de Rougé (q.v.); he married 1. 11 Nov. 1871 Harriet Yapp (*d.*1873), daughter of Edward Yapp, Paris correspondent of the *Daily Telegraph* 2. 1880 Louise Justine Elisabeth Madeleine Thérèse Catherine Balluet d'Estournelles de Constant de Rebecque; he went to Egypt in 1880, as head of an archaeological mission which later became the IFAO, and organised the work of recording scenes and inscriptions in many important tombs, espec. in the Valley of Kings; he was appointed Director of the Bulaq Museum, succeeding Mariette, 1881-6; also of the Antiquities Service; Mariette when dying had been interested in the opening of the smaller pyramids and Brugsch (q.v.) had discovered and copied the texts in Pepi I and Merenre; Maspero continued this work and opened three more; in all he copied and translated 4,000 lines of inscription, making the first edition of these famous Pyramid Texts; he was also involved in the removal of the Deir el-Bahari cache of royal mummies to Cairo Museum, 1881; it is impossible to list all of his great achievements here but the following must be cited: he arranged and catalogued the immense collections in Cairo Museum, regulated excavation throughout Egypt, inaugurated the systematic clearance and preservation of Karnak, and with Lord Cromer's help built up the then embryonic Antiquities Service with five inspectorates for different areas; Maspero returned to France 1886-99, and was again Director in Egypt, 1899-1914, when illness forced him to go back to France in July; under his direction Reisner (q.v.) undertook the Archaeological Survey of Nubia, 1907-9; he acquired many honours, Acad. des Inscriptions, 1883; Hon. Fellow, The Queen's College and Hon. DCL, Oxford, 1887; Hon. KCMG, 1909; Member of the Académie des Inscriptions, 30 Nov. 1883 and Sec. Perpétuel., 1914; his activity, industry and learning were enormous, and he held the premier place in Egyptology in his generation; he edited the gigantic *Cairo Catalogue* which had reached 50 vols. at the time of his death, and the Nubian temples vols. which then numbered 12; he wrote on a very wide variety of subjects and the number of his published works listed in his bibl. exceeds that of any other Egyptologist, *c.*1,200 items; many of these were small or else reviews, his principal works being, *L'Inscription dédicatoire du Temple d'Abydos*, 1867; *Hymne au Nil*, 1868; *Une Enquête judiciaire à Thèbes au temps de la XXe dynastie* (i.e. Papyrus Abbott), 1871; *Des formes de la conjugaison en égyptien antique, en démotique et en copte*, 1871; *Les Pronoms personnels en égyptien*, 1872; *Du genre épistolaire chez les Égyptiens de l'époque pharaonique*, 1872; *Histoire ancienne des peuples de l'Orient*, 1875, and many later eds.; *Mémoire sur quelques papyrus du Louvre*, 1875; *Études Égyptiennes - Romans et poésies du papyrus Harris no. 500 ...*, 1879; *Études Ég. - Étude sur quelques peintures et sur quelques textes relatifs aux funérailles*, with *le conte d'Apôpi et de Soknourî*, 1881; *La Trouvaille de Deir-el-Bahari*, with E. Brugsch, 1881; *Les Contes populaires de l'Égypte ancienne ...*, 1882; *Guide du visiteur au musée de Boulaq*, 1883; *La Trouvaille de Deir-el-Bahari*, 1883; *L'Archéologie égyptienne*, 1887, trans. by A. B. Edwards; *Les Momies royales de Deir-el-Bahari*, fol., 1889; *Trois années de fouilles dans les tombeaux de Thèbes et de Memphis*, fol., 1889; *Catalogue du Musée Égyptien de Marseille*, 1889; *Histoire ancienne Égypte, Assyrie*. 1890, trans. by A. Morton; *Fragments de manuscrits coptes-thébains provenant de la Bibl. du Deir Amba-Shenoudah*. 1892; *Les Inscriptions des pyramides de Saqqarah*, 1894; *Histoire ancienne des peuples de l'Orient classique*, 3 vols., 1895, 1897, 1899, (trans. and ed. A. H. Sayce as *The Dawn of Civilization - Egypt and Chaldea*, 1896; *The Struggle of the Nations - Egypt, Syria and Assyria*, 1896; *The Passing of the Empires*, 1900); *Fouilles autour de la pyramide d'Ounas*, with A. Barsanti, 1900; *Guide du visiteur au musée du Caire*, 1902; and many eds.; *Causeries d'Égypte*, 1907; *Les Mémoires de Sinouhit ...*, 1908; *New Light on Ancient Egypt*, trans. E. Lee, 1908; *Sarcophages des époques persane et ptolémaïque*, Cairo Cat., 1908; *Egypt: ancient sites and modern scenes*, 1910; *Essai sur l'art égyptien*, 1912; *Études de mythologie et d'archéologie ég.*, 8 vols., 1893, 1898, 1900; 1911, 1912, 1913, 1916;

Les enseignements d'Amenemhaît Ier à son fils Sanouasrît Ier, 1914; he also translated Ebers *Egypt*, 1880, 1881, edited the works of Renouf (q.v.) and as a young man transcribed Champollion's *Notices*; his letters were published as *Lettres d'Égypte*, 2003; Maspero's second wife died Paris, 22 Jan. 1953 aged nearly 100; he died in Paris whilst about to address a meeting of the Academy, 30 June 1916.

H. Cordier, *Bibliographie de Gaston Maspero*, 1922, 127-35, enumerates a long list of obituary notices of Maspero, many with portraits; H. Cordier, *Maspero en Amérique*, 1920; *AE* (1916), 145-9 (?W. M. F. Petrie); *ASAE* 16 (1916), 129-40 (portr. Daressy); *BSAC* I (1936) 'Gaston Maspero et les études coptes', 27-36 (portr.) (H. Munier); *CRAIBL* 1918 (1917), 445-82 (R. Cagnat); *EB* 11th ed., 17, 848; *EB* 1968 ed., 14, 1023 (W. R. Dawson); *JEA* 3 (1916), 227-34 (portr.) (É. Naville); *JEA* 33 (1947), 'Letters from Maspero to Amelia Edwards', 66-89 (portr.) (W. R. Dawson); *JMEOS* 1915-16, 104 (W. M. Crompton); *JRAS* 1917, 629-31 (L. W. King); *La Grande Enc.* 23, 362-3 (H. M.); *Larousse* 7, 144 (portr.); *Mélanges Maspero*, 3 vols. (1934-53) Mem. IFAO tom. 66-8; *Nation* 103 New York (1916), 176-7 (J. H. Breasted); Petrie, 27 and passim; *PSBA* 38 (1916), 141-5 (G. F. Legge); *Réc. Trav.* 38 (1916), 211-25 (portr.) (E, Chassinat); *Rev. Arch.* 5e ser., iv (1916), 172-6 (portr.) (E. Naville); *Rev. de l'hist. des religions*, Nov.-Dec. 1916, 264-310 (A. Moret); *Rev. Hist.* 1916, 434-40 (A. Moret); *Sphinx* 21 (1924), 1-11 (G. Jéquier); *WWW* ii, 710; A. C. E. Franquet de Franqueville, *Le Premier Siècle de l'Institut de France*, 1895, I, 395-6; J. Leclant, *CRAIBL* 1998, 1074-1091; E. David, *Gaston Maspero 1846-1916*, 1999; È. Gran-Aymerich, *Dictionnaire biographique d'archéologie 1798-1945*, 2001, incorporated in *Les Chercheurs de passé 1798-1945*, 2007, 977-80; E. David (ed.), *Gaston Maspero. Lettres d'Égypte*, 2003.

MASPERO, (Jacques) Jean Gaston (1885-1915)
French papyrologist; he was born in Paris, 20 Dec. 1885, third son of Gaston M. and his second wife; he showed great interest in archaeology and numismatics at an early age, and was later attached to the IFAO, being assistant to Chassinat (q.v.) for a time; he specialized in Greek papyri, especially those of the Byzantine period, and was engaged by the Catalogue Commission of the Antiquities Service to catalogue the great store of Byzantine papyri in the Cairo Museum; he completed two volumes, but died before the publication of the third, which was seen through the press by his father, who prefixed a portrait and biographical memoir and bibliography; he joined the French forces early in the war, and was killed in action during the French attack on Vauquois in the Argonne, 17 Feb. 1915. [Maspero's second son, Henri, an eminent Sinologist born 15 Dec. 1883, lost his life during the Second World War; he and his wife were deported by the Germans in July 1944; she was imprisoned at Ravensbrück, and he in the concentration-camp of Buchenwald, where he succumbed to brutal treatment aggravated by dysentery, 17 Mar. 1945. See *JEA* 33 (1947), 78; *ZDMG* 101 (1951) 1-2 (portr.).]

G. Maspero in *Papyrus grecs d'époque byzantine,* Cairo Mus. Cat., iii, 1916, pp. i-xxxvi (portr. and bibl.); *JEA* 2 (1915), 119; *Rev. arch.* 1915, 178; È. Gran-Aymerich, *Dictionnaire biographique d'archéologie 1798-1945*, 2001, incorporated in *Les Chercheurs de passé 1798-1945*, 2007, 980.

MASSART, (*Rev.*) **Adhémar Émile Marie Joseph** (1906-1985)
Belgian Egyptologist; he was born at Spy, 31 Oct. 1906, son of Leon M. and Julia Renard; he joined the Jesuits in 1924 and trained for the priesthood studying Coptic under Lefort (q.v.) at the University of Louvain; he was nominated as the successor to Suys (q.v.) as Professor of Egyptology at the Biblical Institute in Rome; he studied under Gunn (q.v.) and Faulkner (q.v.) at Oxford 1939-42, 1946-8 serving as an army chaplain in World War II; he took up his post at Rome in 1948 retiring in 1980; DPhil at Oxford, 1951 with a thesis on a magical papyrus from Leiden; he was editor of *Orientalia* 1965-80 and Dean of the Faculty of Ancient Near Eastern Studies at the Biblical Institute 1966-76, 1978-9; along with nine articles mostly on magic, he published his thesis *The Leiden Magical Papyrus I 343 + I 345*, 1954 and *Notae grammaticae aegyptiacae*, 1965; he died in Rome, 12 Jan. 1985.

Orientalia 54 (1985), 416-8 (portr.) (bibl.), (C. Sturtewagen); *Acta Pontificii Instituti Biblici* 9 (1984-85), 67-9 (C. Sturtewagen).

MATHIESON, Ian James (1927-2010)
British archaeologist and surveyor; he was born in Edinburgh, 23 May 1927, son of James White M., a weapons manufacturer, and Barbara Elizabeth (Daisy) Smith; he was educated at Daniel Stewart's College until 1944; unable to serve in the RAF, he was transferred to the King's Dragoon Guards where he became a tank commander until 1947; he then studied at Heriot Watt College qualifying as a mining surveyor and geologist; he joined the National Coal Board; he became project manager at Hunting Surveys, 1956-72 when he worked in Iraq, Saudi Arabia, 1965-6, and India, and partner and technical director at Survey and Development Services, 1972-86; through his work in Egypt, he became interested in Egyptian archaeology and joined excavations run by the Egypt Exploration Society; he pioneered methods

of surveying and mapping through the use of sound waves and radar; he founded the Saqqara Geophysical Survey Project in 1990 sponsored by the National Museums of Scotland and from 2002 Glasgow Museums; he also established the Scottish Egyptian Archaeological Trust, 2007; FSA Scot; he died in Lauder, 24 June 2010.

Scottish Pharaonic 9 (2010), issue 3, 1-2; *Egyptian Archaeology* 37 (2010), 6 (D. Jeffreys); inf. A. Jeffreys.

MATIEGKOVÁ, Ludmila (1889-1960)
Czechoslovak Egyptologist; she was born in Lovosice, 9 March 1889, daughter of the Professor of Anthropology Jindřich Matiegka (founder of the Institute of Anthropology at Charles University, Prague); she graduated from the Minerva secondary school for women, and later studied history at the Faculty of Arts, Charles University; she attended lectures of the orientalist Rudolf Dvořák, and there began her interest in Egypt; from 1910-11, she attended lectures by Erman (q.v.), Bissing (q.v.) and Hommel (q.v.) in Berlin and Munich; in 1914 she graduated from Charles University; from 1914 she was a teacher at the Minerva secondary school; she maintained contact with the Seminar of Egyptology, especially with František Lexa (q.v.), Jaroslav Černý (q.v.), František Váhala (q.v.), Milada Lexová and Milada Vilímková (q.v.); she visited the library of the Seminar (later the Institute) and worked creatively, writing about mummies and the illnesses of people in ancient Egypt; her publications were *V objetí sfingy*, 1927; *Jakým dojmem působily mumie na první egyptology*, 1929; *Jak vzniklo písmo,* 1930; she died in Mariánské Lázné, 26 Aug.1960.

Inf. J. Ruzová; J. Ruzová, *Gött. Misz.* 152 (1996), 101-2.

MATOUK, Fouad Selim (1902-1978)
Syrian/Lebanese collector; he was born in Damascus in 1902, son of Selim George M., a Christian Arab, and Emily Cressaty; his family emigrated to Egypt when he was a child and he became a successful businessman there; he formed a large collection of antiquities acquiring in 1956 part of the Blanchard (q.v.) collection of scarabs; following the nationalization of business interests in Egypt, he moved to Lebanon with his collection; he published *Corpus du scarabée égyptien* 2 vols., 1971, 1976; he died in Beirut, 13 May 1978; following his death, his entire collection, consisting of 6,124 scarabs, about 100 button seals, 1,800 amulets, and a number of small bronzes, was sold by his son to the Biblisches Institut der Universität Freiburg in Switzerland.

Inf. O. Kraus.

MATTHA, Girgis (1905-1967)
Egyptian demotist; he was born in Cairo, 5 May 1905, son of Mattha Boutros; he was educated at Cairo University, graduating in 1928, and then at the Sorbonne, Institut Catholique in Paris, diploma, 1930, and finally at The Queen's College, Oxford, where he studied under Griffith (q.v.) and Blackman (q.v.); BLitt, 1933; PhD, 1936; he became a lecturer at Cairo University in 1937, later Assistant Professor of philology, Vice-Dean of the Faculty of Letters, 1949-50, and Director of the Institute of Archaeology, 1950-65; his publications included *Demotic Ostraka*, 1945 and *The Demotic Legal Code of Hermopolis West*, with G. R. Hughes, 1975; he died in Cairo, 19 Feb. 1967.

The Queen's College Archives; *The Demotic Legal Code of Hermopolis West*, vii; *The Coptic Encyclopedia* 4, 1141.

MATTHIEU, Militza Edvinovna (1899-1966)
Russian Egyptologist; she was born in Martyshkino 12/24 July 1899, daughter of Edwin M.; she graduated from the Petrograd Institute in 1922 having studied under Turaev (q.v.), Struve (q.v.), and Flittner (q.v.); she was appointed a curator in the Egyptian Dept. of the Hermitage Museum, 23 May 1921 until 1966; she was awarded her doctorate on 30 Nov. 1945 and was appointed Professor at the University of Leningrad, 18 Oct. 1947; she published numerous books and articles in Russian mainly on Egyptian art, notably *Drevneegipetskie Mify (Ancient Egyptian Myths)*, 1956; *Iskusstvo drevnego Egipta (The Art of Ancient Egypt).*with Pavlov, 1961; *In the Times of Nefertiti*, 1965, and with I. Lapis, *Ancient Egyptian Sculpture in the Collection of the State Hermitage*, 1969 as well as a historical novel for young people *Kari, son of an artist*, 1963; she died in Leningrad, 8 April 1966.

JEA 52 (1966), 2; *Great Soviet Encyclopedia* 15, 552; *VDI* 3 (97), 1966, 239-43 (bibl.); 3 (69), 1959, 222-5 (bibl.); M. Korostovtsev in H. Heinen, *Die Geschichte des Altertums im Spiegel der sowjetischen Forschung,* 1980, 31-3.

MAUNIER, Victor Gustvae (otherwise Galli) (1819-1874)
French antiquities dealer and photographer; he was born in Carnoules,17 Dec. 1819, son of Antoine Leandre M., a baker, and Magdelaine Elisabeth Henriette Dejan; he became a jeweller, after abandoning his family, he settled in Athens and then Cairo about 1848 where he became a photographer for the court; at the suggestion of Khedive Abbas I, he went to Upper Egypt in 1852 to photograph ancient monuments and undertook clearances at Luxor,

Karnak, and the West Bank; he is wrongly credited as the French consular agent as he resided for nearly twenty years in the Maison de France at Luxor; Brugsch (q.v.) first met him in 1853 and states that he was a money-lender and dealer in antiquities, well known to all residents and very hospitable to European travellers; he was very helpful to Mariette (q.v.) and superintended his excavations in his absence; it was Maunier who first heard of the discovery of the jewellery of Queen Ahhotep, and he took immediate steps to protect it and inform Mariette of the find; from 1861 he was agent to Halim Pasha, a large landowner, and lived in a fine house at Matana, on the estate; he retired from this service a rich man and returned to France in 1868; he is frequently mentioned in the letters of Lady Duff-Gordon (q.v.), who resided for some years in the Maison de France after he had vacated it; his name is attached to the important Maunier stela (Louvre C. 256), which was in his house at Luxor for many years; he also presented the statues A.125 and A.159 to the Louvre; he is often known as Galli, which was the name of his mistress; he died in Neuilly-sur-Seine, 24 Aug. 1874.

Brugsch, *Mein Leben*, 190-2; Devéria, *Mém. et Fragm.* i, xvi, 336, 357, 358; Duff-Gordon, *Letters from Eg.*, 3rd ed., 138, 145, 154, 160, 163, 184, 235, 265, 271, 279, 371; Maspero, *Bibl. Ég.* 18, p. cii; *Momies royales*, 702, n. 6; *Rec. Trav.* 12. 214; Renouf, *Life-Work*, ii, 3; inf. S. Weens; S. Weens in N. Cooke (ed.), *Journeys Erased by Time*, 2019, 101-14.

MAXWELL, (*Sir*) John, 8th Baronet (1791-1865)
British traveller; he was born at Pollock House, Renfrewshire, 12 May 1791, son of Sir John Maxwell, 7th baronet and Hannah Anne Gardiner; he was educated at Westminster, 1806-9, and Christ Church, Oxford from 1809; he embarked on a tour to the Levant in 1813 with Bramsen (q.v.); he reached Alexandria in July 1815 and met with Buckingham (q.v.); he saw Drovetti's (q.v.) collection in Cairo; he went to Damietta 5 Aug. 1814 before proceeding to the Holy Land; on his return he became MP for Renfrewshire 181-30 and for Lanarkshire 1832-37; he succeeded his father 30 July 1844; he died at Pollock House, 7 June 1865; his unpublished travel diary is in the Mitchell library, Glasgow.

ODNB 37, 519-21; inf B. Moon.

MAXWELL, (*Sir*) John Grenfell (1859-1929)
British army officer and collector; he was born in Toxteth, Liverpool, 12 July 1859, son of Robert M., merchant, and Maria Emma Grenfell; educated Cheltenham; he entered the army, 1879; Lieut., Royal Highlanders, 1881; Capt., 1887; he served in the Egyptian War and was present at Tell el-Kebir, 1882; in Nile expedition, 1884-5 as Staff-Captain; aide-de-camp of Major-Gen. Grenfell (q.v.) in the Egyptian Frontier Field Force, 1884-5; DSO; Dongola, 1896; Major, 1889; Lt. Col., 1896; Col., 1898; he commanded the 2nd Eg. Brigade at Omdurman, and the 14th Brigade, S. Africa, 1900-1; Military Governor of Pretoria; KCB; CMG; Chief Staff Officer, 3rd Army Corps with the rank of Brig. Gen., 1902; he commanded Force in Egypt, 1908-12; served in First World War, 1914-18; KCMG; Commander-in-Chief, Ireland, 1916; GCB; Commander-in-Chief, Northern Cmd. 1916-19; Lord Milner's Mission to Egypt, 1920; he retired 1922; President, EES 1925-9; he had a choice collection of antiquities which was sold at Sotheby's 11-12 June 1928; he died in Cape Town, 21 Feb. 1929.

ODNB 37, 522-4; *JEA* 15 (1929), 103-4 (H. G. Lyons); *WWW* iii, 920.

MAYER, Joseph (1803-1886)
British goldsmith and collector; he was born in Newcastle-under-Lyme, 23 Feb. 1803, son of Samuel M, tanner, sometime Mayor of Newcastle, and Margaret Pepper, and had his business in Liverpool; he was a lifelong collector of coins and antiquities, and his fine collection of Greek coins was sold to the French Govt., 1844; his great collection of Roman, Saxon, Egyptian and other antiquities was exhibited in his private museum in Liverpool until 1867 when he presented it to the City of Liverpool; it was then valued at £75,000, but much of it was destroyed by enemy action in 1940; the Egyptian collection contained among many other first-rate items the two famous judicial papyri that bear his name; he purchased specimens at many sales and from the collections of Lord Valentia (q.v.), Revd H. Stobart (q.v.), Joseph Sams (q.v.), Bram Hertz (q.v.), and others; he was the founder of the Historical Soc. of Lancashire and Cheshire, President, 1866-9; FSA, 1850; he died in Bebington, Cheshire, 19 Jan. 1886; his private collection was sold at Sotheby's 12-13 Feb. 1875 and 21-24 June 1878, and posthumously 23-6 May, 19-21 July and 21-4 July 1887 and at Liverpool 8-10 July 1886 and 15-16 Dec. 1887.

ODNB 37, 573-6 (portr.); *DNB* 37. 149-50; C. T. Gatty, *The Mayer Collection, 1877 2nd ed., 1879;* Liverpool Mus. *Handbook to the Eg. Coll.*, 1st ed. (by Newberry), 1919, 2nd ed. (by Peet), 1932; S. Nicholson and M. Warhurst *Joseph Mayer 1803-1886*, 1982; M. Gibson and S. M. Weight (eds.), *Joseph Mayer of Liverpool 1803-1886*, 1988.

MAYER, Luigi (1755-1803)
German-born Italian-trained artist; he is said to have studied under Piranesi in Rome; he travelled to the Ottoman empire in 1776 apparently in the entourage of Sir Robert Ainslie (q.v.) for who he produced watercolours of the many sites in the Levant; ; he may have visited Egypt in 1776 but definitely travelled there, with others, from 25 Feb.-21 April 1792 under the patronage of Ainslie who commissioned him to make a pictorial record of the

country; his paintings are based around Alexandria and Cairo and were subsequently published as acquatints between 1801-4; he later settled in London and died in 1803; his works are in the British Museum and the Victoria and Albert Museum.

Inf. B. Taylor

MAYNARD, (*Revd***) Thomas Richard** (1823-1897)
British clergyman, born 1823; he was educated at Queens' College, Cambridge; BA, 1852; MA, 1853; he was curate at Aylesford, 1851-3 and at Paddington 1854-5; he was appointed Assistant Chaplain to the Forces, Dover, 1855-67; he lived abroad after his retirement; in 1862 he presented to the British Museum an inscribed fragment from an alabaster seated statue of Akhenaten and Queen Nefertiti from El-Amarna (EA 880); he died in Baden-Baden, 24 Dec. 1897.

Al. Cantab.

MAYSTRE, Charles (1907-1993)
Swiss Egyptologist; he was born in Geneva, 30 Jan. 1907, son of Jean-Louis M., a pastor, and Euphrosina Cretier; he was educated in classical studies at the University of Geneva, graduating in 1925; licence ès lettres, 1930; he studied Egyptology under Moret (q.v.) and Lefebvre (q.v.) at the École Pratique des Hautes Études in Paris; diploma, 1934 for his work on the Book of the Dead; he was attached to the Institut français in Cairo, 1933-40, 1945-7 and took part in the work at Deir el-Medina and Tod; he also worked with Piankoff (q.v.) on texts from the royal tombs in the Valley of the Kings; he obtained his doctorate from the Sorbonne in 1948 with his thesis on the high priests of Ptah; he was appointed lecturer at the University of Geneva, 1948; Extraordinary Professor, 1950; Ordinary Professor, 1962-77; Honorary Professor, 1977-93; he was also responsible for the Egyptian collection in the Musée d'art et d'histoire, Geneva, 1952-78; founder and director of the Centre d'études orientales, later Centre d'études du Proche-orient ancien, 1956-77; he directed excavations at Akasha, 1966-72, Tabo, 1965-75, and Kerma, 1972-5 in Nubia; *Rev. d'Eg.* 44 was dedicated to him; his publications include *La tombe de Nebenmât,*1936; *Les déclarations d'innocence*, 1937; *Le livre des portes,* 1939-46, with Piankoff; *Égypte antique*, 1963; *Akasha* I, 1981; *Tabo* I, 1986; and *Les grands prêtres de Ptah de Memphis*, 1992; he died in Geneva, 11 Sept. 1993.

Journal de Genève 15 Sept. 1993 (M. Valloggia); *BSFE* 128 (1993), 5; *BSEG* 17 (1993), 5-7 (portr.); *Rev. d'Ég.* 45 (1994), 3-9 (portr.) (bibl.) (M. Vallogia) *Voyages en Égypte de l'Antiquité au début du XXe siècle*, 2003, 226-7 (M. Vallogia); *Historisches Lexikon der Schweiz*, 8, 398.

MEAD, Richard (1673-1754)
British collector and physician; he was born in London, 11 Aug. 1673, son of Matthew M., a non-conformist minister, and Elizabeth Walton; he studied at home and then at the University of Utrecht from 1689, the University of Leiden from 1692, and the University of Padua, MD, 1695; MD, Oxford, 1707; he established his practice in London; member of the college of Physicians, 1716; his interest in antiquities was aroused during his stay in Italy and he formed a collection including Egyptian antiquities; about 1734, two coffins from Saqqara were sent to him from Egypt, one of which was presented to the College of Physicians and the other was published by Alexander Gordon (q.v.); Fellow of the Royal Society, 1703, vice-president, 1717; he died in London, 16 Feb. 1754.

ODNB 37 636-41 (portr.); *DNB* 37, 181-6.

MÉCHAIN, Jérôme Isaac (1778-1851)
French astronomer and diplomat; he was born in 1778, son of Pierre François André M., a noted astronomer and mathematician, and Barbe Thérèse Marjou; a member of Napoleon's Commission in Egypt; he left a graffito at Philae; afterwards French Consul at Larnaka, Cyprus and Tangier, retired 1839; he met Champollion (q.v.) in Egypt in 1828; he died in 1851.

Carré, i, 148, 154; Champollion, ii, 36; D. Harlé and J. Lefebvre, *Sur le Nil avec Champollion*, 1993, 52-3.

MEDEM (*Count***) Peter Georg von** (1801-1877)
Baltic traveller and collector; he was born at Mitau, 18/30 Jan. 1801, son of Johann Count von Medem and Louise Countess von der Pahlen; he studied in Berlin 1818 and Heidelberg 1819-20; in 1820-23 he visited the Levant with Baron Alexander von Uxkull (q.v.); they went as far as the Third Cataract in 1822-3 along with Théodore de Lesseps brother of Ferdinand de L. (q.v.); his notebooks were destroyed in 1945; he made a small collection of antiquities which has been in Mitau (now Jelgava), Latvia since 1840; he died in Mitau, 13 March 1877.

Inf. S. Stadnikov; H. Pirang, *Das baltische Herrenhaus*, 1926-30; W. Lenz, *Deutsch-baltisches Biographisches Lexikon 1710-1960*, 1970, 502.

MEESTER DE RAVESTEIN, Emile de (1812-1889)
Belgian collector; he was born at Malines, 24 May 1812, son of Constantin de M. de R. and Caroline de Wargny; he became Belgian ambassador at the Holy See in Rome 1846-59; he bought extensively at sales in Paris and Rome, notably from the collections of Cardinal Lambruschini (q.v.) and Dr. Massari of Naples, Anastasi (q.v.) (1857), Schayes (q.v.) (1859), Raife (q.v.) (1867), and Prince Napoleon (1868); in 1884 he donated his collection to the Musée Royal in Brussels; he died in Ravestein, 20 April 1889.

B. van de Walle et al, *La Collection égyptienne*, 1980, 12-13, 57-8; *Handelingen van de Koninklijke Kring voor Oudheidkunde, Letteren en Kunsten van Mechelen* 54 (1950), 36-8 (B. de Meester de Ravestein); B. van de Walle in *Liber Memorialis, 1835-1985*, 1985, 149-55; A. Tsingarida and A. Verbanck-Piérard (eds), *L'Antiquité au service de la Modernité?*, 2006.

MÉHÉDIN, Léon Eugène (1828-1905)
French architect and photographer; he was born at L'Aigle (Orne), 21 Feb. 1828, son of Armand Dominique M., surveyor, and Emélie Angelique Florine Hébert; he studied architecture in Paris; he later served as an army photographer; inspired by his friend Lottin de Laval (q.v.), he became interested in Egypt and was sent on a photographic mission to Egypt and Nubia in 1860; he also took a squeeze of the obelisk remaining at Luxor; he went on a photographic mission to Mexico, 1864-68; some of his plans and photographs are preserved in the Musée d'Histoire Naturelle, Rouen and the Bibliothèque de Rouen; he died in Bonsecours, 4 May 1905.

M.-A. Dollfus, *BSFE* 80 (1977), 7-20; J.-C. Simoen, *Égypte éternelle-Les voyageurs photographiques au siècle dernier*, 1993, 26.

MEKHITARIAN, Arpag (1911-2004)
Belgian Egyptologist of Armenian extraction; he was born at Tanta, Egypt, 24 Jan. 1911, son of Dikran M. and Rebega Djigamian; he emigrated with his family to Belgium in the 1920s; he studied under Capart (q.v.) who appointed him to the Fondation Égyptologique Reine Élisabeth, 1929 where he became a collaborator in the pharaonic section, 1931, assistant, 1932, Secretary, 1937 and finally Secretary-General, 1947-94; Hon. Secretary-General from 1994; Member of the Administrative Council, 1970; he became curator of Islamic Art at the Musées Royaux d'Art at Brussels; he took part in the Belgian excavations notably at Elkab from 1937 and was resident in Egypt, 1940-6; he was particularly interested in Egyptian art; he published *La peinture égyptienne*, 1954; German ed. *Ägyptische Malerei*, 1954; English ed. *Egyptian Painting*, 1954, 1978; *Introduction à l'Égypte*, 1956; *L'Égypte*, 1964; with others, *Les Chats des Pharaons*, 1989; *La misère des tombes thébaines*, 1994; *Abydos. Sacred Precinct of Osiris*, 1998; he died in Brussels, 27 April 2004.

Jean-Michel Bruffaerts in C. Cannuyer, D. Homès-Frédéricq, F. Mawet, J. Ries (eds*.), Le ciel dans les civilisations orientales - Heaven in the Oriental Civilizations*, Brussels, 1999, XII-XVII (portr.); *Chron. d'Ég.* 80 (2005), 3-8 (J. Bingen and others) (bibl.).

MELLY, André (1802-1851)
Liverpool merchant of Swiss origin, he was born in Geneva, 12 May 1802, son of Jean-Léonard M. and Antoinette-Marguerite Joly; he emigrated to Liverpool and married 1828 Ellen Mary Greg, daughter of Samuel Greg; he visited Egypt and the Sudan with his family, 1850-1, passing through Wadi Halfa and Dongola to reach Khartoum but he died on his return at the village of Gagee, 19 Jan. 1851; his *Lettres d'Égypte et de la Nubie* were published posthumously and privately printed by D. L. and George Prévost, 1852 and his son George M. (born Liverpool, 20 Aug. 1830, *d.*Liverpool, 27 Sept. 1894), MP 1868-74, left an account of the journey, *Khartoum, and the Blue and White Niles*, 1851.

Hill, 236; Hilmy, ii, 29; G. O. Whitehead, *Sudan Notes and Records* 21 (1938), 291-306; S. Sauneron, *BIFAO* 64 (1964), 193-6; J. Galiffe, *Notice généalogiques sur les familles genevoises* 6 (1892), 403-5; Boase 6, 194.

MENASCE, (*Baron*) **Jacques Bekhor Levi de** (1850-1916)
Egyptian financier and collector; he was born in Cairo, Jan. 1850, son of Baron Bekhor David de M. and Allegra Cattaui; he came from a family of wealthy Jewish bankers who had been given citizenship and a title by the Austro-Hungarian Empire; he was educated in Egypt, France and England and worked in the Liverpool, London and Constantinople offices of his family firm before returning to Egypt in 1871; in 1874 he married Adrienne Nahman; he played a prominent part in the business life of Egypt and was involved in several

philanthropic projects; he was head of the Jewish community in Alexandria in 1890-1914; he can be identified with the collector who attempted to sell several objects to the British Museum in 1883 and whose collection was exhibited at the Palais des Arts Libéraux in 1889, the catalogue being drawn up by Georges Legrain (q.v.), and then sold in Paris and 23-24 Feb. 1891 (511 lots); some of these antiquities were acquired by the Louvre; his cousin Baron Jacques Elie de M. (1866- ?) would have been too young to have been the collector, and nothing is known of his other cousin Baron Jacques Moise de M (*b.post* 1862, *d.*1912); he died in Alexandria, 2 June 1916.

A. Wright, *Twentieth Century Impressions of Egypt,* 1909, 448; J. Landau, *Jews in Nineteenth Century Egypt,* 1969, 144-48; G. Kramer, *Minderheit, Millet, oder Nation,* 1982, 146; G. Kramer, *The Jews in Modern Egypt 1914-1952,*1989, 84-5; *Rev. de l'art* 43, 172; Wilbour, 471; BM Departmental Corr. 1883, 72; Lugt 49668.

MENGEDOHT, Henry William (1869-1939)
British orientalist; he was born in London, 9 Aug. 1869, son of John Henry Frederick Hermann M., bookkeeper, originally from Hanover, and Mary Ann Boundy; he studied Egyptology and Assyriology in the Dept. of Eg. and Assyr. Ant. British Museum and gave gallery lectures to the public; he published two short articles in the *Babylonian and Oriental Record,* 5. 136, 151; also *Catalogue of Egyptian Antiquities in the Collection of Sir Herbert Cook,* 1924; he died in London, 21 May 1939.

Inf. George Salby and Margaret Murray.

MERCATI, Michele (1541-1593)
Italian naturalist, doctor, and antiquarian; he was born at San Miniato, 6 April 1541, son of Pietro M., a doctor and papal physician, and Alfonsina Fiamminga; after a medical training, he became interested in minerals and palaeontology; he is famous in Egyptology for his work *Degli obelischi di Roma,* published in 1589, which aroused much interest in ancient Egypt and in hieroglyphs; he died in Rome, 25 June 1593.

DBDI 73, 606-11; *Enc. It.* 22, 878 (portr.); Iversen, 84.

MERCER, (*Revd*) **Samuel Alfred Browne** (1880-1969)
Canadian Egyptologist; he was born in Bristol, England, 10 May 1880, son of Samuel M. and Elizabeth Browne; he was educated in Newfoundland and then obtained B. Div. at the Episcopalian Seminary in Wisconsin, 1904; he then studied Semitic languages at the University of Wisconsin and acquired a degree in civil engineering 1905; he went on to Harvard, BA, 1908 and various universities in Europe: Göttingen, Heidelberg, and Munich where he obtained his PhD, 1910, the Sorbonne studying under Maspero (q.v.), and Berlin where he studied under Sethe (q.v.); he was appointed Professor of Hebrew and Old Testament Literature at the Western Theological Seminary, Chicago, 1910-22, Dean of Bexley Hall Divinity School, 1922-3, Dean of Divinity at Trinity College, University of Toronto, 1923 and then Professor of Semitic Languages and Egyptology there, 1924-46; he wrote numerous articles and books on biblical subjects; his most important works in the Egyptological field were *Growth of Religious and Moral ideas in Egypt,* 1919; *Tutankhamen and Egyptology,* 1923; *Egyptian Grammar,* 1927; *Études sur les origines de la religion de l'Égypte,* 1929; *The Pyramid Texts* 4 vols., 1952; and *Literary Criticism of the Pyramid Texts,* 1956; he died in Toronto, 8 Jan. 1969.

Current Biography 14 (Feb. 1953), 34-7.

MERTZ, Barbara Louise (née Gross) (1927-2013)
American Egyptologist and author; she was born in Canton, Ill., 29 Sept. 1927, daughter of Earl Gross and Grace Tregellas; she was educated at the University of Chicago, studying Egyptology under John Wilson (q.v.); PhB 1947; MA, 1950; PhD, 1952; she married Richard Mertz in 1950 (divorced 1969); she served on the editorial Advisory Board of *KMT*; under the pen name Elizabeth Peters, she wrote a series of mystery novels many set in modern Egypt, she also wrote thrillers under the name of Barbara Michaels; she published two popular books on Egyptology, *Temples, Tombs and Hieroglyphs,* 1964, rev. ed. 2007; and *Black Land, Red Land,* 1966, rev. ed. 2008; she died in Frederick, Md., 8 Aug. 2013.

The Daily Telegraph 29 Aug. 2013; *The Guardian* 13 Aug. 2013; A. Mackova, *ASTENE Bulletin* 57 (2013), 24; *KMT* 24/4 (2013-4), 68-73 (portr.), (D. Forbers); *ARCE Bulletin* 203 (2013), 60-3 (R. Johnson and S. Ikram) (portrs.).

MESSIHA, Hishmat (1917-1995)
Egyptian Egyptologist; he was born in Cairo, 16 May 1917; he obtained a Licence ès Lettres in 1941 and a teaching diploma in 1949; he then studied at the Institute of Archaeology, Cairo, diploma in 1949; he joined the Egyptian Antiquities Service becoming inspector at Saqqara, deputy director of the Coptic Museum, and director-general of Egyptian Antiquities; PhD, 1971; he also taught at the Faculty of Archaeology and the Institut Copte des Hautes Études; apart from works in Arabic, he published *Mallawi Antiquities Museum. A Brief Description*, with M. A. el-Hitta, 1979; and *Finds from Kom Ichkâw*, part 1, 1982; he died 26 Oct. 1995.

BSAC 36 (1997), 181-2 (W. Boutros-Ghali) (portr.), 5-7 (bibl.) (D. Messiha and N. Youssef).

METTERNICH-WINNEBERG, (*Prince*) **Clemens Wenzel Nepomuk Lothar von** (1773-1859)
The famous Austrian Chancellor, statesman, and diplomat who played such a prominent part in European affairs; he was born in Koblenz, 15 May 1773, son of Prince George Karl von M.-W. and Maria Beatrice von Kageneck; his name is associated in Egyptology with the great magical stela found in Alexandria in 1828, and presented to him by Muhammad Ali; this is now in the Metropolitan Museum, New York; it was first published by Golenischeff (q.v.) in 1877, but has since been studied by many others in further publications, e.g. Moret, Sander-Hansen, Nora Scott, etc.; other Egyptian antiquities which once belonged to him are in the Museum of Königswarth, now Kynzvart, Czech Republic; he died in Vienna, 11 June 1859.

EB has Bibl.; *ZÄS* 53, 146.

MEULENAERE, Herman de (1923-2011)
Belgian Egyptologist; he was born in Bruges, 14 May 1923, son of Louis-Emiel de M. and Augusta G. Dewispelare; he was educated at the University of Louvain (Leuven) under Vergote (q.v.); Diplomas in Classical Philology and Oriental Philology, 1946; he also studied at Leiden under de Buck (q.v.), 1946-50 and at Paris under Clère (q.v.), Malinine (q.v.), Posener (q.v.), and Vandier (q.v.), 1950-1; Docteur ès lettres, 1951; he briefly taught Latin at the Athénée Royal in Brussels; he was visiting Professor at Brown University, 1958-9; he took part in the Nubian Rescue campaign; he became Professor at the University of Ghent and Keeper of the Egyptian collection at the Musées Royaux d'Art et d'Histoire in Brussels, 1963; he became assistant in the pharaonic section of the Fondation Égyptologique Reine Élisabeth, 1952, research director, 1956, member of the council, 1971; assistant director, 1973; co-director, 1975-2011 with Bingen (q.v.); editor of the pharaonic section of *Chronique d'Égypte*, 1986-2010; he was also director of Musées Royaux d'Art et d'Histoire, 1984-8; he took part in the American excavations at Mendes, 1964-5, and oversaw the Belgian excavations at Elkab and Thebes, 1965-88; he organized several exhibitions on Akhenaten and Nefertiti in Brussels, 1975; a loan exhibition from Brooklyn in Brussels, 1976-7; and on women in Ancient Egypt in Brussels, 1985-6; he collaborated closely with Bothmer (q.v.) on the Corpus of Late Egyptian Sculpture; he was also co-editor of *Bibliotheca Orientalis*; a volume of studies in his honour *Aegyptus Museis Rediviva* was published in 1993; he published, apart from numerous articles and critical reviews, *Herodotos over de 26ste Dynastie (II, 147-II, 15)*, 1951; with others, *Prosopographia Ptolemaica* III, 1956; with Bothmer and Müller, *Egyptian Sculpture of the Late Period*, 1960; *Le surnom égyptien à la Basse Epoque*, 1966; *Het Leven na de Dood in het Oude Egypte*, 1969; with others, *La chapelle ptolémaïque de Kalabcha*, 1970; *Scarabaeus Sacer*, 1972; *Le Règne du Soleil: Akhnaton et Nefertiti*, 1975; *Égypte Eternelle*, 1976; with P. Mackay, *Mendes* II, 1976; with others, *La collection égyptienne: les étapes marquantes de son développement*. 1981; with L. Limme, *Artibus Aegypti. Studia in honerem Bernardi V. Bothmer*, 1981; with others, *Die spätägyptischen Totenstelen (P. Munro). Index et Addenda*, 1985; with others, *Musées Royaux d'Art et d'Histoire Bruxelles. Antiquité*, 1988, *L'Égypte Ancienne dans la Peinture du XIXe siècle/Ancient Egypt in Nineteenth Century Painting*, 1992; with others, *Écritures de l'Égypte Ancienne*, 1992; with others, *Elkab and Beyond. Studies in Honour of Luc Limme*, 2009; he died in Brussels, 5 June 2011.

L. Limme and J. Strybol, *Aegyptus Museis Rediviva*, 1993 v-vi (F. Van Noten), 7-13 (bibl.) (L. Limme, J. Strybol and N. Vermassen); *BiOr* 68 (2011), 463-4 (L. Limme) (portr.); inf. D. Huyge, L. Limme and P. de Meulenaere; *Chron. d'Ég.* 87 (2012) 2-5 (portr.) (L. Lime and A. Martin); 9-11 (additional bibl.) (L. Delvaux).

MEUX, (*Lady*) **Valerie Susie** (1852-1910)
British collector; she was born in Crokernwell, Drewsteighton, Devon, 27 Feb. 1852 as Susan, daughter of William Langdon, a butcher, and Lydia Jane Ellis; she became briefly an actress in pantomime and then a courtesan in London under the name of Val Reece and later in 1878 wife of Sir Henry Bruce Meux, Bt (1858-

1900), heir of a wealthy brewing family; she was painted by Whistler; her husband had inherited a small collection of Egyptian antiquities which was increased by purchases and in which Lady M. took great interest following her honeymoon in Egypt; it was housed at Theobald's Park, Hertfordshire; she commissioned Budge (q.v.) to catalogue it in 1893; she added considerably to it and in 1895 Budge bought a number of objects in Egypt; a second ed. of the catalogue was published in 1896; Budge also procured for Lady M. a collection of Ethiopic MSS which were sumptuously printed for private circulation; her will offered her collection to the British Museum, but the conditions of the bequest were restrictive and it was declined; after her death the whole collection was sold in 1911, many of the objects being bought by William Randolph Hearst (q.v.) and Sir Henry Wellcome (q.v.); she died in London, 20 Dec. 1910.

Budge, *N. & T.* i, 29; ii, 339; Burke's Peerage; *ODNB Internet Edition*; Budge, *N. & T.* i, 29; ii, 339; Burke's *Peerage*; R. Morrell, *"Budgie..." the life of Sir E. A. T. Wallis Budge*, 2002, 47-50; sale of Theobalds Park by Waring and Gillow, 15-26 May 1911, Lugt, 69914, the Egyptian objects lots 249, 1501-1670; inf. T. Hardwick.

MEYER, Eduard (1855-1930)

German historian and chronologer; he was born in Hamburg, 25 Jan. 1855, son of Eduard M. and Johanna Antoinette Henriette Dessau, and was trained as a historian; he made a special study of the history of the ancient Near East, and became, with Maspero (q.v.) and Breasted (q.v.), the leading historian of this period; he had an excellent approach to his subject and a good style and saw Egypt in the context of surrounding countries; he was the first person in modern times to construct a chronology that would fit all the ancient Near East and not give very early dates for the Old Kingdom, and this, with modifications, is still in use at present, although some of the Sothic dating has had to be abandoned through lack of evidence; his principal works on Egypt and the Near East were, *Set-Typhon: eine religionsgeschichtliche Studie*, 1875; *Geschichte des Alterthums*, 2 vols. 1884-1902, and later edits.; *Geschichte des alten Aegyptens*, 1887; *Aegyptische Chronologie*, 1904, (*Nachträge*, 1907-8), trans. into French by A. Moret and published by the Musée Guimet, 1912; *Aegypten zur Zeit der Pyramidenerbauer*, 1908; *Der Papyrusfund von Elephantine: Dokumente einer jüdischen Gemeinde aus der Perserzeit und das ältest erhaltene Buch der Weltliteratur*, 1912; *Reich und Kultur der Chetiter*, 1914; *Die ältere Chronologie Babyloniens, Assyriens und Ägyptens: Nachtrag zum ersten Bande der Geschichte des Alterthums*, 1925; some of his photographs are in the Griffith Institute, Oxford; he died in Berlin, 31 Aug. 1930.

NDB 17, 309-11; *Bayer. Akad. der Wiss. Jahrbuch*, 1930/1, 43-7; *ZDMG* 85 (1931), 1-24 (W. G. A. Otto); Erman, 112, 169; *Gnomon*, 6 (1930), 622-4 (M. Gelzer); *JEA* 16 (1930), 258; *ZÄS* 66 (1931), 73 (portr.) (G. Steindorff); *Zeit. der Savigny-Stiftung für Rechtgeschichte*, Romantische Ab. 51 (1931), 604-6 (E. Täubler);H. Marohl, *Eduard Meyer,* 1941; K. Christ, *Von Gibbon zu Rostovtzeff*, 1979, 286-333, 370-2; K. Christ, *Römische Geschichte und deutsche Geschichtswissenschaft*, 1982, 930-101; Wm M. Calder III and A Demandt, *Eduard Meyer*, 1990.

MEYRICK, Augustus William Henry (1826-1902)

British army officer and collector; he was born in London, 27 Oct. 1826, son of Col. William Henry M. and Lady Laura Vane; Scots Fusiliers, ensign 1846; Lieut., 1850; Capt., 1855; Colonel, 1868; Major-Gen., 1877; he retired Lieut.-Gen., 1881; he fought in the Crimean War, 1845-6; in 1878 he presented to the British Museum a large collection of oriental arms, Greek, Roman and Egyptian antiquities, most inherited from his second cousin Sir Samuel Rush Meyrick (q.v.), and thence from the Douce collection; the papyrus EA 9969 bears his name; he died at 9 Wilbraham Place, London, 26 March 1902.

Royal United Service Institution Records.

MEYRICK, Sir Samuel Rush (1783-1848)

British antiquary and collector; he was born on 26 Aug. 1783, son of John M. and Harriet Rush; he was educated at The Queen's College, Oxford, BA, 1804, DCL, 1811; he practised in London as an advocate; he wrote on armour and formed an important collection, displayed in Goodrich Court, Herefordshire; he arranged the collections of armour at the Tower of London and Windsor Castle, for which he was knighted, 1832; FSA 1810, co-founder of the British Archaeological Association, 1843; in 1834 he inherited a large proportion of the collection of paintings and antiquities of Francis Douce (q.v.), which included numerous Egyptian objects; his account of the Doucean Museum was published in *The Gentleman's Magazine*, 1836, the Egyptian antiquities described Nov. 1836, 493-4, 598, with the assistance of John Davidson (q.v.); he bequeathed his collections to his cousin Col. William Henry M. (1790-1865); these were variously dispersed by his son Augustus William Henry M. (q.v.); he died at Goodrich Court, 2 April 1848.

ODNB 38, 10-11.

MEZGER, John Maximillian (1867-1935)
British merchant and collector; he was born in Freiburg 11 Oct. 1867, son of Professor Alois M. and Emma Schlatter, both of Swiss origin; he left Germany for Switzerland in 1884 on the death of his father and joined the firm of Bolt and Mezger cotton brokers, with offices at Liverpool, Alexandria, and Khartoum; he was sent to Liverpool in 1887; he became a British citizen in 1909; at one time the largest exporter of Egyptian cotton from Alexandria, 1910-12, he formed a collection of antiquities which sold at Sotheby's, 8 June 1925, lots 1-44; he died in West Kirby, 29 May 1935.

Inf. R. Mezger (son); National Archives; Lugt 88740.

MICHAILIDIS (var. MICHAELIDES), George Anastase (1900-1973)
Greek collector; he was born in Cairo, 18 June 1900, son of Anastase M., civil engineer, and his wife Helen; educated School of Social Studies (Hautes Études Sociales), diploma in journalism, 1927; degree of the School, 1928; degree in Applied Psychology, Paris, 1928; he had a deep interest in hieroglyphs and ancient Egyptian religion; he published numerous essays and pamphlets especially on these topics mostly in *BSAC, BIE* and *BIFAO*; he was an honorary member of the Institut français, Cairo; his Egyptian collecting interests were extremely wide; he possessed ostraca, cylinder seals, bronzes, cuneiform tablets, bas reliefs, scarabs (one of the largest and finest private collections, now in the Egyptian Museum, Berlin), and papyri, ancient Egyptian, Greek, Coptic and Arabic; a large portion of the Greek, Latin, Coptic, and Arabic MSS was acquired by Cambridge University Library, 1977; several examples of Demotic papyri by the British Museum, London, 1976; Coptic, Greek, Latin,and Arabic MSS by the British Library, 1979; and other MSS by the Papyrological Institute at Leiden; a selection from his collection was published by D. S. Crawford, *Papyri Michaelidae: Being a catalogue of the Greek and Latin Papyri, Tablets and Ostraca in the Library of Mr. G. A. Michaelides of Cairo*, Aberdeen, 1955, and H. Goedicke and E. Wente, *Ostraka Michaelides,* 1962; some of his collection was sold at Sotheby's, London, 8 Dec. 1975 lots 123-6 and 23 Feb. 1976 lot 210; some fine flint implements, including a curved knife with gold foil handle from Abu Roash, entered public collections on American West Coast in 1976-7; he died in Athens, 13 July 1973.

Inf. from family in Athens and Peter A. Clayton; S. Clackson, *Zeitschrift für Papyrologie und Epigraphik* 100 (1994), 223-6.

MICHAŁOWSKI, Kazimierz (1901-1981)
Polish classical archaeologist and Egyptologist; he was born in Tarnopol, 14 Dec. 1901, son of Marian M. and Kazimiera Ostrowska; after completing his education at the Tarnopol Gymnasium in 1919, he studied classical archaeology and art history at the Lvov University, 1920-24; from 1923-32 he studied at the Universities and Archaeological Institutes of Berlin, Heidelberg, Münster, Paris, Rome, Athens and Cairo; he participated also in French excavations on the island of Thasos and studied materials coming from Delos; in 1926 he obtained his PhD degree under E. Bulanda at the Lvov University *Les Niobides dans l'art plastique grec*; habilitation, 1929 with a study entitled *Les portraits hellénistiques et romains de Délos*, Vol. XIII, Paris 1932; lecturer at the Lvov University, 1929-30 and at the Warsaw University, 1930-33; named Professor in 1933, ordinarius in 1939; he headed the chair of classical archaeology at the University of Warsaw until 1973; he acted also as the Vice-director of the National Museum in Warsaw, 1939-81; during this time he educated a solid group of specialists in classical, Near Eastern and Egyptian archaeology; his own interest in Egyptology began in 1937-39, taking part in French-Polish excavations at Tell Edfu, organized by him, and published later in three volumes, 1939-50; objects coming from Edfu enriched the collection of the Warsaw National Museum; in Sept. 1939 Michałowski as a Polish officer fought against the Germans obtaining the Virtuti Militari cross; until 1945 he was imprisoned in a camp at Woldenberg; after World War II he participated very actively in the reconstruction of Polish academic life and in building Polish participation in the international programme of studies on Mediterranean cultures; he was the Director of the Institute of Mediterranean Archaeology of the Polish Academy of Sciences, 1956-81; in 1959 he founded in Cairo the Polish Centre for Mediterranean Archaeology, now named after him; he lectured at the University of Alexandria, 1958-59; Michałowski was a specialist in many areas of Egyptian art and archaeology; he directed Polish excavations on many sites: Tell Atrib from 1957; Alexandria from 1960; Dabod, 1961; Faras, 1961-64; Deir el-Bahari from 1961; Dongola from 1964 and wrote many reports and studies connected with his discoveries notably of important paintings in the cathedral of Faras; for the wall-paintings obtained for Poland he organized in Warsaw a special gallery in the National Museum; he was co-editor of *Meander*, and editor of *Études et Travaux, Travaux du Centre*, and of Polish excavation series such as *Faras, Deir el-Bahari, Alexandrie*; 1963-71 he presided over the International Committee of Experts for Rescue of the Abu Simbel temples; apart from in Egypt and Sudan, M. organized and conducted Polish excavations in Mirmekion on the Black Sea 1956-58; Palmyra, Syria, from 1959; Nea Paphos, Cyprus, from 1965; Nimrud, Iraq, from 1974; he was awarded the title of doctor honoris causa of the Universities of Strasbourg, 1962, Cambridge, 1971 and Uppsala, 1977; he was a member of the Polish Academy

of Sciences from 1952; of the Accademia Nazionale dei Lincei, 1967; of the British Academy, 1970 and of many other learned societies; he was honoured with *Mélanges offerts à K. M.*, 1966; his publications included *Tell Edfu 1937-9*, I-III (with others), 1937-50; *Sztuka Starozytna* (Ancient Art in the Warsaw Museum), 1955; *Faras Fouilles polonaises,1961* and *1961-2*, 1962-5; *Faras-Die Kathedrale aus dem Wustensand*, 1967; *Faras. Centre artistique de la Nubie chrétienne*, 1966; *Architektura Faras*, 1966; *Nie tylko piramidy*, 1966 (German trans. *Nicht nur Pyramiden*, 1972); *Faras, Muzeum Narodowe*, 1967; *L'Art de l'ancienne Égypte*, 1968; English trans. *The Art of Ancient Egypt*, 1969 and also German and Spanish trans.; *Das Wunder aus Faras*, 1969; *Karnak*, 1970; *Pyramiden und Mastabas*, 1972; *Faras. Malowidla Scienne w zbiorach Muzeum Narodowego w Warszawie*, 1974; English trans. *Faras. Wall Paintings in the Collection of the National Museum in Warsaw*, 1974; *Od Edfu do Faras*, 1974; editor, *Nubia. Récentes Recherches*, 1975; *Histoire mondiale de la sculpture. Égypte*, 1978; his memoirs *Vspomnienia*, 1986 and collected studies *Opera Minora*, 1990ff were published posthumously; he died in Podkowa Lesna near Warsaw, 1 Jan. 1981.

Nauka Polska 9/10 (1981), 155-70 (M. L. Bernhard); *Meander* 36 (1981), 295-300 (M. L. Bernhard, Z Sztetyllo); *Biogramy uczonych polskich*, 1, 2, Wroclaw 1984, 471-76 (portr.); *50 lat polskich wykopalisk w Egipcie i na Bliskim Wschodzie*, Warszawa 1986, 17-22 (M. L. Bernhard); *Roxzink Muzeum Narodowego w Warszawie* 25 (1981), 7-24 (anon.) (portr.); *Revue Archéologique* (1981), 283-4 (P. Demargne); *AfO* XXVIII (1981-2), 280-1 (H. Brunner); *BSFE* 90 (1981), 3-4 (anon.); *Universalia* (1981), 575-6 (J. Leclant); inf. J. Sliwa; *W kregu wielkich humanistów*, Warsaw, 1991, 155-65, (portr.) (A. Sadurska); *Études et Travaux* 19 (2001), 9-25 (K. Mysliwiec).

MIDDLEMASS, *(Bey)* Arthur Charles (1850-1906)
British naval officer; he was born at Haddington, Scotland, 1 July 1853, son of William M. and Mary Buchanan; he entered the Royal Navy as a Cadet, 1866; he served in the Ashanti War, 1873-4, and the Egyptian War, 1882; Inspector of the Coast Guard at Alexandria, 1884-9; he retired with the rank of Commander, 1896; in 1885 he discovered at Abukir a colossal standard-bearing statue of Middle Kingdom date usurped by Ramesses II; it is now in the Egyptian Museum, Cairo (CG 574), see *Guide* (1915 ed.), no. I; the British Museum purchased from him a number of Coptic (Or. 5638-44) and Arabic (Or. 5645-54) MSS; in retirement he lived in Dorking; he died in Drayton Gardens, S. Kensington, 28 March 1906.

Private inf.; Wilbour, 336-342; inf. Russell McGuirk.

MIDGLEY, Thomas (1874-1954)
British curator and textile scholar; he was born in Bolton, 5 Nov. 1874, son of William Waller Midgley (q.v.) and Martha Calverley; he worked as museum assistant in the Chadwick Museum, Bolton, before being appointed assistant curator in 1890; he succeeded his father as curator in 1906; in 1907 he published the stelae in the Bankfield Museum, Halifax, at the suggestion of Henry Ling Roth (q.v.); like his father, he undertook analyses of textiles from excavations in return for a share of the material; he performed this service for J. L. Starkey's (q.v.) excavations at Karanis; he also published reports on the textiles from Brunton's (q.v.) excavations at Qau, Badari, Mostagedda and Matmar; as a result of this the archaeological textile collections at Bolton are of exceptional depth and scope; he retired in 1934; he died in Shrewsbury, 6 April 1954.

Correspondence in Bolton Museum; A. P. Thomas, 'The Midgleys of Bolton and their Contribution to the Scientific Examination of Ancient Textiles', *Archaeological Textile Newsletter* 45 (Autumn 2007), 21-5 (with bibliography), with the wrong death date; A. P. Thomas in T. Schneider and K. Szpakowska, *Egyptian Stories*, 2007, 428-34.

MIDGLEY, William Waller (1843-1925)
British curator and textile scholar; he was born in Woodhouse in Normanton, Yorks. 17 March 1843, son of William Waller M., a farmer, and Sarah Peace; he was apprenticed to a grocer and worked as a travelling salesman and in other fields before being appointed the first curator of the Chadwick Museum, Bolton in July 1883; he thus oversaw and helped direct the growth of the museum's collections, including Egyptian material acquired through subscription to the EEF and through Annie Barlow (q. v.); as befitted a cotton town this built up particular strengths in material related to the production of textiles; he retired in 1906 and was succeeded as curator by his son Thomas (q.v.); in his retirement he studied and published analyses of linen from Petrie's excavations at Meidum, Tarkhan, and elsewhere; he died in Bolton, 14 Sept. 1925.

Correspondence and research notes in Bolton Museum; *Bolton Evening News*, 18 Sept. 1925; A. P. Thomas, 'The Midgleys of Bolton and their Contribution to the Scientific Examination of Ancient Textiles', *Archaeological Textile Newsletter* 45 (Autumn 2007), 21-5 (with bibliography); A. P. Thomas in T. Schneider and K. Szpakowska, *Egyptian Stories*, 2007, 424-30.

MIEDEMA, Rein (1886-1954)

Dutch Coptologist, archaeologist, and art historian; he was born at Kralingen, 1 Aug. 1886, son of Simon M. and Dirkje de Jong; he studied theology at Leiden, 1907-13; after taking his Doctorate in 1913, he became a Remonstrant clergyman notably pastor at Amersfoort, 1918-51; he also taught as a Privaat-docent in the Universities of Leiden and Utrecht, and was Director of the Institute of Religious and Ecclesiastical Art, Utrecht; he wrote a study *De Heilige Menas*, 1913; a book on Coptic art, *Koptische Kunst*, 1929, and *Karakter-trekken van het Oostersch-Christendom*, 1930; he died in Amersfoort, 27 March 1954.

Inf. Dr. M. Heerma van Voss; *Chron. d'Ég.* 29 (1954), 376 (J. Vergote); D. Nauta (ed.), *Biografisch Lexikon voor de Geschiedenis van het Nederlandse Protestantisme* 2 (1983), 330-2.

MIGLIARINI, Arcangelo Michele (1779-1865)

Italian antiquary and Etruscologist; he was born in Rome, 1779; he was in the service of the Grand Duke of Tuscany; he was appointed Professor of Art and Archaeology in Florence, 1823; Keeper of Egyptian antiquites at Santa Caterina, 1832; and Keeper of Antiquities in the Florence Museum, 1841; he was acquainted with Champollion (q.v.) and well-disposed towards him; he published *Museo di sculture ... Ottavio Gigli*, 1858; *Indication succincte des monuments ég. de Florence*, 1859; also a very full account of the unrolling of a mummy, with notes by Samuel Birch (*Archaeologia*, 36. 161-74), 1855; he died in Florence, 14 Sept. 1865.

Champollion, i, 91, 235, 236, 238; Hilmy, ii, 34; N. Nieri, *Mem. Acad. Lincei*, Ser. 6, 3. 401-543 (1931); *VDI* 4 (162), 1982), 78-86 (A. M. Kulikna).

MILL, *(Revd)* **William Hodge** (1792-1853)

British orientalist and collector; he was born in Hackney, 18 July 1792, son of John Mill and Martha Hodge; he was educated at Trinity College Cambridge, BA, 1813, MA, 1816; he was ordained 1818; in 1821 he was appointed first principal of Bishop's College Calcutta, and became a scholar of Sanskrit and oriental languages; he returned to Britain via Egypt and Nubia, 1837-8; there he acquired a collection of ostraca and small antiquities, given to the British Museum by his daughter, Mrs Webb; he was appointed Regius Professor of Hebrew at Cambridge, 1848; he died in Brasted, Kent, 25 Dec. 1853.

ODNB; travel diaries in Bodleian Library; B. Muhs and T. Vorderstrasse, *JEA* 94 (2008), 223-45.

MILLET, Nicholas Byram (1934-2004)

American Egyptologist; he was born in Richmond, New Hampshire, 28 June 1934, son of Charles Sumner Millet, an American Foreign Service official, and Frances Williamson; his early education was completed abroad; he studied Egyptology at the University of Chicago; BA 1955, MA 1959; Director of the American Research Center in Egypt 1960-63, Director of Excavations 1963-5; he excavated at Toshka and Arminna as assistant director, 1961-2 and as director at Gebel Adda 1962-66 during the Nubian rescue campaign; he then studied at Yale University; PhD, 1968; he was appointed Assistant Professor of Egyptology at Harvard University, 1968-70; he was then named Associate Curator-in-Charge of Egyptian Antiquities at the Royal Ontario Museum in succession to Needler (q.v.) and Associate Professor at the Department of Near Eastern Studies, University of Toronto 1 July 1970; he became Curator, 1974 and Professor, 1981, and retired 30 June 1999 although continuing to teach courses until 2004; President of the Society for the Study of Egyptian Antiquities, 1984-87, Director, 1992; Member of the Editorial Board, 1970-2004; he also undertook a survey in the Dongola Reach, 1976, and excavations at Lahun, 1993-97; he edited *Meroitic Studies*, 1982 and published preliminary reports of his Nubian excavations in *JARCE* 2 (1963), 147-165; 3 (1964), 7-14; 6 (1967), 53-63; he died in Toronto, 19 May 2004.

Inf. R. Shaw and R. Frey, ROM; *Globe and Mail* 21 May 2004, S7; *SSEA Newsletter* Sept. 2004, 1 (portr.) (R. Shaw); *KMT* 15/3 (2004), 19 (R. Leprohon); *Sudan and Nubia* 8 (2004) (portr.) (J. Anderson); *Die Antiken Sudan* 15 (2004), 198-9 (portr.) (K. Grzymski); *JSSEA* 32 (2005), v-vi (portr.) (R. Shaw).

MILLIN DE GRANDMAISON, Aubin Louis (1759-1818)

French antiquarian; he was born in Paris, 18 July 1759, illegitimate son of Adrien Alexandre M. de G. and Noëlle Geslin; he succeeded Barthélmy (q.v) as head of the Cabinet des Médailles, 10 June 1795; he was elected a member of the Institut de France, 23 Nov. 1804 and reconfirmed at the Académie des Inscriptions, 21 March 1816; his publications are concerned chiefly with Roman, French, and other Western monuments, but he was also interested in Egypt and published *Aegyptiaques, ou recueil de quelques monuments égyptiens inédits*, 12 plates of Eg. antiquities, 1816; *Notice des pierres gravées égyptiennes du Museum national des Antiques*; he was a friend and supporter of Champollion (q.v.); he died in Paris, 14 Aug. 1818.

Biographie Universelle 28, 304-6; *NBG* 35, 537-41; Hilmy, ii, 35; A. C. E. Franquet de Franqueville, *Le Premier Siècle de l'Institut de France*, 1895, I, 150; T. Sarmant, *Le Cabinet des Médailles de la Bibliothèque Nationale 1661-1848*, 237-42; È. Gran-Aymerich, *Dictionnaire biographique d'archéologie 1798-1945*, 2001, incorporated in *Les Chercheurs de passé 1798-1945*, 2007, 989-90; G. Espagne and B. Savoy (eds), *Aubin-Loius Millin et l'Allemagne*, 2005.

MILLINGEN, James (1774-1845)

British antiquary and dealer in antiquities; he was born in London, 18 Jan. 1774, son of Michael M, a Dutch merchant, and Elizabeth Coole; he was educated at Westminster School and then worked as a banker; he was imprisoned in Paris during the French Terror, 1792-4; he later lived in Italy, and collected Classical and Egyptian objects, supplying British collectors; he wrote widely on Classical antiquities and coins, being appointed FSA, FRSL, and receiving a civil list pension; he sold a number of Egyptian objects to the British Museum, others being purchased from his estate; he died in Florence, 1 Oct. 1845.

ODNB 38, 250.

MILLINGEN, Julius Michael (1800-1878)

British surgeon and excavator; he was born in London, 19 July 1800, son of James M. (q.v.) and Elizabeth Penny White; he studied at Rome and Edinburgh; MRCS Ed., 1821; he attended Byron in his last illness and settled in Constantinople, 1827, where he was Court Physician to five successive Sultans; he discovered the ruins of Aezani and excavated the temple of Jupiter Urius on the Bosphorus; in Egyptology his name is associated with the Papyrus Millingen, the master-text of the Instruction of Ammenemes; the original is lost, but a good tracing of it which was made in Italy, by Amadeo Peyron it is believed, was first published by Maspero (*Rec. Trav.* ii); he died in Constantinople, 30 Nov. 1878.

ODNB 38, 251; *DNB* 37, 439.

MILNE, Joseph Grafton (1867-1951)

British classical archaeologist, numismatist, and historian; he was born in Bowdon, near Altrincham, Cheshire, 23 Dec. 1867, son of William M. a yarn-agent, and Ellen Grafton; educated at Manchester Grammar School he won a scholarship at Corpus Christi College, Oxford; MA; DLitt; excavated on the site of Megalopolis in Greece, 1890-1; master at Mill Hill School until 1893; Board of Education 1893-1926 when he retired; he ran a Boys Club in West Ham for many years; married Kate Ackroyd, 1896; Deputy Keeper of Coins, Ashmolean Museum, 1931-51; Librarian, Corpus Christi College, Oxford, 1933-46; Milne first visited Egypt 1895-6, spending most of the time with Petrie (q.v.) at Thebes at the time of the Ramesseum excavations, but also visited Grenfell (q.v.) and Hunt (q.v.) at Karanis; copied Greek inscriptions in Cairo, 1899, and in 1905-6 was with Currelly (q.v.) working for the EEF at Deir el-Bahri; he served for many years on the Committee of the EES, and was Treasurer, 1912-19; he published many books and articles on the history and inscriptions of Graeco-Roman Egypt and made a speciality of Greek and Roman numismatics, contributing many articles to *JEA* on Ptolemaic coins; his main works were *History of Egypt under Roman Rule*, 1899, in the Petrie series, the *Greek Inscriptions* in the *Cairo Cat.* 1905, and the Greek material of the *Theban Ostraca*, 1913; the photographs are in the Griffith Institute, Oxford; he died in Oxford, 7 Aug. 1951.

JEA 38 (1952), 112-14 (portr.) (H. Last); *Numismatic Chronicle*, 1951, 115-25 (bibl.); *The Times*, 14 Aug. 1951.

MIMAUT, Jean François (1773-1837)

French diplomat and collector; he was born in Méru (Oise), 24 April 1773, the son of a physician; educated at the Coll. de Beauvais and Paris; he entered the diplomatic service and became Secretary to the Legation in Italy, 1804; Consul-General at Cagliari, 1814; at Cartagena, 1817; at Venice, 1826; in Egypt, 1829; it was through his influence with Muhammad Ali that the obelisk now in the Place de la Concorde was obtained for France; he made a large collection of Egyptian antiquities, which was sold in Paris after his death (18 Dec. 1837, 588 lots), see *Description des antiquités égyptiennes, grecques et romaines de la collection de M. Mimaut*, Paris, 1837; one important piece, the Table of Kings, was obtained by the British Museum (now EA 117); he was friendly to Champollion (q.v.) and his name is attached to a Greek Magical Papyrus in the Louvre (2391); Member of the Légion d'Honneur; he died in Paris, 31 Jan. 1837.

Biogr. notice prefixed to sale cat. by L. J. J. Dubois, Paris, 1837 (portr.); *NBG* 35, 578-9; Carré (see index); Champollion, ii, 248, 407, 412, 420; Lugt 14888.

MINA, Togo (1906-1949)

Egyptian Coptologist and archaeologist; he was born at Asyut, 7 Feb. 1906, son of a pharmacist; he studied locally and then in 1924 went to the University of Cairo where he graduated in archaeology in 1929; he studied in France 1930-34 under Lefebvre (q.v.), Drioton (q.v.) and Moret (q.v.) at the École Pratique, École du Louvre, and Institut Catholique; PhD 1935; he also studied briefly under Sethe (q.v.) at Berlin; on his return to Egypt in

1934 he was appointed assistant to Simaika Pasha (q.v.) at the Coptic Museum and succeeded him as Director in 1944; he excavated the monastery of Saint Menas near Alexandria and made sondages at monasteries in the Theban area in 1948; his publications include his thesis *Le martyre d'Apa Epima*, 1937 and *Inscriptions coptes et greques de Nubie*, 1942; he was in the process of acquiring the Nag Hammadi codices for the Museum at the time of his death in Asyut, 24 Oct. 1949.

BIE 32 (1949-50), 325-9 (É. Drioton); *CHE* serie ii, (1950), 351; *Chron. d'Ég.* 25, 389-90 (J. Doresse).

MINUTOLI, (*Freiherr von*) **(Nicolas) Johann Heinrich Benjamin Menu** (1772-1846)
Prussian army officer; he was born in Geneva, 12 May 1772, son of Daniel Menu and Isabelle Lucadou; he entered the Prussian army in 1784 in which he won distinction and came under the personal notice of the king; he adopted the style von Minutoli; in 1820 he was sent by the Prussian Govt. on a scientific mission to Egypt, and visited Siwa oasis, 1820-1; he undertook excavations at Saqqara and Hermopolis; he published an interesting account, *Reise zum Tempel des Jupiter Ammon in der Libyschen Wüste und nach Ober-Aegypten in den Jahren 1820 und 1821. Nach seinem Tagebuch herausgegeben, und mit Beilagen begleitet von E. H. Toelken. Mit einem Atlas*, fol. 1824; *Nachträge*, pub. 1827; his second wife Wolfardine Auguste Luise (1 Feb. 1794-Berlin 22 Nov. 1868), daughter of Adolf Friedrich Graf von der Schulenburg and Wolfardine von Kampen, published *Mes Souvenirs d'Égypte*, Paris, 1826, English ed., 1827; he collected large quantities of antiquities, some of which were sold in Paris and seen by Champollion (q.v.); others were acquired for the Berlin Museum; part of his collection was lost in a shipwreck off Hamburg; the remainder was retained in the collection of Dr. Alexander von Minutoli (1806-1887), which was sold in Cologne on 25-6 Oct. 1875; he died in Berlin, 16 Sept. 1846.

Hilmy, ii, 36; *Larousse XIXe siècle*, II. 308-9; inf. H. Nehls; H. Nehls, *Der Herold* 12 (1988), 143-200;inf. E. Staehelin; J. Karig in P. and J. Starkey, *Travellers in Egypt,* 1998, 70-4 and D. Manley in *ibid.*, 97-107; È. Gran-Aymerich, *Dictionnaire biographique d'archéologie 1798-1945*, 2001, incorporated in *Les Chercheurs de passé 1798-1945*, 2007, 991; Lugt 35856.

MISSETT, Ernest (*d.*1820)
British army officer and diplomat; 97th Regt. of Foot; Capt. 1799; Major, 1803; Lieut.-Col., 1810; British Consul-General in Egypt, 1803-16, absent Sept. 1807-July 1811; he resigned owing to ill health, and was succeeded by Henry Salt (q.v.) who arrived in early 1816; he died in Florence, 22 Sept. 1820.

Athanasi, 3. 4; Burckhardt, *Travels in Nubia*, 457; *GM* 1821, i, 185; Henniker, 201; Legh, 10 and often; Light, 23, 27, 111, 115, 123; Salt, i, 133, 403, 451, 455, 465; Valentia, iii, 456 and often.

MOGENSEN, Maria Pouline (1882-1932)
Danish Egyptologist; she was born in Copenhagen, 1 Oct. 1882, daughter of Niels M. and Marie Vilhelmine Emilie Dohn; she studied Egyptology under Schmidt (q.v.) and Lange (q.v.); she joined the staff of the Ny Carlsberg Glyptotek, 1910, and succeeded Schmidt as Keeper of the Egyptian Department; she published *Inscriptions hiéroglyphiques du Musée National de Copenhague*, 1918; *Le mastaba égyptien de la Glyptothèque Ny Carlsberg*, 1921; *La Glyptothèque Ny Carlsberg; La Collection égyptienne*, 1930; she died in Copenhagen, 30 Oct. 1932.

Chron. d'Ég. 8 (1933), 140-1; internet *Dansk Kvinde Biografie* (K.-E. Hogsbro); T. Bagh, *Finds from W. M. F. Petrie's Excavations in Egypt in the Ny Carlsberg Glyptotek*, 2011, 9-10.

MOHASSIB, (*Bey*) **Muhammad** (1843-1928)
Egyptian antiquities dealer; he was born in Luxor (?) 1843; he began life as a donkey-boy and served Lady Duff-Gordon (q.v.) who taught him English; he became an itinerant dealer in antiquities, and opened a shop in Luxor in the early 1880s; many important monuments now in museums in Europe and America were procured through him; at one time he fell under suspicion and was arrested by Grébaut (q.v.) when he was Director of the Antiquities Service, but was released as he bore the highest character all his life; he died in Luxor, 1 April 1928.

Andrews Diary; Budge, *N & T* i, 138-9, 143, 145, 150; *JEA* 14 (1928), 184 (P. E. Newberry); Wilbour, 48 and often (see index); F. Hagen and K. Ryholt, *The Antiquities Trade in Egypt 1880-1930*, 2017, 245-7.

MOHR, Herta Theresa (1914-1945)
Austrian Egyptologist; she was born in Vienna, 24 April 1914, daughter of Adolf Israel M., a physician, and Gabriele Kaufmann; she studied Oriental Studies at the University of Vienna, 1937-8; as Jews, her family then fled to the Netherlands where she undertook research at Leiden on the mastaba chapel of Hetepherakhti in the Leiden Museum of Antiquities; she was arrested on 2 Aug, 1942 and eventually deported in 1944 to Auschwitz concentration camp; her manuscript was edited by Jozef Janssen (q.v.) and de Buck (q.v.) and published despite the difficult circumstances of World War II, *The Mastaba of Hetep-her-Akhti*, 1943; she died in the camp of Bergen-Belsen, 15 April 1945.

N. van de Beek in C. Demarée. A. J. Stuart, and V. Verschoor, (eds.), *Imaging and Imagining the Memphite Necropolis. Liber Amicorum René van Walsem*, 2017, 233-8; inf. M. Raven.

MOHSEN, Muhammad (Mohamed) Ahmad (1932-2001)
Egyptian Egyptologist; he was born in Zagazig, 16 Jan. 1932; he was educated at Ain Shams University under Hassan (q.v.) and Fakhry (q.v.), graduating 1957; he joined the Antiquities Service as an inspector in the pyramids area and later the eastern Delta; he took part in the Nubian campaign, 1958 and excavations in Memphis and Saqqara, 1959, and Tell Basta and Abu Yassin, 1960-6; he was appointed curator in the Egyptian Museum, Cairo, 1967; he later became Deputy Director, and Director 1978-15 Oct. 1981; he became Director of the Museums' Section in the Egyptian Antiquities Organization, 1983; he again became Director of the Egyptian Museum 1987-13 Oct. 1991; he was curator at loan exhibitions in Canada, 1985; Memphis, USA, 1987; Japan, 1970, 1978, 1988; Russia, 1974; and France, 1976; he died 14 on July 2001.

Bulletin of the Egyptian Museum 1 (2004), 8; 6 (2009), 9-13 (portr.).

MOKHTAR, Muhammad Gamal-eddin (1918-1998)
Egyptian Egyptologist; he was born in Alexandria, 14 July 1918 son of a Professor of History at Cairo; he was educated at the University of Cairo; BA in geography, 1939; and at the High Institute of Pedagogy, diploma, 1940; he returned to Cairo University to study Egyptology; MA, 1943; he was an assistant at the Institute of Pedagogy in Alexandria, 1946-7; he then obtained a diploma in education at Iowa State Teachers College and a diploma in Educational Guidance at Ain Shams University, 1956; Fulbright Exchange Fellow, 1953-4; PhD in Egyptology, 1957 from Ain Shams University studying under Kees (q.v.) and Badawi (q.v.); he became assistant Professor at the Training Teachers College in Cairo, 1957-8; Scientific Director and Chief Archaeologist of the Centre of Documentation, 1958-1967 when he took part in the Nubian Rescue campaign; Professor of Ancient History, Cairo University in succession to Fakhry, 1967; Under-Secretary of State and Director and later President of the Egyptian Antiquities Organization, 1967-77; Hon. PhD from the Université of Montpellier, 1972; Professor of Archaeology at the University of Helwan, 1977; Professor of Archaeology at King Saud University in Riyadh, 1977-82; Professor emeritus of Archaeology at the University of Alexandria, 1982-95; he served on numerous national and international committees; he was awarded the Légion d'honneur; the French Institute in Cairo published two volumes of studies in his honour *Mélanges Gamal eddin Mokhtar*, 1985; he was the editor of Volume 2 of the UNESCO *General History of Africa*, 1981; he published several studies in Arabic: *Egyptian Civilization*, 1957 (with A. Badawi); *Ancient History of Egypt and the Near East*, 1967; *Education in Ancient Egypt*, 1974 (with A. B Badawi); and was editor of the *Encyclopedia of Egyptian Civilization*, 1975-7; his other published works were *Le Temple de Derr*, 1965 (with Z. el-Kordy and A. Sadek); *Le Mobilier dans l'Egypte Ancienne*, 1965; *Le Speos d'Ellesija*, 1968 (with C. Desroches-Noblecourt and S. Donadoni); *Agriculture in ancient Egypt*, no date; *Dresses in ancient Egypt*, no date; *Ihnasya el-Medineh (Herakleopolis Magna). Its Importance and Its Role in Pharaonic History*, 1983; he died 30 Jan. 1998.

NARCE 88 (1974), 24-5; *GM* 76 (1984), 89-90; *Mélanges Gamal edddin Mokhtar*, vii-xi (portr.) (bibl.); IAE Internet obituary (N. Grimal); *Alexandria Archaeological Society Newsleetter* 3 (1998), 10-12. (M. El Abbadi); *Memnonia* IX (1998), 17-28 (portr), (bibl) (G. A. Gabulla, T. Handoussa, C. Leblanc); *BSAC* 38 (1999), 9-10 (portr.) (W. Boutros-Ghali).

MOLDENKE, Charles Edward (1860-1935)
American Egyptologist; he was born at Lyck, East Prussia, 10 Oct. 1860, son of Revd Eduard Friedrich M. and Agnes Elise Pauline Aurora Harder; his father was a missionary in Wisconsin, USA, 1861-6 and settled permanently in America in 1869; he was educated at Columbia Grammar School 1872-5 and Columbia University; BA 1879; MA 1883; he studied Oriental Languages at the University of Halle, 1880 and Egyptology at Strasbourg under Duemichen (q.v.); PhD 1884; he was ordained in 1885; pastor at Jersey City Heights, 1885-90 and St. Peter's Lutheran Church, New York City, 1890-6; he resigned in 1896 to travel to Europe and the Near East; pastor at Mount Vernon, New York, 1897-1900; he spent the latter part of his life in travel in North and South America and collecting botanical specimens; he was the author of several popular books including *The Language of the Ancient Egyptians*, 1885; *The Egyptian Origin of our Alphabet*, 1886; *Ueber die in altägyptischen Texten erwähnten Bäume und deren Verwerthung*, 1886; *The New York Obelisk*, 1st ed. 1891, 2nd ed. 1935; *The Tale of the Two Brothers*, 1898; *Egyptian Classics* I: *Papyrus d'Orbiney*, 1900; he died in Watchung, New Jersey, 18 Jan. 1935.

The New York Obelisk 2nd ed., iii-xiv (portr.) (H. N. Moldenke).

MOLESWORTH-ST. AUBYN, (*Lady*) **Ingeborg Alfhild** (*née* **MULLER**) (1870–1928)
English draughtswoman of Danish origin; she was born in Jutland in 1870, daughter of Johan Viggo Sigvald Muller (1836–1904) and Anna Schmidt (*d.*1896); her father, a civil engineer, had trained in England, moved to Newquay in the early 1870s and became a naturalised British citizen; she married the Revd St. Aubyn Hender Molesworth-St. Aubyn (1833–1913) on 2 Sept. 1902, who became the 12th baronet in 1912; OBE 1920; made 200 drawings for Valdemar Schmidt's *Levende og døde i det gamle Ægypten: Album til ordnung af Sarkofager, Mumiekister, Mumiehylstre o. lign*, Copenhagen, 1919, including the coffins of Isettayefnakhte in the Royal Cornwall Museum, Truro (1837.23.2–3), in which town she gave lectures in the 1920s; she died in Newquay, Cornwall, 11 Dec. 1928 and was buried in her husband's family vault in the church of St Crewenna, Crowan, Cornwall.

Inf. D.W. Donaldson and A.M. Dodson; note by N. Nail, in Royal Cornwall Museum, Truro.

MÖLLER, Georg Christian Julius (1876-1921)
German Egyptologist; he was born in Caracas, 5 Nov. 1876, son of Martin M., a merchant, and Maria Aminé; he studied at Berlin under Erman (q.v.), 1896-1900; PhD, 1900; he then excavated in Egypt and was attached to the German consulate, 1901-7; he was appointed to the staff of Berlin Museum, later becoming Assistant Director of the Egyptian collections, 1907; Habilitation, 1912; he lectured at Berlin, 1913-6, 1918-22; Professor, 1916; he excavated in Egypt, particularly at Abusir el-Melek; Möller was an all-round Egyptologist and produced an edition of the Rhind Demotic Bilingual Papyri, a vol. on the goldsmith's work in Berlin Museum, and another on Mummy Portraits; but his most important work was in the field of hieratic texts and palaeography; at the time of his death he was preparing works on the graffiti in the Hatnub quarry, hieroglyphic palaeography, and the history of the Libyans; in addition to many articles in journals such as *ZÄS*, he wrote *Ausgrabung bei Abusir el-Meleq, 1906*, 1907; *Hieratische Paläographie: die Aegyptische Buchschrift in ihrer Entwicklung von der fünften Dynastie bis zur römischen Kaiserzeit*, 3 vols. 1909-12, his most important work; *Hieratische Lesestücke für den akademisch-Gebrauch*, 3 pts., 1910-27; *Die beiden Totenpapyrus Rhind des Museum zu Edinburgh*, 1913; *Mumienschilder*, 1913; *Das Mumienporträt*, fol., 1920; posth. *Die Metalkunst der alten Ägypter*, 1924; *Die archeologischen Ergebnisse nach den Aufzeichnungen Georg Möllers, bearbeitet von Alexander Scharff*, 1926; he died suddenly in Uppsala, 2 Oct. 1921.

Aegyptus 2 (1921), 344 (G. Farina); *JEA* 7 (1921), 231; *ZÄS* 57 (1922), 142-4 (portr.) (G. Steindorff); E. Endesfelder, *Die Ägyptologie an der Berliner Universität-Zur Geschichte eines Fachgebietes*, 27-8.

MONCONYS, Balthasar de (1608-1665)
French traveller; he was born in Lyons, 1 March 1608, coming from an old family of Burgundy long connected with judicial affairs; his brother was a collector of antiquities, coins etc., which may have stimulated his interest in the past; he studied at the Jesuits' College, Lyons, and after the plague in 1628 went to the University of Salamanca; he became a royal councillor subsequently and frequented the Academy in Paris that later produced the Academy of Sciences founded by Colbert; he married in 1638 and in 1645 set out on his long-wished journey to the East; he arrived Alexandria 1 Jan. 1647 and remained in Egypt until 13 Oct. when he embarked for Jaffa, returning to Europe in 1649; he later visited England, 1663, meeting many of the savants of the period, and also Italy and the Netherlands, and left a description of the painter Vermeer at work; he succeeded to his brother's judicial office, 1664, meeting Kircher (q.v.) in Rome the same year; his account of his travels was first published in 1665-6; while in Egypt he visited Sinai which he described very thoroughly as he did those antiquities that he saw elsewhere; Monconys liked statistics and always tried to be very exact on dimensions of structures, geographical features and distances; he noted Cleopatra's Needle at Alexandria and Pompey's Pillar, but his illustrations of the pyramids and Sphinx are very poor and unhelpful; in a description of them in a letter home he makes the great pyramid 520 feet high and 682 feet square, but more importantly states that the entrance on the N. side was on the sixteenth step, showing it could not have been much buried at the base to account for the apparent discrepancy in his measurements here; again his reference to the platform at the summit being 16 feet square suggests he climbed it, while in general his is probably the best verbal description of the interior of that period; he gives lengths down to inches and angles of inclination of the passages, as well as detailing the sarcophagus; also good is the account of the Sphinx which he makes 26 feet high as mainly buried then; he further describes the mummy galleries at Saqqara, wood and bronze figures among which he recognized a seated female figure as Isis, and wooden coffins; he bought some antiquities in Cairo for, he said, three piastres; particularly interesting from the Egyptological point of view is the fact that in his letter to M. Bernier written while in Egypt he refers to copying material for Kircher to see; he died in Lyons, 28 April 1665.

Voyage en Égypte de Balthasar de Monconys 1646-1647, ed. and with notes by Henry Amer, 1973, 8th vol. of *Voyageurs Occid, en Égypte*, Cairo; S. Cordier, *Balthazar de Monconys*, Brussels, 1967; Clément, *Les Français d'Égypte aux XVIIᵉ et XVIIIᵉ*, Cairo, 1960; M. Labib, *Pélerins et voyageurs au Mont Sinai*, Cairo, 1961; M. Varille, 'Balthazar de Monconys', *Bull. Soc. Lit. Hist. et Arch. de Lyon*, vol. 13, (1934); Lamy, 109-111.

MOND, (*Sir*) **Robert Ludwig** (1867-1938)
British chemist and excavator; he was born in Farnworth, near Widnes, Lancs., 9 Sept. 1867, eldest son of Dr. Ludwig Mond, FRS, who was of German origin, and Frida Löwenthal; he was educated at Cheltenham and Peterhouse, Cambridge, also at the Universities of Zürich, Edinburgh, and Glasgow; he married firstly in 1898, Helen Edith Levis (who died in Luxor in 1905), and secondly in London, 6 Dec. 1922 Marie Louise Le Manach (born in Belle-Isle-en-Terre 5 Feb. 1869, died there 21 Nov. 1949); Director of the Mond Cos.; of his services and contributions to chemistry and other branches of science, accounts will be found elsewhere; for many years his chief recreation was Egyptian archaeology and he frequently visited Egypt from 1901 onwards; in 1902 he began work on clearing and recording Theban tombs, discovering several new ones; he personally supervised the work, 1902-5 and 1923-6; in this effort he had the assistance of Newberry, (q.v.) Carter (q.v.), E. J. Mackay (q.v.), Emery (q.v.), Frankfort (q.v.), F. W. Green (q.v.), Weigall (q.v.), Yeivin (q.v.) and others; he defrayed the cost of repairing, restoring and safeguarding many tombs and other monuments in Egypt including the tomb of Sety I, and was a generous supporter of many archaeological expeditions in Egypt, and elsewhere; those of the EES, of Garstang (q.v.) in Meroe and in Asia Minor, of the Liverpool Inst. of Archaeology, of Miss Garrod at Athlit and Lydda and of H. Winkler (q.v.) in the Eastern and Libyan deserts; in 1926 he ceased working at Thebes and transferred his activities to Armant, in 1929 handing over the concession to the EES when he was elected President that year; he was also Treasurer of the Palestine Exploration Fund and of the British School of Archaeology in Palestine; he defrayed the cost of many archaeological publications, and presented many antiquities to museums, bequeathing his collections to the British Museum and assisting with the purchase of Petrie's collection by University College London; he was also a great benefactor of the Royal Institution, of the British Institute in Paris, and of many other scientific and cultural bodies; LL.D.; FRSE.; FRS; knighted 1932; a large collection of his notes, photographs, and other material relating to the Theban tombs is now in the Griffith Inst., Oxford; he died in Paris, 22 Oct. 1938.

DNB 1931-40, 622-3; *ODNB* 38, 615-6; *WWW* iii, 954; R. Mond, *Notes for a Biography*, privately printed, 1928; *JEA* 24 (1938), 208-10 (portr.) (P. E. Newberry); *Nature* 142 (1938), 862-3 (C. S. Gibson) 863-5 (P. E. Newberry); *AAA* 25 (1938), 69-70 (A. Blackman); *Chron. d'Ég.* 14 (1939), 140-1 (J. Capart); *OFRS* 7, Jan. 1939 (portr.); *Rev. arch.* 6e sér. 13 (1939), 126-7 (C. Picard); *CRAIBL* 1938, 463-5 (C. Petit-Dutaillis); Lady Mond, *A la Mémoire de Sir Robert Mond (1867-1938)*, privately printed, 1938; I. E. S. Edwards in *BMQ* 13/2 (1939), 41-5 and 14/1 (1940), 1-5 (objects from the collection); P. Delestre, *La vie fabuleuse de Lady Mond*, 1970; inf. C. Coleman; T. Adam, *Transnational Philanthropy: The Mond Family's Support for Public Institutions*, 2016, 207-47.

MONNERET DE VILLARD, Ugo (1881-1954)
Italian archaeologist and orientalist; he was born in Milan, 16 Jan. 1881, son of Enrico M. and Anna Poli; he studied to become an engineer, but became interested in medieval architecture and later in oriental studies; his first visit to Egypt was for the purpose of making a study of the Pharos of Alexandria; he later conducted a long series of excavations in Upper Egypt between 1921 and 1934; he was able to demonstrate that Coptic art was in the Hellenistic tradition and made a special study of the monasteries near Sohag; Christian art in Nubia formed but one of a large number of subjects in which he was interested, his range covered fields as far apart as Persia and Sicily; he published *Les Couvents près de Sohâg*, 2 vols. 1925-6; *Deyr el-Muharraqah*, 1928; *Le iscrizioni del cimitero di Sakinya, Nubia*, 1933; *La Nubia medioevale*, 2 vols. 1929-34; he died in Rome, 4 Nov. 1954.

Les Cahiers coptes, Cairo, 1954, nos. 7-8, 32-7 (bibl.) (U. Scarpocchi); *CRAIBL* 1954, 466-8 (A. Grenier); *Orientalia* 24 (1955), 94 (A. Pohl); *Oriente moderno* 34, nr. 12 (Dec. 1954), 587-90 (bibl.) (E. Rossi) reprinted from; *Kush*, 3 (1955), 112-15 (E. Rossi); *Rivista degli studi orientali* 30 (1955), 172-88 (bibl.) (G. Levi Della Vida); *Syria*, 32 (1955), 394-5 (R. Dussaud); *Chi è* 1948, 614.

MONRO, (*Revd*) **Vere** (1801-1841)
British traveller; he was born at Thaxted, 10 March 1801, son of Revd Thomas M. of Little Easton, Essex and Sarah Jane Hopegood; he was educated at University College, Oxford, BA, 1823; he visited Egypt and Nubia with J. A. St. John (q.v.) 1832-3, whose book is dedicated to him; his name is carved on the rock of Abu Sir, 2nd Cataract; he parted from St. John at Cairo, 31 March 1834, and went on alone to Palestine and Syria; he published *A Summer Ramble in Syria*, London, 1835; he died in Malta, 20 Oct. 1841.

Al. Oxon.; St. John, *Eg. and Moh. Ali*, 1834, i, 79; ii, 344 et passim.

MONTAGU, Edward Wortley (1713-1776)
British traveller and eccentric; he was born in London, 16 May 1713, son of Edward Wortley M. and Lady Mary Pierrepont, the celebrated literary figure; he was educated at Westminster; MP, 1747-68; FRS, 1751; he

led an unconventional life and left England in 1762; he sailed to Egypt in April 1763 from Leghorn in the company of Nathaniel Davison (q.v.) as secretary; he undertook excavations at Alexandria and at Saqqara and journeyed to Palestine through Sinai in 1764 before returning to Europe; he returned to Alexandria in 1766 where he undertook the examination of Pompey's Pillar, published in *Philosophical Transactions* lxi, 1767, 56 and 438, before leaving in 1767; he was in Egypt again in 1771-2 and 1772-3; the objects from his excavations in 1764 were sent to his brother-in-law the Earl of Bute who gave some to King George III, who passed them to the British Museum in 1766 and 1767; Montagu adopted Turkish dress and religion; he died in Padua, 29 April 1776.

Seetzen iii, 382-5; J. Curling, *Edward Wortley Montagu*, 1954; *ODNB* 30, 714-6; *DNB* 38, 237-40.

MONTAGU, John 4th Earl of Sandwich (1718-1792)
British traveller and politician, he was born in London, 3 Nov. 1718, son of Edward Richard Montagu, Viscount Hinchingbroke and Elizabeth Popham; he was educated at Eton and Trinity College, Cambridge although he did not take a degree; in 1738-9 he undertook a grand tour of the Mediterranean including Italy, Greece, Turkey and Egypt where he visited Alexandria, Cairo, Giza, Saqqara, Dahshur and Heliopolis; an account of his travels was later edited by J. Cooke, *A voyage performed by the late Earl of Sandwich round the Mediterranean in years 1738 and 1739*, 1809; while abroad, he formed a collection of antiquities including some Egyptian pieces; he was a founder member and President of the Egyptian Society, 1741-3; FSA, 1746; thereafter he entered politics holding several high offices notably First Lord of the Admiralty, 1771-82, where he supported the voyages of Captain Cook; he gave his name to a popular snack; he died in London, 30 April 1792.

ODNB 38, 744-8 (portr.); *DNB* 38, 254-8; N. Rodger, *The Insatiable Earl*, 1993; *BIFAO* 50 (1952), 99-105.

MONTET, (Jean) Pierre Marie (1885-1966)
French Egyptologist; he was born at Villefranche-sur-Saône, Burgundy, 27 June 1885, son of Jacques M. and Pierrette Vaillant; he studied at the University of Lyons under Loret (q.v.) and then worked at the IFAO in Cairo, 1910-14, during which time he collected material for his thesis, published later as *Les Scènes de la vie privée dans les tombeaux égyptiens de l'Ancien Empire*, 1925; after the First World War Montet left Egypt for a while and excavated the important site of Byblos in Lebanon between 1921 and 1924, where he discovered a temple and many royal tombs dating from the first half of the second millennium BC; these contained much jewellery and were also rich in objects showing contacts with Egypt; Montet's most important archaeological work was at Tanis, where large excavations were conducted in a long series of campaigns from 1929 until after the outbreak of war in 1940, and again 1945-51, and 1955-56; here he cleared the great temple area, discovered the smaller temple of Mut, called by him the temple of Anta, and with the help of his architects made the first plans of the wall remains on the site and the great gateway remains; the discovery of the royal tombs was the most sensational find in Egypt since that of the Tomb of Tutankhamun, and yielded the greatest number of untouched royal burials ever discovered in Egypt; in all Montet found four tombs and two princes as well as kings Psusennes, Osorkon II, and Sheshonk III; the rich objects from these burials are now in Cairo Museum, together with many fine pieces of sculpture and statuary that Montet found at the site; an active teacher and lecturer, Montet subsequently became Professor at the University of Strasbourg; in 1928 he founded the journal *Kêmi* which he used as a medium to publish articles and preliminary reports on his excavations; in fact he contributed so many articles to it (up to 1964 over one third of it was written by himself), that it had a character rather similar to that of Petrie's *Anc. Egypt*; Montet also excavated at Abu Roash where he cleared a considerable number of 1st Dynasty mastaba tombs during the 1930s; he was a very prolific writer and published no fewer than 18 books, nearly 180 articles, 52 book reviews, and 9 obit. notices; *Les Inscriptions hiéroglyphiques et hiératiques du Ouâdi-Hammâmât*, with Couyat, 1912; *Byblos et l'Égypte*, 2 vols. 1928, 1929; *Les Nouvelles fouilles de Tanis*, 1933; *Les Reliques de l'art syrien dans l'Égypte du Nouvel Empire*, 1937; *Le Drame d'Avaris*, 1941; *Tanis*, 1942; *La Vie quotidienne en Égypte au temps des Ramsès*, 1946; *La Nécropole royale de Tanis. I. Les Constructions et le tombeau d'Osorkon II à Tanis. II. Les Constructions et le tombeau de Psoussennes à Tanis. III. Les Constructions et le tombeau de Chéchonq III à Tanis*, 3 vols. 1947, 1951, 1960; this was his most important work; *Les Énigmes de Tanis*, 1951; *Géographie de l'Égypte ancienne*, 2 vols. 1957, 1961; *L'Égypte et la Bible*, 1959; *Eternal Egypt*, 1964; *Le lac sacré de Tanis*, 1966; *Lives of the Pharaohs; Vies des pharaons illustres*, 1985; he died in Paris, 18 June 1966.

Chron. d'Ég. 42 (1967), 124-5 (B. van de Walle); *CRAIBL* 1966 (1967), 343-7 (J. Vandier); *Rev. Arch.* 1966, i. 97-9 (J. Leclant); *Rev. d'Ég.* 19 (1967), 7-9 (portr.) (E. Wolff); 10-20 (bibl.) (F. Le Corsu); *BIFAO* 57 (1958), xi-xxlv (bibl. also but not complete); *Syria* 43 (1966), 335-8 (portr.) (J. Vandier); *Univ. de Strasbourg. Bull. d'information*, 7 (1966), 4-12 (portr.) (P. Derchain); *Kêmi* 18 (1968), 9-15 (portr.) (J. Sauneron); *AfO* 22 (1968-9), 216-7 (portr.) (W. Helck); E. Gran-Aymerich, *Dictionnaire biographique d'archéologie 1798-1945*, 2001, incorporated in *Les Chercheurs de passé 1798-1945*, 2007, 997-8.

MONTSERRAT, Dominic Alexander Sebastian (1964-2004)
British Egyptologist and papyrologist; he was born in Slough, Berkshire, 2 Jan. 1964, son of James Smith and Angela Montserrat, both head-teachers; he studied Egyptology at Durham University and then Classics at University College London, obtaining his MA and Ph.D. with a specialism in papyrology; he held the post of Lecturer in Classics at Warwick University 1992-99 and then Project Development Officer (Classics) at the Open University 1999-2002 when he was obliged to resign due to ill-health; he was a member of the Committee of the EES 1995-8 and 1999-2002; he was one of the editors of *Egyptian Archaeology* 2001-4; he was also a Fellow of the Royal Asiatic Society 1992; he published *Sex and Society in Greco-Roman Egypt*, 1996; and *Akhenaten: History, Fantasy, and Ancient Egypt*, 2000; he also organized an award-winning exhibition *Digging for Dreams* at the Petrie Museum, 2000-1 and was involved in radio and TV productions; he died in London, 23 Sept. 2004

The Independent 13 Oct. 2004 (portr.) (Jane Stevenson); *The Times* 29 Oct. 2004; *The Guardian* 10 Nov. 2004 (Ashley Jones); *Egyptian Archaeology* 26 (2005), 2 (P. A. Spencer); inf. Mrs A. Montserrat; M. Capasso (ed.) *Hermae* II, 2010, 103 (portr.) (D. Thompson).

MOOK, Friedrich (1844-1880)
German antiquary; he was born in Bergzabern, 29 Sept. 1844, son of Konrad M.; he studied theology and philosophy at the University of Tübingen, 1863-5; PhD, 1865; he later studied theology at the University of Utrecht and medicine at the University of Berlin, 1868-9 and the University of Heidelberg, 1873-5; he visited Egypt in 1874 and again in 1877 when he discovered prehistoric remains at Helwan; he returned in 1880 travelling as far as the Sudan; he published *Aegyptens vormetallische Zeit*, 1880; his collection of Egyptian antiquities is in the Munich Museum he died near Jericho in Jordan, 13 Dec. 1880.

Hilmy, ii, 42; *ADB* 22, 206; V. Carl, *Lexikon der Pfälzer Personlichkeiten*, 1995, 418.

MOORE, William (1768-1848)
British army officer; he was born 1768; 2nd W. India Regt. transferred to 14th Foot then in India, 1802; Capt., 1806; Major, 1816; he returned to England with dispatches and went on half-pay, 1819; on his way back from India he stayed in Cairo, visited the Pyramids with Belzoni, and conveyed the latter's report thereon to Lord Aberdeen, Pres. SA; he died, with rank of Lieut.-Col., in London, 7 April 1848.

Army Lists; Belzoni i, 391; *GM* 1848, i. 560; *Journ. Soc. for Bibl. of Nat. Hist.* 2, 57, 59.

MORAND, Charles Antoine Louis Alexis (*Comte*) (1771-1835)
French military officer; he was born in Pontarlier 4 June 1771, son of Alexis François M., a lawyer, and Jeanne Claudine Marie Rousel; he joined the army in 1792 as Captain; he accompanied the French expedition to Egypt and served at the Battle of the Pyramids and later commanded forces in Upper Egypt; he drew the first detailed plans of the temples of Karnak and Luxor; he was promoted to General and later served in Napoleon's campaigns; he was made a count and became Napoleon's ADC at Elba; he fought at Waterloo in 1815 and went into exile until 1830; he died in Paris, 2 Sept. 1835.

NBG 36, 450; *Biographie Universelle* 29, 235-6; C. Rivollet, *Général de Bataille Charles Antoine Louis Morand, Comte d'Empire*, 1963.

MORENZ, (Kurt Karl) Siegfried (1914-1970)
German Egyptologist and Copticist; born in Leipzig, 22 Nov. 1914, son of Emil Karl M., a post official, and Hilde Weisswange; he studied at the Schiller-Gymnasium in Leipzig, 1934-8 and later under W. Wolf (q.v.) and J. Leipoldt (q.v.) reading Theology and Egyptology at the University of Leipzig; with his doctorate, he produced his first major work in the field of Coptic *Die Geschichte von Joseph dem Zimmermann*, 1941; he was then appointed to the staff of the Ägyptologische Institut; with his study *Ägyptens Beitrag zur werdenden Kirche,* he entered the field of history of Egyptian religion and its interaction with the Hellenistic world, 1946; he

was appointed university lecturer the same year; Associate Professor, 1952, Professor of Egyptology, 1954-70; Director of the Egyptological Institute Karl-Marx University, Leipzig, until his death; Director of the Egyptian section of the Staatlichen Museum Berlin, 1952-58; Commissar Director of the Ancient History Dept. of the General History Faculty of Karl-Marx University; Ordinarius for Egyptology and History of Religion in the University of Basel, 1961-66; member, 1955, and Vice President, 1966, of Saxon Akad. der Wiss.; Corr., 1954, ordinary Member, 1957, of the German Arch. Inst.; Dr. Theol. (hon. causa) of the Evangelical-Theological Faculty of the University of Tübingen, 1957; hon. Member of the Czechoslovakian Egyptological Inst. of Charles University, Prague, 1965, also Cairo; Member of the Bavarian Akad. der Wiss., 1968; his speciality was Egyptian religion and it should be noted that Morenz was a trained theologian as well as an Egyptologist and Coptic scholar; this gave him an additional insight into a difficult subject and he invented a curious religo-chronological system to show his own unique view of man's religious development; he also subdivided the 'structure' of Egyptian religion into two classes of material, 'National religion' and 'Cult religion'; while these views have not yet gained general acceptance his book on Egyptian religion has gained considerable popularity and his other works have been influential; he was also co-editor of *ZÄS*, 1954, and *OLZ*, 1952-58; his bibliography lists 221 works, books, articles, reviews etc., the principal ones being, *Nilkultur*, 1947; *Einführung in dass wissenschaftliche Arbeiten*, 1947; *Die Geschichte von Joseph dem Zimmermann: übersetzt, erläutert und untersucht von S.M.*, 1951; *Ägypten und das Berliner Ägyptische Museum*, 1953; *Die Zauberflöte: eine Studie zum Lebenszusammenhang Ägypten - Antike - Abendland*, an interesting book dealing with Schikaneder's libretto for Mozart's opera, 1952; *Heilige Schriften: Betrachtungen zur Religionsgeschichte der antiken Mittelmeerwelt*, with J. Leipoldt, 1953; *Der Gott auf der Blume: eine ägyptische Kosmogonie und ihre weltweite Bildwirkung*, with J. Schubert, 1954; *Ägyptische Religion*, 1960, French version *La Religion égyptienne*, trans. L. Jospin, 1962, English version, *Egyptian Religion*, trans. A. E. Keep, 1973; *Üntersuchungen zur Rolle des Schicksals in der ägyptischen Religion*, with D. Müller, 1960; *Gott und Mensch im alten Ägypten*, 1964; *Altägyptischer jenseitsführer: Papyrus Berlin 3127: Mit Bemerkungen zur Totenliteratur der Ägypter*, 1964; *Die Begegnung Europas mit Ägypten: mit einem Beitrag von Martin Kaiser: Herodots Begegnung mit Ägypten*, 1968; *Prestige-Wirtschaft im alten Ägypten*, 1969; while working on a history of Egypt, of which the last named work was intended to be a preliminary part, he died of a heart attack in Leipzig, 14 Jan. 1970.

NDB 8, 100; *AfO* 23 (1970), 222-3 (portr.) (H. Brunner); *Chron. d'Ég.* 45 (1970), 132-3 (P. Derchain); *Jahrb. Sachsische Akad. der Wiss.* zu Leipzig (1969-70), (1972), 235-9 (R. Meyer); *JEA* 56 (1970), 3-4 (J. Gwyn Griffiths); *Neu Kürchner Zeitung* (31 Jan. 1970) (E. Hornung); *Frankfurter Allegemeine Zeitung* 2 Feb. 1970 (S. Hermann); *ZÄS* 96 (1970), v (F. Hintze); 99 (1972), i-x (portr.) (bibl.) (A. Heller) (E. Blumenthal and F. Hintze).

MORET, Alexandre (1868-1938)

French Egyptologist; he was born at Aix-les-Bains, 19 Sept. 1868, son of Maurice M. and Josephine Félicie Perréard; he was educated at the Lycée de Chambéry, 1880-5, and the Lycée Henri IV at Lyons, 1885-8; studied at the Faculté des Lettres at Lyons under V. Loret (q.v.), 1888-93, with special reference to the history of Egypt; entered the Sorbonne, Paris, 1893, and the École des Hautes Études, 1894-7, where he studied under E. Lavisse and G. Maspero (q.v.); during this period he published his first Egyptological works which related to philology, and then three great studies on the social order in ancient Egypt and legal institutions; *L'Appel au roi en Égypte au temps des pharaons et des Ptolémées*, 1894; *Une Fonction judiciaire de la XIIe dynastie et les chrématistes ptolémaïques*, 1894; *La Condition des féaux en Égypte, dans la famille, dans la société, dans la vie d'outre-tombe*, 1897; he succeeded Loret as Maître de Conférences, Faculté de Lettres, at Lyons, 1897-9, returning to Paris as Director at the École des Hautes Études, 1899-1938; also Director of the Musée Guimet, 1905; Keeper, 1918-38; Professor at the Sorbonne, 1920, and at the Collège de France, 192-38; he published the famous law case of Mes for the first time, *Un Procès de famille sous la XIXe dynastie*, 1901; he was immensely erudite and gained his Doctorat ès-Lettres, 1903, with the unique distinction of being the last Doctor in France who presented his thesis written in Latin, *De Bocchori rege*, on the subject of the Saite law-maker who was burnt by the Ethiopian kings; Moret's other great speciality was in the field of Egyptian religion, and he published in the *Annales* of the Musée Guimet, *Le rituel du culte divin journalier en Égypte*, 1902 dealing with the daily temple services and a central idea in Egyptian thought, namely the sacrifice made to the sun-god of his own daughter, the goddess Maat symbol of justice and balance in the universe; *Du caractère religieux de la royauté pharaonique*, 1902 discussing the priestly office of the king; ten articles formed the basis later of three further religious books, but of a more popular kind, *Mystères égyptiens*, 1913; *Rois et dieux d'Égypte*, 1908, trans. by M. Moret as *Kings and Gods of Egypt*, 1912; *Au temps des Pharaons*, 1908, trans. as *In the Time of the Pharaohs*, 1911; at the time of his death

Moret was preparing a great synthesis of his research into Egyptian religion but was unable to complete it; he was also one of the first Egyptologists to study private rights and the law under the Old Kingdom and with Louis Boulard published an important study *Donations et fondations en droit égyptien*, 1907; he published a series of ten articles in the *Journal Asiatique* on charters of immunity and royal decrees at the end of the Old Kingdom and private ownership in the Middle Kingdom; other popular works were *Des clans aux empires*, with L. Davy a sociologist, 1923, trans. by V. Gordon Childe as *Tribe to Empire*; *Le Nil et la Civilisation égyptienne*, 1926, trans. *The Nile & Egyptian Civilisation*, 1927; a large general history, *L'Égypte pharaonique*, 1932; his historical work was crowned by *Histoire de l'Orient*, the first 2 vols. of the great general history published by G. Glotz, 1929-30; it was the largest history undertaken by one man since Maspero wrote his history forty years earlier and equalled in scale only by the *Cambridge Ancient History* written by a team of scholars, for in this work Moret traced four millennia of history in the Near East; see also, *Catalogue du Musée Guimet. Galerie égyptienne*, 1909; *Sarcophages de l'époque bubastite à l'époque saite*, for *Cairo Catalogue*, 2 pts. 1912; *Metternich Stela*, 1915; *Orient et Grèce (Cours d'histoire)*, with P. Cloché, 1933; Moret received many honours from learned societies; 1926 he succeeded Bénédite (q.v.) in the Institut; Doctor, Universities of Oxford and Brussels, *hon. c.*; member of the Institut d'Ég., and the Acad. Rio de Janeiro; 1935 appointed to the Professorial body of the Oriental Institute, University of Brussels; he lectured widely in Europe, USA, Canada, and S. America; translated Meyer's *Chronologie* and Mahler's *Calendrier* into French; he died in Paris, 2 Feb. 1938.

J. Pirenne, *La Religion égyptienne dans l'oeuvre d'Alexandre Moret*, Brussels, 1937, extract from *Annuaire de l'Institut de Philologie et d'Histoire Orientales et Slaves* (portr.) (bibl. partial); J. Pirenne, *Alexandre Moret. Historien du Droit et des Institutions*, Brussels, 1938, extract from *Archives d'Histoire du Droit Oriental; AfO* 12 (1938), 309 (portr.) (O. Koefoed-Petersen); *CRAIBL* 1938, 48-55 (C. Petit-Dutaillis); *Archiv für aeg. Arch.*, Vienna 1938, year 1, pp. 75-6 (J. Vandier d'Abbadie); *BIÉ* 20 (1938), 155-61 (P. F. A. Jouguet); *BIFAO* 20 (1920), 155; 38 (1938), 273-7 (P. F. A. Jouguet); *Journ. des Savants*, 1938, 38-40 (H. Deherain); *Chron. d'Ég.* xiii (1938), 322; *Rev. Arch.* 1938, série 6, t. II, pp. 327-9 (C. Picard); *Rev. de l'Histoire des Religions*, 1938, t. 117, pp. 137-51 (R. Dussaud); *Rev. Scientifique*, 1938, ann. 76, 177-9 (J. Joleaud); *Rev. d'Ég.* 6 (1951), 179-86 (bibl. 119 nos.); C. Charle and E. Telkès, *Professeurs du Collège de France. Dictionnaire biographique 1901-1939*, 1988, 186-187, no. 70); C. Charlé and E. Telkes, *Les Professeurs du Collège de France, dictionnaire biographique 1910-39*, 1988, 186-7; Jean-Michel Bruffaerts, 'Destins égyptologiques croisés: Alexandre Moret et Jean Capart', in M.-C. Bruwier (dir.), *Livres et archives de l'égyptologue Alexandre Moret (1868-1938) à Mariemont*. Catalogue de l'exposition organisée au Musée royal de Mariemont du 24 mars au 2 juin 2000, 2000, 11-17.

MORGAN, Henri Charles Marie Ferdinand Dieudonné de (1854-1909)

French excavator; he was born at the Château de Biou, Huisseau-sur-Cosson, Loir et Cher, 12 April 1854, son of Eugène de M. and Louise Marie Caroline Henriette de Calonne-Chambord; he and his younger brother Jacques (q.v.) became interested in archaeology as children; he later went to the United States where he represented the dealer Feuardent (q.v.); he then joined his brother in his excavations in Russia in 1888, Egypt, 1892-7, and Persia, 1901; in 1906-7 he undertook a general survey of settlements and cemeteries in southern Upper Egypt from Esna to Edfu sponsored by The Brooklyn Museum; his chief interest was in Egyptian prehistory and in 1907-8 he excavated Predynastic and Archaic sites in his concession at his expense, later selling the finds to The Brooklyn Museum; reports on his survey and excavations were published in *ASAE* 12 (1912), 25-38, and W. Needler, *Predynastic and Archaic Egypt in The Brooklyn Museum*, 1984, 50-66; he also wrote several articles on Egyptian prehistory in *Revue de l'École d'Anthropologie de Paris* 18 (1908), 133-49 and 19 (1909), 128-40, 263-281; objects from his excavations are now in the Cairo Museum, The Brooklyn Museum, and the Musée des Antiquités Nationales at Saint-Germain-en-Laye where his field notebooks are preserved; he died in the Chateau d'Orlienas (Rhone), 13 Nov. 1909.

Needler, *op. cit.*, 46-9; *JSSEA* (1979), 39-58 (W. Needler); *BSAK* 1 (1988), 69-76 (W.Needler).

MORGAN, Jacques Jean Marie de (1857-1924)

French civil engineer, geologist, archaeologist, and prehistorian; he was born in Château de Biou, Huisseau-sur-Cosson, Loir-et-Cher, 3 June 1857, brother of Henri de Morgan (q.v.); he studied at the School of Mines, Paris, 1876-1882; he travelled in Europe, 1880-1 and then explored as a prospector areas in the East Indies, 1882, Malacca, 1884, and Armenia, 1886-8; he then conducted scientific missions in the Caucasus, 1888-9, and in Persia, 1889-1; he was appointed Director-General, Egyptian Antiquities Service, 1892-7; while in Egypt he made important excavations at the pyramids of Dahshur, 1894-5, discovering the magnificent collection of royal jewellery belonging to the 12th-Dynasty princesses Merit and Khnumit now in the Egyptian Museum, Cairo; equally important was the discovery of the great royal tomb of Queen Neithhotep at Naqada, excavated in 1897, which first showed the scale of 1st Dynasty architecture; a predynastic specialist, de Morgan may be said to have been, with Petrie (q.v.), the founder of the study of Egyptian prehistory, linking up the early dynasties with the predynastic period in a form generally followed ever since; he discovered the mastaba of Mereruka at Saqqara, 1893, cleared the temple of Kom Ombo, 1893, and conducted the first scientific expedition to explore Sinai and the Bahr-Bela-Ma, an ancient bed of the Nile; he also inaugurated a huge scheme for cataloguing all the extant monuments in Egypt from the Nubian frontier; several volumes were published but this was not continued by his successors; from 1897-1912 he was working in Persia, notably at Susa where he made his most famous discoveries; he was made an officer of the Légion d' honneur, Grand Cross St. Stanislas of Russia, etc.; his principal works in Egyptology and prehistory were, *Catalogue des monuments et inscriptions de l'Égypte antique*, 3 vols., no 1 is *Nubie à Kom Ombos*, 1894, nos. 2 and 3 *Description du Temple d'Ombos*, 1895-1909 with U. Bouriant and others; *Les Carrières de Ptolémaïs*, with U. Bouriant and G. Legrain, 1894; *Le trésor de Dahchour*, 1894; *Fouilles à Dahchour*, 2 vols. 1895-1903; *Recherches sur les Origines de l'Égypte*, 2 vols. 1896-7; also many maps, *Carte de la nécropole Memphite, Dahcour, Sakkarah, Abou-Sir*, etc., 1897; *Introduction to the guide to Giza Museum*, 1892; *Les Premières Civilisations; L'Humanité préhistorique*, 1921; his great work, *La Préhistoire orientale*, 3 vols., was posth. published, 1929 as were his *Mémoires*, 1997, ed. A. Jaunay; his Egyptian collection is in the Musée des Antiquités Nationales, Saint-Germain-en-Laye; he died in Marseilles, 12 June 1924.

Glyn Daniel, *A Hundred Years of Archaeology* (1950), 199, 207, 266; *Ant. Journ.* 5, 71; *BIÉ* 7 (1925), 173-4 (J. B. Piot); *Dict. National des Contemporains* 2, 337-8; *L'Anthropologie* 34 (1924), 467-71 (M. Boule); Petrie, *Seventy years in Archaeology* (1931), 136, 143, 146, 156, 158; *Rev. anthropologique* 34 (1924), 299-300 (Capitan); *Rev. de synthèse historique* 38 (1924), 5-14 (H. Berr); *Syria* 5 (1924), 373-80 (E. Pottier); *Rev. arch.* 55 (1924), 204-22 (S. Reinach); *KMT* 13/2 (2002), 80-83; A. Jaunay, *Jacques de Morgan, Archéologue 1857-1924*, 2002; *Archéo-Nil* 17 (2007), 39-56 (portr.); E. Gran-Aymerich, *Dictionnaire biographique d'archéologie 1798-1945*, 2001, incorporated in *Les Chercheurs de passé 1798-1945*, 2007, 1000-2; F. Djindjian, C. Lorre, and L. Touret, *Caucase, Égypte et Perse: Jacques de Morgan (1857-1924) pionnier de l'aventure archéologique*, 2009; photograph courtesy of Archives Musée d'Archéologie Nationale, Sainte-Germain-en-Laye.

MORGAN, John Pierpont (1838-1913)
American financier, collector and philanthropist; he was born in Hartford, Connecticut, 13 April 1837, son of Junius Spencer M., a banker, and Juliet Pierpont; he was educated at Göttingen University; his banks financed trade worldwide, and he organized many industrial corporations; he became involved with the Metropolitan Museum in 1871, the year after its foundation, and was its president from 1904 until his death; he oversaw the foundation of the Museum's Department of Egyptian Art in 1906, providing funds for its early fieldwork and the purchase of objects; he made several visits to Egypt; his own collections were of great size, scope, and quality; he had a particular interest in manuscripts, and in 1913 purchased the collection of papyri made by Lord Amherst (q.v.), now in the Morgan Library, New York; in 1917 his son and heir, J. P. Morgan jr. (1867-1943) gave a large part of his collections, including many Egyptian objects, to the Metropolitan Museum; other Egyptian pieces were sold at Parke-Bernet, 22-25 March 1944, lots 1-96; he died in Rome, 31 March 1913.

ONDB 39, 133-4; F. H. Taylor, *Pierpont Morgan as Collector and Patron*, New York, 1957; N. Thomas, 'American Institutional Fieldwork in Egypt, 1899-*The American Discovery of Ancient Egypt*, 1995, 60-64; J. Strouse, *J. Pierpont Morgan:Financier and Collector. Bulletin of the Metropolitan Museum*, 77/3 (Winter 2000); inf. T. Hardwick; J. Stouse, *J. P. Morgan: American Financier*, 1999.

MORISON, Anthoine (1665-?)
French traveller; he was born at Bar-le-Duc, 26 Sept. 1665, son of Anthoine M., a legal counsellor of the Chambre des Comptes, and Marguerite de Gistaulx (or de Hestaux de Nuisement); he entered the priesthood and became in 1679 a canon at the Église St.-Pierre, Bar-le-Duc; he went on a pilgrimage to the Holy Land in 1697 and stopped in Egypt on the way, arriving in Sept. 1697; he visited Alexandria, Cairo, Sinai, Giza and the Pyramids, and Damietta where he left for Acre on 24 Feb. 1698; his account of his journey was published as *Relation Historique d'un voyage nouvellement fait au Mont de Sinai et à Jerusalem*, 1704; he died in Bar-le-Duc at an unknown date.

G. Goyon ed., *Voyage en Égypte d'Anthoine Morison 1697*, 1976; Lamy, 125.

MORRIS, (*Lady*) Gladys Perrie (1889-1958)
British administrator; she was born Bryn Golen, Llanrust, 24 Nov. 1889, daughter of William Hugh W. and Lizzie Williams; she married Sir Rhys Hopkin Morris, QC, MP for Carmarthen, 1942 (he died 1956); OBE; MA; LittD; she held a number of administrative positions, Member of the Central Advisory Council for Education in Wales; i/c admin. work of Vocational Guidance Comm. of S. Wales; Chairman Ministry of Labour, Welfare Advisory Comm. (Wales); Member of the National Parks Comm. and of the Welsh Youth Comm.; she was Hon. Secretary of the Egypt Exploration Society, 1936-57; she died in Cardiff, 13 July 1958.

Inf. Miss M. S. Drower; EES *Report*, 1958, 3.

MORRISON, Walter (1836-1921)
British banker and philanthropist; he was born in London, 21 May 1836, son of James M., a merchant, and Mary Todd; educated at Eton and Balliol College, Oxford; he did the Grand Tour after leaving Oxford in 1858 and visited Egypt; JP; MP for various constituencies, 1874-1900; he was a great benefactor to hospitals, to the University of Oxford, and the Bodleian Library; one of the founders of the PEF he gave £15,000 for the British Museum's Carchemish excavations, and was also a generous supporter of excavations in Egypt financing many costly publications; he was on the Committee of the BSAE, and helped fund the acquisition of Petrie's collection of antiquities by University College London; among donations to Oxford Univ., he gave £10,000 in 1912 for the foundation of a readership in Egyptology, first held by Griffith (q.v.); he died in Sidmouth, 18 Dec. 1921.

ODNB 39, 356-7; *DNB* 1912-21, 388-9; *WWW* ii, 751.

MORTON, Anna Anderson (1867-1961)
British writer; she was born at Kennington, Surrey, 16 July 1867, daughter of Robert Morton, a civil engineer and Susanna Wallace Paterson; a student at University College London, 1884-1902; she translated Maspero's *Au temps de Ramsès et d'Assourbanipal* under the title *Life in Ancient Egypt and Assyria*, 1890; also collaborated with Mary Brodrick (q.v.) on *A Concise Dictionary of Egyptian Archaeology*, 1902; she later interested herself in Eastern religions; she died in Croydon, 9 Oct. 1961.

JEA 33 (1947), 87.

MORTON, Samuel George (1799-1851)
American physician, naturalist and anthropologist; born in Philadelphia, Pa., 26 Jan. 1799, son of George M. and Jane Cummings, and the youngest of nine children; as his father died when he was only six months old his mother removed to Westchester, NY, and he was educated at various Quaker boarding schools; in 1812 his mother married Thomas Rogers and returned to Philadelphia where Morton attended the Quaker school in Westtown; he afterwards studied medicine under Joseph Parrish, 1817; attended lectures in medical dept. University of Pennsylvania, MD, 1820; Memb. Acad. Natural Sciences of Philadelphia, Pres. at time of death; further education Edinburgh University, MD, 1823; he married Rebecca Grellet Pearsall, 1827; he published papers on a very wide variety of subjects, as his researches embraced medicine, geology, vertebrate palaeontology and zoology; Professor of Anatomy, Penn. Coll., 1839; resigned, 1843; from an Egyptological point of view he is of importance from several works that he published on Egyptian ethnography: 'Ancient Egyptian Crania' in *Amer. Journal of Science* 48 (1845), 268; 'Crania Aegyptiaca: or Observations on Egyptian Ethnography, derived from anatomy, history and the monuments' in *Trans. Amer. Philosoph. Soc.* 9 (1844), 93-159; 'Races of Ancient Egypt' in *New Philosoph. Journal* 37, 305; these had considerable influence on Gliddon (q.v.), who supplied him with skulls, and others, but as Morton's anthropological studies led him to the view that the races of man were of different origin, he was attacked by many people, including ministers, who claimed he denied Scriptural authority; he died in Philadelphia, 15 May 1851.

DAB 13, 265-6 (D. M. Fisk); Hilmy, ii, 45-6; detailed biographical sketch in *Types of Mankind ... illustrated by selections from the inedited papers of Samuel George Morton* (1854), xvii-lviii.

MOSCONAS, Demetrius (1839-1895)
Greek orientalist and interpreter; he was born on the Island of Leros, 1839; he went to Egypt as a young man and studied hieroglyphic writing under H. Brugsch (q.v.), having a gift for languages, of which he knew ten; Chief Interpreter to Thomas Cook & Son; he went to USA in 1892 with Egyptian exhibits for the Chicago World's Fair; he knew General Gordon, and his eldest son George, a Lieutenant, served under Hicks Pasha and died fighting the Dervishes; another son, Theodorus Demetrius, was Librarian to the Greek Patriarchate at Alexandria; he died in Alexandria, 1895.

Inf. T. D. Mosconas (son).

MOSS, Robert Johnson (1838-1921)
British businessman; he was born in Liverpool, 30 June 1838, son of William Miles M., steamship owner, and Esther Johnson; he was educated in England and Vevey, Switzerland and then apprenticed to a cotton brokers in Liverpool; in 1860 he went to Alexandria as a cotton broker and in 1861 formed R. J. Moss and Co.; as well as cotton, he engaged in the coal trade and in 1871 took over his father's steamship line; President of the British Chamber of Commerce, 1907-8; during the 1890s the British Museum purchased several important collections of antiquities from his company, and it would appear that he acted as an agent for Budge (q.v.), purchasing and storing objects selected by Budge which the Museum could not immediately

afford and then shipping them when finances became available; his company also handled the shipment of antiquities purchased by Budge from other sources; he died in Alexandria, 17 June 1921.

A. Wright, *Twentieth Century Impressions of Egypt* (London, 1909), 326; BM records; FO.

MOSS, Rosalind Louisa Beaufort (1890-1990)
British Egyptologist and bibliographer; she was born in Shrewsbury, 21 Sept. 1890, daughter of the Revd Henry Whitehead M., Headmaster of Shrewsbury School and Mary Beaufort; she was educated at Heathfield School, Ascot and at St. Anne's College, Oxford where she studied anthropology; Diploma, 1917; BSc, 1922; author of *The Life after Death in Oceania and the Malay Archipelago*, 1925; she took up Egyptology in 1917 and became a pupil of Griffith (q.v.); at his encouragement she became editor of *The Topographical Bibliography of Ancient Egyptian Hieroglyphic Texts, Reliefs, and Paintings* in 1924 with B. Porter (q.v.); she travelled extensively visiting museums and sites with her later assistant Ethel Burney (q.v.); she edited Vols. I-VII, 1927-51 and the second edition of Vols. I-II, 1960-72 of the *Bibliography* and collected material for future volumes up to her retirement in 1970; FSA, 1949; Hon. DLitt from Oxford, 1961; Hon. Fellow, St. Anne's College, Oxford, 1967; a volume of tributes was prepared in her memory, T. G. H. James and J. Malek, *A Dedicated Life,* 1990; she died in Ewell, Surrey, 22 April 1990.

JEA 77 (1991), 150-5 (T. G. H. James) (portr.); *The Times* 27 April 1990; *The Independent* 26 April 1990 (J. Malek); T. G. H. James and J. Malek, *A Dedicated Life*, 1990, 107-8 (bibl.); *ODNB* 39, 480.

MOURSI, Mohamed I. (*d.*1994)
Egyptian Egyptologist; he studied archaeology in the Faculty of Art, Cairo University from 1954 and at the University of Munich under H. W. Müller (q.v.); he then taught at the University of Cairo to which he left his library; apart from articles, he published *Die Hohenpriester des Sonnengottes von der Frühzeit Ägyptens bis zum Ende des Neuen Reiches*, 1972 and, with others, *Denkmäler der Oase Dachla*, 1982; he died in 1994.

Bulletin of the Egyptian Museum 4 (2007), 9-11 (T. Handoussa) (portr.) (bibl.).

MOUSSA, Ahmed Mahmoud (1934-1998)
Egyptian Egyptologist and archaeologist; he was born at Damietta, 15 Aug. 1934; he was educated at the University of Cairo (BA in Egyptology) and at Eötvos Lorand University in Budapest; PhD, 1995; he joined the Egyptian Antiquities Service and served as inspector at various locations, notably at Tomas during the Nubian rescue campaign in 1964, Atfih, Abu Roash, Bahria, Heliopolis and Dahshur; he was best known for his work at Saqqara of which site, together with Giza, he became Director-General; he excavated several important tombs in the Unas causeway, 1964-72 and the Valley Temple of Unas, 1971-80; he later was appointed Director-General of the Permanent Committee of Egyptology; apart from articles in *SAK*, *MDAIK*, and *ASAE*, he published *The Tomb of Nefer and Ka-hay*, with H. Altenmüller, 1971; *Two Tombs of Craftsmen*, with F. Junge, 1975; *Das Grab des Nianchchnum and Chnumhotep*, with H. Altenmüller, 1977; and *Le temple d'accueil du complexe funéraire du rou Ounas*, with A. Labrousse, 1996; *La Chaussée du complex funéraire du roi Ounas*, with A. Labrousse, 2002; he died at Giza, 26 Nov. 1998.

Rev d'ég 51 (2000), 5-8 (portr.) (bibl.) (M. El-Ghandour).

MUELLER, Dieter (1935-1977)
German Egyptologist; he was born at Ruhla, 20 Jan. 1935, son of Edmund Müller and Johanna Gentsch; he was educated at Altenburg and Ohrdruf and then studied classical philology and Egyptology at the University of Leipzig under Morenz (q.v.), 1953-8; he was assistant at the Egyptological Institute at Leipzig, 1958-60; PhD, 1960; assistant at the Egyptological Seminar at Göttingen, 1960-5, and assistant at Würzburg, 1965-6; he then taught German for the Goethe Institute, 1966-8; he emigrated to America in 1968 and joined the staff of the Southern Methodist University, Dallas, Texas, 1968-70 and later was Associate Professor of History at the University of Lethbridge in Alberta, Canada; his interests were Egyptian religion and philology; he published his doctoral thesis *Ägypten und die griechischen Isis-Aretalogien*, 1960 and left *A Concise Introduction to Middle Egyptian Grammar*, 1975 in manuscript; he also reviewed extensively; his promising career was tragically cut short when he was killed in Lethbridge, 19 Feb. 1977.

Inf. C. Müller; *ARCE Newsletter* 101/2 (1977), 1-2 (L. Lesko).

MUHAMMED, Muhammed Abdul-Qader (1920-1985)
Egyptian Egyptologist; he was born Cairo, 13 July 1920, son of Muhammed Mamun; he gained his baccalaureate in 1937 and then studied at the Faculty of Arts, Cairo University; BA in English, 1942; he then joined the Institute of Archaeology, obtaining his diploma in 1945; in 1946 he was appointed an inspector in the Dept. of Antiquities; he studied at the University of Cambridge under Glanville (q.v.) and later Emery (q.v.), 1951-57; PhD, 1957; he was appointed Chief Inspector of Luxor, 1958 and later of Middle, and of Lower, Egypt; he undertook excavations at Luxor and Karnak and cleared the tomb of Kyky at Thebes; in 1964 he became Associate Professor at the Department of Archaeology at Cairo University; Professor of Archaeology, 1970; in 1977 he was appointed President of the Egyptian Antiquities Organization; in 1978 he was made Dean of the Faculty of Arts in Mansura until 1980; apart from articles in ASAE on his excavations, his thesis was published as *The Development of the Funerary Beliefs and Practices displayed in the Private Tombs of the New Kingdom at Thebes*, 1966; he died 20 Feb. 1985.

ASAE 66 (1987), 121; *ASAE* 70 (1984-5), 447-8 (portr.) (M. Mostafa); inf. from Cambridge University.

MÜLLER, Hans Wolfgang (1907-1991)
German Egyptologist; he was born in Magdeburg, 16 Aug. 1907, son of Johannes M., a clergyman, and Maria Luise Schröder; he became interested in ancient Egypt when sorting a collection of photographs of the Near East belonging to a local newspaper the *Magdeburger Feuerversicherung*; from 1926 he studied archaeology, art history, and Egyptology at Göttingen under Kees (q.v.), Berlin under Sethe (q.v.), and Munich under Spiegelberg (q.v.); PhD, 1932 with the thesis *Die Totendenksteine des Mittleren Reich*; he was attached to the Berlin Museum, 1931-7; in 1933-5 he toured the Levant on a fellowship from the Deutsches Archäologisches Institut; in 1937 he accompanied the photographer Richard Hamann to Egypt and the results formed the Egyptian section of the photographic collection of Marburg University; he was dismissed from his post in 1937 because of his non-Aryan wife and obtained employment in an architectural office; he served as an interpreter in North Africa, Italy, and Hungary in World War II; he was awarded his habilitation in 1946 for his monograph on the Middle Kingdom tombs of the nomarchs at Aswan; he was appointed reader at Munich University, 1947, Professor 1947, ord. Professor and Director of the Munich Egyptian Collection, 1958-75; he was the editor of *Ägyptologische Forschungen* from 1961 and the founder and editor of the *Münchner Ägyptologische Studien* from 1962; he was the organizer of the exhibitions *5000 Jahre ägyptische Kunst*, 1960-1 and *Nofretete-Echnaton*, 1976-7; he visited Egypt again in 1966 and was the initiator of the Munich excavations at Minshat Abu Omar which began in 1977; he was a committee member of the Deutsches Archäologisches Institut and a member of the Bavarian Academy; he was an adviser to the Metropolitan Museum of Art, New York; his primary interest was in Egyptian art history and he put together an extensive photographic collection which was acquired by the Library of Heidelberg University in 1986; he published over ninety monographs, articles, and reviews; his principal works were *Die Felsengraber der Fürsten von Elephantine aus der Zeit des Mittleren Reiches*, 1940; *Alt-Ägyptische Malerei, Meisterwerke aussereuropäischer Malerei*, 1959; *Die Sammlung Wilhelm Esch, Duisburg*, 1961; *Ägyptische Kunstwerke, Kleinfunde und Glas in der Sammlung E. und M. Kofler-Truniger*, 1964; *Der Isiskult im antiken Benevent und Katalog der Skulpturen aus den ägyptischen Heiligtümern im Museo del Sannio zu Benevent*, 1969; *Ägyptische Kunst, Monumente alter Kulturen*, 1970; with others, *Die Ägyptische Sammlung des Bayerischen Staates*, 1966; with others, *Staatliche Sammlung Ägyptischer Kunst in der Münchner Residenz am Hofgarten, München*, 1970 and later editions 1972, 1976; *Il Culto di Iside nell'Antica Benevento*, 1971; with S. Lloyd, *Ägypten und Vorderasien*, 1987; *Der Waffenfund von Balâta-Sichem und die Sichelschwerter*, 1987, and *Der "Armreif" des Konigs Ahmose und der Handgelenkschutz des Bogenschutzen im alten Ägypten und Vorderasien*, 1989; he left a volume on Egyptian goldsmiths' work in manuscript, posth. published as *Die Schätze der Pharaonen*, 1998; English ed., *The Royal Gold of Ancient Egypt*, 1999; his photographic collection is available on microfiche; *SAK* 6 (1978) was a Festschrift in his honour by twenty authors; he died in Starnberg, 6 Feb. 1991.

NDB 8, 401-3; *Süddeutsche Zeitung* 9-10 Feb. 1991 (D. Schmidt); *ZÄS* 119 (1992), I-VII (P. Munro) (portr.) (bibl. since 1977); *Jahrbuch der Bayerischen Akademie der Wissenschaften* 1991, 1-7 (J. Leclant) (portr.); *SÄK* 6 (1978), IX-XVI (bibl. to 1977).

MÜLLER, Wilhelm Max (1862-1919)
German-American orientalist; born at Gleissenberg, Bavaria, 15 May 1862, son of Friedrich Justus M., a Sanskrit scholar, and Pauline Barthel; he was a grandson of the poet Wilhelm M. who travelled to Egypt with von Sack (q.v.); he studied at the Universities of Erlangen, Leipzig, Berlin where he was a pupil of Erman (q.v.), and

Munich; PhD; he is said to have been an able Greek and Hebrew scholar, but his fame today rests mainly on his Egyptological works; he emigrated to the USA, 1888, and married Bettie Caspar, 1889; he was appointed Professor of Ancient Languages and Old and New Testament Exegesis at the R.E. Seminary, Philadelphia, 1890-1919; was also assistant Professor of Egyptology in the University of Pennsylvania; most of his large publications were Egyptological, *Asien und Europa nach altägyptischen Denkmälern*, 1893, his first book and also the first authoritative study in this branch of history; *Die Liebespoesie der alten Ägypter*, 1899, Egyptian poems from hieroglyphic and demotic texts; he was sent to Egypt three times by the Carnegie Institute, 1904, 1906, 1910; his results were published in *Egyptological Researches*, 2 vols. 1906, 1910, and vol. 3, ed. H. F. Lutz, 1920; *Egyptian Mythology*, 1918; Müller also wrote articles in journals and contributed various entries to the *Encyclopaedia Biblica*, the *Jewish Encyclopaedia* and revisions of Gesenius' *Hebrew Dictionary*; he was drowned while swimming alone at Wildwood, NJ, 12 July 1919.

DAB 13, 320-1; *WWW* ii, 758-9; *Unsere Zeitgenossen.Wer ist's?*, 7th ed., 1914.

MUNIER, (Adolphe) Henri (1884-1945)
French Coptologist and bibliographer; he was born at Meursault, 12 July 1884, son of Jules M. and Rose Mourès; he became Librarian of Cairo Museum, 1908-25, and succeeded Cattaui Bey as Secretary of the Soc. Royale de Géographie de l'Égypte, 1925-45; he published many articles in journals mainly devoted to Coptic texts and the subject of early Christianity in Egypt; he wrote, *Manuscrits Coptes, Cairo Cat.*, 1916; *Catalogue de la Bibliothèque du Musée Égyptien*, 1928; *L'Égypte Byzantine de Dioclétien à la conquête Arabe*, in Zaky el-Ibrachi's *Precis History*, 1932; *Recueil des listes épiscopales de l'Église Copte*, 1943; he died in Cairo, 20 Aug. 1945.

ASAE 48 (1948), 285-98 (portr. and bibl.) (J. E. Goby); *Bull. Soc. Roy. Géogr.* 21, 313; *The Coptic Encyclopedia* 6, 1698 (A. S. Ayiya).

MUNRO, Peter (1930-2009)
German Egyptologist of Scottish origin; he was born in Hamburg, 8 Jan. 1930; he studied Egyptology and classical archaeology at the Universities of Hamburg under Otto (q.v.), Göttingen and Cairo; PhD. Hamburg, 1957; Habilation in Munich under H. W. Müller (q.v.), 1967; he became a lecturer at the Goethe Institute, 1957-60 and was attached to the University of Munich, 1963-5; he also taught at Ain Shams University, 1963-7; he became director of the Kestner Museum in Hanover, 1970-81 and then Professor of Egyptology at the Free University of Berlin, 1982-95 where he taught Egyptian Art and Archaeology; he arranged the Tutankhamun exhibition in Hanover, 1981; he also undertook excavations at Saqqara around the Unas causeway; he published *Die spätägyptichen Totenstelen*, 1973 and *Der Unas-Friedhof Nord-West* I, 1993; he died in Hanover, 2 Jan. 2009.

Inf. C. Loeben; *ZÄS* 139 (2012), I-VII (bibl.) (portr.) (C. Loeben)

MURCH, (*Revd*) Chauncey (1856-1907)
American missionary and collector; he was born in W. Alexander, Pa., 1 Jan. 1856, son of James M. and Mary Ann Strain; educated Muskingum College; BA, 1876; MA, 1879; after attending various theological seminaries he was sent to Egypt in Oct. 1883 by the United Presbyterian Board of Foreign Missions; while in Egypt, and espec. at Luxor, he formed a collection of antiquities; the large series of scarabs in this was acquired by the British Museum in 1906; all the other items went to the Metropolitan Museum of Art, New York in 1910, a description of them being published by A. C. Mace in 1911; the Art Institute of Chicago bought a collection of scarabs from Murch in 1894; he was very helpful to European travellers and collectors in Egypt, and he negotiated the British Museum's payments for many antiquities and Coptic and Greek MSS obtained in Egypt by Budge (q.v.); he died in Aswan, 15 Oct. 1907.

Andrews Diary; Budge, *N. & T.* i, 87, 135, 411; ii, 33, 148, 154, 341, 347; *WWWA* i. 881.

MURE, William (1799-1860)
British classical scholar; he was born in Caldwell, Ayrshire, 9 July 1799, son of William M. of Caldwell and Anne Hunter Blair; he was educated at Edinburgh and Bonn; he visited Italy and Greece, 1838, and published a large work on Greek language and literature, 1850-7; he was an opponent of Champollion whom he criticized in a work entitled, *Brief Remarks on the Chronology of the Egyptian Dynasties. Shewing the fallacy of the system laid down by Messrs. Champollion, in two letters on the Museum of Turin*, 1829; he also wrote *A Dissertation on the Calendar and Zodiac of ancient Egypt: with Remarks on the first introduction and use of the Zodiac among the Greeks*, 1832; he died in Kensington Palace Gardens, 1 April 1860.

ODNB 39, 823; *DNB* 39, 330; Hilmy, ii, 53.

MURNANE, William Joseph (1945-2000)
American Egyptologist; he was born at White Plains, New York, 22 March 1945, son of William Joseph M.; he was brought up in Venezuela and educated at St. Anselm College, New Hampshire and the University of Chicago; MA; PhD, 1973; he joined the Chicago Epigraphic Survey in Luxor in 1972 as junior epigrapher and later became senior epigrapher and deputy director to 1986; he later taught at the University of California at Berkeley in 1986; he was appointed to the Department of History, University of Memphis, 1987 and was also attached as adjunct Professor at the Institute of Egyptian Art and Archaeology from 1994; he was founder and director of the University of Memphis' Karnak Hypostyle Hall Project from 1990; he edited H. Nelson's *The Great Hypostyle Hall at Karnak*, 1981 and published *Ancient Egyptian Coregencies*, 1977; *United with Eternity: A Concise Guide to the Monuments of Medinet Habu*, 1980; *The Penguin Guide to Ancient Egypt*, 1983; *The Road to Kadesh*, 1985; 2nd ed., 1990; *The Boundary Stelae of Akhenaten*, with C. van Siclen, 1993; *Texts from the Amarna Period*, 1995; a volume of studies in his honour *Causing his Name to Live*, edited by P. J. Brand and L. Cooper, was published in 2009; he died at Memphis, Tenn., 17 Nov. 2000

IAE Internet obit; *The Guardian* 23 Jan 2001 (N. Studwick); *SSEA Newsletter* April 2001, 3 (P. Brand); *PAM* 13 (2001), 9-10 (portr.) (Z. Szafranski); *KMT* 12/1 (2001), 4-66 (L. Corcoran); L. Corcoran in P. J. Brand and L. Cooper, *Causing his Name to Live*, 2009, 5-7.

MURRAY, (*Hon. Sir*) **Charles Augustus** (1806-1895)
British diplomat; he was born in London, 22 Nov. 1806, 2nd son of George M. the 5th Earl of Dunmore and Lady Susan Hamilton; he was educated Eton and Oriel College, Oxford; Fellow of All Souls College, 1827; MA, 1837; called to the Bar, Lincoln's Inn, 1827; Secretary Brit. legation, Naples, 1844; Consul-General in Egypt, 1846-53; he was afterwards in the diplomatic service in other countries; CB, 1848; KCB, 1866; PC, 1875; Murray's name is attached to a fine funerary papyrus in the British Museum purchased in 1861 (EA 10010); he died in Paris, 3 June 1895.

ODNB 39, 877-8; *DNB* Suppl. ii, 313; Brugsch, *Mein Leben*, 152.

MURRAY, George William Welsh (1885-1966)
British surveyor and explorer; he was born in London, 9 Sept. 1885, son of George Robert Milner M., FRS, and Helen Jane Welsh; after his education at Westminster School, 1897-1904, he joined the Survey of Egypt in 1907; he was appointed Director of Desert Surveys in 1932, and of the Topographical Survey in 1937, holding this post until 1947, after which he acted as Technical Expert to the Survey of Egypt until 1951; during the First World War he was political officer Northern Red Sea Patrol, 1915, afterwards serving with the 7th Field Survey Company, RE, in Sinai and Palestine, 1916-19; he was promoted Captain and awarded the MC; he married Edith Cairney, 1926; Murray received the Founder's Medal of the Royal Geogr. Soc. in 1936, and was elected Membre de l'Institut d'Égypte, 1938; Vice-President, 1945-7; he was President of the Cairo Scientific Soc. 1936-8 and a member of the council of the Fouad I Desert Institute, 1950; he published many reports on the Egyptian deserts in scientific journals, and wrote articles in *JEA* and the *Geographical Journal*; he also published a book *Sons of Ishmael*; he died in Aberdeen, 31 Jan. 1966.

The Times, 3 Feb. 1966; *JEA* 52 (1966), 2; *The Records of Old Westminsters* III, 1963, 276.

MURRAY, Margaret Alice (1863-1963)
British Egyptologist; she was born Calcutta, 13 July 1863, daughter of James C. M., an English businessman living in India, and Margaret Carr; she at first intended to go in for a nursing career, and in fact had to act as sister-in-charge of Calcutta General Hospital during an epidemic when only twenty-one, but abandoned this when she did not qualify in England, being too small for acceptance; she became the first full-time woman in Egyptology when she had been trained by Petrie (q.v.); she entered University College London, 1894, and studied under J. H. Walker (q.v.), F. Ll. Griffith (q.v.), and Petrie, becoming a junior lecturer in 1898; she was made lecturer 1899; Fellow of University College, 1922; Assistant Professor 1924-35; Hon. DLitt, 1931; FSA (Scot.); FRAI; she assisted Petrie in his excavations in 1902; excavated in Malta, 1921-3; megalithic remains in Minorca, 1930-1; Nabatean Remains at Petra, 1937; joined Petrie and Mackay (q.v.) at Tell Ajjul, Palestine, 1938; her other great interests were in the field of witchcraft and folklore, she was President of the Folk-Lore Society, 1953-5; she published her first article in *PSBA*, 1895; her bibliography, see below, although not complete, lists over 80 books and articles on ancient Egypt, *Guide to the Collection of Egyptian Antiquities in the Edinburgh Museum of Science and Art*, 1903; *The Osireion*, 1904; *Ancient Egyptian Legends,* 1904; *Saqqara*

Mastabas, 2 vols. 1905, 1937; *Elementary Egyptian Grammar*, 1905; *Elementary Coptic Grammar*, 1911; *The Tomb of Two Brothers*, 1910; *Index of Names and Titles in the Old Kingdom*, 1908; *Handbook of Egyptian Sculpture*, 1930; *Egyptian Temples*, 1931; *Coptic Reading Book*, 1933; *The Splendour that was Egypt*, her best-selling work, 1949; *Egyptian Religious Poetry*, 1949; *Seven Memphite tomb chapels*, with H. F. Petrie, 1952 in addition she wrote sections in Petrie's archaeological reports and was also responsible for a number of the plates in them; she published her last book, *The Genesis of Religion*, 1963, at the time of her centenary party which was held at University College London; she died in Welwyn, Herts., 13 Nov. 1963.

My First Hundred Years, autobiogr., London, 1963; *ODNB* 39, 972-3 (portr.); *AEB* 63377 for refs. to centenary; *AfO* 21 (1966), 279 (H. Brunner); *Antiquity* 146, 37 (1963), 87, 92-5; no. 149, 38 (1964), 1-4 (Glyn Daniel); *Archaeology* 17 (1964), 57 (anon.); *ASAE* 59 (1966), 1-9 (portr.) (H. S. K. Bakry); *JEA* 50 (1964), 1; *Orientalia* 33 (1964), 169 (anon.); *Folklore* 72 (1961), 560-6 (bibl. incomplete) (W. Bonser and A. J. Arkell); R. Janssen, *The First Hundred Years*, 1992, passim; M. Drower in G. Cohen and M. Joukowsky, *Breaking Ground*, 2004, 109-41; È. Gran-Aymerich, *Dictionnaire biographique d'archéologie 1798-1945*, 2001, incorporated in *Les Chercheurs de passé 1798-1945*, 2007, 1010; K. L. Sheppard, *The Life of Margaret Alice Murray. A Woman's Work in Archaeology*, 2013; K. L. Sheppard in W. Carruthers (ed.), *Histories of Egyptology*, 2015, 113-28.

MUSES, Charles Arthur (1919–2000)
American mathematician, writer and excavator; he was born in Jersey City, New Jersey, 28 April 1919, son of Maurice Joseph M. and Paulina Augusta Becker; he was educated at Columbia University; MA, 1947, PhD, 1951; he excavated at Heliopolis and Dahshur 1957 in conjunction with Sami Gabra (q.v.) and Shafik Farid (q.v.); at Dahshur, he discovered the 4th Dynasty mastaba of Ipy and the 13th Dynasty pyramid of Ameny-Qemau; he died 26 Aug. 2000.

A. Dodson, *Kmt* 8, 1997, 60-3; Dodson and N. Swelim, *MDAIK* 45, 1998): 319-34.

MUSTAPHA AGHA AYAT (d.1887)
Egyptian merchant and dealer; he was Consular Agent in Luxor for the United States, Britain from 1850, Belgium, and Russia; he had visited Europe and spoke fluent English, French, and Italian; a man of wealth and influence he conducted a considerable illicit trade in antiquities under cover of diplomatic immunity, and many important papyri and other objects are known to have passed through his hands; he carried out excavations at Thebes; he also played a hidden part in the exploitation of the cache of Royal Mummies for which he was deprived of his Belgian agency; he lived in a house built between the columns of the Temple of Luxor which was demolished after his death; he was exceedingly helpful and courteous to British travellers in Egypt, and spared no expense in entertaining them and providing for them everything they required, especially A. H. Rhind (q.v.) and Lady Duff-Gordon (q.v.); he died at an advanced age in July 1887.

Edwards, *Thousand Miles*, 2nd ed., 144, 455; Lady Duff-Gordon, *Letters*, 3rd ed., passim, esp. 190; Maspero, *Momies Royales*, 513; Myers Diary, 15, 16 Feb. 1884; Wilbour, 73 et passim (see index); H. Hopley, *Under Egyptian Palms*, 1869, 166-94; *Foreign Office Confidential Print*, 768, 113; F. Hagen and K. Ryholt, *The Antiquities Trade in Egypt 1880-1930*, 2017, 251-3; S. Weens in *Memnonia* 27 (2016), 135-47.

MUSZYNSKI, Michel (1951-1977)
Belgian demotist of Polish origins; he was born in Antwerp, 18 April 1951, son of Witold M. and Juliette Weckselman; he studied at the Université Libre de Bruxelles under Théodoridès (q.v.); licencie in history 1973, in Egyptology 1974; his thesis was a study of the Turin Judicial Papyrus, 1975; he became secretary of the Association pour les Études du droit pharonique; apart from a number of articles, he contributed to P. Pestman, *Greek and Demotic Texts from the Zenon Archive*, 1980 and *A Guide to the Zenon Archive*, 1981; in 1976-7 he was a pensionnaire at IFAO in Egypt where he was killed in a motor accident near Balat, 12 April 1977.

Priv. inf.; *BIFAO* 77 (1977), 285; *AfO* 25 (1974-7), 356.

MUYSER, (Mgr.) Jacob Louis Lambert (1896-1956)
Dutch Coptologist; he was born in The Hague, 9 May 1896, son of Jacob John Marcus Egbertus M. and Henriette Antonia Maria Beernink; he studied theology and Egyptology at Fribourg in Switzerland with Eugène Dévaud (q.v.); he went to Egypt as a missionary in 1920; he published a long list of works including *Des vases eucharistiques en verre*, 1937; he died in Rome, 16 April 1956.

BIFAO 64 (1966), 213-23 (bibl.) (G. Viaud); *Ex Oriente Lux* 14. 155-6, 8-9 (J. M. A. Janssen); *The Coptic Encyclopedia* 6, 1749 (M. L. Bierbrier and S. Nasim); G. Viaud, *Le Qommos Jacob Muyser*, 1996.

MYERS, Oliver Humphrys (1903-1966)
British archaeologist; he was born in Shoeburyness, 27 June 1903, son of Alfred Edward Cecil M., Lt-Colonel in the Artillery, and Bertha Maud Cory; he was educated at Wellington College, Berks., afterwards being engaged

in literary and theatrical work in Cambridge; in 1927 Terence Gray (q.v.) introduced him to Brunton (q.v.) then excavating at Mostagedda; as a result he went to work with Petrie (q.v.) at Tell Fara in Palestine thereby starting his career in archaeology; he did not begin his work in Egypt until 1929, in which year he began to study hieroglyphs under Gardiner (q.v.); in 1930 began the highly successful association with Mond (q.v.) at Armant for which he is best remembered; he was made Director of the excavation in 1936, the seasons being conducted until 1938; during the Second World War Myers served in the Intelligence Corps, 1941-6, in Egypt, Libya, Palestine, Syria, Lebanon and Aden, and as official co-ordinator of Intelligence under Field Marshal Wilson and General Collet; he married 1. Mary Irene Cathcart Borer, and following his divorce, 2. 1940 (Mary) Julia Theodora de la Motte; he renewed his association with the Nile Valley in 1946, teaching at Gordon College, Khartoum, and excavated at Abka near Wadi Halfa; he was visiting Professor at the Institute of Ancient Sudanese Studies, Zamalek, 1950, and worked in various countries in the Near East after 1953, afterwards being appointed Senior Lecturer in the University of Ibadan in Ife, Nigeria; he never received the recognition which was his due in England after much careful and thorough work in archaeology; he published, *The Bucheum*, 3 vols. 1934; *The Cemeteries of Armant* I, 2 vols., in which no fewer than 40 specialists were involved, 1937; *The Temples of Armant. A preliminary survey*, 2 vols. 1946; all with Sir Robert Mond; *Some Applications of Statistics to Archaeology*, 1951; his bibl. also lists 33 articles in *JEA* and various Egyptological journals, 20 more on different subjects, and four archaeological reviews; in addition he left three works in MS., *Notes on Water Supply and Rainfall, Cemeteries of Armant* II, and *Neolithic Nubians*, he died in Berkhamsted, 26 Nov. 1966.

E. J. Pinero, *De arqueologia británica en Egipto: la vida y los trabajos de Oliver Myers*, Buenos Aires, 1968 (bibl.); *JEA* 53 (1967), I; N. Lewis, *The World, The World*, 1996, 193-8

MYERS, William Joseph (1858-1899)
British army officer and collector; he was born in London, 4 Aug. 1858, son of Thomas Barron M. and Margaret Slovie Melvill, and lived at Porter's Park, Herts.; educated at Eton; Major in King's Royal Rifles; he served in the Zulu War and the Nile Expedition, being stationed in Egypt 1882-7, and was killed in action in the Boer War, at Farquars, 30 Oct. 1899; he formed a fine collection of Egyptian antiquities, with particular strengths in faience and small objects, which he bequeathed to Eton College, some other objects from it being now in the Victoria and Albert Museum and the National Museum of Scotland; other pieces were sold at Sotheby's, 15-17 July 1918; his diary in 36 vols. is preserved at Eton.

JEA 5 (1918), 145; *Eton Coll. Chron.*, no. 2394, 29 Oct. 1936, 243; Lugt 78031; C.N. Reeves, *Burlington Magazine* June 1988, 482-3; S. Spurr, C. N. Reeves, and S. Quirke, *Egyptian Art at Eton College*, 1999, 1-3.

NAGEL, Georges (1899-1956)
Swiss Egyptologist and Biblical scholar; he was born at Verrières, 22 Nov. 1899; he first studied theology at Neuchâtel; he became interested in Egyptology at that time and studied hieroglyphs under Gustave Jéquier (q.v.); he wrote a thesis on political relations between Egypt and Palestine during the period of Kings, 1924; from then on he specialized on Old Testament studies and Egyptology, going to Berlin to complete his studies under Erman (q.v.), Sethe (q.v.), and Grapow (q.v.); he later went to Paris and worked under Drioton (q.v.) and Lefebvre (q.v.), writing a doctoral thesis entitled, *Un Papyrus funéraire de la fin du Nouvel Empire*, 1929; between 1927 and 1929 and 1938 and 1939 Nagel assisted in the Institut Français excavations at Deir el-Medina where he acquired a very thorough knowledge of this necropolis, writing a report on the excavations at Deir el-Medina North in 1928, and a number of articles for *BIFAO*; he served as a minister at the church at Chaux-du-Milieu in the Haut-Jura, 1931-7, but was appointed to the chair in Hebrew and Old Testament studies at Geneva in 1937; he was administrator of the Centre d'Études orientales, 1944; a very careful and exact worker he produced a number of important studies, especially, *Céramique du Nouvel Empire à Deir el-Medineh*, 1938; *Un aspect de la religion de l'Ancienne Égypte*, 1935, dealing with the personal religious emotions shown on votive stelae of workmen in village and their links with Biblical Psalms; *Le culte du soleil dans l'ancienne Égypte, 1943; Les 'mystères' d'Osiris dans l'ancienne Égypte*, 1944; his photographs are in the Griffith Institute, Oxford; his archives including 600 photographs are in the University of Geneva; he died in Geneva, 25 Nov. 1956.

AfO 18, 1st pt. (1957), 232 (H. Brunner); *BIFAO* 58 (1958), 149-51 (P. Humbert) (portr.); 152-4 (B. Bruyère) (bibl.); *BSFE* 23 (May 1957), 4 (É. Drioton); *Chron. d'Ég.* 32 (1957), 82-3 (A. Mekhitarian); *BASOR* 144 (Dec. 1956), 7-8 (W. F. Albright); *JEA* 43 (1957), vii-viii (R. O. Faulkner); *PEQ* 88 (1956), 65-6 (anon.); M. Patanè, *Gött. Misz.* 145 (1995), 15-8; *Voyages en Égypte de l'Antiquité au début du XXe siècle*, 2003, 225 (M. Vallogia).

NAHMAN, Maurice (1868-1948)
Egyptian antiquities dealer; he was born in Cairo, 26 Jan. 1868, son of Robert Nahman Bey, banker, and Sarina Rossano; he joined the staff of the Credit Foncier Égyptien in 1884, cashier 1898, chief cashier 1908-25 when he retired; he had been interested in antiquities since a boy and in 1890 he began his career as a dealer; in 1913 he acquired the property of 27 Madebegh St. (now Sherif St.) where he displayed his antiquities and conducted business with all the major museums; his visitor's book is now in the Dept. of Egyptian Art, The Brooklyn Museum, while his correspondence is retained by the family; objects from his stock were sold at auction in Paris, 26-7 Feb. 1953; he died in Cairo, 18 March 1948; Robert Nahman, son of the above and Marie Antoinette Viola Cerra, born Cairo, 4 Jan. 1901 carried on his father's business until his death in Cairo, 7 Feb. 1954; another son Robert Viola, by Concetta Viola, became a partner of the widow of Albert Eid (q.v.).

Inf. A. Manessero (daughter) and the Brooklyn Museum; *Chron. d'Ég.* 22 (1947), 300-1; F. Hagen and K. Ryholt, *The Antiquities Trade in Egypt 1880-1930*, 2017, 253-6, 269.

NAJIB, Ahmed (*Bey*) (1847-1910)
Egyptian Egyptologist; he was born in 1847 and studied with Ahmed Kamal (q.v.) in the School of Ancient Egyptian Language founded by H. Brugsch (q.v.); he later served in the Ministry of Education and was appointed a Chief Inspector in the Antiquities Department in 1892, retiring in 1905 because of illness; he translated Brugsch's book on hieroglyphs into Arabic and published in Arabic a history of Egypt, 1895 and an account of a tour in Upper Egypt; he died in 1910.

Inf. G. Mokhtar; D. Reid, *JAOS* 105 (1985), 235-7; G. Maspero, *Rapports sur la marche du Service des Antiquités de 1899 à 1910,* 1912, 169.

NASH, David William (1811-1876)
British barrister-at-law; naturalist, and scholar; he was born in Bristol and was baptized there 21 Feb. 1811, son of William Llewellyn N., surgeon, and Catherine Evans; ALS, 1832, FLS, 1849; he was a member of the Syro-Egyptian Society, and wrote works on the Geology of Egypt, on Egyptian chronology, and on the Pharaoh of the Exodus; his library was sold at Sotheby's, 20 Jan. 1888; he died in Ben-Rhydding, Yorkshire, 16 July 1876.

Private inf. Hilmy, ii, 58.

NASH, (*Revd*) George Denis (1866-1943)
British collector; he was born in Ireland, 11 May 1866, son of Thomas James N. of Rockfield, Tullig House, co. Cork and Seamount, Howth and Finnstown, co. Dublin and Juliet Isabella Grainger; he was educated at Trinity College, Dublin BA, 1890; MA, 1893; BD, 1894; vicar of St. Jude's Dublin 1900-5; Assistant Chaplain, Mountjoy Prison, Dublin, 1908; married 1. Lily (d.8 Feb. 1936) widow of J. D. Bradshaw, 2. 11 Feb. 1939, Amy

Lilian Bennet (d. 9 Feb. 1958); he formed a large collection of antiquities being advised by Shorter (q.v.) and Golenischeff (q.v.) among others; following the death of his widow this collection was sold through Spink in 1959 and 1960, a proportion being acquired by the British Museum (EA 1818-20, 65800-65964, 66071-66100, 66107-66202) including the Nash ostraca published by Gardiner and Černý in *Hieratic Ostraca*, 1957; he died at Hollywood, Los Angeles, California, 29 June 1943 (bur. Dublin).

Inf. from Mrs. R. Rosbottom, grandniece; *Burke's Irish Family Records*, 876; *Crockford's Clerical Directory.*

NASH, Walter Llewellyn (1842-1920)

British medical practitioner in Hong Kong; he was born in London, 26 Oct. 1842, son of David William N. (q.v.) and Helen Frances Fowler; on retirement he took a great interest in ancient Egypt and visited Egypt several times; he often bought antiquities at sales and made up small collections which he sold; many of his own objects he published in *PSBA*; in 1898 he succeeded W. H. Rylands (q.v.) as secretary of SBA and remained in office until the Society was merged in the R. Asiatic Soc.; a small Coptic papyrus, now at Cambridge, bears his name; some of his antiquities were bought by the British Museum after his death; FSA, 1895-1918; he died in London, 8 April 1920.

Inf. P. E. Newberry.

NAUS, (*Bey*) Henri Jules Edgard (1875-1938)

Belgian official and administrator in Egypt; he was born in Hasselt, 27 March 1875, son of (Joseph) Henri Louis Martin N. and Marie Rosalie Rombouts; he held many important administrative posts in Egypt; President of the Fondation Égyptologique Reine Élisabeth, Brussels; he died in Brussels, 22 Sept. 1938.

Chron. d'Ég. 14, 5 (portr.).

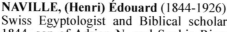

NAVILLE, (Henri) Édouard (1844-1926)

Swiss Egyptologist and Biblical scholar; he was born in Geneva, 14 June 1844, son of Adrien N. and Sophia Rigaud; he prepared himself for his work with unusual thoroughness, being educated at the University of Geneva, King's College, London, and the Universities of Bonn, Paris, and Berlin, 1865-8; he first worked entirely on the philological side and first visited Egypt in 1865, when he copied the Horus texts at Edfu; he studied under Lepsius (q.v.) and was his literary executor, bringing out the 5 vols. of notes to the *Denkmäler* with Borchardt (q.v.), Sethe (q.v.), and other helpers; as a captain in the Swiss army during the Franco-Prussian war he helped to escort prisoners of Bourbaki's army into Switzerland after their defeat by von Werder near Dijon, 1870-1; he next worked on the solar texts and the Book of the Dead, publishing important works in these fields, and later, with Schiaparelli (q.v.), helped Lefébure (q.v.) on the publication of the tomb of Sety I at Thebes; he was the first excavator of the EEF and had already acquired a European reputation when he was invited to dig for the newly founded Society in 1882; he excavated at Tell el-Maskhuta, 1883, the report for this work establishing the format for future publications of this type; he excavated and explored the Wadi Tumilat, 1885-6, the area at the west end of which he identified as the Biblical land of Goshen; excavated at Bubastis, 1886-9; from here and other sites Naville brought back among other objects the colossal granite head of Amenemhat III now in the British Museum (EA 1063), and huge columns and Hathor-capitals which went to Cairo, London, and museums such as Boston in America; excavated at Tell el-Yahudiya, 1887, Saft el-Hinna, 1887, Ahnas (Herakleopolis), 1890-1, Mendes and Tell Mukdam, 1892, in all about 10 Delta sites; he next went to Upper Egypt to excavate Deir el-Bahari, 1893-6, helped by D. G. Hogarth (q.v.), Somers Clarke (q.v.), and H. Carter (q.v.); returning to the field some years later he cleared the Menthuhotep temple with H. R. Hall (q.v.), 1903-7; Naville had been brought up in the old-fashioned school of Mariette (q.v.) and Maspero (q.v.) and liked to work on great temples and large monuments, unlike Petrie (q.v.), but he did make a further examination of the royal necropolis at Abydos, 1910; his last great piece of field-work was the excavation of the Osireion, with G. A. Wainwright (q.v.) and Capt. Gibson, which was left unfinished at the outbreak of war in 1914; he married Marguerite, daughter of Count Alexandre de Pourtalès, 1873, a talented artist who executed the plates for most of his publications; she died 14 Dec. 1930; during his long life he acquired many hons. and distinctions; DCL; LLD; PhD; DLitt; DTheol; Hon. FSA; Fellow of King's Coll. London; for. Assoc. Institute of France; member hist.-philos. class of the Videnskabs - Selskabet of Christiana; For. Member Budapest Acad.; Acad. Vienna; Corr. Acad. of Hist. Madrid; Hon. Member Inter. Comm. Red Cross; Hon. Knight of Grace of Order of St. John of Jerusalem; Commander of the Crown of Italy; Officer Légion d'honneur; Knight of the Red Eagle, Prussia and Polar Star, Sweden; Hon. Prof. University of Geneva; Naville firmly opposed the Berlin School on their views of the Semitic aspect of Egyptian language; he possessed a formidable intelligence and could argue his case extremely effectively; he has been proved right in some controversies such as that with Sethe (q.v.) on the Tuthmoside succession, and his theories on the Exodus and its route still remain fundamental in this subject; he published innumerable articles and reviews in many journals, his principal books being, *Textes relatifs au mythe d'Horus, recueillis dans le temple d'Edfou*, 1870; *La litanie du soleil: inscriptions recueillies dans les tombeaux des rois à Thèbes*, 1875; *Inscription historique de Pinodjem III*, 1883; *Les quatre stèles orientées du Musée de Marseille*, 1880; *The store-city of Pithom and the route of the Exodus*, 1885, and later eds.; *Das aegyptische Todtenbuch der 18. bis 20. Dynastie ...*, fol. 3 vols., 1 vol. text, 1886, a vast project involving hundreds of plates of drawings; *The shrine of Saft el Henneh and the land of Goshen*, *1885*, 1887; *The historical results of the excavations at Bubastis*, 1889; *The Mound of the Jew and the city of Onias. Belbeis, Samanood, Abusir, Tukh el Karmus. 1887*, 1890; *Bubastis, 1887-1889*, 1891; *The route of the Exodus*, 1891; *The Festival-Hall of Osorkon II in the Great Temple of Bubastis, 1887-89*, 1892; *Ahnas el Medineh (Heracleopolis Magna). With chapters on Mendes, the nome of Thoth, and Leontopolis*, 1894; *The Temple of Deir el Bahari, Introductory Memoir*, 1894; *The Temple of Deir el Bahari*, royal fol., 6 vols. 1895-1908; with G. Legrain, *L'Aile nord du pylône d'Aménophis III à Karnak, Les Bas-reliefs*, 1902; *La religion des anciens Égyptiens*, 1906; *The XIth Dynasty Temple at Deir el-Bahari*, 3 vols., with H. R. Hall and others, 1907-13; *Le papyrus hiéroglyphique de Kamara et le papyrus hiératique de Nesikhonsou au Musée du Caire*, 1912; *Archaeology of the Old Testament*, 1913; *The Cemeteries of Abydos*, pt. 1, with T. E. Peet, H. R. Hall, and K. Haddon, 1914; *Le papyrus hiératique de Katseshni au Musée du Caire*, 1914; The Schweich Lectures, *The Text of the Old Testament*, 1916; *L'évolution de la langue égyptienne et les langues sémitiques*, 1920; *The Law of Moses*, 1920; *La haute critique dans le Pentateuque*, 1921; *Le Deutéronome, un livre mosaïque*, 1924; *L'écriture égyptienne: essai sur l'origine et la formation de l'une des premières écritures méditerranéennes*, 1926; *Détails relevés dans les ruines de quelques temples égyptiens ...*, posth. on Abydos, Bahbit el-Higara and Samannud, completed from his notes by Jéquier and notes by M. Naville, 1930; *Papyrus funéraires de la XXᵉ Dynastie*, 2 vols.; he also wrote chapters in *The tomb of Hâtshopsîtsû*, 1906, and *The Funeral Papyrus of Iouiya*, 1908, by T. M. Davis; completed the trans. and commentary in *The Book of the Dead* of Renouf, see Renouf's *Life-Work*, vol. 4, 1907; *Voyage en Égypte (1868-1869)*, ed. J Chappaz, 2012; his correspondence is in the library of Geneva; he died in Malagny, nr. Geneva, 17 Oct. 1926.

BIÉ 9 (1927), 134-5 (H. Gauthier); *Chron. d'Ég.* 3 (1926), 39-41; *CRAIBL* 1926, 246-9 (J. B. Chabot); *JEA* 13 (1927), 1-6 (portr.) (H. R. Hall); *JRAS* 1927, 407-9 (A. M. Blackman); *Rev. Arch.* 25 (1927), 216 (S. Reinach); *Syria* 7 (1926), 421 (R. Dussaud); Hilmy, ii, 58; *WWW* ii, 770; Wilson, 106-7, 109, 110-11, 184-7, 191, 226; E. Endesfelder, Die *Ägyptologie an der Berliner Universität-Zur Geschichte eines Fachgebietes*, 1988, 13-4; D. van Berchem, *L'Égyptologue genevois Édouard Naville*, 1989; È. Gran-Aymerich, *Dictionnaire biographique d'archéologie 1798-1945*, 2001, incorporated in *Les Chercheurs de passé 1798-1945*, 2007, 1013-4; *Voyages en Égypte de l'Antiquité au début du XXe siècle*, 2003, 222-4 (M. Vallogia); D. Maurice-Naville, L. Naville and C. Eggly-Naville, *La Plume, Le Pinceau, La Prière. L'Égyptologue Marguerite Naville (1852-1930)*, 2014; H. Virenque in N. Cooke and V. Daubney, *Every Traveller Needs a Compass*, 2015, 189-96.

NEEDHAM, John Turberville (1713-1781)
British Roman Catholic priest and scientist; he was born in London, 10 Sept. 1713, son of John T. of Hilston and Martha Lucas; he was educated at Douai and became a priest in 1738; he was appointed the director of a literary society in Brussels, later Académie Impériale et Royale des Sciences et Belles-Lettres. 1768-80; he published learned works on a great variety of subjects, and attempted to prove the identity of Egyptian hieroglyphic and Chinese writing; FRS, 1747; FSA; he died in Brussels, 30 Dec. 1781.

ODNB 40, 327-8; *DNB* 40, 157-9; *BIFAO* 5 (1906), 82; *Griffith Studies*, 467; Hilmy, ii, 61.

NEEDLER, Winifred Ellen (1904-1987)
Canadian Egyptologist; she was born in Weimar, Germany, 14 June 1904, daughter of George Henry N., Professor of German at the University of Toronto, and Mary Winifred Chisholm; she studied at the University of Toronto, 1921-26, graduating with a BA with honours in Modern Languages and Philosophy in 1926, the Ontario College of Art for one year, and the School of Fine Arts and Crafts in Boston, 1928-30; she worked as a commercial artist until she joined the staff of the Royal Ontario Museum of Archaeology as a draughtsman/cataloguer, 1935; she concentrated on the Egyptian collection and in 1938-9 spent a year on a fellowship at Yale University studying Egyptian with Bull (q.v.); she devoted herself to identifying and classifying the Egyptian collection and was especially interested in predynastic and early dynastic antiquities; in 1947 she was appointed Deputy Keeper of the Near Eastern Department and became Keeper in 1951; on the division of the department in 1966 she became Curator of Egyptian Antiquities until 1970; on her retirement she was designated Curator Emeritus; Special Lecturer in the Department of Fine Art, University of Toronto, 1953-65 and from l965-70 Associate Professor in the Department of Near Eastern Studies, University of Toronto; in 1947-48 she was in Egypt with Amice Calverley (q.v.) at Abydos and excavated at Jericho in 1956, during which time she visited Egypt, Syria, Iraq, and European museums, and at Buhen in 1962-3; she was awarded a MA from the University of Toronto, 1961 and the degree

of Doctor of Civil Law *honoris causa* at Bishop's University, 1982; she published many articles on objects in the Toronto collection and museum guides; her chief monograph was *Predynastic and Archaic Egypt in The Brooklyn Museum*. 1984; she died in Toronto, 5 Sept. 1987.

JARCE 25 (1988), 1 (R. J. Williams); inf. S. Katary.

NEILSON, Elmer Montgomerie (1874-1958)
British archaeologist; he was born in Edinburgh, 7 Dec. 1874, son of Matthew Montgomerie N., traveller and sportsman, and Mary Isobel Katherine Brody; he later lived in Bedford, Totnes and finally at 'Evelaw', Chudleigh, Devon, and was involved in archaeological work in Exeter; he worked with Petrie (q.v.) in Egypt notably at Abydos in 1921-2; he donated a fragment of a mummy-mask from this site to the Royal Albert Memorial Museum, Exeter, in 1936 (inv. no. 1936.22); his wife Edith Emily Lord died aged 72 in 1938 and his son, Somerville, was killed in action in 1917; he died in Chudleigh, Devon, 29 March 1958.

F. Petrie, *The Tombs of the Courtiers and Oxyrhynkhos*, 1925, 1; inf. A. Dodson.

NELSON, Harold Hayden (1878-1954)
American Egyptologist; born New Orleans, 25 Nov. 1878, son of Aaron N. and Anna Louisa Berry; he took his first degree at Chicago University, 1901; later studied under Breasted, PhD, 1913; he began teaching at the American University in Beirut in 1904 and published his thesis under the title *The Battle of Megiddo*, 1921; in 1924 he became Professor of History and Chairman of the Dept. of History; he was Field Director of the Oriental Institute Epigraphic and Architectural Survey at Luxor, 1924-47 and acting Director of the Oriental Institute, 1942-3; he was appointed a Notable of Egypt by the Egyptian Government for services rendered; he married Lizzie Augusta Bull who died in 1952; his most important work was concerned with the recording of Medinet Habu and he was co-author of *Medinet Habu 1924-28*, 1929; *Medinet Habu Reports*, 1931; *Work in Western Thebes*, 1931-3; he also wrote articles including, *Three Decrees of Ramses III from Karnak*, 1936; *The Identity of Amon-Re of United-with-Eternity*, 1942; *The Naval Battle pictured at Medinet Habu*, 1943 and *The Great Hypostyle Hall at Karnak*, edited by W. J. Murnane, 1981; he died in Chicago, 24 Jan. 1954.

JEA 40 (1954), 2 (R. O. Faulkner); *JNES* 13 (1954), 119 (J. A. Wilson); *WWA* 3,634.

NEROUTSOS, Tassos Demetrios (*Bey*) (1826-1892)
Greek doctor; he was born in Athens in 1826 and settled in Alexandria; he was appointed a member of the Institut Égyptien 1865; in 1879 he became President of Intendance générale sanitaire d'Égypte; he was a competent philologist and recorded archaeological discoveries in Alexandria in several publications and articles including *Archaeological Discoveries in Egypt and Revelations exposed in short*, 1873; *Notice sur les fouilles récentes exécutées à Alexandrie*, 1875, and *L'ancienne Alexandrie*, 1881; he died on 10 Aug. 1892.

Inf V. Chrysikopoulos.

NEUGEBAUER, Otto Eduard (1899-1990)
Austrian-American mathematician; he was born at Innsbruck, Austria on 26 May 1899, son of Rudolf N., a railway construction engineer; he was educated at the Akademisches Gymnasium in Graz and served briefly in World War I, 1917-8; he then studied at the University of Graz, 1919-21; the University of Munich, 1921-2, and the Mathematisches Institut of the University of Göttingen, 1922-7 where he studied under Sethe (q.v.); he became an assistant at the Institut, 1923; special assistant and librarian, 1924; PhD, 1925; Habilitation, 1927; lecturer, 1927; chief assistant, 1930; extraordinarius Professor, 1932; he was dismissed in 1933; he obtained an appointment at the University of Copenhagen, 1934 and became Professor in the Mathematics Dept., Brown University, 1939-69; he was awarded honorary degrees, D. Laws, St. Andrews, 1938; DSc, Princeton, 1957; DSc, Brown, 1971; he was a member of the American Philosophical Society, 1947; the American Academy of Arts and Sciences, the British Academy, Académie des Inscriptions et Belles-Lettres, the Royal Danish Academy, the Royal Belgian Academy, and the Austrian and Irish Academies; his special interest was the history of mathematics and astronomy in ancient Egypt and Mesopotamia although he wrote also on Arabic, Byzantine, and Ethiopic mathematics and calendars; his principal publications concerning Egyptology were his thesis *Die Grundlagen der ägyptischen Bruchrechnung*, 1926; *Vorgriechische Mathematik*, 1934; *The Exact Sciences in Antiquity*, 1952, 2nd ed. 1957; *Egyptian Astronomical Texts* 1-3 (with R. A. Parker), 1960-69; *Egyptian Astronomy*, 1975; in 1984, after his retirement, he was attached to the Institute for Advanced Study in Princeton and died in Lawrenceville, New Jersey, 19 Feb. 1990.

AfO 36/37 (1989/90), 199-200 (H. Hunger) (portr.); *Proceedings of the American Philosophical Society* 137 (1993), 139-165 (N. Swerdlow); *Centaurus* 22 (1979), 257-80 (J. Sachs and G. Toomer), (bibl.); *Journal for the History of Astronomy* 24 (1993), 289-99 (portr.) (N. Swerdlow); R. Krauss, *ZÄS* 144 (2017), 65-85.

NEWBERRY, Essie Winifred (*née* Johnston) (1878-1953)
The wife of P. E. Newberry (q.v.); she was born at Higher Bebington, Cheshire, 30 Sept. 1878, daughter of William Munn Johnston, steamship owner, and Kate Christie; she married P. E. Newberry 12 Feb. 1907; she was a member of the EES from 1920 until her death; she undertook the conservation of the pall of Tutankhamun after its discovery by Howard Carter in 1923; she presented her husband's library to the British Museum, the Edwards Library at University College London, and the Library of Egyptology, Cambridge University; she died in Guildford, Surrey, 21 Feb. 1953.

EES *Report 1953*, 5 (I. E. S. Edwards).

NEWBERRY, John Ernest (1862-1950)
British architect; he was the elder brother of P. E. Newberry (q.v.); he was born Islington, London, 18 March 1862; he visited Egypt in 1881 and again in 1890-3 as draughtsman and assistant to his brother at Beni Hasan, and to Naville (q.v.) at Deir el-Bahri; FRIBA; he died in Ilford, Essex, 28 Dec. 1950.

Newberry Corr.

NEWBERRY, Percy Edward (1868-1949)
British Egyptologist and botanist; he was born in Islington, London, 23 April 1868, son of Henry James N., warehouseman, and Caroline Wyatt; he was educated at King's College School and King's Coll., London, MA; OBE; he studied botany and archaeology and assisted R. S. Poole (q.v.) with the secretarial work of the EEF during its early days, 1884-6; because of his botanical knowledge he was able to be of assistance to Petrie (q.v.) and contributed chapters to *Hawara*, 1889, and *Kahun*, 1890; his first independent work came when he was appointed to take charge of the Archaeological Survey expedition at Beni Hasan and El-Bersha, 1890-4; he next carried out a survey of the Theban Necropolis and superintended excavations for Lord Amherst (q.v.), the Marquis of Northampton (q.v.), Margaret Benson (q.v.), Theodore Davis (q.v.), and Mrs Tytus (q.v.), 1895-1905; he was appointed Brunner Professor of Egyptology in the University of Liverpool, 1906-19; Hon. Reader in Egyptian Art, Liverpool, 1919; Fellow of King's Coll., London, 1908; Professor of Ancient Hist. and Archaeology, Cairo University, 1929-33; President Section H. British Assoc. 1923; Vice Pres. Roy. Anthrop. Inst., 1926; Vice Pres. EES with which he was associated for 65 years; from 1889 onwards he contributed very many articles to *AE, ASAE, JEA, AAA, PSBA*, and *ZÄS*; he married in 1907 Essie Johnston (q.v.); his main works were, *Beni Hasan*, pts. i and ii, with plans by G. Willoughby Fraser, 1893-4; *El Bersheh*, pt. i, plan by G. Willoughby Fraser, pt. ii with F. Ll. Griffith, 1894-5; *The Amherst Papyri, being an account of the Egyptian papyri in the collection of .... Lord A. of Hackney ...*, 1899; *The Life of Rekhmira, Vezîr of Upper Egypt under Thothmes III and Amenhotep II circa 1471-1448 B.C.*, 1900, being only a third of the actual tomb scenes and texts; *A Short History of Ancient Egypt*, with J. Garstang, 1904; *The Tomb of Thoutmosis IV*, with H. Carter and others, 1904; *Scarabs: an introduction to the study of Egyptian Seals and Signet Rings*, 1906; *Scarab-shaped Seals*, Cairo Cat., 1907; *The Timins collection of ancient Egyptian scarabs and cylinder seals*, 1907; *The Tomb of Iouiya and Touiyou*, with H. Carter and others, 1907; *Funerary Statuettes and Model Sarcophagi*, 2 pts., Cairo Cat., 1930-7; he also prepared the inscriptions and translations in *The Temple of Mut in Asher*, 1899; his correspondence and manuscripts are now in the Griffith Institute, Oxford; his library was presented by Mrs Newberry to the Library of Egyptology, Cambridge, the Edwards Library at University College London, and the British Museum; he died in Godalming, 7 Aug. 1949.

AJA 54 (1950), 73-4; *Chron. d'Ég.* 25 (1950), 86; EES *Report* (1949), 4-5; *JEA* 36 (1950), 101-3 (portr.) (W. R. Dawson); *ODNB* 40, 569-70; *DNB* 1941-50, 622-3; *JEA* 76 (1990), 149-55 (bibl.) (D. Magee); P. Whelan in M. Betrò and G. Miniaci, *Talking along the Nile*, 2013, 229-54.

NEWTON, Francis Giesler (1878-1924)
British architect and excavator; he was born in Ipswich, 4 April 1878, son of Francis Edward N., clergyman, and Ellen Giesler; educated Repton, RA Schools and as a student of Sir Aston Webb; he practised as an architect for several years then helped Ashby to plan the Roman ruins at Caerwent, 1906; he next studied monuments in Rome, 1907, and went to Sardinia with Ashby and Duncan Mackenzie to plan *nuraghi*, 1908; he accompanied the latter to Syria and explored Moab in search of megalithic monuments and excavated at Beth Shemesh for the PEF; at

this time he also made the first complete measured drawings of some of the finer rock-tombs and seems to have become acquainted with Egypt; he served in the Hon. Artillery Company during the First World War; he was regularly with the EES expedition to El-Amarna, 1920-4, assisting in the excavation and making plans of a vast area of the city; he also accompanied the joint expedition of the British Museum and Pennsylvania University to Ur of the Chaldees under Woolley (q.v.), 1922-3; in addition he spent several weeks planning and surveying for Sir Arthur Evans (q.v) at Knossos, 1923-4; appointed Director of Excavations at El-Amarna just before his death; although he left no book or major work in his own name much of his results can be found in the *City of Akenaten*, vol. i, and similar publications by other archaeologists who used his excellent drawings and plans which were of an exceedingly high order; his remarkable coloured drawings of the mural paintings at El-Amarna were published as a memorial volume, see below, in 1929; his papers and drawings are in the Griffith Institute, Oxford; Newton was taken ill during an epidemic while directing his last expedition at El-Amarna and died in Asyut, 25 Dec. 1924.

JEA 11 (1925), 70-1 (portr.); *The Mural Painting of El-Amarneh*, ed. H. Frankfort, memoir vii-viii (T. Whittemore) (portr.).

NIBBI, Alessandra (1923-2007)
British-Italian orientalist; she was born in Porto-San-Giorgio, Italy, 30 June 1923, daughter of Gino N., an artist, journalist, and art dealer, and Elvira Petrelli; she was brought up in Australia and attended the University of Melbourne and taught at the University of Sydney; she then returned to Italy to finish her education at the University of Perugia where she studied archaeology and the University of Florence; Dr. Letters, 1965; she settled in Oxford and devoted her considerable energy to Egyptological studies; she published numerous articles, pamphlets, and books espousing unorthodox views on Asiatic settlements and the Delta region; she encouraged excavation in the Delta although the results often disproved her theories; she also wrote on technical subjects including anchors, bellows, and shields; she was the founder and editor of *Discussions in Egyptology* in 1985; she died in Oxford, 15 Jan. 2007.

Personal info; internet obit (C. Vandersleyen).

NICHOLSON, (*Sir*) Charles (1808-1903)
British physician and collector; he was born in Bedale, Yorks, 23 Nov. 1808, son of Charles N. and Barbara Ascough; he studied medicine, MD, Edinburgh, 1833; he emigrated to Australia, 1834, where he practised as a physician; he played a great part in the development of education and the founding of Sydney University, of which he was Provost in 1851 and Chancellor, 1854-62; he returned to England, 1860; knighted, 1852; created baronet, 1859; Hon. DCL Oxford, 1857; Hon. LLD Cambridge and Edinburgh; he made three visits to Egypt 1856-7, 1861 and 1862 and brought back to London a collection of antiquities first described by Bonomi (q.v.) and Birch (q.v.) and published in a catalogue by Bonomi, 1858, reprinted with additional matter as *Aegyptiaca*, 1891 under Nicholson's name; the collection was presented to Sydney University in 1860 with a further consignment in 1864; he died in Totteridge, Herts., 8 Nov. 1903.

ODNB 40, 806-7; *DNB* 1901-11, 11-12; Hilmy, ii, 65; *WWW* i, 525; *Australian Dictionary of Biography* 2, 283-5; R. S. Merrillees, *Living wioth Egypt's Past in Australia*, 1990, 2-6; K. N. Sowada and B. G. Ockinga (eds.), *Egyptian Art in the Nicholson Museum Sydney*, 2006, 1-13..

NIEBUHR, Karsten (1733-1815)
German geographer and traveller; he was born in Lüdingworth, Holstein, 17 March 1733, son of Berthold N., farmer, and Cecilia von Duhn; he had little education, but instructed himself, particularly in mathematics and surveying, and learned Arabic; he joined the expedition sent by Frederick V of Denmark for scientific exploration in Egypt, Arabia, and Syria, which sailed in Jan. 1761; the expedition was in Egypt from 26 Sept. 1761 to 8 Oct. 1762,visiting Alexandria, Rosetta, Cairo, where most time was spent, and then Suez from where Niebuhr was able to visit Mount Sinai; by May 1763 Niebuhr was the only surviving member of the party, the others (including the botanist Forsskål (q.v.)), having died of disease; on his return he lived in Copenhagen, but eventually went back to Germany; he was a careful observer, and his valuable *Reisenbeschreibung nach Arabien und andern umliegenden Ländern* was pub. in 2 vols. in Copenhagen, 1774-8, the third vol. appeared posthumously in 1837; this work contains valuable information on Egypt, including a survey of the Pyramids; Niebuhr also edited Forsskål's work; he died in Meldorf, Holstein, 26 April 1815.

Life, by his son Barthold N., Kiel, 1817; English ed. 1838; T. Hansen, *Arabia felix*, London, 1964; *EB*; Hilmy, ii, 66; *Dansk Biografisk Leksikon* 10, 375-7; È. Gran-Aymerich, *Dictionnaire biographique d'archéologie 1798-1945*, 2001, incorporated in *Les Chercheurs de passé 1798-1945*, 2007, 1018-9; J. Speake (ed.), *Literature of Travel and Exploration*, 2003, 2, 857-9.

NIMS, Charles Francis (1906-1988)
American Egyptologist; he was born at Norwalk, Ohio, 19 Oct. 1906, son of Joel Benjamin N. and Grace Mary Wildman; he was educated at Alma College, Michigan, BA, 1928 and McCormick Theological Seminary, Chicago, B. Divinity, 1931; he was then ordained as a Presbyterian minister and joined the archaeological expedition to Beth Zur in Palestine; in the autumn of 1931 he began his studies in Egyptology at the Oriental Institute, Chicago under Edgerton (q.v.) and Wilson (q.v.) specializing in Demotic studies; in 1934 he was appointed a Research Assistant by Breasted (q.v.); he took part in the expedition to the tomb of Mereruka in 1934-6, and at Luxor 1937-9; PhD 1937; from 1940-3 he was the pastor of the First Presbyterian Church in Eldorado, Ill. and was an army chaplain in France 1943-6; in 1946 he became a photographer and epigraphist on the Epigraphic Survey 1964-30 June 1972; research associate, Oriental Institute, Chicago 1948-67, associate Professor 1967-70, Professor 1970-72; he wrote numerous articles notably on his Demotic studies; he was the author of *Thebes of the Pharaohs. Pattern for Every City*, 1965 and was co-author of *The Mastaba of Mereruka*, 1938; *Medinet Habu* IV-VIII, 1940-1970, *Reliefs and Inscriptions in Karnak* III, 1954; *Grand temple d'Abou Simbel. La Bataille de Qadesh*, 1971; *The Temple of Khonsu* I-II, 1979-1981; and the *The Tomb of Kheruef*, 1980; volume 6 of *Serapis* was dedicated to him; he died in Chicago, 19 Nov. 1988.

Oriental Notes and News 119, 5 (portr.) (G. Hughes); *Serapis* 6 (1980), 1-5 (portr.) (bibl.); *Varia Aegyptiaca* 4 (1988), 191; *Who's Who in the Midwest 1976-1977*, 532.

NIZZOLI, Giuseppe Gaetano Antonio (1792-1858)
Italian diplomat and collector; he was born in Modena, 23. Jan 1792, son of Nicola N., a barber, and Isabella Passerini; after his education in Modena, he left for Milan in 1813 where he joined a law firm; he was named Chancellor of the Austrian Consulate in Egypt in Cairo, 1818-26 and later Alexandria, 1826-7 when he left after personal differences with Acerbi (q.v.); he married firstly in Cairo 30 Jan. 1820 Amalia (1805-1845/9), daughter of Giacomo Sola and Orseola Mancuso,who supervised excavations at Saqqara, April-May 1826; he married secondly in Zante 1849 Maria Coliva; he was appointed Vice-Consul in Zante, 1835-45, Consul in Sira, 1845-51 and finally Salonica, 1851-58 with the personal title of Consul-General; he made considerable collections of Egyptian antiquities; the first part was purchased in 1821 for the Vienna collection, the second in 1824 by the Grand Duke of Tuscany, now in Florence, the third by Palagi (q.v.), now in Bologna, in 1831, and a fourth purchased by Malaspina (q.v.), now in Padua; he met Champollion (q.v.) in Italy in 1824, and a catalogue of the Nizzoli collection compiled by Champollion was published by Pellegrini (q.v.) in 1903 (*Bessarione*, ser. 2, 5. 187); a catalogue of his third collection was published by S. Pernigotti, *Aegyptiaca Bononiensia* I (1991), 46-84; his wife wrote *Memorie sull'Egitto*, 1841; he died in in Salonica, 28 Nov 1858.

Champollion, i, 24, 39, 61, 181, 393; *JEA* 24 (1938), 12; S. Pernigotti, *Aegyptiaca Bononiensia* I (1990), 3-84; S. Daris, *Giuseppe Nizzoli, un impiegato consolare Autriaco nel Levante agli Albori dell'Egittologia*, 2005; L. Gabrielli in *Ricerche di Egittologia e di Antichità Copte* 1 (1999), 55-75; S. Daris in *Studi di Egittologia e di Papirologia* 10 (2013), 151-5; C. Rindi in *Studi di Egittologia e di Papirologia* 11 (2014), 129-47; C. Rindi and M. Guidotti in *Studi di Egittologia e di Papyrologia* 11 (2014), 149-63; S. Pernigotti in M. Betrò and G. Miniaci, *Talking along the Nile*, 2013; 177-85; D. Picchi in N. Cooke and V. Daubney, *Every Traveller Needs a Compass*, 2015,131-42.

NOLAN, (*Revd*) **Frederick** (1784-1864)
Irish scholar and antiquary; he was born Old Rathmines Castle Co. Dublin, 9 Feb. 1784, son of Edward N and Florinda his wife; he was educated at Exeter College, Oxford; DCL, 1825; he was ordained 1806 and made vicar of Prittlewell, Essex in 1822; FRS, 1835; he contributed papers to the *Trans. Royal Soc. Literature* and other journals; he wrote a study on Egyptian chronology and also published a work on harmonizing the grammar of ancient and modern languages; he died in Geraldstown House Co. Navan, 16 Sept. 1864.

ODNB 40, 981; *DNB* 41, 95; Brabrook, *Hist. Royal Soc. Lit.* (1897), 17; Lepsius, *Life*, 174; Hilmy, ii, 73.

NORDEN, Frederik Ludwig (1708-1742)
Danish naval captain and traveller; he was born in Glückstadt, Holstein, 22 Oct. 1708, son of Jørgen N. and Catherine Henrichsen; he entered the Danish navy, 1722; a man of exceptional ability he was sent by Christian VI to Egypt in 1738 to obtain a full and accurate account of the country, and stayed about a year; afterwards attached to the British navy and resided in London; FRS, 1740; a member of the (First) Egyptian Society; his *Travels*, first

published in 1751, were reissued several times and translated into English, French, and German; his drawings were published in 1993; he died in Paris, 21 Sept. 1742.

Nichols, *Lit. Anecd.* ii, 297; Hilmy, ii, 73; *JEA* 23 (1937), 259 *Dansk Biografisk Leksikon* 10, 547-9; M.-L. Buhl and T. Holck Colding, *The Danish Naval Officer Frederik Ludwig Norden*, 1986; M.-L. Buhl, *Les dessins archéologiques et topographiques de l'Egypte ancienne faits par F. L. Norden 1737-1738*, 1993; Lamy, 170-5.

NOROV, Avram Sergeievitch (1795-1869)
Russian explorer, traveller, and public official; he was born in Klychi, 2 Nov. 1795; he served in the military until 1823; he joined the Ministry of the Interior in 1827-50 and the Ministry of Public Instruction from 1850; he became Minister of Public Instruction, 1855-8; he visited Egypt in 1834-5 and again in 1861-2; on his first voyage he brought back to Russia a monumental statue of Sakhmet from the temple of Mut in Luxor inscribed with names and titles of Amenhotep III, which was in the collection of the Academy of Arts and from 1852 in the Hermitage Museum, St. Petersburg (No. 148); author of *A Voyage to Egypt and Nubia in 1834 and 1835* (in Russian), Part 1 and 2, St. Petersburg 1840, 2nd ed. 1853, and *Jerusalem and Sinai*, St. Petersburg, 1878; he died in St. Petersburg, 4 Feb. 1869.

N. Landa, I. Lapis, *Egyptian Antiquities in the Hermitage,* St. Petersburg 1974, pls. 36-37; A. Volkoff, *Voyageurs Russes en Égypte*, 1972, 101-24 (portr.); B. M. Dantsig, *Blizhny Vostok v russkoy nauke i literature,* Moscow 1973, 193-96; inf. J. Śliwa.

NORTHAMPTON, Marquis of *see* **COMPTON**

NOTT, Josiah Clark (1804-1873)
American physician and ethnologist; he was born in Columbia, SC, 31 March 1804, son of Abraham N. and Angelica Mitchell; educated South Carolina College, grad. 1824; he graduated in medicine University of Pennsylvania, 1827; demonstrator for two years, then in private practice in Columbia; studied in Paris, 1835; settled in Mobile, Ala.; Professor of Anatomy, University of Louisiana, 1857-8; Professor of Surgery, Medical Coll. of Alabama, 1858; moved to Baltimore, 1867 and New York, 1868; in the field of ethnology he published with Gliddon (q.v.) *Types of Mankind* (1854) which ran to ten editions, and in which the authors using material gathered by Morton (q.v.) sought to prove that each of the different races sprang from a fixed type, a doctrine contradicted by Darwinian theory; also *Indigenous Races of the Earth*, 1857; he died in Mobile on his birthday, 31 March 1873.

DAB 13, 582-3 (G. H. Ramsey).

NUGENT, Baron *see* **GRENVILLE**

NUR EL-DIN, Muhammad Abdel-Halim (1943-2016)
Egyptian Egyptologist; he was born in al-Ramlah, Benha, 1 July 1943, son of Ahmad Muhammad Nur-el-Din and Fatima Ismail Haggag; he was educated at the Faculty of Arts, Cairo University; BA in Egyptian Archaeology, 1963; MA, 1966; he then studied at the University of Leiden; PhD, 1974; he became assistant professor at the Faculty of Archaeology, Cairo University; associate professor, 1980; full professor, 1986; he was visiting professor at the University of Leiden, 1979; he became Chairman of the Faculty of Archaeology at the University of Sanaa, Yemen, 1982-6; he was Vice-Dean for Educational Affairs at the Dept. of Egyptology, Cairo University, 1988-93; he was appointed Chairman of the Egyptian Antiquities Organization and, after a reorganization, Secretary-General of the Supreme Council of Antiquities, 1988 and 1993-6; he became a Chairman of the Department of Egyptology, Cairo University, 1996-2002; he also served as Head of Arab ICOM, 1995-2001; Director of the Calligraphy Center of the Alexandria Library, 2003-6; and Dean of the Faculty of Archaeology, Cairo University, Fayoum Branch, 2000-5; he was then appointed Dean of the Faculty of Archaeology and Touristic Guidance, Misr University for Science and Technology, 6th October City, 2010-16, and adjunct professor at Cairo University; the *Horizon Studies in Egyptology in Honour of M. A. Nur el-Din*, edited by B. S. el-Sharkawy, was published in 2009; apart from articles, he published *The Demotic Ostraka in the National Museum of Antiquities at Leiden*, 1974; and with G. Wagner, *Stèles funéraires de Kom Abou Billo*, 1985; he edited *The Role of Women in Ancient Egyptian Society*, 1995; he died 16 Nov. 2016.

Internet obit.

OBBINK, Hendrik Willem (1898-1979)
Dutch orientalist; he was born at Smilde, 20 March 1898, son of Herman Theodorus O., Professor of History of Ancient Religions at Utrecht, and Jeantine Gerardine ten Kate; he was educated at Amsterdam and Utrecht and studied at the Universities of Utrecht and Groningen under van der Leeuw (q.v.); Dr. theol. from Utrecht 1925; he was a pastor in several towns and from 1932-9 lecturer in Hebrew and Arabic at the University of Utrecht; he became Professor of the History and Phenomenology of Religion and also Egyptian literature, 1939-68; his chief Egyptological work was his thesis *Die magische beteekenis van den naam inzonderheid in het oude Egypte*, 1925; he died in Zwolle, 14 Sept. 1979.

Nederlands Theologisch Tijdschrift 34 (1980), 64-5 (D. J. Hoens); inf. Prof. Heerma van Voss.

O'CALLAGHAN, (*Revd*) **Roger** (S. J.) (1912-1954)
American orientalist and archaeologist; he was born New York, 13 Oct. 1912; he studied at the Jesuit Seminary in Toronto, 1933-6, and at the Univ. Gregoriana, Rome, 1936-40; in 1942 he entered the Oriental Seminary of Johns Hopkins University receiving a doctorate in 1946; Professor at the Pontifical Biblical Institute, Rome; he was engaged with M. Dunand on archaeological work at Byblos, 1946-50; he wrote a number of articles on a wide variety of Near Eastern subjects, including *Aram Naharaim; The Word* ktp in *Ugaritic and Egypto-Canaanite Mythology*; he was killed in a car accident Baghdad, Iraq, 5 March 1954.

BASOR 133 (Feb. 1954), 30 (W. F. Albright); no. 134 (April 1954), 3-4 (G. S. Glanzmann); *Biblica* (1954), 258-9 (bibl.) (E. Vogt); *Orientalia* 23 (1954), 253-4 (A. Pohl).

OGDON, Jorge Roberto (1954-2007)
Paraguayan-Argentinian Egyptologist; he was born in Asuncion, Paraguay, 23 April 1954, son of Guy Toberto O., a business man of British origins, and Balsia Emelina Aquino; he was educated in Buenos Aires, studying anthropology at the University of Buenos Aires, 1972-3 and Egyptology at the Instituto Argentino de Egiptologia (AIE), graduating 1974; he lectured at AIE, 1975-6 and became its Secretary-General, 1975-7; he was the sole South American representative at the first International Congress of Egyptology at Cairo, 1976; he was editor of *Aegyptus Antiquus* from 1974-9; he left the IAE in 1978; he became director of Centro de Estudios del Antiguo Egipto, 1995-2005; he was also editor of *Revista de Egiptologia-Isis*, 2001-3; he was the author of numerous articles in Spanish and English and *Observaciones sobre los entes llamados Tekenu*, 1977; *The Celestial Ferryman in the Pyramid Texts*, 1977; 2nd ed., 1980, 3rd ed., 1984; *Las manipulaciones magicas en el antiguo Egipto*, 1979; *Un Analisis Lietario del 'Himno Canibal' en los Textos de las Piramides-Bilingual Edition*, 1986, 2nd ed., 2000; *Nuevas perspectivas sobre el fenomeno de la Posesion en el antiguo Egipto*, 1997; english version *Sharing New Ideas on the Phenomenon of Possession in ancient Egypt*, 1997; *The Protection of Life. An Everyday Magical Practice in ancient Egypt*, 1997; *Literatura Egipcia Antigua. Textos Religiosos*, 1998; *Nociones de Epigrafia Jeroglifica*, 1998; *Literatura Egipicia Antigua. El genero epistolar*, 2000; *Estudios de Epigrafia Arcaica*, 2000; he died in Asuncion, 30 Nov. 2007.

Internet obit. Amigos de la Egiptologia; internet bibl.

OKAJIMA, Seitaro (1895-1948)
Japanese Egyptologist; he was born at Osaka, 20 Feb. 1895, son of Tosuke O., an importer, and his wife Kiku; he first followed a commercial career in his father's business, but in 1918 he went to London for a year where he visited the British Museum and began to teach himself Egyptology; on his return to Japan, he studied at the University of Kyoto and continued his Egyptian studies encouraged by Professor Hamada (q.v.); on his graduation he was appointed Professor of the Nara Women's High Normal School; from 1931 he taught a course in Egyptian history at Kyoto; among his many publications in Japanese are *Small Egyptian Grammar*, 1940; *History of Ancient Egypt*, 1940; *Small Coptic Grammar*, 1942, the first works of their kind in Japan; he died in Nara, 6 May 1948.

M. Suzuki, 'La Collection égyptienne de l'Université de Kyoto', *Chichukai-Gakkai* 3 (1980), 62-3; D. Sakai, *Causeries on Egyptology*, 1982 (in Japanese); T. Sakamoto and K. Zenhiro, *Oriento* 61-2 (2018), 163-73 (in Japanese).

OKASHA, Sarwat (1921-2012)
Egyptian politician; he was born in Cairo, 18 Feb. 1921, son of a military officer; he studied at a military academy until 1939 and at the Higher Military School, 1945-7; he obtained a diploma in journalism from the University Fuad I (now University of Cairo), 1951 and later a PhD. from the Sorbonne, 1960; he was one of the military officers who participated in the coup of 1952; he became a military attaché at Bern and Paris, 1953-6 and then ambassador to Italy, 1957-8; he served as Minister of Culture, 1958-62 and 1966-70 with rank of Deputy PM, and Assistant President for Cultural Affairs, 1970-2; he was instrumental in the Nubian rescue campaign in the 1960s, beginning with an appeal to UNESCO 8 March

1960; he served on UNESCO's Executive Board and as Chairman of the Advisory Committee on Culture, Arab World Institute in Paris, 1990-3; he was Visiting Scholar at the Collège de France, 1973; Corresponding Fellow of the British Academy, 1975; he died in Cairo, 27 Feb 2012.

A. Hélal-Giret in R. Legros, *50 Ans d'Éternité*, 2015, 265-70; Internet obit.

O'LEARY, (*Revd*) **De Lacy Evans** (1872-1957)
Anglo-Irish Copticist; he was born at Cullompton, Devon 3 Oct. 1872, son of Henry Joseph Evans O. (1831-1908) and Julia Lovelock (d.1884); the family settled in Bristol in the 1880s, and he was educated at Bristol Grammar School, 1884-7; he converted to Roman Catholicism from Anglicanism in 1888 and trained for the priesthood, but left his seminary in 1890 and returned to the Church of England; assistant master at private schools in Portishead and Cheltenham 1890-95; external student at the University of London, BA, 1895; Cambridge Preliminary Theologi cal Paper 1896; ordained deacon by the bishop of Bath and Wells, 1896 and served as curate of a series of Bristol parishes during 1899-1903, studying simultaneously as an external student of Trinity College Dublin, BA, 1902; MA, 1905; BD, 1908; DD, 1911; he was awarded an extra prize in the Elrington Theological Prize in 1903 and the Elrington Theological Prize in 1904; Diocesan Inspector of Schools in Bristol,1908; Vicar of Christ Church, Barton Hill, 1909-1946; Reader in Aramaic and Syriac, and Chairman of Department of Semitic Studies, University College Bristol, 1908; Special Lecturer in Aramaic and Syriac, University of Bristol, 1909–57; President of University Oriental Society; Chairman of Convocation 1910–28; represented University of Bristol at the 17th International Congress of Orientalists in 1928; he also taught at Bristol Baptist College and at Western College, Bristol; served as a chaplain to the 6th Mounted Brigade of the Egyptian Expeditionary Force, at Ain Moussa, 1916-17; he was entrusted in 1922 by Evelyn-White (q.v.) with the publication of Coptic manuscripts from the Monastery of Saint Macarius in the Wadi Natrun and contributed material to Evelyn-White's final publication; he also translated some fragmentary hymns given to Bristol City Art Gallery by Henry Liddon (q.v.) in 1925; editor of annual bibliography of Christian Egypt in *JEA*, 1922–39, also contributing many reviews; he published over 20 books, his Coptic publications including *The daily office and* Theotokia *of the Coptic Church*, 1911; *The Coptic* Theotokia*: text from Vatican Cod. Copt. xxxviii, Bib. Nat. Copte 22, 23, 35, 69 and other MSS, including fragments recently found at the Dêr Abû Makâr in the Wadi Natrun*, 1923; *Fragmentary Coptic hymns from the Wadi n-Natrun*, 1924; *The* Difnar (Antiphonarium) *of the Coptic Church*, 1926-30; *The Saints of Egypt*,1937; *A primary guide to Coptic literary material*, 1938; retired to Weston-super-Mare, Somerset, in 1946 and died there on 22 July 1957.

A. Dodson and M. Crossley Evans in Dodson, J. J. Johnston and W. Monkhouse (eds) *Studies in Honour of W. J. Tait*, 2014, 67-88; C. Stacey, *Men of the West*, 1926, 48b; *Crockford's Clerical Directory*.

OLENIN, Alexei Nikolaevitch (1763-1843)
Russian historian, archaeologist and artist; he was born in Moscow, 9 Dec. 1763; using the publications of Champollion (q.v.), he tried to read Egyptian hieroglyphs, such as the name and titles of Amenhotep III engraved on the stone statue of Sakhmet brought from Egypt by A. S. Norov (q.v.) in 1835; two letters of Champollion to Olenin are preserved, published by A. V. Atchinsky in 1934; from 1811 Olenin was director of the Imperial Public Library in St. Petersburg; honorary member of the Academy of Arts, 1804; President, 1817; he died in St. Petersburg, 17/29 April 1843.

Palestinskiy Sbornik 5 (68), 1960 (I. G. Lifschitz); *Greater Soviet Encyclopedia* 18, 1974, 430; inf. J. Śliwa.

OLLIVIER-BEAUREGARD, Gratien-Michel (1814-1901)
French Orientalist; he was born in Cognac, 17 March 1814, son of Jean-Laurent O. and Jeanne Tourtavel; he was educated in Cognac and travelled abroad for business; as a family friend of Godard (q.v.), he took on the task of managing his literary estate, and became interested in Egyptology and Oriental cultures; he published Godard's collection of antiquities in *Simples observations sur l'origine et le culte des divinités égyptiennes, à propos de la collection archéologique de feu le Docteur Ernest Godard*, 1863, expanded and revised as *Les divinités égyptiennes: leur origine, leur culte et son expansion dans le monde*, 1866; he presented papers at some of the Congresses of Orientalists, and to other academic meetings; his publications included *La caricature égyptienne*, 1894; *Chez les Pharaons: études égyptiennes*, 1896, a book of essays containing lengthy rebuttals of criticisms of *La caricature égyptienne*; and *La vigne et le vin dans l'antiquité égyptienne*, 1898; member of the Société d'anthropologie de Paris, 1879, President 1897; he died in Paris, 14 Jan. 1901.

Hilmy, i, 57; *Bulletin de la Société d'anthropologie de Paris* 5th series, 2 (1901), 54-6; inf. T. Hardwick.

OMLIN, Joseph A (1906-1976)
Swiss Egyptologist; he was born in Basilea, 10 April 1906; he trained as a medical doctor but his interest in Egyptology led him to study under Schott (q.v.) and Otto (q.v.) at Heidelberg obtaining his doctorate in 1962; his published works are *Amenemhet I und Sesostris I*, 1962, his doctoral dissertation, and an edition of the Turin Erotic Papyrus, *Der Papyrus 55001 und seine satirisch-erotischen Zeichnungen und Inschriften*, 1973; he died in Locarno, 15 Feb. 1976.

Aegyptus 58 (1978), 222 (S. Curto); *ZDMG* 126 (1976), 96*.

OPPENHEIMER, Henry (1859-1932)
American banker and art-collector; he was born in Washington, DC, 1859, son of Morris O. and his wife Joanna; he was educated in Frankfurt and became a partner in the London house of Speyer Bros.; he collected antiquities and works of art, and in 1912 purchased a large number of Heseltine's drawings by the old masters; he also purchased Egyptian antiquities at the Rustafjaell (q.v.) and other sales; his collections were sold at Christie's 22-3 July 1936; some of the Egyptian antiquities were bought by E. L. Paget and resold at the Paget sale, Sotheby's, 18 Oct. 1949; Oppenheimer was elected FSA in 1914; he died in London, 23 March 1932.

Sale cat. preface; South African Records.

OPPERT, Jules Samuel (1825-1905)
French Assyriologist of German-Jewish origin; he was born in Hamburg, 9 July 1825, son of Eduard O. and Henriette Gans; he studied at the Universities of Heidelberg, Bonn, and Berlin; PhD, from Kiel; he then settled in Paris, 1847 and was naturalized in 1856; a leading Assyriologist of the day, he taught German, 1848-51; he then went on a mission to Mesopotamia, 1851-4; Professor of Sanskrit at Imperial Library, 1857; Professor of Philology and Archaeology at the Collège de France from 1874, he was elected of the Académie des Inscriptions, 18 March 1881; he is remembered in Egyptology for an important work presented to the Acad. des Inscr., *Mémoire sur les rapports de l'Égypte et de l'Assyrie*, 1869; he died in Paris, 21 Aug. 1905.

Budge, *R & P*, 206 (portr.); *Rev. arch.* 4e serie, 6 (1905), 338-9; Vapareau; A. C. E. Franquet de Franqueville, *Le Premier Siècle de l'Institut de France*, 1895, I, 387; E. Gran-Aymerich, *Dictionnaire biographique d'archéologie 1798-1945*, 2001, incorporated in *Les Chercheurs de passé 1798-1945*, 2007, 1029-30.

ORCURTI, Pietro Camillo (1822-1871)
Italian Egyptologist; he was on the staff of Turin Museum 1849-60, Director 1861-70, and published a catalogue of the Egyptian collection, *Catalogo illustrato dei monumenti egizii del R. Museo di Torino*, etc., 1852; he died in 1871.

Brugsch, *Mein Leben*, 104; Hilmy, ii, 81; S. Curto, *Storia del Museo Egizio di Torino*, 1976, 40.

ORIGNY, Pierre Adam d' (1697-1774)
French writer; he was born at Reims in 1697, son of Adam d'O., merchant draper, and Andriette Thérèse de Pinteville de Cernon; he served as a soldier and then retired from the army to concentrate on research; he wrote on Egyptian history, religion, and chronology; he rejected Warburton's theory on hieroglyphic writing and continued to argue for their symbolic meanings which influenced Zoega (q.v.); his studies were in turn criticized by de Pauw (q.v.); he published *Dissertations où l'on examine quelques questions appartenant à l'Histoire des Anciens Égyptiens*, 1752; *L'Égypte ancienne*, 1762; and *Chronologie des Rois du grand empire des Egyptiens*, 1765; he died at Paris, 9 Sept. 1774.

NGB 38, 798; *Biographie Universelle* 31, 349-50; E. Iversen, *The Myth of Egypt and its Hieroglyphs*, 1961, 119.

ORT-GEUTHNER, Georges (Jiří) (1900-1941)
Czech Demotist and publisher; he was born in Prague, 28 July 1900, son of Vojtech Ort and Valburga Katerina Aneska Seidel (who married secondly the oriental publisher Paul Geuthner); he studied at the Karl-Ferdinands University, Prague 1918-9 under N. Reich (q.v.); in 1919 he studied Egyptology in Paris at the École des Hautes Études, École du Louvre and the Institut Catholique; from 1921-6 he studied Egyptology at the Charles University, Prague under Lexa (q.v.), PhD, 1926; he worked as an editor in his stepfather's firm in Paris as an editor, chief editor 1930, and Director-General 1940; he published *Grammaire démotique du papyrus magique de Londres et Leyde*, 1936; he died in Paris, 11 Jan. 1941.

W. B. Oerter in *Gött. Misz.* 77 (1984), 85-92; *Kemi* 9 (1942), 107 (P. Montet); *Syria* 22 (1941), 103-4 (R. Dussaud); *Chron. d'Ég.* 17 (1942), 253; inf. W. B. Oerter; W. Oerter, *Die Ägyptologie an der Prager Universitäten 1882-1945*, 2010, 1-5.

OSBORN, Dale James (1922-2004)
American zoologist; he was born in Hemet, California, 10 May 1922; following naval service, he studied at Colorado State College; BSc, 1948, he then attended the University of Wyoming; MSc, 1949; PhD, McGill University, 1957; he was employed as an Instructor in Zoology at the University of Wyoming, Instructor in Biology at Boston University, and Demonstrator in Zoology at McGill University; he served as Asst Professor and Head of Natural Science at Robert College, Istanbul, 1957-61, Asst Professor in Zoology at Texas Technical College, Lubbock, 1960-1, and Teacher of Zoology at Anatolia College, Thessaloniki, 1961-4; he became Field Associate at the Field Museum of Natural History, Chicago, 1964-70 when he was stationed in Cairo and conducted field surveys; he later obtained the post of curator at the Chicago Zoological Park before settling in 1980 in Prague; he published *Animals of the Pharaohs*, 1977, rev. 1978 and, with his wife, *The Mammals of Ancient Egypt*, 1998; he died in Prague, 20 Aug. 2004.

Lynx 36 (2005), 149-152 (V. Hanak and M. Kosina) (portr.) (bibl.).

OSBURN, William (1793-1875)
British antiquarian and historian; he was born at Leeds, baptized 23 July 1793, son of William O., wine merchant; he was educated at Leeds Grammar School; FRSL; Member of the Arch. Inst.; his earliest Egyptological work, the description of the 'Leeds Mummy', 1828, is very good for its time; he visited Egypt 1847-8; his later works are mainly devoted to the relations of Egypt and the Bible, on which he published three books, 1846-54, and the *Monumental History of Egypt*, 2 vols. 1854; he died in New Wortley, Yorkshire, 26 Feb. 1875.

Hilmy, ii, 82; Boase 6, 332-3.

OSMAN, (*Effendi*) (*c*.1791-1835)
British soldier and adventurer; the name was adopted by William Thomson, son of a tradesman from Perth who died when his son was young; he has been incorrectly identified as Donald Thomson and Donald Donald; he went to live in Inverness where, following a brawl in which he believed that he had killed an opponent, he enlisted as a drummer-boy or medical attendant in the British Army; he went to Egypt with the British forces under General Alexander Mackenzie Fraser in 1807; he was taken prisoner and, after suffering great hardships, was given the choice of death or becoming a Muslim; he chose the latter and assumed the religion of Islam, also wearing Turkish dress for the rest of his life; he took part in the Egyptian campaign in Arabia where he met Burckhardt (q.v.); Legh (q.v.) met him at Minya in 1814, and offered to pay the ransom for his release and to convey him to England, but his master married him to one of the women in his harem and as he showed no inclination for release, he remained in Egypt; he was freed *c*.1815 on the intervention of the British consul Henry Salt (q.v.) prompted by Burckhardt; he was afterwards in the service of Burckhardt until the death of the latter in 1817; he then settled in Cairo where he prospered and owned a number of houses; he was for some years interpreter and guard at the British Consulate, and was very helpful to British travellers in Egypt, Robert Hay (q.v,) being especially indebted to him on his first arrival in Cairo; Kinglake (q.v.) was entertained by him during his visit to Cairo; he died of dysentery in Cairo, 8 Nov. 1835.

ODNB 42, 56-7; Bonomi Diary, 1833, 27 May; Hay Diary, 1824, 24 Nov. *et seq.*; Kinglake, *Eothen*, ch. 18; Legh, 129; Letter from Fulgence Fresnel, Cairo, 13 Nov. 1835, Lane Corr. 16; Madden, *Travels*, i. 345; Madox, i. 107, 115, 255; ii, 4; Sherer, 160, 176; Westcar Diary, 258, 270; etc.; *Cairo Today* 6 Oct 1987, 48-51; J. Thompson, *Journal of World History* 5 (1994), 99-123; J. Thompson in Jill Edwards, *Historians in Cairo*, 2002, 81-106; J. Thompson, *Edward William Lane 1801-1876*, 2010, 44-6, 372-3.

OTREPPE DE BOUVETTE, (*Baron*) **Albert d'** (1787-1875)
Belgian collector; he was born in Namur, 16 Nov. 1787, son of Philippe Théodore Jean d'O., seigneur de Bouvette and Marie Anne Victoire Mincé du Fontbaré; he studied law in Paris and was appointed to a legal post at Amiens in 1811; he returned to Belgium in 1816 and took up a similar post at Liège, retiring in 1832; he was much interested in archaeology and helped to found the Institut Archéologique Liégeois of which he was the first President; on 7 Dec. 1865 he donated a number of Egyptian objects to the Musée Curtius, Liège including coffins and stelae, most, if not all, of which had been acquired at the sale Antoine Schayes in Brussels 6-8 Dec. 1859 via the Anastasi sale in Paris in 1857; several smaller objects were given to the Museum in 1873; he died in Liège, 14 Nov. 1875.

J. Alexandre, *Tablettes liégeoises* (1875); *Bulletin de l'Institut archéologique liégeois* 12 (1874), 161-4; *Chronique archéologique du pays de Liège* 18 (1927), 89 (F. Magnette); M. Malaise, *Antiquités égyptiennes et verres du Proche-Orient ancien des Musées Curtius et du verre à Liège* (1971), 14-5; E. Warmenbol, *La Caravane du Caire*, 2006, 99-117.

OTTO, Eberhard (1913-1974)
German Egyptologist; born in Dresden, 26 Feb. 1913, son of Hermann O., a law court director, and his wife née Leplow; he studied Egyptology and Semitic Languages, 1932-7 at Leipzig, Munich, and Göttingen; Dr. Phil. Göttingen University, 1937; he was assistant to Kees (q.v.) in Göttingen, 1937-40, Habilitation, 1944;

he married Gudrun Stumpp, 1941; Lecturer Göttingen, 1943; Assistant Professor Hamburg, 1952; Professor Heidelberg, 1955; Member Heidelberg Akad. der Wissenschaften, 1957; German Archaeological Institute, 1958; Hon. Professor Instituto Sudamericano de Asuntos Legales, Buenos Aires; Otto's specialities were threefold, in the fields of religion, psychology and ancient Egyptian ideology, and he began his career by producing an important study on the history of the bull cult, 1938; later he turned to geographical matters and wrote an account of the topography of the Theban nome; yet another interest was late texts; in all these departments he produced significant works; his principal publications were, *Beiträge zur Geschichte der Stierkulte in Aegypten*, 1938, also 1964; *Topographie des Thebanischen Gaues,* 1952; *Ägypten, der Weg des Pharaonen-Reiches*, 1953, 1958; *Die Biographischen Inschriften der Ägyptischen Spatzeit, ihre geistes geschichtliche und literarische Bedeutung*, 1954; *Kleines Wörterbuch der Ägyptologie*, with H. W. Helck, 1956; *Das Ägyptische Mundoffnungsritual,* 1960; *Ägyptologische Abhandlungen*, etc., 1960, with H. W. Helck; *Aus der Sammlung des Ägyptologischen Institutes der Universität Heidelberg,* (illustrated catalogue) 1964; *Gott und Mensch nach den Ägyptischen Tempelinschriften der Griechisch-Römischen Zeit. Eine Untersuchung zur Phraseologie der Tempelinschriften*, 1964; *Die Religion der alten Ägypter* in *Handbuch der Orientalistik* Abt. 1 Bd. 8, Lfg 1., 1964; *Osiris und Amun: Kult und heilige Statten*, trans. as *Egyptian arts and cults of Osiris and Amon ...* by Kate Bosse Griffiths, 1968; he contributed a short study entitled *Götter und Tempel* to K. Lange and M. Hirmer's *Ägypten* trans. as *Egypt*, 1967; a final project was the vast encyclopaedia of Egyptology undertaken with H. W. Helck (q.v.) as co-editor and with a large team of specialist writers, *Lexikon der Ägyptologie*, appearing in fascicles from 1972; Otto also wrote *Das Verhältnis von Rite und Mythus im Ägyptischen* etc., and a précis history, 1954; he died in Mülben, Up. Eberbach, 11 Oct. 1974.

Inf. Otto family; *BSFE* 70-71 (1974), 8; *Kürschner* 11th ed. (1970), 2188; *Wer ist Wer*? 17th ed. (1971-3), 800; *WW in Germany* 5th ed. (1974), 1250; *Frankfurter Allegemeine Zeitung* 25 Oct. 1974; *SAK* 2 (1975), v-xviii (H. W. Helck) (bibl.); *ZÄS* 103 (1976), v-vii (portr.) (E. Lüddeckens); *ZDMG* 126 (1976), 1-4 (portr.) (H. Brunner); *Saeculum* 25 (1974), 291-2 (J. Krecher); J. Assmann et al, ed., *Problems and Priorities in Egyptian Archaeology*, 1987, 23-7.

OUARDÉ, Antoun *see* **WARDI**

PACHO, Jean Raymond (1794-1829)
French traveller; he was born in Nice, 3 Jan. 1794; he was educated at the Collège de Tournon; he visited Italy and came to Paris in 1816; his first interests were drawing and botany, but in 1818 he went to Egypt with the intention of exploring that country; as he was unable to obtain the necessary funds he returned to Paris and made a living by painting portraits and journalism until the end of 1820; he then returned to Egypt, funds having been provided by a French merchant in the service of the Pasha; he explored Lower Egypt, making drawings of the monuments and collecting plants; the death of his patron in 1823 interrupted his explorations, but another supporter having appeared, he continued them for another year; returning to Cairo, he planned the exploration of Cyrenaica, which he accomplished between Nov. 1824 and July 1825; on the recommendation of Letronne (q.v.) he received a grant for further exploration, but his mind gave way and he took his own life; he published an account of his travels, Paris, 1827-9, with a large folio vol. of plates; he died in Paris, 26 Jan. 1829.

NBG 39, 12; Champollion, i, 271, 295; ii, 74.

PAGE, Anthea Briane (1932-2001)
British publisher; she was born at Hornchurch 3 July 1932, daughter of Archibald Henry Page, a solicitor, and Marjorie Agnes Butler; she worked as a secretary in the British Foreign Office and served in Rome and Athens; she took an extramural diploma in archaeology at University College London specializing in Egyptology; as a result of her interest, she became secretary at the Department of Egyptology, University College London, 1967; Harry Smith, later Professor, encouraged her interest in Egyptology and suggested the publication of objects in the Petrie Museum; she eventually left the Department in 1981 and founded her publication company The Rubicon Press specializing in Egyptological and classical subjects; she published *Egyptian Sculpture Archaic to Saite from the Petrie Collection*, 1976 and *Ancient Egyptian Figured Ostraca in the Petrie Collection*, 1983; she died in London, 25 Nov. 2001

Inf. A. Phillips and H. S. Smith; *Bulletin of ASTENE* 13 (2002), 10.

PAGET, Rosalind Frances Emily (1844-1925)
English copyist; she was born at Elford, 5 Jan. 1844, daughter of Revd Francis Edward P., Rector of Elford, Staffs, and Fanny Chester; he was a student at University College London, 1893-8; she went to Egypt 1895-6 with Miss Pirie (later Mrs Quibell, q.v.) for the Egyptian Research Account and copied the scenes in the tomb of Ptahhotep at Saqqara, published in the memoir *The Ramesseum*, 1896; she visited the temple of Deir el-Bahri and made many coloured facsimiles which were used by Griffith in his *Hieroglyphs*, 1898; these watercolours are in the Griffith Institute, Oxford; she died unmarried in Wells, 29 Jan. 1925.

Burke's Landed Gentry; Petrie, 158.

PALAGI, (Filippo) Pelagio (1775-1860)
Italian painter, sculptor, and architect; he was born in Bologna, 25 May 1775, son of Baldassare Michele Franceso P. and Giuliana Raffanini; he worked mainly in Rome, and collected works of art and antiquities, which he bequeathed to his native town of Bologna; the Egyptian antiquities were purchased from the collection of Nizzoli (q.v.) in 1831, and were therefore brought from Egypt between 1817 and 1828; he died in Turin, 6 March 1860.

DBDI 80, 382-5; *Enc. It.* 25. 943; Ducati, *Guida del Museo di Bologna*, 1923. 6; R. Grandi and C. Morigi Govi, *Pelagio Palagi i artisti e collezionista*, 1976; C. Morigi Govi and G. Sassatelli, *Dalla stanza delle antichità al Museo Civico*, 1984, 191-210; C. Poppi, *Pelagio Palagi. Dipinti dale raccolte del Commune di Bologna*, 1996; D. Picchi in *EDAL* 1 (2009), 35-40.

PALANQUE, (Henri Amédée) Charles (1865-1909)
French Egyptologist; he was born at Auch, 21 Dec. 1865, son of Louis P. and Marie Mesté; he studied under Guieysse (q.v.) and Moret (q.v.); member of the IFAO Cairo 1900-3; he excavated at El-Der, near Abu Roash, 1900-2, Bawit 1902-3 and at Asyut, 1903; he contributed to the *Bull.* and *Mem.* of the Institute; he died in Auch, 9 Dec. 1909.

BIFAO 7 (1910), 177; C. Meurice, *Bulletin de la Société Archéologqiue Historique, Littéraire et Scientifique de Gers* 399 (2011), 64-78.

PALERNE, Jean (1557-1592)
French poet and traveller; he was known as 'Forésien' because born in Fouillouse, near St. Étienne-en-Forez, 1557, son of Clément P. and Antoinette Guichard; at the age of nineteen he followed François Duke of Alençon, the fourth son of Henri II of France, on various journeys in Flanders and England as a secretary, 1576-7; he then went on his own to Spain, but little is known of this trip or its purpose; he toured the Levant in 1581-3, arriving at Alexandria, 20 July, 1581, remaining in Egypt until 18 Sept.; he visited Rosetta, crossed the Delta by boat to Cairo where he visited Mataria, the Pyramids and Sphinx, and probably Saqqara, then travelled to Sinai by

the desert route, Suez and the shores of the Red Sea, returning to Damietta by the other branch of the Nile and embarking for the Holy Land; his account of his voyage entitled *Pérégrinations*, etc., was published 1606 and provides the best description of ancient Egyptian monuments and antiquities before Greaves (q.v.); he gives a very full description of the visible antiquities in Alexandria, mentioning the two obelisks, their dimensions and hieroglyphic inscriptions; he describes the garden of Mataria and the obelisk nearby which he did not have a chance to see at close quarters; there is a long and detailed description of the Sphinx and the pyramids, which he noted were wrongly called granaries of Pharaoh by the Jews; he correctly states that the pyramids were built as tombs by the Pharaohs, and gives the measurements of the Great Pyramid; he described the galleries inside, giving a good account of the burial chamber and sarcophagus, and a very brief account of the second and third Giza pyramids and mastabas as well as the various smaller pyramids and burial places where mummies were found, five or six miles away; he gives a brief account of mummification, and interestingly refers to figurines of men and animals found with the mummies; his description of Sinai is also detailed; he held a financial post at Orleans, 1587-92 and died there in 1592.

Voyage en Égypte de Jean Palerne Forésien 1581, ed. Serge Sauneron, 1971, 2nd vol. of *Voyageurs Occid. en Égypte, IFAO* Cairo; *Biogr. Univ.* 32, 11; *NBG* 39, 77-8.

PALIN, Nils Gustaf (1765-1842)
Swedish orientalist and diplomat; he was born Stockholm, 15 Aug. 1765, son of Nils P. and Catharina Ahman; Swedish ambassador in Constantinople 1814-24, he travelled in Egypt and the Near East; he formed a rich collection of Egyptian antiquities, part of which was lost in a fire at Pera in 1818; he received John Lee (q.v.) in Constantinople and went with him to Thebes, 1810; an unsuccessful precursor of Young (q.v.) and Champollion (q.v.), he claimed to have deciphered hieroglyphs and wrote several books on the decipherment of Egyptian writing, as early as 1802 and 1804 on the Rosetta Stone and later more elaborate works, 1812; today these memoirs are only of historic interest as they contain no real discoveries; his later life was spent in Italy, he retired from official life to a mansion at Rome, where he was murdered, 16 March 1842 and many of his antiquities were stolen; his remaining collections were sold in Paris, 18-19 April 1859, many being acquired by the Louvre; the unillustrated catalogue, *Catalogue des objets contenus dans le cabinet d'antiquités de feu M. le Chevalier de Palin*, produced at Rome about 1842, lists 226 Egyptian items; there is a copy in the Royal Library in Stockholm with drawings of some of the objects in the margins.

Lee MSS; *Rev. de l'Art*, 43. 168; *BIFAO* 5 (1906), 84; Hilmy, i, 175; *Svenska Män och Kvinnor* 6, 5-6; Lugt 24842.

PALMER, Edward Henry (1840-1882)
British orientalist; born Cambridge, 7 Aug. 1840, son of William Henry Palmer and Mary Sword; he was made Fellow of St. John's Coll. 1867; MA, 1870; he married firstly Laura Davis 1871; having mastered a number of oriental languages he wished to visit the east and was able to do so when he was chosen in 1868 to accompany Sir Charles Wilson, Capt. Henry Spencer Palmer, and the Revd F. Holland on their survey of Sinai for the PEF, which had already been visited by Holland; Palmer's principal duty was to collect the correct place-names from the Bedouin so that an accurate nomenclature of the Sinai peninsula could be established for the first time; this expedition proved successful and the following year Palmer and Chas. Francis Tyrwhitt Drake walked the six hundred miles from Sinai to Jerusalem, on foot without any escort, a formidable feat in those days; they discovered no inscriptions, but they explored for the first time the 'Desert of the Wanderings called Tih'; Palmer published an account *The Desert of the Exodus* in 2 vols., 1871, in which he mentions Major Macdonald (q.v.) and his work; still restless, in 1881 he gave up his university work and became a journalist working for the *Standard*; he went to Egypt on a secret mission in 1882, apparently he was sent by Gladstone's government to detach the Arab tribes of the Sinai area from the side of the Egyptian rebels, with English gold he was to try to obtain help from the Bedouin sheikhs in securing the immunity of the Suez Canal and its repair if damaged by the followers of Arabi; from now on he acted the part of an adventurer in the Suez area with some success at first, but was later shot, probably by robbers, 11 Aug. 1882; Palmer was buried in St. Paul's Cathedral crypt, 1883.

ODNB 42, 484-6; *DNB* 43, 122-6; W. Besant, *The Life and Achievements of Edward Henry Palmer*, 1883 (portr.); Capt. A. E. Haynes, *Man-hunting in the Desert*, 1894.

PALMER, William (1811-1879)
British Roman Catholic theologian and chronologist; he was born at Mixby, 12 July 1811, son of William Jocelyn P. and Dorothea Richardson Roundell, and was the brother of the 1st Earl of Selbourne; he was educated Magdalen College, Oxford; MA, 1833; he visited Egypt 1853-4, and published *Egyptian Chronicles with a Harmony of Sacred and Egyptian Chronology*, 2 vols. 1861; he died and was buried in Rome, 5 April 1879.

ODNB 42, 543-4; *DNB* 43, 167-9; Hilmy, ii, 89.

PANCKOUCKE, Charles Louis Fleury (1780-1844)
French publisher and collector; he was born in Paris 26 Dec. 1780, son of Charles-Joseph P., publisher of Diderot's *Encyclopédie* and friend of Voltaire and Rousseau, and Thérèse Couret de Villeneuve; he succeeded his father in the family firm; in 1820 he petitioned Louis XVIII to be allowed to publish a second edition of the *Description de l'Égypte*, due to the success and small print run of the first edition (itself not completed until 1828); this began in 1821, and was completed in 1830; this second edition of the *Description* is often called the 'Panckoucke edition'; he also published Dubois's (q.v.) catalogue of the Mimaut (q.v.) collection; he formed a collection published as *Collection d'antiquités égyptiennes, grecques et romaines, d'objets d'art du XVe siècle, vases et coupes grecs, manuscrits, tableaux et gravures, réunis et classés par C.-L.-F. Panckoucke* (1841); he bequeathed this to the town of Meudon to form a museum but his will was overturned by his son; a granite offering table, discovered in 1942 in the parkland of his house, is now in the Meudon Museum; other Egyptian objects from his collection were sold in Paris, Drouot, 25 March 1926; he died at Fleury Sous Meudon, 11 July 1844.

La littérature française contemporaine 1827-1849 V, 1854, 583; A. Charron, *RdE* 42 (1991), 253-5; inf. T. Hardwick.

PARAVEY, Charles Hippolyte de (1787-1871)
French civil servant and writer; he was born in Fumay, 25 Sept. 1787, son of Georges P. engineer, and Charlotte Mathis; he was educated at the École Polytechnique and was an officer in the Corps de Ponts et Chaussées; he wrote many works on Egyptian hieroglyphs and the Zodiac of Dendera and sought to find therein references to the Noachian Deluge and other biblical narratives; he claimed to have established a common hieroglyphic origin of all forms of writing in his *Essai sur l'origine unique et hiéroglyphique des chiffres et des lettres de tous les peuples*, etc., Paris, 1826; he was de Rougé's (q.v.) first instructor in Egyptology; he died in St-Germain-en-Laye, 15 May 1871.

NBG 39, 187; Chabas, 47; Hartleben, ii, 137; Hilmy, i, 175; *Larousse* XIXe, 12, 2-3.

PARISET, Étienne (1770-1847)
French physician; he was born at Grand, 5 Aug. 1770, son of Claude P.; Sec. perpétuel of the Acad. de Med., Paris; he visited Egypt in 1828 intending to accompany Champollion (q.v.) on his journey to Upper Egypt, but remained in Cairo to study the plague; he studied the technique of mummification and published *Lettre sur les Embaumements*, 1827; he died in Paris, 6 July 1847.

NBG 39, 214-6; Carré, i, 220; Champollion, ii, 214 and often; E. F. Dubois, *Histoire des Membres de l'Académie Royale de Médecine*, 1850, I, ix-xxxii, 1-20 (bibl.); G. Sussman, *Journal of the History of Medecine and Allied Sciences* 26 (1971), 52-71; S. Salzgeber, *Biographie d'Étienne Parsiet*, 2006.

PARKE, Henry (1790-1835)
British architect; he was baptized in London, 25 Dec. 1790, son of John P., musician, and his wife Hannah Maria; he visited Egypt and ascended the Nile to Wady Halfa, with J. J. Scholes, and the Levant, 1824; on the journey to Upper Egypt they travelled in company with Frederick Catherwood (q.v.) and Henry Westcar (q.v.); Parke published a map of Nubia which is rare and indicates the positions of all the temples, rock tombs, and important buildings on the banks of the river; his large collection of architectural drawings from antique subjects is in the library of the Royal Institute of British Architects; he died in London, 5 May 1835.

ODNB 42, 647; *DNB* 43, 225-6; Hay Diary 1824, Sept. 11; Westcar Diary, passim.

PARKER, John Henry (1806-1884)
British writer on architecture; he was born in London, 1 March 1806, son of John P. and Catherine Elizabeth Ryder; he succeeded his uncle Joseph in the well-known book-selling and publishing house at Oxford; FSA, 1849; CB, 1871; he published *The Twelve Egyptian Obelisks in Rome*, Oxford, 1879, with translations of the texts by Samuel Birch; he died in Oxford, 31 Jan. 1884.

ODNB 42, 697-8; *DNB* 43, 250-1; Hilmy, ii, 93.

PARKER, Richard Anthony (1905-1993)
American Egyptologist; he was born in Chicago, 10 Dec. 1905, son of Thomas Frank P. and Emma Ursula Heldman; he graduated from Dartmouth College, BA, 1930 and studied at the Oriental Institute, University of Chicago from 1934; PhD, Aug. 1938; he became research assistant at Chicago, 1 July 1938-42; research associate, 1 July 1942-6; and Assistant Professor of Egyptology, 1 July 1946-9; he served as an epigrapher with Chicago's Epigraphic Survey at Luxor 1 Oct. 1938-April 1940 when work was halted due to World War II; assistant Field Director, 1 July 1946-7; Director, 1947-31 Dec. 1948; Consultant Field Director, 1 Jan.-30 June

1949; he was appointed the first Charles Edwin Wilbour Professor of Egyptology and chairman of the Department of Egyptology at Brown University, Providence, Rhode Island on 1 July 1948 and held the positions until his retirement in 1972; he was a founder member of the American Research Center in Egypt, Trustee, 1948-74 and a founder of the *Annual Egyptological Bibliography*; he was a member of the visiting committees, Department of Middle Eastern Civilization, Harvard, 1950-61 and Department of Egyptian Art, Boston Museum of Fine Arts from 1950; he was a specialist in Demotic studies, Egyptian mathematics, astronomy, and chronology; his principal publications were *Medinet Habu* IV-VII, 1946-64; *Reliefs and Inscriptions at Karnak* III, 1957; *The Temple of Khonsu* I, 1979, all as part of the Chicago Epigraphic Survey; *Babylonian Chronology 626 B.C.-A.D. 75* 1942, rev. 1946, 1956 with W. H. Dubberstein; *The Calendars of Ancient Egypt*, 1950; *The Calendar: Past, Present and Future,*1955, with C. R. Decker and Q. Wright; *A Vienna Demotic Papyrus on Eclipse and Lunar Omina*, 1959; *Egyptian Astronomical Texts* 1-3, 1960-69, with O. Neugebauer; *A Saite Oracle Papyrus from Thebes in The Brooklyn Museum (Pap. Brooklyn 47.218.3)*, 1962; *Demotic Mathematical Papyri*, 1972; *The Edifice of Taharqa by the Sacred Lake of Karnak*, 1979, with J. Leclant and J. C. Golvin; and *Denkmäler der Oase Dachla aus dem Nachlass von Ahmed Fakhry*, 1982, with O. Neugebauer and D. Pingree; a volume of papers *Egyptological Studies in Honor of Richard A. Parker*, edited by L. H. Lesko was published in 1986; he died in Providence, 3 June 1993.

WWA 1990-1, 2524; Lesko, *op. cit.*, ix-xiv (portr.) (bibl.); *JEA* 79 (1993), ix; *The Oriental Institute Annual Report 1992-1993*, 8-10 (J. Larson and J. Johnson); *JARCE* 31 (1994), i-ii (L. H. Lesko)

PARRISH, Dillwyn (1840-1899)
American collector; he was born in Philadelphia 10 June 1840, son of William Dillwyn P. and Elizabeth Miller; later of Bickley, Kent, he formed a collection of antiquities and *objets d'art*; on the Committee of the EEF, 1893-8; his collections were sold at Sotheby's, 5 June 1928; the Egyptian objects (lots 55-63) included the four canopic jars of Princess Eskhons (Neskhons) from the royal cache of Deir el-Bahri, which he obtained in 1874 from Andrew MacCallum (q.v.); these were withdrawn from the sale and were presented to the British Museum in 1929 by the Misses Parrish (EA 59187-59200; see *BMQ* 4, 2.); he presented some objects to the Pennsylvania University Museum; he died in Châtel-Guyon, France, 11 Aug. 1899.

Maspero, *Momies Royales*, 712; *Rec. Trav.* 4, 79.

PARTHEY, Gustav Friedrich Constantin (1798-1872)
German Coptologist and classical scholar; he was born in Berlin, 27 Oct. 1798, son of Daniel Friedrich P. and Wilhelmine Nicolai; educated at Berlin and Heidelberg, graduating 1820; he visited England, Italy, and Egypt, 1820-4; he published a number of Greek and Coptic texts, and several books, the best-known of which is *Vocabularium Coptico-latinum et Latino-copticum*, which remained the best Coptic dictionary for many years until it was superseded by more modern works; his *Wanderungen durch Sicilien und die Levant*, 1833-40, deals with Egypt in the second part; Member of the Berlin Acad., 1857; he died in Rome, 2 April 1872.

Hilmy, ii, 94; *ADB* 25, 189-91.

PARTRIDGE, Robert Bernard (1951-2011)
British Egyptologist; he was born on a British Airforce base in Rinteln, Germany. 10 April 1951, son of Bernard P., who was serving in the RAF at the time, and his wife Mary Andrews; he was educated at Churston Ferrers Grammar School, Brixham, Devon; he worked for Barclays Bank from 1969-1999, in a variety of roles including that of a Branch Manager in Devon and from 1984 as a Systems Consultant in Knutsford, Cheshire; he studied at the University of Manchester under Rosalie David gaining the Certificate in Egyptology with distinction in 1989; he was chairman of the Manchester Ancient Egypt Society 1994-2011 and editor of *Ancient Egypt* magazine, 2004-2011; he was a trustee of the EES, 2009-10; he lectured in Egyptology at the Centre for Continuing Education at the University of Manchester; he was the owner of the *Ancient Egypt Picture Library*, a collection of over 30,000 photographic slides and digital images of Ancient Egyptian sites and artefacts; his principal published works were *Faces of Pharaohs. Royal Mummies and Coffins from Ancient Thebes*, 1994; *Transport in Ancient Egypt*, 1996; *Fighting Pharaohs. Weapons and Warfare in Ancient Egypt*, 2002; he died in Knutsford, Cheshire, 10 July 2011.

Inf. J. P. Phillips; *Ancient Egypt* 12/1 (2011), 63 (portr.), (P. Phillips).

PASLEY, (*Sir*) Charles William (1780-1861)
British military engineer; he was born at Eskdalemuir, Dumfries, 8 Sept. 1780, son of Charles P., merchant of London, and Jane Carlyle; he was educated at Selkirk and the Royal Military Academy, Woolwich from Aug. 1796; he was commissioned as 2nd Lt. in the Royal Artillery, 1 Dec. 1797 but was transferred to the Royal Engineers on 1 April 1798; he was promoted to 1st Lt. 28 May 1799; he served in Minorca and Malta and in 1802 undertook a private visit to Egypt on leave; his diary of the visit with plans of the monuments is now in the British Library (Add. MSS 41973); in his later career he became Director of the School of Military Engineering at Chatham 1812-41, Major-General, 1841, Inspector-General of the Railways, 1841-46; KCB, 1846, Col-Commandant of the Royal Engineers, 1853, and General, 1860; he died in London, 19 April 1861; his papers are now in the British Library (Add. MSS 41961-41995).

ODNB 42, 969-71 (portr.); *DNB* 43, 439-42 (R. H. Vetch); Boase 2, 1375-6; P. H. Kealy, *General Sir Charles William Pasley*, 1930.

PASSALACQUA, Giuseppe Gaspare Ludovico (1797-1865)
Italian excavator and collector; he was baptized in Trieste, 26 Feb. 1797, son of Pietro P., a merchant from Messina, and Regina Marchetti; he went to Egypt in 1820 as a horse-dealer, but as this business did not prosper, he took to excavating and collecting antiquities; he made a large and very important collection at Thebes and other sites and brought it to Paris in order to sell it; it was exhibited at 52, Passage Vivienne in 1826, and was offered to the French government for 400,000 francs, but this offer was rejected and it was afterwards bought for 100,000 francs by Friedrich Wilhelm IV of Prussia for the Berlin Museum in 1827; Passalacqua was in consequence installed as Conservator of the Egyptian Collections in 1828, a position he held until the end of his life, when Lepsius, who from 1855 had been Assistant Conservator, succeeded him; the collection was described in the *Catalogue raisonné et historique des antiquités découvertes en Égypte par J. Passalacqua*, 3 pts. 1826; he died in Berlin, 1865.

Brugsch, *Mein Leben*, 25-49, 189; Champollion, i, 297; Ebers, *Richard Lepsius* (trans. Underhill), 183; Hilmy, ii, 95; Madox, i, 278 and passim; Westcar Diary, 274; E. Gran-Aymerich, *Dictionnaire biographique d'archéologie 1798-1945*, 2001, incorporated in *Les Chercheurs de passé 1798-1945*, 2007, 1043; P. Tedesco, *Aegyptus* 97 (2017), 209-243.

PATERSON, Emily (1861-1947)
Friend and associate of Amelia Edwards (q.v.); she was born at Edgbaston, Birmingham, 11 March 1861, daughter of Alfred Sweet P. and Sarah Clark; she was her private secretary, 1888-92, and succeeded her as General Secretary, EEF, 1892; she retired, 1919, and in recognition of her work was made a Life Member and awarded a pension; she attended Griffith's classes at University College London, and gave lectures for the Fund, to whose library she was also a donor; she died in Redruth, Cornwall, 3 Sept. 1947.

EES *Ann. Rep.* 1947, 7; *JEA* 33 (1947), 2; Newberry Corr.

PAUTHIER, Jean Pierre Guillaume (1801-1873)
French orientalist; born in Mamirolle, 4 Oct. 1801, son of Pierre François P., farmer, and Jeanne Baptiste Bideaux; he published works on Far Eastern languages and Egyptian, *Sinico-Aegyptiaca: Essai sur l'origine et la formation similaire des écritures figuratives Chinoise et Égyptienne, composé principalement d'après les écrivains indigènes, traduits pour la première fois dans une langue européenne*, 1842; *Hymnes Sanscrits, Persans, Égyptiens, Assyriens et Chinois. Le Chi-King ou livres des vers, traduit par G.P.*, 1872; he died in Paris, 11 March 1873.

NBG 39, 418-9; Hilmy, ii, 99; *La Grande Enc.* 26, 144; Vapereau, 1222.

PAUW, Cornelius de (1739-1799)
Dutch writer; he was born in Amsterdam, 19 Aug. 1739, son of Antonius P. of a literary and diplomatic family, and Quirina van Heijningen; he was educated at Liège and Göttingen in anticipation of a church post; he was appointed a canon at Xanten, 1763; he wrote studies on Greeks, Americans, and Germans as well as *Recherches philosophiques sur les Égyptiens et les Chinois*, 1773, new ed., 1774 which was translated into English and German; he criticized the views of d'Origny (q.v.) and de Guignes (q.v.) in linking the Chinese and the Egyptians; he also defended the originality of Egyptian art; he died in Xanten, 7 July 1799.

NGB 39, 419; *Biographie Universelle* 32, 321-2; C. Traunecker in *Égypte Afrique & Orient* 58 (2010), 3-8.

PAVLOV, Vsevolod Vladimirovitch (1898-1972)
Russian Egyptologist and art historian; he was born in Buryn 20 Jan./Feb. 1, 1898, son of Vladimir Vladimirovitch P. and Lydia Dmitrievna Vadbolsky; he studied in Moscow, and there he was active at the Museum and later also as Professor at the University; for more than 30 years he devoted his efforts to studies and publications of the

resources of the Pushkin Museum; he was the author of many catalogues and studies on Egyptian art in Russian *Ocherki po iskusstvu drevnego Egipta (Studies on the Art of ancient Egypt)*, 1936; *Egyptian Sculpture. Small objects*, Moscow 1949; *Chudozhestvennoe remeslo drevnego Egipta (Artistic Handicraft of Ancient Egypt)*, with S. I. Hodjash, 1959; *Fayumsky portret (The Fayum Portraits)*, with R. Shurinova, 1965; *Egipetsky portret I-IV vekov (Egyptian Portraits of I-IV cent.)*, 1967 and *Egyptian Small Sculpture*, with S. I. Hodjash, 1985 (posth.); he died in Moscow, 16 Feb. 1972.

VDI 2 (124), 1973, 205-8 (N. A. Pomerantseva); inf. J. Śliwa.

PAYNE, Joan Crowfoot (1912-2002)
British archaeologist; she was born at Giza, 16 Jan. 1912, daughter of John Crowfoot (q.v.) and Grace Hood Crowfoot (q.v); she excavated in England and Palestine under her father, Garstang (q.v.), and others, specializing in lithics; she catalogued and organized the display of lithics in the Palestine Archaeological Museum, Jerusalem; she gave up her career on marriage in 1937; she was appointed Cataloguer at the Ashmolean Museum, Oxford, 1957, Departmental assistant, 1965-79; she created a card catalogue of the Egyptian and Nubian antiquities at the museum; she focused her research on prehistoric Egypt, designed a new predynastic gallery, and collaborated with Baumgartel (q.v.) editing her publication on Naqada; she was awarded an honorary MA, 1980; she published *Catalogue of the Predynastic Egyptian Collection in the Ashmolean Museum*, 1993; republished with addenda, 2000; she left her files to the Griffith Institute; she died in Purbrook, Hampshire, 4 Oct. 2002.

Inf. H. Whitehouse and S. Payne; *The Ashmolean* 44 (2003), 20-1 (portr.) (P. R. S. Moorey); *Levant* 35 (2003), iv-v (P. R. S. Moorey).

PEACOCK, David Philip Spencer (1939-2015)
British excavator; he was born at Stamford, 14 Jan. 1939, son of Philip Frederick P., a carpenter and later clerk of works at RAF Wittering, and Agnes Taylor; he was educated at Stamford School for Boys and then studied geology at the University of St. Andrews; B.Sc.; PhD; he became a research fellow in the application of science to archaeology at the University of Birmingham, 1965-8; he was appointed research fellow at Southampton University, 1968; later reader and professor of archaeology, 1990-2004, head of the Dept. of Archaeology, 1998-2003, and Deputy Dean of the Faculty of Humanities, 2000-1; he was an expert on the Red Sea trade in the Roman period; he directed excavations at Mons Claudianus, 1987-93, Mons Porphyrites, 1994-8, Quseir el-Qadim, 1999-2003, and at the Ethiopian site of Adulis, 2004-5; FSA, 1974; he was awarded the Kenyon medal by the British Academy, 2012, and the Pommerance medal by the American Institute of Archaeology, 2012; his publications included *Pottery and Early Commerce*, 1977; *Pottery in the Roman World*, 1982; *Amphorae and the Roman Economy*, with D. F. Williams, 1991; *The Roman Imperial Porphyry Quarries, Interim Reports*, with V. Maxfield, 1994-8; *Survey and Excavation at Mons Claudianus* I, with V. Maxfield, 1997; II, 2001; III, 2006; *The Roman Imperial Quarries*, with V. Maxfield, 2001; II, 2007; *Food for the Gods*, 2006; *Myos-Hormos-Quseir el-Qadim* I, with L. Blue, 2006; II, 2011; *The Ancient Red Sea Port of Adulis*, with L. Blue, 2007; *Bread for the People*, with D. F. Williams, 2011; *The Stone of Life*, 2013; he died at Winchester, 15 March 2015.

The Times 17 June 2015; *Times Higher Education* internet obit; inf. Prof. A. Peacock.

PEASE, Thomas (1816–1884)
English traveller and collector; he was born in Park Place, Leeds, 31 Jan. 1816, only surviving son of Thomas Benson Pease (1782–1846), a wealthy Quaker stuff merchant, and Martha Whitelock (*d*.1828); he was educated at Darlington School, County Durham, he joined the family firm and married Lucy Fryer (1820-44) in 1842, and had two daughters; after his wife's death, he spent the winter of 1845–6 in Egypt, where he began a collection of small antiquities that ultimately went to Plymouth City Museum and Art Gallery in 1919; he met there George John Browne, 3rd Marquis of Sligo (1820–96), turning down his invitation to accompany him on a trip to Palestine; inherited Chapel Allerton Hall, Leeds, on death of his father; made a further visit to Lower Egypt (only) in the winter of 1846–7, accompanied by his younger sisters, Susan (1817–73) and Louisa Ann (*b*.1820); married Martha Lucy Aggs (1824–53) in 1850, with whom he had two daughters and a son, Thomas Ormston Pease (1853-1937), to whom his Egyptian collection passed in 1917; he moved to Bristol in the summer of 1852, taking up residence in Westbury-on-Trym, where he later became acquainted with Amelia Edwards (q.v.); he married Susanna Ann Fry (1828–1917) in April 1856, with whom he had ten children; Vice-Chairman, Poor Law Board of Guardians; Fellow of the Geological Society of London 1860; member Bristol Institution for the Advancement of Science and Art 1860; founder member of the Bristol Naturalists' Society in 1862 (Vice-President 1864–71); Joint Secretary of Finance of the Bristol Museum & Library Association in 1871; he died at the Quaker Meeting House, Bristol, 15 Jan. 1884.

A. Dodson, *JEA* 94 (2008), 107–138.

PECK, Caroline Nestmann (1921-1987)
American Egyptologist; she was born at Wheeling, West Virginia, 27 June 1921, daughter of Carl Nestmann and Louise Webb; she married Russell Alan Peck, 1952; she studied at the Oriental Institute, Chicago 1942-49; MA 1949, and Brown University, Providence 1949-58; PhD 1958; she wrote her thesis on *Some Decorated Tombs of the First Intermediate Period at Naga ed-Deir*; she became a teaching associate in Egyptology at Brown University; she died in Providence, RI, 9 Sept. 1987.

Varia Aegyptiaca 3 (1987), 187-8 (C. Van Siclen).

PEET, (Thomas) Eric (1882-1934)
British Egyptologist and archaeologist; he was born in Liverpool, 12 Aug. 1882, son of Thomas P. and Salome Fowler; he was educated at Merchant Taylors' School, Crosby, and afterwards studied Mathematics and Classics at The Queen's College, Oxford; Jodrell Scholar; Craven Fellow, 1906, with which he went to Italy to study archaeology; Pelham Student, British School in Rome; he excavated in Italy, 1909, and afterwards published his first major work, *The Stone and Bronze Ages in Italy and Sicily*; it was through his friendship with MacIver (q.v.) that he first became interested in and then entered Egyptology, and Newberry (q.v.) arranged for him to work under Garstang (q.v.) at Abydos and also took him with him to the Delta, 1909; he transferred to the EEF the same year, and worked at Abydos, 1909-13, at first under Naville (q.v.) but later independently; at this time he married Mary Florence Lawton, 1910, and was made Lecturer in Egyptology in the University of Manchester, 1913-28; he met Gardiner (q.v.) in the library of Cairo Museum and afterwards began to study Egyptian with him, 1911, but was in fact mainly self-taught in this as in Coptic and Demotic; he became a philologist of high calibre and made important contributions to the study and translation of papyri dealing with mathematics and with the tomb-robberies at Thebes under the late Ramesside kings; he served during the First World War in the RASC in Salonica and in France; after the war he was made Director of the EES excavations and although this work was not really his forte he inaugurated the important series of excavations at El-Amarna with the help of Newton 1921; he was made Laycock Student in Egyptology at Oxford, 1923, and Brunner Professor of Egyptology in Liverpool University, 1920-33; he became Reader and Professor designate in Egyptology at Oxford, 1933-4, but died before the latter appointment was confirmed; Fellow of The Queen's College, Oxford, 1933; Peet was also the editor of the *Liverpool Annals of Art and Archaeology* from 1921 onwards, and the *JEA* from 1923, to which he contributed many articles and reviews; he delivered a course of lectures at Cairo University, 1929, and the Schweich lectures for the British Academy the same year; his bibl. lists 75 books and articles on Egyptological subjects but is not complete; he wrote *The Cemeteries of Abydos*, pt. i with E. Naville, 1914, pt. ii, 1914, pt. iii, with W. L. S. Loat, 1913; *The Inscriptions of Sinai ...*, pt. i fol., with A. H. Gardiner, 1917; *The Mayer Papyri A. and B, Nos. M. 11162 and M. 11186 of the Free Public Museums, Liverpool*, 1920; *Egypt and the Old Testament*, 1922; *The Rhind Mathematical Papyrus, British Museum 10057 and 10058*, 1923; *The City of Akhenaten* I, with C. L. Woolley and others, 1923; *I Papiri ieratici del Museo di Torino: Il Giornale della necropoli di Tebe*, with G. Botti, 1928; *The Great Tomb-Robberies of the Twentieth Egyptian Dynasty*, 1930; *A comparative Study of the Literatures of Egypt, Palestine and Mesopotamia* (Schweich Lectures), 1931; also an inaug. lecture, *The Present Position of Egyptological Studies*, 1934, and chapters in the *Cambridge Anc. Hist.*; his papers and drawings are in the Griffith Institute, Oxford; he died in Oxford, 22 Feb. 1934.

AAA 21 (1934), 3-4 (J. P. Droop); *AE*, T (1934), 63-4 (S. R. K. Glanville); *Bull. John Rylands, Lib.* Manchester, 18 (1934), 259-60; *Chron. d'Ég.* 9 (1934), 323; *DNB* 1931-40, 685-6 (G. Battiscombe Gunn); *Eg. Rel.* 2 (1934), 155-60 (portr.) (bibl.) (H. W. Fairman); *JEA* 20 (1934), 66-70 (portr.) (A. H. Gardiner); *WWW* iii, 1061; *ODNB* 43, 435.

PEIRESC, Nicolas Claude Fabri de (1580-1637)
French antiquarian; he was born at Beaugensiers 1 Dec. 1580, son of Reynaud Fabri, an official, and Marguerite de Bompar; he studied at Padua and devoted himself to the collection of antiquities and natural curiosities carrying out an extensive correspondence with like-minded collectors and scholars; he was interested in Egyptian objects which he acquired through his agent Père Theophile Minuti who visited Egypt, and from French officials in Egypt; he wrote an unpublished essay on Egyptian antiquities; his collection was eventually acquired in part by the Bibliothèque Sainte-Geneviève in Paris and later passed into the French national collections; he died at Aix-en-Provence, 24 June 1637.

G. Cahen-Salvador, *Un Grand Humaniste Peiresc*, 1951; J. Hellin, *Nicolas-Claude Fabri de Peiresc 1580-1637*, 1980; S. Aufrère, *La Momie et la tempête*, 1990; M.-P. Foisy-Aufrère, *Egypte et Provence*, 1985, 182-7; J. Chamay and S. H. Aufrère, *Antike Kunst* 39 (1996), 38-51.

PELIZAEUS, (Friedrich) Wilhelm (1851-1930)
German businessman and collector; he was born at Hildesheim, 6 Sept. 1851, son of Clemens P., legal counsellor, and Emilie Schwarz; he joined his uncle's firm in Alexandria in 1869-78 and resided in Cairo 1878-1914; from 1885 he formed an extensive Egyptian collection; he also financed the excavations of the University of Leipzig 1903-6 and the Vienna Academy 1912-4, 1925-9; in 1907 he founded the Pelizaeus Museum, a rich collection with many fine Old Kingdom pieces of sculpture, opened in 1911; Hon. PhD Göttingen, 1921; in 1911 he was made an Hon. citizen of Hildesheim where he died, 14 Oct. 1930.

Chron. d'Ég. 11 (1931), 134; *Die Denkmäler des Pelizaeus Museums zu Hildesheim*, 1921 G. Roeder; H. Kayser, *Das Pelizaeus-Museum in Hildesheim*, 1966, 5-15; B. Schmitz *Das Alte Reich*, 1986, 6-7; A. Eggebrecht, *Pelizaeus-Museum, Hildesheim*, 1979, 9-13 (portr); *NDB* 20, 164 (B. Schmiz); inf. B. Schmitz.

PELLEGRINI, Astorre (1844-1908)
Italian Egyptologist; he was born in Leghorn, 5 June 1844; he was educated at Pisa University; afterwards at Florence, he published many short articles, chiefly in *Bessarione* from 1906 onwards; he published a papyrus with a new text of the Book of Breathings, and some short Coptic texts; he died in Florence, 22 Feb. 1908.

Sphinx 12, 152 (bibl.); *Bessarione* 12 (1908), 219-20.

PENDLEBURY, John Devitt Stringfellow (1904-1941)
British archaeologist and Cretan excavator; he was born in London, 12 Oct. 1904, son of Herbert Stringfellow P., a surgeon, and Lilian Dorothea Devitt; he was educated at Winchester, 1918-23, and Pembroke College, Cambridge, 1923; Exhibitioner, Shoolbred and Beatson Scholar; BA, 1927; MA; FSA; FRSA; Cambridge University Student at the British School of Arch. in Athens, 1927-8; Member of the Arch. expedition of Macedonia, 1928; also excavated in Crete; married Hilda Winifred White, 1928; he joined the EES expeditions to Armant and El-Amarna, 1928-9, and then directed the Amarna expedition 1930-1; he was appointed Curator of Knossos in Crete, 1930-4, and was the successor of Sir Arthur Evans (q.v.) in this work; he spent the summer months working in Crete and continued the Amarna excavations until 1936; he later excavated at Mount Dikte and other sites in Crete until the war, 1936-9; British Vice-Consul, Candia, Crete, 1941; although his work was primarily in Crete and Minoan archaeology and history, Pendlebury did much important work at El-Amarna, clearing and re-examining the central city and the important government buildings, as well as excavating many houses; he was able with the help of R. Lavers, to reconstruct the layout and much of the plan of the great Aten temple and the main palace, and also locate the records office and other administrative areas; another important contribution was the classification and study of objects showing contacts and connections between the Aegean and Egypt; besides articles in journals he published, *Aegyptiaca, a Catalogue of Egyptian objects in the Aegean Area*, 1930; *A Handbook to the Palace of Minos*, 1933; *The City of Akhenaten* II. *The North Suburb and the Desert Altars*, with H. Frankfort, 1933; *The City of Akhenaten* III. *The Central City and Official Quarters*, 2 pts., posth. with H. W. Fairman and others, 1951; *Tell el Amarna*, 1935; *The Archaeology of Crete*, 1939; in 1939 he joined the forces in Crete, Capt. 18th Infantry Brigade, and in May 1941 was severely wounded in action; he was looked after in a nearby house which was later entered by German paratroopers; he came from his bed to protect the lady of the house and, according to one version, was shot dead or alternatively he suffered a fatal internal haemorrhage in Kaminia near Heraklion, on or about 22 May 1941.

Chron. d'Ég. 18 (1943), 272-3 (J. Capart); *JEA* 28 (1941), 61-3 (portr.) (S. R. K. Glanville); *WWW* iv, 903; *Annual of the British School at Athens* XLI (1940-5), 5-8 (portr.); È. Gran-Aymerich, *Dictionnaire biographique d'archéologie 1798-1945*, 2001, incorporated in *Les Chercheurs de passé 1798-1945*, 2007, 1043-4; I. Grundon, *The Rash Adventurer*, 2007; R. Janssen, *Gött. Misz.* 225 (2010), 75-81; C. Naunton, *KMT* 21, 3 (2010), 45-53.

PENEY, Alfred (1817-1861)
French physician and explorer; he was born at Saint-Genix, 3 Aug. 1817; he was educated at Montpellier and Paris; he became secretary of A. B. Clot-Bey (q.v.), and was appointed chief medical officer to the troops in the Sudan; he went on an exploration expedition to the country beyond Gondokoro, but as he did not return, a search-party was sent and found him dying at Gondokoro, 26 July 1861.

Hill, 304; Lepsius, 196, 199, 205; Bayard Taylor, 293; *BIÉ* 1st ser. 7 (1862), 30-40.

PENNETHORNE, John (1808-1888)

British traveller, architect and mathematician; he was born at Worcester, 4 January 1808; son of Thomas P., the younger brother of Sir James Pennethorne; he entered the office of the architect John Nash in London becoming his favourite pupil; he made a study tour of Europe and Egypt 1830-5; visiting Athens in 1832 he observed the curvature of the horizontal lines of the Parthenon; spending the winter of 1833 at Thebes he made studies of the mouldings and coloured decoration of the temples and particularly the curved lines of the Temple at Medinet Habu; he met Burton (q.v.) at Thebes 13 Nov. 1833 and Hay (q.v.) at Karnak 2 Jan. 1834, having met him before at Cairo; he returned to England in 1835 but revisted Athens in 1837 to take additional measuremenets and make further observations; similar discoveries were made by Joseph Hoffer and published in C.F.L Förster's *Allgemeine Bauzeitung* 1838; he published in 1844 a pamphlet *The Elements and Mathematical Principles of Greek Architecture and Artists, recovered by an Analysis and Study of the remaining works of Architecture designed and erected in the age of Pericles* that were further pursued by F. C. Penrose who in 1851 published *Investigations of the Princples of Athenian Architecture*; he published *The Geometry and Optics of Ancient Architcture, illustrated by examples from Thebes, Athens and Rome* with 56 plates in 1878; in Feb. 1879 he contributed to the *Transactions of the Royal Institute of British Architects* a paper on 'The Connection between Ancient Art and the Ancient Geometry, as Illustrated by works of the age of Pericles'; he died at Hampstead, his residence at Yarmouth on the Isle of Wight, 20 Jan. 1888.

Inf. N. Cooke

PERC, Bernarda (1929-1983)

Yugoslav Egyptologist; she was born in Celje, Slovenia, 9 Nov. 1929; she studied archaeology and prehistory at the University of Ljubljana, 1949-54; she was appointed Keeper and later Director of the Regional Museum in Ptuj; in 1959 she became interested in Egyptology as a result of attending a seminar in Cairo; she studied under Fakhry (q.v.), Abu Bakr (q.v.) and Bakir (q.v.) at the University of Cairo 1959-61 and at Munich under Müller (q.v.), von Beckerath, and Westendorf 1963-68; she was awarded her doctorate for her work on Egyptian cults in the Balkans in the Roman period, *Beitrage zur Verbreitung Ägyptischer Kulte auf dem Balkan und in den Donauländern zur Römerzeit*, 1968; a post in Egyptology was created for her in Ljubljana; she died in Ljubljana, 30 May 1983.

Gött. Misz. 73 (1984), 7-11 (bibl.) (portr.) (A. Nibbi); *Argo* 22 (1983), 152-3 (I. Curk).

PERCIVAL, Francis William (1843-1929)

British traveller; he was born Northampton, 24 Sept. 1843, son of Samuel P. and Jane Goodchild; he was educated at The Queen's College, Oxford; MA; FSA; he was a lifelong friend of Sayce (q.v.) and travelled frequently with him in Egypt and elsewhere; he joined the EEF in 1886 and served on the Committee from 1894; Hon. Librarian, 1919; he died in London, 21 Feb. 1929.

Sayce, passim.

PERCY, (*Lord***) Algernon, 1st Baron Prudhoe and 4th Duke of Northumberland** (1792-1865)

British collector; he was born in Syon House, 15 Dec. 1792, second son of Hugh Percy, 2nd Duke, by his second marriage to Frances Julia Burrell; he entered the Navy, 1805; retired Captain, 1815; Rear-Admiral, 1850; Vice-Ad., 1857; Admiral, 1862; he was created Baron Prudhoe, 1816; from 1826 he travelled in the East for some years with Major Orlando Felix (q.v.) and met Champollion (q.v.) in Cairo in Sept. 1828 and again in Nubia in Jan. 1829; he reached Sennnar in 1829 and removed two granite lion statues from Gebel Barkal which were later presented to the British Museum (EA 1 and 2); he formed an extensive collection of Egyptian antiquities (over 2,000 objects), added to by his descendants, of which a catalogue by Samuel Birch was published in 1880; he accompanied Sir John Herschel's expedition to the Cape, 1834; DCL, Oxford, 1841; FRS; FSA; FGS; FRAS; he financed E. W. Lane's Arabic *Lexikon* and sent him to Egypt to collect materials; his wife, née Lady Eleanor Grosvenor, continued to support Lane after the Duke's death; he succeeded as 4th Duke, 1847; he also restored Alnwick Castle and greatly improved the estate; First Lord of the Admiralty, 1852-3; a Trustee of the British Museum; the bulk of the Alnwick collection of antiquities were purchased by the University of Durham in 1950, but some pieces were sold at the same time to the British Museum; his papers are at Alnwick Castle; he died in Alnwick, 12 Feb. 1865, and was buried in the Percy Chapel.

ODNB 43, 684-6; *DNB* 44, 390; *Ann. Register*, 1865, 19-21; J. Ruffle in P. and J. Starkey, *Travellers in Egypt*, 1998, 75-84; J. Ruffle in J. Thompson (ed.), *Cairo Papers* 23/3 (2000), 80-9.

PERCY, (*Earl*) Henry Algernon George (1871-1909)
British collector; he was born in London, 21 Jan. 1871, eldest son of Henry Percy, 7th Duke of Northumberland and Lady Edith Campbell; he was educated at Eton, 1884-9 and Christ Church, Oxford; BA, 1893; MP, 1895-1909; Under Secretary of State for India, 1902-3, of Foreign Affairs, 1903-5; he visited Persia in 1895, Turkey in 1897 and 1899, and Egypt in 1908; he studied hieroglyphs and formed a choice collection of Egyptian antiquities consisting largely of scarabs; a statuette of Meryankhre Mentuhotep from this collection was acquired by the British Museum in 1949 (EA 65429); the rest was dispersed in sales at Sotheby's, 9 July 1974, 21 April 1975, and 14 July 1975; the Northumberland papyri were acquired by the British Museum in 1991 (EA 73664-73); he died in Paris, 30 Dec. 1909.

ODNB 43, 720-1; *DNB Suppl.* 2, vol. 311, 103-4 (D. G. Hogarth); *WWW* i, 558; *The Complete Peerage* 9, 750.

PERDRIZET, (Émile) Paul Frédéric (1870-1938)
French classicist; he was born at Montbéliard, 22 July 1870, son of Paul David Frédéric P. and Adèle Emma Heitz; he studied at the École Normale from 1890 and was attached to the French School at Athens from 1893; he took part in French excavations in Greece and visited the Levant notably Egypt in 1909 when he met the collector Fouquet (q.v.) whose collection he helped to publish; from 1899 he was a member of the staff of the University of Nancy; he served in World War I; in 1919 he was named Professor of Archaeology at Strasbourg; he visited Egypt again in 1928 and 1933 and acted as advisor to the excavations at the tomb of Petosiris at Tuna el-Gebel; he was elected a member of the Académie des Inscriptions 1934; his publications which concern Egyptology include *Les Bronzes grecs d'Égypte de la collection Fouquet*, 1911; *Les Graffitis grecs du Memnonion d'Abydos,* 1919 with G. Lefebvre; and *Les Terres-cuites d'Égypte de la collection Fouquet*, 1921; he died in Nancy, 4 June 1938.

Rev. arch. 1938, 236-9 (C. Picard) (portr.) (bibl.); *CRAIBL* 1938, 270-80 (C. Picard); *Chron. d'Ég.* 14 (1939), 206-7 (C. Preaux); È. Gran-Aymerich, *Dictionnaire biographique d'archéologie 1798-1945*, 2001, incorporated in *Les Chercheurs de passé 1798-1945*, 2007, 1046-7.

PEREPELKIN, Yuri Yakovlevitch (1903-1982)
Russian Egyptologist; he was born at St. Petersburg, 1 June 1903, son of Yakov Nikolaevitch P., an engineer, and Maria Alexeievna Schjetin; he studied physics, mathematics, and history at the University of the Crimea and later Egyptology at the University of Leningrad until 1927; he then became a teacher of German; on 1 Feb. 1931 he became a member of the Academy of Sciences of USSR and was also a scientific assistant at the Museum (later Institute) for Books, Documents, and Manuscripts, Institute of History, and Institute for Oriental Studies; he presented his thesis for the degree of candidate of literature on 25 Oct. 1935 on the subject *Periods of evolution in the literary monuments of El Amarna*; he was lecturer and later guest Professor of Egyptology at the University of Leningrad 1935-6 and guest Professor at the University of Tashkent 1943-5; he became Doctor of Historical Sciences, 3 Oct. 1969; his principal interests were the history of the means of production in the Old Kingdom and the history of the Amarna period; his publications included *"Dom snau" v Starom carstve*, 1960, German trans. *Das Snau-Haus im Alten Reich*, 1960; *Perevorot Amen-chotpa IV*, 2 vols. 1967, 1984; *Taina zologogo groba*, 1968 2nd ed. 1970, English trans. *The Secret of the Gold Coffin*, 1978; *Keie i Semnech-ke-re*, 1979; and a German trans. of a monograph in *Palestinskii Sbornik* 16 (1966), *Privateigentum in der Vorstellung der Ägypter des Alten Reichs*, 1986 and his posthumous *Khozyaystvo staroegipetskikh velmozh*, 1988; *Istoria Drevnego Vostoka*, 1988; he died in Leningrad, 7 March 1982.

BSFE 93 (1982), 3; J. J. Perepelkin, *Privateigentum...* vii-x (bibl.) (R. Müller-Wollermann); S. D. Miliband, *Biobibliographical Glossary of Soviet Orientalists* (in Russian), Moscow, 1975, 425; *VDI* 161 (1982), 203; inf. J. Śliwa.

PERICHON, (*Bey*) Jean André (1860-1929)
French industrialist; he was born at Petites Magnelles, Bessines near Limoges, 17 Feb. 1860, son of Pierre François P. and Geneviève Clément; educated at the École des Arts et Métiers d'Angers; he worked for five years for the firm of Cail, Paris, and was sent by them to Egypt, where he directed the Khedive's sugar factory at Roda for 22 years; while in Egypt he formed a collection of antiquities, being assisted by Maspero (q.v.) and Lefébure (q.v.); this collection was bequeathed to the town of Limoges and since 1931 has been exhibited in the Musée Municipal; he died 1929.

Limoges Museum, Guide-Catalogue, 9; *Chron. d'Ég.* 14, 150.

PERNETTY, Antoine Joseph (1716-1796)
French Benedictine monk; he was born at Roanne, 12 Feb. 1716; he published a work on Egyptian and Greek fables and an attempt to decipher hieroglyphs, 2 vols., Paris, 1758, reissued in 1786; he died at Avignon, 16 Oct. 1796.

NBG 39, 619-21; *BIFAO* 5 (1906), 82; Hilmy, ii, 104.

PEROFFSKY (PEROVSKY), Vassili Alexeievitch (1784-1857)
Russian general; he was born in Pochop 20 Feb. 1795, illegitimate son of Count Alexei Kirillovitch Rumiantsev; he was greatly censured for his retreat in the Khivan expedition, 1839-40, but was vindicated by the Duke of Wellington whose opinion had been requested by the Czar; Governor of Orenburg; 1832-42, 1851-7; his name is remembered in Egyptology by the 'Pierre Peroffsky', a large stone inscribed with the 64th Chapter of the Book of the Dead; it was given to P. by Czar Nicholas and presented by his family to the Hermitage Museum in 1861; he died in Alupka in the Crimea, 20 Dec. 1857.

Golenischeff, *Herm. Eg. Coll.*, p. 169, no. 1101; Maspero, *Études de Myth* i, 368, n. l; *Larousse, XIXe siècle*, 12. 647; A. Geikie, *Life of Sir Roderick Murchison*, i. 344; *Greater Soviet Encyclopedia*, 19, 450.

PERRING, John Shae (1813-1869)
British civil engineer; he was born in Boston, Lincs, 24 Jan. 1813; he was educated Dorrington Grammar School and articled to a surveyor; he came to London in 1833, and afterwards went to Egypt in March 1836 under directions of Galloway Bros. of London, as assistant to Galloway Bey, manager of public works for Muhammad Ali, and was engaged on various works; in Jan.-Aug. 1837 he assisted Col. Howard Vyse (q.v.) in his survey and exploration of the pyramids of Giza; he published a work *On the Engineering of the Ancient Egyptians*, 1835; also *The Pyramids of Gizeh*, a large oblong folio, 1839; part i of this deals with the Great Pyramid, part ii with the other Giza pyramids, and part iii with the pyramids south of Abu Roash, those of Middle Egypt, and Campbell's Tomb; Perring's work was acknowledged by Howard-Vyse in his own publication; he returned to England in 1840, and was thereafter employed in railway and other engineering works; some of his papers are in the Dept. of Ancient Egypt and the Sudan, British Museum; he died in Manchester, 16 Jan. 1869 and was buried in London, Kensal Green cemetery.

ODNB 43, 799; *DNB* 45, 15-16; Hilmy, ii, 104; Vyse, *Pyramids*, passim (portr. vol. iii frontispiece); P. Usick in *Gott. Misz.* 180 (2001) (103-6.

PERROT, Georges (1832-1914)
French classical scholar and writer on ancient art and architecture; he was born in Villeneuve-Saint-Georges, 12 Nov. 1832, son of Georges P. and Caroline Joséphine Eugénie Dornès; he joined the French School at Athens and visited Greece, 1855-8; he was employed in educational work at Angoulême, Orleans, and Versailles, 1858-60; he went on a mission to Asia Minor, 1860-2; he was appointed lecturer in ancient history at the École des Hautes Études, 1874; Director of École Normale supérieure, 1883; he was elected to the Académie des Inscriptions, 18 Dec. 1874; his principal work is the monumental *Histoire de l'art dans l'antiquité*, written in collaboration with Charles Chipiez (q.v.), the first volume of which deals with Egypt and appeared in 1881; he was elected to the Académie des Inscriptions, 18 Dec. 1874; Sec. perpétuel, 1904-14; he died in Paris, 30 June 1914.

Maspero, *Notice sur ... M. Georges Perrot (Mem. Acad.* 1915) (portr.); Hilmy, ii, 104; A. C. E. Franquet de Franqueville, *Le Premier Siècle de l'Institut de France*, 1895, I, 365; È. Gran-Aymerich, *Dictionnaire biographique d'archéologie 1798-1945*, 2001, incorporated in *Les Chercheurs de passé 1798-1945*, 2007, 1051-3.

PERRY, Charles (*c*.1698-1780)
British traveller and medical writer; he graduated from Leiden, 1723 and also studied at Utrecht; he visited Constantinople, Egypt, Palestine, and Greece, 1736-42; he was a member of the Egyptian Society, 1741-3; he published medical works and an account of his travels, *View of the Levant*, 1743, which contains a great deal of interesting information on Egypt; the mummy described and figured in that work passed into the hands of Richard Cosway, RA, at the sale of whose effects, it was acquired by Pettigrew (q.v.), who examined and published it; the coffin was acquired by John Lee (q.v.), and then by Lord Amherst (q.v.), lot 348 in the 1921 sale; Perry died in 1780.

ODNB 43, 819; *DNB* 45, 29; *JEA* 20 (1934), 170; *Hartwell Cat.*, nos. 589, 590; Hilmy, ii, 108; Pettigrew, *Hist. Eg. Mummies*, p. xvii; Lamy, 156-7; R. Finnegan, *English Explorers in the East (1738-1745)*, 2019, *passim*.

PERRY, William James (1887-1949)
British anthropologist and diffusionist; born in Lower Edmonton, N. London, 18 Sept. 1887, son of Revd Dr. William James Perry and Sarah Bate; his father taught at the Grocers' Co. School, Hackney Downs and was later Headmaster and Chaplain of the Royal St. Anne's School, Redhill Surrey, where Perry attended as a pupil until he gained a scholarship to the City of London School; he afterwards gained a mathematical scholarship to Selwyn College, Cambridge, 1906; at this time he also attended anthropology lectures given by A. C. Haddon and W. H. R. Rivers; MA; DSc; from 1911 he became a schoolmaster at Pocklington, Yorks.; he married Gwynllyan Lilian, daughter of D. Wykeham-Williams, 1915; Reader in Comparative Religion Manchester University, 1919-23; Upton Lecturer in History of Religions, Manchester College, Oxford, 1924-27; Reader in Cultural Anthropology,

University College London, 1923-39; from his appointment at London he suffered from Parkinson's disease and retired prematurely, but was also able to give University Extension lectures at Morley College, Lambeth, for some years; Perry became linked with Elliot Smith (q.v.) and Rivers in the so-called 'Diffusion' theory from 1915 onwards; this 'Heliolithic' view of history and archaeology derived all subsequent civilization from Egypt and traced the spread of sun-worshipping peoples all over the world; Perry in his first major work linked megalithic monuments in France and Iberia with adjacent mineworkings and metal washing, see his paper *The Relationship between the Geographical Distribution of Megalithic Monuments and Ancient Mines* (in Mems. & Proc. Manchester Lit. & Phil. Soc. vol. 60, 1915-16); for his next work *The Megalithic Culture of Indonesia*, 1918, he taught himself Dutch in order to read all the material; his most famous work *The Children of the Sun*, 1923, carried Elliot Smith's views to the most extreme point, and became the archetypal book of this school; *The Growth of Civilization*, 1924, and *Gods and Men*, 1927, as well as *The Origin of Magic and Religion*, 1923, all continued the theme; *The Primordial Ocean*, 1935, took the view that all civilization derived from the primeval waters, often referred to in Egyptian religious texts, i.e. the Nile flood; he died in Roydon-by-Ware, Herts., 29 April 1949.

Inf. Mrs Margaret Halsen (daughter) and Miss Nora Perry (sister); Glyn E. Daniel, *A Hundred of Archaeology*, 1950, 247, 317; *WWW* iv, 906.

PERSIGNY, (*Duc de*) **Jean Victor Gilbert Fialin** (1808-1872)
French statesman; he was born St. Germain L'Espinasse, 11 Jan. 1808, son of Henry F. and Anne de Girard de Charbonnière; he was educated at Limoges and became an officer in the Hussars, 1828; he was dismissed for the share taken by the regiment in the revolution of 1830; he became a Bonapartist and was imprisoned during which time he wrote *De la destination et de l'utilité des pyramides d'Égypte*, Paris, 1845, a work in which he sought to prove that the pyramids were built as screens against the desert sand to prevent the Nile from silting; he became Minister of the Interior, 1852-4, and 1860-3; he was exiled in 1870, and died in Nice, 11 Jan. 1872.

Carré, ii. 120; Delaroa, *Le Duc de Persigny*, 1865.

PESTMAN, Pieter Willem (1933-2010)
Dutch demotist and papyrologist; he was born in Amsterdam, 28 April 1933, son of Pieter Dirk P. and Wilhelmina Koster; he studied law at the University of Utrecht, graduating in 1953 and then papyrology and Egyptian law under de Buck (q.v.) at Leiden; PhD, 1956; habilitation, 1961; he studied demotic in Paris under Malinine (q.v.), 1960-1; he was attached to the Papyrologisch Instituut from 1961; he became a leading authority in the publication of texts of the Hellenistic period; he was the editor of *Papyrologica Lugduno-Batava* from 1978, *Studia et Documenta ad Iurea Orientis Antiqui Pertinentia* from 1969, and *Studia Demotica* from 1987; a volume in his honour A. M. F. W. Verhoogt and S. P. Vleeming (eds), *The Two Faces of Graeco-Roman Egypt. Greek and Demotic and Greek-Demotic Texts and Studies Presented to P. W. Pestman* was issued in 1998; apart from his numerous articles and volumes edited by him, he published *Marriage and Matrimonial Property in Ancient Egypt*, 1961; *Chronologie égyptienne d'après les textes démotiques ...*, 1967; *Over vrouwen en voogden in het Oude Egypte*, 1969; with others, *Berichtigungsliste der Griechischen Papyrusurkunden aus Ägypten*, 6 (1976), 7 (1986), 8 (1992), 9 (1995), 10 (1998); with others, *Recueil de textes démotiques et bilingues*, I-III, 1977; *A Guide to the Zenon Archive*, I-II, 1981; *L'archivio di Amenothes, figlio di Horos (P. Tor. Amenothes), 1981; Les archives privées de Dionysios, fils de Kephalas*, with E. Boswinkel, 1982; *Een kraakpand in het Oude Egypte?*, 1982; *Familiearchieven uit het land van Pharao*, 1989; *The New Papyrological Primer*, 1990, rev. ed., 1994; *Il processo di Hermias e altri documenti dell'archivio dei choachiti (P. Tor. Choachiti). Papiri greci e demotici conservati a Torino e in altre collezione d'Italia*, 1992; *The Archive of the Theban Choachytes (Second Century B.C.). A Survey of the Demotic and Greek Papyri Contained in the Archive*, 1993; *Les papyrus démotiques de Tsenhor (P. Tsenhor). Les archives privées d'une femme égyptienne du temps de Darius Ier*, 1994; he died in Pancalieri, Italy, 14 May 2010.

Internet obit; inf. M. Pestman.

PETERSON, Enoch Ernest (1891-1978)
American archaeologist; he was born in Liberty Pole, Franklin, Wisconsin 24 Sept. 1891, son of Knute P. and Anna Hoffand; he was educated at Luther College in Deborah, Iowa; BA, 1912; he then taught Latin there; in 1921 he studied at the University of Michigan; MA, 1922; he did research at the University of Edinburgh, 1923-25, under Sir William Ramsay; he undertook field research for the University of Michigan at Antioch in Pisidia, 1924, Carthage, 1925, and Karanis, 1925-6, under Starkey (q.v.); from 1927-35 he was the Director of the Karanis expedition and also excavated at Dime and Teremouthis; in 1935 he was appointed Egyptian Curator

of the Kelsey Museum of Art and Archaeology at Ann Arbor; he was awarded an honorary Doctor of Letters from Luther College in 1941; he became Museum Director 1950-61; he published *Karanis topographical and architectural report of excavations during the seasons 1924-28*, with A. R. Boak, 1931 and *Coins from Karanis*, with R. A. Haadvedt and E. Husselman, 1964; he also prepared a detailed archaeological report which was edited by E. Husselman, *Karanis Topography and Architecture*, 1979; he died in Fargo, North Dakota, Sept. 1978.

Inf. Kelsey Museum, Ann Arbor.

PETHERICK, John (1813-1882)
British traveller and writer; usually known as 'Consul Petherick'; he was born at Merthyr Tydvil, Wales 9 May 1813, son of John P. and his wife Martha; he trained as an engineer; he visited Egypt and entered the service of Muhammad Ali as an engineer, 1845; in 1848 he left Egypt and established himself in Kordofan and thereafter explored Central and East Africa; he served as consul for the Sudan, 1850-63; he published *Egypt, the Sudan and Central Africa*, 1853-8; he died in London, 15 July 1882.

DNB 21, 305; *Proc. R. Geogr. Soc.* 4, 700; Hilmy, ii, 109; Boase 2, 1479; T, Baber in N. Cooke and V. Daubney (eds.), *Lost and Now Found*, 2017, 27-8.

PETRAEUS, Theodor (*c*.1630-1672)
Danish orientalist; he was born *c*.1630 in Flensburg, son of Peter Dirksen, and was educated in Denmark, afterwards studying oriental languages in Leiden, 1650; he went to the Near East and visited Syria, Palestine and Egypt, 1656; here he continued to study Arabic, Ethiopic, Coptic, Persian, and Armenian; he afterwards published Coptic texts with phonetic transcription and brought back with him many of the Coptic books which are now in the Prussian State Library in Berlin; his papers are in the Royal Library in Copenhagen; he died in Copenhagen, 1672.

Inf. E. Iversen; *Bricka Dansk Biogr. Leksikon*, 18, 292-3.

PETRIE, (*Lady*) **Hilda Mary Isabel** (1871-1956)
British Egyptologist; she was born in Dublin, 8 June 1871, daughter of Richard Denny Urlin and Mary Addis; a family friendship with Professor Seeley led her to be first interested in geology; at this time she posed as one of the companions in the pre-Raphaelite painting by Henry Holland depicting the meeting of Dante and Beatrice; she became interested in Egyptology and married Flinders Petrie (q.v.) in 1896; she served as Hon. Secretary of the British School of Archaeology in Egypt for many years, and not only helped her husband on the actual excavations in the field, but also assisted him in much of the detailed work, measuring and drawing; she accompanied her husband to many of the sites he excavated in Egypt, and joined his expedition to Sinai as well as to Palestine; she was constantly engaged in administrative work, raising much of the funds provided for this work through the Egyptian Research Account; after Petrie's death she prepared and published his remaining manuscripts, among them *Ceremonial Slate Palettes*, 1953; she helped M. Murray excavate the Osireion at Abydos, 1902-33; she was responsible for the specialized archaeological Petrie Library going to the Sudan Antiquities Service in Khartoum; her own two original works were, *Egyptian hieroglyphs of the First and Second Dynasties*, 1927 and *Seven Memphite tomb chapels*, 1952, dealing with her work at Saqqara; she also published *Side Notes on the Bible from Flinders Petrie's Discoveries*, 1933; she died in London, 23 Nov. 1956.

Archaeology 10 (1957), 141 (anon.); *AfO* 18, 1st pt. (1957), 233-4 (E. Weidner); *JEA* 43 (1957), vii (R. O. Faulkner); *Kush* 5 (1957), 105-6 (O. H. Myers); *Orientalia* 26 (1957), 157 (A. Pohl); *PEQ* 89 (1957), (O. Tufnell); W. M. F. Petrie, *Seventy Years in Archaeology*; M. S. Drower, *Letters from the Desert*, 2004; È. Gran-Aymerich, *Dictionnaire biographique d'archéologie 1798-1945*, 2001, incorporated in *Les Chercheurs de passé 1798-1945*, 2007, 1053.

PETRIE, (*Sir*) **William Matthew Flinders** (1853-1942)
British Egyptologist; he was born in Charlton, Kent, 3 June 1853, the son of William P. a civil engineer and surveyor, and Anne daughter of Capt. Matthew Flinders, the explorer of Australia; as a boy he collected coins and was later introduced by R. W. Poole (q.v.) to Amelia Edwards (q.v.); his interest in ancient Egypt was first aroused at the age of thirteen by Piazzi Smyth's (q.v.) book on the Great Pyramid; he attended no schools or college and this lack of formal education was both his strength and weakness in later life, for while he pursued his aims directly and was not given to accepting out-of-date methods or theories, he also ignored the views of many who were making valuable contributions to Egyptology and archaeology; he received a considerable training in British archaeology and prehistory, and with his father surveyed Stonehenge in 1872; from this period also dated his lifelong interest in weights and measures; he next surveyed a great many earthworks and archaeological remains

in southern England, 1875-80, making a large number of plans of these; he first went to Egypt to make a survey of the Pyramids, 1880-2; he dug for the EEF, 1884-6; he quarrelled with them and decided to set up an archaeological body of his own and thus be completely independent of all outside control; he had a hard struggle at first but from 1887 excavated regularly with the help of J. Haworth (q.v.) and M. Kennard (q.v.); he founded the Egyptian Research Account, 1894, later enlarged as the British School of Archaeology in Egypt; he rejoined the EEF and worked for them again, 1896-1905; by the wish of Miss Edwards he was appointed to the first chair in Egyptology in England, Edwards Professor, University College London, 1892-1933; Emeritus Prof. 1933-42; Kt., 1923; FRS, 1902; FBA, 1904; DCL, Oxford, 1892; LittD Cantab, 1900; LLD, Edinburgh, 1896, Aberdeen, 1906; DLitt, DSc, PhD, Strass., 1897; Member of the Royal Irish Acad., and the Amer. Philos. Soc.; he married Hilda Urlin (see above), 1897; he inaugurated the first systematic archaeological work in the Near East, and during 42 years excavated more sites than Mariette (q.v.); he dug at the following places, Tanis, 1884; Naukratis, 1884-5; Daphnae, 1886; Nebesha, 1886; Hawara, Biahmu, and Arsinoe (Crocodilopolis), 1888, and Hawara, 1910-11; Illahun-Kahun, 1889-90, 1914-19; Gurob, 1889-90; Maidum, 1891, 1909; El-Amarna, 1891-2; Koptos, 1893-4; Naqada and Ballas, 1895; Thebes - Ramesseum, etc., 1895-6; Qurna, 1908; Deshasha, 1897; Dendera, 1897-8; Abadiya-Hu (Diospolis), 1898-9; Abydos, 1899-1903, 1921; Ehnasya, 1903-4; Buto, 1904; Sinai - Wadi Maghara and Serabit, 1904-5; Tell el-Yahudiya, 1905-6; Tell er-Reteba, 1905-6; Saft el-Hinna, 1906; Giza and Rifa, 1906-7; Athribis, 1907; Memphis, 1908-13; Tarkhan, 1911-13; Sidmant, 1920-1; Haraga; Shurafa, 1911; Heliopolis, 1912; Qau, 1923-4; he also dug for a season in Palestine in 1890, and later abandoned Egypt in 1926 to work until 1938 on Hyksos and other sites in Palestine notably Gaza, 1927-34; he made more major archaeological discoveries than any other archaeologist, the city of Naukratis whose whereabouts had been unknown, the site of Kahun, many fine objects from El-Amarna, the great predynastic cemetery at Naqada, archaic material from the royal tombs of Abydos, the Israel stela of King Mereneptah and the magnificent jewels from Lahun, to list but a few; Petrie advanced the whole approach to archaeology, his methods and techniques being revolutionary in the Near East at the time; he took Furtwängler's method of dating painted and decorated pottery as an archaeological chronometer and expanded it so that it could be used for all types for the first time, systematically arranging predynastic Egyptian material, and thus inventing sequence dating; in 1891 he established synchronisms through pottery with Greece aided by his former pupil E. Gardner (q.v.), again evolving a new method; he also discovered the first texts in the Sinaitic script; his greatest contribution was his emphasis on the importance of observing *everything* found, and his insistence on the typological study of all objects, however humble; he exercised a profound influence on all museums during the 1880s which at that time did not know how to conserve antiquities properly; his method of fund-raising through the sale of antiquities to museums gained him his independence and also provided him with a much wider variety of objects for study; his other great contribution was the discovery of the earliest historical and predynastic periods, hitherto unsuspected; Petrie trained many assistants who continued his work; every year he held exhibitions to arouse public interest in discovering more sites; he amassed a very great collection of antiquities, which is housed at University Coll. London; this collection was bought from him in 1913 by public subscription, the donors including Walter Morrison and Robert Mond (q.v.); he founded the journal *Ancient Egypt* in 1914, and edited it for twenty years; Petrie published about 1,000 books, articles, and reviews (see below), the most important works being, *Inductive Metrology*, 1877; *The Pyramids and Temples of Gizeh*, 1883; *Tanis. Part I, 1883-4*, 1885; *Naukratis. Part I, 1884-5*, with E. Gardner and others, 1886; *Racial Photographs from the Egyptian Monume*nts, 1887; *Tanis, Part II. Nebesheh (Am) and Defenneh (Tahpanhes)*, with A. S. Murray and others, 1888; *A Season in Egypt*, 1888; *Two Hieroglyphic Papyri from Tanis. Part II. The Geographical Papyrus (An Almanack)*, with H. Brugsch, 1889; *Hawara, Biahmu and Arsinoe*, 1889; *Historical Scarabs*, 1889; *Kahun, Gurob and Hawara*, with F. Fl. Griffith and others, 1890; *Illahun, Kahun and Gurob, 1889-90*, with A. H. Sayce and others, 1892; *Ten Years Digging in Egypt, 1881-1891*, 1892; *Tell el Amarna*, with A. H. Sayce and others 1894; *A History of Egypt*, 1st ed., 3 vols., 1894-1905; *Egyptian Decorative Art*, 1895; *Egyptian Tales*, 2 vols., 1895; *Koptos*, with D. G. Hogarth, 1896; *Naqada and Ballas, 1895*, with J. E. Quibell and others, 1896; *Six Temples at Thebes*, 1896, with W. Spiegelberg, 1897; *Deshasheh, 1897*, with F. Ll. Griffith, 1898; *Religion and Conscience in Ancient Egypt*, 1898; *Syria and Egypt, from the Tell el Amarna Letters,* 1898; *Dendereh, 1898*, 2 pts., with F. Ll. Griffith and others, 1900; *The Royal Tombs of the First Dynasty, 1900*, pt. i, 1900; *The Royal Tombs of the Earliest Dynasties, 1901*, pt. ii, with F. Ll. Griffith, 1901; *Diospolis Parva. The cemeteries of Abadiyeh and Hu, 1898-9*, with A. C. Mace, 1901; *Abydos*, pt. i, with A. E. Weigall, 1902; *Abydos*, pt. ii, with F. Ll. Griffith, 1903; *Ehnasya, 1904*, with C. T. Currelly, 1904; *Methods and Aims in Archaeology*, 1904; *Roman Ehnasya (Herakleopolis Magna) 1904*, 1905; *Hyksos and Israelite Citie*s, with J. G. Duncan, 1906; *The Religion of Ancient Egypt*, 1905; *Researches in Sinai*, with C. T. Currelly, 1906; *Gizeh and Rifeh*, with Sir H. Thompson and W. E. Crum, 1907; *Athribis*, with J. H. Walker and others, 1908; *The Arts and Crafts of ancient Egypt*, 1909; *Memphis I*, with J. H. Walker, 1909; *The Palace of Apries, (Memphis II)*, with J. H. Walker, 1909; *Personal Religion in Egypt before Christianity*, 1909; *Qurneh*, with J. H. Walker, 1909; *Meydum and Memphis III*, with E. Mackay and others, 1910; *Historical Studies*, with E. B. Knobel and others, 1911; *Roman Portraits and Memphis IV*, 1911; *Egypt and Israel*, 1911; *The Revolutions of Civilization*, 1911; *The Formation of the Alphabet*, 1912; *The Labyrinth, Gerzeh and Mazghuneh*, with G. A. Wainwright and others, 1912; *The Hawara Portfolio*, 1913; *Tarkhan and Memphis V*, with G. A.

Wainwright and others, 1913; *Tarkhan II*, 1914; *Amulets*, 1914; *Handbook of Egyptian antiquities collected by Flinders Petrie, exhib. at University Coll. Gower St*, 1915; *Heliopolis, Kafr Ammar and Shurafa*, with E. Mackay and others, 1915; *Scarabs and Cylinders with names*, 1917; *Tools and Weapons*, 1917; *Eastern Exploration. Past and Future*, 1918; *Some Sources of Human History*, 1919; *Prehistoric Egypt*, 1920; *Corpus of Prehistoric Pottery and Palettes*, 1921; *Lahun II*, with G. Brunton and others, 1923; *Social Life in Ancient Egypt*, 1923; *Sedment*, 2 vols. 1924; *Religious Life in Ancient Egypt*, 1924; *Ancient Egyptians*, Div. I, no. 11 of *Descriptive Sociology*, fol., 1925; *Buttons and design scarabs*, 1925; *Tombs of the Courtiers and Oxyrhynkhos*, with A. H. Gardiner and others, 1925; *Ancient Weights and Measures*, 1926; *Glass Stamps and Weights*, 1926; *Objects of daily use*, 1927; *Qau and Badari. I*, 1927; *Gerar*, 1928; *Beth-Pelet I (Tell Fara)*, with O. Tufnell, 1930; *Antaeopolis. The tombs of Qau*, 1930; *Decorative patterns of the Ancient World*, 1930; *Ancient Gaza. Tell El Ajjul*, 5 vols. 1931-52; *Seventy Years in Archaeology*, 1931; *Measures and Weights*, 1934; *Shabtis*. 1935; *Anthedon. Sinai*, with J. C. Ellis, 1937; *The Funeral Furniture of Egypt*, 1937; *Egyptian Architecture*, 1938; *The Making of Egypt*, 1939; *Wisdom of the Egyptians*, 1940; posth. pub., *Ceremonial Slate Palettes. Corpus of Proto-Dynastic Pottery*, with H. Petrie and M. A. Murray; 66 of these are quarto vols.; his most important finds are in the Egyptian Museum, Cairo and other museums in England and America, but his collection of Palestinian pottery is in the Institute of Archaeology, London, with whose foundation he was involved; 113 of his notebooks and his distribution lists are kept in the Petrie Museum, University Coll. (B. Adams, *JEA* 61 (1975), 108, 110-1) and other papers are in the Griffith Institute, Oxford (*ibid.*, 109) and the EES Lucy Gura Archive; portraits by P. A. de Lászlo are in Univ. Coll. Old Refectory and the Petrie Collection, others by G. F. Watts and de Lászlo in the National Portr. Gallery and the Ashmolean Museum, and a small one by Mrs Brunton in the Edwards Library; Petrie died in Jerusalem, 28 July 1942.

Autobiogr. *Seventy Years in Archaeology*, 1931; M. S. Drower, *Flinders Petrie*, 1985; *The Archaeology of Palestine*, Centenary Exhibition, Occasional Paper no. 10 of the Institute of Archaeology, London, 1953; W. F. Albright, *The Archaeology of Palestine*, 1949, 29 and passim (portr.); Glyn E. Daniel, *A Hundred Years of Archaeology*, 1950, 174-7 and passim; C. M. Daugherty, *The Great Archaeologists*, 1962; M. A. Murray, *The Splendour that was Egypt*, 1949, 314-17 (portr.); *My First Hundred Years*, 1963, 93 and passim; Sir R. E. M. Wheeler, *Archaeology from the Earth*, 1954, 29-30 and passim; *AfO* 15 (1945-51), 187 (A. Scharff); *AJA* 46 (1942), 546-7 (S. B. Luce); *BASOR* 87 (1942), 6-7 (Nelson Glueck); *Chron. d'Ég.* 35 (1943), 120; 39 (1945), 120 (Habib Jamati); *ODNB* 43, 920-3 (portr.); *DNB* 1941-50, 666-7 (C. L. Woolley); *EB* 1968 ed., 17.756 (W. R. Dawson); *JEA* 29 (1943), 67-70 (portr.) (P. E. Newberry); *JRAS* 1942, 263; *Man*, 43 (1943), no. 9, 20-1 (J. L. Myres); *Nature* 1942, Aug. 15, (A. H. Gardiner); *PEQ* 1943, 5-8 (O. Tufnell); *PBA* 28 (1942), 307-24 (portr.) (S. Smith); *WWW* iv, 908; *JNES* 31 (1972), 158-60, 356-79 (bibl.) (E. Uphill); *Biblical Archaeology Review* 6 (Nov./Dec. 1980), 44-55; R. Janssen, *The First Hundred Years*, 1992, 1-26; *KMT* 15/1 (2004), 66-68; E. Gran-Aymerich, *Dictionnaire biographique d'archéologie 1798-1945*, 2001, incorporated in *Les Chercheurs de passé 1798-1945*, 2007, 1054-6; M. S. Drower, *Letters from the Desert*, 2004; B. T. Trope et al., *Excavating Egypt: Great Discoveries from the Petrie Museum of Egyptian Antiquities*, 2005; P. Spencer in P. Spencer, *The Egypt Exploration Society. The Early Years*, 2007, 33-65; *Archaéonil* 17 (2007), 53-6 (portr.); M. Capasso (ed.), *Hermae*, 2007, 53-6 (C. Römer); S. Quirke in D. Magee, J. Bourriau and S. Quirke, *Sitting Beside Lepsius*, 2009, 439-462; P. Spencer, in E. Teeter, *Before The Pyramids*, 2011, 17-24; S. Quirke, *Hidden Hands*, 2010, passim.; T. Bagh, *Finds from W. M. F. Petrie's Excavations in Egypt in the Ny Carlsberg Glyptotek*, 2011, 10-13; P. del Vesco in M. Betrò and G. Miniaci, *Talking along the Nile*, 2013, 83-92.

PETROVSKY, Nicholas Sergeievitch (1923-1981)
Russian Egyptologist; he was born in Leningrad, 9 April 1923, son of Sergei Nikolaievitch P. and Maria Nikolaievna Kozlovsky; he was educated in the Faculty of History at the University of Leningrad finishing in 1948; in 1957 he was appointed lecturer at the Faculty of Oriental Studies, University of Leningrad and in 1968 professor; he specialized in the philology of ancient Egyptian and was the first to publish a grammar of classical Egyptian in Russian, *Egipetskii iazyk*, 1958, and also *Sochetaniya slov v egipetskom iazyke*, 1970; he died in Leningrad, 15 Aug. 1981.

Gött. Misz. 49 (1981), 7-8 (portr.); inf. from A. Elanskaya.

PETTIGREW, Thomas Joseph (1791-1865)
British surgeon and antiquary; he was born in London, 28 Oct. 1791, the son of William P., a naval surgeon and medical supervisor of a workhouse, and Elizabeth Cranford; he practised as a surgeon in Savile Row; in his capacity of surgeon to the Duke of Kent he vaccinated Queen Victoria; he was also Librarian to the Duke of Sussex; FRCS; FRS; FSA; Hon. Member, Inst. Ég.; he took an active part in most of the literary and archaeological movements of his time, and was one of the founders of the British Arch. Assn.; he first became interested in Egyptology through meeting Belzoni in 1818, and afterwards studied the language etc. with assiduity; his special interest was mummification, and he published *History of Egyptian Mummies and an Account of the Worship and Embalming of the Sacred Animals*, 1834; also *Encyclopaedia Aegyptica*, 1842, and many shorter papers besides many works on other subjects; he unrolled and gave demonstrations on a large number of mummies;

he had a collection of Egyptian antiquities, some of which were sold 23 Aug. 1905, lots 205-12, but the principal items had already been disposed of during his life-time; he died in London, 23 Nov. 1865.

Autobiography up to 1840, in *Medical Portrait Gallery*, iv; *ODNB* 43, 940-1; *DNB* 45. 108-9; W. R. Dawson, *Memoir of T. J. Pettigrew*, N.Y., 1931 (portrs. and bibl.); *JEA* 20 (1934), 170 (portr.); Lugt 63616; Dawson MSS 18, ff. 120-32; 27, ff. 39, 42; 30, ff. 1-269; 39, f. 97; 40, ff. 174, 199; 63, ff. 96-143; Hilmy, ii, 113; S. Sobhi Abdel-Hakim in P. Starkey and N. El Kholy (eds.), *Egypt through the Eyes of Travellers*, 2002, 130-9; J. Buikstra and C. Roberts (eds.), *The Global History of Palaeopathogy. Pioneers and Prospects*, 2012, 210 (B. Baker and M. Judd); G. Moshenska in W. Carruthers (ed.), *Histories of Egyptology*, 2015, 201-14; J. Taylor, *Ancient Egypt* 19 (2018), 40-5 (portr.).

PEYRON, Amedeo Angelo Maria (1785-1870)
Italian Coptologist and Greek scholar; he was born in Turin, 2 Oct. 1785, son of Bernardino P. and Teresa Marchetti, the youngest of 11 brothers; in 1800 he attended Greek classes and others in oriental literature given at the University of Turin by the Abbot of Caluso, who remained a good friend to him; he was ordained priest about 1810; he taught oriental languages from 1803, and was assistant in the library of Turin Univ., 1814; Professor, 1815, also teaching Greek; he was employed by Count Balbo to collect ancient MSS; Member of Turin Acad., 1816, and of Inst. de France, 1854 on the recommendation of Cardinal Mai (q.v.) with whom he had been acquainted since 1820; at an early age he began to collect materials for his Coptic dictionary, this being his chief preoccupation from 1825 to 1835; he arranged the words under radicals instead of the usual alphabet, a feature criticized by Letronne and Silvestre de Sacy, though they praised the final result; in 1835 his *Lexicon Linguae Copticae* was published at the expense of the King; Peyron did little Coptic after this but turned his attention to Greek; he died in Turin, 27 April 1870.

Atti R. Acad. Scienze Torino, 5. 778-807; Hilmy, ii, 113; *The Coptic Encyclopedia* 6, 1952 (A. S. Atiya); S. Curto (ed.), *Giornata di studio in onore di Amadeo Peyron*, 1998; M. Capasso (ed.), *Hermae* II, 2010, 11-15 (portr.) (N. Pellé).

PHILIP, L. Paul (*fl.* 1887-1909)
French antiquities dealer in Egypt and France; he was originally a carpenter's apprentice who turned to dealing in antiquities; he excavated at Heliopolis, 1892-3; his antiquities were sold in Paris 10-12 April 1905.

EEF Arch. Report (1892-3), 25; *Journal des Savants* Jan.-June 1992, 162-3, 165-6; F. Hagen and K. Ryholt, *The Antiquities Trade in Egypt 1880-1930*, 2017, 257-8.

PIANKOFF, Alexandre (1897-1966)
Egyptologist of Russian origin; he was born in St. Petersburg, 18 Oct. 1897, son of Nicholas P.; as a boy he became interested in Egypt when he saw the Golenischeff Egyptian collection in the Hermitage; he studied classics but the war interrupted his academic career and he served with the French forces at Salonika, 1917; he went to Berlin and studied Egyptian philology under Erman (q.v.) and Sethe (q.v.), 1920; he settled in Paris 1924-39, where he continued his classical studies at the Sorbonne, 1927; he also learnt Turkish, Arabic, and Persian; he gained his Doctorate at the University of Paris with a thesis entitled, *Le coeur dans les textes égyptiens*, 1930; from then on he specialized in philology and religion; attached to the Byzantine Institute as a specialist in Arabic and Coptic, 1928-39; served again with the French forces, 1939-40, from then on being mainly in Cairo where he worked for the French Institute, the Bollingen Foundation with the help of Rambova (q.v.) and Thomas (q.v.) and the Centre National de la Recherche Scientifique; he undertook research on the texts and religious scenes in the royal tombs at Thebes; he published a large number of articles and books on Egyptian religion among which were, *Livre de l'Am-Douat*, with trans.; *Livre des portes*, 1939-62, all the known versions with Ch. Maystre and on his own; *Le Livre du jour et de la Nuit*, 1942; *Livre des Quererts*, 1946, with trans.; *Livre de la vache divine; Litanies du Soleil; Les chapelles de Tout-Ankh-Amon*, fol. 1952; *La création du disque solaire*, 1952; for the Bollingen Foundation, *The Tomb of Rameses VI*, 2 vols. 1954; *The Shrines of Tut-ankh-amon*, 1955; *Mythological Papyri*, with N. Rambova, 2 vols. 1957; *The Litany of Re*, 1964; and posthumously *The Pyramid of Unas*, 1968; *The Wandering of the Soul*, 1972; he was made Maître de Recherches, 1964, and awarded a silver medal; he died in Brussels, 20 July 1966.

BIFAO 65 (1967), 227-30 (portr.) (F. Daumas); *JEA* 52 (1966), 1-2; *Chron. d'Ég.* 43 (1968) 104-10 (bibl.) (D. Abou-Ghazi); *The Pyamid of Unas*, 117-8.

PICCININI, --- (*fl.*1819-1829)
Italian excavator; he was a native of Lucca who excavated in Egypt and also bought antiquities for Giovanni Anastasi (q.v.); he had a house at Thebes at the S. end of Dra Abu el-Naga, close to the tomb now numbered 161; nothing is known of his previous or later history, but he is frequently mentioned by early travellers in Egypt, and was at Thebes some years earlier than Winlock (*JEA* 10, 231, n. 1) suggests.

Champollion, ii, 149, 245; Hartleben, ii, 292, 320; Hay Diary; Westcar Diary, 72.

PIEHL, Karl Fredrik (1853-1904)
Swedish Egyptologist; he was born in Stockholm, 30 March 1853, son of Carl Theodor P. and Carolina Cecilia Skarstedt; he at first worked with Lieblein (q.v.) in Christiania and in various continental museums, joining Maspero (q.v.) in Paris in 1878; he took Fil. dr. 1881 and was made lecturer at the University of Uppsala the same year; he visited Egypt several times, 1882-3, 1883-4, 1887-8; was appointed Professor of Egyptology in Uppsala, 1893; in 1889 he founded a museum of Egyptian antiquities in Uppsala, which from 1895 bore the name Victoriamuseet; Piehl also founded the journal *Sphinx*, 1896, which he edited until his death; his studies deal mainly with grammatical and lexicographical problems; an eminent philologist he made a special study of texts of the Late and Ptolemaic periods; in his *Petites études égyptologiques*, 1881, Piehl began the work which made him famous among his contemporaries; his next publication was the *Dictionnaire du papyrus Harris No. I, etc.*, 1882, followed by what was probably his greatest achievement, *Inscriptions hiéroglyphiques recueillies en Europe et en Égypte*, 1884-1903, a large-scale work in 6 pts.; in this he collected a mass of mostly unpublished texts; in addition he wrote a large number of small articles and reviews in scientific journals, many in *Sphinx*, and his bibl. lists about 206 articles and books and 112 reviews although not complete; among contemporary Egyptologists he showed an extreme antipathy towards the Berlin school, this being expecially marked in his reviews; despite this idiosyncrasy Piehl was a brilliant scholar and achieved much for Egyptology in Sweden; he was known as a clever lecturer and he imparted some of his enthusiasm for his subject to the public in entertaining books in Swedish; he left his library to the University of Uppsala; he died in Sigtuna near Uppsala, 9 Aug. 1904.

Inf. B. J. Peterson and L. Troy; *Sphinx* 8, 117-34 (portr.) (E. Andersson); 9, 104-19 and 137-57 (bibl.); *Rec. Trav.* 27 (1905), 134-6 (E. Naville); Hilmy, ii, 116; *Svenska Männ och Kvinnor* 6, 124-5.

PIEPER, Max (1882-1941)
German Egyptologist; he was born in Magdeburg, 9 April 1882, son of Rudolf P., a bank official; he was educated at Berlin University under Erman (q.v.); PhD, 1904; he served as a lecturer at various gymnasiums in Berlin and elsewhere until 1934; he published, with Max Burchardt, *Handbuch der aegyptischen Königsnamen*, 1912; *Die ägyptische Literatur*, 1927; *Die grosse Inschrift des Königs Neferhotep in Abydos*, 1929; and *Das ägyptische Märchen*, 1935; he died in Berlin, 31 May 1941.

Chron. d'Ég. 18. 273; Kürschner; *AfO* 14 (1941-44), 236; inf. E. Hornung; E. Endesfelder, *Die Ägyptologie an der Berliner Universität-Zur Geschichte eines Fachgebietes*, 1988, 27.

PIER, Garrett Chatfield (1875-1943)
American archaeologist and museum official; he was born in London, 30 Oct. 1875; son of Garrett Ryckman P. and Eleanor Blackman; he studied at Columbia University, New York, 1896-8, and then in European and Egyptian museums for four years; also Egyptology and Assyriology at Chicago University, 1906; Assistant Curator of Decorative Arts MMA, 1907-10; he married 1. Adelaide Wilson, 1902 (d.1926), 2. Riva Greenwood, 1927; he visited Japan, China, and the Far East to buy for the MMA, 1911-14; he served in the First World War, 1918-19, and was attached to US State Dept. and the Peace Commission, 1919-21; Pier formed a considerable collection of Egyptian antiquities and published an account of them, *Egyptian Antiquities in the Pier Collection*, 1906; he loaned his collection of small objects to Yale University, 1930, but had to sell them at auction at the American Art Association, New York, 6-7 March 1936, at which time the University purchased seventy objects; he also published *Inscriptions of the Nile Monuments*, 1908; *Pottery of the Near East*, 1909; in addition, works on antique guns and fiction; he died in St. Petersburg, Florida, 30 Dec. 1943.

Inf. Dows Dunham; L. Bull, *Egyptian Antiquities in the Pier Collection, Bull. Assoc. in Fine Arts Yale University*, June 1936, 30-4; *WWA* ii, 424.

PIERCE, Richard Holton (1935-2019)
American-Norwegian demotist, Nubiologist and Classical philologist; he was born Westwood, Mass., in 1935, the son of Frank P, and his wife Ruth; he developed an interest in Egyptology from visits to the Museum of Fine Arts, Boston; he studied Egyptology and Classics at Brown University and the Queen's College, Oxford; PhD Brown, on demotic papyri in Brooklyn, 1963; he married his Norwegian wife Wenche, whom he had met in Oxford, 1958; he worked in Nubia 1963-4, and moved to Bergen in 1966, first on a scholarship, and then as a lecturer in Greek; personal chair in Egyptology 1971; he had a wide range of interests, but was particularly interested in Nubia, being Visiting Professor in Khartoum 1976, undertaking various pieces of fieldwork and being one of the editors of the *Fontes Historiae Nubiorum*, 1994-2000; he retired in 2005, but continued to undertake research, making his last visit to the Sudan in 2017; two volumes of studies were published in his honour, *Understanding and History in Arts and Sciences*, edited by R. Skarsten, E. J. Kleppe and R. Bjerre Finnestad, 1991, and *From the Fjords to the Nile*, edited by P. Steiner, A. Tsakos and E. Heldaas Seland, 2018; he published various articles and

reviews, together with *Three Demotic Papyri in the Brooklyn Museum: a contribution to the study of contracts and their instruments in Ptolemaic Egypt*, 1972.

Internet obits.

PIERRET, (Charles) Paul (1836-1916)
French Egyptologist, he was born at Rambouillet, 25 June 1836, son of Charles Joseph P. and Charlotte Sophie Aubry; he was a student of de Rougé (q.v.); conservator of the Egyptian collections of the Louvre in succession to de Rougé until 1 Oct. 1907; he did much to popularize Egyptology in France; he published a translation of the Book of the Dead, a hieroglyphic vocabulary and books on Egyptian mythology; he died in Versailles, 10 Jan. 1916.

AE 1916, 187; Hilmy, ii, 117; *Rev. arch.* serie 3 (1916), 154.

PIÉTREMENT, Charles Alexandre (1826-1906)
French naturalist and ethnologist; he was born at Esternay, 15 Feb. 1826, son of Pierre Alexandre P. and Marie-Anne Genereuse Garnier; he made a special study of the history of the domestication of animals, in particular the horse; he published, *Les Chevaux dans les temps préhistoriques et historiques*, Paris, 1868; also on the horse in Egypt, *Rev. d'Éthnographie*, 3. 396-88, and *Les origines du cheval domestique, d'après la paléontologie, la zoologie, l'histoire et la philologie*, Paris, 1870; he died in Paris, 1906.

Hilmy, ii, 117-18; *Larousse XXᵉ* 5, 582.

PIETRO DELLA VALLE *see* **VALLE**

PIETSCHMANN, (Ludwig Wilhem Erdmann) Richard (1851-1923)
German Egyptologist; he was born in Stettin, 24 Sept. 1851, son of Eduard P. and Leopoldine Post; he studied at the Universities of Berlin and Leipzig; he became librarian successively at Breslau 1876-87, Marburg 1888, Göttingen 1888-99, Greifswald 1899-1902, Berlin 1902-3; Professor of Egyptology and Oriental History, Göttingen 1889-99, Professor of Bibliography and Egyptology 1903-23, and Director of the Univ. Library, Göttingen, 1903-21; he died in Göttingen, 17 Oct. 1923.

Chronik der ... Univ. Göttingen, 1921-3; Hilmy, ii, 119; Kürschner; *Zentralblatt für Bibliothekswesen* 43 (1926), 213-35 (portr.) (G. Leyh); *Gött. Misz.* 28 (1978), 12, 15; *DBE* 9, 492; *Wer ists's* 1911, 1093; T. Gertzen in J. Arp-Neuman and T. Gertzen (eds.), *'Steininschrift und Bibelwort'*, 2019, 25-30.

PIGNORIA, Lorenzo (1571-1631)
Italian antiquary; he was born in Padua, 12 Oct. 1571, son of Antonio P., agent for the monastery of S. Lorenzo; he received a Jesuit education; he studied philosophy and law at Padua University, matric. 1591; he took holy orders, 1602, Canon of S. Lorenzo, Padua, 1609, Canon of Treviso, 1630; he worked as secretary for Marco Cornaro, Bishop of Padua, living in Rome 1605-7; returning to Padua he served as parish priest and became an important intellectual figure in the town, writing occasional verse; he was a correspondent of Galileo, Cassiano dal Pozzo, Prosper Alpini (q.v.), and Peiresc (q.v.) among others; his interests were wide-ranging, covering many aspects of ancient cultures and science; he studied the bronze "Mensa Isiaca" in the collection of the Duke of Mantua (now in the Museo Egizio, Turin), and published *Mensa Isiaca Vetustissimae tabulae aeneae sacris Aegyptiorum...*, 1605 (and subsequent editions); this eschewed neo-Platonic, allegorical interpretations of the table in favour of empirical observation based on comparison with classical texts and ancient objects known to him; he produced a new edition of Vincenzo Cartari's *Le imagini degli dei degli antichi*, 1615, which compared Egyptian, Classical, Indian, and Mexican deities, an early example of comparative theology taken up by Kircher (q.v.) in his *Oedipus Aegyptiacus*; he died of pestilence in Padua, 15 June 1631.

F. Zen Benetti, 'Per la biografia di Lorenzo Pignoria, erudito padovano', in M. Billanovich et al. (eds) *Viridiarium Floridum: Studi di storia veneta offerti dagli allievi a Paolo Sambin*, 1984, 317-336.

PILLAVOINE, Alexandre (1756-1838)
French merchant and diplomat; he was born 22 Jan. 1756; he emigrated at the Revolution and took refuge in Aleppo, where he carried on his business until the time of the French expedition to Egypt; he was made prisoner by the Turks, robbed, and tortured, 1799, but was set at liberty the same year for a large ransom which ruined him; French Consul at Saint-Jean d'Acre, 1802; Consul-General in Egypt, July 1819-21 in succession to Roussel (q.v.); afterwards Consul at Baltimore, 1821, Philadelphia 1825, and Larnaca, 1829; he retired, 1831; in 1820 he received Lelorrain (q.v.) and procured facilities for him to remove the Dendera Zodiac; he died 4 Oct. 1838.

French FO Records; Lelorrain, 15.

PILLET, Maurice Louis Ernest (1881-1964)
French architect and archaeologist; born at Mantes-sur-Seine, 31 Oct. 1881, son of Émile Ferdinand P. and Marie Amélie Félicité Gouin; he studied mathematics and graduated from the École des Beaux-Arts, 1911; he was then attached to the IFAO in Cairo and served with the expedition to Persia, excavating the palace of Darius I at Susa; during the First World War he served in France and after being wounded went to Morocco, 1916; here he was appointed Director of the Antiquities Service and the Beaux-Arts at Marrakesh, 1916-17; he was then appointed Director of Works for the Egyptian Antiquities Service at Karnak after the death of Legrain, 1920-5; Pillet later worked in the Lebanon, where he recovered the plan of one of the temples of Byblos, and then directed the excavations at Dura-Europos; he returned to work in Egypt in 1948, excavating at Dara with R. Weill; he contributed to many architectural and archaeological reports on western Asia, and also wrote many articles on the restoration of Egyptian buildings and on consolidation work, in *ASAE, Rev. de l'Égypte ancienne*, and *BIFAO*; his photographic archives are now at the Maison de l'Orient et de la Mediterranée-Jean Pouilloux at Lyons and available on the internet; he died in Versailles, 10 March 1964.

Syria 41 (1964), 385-6 (portr.) (A. Parrot); M. Azim, *Inventaire de la collection M. Pillet*, 1999; È. Gran-Aymerich, *Dictionnaire biographique d'archéologie 1798-1945*, 2001, incorporated in *Les Chercheurs de passé 1798-1945*, 2007, 1064; inf. M. Azim.

PINCIA, Pietro Lorenzo (1682-1755)
Italian priest and traveller; he was born at Ivrea 19 Sept. 1682, son of Giovanni Domenico Pinchia and Angela Francesca Moritta; from 1702 he studied in Rome at the Congregazione della Missione; he became a priest in 1705; he travelled to the Levant from 1719-21, being in Egypt from 16 Sept. 1720 until 9 July 1721; he visited numerous sites, going up the Nile as far as Philae with Sicard (q.v.) from 8 Nov. 1720 until 21 Jan. 1721 and visiting Sinai from 11 March to 9 April 1721; he was appointed deputy provost at the Cathedral at Ivrea in 1727, succeeding to the post of provost in 1729; he died at Ivrea 21 Feb. 1755 leaving a manuscript account of his voyage published in 1998.

G. Beraltino et al, *In Egitto Primo di Napoleone*, 1998; inf. M. Azim and P. Boaglio.

PIOTROVSKY, Boris Borisovitch (1908-1990)
Russian archaeologist; he was born in St. Petersburg, 14 Feb. 1908, son of Boris Bronislavovitch P., a teacher of mathematics and engineering and Sophia Alexandrovna Zavadsky; in 1922 he began the study of hieroglyphs under Flittner (q.v.) and from 1925-30 attended the historical-linguistic faculty of Leningrad State University specializing in Egyptology and archaeology; in 1929 he joined the Academy of the History of Material Culture as a junior research assistant and thereafter concentrated on the study of Urartu; research assistant at the Hermitage, 1931; from 1939-71 he undertook important excavations at Karmir-Blur in Armenia; corresponding member of the Academy of Sciences of the Armenian SSR 1945, member 1968; member of the Academy of Sciences of the USSR 1970; Director of the Leningrad section of the Institute of Archaeology 1953-64; Director of the Hermitage Museum from 1964 until his death; head of the sub-department of the history of the ancient East at the Leningrad State University 1966; from 1981 he directed the Department of the Ancient East at the Oriental Institute of the Academy; corresponding member of the Bavarian Academy, the British Academy, and the Académie des Inscriptions et Belles Lettres, Paris; in 1961-3 he led the expedition of the Academy of Sciences in the Nubian rescue campaign and recorded inscriptions in the Wadi Allaki; he organized the Tutankhamun exhibition in the USSR, 1973-5; apart from two early articles, his publications in Egyptology concentrated on his Nubian work and Tutankhamun including *Drevnaia Nubia*, 1964; *Sokrovisca Tutanchamona*, 1973; *Tutanchamon i ego vremia*, 1976; *Vadi Allaki. Putku zlotom rudnikom Nubii*, 1983; he edited *Egyptian Antiquities in the Hermitage*, 1974; he died in Leningrad, 15 Oct. 1990.

Great Soviet Encyclopedia 19,551; *Soviet Archaeology* 1991/3 (in Russian), 108-14 (portr.); *VDI* 185-2 (1988), 241-2; 203 (1992), 145-166; Y. Alyanski, *Boris Piotrovsky: the Chief Curator of the Hermitage*, 1988; inf. J. Śliwa; *VDI* (1992), 145-7 (O. Pavlova, G. Bongard-Levin, and A. Zubov); 158-60 (J. Werner), 160-3 (J. Leclant); Bundesarchiv, B 145 Bild-F078401-0011 / Engelbert Reineke / CC-BY-SA 3.0 (image).

PIRENNE, (*Comte*) **Jacques** (1891-1972)
Belgian Egyptologist; he was born at Ghent, 26 June 1891, son of Henri P., the historian and Jenny van der Haeghen; he studied law and history at the University of Ghent; PhD, 1914; he obtained his doctorate in law in 1918 after serving in World War I; he practised law in Brussels until 1936, but soon showed interest in the study

of the history of law in ancient Egypt, encouraged by Capart (q.v.); tutor to the future King Leopold III, 1921-4; lecturer on the history of law at the Université Libre de Bruxelles in 1921, Professor 1925; he took part in the creation of the Institut de philologie de d'histoire orientales et slaves in 1930 and founded the review *Archives d'Histoire du droit oriental* in 1937; in 1936 he gave a course on Egyptian law at the Collège de France, Paris and he lectured in 1939 at the University of Cairo; he gave further courses at the University of Grenoble in 1940-1 and the University of Geneva, 1941-4; after World War II he became secretary to King Leopold III until his abdication; his principal works on Egyptology were *Histoire de la Civilisation de l'Égypte ancienne*. 3 vols. (with A. Mekhitarian), 1961-3; *La Religion et la Morale dans l'Égypte antique*, 1965; he died in the Château de Hierges, Ardennes, France, 7 Sept. 1972.

BSFE 65 (1972), 9; *Recueils de la Société Jean Bodin* 36 (1973), i-xxiii (portr.), (bibl.) (J. Gilissen); *Revue Internationale des Droits de l'Antiquité* 19 (1972), I-XVII (portr.) (A. Théodoridès); *WW in Belgium* 1962, 811.

PIRIE, Annie Abernethie *see* **QUIBELL**

PISTELLI, Ermenegildo (1862-1927)
Italian classical scholar, writer, and journalist; he was born at Camaiore 15 Feb. 1862 , son of Alfonso P. and Clelia Benedetti; he was educated in Florence and entered the priesthood in 1884; he taught classics at schools in Florence, notably from 1903 at the Istituto di Studi superiori; he became a colleague of Vitelli (q.v.); he carried out excavations in Egypt at Oxyrhynchus, 1910, 1912-4; he died in Florence, 14 Jan. 1927.

DBDI 84, 260-3; *Aegyptus* 8 (1927), 108-111 (M. Norsa); M. Capasso (ed.), *Hermae*, 2007, 77-80 (P. Prunetti); *Ency. It.* 27, 24-5; G. Bastianini and A. Casanova, *100 Anni di Istituzioni Fiorentine per la Papirologia*, 2009, vii.

PITCAIRN, John (1841-1916)
American businessman and benefactor; he was born in Johnstone, Scotland, 10 Jan. 1841, son of John P. and Agnes McEwen; he amassed a fortune through a career in the railroad and oil industries and was a co-founder of the Pittsburgh Plate Glass Company; he was a member of the Swedenborgian General Church of the New Jerusalem, based in Bryn Athyn, Pennsylvania; he travelled in Egypt with Revd William H. Benade in 1878, collecting Egyptian antiquities; that same year he purchased for the Academy of the New Church museum (now Glencairn Museum) a collection of approximately 1,300 small objects formed by Rodolfo Lanzone (q.v.); he died in Bryn Athyn, 22 July 1916.

Family archive and Egyptian travel diary in Glencairn Museum Archives; R. Gladish, *John Pitcairn: Uncommon Entrepreneur*, 1989; E. Gyllenhaal, 'From Parlor to Castle: The Egyptian Collection at Glencairn Museum' in *Studies in Honor of David P. Silverman*, 2010.

PITCAIRN, Raymond (1885-1966) **and Theodore** (1893-1973)
American collectors, sons of John Pitcairn (q.v.) and Gertrude Starkey; Raymond was born in Philadelphia, 18 April 1885; Theodore, also in Philadelphia, 5 Nov. 1893; they inherited money from their father; both were art collectors and purchased Egyptian and mediaeval art, much from Joseph Brummer (q.v.); Theodore also collected European paintings; Raymond supervised the construction of the Gothic and Romanesque style Bryn Athyn Cathedral; in the 1930s Theodore became leader of The Lord's New Church Which is Nova Hierosolyma, resigning from The General Church of the New Jerusalem; the estates of both men gave Egyptian material to the Academy of the New Church museum (now Glencairn Museum); some of Theodore's major Egyptian pieces were sold at Christie's (London, 6 July 1976, lot 117; New York, 14 June 1979, lots 189-190); Raymond died in Abington, Pennsylvania, 12 July 1966, while Theodore died in Bryn Athyn, Pennsylvania, 17 Dec. 1973.

Family archive and material relating to collections in Glencairn Museum Archives; E. Gyllenhaal, 'From Parlor to Castle: The Egyptian Collection at Glencairn Museum' in *Studies in Honor of David P. Silverman*, 2010, 175-203; inf. T. Hardwick.

PITT RIVERS, (*Lt.-Gen.*) **Augustus Henry Lane-Fox** (1827-1900)
British collector and archaeologist; he was born at Hope Hall, Bramham Park, Yorkshire, 14 April 1827, son of William Augustus Lane-Fox and Lady Caroline Douglas; he was educated at Sandhurst and joined the Grenadier Guards in 1845 as a Lt.; Capt. 1850, Brevet-Major 1854, Major 1857, Lt.-Col. 1867, Maj.-Gen. 1877, Lt.-Gen. 1882; he served in the Crimean War; in 1880 he adopted the name Pitt Rivers after succeeding to the family estates of his great-uncle Baron Rivers; he formed a large ethnographical collection which he gave to the University of Oxford, now the Pitt-Rivers Museum; he conducted many archaeological excavations in England and Ireland; FSA, 1864; FRS, 1876; Hon. DCL from Oxford, 1886; he was appointed first Inspector of Ancient

Monuments in 1882; he visited Egypt in 1881 and was the first to discover flint implements in stratified levels near Thebes; he formed his archaeological collection into a private museum at Farnham, Dorset, now dispersed, some of the Egyptian objects being sold at Sotheby's 8 Nov. 1976 and 4 Dec. 1978, and others through K. J. Hewett (q.v.); the British Museum acquired the Pitt-Rivers knife (EA 68512) and a wooden stela (EA 66842); he died in Rushmore House, Cranborne Chase, 4 May 1900.

ODNB 47, 43-4 (portr.); *DNB* Suppl. 3, 268-70; *WWW* 1, 257; Boase, Suppl. VI, 402-3; L. H. Buxton, *The Pitt-Rivers museum Farnham*, 1929, 17-23 (portr.); M. Bowden, *General Pitt-Rivers: Father of Scientific Archaeology*, 1984; M. Bowden, *Pitt-Rivers*, 1991; È. Gran-Aymerich, *Dictionnaire biographique d'archéologie 1798-1945*, 2001, incorporated in *Les Chercheurs de passé 1798-1945*, 2007, 1066-9; A. Stevenson, *Egyptian Archaeology* 37 (2010), 41-3.

PLENDERLEITH, Harold James (1898-1997)
British conservator; he was born in Coatbridge, Lanarkshire, 19 Sept. 1898, son of Robert James P., art teacher, and Lucy Bell; he was educated at the Harris Academy in Dundee and went to University College of St. Andrews in 1916 to study science; he left to serve in World War I where he earned a MC in 1918 and then completed his education at University College, Dundee; BSc,1921; PhD, 1923; in 1924 he joined the laboratory of the Department of Scientific and Industrial Research at the British Museum which became the Research Laboratory of the British Museum in 1931; Assistant Keeper, 1931-8; Deputy Keeper, 1938-49; Keeper, 1949-59; Professor of Chemistry, Royal Academy of Arts, 1936-58; Director, International Centre for the Study of the Preservation and Restoration of Cultural Property, 1959-71; President of the International Institute for the Conservation of Museum Objects, 1965-8; CBE, 1959; he worked on the scientific analysis of objects from the tomb of Tutankhamun and was responsible for the care of the objects evacuated from the British Museum during World War II; his principal publication was *The Conservation of Antiquities and Works of Art*, 1956; revised ed., 1971; he died in Inverness, 2 Nov. 1997.

Who's Who 1995, 1527; *The Independent* 6 Nov. 1997 (portr.) (A. Oddy); *The Times* 11 Nov. 1997 (portr.), 25; *The Guardian* 12 Dec. 1997 (portr.) (A. Oddy); *SSCR Journal* 9 (FE. 1998), 5 (A. Oddy and G. de Guichen); *Bulletin of the International Institute fro the Conservation of Historic and Artistic Works* 6 (1997), 1-2 (A. Oddy).

PLEYTE, Willem (1836-1903)
Dutch Egyptologist; he was born in Hillegom, 26 June 1836, son of Cornelis Marinus P. and Gesina Marina van Voorthysen; he was educated at Zalt-Bommel and studied theology at the University of Utrecht; he was appointed conservator of the Egyptian collections at Leiden, 1 Feb. 1869; Director of the Leiden Museum, 1891-1903; D. ès Lettres *hon. c.*, Leiden, 1873; also Member of the Royal Acad. of Sciences, Amsterdam, 1882; Pleyte made hieratic his special field and was responsible for the making of a fount for it; he published many of the hieratic papyri in the museums of Leiden, Paris, and Turin, of the last in collaboration with Francesco Rossi; his main works were, *Catalogue raisonné de types égyptiens hiératiques de la fonderie de N. Tetterode à Amsterdam*, 1865; *La Religion des pré-Israélites: recherches sur le dieu Seth*, 1865; *Études égyptologiques*, 1866; *Les Papyrus Rollin, de la Bibliothèque Nat. de Paris*, fol. 1868; *Papyrus de Turin. Fac-similés par F. Rossi, et pub. par W. Pleyte*, 6 pts., 1869-76; *Chapitres supplémentaires du Livre des Morts 162 à 174. Publiés d'après les Monuments de Leide, du Louvre, et du Musée Britannique*, 3 vols., autographed by T. Bytel, 1881-2; *Over drie handschriften op papyrus bekend onder de titels van 'Papyrus du Lac Moeris du Fayoum et du Labyrinthe'*, 1884; *Manuscrits Coptes du Musée d'Antiquités des Pays-Bas à Leide*, with P. A. A. Boeser, 1897; he died in Leiden, 11 March 1903.

Sphinx 7 (1903), 175-6 (portr.) (K. Piehl); Hilmy, ii, 122 *Levensberichten der Maatschappij van Nederl. Letterkunde* (1904), 91-108 (P. Boeser); *Nieuw Nederlandsch Biografisch Woordenboeck* 4, 1087 ff; D. J. Van Wijngaarden, *Van Hiernius tot Boeser*, 1935, 12-5; *OMRO* 67 (1987), 93-9 (H. Hasselbach) (bibl.); inf. M. Raven.

PLUMLEY, (*Revd*) Jack Martin (1910-1999)
British Egyptologist; he was born in Peverell, Devon, 2 Sept. 1910, son of Arthur Henry P., an oil company employee, and Lily Martin; he was educated at Merchant Taylors' School, London where he showed an aptitude for ancient languages and from 1929 St. John's College, Durham where he read theology and Hebrew; BA; M. Litt.; he was ordained a deacon in 1933 and priest in 1934; he then served in various parishes including Hoxton, 1942-5 and Tottenham, 1945-7; while in London, he attended classes given by Glanville (q.v.) and also was befriended by Černy (q.v.) who encouraged his interest in Egyptology especially Coptic studies; when Glanville moved to Cambridge, he arranged for Plumley's appointment as rector and vicar of Milton near Cambridge, 1948-57; Plumley also became associate lecturer in Coptic at Cambridge University, 1948-57, and

served as secretary of the Oriental Languages Faculty; he succeeded Glanville as Herbert Thompson Professor of Egyptology at Cambridge, 1957-77; Fellow of Selwyn College, 1957; Member, Council of Senate of the University, 1965-70; Acting Dean, Pembroke College, 1981-2; Glanville Memorial lecturer, 1982; Priest-in-Charge, Longstowe, 1981-95; FSA, 1966; Fellow of the Institute of Coptic Studies, 1966, and corresponding member of the German Institute of Archaeology, 1966; he directed the excavations at Qasr Ibrim during and after the Nubian rescue campaign, 1963-4, 1966, 1969, 1972, 1974, 1976; Chairman of the British Committee of the International Critical Greek New Testament Project, 1963-87; President of the International Society for Nubian Studies, 1978-82 and thereafter Patron; he married 1.1938 Gwendolen Alice Darling (*d*.1984) who wrote an account of the 1974 expedition to Qasr Ibrim, *A Nubian Diary*, 1977; 2. 1986 Ursula Clara Dowle; apart from preliminary archaeological reports and other articles, he published *Introduction to Coptic Grammar*, 1948; *The Scrolls of Bishop Timotheos*, 1975; with G. Browne, *Old Nubian Texts from Qasr Ibrim* I, 1988; and edited *Nubian Studies*, 1982; he died at Cambridge, 2 July 1999.

Who's Who 1998, 1584; *The Times* 23 July 1999; *The Independent* 15 July 1999 (B. Kemp); *The Daily Telegraph* 17 July 1999; *Sudan and Nubia* 3 (1999), 90-1 (J. Alexander).

POCOCKE, (*Revd*) **Richard** (1704-1765)
British traveller and divine; he was born in Southampton, 1704, bapt. 30 Nov, son of Richard P. and Elizabeth Milles; he studied at Corpus Christi College, Oxford; BA, 1725; DCL, 1733; he visited Egypt 29 Sept. (10 Oct. new style) 1737-March 1738, ascending the Nile as far as Philae, and then visited Palestine, Asia Minor, returning to Egypt Dec. 1738-July 1739 when he visited Sinai, and Greece, 1739-40; he explored Switzerland, 1741; Bishop of Ossory, 1756-65, of Meath, 1765; he published an account of his eastern travels, *A Description of the East, and some other countries*, fol. 2 vols. 1743-5; this is a most important work as it gives detailed and comprehensive descriptions of many sites and places as they existed long before the later visitors made their full recordings of the monuments; thus much existing then had already disappeared by the early years of the next century; a MS journal of these travels still exists, British Library Add. MSS 22995, 22997-8; Pococke was a member of the first Egyptian Society founded 1741, Secretary 1742-3; he died while on a visitation, in Charleville, nr. Tullamore, Ireland, 25 Sept. 1765.

ODNB 44, 667-9; *DNB* 46, 12-14; Hilmy, ii, 124; *JEA* 23 (1937), 260; M. McCarthy, *Apollo* (May 1996), 25-30; J. Speake (ed.), *Literature of Travel and Exploration*, 2003, 2, 968-70; Lamy, 176-9; R. Finnegan, *Journal of the History of Collections* 27 (2015), 33-48; R. Finnegan, *ASTENE Bulletin* 68 (2016), 20-1; R. Finnegan, *English Explorers in the East (1738-1745)*, 2019, *passim*.

POCZOBUT-ODLANICKI, Marcin (1728-1810)
Polish astronomer; he was born at Slomiance, 30 Oct. 1728, son of Casimir P. and Helen Hlebowiczow; he became a member of the Jesuit order and trained as an astronomer at Prague; he built an observatory at Vilna, 1756-8, and then undertook further training in France and Italy; director of the Vilna observatory from 1761; he wrote papers on the Dendera zodiac, *Essais sur l'époque de l'antiquité du zodiaque de Denderah (Tinthyris)*, 1803 with editions in Polish, German and Russian; *Recherches sur l'antiquité du zodiaque de Denderah (Tintyris)*, 1805; he died at Dyneburg, 8 Feb. 1810.

Polski Slownik Biograficzny 27, 52-62; inf. J. Śliwa.

POINSINET DE SIVRY, Louis (1733-1804)
French writer and classical scholar; he was born in Versailles, 20 Feb. 1733, son of Pierre P., an official of the Duke of Orleans, and Magdelene Victoire Chappard; he wrote several tragedies and translated Sappho, Anacreon, and Bion (1758); Pliny (1781); Aristophanes (1784); published a work, *Nouvelles recherches sur la science des médailles, inscriptions et hiéroglyphes antiques*, 1778, in which he claimed to be able to read the hieroglyphs on the Turin bust, previously studied by Needham (q.v.), Stukeley (q.v.), and others, which is in fact a manifest forgery; he died in Paris, 11 March 1804.

NBG 40, 559-60; *Mem. IFAO*. 66. 367 (*Mélanges Maspero*); Hilmy, ii, 125.

POITEVIN, Éphraim (*fl.* 1853-1855)
French Egyptologist; he contributed articles to *Rev. arch.*, 1853-5, on the Table of Abydos, the inscription of Ahmose, and the town of Avaris; at his instigation a monument to Champollion was erected at the Collège de France.

Hartleben, ii. 606; Hilmy, ii, 125.

POITOU, Eugène Louis (1815-1880)

French poet and publicist; he was born in Angers, 9 Feb. 1815, son of Jean Louis P., a judge, and Marie Rosalie Beaumont; he studied law in Paris and became a judge at Angers in 1848; he was named as an imperial counsellor in 1856; he visited Egypt in 1857 where he met Clot-Bey (q.v.), and travelled with him as far as the Cataracts; he published *Un Hiver en Égypte*, 1859, which was translated into English and reached a fourth edition; he was the first Frenchman to describe the Serapeum at Saqqara; Légion d'Honneur 1862; he died 1880.

Carré, ii, 251-3; Hilmy, ii, 125; *Larousse XIXe siècle* 12, 1279; Vapereau, 1436.

POLOTSKY, Hans Jacob (1905-1991)

Israeli Egyptologist and philologist; he was born in Zurich, 13 Sept. 1905, son of Russian parents Abraham P. and Esther Rode who settled in Berlin; he was educated from 1924-28 at the Universities of Berlin under Sethe (q.v.) and Göttingen under Kees (q.v.) specializing in Egyptology and Semitic languages; PhD 1928; he became an assistant at Göttingen involved with the publication of Coptic Manichean texts; he emigrated from Germany in 1934; Instructor in Egyptology, Hebrew University of Jerusalem, 1934-51; Professor of Egyptology and Semitic Linguistics, 1951-72; Visiting Professor at Chicago 1952, Brown University 1959-60, Copenhagen 1967-8, Yale 1985, and Berlin 1990; Hon. PhD from Manchester University; Founder Member of the Israel Academy of Sciences and Humanities; Corresponding Fellow of the British Academy and the School of Oriental and African Studies; Hon. Fellow of the Royal Asiatic Society; he was the leading philologist of his generation and revolutionized the study of ancient Egyptian and Coptic grammar with his work on second tenses; a volume of eleven studies was dedicated to him *Studies in Egyptology and Linguistics in Honour of H. J. Polotsky*, 1964 and a further volume of twenty-nine studies in philology was written for him by various authors in D. W. Young, *Studies Presented to Hans Jakob Polotsky*, 1981; his articles on Egyptian and other languages up to 1965 were published in his *Collected Papers*, 1971, and further articles were collected in *Scripta Posteriora on Egyptian and Coptic,* edited by V. Lepper and L. Depuydt, 2007; his Glanville lecture was published by J. Ray, *Lingua Sapientissima*, 1987; his monographs on Egyptian philology were his thesis *Zu den Inschriften der 11. Dynastie*, 1929; *Manichäische Homilien*, Vol. I, 1934; *Études de syntaxe copte*, 1944 reprinted in Collected Papers; *Essays on Egyptian Grammar*, with J. P. Allen, L. Depuydt, and D. Silverman, 1986; *Grundlagen des Koptischen Satzbaus*, 1987, 1990; some of his correspondence was edited by E. Ullendorff, *Ausgewählte Briefe*, 1992; he died in Jerusalem, 10 Aug. 1991.

The Times 14 Aug. 1991; *The Independent*, 29 Aug. 1991 (A. K. Irvine);*ZÄS* 120 (1993), I-V (portr.), (J. Osing); *Orientalia* 61 (1992), 208-13 (A. Shisha-Halevy); *Rassegna di Studi Etiopici* 34 (1992), 115-125 (S. Hopkins); *Journal of the Royal Asiatic Society* 3rd ser. 4 (1994), 3-13 (E. Ullendorff); *NDB* 20, 608-9; M. Müller in J. Arp-Neuman and T. Gertzen (eds.), '*Steininschrift und Bibelwort*', 2019, 73-8.

POMERANCE, Leon (1907-1988)

American businessman, collector and benefactor; he was born in Brooklyn, 2 Aug. 1907, son of Michael P., founder of the Forest Paper Co., and Esther Meyer; he attended New York University; he worked for the family business, Forest Paper Company; he endowed awards and scholarships at the American Institute of Archaeology and funded its excavations at the Cretan site of Kato Zakros, 1969-72; he published on Bronze Age Aegean chronology and its relationship with Egypt; he formed a collection of antiquities, exhibited at the Brooklyn Museum in 1966; some objects were sold at Sotheby's (New York, 11 Dec. 1980; 22 May 1981; 29 May 1987), others were dispersed privately from family possession; his papers are in the University of Florida Smathers Libraries; he died in New York City, 11 Nov. 1988.

J. L. Keith (ed.), *The Pomerance Collection of Ancient Art*, 1966; C. Finch, 'The Archaeophiles: Leon and Harriet Pomerance' *Auction* 4/5 (Jan 1971), 35-38; J. W. Shaw in *AJA* 93/3 (July 1989), 459-60; info. T. Hardwick.

PONIATOWSKI, (*Prince*) Stanislaus (1754-1833)

Polish statesman and general, he was born in Warsaw, 23 Nov. 1754, son of Prince Casimir P. and Apollonia Usztrycka; he retired in 1793 and settled in Vienna and afterwards in Rome where he formed his famous collection of engraved gems in his house in the Via Flaminia; he died in Florence, 13 Feb. 1833; the collection was sent to London for disposal and the gems were sold at Christie's in a sale of 2339 lots, 29 April-21 May 1839; it included many fine scarabs and gnostic gems from Egypt; the authenticity of his gem collection has often been questioned; in reality a great part was modern, executed according to his request with application of ancient motifs mainly inspired by literary sources; the collection before the sale was copied piece by piece; one set of plaster casts was bought by the University of Tübingen; the second one is now in the collection of the Royal Castle at Warsaw; he died in 1833.

C. W. King, *Handb. of Engraved Gems*, 2nd ed., 193-7; Lugt 15422; M. Brandys, *Nieznany ksiaze Poniatowski,*

Warsaw 4 1970; A. Busiri Vici, I *Poniatowski e Roma*, Florence 1971, 313-365; J. Kolendo in *Studia Archaeologiczne* 1 (1981), 81-99; *Polski Słownik Biograficzny* 27, 481-7; inf. J. Śliwa.

PONTCHARTRAIN, (*Comte*) **Jérôme Phélypeaux de** (1674-1747)
French statesman and collector; he was born in Paris, March 1674, son of Louis P. and Marie de Maupeou; he succeeded his father as Secretary of State, 1693, but resigned office in 1715 in favour of his son; he owned a collection of Egyptian antiquities, probably sent by B. de Maillet (q.v.), French Consul-General in Egypt; among them was a mummy, which was described and reproduced in an elaborate MS by Florimond, now in the library of King's College, Cambridge; this mummy was given to the Convent of the Petits Pères, Paris, which was destroyed during the Revolution, and the mummy which was believed to be that of Cleopatra, was buried in the convent garden; he died in Paris, 18 Feb. 1747.

Inf. Mme Noblecourt; Carré, i, 42, 57; Dawson MS 15, ff. 238-42; Florimond MS

POOLE, Reginald Stuart (1832-1895)
British orientalist and numismatist; he was born in London, 27 Feb. 1832, younger son of Revd Edward Richard P. and his wife Sophia, sister of E. W. Lane (q.v.); as a boy he went to Egypt where he began the study of Egyptian monuments and antiquities and twice ascended the Nile under the guidance of his uncle Lane; he was thus able to contribute articles to the *Literary Gazette* before he was 17, these being republished as *Horae Aegyptiacae, or the Chronology of Ancient Egypt*, 1851; he entered the service of the British Museum, Feb. 1852; he married Eliza Christina Forlonge, 1861; appointed Keeper of Coins and Medals, 1870; retired 1893; he frequently wrote articles on Egyptian subjects and lectured on Egyptological topics; he published *Cities of Egypt*, 1882; on coins *Ptolemaic Kings of Egypt*, 1883; *Alexandria*, 1892; also articles in *Smith's Dictionary of the Bible* and *Enc. Britannica*; he vindicated Champollion (q.v.) against the attacks of Sir G. Cornewall Lewis (q.v.) (*Archaeologia*, 39, 471), and took an active part with Amelia Edwards (q.v.) in founding the EEF, 1882 as joint Hon. Secretary and later Vice-President; Hon. LLD Cambridge, 1880; Professor of Classical Archaeology, University College London, 1889; Hon. Sec. EEF; Corresponding Member of the Académie des Inscriptions, 22 Dec. 1876; he died in W. Kensington, London, 8 Feb. 1895.

ODNB 44, 845-7; *DNB* 46, 101-3; Hilmy, ii, 128; *JEA* 33 (1947), 72; Newberry Corr.; A. C. E. Franquet de Franqueville, *Le Premier Siècle de l'Institut de France*, 1895, II, 299.

POOLE, Sophia (1804-1891)
British writer; she was born in Hereford, 16 Jan. 1804, daughter of Revd Theopilus Lane and Sophia Gardiner, and was the sister of E. W. Lane (q.v.); she married Edward Richard Poole, 1829; while living in Egypt with her brother, 1842-9, she published *The Englishwoman in Egypt*, 2 vols. 1844, second series vol. iii, 1846, new ed. (ed. A. Kararah), 2003; she spent her last years in her son's official house at the British Museum where she died 6 May 1891.

ODNB 44, 849; *DNB* 46, 104; Hilmy, ii, 130; Romer, ii, 3; J. Thompson, *Edward William Lane 1816-1876*, 2010, *passim*.

PORTAL, (*Baron*) **Pierre Paul Frédéric de** (1804-1876)
French archaeologist; born in Bordeaux, 7 Nov. 1804, son of Pierre Barthélémy P. and Elisabeth Marguerite Bergès; he published *Les symboles des Égyptiens comparés à ceux des Hébreux*, 1840; he died in Paris, 1876.

La Grande Enc. 27, 356 (E. Babylon).

PORTER, Bertha (1852-1941)
Egyptological bibliographer; she was born in London, 9 April 1852, daughter of Frederick William P., architect and Sarah Moyle; her tastes were literary and she was acquainted with Dickens, Carlyle, and the Brownings; she was also interested in psychical research; she studied Egyptology under Griffith (q.v.) and under Sethe (q.v.) at Göttingen, after which she spent many years in amassing the material for the *Topographical Bibliography of Ancient Egyptian Hieroglyphic Texts, Reliefs and Paintings*, the first volume of which, dealing with the Theban Necropolis, appeared in 1927; this was produced with the collaboration of Rosalind Moss (q.v.), who produced many subsequent volumes; her MSS are in the Griffith Institute; she died in Oxford, 17 Jan. 1941.

The Times, 22 Jan. 1941.

POSENER, (Henri) Georges (1906-1988)

French Egyptologist; he was born in Paris, 12 Sept. 1906, son of Solomon Pozner, a Russian lawyer and journalist who left his country in 1905, and Esther Sidersky; the family returned to Russia after the 1917 Revolution but again emigrated to France in 1921; he was educated at the Lycée Russe in Paris, the Sorbonne where he studied history and geography, and the École Pratique des Hautes Études where he studied Egyptology under Sottas (q.v.), Lefebvre (q.v.), Weill (q.v.), and Moret (q.v.) from 1925-31; he was awarded his diploma in 1933 with a thesis on the texts of the Persian period; he exhibited a deep interest in Egyptian philology and literature; from 1931-9 he was attached to the French Institute in Cairo and took part in the excavations at Tod and Deir el-Medina; he was assigned the publication of the literary hieratic ostraca from Deir el-Medina, a task which was to become his life's work and allowed him to reconstruct many ancient Egyptian literary texts; he served in the French army at the beginning of World War II, was taken prisoner and escaped in 1940, and spent the rest of the war in hiding in Paris where he took part in the Resistance; in 1945 he was appointed Director of Studies in history and Egyptian archaeology at the École Pratique until 1976; Professor of Egyptian Philology and Archaeology at the Collège de France 1961-78; Visiting Professor Brown University 1952-3; Member of the Académie des Inscriptions et Belles-Lettres 1969; President of the Société Française d'Égyptologie 1963-71 and editor of *Revue d'Égyptologie* until 1985; Professor honoris-causa of the University of Heidelberg; Corresponding Member of the British Academy; Member of the German Archaeological Institute and the Academies of Sciences in Göttingen and Munich; he wrote nearly a hundred books and articles covering a wide range of subjects especially history, religion, and literature; his principal works were *Catalogue des ostraca hiératiques littéraires de Deir el Médineh* I-III, 1934-80; *La Première domination perse en Égypte, recueil d'inscriptions hiéro-glyphiques*, 1936; *Princes et pays d'Asie et de Nubie, textes hiératiques sur des figurines d'envoûtement du Moyen Age*, 1940; *Littérature et politique dans l'Égypte de la XIIe dynastie*, 1956; *Dictionnaire de la civilisation égyptienne*, 1959; *De la divinité du pharaon*, 1960; *Leçon inaugurale ... au Collège de France*, 1961; *Catalogue des stèles du Sérapéum de Memphis* I, with M. Malinine and J. Vercoutter, 1968; *L'Enseignement loyaliste*, 1976; *Le papyrus Vandier*, 1985; *Cinq figurines d'envoûtement*, 1987; he died in Garaches, 15 May 1988.

BIFAO 88 (1988), vii-xxviii (portr.) (bibl.) (J. Yoyotte and O. Perdu); *Rev. d'Ég.* 39 (1988), i-iii (A. Mekhitarian); *BSFE* 112 (1988), 4-10 (J. Assmann).

POSENER-KRIÉGER, Paule Violette (1925-1996)

French Egyptologist; she was born in Paris, 18 April 1925, daughter of Lucien K., an engineer, and Elise Beyer; she initially obtained a science degree to study for medicine but then studied Egyptology at the Sorbonne and the École Pratique des hautes études under Posener (q.v.), Clère (q.v.), and Malinine (q.v.), graduating in 1951; she was attached to the Louvre, 1948-58 and to CNRS, 1953-78; she married Georges Posener in 1960; she succeeded her husband as Directeur des Études at the École Pratique in 1978, teaching there from 1979-81 and 1990-3; she was director of the Institut français d'archéologie orientale in Cairo, 1981-Jan. 1990; she specialized in the study of Egyptian palaeography of the Old Kingdom notably hieratic texts from Abusir and Gebelein; her publications included *Catalogue de l'exposition France-Égypte*, 1949; *Catalogue de la collection égyptienne du Musée Municipal de Limoges*, 1958; with J. de Cenival, *The Abu Sir Papyri*, 1968; and *Les archives du temple funéraire de Néferirkarê,-Kakaï*, 1976, and posthumously *I papiri di Gebelein. Scavi G. Farina 1935*, 2004; she also translated H. Frankfort, *Kingship and the Gods* as *La royauté et les dieux*, 1951 and S. Schott, *Die altägyptische Liebeslieder* as *Les chants d'amour de l'Égypte ancienne*, 1956; she died in Paris, 11 May 1996.

Rev. d'Ég. 48 (1997), 5-14 (portr.) (bibl.) (J. Yoyotte); *BSFE* 136 (1996), 3; IAE Internet obituary (J. Yoyotte); inf. E. Delange.

POSNO, Gustave (*fl.* 1874-1883)

Dutch collector; a catalogue of his antiquities, *Collection de M. Posno*, Cairo, 1874, was issued; the objects described were mostly Graeco-Roman, and the collection was sold in Paris 22-28 May 1883 (cat. with plates by Rollin (q.v.) and Feuardent (q.v.)), some bronzes being bought for the Louvre; other objects are now in the Palais des Beaux-Arts, Paris, Berlin (8438-9), and Copenhagen (A99).

Inf. Dr. R. Moss; *Rev. de l'Art*, 43. 171; L Stern in *Zeitschrift für die gebildete Welt* 3 (1883), 285-8; Lugt 43062.

POTOCKI, (*Comte*) Jan (1761-1815)

Polish writer and traveller; he was born in Pikow, Ukraine, 8 March 1761, son of Joseph P. and Anne Therese Countess Ossolinska; he visited Egypt in 1784 and published an account of his journey, *Voyage en Turquie, en Égypte, fait en*

1784, 1788; also works on chronology, *Dynasties du second livre de Manéthon*, 1805; *Examen critique du fragment égyptien connu sous le nom de l'ancienne chronique*, 1808, etc.; he died in Ohladowka, 11 Dec. 1815.

Hilmy, ii, 133; *Larousse XIXe siècle* 12. 1521; *NBG* 40, 900; *PSL* 28, 36-42; inf. J. Śliwa; Lamy, 214-6.

POURTALÈS-GORGIER, (*Comte*) **James Alexandre de** (1776-1855)
French collector; he was born in Neuchatel, 28 Nov. 1776, son of Jacques Louis de P. and Rose Augustine de Luze; chamberlain to the King of Prussia who awarded him the title of count in 1814; he formed a gallery of antiquities and works of art in Paris including a mummy and coffins from the Thédénat-Duvent (q.v.) sale which he presented to the Berlin Museum in 1825; for his collection see T. Panofka, *Antiques du cabinet du Comte de Pourtalès-Gorgier*, 1834; he died in Paris, 24 March 1855; his collection was sold 6 Feb.-21 March 1865 when many of the more important pieces among the Egyptian objects were bought by Amherst (q.v.); he has been confused with his cousin Albert Alexandre Comte de Pourtalès (1810-1883) who was the father of Marguerite, wife of Édouard Naville (q.v.).

Inf. P. E. Newberry; L. Malzac, *Les Pourtalès*, 1914; *Dictionnaire Historique et Biographique de la Suisse* 5, 333; Lugt 28257; inf. J. Taylor.

PRAKHOV, Adrian Viktorovitch (1846-1916)
Russian art historian and collector; he was born in Mstislavl 16 March 1846, son of Viktor P.; he was the author of a study entitled *Critical Observations on the Forms of Fine Arts. Part I: The architecture of ancient Egypt*, St. Petersburg 1880 (in Russian); he formed in Egypt in 1881 an interesting collection of Egyptian antiquities of which 217 items purchased from his son in 1935-40 are now in the Pushkin Museum in Moscow, including also a papyrus of the Late Period, named after him; the Papyrus Prakhov, concerning some economic problems, was later in the possession of B. A. Turaev (q.v.) who published the text in 1921 and 1927 (posth.) and is now in the collection of the State Hermitage, Leningrad; he died at Yalta, 14 May 1916.

Ocerki po istorii russkogo vostokovedeniya, Vol. III, Moscow 1960, 111-18 (M. A. Korostovtsev and S. I. Hodjash); inf. J. Śliwa.

PRATT, Edward Roger (1789-1863)
British traveller and collector; he was born in Ryston Hall, Norfolk, 26 Sept. 1789, son of Edward Roger P., landowner, and Pleasance Browne; he was educated at Trinity College Cambridge; BA, 1812, MA, 1815; he travelled in the Mediterranean and visited Egypt, Dec. 1833-May 1834; he formed a collection of Egyptian objects, some purchased from the d'Athanasi (q.v.) collection, others perhaps in Egypt; objects were sold at Sotheby's New York, 17 Dec. 1998 and 6 Dec. 2006; two stelae were sold privately to the British Museum, EA 74847 and 77395; he was High Sheriff of Norfolk, 1850; he died at Ryston Hall, 28 May 1863.

Al. Cantab.; travel journal in family possession.

PRÉVOST-PARADOL, Lucien Anatole (1829-1870)
French scholar; he was born in Paris, 8 Aug. 1829, son of Vincent François Prévost and Anne Catherine Lucinde Paradol; he was educated at the Collège Bourbon and École Normale; he was appointed Professor of French Literature at Aix, 1855; elected to the Acad. Française in the vacancy caused by the death of Ampère on whom he published an *Éloge*, 1865; he visited Egypt in 1865 being accompanied to Thebes by Arakel Bey (q.v.), but although declaring himself to be 'intoxicated with Egypt' he published no account of his journey; later appointed envoy to USA he soon after died by his own hand in Washington, 20 July 1870.

EB 22, 312; Carré ii, 265-6; Lady Duff Gordon, *Letters*, 334; A. Aubert, *Un Grand Liberal*, 1931.

PRICE, (Frederick George) Hilton (1842-1909)
British banker and antiquary; he was born London, 20 Aug. 1842, son of Frederick William P., a banker, and Louisa Tinson; he entered Child's Bank in 1860 and eventually became senior partner; FSA, 1882, and Director, SA, 1894-1909; VP, Soc. Bibl. Arch.; President, EEF, 1906-9; he married Christina Bailey, 1867; he published several antiquarian works, and formed a large collection of antiquities, those relating to London later forming the basis of the London Museum; his Egyptian antiquities were very numerous and choice, many of them he himself described in *PSBA*, and the whole collection was luxuriously catalogued in sumptuous volumes (2 vols. 1897-1908); the collection was sold at Sotheby's, 12-21 July 1911, and realized £12,040; his numismatic library sold at Sotheby's, 20 April 1911; he died in Cannes, 14 March 1909.

AAA 2, 94; *WWW* i, 575; *ODNB* 45, 293-4; Lugt 70122.

PRICHARD, James Cowles (1786-1848)
British physician and anthropologist; he was born in Ross-on-Wye, 11 Feb. 1786, son of Thomas P., Quaker and businessman, and Mary Lewis; MD, Edinburgh, 1808; he matriculated at Trinity College, Cambridge, 1808, and afterwards at St. John's and Trinity Colls., Oxford, but did not graduate at either University; Physician to St. Peter's Hospital, Bristol, 1811, and to Bristol Infirmary, 1814; a Commissioner of Lunacy, 1845; apart from his valuable contributions to anthropology of which his *Physical History of Mankind* and *Natural History of Man* are the most important, he seriously studied Egyptian history, chronology, and religion; he published *Analysis of Egyptian Mythology* (1st ed. 1819, trans. into German, 1837); he died in London, 22 Dec. 1848.

ODNB 45, 329-32; *DNB* 46, 344-6; Haddon, *Hist. of Anthropology*, 104 (portr.); Hilmy, ii, 135; *Man*, 1949, § 163 (portr.).

PRIESE, Karl-Heinz (1935-2017)
German Egyptologist; he was born in Ziesar, 25 June 1935; he studied Egyptology and Semitic Studies at the Humboldt University in Berlin under Hintze (q.v.), 1954-8; BA, 1958; PhD, 1964; Habilitation, 1974; he became an assistant at the university from 1958; he succeeded Morenz (q.v.) at Leipzig; he joined the Egyptian Museum in Berlin as research assistant, 1978-83; Keeper, 1983-8; Director 1988-2000; Hon. Professor, Humboldt University, 1993; he took part in the Burtana expedition, 1960-9 and the excavations at Musawwarat es-Sufra in the Sudan from 1960; apart from articles, he published *Die Opferkammer des Merib*, 1984; with others, *Das Ägyptische Museum*, 1989 and 1991; *Das Gold von Meroe*, 1992; English ed., *The Gold of Meroe*, 1993; he died in Berlin, 27 Jan. 2017.

Der Antike Sudan 28 (2017), 135-8 (S. Wenig) (portr.) (bibl.); inf. S. Wenig.

PRINGLE, John Watson (1790-1861)
British army officer and traveller; he was baptized at Earlston, Berwick, 12 Oct. 1790, son of Col. George P. and Margaret Watson; entered Royal Engineers, Lieut., 1811; he fought and was wounded at Waterloo; on half-pay as Captain, 1817; he visited Egypt en route for Ceylon, 1824, and published *Route de l'Inde par l'Égypte et la Mer Rouge* in *Bull. Soc. Géogr. Paris*, 1826, 651; he died in Bath, 12 Oct. 1861.

C. Dalton, *Waterloo Roll Call*, 2nd ed., 229; Madox, ii, 28, 33; Westcar Diary, 191-6, 200, 207, 218, 221.

PRISSE D'AVENNES, Achilles Constant Théodore Émile (1807-1879)
French Egyptologist; he was born in Avesnes-sur-Helpe, 27 Jan 1807, son of Constant P., an inspector of the woods belonging to the Prince of Talleyrand who died of typhus in 1814, and Claire Constance Theresa Victoire Pillot; despite the apparent connection of his name with this place, Carré states that he himself believed in a romantic descent from an old British family who emigrated to Flanders under Charles II, and that he considered it was the Welsh Price of Avon and Carnarvon; he was brought up by a local curé after this, and was educated at Châlons-sur-Marne, 1822-5, where he obtained the diploma of Engineer-Architect; he took part in the Greek War of Independence, 1826, and then went to Egypt in 1827 where he obtained an appointment as engineer and lecturer in military schools under Muhammad Ali which lasted until 1836; from 1836-1844 he undertook the copying of Egyptian monuments; he is the most mysterious of all the great pioneer figures in Egyptology and in fact far less is known about his career than the others, while his disposition did not encourage friendships with many of his colleagues; his work is of major importance nevertheless, and he not only did a great deal of work for others but also produced single-handed the largest series of illustrated records of Egyptian monuments of any Frenchman since Champollion (q.v.); in 1842 he founded with Henry Abbott (q.v.) the Association Littéraire in Cairo; he cut out the Table of Kings at Karnak in 1843 and overcoming great difficulties removed it to France; he revisited Egypt in 1858-60 with Testas (q.v.); his name is particularly associated with the famous papyrus in the Bibl. Nationale (Cartons 183-94) and with the Table of Kings; Prisse was an outstandingly brilliant observer and was one of the first to note the Aten blocks in the Horemheb pylons at Karnak, 1839, and wrote to Wilkinson (q.v.) about them at a time when they were scarcely understood; he copied much that has since gone, when rooms were being cleared in temples or walls destroyed for masonry; he adopted the name Idris-Effendi and although known to many visitors to Egypt, received little recognition in his lifetime except for the award of the rank of Chevalier of the Légion d'honneur; the splendid series of publications, included, besides the facsimile of his papyrus discovered in 1843, *Les Monuments égyptiens*, fol. 1847, to complement Champollion's work; *Oriental Album. Characters, costumes and modes of life in the Valley of the Nile illustrated from designs taken on the spot by E. Prisse, with descriptive letter-press by James Augustus St. John*, 1848-51; *Atlas de l'histoire de l'art égyptien, d'après les monuments,*

depuis les temps les plus reculés jusqu'à la domination romaine, atlas in 2 vols. fol. 1858-77, reprint, 1991; *L'Art arabe, d'après les monuments du Caire, depuis le VIIe siècle jusqu'à la fin du XVIIIe siècle,* 3 vols. fol. 1867-79; his MSS and drawings are in the Bibl. Nat. (Nouv. Acq. Fr. 20416-49), while other papers were in the possession of his son (*d.*1919) from whom they were acquired by the Archaeological Soc. of Avesnes, some of these papers and the portrait of Prisse being stolen by the Germans from Avesnes in 1918 and have not been recovered; yet others of his many MSS were sold in London, where his library was sold at Sotheby's, 17 Feb. 1879; he died in Paris, 10 Jan. 1879.

Carré, i, 301-23 (bibl.); Hilmy, ii, 138; *Notice biographique sur Émile Prisse d'Avenne,* 1896; M. Dewachter, *BSFE* 101 (1984) 49-71; *Aramco World* Nov./Dec. 1990, 39-47; M Dewachter, *Un Avesnois: l'égyptologue Prisse d'Avennes (1807-1879),* 1988; M. J. Raven (ed.) W. de Famars Testas, *Reischetsen wit Egypte (1858-1860),* 1988; M. Raven in *Atlas de l'histoire des l'art égyptian,* reprint 1991, 1-6; È. Gran-Aymerich, *Dictionnaire biographique d'archéologie 1798-1945,* 2001, incorporated in *Les Chercheurs de passé 1798-1945,* 2007, 1079-81; Y. Thibaudault in *Égypte Afrique & Orient* 44 (2006), 15-22; M. Volait, *Émile Prisse d'Avennes. Un artiste-antiquaire en Égypte au XIXe siècle,* 2013.

PROKESCH VON OSTEN, *(Count)* **Anton Franz** *(the elder)* (1795-1876)
Austrian diplomat; he was born at Graz, 10 Dec. 1795, son of Maximilian Franz P. and Anna Stadler, and began a military career by serving as an officer 1813-15, becoming aide-de-camp to Schwarzenberg, 1818; he visited Egypt, 5 Oct. 1825-30 March 1827; he was later sent on missions to Greece and the Levant, 1828, and was sent to negotiate peace between the Viceroy of Egypt and the Sultan in 1833; m. 1832 Irene Kieswetter von Wiesenbrunn; he later served as ambassador to Berlin and held other high posts; he published *Erinnerungen aus Aegypten und Kleinasien,* 3 vols. 1839-31; *Das Land zwischen den Katarakten des Nil,* 1831; he died at Vienna, 26 Oct. 1876; his son Anton, born Athens, 19 Feb. 1837 published an account of his own trip to Egypt, *Nilfahrt bis zu den zweiten Katarakten, Führer durch Aegypten und Nubien,* 1874; he died in Gmunden, 12 March 1919.

ADB 26 (1888), 631-45 (von Zeissberg), see espec. pp. 635-6. *Der Grosse Brockhaus,* 9 (1956), 414; *La Grande Enc.* 27. 759; *Larousse, XIXᵉ siècle* 13, 230; *Nouveau Larousse illustré; Dict. Universel Encycl.* 7 (n.d.), 47 (a-b) also deals with his son; *Espasa-Calpe Enciclopedia Universal Illustrada europeo-americana.* 47 (1922), 851-2; D Bertsch, *Anton Prokesch von Osten (1795-1876): Ein Diplomat Österreichs in Athen und and der Hohen Pforte,* 2005; E. Czerny in N. Cooke (ed.), *Journeys Erased by Time,* 2019, 139-56.

PRUDHOE, Lord *see* **PERCY**

PRUNER, *(Bey)* **Franz Ignaz** (1808-1883)
German physician and anthropologist; he was born in Pfreimdt, Bavaria, 8 March 1808, son of Ignaz P., an administrator, and Katherine Horchler; he was educated in medicine at Munich, and later studied in Paris, 1860-70, under Grossi; he went to Egypt to assist Clot-Bey (q.v.) in the medical service; Dir. of the Military Hospital, 1833, and later of the Central Hospital and Kasr el-Aini Hospital; he was created a Bey in 1839; he left Egypt in 1860; in addition to his medical writings, Pruner wrote on the Egyptian race and its origin, on Neanderthal Man, and on the general problems of race; he took hair to be the test of racial purity; President, Soc. Anthr. Paris, 1865; Hon. FRAI, 1863; he died in Pisa, 29 Sept. 1883.

BIE 2nd ser. 1883, 81; Brugsch, *Mein Leben,* 159; Clot-Bey, *Aperçu,* ii, 417; Hilmy, ii, 144; *JAI* 12, 561; Lepsius, 47, 98; *NDB* 20, 747-8.

PUGIOLI, Pietro (1831-1902)
Italian collector of Alexandria; he was born in Bologna, 1831 and carried out excavations in Alexandria; his collection of antiquities was seen by Wilbour in 1884; a collection of vases from Pugioli was acquired by Cairo Museum in 1888; he sold objects to Bologna, Vienna, and New York, and donated others to the Graeco-Roman Museum in Alexandria; he published *Esposizione del governo di S.A. Ismail Iᵉʳ,* Alexandria, 1874; he died in 1902.

BIE 9 (1888), pp. iv-xii; Hilmy, ii, 145; Wilbour, 313, 386; T. Schreiber, *Daheim* 34 (1902), 14-16; F. Hagen and K. Ryholt, *The Antiquities Trade in Egypt 1880-1930,* 2017, 258.

PÜCKLER-MUSKAU, *(Prince)* **Hermann Ludwig Heinrich** (1785-1871)
German traveller and author; he was born in Muskau, Lusatia, 30 Oct. 1785, son of Ludwig Johannes Carl Erdmann P. and Clementine Cunigunde Charlotte Olympia Luise, Countess von Callenberg, heiress of Myskau; after military service he settled on his estates, then travelled extensively in England, America, Asia Minor, and Egypt and the Sudan in 1837; his account of his journey in Egypt was translated into English by H. E. Lloyd under the title *Travels and Adventures in Egypt,* 2 vols. 1845; he visited Vyse during his operations at the Pyramids;

he had a long correspondence with Sarah Austin, mother of Lucie Duff Gordon (q.v.); he died in Branitz, 4 Feb. 1871.

EB 22, 632; *Vyse*, i, 170, 172; Hilmy, ii, 145; *ADB* 26, 692-5; *Unsere Zeit* 7, no 8 (1871), 550-8; L. Assing-Grimelli, *Fürst Hermann Pückler-Muskau*, 1873; L. Assing-Grimelli, *Pückler-Muskaus Briefwechsel und Tagebucher*, 9 vols., 1873-6; P. Bowman, *The Fortune Hunter: A German Prince in Regency England*, 2010.

QUAEGEBEUR, Jan (1943-1995)

Belgian Egyptologist and Demotist; he was born in Tielt, 14 Dec. 1943, son of Georges Q. and Hélène Vergote and nephew of Jozef Vergote (q.v.); he studied classical philology and Egyptology at the University of Leuven, 1962-7, and at the University of Ghent under De Meulenaere, 1969; he was a foreign pensioner at IFAO, 1970-1 and later studied in Paris at the École Pratique des Hautes Études and the Collège de France, 1971-2 and at the University of Leiden under P. W. Pestman; PhD from Leuven, 1973; he became a researcher at the Belgian National Fund for Scientific Research, 1967-77; Lecturer in the Faculty of Arts at the K. U. Leuven from 1978; Assistant Professor from 1986; Professor from 1988; associate director of studies at the École Pratique in Paris, 1988; he took part in the Belgian excavations at Thebes from 1970 and Elkab from 1975; founder and director of the Belgian-French excavations at Shenhur from 1991; he was on the editorial board of *OLP* (Leuven) and *Studia Demotica* (Leiden) and directed the series *Orientalia Lovaniensia Analecta* for many years; he was a specialist in the Demotic language, the history and religion of Late Period and Graeco-Roman Egypt, and Graeco-Egyptian onomastics and published several Demotic papyri; he held a fellowship at the Metropolitan Museum of Art, New York in 1994; he delivered the Glanville Memorial Lecture in Cambridge in 1993 and the Raymond and Beverly Sackler Distinguished Lecture in Egyptology at the British Museum in 1995; a memorial lecture was established in his honour at Leuven; he published over 170 articles as well as his thesis *Le dieu égyptien Shai*, 1975; with P. Pestman and R. Vos, *Recueil de textes démotiques et bilingues*, 1977; and with M. Coenen, *De Papyrus Denon in het Museum Meermanno-Westreenianum, Den Haag, of het Boek van het Ademen van Isis*, 1995; a volume of essays edited by W. Clarysse, A. Schoors, and H. Willems, *Egyptian Religion. The Last Thousand Years*, 1998, was published in his memory; *La naine et le bouquetin ou l'énigme de la barque en albâtre de Toutankhamon*, 1999; he died in Leuven (Louvain), 10 Aug. 1995.

JEA 81 (1995), v; *BSFE* 134 (1995), 8-9 (C. Traunecker); *Phoenix* 41 (1995), 95-6 (portr.) (W. Clarysse); *Rev. d'Eg.* 47 (1996), 5-7 (C. Traunecker); *CRIPEL* 18 (1997), 13-5 (D. Valbelle); *Aegyptus* 76 (1996), 173-7 (H. Hauben); W. Clarysse et al., *Egyptian Religion*, 1998, xxv-xxx (C. Vandersleyen); *Acta Orientalia Belgica* XI (1998), xiv-xv (portr.) (C. Vandersleyen).

QUATREMÈRE, Étienne-Marc (1782-1857)

French classical scholar and antiquary; born in Paris, 12 July 1782, son of Marc Étienne Q. and Suzanne Sophie Lesueur-Florent; he was appointed to the MSS. Dept. of the Bibl. Nationale, 1807; Professor of Greek literature at Rouen, 1809; Professor of Hebrew Literature, Collège de France, 1819-57; Member of the Académie des Inscriptions, 23 June 1815; while his work was mainly classical, he studied Egyptian history and published *Recherches critiques et historiques sur la langue et la littérature de l'Égypte*, Paris, 1808; *Mémoires géographiques et historiques sur l'Égypte et sur quelques contrées voisines*, etc., Paris, 1811, based on Coptic and Arabic manuscripts; he died in Paris, 18 Sept. 1857; his cousin Antoine Chrysostome Q. de Quincy (*b.* Paris 21 Oct. 1755, *d.* Paris 28 Dec. 1849), son of François-Bernard Q. de l'Épine, a cloth merchant and Marie-Anne Bourjot, was a Professor of Archaeology, editor of the Journal des Savants; Member of the Académie des Beaux-Arts, 16 Feb. 1804, reconfirmed 21 March 1816 and secretary, 1816-39; he was the author of *De l'architecture égyptienne considérée dans ses origines*, 1803.

Hartleben (see index); Hilmy, ii, 147; *La Grande Enc.*, 27, 1122-3; *NGB* 41, 286-7; A. C. E. Franquet de Franqueville, *Le Premier Siècle de l'Institut de France*, 1895, I, 149 and 180-1; R. Schneider, *Quatremère de Quincy et son intervention dans les arts (1788-1830)*, 1910; Lamy, 299; È. Gran-Aymerich, *Dictionnaire biographique d'archéologie 1798-1945*, 2001, incorporated in *Les Chercheurs de passé 1798-1945*, 2007, 1083-4; V. Petridou in C. Grell, *L'Égypte imaginaire*, 2001, 173-186.

QUIBELL, Anne Abernethie (*née* Pirie) (1862-1927)

British artist and archaeologist; she was born at Aberdeen, 5 Dec. 1862, daughter of Revd Prof. William Robertson P. of Aberdeen and Margaret Chalmers Forbes; she studied at University College London; she went to Egypt in 1895 as an assistant to Petrie (q.v.) in copying reliefs at Saqqara and Thebes; she married J. E. Quibell (q.v.) in 1900; she later assisted her husband in his archaeological work at Elkab, Hierakonpolis, and Saqqara; her drawings of hieroglyphs from the tomb of Paheri at Elkab were used by Griffith in his monograph *Hieroglyphs*, 1898; she published two popular books, *Egyptian History and Art*, 1923; *A Wayfarer in Egypt*, 2nd ed., 1926; she arranged the Grant-Bey Collection in Aberdeen; she died in Cambridge, 26 Dec. 1927.

Inf. Aberdeen Univ.; Petrie, 158; R. Janssen, *The First Hundred Years*, 1992, 1992, 13; *Ancient Egypt* 14/4 (2014), 16-23 (L. Young).

QUIBELL, (James) Edward (1867-1935)

British Egyptologist; he was born in Newport, Shropshire, 11 Nov. 1867, son of John Q. and Catherine Susannah Smith; he graduated at Christ Church, Oxford, after which he assisted Petrie (q.v.) on a number of his excavations;

he was at Coptos, 1893, a site which first opened up the history of Egypt as far back as the First Dynasty, and the following year went to Naqada and Ballas which produced the first and probably the greatest collection of predynastic material ever discovered and also revealed new vistas in the story of Egypt; Quibell is said to have been the first person to recognize, although not publicly to state, that the remains found at Ballas were predynastic, not *New Race* of the First Intermediate Period; thorough training under Petrie had made him the best-equipped excavator of early sites at that time, and he next excavated the town and area of Hierakonpolis for the ERA with results which are famous in the annals of Egyptian archaeology; with Green (q.v.) and Somers Clarke (q.v.) he discovered the 'Main Deposit' containing the Narmer palette, many carved mace-heads and ivories and other important proto-dynastic objects, and in the remains of an early temple the archaic statuettes of King Khasekhem etc.; he cleared the area of the Ramesseum, a very different kind of work, finding important Middle Kingdom papyri and a wealth of inscribed material such as jar sealings; he was appointed to the staff of the Antiquities Service and worked on the Cairo Cat. 1899, becoming Inspector in Chief of Antiquities in the Delta and Middle Egypt, 1899-1904 and Luxor 1904-5; at Luxor he discovered the tomb of Yuia and Tuiu, 1905; on becoming Chief Inspector at Saqqara in 1905 he excavated the magnificent monastery of St. Jeremias, many archaic mastabas, and a very great quantity of Early Dynastic cemetery material, notably the tomb of Hesire; this work went on for many years and gained the Egyptian Museum, Cairo a wealth of fine objects of all periods; in all this work he was assisted by his very able wife, Annie A. Quibell (q.v.) who made copies in outline and colour for his publications; from 1 Jan. 1914 to 1923 he served as Keeper of the Egyptian Museum and during this time greatly improved its decoration and installation; he was appointed Secretary-General of the Antiquities Dept., 1923 and retired, 1 April 1925; in fact he continued to work and carried out further excavations at first as assistant to Firth (q.v.) who had succeeded him at Saqqara, then after 1931 as director on the Step Pyramid site; this was his largest excavation although not the one which is best known, and involved the recovery and restoration of an immense number of objects; Quibell continued the work of Petrie successfully and refined it, improving the standard of publications throughout his career; he contributed to or else wrote no fewer than 18 quarto vols. in all; *Naqada*, with W. M. F. Petrie, 1895; *Ballas*, with chapters by W. M. F. P., 1896; *El Kab*, with Somers Clarke and J. J. Tylor, 1898; *The Ramesseum*, with W. Spiegelberg, 1898; *Hierakonpolis*, 2 vols., with W. M. F. P. and F. W. Green, 1900-2; *Archaic Objects*, 2 vols., Cairo Cat., 1904-5; *The Tomb of Yuaa and Thuiu*, Cairo Cat., 1908; *Excavations at Saqqara*, (1905-6), (1906-7) with a section of religious texts by P. Lacau, (1907-8) and other sections by Sir Herbert Thompson and W. Spiegelberg, 3 vols. 1908-9; *The Monastery of Apa Jeremias: the Coptic inscriptions edited by Sir Herbert Thompson*, 2 vols. 1912; *Excavations at Saqqara 1911-12. The Tomb of Hesy*, 1913; *Excavations at Saqqara 1912-14. Archaic Mastabas*, 1923; *Teti Pyramid, north side*, with A. G. K. Hayter, 1927; *The Step Pyramid*, with C. M. Firth and J. P. Lauer, 2 vols. 1935; part of his archive passed to Varille (q.v.) and then to the Università degli Studi in Milan; he died in Hertford, 5 June 1935.

AE U (1935), 125 (M. A. Murray); *Chron. d'Ég.* 11 (1936), 100-1; E.E.S. *Report*, 1935, 9; *JEA* 21 (1935), 115-16; Petrie, 144, 148; Sayce, 298, 322; *KMT* 12/1 (2001), 78-80; È. Gran-Aymerich, *Dictionnaire biographique d'archéologie 1798-1945*, 2001, incorporated in *Les Chercheurs de passé 1798-1945*, 2007, 1084-5; P. Piacentini, *Egypt and the Pharaohs from the Sand to the Library*, 2010, 82-90. Photograph courtesy of the Lauer family.

QUINTINO, Giulio de San *see* **CORDERO DI SAN QUINTINO**

RADDI, Giuseppe (1770-1829)

Italian botanist; he was born in Florence, 9 July 1770, son of Stefano R. and Orsola Pandolfini; he was employed at the Museum of Natural History in Florence; he visited Brazil about 1820 and published papers on Brazilian Cryptograms, 1822-3; he accompanied Rosellini in Champollion's expedition to Egypt in 1828 but was taken ill; he died in Rhodes on his way back to Florence, 7/8 Sept. 1829.

DBDI 86, 95-7; *Atti Acad. Geografili, Firenze*, 8 (1830), 304-9; Champollion, ii, vii, 9, 16, 47, 398.

RADZIWILL, (*Prince*) **Nicholas Christopher called Orphan** (1549-1616)

Polish nobleman and official of high rank, traveller and diarist; he was born at Czmielow, 2 Aug. 1549, son of Nicholas R. and Elizabeth Szydlowiecka; as a descendent of Lithuanian noble family, count of Olyka and Nieswiez, he was very carefully educated; he travelled to Strasbourg 1563-65 and to Italy and France 1565-67; during the years 1582-84, he undertook a pilgrimage to the Holy Land, giving in his later account an interesting description of his stay in Egypt in the course of this enterprise; he spent about two months in 1583 in Egypt; he stayed at the house of Marian, French consul in Cairo, and with his assistance he undertook some excursions; he gave a quite detailed description of Cairo, its gates and mosques; he was at the Pyramids, climbing to the top of the Cheops Pyramid; according to the tradition, the Sphinx in his opinion was the head of the princess Rhodopis; he also described the cemeteries at Memphis; visiting Alexandria, he purchased a zoological collection and two mummies; on 9 Oct. 1583 he sailed from Alexandria to Crete carrying on board the two mummies, each divided into three parts "because they were much used also as drugs", during a violent storm R. was forced to throw the mummies overboard, because of the demands of his superstitious comrades who were sure that the mummies caused the storm; he wrote up his travels about 1590; in 1592 the text was going round from hand to hand; a Latin translation was made, which appeared as *Hierosolymitana peregrinatio*, 1601 and subsequent editions; the first Polish edition, Cracow 1607, was made not from the handwritten original, but from the Latin translation; only the critical editions of 1925 and 1962 are based on the four preserved manuscripts; German editions appeared in 1603 and 1605, Russian in 1787; he died in Nieswiez, 28 Feb. 1616.

J. Bystron, *Polacy w Ziemi Swietej, Syrii i Egipcie,* Cracow, 1930, 28-40; *Mikolaja Krzysztofa Radziwilla peregrynacja do Ziem i Swietej (1582-1584),* ed. J. Czubek, Cracow, 1925; *Mikolaj Krzysztof Radziwill "Sierotka", Podróz do Ziemi Swietej, Syrii i Egiptu* 1582-1584, ed. L. Kukulski, Warsaw, 1962; *Archeologia* XIX, 1968 (1969) 109-115 (B. Rutkowski); *Polski Slownik Biograficzny* 30, 349-361 (H. Lulewicz); *ZÄS* 117 (1990), 157-171 (T. Schneider); inf. J. Śliwa.

RAFFAELLI, Giuseppi (1750-1826)

Italian jurist, writer and collector; he was born at Catanzaro 20 Feb. 1750, son of Francesco R. and Elisabetta Calabretti; a liberal thinker, he was banished from Naples to Turin and Milan, 1799-1808; he died in Naples, 26 Feb. 1826; at the sale of his collection of antiquities in Paris, 5 April 1824, Champollion (q.v.) secured some items for the private collection of the Duc de Blacas (q.v.).

DBDI 86, 139-42; Champollion, i, 8; *Rec. Champ.* 5; Valentia, iii, 438; L. Aliquo Lenzi and F. Aliquo Taverriti, *Gli Scrittori Calabresi*, 1955, 3, 136-8; Lugt 10640.

RAGUSE, (*Duc de*) *see* **MARMONT**

RAIFÉ, Alphonse (1802-1860)

French collector; he bought antiquities at the principal sales, particularly that of Anastasi (q.v.) in Paris, 1857; two important papyri in the Louvre bear his name (4889-90); his collections were catalogued by Lenormant (q.v.) and sold in Paris, 10-23 March 1867 (Egyptian antiquities lots 1-446) fetching high prices.

Sale cat. pp. v-xv (portr.); *Bibl. Ég.* 17, xliii-lv; *Rev. de l'Art*, 43, 168; Lugt 29623.

RAINER, (*Archduke*) **Ferdinand Maria Johan Evangelist Franz Ignaz** (1827-1913)

Austrian collector; he was born at Vienna, 11 Jan. 1827, a prince of the House of Hapsburg and 4th son of the Archduke Rainer (1784-1864), Viceroy of Lombardy-Venetia, grandson of the Emperor Leopold II (1747-92) and Princess Elisabeth of Savoy; he made a large collection of papyri, hieratic, Demotic, Coptic, Greek, and Arabic; the collection originated with a large find at Arsinoë in 1877-8 which was purchased from the dealer T. Graf (q.v.) in 1884; many subsequent additions were made, notably two large finds from El-Ashmunein and Akhmim; the collection was acquired by the Imperial Library of Vienna, and in 1892 an account of it was published; *Papyrus Erzherzog Rainer: Führer durch die Ausstellung*; the Archduke was Patron of the Arts and Crafts Museum, 1862-98, and Curator of the Acad. of Sciences, 1861-1913; he died in Vienna, 27 Feb. 1913.

EB ed. 12, 32. 241.

RAINIER, Peter (1784-1836)
British naval officer; he was born in London, 1 Aug. 1784, son of John R., banker of Hackney, and Susannah Burrell; he was the nephew of the famous Admiral of the same name; Capt. RN, 1806; he was on active service throughout the Napoleonic wars; CB, 1815; naval aide-de-camp to William IV, 1830; he went up the Nile as far as Abu Simbel in 1828 and met Champollion in Nubia (C. mis-spells his name as Reynier); his name is carved on the rock of Abu Sir; he died in Southampton, 13 April 1836.

Champollion, ii, 19, 191; O'Byrne, *Naval Biog.* 949; C. Calvert, *Genealogy of the Rainier Family*, 1903.

RAMBOVA, Natacha (*née* **Shaugnessy**), **(Winifred Kimball)** (1897-1966)
American designer and researcher; she was born in Salt Lake City, 19 Jan. 1897, daughter of Col. Michael S., a federal marshal, and Winifred Kimball of a noted Mormon family (she had been married to a Mr Butts and subsequent to her divorce from Michael S., she married Edgar de Wolfe and Richard Hudnut who adopted her daughter); she was educated in London and then attended a ballet school in New York and then joined the dance company, adopting the name Natacha Rambova; she accompanied the troupe to Hollywood where she became a costume and set designer; she married Rudolph Valentino (*d.*1926) in 1922 (illegally) and 1923 (legally) and in 1932 Count Alvaro de Urzaiz; she became a spiritualist and went to Egypt in 1936 where she met Carter (q.v.) and developed an interest in Egyptology; she was attracted to mythology and religious symbolism; she studied briefly under Glanville (q.v.); she obtained a grant from the Bollingen Foundation to study the symbolic material on scarabs in 1946; while in Egypt, she met Piankoff (q.v.) and changed her project to record the religious texts in the royal tombs under his direction and with the help of Elizabeth Thomas (q.v.); she worked in Egypt until 1955 and helped with the publication of the results; Egyptian objects from her collection were sold at Sotheby's New York, 5 Dec. 2007; her papers are preserved at Yale University; she died in Pasadena, California 5 June 1966.

M. Morris, *Madam Valentino*, 1991; R. Janssen, *Gött. Misz.* 153 (1996), 5-16 and 156 (1997), 67-72; M. Morris and E. Zumaya, *Beyond Valentino*, 2017.

RAMOND, Pierre (1917-1983)
French Egyptologist; he was born at St. Affrique, 6 June 1917, son of Louis R., postmaster, and Caroline Binder; he was educated at the seminary of Valence d'Albigeois where he studied philosophy and oriental languages; he became an employee of the Mutualité Sociale Agricole at Marseille and then Albi, retiring in 1973; his interest in Egyptology was encouraged by Sainte-Fare-Garnot among others and he collaborated in various Egyptological publications and conferences; he concerned himself principally with the publication of the Egyptian objects at Toulouse; *Musée Georges Labit. Antiquités égyptiennes* (with J. C. Guillevic), 1971; *Le Papyrus Varille* (with J. C. Guillevic), 1975; *Les Stèles égyptiennes du Musée G. Labit à Toulouse*, 1977; he died in Albi, 27 Feb. 1983.

Inf. Mme. P. Ramond.

RAMSAY, William Wardlaw (1812-1837)
British traveller; he was born in 1812, the son of Robert Wardlaw R. and Lady Anne Lindsay, daughter of 6th Earl of Balcarres and 23rd of Crawford; he accompanied Lord Lindsay to Egypt, 1836-7 and died during the journey; his name is carved on the rock of Abu Sir; he kept a journal from which many extracts are quoted in Lord Lindsay's book; he died in Damascus, 1837.

Lindsay, pref. vi. 134, and passim; E. Warburton, *The Crescent and the Cross*, 1, 315.

RANKE, (Heinrich Johannes) Hermann (1878-1953)
German Egyptologist and Assyriologist; he was born Balgheim near Nördlingen, 5 Aug. 1878, son of Leopold Friedrich R., a pastor, and Julia Bever; he studied theology in Lübeck, in Göttingen, 1897, Greifswald, 1897 and Munich, 1899 with Hommel (q.v.) and Dyroff (q.v.), specializing in Semitic language and Assyriology; PhD, 1902; Habilitation at the University of Heidelberg, 1910; he was a research fellow at Philadelphia, 1902-5; he later studied Egyptology in Berlin with Adolf Erman (q.v.) and joined the Berlin Museum in 1905; he became Associate Professor at the University of Heidelberg, 1911; Professor, 1923-37; Visiting Professor, University of Wisconsin, 1932-3; as his position in Germany became untenable during the Nazi period due to his half-Jewish wife, he went to America in 1937; there he became visiting Professor at the University of Wisconsin, 1938 and the University of Philadelphia, 1938-42 where he was closely associated with Philadelphia Museum; he returned to Heidelberg, 1942; he resumed

teaching after the war as lecturer at Heidelberg, 1946-8; Dean of the Philosophical Faculty, 1947-8; he then returned to Philadelphia and was also Visiting Professor at the University of Alexandria, 1950-2; he took part in the excavations at Amarna under Borchardt (q.v.), 1912-13 and with Junker (q.v.) at Merimde Beni-Salame; he undertook his own excavation at el-Hibeh/Qarara, 1913 where he was succeeded by Bilabel (q.v.); objects from Merimde and el-Hibeh enlarged the Egyptian collection, founded by Ranke in 1910, of the Heidelberg Institute; he produced *Die Personennamen in den Urkunden der Hammurabi-Dynastie*, 1905; *Babylonian Legal and Business Documents from the Time of the First Dynasty of Babylon*, 1906; and wrote *Keilschriftliches Material zur altägyptischen Vokalisation* in which his training in Semitic languages proved useful; Ranke helped Erman with many of his major projects and works such as *Ägypten und ägyptische Leben im Altertum*, 1923; the great *Wörterbuch der ägyptischen Sprache* and others; his output was considerable especially important being *Die ägyptischen Personennamen*, 2 vols. 1935-52; he also published *Die altägyptische Schlangenspiel*, 1920; *Koptische Friedhöfe bei Karâra und der Amontempel Scheschonks I bei El Hibe*, 1926; *The Art of Ancient Egypt*, 1936; *Meisterwerke der ägyptischen Kunst*, 1948; he died in Freiburg, 22 April 1953.

NBG 21, 144-5; *Wer Ist's* 1935; *AfO* 16 (1953), 393-4 (portr.) (W. Wolf); *Chron. d'Ég.* 28 (1953), 320-21 (anon.); *JEA* 39 (1953), 2 (R. O. Faulkner); *Orientalia*, 22 (1953), 431 (A. Pohl); *The Univ. Museum Bulletin. Philadelphia.* vol. 17, no. 4 (Dec. 1953), 57-9 (portr.) (R. Anthes); *ZDMG* 105 (1955), 17-26 (S. Schott/E. Edel) (portr.) (bibl.); inf. W. Habermann, Univ. of Frankfort a. M. and T. Schneider.

RANKIN, John (1845-1928)

Shipowner and philanthropist; he was born in Greenbank, New Brunswick, Canada, 14 Feb. 1845, son of James R., formerly of Mearns, Renfrewshire, who emigrated to New Brunswick where the Rankin family founded a successful timber and later shipping business, and Marion Ferguson; he was sent to be educated at Dr. Ihne's, Liverpool and the University of St. Andrews, 1860-1; he joined the branch of the family firm in Liverpool, later becoming Chairman, Rankin Gilmour & Co. Ltd.; Director of the Bank of Liverpool, 1900, Chairman, 1906-9; Member of the Council of Liverpool University, 1902-7; High Sheriff, Westmorland, 1910; Governor of Sedbergh School, 1911; LLD, University of Liverpool, 1920; he had the Hon. Freedom of the City of Liverpool conferred upon him in 1921; Treasurer and Vice-President of the Liverpool Institute of Archaeology; he was a member of the Financing Committee and a benefactor of John Garstang's (q.v.) excavations in Egypt from 1900 onwards from which he received a considerable collection of Egyptian artefacts; he later donated these to several institutions including Sedbergh School, Liverpool Museum and Kendal Museum; he spent his time between residences at Hill Top, New Hutton and St. Michael's Mount, Liverpool, where he died 23 Dec. 1928.

J. Rankin, *A History of Our Firm: Some Account of Pollock, Gilmour & Co. and its Connections*, 1908, 304; *WWW* ii, 869; W. T. Pike, *Liverpool and Birkenhead in the Twentieth Century*, 1911, 172; D. Jeremy, *Dictionary of Business Biography*, 4, 837-40; inf. A. Garnett.

RANTZAU, Hendrik (1599-1674)

Danish traveller; he was born 26 Jan. 1599, son of Frants R. and Anne Rosenkrantz; he studied in Geneva from 1618, Orleans, Padua in 1621, and Siena in 1622; he then embarked on a tour to the Levant, visiting Egypt in 1623; he reached Cairo and saw the Pyramids and Sphinx and unwrapped a mummy; he published an account of his travels, *Reise-Buch auf Jerusalem, Cairo und Constantinopel*, 1669; later counsellor of Frederick III; he died on 16 Jan. 1674.

Dansk Biografisk Leksikon 11, 627; M.-L. Buhl, *Les dessins archéologiques et topographiques de l'Égypte ancienne faits par F. L. Norden 1737-1738*, 1993, 22.

RAPER, Matthew (1740-1826)

British antiquarian; born 1740, son of William R., of Wendover Dean, Bucks., a Director of the Bank of England; he lived at Ashlyn's Hall, Herts.; FRS, 1783; FSA, 17 Nov. 1785 later Director, 23 April 1810-3, and Vice Pres., 1813-26; Sheriff of Herts, 4 Feb. 1791; an ardent supporter of Thomas Young, he was one of the founders and managers of the latter's Egyptian Society; he wrote an introductory note to the publication of the Rosetta Stone in *Archaeologia* 16 (1812), 205-11; he died in his London home, 86 Wimpole St., 26 Nov. 1827.

Sir E. Brabrook, *Archaeologia* 62 (1911), 72-3 and *Proceedings of the Society of Antiquaries* 29 (1916/7), 67; Geikine, *Annals of the R. S. Club*, 178, 217, 290.

RAPHAEL, Maurice (1905-?)
Egyptian Egyptologist; he was born in 1905 and studied archaeology at the University of Cairo and abroad; he joined the Antiquities Service as an inspector and was later a curator of the Egyptian Museum, Cairo; he published a few objects in *ASAE* 37 (1937), 79-80, *ASAE* 38 (1938), 117-24; and *MIFAO* 66 (1935-8), 509-12; he succeeded Moharram Kamal (q.v.) as Director of the Egyptian Museum in 1957 and retired in 1960.

Inf. D. Abou-Ghazi; *Bulletin of the Egyptian Museum* 1 (2004), 8.

RAPHAEL, Oscar Charles (1874-1941)
British collector; he was born in London, 1 March 1874, son of Geroge Gershon Charles R., a banker, and Charlotte Hanne Melchior; he was educated at Wellington College , 1887-92 and Pembroke College, Cambridge; FSA; he served as a voluntary assistant at the British Museum and Hon. Curator of Oriental Art at the Fitzwilliam Museum, Cambridge; he collected Egyptian antiquities as a child and maintained and deepened his interests as an adult, forming a large collection of Oriental ceramics and sculptures; the finest Egyptian object in his collection was a head of Amenemhat III from the collection of Lord Grenfell (q.v.), now in the Fitzwilliam Museum; he lent this to and was on the organizing committee for the 1921 Burlington Fine Arts Club exhibition of Egyptian art; he bequeathed his collections to the British Museum and the Fitzwilliam Museum; he died at Northwick Park, Blockley, Gloucs., 6 Sept. 1941.

The Times, 10 Sept. 1941; *Ars Islamica* 9 (1942) 237-7 (B. Gray); inf. T. Hardwick.

RAWLINSON, (*Revd*) **George** (1812-1902)
British clergyman and historian; he was born in Chadlington, Oxfordshire, 23 Nov. 1812, son of Abram Tyzack R., a landowner, and Elizabeth Eudocia Creswicke, and was the younger brother of Sir Henry C. R. the pioneer of Assyriology; he was educated Trinity College, Oxford; BA, 1838; MA, 1841; Fellow of Exeter College; Camden Professor of Ancient History, 1861-89; Canon of Canterbury, 1872; he published *History of Ancient Egypt,* 2 vols. 1881, a work criticized by Amelia Edwards; *Egypt and Babylon, from Scripture and profane sources*, 1885; *Ancient Egypt*, with A. Gilman, 1887; *Moses, his life and times*, 1887; he also edited Herodotus and wrote many books on Assyria and the ancient history of the Near East, as well as assisting his brother; he died in Canterbury, 6 Oct. 1902.

ODNB 46, 154-5; Hilmy, ii, 152; *JEA* 33 (1947), 71; *WWW* i, 588.

RAWNSLEY, (*Revd*) **Hardwicke Drummond** (1851-1920)
British clergyman and author; he was born at Shiplake Vicarage, Henley-on-Thames, 28 Sept. 1851, son of Canon Robert Drummond Burrell R. and Catherine Ann Franklin; educated Uppingham and Balliol College, Oxford; MA, 1875; he was ordained 1875 and was head of the Clifton College mision in Bristol before holding benefices in the Lake District; Canon of Carlisle; he took a leading part in the foundation of the National Trust, and was interested in many social, cultural, and educational movements; he visited Egypt, Syria, and Palestine, 1875, and Egypt again in 1890; he published *Notes for the Nile*, 1892, a travel book which enjoyed great popularity; in 1896 he published *Life of Bishop Harvey Goodwin,* brother of Charles Wycliffe G. (q.v.), which contains valuable information on the latter; a voluminous writer on many subjects; he died in Grasmere, 28 May 1920.

Life, by E. F. Rawnsley, 1923 (portr.); *WWW* ii, 872; *ODNB* 46, 169-71.

RAYET, (Paul Daniel) Olivier (1847-1887)
French classical archaeologist; he was born in Puy L'Evêque (Lot), 23 Sept. 1847, son of Pons Pascal Célestin Desiré R. and Elisabeth Mantz; he was educated at the École Normale from 1866 and went out to the French School in Athens in 1869; he excavated at Miletus, 1873; he was Répétiteur for Greek antiquities at the École des Hautes Études, 1876, and Directeur-adjoint, 1878; he became Professor of Ancient Art at the Collège de France, 1879 and succeeded Lenormant (q.v.) as Professor of Archaeology at the Bibliothèque Nationale, 1884; he published *Monuments de l'Art Antique*, which appeared in parts and was completed in 2 fol. vols. with 90 plates, Paris, 1884; Maspero (q.v.) contributed eleven important articles to this collection between 1879 and 1883; his collection was sold in Paris, 4-5 April 1879; Member of the Légion d'Honneur; he died in Paris, 19 Feb. 1887.

Annuaire Éc. des H.É., 1897, 53, 55; Hilmy, ii, 152; È. Gran-Aymerich, *Dictionnaire biographique d'archéologie 1798-1945*, 2001, incorporated in *Les Chercheurs de passé 1798-1945*, 2007, 1085-7.

REA, *(Rt. Hon.)* **Russell** (1846-1916)
British collector; he was born at Salford, 11 Dec. 1846, son of Daniel K. R. of Eskdale, Cumberland, and Elizabeth Russell; he was a merchant of Liverpool; he visited Egypt, 1907-8, and in subsequent years purchased a considerable number of antiquities chiefly from Muhammad Mohassib (q.v.), under the guidance of Howard Carter (q.v.) and Harold Jones (q.v.); he subscribed to excavations at Abydos and other sites; many of his antiquities were presented to the British Museum by his widow; he died in Dorking, 5 Feb. 1916.

Inf. P. E. Newberry; *JEA* 14 (1928), 46; *WWW* ii, 874.

READY, William Talbot (1857-1914)
British antiquities dealer; he was born at Lowestoft, Suffolk, 18 Aug. 1857, son of Robert Cooper R., sigillarist and electrotypist, who was employed in the British Museum from 1860-97, and Susan Papworth; he was first employed as a cleaner and repairer of antiquities in the British Museum in 1879; in 1886 he established himself as an antiquities dealer at 55 Rathbone Place, off Oxford St, until 1909 when he is listed at 6 Bloomsbury St. and from 1910 at 66 Great Russell St.; both these latter addresses were also occupied by the dealers Rollin (q.v.) and Feuardent with whom Ready probably was associated from 1909; he sold objects to the British Museum and the Royal Scottish Museum among others and also acted as an agent for the British Museum at antiquities sales; he was also involved in the production of sale catalogues for Sotheby's notably the Stanton sale catalogue, 26 July 1894 and the Hilton Price, Kennard and Rustafjaell collections (q.q.v.); his own collection was sold at Paris, Hotel Drouot, 14 and 15 March 1919; he died in London, 14 Jan. 1914.

BM archives; *The Times* 15 Jan 1914; Lugt 78621.

REICH, Nathaniel Julius (1876-1943)
American Egyptologist; born Savar, Hungary, 29 April 1876, son of Wilhelm R., later Chief Rabbi of Baden near Vienna, and his wife Sidonie; he attended primary and secondary school in Baden, graduating 1897; he enrolled in 1897 at Vienna University where he studied Semitic languages and Egyptian under Reinisch (q.v.) and Coptic and Demotic under Krall (q.v.) from 1900; he studied at Berlin University during the winter semester 1898/9 and at the Vienna University of Technology, autumn 1900-1; PhD, Vienna University, 1904; he worked with Spiegelberg (q.v.) in Strassburg, 1907-8 and Griffith in Oxford, 1909; his application for a lectureship in Egyptology with special reference to Demotic at Vienna University was rejected in 1910; he became lecturer at k. k. Deutsche Karl-Ferdinands-University in Prague, 1913-8; he was appointed to a lectureship for Demotic Egyptian at Vienna University, 1920-22; he emigrated to USA Jan. 1922; he became assistant curator at the University Museum of the University of Pennsylvania, 1922; he was Associate Professor of Egyptology, Papyrology, and Ancient Oriental Studies at Dropsie College, Philadelphia from 1925-34; Research Professor from 1934; he was also reader at John Hopkins University from 1926; he was the editor of the journal *Mizraim* which dealt with Papyrology, Egyptology and Ancient Law, and to which he contributed a large number of articles and reviews; his published work included *Demotische und griechische Texte auf Mumientäfelchen in der Sammlung der Papyrus Erzherzog Rainier*, 1908, repr. 1923; *Papyri juristischen Inhalts in hieratischer und demotischer Schrift aus dem British Museum*, 1914; *An abbreviated demotic Book of the Dead (BM, EA 10072)*, 1931; he died in Philadelphia, 5 Oct. 1943.

AfO 15 (1945-51), 199; *NY Times* for 6 Oct. 1943; *Gött. Misz.* 214 (2007) 91-3 (W. B. Oerter); *Nathaniel Julius Reich Collection, University of Pennsylvania*; W. B. Oerter in J. Holaubek, H. Navrátilová and W. B. Oerter (eds), *Egypt and Austria* III, Prague, 2007, 183-90; inf. W. B. Oerter; W. Oerter, *Die Ägyptologie an der Prager Universitäten 1882-1945*, 2010, 96-111, 117-21, 139-54.

REIL, Wilhelm (1820-1880)
German physician; he was born in Schönwerda, Thüringen, 8 April 1820; he settled in Cairo about 1850 and practised amongst the European population; in 1860 he opened a sanatorium for the treatment of chest complaints; he was made physician to the Viceroy; he was interested in antiquities and carried out excavations, being known to Mariette (q.v.) and other European excavators; he greatly damaged the scenes in the Tomb of Ti by taking wet squeezes which removed the colours; he published *Aegypten als Winteraufenthalt für Kranke*, 1859; he died in Cairo, 14 Jan. 1880.

Bibl. Ég. 18, pp. cx, clxxx; 21, p. lxxxvi; Hilmy, ii, 159.

REINEKE, Walter Friedrich (1936-2015)
German Egyptologist; he was born near Eisenach, 22 July 1936; he studied at the Humboldt University in Berlin under Hintze (q.v.) and Morenz (q.v.), 1954-8; Diploma, 1958; PhD., 1965; Habilitation, 1986; he became a research assistant at the Deutsche Akademie der Wissenschaften where he worked on the Berlin *Wörterbuch*

project, 1958; Chief Editor, 1969; Head of the reconstituted project, 1992-8; he was appointed Professor at the East Berlin Academy, 1987; his principal interests were in the mathematics and sciences in ancient Egypt; he took part in the epigraphical campaigns at the Second Cataract and excavations at Musawarat es Sufra, 1959-66, and at Tell Basta, 1979-90; he edited *Acts of the First International Congress of Egyptology. Cairo October 2-10 1976*, 1979; and *Mitteilungen aus der Arbeit am Wörterbuch der ägyptischen Sprache*, 1-5 (1993-6); a volume of studies was dedicated to him and others edited by C.-B. Arnst and others, *Begegnungen. Antike Kulturen im Niltal*, 2016; he published *Wörterbuch der ägyptischen Sprache* 7, 1963; with others, *Ägypten und Kusch*, 1977; with others, *Urkunden des ägyptischen Altertums* IV, 5-16=*Urkunden der 18. Dynastie. Übersetzung zu den Heften 5-16*, 1984; with A. Burkhardt, *Adolf Erman - Akademieschriften (1880-1920)*, 1986; with K. Freier, *Karl Richard Lepsius (1810-84)*, 1988; with F. Hintze, *Felsinschriften aus dem sudanesischen Nubien*, 1989; with M. Bakir, *Tell Basta* I, 1992; with others, *Erklärendes Wörterbuch zur Kultur und Kunst des alten Orients*, 1995; he died in Berlin, 23 Feb. 2015

Internet bio.; L. Mertens, *Das Lexikon der DDR-Historiker*, 2006, 500; C.-B. Arnst and others, *Begegnungen. Antike Kulturen im Niltal*, 2001, XXVI (portr.), XXVII-XXXII (bibl.) (A. Burkhardt); *ZÄS* 143 (2016), 1-4 (K.-H. Priese) (portr.), inf. I. Hafemann and S. Wenig.

REINISCH, Simon Leo (1832-1919)
Austrian philologist; he was born in Osterwitz, Styria, 26 Oct. 1832, son of Josef R., farmer, and Elisabeth Spieler; he studied at Vienna 1854-7, habil. 1861; Professor at Vienna University, 1868-1903; adviser to the Miramar Egyptian Collection; he made several expeditions to Egypt, and for the last thirty years of his life he studied the languages of NE Africa, especially the Cushite group; he made many contributions to Egyptological literature, see *Die Aegyptischen Denkmäler in Miramar*, 1865; *Aegyptische Chrestomathie*, 2 vols. 1873-5; a bronze portrait medal was issued in 1902; he died in Maria Lankouitz, 24 Dec. 1919.

EEF *Arch. Rep.* 1902-3, 37; Hilmy, ii, 160; inf. H. Satzinger.

REISNER, George Andrew (1867-1942)
American Egyptologist; he was born in Indianapolis, 5 Nov. 1867, son of George Andrew R., partner in a shoe store, and Mary Elizabeth Mason; the family was of German origin, coming from Worms; he was educated at Indianapolis Classical High School, and Harvard University, AB; AM; PhD; he at first studied law but this did not appeal to him and he became a travelling Fellow of Harvard University, 1893-6; at this time he went to Berlin to study Semitics and work on texts from Assyria and Babylonia, but instead of becoming an Assyriologist he was drawn to Egyptology, studying Egyptian at the University under Erman (q.v.) and Sethe (q.v.), 1894-7; he was a temporary assistant in Berlin Museum, 1895-6; on his return to America he was appointed Instructor in Semitics, Harvard University, 1896-7; Director of the Hearst Egyptian Expedition of the University of California and Hearst Lecturer, 1899-1905; Director of the Harvard-Boston Eg. Expedition, and Assistant Professor of Egyptology, Harvard University, 1910; Archaeological Director of Nubian Archaeological Survey by the Egyptian Government, 1907-9; Director of the Harvard Excavations at Samaria, Palestine, 1909-10; Curator of the Egyptian Dept. of Museum of Fine Arts, Boston, 1910-42; assistant Professor of Semitic Archaeology, 1905-10; Professor of Egyptology, Harvard, 1914-42; Reisner's meeting with Mrs. P. A. Hearst (q.v.) marked a turning-point in his career as an archaeologist, and with her support he began a long series of excavation campaigns; he dug at Deir el-Ballas in Middle Egypt, Naga-ed-Der, Giza Pyramids, 1899-1905; in Nubia, 1907-9, and at Samaria, 1909-10; he also worked at Zawiyat el-Aryan, Kerma, Gebel Barkal, Nuri, Kurru, Begarawiya, Semna, and at the Giza pyramids again; he made many major discoveries relating to the history of Lower Nubia, the pyramids of 68 Ethiopian kings and those of five more of the 25th Dynasty, the valley temple of King Mycerinus, and many tombs at Giza; he married Mary Putnam Bronson, 1892; he was a Corr. Member of the Saxon Acad., 1929; an Ordinary member of the Arch. Inst. of the German State; hon. DLitt, Harvard 1939; Reisner was the first person to make fully systematic excavations in Egypt, exploiting the technique of recorded digging much further than Petrie (q.v.) and earlier archaeologists had done; this attention to every detail and the scrupulous care taken meant, however, that although his reports were much fuller than those of his predecessors, they also required much more time for preparation, resulting in a great part of his work remaining incomplete and unpublished at his death; his publications were nevertheless of great importance and of truly monumental proportions, with a detailed study unknown before his time; his most important discovery was the tomb of Queen Hetepheres at Giza; for the Cairo Cat. he did work on models of ships and boats, amulets (partly published), Canopic vases and Cuneiform tablets (unpublished); Reisner wrote many articles as well, some being important studies in their own right; his bibl. lists 80 items, *Sumerisch-Babylonische Hymnen; Tempel Urkunden aus Telloh; The Hearst medical papyrus*, 1905; *Amulets*, Cairo Cat., 1907; *The early dynastic cemeteries of Naga-ed-Dêr*, part i. part ii by A. C. Mace, 1908-9; *Archaeological Report, 1907-8, Arch. Survey of Nubia*, 2 vols. 1910; *The Egyptian concept of immortality*, 1912; *Models of Ships and Boats*, Cairo Cat., 1913; *Excavations at Kerma*, Harvard African Studies, vols. 5 and 6, 1923;

Mycerinus: the temples of the Third Pyramid at Giza, 1931; *A Provincial Cemetery of the Pyramid age: Naga-ed-Dêr*, part iii, 1932; *The Development of the Egyptian tomb down to the accession of Cheops*, 1936; *A History of the Giza Necropolis*, 2 vols., vol. 2 *The Tomb of Hetep-heres, the mother of Cheops*, 1942 and posth. 1955; *Semna Kumma,* posth. Dows Dunham and J. M. A. Janssen, 1960; *The West and South Cemeteries at Meroe*, posth. compiled Dows Dunham, 1963; *Uronarti Shalfak Mirgissa*, posth. Dows Dunham, 1967; *The Barkal Temples,* posth. Dows Dunham, 1970; *Excavations at Kerma VI,* posth. Dows Dunham, 1982; he died at Giza, 6 June 1942.

AfO 15 (1945-51), 187-8 (A. Scharff); *AJA* 46 (1942), 410-12 (portr.) (Dows Dunham); *Amer. Phil. Soc. Year Book*, 1942, 369-74 (H. E. Winlock); *ASAE* 41 (1942), 11-18 (portr. and bibl.) (G. Brunton); *Chron. d'Ég.* 36 (1943), 268-70; *Man* 42 (1942), no. 76, 1837 (J. L. Myres); *Nature* 150 (1942), 84 (A. H. Gardiner); *WWW* iv, 964; *WWWA* 2, 443; *DAB* Supplement 3, 626-8; È. Gran-Aymerich, *Dictionnaire biographique d'archéologie 1798-1945*, 2001, incorporated in *Les Chercheurs de passé 1798-1945*, 2007, 1101-2.

RENAN, Joseph Ernest (1823-1892)
French philosopher and orientalist; born in Tréguier, 28 Feb. 1823, son of Philibert François R. and Magdelaine Josèphe Féger; he is now best remembered for his critical and historical works on the Bible, and for his *Vie de Jésus* translated into English by Wilbour (q.v.); he carried out excavations in Syria and in 1864 he visited Egypt while Mariette (q.v.) was actively excavating; he was much shocked by the destruction of monuments under the Viceroys for building material and welcomed the inauguration of excavation and conservation by Mariette; it was at Renan's suggestion that the Mission Archéologique (afterwards the IFAO) was established in Cairo; from 1874 onwards he corresponded with Maspero (q.v.); he died in Paris, 2 Oct. 1892.

EB 23. 93-5; Carré, ii, 234-49; *Correspondance de Renan,* Paris, 1926-8; J. Darmesteter, *Notice sur la vie et l'oevure de M. Renan*, 1898; È. Gran-Aymerich, *Dictionnaire biographique d'archéologie 1798-1945*, 2001, incorporated in *Les Chercheurs de passé 1798-1945*, 2007, 1102-6.

RENOUARD, *(Revd)* **George Cecil** (1780-1867)
British clergyman and orientalist; he was born in Stamford, Lincs., 7 Sept. 1780, son of Peter R. adjutant in the Rutland militia, and Mary Ott; educated at St. Paul's School, Charterhouse, and Sidney Sussex College, Cambridge; BA, 1802; ordained, 1804; Chaplain to the British Embassy, Constantinople, 1804-6, 1811-14; Professor of Arabic, Cambridge, 1815; Rector of Swanscombe, 1818-67; he studied Hebrew, Arabic, Egyptian, and Berber languages; Foreign Sec., RGS, 1836-46; he was a constant correspondent of E. Hincks and other orientalists, and had a large oriental library, which was sold at Sotheby's with that of Hincks, 12 Nov. 1867; he died in Swanscombe, 15 Feb. 1867.

ODNB 46, 490-1; *DNB* 48, 22; Hincks, passim (see index).

RENOUF, Ludovica Cecilia (*née* **Brentano la Roche**) (1836-1921)
Wife of Sir Peter Le Page R.; she was born in Marienburg, 3 Nov. 1836, the daughter of Christian B. and Emily Anna Nizza Genger; she married at Aschaffenburg, 25 July 1857; she collected all her husband's Egyptological works and republished them in four vols., after his death; she died in London, 8 Feb. 1921.

Inf. Miss E. Renouf (daughter) and Paul Renouf.

RENOUF, *(Sir)* **Peter Le Page** (1822-1897)
Egyptologist and orientalist; born Guernsey, 23 Aug. 1822, son of Joseph R. and Mary Le Page; educated at Elizabeth College, Guernsey, and Pembroke College, Oxford, 1840, where he read Hebrew and left before taking a degree having become a Roman Catholic; he then went abroad, later becoming Classical tutor, Oscott College; appointed Professor of Ancient History and Oriental languages, Catholic University, Dublin, 1855-64; HM Inspector of Schools, 1864-85; while in Ireland became interested in Egypt through the funerary papyri preserved at Trinity College, Dublin; encouraged by Hincks (q.v.) he now began to publish Egyptological articles in the periodical *Atlantis*; he visited Egypt with his wife, Ludovica, daughter of Christian Brentano la Roche, 1875, going via Syria-Lebanon; Hibbert Lecturer, 1879; he succeeded Birch (q.v.) as Keeper of Oriental Antiquities, British Museum, 1 May 1886-3 Dec. 1891; he was President Soc. Bibl. Arch., 1885-97; knighted 1896, he made many contributions to Egyptology and published many articles in journals espec. *PSBA*; his main works were, *An Elementary Grammar of the Ancient Egyptian Language*, pt. i only pub., 1875; *Lectures on the Origin*

and Growth of Religion, as illustrated by the Religion of Ancient Egypt, 1880; *Assyrian Antiquities. Guide to the Nimroud Central Saloon of the British Museum*, 1886; *The Book of the Dead. Facsimile of the Papyrus of Ani in the British Museum*, 1890; his most important work, the translation of the Book of the Dead, was unfinished at his death and was completed by Naville; his writings were collected and republished by his wife under the title *The Life-work of Sir P. Le Page Renouf*, 4 vols. 1902-7; his letters have been edited and published by J. Cathcart, *The Letters of Peter le Page Renouf (1822-1897)*, 2002-4, in 4 volumes; during Renouf's period as Keeper the work of arrangement, modernisation, and enlarging the Egyptian collections was actively carried on, and many famous pieces were added; his correspondence is in the Griffith Institute, Oxford; he died in London, 14 Oct. 1897.

WWW i, 594; *PSBA* 19, 271-9 (bibl.) (portr.); *ZÄS* 35, 165; Biogr. (by his daughter), in *Life-work*, iv, pp. i-cxxxiii; Correspondence, Dawson MS, 18, ff. 1-94; *ODNB* 46, 491-2; K. Cathcart (ed.), *The Letters of Peter le Page Renouf*, 4 vols, 2002-4.

REUVENS, Caspar Jacob Christiaan (1793-1835)
Dutch scholar and archaeologist; he was born in The Hague, 22 Jan. 1793, son of Jan Everard R. and Maria Susanna Garcin; he studied law at the Athenaeum, Amsterdam, 1808, and at the University of Leiden, 1810, afterwards going on to Paris, 1813; he became interested in archaeology and Egyptology and was appointed Director of the Leiden Museum of Antiquities, 1818-35; also Professor of Archaeology at Leiden University, 1820-35; he was anxious to build up its collections so that it should become one of the most important in Europe, and many pieces were added at this time, the Anastasi collection being acquired during his directorship; he studied Greek and Demotic papyri and corresponded with leading Egyptologists of the day; his main published works were, *Over het verband der Archaeologie met de hedenhaagsche Kunsten*, 1827; *Lettres à M. Letronne sur les papyrus bilingues et grecs, et sur quelques autres monuments gréco-égyptiens du Musée d'Antiquités de l'Université de Leide*, 1830; he died in Rotterdam, 26 July 1835.

Chron. d'Ég. 11 (1936) 472-7 (portr.) (W. D. Van Wijngaarden); *NNBW* iv, 1144-5; Hilmy, ii, 162-3; *Tijdspiegel* 1918, 1-7 (J. H. Holwerda); W. D. Van Wijngaarden, *Van Heurnius tot Boeser*, 1935, 5-8; H. Schneider, *De Laudibus Aegyptologiae. C. J. C. Reuvens als verzamelaar van Aegyptiaca*, 1985; H. Schneider in C. Morigi Govi, S. Curto, and S. Pernigotti, *L'Egitto fuori dell'Egitto*, 1991, 391-402; R. B. Halbertsma, *Scholars, Travellers and Trade: the pioneer years of the National Museum of Antiquities in Leiden, 1818-40*, 2003, 21-30, passim.; M. Hoijtink, *Exhibiting the Past. Caspar J. C. Reuvens and the Museums of Antiquities in Europe 1800-1840*, 2012.

RÉVÉREND *(Abbé)* **Dominique (1648-1734)**
French physician; he was born at Rouen, 14 Nov. 1648; he was named Dean of the Chapter of St. Cloud, 1681; he was greatly interested in supposed Egyptian mystical writings and wrote *Lettres à Monsieur H*** sur les premiers dieux ou rois d'Égypte* 1st ed. 1712, enlarged ed. 1733; he died in Paris, 26 July 1734.

NBG 42, 66-7.

REVILLOUT, (Charles) Eugène (1843-1913)
French Egyptologist; he was born at Besançon, 2 May 1843, son of Victor R., a doctor, and Caroline Philippine Octavie Revillout; he first intended to join the Dominican order in 1865 but left in 1867; he became very interested in Coptic and Egyptian, and studied oriental languages and Egyptology at the École Pratique des Hautes Études under de Rougé (q.v.), 1868-71; he also studied Arabic, 1869; he later took up Demotic, 1876; he was appointed curator at the Louvre, 1872, promoted to assistant keeper, 1876-1 Oct. 1907; he was appointed Professor of Demotic, Coptic, and Egyptian Law at the École du Louvre; he taught at the Institut catholique, 1 Feb. 1908-16 Jan. 1913; Revillout copied most of the Demotic material available in his day and published an enormous quantity of texts and articles, but he was erratic and unsystematic and his work often has inaccuracies; he did nevertheless make known to scholars a very great amount of textual material, and opened up the field of Egyptian law, as well as Demotic, at a time when it was not well defined, thereby doing a service to later students in these fields; with Brugsch (q.v.) and Chabas (q.v.) he founded the *Revue Égyptologique* in 1880, the greater part of which he wrote himself; he was made a Chevalier of the Légion d'honneur and was also for many years Conservateur-Adjoint in the Egyptian Dept. of the Louvre; his output was prodigious and he had produced over 70 major books and studies by 1900; he was equally prolific in the sphere of articles and published hundreds in all the leading journals, but his major contribution here was to the *Rev. Ég.* for which he wrote about 230 articles, 19 bibls. and reviews, and seven obituaries; from this immense output the following may be cited, *Le Concile de Nicée d'après les textes Coptes*, 2 vols. 1873-1918; *Mémoire sur les Blemmyes, à propos d'une inscription copte trouvée à Dendur*, 1874; *Apocryphes Coptes du Nouveau Testament: textes*, 1876;

Actes et contrats des Musées Égyptiens de Boulaq et du Louvre, 1876; *Le Roman de Setna: étude philologique et critique, avec traduction mot à mot du texte démotique, introduction historique et commentaire grammatical*, 1877; *Nouvelle Chrestomathie démotique: mission de 1878, contrats ...*, 1878; *Rituel funéraire de Pamonth en démotique, avec les textes hiéroglyphiques et hiératiques correspondants*, 1880; *Chrestomathie démotique*, 4 vols. 1880; *Cours de langue démotique, leçon d'ouverture*, 1883; *Cours de droit égyptien*, 1884; *Le procès d'Hermias ...*, 2 fasc. 1884-1903; *Corpus papyrorum Aegypti*, 3 vols. in 4, with A. Eisenlohr, 1885-92; *Un Poème Satyrique, composé à l'occasion de la maladie du poète musicien hérault d'insurrection, Hor-Uta ... Papyrus de Vienne*, 1885; *Les obligations en droit égyptien comparé aux autres droits de l'antiquité ... suivies d'un appendice sur le droit de la Chaldée au 23ᵉ siècle et au 6ᵉ siècle avant J.-C.*, with V. Revillout, 1886; *Second mémoire sur les Blemmyes, d'après les inscriptions démotique des Nubiens*, 1887; *Musée du Louvre: catalogue de la Sculpture égyptienne*, 1889; *Notice des papyrus démotiques archaïques et autres textes juridiques ou historiques traduits et commentés ...*, 1896; *Les drames de la conscience: études sur deux moralistes égyptiens inédits des deux premiers siècles de notre ère*, 1901; *Le syllabaire démotique*, 2 fasc. 1912-13; he died in Paris, 16 Jan. 1913.

Proc. Acad. des sciences, belles-lettres et arts de Besançon- verb. and mem. 1913 'L'Égyptologue Eugène Revillout', 261-319 (portr.) (C. Baille); *Bull. Soc. d'Ethnogr.* Paris, 1913, N.S. I, 81-3 (O. Guérin); Curinier, *Dict. des Contemporains*, 2. 196-8; *La Grande Enc.* 28, 543; *Rev. Arch.* Ser. 4, 21 (1913), 243-4 (S. de Ricci); *Rev. Ég.* N.S. I. (1919), 101-3 (H. Sottas); *Stud. Pal. und pap.* 13 (1913), 10-18 (bibl.) (K. F. J. Wessely); S. Sagay in G. Widmer and D. Devauchelle (eds), *Actes du IXe Congrès International des Études Démotiques*, 2009, 317-329.

REYMOND, Eva Anne Elisabeth (*née* Jelínková) (1923-1986)
Czech-British demotist; she was born in Prague, 5 Sept. 1923; she studied at Charles University, Prague under Lexa (q.v.); BA, 1942 in Classics and History; Diploma in Education, 1943; degree in Ancient History and Egyptology, 1946; she was assistant lecturer at Charles IV University before emigrating to Western Europe in 1946; she then studied Demotic under Gunn (q.v.) at Oxford, 1946 and then in Paris, diploma of ancient oriental languages, École des langues orientales anciennes 1948 and diploma from the Sorbonne, 1949; she was attached to CNRS as a research assistant, 1950-7; she was also a research assistant at Cambridge under Glanville (q.v.), 1955-60; she studied at the University of Liverpool under Fairman (q.v.), 1957-60; PhD, 1960; she was appointed lecturer in Coptic at the University of Manchester in 1960 and later reader; she adopted her mother's maiden name Reimonová; her interest was in Demotic and she published papyri in Manchester, Oxford, and Vienna; she developed a special method for handling papyri; her principal publications were *Les inscriptions de la statue guérisseuse de Djed-her le Sauveur*, 1956; *The Mythical Origin of the Egyptian Temple*, 1969; *Catalogue of Demotic Papyri in the Ashmolean Museum* I, 1973; *Four Martyrdoms from the Pierpont Morgan Coptic Codices*, with John Barns, 1973; *From the Contents of the Libraries of the Suchos Temples in the Fayyum*, 2 vols. 1976-7; and *From the Records of a Priestly Family from Memphis*, 1981; her papers are preserved in the University of Manchester Library; she died in Oxford, 27 Sept. 1986.

JEA 73 (1987), ix and private inf; J. Ruzová, *Gött. Misz.* 152 (1996), 95-6 (portr.); inf. J. Ruzová.

REYMOND, René Jean (1885-1908)
French artist; he was born at Tocagne Saint-Apre, Dordogne, 25 May 1885; he was attached to the French Institute from 1906; an excellent copyist and colour reproducer he died in Cairo before he was able to complete his collection of hieroglyphic signs, 7 July 1908.

BIFAO 6, 196 (É. Chassinat).

RHIND, Alexander Henry (1833-1863)
British excavator; he was born in Wick, Caithness, 26 July 1833, son of Josiah R. a banker, and Henrietta Sinclair; he was educated at Pultneytown, Caithness, and Edinburgh University, 1848-50 where he studied literature; he conducted archaeological excavations in Scotland; he abandoned his studies owing to ill health and was obliged to winter in the south; he visited Egypt, 1855-6 and 1856-7; also travelled in Spain, France, and Italy, 1858-62; FSA Scot., 1852; he excavated at Thebes, Giza, and Elephantine with Stobart (q.v.) and acquired a fine collection of antiquities which he bequeathed to the National Museum of Antiquities, Edinburgh (now the National Museums of Scotland); he published *Thebes; its tombs and their tenants*, 1862; *Egypt: its Climate, Character, and Resources as a Winter Resort: with an Appendix of Meteorological Notes*, 1856; by his will Rhind bequeathed £5,000 for two scholarships at Edinburgh, £7,000 for an orphanage at Wick, £400 to the Soc. Ant. Scot., and his large library and collections, together with a substantial sum to found an annual series of lectures in archaeology in Edinburgh, which began in 1874 and still continues; Rhind's name is associated with the Egyptian collection at Edinburgh, with the lectureship, and especially with certain important papyri; the two bilingual Hieratic-Demotic papyri at Edinburgh (908-9), and in the British Museum the Mathematical Papyrus (EA 10057-8), and the leather roll (EA 10250), as well as the long magical

papyrus generally called Bremner-Rhind (EA 10188); the papyri now in the British Museum for some unknown reason were not sent to Edinburgh Museum with the rest of the collection, but were sold by David Bremner (q.v.), Rhind's executor; while most of his collection was transferred to the Royal Scottish Museum (now National Museum of Scotland), some of his collection of archaeological material was transferred to the Paisley Museum (officially accessioned in 1955); his papers are in the Society of Antiquaries of Scotland; he revisited Egypt, 1862-3, where he had a serious illness and died on the way home in La Majolica, on Lake Como, 3 July 1863.

Inf. obtained in Edinburgh and Miss C. Gilmour; J. Stuart, *Alexander Henry Rhind of Sibster*, 1864; *ODNB* 46, 590; *DNB* 48, 82-3; Hilmy, ii, 171; A. Dodson, *KMT* 19/4 (2008), 38-54 (portr.); R. Irving and M. Maitland in N. Cooke and V. Daubney, *Every Traveller Needs a Compass*, 2015, 87-100.

RHONÉ, Arthur (1836-1910)

French author and traveller; he was born in Paris, 14 March 1836, son of Léon R., Master of Requests, and Fanny Bernard; he was a close friend of Mariette (q.v.) and frequently accompanied him on his tours of inspection in Upper Egypt, as he also did with Maspero (q.v.); he thus made many journeys between 1865 and 1882; in 1881 he was attached to the Mission Arch. in Cairo; he contributed many accounts of discoveries in Egypt to the *Gaz. des Beaux Arts, le Temps, Mag. Pittoresque*, etc., and published a travel book, *L'Égypte à petites journées*, which enjoyed great popularity, running to several editions; his correspondence is in the Griffith Institute, Oxford; he died in Paris, 7 June 1910.

Hilmy, ii, 171; *Rev. arch.* Sér. 4, 16. 152; Wilbour, 64, 92, et passim.

RIAD GHABUR, Henry (1913-2000+)

Egyptian Egyptologist; he was born in 1913; he studied archaeology at the University of Cairo graduating in 1941; he joined the Antiquities Service as inspector of Middle Egypt, 19 Aug. 1941 but was soon transferred to the museum branch, becoming assistant to the administrative manager, 17 Nov. 1941; he was appointed administrative director of the Cairo Museum, 21 April 1944; he then became inspector in the Fayum; he continued his studies in France; PhD, 1957; he became curator in the Graeco-Roman Museum in Alexandria, 1957 and Director, 1958-67; he then transferred to the Egyptian Museum, Cairo as curator and then Director, 11 Feb. 1967-14 Feb. 1973; he later served as resident Egyptologist at Chicago House in Luxor whose library was renamed the Henry Riad Memorial Library; he excavated in Ashmunein, 1944; he contributed to the volumes *Mummification in Ancient Egypt and the Celebration of the Hundredth Anniversary of the Discovery of the Royal Mummies in the Valley of the Kings at Thebes*, 1973, and *General History of Africa* I, 1981; he died after 2000.

Bulletin of the Egyptian Museum 1 (2004), 8.

RICARDI, Francesco (*fl.*1821-1843)

Genoese writer; he claimed to have discovered the method of decipherment of hieroglyphs, and published a number of pamphlets between 1821 and 1843 attacking Champollion's system and defending his own.

Champollion, i, 41, 67, 72; Hartleben, i, 545, 58; Hilmy, ii, 172.

RICCI, Alessandro (1792/95-1834)

Italian physician, explorer, and collector; he was born in Siena, *c.*1792/5, son of Angelo R. and Rebecca Gabrielli; he was a native of Siena and accompanied Bankes (q.v.) in his travels in Egypt, 1818-19; he was employed by Bankes to draw the scenes at Beni Hasan, and was also associated with Belzoni (q.v.) for whom he made drawings in the tomb of Sety I; he made several journeys through Egypt and Nubia, 1818-21, and visited the Oasis of Ammon; he accompanied Linant (q.v.) to Sinai, 1820, and was later a member of the Champollion (q.v.)-Rosellini (q.v.) expedition to Egypt, 1928-29; Ricci's collections are partly in Florence and partly in Dresden; his journal and documents relating to him have been published by the Soc. Royale Géogr., edited by Angelo Sammarco, 2 vols., Cairo, 1930, where full references will be found; a copy of the journal was discovered in 2009 and has been published by D. Salvodi, *Viaggi del dottore Alessandro Ricci fatti negli ann I 1818, 1819, 1820, 1821, 1822 in Nubia, al Tempio di Giove Ammone, al Monte Sinai, el al Sennar*, 2011; he died in Florence, 11 Jan. 1834.

DBDI 87, 231-3; Athanasi, 25, 27; Belzoni, i, 371, 388; ii, 24, 38, 105; Champollion, passim; Finati, ii, 301, 335, 344, 357, 394; Hartleben (see index); Hay Diary, 1825, Dec. 1; Linant Diary to other refs. in Sammarco ut supra; È. Gran-Aymerich, *Dictionnaire biographique d'archéologie 1798-1945*, 2001, incorporated in *Les Chercheurs de passé 1798-1945*, 2007, 110; M. Pezin in M. Dewachter and A. Fouchard, *L'Égyptologie et les Champollions*, 1994, 181-9; P. Usick, *Gött. Misz.* 162 (1998), 73-92; P. Usick in W. V. Davies, (ed.), *Studies in Egyptian Antiquities to T. G. H. James*, 1999, 115-21; D. Salvodi, *From Siena to Nubia*, 2018.

RICCI, Seymour Montefiore Robert Rosso de (1881-1942)

British bibliographer and antiquary; he was born in Twickenham, 17 May 1881, son of James Hermann de R. and Hélène Montefiore; he resided chiefly in Paris, and published many bibliographical works on rare books and

MSS; he had a fine library and his knowledge of book collectors and sales of books and MSS was unrivalled; he visited Egypt several times and obtained many important papyri, chiefly Greek, some of which he published; Sandars Lecturer, Cambridge, 1929-30; he published a bibliography of Egyptology (*Rev. Arch*, v-viii, 1917-18), and of Champollion (*Rec. Champ.* 763-84); his papers and library are in the Collège de France; he died in Paris, 25 Dec. 1942.

ODNB 46, 638-40; *Chron. d'Ég.* 18 (1943), 326-30 (C. Preaux), 19 (1944), 96-7 (J. Capart); *JEA* 31 (1945), 1; *The Library,* (1943-4), 187-94; *Rev. arch.* sér 6, 24 (1945), 118-120 (C. Picard); M. Capasso (ed.), *Hermae* IV, 2015, 39-42 (portr.) (N. Carling).

RICE, (Arthur) Michael Penarthur Merrick (1928-2013)
British author; he was born in London, 21 May 1928, son of Arthur Vincent R., later of Penarth, Glamorgan, a banker, and Dora Kathleen Blacklock; he was educated at Challoner School in Finchley and served in World War II; he then joined the International Wool Secretariat; he founded his own public relations firm, 1957-2005; his company specialized in museum planning and design in the Arab world, notably Bahrain, Oman, and Saudi Arabia; he also had a great interest in Egyptology; CMG, 2002; Chairman of the Bahrain Society, 1997-2008; founder of the Public Relations Consultants' Association, 1969; Chairman, 1978-81; among his publications were *Egypt's Making*, 1990, rev. 2004; *Egypt's Legacy*, 1997; *Who's Who in Ancient Egypt*, 1999; *Consuming Ancient Egypt*, 2003; *Swifter than the Arrow: the golden hunting hounds of Ancient Egypt*, 2006; he died 1 Oct. 2013.

Who's Who 2012, 1934; *Debrett's People of Today* 2012 1380; *The Daily Telegraph* 18 Nov. 2013.

RICHARDS, Thomas Bingham (1780-1857)
British agent; he was born in Birmingham, 29 Nov. 1780, son of Theophilus R., toymaker, silversmith, and gun manufacturer, and Mary Bingham; he was the London agent of Henry Salt (q.v.); of Lamb's Conduit Place, London, and Langton, Tunbridge Wells; he carried out the prolonged and difficult negotiations with the Trustees of the British Museum for the purchase of Salt's collections, 1821-4; he died in Langton, Tunbridge Wells, 30 April 1857.

GM 1857, i, 740; Salt, i, 413; ii, 40 et passim.

RICHARDSON, Robert (1779-1847)
British physician and traveller; he was born in Stirling, 1779, son of James R., a farmer, of Doune, Perthshire; he was educated at the University of Glasgow from 1796 and at the University of Edinburgh; MD, 1807; LRCP, 1815; he was travelling physician to Viscount Mountjoy and to the Earl of Belmore (q.v.) with whom he travelled in Egypt as far as the Second Cataract, and in Palestine, 1816-18; he practised in London; he published the narrative of Lord Belmore's travels, 2 vols. 1822; his library was sold at Sotheby's, 11 April 1849; he died in Gordon Square, Bloomsbury, 5 Nov. 1847, and was buried in Highgate Cemetery.

ODNB 46, 845; *DNB* 48, 242; Belzoni, i, 386, 436; ii, 292; Cailliaud, *Oasis*, 51; Hilmy, ii, 172; Lindsay, 114; Munk, *Roll Coll. of Phys.* iii, 134; Westcar Diary, 250; W. Addison, *The Matriculation Albums of the University of Glasgow from 1728 to 1858*, 1913, 181 No, 5774.

RICHTER, Otto Friedrich von (1792-1816)
Baltic traveller and collector; he was born at Neu-Kusthof (now Vaste-Kuuste) near Dorpat (now Tartu in Estonia), 6 Aug. 1792, son of Otto Magnus Johann von R. and Anna Augusta Charlotte von Engelhardt; he studied Oriental languages at the University of Heidelberg from 1809-13; he undertook a journey to Constantinople in 1814 where he met Lidman (q.v.) and accompanied him to Egypt and Nubia 12 April-20 Aug. 1815 as his secretary; he then travelled through Palestine and Anatolia and was on the point of proceeding to Persia when he died; his papers and collection of antiquities were returned to his family; his papers were edited and published by J. P. G. Ewers, *Wallfahrten im Morgenlande*, 1822; his antiquities were presented to the University of Dorpat, but during World War I they were transferred to the Museum of Fine Arts, Voronezh; his notebooks are in the State Historical Central Archive of Estonia; he died in Smyrna, 13 Aug. 1816.

G. Ewers, *Dörpatische Beyträge für Freunde der Philosophie, Literatur und Kunst* 2 (1819), 451 ff.; S. Stadnikow, *Alt-Orientalische Forschungen* 18 (1991), 195-203; *Deutsch baltisches Biographisches Lexikon 1710-1960*, 1970;F. Hinkel, *Altorientalische Forschungen* 19 (1992), 230-46; F. Hinkel, *Études Nubiennes* II, 1994, 49-51; V. Solkin, *KMT* 27 (2016), 52-6 (portr.).

RICKE, Herbert Rüdiger (1901-1976)
German architect and Egyptologist; he was born at Linden near Hanover, 27 Sept. 1901, son of George R., a merchant, and Elise Mackenroth; he was educated at the Polytechnical School in Hanover 1920-5 as an architect; he was sent to Egypt in 1926 to assist Borchardt (q.v.) in the publication of the German excavations at El-Amarna; on his return to Hanover, he completed his dissertation on Amarna domestic architecture under Hölscher (q.v.) at the Abteilung für Architectur at the Technische Hochschule; PhD, 1931; he went back to Egypt in 1931 as

Borchardt's assistant in his new Institute which later, in 1950, became the Swiss Institute of whih he became Director after Borchardt's death in 1938 until 1970; he undertook excavations at the mortuary temple of Thutmose III at Thebes, 1934-7; at the Temple of Kamutef in Karnak, 1938, 1952-4; at the sun temple of Userkaf at Abusir, 1954-7; at the temple of Nectanebo II at Elephantine, 1938, 1954, 1958; in Nubia, 1960-1; at the Harmachis temple of Chephren in Giza, 1965-7; and at the mortuary temple of Amenhotep III at Thebes, 1964 and 1970; he was the editor of *Beiträge zur Ägyptischen Bauforschung und Alterumskunde* where most of his reports were published; a volume of studies in his honour was published in this series in 1971; his main publications were *Ägypten*, with Borchardt, 1929; *Der Gundriss des Amarna-Wohnhauses*, 1932; *Der Totentempel Thutmoses' III*, 1939 (in *Beiträge* 3); *Das Kamutef-Heiligtum in Karnak*, 1954 (ibid.); *Bemerkungen zur ägyptischen Baukunst des alten Reich*, 1944-50 (in *Beiträge* 5-6); *Die Tempel Nectanebos' II in Elephantine*, 1960 (in *Beiträge* 6); *Das Sonnenheiligtum des Königs Userkaf* I-II, 1965-9 (in *Beiträge* 7-8); *The Beit el-Wali Temple of Ramesses II*, with G. Hughes and E. Wente, 1968; *Ausgrabungen vor Khor-Dehmit bis Beit el-Wali, Der Harmachistempel des Chefren in Giseh*, 1970 (in *Beiträge* 10); and *Untersuchungen im Totentempel Amenophis' III*, 1981 (in *Beiträge* 11); he died in Diessen, 22 March 1976.

Beiträge 12 (1971), xiii-xiv (portr.) (B. Peyer): *Informationsblatt der deutsch-sprachigen Ägyptologie* 12 (1976), 3 (P. Derchain); *NDB* 21, 547-8; P. Speiser, *MDAIK* 70/1 (2014/2015), 415-22.

RICKETTS, Charles de Sousy (1866-1931)

British artist and collector; he was born in Geneva, 2 Oct. 1866, son of Charles Robert R. and Hélène Cornélie de Soucy; he trained as an engraver; with his partner, the artist Charles Haslewood Shannon (born at Quarrington, Lincs., 26 April 1863, son of Frederick William S. and Catherine Emma Manthorp, died at Richmond, 18 March 1937), he founded the Vale Press, designing and printing books; he worked as a theatrical designer and art critic, while Shannon was a renowned portraitist; they formed a large and various collection of works of art, including Egyptian material purchased in Egypt and at the Hilton Price (q.v.) and MacGregor (q. q. v.) sales and elsewhere; they loaned Egyptian objects to the 1921 Burlington Fine Arts Society exhibition of Egyptian art; their collections were bequeathed to the Fitzwilliam Museum, Cambridge; he died in London, 7 Oct. 1931.

ODNB 46, 891-3; 49, 987-9; C. Lewis (ed.), *Self Portrait: Taken from the letters & journals of Charles Ricketts R. A.*, 1939; J. Darracott (ed.), *All for Art: the Ricketts and Shannon Collection*, 1979.

RIEFSTAHL, Elisabeth (*née* Titzel) (1889-1986)

American Egyptologist; she was born in Butler, Pa., 8 March 1889, daughter of Dr. Walter Randolph Titzel and Molly Davis; she was educated at the University of Chicago and then went into editorial work for the periodicals *Asia* and *Dial*; in 1924 she married Rudolf Riefstahl, later Professor of Islamic Art and Culture at New York University (*d.*1936); in 1936 she became the first librarian of the Wilbour Library of Egyptology at The Brooklyn Museum, acting as curator of Egyptology during the absence of Cooney (q.v.) on military service, 1942-6, associate curator of Egyptology, 1947, retiring 1955; she helped to revitalize and expand the library and published many objects from the Brooklyn collection mainly in the *Brooklyn Museum Bulletin*; her principal publications were *Pagan and Christian Egypt*, with J. D. Cooney, 1941; *Toilet articles from ancient Egypt from the Charles Edwin Wilbour memorial collection of The New York Historical Society in the Brooklyn Museum*, 1943; *Patterned Textiles in pharaonic Egypt*, 1944; *Glass and glazes from Ancient Egypt*, 1948; *Thebes in the time of Amunhotep III*, 1964; and *Ancient Egyptian glass and glazes in The Brooklyn Museum*, 1968; she died in Southfield, Michigan, 15 Sept. 1986.

BES 2 (1980), 33-5 (J. D. Cooney), 121-4 (bibl.) (D. Guzman); inf. D. Guzman.

RIFAUD, Jean Jacques (1786-1852)

French sculptor and excavator; he was born in Marseilles, 28 Nov. 1786, son of Joseph R., a gilder, and Anne Seneq; he was trained as a sculptor but was conscripted into the French army and fought in Spain where he was either taken prisoner or deserted; he then travelled to the Levant, arriving in Egypt in Jan. 1814 where he carried out excavations for Drovetti (q.v.), whom he accompanied to the Second Cataract in 1816; he remained in Egypt until 15 Aug. 1826; here he carried out an immense amount of digging, at Thebes, 1817-23, in the Fayum, 1823-4, and in the Delta, 1824-6; his work, however, was hasty and unscientific as so often the case during that period, for his only object was the acquisition of portable antiquities; on his return to Europe, he was awarded the Legion d'honneur, 1831 and visited various cities in an unsettled life; he planned to publish *Voyage en Égypte, en Nubie et lieux circonvoisins, depuis 1805 jusqu'en 1827*, 5 vols. 8vo and large fol. vol. of plates but only the fol. vol.

of plates appeared incompletely in Paris 1830-4 and a later enlarged ed. in Munich; it was finally published by M.-C. Bruwier, W. Claes and A. Quertinmont, 2014; he did publish *Tableau de l'Égypte, de la Nubie et des lieux circonvoisins: ou itinéraire à l'usage des Voyageurs*, etc. 1830; *Rapport faits par les diverses Académies et Sociétés savantes de France sur les ouvrages et collections rapportés de l'Égypte et de la Nubie*, 1829; many of the antiquities found by Rifaud are in the Drovetti Collection at Turin, but others are dispersed in many museums; he sometimes carved his name on the statues he found, and the date, e.g. three at Turin and one at Munich; his papers are now in the Department of Manuscripts of the Bibliothèque Publique et Universitaire of Geneva; he died in Geneva, 9 Sept. 1852, and his property was sold there on 26 March 1853.

Carré, i, 176, 201, 227, 244; Devéria, *Mém. et Fragm.* i, 276-9; Hartleben, ii, 192, 414, 426; Hilmy, ii, 173; Irby, 5; Richardson, ii, 92 (as 'Ripaud'); Sherer, 81, 84, 91, 113; A.- M. Pfister, *Musées de Genève* 17 (1961), 8-10; 18 (1961), 15-17; M. Patanè, *Gött. Misz.* 135 (1993), 73-5; J.-J. Fiechter, *La moisson des dieux*, 1994, *passim*; M. Azim, *Gött. Misz.* 143 (1994), 7-19; M. Patanè in M. Dewachter and A. Fouchard (eds.), *L'égyptologie et les Champollion*, 1994, 91-4; M.-C. Bruwier, *L'Égypte au regard de J.-J. Rifaud*, 1998; M.-F. Tilliet-Haulot and M.-C. Bruwier, *Explorer. Égypte et la Nubie au début du XIXᵉ siècle*, 1999; inf. M. Azim; *Pascal Coste. Toutes les Égypte*, 1998, 221-34; E. Gran-Aymerich, *Dictionnaire biographique d'archéologie 1798-1945*, 2001, incorporated in *Les Chercheurs de passé 1798-1945*, 2007, 1113-14; *Voyages en Égypte de l'Antiquité au début du XXe siècle*, 2003, 87-97 (J. Yoyotte); M.-C. Bruwier in N. Cooke and V. Daubney, *Every Traveller Needs a Compass*, 2015, 53-64.

RINALDI, (Ambrogio) Celeste (1902-1977)
Italian civil engineer; he was born in Turin, 7 Nov. 1902; he was trained as a civil engineer graduating in 1926 and had a successful career as an architect enabling him to finance his interest in ancient Egyptian architecture; he studied informally with Botti (q.v.); in 1946 he met Vita Maragiolio (q.v.) who became his collaborator in a project to document the architecture of the pyramids in the Memphite region; he also took part in the work of the Turin Museum during the Nubian rescue compaign, 1961-5; his publications with Maragiolio were *Notizie sulle piramidi di Zedefra, Zedkara Isesi, Teti*, 1962; *L'Architettura della Piramidi Menfite*, ii-viii, 1963-1977; and with S. Curto and others, *Kalabsha*, 1965; *Dehmit* 1973; and *Korosko-Kasr Ibrim. Incisioni Rupestri Nubiane*, 1987; and posthumously *Le Piramidi*, 1983; he died 5 March 1977.

BSFE 79 (1977), 4; *Aegyptus* 58 (1978), 222-4 (S. Curto); inf. S. Curto; F. L. Oscott, *Il segreto della Sfinge*, 1998, 239.

RIPAULT, Louis Madeleine (1775-1823)
French antiquary; he was born in Orléans, 29 Oct. 1775, son of François R., grocer, and Marie Françoise Bouguet; he was a member of Napoleon's Commission in Egypt; afterwards librarian to the Imperial Palace; he took part in the Commission's expedition to Upper Egypt and published reports on the monuments; he died at La Chapelle Saint Mesmin, 12 July 1823.

NBG 42, 311-2; Carré, i, 149, 150, 154; Hartleben, i, *passim* (see index); Hilmy, ii, 174; *Chron. d'Ég*, 17 (1942), 207.

RIQUET, Adolphe de *see* **CARAMAN**

RIZKANA, Ibrahim (1912-1997)
Egyptian archaeologist; he was born on 25 April 1912; he was studied geography in the Faculty of Arts at Cairo University, graduating in 1934; he subsequently became a Professor in the Geography Department there; he undertook excavations with Amer (q.v.) at the sites of Maadi, 1935-48, and Wadi Digla, 1951-3; he later taught abroad in Libya, Saudi Arabia and Algeria before returning to Cairo in 1985; he published, with J. Seeher, *Maadi I-IV*, 1987-90; he died 28 Jan. 1997.

IAE Internet obituary (anon.).

ROBERTS, David (1796-1864)
British artist and traveller; he was born in Stockbridge, near Edinburgh, 24 Oct. 1796, son of John R., a shoemaker, and Christina Ritchie; he was apprenticed to a house-painter, and began his artistic career as a scene-painter; he came to London, 1822, and began to exhibit in the Royal Academy and British Inst., 1826; he visited the East, 1838-9; ARA, 1838; RA, 1841; his oriental drawings were lithographed and published in a series of volumes, *Egypt and Nubia*, 3 vols. 1846-9; *The Holy Land, Syria, Egypt and Nubia*, 1842-9, with text by the Revd George Croly; another ed. with 250 plates, 1885; his remaining works were sold at Christie's, 13-19 May 1865 (1040 lots) and his library 20 May (305 lots); an Art Union of London portrait medal was issued in 1875; he died in London, 25 Nov. 1864 and was buried in Norwood cemetery, south London.

Life, by James Ballantine, 1866; *DNB* 48, 376; Hilmy, ii, 176; Lugt 28518, 28536; H. Guiterman, *David Roberts*, 1978; K. Sims, *David Roberts*, 1984; W. Peck, *KMT* 12/2 (2001), 68-83.

ROBICHON, Clément Pierre Victoire Louis (1906-1999)
French excavator; he was born at Saint-Malo, 5 Nov. 1906, son of Henri Marie Pierre Louis R., architect, and Marie Louise Magdelaine Monrouzeau; he studied architecture and graduated in 1928; he joined IFAO on 1 Nov. 1929 and worked as architect on the excavations until 30 Sept. 1946 apart from absence due to military service and work in France, 1941-45; he succeeded Bruyère (q.v.) as chief architect, 9 Nov. 1946; he joined CNRS on 1 Oct. 1960 and was promoted to director of research, Jan. 1971; he undertook work at Medamud, 1929-39, the tomb of Amenhotep son of Hapu, 1934-7, the mortuary temple of Ramesses IV, 1936-37, at Karnak-Nord, 1949-51, and Soleb from 1957-78, and also at Sedeinga; he published *En Egypte*, 1937, new ed. 1955, trans. *Eternal Egypt*, 1955; *La Tombe du Scribe Royal Amenhotep fils de Hapou*, 1936; *Description sommaire du temple primitif de Médamoud*, 1945, with Barguet; *Karnak-Nord* IV, with Barguet and Leclant; and *Soleb* I-V, with Giorgini (q.v.) and Leclant, 1965-2003; he died in Neuilly-sur-Seine, 6 July 1999.

Inf. J. Leclant.

ROBINOW, Max Emil (*c.*1844-1900)
British businessman, collector, and benefactor; he was born in Hamburg about 1844; he emigrated to England and became a member of the firm of Gottschadk & Co., shippers of Manchester, he wintered in Egypt 1895-6; he became a British citizen 1875; he formed a collection of Egyptian antiquities acquired from Reinhardt and other dealers; he was also an active member of the Lancashire and Cheshire Archaeological Soc.; his collections are now in Manchester Museum; he died in Didsbury, Manchester, 3 Feb. 1900.

Manchester Guardian, obit. 6 Feb. 1900; Myers Diary, 18 April and 16 June 1896; National Archives.

ROBIOU DE LA TRÉHONNAIS, Félix Marie Louis Jean (1818-1894)
French classical scholar and orientalist; commonly called Félix Robiou; he was born in Rennes, 10 Oct. 1818, son of Félix R. and Marie Noemi Corquat; he studied at the École Normale, teaching diploma, 1847; he held various posts before becoming Assistant Director of Ancient History, École des Hautes Études, 1871, resigned 1874; he later held posts at Nancy and Rennes, 1875; he was elected a corresponding member of the Académie des Inscriptions, 29 Dec. 1882; he wrote a great deal on Egyptian and Greek chronology, religion, and history, and also contributed the text to F. Lenormant's *Chefs-d'oeuvre de l'Art Antique*, Paris, 1867; he died in Rennes, 30 Jan. 1894.

Annuaire Éc. Hautes Études, 1897, 5, 54; Hilmy, ii, 177; Vapereau, 1349; A. C. E. Franquet de Franqueville, *Le Premier Siècle de l'Institut de France*, 1895, II, 315.

ROCHEMONTEIX, (*Marquis de*) **(Frédéric Josephe) Maxence René de Chalvet** (1849-1891)
French Egyptologist; he was born in Clermont-Ferrand, 5 Feb. 1849, son of Charles Marie Hippolyte de C. de R. and Marie Claire Baucheron de Lécherolle; he was educated at the Lycées St. Louis, Louis-le-Grand, and d'Alger; he learned Arabic and various African languages including Berber and Nubian, and also studied Egyptology; he began life in a bank, but his linguistic tastes made him seek employment in Egypt; he was sent to Egypt by the Ministry of Public Instruction in 1875 where he joined Mariette (q.v.); he visited many sites and settled at Edfu on his second journey, 1877; he returned to Egypt in 1879 with a civil appointment (Sous-Administrateur de la Commission des Domaines de l'État) and retired in 1885; he studied under Maspero (q.v.) at the Collège de France and began the publication of the Temple of Edfu which was continued and completed by Chassinat (q.v.) after his death; *Le Temple d'Edfou*, pt. i, 1892; his lesser works were collected by Maspero and published in the *Bibl. Ég.* series, see below, in 1894; he died in Paris, 30 Dec. 1891.

Oeuvres Diverses 1894, *Bibl. Ég.* 3, pp. xi-xxxix (biogr. and portr.) (G. Maspero); Wilbour, pl. facing p. 240 (portr.); E. David, *Mariette Pacha 1821-1881*, 1994, 237-8, 242-3; È. Gran-Aymerich, *Dictionnaire biographique d'archéologie 1798-1945*, 2001, incorporated in *Les Chercheurs de passé 1798-1945*, 2007, 1118-9.

ROCHETTE, Désiré Raoul also known as RAOUL-ROCHETTE (1790-1854)
French classicist; he was born in Saint Amand, 9 March 1790, son of a doctor; he succeeded Millin (q.v.) as head of the Cabinet des Médailles, 26 Aug. 1818-1 March 1848 when he was dismissed; he became a Membre de l'Institut, 19 Jan. 1816, and Sécrétaire perpetual de l'Académie des Beaux-Arts, 29 June 1839; he was the author of *Histoire des Colonies Grecques*, 1813; he translated Baroness Minutoli's *Mes Souvenirs d'Égypte*, 1826; he

was an opponent of Champollion's claims and sided with Quatremère (q.v.) and Jomard (q.v.) against Silvestre de Sacy (q.v.) and the Duc de Blacas (q.v.); he died in Paris, 5 July 1854; his antiquities were sold in Paris, 30 April-1 May 1855.

NBG 42, 464-6; *Rev. arch.* 3, 118, 194; Champollion, i, 45, 129, 324; ii, 250; Hilmy, ii, 151; A. C. E. Franquet de Franqueville, *Le Premier Siècle de l'Institut de France*, 1895, I, 181-2; G. Perrot, *CRAIBL* 1906, 638-701; T. Sarmant, *Le Cabinet des Médailles de la Bibliothèque Nationale 1661-1848*, 265-73, 278-80; È. Gran-Aymerich, *Dictionnaire biographique d'archéologie 1798-1945*, 2001, incorporated in *Les Chercheurs de passé 1798-1945*, 2007, 1089-92.

ROCKEFELLER, John Davison (Jr.) (1874-1960)
American oil magnate and philanthropist; he was born at Cleveland, Ohio, 29 Jan. 1874, only son of John Davison R. the 'Oil King' and first billionaire, and Laura C. Spelman, his wife; he was educated at Brown University, BA; MA; LLD; he married 1. Abby Green Aldrich, 1901, (*d.*1948), 2. Martha Baird Allen, 1951; Rockefeller was associated with his father in all his vast business, philanthropic, and educational enterprises, and was Chairman of the Board of the Rockefeller Foundation; he took a keen interest in Egyptology through the influence of Breasted; in all, his benefactions reached the stupendous total of over four hundred million dollars, worth many times as much at present-day values; he was undoubtedly the greatest benefactor to Egyptology there has ever been, and through Breasted (q.v.) gave very great financial help to the University of Chicago, for the Oriental Institute and, in Egypt, Chicago House and other Egyptological projects including an unsuccessful proposal to rebuild the Cairo Museum; many sumptuous vols. such as the *Temple of King Sethos I at Abydos*, I-IV would not have been published without his aid; Rockefeller visited Egypt in order to see the work being done by the Oriental Institute; he died in Tucson, Arizona, 11 May 1960.

Literature on the Rockefeller family is large and varied; the following sources are particularly relevant; *WWW* 5, 941; EB 19. 403-4; R. B. Fosdick, *John D. Rockefeller Jr.*, 1956; A. Nevins, *Study in Power*, 2 vols., 1953; S. Loebl, *America's Medicis: the Rockefellers and their astonishing cultural legacy*, 2010.

RODIN, Auguste (1840-1917)
French sculptor and collector; he was born in Paris, 12 Nov. 1840, son of Jean-Baptiste R. and Marie Cheffer; he was the best-known and most regarded sculptor of the nineteenth and early twentieth centuries; he was conscious of the influence of Classical and ancient sculpture on his work, and collected Classical, Egyptian, and Oriental art, incorporating ancient pieces into some of his studies; he was supplied by Aslanian, Altounian, and Brummer (q. q. v.) among others, and for a time employed Brummer in his workshop; he donated his collections and studio to the French state, to form the Musée Rodin, Paris; this includes around 1,000 Egyptian objects; he died in Meudon, 18 Nov. 1917.

Grove Dictionary of Art 26, 508-515; B. Garnier, *Rodin: Antiquity is my youth, a sculptor's collection*, 2002; B. Garnier, *Rodin, Freud, Collectionneurs: la passion à l'œuvre*, 2009; N. Kayser-Lienhard and B. Garnier in *EDAL* 1 (2009), 77-82.

ROEDER, (Ernst) Günther (1881-1966)
German Egyptologist; he was born at Schwiebus, 2 Aug. 1881, son of Ernst R., pharmacist, and Meta Wahrburg; he studied at the University of Jena and then Berlin under Erman (q.v.), gaining his doctorate at Friedrich-Wilhelm University, 1904; he helped with the classification of objects in the Egyptian Department of Berlin Museum, becoming a methodical and very systematic worker; he also published the inscriptions in the museum, and at this time also helped with the *Wörterbuch*, 1900-7; he joined the Egyptian Antiquities Service, 1907-11; for Maspero (q.v.) he copied the reliefs and inscriptions in three Nubian temples, Debod, Kalabsha, and Dakka, and for Cairo Museum also published the *Naos* vol. of the *Cairo Cat. General*; he completed his habilitaion at the University of Beslau, 1914; he then became a lecturer at Breslau, 1914; Professor, 1916; he was Director of the Hildesheim Museum which had been founded shortly before by W. Pelizaeus (q.v.), 1915-1945 and Director of the Berlin Museum, Dec. 1940-45 when he was dismissed from his posts as a supporter of the Nazi government; he published a catalogue of this collection; between 1929 and 1939; he directed the excavations at Hermopolis, 1930-39, for which he became famous, clearing much of the vast site of the Thoth temple and the associated buildings,

and finding many blocks with scenes of the Aten which apparently came from El-Amarna; he was appointed Director in the Berlin Museum, 1940-45; Roeder made a special study of Egyptian mythology and religion and also certain types of object, his wide variety of interests being shown in his publications; he was a very prolific writer: *Die Praeposition* r *in der Entwicklung der aegyptischen Sprache*, 1904; *Naos*, 1914; *Urkunden zur Religion des alten Ägypten*, 1915, rev. 1923; *Debod bis Bab Kalabsche*, 2 out of 3 vols. 1911-12; *Die Denkmäler des Pelizaeus-Museums zu Hildesheim*, 1921; *Aegyptische Inschriften aus den königlichen Museen zu Berlin*, 1924; *Ägyptisch: praktische Einführung in die Hieroglyphen und die ägyptische Sprache mit Lesestücken und Wörterbuch*, 1926; *Altägyptische Erzählungen und Märchen; ... von G. R.*, 1927; *Die Mastaba des Uhemka im Pelizaeus-Museum zu Hildesheim*, 1927; *Ein namenloser Frauensarg des mittleren Reichs, um 2000 v. Chr. aus Siut, ... zu Bremen*, 1929; *Der Tempel von Dakke*, 2 out of 3 vols. 1930; *Statuen ägyptischer Königinnen in Anschluss an den Torso Amon-Erdas II. in Sydney untersucht*, 1932; *Ägyptische Bronzewerke*, 1937; *Der Felsentempel von Bet el-Wali*, 1938; *Ägyptische Bronzefiguren*, 2 pts., 1956; *Volksglaube im Pharaonenreich*, 1952; *Hermopolis, 1929-1939; Ausgrabungen ...*, 1959; *Die ägyptische Religion in Texten und Bildern*, 4 pts. 1959-61, an immense study; and posthumously *Amarna-Reliefs aus Hermopolis. Ausgrabungen der Deutschen Hermopolis-Expedition 1929-39* II, 1969; he also published articles in journals and contributed many items to the Pauly-Wissowa-Kroll and Roescher encycs.; his papers are preserved in the state archives in Hildesheim; he died in Cairo, 6 Nov. 1966.

Chron. d'Ég. 42 (1967), 125-8 (B. van de Walle); *WW Germany; AfO* 22 (1968-9) 218-9 (portr.) (H. Brunner); *Wer Ist's* 1935; H. Reyer in A. Spiekermann (ed.), *"Zur Zierde gereicht...."*, 2008, 187-216; Bettina Schmitz and Antje Spiekermann, 'Der Roeder-Hanke-Nachlass im Stadtarchiv Hildesheim (Bestand 364). Ein erster Überblick' in *Hildesheimer Jahrbuch für Stadt und Stift Hildesheim* 80, 2008, 273-289; inf. B. Schmitz; B Schmitz in *Gott. Misz.* 224 (2010), 7-8; inf. T. Schneider; C. Bayer in J. Arp-Neuman and T. Gertzen (eds.), '*Steininschrift und Bibelwort*', 2019, 85-92.

ROGERS, (*Bey*) Edward Thomas (1830-1884)
British Consular official; he was born in London, 14 Aug. 1830, son of William Gibbs R., a noted woodcarver, and Mary Johnson; he entered the Consular Service in 1848 as British Vice-Consul in Jerusalem; Vice-Consul at Haifa, 1855-7; Vice-C. at Beirut, 1857; was engaged in several special missions to the East, 1857-61; Consul-General at Damascus, 1861-7; Acting Consul-General in Syria, 1867-8; Consul at Cairo, 1868-75; in 1875 this consulate was abolished and Rogers returned to England, acting for a short time as agent for the Egyptian Govt., after which he returned to Egypt and was appointed Director of the Ministry of Public Instruction; he was interested in oriental art and collected antiquities and Arabic coins; he contributed to *Academy, Art Journal*, and *BIE*; his name is associated with the 'Tablette Rogers', a hieratic text of Dyn. XXI from the cache of Royal Mummies, published by Maspero, *Rec. Trav.* 2. 13-18, and afterwards acquired by the Louvre; his collection was sold at Sotheby's, 29-9 March 1899; he died in Cairo, 10 June 1884.

Academy, 14 and 28 June, 1884; *Athenaeum*, 14 June and 22 Sept. 1884; Hilmy, ii, 179; Westminster Archives; Lugt 57033; *ASTENE* Bulletin 65 (2015), 23-4.

ROLLIN, Claude Camille (1813-1883)
French dealer; he was born in Paris, 28 Feb. 1813, son of Charles Louis R., a coin dealer, and Adelaide Sagoust; he assisted in and took over his father's business located from 1834 at 12 rue Vivienne; he dealt in coins, gems, and antiquities in Paris, he later took into partnership in 1859 his son-in-law Félix Feuardent (q.v.), opening a branch in London, 1867, at 27 Haymarket, later removed to 10 Bloomsbury Street, under the name of Rollin & Feuardent; on the death of his son Charles Rollin on 13 Sept. 1906, the firm continued as Feuardent Frères in 4 Rue Louvois, Paris, until 1935; it supplied the leading museums, in 1872 selling to the Louvre a gold collar of Osorkon II for 25,000 francs; Rollin's name is attached to papyri in the British Museum (EA 10257, 10371) and to several others in the Bibl. Nat., Paris, viz. a portion of the Harem Conspiracy texts (part of pap. Lee, BN 195), a group of account papyri of the XIXth Dyn., pub. by Pleyte and Spigelberg (BN 203-213); he died in Brussels, 4 July 1883.

E. Babelon, *Traité des Monnaies gr. et rom*, pt. i, t. i, Paris, 1901; *Rev. de l'Art*, 43, 170; inf. R. Merrillees.

ROMANO, James (1947-2003)
American Egyptologist; he was born at Far Rockaway, New York 12 April 1947, son of Vincent R. and Mary Hornick; he studied Egyptology at SUNY Binghampton under Gerald Kadish (BA, 1969) and at the Institute of Fine Arts, New York University under Bothmer (q.v.) and Fischer (q.v.); MA, 1972; PhD in Ancient Near Eastern and Egyptian Art and Archaeology, 1989; he held appointments as chief Researcher in Egyptology at the C. G. Jung Foundation and Research Intern at The Metropolitan Museum of Art, 1972-74; he joined the Department of Egyptian, Classical, and Ancient Middle Eastern Art at the Brooklyn Museum, 1 March 1976, curator 1988-2003; he also served as Adjunct Lecturer in the Art History Department at Queens College; he was project director in the reinstallation of the Egyptian galleries in the Brooklyn Museum completed in 2003; he acted as consultant for the gallery installations at the Dallas Museum of Art, the Indianapolis Museum of Art, the Walters Art Gallery,

the Luxor Museum, and the Carnegie Museum of Natural History; he was a specialist in the study of Egyptian sculpture and art; he edited *The Bulletin of the Egyptological Seminar* 1984-87, 1991-93; he published *Catalogue of the Luxor Museum of Egyptian Art*, 1979; *Daily Life of the Ancient Egyptians*, 1990; *Death, Burial and Afterlife in Ancient Egypt*, 1990; *Art for Eternity: Masterpieces from Ancient Egypt*, with others, 1999; *In the Fullness of Time:Masterpieces of Egyptian Art from American Collections*, 2002; a volume of studies in his honour was published in *BES* 17 (2007); he was killed in a motor accident at Lynbrook, NY, 11 Aug. 2003.

SSEA Newsletter, Sept 2003, 1; *Daily Life of the Ancient Egyptians*, iv; *NY Times* 16 Aug. 2003; *Egyptian Archaeology* 23 (2003), 44; *KMT* 14/4 (4) (2003/4), 19-20 (portr.) (E. Russmann); *JARCE* 41 (2004), 1-3 (portr.) (R Fazzini); *BES* 17 (2007), 1-2 (Diana C. Patch), 227-9 (bibl.) (Diane Bergman).

ROMER, Isabella Frances (1798-1852)
British miscellaneous writer; she was baptized in Marylebone, London, 21 June 1798, daughter of Major-General John William Angus R. and Marianne Cuthbert; she married Major William Medows Hamerton of the 67th Foot but soon after separated; she travelled in the East and published *A Pilgrimage to the Temples and Tombs of Egypt, Nubia and Palestine*, 2 vols. 1846, 2nd ed. 1847; she died in London, 27 April 1852.

ODNB 47, 658-9; *DNB* 49, 184; Hilmy, ii, 181.

ROMIEU, Auguste (*fl.* 1866-1902)
French scientist and mathematician; he was Professor of Hydrography at the Coll. d'Agde (Hérault); a disciple of Chabas (q.v.), he wrote articles on Egyptian astronomy and calendar in *Rec. Trav.* and *ZÄS* and published a memoir on the calendar, 1902.

Chabas, lviii; Hilmy, ii, 181.

ROSA, Virginio Michele (1886-1912)
Italian excavator; he was born in Pinerolo, 30 Sept. 1886, son of Giovanni Battsita R., an army officer, and Enrichetta Pianazzi; he studied classics and botany at Turin and developed an interest in photography and Egyptology which he pursued privately; he obtained a post at a botanical garden in Sardinia, 1909; he was appointed assistant to Schiaparelli (q.v.) to replace Ballerini (q.v.), 1910; he conducted the excavations at Gebelein and Asyut, 1911; he died at Varese, 20 Feb. 1912.

B. Moisio, *EDAL* III (2012), 77-96; P. del Vesco et al.: *Missione Egitto 1903-1920*, 2017, 271-9.

RÖSCH, Friedrich (1883-1914)
German Copticist; he was born at Backnang, Würtemberg, 1 Aug. 1883; after he completed his studies he worked in the Egyptian Department of the Berlin Museum and was also an assistant at the German Egyptological Institute in Cairo, in which capacity he took part in the excavations at El-Amarna; he was interested in Berber dialects as well as Coptic; Rösch published *Vorbemerkungen zu einer Grammatik der achmimischen Mundart*, 1909; *Bruchstücke des ersten Clemensbriefes, nach dem achmimischen Papyrus der Strassburger Universität ...*, 1910; he was killed in the First World War at Raon l'Étape, France, 29 Aug. 1914.

ZÄS 52 (1914), 131 (G. Steindorff).

ROSELLINI, (Niccolo Francesco) Ippolito Baldessare (1800-1843)
Italian Egyptologist; he was born in Pisa, 13 Aug. 1800, son of Giambattisto R., a merchant, and Angiola Biagetti, his family being from Pescia; he was educated at the school of Padri Serviti di S. Antonio etc., and afterwards studied Hebrew at the University of Pisa, 1817-21; he began the study of oriental languages under Mezzofanti at Bologna, 1821-4; he was appointed Professor of Oriental Languages at Pisa, 1824; Rosellini was the first Egyptologist in Italy and the founder of Egyptology in Italy through his support of Champollion (q.v.) and also through his own great efforts; he met C. when the latter was visiting the Italian collections and this led to his exploring Egypt as head of the Tuscan delegation in Champollion's expedition to Egypt, 1828-9; on his return he published his results in the great work on the monuments of Egypt and Nubia; in Paris in 1827 he married Zenobia, daughter of the famous composer Cherubini; his most important published works had great influence at the time of their appearance and were fundamental to the development to the subject, they were, *Di un bassorilievo egiziano della I.e R. Galleria di Firenze*, 1826; *Breve notizia degli oggetti di antichità Egiziane riportate dalla spedizione letteraria Toscana in Egitto e nella Nubia, eseguita negli anni 1828-29 ed esposte al publico nell'Accademia delle arti e mestieri in Sta. Caterina*, 1830; *I Monumenti dell'Egitto e della Nubia, disegnati dalla spedizione scientifico-letteraria Toscana in Egitto: distribuiti in ordine di materie, interpretati ed*

illustrati, this vast work consists of three separate parts, I. *Monumenti storici*, 5 vols. and atlas, II. *Monumenti civili*, 3 vols. and atlas, III. *Monumenti del culto*, 1 vol. and atlas, with a total of 395 plates of the largest fol. size and 3,300 pages of text, 1832-44; *Elementa Linguae Aegyptiacae, vulgo Copticae*, ed. L. M. Ungarelli, 1837; his papers and journals are in the Library of Pisa University, and from the material that he left came a posth. publication, *Giornale della Spedizione letteraria toscana in Egitto negli anni 1828-9*, brought out by G. Gabrieli, 1925; his collection of Egyptian antiquities is mainly in Florence, but other objects are in the Museo dell'Opera Primaziale and the Museo di Ateneo in Pisa; he died in Pisa, 4 June 1843.

DBDI 88, 460-2; G. Bardelli, *Biografia del Prof. Ippolito Rosellini*, 1843; G-Dei, *Biografia del Cav. Prof. Ippolito Rosellini*, 1843; *Scritti dedicati alla memoria di Ippolito Rosellini nel primo centenario della morte*, Florence, 1945, 1-19 (portr.) (E. Breccia); *Studi in memoria di Rosellini nel primo centenario della Morte*, Pisa, 2 vols. 1949-55, xv-116 (bibl.) (portr.) (G. Botti and others); G. Gabrieli, *Ippolito Rosellini e il suo giornale della spedizione letteraria Toscana in Egitto negli anni 1828-1829*, 1925, new ed. with intro., 1995; Champollion, ii, passim; Hartleben, passim; *Aegyptus* 5 (1925), 65; Hilmy, ii, 182-93; Atti del Convegno 'Ippolito Rosellini: passato et presente di una disciplina, 1982, passim; M. P. Cesaretti in C. Morigi Govi, S. Curto, S. Pernigotti, *L'Egitto fuori dell'Egitto*, 1991, 69-82; È. Gran-Aymerich, *Dictionnaire biographique d'archéologie 1798-1945*, 2001, incorporated in *Les Chercheurs de passé 1798-1945*, 2007, 1125-6; M. A. Guidotti in M. Betrò and G. Miniaci, *Talking along the Nile*, 2013, 131-6; G. Miniaci in *ibid.*, 151-61; P. Piacentini in *ibid.*, 187-95.

ROSENVASSER, Abraham (1896-1983)
Argentinian Egyptologist; he was born at Carlos Casares, 20 June 1896, son of Solomon R. and Rose Weisman; he studied history in the Instituto Nacional del Profesorado Secundario graduating in 1918, and law at the University of Buenos Aires graduating in 1919; PhD University of Buenos Aires; he was self taught in Egyptology; Professor of Ancient History, University of La Plata, 1939-42, 1955-57; Director of the Instituto de Historia Antigua, 1958-65; Professor of History of the Ancient Near East, University of Buenos Aires, 1955-69; founder and Director of the Instituto de Historia Antigua y Oriental, University of Buenos Aires 1963-83; co-Director of the Franco-Argentine Archaeological Expedition at Aksha in Nubia, 1961-3; he was the author of numerous books and articles including *Escritura, escribas y literatura del Antiguo Egipto*, 1930; *Nuevos textos literarios del Antiguo Egipto*, 1936; *Las ideas morales en el Antiguo Egipto*, 1938; *Procesis criminales en el Antiguo durante la dinistia XX*, 1938; *La poesia amatoria en el Antiguo Egipto*, 1945; *Torneo de acertijos en la literatura del Antiguo Egipto*, 1947; *Politica y religion en la historia antigua de Egipto e Israel*, 1973; *La religion de El Amarna*, 1973; *Aksha, arqueologia de la Nubia*, 1977; he died in Buenos Aires, 9 June 1983.

Inf. P. Fuscaldo; *Revista des Estudios de Egiptologia* 1 (1990), 6-11 (portr.), 13-15 (bibl.) (P. Fuscaldo).

RÖSER, Jacob von (1799-1862)
German traveller; he was born in Ellingen, 3 June 1799, son of Maximilian Justin R., a physician who had the title Hofrath, and Elisabeth Bona; he studied medicine in Würzburg and Tübingen, where he received his PhD, 1819; for a short period he practiced together with his father in Mergentheim, before he became personal physician of Count zu Hohenlohe-Bartenstein in 1823; in 1834 he set off on his journey to the East, starting at Venice; he visited various places (Patras, Athens and some historical sites) in Greece, and then his travel route led him from Smyrna to Bursa and Constantinople, and back to Nauplia where he took a post boat to Alexandria; he then travelled on to Cairo with visits of the Pyramids of Giza and a hospital five hours north-east of Cairo; the last part of his journey was the Holy Land, starting in Jaffa with the final destination of Jerusalem, where he dedicated himself to the treatment of plague patients; he returned via Beirut, Cyprus, and Rhodes; he spent some time in Greece again, before he reached Trieste in Feb. 1835; he published *Tagebuch meiner Reise nach Griechenland, in die Türkei, nach Ägypten und Syrien, im Jahre 1834 bis 1835*, 1836; and *Über einige Krankheiten des Orients*, 1837; he died in Bartenstein, 25 April 1862.

ADB 29, 236-7; inf. Dr. J. Gierlichs.

ROSIGNANI, Joseph (*fl.*1818-1834)
French-Italian adventurer from Turin; he served in the French army in Egypt and remained behind; he entered Drovetti's service in 1811; agent for Drovetti (q.v.) at Thebes where he worked with Antonio Lebolo (q.v.) and joined him in hostile acts against Belzoni (q.v.), who always called him 'the renegade'; guide to the French excavations in Deir el-Medina 1834 when the sarcophagus of Ankhesnesneferibre was recovered.

Belzoni, i, 385; ii, 129, 132, 235, 237; Salt, ii, 23; inf. M. Dewachter; F. Caillaud, *Voyage a l'oasis de Thèbes*, 56.

ROSS, Justin Charles (1841-1896)
British army officer and irrigation engineer; he was born in Calcutta, 10 Dec. 1841, son of Alexander R., civil servant, and Isabella McCarty; Bengal Engineers, Lieut., 1860; Capt., 1873; Major, 1881; retired at Lieut.-Col., 1888; he served as Inspector of E. Delta, 1855; Inspector General of Irrigation for all Egypt; retired,

1893; CMG; LLD; he was on the committee of the EEF, 1894-6; he studied Egyptology and as he spoke Arabic fluently, Petrie (q.v.) endeavoured to have him appointed Director of the Antiquities Service; he died in Bournemouth, 17 Aug. 1896.

RE Journal, 20 Aug. 1896; *Scottish Geogr. Journ.* ix (1893), 169-93; Wilbour, 345, 576, 578; Colvin, 94, 199; Griffith Corr., nos. 202, 204, 207, 462, 463.

ROSSETTI, Carlo (1736-1820)
Italian merchant; he was from Milan and came to Egypt in the time of Ali Bey where he traded under Venetian protection; in 1776 he renounced Venetian nationality for Austrian engaging in trade with Trieste; Austrian Consular Agent, 1793-1805; Consul-General in Egypt for Prussia and other powers; he gained the confidence of Murad Bey whom he warned of Napoleon's impending invasion of Egypt; Napoleon employed him in various missions during the French occupation; the Rossetti who received Champollion (q.v.) in 1828 was his son, and was Consul for Tuscany; the elder R. died, blind and paralysed, in his palace at Bulaq, 19 Feb. 1820.

Athanasi, 15; Champollion, ii, 21, 22, 24, 36, 62, 64; Clot-Bey, ii, 174; G. Guimard, *Les Reformes en Égypte*, Cairo, 1936, 65 n.; Hamilton, *Aegyptiaca*, 343; Minutoli, 29, 37-8, 49, 11; R. Agstner, *Von k.k. Konsularagentie zum Österreichischen Generalkonsulat*, 1993.

ROSSI, Francesco (1827-1912)
Italian Egyptologist; he was born in Turin, 8 May 1827; after taking his degree in Philosophy, 1854, he became an assistant in the Egyptian Museum, Turin, 1865; he was made Vice-Director, 1867; he was appointed Professor Extraordinary in 1876-7, and Professor in Ordinary, 1906-9; he helped to compile the museum catalogue; the major part of his studies appeared in the *Atti* of the Reale Accademia delle Scienze di Torino, vols. xxxv-xliii; besides producing many long articles he wrote, *Papyrus de Turin facsimilés par F. Rossi de Turin et publiés par W. Pleyte de Leide*, 2 vols. 1869-76; *Catalogo illustrato delle antichità egiziane del museo di Bologna*, 1871; *Grammatica copto-geroglifica con un'appendice dei principali segni sillabici e del loro significato illustrati da esempi ...*, 1877; *R. Museo di Torino, Antichità egiziane*, 2 vols. with A. Fabretti and R. V. Lanzone, 1882-8; *I Monumenti Egizi del museo d'antichità di Torino*, 1884; *I papiri copti del Museo Egizio di Torino transcritti e tradotti da F. Rossi*, 2 vols. 1887-8; *Grammatica Egizia nelle tre scritture geroglifica, demotica e copta*, 1901; he died in Turin, 11 Jan. 1912.

Enc. It. 30. 142-3 (G. Farina); Hilmy, ii, 194.

RÖSSLER-KÖHLER, Ursula (1947-2019)
German Egyptologist; she was born 3 Aug. 1947 in Cassel; she studied Egyptology, Prehistoric Archaeology, and Cultural Anthropology at Georg August University in Göttingen; PhD, 1973; Habilitation, 1988; she was appointed Professor at the Rheinische Friedrich Wilhelms University in Bonn, 1991-2011; she was the founder and director of the Totenbuch Project; she was the editor of the series *Handschriften des altägyptischen Totenbuches* and *Studien zum altägyptischen Totenbuch*; she also edited the series *Ägyptologische Abhandlungen*; she undertook a survey of the 12th nome, 1980-1 and excavations at Maabda; she was the founder of the Egyptian Museum in Bonn, 2001; a volume of studies in her honour was produced by A. El-Harawy and D. Morenz, *Weitergabe*, 2015; she published *Der Imiut*, 1973; *Kapitel 17 des ägyptsichen Totenbuches*, 1979; *Individuelle Haltungen zum ägyptischen Königtum der Spätzeit*, 1987; with D. Kurth, *Zur Archäologie des 12. Oberägyptischen Gaues*, 1987; and *Zur Tradierungsgeschichte des Totenbuches zwischen der 17. und 22. Dynastie (Tb 17)*, 1999; with T. Tawfik, she edited *Die Ihr Vorbeigehen werdet... Wenn Gräber, Tempel und Statuen sprechen*, 2009; she died in Meckenheim near Bonn, 11 March 2019.

Inernet obit., Bonn University.

ROSTOVITZ, Alexandros (d. 1919)
Greek collector; he was born in Constantinople or Macedonia and settled in Cairo where he was associated with the Thomas Cook travel company; he became their chief agent in Egypt before founding his own travel company in 1889; he also was involved in various other business ventures in Egypt; he is frequently mentioned in Wilbour's diary; in 1904 he donated to the National Museum at Athens his collection of 2,237 Egyptian antiquities which included a cup from the royal cache; he was President of the Greek Community of Cairo and was awarded the title of Bey by the Khedive; he died in Cairo, 1919.

Inf V. Chrysikopoulos; Wilbour, *passim*.

ROTH, Henry Ling (1855-1925)
British curator and weaving expert; he was born in London, 3 Feb. 1855, son of Matthias R., a doctor, and Anna Maria Collins; he was a man of wide interests and wrote several valuable articles in *JAI*, and studied ancient textiles; he published a handbook on ancient Egyptian and Greek looms for the Bankfield Museum, Halifax, of which he was Curator, and with G. M. Crowfoot (q.v.) contributed an article on the same subject of *AE* 1921, 97-101; he died in Leeds, 12 May 1925.

JEA 11 (1925), 333; *Man* 1925, 97 (portr. and bibl.).

ROUELLE, Guillaume François (1703-1770)
French chemist; he was born at Mathieu, 16 Sept. 1703, son of Jacques R., a farmer, and Marie Bougon; he began life as an apothecary, and was appointed Demonstrator in Chemistry, Jardin du Roi, Paris, 1742, where Lavoisier was one of his pupils; his most important work was that on the *salts* which form the basis of the modern chemical acceptation of that term; in 1750 he communicated to the Acad. des Sciences a memoir on Egyptian embalming which contains some good observations and is very creditable for its period; he died at Paris, 3 Aug. 1770.

Hilmy, ii, 195; *Mem. I.É.*, 13, 38.

ROUGÉ, (*Vicomte*) (Alexis Hervé) Jacques de (1842-1928)
French Egyptologist; he was born in Paris, 17 Feb. 1842, eldest son of E. de Rougé (q.v.) and Valentine Marie de Ganay; he studied under his father in Paris, and accompanied him on his expedition to Egypt, 1863-4; he edited and published the inscriptions copied on this journey, of special interest being those gathered by the father at Edfu, 4 vols. 1877-9; he himself wrote some important studies, see *Monnaies des nomes de l'Égypte*, 1875; *Inscriptions hiéroglyphiques copiées en Égypte* ... (tome 3) 2 vols. 1877-8; *Géographie ancienne de la Basse-Égypte*, 1891; he also contributed an important series of articles on the Edfu geographical texts to *Rev. Arch.*; at the age of 80 he attended the Champollion centenary celebrations in 1922; he died at the Chateau de Précigné, 9 Oct. 1922.

Chron. d'Ég. 13, (1938) 327; Hilmy, i, 177.

ROUGÉ, (*Vicomte*) Emmanuel Charles Oliver Camille de (1811-1872)
French Egyptologist; he was born in Paris 11 Apr. 1811, son of Augustin Charles Camille de R., a noble cavalry officer, and Adélaide Charlotte Colombe de la Porte de Riantz; he was educated by the Jesuits at the Coll. de Saint-Acheul, intending to enter a career in the Council of State, but the revolution of 1830 led to his father's retirement to his château of Précigné, Sarthe, and he decided to follow an academic life; not wishing to live in the country he studied Arabic and Hebrew in Paris, but was turned from a career in Semitics by reading Champollion's *Grammaire* in 1839, subsequently working on the decipherment of hieroglyphic texts; de Rougé has been called the founder of Egyptian philology by Naville (q.v.), and was the first person to translate a running text; his first published work was a masterly refutation of certain theories put out by Bunsen (q.v.) partly influenced by Lepsius, *Examen de l'ouvrage du Chevalier de Bunsen, la place de l'Égypte dans l'histoire du monde*, 1846-7; he next wrote *Lettres à M. de Saulcy sur les éléments de l'écriture démotique*, 1848; *Lettres à M. Leemans*, 1849; he was appointed Conservator of the Egyptian collection at the Louvre, 1849, and made an inventory of the collections in the same year, *Notice des monuments exposés dans la galerie d'antiquités égyptiennes au Musée du Louvre*, which went through many later eds; at this time he visited Turin, Berlin, Leiden and London; in *Mémoire sur l'inscription du tombeau d'Ahmès*, 1849, and 'Étude sur une stèle ég. appartenant à la Bibl. imperiale', *Journal asiatique,* VIII, X, XII, 1856-8, he laid down for the first time correct rules for reading and making translations of hieroglyphic texts; with the *Tale of Two Brothers* and *Poème de Pentaour*, 1856, he revealed for the first time the great wealth of Egyptian literature preserved in hieratic books; he succeeded Lenormant (q.v.) in Champollion's chair, 1860; he visited Egypt with his son Jacques, 1862-3; he also published, *Catalogue des signes hiéroglyphiques de l'Imprimerie nationale,* 1851; *Recherches sur les monuments qu'on peut attribuer aux premières dynasties de Manéthon,* 1864-5, which put the study of the succession of the Old Kingdom kings on a firmer base; *Rituel funéraire des anciens Égyptiens*, 1861-3; *Album photographique de la Mission remplie en Égypte par le vte. E. de Rougé... 1863-1864*, 1865; *Chrestomathie égyptienne*, 4 vols. 1867-76, his largest work, the last two parts posthumous; he was made Senator, 1870; he taught many French Egyptologists, notably Maspero (q.v.), who collected his lesser works and published them in *Bibl. Ég.* 6 vols.; his importance in the story of Egyptology is concisely summed up by Maspero, 'Champollion deciphered the texts... de Rougé gave us the method which allowed us to utilize and bring to perfection the discovery of Champollion'; he died at the Chateau de Précigné, Bois-Dauphin, Sarthe, 27 Dec. 1872.

Maspero, 'Notice Biogr.' *(Bibl. Ég. 21)* 1907, pp. i-clvi (portr.); Maspero, *La Grande Encyc.* 28. 1011-12; A. C. E. Franquet de Franqueville, *Le Premier Siècle de l'Institut de France*, 1895, I, 611; H.A. Wallon, *Notice historique sur la vie et les travaux de M. le vte. Emmanuel de Rougé*, 1878; *JEA* 3 (1916), 227-8 (E. Naville); Hilmy, i, 177; È. Gran-Aymerich, *Dictionnaire biographique d'archéologie 1798-1945*, 2001, incorporated in *Les Chercheurs de passé 1798-1945*, 2007, 1128-32.

ROUSSEL, Joseph Jean Baptiste Hercule de (1785-1835)
French diplomat; he was born at Bagnols-sur-Cèze, 17 or 19 Sept. 1785, son of Alexis Gabriel de R., a lawyer, and Rose Migne; he was attached to the French embassy at Constantinople, 1778; he served as vice-consul at the Dardenelles, 1779-85, and at Coron, 1786-93, and then as consul at Nauplia, 1793-1802, Khania, 1802-7, and Patras, 1810-14; he was appointed French Consul-General in Egypt, 25 Sept. 1814 in succession to Drovetti (q.v.), but only arrived in Egypt on 25 Aug. 1816; he held office in the interval between the two periods of the consulship of Drovetti and was much under his influence; he left Egypt by May 1819; Pillavoine (q.v.) served as acting Consul from 28 July 1819 until Drovetti's reappointment in 1821; he died at Bagnols-sur-Cèze, 14 May 1835.

Belzoni, ii, 235; Cailliaud, 65; J.-J. Fiechter, *La moisson des dieux*, 1994, 45, 159; R. T. Ridley, *Napoleon's Proconsul in Egypt*, 1998, *passim*; *Bulletin des lois de la République Française*, 6 March 1822 (birthdate 17 Sept.); L. Alègre, *Notices biographiques du Gard*, 1880, II, 239-46 (birthdate 19 Sept.); A. Mézin, *Les Consuls de France au siècle des lumières (1715-1792)*, 1998, 531 (birthdate 19 Sept.); A. Favre d'Arcier, *Les oubliés de la liberté*, 2007, 235 (birthdate 19 Sept.).

ROUSSET, (Charles Anne) Jules (*Bey*) (1802-1881)
French accountancy expert; he was born in Flavigny-sur-Ozerain, 9 Oct. 1802, son of Charles Philippe R., a financial official, and Jeanne Marguerite Joséphine Harpin; he was attached to the Ministry of Finance, 1832-43; he was sent to Egypt about 1845 to audit the Egyptian government accounts and finances; while in Egypt, he formed a collection of antiquities; he was awarded the title of Bey in 1847; Prefect of Loire, 1848-51; Counsellor at the Cour des Comptes, 1852; his collection was sold in Paris, 15 July 1868 (1,208 lots); all of these antiquities were acquired by the Louvre; he died at Arc-les-Gay, 21 Oct. 1881.

Internet *Dictionnaire historique, génealogique et biographique (1807-1947)* from Cour des Comptes.

ROWE, Alan Jenvey (1890-1968)
British Egyptologist and archaeologist; he was born in Deptford, 29 Oct. 1890, son of Lewis Oxley R., accountant, and Florence Emily Jenvey; he became interested in Egyptology in early life through studying the collections in the British Museum; subsequently while working as a journalist he emigrated to Adelaide, South Australia in 1912 where he enlarged his experience by working voluntarily in museums in Sydney and Adelaide and lecturing in history in the University of Adelaide; after failure to obtain a museum post in Australia, he left Australia in 1922; Rowe's first archaeological field-work was as archaeological assistant to C. S. Fisher (q.v.) with the University Museum of Pennsylvania expedition to Palestine at the site of Beth Shan, an important Egyptian town in the New Kingdom, 1922; he also helped in the recording of objects at Memphis previously discovered by the Univ. of Pennsylvania expedition; from 1923 to 1925 he was chief archaeological assistant to Reisner (q.v.) with the joint Harvard-Boston expedition to Giza, where during the absence of Reisner in America he was directing work at the time of the discovery of the 'tomb' of Hetepheres the mother of King Khufu; at this period he directed work on many sites in Egypt and Palestine, Girga (Upper Egypt), Semna and Kumma (Sudan), Beth Shan (Palestine); his assistant in Egypt was T. R. D. Greenlees; this work was followed by excavation at the pyramid of Maidum 1929-32, Gezer (Palestine) and Benha (Athribis), 1925-34; Benha yielded interesting discoveries, 1938, the expedition being financed by Sir Robert Mond (q.v.); he was appointed Curator of the Graeco-Roman Museum in Alexandria, 1940-9; while in this post he made further discoveries in the Western Desert, notably the Ramesside fortress at Zawyet Umm el-Rakham, 1946; he also excavated the Catacombs of Kom el-Shuqafa, Alexandria, 1941-2; the Serapeum or remains of the temple of Serapis, 1943-5; in 1943 the War Office asked him to make a special report on damage to monuments in the war zone in Cyrenaica; he was appointed Special Lecturer in Near Eastern Archaeology in the University of Manchester, 1950-52, and Lecturer, 1952-8; his last four expeditions were made to the tombs and cemeteries of Roman Cyrene where he discovered remarkable statues of the goddess Persephone 1952-57; he married secondly in 1947 Mrs Olga Serafina Wilson (1905-15 Sept. 1958), daughter of Antonio Cucinotta, who helped him in his archaeological field-work until her death; he published several articles in Australia on Egyptian and other antiquities and left in manuscript a catalogue of the Egyptian antiquities in the South Australian Museum; in addition to numerous other articles in journals he wrote, *A Catalogue of Egyptian Scarabs, Scaraboids, Seals and Amulets in the Palestine Archaeological Museum*, 1930; *The Topography and History of Beth-Shan, with details of Egyptian and other inscriptions found on the site*, 1930; *The Eckley B. Coxe, jr., Expedition excavations at Meydum (1929-30)*, 1931; a trans. of Leibovitch's *Ancient Egypt*, 1938; *The Four Canaanite Temples of Beth-Shan*, pt. i., 1940; *Discovery of the Famous Temple and Enclosure of Serapis at Alexandria*, see *ASAE* 1946; *New Light on Aegypto-Cyrenaean Relations. Two Ptolemaic statues found in Tolmeita*, 1948; *A Contribution to the Archaeology of the Western Desert*, see *Bull. of the John Rylands Library*, vol. 36. 128, 484, 1951; vol. 38. 139, 1953; some of his papers are in the Griffith Institute, Liverpool University, and the South Australian Museum, Adelaide; he died in Manchester, 3 Jan. 1968.

Private inf.; *The Times*, 12 Jan. 1968; *PEQ* 100 (1968); 76-7; *Expedition* 21 (1979), 27-9; A. Rowe, *Some Details of the Life of Olga Serafina Rowe (A.D. 1905-1958)*, ms, 1960; R. S. Merillees, *Living with Egypt's Past in Australia*, 1990, 34-9; J. C. Thorn, *Libyan Studies* 27 (2006), 71-83; R. S. Merrillees in Z. A. Hawass and J. Richards (eds.), *The Archaeology and Art of Ancient Egypt. Essays in Honor of David B. O'Connor* II, 2007, 161-9; inf. J. C. Thorn and R. Grandison.

RUBENSOHN, Otto (1867-1964)
German archaeologist; he was born in Kassel 24 Nov. 1867 son of Hermann R., a merchant, and Rosa Herrlich; he studied in Berlin and Strasbourg, PhD, 1892; he excavated in Greece 1897-9; he was attached to the papyrus section of the Berlin Museum, 1901-7, and conducted excavations for papyri at Elephantine, 1906-7, and Abusir el-Meleq, 1902-7; in Egypt he met Pelizaeus (q.v.) who arranged his appointment as assistant in his museum at Hildesheim in 1907; he became Director, 1909-15; for the opening of the Pelizaeus Museum, he published *Hellenistisches Silbergerät in antiken Gipsabgüssen*, 1911; he returned to Berlin as a teacher in 1915; he emigrated to Switzerland in 1939; he died in Hochenschwand, 9 Aug. 1964; his papers are now in the Jüdisches Museum, Berlin.

R. Lillies and W. Schiering, *Archäologenbildnisse,* 1988 (K. Schefold) (portr.) inf. B. Schmitz; *Wer ist's* 1935; M. Capasso (ed.), *Hermae* III, 201, 41-56 (portr.) (J. Kuckertz).

RUBINSTEIN, Rebekka Ionovna (1899-1982)
Russian Egyptologist; she was born at Krementchug, Ukraine, 11 Oct. 1899, daughter of Iona Yakovlevitch R. and Maria Borisovna Rabinovitch; she was educated at Moscow University and later the University of Leningrad under Struve (q.v.) and Flittner (q.v.) graduating in 1924; she became scientific assistant at the Hermitage Museum, 1924-34, and teacher at the A. I. Herzen State Pedagogical Institute; she became a Candidate of Historical Sciences in 1940 and docent in 1941; from 1944 she worked at the Oriental Science Institute (Moscow Branch) and taught in the Moscow Region Pedagogical Institute; from 1949 she was a scientific associate of the Ancient Oriental Department of the Pushkin State Museum of Fine Arts, Moscow; she published many articles concerning Egyptian objects in the Hermitage and the Pushkin Museums; she was also interested in the art and archaeology of Urartu, writing *At the Walls of Teyshebaini* (Russ.), Moscow, 1975; she married the orientalist Nicholas Alexandrovitch Sholpo (1903-41); she died in Moscow, 10 April 1982.

S. D. Miliband, *Bibliograficeskiy slovar' sovetskikh vostokovegov*, 1975, 484; family inf.

RUFFER, (*Sir*) Marc Armand (1859-1917)
British-Swiss pathologist; he was born at Lyons, 29 Aug. 1859, son of Baron Alphonse Jacques de Ruffer, a banker, and his wife Caroline; he was educated at Brasenose College, Oxford, 1878-81 and University College London; BA, 1882; B. Med. and MA, 1887; he was naturalized 14 Nov. 1890; he became the first director of the Lister Institute, London, 1891; he contracted diphtheria in the course of his research, and was obliged to resign his position and convalesce in Egypt; there he became Professor of Bacteriology, Cairo Medical School; President, Sanitary and Quarantine Council of Egypt; FLS; CMG, 1916; Head of the Red Cross in Egypt, 1914; he investigated traces of ancient disease in Egyptian mummies and skeletons and published a number of important articles on this subject which were collected after his death as *Studies in the Palaeopathology of Egypt*, ed. by Roy L. Moodie, 1921; he died when his ship was torpedoed at sea off Salonica, 15 April 1917.

WWW ii, 915; Al. Oxon; *Medical History* 11:2 (April 1967), 150-6 (A. T. Sandison), reprinted in J. Buikstra and C. Roberts (eds.), *The Global History of Paleopatholgy. Pioneers and Prospects*, 2012, 106-10 (bibl.); *ibid.*, 212 (B. Baker and M. Judd).

RUMIANTSEV, (*Count*) Nikolai Petrovitch (1754-1826)
Russian statesman and diplomat, eminent collector; he was born in St. Petersburg, 3/14 April 1754, son of Count Peter A. R. and Princess Catherine Galitzine; in 1774-76 he travelled in Europe, studying for some months at the University of Leiden; from 1776-95 in diplomatic service abroad; he once again travelled in Europe from 1798-1801; 1806 Senator, 1807-14 Foreign Minister; he formed in St. Petersburg a large collection of manuscripts, books, coins, ethnographic objects, Egyptian antiquities, etc., which became after his death the basis of a state museum formed in 1831; in 1861 the collection was transferred to Moscow, known as the Roumiantsev Museum there; Egyptian objects from this collection are now in the Pushkin Museum in Moscow; he died in St. Petersburg, 15 Jan. 1826.

Sovetskaia Istoriceskaia Enciklopedia 12/307-308; *Great Soviet Encyclopedia* 22, 367; inf. J. Śliwa.

RÜPPELL, Eduard Wilhelm Peter Simon (1794-1884)
German naturalist, geographer, cartographer, ethnographer and traveller; he was born in Frankfurt, 20 Nov. 1794, son of Simon R., postmaster and banker (1759-1812), and Elisabeth Arstenius (*d*.1812); destined to be a merchant in London, he went to Egypt in 1817 for his health; there he met Salt (q.v.), for whom he made drawings at Giza, and Burckhardt (q.v.) who encouraged him to become an independent explorer; he visited the Nile Valley from Cairo to Aswan and the Sinai, 1817-8; he returned to Europe to study at Pavia and at Genoa under the astronomer F. von Zach, 1818-21; he went back to Egypt as a founder member of the Senckenbergische Naturforschende Gesellschaft (SNG) and visited Nubia, the Sudan, the Red Sea coast, 1822-27; he undertook another major expedition mainly to Abyssinia, 1831-34 and revisited Egypt again in 1849-50; he made great contributions to the knowledge of the fauna of those regions, a great many specimens of which were sent back to Senckenberg for its Museum of Natural History; he was awarded a votive medal by the Frankfurt Senate, 1829; he was also awarded an honorary degree of Doctor of Medicine by the University of Giessen, 1827; he was the first foreigner to be given the Gold Medal of the Royal Geographical Society in 1839; in 1835 he became head of the numismatic collection in the municipal library (now Universitätsbibliothek Johann Christian Senckenberg) in Frankfurt to which he presented his own collections of coins (*c*.10,000 items) and antiquities (*c*.350 items) and which still houses some papyri, Ethiopic manuscripts, and eight plates of drawings illustrating a great number of his Egyptian antiquities collected before 1828; the collection was later transferred to the Historical Museum in 1878 and the antiquities were finally assigned to the Liebieghaus Museum in 1919 apart from some animal mummies in the Senckenberg Museum; two accounts of his travels were published, *Reisen in Nubien, Kordofan und dem peträischen Arabien*, 1829, and a large atlas of plates, 1826-31; and *Reise in Abyssinien*, 1838-40, 2 vols. and atlas; he also published *Systematische Uebersicht der Vögel Nord- Ost-Afrika's*, 1845; *Neue Wirbelthiere zu der Fauna Abyssinien gehörig*, 1835-40; and several minor works and papers including a letter with some archaeological remarks and drawings 'Auszug eines Schreibens…' in J. von Hammer, *Fundgruben des Orients* 5 (1816) (sic), 427-33; in his honour the Rüppellstiftung zur Förderung wissenschaftlicher Reisen was founded at Frankfurt-a-M. in 1871; his manuscripts and drawings are preserved in the SNG archives in Frankfurt; he died in Frankfurt, 10 Dec. 1884 and a small obelisk was erected over his still extant grave.

Hilmy, ii, 200; Irby, 38, 39, 41, 48; Westcar Diary, 174; *Proceedings of the Royal Geographical Society* 8 (1886), 654; R. Mertens, *Eduard Rüppell*, 1949; *ADB* 29, 707-14; *NDB* 22, 226-7; W. Klausewitz, *Natur und Museum* 114/12 (1984), 337-356 and 132/5 (2002), 157-69; B. Gessler-Löhr; *Ägyptische Bildwerke* I. Liebieghaus Museum alter Plastik ,1990, 13-5; H.-C. Noeske et al., *Die Münzen der Ptolemäer. Schriften des Historischen Museums Frankfurt am Main* 21 (2000), 7; W. Klausewitz, 'Die Rüppell-Medaille und Goethe', in H.-C. Noeske, *op. cit.*, 8-11; P. Usick and D. Manley, *The Sphinx Revealed*, 2007, 10, 14, 53; inf. B. Gessler-Löhr; B. Gessler-Löhr in M. Betrò and G. Miniaci, *Talking along the Nile*, 2013, 101-23.

RUSTAFJAELL, Robert de (1859-1943)
British-American collector, dealer and author; he was born in St. Petersburg, Russia, 10 Dec. 1859, son of Nicholas Classen Smed (to whom the surnames Smith and de Rustafjaell were later attributed), an engineer of Norwegian extraction, and Maria Tamara Orbeliani although he later claimed to have been born in Birmingham and an obituary notice quotes his year of birth as 1876; few of his often extravagant claims about his ancestry and life can be externally verified; he claims to have been brought to England in 1861 by his parents and to have been educated at Harrow and Oxford, and in Sweden and Germany; he travelled overseas after 1877, spending time in America before returning to England in 1887; he was first known by the surname Smith or Fawcus-Smith although he was using that of de Rustafjaell by 1892 and formally changed to the latter on 9 Oct. 1894; he appears to have married a Swedish lady Carolina Amalia Arfwidson in 1892, with whom he had a son soon afterwards; he was married again in 1895 to Harriet Sarah Wilkinson, but was in the company of his first wife and son in the 1901 census; by 1905 he was married to an American, Mary Davis, perhaps the mother of his daughter Tamara, born in southern Russia in 1907; he excavated at Cyzicus in Turkey in 1901; he lived for some time in Egypt as a geologist, mining engineer and owner of the Luxor Trading Co. which also sold antiquities; he was elected a Fellow of the Royal Geographic Society in 1899, of the Zoological Society in 1901, and the Royal Numismatic Society in 1904; he formed a collection of Egyptian antiquities, mainly Predynastic, but also acquiring a number of New Kingdom votive cloths from the Hathor shrine at Deir el-Bahari, fragments from the walls of Theban tombs including that of Nebamun, and two groups of papyri and codices; in addition to short notices on his collection in newspapers and journals, he published *Palaeolithic Vessels of Egypt or the Earliest Handiwork of Man*, London, 1907; *The Light of Egypt from Recently Discovered Predynastic and Early Christian Records*, etc., 1909; *The Stone Age in Egypt: a record of recently discovered implements and products of the archaic Niliotic races inhabiting the Thebaid*, 1914; he was declared bankrupt in London in 1914 and emigrated to America; at one period he changed his name to Col. Prince Roman Orbeliani (as well as other variants); his collections were dispersed in five sales: Sotheby's, 19-21 Dec. 1906 (550 lots), 9-10 Dec. 1907 (245 lots), 20-24 Jan. 1913 (1051 lots), Paris 29 May 1914, and New York, 29 Nov.-1 Dec 1915 (745 lots); the first sale produced £1,843, the second £308-12, the third £2,748, and the fifth $12,760; a posthumous sale took

place in New York, 13-14 Dec. 1949; Wellcome (q.v.) was a major purchaser at his sales, and other groups of some objects from his collections are in the British Museum, British Library, Berlin Museum and the Louvre; he died in New York, 10 Feb. 1943.

Inf. T. Hardwick and A. Dodson; R. Geogr. Soc.; National Achives, Kew (Naturalization papers); *Les Donateurs du Louvre*, 1989, 313; New York Times, various issues; Lugt 64969, 65946, 72085, 74476, 75285; A. Muls, *In de Kaukasus:dagboek van August Muls, een Antwerps mijnexploitant 1917-1918*, 1990, 186-7; F. Hagen and K. Ryholt, *The Antiquities Trade in Egypt 1880-1930*, 2017, 259.

RUSZCZYC, Barbara (1928-2001)
Polish archaeologist and art historian; she was born in Vilnius, 18 Sept 1928, daughter of Ferdinand R., a noted painter, and Regina Rouck; she studied classical archaeology in Warsaw under Michalowski (q.v.); MA, 1955; PhD, 1972; she joined the staff of the National Museum in Warsaw, 1949 as a guide and was transferred to the Department of Ancient Art, 1950; senior curator, 1973-90; she helped to publish the collection and organise exhibitions; she also lectured in ancient art at Warsaw University in the absence of Professor Michalowski and at the Academy of Catholic Theology in Warsaw, 1973-93; she undertook fieldwork in Egypt and the Sudan, notably as field director at Benha (Tell Atrib), 1969-84 as well as at Faras and Alexandria; she retired from the museum in 1990 but continued as a volunteer; apart from articles and excavation reports, she published *Kościół pod wezwaniem Świetejh Dziewicy w Tell Atrib*, 1997; she died in Warsaw, 11 Sept. 2001.

PAM 13 (2001), 11-12 (portr.). (J. Lipinska).

RYLANDS, William Harry (1847-1922)
British archaeologist; he was born in Warrington, 20 Dec. 1847, son of Thomas Glazebrook R., manufacturer, and Jane Chapman Ragg; MRAS.; he contributed a few papers on Egyptian subjects to the Society's *Proceedings*, and a memoir and bibl. of Renouf; he was also interested in heraldry and edited some of the visitation vols. for the Harleian Society; he died London, 8 Sept. 1922.

JEA 9 (1923), 223; *JRAS* 1922, 637; *PEFQS* 1923, I.

SAAD, Ramadan Mustafa Hasan (1935-1974)
Egyptian archaeologist; he was born in Shibin el-Kom, Menufiya Province, 8 Dec. 1935; he was educated at Cairo University under Abu Bakr (q.v.) and Fakhry (q.v.); he was inspector at Luxor and resident Egyptologist at the Centre Franco-Egyptien at Karnak, 1969-71; he obtained a doctorate at the University of Lyons under Barguet, 1972 with a thesis entitled *Les Martelages de la XVIIIe dynastie dans le Temple d'Amon-Re à Karnak*; he became chief inspector of Upper Egypt 1972; he died in Cairo, 4 Sept. 1974.

Inf. from L. Manniche and J. C. Goyon; *BSFE* 70-1 (1974), 9; *JEA* 61 (1975), 4.

SAAD, Zaki Youssef (1901-1982)
Egyptian archaeologist; he was born in Mit Ghamr, Daqahliya Province, 13 Aug. 1901; he studied in his province and then at Cairo University, diploma, 1930; he was appointed assistant to the Mission Archéologique in Nubia, 1931-34 and then assisted Emery (q.v.) in his excavations at Saqqara, 1934-40; he became Director of Works at Saqqara, 1940-1 and then Chief Inspector of Saqqara and Giza, 1941 and a Keeper in the Cairo Museum, 1944; he carried out excavations at Saqqara, 1939-42, in the area between the Step Pyramid and the Unas causeway and near the Teti Pyramid; he also excavated extensively at Helwan, 1942-54 although his results are largely unpublished; he became Director of the Inspectorates of the Service, 1954-60; he took part in the Nubian campaign at Qustul in 1958; apart from his preliminary reports in *ASAE*, his published works include *The Tomb of Hemaka* (with W. B. Emery), 1938; *The Tomb of Hor-Aha* (with W. B. Emery), 1939; *Royal Excavations at Saqqara and Helwan*, 1947; *Royal Excavations at Helwan*, 1951; *Ceiling Stelae in the Second Dynasty Tombs*, 1957; *The Excavations at Helwan*, (with J. F. Autry), 1969; he died at Raleigh, North Carolina, USA, 18 Sept. 1982.

Grandes Découvertes, 5; *GM* 76 (1984), 86 (H. Attiatalla); *ASAE* 69 (1983), 379-80 (portr.) (L. Habachi); *Archaéonil* 17 (2007), 107-14 (E. Köhler).

SABATIER, Raymond Gabriel Baptiste (1810-1879)
French diplomat and collector; he was born in Béziers (Hérault), 11 Jan. 1810, son of Jean Baptiste S. and Marguerite Baptiste Crebassau; Attaché and later Captain in the Corps d'État Major; sent on a mission to the Morea, 1836; he visited the east including Egypt and Nubia, 1840-1; Consul-General for France in Egypt, 1852; minister plenipotentiary, 1862; resigned 1864; Commander of the Légion d'honneur, 1854; he had the Viceroy's permission to excavate in Egypt and was able to amass a large collection of antiquities for which a special gallery was constructed in his house, 35 Avenue Hoche, Paris; this collection was sold at Hôtel Drouot, Paris (31 March-4 April 1890) (615 lots); many items were acquired for the Ny Carlsberg Glyptotek in Copenhagen, but some went elsewhere (e.g. the stela BM, EA 656); a papyrus not in the sale, was later acquired by the Louvre in 1945 from his grandson the Comte de Jumilhac, after whom it was named (Louvre E 17110); he died in Paris, 12 Jan. 1879.

Inf. Comte de Jumilhac (grandson); *Bibl. Ég.* 18. p. xlix; Carré, i. 43; Lugt 48962; E. David, *Mariette Pacha 1821-1881*, 1994, 88, 96, 101.

SACHS, Curt (1881-1959)
German-American musicologist; born Berlin, 29 June 1881, son of Louis Eduard S., a manufacturer, and Anna Frohlich; he was educated at Berlin University, and appointed Professor of Musicology there; Curator of the Museum of Musical Instruments, Berlin, 1919-33; he went to America as Visiting Professor at New York University, 1937 and then worked in the New York Public Library; he became Professor at Columbia University from 1953 and then at the New York University from 1957; he was musical consultant to the Egyptian Government in Cairo, 1930; a world famous authority on ancient music and musical instruments, he wrote several books dealing with this subject, *Die Musikinstrumente des alten Aegyptens*, 1921; *Musik des Altertums,* 1924; *The Rise of Music in the Ancient World*, 1944; he died in New York, 5 Feb. 1959.

AfO 19 (1959-60), 271; *NDB* 22, 335-6.

SACK, (Sebastian) Albert (*Graf*) **von** (1757-1829)
German traveller; he was born in Eichholz, Liegnitz, Silesia in 1757 into a Prussian noble family; originally a baron, he was created count in 1821; he undertook voyages to Surinam, 1805-7 and again 1810-2; he travelled

to the Levant from 1818-20, visiting Egypt, Cyprus, and Greece; he was in Egypt, 1818-9, and obtained two Sakhmet statues from Belzoni (q.v.) which he later presented to the Berlin Museum; he later visited Mexico in 1824-5; he died in Berlin, 7 Aug. 1829.

H. Nehls, *Museums Journal (Berlin)* 15 (2001), 20-3.

SADEK, Abdel Aziz Fahmy (1933-1995)
Egyptian Egyptologist; he was born in Cairo, 24 March 1933, son of Fahmy Sadek and Ihsan Hassan Sabry; he studied at the University of Cairo, graduating in 1959 when he was employed in the Egyptian Antiquities Service; he first served at Tura al-Asmant and then at the Centre of Documentation as assistant Egyptologist, 1959-62; he later studied at Prague, 1962-3, and at Lyons under Barguet, 1973-6; PhD, 1976; he was in charge of the Centre's Documentation Section, 1965-70 and the Western Desert Project, 1964-93; Director of Publications, 1970-76 as well as of Scientific Affairs, 1976-82; Senior Egyptologist in 1983; Acting Director-General of the Centre, 1983-9; Director-General, 1989-93; he studied the papyri of the Amduat in Louvre in Paris, 1991; he taught at the University of Helwan and the University of Alexandria from 1980; he took part in archaeological work at Tura al-Asmant, 1959-60, the Nubian campaign where he copied many temple reliefs, western Thebes where he copied graffiti, 1969-89, and Dakhla, 1969-70, and the Valley of the Queens, 1986-89; he contributed to the following publications of the Collection Scientifique of the Centre, *Temple de Derr*, 1965; *Graffiti de la Montagne thébaine*, III, 1970-7, IV, 1970-83 and *Gerf Hussein*, II-IV, 1970-83 and published his thesis *Contribution à l'Étude de l'Amduat*, 1985; two volumes of studies in his memory were published in *Varia Aegyptiaca* 10/2-3 (1995) by C. C. Van Siclen III (ed.), *Iubilate Conlegae*, 1995 [1997]; he died in Cairo, 4 March 1995.

KMT 6 No. 2(1995), 2-3; *Memnonia* 6 (1995), 14-22 (portr.) (J. Goyon), 28-32 (bibl.) (G. Mokhtar); *Varia Aegyptiaca* 10/ 2-3, iii-x (portrs.) (C. Sheikholeslami), xi-xiii (A. Fakhry); xiv-xvi (bibl.) (C. Leblanc).

SAGAN, Jarosław John (1903-1979)
Polish naturalist, amateur archaeologist, and collector; in 1929-39 co-creator and custodian of the Regional Drohobycz Museum in Truskawiec; after the defeat of Sept. 1939, as a soldier, he was confined in Hungary from where in the middle of 1940 he reached the Polish army in Syria; during his stay in the Near East he collected historical, archaeological and zoological objects; his great passion was officially confirmed when the Field Museum No. 2 attached to the Independent Brigade of Carpathian Riflemen fighting in the Near East was created 20 May 1943, and he was named its curator; member of the Royal Naturalist Society in Egypt; shortly before the end of the war, he was sent to Egypt, where he enlarged his collection, through stray finds and purchases from his own salary from such Cairo dealers as Mohareb Zaki, Albert Eid (q.v.), E. A. Abemayor (q.v.) and in Luxor, Sayed Mollatam; he also contacted the authorities of the Egyptian Museum in Cairo, obtaining from there a considerable amount of material in part return for his conservator's services for the Museum, arranged by Hamza (q.v.); part of the collection was formed also by finds gathered during military fortification works in Heliopolis and in Abu Rawash; in 1947 the whole collection reached London from where the greater part went to Cracow in 1948; his archaeological and numismatic collection of about 3,000 specimens, together with the old collection and with items sent to Cracow in 1908 by Smolenski (q.v.), comprise the Cracow Archaeological Museum; only a part of this collection is published in volumes of *Materially Archeologiczne*, but the more important objects are exhibited in the Museum; he died in Cracow, 8 April 1979.

R. Wójcik, *Odmiency, Warsaw*, 1974, 210-245; *Materially Archeologiczne* XXI, 1981, 179-80 (M. Zaitz); J. Śliwa, *Scarabs,* 1985, 12-13.

el-SAGHIR, Mohamed (1939-2006)
Egyptian archaeologist; he was born in Sohag in 1939; he studied archaeology at Cairo University; BA, 1962; MA, 1976; he obtained his PhD from Assiut University, 1986; he joined the Antiquities Service and served as inspector at various sites notably Saqqara, Giza, and Helwan, 1963-73; he was promoted to Chief Inspector, East Delta in 1974 and Chief Inspector, Upper Egypt, 1974-78; he was appointed Director of Upper Egyptian Antiquities, 1979-84, then General Director of Upper Egyptian Antiquities, 1984-94, Head of the Central Directorate of Upper Egyptian Antiquities, 1994-97, and Head of the Pharaonic and Graeco-Roman Sector, 1997-2000; he served on several committees notably the Permanent Committee for Egyptian Antiquities of the Supreme Council of Antiquities and the Franco-Egyptian Centre for the Conservation of the Karnak Temple; he undertook excavations at Komir near Esna, 1979, Sohag and Luxor where he supervised the unearthing of the Luxor cache of statues, 1989; his publications included, with others, *Guide de Karnak*, 1989 and *Das Statuenversteck im Luxortempel*, 1992; English version, *The Discovery of the Statuary Cachette of Luxor Temple*, 1992; he died 30 July 2006.

Bulletin of the Egyptian Museum 5 (2008), 9-13 (Z. Hawass) (portr.) (bibl.).

ST. ASAPH, Viscount *see* **ASHBURNHAM**

SAINT-FERRIOL *see* **SIBEUD**

ST. JOHN, Bayle (1822-1859)
British author; he was born in Kentish Town, London, 19 Aug. 1822, son of the following; he visited Egypt in 1846 and 1851, and published *Adventures in the Lybian Desert and the Oasis of Jupiter Ammon*, 1849, new ed., 1853; he also wrote works on modern Egypt; he died in St. John's Wood, London, 1 Aug. 1859 and was buried in Kensal Green.

ODNB 48, 612; *DNB* 50, 128; Hilmy, ii, 204; Maspero, *Et. de Myth.* vi. 265.

ST. JOHN, James Augustus (1801-1875)
British author and traveller; he was born in Laugharne, Carmarthenshire, 24 Sept. 1801 as James John, son of Gelly John and Rachel William; he married Eliza Caroline Agar Hanzard, 1819, and was father of the above; he assisted James Silk Buckingham (q.v.) in the editorship of the *Oriental Herald*, 1824; he travelled extensively in Egypt and Nubia, mostly on foot, 1832-3; published *Egypt and Mohammed Ali*, 2 vols. 1834; *Egypt and Nubia*, 1845; he wrote the text of Prisse's *Oriental Album*, 1848; he died in London, 22 Sept. 1875 and was buried in Highgate Cemetery.

ODNB 48, 628-9; *DNB* 50, 145; Hilmy, ii, 204; Vyse, ii, 310.

SALLES, Eusèbe François (*Comte*) **de** (1796-1873)
French traveller; he was born in Montpellier, 16 Dec. 1796, son of Jacques de Salles and Marie Brunel; he studied medicine at Montpellier, graduating in 1816, and then oriental languages at the College de France; he became chief interpreter for the French army in Algeria, 1830-33; he was later appointed Professor of Arabic at Marseillies, 1835-67; he visited the Levant in 1837-9 including Egypt where he went up the Nile as far as the second cataract; he met there Pückler-Muskau (q.v.); he published *Peregrinations en Orient*, 1840; he died in Montpellier, 1 Jan. 1873.

Vapereau, *Dictionnaire Universel des Contemporains*, 5th ed., 1880, 1610-1; inf. M. Azim.

SALLIER, François (1764-1831)
French Revenue official and collector; he was born in 1764, son of Philippe S. and Lucrèce Lache; he lived at Aix-en-Provence, of which town he was Mayor, 1802-6; he rendered many important public services to his native town, but is remembered today for his collection of antiquities, now in the Aix Museum, and for five papyri, four of which, known as Sallier I-IV, are historic in the annals of Egyptology and were first studied by Champollion (q.v.) who twice visited Sallier, in July 1828 and Jan. 1830; these papyri were purchased by the British Museum in 1839 (EA 10181-2, 10184-5 and a demotic pap. 19226); objects from his collection were purchased for the Louvre in 1816 and the Musée Calvet, Avignon in 1833; he died in Aix, 20 Feb. 1831.

JEA 35 (1949), 160; M. P. Foissy-Aufrère, *Égypte et Provence*, 1985, 259-71.

SALT, Henry (1780-1827)
British diplomat and collector; he was born in Lichfield, 14 June 1780, son of Thomas S. and Alice Butt; he was trained as a portrait-painter and went to London in 1797 as a pupil of Joseph Farington, R.A., and afterwards of John Hoppner, RA; in 1802 he accompanied George Annesley, Visct. Valentia (q.v.), as secretary and draughtsman, on a long tour in the East, visiting India, Ceylon, Abyssinia, and Egypt, and returned 1806; he made many drawings to illustrate Lord V.'s *Voyages and Travels*, 1809; he was sent by the Govt. on a mission to Abyssinia, 1809-11, and published an account, *Voyage to Abyssinia*, 1814; in 1815 he was appointed to succeed Missett (q.v.) as British Consul-General in Egypt and arrived there in 1816; he carried out much excavation in Egypt with the intention of procuring antiquities for the British Museum, and in the process amassed enormous quantities on his own account; through Belzoni (q.v.) and Burckhardt (q.v.) he removed the colossal bust of Ramesses II from Thebes and presented it to the British Museum (EA 19), 1817; he employed Belzoni at Thebes and also financed his excavations in Nubia, and those of Caviglia (q.v.) at the Pyramids; in 1819, d'Athanasi (q.v.) excavated at Thebes under his direction; from 1818-21, he sent a large collection of antiquities to the British Museum, but the Trustees objected to the price demanded, and after protracted delay, they gave only £2,000 (less than the cost of excavation and transport) for the collection, but rejected the finest piece - the sarcophagus of Sety I - which was subsequently bought by Sir John Soane for his museum for £2,000; in private Salt attempted to place blame for the high excavation costs on Belzoni's extravagance; he had better luck with his second collection, formed 1819-24, which was reported upon

by Champollion (q.v.) and bought by the King of France for £10,000; his third collection was sold at Sotheby's 29 June-8 July 1835; it had been formed 1824-7, and was auctioned in 1,283 lots for £7,168; many objects were bought by the British Museum; an anonymous sale of Egyptian antiquities held at Sotheby's, 15-16 March 1833, has also been attributed to Salt's estate (258 lots); besides a rather tedious poem on the Nile, Salt published an *Essay on Dr. Young's and M. Champollion's Phonetic System of Hieroglyphics, with some additional discoveries*, etc., 1825; FRS, 1812; FLS; his papers and drawings are in the British Museum and the Griffith Institute, Oxford; he died at Desuke village near Alexandria, 30 Oct. 1827, and was buried in Alexandria.

Biogr. by J. J. Halls, 2 vols. 1834 (portr.); *DNB* 50, 212-13; *ODNB* 48, 749-50; *GM* 1835, ii, 187; Hilmy, ii. 208; References to Salt, many of them important, abound in the diaries and books of travel of his period; Minutoli, 16-17; *JEA* 2 (1915), 133-40 (H R H Hall) but rather unjust; Lugt 13273 and 14046; *Bulletin of the John Rylands University Library* 57 (1974-5), 69-91 (C. Bosworth); *Apollo*, 108, (1978) 224-31; C.E. Bosworth, *Bulletin of the John Rylands Library*, 57 (1974-5,) 69-91; D, Manley and P. Rée, *Henry Salt*, 2001; È. Gran-Aymerich, *Dictionnaire biographique d'archéologie 1798-1945*, 2001, incorporated in *Les Chercheurs de passé 1798-1945*, 2007, 1140-1; G. D. Scott in S. D'Auria (ed.), *Servant of Mut: Studies in Honor of Richard A. Fazzini*, 2007, 226-7 (on the 1833 sale); A. Bednarski in W. Carruthers (ed.), *Histories of Egyptology*, 2015, 86-7.

SALVOLINI, Francesco (1809-1838)
Italian orientalist; he was born in Faenza, 9 March 1809, son of Luigi D. and Luigia Bandini; he studied oriental languages at Bologna under Mezzofanti, and went to Paris in 1830 as a student of Champollion (q.v.); he visited Leiden to copy papyri, 1834; after Champollion's death certain important MSS of his were found to be missing, and an appeal was made for their return; it was eventually alleged that Salvolini had stolen them, and after his benefactor's death, published the discoveries contained in them as his own; a summary of the standard version of this episode will be found in the Introduction to Budge's *Egyptian Hieroglyphic Dictionary* (1920), pp. xxii-xxv, although it has also been suggested that this was not actually the case; his papers are preserved in the Bibliotheca Communale di Faenza; he published in his lifetime, *Campagne de Rhamsès le Grand (Sésostris) contre les Scheta et leurs alliés. MS. hiératique égyptien, appartenant à M. Sallier, à Aix en Provence, Notice sur ce manuscrit*, 1835; *Analyse grammaticale raisonnée de différents textes anciens égyptiens. Vol. i, Texte hiéroglyphique et démotique de la pierre de Rosette. Vol. ii. Plates*, 1836; also see *Papiers de Salvolini (sur l'Égypte) conservés dans la Bibl. Nationale, Paris*, 5 vols.; he died in Paris, 24 Feb. 1838.

A. Montanari, *Uomini Ilustri di Faenza*, vol, I, 1883, 167-76; *Enc. It.* 30, 589; Hartleben, see index; Hilmy, ii, 209; *Rev. d'Ég.* 39 (1988), 213-27; J. Kettel, *Jean-François Champollion le Jeune*, 1990, 212-5 (bibl.); A. Cassani, *Manfrediana* 22 (1987), 8-18, 23 (1989), 11-32, and 24 (1990), 26-43; F. Merletti, *Bolletino Società di studi storici faentini* 1 (2001), 20-7; F. Merletti, *Manfrediana* 35-6 (2001-2002), 49-54 and 38-9 (2004-2005), 3-12; F. Merletti, *Studi Piemontesi* 32 (2003), 137-43; F. Merletti *Gott. Misz.* 208 (2006), 57-73 (suggesting S. took MSS with Champollion's knowledge); F. Merletti, *Francesco Salvolini da Faenza a Parigi*, 2011.

SAMS, JOSEPH (1784-1860)
British bookseller and antiquities dealer; he was born in Wellington, Somerset, 26 Feb. 1784, son of Joseph S. and his wife Esther, Quakers; he settled in Darlington where he opened a school, but soon closed it and opened a bookseller's shop; he visited Egypt and Palestine, 1832-3, and brought back a valuable collection of antiquities, many of which were purchased by the British Museum with a Parliamentary grant of £2,500 in 1834; among these were many papyri and the coffin of Amau (EA 6654); his remaining collections augmented by purchases at the Salt sale, 1835 and from Charles Bogaert of Bruges, were exhibited in London and a catalogue issued; many important items were bought by Joseph Mayer (q.v.) of Liverpool; Sams also dealt in MSS, and many famous specimens passed through his hands, including a number in Coptic, purchased by the British Museum; his books, pictures, tapestries, and other antiquities were sold at Puttick & Simpson's in two sales, 2-3 Nov. 1860, and 18 Feb. 1861; he died in Darlington, 18 March 1860.

ODNB 48, 807; *DNB* 50, 236-7; Athanasi, 127; Edwards, *Lives of the Founders*, 34; *GM* 1833, 103, pt. 1, 312-14; Hilmy ii, 209; Lugt 25779 (second sale not in Lugt); N. Penney in *The Journal of the Friends Historical Society* 20 (1923), 24-7; E. Milligan, *Biographical Dictionary of British Quakers in Commerce and Industry 1775-1920*, 2007, 387.

SAMSON, Julia Ellen (née Lazarus) (1910-2002)
British archaeologist; she was born in Perth, Western Australia, 7 June 1909, daughter of Emanual Lazarus and Esther Hallé; she visited Egypt with her family en route to London where they later settled; she studied under Glanville (q.v.) at University College London, 1933-36; Diploma in Archaeology, 1936; she took part in Pendelbury's (q.v.) excavations at Amarna, 1936; she later joined the civil service as a press officer in the Ministries of Food and Health; on retirement she worked at the Petrie Museum from 1967 as Hon Research Assistant to catalogue the finds from Amarna; she joined the Egypt Exploration Society in 1924 inspired by the discovery of the tomb of Tutankhamun and was its oldest member at her

death; she served on its committee 1948-9; she published a chapter in Pendelbury's *City of Akhenaten* III, 1951; *Amarna: City of Akhenaten and Nefertiti:Key Pieces in the Petrie Museum*, 1972, rev. 1978, and *Nefertiti and Cleopatra*, 1985; she died in London, 6 April 2002.

Friends of the Petrie Museum Newsletter 25 (2002), 6 (portr.) (H. Smith).

SANDER-HANSEN, Constantin Emil (1905-1963)
Danish Egyptologist; born Lillerod, 13 Nov. 1905, son of Hans Peter Alfred H. and Constantia Emilié Sander; he studied under H. O. Lange (q.v.) at Copenhagen; as a young man he was chosen by K. Sethe (q.v.) to act as assistant in the great project of publishing all the Pyramid Texts, and after Sethe's death in 1934 was entrusted by the Commission with the work of bringing out all the as yet unpublished commentaries based on Sethe's notes; the last two vols. appeared in 1962 only just before Sander-Hansen's own death; in 1937 he gained his PhD at the University of Copenhagen with a thesis devoted to the inscriptions on the sarcophagus of the Divine Adoratrice of Amun, Ankhnesneferibre; he succeeded to Lange's chair, 1946, and was editor of *Acta Orientalia*; he also directed the Egyptological Institute attached to the university; his main published work was in the field of philology, *Historische Inschriften der 19. Dynastie*, in the *Bibl. Aeg.* series, 1933; *Das Gottesweib des Amun*, 1940; *Studien zur Grammatik der Pyramidentexte*, 1956; *Die Texte der Metternichstele*, 1956; *Über die Bildung der Modi im altägyptischen*, 1941; *Ägyptische Grammatik*, 1962; he died in Copenhagen, Frederiksberg, 31 Jan. 1963.

Acta Orientalia, 27 (1963), 75-7 (W. Erichsen); *Chron. d'Ég.* 38 (1963), 113-15 (B. van de Walle); *AfO* 21 (1966), 268-9 (H. Brunner); *Det Kongelige Danske Videnskasomhed*, 1962-3 (Copenhagen 1963), 1-11 (W. Erichsen); *Jahrbuch der Bayerischen Akad. der Wissenschaften*, 1963 (Munich 1963), 213-15 (H. W. Müller); *Dansk Biografisk Leksikon* 12, 609-10 (T. Holm-Rasmussen).

SANDFORD, Kenneth Stuart (1899-1971)
British geologist and prehistorian; he was born at Gravesend, 9 Dec. 1899, son of Horatio S., a marine engineer, and Lizzie Adlington; he was educated at University College, Oxford; BA, 1923; MA, 1925; DSc, 1934; he undertook geological research in the Nile Valley, 1925-33 for the British School of Archaeology in Egypt and the University of Chicago and in Libya, 1932; University Demonstrator in Pleistocene Geology, Oxford, 1927; and in Geology, 1935; Reader, 1948; Fellow of the Geological Society of London, 1924; Council Memb., 1943-7, 1950-4; Fellow of the Royal Geographical Society, 1932; Council Memb., 1934-7, 1939-41, 1962-66; Vice-Pres., 1967-71; editor of Geologists' Assoc., 1945-51, 1968-71; he published *First Report of the Prehistoric Surevey Expedition*, with Arkell (q.v.), 1928; *Palaeolithic Man and the Nile- Faiyum Divide*, 1928; *Palaeolithic Man and the Nile Valley in Nubia and Upper Egypt*, 1933; *Palaeolithic Man and the Nile Valley in Upper and Middle Egypt*, 1934; *Palaeolithic Man and the Nile Valley in Lower Egypt*, 1939; he died in Oxford, 18 Nov. 1971.

WWW VII, 702; *Proceedings of the Geologists' Association* 83 (1972), 117-9.

SANDYS, George (1578-1644)
British traveller and antiquarian; he was born at Bishopthorpe Palace, York, 2 March 1578, seventh and youngest son of Edwin Sandys, Archbishop of York, and Cicely Wilford; he matriculated at St. Mary Hall, Oxford, 1589, later at Corpus Christi, but does not appear to have taken a degree; he went on an extended tour, 1610, visiting France, Italy and spending a year in Turkey, Egypt, and Palestine; he returned via Rome and published an account of his travels, *The Relation of a Journey begun An. Dom. 1610, in Four Books*, 1615; in this Sandys quoted the classical authors and stated that the medieval tradition that the pyramids were built by the Jews was wrong, and also that they were not the granaries of Joseph, but the burial places of Egyptian kings, citing the tradition of the soul returning to the preserved body after a period of 36,000 years; his estimate of the Great Pyramid base as a square of eight acres was much too small and his general description although better than many others of the period is most inadequate when compared with that of Greaves (q.v.); he also confused the Tura quarries with the Trojans whom he thought lived there as captives, but he climbed the Cheops pyramid and gave a graphic description of the interior as well as an account of the second and third pyramids at Giza; Sandys was also a poet and his verse written after a visit to the holy sepulchre at Jerusalem influenced Milton; he later became interested in colonial expansion and was connected with Virginia and the Bermudas Company; he went to America in 1621 and acquired a plantation, but returned to England after various quarrels; he continued to write and be a courtier until his death at Boxley Abbey, near Maidstone, 1644, buried 7 March at Boxley; his papers eventually went to the Ashmolean Museum with the Tradescant collection.

ODNB 48, 929-32 (portr.); *DNB* 50, 290; Vyse, *Operations carried on at the pyramids of Gizeh in 1837*, vol. ii; R. B. Davis, *George Sandys, Poet-Adventurer*, 1955.

SAN QUINTINO *see* **CORDERO DI SAN QUINTINO**

SANTONI, Pietro (*fl.* 1820-1830)
Italian banker; he was from Leghorn and brother-in-law to Henry Salt (q.v.); he negotiated the sale of Salt's second collection to the French Govt., in 1825; he met Champollion (q.v.) in Alexandria in 1828.

Champollion, i, 239 and passim; ii, 22, 37; Salt, ii, 250 etc.

SAULCY, Louis Félicien Joseph Caignart de (1807-1880)
French museum keeper and numismatist; he was born in Lille, 19 March 1807, son of Félicien Joseph C. de S. and Marie Rose Suzanne Liaubon; Keeper of the Artillery Museum, Paris, 1840; Senator, 1854; Member of the Acad.; he wrote many important numismatic works, also wrote on ancient Egyptian language, especially Demotic; he travelled in Egypt in 1863 and 1869, the MS journal of these voyages is in the library of the Inst. Fr. (2259-63); he died in Paris, 4 Nov. 1880

CRAIBL ser. 4, 9 (1881), 331-70 (bibl.) (H. Wallon); Brugsch, *Mein Leben*, 54 88, 91; Hilmy, i, 180; Larousse, *XXᵉ siècle* 6. 206; F. Bassan, *L. F. Caignart de Saulcy-Carnets de Voyage*, 1955; *F. de Saulcy et la Terre Sainte*, 1982; Gaillardot Bey, *BIE*, 2e série, II (1881); *Archeologia*, 220 (1987), 65-75; *ibid.*, 222 (1987), 14; È. Gran-Aymerich, *Dictionnaire biographique d'archéologie 1798-1945*, 2001, incorporated in *Les Chercheurs de passé 1798-1945*, 2007, 1143-6.

SAULNIER, Sébastien Louis (1790-1835)
French collector and antiquarian; he was born in Nancy, 29 Jan. 1790, son of Pierre Dieudonné Louis S., prefect and Marie Lacratelle; he held several prefectures, including that of Tarn-et-Garonne 1815, l'Aude 1815, Mayenne 1830-1, and Loiret 1831-35; he was also briefly prefect of Police 1830-1; he financed explorations in Egypt and imported antiquities; he sent Lelorrain (q.v.) to take down and bring to Paris the Circular Zodiac of Dendera, now in the Louvre, and hoped that his Egyptian collections would be acquired for this museum; but at the sale in Paris in 1839, most of them were acquired by Berlin; he published works on roads and railways and an account of the Lelorrain expedition, *Notice sur le voyage de M. Lelorrain en Égypte: et observations sur le Zodiaque circulaire de Dendérah*, 1822; he died in Saint-Jean-de-la-Ruelle, 23 Oct. 1835.

Champollion, i, 6, 11; ii, 155; Hartleben, i, 395, 547; ii, 473; Hilmy, ii, 213; Larousse 14, 263; 263; J. Z. Buchwald and D. G. Josefowicz, *The Zodiac of Paris*, 2010, passim; sale not in Lugt.

SAUNERON, Serge Louis Charles (1927-1976)
French Egyptologist; he was born in Paris, 3 Jan. 1927, son of Fernand S. and Paule Wolber; he was educated at the Lycée Henri IV and the École Normale Supérieure; he became interested in Egyptology in 1941 and in 1949 he went to Egypt with Montet (q.v.) as his photographer; he was attached to the French Institute in Cairo where he made his career; pensionnaire 1950-61; director of excavations 1961; librarian 1962-7; secretary-general 1967-9 and finally Director 1969-76; he was also co-director of the Centre Franco-Égyptien de Karnak from 1967; Corresponding Member of the Académie des Inscriptions et Belles-Lettres and Member of the Institut d'Égypte; he was interested in all phases of Egyptian culture but concentrated on the publication of hieratic texts and the excavation and publication of the Esna temple; he initiated the publication of the accounts of the early European travellers to Egypt; his bibliography covers over two hundred books and articles; his monographs included *Rituel de l'embaumement*, 1952; *Les prêtres de l'ancienne Égypte*, 1957; English ed., 1960; *Catalogue des ostraca hiératiques non littéraires de Deir el-Médineh (nos. 550-623)*, 1959; *Quatres campagnes à Esna (Esna I)*, 1959; *Les fêtes religieuses d'Esna aux derniers siècles du paganisme* (Esna V), 1962; *Le Temple d'Esna (Esna II)*, 1963; *Nous partons pour l'Égypte*, 1965; *Le Temple d'Esna (Esna III)*, 1968; *L'Égyptologie*, 1968; *Le Temple d'Esna (nos. 399-472) (Esna IV/1)*, 1969; *Le papyrus magique illustré de Brooklyn*, 1970; *Annuaire de l'Égyptologie*, with P. Derchain, 1971; *Les ermitages chrétiens du desert d'Esna*, vols. 1-2 with J. Jacquet, vol. 4, 1972; *Villes et légendes d'Égypte, 1974*, 2nd ed. 1983; *Travaux de l'Institut français d'archéologie orientale 1969-1974*, 1974; *Le temple d'Esna (nos. 473-546) (Esna VI/1)*, 1975; *Edfou et Philae, derniers temples d'Égypte*, with H. Stierlin, 1975; *L Écriture figurative dans les textes d'Esna (Esna VIII)*, 1982; *La Porte ptolémaique de l'enceinte de Mout à Karnak*, 1983; and *Un traité égyptien d'ophiologie*, 1989; he also edited and introduced vols. 1-4, 6, 10 and 11 in his series *Voyageurs occidentaux en Égypte*, 1970-4; a two volume collection of studies was published in his memory, 1979; he was killed in an automobile accident on the Cairo to Alexandria road, 3 June 1976.

BIFAO 77 (1977), 1-21 (bibl.) (portr.) (J. Yoyotte); *AfO* 25 (1974-7), 351 (H. Brunner); *Aegyptus* 56 (1976), 295-6 (E. Bresciani); *BSFE* 76 (1976), 3-4; *WWF* 1973-4, 1458; inf. L. Marucchi.

SAUVAJOL, Henri (*d.* 1860)
French commissariat official in Algeria; he communicated to Devéria (q.v.) some Egyptian antiquities discovered in Algeria; died 1860.

Devéria, *Mém. et Fragm.* i. 143.

SAVARY, Claude Etienne (1750-1788)
French orientalist and traveller; he was born at Vitré in 1750 and was educated at the College in Rennes; he visited Egypt, 1777-9, as part of the Tott (q.v.) mission and wrote enthusiastically about the country; accompanied in part by Adanson (q.v.), he appears only to have visited Lower Egypt but gives the impression that he visited Upper Egypt when in fact his account of that area is based on previous travellers notably a French officer Chevalier; he published his travels *Lettres sur l'Egypte*, 1785-6; *Vie de Mahomet*, 1783, *Morale de Mahomet*, 1784, and posthumously *Grammaire arabe*, 1813; he died in Paris, 4 Feb. 1788.

Biographie Universelle 38, 108-9; Carré i, 80-104; Lamy, 221-4; È. Gran-Aymerich, *Dictionnaire biographique d'archéologie 1798-1945*, 2001, incorporated in *Les Chercheurs de passé 1798-1945*, 2007, 1149.

SÄVE-SÖDERBERGH, Torgny (1914-1998)
Swedish Egyptologist; he was born in Lund, 14 June 1914, son of Professor Gotthard Soderbergh and Inga Säve; he studied Egyptology at the Universities of Uppsala and Göttingen; PhD, Uppsala, 1941; he took part in the Swedish excavation at Abu Ghalib in 1935; during World War II, he served as a Red Cross delegate in Greece from 1943; he was appointed Professor at the University of Uppsala, 1950-80; he undertook the publication of Theban tombs begun by N. de Garis Davies (q.v.) and completed two field seasons in Egypt; he was Swedish delegate to the UNESCO Executive Committee in charge of the Nubian rescue campaign, 1962-80, and served as field director of the Scandinavian Joint Expedition to Sudanese Nubia, 1961-4; he later edited the eleven volumes of publications completed in 1991; he also served as field director in 1975 of the expedition recording the tombs of the Nag Hammadi necropolis; he was a member of the committee which accomplished the publication of the Nag Hammadi Codices, 1970-83; he was President of the International Association of Egyptologists, 1976-82, and of the Royal Swedish Academy of Letters, History and Antiquities, 1978-84; Hon. President of the International Association for Coptic Studies and the Association of Nubian Studies; Corresponding member of the Académie des Inscriptions et Belles-Lettres, 10 March 1979; a volume of essays edited by R. Holthoer and T. Linders, *Sundries in honour of Torgny Säve-Söderbergh* was published in 1984; apart from many articles, his principal publications were his thesis *Ägypten und Nubien*, 1941; *Einige ägyptische Denkmäler in Schweden*, 1945; *The Navy of the XVIIIth Egyptian Dynasty*, 1946; *Studies in the Coptic Manichean Psalm Book*, 1949; *On Egyptian Representations of Hippopotamus Hunting as a Religious Motive*, 1953; *Four Eighteenth Dynasty Tombs*, 1957; *Faroner och människor*, 1958; translated as *Pharaohs and Mortals*, 1963; *The Scandinavian Joint Expedition to Sudanese Nubia*, 1979; with G. Englund and H.-A. Nordstrom, *The Scandinavian Joint Expedition to Sudanese Nubia. Vol. 6. Late Nubian Cemeteries*, 1981; *Temples and Tombs of Ancient Nubia*, 1987; with L. Troy, *The Scandinavian Joint Expedition to Sudanese Nubia. Vols. 5.2-3. New Kingdom Pharaonic Sites*, 1991; *The Old Kingdom Cemetery at Hamradom (El-Qasr wa es-Saiyad)*, 1994; he died in Uppsala, 21 May 1998.

IAE Internet obituary (L. Troy); *AEB* 1995, viii; *CRAIBL* 1998, 457-8 (G. Le Rider); *Vem Ar Det*, 1995, 1079.

SAVILE, (*Revd*) **Bourchier Wrey** (1817-1888)
British clergyman and author; he was born in London, 11 March 1817, son of Albany S. and Elizabeth Wrey; he entered Westminster School in 1828, scholar, 1831; Emmanuel College, Cambridge, 1835; BA, 1839, MA, 1842; he married Mary Elizabeth Whyte, 1842; while holding various appointments in Devonshire he wrote over 40 books in all; see *Anglo-Israelism and the Great Pyramid*, 1880, which exposed fallacies of the theory of the Jewish origin of the English; also *Israel in Egypt*, 1864, a study relating the monuments to the sojourn in Egypt; *Egypt's Testimony to Sacred History*, 1866, and theological works; he died in Shillingford, 14 April 1888.

ODNB 49, 98-9; *DNB* 50, 355-6; Hilmy, ii, 215.

SAWI, Ahmad Abdel-Qader el- (1932-2017)
Egyptian Egyptologist; he was born in Warakel Hadar, Imbaba, Giza, 12 May 1932, son of Abdel-Qader el-Sawi, a local mayor; he studied Egyptology at Ain Shams University; BA, 1957, and later at Charles University, Prague under Hintze (q.v.); PhD, 1978; he first joined the Antiquities Service as inspector, later chief inspector, director of the Technical Office, director of Documentation, and director of Excavations and Inspectorates, rising to become Undersecretary of State for the Egyptian Archaeology Section and a member of the Permanent Committee; he left the service to become lecturer in the Department of Egyptology at the University of Sohag, 1979; assistant

professor, 1983; professor, 1988-92; head of dept., 1989, dean of the faculty, 1990; he became dean of Al-Alsun Institute of Tourism, 1993; he also taught at the Universities of Asyut and of Tanta; he was a consultant at the Tutankhamun exhibition in Chicago, 1977; he undertook excavations in Nubia at Qustul and Ballana, 1962-4, at Tell Basta, 1964-71, and Kom Abu Billo, 1971-5 and at the temple of Sety I at Abydos; a volume of essays in his honour was edited by K. Daoud and S. Abd el-Fatah, *The World of Ancient Egypt*, 2007; he published *Excavations at Tell Basta: Report of Seasons 1967-71*, 1979; he died 30 Sept. 2017.

K. Daoud and S. Abd el-Fatah (eds.), *The World of Ancient Egypt*, 1979, 10-8 (Z. Hawass) (portr.), 14-5 (bibl.); *Pražské Egyptologické Studie* 19 (2017), 84-6 (Z. Hawass), 87-9 (M. Verner); inf. H. Bassir.

SAXONY (*Prince of*), **Johann Georg Pius Karl Leopold Maria Januarius Anacletus** (1869-1938)
German prince; he was born at Dresden, 10 July 1869, son of King Georg of Saxony and Infanta Maria Anna of Portugal; he was educated privately to 1881 and then undertook military training; he studied law at the University of Freiburg, 1889-90 and then history and art at the University of Leipzig; Hon. PhD, 1909; he was a well-known art collector whose collection included objects from ancient Egypt; he published *Streifzüge durch die Kirchen und Klöster Ägyptens*, 1914; he died at Schloss Altshausen, 24 Nov. 1938.

B. Heide and B. Thiem, *Sammler-Pilger-Wegbereiter. Die Sammlung des Prinzen Johann Georg von Sachsen*, 2004; inf. Dr. K. Konrad.

SAYCE, (*Revd***) Archibald Henry** (1845-1933)
British Assyriologist; he was born in Shirehampton, Gloucs., 25 Sept. 1845, son of Revd Henry Samuel S., vicar of Shirehampton, and Mary Anne Cartwright; he was educated at Grosvenor Coll. Bath and The Queen's Coll. Oxford; Professor of Assyriology, University of Oxford, 1891-1919; DLitt; LLD; DD; Hon. FBA; member of the OT Revision Company, 1874-84; Hibbert Lecturer, 1887; Gifford Lecturer, 1900-2; Rhind Lecturer, 1906; Huxley Lecturer, 1931; he did important and pioneer work on the Carian script and on the Hittite language and texts; he published many books and studies in the field of Assyrian and Western Asian archaeology and philology; although not an Egyptologist he was intimately connected with Egypt for over half a century, and travelled extensively in Egypt where he spent many winters in his own boat on the Nile, copying inscriptions etc.; he had a wide circle of friends among Egyptologists and published his interesting *Reminiscences* in 1923; the following relate to Egypt, *The Ancient Empires of the East*, 1884; *The Egypt of the Hebrews and Herodotos,* 1895; *Egyptian and Babylonian Religion*, 1903; *Aramaic papyri discovered at Assuan*, 1906; he also edited *Murray's Handbook to Egypt*, 1896; his papers are in the Griffith Institute, Oxford; he bequeathed his library to The Queen's College, Oxford, and his collections of Egyptian antiquities and Oriental ceramics to the Ashmolean Museum; he died in Bath, 4 Feb. 1933.

Budge, *R & P,* 185 (portr.); *DNB* 1931-40, 786-88; *ODNB* 49, 158-60; *JEA* 19 (1933), 65-6 (F. Ll. Griffith); autobiogr., *Reminiscences*, 1923 (portr.); *WWW* iii, 120; P. Ward in *KMT* 10/3 (1999), 79-83.

SAYED, Abdel Moneim Abdel Halim (1926-2011)
Egyptian Egyptologist; he worked as a teacher in Somalia, 1957 and in Yemen, 1959; he studied at the University of Alexandria, MA, 1968; PhD, 1973; he then joined the staff of the History Dept., University of Alexandria; he carried out excavations at Wadi Gawasis on the Red Sea, 1976-7, discovering an Egyptian port of the Middle Kingdom; he published a number of articles about his discoveries in *Rev d'Ég* 29 (1977), 138-78 ; *JEA* 64 (1978), 69-71; *JEA* 66 (1980), 154-7; and *Chron. d'Ég*, 58 (1983), 23-37; The *Festschrift* Volume of Abdel Moneim Sayed was published in 2006; he died in 2011.

BSFE 180 (2011), 2.

SCAMUZZI, Ernesto (1899-1974)
Italian Egyptologist; he was born in Rome, 1899; following his Egyptological studies during which he wrote a thesis on the Pyramid Texts, he joined the staff of the Turin Museum in 1929; he was transferred to Florence in 1939 and then appointed Director of the Museo Egizio in 1943 in succession to Farina (q.v.), holding the post until 1964; he was responsible for the restoration of the Museum after World War II; his principal publications were *La Mensa Isiaca*, 1939; *Museo Egizio di Torino*, 1964; he died in Turin, 21 July 1974.

Aegyptus 54 (1974), 203-5 (bibl.) (S. Curto).

SCHACK-SCHACKENBURG, (*Count*) **Hans** (1852-1905)
German Egyptologist; he was born in Schackenburg, 12 Dec. 1852, son of Count Otto Dietrich S-S., a large landowner, and Friederike Rosine Juliane von Kragh; he took over the management of his paternal estates as the age of 21; educated at the Universities of Dresden and Göttingen; he devoted all his leisure to Egyptology in which he was self-taught, but was not a mere amateur, for all his work was thorough and scholarly; his first publications date from 1883, and he devoted special attention to the Pyramid Texts of which he coordinated and numbered the sections (*ZÄS* 42, 87); he served on the *Wörterbuch* Commission from 1898, and collated many mathematical and astronomical texts, as well as the mythological texts in the Tombs of the Kings; in later years, he was confined by a long illness, but continued to work to the end; he published *Aegyptologische Studien*, 1902; *Das Buch von den zwei Wegen des seligen Toten (Zweiwegebuch)*, 1903; his collection was sold in Aarhus in Sept. 1992; he died in Schackenburg, 28 Jan. 1905.

EEF *Arch. Rep.* 1905-6, 51; *ZÄS* 42, 87.

SCHADEN, Otto John (1937-2015)
American Egyptologist; he was born 26 Aug. 1937, son of John S. and his wife Irma, originally from Austria; he was educated at the University of Illinois, 1955-7, the Oriental Institute of the University of Chicago, 1957-66; BA, 1959; MA, 1966; and finally the University of Minnesota, 1966-77; PhD, 1977 with a thesis on the God's Father Ay; he was a teaching assistant at the same university, 1968-75, a lecturer at Minneapolis College of Art, 1977 and at the University of Minnesota, 1979; he became a research fellow at its computer centre, 1979-80 and Hon. Fellow of the Center for Ancient Studies, University of Minnesota, 1983-7; he was appointed adjunct Professor at the University of Memphis, 1995-2006; he took part in the University of Chicago expedition to Nubia, 1962-3 and its expedition to Sudan, 1963-4; he undertook work at Karnak, 1971, 1978 and 1984, 1985-6 and at Giza under Goedicke (q.v.), 1974; he excavated in the Valley of the Kings, 1972-2015, clearing KV23 (Tomb of Ay), KV24-5, and from 1992-2001, 2003-15 KV10 (Tomb of Amenmesse); he discovered KV63 in 2005 and cleared it, 2006-10; he only published preliminary articles about his discoveries; he died in Chicago, 23 Nov. 2015.

KMT 27 (2016), 18-20 (portr.), 20-1 (bibl.) (E. Ertman).

SCHÄFER, (Johann) Heinrich (1868-1957)
German Egyptologist; born in Berlin, 29 Oct. 1868, son of Heinrich S., a merchant, and Auguste Eichelkraut; he studied classical philology and later Egyptology under Erman (q.v.), 1887; he then worked on Papyrus Ebers; PhD, 1892; he was appointed to a post in the Berlin Egyptian Museum, becoming Acting Director, 1909 and Director, 1914-35; from this time on Schäfer was responsible for a great amount of reorganization and cataloguing of this great collection; on his first visit to Egypt with Ulrich Wilcken (q.v.) they found a papyrus at Ihnasya, 1899; Schäfer assisted at the excavation of Niuserre's sun temple and with Junker's (q.v.) survey of Philae, collecting Nubian Texts; on the philological side he worked on texts of the Ethiopian period and those in the Berlin Museum, and with Junker on texts in the Kenzi dialect; he also published the Coptic Cambyses story; he was a corresponding member of the Gesellschaft der Wissenschaften, Göttingen, and an hon. member of the Russian Institute of Art History, Leningrad, a corresponding member of the Commission of the Royal Belgian Museum, and the Vienna Akad. der Wissenschaften; his list of works is a very large one, 212 nos. in the bibl. of 1938, and covers the fields of Egyptian art, archaeology and philology; *Commentationes de papyro medicinali Lipsiensi*, (Pap. Ebers), 1892; *Aeg. Abteilung Amtliche Berichte aus den König. Kunstsammlungen*, 1895-1907; *Die äthiopische Königsinschrift des Berliner Museums*, 1901; *Grab- und Denksteine des Mittleren Reichs im Museum von Kairo*, with H. O. Lange, 1902-25; *Ein Bruchstück altägyptischer Annalen*, with L. Borchardt and K. Sethe, on the Palermo stone, 1902; *Die Lieder eines ägyptischen Bauern*, 1903; *Die altägyptischen Prunkgefässe mit aufgesetzten Randverzierungen*, on the art of the goldsmith, 1903; *Die Mysterien des Osiris in Abydos unter König Sesostris III* (Ikhernofret stela), 1904; *Urkunden der älteren Äthiopenkönige*, 1905; *Priestergräber und andere Grabfunde vom Ende des Alten Reiches bis zur griechischen Zeit vom totentempel des Ne-user-rê*, 1908; *Ägyptische Goldschmiedearbeiten*, with G. Möller and W. Schubart, 1910; *Aegyptische Inschriften aus den Königlichen Museen zu Berlin*, pt. i, *Inschriften von der ältesten Zeit bis zum Ende der Hyksoszeit*, 1913; *Ägyptische Kunst*, 1913; *Nubische Texte im Dialekte der Kunûzi*, 1917; *Von ägyptischer Kunst, besonders der Zeichenkunst*, 1919, 1922; *Die Religion und Kunst von El-Amarna*, 1923; *Die Kunst des alten orients*, with W. Andrae, 1925; *Ägyptische und heutige kunst und Weltgebäude der alten Ägypter*, 1928; *Das altägyptische Bildnis*, 1936; he died in Hessisch-Lichtenau, 6 April 1957.

Almanach der Österreichischen Akad. der Wissenschaften, 107, Vienna (1957), 357-62 (H. Junker); *AfO* 18, 1st pt. (1957), 225-6 (portr.) (H. Brunner); *ZÄS* 75 (1939), 1-16 (bibl.); 82 (1957), i-iv (W. Wolf); *NDB* 22, 507-8;

Wer ists's 1935; T. Gertzen, *Boote, Burgen, Bischarin,* 2014; S. Voss Kern, *ZÄS* 143 (2016), 244-52; S. Peuckert, *ZÄS* 144 (2017), 108-38; M. Eaton-Krauss, *Gött. Misz.* 253 (2017), 11-14

SCHARFF, Alexander (1892-1950)
German Egyptologist; he was born in Frankfurt, 26 Feb. 1892, son of Julius S., a merchant, and Caroline Fellner; he was educated in Halle and in Berlin under Erman (q.v.) and Sethe (q.v.); PhD, 1920; Habilitation from the University of Halle, 1928; he was appointed Assistant Professor of Egyptology in the University of Munich, 1923; Professor, 1932-50; he was interested in literary, religious, and philosophical texts and began to publish works in these fields, but later turned to what were his main specialities, predynastic and archaeological subjects; he was interested in Egyptian chronology and stressed in his books the synchronisms with Western Asia; he reduced Meyer's date for the accession of Menes and the foundation of a united Egypt to *c.*3000 BC which has found a wide acceptance among historians but is also rejected by others; Scharff wrote over 200 publications in all, the most important were, *Aegyptische Sonnenlieder. Übersetzt und eingeleitet von A. S.,* 1922; completed and brought out G. Möller's *Die archaeologischen Ergebnisse des vorgeschichtlichen Gräberfeldes von Abusir el-Meleq,* 1926; *Grundzüge der ägyptischen vorgeschichte,* 1927; *Die Altertümer der Vor- und Frühzeit Ägyptens,* 2 pts., 1929, 1931; *Ägyptologische Forschungen,* fol. 1936; *Der historische Abschnitt der Lehre für König Merikarê,* 1936; *Der Bericht über das Streitgespräch eines Lebensmüden mit seiner Seele,* trans. of the hieratic text with commentary, 1937; *Einführung in die ägyptische Rechtsgeschichte bis zum Ende des neuen Reiches,* with Erwin Seidl, fol. 1939; *Die frühkulturen Ägyptens und Mesopotamiens, Ein Vortrag, etc.,* 1941; *Archäologische Beiträge zur Frage der Entstehung der Hieroglyphenschrift,* 1942; *Wesensunterschiede ägyptischer und vorderasiatischer Kunst. Ein Vortrag, etc.,* 1943; *Das Grab als Wohnhaus in der ägyptischen Frühzeit, etc.,* 1947; *Ägypten und Vorderasien im Altertum,* with A. Moortgat, 1950; also articles in *ZÄS* and other journals; some of his papers are in the Griffith Institute, Oxford; he died in Munich, 12 Nov. 1950.

AfO 15 (1945-51), 186-7 (H. Stock); *JEA* 37 (1951), 2; Kürschner, 1950, 1759; *ZÄS* 79 (1954), x-xvi (portr.) (H. Stock); *ZDMG* 101 (Neue Folge 26, 1951), 11-14 (portr.) (R. Anthes); E. Endesfelder, *Die Ägyptologie an der Berliner Universität-Zur Geschichte eines Fachgebietes,* 1988, 26-7.

SCHAYES, Antoine Guillaume Bernard (1808-1859)
Belgian collector; he was born in Louvain, 11 Jan. 1808, son of Lambert S., an architect, and Jeanne Marie Gabrielle de Barneige; he studied at the University of Louvain; he became archivist of Flanders , Jan. 1843 and curator of the Museé Royal d'Artillerie, d'Armures et d'Antiquités in Brussels, later Musées Royaux, March 1847; Member of the Académie royale des Sciences, Lettres et des Beaux-Arts; he bought many lots at the Anastasi sale in 1857 and his own collection was sold in Brussels 6-8 Dec. 1859 when pieces were acquired by Otreppe (q.v.) and Meester de Ravenstein (q.v.); he died in Ixelles, 8 Jan. 1859.

Biographie Nationale de Belgique 21, 1911-3; E. Warmenbol, *La Caravane du Caire,* 2006, 103-5.

SCHEIL, (*Père*) **Jean Vincent** (1858-1940)
French Assyriologist; he was born in Königsmacker, Lorraine, 10 June 1858, son of Pierre S. and Catherine Jaminet; in his early career he studied Egyptology in Paris under Maspero (q.v.), 1887-9 and joined the Mission Arch. at Cairo, 1890-2; he was mainly employed in copying Theban tombs, some of which he published in *Mém. Miss. Arch.* t. 5; he then concentrated on Assyriology and became eminent in that field, spending the rest of his life in it; he died in Paris, 21 Sept. 1940.

AfO 13, 353; Budge, *R & P,* 215 (portr.); *Orientalia* N.S. 11. 80 (bibl.); *Rev. d'Assyr.* 37. 81; *Syria* 21 (1940), 361; È. Gran-Aymerich, *Dictionnaire biographique d'archéologie 1798-1945,* 2001, incorporated in *Les Chercheurs de passé 1798-1945,* 2007, 1153-4.

SCHENCKE, Johann Friederich Wilhelm (1869-1946)
Norwegian orientalist; he was born in Kristiania, 9 Jan. 1869, son of Friederich Wilhelm S. and Marie Edvardine Bohm; he read theology at the University of Kristiania, studying semitic languages and Egyptology under Lieblein (q.v.), graduating 1894; he joined the University as a research fellow in history of religions, 1901; PhD, 1904 with a thesis on Amun-Re; he was awarded the Fridtjof Nansen award, 1905; he was appointed Professor of Religious History at the University, 1914-39; he died at Grabkammen, Aker, 29 June 1946.

Norsk Biografisk Lexikon 12, 328-30; S. A. Naguib in S. Hjelde, *Man, Meaning and Mystery,* 2000, 106-9.

SCHEURLEER, Constant Willem Lunsingh (1881-1941)

Dutch collector; he was born in The Hague, 7 Sept. 1881, son of Daniel François Lunsingh S. and Maria Elsina Petronella Lunsingh Tonckens; he was a banker and private collector with his own Museum Scheurleer in The Hague; he purchased part of the von Bissing (q.v.) collection in 1921; when his private museum closed in 1934, part of his collection was acquired by the Allard Pierson Museum in Amsterdam, some other pieces being acquired by Brooklyn Museum;; he occupied a private chair of Greek archaeology in the University of Leiden from 1936; he died in The Hague, 3 March 1941.

Inf. Prof. Heerma van Voss.

SCHIAPARELLI, Ernesto (1856-1928)

Italian Egyptologist; he was born in Occhieppo Inferiore, Biella, 12 July 1856, son of the historian Luigi S. and Francesca Corona, and cousin of the astronomer Giovanni S. and the fashion designer Elsa S.; he studied Egyptology under F. Rossi (q.v.) at the University of Turin and then under Maspero (q.v.) in Paris, 1877-80; he was made Director of the Egyptian section of the Florence Museum, 1881-94 and afterwards was for many years Director of the Turin Museum, 1894-1928; he also was in charge of the Italian Arch. Mission excavations for 12 seasons between 1903 and 1920; this involved work at sites all over Egypt, and he dug at Heliopolis, where he found important reliefs from a temple built by King Zoser, at the Khufu pyramid at Giza and among the mastabas there finding more important material; at the former site he discovered traces of the predynastic age and the ruins of the Mnevis temple; he also worked at Hermopolis Magna and Asyut, 1906-13, where he excavated the cemeteries, as also at Qau el-Kebir, and cleared the tomb of the high-priest of Seth; El-Hammamia was also dug, and the Valley of Queens in western Thebes, where Schiaparelli opened the tombs of Queen Nefertari, Khaemwese and Amenherkhepshef, son of Ramesses III; at Gebelein he worked at the sanctuary of Hathor and on the cemetery, and then in the necropolis at Aswan where he excavated the important tomb of Harkhuf; his most important find, which brought him fame, was at Deir el-Medina, where he had the good fortune to find the intact tomb of the architect Kha and his wife; almost all the objects from this tomb, which give a fine picture of ancient Egyptian life and civilization, are now in Turin Museum; his other most important work was on the funerary papyri and the Book of the Dead, many facsimiles of which he published in a huge three-volume work which rivals that of Naville in scope; he was engaged in preparing reports of his excavations at the end of his life, and two vols. had appeared by 1927, the rest remaining unpublished; Schiaparelli was a senator of the National Parliament; his principal works were, *Del sentimento religioso degli Egiziani*, 1877; *Il Libro dei Funerali degli antichi Egiziani, ricavato da Monumenti inediti. Tradotto e commentato da E.S.*, 3 vols., fol. 1881-90; *Museo Archeologico di Firenze. Antichità egizie, ordinate e descritte da E.S.*, pt. i, 1887; *Les Hypogées Royaux Thèbes. 2nd Div.*, with E. Lefébure and É. Naville, 1889; *La catena orientale dell'Egitto*, 1890; *La geografia del'Africa orientale, secondo le indicazioni dei monumenti egiziani*, fol. 1916; *Relazioni sui lavori della Missione Archeologica italiana in Egitto, anni 1903-1920. I. Esplorazione della 'Valle delle Regina' nella necropoli di Tebe*, fol. 1924; *II. La Tomba intatta dell'architetto Cha nella necropoli di Tebi*, fol. 1927; he died in Turin, 17 Feb. 1928.

DBDI 91, 441-5; *Aegyptus* 8 (1927), 337-8 (A. Calderini); *AE* N (1928), 52-4 (A. Tulli, trans. A. Petrie); *Enc. It.* 31. 77 (G. Farina); *Chron. d'Ég.* 4 (1928), 210; *JEA* 14 (1928), 181; Museo Egizio di Torino, *Guido allo Statuario e alle Sale del primo piano*, pp. 4-5, 11, 12, 15, 18, 20, 23, 24, 25; R. Paribeni, *Commemorazione di E. Schiaparelli*, Reale Accad. Naz. dei Lincei, Scienze morali, storiche e filologiche classe, Rome 1928, ser. 6, vol. 4, 197-204; Hilmy ii, 218; *Illustrazione Biellese* 111 (1941), 9-23; È. Gran-Aymerich, *Dictionnaire biographique d'archéologie 1798-1945*, 2001, incorporated in *Les Chercheurs de passé 1798-1945*, 2007, 1155-6; P. del Vesco et al., *Missione Egitto 1903-1920*, 2017, 37-55.

SCHIMMEL, Norbert (1904-1990)

American collector; he was born in Berlin, 2 Sept. 1904; he worked in the antiquarian book trade for a time; in 1938 he emigrated to America and developed the New Hermes Engraving Machine Corporation; he was encouraged to collect antiquities by Pomerance (q.v.) and Cooney (q.v.) whom he met about 1947; he formed an important collection of Near Eastern objects notably reliefs in the Amarna style; he contributed to exhibitions at Queen's College, New York, 1958 and the Metropolitan Museum, 1959; his own collection was exhibited at the Fogg Museum, Harvard University, 1964-5 *The Beauty of Ancient Art*, ed. H. Hoffmann, 1964; again in Cleveland, Dallas, New York, and the Israel Museum 1974-7 *Ancient Art. The Norbert Schimmel Collection*, ed. O. White Muscarella, 1974; it was shown in Berlin, Hamburg and Munich 1978-9 *Von Troja bis Amarna*, ed. J. Settgast, 1978; he served on the visiting committees of several departments of the Metropolitan Museum of Art of New York and the Fogg Museum of Art; he joined the Board of Trustees of the Metropolitan Museum, 1976-89; he was a founder and honorary fellow of the Israel Museum and president of its American friends; he was a trustee of the Archaeological Institute of America; from 1981-9 he donated large parts of his collection to the Metropolitan Museum including the Amarna reliefs, while other pieces went to the Israel Museum and the Arthur

M. Sackler Museum, Harvard in 1991; the residue of the collection was sold at Sotheby's New York 16 Dec. 1992; he died in Longboat Key, Florida, 16 Feb. 1990.

The Metropolitan Museum of Art Bulletin Spring 1992, 2-4 (J. R. Mertens); *The New York Times* 22 Feb. 1990, B11.

SCHLICHTEGROLL, (Adolf Heinrich) Friedrich (1765-1822)

German antiquary; he was born in Waltershausen near Gotha, 8 Dec. 1765, son of Daniel S., an administrator, and Maria Boemhardt; he studied law at Jena and philology at Gottingen, 1783-7; he became a teacher at Gotha, 1787-1800 and then worked in the Ducal library; Librarian, 1802; he became General Secretary of the Akademie der Wissenschaften in Munich, 1807; he published a work on Egyptian, Greek, and Roman divinities, 1792-8, and a work on the Rosetta Stone with German translation and 7 plates, Munich, 1818; he died at Munich, 4 Dec. 1822.

ADB 31, 484-7; *NDB* 23, 72-3; *BIFAO* 5 (1906), 85; Hilmy, ii, 219.

SCHMIDT, Carl (1868-1938)

German Coptologist; he was born in Hagenow, Mecklenburg, 26 Aug. 1868, son of Johann Heinrich Friedrich S., a teacher, and Elisabeth Elenore Friedericke Schneider; he studied at the Universities of Leipzig and Berlin, 1887-94; Privat-docent, Berlin, 1899; Professor Extraordinary, 1909; Hon. Professor, 1921; Professor, 1928; retired, 1935; he edited and published many important Coptic texts, and in 1930 discovered the famous Manichaean papyri; he visited Egypt several times to obtain Coptic MSS; some of his MSS went to Louvain, and were edited by Lefort (q.v.), but most of them were later destroyed by enemy action; the rest were sold to Michigan University after his death; he died in Cairo, 17 April 1938.

BSAC 4, 195; *Chron. d'Ég.* 13. 335; *JEA* 24 (1938), 135; *ZÄS* 74 (1938), 69-70 (W. Schubert); *The Coptic Encyclopedia* 7, 2106-7 (A. S. Atiya).

SCHMIDT, Valdemar (1836-1925)

Danish Egyptologist; he was born in Hammel, N. Jutland, 7 Jan. 1836, son of Jens Christian S. and Ane Catherine Marie Alvilda Meyer; he had a brilliant University career and was a great linguist, and knew, it was said, 28 languages; he studied at Berlin under Brugsch (q.v.) and Paris under de Rougé (q.v.); PhD, 1873; he visited Greece, Western Asia, and Egypt, 1860-9; he was secretary to the Arch. Congress at Copenhagen, 1869; he was appointed Professor at Copenhagen University, 1883-1921, and for many years was also Hon. Keeper of the Ny Carlsberg Glyptotek Egyptian collection; he visited Egypt several times and went to England almost annually; he published many archaeological works, including a history of Assyria, 1874, and of Egypt, 1877; his last important work was an elaborate study of Egyptian sarcophagi; see, *Den aegyptiske samling: Ny Carlsberg Glyptotek*, 1899; *Choix de monuments égyptiens faisant partie de la Glyptotèque Ny-Carlsberg*, 2 pts., 1906-10; *Collection de stèles égyptiennes léguées à l'évêché de Copenhague par feu Frédéric Münter ... et actuellement conservées à la Glyptothèque Ny Carlsberg, à Copenhague*, 1910; *Levende og Døde i det gamle Aegypten: album til ordning of sarcofager, mumiekister, mumiekylstre o. lign*, 1919; he died in Copenhagen, 26 June 1925.

JEA 13 (1927), 80-1 (portr. pl. ii); *L'Anthropologie* 36, 168; *Dansk Biografisk Leksikon* 13, 198-9.

SCHMIDT-CIĄŻYŃSKI, Constantine Alexander Victor (1817-1889)

Polish art collector and dealer in antiquities; he was born in Gorizia, 18 Feb. 1817, son of Louis S., a physician of Napoleon's army from Lorraine, and Louisa Rosalia Ciążyńska; he studied at the University of Dorpat about 1835-39, and until 1851 he resided in St. Petersburg; from 1851-69 he lived mainly in France, travelling to Italy and England in search for art objects; he was the owner of a fine collection of scarabs and gnostic gems from Egypt; as a dealer he was renowned; his shop on Quai Voltaire in Paris was well-known; he also owned two branches in Vichy and Nice; in 1863 he was named purveyor by appointment to Napoleon III; from 1869 he resided in London, retiring gradually from business, but still interested in his private collection of scarabs, gems and cameos; in his old age he decided to offer some of his art objects to Polish museums; in 1883 he presented his paintings and engravings to Poznan and in 1886 his glyptic collection of 2517 items was transferred to the National Museum of Cracow; in 1884 his gems and scarabs were temporarily exhibited in the Cloth Hall; now they are kept in the Department of Artistic Handicraft; he died in Gorizia, Italy, 5 Jan. 1889.

J. Śliwa, *Egyptian Scarabs and Magical Gems from the Collection of Constantine Schmidt-Ciążyński*, Cracow, 1989, 14-33.

SCHOLZ, (Johann Martin) Augustin (1794-1852)
German orientalist and theologian; he was born in Kapsdorf near Breslau, 8 Feb. 1794; he studied at the University of Breslau, 1818-21; in 1820 he accompanied Minutoli (q.v.) on his trip to Egypt and later went on to Palestine and Syria; he was appointed Professor at Bonn, 1821, and Professor of Old Testament and Church History, 1823; he published an account of his travels *Reise in die Gegend zwischen Alexandrien und Parätonium, die Libysche Wüste, Siwa, Egypten, Palästina und Syrien in den Jahren 1820-1821*, 1822; he died in Bonn, 20 Oct. 1852.

ADB 32, 226-7;*DBE* 9, 172.

SCHOTT, Siegfried Hugo Erdmann (1897-1971)
German Egyptologist; he was born in Berlin, 20 Aug. 1897, son of Walther S. and Elli Blank; he studied Egyptology under Ranke (q.v.) at Heidelberg, 1924; later with Junker (q.v.) and Sethe (q.v.); PhD, 1926; he also studied under Kees (q.v.) at Gottingen; Habilition, 1932; his inaugural dissertation *Untersuchungen zur Schriftgeschichte der Pyramidentexte* was published at Heidelberg, 1926; he was at first an assistant in Berlin Museum and also worked as assistant with the German Archaeological Institute in Cairo, 1 Oct. 1929-30 Sep. 1931, at this time undertaking the translations of inscriptions for the German E. Delta expedition of 1929 (see *MDAIK* 1 (1930), 28); he also acted as an epigrapher for the Americans at Chicago House, Luxor, 1931-37; he married Erika Fischmeister who assisted him afterwards in his work; he became a lecturer at Heidelberg during Ranke's absence in America; Lecturer University of Göttingen, 1943; Associate Professor, University of Heidelberg, 1943-5; Professor of Egyptology, 1952-6; he succeeded Kees as Professor at Göttingen, 1956-65; Director of Egyptological Seminar; Professor (emeritus) Göttingen, 1965-71; Mem. Akad. der Wiss. Göttingen; also Mainz; Mem. Deutsche Arch. Inst.; Corr. mem. Acad. des Inscriptions et Belles Lettres; Schott's main interests were in Egyptian poetry and especially in religious texts, subjects relating to ancient Egyptian religion in general form the major part of his published output which often dealt with highly specialized subjects; his study of the role of the pyramid temple and the religious functions and symbolic meaning of the different parts of an Old Kingdom funerary complex, published in conjunction with Ricke's architectural study, became something of a classic and was very influential; other fundamental works relate to many of the important religious festivals and rites as enacted at Thebes and Memphis; his thoroughness is demonstrated by the fact that he copied all the late religious papyri for part of *Urkunden Mythologischen Inhalts* (Urk. VI, 1929/30); a Festschrift to mark his 70th birthday, ed. by W. Helck, was published in 1968; his principal works from a numerous list are, *The Feasts at Thebes* in H. Nelson, *Work in Western Thebes 1931-1933*, 1934; *Mythe und Mythenbildung im alten Ägypten*, 1945; *Altägyptische Liebeslieder mit Märchen und Liebesgeschichte*, 1950; *Altägyptische Festdaten*, 1950; *Bemerkungen zum ägyptischen Pyramidenkult*, in *Beiträge zur Ägyptischen Bauforschung und Altertumskunde* 5, 1950; *Hieroglyphen: untersuchungen zum Ursprung der Schrift*, 1951; *Das Schöne Fest vom Wüstentale: Festbräuche einer Totenstadt*, 1953; *Deutung der Geheimnisse des Rituals für die Abwehr der Bösen*,1954; *Fragmente memphitischer theologie in demotischer schrift (Pap. demot. Berlin 13603)*, with W. Erichsen, 1954; *Krönungstag d. Köningen Hatschepsut*, 1955; *Wall scenes from the Mortuary Chapel of the Mayor Paser at Medinet Habu*, trans. E. B. Hauser, 1957; *Die Reinignung Pharaos in einem memphitischen Tempel*, 1957; *Die Schrift der verborgenen Kammer in Königsgräbern der 18. Dynastie: Gliederung, Titel und Vermerke*, 1958; *Kanais. Der Tempel Sethos I im Wâdi Mia*, 1961; *Der Denkstein Sethos' I für die Kapelle Ramses I in Abydos*, 1964; *Die Eine ägyptische Schreibpalette als Rechenbrett*, 1967; *Ägyptische Quellen zum Plan des Sphinxtempels* in *Beiträge zur Ägyptischen Bauforschung und Altertumskunde* 10, 1970; and posthumously *Bücher und Bibliotheken im Alten Ägypten,* 1990; his photographs of Theban tombs are in the Griffith Institute, Oxford; he died in Innsbruck, 29 Oct. 1971.

AfO 24 (1973), 249-50 (portr.) (H. Brunner); *BSFE* 63 (1972), 5 (J. Leclant); *Chron. d'Ég.* 46 (1971), 310-12 (P. Derchain); *Informationsblatt der Deutschs. Agyptologie* 3 (Jan. 1972), 3 (anon); *JEA* 58 (1972), 4 (anon); *Wer ist Wer?* 16 (1969/70), 1180; *WW in Germany* 4th ed. (1972), 1345; *ZDMG* 122 (1972), 19-21 (W. Westendorf); *Gött. Misz.* 57, (1982), 79-87; (bibl.) (E. Schott and A. Grimm); *NDB* 23, 496-7;inf. T. Schneider; S. Voss, *Die Geschichte der Abteilung Kairo des DAI im Spannungsfeld deutscher politischer Interessen* (Band 2), *1929-1966*, 2017, 117-20; L. Theermann in J. Arp-Neuman and T. Gertzen (eds.), 'Steininschrift und Bibelwort', 2019, 79-84.

SCHOW, Niels Iversen (1754-1830)
Danish classical scholar; he was born in Copenhagen, 16 June 1754, son of Iver Nielson S. and Dorthe Catherine Clemensdatter; he was a student of C. G. Heyne (q.v.); Professor of Archaeology, Copenhagen University, 1805; Professor of Greek, 1813-27; he was a friend of Zoega (q.v.); on a visit to Rome he was given the first Greek papyrus from Egypt in the Borgia (q.v.) collection to edit, which he published as *Charta papyracea Graece scripta in Musei Borgiani Velitiris*, etc., Rome, 1788; he died in Copenhagen, 18 Oct. 1830.

Preisendanz, *Papyrusfunde und Papyrusforschung*, 1933, 72; *Chron. d'Ég.* 7, 324; Hilmy, ii, 222; *Dansk Biografisk Leksikon* 13, 156-7; M. Capasso (ed.), *Hermae*, 2007, 19-28 (portr.) (M. Capasso).

SCHUBART, (Friedrich) Wilhelm Ludwig (1873-1960)

German papyrologist; he was born at Leignitz, 21 Oct. 1873, son of Ernst Heinrich Friedrich S., an official, and Theodore Wilhelmine Sophie Rudolf; he studied from 1891 at Tubingen, Halle, Berlin and Breslau under Wilcken (q.v.); PhD, 1900; he worked as a teacher in Berlin, 1898-1900; he was appointed to the Berlin Museum, 1900, later head of the Papyrus Collection, 1909-37; he also became Professor in 1912-37; he excavated at Dime (Soknopaiu Nesos) and Medinet Madi (Narmuthis), 1909-10 with Zucker (q.v.); their dig diary was published in *Archiv für Papyrusforschung* 21 (1971), 5-55; apart from articles, he edited numerous works on Papyrology and published *Aegypten von Alexander der Gross bis auf Mohammed*, 1922; *Die Papyri als Zeugen antiker Kultur*, 1925; *Die Griechen in Aegypten*, 1927; and *Verfassung und Veerwaltung des Ptolemäerreiches*, 1937; he died at Halle, 9 Aug. 1960.

Chron. d'Eg. 36 (1961), 423-7 (C. Préaux); M. Capasso, *Hermae*, 2007, 193-206 (G. Poethke).

SCHULMAN, Alan Richard (1930-2000)

American Egyptologist; he was born in Brooklyn, New York, 14 Jan. 1930, son of Jacob Theodore S. and Hilda Tannebaum; he studied at the City College of New York; BA in Classical Languages and Ancient History, 1952; he then served in the Korean war; he undertook graduate work at the Oriental Institute of the University of Chicago under Wilson (q.v.) and Edgerton (q.v.); MA in Egyptology, 1958; he then studied at the University of Pennsylvania under Anthes (q.v.); PhD in Egyptology, 1962; he worked as an assistant in the Egyptian section of the University Museum of Pennsylvania, 1962-63; he was a Visiting Associate Professor at Columbia University, 1965; Dropsie University, 1966-8; and Tel Aviv University, 1969-70; he was appointed Professor of Ancient and Military History at Queen's College, New York and at the Graduate Center of the City University of New York, 1965; he was editor of *JARCE*, 1966-70; he was a founder of the Egyptological Seminar of New York and *BES* 10 was dedicated to him; he was co-founder and co-editor of the *New Kingdom Memphis Newsletter*; he was particularly interested in Egyptian New Kingdom history and foreign relations and military history; apart from numerous articles, he published his doctoral thesis *Military Rank, Title, and Organization in the Egyptian New Kingdom*, 1964 and *Ceremonial Execution and Public Rewards*, 1988 as well as many articles notably on military history; he died in Tel Aviv, 20 July 2000.

A. R. Schulman, *Ceremonial Execution and Public Rewards*, 1988, ii; *BES* 10 (1989/90), 4-7 (portr.) (J. F. Romano), 8-13 (bibl.) (D. Guzman); IAE internet obituary (R. Fazzini); *JSSEA* 28 (2001), vi-x (portr.) (R. Delia).

SCHWEINFURTH, Georg August (1836-1925)

German explorer and botanist; of Baltic German origin, he was born in Riga, 29 Dec. 1836, son of Georg Adam S., a merchant, and Luise Mauer; he was educated at the Universities of Heidelberg, Munich, and Berlin, 1856-62; he specialized in botany and palaeontology; he explored the shores of the Red Sea, Egypt, and the Sudan as far as Khartoum, 1863-6; he afterwards explored the interior of Africa, 1869-71, when he made many important geographical and scientific discoveries, but his collections were lost by fire; he next explored the Libyan Desert with Rohlfs, 1873-4; in 1875 he settled in Cairo, and founded the Geographical Society there under the auspices of the Khedive; between 1876 and 1888 he explored the Arabian Desert and conducted botanical and geological researches in the Fayum and the Nile Valley, publishing many valuable articles thereon; he removed to Berlin, 1889 where he died 19 Sept. 1925.

NDB 24, 50-1; *Aegyptus* 6. 251; *Bull. Soc. Geogr. Eg.* 14. 65 (portr.); 72 (bibl.); 129; 135; 139; Hilmy, ii, 224; *JEA* 12 (1926), 304; *OLZ* 29 (1926), 1; *Rev. arch.* 23, 124; Max Linke, *Petermans Geographische Mitteilungen* 121, 4 (1977), 247-51; *Wer ists's 1911*, 1339-40.

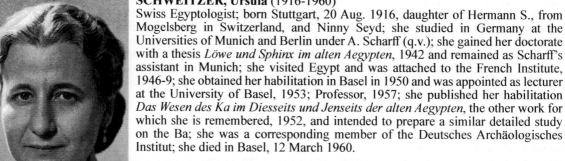

SCHWEITZER, Ursula (1916-1960)

Swiss Egyptologist; born Stuttgart, 20 Aug. 1916, daughter of Hermann S., from Mogelsberg in Switzerland, and Ninny Seyd; she studied in Germany at the Universities of Munich and Berlin under A. Scharff (q.v.); she gained her doctorate with a thesis *Löwe und Sphinx im alten Aegypten*, 1942 and remained as Scharff's assistant in Munich; she visited Egypt and was attached to the French Institute, 1946-9; she obtained her habilitation in Basel in 1950 and was appointed as lecturer at the University of Basel, 1953; Professor, 1957; she published her habilitation *Das Wesen des Ka im Diesseits und Jenseits der alten Aegypten*, the other work for which she is remembered, 1952, and intended to prepare a similar detailed study on the Ba; she was a corresponding member of the Deutsches Archäologisches Institut; she died in Basel, 12 March 1960.

AfO 19 (1959-60), 268 (H. Brunner); *Chron. d'Ég.* 35 (1960), 195-7 (A. Mekhitarian); *ZÄS* 85 (1960), iv (portr.) (H. Stock); *ZDMG* 6 112 (1962), 1-5 (bibl.) (P. Kaplony); inf. E. Staehelin.

SCOLES, Joseph John (1798-1863)
British architect; he was born in London, 27 June 1798, son of Matthew S., a joiner, and Elizabeth Starling; he studied in Italy with Bonomi (q.v.), and practised in London; pupil of Joseph Ireland, and FRIBA, 1835; he published architectural works; he and Henry Parke (q.v.) accompanied Henry Westcar (q.v.) and Frederic Catherwood (q.v.) up the Nile as far as Wadi Halfa, and afterwards visited the Levant with Parke; recommended Francis Arundale (q.v.) to Robert Hay (q.v.) as replacement artist for Charles Laver (q.v.); in 1840s designed many RC churches for the Jesuit Order in a variety of architectural styles from Gothic to neo-classical; he died in London, 29 Dec. 1863.

ODNB 49, 314-6; *DNB* 51, 3; Hilmy, ii, 225; Westcar Diary, 27 et passim; Bodley MS Eng. lett. d. 165 f.45

SCOTT, Nora Elizabeth (1905-1994)
British-American Egyptologist; she was born at Prestwick, Scotland, 14 July 1905, daughter of Ernest Findlay Scott, Professor of New Testament Literature, Queen's College, Kingston, Ontario, 1908-1919 and then Professor of Biblical Theology, Union Theological Seminary, New York, and Annie Roxburgh Dunlop; she was educated at Horace Mann School, Barnard College; BA in Classics; she then studied Egyptology at Oxford University under Griffith (q.v.) and Blackman (q.v.); MA; she excavated at Armant, 1929-30; she joined the staff of the Dept. of Egyptian Art, Metropolitan Museum, New York, 1931, becoming assistant curator, associate curator, and Curator of the Dept., 1970-3; she was also Adjunct Professor at Columbia University; she published *Egyptian Statues*, with C. Sheeler, 1945; *Egyptian Statuettes*, with C. Sheeler, 1946; *The Home Life of the Ancient Egyptians*, 1947, revised as *The Daily Life of the Ancient Egyptians,* 1973; and many articles in *BMMA*; she died in Kennett Square, Pennsylvania, 5 April 1994.

Inf. V. Burton.

SCOTT-MONCREIFF, Philip David (1882-1911)
British Egyptologist; he was born in London, 27 Feb. 1882, son of William Dundas S-M., engineer and designer of the Cutty Sark, and Emily Mary de Gilibert; he was educated at Charterhouse and Christ's College, Cambridge where he studied Semitic languages; BA, 1903; MA, 1907; he was appwointed an assistant in the Dept. of Egyptian and Assyrian Antiquities, British Museum, 3 Dec. 1903; in Oct.-Nov. 1905 he helped Crowfoot (q.v.) to clear and repair the Temple of Buhen on which he published brief notes in *PSBA* 29 (1907) and visited the sites of Musawwarat El-Sufra and Naga, published in *PSBA* 30 (1908); apart from some articles, he was the author of *Paganism and Christianity in Egypt*, 1913 and began the series of *Hieroglyphic Texts from Egyptian Stelae and etc. in the British Museum* completing Vol. 1, 1911 and part of Vol. 2, 1912; he died in Egham, 8 Feb. 1911.

Al. Cantab.; *Paganism and Christianity in Egypt*, v-viii (N. McLean); *Burke's Landed Gentry* 18th ed., part 2, 1969, 447; *The Times* 11 Feb. 1911, 11.

SCOTTO, Antonio (*d.* 1821)
Italian physician from Genoa; he arrived in Egypt in 1814, and was employed by Ibrahim Pasha as his personal physician in the Arabian War, 1816-18, and during the Sennar expedition, 1821; he travelled through the Sudan with Linant (q.v.), and Light (q.v.) met him at Asyut in 1814; he died in Sennar, 1821.

Hill, 334; Belzoni, i, 47; Light, 42; Linant Diary.

SEELE, Keith Cedric (1898-1971)
American Egyptologist and educator; born in Warsaw, Indiana, 13 Feb. 1898, son of Henry D. S. and Ora Capitola Dick; the family moved to Elkhart, Ind., and as a youth he helped the family's finances by working in a factory there during the summer; BA College of Wooster, 1922; his first contact with Egypt was when he taught English at Assiut College, 1922-23; after graduating he was ordained in the ministry of the Presbyterian Church (USA); BD, McCormick Theol. Sem., 1926; he gained the T.B. Blackstone Fellowship in New Testament studies, and studied Egyptology at the University of Berlin under Sethe (q.v.), 1926-8; Fellow Inst. Internat. Educ., Berlin, 1926-7; he joined the University of Chicago and the staff of the Oriental Institute, 1928; his first work was on objects and records collected by Breasted (q.v.), which formed the nucleus of the later OI Museum; he married Diederika A. H. Millard, 29 June 1929, who afterwards accompanied him to Egypt and later assisted him in the editing of *JNES*; further study in Berlin followed, 1930; he was a member of the epigraphic survey expedition of the OI of Chicago University at both Luxor and Saqqara, 1929-36; he also systematically visited and compiled his own photographic record of Theban tombs, notably that of Tjanefer, the material from this in fact forming the subject for his doctoral dissertation; PhD University of Chicago, 1938; having returned to the USA he was appointed Instructor in Egyptology, 1936-41; during the war he served in the US Army Signal Corps working in 1st Intelligence in Washington, DC, 1942-44; Assistant Professor in Egyptology University of Chicago, 1941-6;

Assoc. Prof. 1946-50; Professor, 1950-64; Emeritus Prof., 1964-71; LHD, 1947; Phi Beta Kappa; Corr. Mem. Instit. d'É.; Mem. Deutsches Arch. Inst.; Mem. Soc. Franc. Eg.; Mem. EES; Lt. Amer. Orient. Soc.; Del. UN Conference Conservation and Utilization Resources, Lake Success, NY 1949; Director of the OI Nubian expedition in connection with the Aswan High Dam programme, 1960-64; he excavated in the Bab Kalabsha area, 1960-61 and at Qustul, Ballana, Arminna, 1962-4; he was editor of *JNES*, 1948-71; he translated Steindorff's *Die Blütezeit des Pharaonreichs* into English, but with extensive revisions, 1942; in addition to articles in journals his principal Egyptological publications and those of which he was co-author were, *Medinet Habu* II: *Later Historical Records of Ramses III*, with H. H. Nelson and J. A. Wilson, 1932; *Medinet Habu* III: *The Calendar, the Slaughterhouse, and Minor Records of Ramses III*, with Nelson, Wilson and S. Schott, 1934; *Reliefs and Inscriptions of Karnak I: Ramses III's Temple within the Great Enclosure of Amon and Ramses III's Temple in the Enclosure of Mut*, with Nelson and Schott, 1936; *The Mastaba of Mereruka*, 2 vols., with P. Duell, C. F. Nims, 1938; *Festival Scenes of Ramses III*, with Nelson and others, 1940; *The Coregency of Ramses II with Seti I and the Date of the Great Hypostyle Hall at Karnak*, 1940; *When Egypt ruled the East*, with G. Steindorff, 1942, rev. ed. 1957; *Reliefs and Inscriptions at Karnak* III: *The Bubastite Portal*, with Schott, G. R. Hughes and others, 1953; *Medinet Habu* V: *The Temple Proper, Part I*, with G. R. Hughes and others, 1957; *The Tomb of Tjanefer at Thebes*, 1959; *The Beit el-Wali temple of Ramesses II*, with Hughes and E. F. Wente, 1967; *Ausgrabungen von Khor-Dehmit bis Bet el-Wali*, with H. Ricke, L. Habachi, L. V. Zabkar, 1967; he also edited the very comprehensive prehistory section of Hayes' (q.v.) uncompleted history of Egypt under the title *Most Ancient Egypt*, 1964; he also was editor of *Blackfeet and Buffalo, memories of Life among the Indians*, 1962 as he had an interest in native American culture; he died in Chicago, 23 July 1971.

AfO 24 (1973), 255 (H. Brunner); *BSFE* No. 62 (1972), 4-5 (anon.); *Dir. of Amer. Scholars* 1 (4th ed.) 1963, 270; *JNES* 32 (1973), 1-3 (portr.) (anon.) in memoriam no.; *WWA* 37th ed. vol. 2 (1972-3), 2840-1; *Wooster College Alumni Mag.*, Wooster Ohio, (Nov.-Dec. 1971), 27-8.

SEETZEN, Ulrich Jasper (1767-1811)

German explorer; he was born in Sophiengroden, 30 Jan. 1767, son of Ulrich Jasper S., a farmer, and Trienke Otten; he studied medicine and natural history at Göttingen under Blumenbach (q.v.); he set off to explore the Middle East in 1802 with the support of Duke Ernest II of Gotha and his son with the request to obtain objects for the Gotha collection; he went first to Syria and from May 1807-March 1809 visited Egypt including Giza, Saqqara, Heliopolis, the Fayum, and Sinai where he was the first European to view Wadi Maghara; he passed himself off as a Muslim, Musa el-Hakam; he formed a large collection of 1574 manuscripts and 3536 antiquities which he sent back to Gotha in 1809; he left Egypt in 1809 for Arabia but died in mysterious circumstances near Mocha in Sept. 1811; his diaries *Ulrich Jasper Seetzens Reisen* were published in 1854-9.

ADB 33, 590-2; R. Hallett, *The Penetration of Africa to 1815* (1965), 379-80; *Ulrich Jasper Seetzen (1767-1811). Leben und Werk*, 1995; U. Wallenstein, *Ägyptische Sammlung*, Gotha, 1996; U. Wallenstein in H. Erkenbrecher and H. Roob (eds.), *Die Residenzstadt Gotha in der Goethe-Zeit*, 1998, 203-221; U. Wallenstein in *Vernisage* 17 (1999), 24-35; J. Schienerl, *Der Weg in den Orient. Der Forscher Ulrich Jasper Seetzen: Von Jever in den Jemen (1802-1811)*, 2000; inf. U. Wallenstein; C. Walbiner in N. Cooke and V. Daubney, *Every Traveller Needs a Compass*, 2015,197-204.

SEGAL, Walter (1907-1985)

German-British architect; he was born in Berlin, 15 May 1907, son of Arthur Segal and Ernestine Chavas, artists of Jewish-Romanian origin; he studied architecture in Berlin and Zurich, 1929-32; he worked as architect under Ricke (q.v.) for the Borchardt Institute's excavation of the mortuary temple of Thutmose III at Thebes, 1934-5; he then spent the summer and autumn of 1935 studying and making technical drawings of chairs and stools in the Cairo Museum; he recorded objects in the Naples and British Museums, 1936, but never published his work which remained in a safe-deposit box until 1984; portions have been edited and published by Marianne Eaton-Krauss, *JEA* 75 (1989), 77-88, and *The Thrones, Chairs, Stools, and Footstols from the Tomb of Tutankhamun*, 2008; his papers dealing with the Tutankhamun material are now in the Griffith Institute; he settled in Britain, 1936, practising as an architect and teaching architecture at University College London and elsewhere; he died in London, 27 Oct. 1985.

ODNB 49, 679-80 (place of birth incorrectly given as Ascona, Switzerland); J. McKean, *Learning from Segal. Walter Segal's Life, Work and Influence*, 1989; M Eaton-Krauss, *JEA* 75 (1989), 77-8; inf. T. Hardwick.

SEGATO, Girolamo (1792-1836)

Italian chemist, explorer, draughtsman, and cartographer; he was born in Vadana nel Bellunese, 13 June 1792, son of Benedetto S. and Giustina Lante; he went to Egypt for a commercial firm in 1818; he excavated at Saqqara for Minutoli (q.v.) in 1820; in company with Lorenzo Masi, an engineer in the service of the Pasha, he explored and

mapped a large region of the country south of Wadi Halfa and the Blue and White Niles, 1821-2; after returning to Italy he published *Saggi pittorici ... sull'Egitto*, 1827; he became a friend of Champollion (q.v.) whom he met in Florence; he died in Florence, 3 Feb. 1836.

Garollo, *Diz. Biogr. Univ.; Enc. It.*; Hill, 335; Champollion, i, 336; Hilmy, ii, 227; R. Almagia, *L'opera degli Italiani per to conoscenza dell'Egitto*, 1926, 5, 18 (bibl.) C. della Valle, *Girolamo Segato (1792-1836)*, 1934; Gino Pieri, *Girolamo Segato (1792-1836)*, 1936, 214-21, (bibl.); O. Millo, *Ricordo di Girolamo Segato, Dolomiti*, IV, 4 (1981), 39-46; *Il Nilo sui Lungarni*, 1982, 16-17; A. Siliotti, ed., *Viaggiatori veneti alla scoperta dell'Egitto*, 1985, 113-6; E. Bresciani in M. Betrò and G. Miniaci, *Talking along the Nile*, 2013, 59-67.

SEIDEL, Matthias Lothar (1948-2013)

German Egyptologist; he was born in Osterode, 18 Aug. 1948; he studied Egyptology, archaeology, and art history at the Free University, Berlin and the Ludwig Maximilians University, Munich; he specialized in art history; he taught at various universities in Germany and the USA and was adjunct professor at Johns Hopkins University; he was associated with Egyptian collections in Berlin and Munich and was a research associate at the Roemer and Pelizaeus Museum, Hildesheim, 1984-2001 and 2011-13 where he participated in exhibition projects and catalogues; he published his thesis *Die königlichen Statuengruppen: Die Denkmäler vom Alten Reich bis zum Ende der 18. Dynastie*, 1996; with Regina Schulz, *Egypt. The World of the Pharaohs*, 1998; *Ägypten*, 2001; Eng. trans., *Egypt. Art and Architecture*, 2010; *Khepereru-Scarabs: Scarabs, Scaraboids and Plaques from Egypt and the Ancient Near East in the Walters Art Museum*, 2007; and *Egyptian Art - The Walters Art Museum*, 2009; he died in Hildesheim, 19 May 2013.

Inf. R. Schulz.

SEIDL, Erwin Oskar Friedrich (1905-1987)

German classicist and Egyptologist; he was born in Munich, 6 Nov. 1905, son of Oskar S. and Marie Buchmann; he studied ancient law and also Egyptology under Spiegelberg (q.v.); PhD, 1929; Habilitation, 1932; he taught Roman and ancient law at the Universities of Greifswald, 1937-42; Erlangen, 1942-58 where he was Professor of Roman Law; and at Cologne, 1958-70 where he held the same position; he specialized in the history of law in Egypt in all periods; a volume of essays was prepared in his honour in *Studia et Documenta Historiae et Iuris* 43 (1977); of his over 200 articles and books, the prinicpal works concerned with Egypt were *Der Eid im römisch-ägyptischen Provinzialrecht*, 1933-8; *Einführung in die ägyptische Rechtsgeschichte bis zum Ende des Neuen Reiches*, 1939, 2nd ed.,1951; *Ägyptische Rechtsgeschichte der Saiten- und Perserzeit*, 1956, 2nd ed., 1968; *Ptolemäische Rechtsgeschichte*, 1962; *Rechtsgeschichte Ägyptens als romischer Provinz*, 1973; he died in Jettingen, 4 April 1987.

NDB 24, 182-3; *Aegyptus* 68 (1988), 205-6 (J. Mélèze-Modrzejewski); *Revue historique du droit français et étranger* 65 (1987), 1 (J. Mélèze-Modrzejewski); *Studia et Documenta Historiae et Iuris* 43 (1977), 565-73 (bibl.) (J. Mélèze-Modrzejewski).

SEKOWSKI, Józef Julian (Osip Ivanovitch) (1800-1858)

Polish orientalist; he was born at Antagolony near Vilna, 31 March 1800 son of Jan S.; he was educated at the University of Vilna; in 1819 he travelled to Istanbul where he obtained an appointment as dragoman of the Russian mission; in 1820 he travelled with a Swedish priest Jakob Berggren to Syria and Egypt as far as Abu Simbel returning in 1821; in Aug. 1822 he was appointed Professor in Oriental Languages at the University of St. Petersburg retiring 1847; he published an account of his travels in *Petersburger Zeitung*, 1822; in 1825 he published an account of Egyptian antiquities in St. Petersburg in *Severnaya Pcela* No. 9; he was awarded a PhD by Cracow University in 1826; he presented a Demotic papyrus to the Library of the Jagellonian University of Cracow which was published by the St. Petersburg Academy, *Exemplum Papyri Aegyptiacae*, 1826; he also published a number of works under the pseudonym Baron Bambreus; he died in St. Petersburg, 16 March 1858; his collected works were published by the Academy of Sciences in nine parts *Sobranie Socinenii Senkovskago (Barona Bambreusa)*, St. Petersburg, 1858.

Hartleben, ii, 111; Hilmy, ii, 228; inf. from R. Holthoer and J. Śliwa; *Gött. Misz.* 22 (1976), 7; L. Pedrotti, *Jósef-Julian Sekowski. The Genesis of a Literary Alien* (University of California Publications in Modern Philology, Vol. 73), 1965; T. Andrzejewski, 'U poczatków polskiego kolekcjonerstwa egiptologicznego' in: *Szkice z dziejów polskiej orientalistyki* II, 1966, 55-77; *ZÄS* 99 (1973), 25-9 (A. Szczudlowska); *Rocznik Orientalistyczny* XLI (1980), 131-8 (A. Szczudlowska).

SELIGMAN, Charles Gabriel (1873-1940)

British ethnologist; he was born in London, 24 Dec. 1873, only child of Hermann Seligmann (the final 'n' of the surname ceased to be used after 1914), a wealthy wine merchant, and Olivia Mendez da Costa; he qualified in medicine (pathology), but became involved in anthropology through the Cambridge anthropological expedition to the Torres Strait in 1898; he became a lecturer in ethnology at the London School of Economics, 1910, and Professor (part-time), 1913, a position that he held until 1934, but he also taught anthropology for Petrie's (q.v.) Egyptology diploma course at University College London; he was very widely traveled but is known especially for his fieldwork in Papua New Guinea and Sudan; with his wife, Brenda Zara Salaman (1883-1965), he first visited Egypt in 1908-9 where he spent a considerable amount of time with Petrie at his camp in Thebes; they visited Egypt again in 1913-14 and collected a large number of lithics from surface deposits and through excavation around Abydos and Thebes; he and his wife undertook a survey of Nilotic groups with funding from the government of Anglo-Egyptian Sudan, 1909-10, 1911-12, 1921-2; he saw in the pastoral tribes of the Upper Nile Province, a corrupted remnant of prehistoric Caucasian immigrants, whose arrival in Africa had precipitated the rise of ancient Egypt dynastic society, a now discredited idea; apart from several articles including the extensive 'Some aspects of the Hamitic problem in the Anglo-Egyptian Sudan', *Journal of the Royal Anthropological Institute of Great Britain and Ireland* 43 (1913), 593-705 and 'The older palaeolithic age in Egypt', *ibid.*, 51 (1921), 115-3, he published *Egypt and Negro Africa: a study in divine kingship*, 1934; he died in a nursing home in Oxford, 9 Sept. 1940.

ODNB 49, 709-11 (portr.); *American Anthropologist* 43 (1941), 437-9 (Melville J. Herskovits); inf. A. Stevenson.

SELIKOVITSCH, Goetzel (1863-1926)

Russian-American Egyptologist, orientalist, and journalist; born in Rietavas, Lithuania (Russia), 23 May 1863, son of David S. and Rachel Zundelewitz; he won a reputation as a boy prodigy in Hebrew and Talmudic studies; in 1879 he went to Paris and studied oriental languages at the École des Hautes Études, learning Egyptian, Ethiopic, Arabic, and Sanskrit; he graduated, 1884 and was attached for a short time to the Bibliothèque Nationale; in 1885 he acted as chief interpreter to Lord Wolseley for Arabic and Nubian dialects during the British expedition to relieve Khartoum, but was released from his duties when he was suspected of being sympathetic to the local imhabitants; before returning to France he visited Ethiopia, Morocco, Algeria, and Asia Minor, learning the local languages and customs of the natives and publishing the results in French and Hebrew journals; he emigrated to the USA in 1887, and lectured on hieroglyphs and Egyptology at the University of Pennsylvania and at the Franklin Institute, Philadelphia; unable to follow an academic career as he wished, he had to take up Yiddish journalism; he seems to have been unable to concentrate his abilities in any one subject for long, but he published *The Dawn of Egyptian Civilization*, 1887; he died in New York, 27 Nov. 1926.

DAB 16, 573-4.

SELIM, Abdel Kader (1922-2002)

Egyptian Egyptologist; he was born in Tanta 18 July 1922; he was educated at Cairo University; BA, 1945; he then studied Egyptology in Paris at the Ecole Pratique des Hautes Etudes at the Sorbonne, diploma 1948 and the Institut Catholique, diploma in hieroglyphic, 1948 and Coptic,1949; he obtained at doctorate in archaeology at the University of Brussels, 1950; he was appointed assistant curator at the Egyptian Museum in Cairo, becoming later first curator, 1966; Deputy Director, 1970; and finally Director from 15 Feb. 1973 to 19 April 1977; he also held the post of Director General of the Nubian Monuments Salvage Fund, 1973-77; he became Director-General of the Pharaonic Section of the Antiquities Service, 1977; Undersecretary of State for the Pharaonic and Museums Section, 1979; Acting Chairman of the Egyptian Antiquities Service, Jan. 1982-July 1982; he was involved in various major exhibitions including the Tutankhamun exhibition in London, 1972, and the Akhenaten exhibition in European venues, 1975-6; he died 2002.

Bulletin of the Egyptian Museum 1 (2004), 8; 3 (2006), 9 (portr.).

SENKOWSKI *see* **SEKOWSKI**

SETHE, Kurt Heinrich (1869-1934)

German Egyptologist; he was born in Berlin, 30 Sept. 1869, son of Heinrich Christoph S. and his wife Auguste Gertrud; he studied Egyptology under Erman (q.v.) at Berlin University, 1888-92; PhD, 1892; Habilitation, 1895; he lectured at Berlin University, 1895-1900; he was later appointed to the University of Göttingen, 1900; Professor, 1907; afterwards succeeding Erman at Berlin, 1923; Sethe was with Erman the greatest figure in Egyptian

philology in the twentieth century; his achievement has been said to have been comparable with that of Brugsch (q.v.) or even Champollion (q.v.) in some fields; he made discoveries in all philological branches and also in history, geography, religion, mathematics, and chronology; his range was comprehensive, covering all texts from those of the Early Dynastic period to Demotic and Coptic, making important discoveries in all; he was a voluminous writer; of his many grammatical works the great *Verbum* was the most important; he collated and re-edited the Pyramid Texts, first published by Maspero (q.v.); he founded and edited the *Untersuchungen zur Geschichte und Altertumskunde Aegyptens* to which he made many important contributions from 1896 onwards; he visited Egypt, 1904-5, and copied and collated a large number of historical texts which he pub., 1906-9, as *Urkunden der 18. Dynastie*; his many works defined the Egyptian language in a way never before achieved and made the study of grammar more exact; these contributions appeared in *ZÄS* and other journals and as separate publications; his principal works were, *Die Thronwirren unter den Nachfolgern Königs Thutmosis I, etc.*, 1896; *Das Aegyptische Verbum in Altaegyptischen, Neuaegyptischen und Koptischen*, 3 vols. 1899-1902; *Dodekaschoinos: das Zwölfmeilenland an der Grenze von Aegypten und Nubien*, 1901; *Beiträge zur ältesten Geschichte Ägyptens*, 1905; *Urkunden des Alten Reichs*, 4 pts., 1903-33; *Urkunden der 18. Dynastie*, 16 pts., 1906-9; *Hieroglyphischen Urkunden der Griechisch-Römischen Zeit*, 3 pts., 1904-16; *Die Altaegyptischen Pyramidentexte*, 1 and 2, Text, vol. 3, Kritischer Apparat, 4, Epigraphik, 1908-22, his greatest work; *Die Einsetzung des Veziers unter der 18. Dynastie: Inschrift im Grabe des Rech-mi-Re zu Schech Abd el Gurna*, 1909; *Sarapis und die sogenannten 'Katochoi' des Sarapis: zwei Probleme der Griechisch-Aegyptischen Religionsgeschichte*, 1913; *Der Nominalsatz im Ägyptischen und Koptischen*, 1916; *Von Zahlen und Zahlworten bei den alten Ägyptern und was für andere Völker und Sprachen daraus zu lernen ist ...*, 1916; *Die Zeitrechnung der alten Aegypter im Verhältnis zu der andern Völker*, 2 pts., 1919-20; *Demotische Urkunden zum ägyptischen Bürgschaftsrechte, vorzüglich der Ptolemärzeit, etc.*, 1920, a huge work of over 800 pages; *Aegyptische Lesestücke ... Texte des Mittleren Reiches*, 2 pts., 1924-7; *Dramatische Texte zu Altaegyptischen Mysterienspielen*, 1928; *Urgeschichte und älteste Religion der Ägypter*, 1930; *Das Hatschepsut-Problem noch einmal untersucht*, 1932; *Historisch-biographische Urkunden des Mittleren Reiches*, with W. Erichsen, 1935; *Übersetzung und Kommentar zu den Altägyptischen Pyramidentexten*, 6 vols. with W. Erichsen, 1935-62; *Thebanische Tempelinschriften aus Griechisch-Römischer Zeit*, posth., 1957; Sethe edited the text of Lepsius' *Denkmäler* which was supplied by Naville (q.v.) and collaborated with Gardiner (q.v.) in *Egyptian Letters to the Dead*; he visited Egypt for a second time in 1925; he died in Berlin, 6 July 1934.

NDB 24, 274-6; *Bayerische Akad. der Wiss. Jahrbuch*, 1934/5, 32-9 (A. Scharff); *Chron. d'Ég.* 10 (1935), 77-8 (J. Capart); *Eg. Rel.* 3 (1935), 116-18 (A. Scharff); *Ges. der Wiss. zu Göttingen Nach. Jahresbericht.* 1934/5, 66-74 (H. A. H. Kees); *JEA* 20 (1934), 213-14; *ZÄS* 70 (1934), 132-4 (portr.) (? Steindorff); *Zeitschrift für Eingeborenen-Sprachen* 25 (1934), 78 (E. Zyhlarz); *FuF* 10 (1934), 283-4 (H. Grapow); *Enchoria* 5 (1975), 135-50 (bibl.); 'Gedächtnisrede des Hrn. Erman auf K. Sethe' in W. Peek (ed.), *Opuscula. Sammelausgaben seltener und bisher nicht selbstständig erschienener wissenschaftlicher Abhandlungen*, 1976, cxi-cxvi; E. Endesfelder, *Die Ägyptologie an der Berliner Universität-Zur Geschichte eines Fachgebietes*, 1988, 26-7; 32-41; W. Westendorf in K. Arndt et al. (ed.), *Göttinger Gelehrte. Die Akademie der Wissenschaften zu Göttingen in Bildnissen und Würdigungen 1751-2001*, 1 (2001), 344-5.; È. Gran-Aymerich, *Dictionnaire biographique d'archéologie 1798-1945*, 2001, incorporated in *Les Chercheurs de passé 1798-1945*, 2007, 1165-6; T. Gertzen in J. Arp-Neuman and T. Gertzen (eds.), '*Steininschrift und Bibelwort*', 2019, 45-50; inf. T. Gertzen.

SETON-KARR, Heywood Walter (1859-1938)
British explorer; he was born in Belgaum, Bombay, 2 June 1859, son of George Berkeley Seton-Karr, a civil servant in India, and Eleanor Osborne; he was educated at Eton, 1873-7, Oriel College, Oxford, 1878, and Sandhurst; Lt.,1882; he served in the army until 1884 including several years in Egypt; in 1896 he discovered the ancient flint mines in the Wadi el-Sheikh reported in *The Journal of the Anthropological Institute* 27 (1897); he donated flint assemblages to various museums including the Cairo Museum, the British Museum, Brussels, and Italian collections; he died in London, 13 Jan. 1938.

ODNB 30, 884-5; *Chron. d'Eg.* 13 (1938), 327; *WWW* iii, 1218.

SETON-WILLIAMS, (Marjory) Veronica (1910-1992)
British-Australian archaeologist; she was born in Melbourne, 20 April 1910, daughter of Seton Gordon Nixon Williams, a lawyer, and Eliza Mary Staughton; she was educated at home, Clyde Girls Grammar School, and the University of Melbourne where she studied history and political science as there were no courses in archaeology or Egyptology which were her chief interests; she graduated in 1934 and went to England to study Egyptology and later prehistory at University College London; Diploma in Prehistory; PhD, 1957; she excavated with Mortimer Wheeler at Maiden Castle, 1934-6; with Petrie (q.v.) at Sheikh Zuweyed in the Sinai, 1935-6, with Garstang (q.v.) in Palestine and Turkey, 1936-7, and with Starkey at Tell el-Duweir, 1937-8; during World War II

she worked in the Ministry of Information; she later taught at the Institute of Archaeology, the City Literary Institute, and in the Department of Extra-Mural Studies, University of London until 1977; FSA, 1947; she excavated in Syria, 1956-60 and was field director of the Egypt Exploration Society's excavation at Tell el-Farain (Buto), 1964-8; from 1963 she was a regular lecturer for Swan's Nile cruises; her publications were *Britain and the Arab States*, 1948; *Ptolemaic Temples*, 1978; *Les Trésors de Tutankhamon*, 1980; *Les Trésors de Babylone*, 1981; *Blue Guide to Egypt*, with Peter Stocks, 1983, rev. 1988; *El-Amarna*, 1984; *Egyptian Poems*, 1987; *Egyptian Stories and Legends*, 1988; her autobiography *The Road to El-Aguzein*, 1988; and *A Short History of Egypt*, 1989; she died at St Helier, Jersey, 29 May 1992.

The Times 4 June 1992; *The Guardian* 4 June 1992 (M. Drower); *The Independent* 4 June 1992 (H. S. Smith); *The Daily Telegraph* 11 June 1992; R. S. Merrillees, *Living with Egypt's Past in Australia*, 1990, 43, 46; *Buried History* 49 (2013), 17-22 (portr.) (R. Merrillees).

SETTGAST, Jürgen (1932-2004)
German Egyptologist; he was born at Wismar 21 March 1932; he studied at the University of Heidelberg (PhD, 1960); he then joined the German Archaeological Institute in Cairo and took part in excavations at Thebes in 1966; he was appointed Director of the Ägyptische Museum at Charlottenburg in West Berlin 1 Sept. 1968; he organized a series of succesful exhibitions *Echanton-Nofretete*, 1976; *Tutanchamun*, 1980, and Nofret, 1985 and opened up new galleries; he was obliged to resign in 1988 due to ill health; he died in Berlin, 31 Jan. 2004.

Amun 21 (2004), 34 (portr.) (D. Wildung); *ZÄS* 132 (2005), XII-XIII (portr.) (D. Wildung).

SEVILLA, Covadonga (1964-2016)
Spanish Egyptologist; she studied Egyptology at Brussels under Tefnin (q.v.) and de Meulenaere (q.v.); PhD.; she then became a lecturer in Egyptology at the Universidad Autónoma in Madrid; her main interest was the study of female royal aspects in the Third Intermediate and Late Periods; she was a co-founder of the journal *Trabajos de Egiptologia* and was a co-ordinator of the First Conference of Iberian Egyptology, 1998; she excavated at Ihnasya el-Medina (Herakleopolis) and as well as at Madam in the UAE and was co-director of research on Tomb 20-9 in Luxor; she died in Madrid, 23 June 2016.

Inf. J-R. Perez-Accino.

SEYFFARTH, Gustavus (1796-1885)
German-American orientalist, archaeologist and theologian; he was born at Uebigau near Torgau, Germany, 13 July 1796, son of Traugott August S., a Lutheran clergyman, and Johanna Dorothea Hertel; he studied classics at St. Afra, the Fürstenschule at Meissen, and at the University of Leipzig, 1815-19 under Spohn (q.v.); PhD; AM Phil. and Theol. Dr.; he was later appointed Docent and, as he knew Coptic as well, was given the task of completing the two vols. of Spohn's *De lingua et literis veterum Aegyptiorum ...*, 1825-31; to do this he visited many European collections, 1826-8, and made over 10,000 copies and impressions from Egyptian monuments and Coptic MSS; this vast corpus of material *Bibliotheca Aegyptiaca Manuscripta*, filled 14 royal folio vols., not including an index in quarto, and was bequeathed by him at his death to the New York Historical Soc.; in 1830 he was appointed to the first Professorship in archaeology at Leipzig University; it is at this period that he began his lifelong struggle with Champollion (q.v.) and his followers; Seyffarth claimed that Egyptian was based on what has been termed ancient Coptic, which was related to Hebrew, which in turn was the mother of all languages; that hieroglyphs, were thus mainly phonograms, or syllabic writing; that the signs represented syllabic composites derived from Noah's alphabet, which consisted of eighteen consonants and seven vowels representing the zodiac, all other alphabets deriving from this one; by the Egyptian alphabet he meant 630 hieroglyphic signs, however, and he appears to have denied the existence of determinatives; as the Champollionists gained ground in Germany Seyffarth's position became impossible and he found it increasingly hard to get his numerous and extraordinary works published or to found a proper school, so that he resigned his chair and emigrated to the USA in 1854, where he taught for three years without payment at Concordia Coll., St. Louis; he moved to New York, 1859, where he worked at the Astor Library, and also preached at Yorkville; he vainly tried with

others to found a theological seminary at Donsville, and attacked slavery; Seyffarth's life is perhaps the most tragic example in all Egyptology of a brilliant mind, perhaps genius, led astray by fantastic notions; he had vast erudition and incredible industry, but was obsessed with astronomical ideas and linguistic heresies; had he used his very great intellectual powers alongside Champollion, Lepsius (q.v.), Brugsch (q.v.) and Ebers (q.v.) whom he fought for sixty years, his contributions to Egyptology might have been immense; the Assyriologist F. Delizsch who was once his student in Hebrew had a very high regard for his knowledge of Semitics; he claimed to be the first decipherer of hieroglyphs, and that all other figures connected with decipherment had after Young (q.v.) been merely using his discoveries, often wrongly; his bibl. lists about 113 published books and articles and 31 unpublished works, and the list of his works is a very long one, many being in Latin, *Rudimenta Hieroglyphices ...* , 1826 is perhaps the best-known; also *De Hieroglyphica Aegyptiorum scriptura*, 1825, *Clavis Aegyptiaca*, his most mature work; *Thesaurus Copticus*, 4 vols. 1829; Seyffarth did have a certain following, Uhlemann (q.v.) and Wuttke were his pupils, Knortz his biographer went so far as to state that the translation of the Rosetta Stone was only made possible through his system; the arrangement of the fragments of the canon of Kings at Turin is mainly due to him; his papers papers bequeathed to the New York Historical Society are now in the Brooklyn Museum; he died in New York, 17 Nov. 1885.

The Literary Life of Gustavus Seyffarth, 1886, autobiogr, (bibl.); Knortz, *Gustav Seyffarth: eine biographische Skizze*, 1886; *NDB* 24, 296-7; *ZDMG* 41 (1887), 193-231, a critical estimate (G. Ebers); DAB 17. 4-5; Hartleben, passim; Renouf, *Life-Work*, i. 1-80 (selective bibl.); Hilmy, ii, 229; Champollion, i, 119 and often; E. Blumenthal, *Altes Ägypten in Leipzig*, 1981 3-7; E. Blumenthal in P. Nagel (ed.), *Carl-Schmidt-Kolloquium an der Martin-Luther-Universität Halle-Wittenberg 1988*, 1990, 96-9; W. Wolze in J. Arp-Neuman and T. Gertzen (eds.), 'Steininschrift und Bibelwort', 2019, 31-8.

SEYMOUR, Henry Danby (1820-1877)
British author and politician; he was born in London, 1 July 1820, son of Henry S. and Jane Hopkinson; he lived at 39 Upper Grosvenor Square, London; MP for Poole; previously Under-Secretary of State for India; he published *Russia and the Black Sea*, 1855; he translated Brugsch's History under the title *Egypt under the Pharaohs*, 2 vols. 1879, but died just before completing it; in 1869 he presented to the British Museum four fragments of Theban tomb paintings (EA 919-22) which were published by Budge, *Wall Decorations of Egyptian Tombs*, (1914), 14-15, other objects of his, formerly in the Blackmore Museum, Salisbury, are now in the Bournemouth Natural History Society; a foundation-member of the Soc. Biblical Arch.; he died in Brymore, Somerset, 4 Aug. 1877.

Boase 3, 505.

SHANNON, Charles Haslewood *see* RICKETTS, Charles de Sousy.

SHARPE, Samuel (1799-1881)
British banker, antiquary, and Biblical scholar; he was born in King St., London, 8 March 1799, son of Sutton S., a brewer, and Maria his 2nd wife who was the sister of Samuel Rogers the poet; he entered the banking house of Samuel and Henry Rogers, 1814, becoming a partner, 1821-61; much of his spare time was devoted to studies for which he is best remembered today; his interest in Egyptology in which his work went far beyond that of an amateur, was aroused by the work of T. Young (q.v.), and he studied the works of Champollion (q.v.) and Wilkinson (q.v.) and learned Coptic as well; at the same time his interest in ancient history and Biblical studies was also cultivated and he afterwards published works in these fields; he married his cousin Sarah S., 1827, and shortly afterwards began to publish a long series of popular books on Egypt; *The Early History of Egypt*, 1836; *Egyptian Inscriptions*, series 1 and 2, 1837, 1841 and 1855, was the largest body of hieroglyphic writing published until then, and was of great importance as it made available a large mass of material to students; *Rudiments of a Vocabulary of Hieroglyphics*, 1837; *History of Egypt under the Ptolemies; History of Egypt under the Romans*, 1842; (all three of these histories were incorporated as the *History of Egypt*, 1846, 1852, and later editions); *The Chronology and Geography of Ancient Egypt*, 1849, with Bonomi; *The Triple Mummy Case of Aro-eri-Ao*, 1858 with drawings by Bonomi; *Egyptian Hieroglyphics*, 1861; *Egyptian Antiquities in the British Museum described*, 1862; notes in Bonomi's *Egypt, Nubia and Ethiopia*, 1862; *Egyptian Mythology and Egyptian Christianity*, 1863; *The Alabaster Sarcophagus of Oimenepthah*, 1864; *Texts from the Holy Bible explained*, 1866 (with drawings by Bonomi); *The Decree of Canopus*, Egyptian and Greek, 1870; *The Rosetta Stone*, Egyptian and Greek, 1871; from 1840 on he published a Hebrew Grammar and a new translation of the Bible; he bought and presented to the British Museum the statue of Prince Khaemwese (EA 947) because he believed he was the chief of the magicians who opposed Moses; Sharpe did a great service by his publications as he helped to arouse widespread interest in the subject at a time when popular and semi-serious works were still rare; he was a benefactor of University College London, and some of his books were later presented to the Edwards Library, UCL by his daughter; he died in Highbury Place, London, 28 July 1881.

Life by P. W. Clayden, 1883; *ODNB* 50, 57-8; *DNB* 51, 425-7; Hilmy, ii, 231; E. Bernand in *ZPE* 91 (1992), 217-20.

SHAW, (*Revd*) Thomas (1694-1751)

British traveller and antiquary; born Kendal, 4 June 1694, son of Gabriel S., a dyer, and his wife Agnes; he was educated at Kendal Grammar School, and entered The Queen's College, Oxford, 1711; BA, 1716; MA, 1720; Fellow of The Queen's College, 1727; DD, 1734; FRS, 1734; he went as chaplain to the English factory at Algiers in 1720, and subsequently visited Egypt, Sinai and much of North Africa; he married Joanna, widow of Edward Holden the consul in Algiers, and returned to England in 1733; he published *Travels or Observations relating to several parts of Barbary and the Levant*, 1738, an account that was extremely well illustrated with maps and plates; in this work he described his visit to the Pyramids and makes observations on Egypt; a most careful scholar he described 640 species of plant that he saw in the east; he was made Principal of St. Edmund Hall, 1740; Regius Professor of Greek in the University of Oxford, 1741; he bequeathed his papers and antiquities (subsequently transferred to the Ashmolean Museum) to the Bodleian Library; he died Bramley, 15 Aug. 1751, and was buried in Bramley Church, Hants.

ODNB 50, 124-5; *DNB* 51, 446-7; Vyse, *Operations carried on at the pyramids of Gizeh in 1837*, vol. ii, 237-41; H. Whitehouse *JEA* 88 (2002), 237-42; R. Finnegan, *English Explorers in the East (1738-1745)*, 2019, *passim*.

SHELLEY, George Ernest (1840-1910)

British ornithologist; he was born at Wotton, Surrey, 15 May 1840, son of John S. and Elizabeth Bowen; Capt. Grenadier Guards; he made four expeditions to Egypt and published his standard work, *The Birds of Egypt*, 1870, which has been extremely valuable to Egyptologists in determining the species represented on the monuments; African birds being his special study, he visited the Gold Coast, Natal, etc.; his large collections are now in the Natural History Museum; he died in Bournemouth, 29 Nov. 1910.

Hist. Coll. B.M. Hist. ii, 484; *Ibis*, 9th ser. 5, 369.

SHELTON, William Arthur (1875-1959)

American theologian; he was born in Azusa, California, 6 Sept. 1875, son of Leroy S. and Sarah Rogers; he was educated at Yale, BD and MA; he was Professor of Hebrew and Old Testament Literature at Emory College 1914-30, and founded the University's archaeological museum, now the Michael C. Carlos Museum; he spent the year 1915-16 studying under J. H. Breasted (q.v.) at Chicago; in 1920 he visited Egypt and the Middle East as part of a mission led by Breasted, collecting objects for his museum and publishing an account of his journey; his diaries and photographs from the journey are also in the museum; he died in Atlanta, 22 Feb. 1959.

Inf. Michael C. Carlos Museum; W. A. Shelton, *Dust and Ashes of Empires*, 1922; B. M. Bowen, *The Candler School of Theology*, 1974, 172-3; G. Robins, *Monuments and Mummies: the Shelton expedition to Egypt*, 1989; G. Emberling (ed.), *American Archaeologists in the Middle East 1919-1920*, 2010; *WWWA* 5, 657.

SHENUDA MAKARIOS (1837-1904)

Austrian Consular Agent and French consul at Luxor; he was born in 1837; he was a Catholic Copt of Luxor, who acted as the Austrian consular agent in Luxor from 25 May 1869 until 1904; he offered his services to de Rougé (q.v.) as a copyist during his voyage to Egypt, but the offer was declined as de R. had seen a stela in a collection in Cairo which was ascertained to have been fabricated by Shenuda; apparently he or a relation, Makarios Shenuda, acquired objects of Egyptian art for Prince W. Czartoryski (q.v.), and "managed" the excavations at Akhmim, 1882-4; he is mentioned as Shenuda by Bouriant (q.v.) and Wilbour (q.v.); Shenuda Makarios carried out excavations in the Valley of the Kings, 1900; he died in 1904 and was succeeded as Austrian consular agent by his son Iskander Shenuda from 29 Jan. 1905 until 10 Sept. 1914.

Inf. P. E. Newberry; *ASAE* 2 (1901), 196; letters of Sh. to Prince Czartoryski from the years 1882-6, Czartoryski Library in Cracow, No. EW 2113; *Prace Archeologiczne* 14 (1972) 85-104 (Moczulska and Śliwa), 105-14; inf. J. Śliwa; *Rec Trav* 7 (1886), 128; Wilbour, 292; R. Agstner, *Der Ballhausplatz und Nordafrika,* 1995, 151-2; F. Hagen and K. Ryholt, *The Antiquities Trade in Egypt 1880-1930*, 2017, 262-3.

SHERER, (Joseph) Moyle (1789-1869)

British army officer and traveller; he was born in Southampton, 18 Feb. 1789, youngest son of Joseph S.; Major in the 34th Foot (Cumberland); he served in the Peninsular War and was taken prisoner at Puerta de Mayer, 1813; he afterwards went to India and returned by the overland route; he published *Sketches in India*, 1821; *Scenes and Impressions of Egypt and Italy*, 1824 (2nd ed. 1825) (selections from both these works republished in one vol. 1825), and other works; he died in Southampton, 18 Feb. 1869.

ODNB 50, 288-9; *DNB* 52, 73-4; Hilmy, ii, 233.

SHERIF, Negm el din Mohammed (1927-1994)

Sudanese archaeologist; he was born at Kyekka near Abri, 1927; he was educated at the University of Khartoum and at Durham under Macadam (q.v.); he joined the Sudan Antiquities Service as inspector at Wadi Halfa where he oversaw salvage excavations during the Nubian rescue campaign; he became Director-General of Antiquities and the National Museums and editor of *Kush* in succession to Thabit (q.v.), 1970-87; he had to retire early due to injuries sustained in a motor accident in 1980; he died in Khartoum, 19 Sept. 1994.

The Sudan Archaeological Research Society Newsletter 7 (1994), 29-30 (L.P. Kirwan); *BSFE* 131 (1994), 5-6; *Kush* 17 (1997), 379-80; *Archéologie du Nil Moyen* 7 (1995), 3 (portr.); inf. W. Adams.

SHINNIE, Margaret Blanche Elizabeth (*née* Cloake) (1918-1995)
British archaeologist; she was born Harston, Cambridgeshire, 29 Oct. 1918, daughter of Philip Cyril Cloake, Professor of Neurology, Birmingham University, and Letitia Blanche Macdonald; in 1940 she married Peter Shinnie (q.v.), later Commissioner for Archaeology in the Sudan; she took part in the excavations at Amara West, Soba, Tanaqasi, Ghazali, Debeira West, and Meroe; following her divorce, she retained her interest in Sudanese archaeology and served on the council of the British Institute in Eastern Africa; assistant editor of the Journal of the Royal Geographic Society; she published *Linant de Bellefonds, journal d'un voyage à Méroé dans les années 1821 et 1822*, 1958; *Ancient African Kingdoms*, 1966; and with her former husband *Debeira West*, 1978; she died at Ashwellthorpe, Norfolk, 10 Jan. 1995.

The Sudan Archaeological Research Society Newsletter 8 (1995), 47-8 (J. Alexander); 9 (1995), 24-5 (P. Shinnie).

SHINNIE, Peter Lewis (1915-2007)
British archaeologist; he was born in Wimbledon, London 18 Jan. 1915, son of Andrew James Shinnie OBE, MD, Medical Officer for Westminster, and Olive Victoire Lewis; he was educated at Westminster School and Christ Church Oxford, 1934-38, studying under Gunn (q.v.); BA 1938; MA; he undertook his first excavation under Sir Mortimer Wheeler at Maiden Castle; President of the Oxford University Archaeological Society; he worked as a temporary assistant at the Ashmolean Museum before serving in world WAR II in the RAF; he was appointed temporary Assistant Keeper at the Ashmolean Museum, 1945-6, and then Assistant Commissioner for Archaeology in the Sudan, 1946-8 under Arkell (q.v.) and Commissioner, 1948-55; he returned temporarily to the Ashmolean Museum 1955-6 and then became Director of Antiquities, Uganda, 1956-8, Professor of Archaeology, University of Ghana, 1958-66, University of Khartoum, 1966-70, and finally University of Calgary, 1970-80; FSA, 1948; Corresp. FBA, 1999; Hon LLD, Calgary, 1983; he excavated at Amara West, 1948-51, Soba, 1950-52, Tanqasi, 1953-54, Ghazali, 1953-54; Debeira West, 1961-64, and Meroe, 1965-84; he founded the journal *Kush* in 1953 and later *Nyame Akuma* for Africanists; *JSSEA* 17 (1990) was dedicated to him and a volume of studies was produced in his honour *An African Commitment. Papers in Honour of Peter Lewis Shinnie*, edited by Judy Sterner and Nicholas David, 1992; he was awarded Sudan's Order of the Two Niles in 2006; apart from work on sub-Saharan Africa, his publications included *Excavation at Soba*, 1955; *Medieval Nubia*, 1954; *Ghazali: A Monastery in Northern Sudan*, 1960; *Meroe. A Civilization of the Sudan*, 1967; *Debeira West. A Medieval Nubian Town*, 1978, with Margaret Shinnie (q.v.); *The Capital of Kush* 1, 1980, R. J. Bradley; *Ancient Nubia*, 1996, *The Capital of Kush* 2: *Meroe Excavations 1973-4*, 2004; he died in Calgary, 9 July 2007.

An African Committment, 1992 xv-xxii (portr.) (N. David), 241-6 (bibl.); P. Shinnie in P. Robertshaw (ed.), *A History of African Archaeology*, 1990, 221-235; *Who's Who* 2007; *The Times* 11 Oct. 2007; *The Records of Old Westminsters* III, 1963, 347; *Egyptian Archaeology* 31 (2007), 44; *Sudan and Nubia* 11 (2007), 129-30 (portr.) (N. Grzymski); *Der Antike Sudan* 18 (2007), 211-13; *Newsletter of SSEA* (2008), 1-2 (portr.) (N. David).

SHORE, Arthur Frank (Peter) (1924-1994)
British Egyptologist and Demotist; he was born in Aldbury, Herts., 14 Nov. 1924, son of Harry S., schoolmaster, and Gertrude Emma Cross; he was educated at Cardinal Vaughan Memorial School, London, 1934-42, and King's College, Cambridge from Jan. 1943; his studies were interrupted by war service in the Royal Corps of Signals, and illness; he returned to Cambridge in 1947 and studied Demotic under Glanville (q.v.); BA, 1949; MA, 1952; he held a studentship in Oriental languages at Cambridge, 1949-55; he undertook research in Egypt from Dec. 1953 to May 1954 for his proposed thesis on mines and quarries; Fellow of King's College, Cambridge, 1955; temporary lecturer in Egyptology, University of Liverpool, Oct. 1955-Dec. 1956; Assistant Keeper, Department of Egyptian Antiquities, British Museum, 1 Jan. 1957-30 Sept. 1974; Brunner Professor of Egyptology, University of Liverpool in succession to Fairman (q.v.), 1 Oct. 1974- June 1991; Chairman of the Egypt Exploration Society, 1989-94; he took part in the Polish excavations at Faras during the Nubian rescue campaign, 1963; he specialized in the study of Demotic and Coptic texts and material remains from the post-pharaonic and Coptic periods; a volume of studies in his honour *The Unbroken Reed* was published in 1994; apart from his articles, his publications included *Portrait Painting from Roman Egypt*, 1962, revised 1972; with I. E. S. Edwards and R. Pinder-Wilson, *5000 Years of Egyptian Art*,

1962; with I. E. S. Edwards and T. G. H. James, *A General Introductory Guide to the Egyptian Collections in the British Museum*, 1964; and *Joshua I-VI and other passages in Coptic*, 1963; his catalogue of Demotic papyri from Gebelein remained unpublished at his death; he died in Southport, 27 Nov. 1994.

BM Archives; *The Times* 3 Dec. 1994 (T. G. H. James); *The Independent* 2 Dec. 1994 (C. Eyre); *The Sudan Archaeological Research Society Newsletter* 8 (1995), 48-9; *JEA* 81 (1995), 196-200 (portr.) (C.J. Eyre).

SHORTER, Alan Wynn (1905-1938)
British Egyptologist; he was born in London, 8 June 1905, son of Wilfred Wynn S. and Mary Adams; he was educated at St. Paul's School and in 1922 attended evening classes given by Margaret Murray at University College London; he then gained a classical exhibition to The Queen's College, Oxford, 1924; he read Egyptian and Coptic and in 1928 was on the expedition to El-Amarna and Armant when the EES excavated the Bucheum; he was appointed Assistant Keeper in the Egyptian Dept. of the British Museum, 1929-38; he married Joan Dove, 1931; his chief interest was in religion and funerary papyri and he published several popular books on life in ancient Egypt and mythology, and was engaged on the production of a catalogue of the BM papyri of the Book of the Dead, one part of which he had completed at his death; he wrote, *An Introduction to Egyptian Religion: an account of religion in Egypt during the Eighteenth Dynasty*, 1931*; Everyday Life in ancient Egypt*, 1932; *The Egyptian Gods*, 1937; *Catalogue of Egyptian religious papyri in the British Museum. Copies of the book PR(T)-M-HRW, from the xviiith to the xxiind Dynasty*, 1938; he died in London, 31 May 1938.

Archiv für Aeg. Arch. 1 (1938), 188 (E. Ritter von Komorzynski); *Chron. d'Ég.* 13 (1938), 339; *JEA* 24 (1938), 211-12 (A. M. Blackman); R. Janssen, *The First Hundred Years*, 1992, 23.

SHOUKRY, Muhammad Anwar (1905-1987)
Egyptian Egyptologist; he was born in Alexandria, 27 March 1905, son of Muhammad S., a railway inspector; he was educated at the Higher Training College, Cairo, 1924-8, diploma in 1938 and then at the Institute of Archaeology, University of Cairo, 1931-4, BA, 1934; in 1936 he was sent to study at Göttingen under Kees (q.v.), but his studies were interrupted by the outbreak of World War II; he finished his doctorate in the University of Cairo, PhD, 1942; he was then appointed lecturer and later Professor at the University of Cairo; he was subsequently first curator at the Cairo Museum, 1952-6; sub-director at the Centre of Documentation, 1956-9; Head of the Department of Egyptian Antiquities, 1959-60; and Director-General of the Antiquities Service, 1960-4; in 1964 he was transferred to manage the rescue of Nubian Monuments; he retired in 1965 but continued with his Nubian work for another year; he took part in excavations at Giza, Ashmunein, and Aniba and supervised work at Abu Simbel; following his retirement he taught at universities in Algeria and Saudi Arabia; apart from some articles in German and Arabic, he published his thesis *Die Privatgrabstatue im Alten Reich*, 1951; he died in 2 June 1987.

Gött. Misz. 76 (1984), 85; inf. Dia Abou-Ghazi.

SIBEUD, Jacques Marie Louis Xavier de, Comte de Saint-Ferriol (1814-1877)
French collector; he was born in Château de Clelles (Isère), 9 May 1814, eldest son of Joseph Gaspard Armand Vincent-de-Paule de S. and Madeleine Françoise de Gallien de Chabons; he was educated at Fribourg and Paris; he inherited the Château d'Uriage from the Marquise de Gautheron, 1828; he travelled in Germany and Russia, 1839-40, and in Egypt and Nubia, Dec. to Aug. 1841-42; he made a choice collection of antiquities, of which the famous stela of Quban is the most important; this collection, long in the Château d'Uriage is now mainly in the Museum of Grenoble, to which it was presented in 1916; the count left a MS journal of his voyage to Egypt; he died suddenly at Évian (Haute-Savoie), 26 April 1877, and was buried at Saint-Martin d'Uriage; his travel diary is at the Bibliothèque Municipale de Grenoble and other papers are in the Institut d'égyptologie at Lyons.

Carré, i, 351-9; P. Tresson, *Bull. Acad. Delphinale*, Grenoble, 1928; *Rev. Ég.* N.S. i. 1; *BSFE* 89 (Oct. 1980), 12.

SIBREE, Ernest (1859-1927)
British philologist; he was born in Painswick, Gloucs., 2 Jan. 1859, son of John S., schoolmaster and Anna Cash; he studied at the University of Bonn, University College London, and Oxford; BA, 1887; MA, 1890; he held the post of Assistant Keeper at the Indian Institute, Oxford, 1888-94; he then became Lecturer in Oriental Languages and Literature (later in 1896 Oriental Languages and in 1905 Egyptian and Assyrian) at University College Bristol, 1896 and also Hon Arts and Science Librarian, 1901; Secr. of the Oriental Languages Dept. (renamed in 1906 Dept. of Semitic Studies), 1906; Lecturer in Oriental Languages at the University of Bristol, 1909; Hon. Sec. of the University Oriental Soc.; he retired in 1923 but was named part-time lecturer in Comparative Philology; among his pupils were Wainwright (q.v.) and Mackay (q.v.); he died in Bristol, 29 March 1927.

JEA 93 (2007), 247-53 (portr.) (A. Dodson)

SICARD, (*Père*) **Claude** (1677-1726)
French Jesuit and traveller; he was born at Aubagne, 4 May 1677 and joined the Jesuits in 1692; he was Professor at Lyons for a time, then went as a missionary to Syria in 1700; in 1712 he transferred to Cairo where he remained for the rest of his life; he made extended tours to Upper Egypt, 1714, 1716, 1718, 1720-1, and 1726; to the Fayum in 1717; to Sinai in 1720; and to Middle Egypt and the Delta in 1723; his principal object was to make converts amongst the Copts, but he was ordered by the Regent, Philippe of Orleans, to survey the ancient monuments and to make plans and drawings of them; he was the first European traveller known to have reached Aswan and to describe Philae, Elephantine, and Kom Ombo; his papers were mostly lost, a matter for great regret as he shows himself, in such papers as have survived, to be an excellent observer; he did leave a complete list of all the monuments and sites he explored, both Christian and pagan; his surviving accounts were published by Sauneron and Martin, *Oeuvres* I-III, Cairo, 1982; he died of plague in Cairo, 12 April 1726.

Carré, i, 67-70; (bibl.) 75; Hilmy, ii, 233; Martin, *BIFAO* 87 (1987), 265-8; Lamy, 138-69.

SICKLER, Friedrich Karl Ludwig (1773-1836)
German antiquary; he was born in Gräfentonna, 3 Nov. 1773, son of Johann Volkmar S.; he studied theology and philosophy in Jena, 1791-4 and philology in Göttingen, 1794-5; PhD from Jena, 1798; he visited Rome where he acted as a tutor, 1805-11; he became the director of the gymnasium in Hildburghausen, 1812; he wrote between 1820 and 1832 on the hieroglyphs in the astronomical texts at Dendera, on mummy-cases in the Hammer-Purgstall (q.v.) collection, a work on Egyptian and Ethiopian hieroglyphic writing etc.; he died at Hildburghausen, 8 Aug. 1836.

BIFAO 5 (1906), 86; Hilmy, ii, 234; *DBE* 9, 425.

SIEBER, Franz Wilhelm (1789-1844)
Czech doctor; he was born in Prague, 30 March 1789; he visited the Levant in 1817-8 including Egypt where he formed a collection of antiquities which he later sold to the Akademie der Wissenschaften, Munich; he was a member of the Munich Akademie and also the Academy in Moscow; he published an account of his travels and a report on a mummy in 1820; he died in Prague, 17 Dec. 1844.

ADB 34, 177-9; Inf. S. Stadnikov.

SILVESTRE DE SACY, (*Baron*) **Antoine Isaac** (1758-1838)
French orientalist and the professor of Champollion (q.v.); he was born in Paris, 22 Sept. 1758, son of Abraham Jacques Silvestre de S., notary of Châtelet, who died 1765, and Marie Marguerite Judde; young de Sacy's education was superintended by his mother, an intelligent and capable woman; she died in 1819 aged 86; it is uncertain how he first became an orientalist; his teachers are not known, but he studied Hebrew in order to control the Latin and French versions of the Bible; to this he later added many other Semitic languages, and he later taught Persian; something of a prodigy he learnt German, English, Spanish, and Italian as well; in 1780 he published a notice on a Syriac manuscript in the Royal Library, but his studies at this period had to be done in his spare time from his duties as a civil servant; in 1781 he was appointed to the council of the mint; in 1785 he became one of the eight resident free Academicians in the Acad. des Inscriptions et Belles-lettres; his civil service duties ceased with the revolution; he married 1786; he published *Mémoires sur les antiquités de la Perse*, 1793; Arabic was not his special study until later in life; at this time he ran great risk as a royalist and staunch supporter of the church by having church services publicly celebrated in his house when worship was discouraged in churches; he was made Professor of Arabic at the École des langues orientales vivantes at the Bibl. Nationale 1795/6, to which Persian was afterwards added, but he again refused to propagate political ideas as all lecturers were expected to do by the government at the time; for his eldest son he wrote a child's grammar to all languages, 1799; de Sacy had completed his major work by 1805, the monumental *Grammaire arabe*, 2 vols. 1810, and the great *Chrestomathie arabe*, 3 vols. 1806; he later published further Arabic works; as a scholar his reputation had become so great by 1814 that von Humboldt saw to it that the invading allied armies respected all his property; he was appointed royal censor by Louis XVIII, 1814, and Rector of the University of Paris, 1815; he founded with Rémusat the Soc. Asiatique and the *Journal Asiatique*, 1822, and was the first President; he was also Administrator of the Collège de France, 1823, and the School of Oriental Languages, 1824; made Inspector of oriental types at the Royal Print, Conservator of oriental manuscripts of the Royal Library, and Perpetual Secretary of the Acad. des Inscr. (in succession to Dacier), from 1832; Chevalier of the Légion d'honneur, 1803, Officer, 1814, Commander, 1822, and Grand Officer 1837; he was elected to at least 20 learned societies and academies, being a member of Göttingen, Copenhagen, Amsterdam, Frankfurt, Naples, Munich, Berlin, Uppsala, London, St. Petersburg, Worcester (Massachusetts) and Calcutta among others; his greatest claim to fame is probably the work he did on the Rosetta Stone and in encouraging others to work on the decipherment

of hieroglyphs; de Sacy was the first person to read any ancient Egyptian words, albeit in a small way, for he recognized and translated three names in the Demotic version, starting with Ptolemy, 1802; he thought at this time that it was, like Arabic, an alphabetic script and without ideograms, which led him to classify the signs into 25 groups after the 25 letters of the Egyptian alphabet mentioned by Plutarch; because of this mistaken notion and the empirical approach involved, de Sacy, like his follower Åkerblad (q.v.), could get no further; a very busy man with innumerable other duties he soon abandoned work on the stone; he remained, however, at the centre of all the controversies and discussion that went on over the next thirty years, taking a fatherly interest in the progress of Egyptology; a man of great erudition and free from personal bias, he was at first not impressed by Champollion's claims to have discovered the answer to deciphering the texts, and in fact corresponded and encouraged Young (q.v.) when he was making progress; but he later swung round to Champollion's side when it became evident that he was evolving the correct system, and he lived long enough to see him vindicated; de Sacy liked to encourage all young scholars in oriental studies and must be judged on the whole of his life's work and not on his partial work on Egyptian Demotic; his library was sold in Paris by Romain Merlin, the sale catalogue, *Bibliothèque de M. le Baron Silvestre de Sacy*, 1842-7; he died in Paris, 21 Feb. 1838 and was buried in Père Lachaise cemetery.

H. Dehérain, *Silvestre de Sacy*, 1938; Hartwig Derenbourg, *Silvestre de Sacy*, 1895 (portr.); Centenary hommage by his family, 1938; *EB* ed. xi, 25, 119; Hartleben (see index); Hilmy, ii, 235; Renouf, *Life-Work*, i. 44, 88, 151, 167-9; *CRAIBL* 1936, 64-73; Lamy, 300-2; E. Gran-Aymerich, *Dictionnaire biographique d'archéologie 1798-1945*, 2001, incorporated in *Les Chercheurs de passé 1798-1945*, 2007, 1169-71.

SIMAIKA, Marcus (*Pasha*) (1864-1944)
Egyptian administrator and collector; he was born in Cairo, 28 Feb. 1864, son oft Hana S. and Bamba al-Birmani; from 1883 he served in the Egyptian State Railways and other bodies; member from 1906 and later chairman of the Commission for the Preservation of Arab Monuments, under which he placed the ancient Coptic churches; he was the founder and first Director of the Coptic Museum in 1908, taken over by the government in 1931; Bey, 1899; Pasha, 1915; CBE, 1932; Légion d'Honneur, 1937; FSA; he undertook the cataloguing of Coptic manuscripts in Egypt; he died in Alexandria, 2 Oct. 1944.

BSC 10 (1944), 207 (M. B. Ghali); *The Coptic Encyclopedia* 6, 1700; *Kemet* 2 no. 2 (1993), 22-3; Samir M. Simaika, *Marcus Simaika*, 2017.

SIMON, (Henri) James (1851-1932)
German businessman and benefactor; he was born in Berlin, 17 Sept. 1851, son of Izaak S. and his wife Adolphine; he was a partner in the family business of Simon Brothers, a successful textile firm; he was a collector and substantial donor to Berlin's museums, to which he gave many valuable paintings; he also purchased objects for the Ägyptisches Museum Berlin, including the 'Berlin Green Head' and the wooden head of Queen Tiye said to come from Gurob; in 1898 he helped found the Deutsche Orient-Gesellschaft, and sponsored its excavations including those at Babylon, Boğazköy, Abusir and Amarna; he thus became the owner of the bust of Nefertiti and much other Amarna material, which he donated to the Ägyptisches Museum in 1920; he also supported numerous social charities; he died in Berlin, 23 May 1932.

O. Matthes, *James Simon: Mäzen im wilhelminischen Zeitalter*, 2000; B. Schultz (ed.), *James Simon: Philantrop und Kunstmäzen / Philanthropist and Patron of the Arts*, 2007; R. Dreyfus and O. Matthes, *The State Museums of Berlin and the Legacy of James Simon*, 2008; D. Strauch, *James Simon*, 2010.

SIMONIDES, Constantine (1824-1867)
Greek forger of papyri and manuscripts; he himself gave the place and date of his birth as Hydra, 11 Nov. 1824, but subsequently 'emended' this to 5 Nov. 1820 so as to justify his claim that he wrote the *Codex Sinaiticus* in 1839; he was a monk at Mount Athos; he was in Britain in 1853, when he sold manuscripts of varying authenticities to the British Museum and Sir Thomas Phillipps; he was in Europe from 1854, and in 1855 he created a history of Egypt by Uranius, initially accepted by Lepsius (q.v.) and Dindorf, and edited and published by the latter as *Uranii Alexandrii de regibus Aegyptiorum libri tres*, 1856; it was subsequently rejected by Lepsius, who instigated his arrest for forgery; S. was made to repay the money he received for the forged Uranius, and was briefly detained in Berlin; he returned to Britain in 1858, and in 1860 introduced himself to Joseph Mayer (q.v.) to whom he had dedicated his *A Brief discussion on Hieroglyphic Letters*, 1860, which opposed Champollion's (q.v.) decipherment of hieroglyphs in favour of a symbolic system; he unrolled papyri in Meyer's collection, including the Tomb Robbery papyri, and created forgeries, such as unbelievably early versions of the gospels, from some of them; a committee of the Royal Society of Literature investigated the matter in 1863, and C. W. Goodwin (q.v.) detected the forgery; in 1862 S. himself declared that the *Codex Sinaiticus* was a forgery made by himself in 1839, an absurdity exposed by Henry

Bradshaw; he published a work on Horapollo, *Concerning Horus of Nilopolis*, 1863, in which he claimed to have discovered Horapollo's funerary stela and further volumes of his works, and a translation of the *Periplus of Hanno*, 1864, also of dubious worth; he left Britain in 1864; he died in Alexandria, 1867.

Charles Stewart, *Biogr. Memoir of Constantine Simonides*, London, 1859; J. A. Farrer, *Literary Forgeries*, 39-66; Ebers, *Richard Lepsius* (trans. Underhill), 194-5, 335 *The Athenaeum* Feb. 16, 1856, 201; *Report of the Council of the Royal Society of Literature on some of the Mayer Papyri and a Palimpsest Manuscript. of Uranius*, 1863; F. Ritschl, *Rhein. Mus.* 27. 114-26; H. Bradshaw, *Guardian*, 26 Jan. 1863; two collections of press-cuttings on S.'s career in England, BL Press-marks 1700 b. 4 and 11899 g. 42; *The Mount Sinai MS. of the Bible* (BM pamphlet) 4th ed. 1935, 11-15; corresp. on the forged papyri, BL Add. MS 34098; corresp. on other forgeries, with some actual specimens of them, Add. MS 42502; Hilmy, ii, 237; A. N. L. Munby, *Phillipps Studies*, 8v. 114-31 (portr.); M. Jones (ed.), *Fake? The Art of Deception*, 1990, 172; O. Masson, *Revue des Études Grecques* 105 (1992), 234-5; O. Masson, *The Griffon* 3 (1993), 7-15; inf. O. Masson and T. Hardwick.

SIMONS, Jan Josef (1899-1969)
Dutch scholar; he was born at Tilburg, 24 Nov. 1899 and joined the Jesuit order in 1918; he studied philosophy at Jersey where he obtained his doctorate and at the Institut Biblique at Rome; he then studied under Mallon (q.v.) at Jerusalem when he took part in excavations and developed an interest in topography; he completed his studies at Maastricht and later became a lecturer at the Institut Biblique; his chief publication was *Handbook for the Study of Egyptian Topographical Lists relating to Western Asia*, 1937 apart from other works on Palestinian topography; he died at Nijmegen, 3 Jan. 1969.

Bib. Or. 26 (1969), i-ii (portr.) (P. Cools)

SIMPSON, (William) Kelly (1928-2017)
American Egyptologist; he was born in New York, 3 Jan. 1928, son of Kenneth Farrand S., a lawyer and later congressman, and Helen Louise Knickerbacker Porter; he was educated at Yale University, 1943-54; BA in English, 1947; MA, 1948; PhD, 1954; Hon Doctor of Humane Letters from the American University in Cairo, 2001; he served as curatorial assistant at the Metropolitan Museum of New York in the Egyptian Dept. under Hayes (q.v.) and Lansing (q.v.), 1949-54, while working for his doctorate under Bull (q.v.); he received a Fulbright Fellowship to visit Egypt, 1954-6; he became a research fellow at Harvard University, 1956-8; he was appointed assistant professor in the Dept. of Near Eastern Languages and Literature at Yale University, 1958; associate professor, of Egyptology, 1963; professor, 1965-2004 and then emeritus; he also served as chairman of the Dept., 1967-70; in addition to his post at Yale, he became curator of of the Dept. of Egyptian and Ancient Near Eastern Art at the Museum of Fine Arts, Boston, 1970-86; consultative curator from 1986; he also lectured at Harvard University, the University of Pennsylvania, the Institute of Advanced Studies at Princeton University, the Collège de France, and the Calouste Gulbenkian Foundation at Lisbon; he served three terms as president of the International Association of Egyptologists, 1982-91; he held the position of vice-chairman of the Boards of the American University in Cairo and trustee of the Archaeological Institute of America and the American Research Center in Egypt; he was awarded the Distinguished Achievement Award from the American Research Center, 1998; Medal for Distinguished Service to Egyptology from the Egyptian Ministry of Culture, 2000; and the Augustus Graham Medal by Brooklyn Museum, 2003; he excavated at Giza under Fakhry (q.v.) and Memphis under Anthes (q.v) and organized the Yale-Pennsylvania expedition to Nubia, excavating at Toshka and Arminna, 1960-3 and co-directed the subsequent work at Abydos; he also undertook epigraphic work at Giza; *Studies in Honor of William Kelly Simpson* in two volumes were edited by P. Der Manuelian, 1996; apart from over 150 articles, he published *Papyrus Reisner* I, 1963; *Heka-Nefer and the Dynastic Material from Toshka and Arimma*, 1963; *Papyrus Reisner* II, 1965; *Papyrus Reisner* III, 1969; with D. Dunham, *The Mastaba of Queen Mersyankh* III. *G 7530-7540*, 1970; with W. Hallo, *The Ancient Near East. A History*, 1971; with R. Faulkner and E. Wente, *The Literature of Ancient Egypt*, 1972; 2nd ed. 1973; *The Terrace of the Great God at Abydos*,1974; *The Mastabas of Qar and Idu. G7101-7102*, 1976; *The Face of Egypt. Permanence and Change in Egyptian Art*, 1976; *The Offering Chapel of Sekhem-ankh-ptah in the Museum of Fine Arts Boston*, 1976; *The Mastabas of Kawab, Khafkufu I and II. G7110-7120, 7130-7140, 7150*, 1978; *Mastabas of the Western Cemetery* I, 1980; *Papyrus Reisner* IV, 1986; *The Offering Chapel of Kayemnofret in the Museum of Fine Arts Boston*, 1992; and *Inscribed Material from the Pennsylvania-Yale Excavations at Abydos*, 1995; he died in New York, 24 March 2017.

NY Times 31 March 2017; Yale Univ. Dept. of Near Eastern Languages and Civilizations (photo).

SIMPSON, (Revd) William Sparrow (1828-1897)
British antiquary and historian; he was born in Chelmsford, Essex, 24 Jan. 1828, son of William S. and Jane Sparrow; he was educated at Queens' College, Cambridge; BA, 1851; MA, 1854; became Rector of St. Vedast, City of London, 1857-97; DD, 1873; FSA Librarian and Sub-dean of St. Paul's; Hon. Librarian to the Archbishop

of Canterbury; he published many archaeological books and papers; vice-Pres. Brit. Archaeological Association; in 1867 he bought from the dealer W. S. Lincoln a bronze axe with the cartouche of King Kamose of Dyn. XVII and published it (*J. Br. Arch. Assn.* 23. 293 and pl. 15); he presented it to the British Museum in 1875 (EA 36772); he died in London, 28 March 1897.

Al. Cantab.; JEA 10, 264; W. J. Sparrow Simpson, *Memoirs of the Rev. W. Sparrow Simpson, D.D.,* 1899.

SKRINE, (*Revd*) Vincent Eccles (1850-1925)
British benefactor; he was born at Bath, 24 Aug. 1850, son of Henry Duncan S and Susanna Caroline Mills; Corpus Christi College, Oxford; BA, 1875; MA, 1877; he was ordained, 1875; Vicar of Itchen Stoke, Hants, and finally Rector of Claverton, Bath, where he died in 1925; he presented a collection of papyri to the Bodleian Library in 1913; some of these came from the great find of mummies cleared by Grébaut (q.v.) in 1891, and as they were obtained by the donor's brother-in-law Col. Vivian at the time of the Battle of Tell el-Kebir in 1882, it proves that the site was being exploited by the local diggers for some years before they disclosed the secret; he died at Claverton, 29 Nov. 1925.

Clergy Lists; JEA 4 (1917), 122; 5 (1918), 24.

SLOANE, Charles (*fl.*1820-1838)
British diplomat and excavator; he was British Consular official in Cairo; Secretary and later Chancellor of the British Consulate, 1824-38; with Caviglia (q.v.) he discovered the colossus of Ramesses II at Mit Rahina, 1820; he joined with Salt (q.v.), Vyse (q.v.), Briggs (q.v.), and others in financing Caviglia's excavations.

Bonomi Diary, Nov. 27, 1831; FO Records; Hay Diary, 1824, Nov. 28 and Dec. 3; Lindsay, 39; Westcar Dairy, 243, 264, 275, 280.

SLOANE, (*Sir*) Hans, Baronet (1660-1753)
British physician and collector; he was born at Killileagh, Co. Down, Ireland, son of Alexander S., receiver-general of taxes, and Sarah Hicks; he studied medicine at Paris and Montpelier; MD University of Orange, 1683; he settled in London where he became a successful physician and moved in scientific circles; Fellow of the Royal Society, 21 Jan. 1685; member of the College of Physicians, 12 April 1687; Secretary of the Royal Society, 1693-1712; MD from the University of Oxford, 19 July 1701; Baronet, 3 April 1716; President of the College of Physicians, 1719-35; President of the Royal Society, 1727-41 in succession to Newton; he was also a member of the Academies of Science in Paris, St. Petersburg and Madrid; he formed a large collection of antiquities and other curiosities which by his will were offered to the nation at a bargain price of £20,000; their purchase resulted in the foundation of the British Museum in 1753; his original collection included a number of Egyptian antiquities; he died in Chelsea, 11 Jan. 1753.

ODNB 50, 943-9 (portr.); *DNB* 52, 379-80 (N. Moore); A. MacGregor (ed.), *Sir Hans Sloane,* 1994; M. L. Bierbrier, 'The Sloane Collection of Egyptian Antiquities' in L. Limme and J. Strybol (ed.), *Aegyptus Museis Rediviva,* 1993; J. Delbugo, *Collecting the World,* 2017.

SLOLEY, Robert Walter (1879-1958)
British scientist; born at Lewisham, 21 June 1879, son of Robert Hugh S., accountant, and Elizabeth Maxted; he graduated from St. John's College, Cambridge, and then joined the staff of Liverpool College; during the First World War he went to the Department of Instrument Inspection of the Air Ministry, and afterwards continued at Kidbrooke depot; while there he wrote a book on aircraft instruments which went through several editions; he travelled extensively and visited S. Africa and India; for a year or two he studied Egyptian at University College London, and was a member of the EES for over thirty years until his death; he also served on the Committee for many years and gave lectures to the Society, wrote book reviews and contributed to bibliographies in *JEA*; Sloley's great interest lay in ancient Egyptian mathematics and science, in particular astronomy and methods of measuring time, on which subject he was an expert; he wrote the chapter on 'Science' in *The Legacy of Egypt,* and contributed an important article on methods of measuring time to *JEA* 17, and another in *Ancient Egypt* for 1924; Sloley lectured to schools and broadcast a talk entitled 'A Day in the Life of an Egyptian Schoolboy', his papers are in the Griffith Institute, Oxford; he died at Amersham, Bucks., 18 Aug. 1958.

EES *Report* (1958), 4 (R. O. Faulkner); *Nature* 182 (1958), 1128 (R. O. Faulkner).

ŚMIESZEK, Antoni Józef (1881-1943)
Polish Egyptologist and linguist; he was born in Oswiecim, 22 May 1881; he studied linguistics and classical philology at the University of Cracow, 1901-5 and later at the Universities of Munich, Berlin, and London, 1907-10; after World War I he obtained a post teaching linguistics at the University of Tomsk, 1918-21; a chair of Egyptology was created for him at Poznan, 1921-33 and later at Warsaw, 1934-9; he wrote on Egyptian religion and linguistics in Polish periodicals and general collective works; he committed suicide in Göttingen, 12 Jan. 1943.

Biographies of Polish scholars, 1985, I, 3; inf. J. Śliwa

SMITH, (*Sir*) Charles Holled (1846-1925)

British army officer and excavator; he was born at Germyns, Romsey, 12 Sept. 1846, son of Charles Sergison S. of Consall Hall, Leek, Staffs. and Georgiana Gardner; educated Shrewsbury School; he entered the Army, 1865; Capt., 1877; retired, Major-General, 1900; KCMG, 1892; CB; he served in the Zulu and Boer Wars, 1879-81; in the Sudan, 1885-6, Suakin, 1888, Tollar, 1891; Governor of the Red Sea Littoral and Commandant at Suakin, 1888-92; he excavated at Aswan, 1887-8; in 1887 he presented to the British Museum some important stelae and other sculptured monuments (EA 1015, 1019, 1021-2, 1055, 1188-9); he died at Hove, Sussex, 18 March 1925.

Budge, *N & T* i, 94, 100, 132; *WWW* ii, 970.

SMITH, Earl Baldwin (1888-1956)

American architect and archaeologist; born Topsham, Maine, 25 May 1888, son of Frank Eugene S. and Nellie Frances Baldwin; he graduated from Pratt Institute, Brooklyn, 1906; AM Princeton University, 1912; PhD Princeton, 1915; he joined the Department of Art and Archaeology, Princeton, 1916, and became Professor of the History of Architecture, 1931; he was Chairman of the Dept. 1945-54; he wrote a study *Egyptian Architecture as Cultural Expression*, 1938, which was the first such analysis of architecture as representing ancient Egyptian life since Perrot (q.v.) and Chipiez (q.v.) produced their important survey; he died at Princeton, 7 March 1956.

AJA 60 (1956), 285-7 (E. Sjoqvist); *AfO* 18 (1957), 234 (E. Weidner); *WWWA* 3, 794.

SMITH, Edwin (1822-1906)

American adventurer and dealer; he was born in Bridgeport, Connecticut, 27 April 1822, son of Sheldon S.; he settled in Egypt in 1858 and resided at Luxor until 1876, carrying on the business of a money-lender and antiquities dealer; he acquired two important medical papyri in Jan. 1862, one of which he sold to Ebers and the other he retained until his death, when his daughter Leonora presented it, with other objects from his collection, to the N-Y Historical Society; the Edwin Smith Papyrus was published in a sumptuous edition by Breasted in 1930, and is now in the New York Academy of Medicine; the rest of his collection is now in the Brooklyn Museum; Smith had considerable knowledge of hieroglyphic and hieratic writing and Naville stated that he used that knowledge to assist the local inhabitants to make forged antiquities, and according to Adams (q.v.), he was a forger himself; he died in Naples, Italy, 23 April 1906.

A. L. Adams, *Notes of a Naturalist in the Nile Valley*, 56-8; Breasted, *Edwin Smith Surgical Papyrus*, 20; Devéria, *Mém. et Fragm.* i, 358; Wilson, 52-7; R. F. Hagen and K. Ryholt, *The Antiquities Trade in Egypt 1880-1930*, 2017, 263-4.

SMITH, (*Sir*) Grafton Elliot (1871-1937)

Australian anatomist and anthropologist; he was born in Grafton, NSW, Australia, 15 Aug. 1871, son of Stephen Sheldrick S., a teacher, and Mary Jane Evans; he studied at the Universities of Sydney and Cambridge; Fellow (later Hon. Fellow) St. John's College; he was appointed Professor of Anatomy in the Cairo School of Medicine, 1900-9; he later held appointments at Manchester, 1909, and University College London, 1919-36; MA; LittD; DSc; MD; LRCP; FRS; knighted 1934; he married Kathleen daughter of William Macredie 1900; Elliot Smith was one of the foremost authorities on the brain and the evolution of man; while working in Egypt he examined the human remains and mummies found at many sites, in particular those discovered in the Arch. Survey of Nubia; he was the first person to make a systematic examination of all the Royal Mummies in Cairo Museum, and from this information and material derived from a study of many others, he explained and defined the technique of embalming in Egypt and corrected many long-standing errors; it was the most important work done on this subject until Lucas re-examined the evidence; in his other Egyptological and anthropological studies his views had not the same value; his ideas became increasingly eccentric and he put forward the hypothesis that Egypt was the original home of most of the customs and beliefs of civilized mankind, which spread throughout the entire world; this provoked controversy and was evolved into the Diffusionist Theory which gained some following at the time, but which was never widely accepted; a collection of his Egyptian antiquities was donated to the Nicholson Museum, Sydney in 1984; he published valuable works on mummification, *A Contribution to the study of mummification in Egypt with special reference to the measures adopted during the ... 21st Dynasty for moulding the form of the body*, 1906; *Archaeological Survey of Nubia, 1907-8. 2. Report on the human remains*, 2 vols. with F. Wood Jones, 1910; *The Royal Mummies*, Cairo Cat., 1912; *The Ancient Egyptians and the origin of civilization*, new ed., 1923; *Tutankhamen and the discovery of his tomb by the late Earl of Carnarvon and Mr. Howard Carter*, 1923; *Egyptian Mummies*, with W. R. Dawson, 1924; he also contributed a paper on the physical characters of the mummy of Thutmose IV to the Davis report, and wrote articles in journals; he died in London, 1 Jan. 1937.

Sir Grafton Elliot Smith. A Biogr. Record by his Colleagues, ed. W. R. Dawson, 1938 (portr. and bibl., pp. 219-53); *American Anthropologist.* NS 39 (1937), 523-6 (T. W. Todd); *Bull. John Rylands Lib* 21 (1937), 4-6 (T. H.

435

Pear); *BMJ*, Jan. 1937, 99; *Chron. d'Ég.* 12 (1937), 231-2 (J. Capart); *Lancet*, Jan. 1937, 113; *Nature*, 9 Jan. 1937, 57; *Science*, NS 85, New York, 1937, 66-8 (W. K. Gregory); *WWW* iii, 1253; A. P. Elkin and N. W. G. Macintosh (eds.), *Grafton Elliot Smith. The Man and his Work*, 1974; R. S. Merrilllees, *Living with Egypt's Past in Asutralia*, 1990, 28-29; *ODNB* 51, 156-7; È. Gran-Aymerich, *Dictionnaire biographique d'archéologie 1798-1945*, 2001, incorporated in *Les Chercheurs de passé 1798-1945*, 2007, 1174-5; V. G. Callender in K. N. Sowada and B. G. Ockinga (eds.), *Egyptian Art in the Nicholson Museum, Sydney*, 2006, 57-79; J. Buikstra and C. Roberts, *The Global History of Palaeopathology. Pioneers and Prospects*, 2012, 213-5 (B. Baker and M. Judd).

SMITH, Joseph Lindon (1863-1950)
American artist and copyist; he was born at Pawtucket, Rhode Island, 11 Oct, 1863, son of Henry S., a wholesale lumber merchant, and Emma Greenleaf; he was trained as an artist at MIT, Museum School of the Boston Museum of Fine Arts and in Paris; he returned to Boston in 1885 and earned his living as a painter and lecturer in art; his work had an extraordinary realism and he aimed to get his reproductions of Egyptian scenes and reliefs as like the original as it was possible, with much three dimensional treatment; he was painting in Egypt and Nubia in 1898 when he aroused the interest of Phoebe A. Hearst (q.v.) and later of Reisner (q.v.) whose expeditions he joined, 1916-39; he later became a trustee and honoraray curator at the Boston Museum, to which he gave numerous objects, and where the largest group of his pictures can be found; he was a founding member of ARCE, 1948; he exhibited his work at the Cairo Museum, 1948-50, and taught at the Egyptian Ministry of Education; in an amusing account of his life, *Tombs, Temples and Ancient Art*, edited by his wife, Corinna Lindon Smith, 1956, he gives excellent descriptions of the discovery of tombs such as that of Yuya and Tuya, and also many anecdotes of archaeologists in Egypt; he also painted scenes in Iraq, Iran, Syria and Phoenicia, the Far East, and Maya lands; he died in New York, 18 Oct. 1950.

Tombs, Temples and Ancient Art, 1956; *WWWA* 3, 797; M. M. Allam, *Joseph Lindon Smith: The man and the artist*, 1949; C. Lindon Smith, *Interesting People*, 1962; B. Lesko et al., *Joseph Lindon Smith: Paintings from Egypt*, 1998.

SMITH, (Lars) Otto (1864-1935)
Swedish collector; he was born in Stockholm, 29 Jan. 1864, son of Lars Olsson S., a wine merchant, and Marie Louise Collin; he studied at the universities of Uppsala, Leipzig, and Tübingen; PhD, 1886; he then entered the family business becoming managing director of Karlshamn Spirituous Liquor Co.; he formed a collection of Egyptian antiquities which is now in the Linköping Museum, Sweden; he died in Karlshamn, 27 May 1935.

Svenska Man och Kvinnor 7, 109-110; G. Björkman, *A Selection of the Objects in the Smith Collection of Egyptian Antiquities at the Linköping Museum, Sweden*, 1971.

SMITH, Ray Winfield (1897-1982)
American businessman and collector; he was born in Marlboro, New Hampshire, 4 June 1897, son of John Henry S. and Ellen Maria Stone; BSc Dartmouth College 1918; he served in the American army 1918-9 and then worked for the Sinclair Oil Company 1922-36 during which time he began an important glass collection; he ran his own export-import firm 1936-42; he served in the US Air Force 1944-5 and then became a government official 1946-55 notably economic adviser to the US army in Berlin 1951-2; chairman of the International Committee on Ancient Glass 1948-68; trustee of the Archaeological Institute of America 1957-66; D. of Humane Letters (hon.), Dartmouth College 1958; Director, ARCE, Cairo 1963-5; founder and director of the Akhenaten Temple Project 1965-72; his glass collection, now in the Corning Museum of Glass, was sold in 1975; he was co-author of *The Akhenaten Temple Project. Vol. I: The Initial Discoveries*, 1976; he died in Houston, Texas, 17 April 1982.

WWWA 1982-3, 3128; *NY Times* 19 April 1982.

SMITH, Sidney (1889-1979)
British Assyriologist; he was born in Leeds, 29 Aug. 1889, son of Sidney S., a journalist who moved to London, and Ellen Crouch; he was educated at the City of London School and Queens' College, Cambridge, 1907-11; BA, 1911; he became a schoolteacher and attended classes at Berlin in Oriental studies; he was appointed an Assistant in the Department of Egyptian and Assyrian Antiquities, British Museum, 8 July 1914, but did not take up his post until 1919 following war service; Director of Antiquities in Iraq and Director of the Iraq Museum, 1926-31; Keeper of Egyptian and Assyrian Antiquities, British Museum in succession to Hall (q.v.), Jan. 1931-30 Sept. 1948; Hon. Lecturer in Accadian Assyriology, King's College, London, 1924-38; Hon. Lecturer in Near Eastern Archaeology, Institute of Archaeology, University of London, from 1934; Hon. Professor, 1938-46; LittD, Cambridge, 1941; Fellow of the British Academy, 1941; Professor of Ancient Semitic Languages and Civilization, School of Oriental and African Studies, University of London, 1948-55; he died at Barcombe, 12 June 1979.

PBA LXVI (1980), 463-71 (D. J. Wiseman) (portr.).

SMITH, William Stevenson (1907-1969)

American Egyptologist; he was born in Indianapolis, Indiana, 7 Feb. 1907, son of Louis Ferdinand S. and Edna Wirth Stevenson; he was educated at the University of Chicago, 1924-6, BA, and graduated from Harvard University, 1928; PhD Harvard, 1940; he joined the staff of the Museum of Fine Arts, Boston, 1928; from 1930 to 1939 he was a member of the joint expedition of Harvard and the Boston Museum in Egypt at the Giza Pyramids working as assistant museum curator under G. A. Reisner (q.v.); he returned to Egypt after the war to close down the Harvard-Boston expedition, 1946-7; Lieut. Commander in the United States Naval Reserve during the war, active service 1942-6; during this period he continued to be Assistant Curator in the Department of Egyptian Art in Boston, 1941-54; Associate Curator 1954-6; Curator 1956 until his death; lecturer in European art in the Fine Arts Department of Harvard University from 1948; in 1951 he spent an additional year in Egypt researching under a Fulbright grant and served as Director of the American Research Center in Egypt, Cairo, holding this post until his resignation in 1966; he continued as a member of the Board of governors and the executive committee of the Center, and was also a member of the American Academy of Arts and Sciences, the German Archaeological Institute of America, the American Oriental Soc., and the Cambridge Historical Soc.; Stevenson Smith was primarily interested in history and archaeology, making Egyptian art his special study; his principal published works were, *Ancient Egypt as represented in the Museum of Fine Arts*, 1942 (4th rev. ed. 1960), a handbook to the Collections; *A History of Egyptian Sculpture and Painting in the Old Kingdom*, 1946, revised ed.,1981, a monumental study of this subject; *A History of the Giza Necropolis*, vol. 2, *The Tomb of Hetep-heres*, with Reisner; *The Art and Architecture of Ancient Egypt* (Pelican Hist. of Art), 1958; *Interconnections in the Ancient Near East*, 1965; he also contributed a chapter on 'The Old Kingdom in Egypt' to the revised ed. of the *Cambridge Anc. Hist.*, 1962, and to journals various articles, see *Bull. BMFA.; JARCE; JEA; JNES; ZÄS*, etc.; he died in Cambridge, Massachusetts, 14 Jan. 1969.

Inf. Museum of Fine Arts, Boston; *WWA* 1968-9, 2046; *AfO* 23 (1970), 223-4 (portr.) (H. Brunner); *AJA* 73 (1969), 275; *Boston Museum Bulletin* 66 (1968), 167-8 (portr.), (D. Dunham); *ibid*, 68 (1970), 270-273 (bibl.). Photograph ©2011 Museum of Fine Arts, Boston.

SMITHER, Paul Cecil (1913-1943)

British Egyptologist; born Chiswick, 5 Dec. 1913, son of Arthur Cecil S. and Elizabeth Jones; he entered The Queen's College, Oxford, 1936, where he studied under Gunn (q.v.); BA, 1939; during World War II, he was aatched to the Foreign Office, serving as a code-breaker at Bletchley Park where he worked until his death; he specialized in Middle Egyptian, particularly in the hieratic script of the period, and in spite of illness was able to complete much of the work on an important article, 'The Semnah Despatches', see below; his papers are in the Griffith Institute, Oxford; he died, Oxford, 2 Sept. 1943.

JEA 29 (1943), 1; 31 (1945), 3-10 (B. G. Gunn)); S. Joinson (daughter) in *St Helen's Window*, newsletter of St Helen's Church Abingdon, 12/7 (May 2009), 3.

SMOLEŃSKI, Tadeusz Samuel (Thadée) (1884-1909)

Polish Egyptologist; he was born at Jaworze, Silesia, 16 Aug. 1884, son ofStanislaw S., a doctor, and Helena Babirecka; he was educated at the Sobieski school in Cracow and in 1902 entered the Jagellonian University; after research work on the history of Poland he was sent to Egypt for his health, 1905; here he learned Arabic but after visiting Cairo Museum and seeing the monuments he decided to make Egyptology his career; he applied to Maspero (q.v.) and obtained a post in the library of the French Institute and studied Egyptian during the evenings; he was later able to devote himself entirely to study, his first Egyptological work being, *État actuel des recherches égyptologiques*, 1906; for Back (q.v.), he directed an archaeological expedition to Sharuna near Oxyrhynchus and another necropolis at El-Gamhud, 1907-8, discovering a huge necropolis of various periods, see his article on the tomb of a 6th Dynasty prince in *ASAE* 8; besides other articles in journals he also wrote a doctoral dissertation, *Les peuples maritimes du nord à l'époque de Ramsès II et de Menephtah*, published after his death, 1912; Smolenski was the real pioneer of Polish Egyptology and excavation, and his early death cut short a career of great promise; he died in Cracow, 29 Aug. 1909.

ASAE 10 (1910), 91-96 (bibl.) (G. Maspero); J. Pilecki, *Tadeusz Samuel S. (1884-1909), Étude sur la vie et l'activité scientifique du premier égyptologue polonais*; *Folia Orient* 2 (1960), 231-48 (portr.) (J. Pilecki); *AE* (1916) 38 (W. M. F. Petrie?); J. Śliwa in *Studia Aegyptiaca* XVII (2002), 435-42.

SMYTH, Charles Piazzi (1819-1900)
British astronomer; he was born in Naples, 3 Jan. 1819, son of Admiral William Henry S., FRS, a friend of John Lee (q.v.), and Annarella Warington, and was named after the Sicilian astronomer Giuseppe Piazzi; he was educated at Bedford Grammar School, and went out as assistant in the Royal Observatory at the Cape, 1835; here he did distinguished work and also as Astronomer Royal of Scotland, although the latter position brought him little chance of actual astronomical observation as it was mainly nominal; Professor of Astronomy, Edinburgh University, 1845; he married Jessie Duncan, 1855; FRS, 1857; he visited and surveyed the Great Pyramid, 1865, and took some of the earliest photographs; he published the standard Pyramidological work, *Our Inheritance in the Great Pyramid*, 1864; *Life and Work at the Great Pyramid*, 3 vols. 1867; in these books he made quite fantastic deductions from his measurements following the theories first enunciated by John Taylor, and propounded a theory that the builders could never have conceived or acted upon; these ideas, nevertheless, had a profound influence on young Petrie (q.v.); he resigned from the Royal Society in 1874, the only Fellow ever then to have done so, on the Society's refusing to accept a paper by him on his interpretation of the design of the Great Pyramid; he retired in 1888, and died at Ripon, Yorks., 21 Feb. 1900.

ODNB 51, 428-9; *DNB* Suppl. 3.350; Hilmy, ii, 239; Lauer, *Le Problème des Pyramides d'Égypte*, 114-16 and passim; H. A. and M. T. Brück, *The Peripatetic Astronomer*, 1988.

SOCIN, Albert (1844-1899)
German orientalist; he was born in Basel, 13 Oct. 1844; he studied oriental languages under J. H. Petermann; Professor at Tübingen University; he published a Grammar of Classical Arabic in the Porta Linguarum Orientalium series, which was translated into English by T. Stenhouse; he contributed the chapter on the religion of Islam to Baedeker's *Egypt*; he died in Leipzig, 24 June 1899.

Larousse XXe siècle 6, 386.

SOLDI COLBERT DE BEAULIEU, Émile Arthur (1846-1906)
French sculptor, he was born in Belleville-Paris, 27/29 May 1846, son of David S., Professor of Modern Languages; he studied Egyptology under Maspero (q.v.) and Guieysse (q.v.) at the École des Hautes Études, Paris, 1895-7; he published works on Egyptian and oriental art and sculpture, 1874-83; he died in Rome, 14 March 1906.

Annuaire École des H. É., 1897; Hilmy, ii, 244; E. Benezit, *Dictionnaire des peinturs, sculpteurs, dessinateurs et graveurs*, 12, 954; *The Jewish Encyclopedia* 11, 434.

SONNINI DE MANONCOURT, Charles Nicolas Sigisbert (1751-1812)
French naturalist and traveller; he was born in Lunéville, Lorraine, 1 Feb. 1751, son of Nicolas Charles Philippe S., an Italian in the service of Lorraine; he trained as a lawyer at Nancy, but soon abandoned law and entered the Navy as Officier-Ingénieur; he visited America and west Africa, 1772-5; he retired from the navy and devoted himself to natural history, which had always been his main interest, and studied under Buffon; in 1777 he arrived in Alexandria as part of the Tott (q.v.) mission and spent three years exploring Egypt as far as Aswan, accompanied in part by Adanson (q.v.), and then the Levant; he returned to Paris, and produced a new edition of Buffon's great work in 127 vols., of which nearly 80 contained new matter contributed by himself, 1789-1808; his *Voyage dans la Haute et Basse Égypte, fait par ordre de l'ancien gouvernement (de 1777 à 1780), et contenant des observations de tous genres*, etc., 3 vols., fol. Atlas, did not appear until 1799; this deals largely with the natural history and physical features of the country, but he visited and described many ancient sites; the work was very successful and was translated into English, German and Russian; he died in Paris, 29 May 1812.

NBG 44, 180-2; *Biographie Universelle* 39, 613-5; Carré, i, 108-115; Hilmy, ii, 245; Lamy, 217-20.; S. Aufrère in *Égypte Afrique & Orient* 58 (2010), 9-24; S. H. Aufrère, *Égypte Afrique & Orient* 58 (2010), 9-24.

SOPWITH, Thomas (1803-1879)
British mining engineer; he was born in Newcastle-upon-Tyne, 3 Jan. 1803, son of Jacob S., builder and cabinet-maker, and Isabella Lowes; he married 1. Mary Dickenson, 1828, 2. Jane Scott, 1831, 3. Anne Potter, 1855; FRS; he visited Egypt and afterwards published *Notes on a Visit to Egypt*, 1857; he died at his home in Westminster, 16 Jan. 1879.

ODNB 51, 641-2; *DNB* 53, 263-4.

SOTTAS, Henri (1880-1927)

French Egyptologist; he was born at Rennes, 10 March 1880, son of Jules S. and Marie Éléonore Fléchelle; intended for a military career he was trained at the college of Saint-Cyr, 1898; Second Lieut. in the army, 1900, Lieut. 1902, but left the service through ill health, 1910; he took up Egyptology and entered the École des Hautes Études where he studied under P. Guieysse (q.v.) and A. Moret (q.v.), 1909-13; he published his first article in 1912 and gained his diploma with a thesis on funerary endowments, 1913; he visited Egypt that same year but his career was now interrupted by the war; he was wounded in 1914 and ill for two years after, then served at the War Ministry until 1918; chevalier of the Légion d'honneur and Croix de Guerre; he succeeded Guieysse as Professor of Egyptian Philology at the École, 1918, and took up teaching duties the next year; Sottas specialized in texts of the Late Period and in Demotic which he also taught at the École du Louvre; his bibl. is not extensive, about 38 books and articles and 5 reviews, but it includes important studies, *La Préservation de la propriété funéraire dans l'ancienne Égypte*, thesis, 1913; *Papyrus Démotiques de Lille*, 1921; *Lettre à M. Dacier*, centenary ed., 1922; *Introduction à l'étude des hiéroglyphes*, with É. Drioton, 1922; *Un Décret trilingue en l'honneur de Ptolémée IV*, with H. Gauthier, 1925; he died of influenza at the height of his achievement, 2 Jan. 1927.

Aegyptus 8 (1927), 112-13 (P. F. A. Jouguet); *Chron. d'Ég.* 2 (1927), 97-9 (A. Moret); *JEA* 13 (1927), 81; *Rev. arch.* sér. 5, 25 (1927), 219-20; *Rev. de l'Ég. Anc.* 2 (1929), 121-7 (bibl.) (R. Weill).

SPARROW *see* **SIMPSON**

SPELEERS, Louis (1882-1966)

Belgian Egyptologist; he was born at Antwerp, 4 Nov. 1882, son of Lambert Victor S. and Catherine Masschelier; after study in universities in Belgium, he completed his training in oriental languages in Germany, 1906-9; gained doctorate in History of Art and Archaeology at Brussels; he joined the Near Eastern Department of Museum of Art and History, 1912, Hon. Conservator, 1947; he was also Lecturer in Egyptian art and philology at the University of Ghent, 1920, and was Professor of Egyptology; his list of works is long; among the most important are, *Le papyrus de Nefer Renpet; un Livre des Morts de la XVIIIme dynastie, aux Mus. Roy. du Cinquantenaire à Bruxelles,* 1917; *Recueil des inscriptions égyptiennes des Mus. Roy. du Cinquantenaire à Bruxelles,* 1923; *Les Textes des pyramides égyptiennes: 1. traduction, 2. vocabulaire,* 2 pts, 1923-4, perhaps his most important work; *Le costume oriental ancien,* 1923; *Les figurines funéraires égyptiennes,* 1923; *Catalogue des intailles et empreintes égyptiennes des Musées Royaux du Cinquantenaire à Bruxelles,* 1934; *Comment faut-il lire les textes des pyramides égyptiennes?,* 1934; *La fin du chapitre V du Livre des Morts et le 415c des Textes des Pyramides; réponse à un correcteur,* 1940; *Le chapitre V du Livre des Morts; seconde réponse à un correcteur,* 1941; he also wrote a work dealing with the first two vols. of the Coffin Texts, *Texte des cercueils du Moyen Empire,* 1946, and various articles; he died in Etterbeek, 22 Sept. 1966.

Chron. d'Ég. 42 (1967), 128-30 (H. De Meulenaere).

SPENCER, Paul (*d.*1767)

Irish antiquary; he travelled considerably in the East, and 'in the year 1721 he drew with his own hand draughts of all the Egyptian pyramids, obelisks, etc. and most of all the curious remains of antiquity in these foreign countries, which are greatly valued'; he died in Muff, Co. Londonderry, 11 Sept. 1767; his drawings etc. have not been traced.

Lloyds Evening Post 21, 318 (1767).

SPENCER CHURCHILL, (*Capt.***) (Edward) George** (1876-1964)

British soldier and collector; he was born in London, 21 May 1876, son of Lord Edward Spencer C., DL, and Augusta Warburton, his wife, being thus cousin to Sir Winston Churchill; he was educated at Eton and Magdalen College, Oxford; BA, 1898; Capt. in Grenadier Guards; JP and DL for Worcestershire; he inherited Northwick Park, Gloucs., and its collections from his maternal grandmother in 1912; he travelled a great deal and published *Tarpon Fishing in Mexico and Florida*, 1906; he greatly enlarged his collections especially in the field of antiquities and small objects, until it became of national importance; catalogues were published of the pictures and some of the very varied objects in his lifetime, see R. Allatine, *Collections de ... Monnaies grecques et romaines*, 1928, etc.; his interest in Egypt was first aroused when he was sent there as a boy of 13 for his health's sake; at the time of his death his collections were valued at over £2,000,000 but this was purely nominal; while the paintings formed by far the most valuable group, (he had inherited a huge collection of 400 pictures and added 200 more), the Egyptian, Near Eastern, and Classical antiquities were of considerable importance; his will provided for the British and Ashmolean Museums to have first choice from his antiquities before their sale, and a number of fine Egyptian pieces were thus acquired, notable among these being the stone Early Dynastic frog (BM EA 66837); before the sale, which caused great interest, a special exhibition of some of the paintings and works of art was held at Christies, 31 Dec. 1964 to 14 Jan. 1965; the sale of his antiquities lasted three days, 21-3 June 1965, and consisted of 551 lots; the Egyptian objects (mainly lots 83-200) fetched over £10,000; he died in Roehampton, 24 June 1964.

Private inf.; *Christie's Catalogue; The Times*, June 25, 1964; Walford's *County Families of the U.K.,* 16th ed. 1920, 266; Ashmolean Museum, *Exhibition of Antiquities and Coins purchased from the collection of the late Captain E. G. Spencer-Churchill*, 1965.

SPIEGEL, Joachim Bruno (1911-1989)
German Egyptologist; he was born in Berlin, 16 June 1911, son of Paul S. and Baroness Justine von Seydlitz-Kurzbach; he studied Egyptology at Berlin under Sethe (q.v.), 1929-34; PhD, 17 May 1934 which he published in *ZÄS* 71 (1935), 56-81; he was an assistant on the *Wörterbuch* project, March 1930-31 Dec. 1934; he was an assistant to Wolf (q.v.) at Leipzig, 1 Jan. 1935-31 Dec. 1936; he obtained his habilitation at Leipzig, 3 Dec. 1937; he was attached to the Deutsches Archäologishes Institut, 1 Jan. 1937-31 July 1940; he served at first in Egypt working at Merimda with Junker (q.v.), at Medinet Madi with Vogliano (q.v.), and at Giza with Selim Hassan (q.v.); he was obliged to leave Egypt on the outbreak of World War II; he served in the German Foreign Office as an Arabic expert, 1 Aug. 1940-8 May 1945; he became a lecturer at the University of Göttingen from 5 Dec. 1945; Associate Professor, 14 Sept. 1957; Professor, 22 Dec. 1966-30 Sept. 1976; he was particularly interested in aspects of Egyptian religion; his principal publications were his habilitation *Die Erzählung vom Streite des Horus und Seth*, 1937; *Soziale und weltanschauliche Reformbewegungen im alten Ägypten*, 1950; *Das Werden der altägyptischer Hochkultur*, 1953; *Das Auferstehungsritual der Unas-Pyramide,* 1971; *Die Götter von Abydos*, 1973; *Die Idee vom Totengericht in der ägyptischen Religion*, 1976; he died in Nürtingen, 1 Nov. 1989.

Inf. H. Behlmer.

SPIEGELBERG, Wilhelm (1870-1930)
German Egyptologist and Demotist; he was born in Hanover, 25 June 1870, son of Eduard S., a banker, and Antonie Dux; educated at the Universities of Strassburg, Berlin and Paris where he studied under Dümichen (q.v.), Erman (q.v.) and Maspero (q.v.), 1888-94; PhD, 1891 and Habilitation, 1894 at Strassburg; he travelled to Egypt several times, 1895-99; he was appointed Lecturer of Egyptology at the University of Strassburg in 1899 in succession to Duemichen; Professor, 1907-1918; he left Strassburg in 1918 when it was returned to France and became Hon. Prof. in Heidelberg, 1920; he became lecturer in Munich in 1923; his earlier work was mainly on hieratic papyri and he made a special study of the juristic texts on which he did valuable research, many texts and inscriptions being published by him from a great many sources; he later turned chiefly to Coptic and Demotic studies, becoming the leading exponent of the latter in Germany and, with Griffith, the foremost in Europe; he published very many important literary texts, hitherto neglected, from collections all over Europe, and also a useful Demotic grammar; in 1921 he brought out his Coptic Dictionary, a work of great value only superseded by the great Coptic Dict. of Crum (q.v.); Spiegelberg was also interested in archaeology and art, writing works in these fields as well as in philology; master of the short article, Spiegelberg wrote hundreds for all the leading journals of his day, contributing more to *ZÄS* than any other author, 159 in all; he was made a member of the Bav. Akad. 1924; his main works from a very large total were, *Studien und Materialien zum Rechtswesen des Pharaonreiches der Dynast. XVIII - XXI, c.1500 - 1000 v. Chr. ...,* Inaug. dissertation, 1892; *Correspondance du temps des Rois-Prêtres ...,* 1895; *Hieratic ostraka and papyri found by J. E. Quibell* in J. Quibell, *The Ramesseum*, 1898; *Rechnungen aus der Zeit Setis I., circa 1350 v. Chr., mit anderen Rechnungen des Neuen Reiches,* fol., 2 vols. 1896; *Die Aegyptische Sammlung des Museum-Mermanno-Westreenianum im Haag,* 1896; *Die Novelle im alten Aegypten: Ein litterar-historischer Essay,* 1898; *Aegyptische und griechische Eigennamen aus Mumienetiketten der Römischen Kaiserzeit, auf Grund von grossenteils unveröffentlichem Material ...,* 1901; *Demotische Papyrus aus den Königlichen Museen zu Berlin,* fol. 1902; *Die Demotischen Papyrus der Strassburger Bibliothek,* 1902; *Aegyptische Grabsteine und Denksteine aus süddeutschen Sammlungen,* 3 pts., 1902-6; *Geschichte der Ägyptischen Kunst bis zum Hellenismus,* 1903; *Aegyptologische Randglossen zum Alten Testament,* 1904; *Der Aufenthalt Israels in Aegypten im Lichte der Aegyptischen Monumente,* 1904; *Die Demotischen Denkmäler,* 3 pts. in 4 vols., Cairo Cat. 1. *Die Demotischen Inschriften,* 1904, 2. *Die Demotischen Papyrus,* 1906-8, 3. *Demotische Inschriften und Papyri: Fortsetzung,* 1932; *Demotische Papyrus von der Insel Elephantine. I. Nr. 1-13,* 1908; *Ausgewählte Kunst-Denkmäler der Aegyptischen Sammlung der Kaiser-Wilhelms-Universität Strassburg,* 1909; *Die Demotischen Papyrus der Musées Royaux du Cinquantenaire,*1909; *Der Sargenkreis des Königs Petubastes,* 1910; *Demotische Texte auf Krügen,* 1912; *Die Demotischen Papyri Hauswaldt: Verträge der ersten Hälfte der Ptolemäerzeit ... aus Apollinopolis,* 2 pts., 1913; *Die sogenannte Demotische Chronik des Pap. 215 der Bibl. Nationale zu Paris ...,* 1914; *Die Prinz-Joachim-Ostraka: Griechische und Demotische Beisetzungsurkunden für Ibis- und Falkenmumien aus Ombos,* with F. Preisigke, 1914; *Ägyptische und Griechische Inschriften und Graffiti aus den Steinbrüchen des Gebel Silsile (Oberägypten),* with F. Preisigke, 1915; *Der Ägyptische Mythus vom Sonnenauge, der Papyrus der Tierfabeln 'Kufi', nach dem Leidener Demotischen Papyrus I 384,* 1917; *Ägyptische und andere Graffiti, Inschriften und Zeichnungen, aus der Thebanischen Nekropolis: Text-Atals,* fol. 1921; *Koptisches Handwörterbuch,* 1921; *Demotische Grammatik,* 1925; *Die Demotischen Urkunden*

des Zenon-Archivs, 1929; *Die Demotischen Papyri Loeb,* 1931; see also his chapter in Petrie *Six Temples at Thebes*, 1896; appendices in Sayce *Aramaic papyri discovered at Assuan*, 1906; he contributed to Lexa, *Demotisches Totenbuch*, 1910; some of his papers and squeezes are in the Griffith Institute, Oxford; he edited part of Dümichen's *Geography*; he died in Munich, 23 Dec. 1930.

NDB 24, 682-4; *Aegyptus* 11 (1931), 195-201 (E. Seidl); *AJSL* 47 (1931), 297-8 (W. F. Edgerton); *Bayerische Akad. der Wiss. Jahrbuch*, 1931, 27-34 (G. Bergsträsser); *Byzantion*, 6 (1931), 971 (M. Meyerhof); *Chron. d'Ég.* 7 (1932), 116-17 (J. Capart), 117-18 (C. Préaux); *JEA* 17 (1931), 144; Newberry Corr.; *ZÄS* 66 (1931), 74-5 (portr.) (G. Steindorff); *AfP* 10 (1932), 98-9 (L. Wenger); 315 (U. Wilcken); *Byzantinische Zeitschrift* 32 (1932) 255-6 (E. Seidl); *Klio* 24 (1931), 531-2 (C. Lehmann-Haupt); *Zeitschrift der Savigny-Stiftung für Rechtsgeschichte* 51 (1931), 606-8; W. Spiegelberg in *Elsaß-Lothringen, Sonderheft der Zeitschrift Deutsches Vaterland* (1922), 47-49; *Zum Andenken an Wilhelm Spiegelberg*, 1930; *Enchoria* 4 (1974), 95-139 (bibl.); *Enchoria* 11 (1982), 85-97; A. Grimm and S. Schoske, *Wilhelm Speigelberg als Sammler, R.A.M.S.E.S.* 1, München (1995); St. Rebenich in M. Mülke, *Wilamowitz und kein Ende*, 2003, 189-207; inf. T. Gertzen; P. Whelan in M. Betrò and G. Miniaci, *Talking along the Nile*, 2013, 229-54; R. Spiegelberg, *Wilhelm Spiegelberg. A Life in Egyptology*, 2015 (on internet only); R. Spiegelberg in J. Arp-Neuman and T. Gertzen (eds.), '*Steininschrift und Bibelwort*', 2019, 51-7; T. Gertzen, *Wilhelm Leeser Spiegelberg (1870-1930)*, 2018.

SPINETO *see* **DORIA**

SPITTA, (*Bey*) **Wilhelm** (1853-1883)
German orientalist; he was born in Wittingen, 14 June 1853, son of Karl Johann Philipp S., a clergyman and composer of hymns, and Johanne Maria Hotzen; after his father's death, he spent his childhood and youth in Hildesheim; he went to Göttingen University in 1871 to study philosophy and Arabic; he was Librarian of the Vice-Regal Library, Cairo; he retired in 1882 and returned to Germany; he published many Arabic works, and *Contes Arabes Populaires*, 1882, a collection of stories with many ancient Egyptian parallels, and a grammar of the Egyptian Arabic dialect *Grammatik des arabischen Vulgärdialectes von Aegypten*, 1880; he died 6 Sept. 1883.

Centralblatt f. Bibliothekwesen, 1884, 105-12; Hilmy, ii, 256; Wilbour, passim (see index); G. Ebers, *Aegypten in Bild and Wort*, I-II, 1879-80, passim; archives of the Pelizaeus-Museum, Hildesheim; inf. B. Schmitz.

SPOHN, Friedrich August Wilhelm (1792-1824)
German orientalist; born in Dortmund, 16 May 1792, son of Theophilus Lebrecht S., Professor, and Christiana Rosina Wilhelmina Nettonain; he became Professor of Greek and Roman Literature at Leipzig in 1819; he claimed to have discovered how to decipher hieroglyphics; an elaborate work with plates, *De Lingua et Literis veterum Aegyptiorum* was posthumously edited by Seyffarth (q.v.), 1825-31, he died in Berlin, 19 March 1824.

Champollion, i, 166, 255, 264, 390; Hilmy, ii, 256; E. Blumenthal, *Ältes Agypten in Leipzig*, 1981, 3; E. Blumethal, *Ein Leipziger Grabdenkmal im ägyptischen Stil und der Anfänge der Ägyptologie in Deutschland*, 1999.

SPURRELL, Flaxman Charles John (1842-1915)
British geologist and antiquary; he was born in London, 8 Sept, 1842, the son of Flaxman S., surgeon of Bexley Heath, and Ann Spurrell; he was educated at Epsom College, 1855-6; he was a medical man but did not practise; he collected flint implements and fossils, a large collection of which from the Crayford Deposits he gave to the British Museum (Nat. Hist.) in 1895; he contributed a chapter on flint implements to Petrie's *Naqada* and another to his *Tell el Amarna*; he published articles in *Arch. Journ.* and *Quarterly Journal of the Geological Society*; he retired to Norfolk, where he died in Bessingham, 25 Feb. 1915.

AE 1915, 93; *Epsom Coll. Registers*; *JEA* 2 (1915), 251; Newberry Corr.; Petrie, 17, 107, 128.

STADELMANN, Rainer (1933-2019)
German Egyptologist; he was born in Oettingen, Bavaria, 24 Oct. 1933; he studied Egyptology, Near Eastern, and Classical Archaeology at the University of Munich, 1953-7 and the University of Heidelberg, 1957-67; PhD, 1960; Habilitation, 1967; he served as assistant at Heidelberg until 1967; lecturer, 1967-8; he was appointed deputy director of the German Archaeological Institute in Cario, 1968-89; Director, 1989-98; hon. professor at Heidelberg, 1975; he excavated at the sun-temple of Userkaf, 1955-6; at Elephantine, 1969-71; Dahshur from 1975; and the mortuary temple of Sety I at Gurna from 1970 and the mortuary temple of Amenhotep III at Kom el-Hetan; *Stationen*, a volume of studies in his honour, was edited by H. Guksch and D. Polz, 1998; apart from numeorus articles, he published *Die ägyptischen Pyramiden*,1985; he died 14 Jan. 2019.

H. Guksch and D. Polze, *Stationen*, 1998, XIII-XVII (bibl.) (portr.).

STADNIKOV, Sergei (1956-2015)
Estonian Egyptologist; he was born in Parnu, 26 July 1956; he was educated in Tallin and then at the State University of Tartu, 1977-82 where he began his study of Egyptian language; he then studied Egyptology at the University of Leningrad under Igor Vinogradov; he was a lecturer at the Institute of History in Tallin; he specialized in the study of Middle Kingdom literature and the history of Estonian travellers to Egypt; he published numerous translations of Egyptian texts in Estonian; he died in Tallin, 26 June 2015.

Newspaper obits.

STANTON, (*Sir*) **Edward** (1827-1907)
British army officer, diplomat, and collector; he was born 19 Feb. 1827, baptized 26 March at Painswick, Gloucestershire, son of William Henry S. of Thrupp and Jane Smith; educated Woolwich Acad.; he entered the Royal Engineers, 1844, and served at the Cape, 1847-53; Crimea, 1854-5; retired, 1859; General, 1881; Consul-General at Warsaw, 1860, and Egypt, 1865-76; Chargé d'aff., Munich, 1876; CB, 1857; KCMG, 1882; KCB, 1905; he had a collection of Egyptian antiquities which was sold at Sotheby's, 26 July 1894; the British Museum bought the hieratic papyrus of Queen Nodjmet (EA 10490); he procured for the Duke of Sutherland the mummy unrolled by Birch at Stafford House in 1875; he died in Stroud, Gloucs., 24 June 1907.

Khedives and Pashas, 167, 169, 214-18; *WWW* i, 671; Wilbour, 148; Lugt 52832.

STARKEY, (James) Leslie (1895-1938)
British archaeologist; he was born in London, 3 Jan. 1895, son of James S., architect and surveyor, and Louisa Pike, widow of William Brown; he lacked a formal education but showed an interest in antiquity, working for an antique dealer near the British Museum; he served in the Royal Navy Air Service in World War I; he then studied Egyptology in evening classes at University College London under Petrie (q.v.) and Margaret Murray (q.v.); he joined Petrie's excavation team, working at Qau under Brunton (q.v.), 1922-4 and 1925 where he discovered important Coptic mansucripts; he was appointed field director at the University of Michigan's excavation at Karanis, 1924-6; he rejoined Petrie when he moved to Palestine and took part in work at Wadi Ghazzeh, 1926, Tell Jemmeh, 1926-7, Tell el-Fara, 1928-9, and Tell el-Ajjul, 1930-2; he became director of excavations at Lachish, 1932-8; FSA; member of the executive committee of the Palestine Exploration Fund; his articles and publication dealt with his work in Palestine; he was murdered by bandits near Hebron, 10 Jan. 1938 and was buried on Mount Zion, Jerusalem.

W. Slaninka, *'Not for the Greed of Gold'*, 2010.

STEFANI, Antonio (*fl.*1815-1835)
Albanian merchant; he settled in Khartoum about 1815; in 1834 he entered into partnership with Giuseppe Ferlini (q.v.) to excavate at Meroë.

Budge, *Eg. Sudan*, i, 285.

STEGEMANN, Viktor (1902-1948)
German scholar in Classics and Coptology, he was born in Aachen, 17 Jan. 1902, son of a school director; he was educated at secondary school in Aachen to 1921; he then enrolled in Classics, Ancient History, Egyptology and Coptic at the Universities of Heidelberg and Munich; thanks to Franz Boll, he later on specialized in ancient astrology; PhD, 1925; he then worked as a teacher first in a private school in Heidelberg, then at several municipal schools, and finally at the famous country boarding-school at castle Salem where he was responsible for education in Classics; with his study on Dorotheos of Sidon he obtained the qualification for a lectureship (Habilitation), 1937; lecturer in Classics at Würzburg University, 1938, and in 1939 he had to be confirmed as lecturer of the new order; his real university career started in Oct. 1940, when he was transferred to Deutsche Karls-Universität at Prague where he worked together with Hopfner (q.v.); he was rewarded with the title of Hon. Professor in Classics, 1943; in 1945, after World War II, he left Prague for Germany, where some years later he was given a lectureship in Classics at Philosophisch-Theologische Hochschule Regensburg, the later University of Regensburg; he published among others: *Die koptischen Zaubertexte der Sammlung papyrus Erzherzog Rainer in Wien*, 1933/34; *Die Gestalt Christi in den kopt. Zaubertexten*, 1934; *Koptische Paläographie*, 1936; he died at Gräfelfing, Germany, 2 March 1948.

Gymnasium 56/1 (1949), 74-7 (H. Haas); *Eikasmos* IV (1993) 206-11 (F. Brunhölzl); XIV (2003), 416-19 (M. Sicherl); *Proceedings Papyrology*, Helsinki, 2007, 827-38 (W. B. Oerter); W. Oerter, D*ie Ägyptologie an der Prager Universität 1882-1945*, 2010, 137-8.

STEINBÜCHEL von RHEINWALL, Anton (1790-1883)
Austrian orientalist and antiquary; he was born in Krems, Lower Austria, 4 Dec. 1790, son of Jakob S., a military doctor who was ennobled; he studied at the University of Vienna, 1807-11; DPhil, 1811; he was appointed Assistant Keeper of of Coins and Antiquities, 1811; Assistant Director, 1816; Director, 1819-40; Professor of Archaeology and Numismatics, Vienna University, 1817-34; member of the Academies of Vienna, Rome, Naples, and others; he published an account of the scarabs in the museum, 1824, and a handbook of the Egyptian collection, 1826; he died at Innsbruck 28 Dec. 1883.

Hilmy, ii, 259; *Oesterr. Nat.-Enzyc.* 5, 138; *ŐBL* 13, 163.

STEINDORFF, Georg (1861-1951)
German Egyptologist and Copticist; he was born in Dessau, 12 Nov. 1861, son of Ludwig S., a merchant, and Helen Ehrmann; he was educated at the Universities of Berlin, 1881-2 and Göttingen, and was Erman's (q.v.) first student; PhD Gött., 1884; habilitation, Berlin, 1891; he lectured at Berlin University, 1891-3 afterwards appointed assistant in Berlin Museum, 1885-93; Associate Professor of Egyptology at Leipzig in succession to Ebers (q.v.), 1893; Professor, 1904-1934; he founded the Egyptian Institute in Leipzig and filled it with objects from his excavations in Egypt and Nubia; Dean of the Philosophical Faculty, 1918-9; Rector, 1923-4; Steindorff made a special study of Coptic and was with Crum (q.v.) the leading authority in the world during his lifetime; he was also interested in art and published books and articles on this subject as well as on Egyptian religion; he explored the Libyan Desert, 1899-1900; excavated at Giza, 1903, 1905-6, 1909-10, and in Nubia, 1912-14 and 1930-1; he edited the *ZÄS* for 40 years until 1937 and contributed many articles to it; his studies in Coptic were of the utmost importance and his Coptic Grammar still remains a standard work of reference and perhaps the most popular ever written in this field; in philology as a whole he was in the first rank and established the rules which are generally accepted for the vocalization of Egyptian; in 1939 he was forced to emigrate to America when the Nazis were in power in Germany, and started another career there at the age of nearly eighty; he continued his studies in the museums of New York, Boston, and Baltimore and the Oriental Institute of Chicago; Hon. Member of American Oriental Soc.; at Baltimore he compiled a 12-vol. MSS Catalogue of Egyptian antiquities in the Walters Art Gallery, which formed the basis for a later published work; both his 70th and 80th birthdays were the subject of tributes, see below; his published works are very numerous and his bibl. lists about 250 books, articles, and reviews, the first of which appeared in 1883, the last in the year of his death nearly 70 years later; *Sassanidische Siegelsteine*, with P. Horn, 1891; *Koptische Grammatik mit Chrestomathie, Wörterverzeichnis und Literatur*, 1894, rev. ed. 1904; *Grabfunde des Mittleren Reiches in den Königlichen Museen zu Berlin. I. Das Grab des Mentuhotep*, 1896; *Die Apokalypse des Elias, eine unbekannte Apokalypse und Bruchstücke der Sophonias-Apokalypse. Koptische Texte, Übersetzung, Glossar*, 1899; *Die Blütezeit des Pharaonenreiches*, 1900, rev. ed. 1926; *Grabfunde des Mitt. Reiches in den Königlichen Museen zu Berlin, II. Der Sarg des Sebk-o. Ein Grabfund aus Gebelên*, 1901; *Durch die Libysche Wüste zur Amonoase*, 1904; *The Religion of the Ancient Egyptians*, 1905; *Koptische Rechtsurkunden des Achten Jahrhunderts aus Djême, Theben*, with W. E. Crum, 1912; *Das Grab des Ti. Veröffentlichungen der Ernst von Sieglin Expedition in Ägypten*, vol. 2, 1913; *Aegypten in Vergangenheit und Gegenwart*, 1915; *Kurzer Abriss der Koptischen Grammatik mit Lesestücken und Wörterverzeichnis*, 1921; *Die Kunst der Aegypter: Bauten, Plastik, Kunstgewerbe*, 1928; *Aniba*, I. Band with R. Heidenreich, F. Kretschmar, A. Langsdorff, and W. Wolf, II. Band with M. Marcks, H. Schleif, and W. Wolf, 1935-7; *Die Thebanische Gräberwelt*, with W. Wolf, 1936; *When Egypt Ruled the East*, with K. C. Seele, 1942; *Egypt*, text of Hoyningen-Huene, 1943; *Catalogue of the Egyptian Sculpture in the Walters Art Gallery*, 1946; *Lehrbuch der Koptischen Grammatik*, 1951; while in America he also wrote a *Coptic-Egyptian Etymological Dictionary*; *The Origin of the Coptic Language and Literature: Prolegomena to the Coptic Grammar*; *The Proverbs of Solomon in Akhmimic Coptic according to a Papyrus in the State Library in Berlin*, with a Coptic-Greek Glossary compiled by Carl Schmidt; he also edited many editions of Baedeker's *Egypt*, making it a standard work for all travellers and the best general guide available; he died in North Hollywood, California, 28 Aug. 1951.

NDB 25, 173-5 (E. Blumenthal); *AEB* 28, 29; *Bulletin Issued by the Egyptian Educ. Bureau, London*, no. 58, Sept. 1951. 25 (anon.); *Chron. d'Ég.* 27 (1952), 391; *JAOS* 61 (1941), 288-9, *Eightieth Anniversary of Prof. Steindorff*, J. H. Breasted Jnr.; 66 (1946), 76-87, *The Writings of Georg Steindorff*, J. H. Breasted Jnr.; 67 (1947), 141-2, 326-7; *JEA* 38 (1952), 2; Kürschner; Newberry Corr.; *The Times*, 30 Aug. 1951; *ZÄS* 67 (1931), 1, Seventieth Birthday Tribute; *ZÄS* 79 (1954), V-VI (portr.) (S. Morenz); E. Blumenthal, *Altes Ägypten in Leipzig*, 1918, 15-31; E. Endesfelder, *Die Ägyptologie an der Berliner Universität-Zur Geschichte eines Fachgebietes*, 1988, 26-7; H. Strauss and W. Röder, *International Biographical Dictionary of Central European Emigrés 1933-45*, II, part 2, 414-5; A. Spiekermann and F. Kampp-Seyfried, *Giza. Ausgrabungen im Friedhof der Cheopspyramide von Georg Steindorff*, 2003; inf. T. Schneider; S. Voss Kern, *ZÄS* 143 (2016), 244-52; S. Voss and D. Raue, *Georg Steindorff und die deutsche Ägyptologie*, 2016; T. Gertzen in J. Arp-Neuman and T. Gertzen (eds.), '*Steininschrift und Bibelwort*', 2019, 39-44.

STEPHENS, John Lloyd (1805-1852)
American traveller; he was born in Shrewbury, New Jersey 28 Nov. 1805, son of Benjamin S. (Benoni Stephenson), a merchant, and Clemence Lloyd; he was educated at Columbia University, 1818-22 and became a lawyer in New York; he travelled to Europe in 1834 and then on to Egypt in Dec. 1835; he went up the Nile in 1836 and then went on to Petra and the Holy Land before returning to Egypt and then Europe and New York; he met Catherwood (q.v.) in London in 1836 and the two became pioneers of the exploration of Mayan ruins in South America from 1839; he wrote *Incidents of Travel in Egypt, Arabia Petraea, and the Holy Land*, 1837; he died in New York, 13 Oct. 1852.

V. von Hagen, *Maya Explorer*, 1947; V. von Hagen, *Search for the Maya*. 1973; *DAB* 17, 579-80.

STERN, Kurt Joseph (*d.*1973)
German-British doctor and collector; he was born in Germany, son of Harry and Julia S.; he was trained as a gynaecological surgeon; MD Freiburg, 1927; LRCP, LRCS, Edinburgh, LRFRS, Glasgow, 1935; sometime on the staff of the University Hospital, Frankfurt; he emigrated to England and later had a practice in Harley St. in London; he formed a collection of about 4,000 antiquities, mainly Egyptian including sculpture, amulets and scarabs which he left to the Israel Museum in Jerusalem; he died 29 July 1973.

Israel Museum News 12 (1976), 37.

STERN, Ludwig Julius Christian (1846-1911)
German Egyptologist, orientalist, and Celtic scholar; he was born in Hildesheim, 12 Aug. 1846, son of Christian Ferdinanad S., a police official, and Johanne Bartels; he was educated at Hildesheim, 1854-65 and the University of Göttingen, 1865-9; he had great aptitude for languages and in his youth, in addition to the modern languages taught at school, he mastered, self-taught, Italian, Spanish, and Slavonic languages, especially Russian; at Göttingen he studied under Lotje, Teichmüller Wiesler, and Th. Müller, but specialized in oriental languages under Ewarl, Berteau, and Benfrey; in addition to Hebrew, Arabic, and Ethiopic, he turned to Egyptology under H. Brugsch (q.v.), 1868, and from 1869 onwards continued his studies in the Egyptian Dept. of Berlin Museum under Lepsius (q.v.); in 1872 he accompanied Ebers (q.v.) to Egypt, and was appointed librarian of the Viceregal Library at Cairo, 1873; in 1874 he was appointed to the staff of the Egyptian Dept. of Berlin Museum, and at the same time prepared a catalogue of the oriental MSS in the Royal Library; after the death of Lepsius in 1884, Stern found himself unable to work under his successor, and he thereupon completely renounced Egyptology and became Keeper of Manuscripts in the Royal Library, 1886, and began the study of Celtic languages in which he became a recognized authority; he was a co-founder and joint-editor of the *Zeitschr. für Celtische Philologie*; his best-known Egyptological work was his valuable *Koptische Grammatik*, 1880; he also compiled *Hieroglyph.-Lat. Glossar zu Papyrus Ebers*, 1875; he contributed to *Records of the Past* and wrote many articles in *ZÄS*; he died in Berlin, 9 Oct. 1911.

Hilmy, ii, 260; *Zeitschr. f. Celt. Philol.* 8 (1912), 583-7 (portr.); *Zentralbl. f. Bibliothekswesen*, 36-41; E. Blumenthal in P. Nagel (ed.), *Carl-Schmidt-Kolloquium an der Martin-Luther-Universität Halle-Wittenberg 1988*, 1990, 99-104; K.-Th. Zauzich in *Gött. Misz.* 210 (2006), 105-107; S. Mangold in *ZDMG* 157 (2007), 51-58; inf. T. Gertzen; *NDB* 25, 278.

STEUART, John Robert (1780-1848)
British numismatist and collector; he published *Description of the Ancient Monuments in Lydia and Phrygia*, fol. 1842; his numismatic collections were sold in three sales at Sotheby's, 30 Jan. 1840 (15 days), 19 July 1841, and 3 May 1844, the last anonymous; many items were bought by the British Museum; his library was sold, 25 Nov. 1846, and his antiquities, which included many Egyptian objects, in June 1849; he travelled in the East, 1826, and was elected FRS, 1829; he died in Hampstead, 16 Dec. 1848.

STEVENSON, Sara (*née* **Yorke**) (1847-1922)
American museum curator; she was born in Paris, 19 Feb. 1847, daughter of Edward Yorke, banker, and Sarah Hanna; she was brought up in Paris and in Mexico; in 1870 she married Cornelius Stevenson of Philadelphia; in 1889 she helped to found the Archaeological Association of the University of Pennsylvania from which the University Museum originated; in 1890 she was appointed first curator of the Egyptian and Mediterranean section of the Museum; she supported the excavations of Petrie and the Egypt Exploration Fund in return for objects; she was a founder member of the American Exploration Society in 1897; in 1898 she went to Egypt to arrange independent excavations, and although largely unsuccessful, brought back a large number of antiquities; she resigned in 1905 and later became a newspaper columnist and curator at the Philadelphia Museum of Art; she died in Philadelphia, 14 Nov. 1922.

DAB 17, 635-6; *WWWA* i, 1133; Expedition 21 (Winter 1979); *BES* 6 (1984), 7-9.

STEWART, William Arnold (1882-1953)
British artist and designer; he was born in Ilkley, Yorkshire, 17 July 1882, son of John Reich S. and Naamah Arnold; he was educated at Bradford Technical College and the Royal College of Art; he became chief designer of Lister and Co. in Bradford; in 1911 he took up a teaching post in the Department of Arts and Crafts in the Egyptian Ministry of Education, becoming Principal of the School of Arts and Crafts, Cairo; from 1927-9 he reconstructed the furniture of Queen Hetepheres found by Reisner (q.v.) at Giza; in 1930 he was appointed Supervisor of Technical Education to the Palestine Government and later Controller of Light Industries, retired 1947; his diary and working papers concerning his work for Reisner are now in the Griffith Institute, Oxford; he died at High Wycombe, 18 Jan. 1953.

DNB Missing Persons, 663-4; *ODNB* 52, 769; inf. J. Malek and Stewart family.

STIBBERT, Frederick (1838-1906)
British traveller and collector; he was born in Florence, 9 Nov. 1838, son of Thomas S., a wealthy nabob's son, and Giulia Cafaggi; he was educated at Magdalene College, Cambridge; he returned to Italy and served under Garibaldi in the Italian struggle for independence; he travelled widely, and visited Egypt in 1869; he formed a large collection of arms and armour, but also collected Egyptian antiquities, including three sarcophagi; he designed and decorated an Egyptian-style building in the grounds of his Florentine villa; after his death the villa and collections were given to the city of Florence to form the Stibbert Museum; he died at Montughi near Florence, 10 April 1906.

Drawings of Egypt in the Stibbert Museum; *Frederick Stibbert: Gentiluomo, collezionista e sognatore*, 2000; G. Rosati ,'Neo-Egyptian Garden Ornaments in Florence during the 19th Century', in J.-M. Humbert and C. Price (eds) *Imhotep Today: Egyptianizing Architecture*, 2003, 225-7.

STOBART, (*Revd*) **Henry** (1824-1895)
British clergyman and collector; he was born in Chester-le-Street, Co. Durham, 26 April 1824, second son of William S., coal owner, and Barbara Haytor; he was educated at The Queen's College, Oxford from 1842; BA, 1847; MA, 1848; ordained, 1849; he held various curacies, 1849-64; Rector of Warkton, Northants., 1865-81, where he completely restored the church; he visited Egypt, 1854-5, and brought back some important antiquities; some of these were published in a fol. vol. without letterpress, *Egyptian Antiquities collected on a voyage made in Upper Egypt in the years 1854 and 1855 ...*, 1855; most of the antiquities were bought by Joseph Mayer (q.v.) of Liverpool, including the papyri, now famous as 'Mayer A & B'; the British Museum bought the Coptic and Greek papyri, one of which had on the *verso* the Funeral oration of Hypereides, edited by Churchill Babington; the remainder were given to the Bristol Museum by Miss Stobart in 1927; his squeezes are in the Griffith Institute, Oxford; he retired to Wykeham Rise, Totteridge, Herts. in 1881, and died at Funchal, Madeira, 30 Dec. 1895.

Inf. relatives; Hilmy, ii, 261; *JEA* 35 (1949), 163; 19, 143; *ZÄS* 38, 17.

STOCHOVE, Vincent (1605-1679)
Belgian traveller; he was born in Bruges, 25 Feb. 1605, son of Jean S. and Marie Reyvaert; he was well educated in classical studies; in 1630 he set off for a tour to the Levant going firstly to Constantinople, Syria, and Palestine; he reached Damietta in Sept. 1631 and proceeded to Cairo where he described the pyramids at Giza and the tombs at Saqqara which he entered to examine the mummies; he also visited Sinai; he left Egypt in Oct. 1631 and returned to Bruges in Sept. 1632; he published an account of his voyage in French in Brussels, 1643 which went through several editions and in Flemish, 1658; an edition of the Egyptian section was published by B. van de Walle (q.v.), 1975; he was later elected burgomaster of Bruges 1654 and 1664; he died in Bruges, 26 Dec. 1679.

Bibliographie Nationale de Belgique 24, 43-6; B. van de Walle (ed.), *Voyage en Égypte 1631*, 1975, ii-xvi; Lamy, 114-16.

STOCK, Hanns (1908-1966)
German Egyptologist; he was born at Pfaffenhofen, Upper Bavaria, 7 Oct. 1908, son of Johann S. and Genoveva Schreier; he was educated in Turin and Rome and later at the University of Munich from 1934; PhD, 1940; he worked at Munich until 1940, and was assistant in the Berlin Museum, 1940-1; he married Ines Mion, 1945; after the war he was appointed assistant in the Egyptian Department of the State collections at Munich, 1946-50; also Director of Studies and later Professor in the University, 1947, 1952; Director of the Egyptian collections, 1955; in 1957 he was made first Director of the German Archaeological Institute, Cairo, 1955; in addition to articles in journals, Stock published two studies on his special subject, the Intermediate Periods, *Studien zur Geschichte und Archäologie der 13. bis 17. Dynastie Ägyptens, unter besonderer Berücksichtigung der Skarabäen dieser Zwischenzeit*, 1942; *Die erste Zwischenzeit Ägyptens*, 1949; he was killed in an automobile accident near Bad Tölz, 23 July 1966.

MDAIK 21 (1966) (portr.); *ZÄS* 95 (1968), v-vi (H. W. Müller); *Frankfurter Allegmeine Zeitung* 27 July 1966; *AfO* 22 (1968-9), 219-20 (portr.) (W. Helck); inf. T. Schneider.

STOCLET, Adolphe (1871-1949)

Belgian civil engineer, financier and collector; he was born in Brussels, 30 Sept. 1871, son of Victor S. and Ann Caspers; he worked in Paris, Milan, Vienna, and Brussels; with his wife Suzanne (née Stevens, April 24 1874 - Nov. 16 1949) he formed a large collection of early Renaissance paintings, Mediaeval enamels, and ancient Near Eastern, pre-Columbian, Chinese, tribal African, and Egyptian objects; this was housed in the modernist Palais Stoclet in Brussels, designed by the Vienna Secession architect Josef Hoffmann, with murals by Gustav Klimt; some of the Egyptian objects were published by Frankfort (q.v.), although a number of the more impressive pieces discussed are generally considered forgeries made by Aslanian (q.v.) and other inter-war craftsmen; after his death his collections were divided among his heirs; some Egyptian and Near Eastern pieces were sold at auction in London (Sotheby's, 28 June 1965, lots 156-171); a Middle Kingdom statue of a vizier is now in the St. Louis Art Museum; he died in Brussels, 3 Nov. 1949.

Family information; H. Frankfort, 'Egyptische beeldhouwwerken uit de verzameling A. Stoclet te Brussel', *Maandblad voor Beeldende Kunsten* 7/3 (March 1930); J. P. van Goidsenhoven, *Adolphe Stoclet Collection* I (Brussels, 1956); Eskenazi, *Chinese Works of Art from the Stoclet Collection*, 2003 5-9; J.-J. Fiechter, *Faux et Faussaires en art Égyptien*, 2005, 21-26, 35-6; info. T. Hardwick and J.-M. Bruffaerts.

STOPPELAERE, Alexandre Marie Jean Baptiste (1890-1978)

French artist; he was born in St.-Paul-de-Fenouillet, 15 May 1890, son of Jean Baptiste Simon Louis S. and Marie Christine Antoinette Rives; he went to Egypt in 1938 to give a series of seminars on painting techniques and restoration; he was mobilized in the Middle East in 1939-40 and then put in charge of the restoration of the Theban tombs until 1952; he wrote an article on Theban tomb painting in *Valeurs* No. 7-8 (1947); he died in Issy-les-Molineaux, 13 April 1978.

BSFE 82 (1978), 4-5; inf. A. Mekhitarian.

STOREY, Samuel (1840-1925)

British politician; he was born in Sherburn, Co. Durham, 13 Jan. 1840, son of Robert S., a farmer and Mary Ann Craggs; MP for Sunderland, 1881-95 and 1910; DL; JP; he visited Egypt in 1884 and bought antiquities, including two mummies; he died in Chester-le-Street, 18 Jan. 1925.

WWW ii, 1004; Wilbour, 292.

STRACHAN-DAVIDSON, James Leigh (1843-1916)

British scholar; born Byfleet, Surrey, 22 Oct. 1843, son of James S.-D. and Mary Anne Richardson; Balliol College, Oxford; LL.D.; MA; Master of Balliol, 1907-16; he visited Egypt 1886-7; he presented to the Pitt-Rivers Museum a cup with a hieratic inscription, 1887, published by Griffith, *PSBA* 14, 328; he presented other Egyptian objects to the Ashmolean Museum; he died in Balliol College, Oxford, 28 March 1916.

ODNB 15, 306; *DNB* 1912-21, 512-13; *WWW* ii, 1006.

STRACMANS, Maurice (1895-1990)

Belgian Egyptologist; he was born on 30 Nov. 1895; he studied at the University of Liège under Capart (q.v.) and wrote his thesis on *Histoire et Littérature orientales*; he also studied ethnology in Paris; he became Professor of Egyptology at the Université Libre de Bruxelles in Brussels, 1934-65; he assisted Pirenne (q.v.) in his work on Egyptian law and wrote numerous articles in *Chronique d'Égypte* and other journals on Egyptian religion and circumcision; he took part in the excavations at Dara in Upper Egypt, 1945-7; he died in Brussels, 24 Oct. 1990.

Inf. J. Quaegebeur and A. Théodoridès.

STRATON, (*Sir***) Joseph** (1777-1840)

British army officer and traveller; he was baptized at Torryburn, Fife, Scotland 20 Nov. 1777, son of Col. William Muter and Janet Straton, but assumed the name of Straton about 1816 on succeeding to the property of his aunt, near Montrose; he was an officer in the 6th Inniskilling Dragoons; he commanded the Union Brigade at Waterloo on the death of Sir Wm. Ponsonby and was wounded; Lieut.-Col., 1814; CB; KCH; FRSE; he left about £70,000 to Edinburgh University; he visited Salt (q.v.) after a tour in Palestine, 1817, and accompanied Irby (q.v.) and Mangles (q.v.) to the Pyramids, Sept, 1817, then went as far as Abu Simbel, a description of which he sent to

Dacier; he published 'Account of the Sepulchral Caverns of Egypt' (*Edinb. Philos. Inst.* 3. 345); Lieut.-General; he died in London, 23 Oct. 1840.

C. Dalton, *Waterloo Roll Call*, 2nd ed. 62; Hilmy, ii, 262; Finati, 215; Irby, 49, 51, 58; Salt, ii, 45; *BIFAO* 65 (1967), 169-75); *BSFE* 45 (1966), 19-32.

STRICKER, Bruno Hugo (1910-2005)
Dutch Egyptologist; he was born in Rotterdam 23 Aug. 1910, son of Dr. Willem Frederik Otto S. and Cato Scheffer; he was educated at the University of Leiden under de Buck (q.v.) from 1928 and also at the University of Berlin under Erman (q.v.); he obtained his doctorate from Leiden in 1945 with his thesis *Die Indeling der Egyptische Taalgeschiedenis*; he became research assistant in the Rijksmuseum van Oudeheden, 1940-8 and Keeper of the Egyptian Dept, 1948-75; he is principally known for his interest in Egyptian religion; a series of essays was published in his honour in *Hermes Aegyptiacus*, ed. T. Duquesne, 1985; apart from his many articles, he published *De groote zeeslang*, 1953; *Gids voor de verzameling van Egyptische beeldhouwwerken*, 1953; *Die overstroming von der Nijl*, 1956; *De brief van Aristeas*, 1956; *De Geboorte van Horus*, 1963-89; *De maat der dingen*, 1976, and *Het Oude Verbond*, 1984; he died at Oegstgeest, 18 Sept. 2005.

Koninklijke Nederlandse Akademie van Wetenschappen. Levensberichten en herdenkingen (2007), 88-92 (portr.) (J. F. Borghouts); *Phoenix* 52 (2006), 44 (M. Heerma van Voss); T. Duquesne (ed.) *Hermes Aegyptiacus*, 1985, (portr.), 9-17 (bibl.); inf. H. van Voss and M. Raven.

STROGANOV, (*Count*) **Grigori Sergeievitch** (1829-1910)
Russian nobleman and collector; he was born in St. Petersburg, 16 June 1829, son of Count Sergei Grigorievitch S. and Princess Natalia Pavlovna née Stroganov; a catalogue of his collection of antiquities *Catalog der Sammlung ägyptischer Alterthümer des Grafen Gregor Strogonoff* was published in Aachen in 1880, without the author's name, but it is known to be by Émile Brugsch (q.v.) from the third unnumbered page; there is another publication of the collection by L. Pollak, *Les Antiquités. Pièces de Choix de la Collection du Comte Grégoire Stroganoff à Rome*, 1911; some of the collection is in the Suermondt-Ludwig Museum in Aachen and the rest is dispersed in various museums and private collections; he lived partly in Rome where he housed part of his collection; he died in Paris, 27 July 1910; he has been confused in earlier editions with his cousin Count Grigori Alexandrovitch Stroganov (1823-1879).

Hilmy, ii, 263; Vapereau, 1682; M. Hill, *Metropolitan Museum Journal* 40 (2005), 163 and note 3; G. Meurer, *Newsletter of the International Association of Egyptologists. Museums and Collections* 24 (2004), 2-3; V. Kalpakcian, *Études Lausannoises d'Histoire de l'Art. La Russie et l'Occident* 2009; V. Kalpakcian in L. Tonini (ed.), *Il collezionismo in Russia da Pietro I all'Unione Sovietica*, 2009; M. Hill, G. Meurer and M. Raven, *Journal of the History of Collections*, 22 (2010), 289-306.

STROUHAL, Eugen (1931-2016)
Czech anthropologist; he was born in Prague, 24 Jan. 1931, son of Eugen S., a medical doctor, and Antonia Ipoltová; he graduated from the Faculty of Medicine, Charles University, 1956, and the Faculty of Arts in archaeology, 1959; he obtained the degree of candidate of biological sciences, 1968; DSc, Charles University, 1991; Hab, Faculty of Archaeology, Warsaw University, 1991; Hab, Faculty of Natural Sciences, Charles University, 1992; he worked as a doctor at a spa, 1956-7; he became lecturer at the Institute of Biology in the Medical Faculty of Charles University in Pilsen, 1957-60; he then lectured at the Research Institute of Endocrinology at the Motol Hospital in Prague, 1960-9 and was also lecturer in archaeology and anthropology at the University of 17 Nov. in Prague and an assistant at the Medical Faculty of Charles University, 1961-8; he became a staff member of the Náprstek Museum, 1969-92 where he established a department of archaeology of North Africa and the Middle East; he was appointed lecturer at Charles University in the Medical Faculty, 1989 and director of the Institute for the History of Medicine, 1993; he served as Professor of History of Medicine, Charles University, 1995-2004 ; he also lectured at the West Bohemian University, Pilsen and the University of Third Age (Continuing Education) from 1993; he worked on anthropological collections in the USA, 1972-3 and in Vienna, 1969-70, 1985, 1989; he took part in Czech excavations in Nubia, 1960-5, and Abusir, and Anglo-Dutch excavations at Saqqara, 1976, 1979, 1982 and from 1991; he was awarded the Hrdlicka Commemorative Medal, 1981; Michałówski Medal from the University of Warsaw, 1987, Charles University Medical Faculty Medal, 1998; the Charles University Medal (Hradec Králové), 2001, and the Charles University Medical Faculty (Pilsen) Medal, 2005; he was a Hon. Memb. of the Austrian Anthropological Society, 1969; the Spanish Anthropological Society, 1980; the Swedish Society for the History of Medicine, 1985; the Polish Anthropological Society, 1988; the Austrian Archaeological Institute, 1991; the Society for the History of Science and Technology, Prague, 2001; and the Czech Anthropological Society, 2006; apart from over 400 articles in various languages, he published, with L. Vyhnánek, *Egyptian Mummies in Czechoslovak Collections*, 1980; with J. Jungwirth, *Die anthropologische Untersuchung der C-Gruppen- und Pan-Gräber-Skelette aus Sayala, Ägyptisch-*

Nubien, 1984; with others, *Wadi Qitna and Kalabsha-South*, 1984; *Life of the Ancient Egyptians*, 1992 ; with L. Bares, *The Secondary Cemetery in the Mastaba of Ptahshepses at Abusir*, 1993; with L. Bares and K. Smoláriková, *Abusir IV. The Shaft Tomb of Udjahorresnet at Abusir*, 1999; with others, *Abusir V. The Cemeteries at Abusir South* I, 2001; with others, *Abusir VI. Djedjare's Family Cemetery*, 2002; *The Memphite Tomb of Horemheb, Commander-in-chief of Tutankhamun. Human Skeletal Remains*, 2008; with others, *Abusir XX. Lesser Late Period Tombs at Abusir*, 2009; with others, *The Medicine of the Ancient Egyptians* I, 2014; with Y. Coppins, he edited *Actes du premier colloque international d'anthropologie physique des anciens Égyptiens*, 1981; his papers are in the National Museum in Prague; he died in Prague, 20 Oct. 2016.

Kdo Je Kdo, 1998, 561; *Anthropologie* XLVIII/2 (2010), 69-90 (bibl.); J. Buikstra and C. Roberts (eds.), *The Global History of Palaeopathology. Pioneers and Prospects*, 2012, 126-130 (A. Zink) (bibl.); *Ägypten und Levante* XXVI (2016),14-16 (M. Bietak) (portr.); inf. H. Navratilova.

STRUVE, Vasili Vasilevitch (1889-1965)
Russian Egyptologist and Assyriologist; he was born in St. Petersburg, 2 Feb. 1889; the son of Vasili S. he first studied classical Philology and then Egyptology under Turaev (q.v.), graduating in 1911 from the History and Philological Faculty of St. Petersburg University; he studied briefly at Berlin under Erman (q.v.), 1914; appointed Lecturer and began teaching, 1916; Professor University of St. Petersburg, 1920-65; he produced a doctoral dissertation *Manetho and his Time*, 1928; he had already become interested in Semitics and as a lecturer studied Assyriology under Kokowtzov; head of Egyptian section, State Hermitage Museum, 1981-33; historian, Doctor of Historical Sciences, 1934; he was elected full member of the USSR Acad. of Sciences, 1935; from 1937 onwards corr. member of the Prague Acad. of Sciences; Director of Institute of Oriental Studies, 1941-50; Director of the Institute of Anthropology and Ethnography, 1935-50; Director of Dept. of Ancient East at the Academy of Sciences, 1958-65; Chairman of the newly organized Eastern Commission of USSR Geographical Society, Dec. 1955; Bureau member, Department of Historical Sciences, USSR Acad of Sciences, Feb. 1957; Honoured Science Worker of Uzbek SSR, 1943; Marxist historian; Order of Lenin, 1945; Struve's speciality was in subjects relating to the history of the ancient East, in which context he refuted the theory of "age-old feudalism" in the east, replacing it with another theory of "slave-holding society"; his studies may be said to have started from the analysis of Manetho, and later embraced a wide range of subjects, in particular the mathematical papyri in the museums in Moscow and Leningrad for which he is probably best remembered; they also included domestic problems of the Third Dynasty of Ur and matters connected with ancient Iranian religion; his works were very numerous and the bibl. covering the years 1912-61 lists about 273 items; from among these many historical items may be cited, *The Ownership Rights for Arable and Vineyard Land in Ptolemaic Egypt*, 1915; *Israel in Egypt*, 1920; 'Ort der Herkunft und Zweck der Zusammenstellung des grossen Papyrus Harris' in *Aegyptus* 7, 1926; *Manefon i ego vremia*, 1928-30; *Mathematischer Papyrus des Staatlichen Museums der Schönen Künste in Moskau* 1930; *Ipuwer's Words, Leiden Papyrus No. 344, The Social Revolution in Egypt at the End of the Middle Kingdom (circa 1750 BC)*, 1935; *Istoria drevnego vostoka (History of the Ancient Near East)*, 1941; and posthumously *Etiudy po istorii Severnogo Prichernomorya, Kavkaza i Srednei Azii*, 1968 with a publication of the stelae in the Hermitage; he also contributed to the great Encyclopaedia of World History,*Vsemimaja istoria* I, II, 1955-56; for his services to scholarship he was awarded the Order of the Red Banner of Labour, 1959; he died in Leningrad, 15 Sept 1965.

Akademiku Vasiliyu Vasilèvich Struve: drevnii Mir, sbornik statée, Moscow 1962, (bibl. covers 1912-61); *AEB* 1964, 64305; *BiOr* 23 (1966), 347-8 (J. Klima); Festschrift vol. on occasion of 75th birthday, 128 pages entitled *Assiriologijai Egiptologija*, 1964, has biogr. (L. Al Lipin); *Drevniy Egipet; Drevnyaya Afrika. Sbornik Statei Posviaskchennny Pamiati Akademika V. V. Struve*, 1967, 3-7; (*Ancient Egypt and Ancient Africa. Volume of Articles. Dedicated to the Memory of Academician V. V. Struve*); *Narody Afriki: Azii* 6 (1965), 341-2 (*Peoples of Africa and Asia* 6); *Palestinsky Sbornik* 15 (1966), 3-4; *Prezglad Orientalistyczny* 1 (57) (1966), 66-7 (B. Nadel); *Biographic Directory of the U.S.S.R.* 1965-66, 2nd ed., New York, 821-2. *VDI* 92, 1966, 3-8; *VDI* 1 (188), 1989, 244-9; M. Korostovtsev in H. Heinen, *Die Geschichte des Altertums im Spiegel der sowjetischen Forschung*, 1980, 20-5.

STRZYGOWSKI, Josef (1862-1941)
Austrian Byzantinist; he was born at Biala near Bielitz, 7 March 1862; originally destined to take over his father's textile business, he opted for academic studies at Munich, PhD 1885; he studied in Rome for four years and then spent a year in Greece and visited Constantinople; Professor at Graz 1892 and at Vienna 1909; he visited Egypt in 1894-5 and again in 1900 when he collected Coptic items for Berlin Museum and was asked by Maspero (q.v.) to prepare the catalogue of the Coptic collection in the Cairo Museum, *Koptische Kunst*, 1904; he died in Vienna, 7 Jan. 1941.

Byzantion 15 (1940-41), 505-10.

STUART, Henry Windsor Villiers (1827-1895)

British politician, traveller, and writer; he was born probably in Dromana, Ireland, 13 Sept. 1827, son of Henry V., Baron Stuart de Decies and Theresia Pauline Ott; he was educated at Durham University; ordained, 1850, but seceded from the Church, 1873; MP for Waterford, 1873-4, 1880-5; as he could not prove that his parents were married he was unable to succeed to the peerage; he went to Egypt on a social and political mission, 1883-4, the reports of this visit being published as a blue book; he also wrote *Nile Gleanings, concerning the Ethnology, History, and Art of Ancient Egypt, as revealed by Egyptian Paintings and Bas-Reliefs. With descriptions of Nubia and its Great Rock Temples to the Second Cataract*, 1879; *The Funeral Tent of an Egyptian Queen*, 1882; other works including articles in *PSBA*; he died by drowning off Villierstown Quay on the river Blackwater, 12 Oct. 1895; his collection was sold at Christie's 17 April 1970, lots 55-84.

ODNB 53, 158-9; *DNB* 55, 85; Hilmy, ii, 263-5; Wilbour, 212, 246, 287, 295.

STUKELEY, William (1687-1765)

British antiquarian; he was born at Holbeach, Lincolnshire, 7 Nov. 1687, son of John S., an attorney, and Frances Gullen; he was educated at Corpus Christi College, Cambridge 1703-8, MB, 1708; he studied medicine and went into private practice; FRS, 1718; MD, 1719; founder member of the Society of Antiquaries 1718; he was later a clergyman at Somerby-by-Grantham and Stamford and finally in 1747 rector of St. George-the Martyr, London; he was secretary of the short-lived Egyptian Society in 1741 and wrote on hieroglyphs in opposition of Needham (q.v.); he died in London, 27 Feb. 1765.

ODNB 53, 231-35 (portr.); *DNB* 55, 127-9; *GM* May 1765, 211ff.; *Al. Cantab.*; W. R. Dawson, *Studies Presented to F. Ll. Griffith*, 1932, 465-73; S. Piggot, *William Stukeley: an eighteenth-century antiquary*, rev. ed., 1985.

STURROCK, John (1832-1888)

Scottish engineer and surveyor to Lloyd's Registry of Shipping; he was born in Slap, 20 Dec. 1832, son of James S. and Elizabeth Nicol; in private life he was an enthusiastic antiquary and formed a private museum of antiquities which he had personally excavated or purchased at sales; the collection was sold in 1889 and many items were bought by the Soc. of Antiquaries of Scotland; among the Egyptian items, the finest specimen was the sword of King Kamose which was acquired by Sir John Evans (q.v.), who presented a cast of it to the British Museum (EA 36808); the sword was exhibited in the Burlington Fine Arts Club in 1922 (see *JEA* 10 (1924), 263 n. 7) and is now in the Ashmolean Museum; Sturrock died in Oakbank, Monikie, 25 Dec. 1888.

Inf. C. Aldred.

SUEFI (*var.* **SWAYFI**), **Ali Muhammad** (*fl.* 1891-1925)

Egyptian workman; he came from el-Lahun; he was employed by Petrie (q.v.) and soon became his chief excavator; he later worked for Brunton (q.v.); he excavated at Meidum, 1890-1; Amarna, 1891-2, Coptos, 1893-4; Naqada, 1894-5, Oxyrhynchus, 1896-7; Hu, 1897-8; Abydos, 1899-1901, Saft and Suwa, 1905-6; Meidum, 1909-10; al-Riqqa, 1912; Haraga, 1913-4; Medinat al-Ghurab, 1919-20; and Qau and Badari, 1922-5.

S. Quirke, *Hidden Hands*, 2010, 303-4.

SUYS, (*Père*) **Émile Joseph Auguste** (1894-1935)

Belgian Egyptologist; he was born at Anderlecht, 6 Dec. 1894, son of Pierre S. and Elisabeth Stockmans; he trained for the priesthood at Tronchiennes, 1912, and became a Jesuit; when the First World War broke out, he was evacuated to England where he studied philosophy; he later served as a stretcher-bearer at the front; Professor of Flemish at Saint-Servais college at Liège, 1920-22, and also served as priest; he began the study of Egyptology under Capart (q.v.) and worked at Fondation Égyptologique Reine Élisabeth in Brussels; he later succeeded Mallon (q.v.) as Professor at the Pontifical Biblical Institute, Rome; at this time he wrote a small hieroglyphic grammar for his students, 1929, and edited texts for their exercises, 1929-30; he gave public tuition on Egyptian art and civilization, helping to arouse popular interest in Egyptology; he visited Egypt in 1930; Suys specialized in Egyptian literature and presented the discoveries of Lefebvre (q.v.) at the tomb of Petosiris in popular form in this first large published work, *Vie de Petosiris, grand prêtre de Thot à Hermopolis la Grande*, 1927; he also published a book on the Eloquent Peasant, *Étude sur le conte du fellah plaideur*, 1933; *La Sagesse d'Ani*, 1935; in addition he wrote articles in a number of journals including *Egyptian Religion*, contributed to encyclopedias, and made a study of Amenemope; he died at Vaulx-en-Vélin near Lyons, 19 Dec. 1935.

Chron. d'Ég. 11 (1936), 459 (G. Lambert).

SUZUKI, (Hachisi) Madoka (1945-2018)
Japanese Egyptologist; she studied at the University of Tokyo and the École de Louvre under Desroches-Noblecourt (q.v.) and the University of Paris-Sorbonne under Leclant (q.v.) and later Grimal; MA, 1979; she was appointed researcher at the Heian Museum of Ancient History; she became a professor at the University Hijiyaqma, 1991-2001, and at the University of Sciences and Arts of Kurashiki, 2001-18; she was also a researcher at National Museum of Tokyo, 1994-2011; she excavated at Akoris, 1981-4; apart from numerous articles concerning Egyptian collections in Japan, she published *Excavations of Akoris in Middle Egypt*, 1983; she died in a traffic accident, 17 Jan. 2018.

CIPEG Journal 2 (2018), 1-2 (T. Sakamoto).

SWELIM, Nabil (1935-2015)
Egyptian archaeologist and naval officer; he was born *c*. 1935; he served in the Egyptian navy and studied at the Naval Academy; BSc., 1952 and then the Naval Institute, Ismailia; MSc, 1963; on leaving the navy, he became interested in Egyptology and obtained PhD, Eotvos Lorand University Budapest, 1981; he was a specialist in pyramid studies; he undertook archaeological investigations at Abydos, Saqqara, Seila, Abu Rawash and Mazghuna; apart from articles, he published *Some Problems on the History of the Third Dynasty*, 1983; and *The Brick Pyramid at Abu Rawash*, 1987; he died 23 Sept. 2015.

Internet obit.

SZCZEPAŃSKI, (*Revd*) **Władysław** (1877-1927)
Polish Biblical scholar, orientalist and archaeologist; he was born in Biala, 20 May 1877; member of the Jesuit order, taking holy orders in Cracow, 1903; he studied philosophy and theology at Cracow University, 1900-04, later archaeology and oriental languages at St. Joseph University in Beirut, 1904-7 and Assyriology in Innsbruck, 1907-09; specialist in the field of ancient history of the Near East and of the historical geography of Palestine; also an expert of canonical law; professor of Semitics at the Gregorian University, Rome, 1909-15 and director of the Museum of the Pontificio Istituto Biblico; professor at Warsaw University, 1918-27 and rector of the Warsaw Theological Seminary simultaneously; he was much interested in ancient Egypt; in 1906 he published his *Turquoise Mines on Sinai Peninsula*; he was also concerned with the topography of the Exodus, notably with the details of crossing the Red Sea by the Israelites; he is also an author of a vast textbook *Egypt*, 1922 in the series *Most Ancient Civilizations of the Classical East*; he died in Innsbruck, 30 May 1927.

Biograms of Polish Scholars 1, 3, 1985, 344-346; inf. J. Śliwa.

TABERNA, Vincenzo (*fl.*1788-1814)
Italian interpreter of Piedmontese origin; he was captured by Tunisian pirates and sold to Ali Pasha, later ruler of Tripoli, becoming his treasurer; on the overthrow of Ali Pasha in 1795, he followed his master into exile in Egypt and visited Mecca with him, being known as Sheikh Mansur; he later fought on the side of the Mamlukes against the French forces; on the departure of Ali Pasha for Constantinople in 1800, he joined the British forces as interpreter to Sir Sidney Smith, and secretary to Col. Missett (q.v.), British Consul-General in Egypt; he was given the rank of captain and later major; he was wounded during the British intervention in 1807 but returned to Egypt with Missett in 1811; he rendered much assistance to British travellers in Egypt such as Legh (q.v.) and Light (q.v.).

Hamilton, 344-5; Legh, 16, 132, 154; Valentia, iii, 405; G. Guémard in *Bulletin de la Société royale d'archéologie d'Alexandrie*, 27-38.

TAHTAWI, Rifa'a Rafi el- (1801-1873)
Egyptian scholar; he was born in Tahta, between Sohag and Asyut, 14 Oct. 1801, son of Badawi al-Husayni al-Qasimi, a tax farmer who was ruined by Muhammad Ali's reforms, and Fatima al-Farghali al-Ansari; he was educated at al-Azhar University in Cairo, 1817-23, and then became a teacher there; he served as a chaplain to a group of students sent to study in Paris by Muhammad Ali, 1826-31 where he studied under Agoub (q.v.); he then worked as a translator at the Medical School, 1831-3 and the Artillery School, 1833-4; in 1835 he became director of the School of Languages where he translated many European books into Arabic; he fell into disfavour under Abbas I in 1849 when his school was closed but was restored to government posts under by later rulers; he developed an interest in Egyptology and supervised the translation of a French work on ancient Egyptian history as *Bidayat al-qudama*, 1838; he also submitted a plan to preserve ancient Egyptian antiquities in 1835 and set up a museum in his school; among his own works was an account of his time in Paris, *Takhlis al-ibriz fi takhlis Baris*, 1834, translated by D. Newman, *An Imam in Paris*, 2004, and *Anwar tawfiq al-jalil fi akhbar Misr wa-tawthiq Banu Ismail*, a history of Egypt up to the Islamic conquest, 1868; he died in Cairo, 27 May 1873.

D. Reid, *Whose Pharaohs?*, 2002, 50-4, 108-112; D. Newman, *An Imam in Paris*, 2004, 29-67.

TAIT, George Aidan Drury (1902-1970)
British educator and curator; he was born in Birkenhead, 9 June 1902, son of Revd. Arthur James T. and Jane Dumergue Drury; he became assistant master at Eton College, 1927-62 and curator of the Myers (q.v.) collection which he was instrumental in saving from dispersal; he later acted as adviser for the Wainwright (q.v.) Essay Prize; he published 'The Egyptian Relief Chalice', *JEA* 49 (1963), 93-139; he died at Fordingbridge, 22 Nov 1970.

JEA 57 (1971), 2 (T. G. H. James); inf. J. Reade.

TALBOT, William Henry Fox (1800-1877)
British inventor and collector; he was born in Melbury, Dorset, 11 Feb. 1800, son of Willian Davenport T. and Lady Elisabeth Theresa Fox-Strangways; he was educated at Harrow from 1811 and at Cambridge, 1819-21; BA, 1821; MA, 1825; he settled at his ancestral home Lacock Abbey, Wiltshire in 1827; he invented the calotype process in photography; he had an interest in ancient languages and studied hieroglyphs; he collected some Egyptian stelae, now at Lacock, and hosted Lepsius (q.v.) on a visit; he published a pamphlet in 1846 *The Talbotype applied to Hieroglyphics*, using his photographic process to illustrate a drawing of the Ibrim stela of Sety I; he later turned to a study of cuneiform; his papers are now in the British Library; he died at Lacock Abbey, 17 Sept. 1877.

ODNB 53, 730-33 (portr.); *DNB* 55, 339-341; R. Caminos, *JEA* 52 (1966), 65-70; È. Gran-Aymerich, *Dictionnaire biographique d'archéologie 1798-1945*, 2001, incorporated in *Les Chercheurs de passé 1798-1945*, 2007, 1183.

TANO, Marius (*fl.*1870-1906)
Cypriot dealer of Greek origin; he was born in Larnaca, Cyprus, the son of Nicholas Constantinos T., a French subject, whose father Constantinos T. had emigrated from Ayia Mavra (Lefkas) about 1774 and held the post of Vice-Consul of Denmark in 1816; Marius T. is said to have studied architecture in France; he emigrated to Egypt and founded the first steamship office in Alexandria; later he owned an antiquities shop in Cairo founded in 1870; Tano carried on business simultaneously in Larnaca, Cyprus; he sold objects to Golenischeff (q.v), now in Russian museums; in 1884 he offered two mummies to the Cyprus museum; he sold some of the Amarna tablets to Daninos

(q.v.); in 1889 he offered to the collection of Rouen several Egyptian alabaster vessels, and in 1908 an assemblage of 132 flints of the Fayum Neolithic collected personally by him; he was the source for other antiquities in the Louvre, the Nicosia Museum, and the Museums at Athens, Marseilles and Lyons; he exhibited objects at the Paris exposition in 1889 and shortly thereafter retired to Larnaca; in 1892-1893 he was also in contact with Prince Wladysaw Czartoryski (q.v.) offering his Museum some Cypriote objects which were purchased and some plaster masks from the Fayum; some of the masks had already been bought by U. Bouriant (q.v.) and some were destined for Denmark; he also supplied Golenischeff (q.v.) and Dimitriou (q.v.); he was appointed to a post a the French consulate in Larnaca; he died *c.*1906 when his business was taken over by his nephew Nicolas Tano (q.v.).

Rev. Arch. 1885, II,342 (S.Reinach); *BCH* 101 (1977), 313-323 (O.Masson); *Folia Orientalia* XIX (1978), 191-200 (K.Moczulska); S. Aufrère, *Collections des Musées départementaux de Seine Maritime*, 1987; inf. J Śliwa and O Masson; R. Merrillees, *The Tano Family and Gifts from the Nile to Cyprus*, 2003, 6-8; F. Hagen and K. Ryholt, *The Antiquities Trade in Egypt 1880-1930*, 266.

TANO, Nicolas (1866-1924)
Cypriot dealer and collector of Greek origin; he was born in 1866, son of Georgios Nicholas T., a landowner and businessman at Patriki in the Karpas, brother of Marius Tano Panayiotis (q.v); he was a dealer in Egyptian antiquities in Cairo at 53 Sh. Ibrahim Pasha, formerly at 7 Sh. Kamel, opposite old Shepheard's Hotel, succeeding his uncle Marius T. (see above) about 1889; his collection was sold at Sotheby's in June 1928; he died in Cairo 1924; after his death his business was continued by his son Georgios Tano (*b.*1908, *d.*London 1977), who retired in the 1940s and his cousin Phocion Jean T. (*b.*1898, *d.*1972), son of Jean T., brother or cousin of Marius, who was involved in the sale of the Nag Hammadi Papyri, the Dishna Papers, and the Tebtunis library; the business was sold in 1972 and the remaining collection lost in the Turkish invasion of Cyprus in 1974.

Inf. L. Keimer and O. Masson; Wilbour, 170, 340, 439, 441, 461; *Bulletin de Correspondance Hellénique* 101 (1977), 315-7; R. Merrillees, *The Tano Family and Gifts from the Nile to Cyprus*, 2003, 8-21; F. Hagen and K. Ryholt, The Antiquities Trade in Egypt 1880-1930, 2017, 265-7.

TASSIE, Geoffrey John (1959-2019)
British archaeologist; he was born in Croydon, Surrey, 17 April 1959, son of Rowland John T., a motor mechanic, and Vera J. Thunder; he was educated at Birkbeck College, University of London, 1988-92; Diploma in Archaeology (Hons), 1992; and at University College London, 1992-2009; BA (Hons.) in Egyptian Archaeology 1995; MA in World Archaeological Method and Practices, 1997; and PhD, 2009; he became Managing Director, Egyptian Cultural Heritage Organization, Sept. 1998-2019 and Director of Archaeology, Qatar Museums Authority, 2006-8; he was appointed Hon. Research Fellow, University of Winchester, May 2010-19 and Postdoctoral Research Fellow, Free University of Berlin, Sept. 2013-July 2018 and the University of Edinburgh, Sept. 2017-8; he was a tutor at SOAS, 2001-2 and lecturer, 2007-8, 2014; he was a specialist in lithics and field methods; he undertook excavations at Kafr Hassan Dawood, 1995-9; the Fayum, 2002-4; Minufiyeh Archaeological Survey, 2006-19; Sais, 2006-7; Quesna, 2011-12;Imbaba Prehistoric Survey including Merimde Beni Salama 2013-19; and Naqada as Project Director, 2018-19; he published, with T. Duquesne and others, *The Salakhana Trove*, 2009; with others, *Managing Egypt's Cultural Heritage*, 2009; with L. Owens, *Standards of Archaeological Excavation*, 2010; *Prehistoric Egypt*, 2014; with P. Wilson, *Sais* II, 2014; he died in Cairo, 28 March 2019.

Inf. Joanne Rowland; *The Guardian* 10 April 2019 (Jacky Rowland).

TATTAM, (*Ven.*) Henry (1788-1868)
British Coptologist; he was born at North Marston, Bucks., 28 Dec. 1788, son of John T. and Jane Gurney; he was educated at Christ's College, Cambridge; Rector of St. Cuthbert, Bedford, 1822; Rector of Great Woolstone, Bucks., 1831; he held both livings until 1849 when he was presented to the benefice of Stanford Rivers, Essex; Archdeacon of Bedford, 1845-66; Chaplain-in-Ord. to Queen Victoria; FRS, 1835; Hon. LLD Trinity College, Dublin, 1845; DD Göttingen; PhD, Leiden; he visited Egypt and Syria, 1838-9, to obtain oriental MSS and brought back a considerable number of Coptic MSS, and also antiquities for John Lee (q.v.); he was one of the pioneers of Coptic studies in England and probably the most distinguished figure in this field at that time; he published many important works, see especially, *A Compendious Grammar of the Egyptian Language as contained in the Coptic and Sahidic Dialects: with Observations on the Bashmuric: together with alphabets and Numerals in the Hieroglyphic and Enchorial Characters, and a few explanatory observations with an Appendix consisting of the Rudiments of a Dictionary of the ancient Egyptian Language in the enchorial character by Th. Young*, 1830; *Lexicon Aegyptiaco-Latinum ex veteribus linguae Aegyptiacae Monumentis et ex operibus La Crozii, Woidii et aliorum summo studio congestum cum indice vocum Latinorum*, 1835; *Duodecim Prophetarum libros in lingua Aegyptiaca vulgo Coptica seu Memphitica ex manuscript. Parisiensi descriptos*, 1836; *The Apostolic Constitutions, or Canons of the Apostles in Coptic, with an English translation*, 1848; *Prophetae Majores, in dialecto linguae Aegyptiacae Memphitica seu Coptica, edidit cum*

versione Latina, 2 vols. 1852; his own Coptic MSS were acquired by the British Museum, now British Library (MSS Or. 422-42); his library was sold at Sotheby's, 16 June 1868; he died at Stanford Rivers, 8 Jan. 1868.

ODNB 53, 836-7; *DNB* 55. 386-7; Edwards, *Lives of the Founders*, 613; Hilmy, ii, 277; Hincks, 13, 69, 160, 179; Boase 3, 882, *A1. Cantab.*; *The Coptic Encyclopedia* 7, 2202 (A. S. Atiya).

TAWFIK, Ahmed Sayed (1936-1990)
Egyptian Egyptologist; he was born in Cairo, 29 July 1936, son of Tawfik Ahmad el-Zir, a manufacturer of sweets, and Aziza Osman Eid; he was educated at the Faculty of Arts, Cairo University, 1955-9, under Bakir (q.v.), Abu Bakr (q.v.), Mattha (q.v.), and Fakhry (q.v.); BA in Egyptology, May 1959; he was awarded the Lepsius scholarship in 1960 and studied at Göttingen University under Schott (q.v.), 1961-6; PhD in Egyptology, April 1966 with his thesis *Untersuchung zur Grossen Liste der Weihgeschenke Thutmosis III*; he obtained a teaching post in Cairo University, 1966; he was associated with the Akhenaten Temple Project, 1966-72, and wrote a series of studies on the Amarna period; he became assistant Professor in the Faculty of Archaeology, Cairo University, 1973; Professor, July 1979; Vice-Dean of the Faculty, 1980; Dean of the Faculty, 4 Oct. 1981-3 Oct. 1987; Head of the Egyptology Dept., Oct. 1987-Dec. 1988; he was appointed Chairman of the Egyptian Antiquities Organization, Dec. 1989; he was in charge of the Cairo Faculty of Archaeology excavations at Saqqara from 1984; a memorial volume of studies *Die Ihr vorbeigehen werdet... Wenn Gräber, Tempel und Statuen sprechen* was edited by U. Rössler-Köhler and T. Tawfik, 2009; he contributed to R. Smith and D. Redford, *The Akhenaten Temple Project* I, 1976 and wrote in *MDAIK* 25 (1969), 27 (1971), 29 (1973), 31 (1975), 32 (1976), 35 (1979), 37 (1981) and *Gott. Misz.* 26 (1977), 29 (1977), 29 (1978), and 30 (1978); he died in Cairo, 20 Dec. 1990.

Inf. V. Teague, British Council, Cairo and C. Müller, Göttingen University; *JEA* 77 (1991), xi; *BSFE* 120 (1991), 3; *ASAE* 72 (1992-1993), 193-6 (bibl.) (portr.) (T. Handoussa); U. Rössler-Köhler and T. Tawfik, *Die Ihr vorbeigehen werdet... Wenn Gräber, Tempel und Statuen sprechen*, 2009, IX-X (T. Tawfik).

TAYLOR, Bayard (1825-1878)
American traveller and diplomat; he was born in Kennett Square, Pennsylvania, 11 Jan. 1825, son of Joseph T. and Rebecca Bauer Way; he visited Egypt and the Sudan, 1851-2 and 1874; afterwards became US Ambassador in Berlin 1877; he published *Life and Landscapes from Egypt to the ... White Nile*, 1854, *Egypt and Iceland in the Year 1874*, 1902 and other works; he died in Berlin, 19 Dec. 1878.

Life and Letters, by his wife, 1884; Hill, 357; Hilmy, ii, 278; *DAB* 18, 314-16; H. G. Bastalick, J. B. Taylor and R. L Taylor, *Kennett Square,* 1987; C. Vivian, *Americans in Egypt 1770-1915*, 2012, 125-39.

TAYLOR, (Baron) Isidore Justin Séverin (1789-1879)
French antiquarian and author; he was born in Brussels, 5 Aug. 1789, son of Hélie T., Professor at Leiden, and Marie-Jacqueline Antoinette Walwein; Inspecteur des Beaux Arts, 1838; he was the founder of Soc. des Gens de Lettres in 1830 he went to Egypt in 1828 to examine the possibility of obtaining an obelisk for France; he was sent to Egypt in 1830 by Charles X to arrange for the transfer of the Luxor Obelisk to Paris; he was presented by Mimaut (q.v.) to Muhammad Ali, and gave him a copy of the *Description de l'Égypte* and other gifts; the removal of the obelisk having been authorized, he returned to France on news of the July Revolution; he published *L'Égypte*, a descriptive work, under the pseudonym of R. P. Laorty Hadji, 1857, and had previously collaborated with Louis Reybaud in *La Syrie, l'Égypte, la Palestine et la Judée*, 2 vols. 1839; he died in Paris, 6 Sept. 1879.

Carré, i, 212-21.; Hilmy, ii, 278; A. Jubinal, *Revue du Midi*, 2 serie, 2 (1844), 115-22, 146-61; E. Maingot, *Le Baron Taylor*, 1963; M. Dewachter, *Chron. d'Ég.* 55, (1980), 39-42; J. Bulté, *Catalogue des collections égyptiennes du Musée National de Céramique à Sèvres*, 1981, 16-17; J. Plazaola, *Le Baron Taylor*, 1989; E. Gaddy, *Chron. d'Ég.* 81 (2006), 25-44.

TEFNIN, Roland (1945-2006)
Belgian Egyptologist; he was born at Spa, Ardennes, 29 April 1945, son of Raymond T. and Anny Magnée; he studied at the Université Libre, Brussels from 1962, firstly classical philology for which he obtained a diploma in 1966, and also Egyptology under Gilbert (q.v.); Diploma in the History of Art and Archaeology, 1968 and

in Philology and Oriental History, 1969; PhD, 1973; he taught at the Université Libre, Brussels from 1966 and succeeded Gilbert, 1 Oct. 1974; Professor 1 Oct. 1982; Full Professor 1 Oct. 1985; he excavated in Syria, 1970-86, at Elkab, 1974, and at Tanis, 1990-7; he led a team from his university in recording private tombs TT 29 and TT 96 on the West Bank at Luxor from 1998; he was a member of the Fondation Égyptologique Reine Élisabeth from 1964 and a member of its excavation committee from 1988; he founded in 1992 the Centre pour l'Étude et la Sauvegarde de la peinture égyptienne ancienne; he published *La statuaire d'Hatshepsout à Deir el-Bahari. Portrait royal et politique sous la 18e dynastie*, 1979; with Jean-Marc Doyen et Eugène Warmenbol, *Les niveaux supérieurs du Tell Abou Danné. Chantier A, 1977-78*, 1980; *Statues et statuettes de l'ancienne Égypte*, 1988; *Art et magie au temps des pyramides*, 1991; *La peinture égyptienne ancienne*, 1997; *Mastabas de Saqqara. Textes et commentaire. La chapelle de Mererouka*, 1998; *Tombes thébaines privées et mastabas de Saqqara. La chapelle de Nakht TT 52*, 2003; *Le regard de l'image, des origines jusqu'à Byzance*, 2003; he also edited *La peinture égyptienne ancienne. Un monde de signes à préserver*, 1994; 2nd ed., 1997; and *La peinture égyptienne ancienne. Un monde de signes à préserver. Actes du Colloque International de Bruxelles 1994*, 1997; a volume *Chron. d'Ég.* 81 (2006) was dedicated to him and a volume of studies was published in his memory, E. Warmenbol and V. Angenot, *Thèbes aux 101 portes. Mélanges à la mémoire de Roland Tefnin*, 2010; he died while on holiday at Auroville, near Pondicherry, India, 13 July 2006.

E. Warmenbol and V. Angenot (edd.), *Thèbes aux 101 portes. Mélanges à la mémoire de Roland Tefnin*, Brussels, 2010, XI-XX (portr.), XXI-XXVII (bibl.); inf. E. Warmenbol; *Égypte Afrique & Orient* 45 (2007), 3-4 (portr.) (V. Angenot).

TERRACE, Edward Lee Bockman (1936-1973)
American Egyptologist and art historian; he was born at Anacortes, Washington 1 Oct. 1936, son of Edward J. T. and Ruth Bockman; he was educated at Dartmouth, BA, 1957 and Harvard University, BA, 1963; PhD, 1968; he also studied at The Queen's College Oxford, 1957-8; his interest was primarily in Egyptian art, and his publications were *Art of the Ancient Near East in Boston*, 1962; *Egyptian Paintings of the Middle Kingdom*, 1968; *Treasures of Egyptian Art from the Cairo Museum*, 1970; his career was cut tragically short when he was murdered in Cairo, 13 Nov.1973.

NARCE 88 (1974), 1-3 (L. Habachi); *The Times* 21 Nov. 1973 (M. Rice).

TERSAN, (*Abbé*) **Charles Philippe Campion de** (1737-1819)
French antiquarian and collector; he was born in Marseilles 8 Aug. 1737, son of Charles Joseph Campion, a banker, and Elisabeth David; he became an abbé about 1762; he was an amateur engraver; following a visit to Italy in 1766, he formed a collection of antiquities including some from Egypt; he interested himself in the decipherment of hieroglyphs and assisted Champollion (q.v.) in his research; his collection was sold in Paris, 8-30 Nov. 1819, the catalogue being drawn up by Grivaud de la Vincelle (q.v.); he died in Paris, 11 May 1819.

Bio. Univ. 41,181-2; inf. J. Kettel; Lugt 9679; F. Arquié-Bruley, *Bulletin de la Société Nationale des Antiquitaires de France*, 1998, 114-34.

TESTAS, Willem de Famars (1834-1896)
Dutch artist; he was born in Utrecht 30 Aug. 1834, son of Hendrik Johan T., an army officer, and Marij Frederica Duim; he accompanied Prisse (q.v.) to Egypt in 1858-60 and was responsible for some of the drawings in Prisse's *Art Égyptien* and *Art Arabe;* he returned to Egypt in Jan-July 1868 visiting Alexandria, Cairo and the Fayum; his paintings and drawings are preserved in various Dutch collections; he lived in Brussels from 1873-91; the diaries of his trips were edited by M. J. Raven, *Reisschetsen uit Egypte 1858-1860,* 1988; and *De schilderskaravaan, 1868,* 1992; he died in Arnhem, 24 March 1896.

M. J. Raven *op. cit.,* 9-12, 18-25.

TEUF(F)EL VON GUNDERSDORF, (*Baron*) **Hans Christoph** (1567-1624)
Austrian traveller; born 23 Dec. 1567, son of Christoph T. and Susanna von Weissprich; he was educated at the Universities of Padua, Bologna and Siena, 1585-6; he left for the Levant in 1587 and returned 1590/1, visiting Egypt 19 Sept.-9 Dec. 1588; he later served under the emperors Matthias and Ferdinand II; he published an account of his travels in 1598; his stay in Egypt during which he toured Alexandria, Cairo, Giza and Saqqara, was too short to be of use for new antiquarian material; he died in Qazvin, Persia on a further trip, 24 Aug. 1624.

Voyages en Égypte pendant les années 1587-1588 trans. from the German by Ursula Castel, notes by S. Sauneron, 1972.

TE VELDE, Herman (1932-2019)
Dutch Egyptologist; he was born in Colmschate near Deventer, 3 Oct. 1932, son of Hendrik te V. and Aaltje Klaziena in 't Hof; he studied theology, religious history, and and Egyptology at the University of Groningen under Th. P. van Baaren, 1952-8, and Egyptology at the University of Marburg under Helmuth Jacobsohn, 1956-7; PhD from Groningen, 1967; he became lecturer at Groningen, 1970-80; Professor of Ancient Religions and Egyptian Language and Literature, 1980-97; he took part in IFAO excavations at the Temple of Montu at Thebes, the University of Pennsylvania work in the tombs at Dra Abu el-Naga, and the Brooklyn Museum excavations at the Temple of Mut at Karnak; a volume of articles was produced for him, *Essays on Ancient Egypt in Honour of Professor Herman Te Velde*, edited by J. van Dijk, 1997; he specialized in Egyptian religion; apart from over 50 articles and reviews, he published his thesis *Seth, God of Confusion*, 1967, reprint 1977; and *De Goede Dag der Oude Egyptenaren*, 1971; he died in Eelde, 26 May 2019.

Inf. J. van Dij; J. van Dijk, *Phoenix* (2014), 35-45.

TEXTOR DE RAVISI, (*Baron*) **Anatole Arthur** (1822-1902)
French Colonial Administrator; he was born at Bourges, 15 June 1822, son of Louis Édouard T., an army officer, and Marie Arzena Guenot de Rongegoutte; he served in La Réunion, 1847-52, and in India, 1853-63; he was very interested in oriental studies and published works on Hindu and Buddhist architecture; in later life he became interested in Egyptology, and made many communications to the Congress of Orientalists at Paris, 1880, and Saint-Étienne, 1883; he died in Paris, 10 Jan. 1902.

Hilmy, ii, 281.

TEYNARD, Félix (1817-1892)
French engineer; he was educated at Grenoble; he visited Egypt in 1851 and 1869; he published *Égypte et Nubie, Sites et Monuments les plus intéressants pour l'étude de l'art et de l'histoire, etc.*, 1858, in 2 vols.; this was a large and sumptuous collection of plates intended as a supplement to the *Description de l'Égypte*.

Carré, ii, 324, 361; Hilmy, ii, 282.

THABIT, Thabit Hassan (*d.*1996)
Sudanese archaeologist; he served as deputy to Vercoutter (q.v.) in the Sudan Antiquities Service; he was appointed first Sudanese Director-General of the National Museums and Commissioner for Archaeology and editor of *Kush*, 11 Nov. 1961-1970 when he was succeeded by Sherif (q.v.); he oversaw the Nubian Rescue campaign in Sudanese Nubia and conducted excavations at the tomb of Djehutyhotep at Debeira East; he died on 2 June 1996.

Kush 17 (1997), 379; inf. W. Adams.

THACKER, Thomas William (1911-1984)
British orientalist; he was born in Bodicote, Oxfordshire, 6 Nov. 1911, son of Thomas William T. and Edith Maud Clarke; he was educated at the City of Oxford School and St Catherine's College, Oxford; BA, 1933; he studied at Berlin University, 1933-6 and took part in the excavation of El-Amarna, 1935; Senior Student, Oxford, 1935-7; Mark Quested Exhibitioner, Oxford, 1937-9; he was appointed assistant lecturer in Semitic Languages, University College of N. Wales Bangor, 1937 and then became reader in Hebrew, University of Durham, 1938-45 except for 1940-5 when he served in the Foreign Office; Professor of Hebrew and Oriental Languages, Durham, 1945-51; in 1951 he became the first Director of the School of Oriental Studies at Durham as well as Professor of Semitic Philology until his retirement in 1977; his main contribution to Egyptian philology was *The Relationship of the Semitic and Egyptian Verbal System*, 1954; he died in Durham, 23 April 1984.

WW 1984

THAUSING, Gertrud Maria Elisa (1905-1997)
Austrian Egyptologist; she was born in Vienna, 29 Dec. 1905, daughter of Victor Julius T. and Elsa Rosa Maria Ripka Edle von Richthofen; she studied Egyptology at the University of Vienna under Junker (q.v.) and Czermak (q.v.); PhD, 1930; she then became an assistant in the university, 1941; lecturer in place of Balcz (q.v.) from 1942; she produced her habilitation in 1943; Director of the Institut für Ägyptologie und Afrikanistik, 1953-77; then lecturer to 1995; her main interest was in Egyptian religion and Egyptian and African languages; a volume of studies was produced in her honour *Zwischen den beiden Ewigkeiten*,

1994; her chief works were *Der Auferstehungsgedanke in ägyptischen religiösen Texten*, 1943; with T. Kerszt-Kratschmann, *Das grosse ägyptische Totenbuch (Papyrus Reinisch) der Papyrussammlung der Österreichischen Nationalbibliothek*, 1969; with H. Goedicke, *Nofretari. Eine Dokumentation der Wandgemälde ihres Grabes*, 1971; *Sein und Werden. Versuch einer Ganzheitsschau der Religion der Pharaonenreiches*, 1971; and her autobiography *Tarudet. Eine Leben für die Ägyptologie*, 1989; she died in Vienna, 4 May 1997.

IAE Internet obituary (H. Satzinger); *Mittleilungen der Antropologische Gesellschaft in Wien* 128 (1990), 175-7 (portr) (M. Bietak); R. Teichl, *Österreichcher der Gegenwart*, 1951, 307.

THÉDÉNAT-DUVENT, Pierre Paul (1756-1822)
French diplomat; he was born at Uzès, 7 April 1756, son of Pierre T. and Isabeau Roussel; French Vice-consul at Cairo; he arrived on 14 Nov. 1815 taking over from Drovetti (q.v.) until the arrival of Roussel (q.v.); Acting Consul-General, May-July 1819; he made two large collections of Egyptian antiquities which were sold in Paris, 23-24 Dec. 1822 (cat. by Dubois); he wrote a history of contemporary Egypt, *L'Égypte sous Méhémed Ali*, which was posthumously published by F. J. Joly, 1822; the important stela, Louvre C. 14, was found by him at Abydos; at the sale it was acquired by Rollin (q.v.) for Cousinéry (q.v.), by whom it was sold to the Louvre; a papyrus in the Bibl. Nat. bears his name.

Hilmy, ii, 283; *TSBA* 5, 555; Lugt 10302; R. T. Ridley, *Napoleon's Proconsul in Egypt*, 1998, *passim*.

THÉODORIDES, Aristide (1911-1994)
Belgian Egyptologist of Greek extraction; he was born in Westende, 30 June 1911; he studied history at the Université Libre in Brussels, licentiate, 1937, and then philosophy, 1938, and oriental studies at the Institut de Philologie et d'Histoire orientales et slaves, 1939; he obtained a post teaching at a secondary school in Uccle, 1940, and, after World War II, was able to study Egyptology part-time in Paris at the École Pratique des Hautes Études with Posener (q.v.), Clère (q.v.), and Malinine (q.v.); at the Sorbonne with Alliot (q.v.) and Garnot (q.v.); and at the Faculté Catholique with Drioton (q.v.); PhD at Brussels, 1958 with a thesis on the juridical stela of Karnak; he obtained a fellowship through the influence of Pirenne (q.v.) to study at Oxford with Černý (q.v.), 1959 and briefly in 1960 and 1961 and later funds to travel to Egypt; Agrégation de l'enseignement supérieur, 1962; he edited Pirenne's *Histoire*; he was attached to the Fondation Égyptologique Reine Élisabeth, section on institutions and law from 1960; head of section, 1975; and also to the Université Libre, Brussels in 1963; lecturer, 1964, Professor, 1966-81; Professor of Egyptian Language and Civilization at the Institut des Hautes Études in Brussels; President of the Société Belge d'Études Orientales; Director of the Section d'Institutions et de Droit at the Fondation Égyptologique Reine Élisabeth; he was a specialist in ancient Egyptian law; he organized a colloquium on the subject in Brussels in 1974, published as *Le droit égyptien ancien*, 1976 and wrote extensively on legal matters in various journals notably the *Revue Internationale des Droits de l'Antiquité;* a volume in his honour *Individu, Société et Spiritualité dans l'Égypte pharaonique et copte*, edited by C. Cannuyer and J.-M. Kruchten, was published in 1993; he died in Uccle, 4 Feb. 1994.

C. Cannuyer and J.-M. Kruchten, *op. cit.*, vii-xv (J.-M. Kruchten) (bibl.); family inf.; *Acta Orientalia Belgica* 8 (1993), 1-7 (J. Ries), 11-15 (J. Tempels); *Chron. d'Ég.* 70 (1995), 5-8 (A. Mekhitarian); *Revue internationale des droits de l'Antiquité* 41 (1994), IX-XII (portr.) (M. Nuyens).

THÉVENOT, Jean de (1633-1667)
French traveller; he was born in Paris, 16 June 1633, the nephew of Melchisédech T.; in 1656 he left Turkey for Egypt, remaining there from Jan. 1657 to Jan. 1659, going up the Rosetta branch of the Nile to Bulaq and visiting Giza and Saqqara; he also made a journey to the Suez area; he went on a second trip to the east in 1663, visiting Saida, Damascus, Mosul, and Baghdad, after which he went to Persia; he published *Voyage au Levant,* 1664; after his death the *Voyages de M. Thévenot,* 5 vols. 1689, was published; he left an interesting description of the pyramids; he died in Miana in Persia, 28 Nov. 1667.

La Grande Enc. 31, 8; Vyse, ii, 215-17; Lamy, 126-31; J. Speake (ed.), *Literature of Travel and Exploration*, 2003, 3, 1174-5.

THEVET, André (*c.*1516-1592)
French geographer and traveller; he was born at Angoulême about 1516 and joined a religious order in that town; in 1549 he embarked on a tour of the Levant visiting Egypt in 1551-2 where he proceeded as far as Cairo before crossing the Sinai to Palestine; he published his account of his travels *Cosmographie de Levant* in 1554;

in 1555 he joined the short-lived French colony in Brazil; on his return he became almoner to Queen Catherine de Medici and royal cosmographer and guardian of the royal cabinet of curiosities at Fontainebleau; he died in Paris, 23 Nov. 1592.

Bulletin de géographie historique et descriptive II (1888), 166-201 (P. Gaffarel); *Mémoires de la Société Archéologique et Historique de la Charente* VII (1907-8), 1-47 (D. Touzard); J. Adhémar, *Frère André Thevet, 1947*; F. Lestringant, *Voyages en Egypte 1549-1552, 1984*; C. Cannuyer, *DIE* 3 (1985), 7-20; Lamy, 70-3; F. Lestringaut, *Sous la Leçon des Vents*, 2003.

THISSEN, Heinz-Josef (1940-2014)
German demotist; he was born at Neuss, 13 March 1940; he studied classical philology, 1959-65 and Egyptology, 1961-5 at the University of Cologne under Hermann (q. v.); PhD, 1965; he undertook further studies in Egyptology at the University of Würzburg under Lüddeckens (q.v.), 1965-70; Habilitation at Cologne, 1985; he worked as an assistant in the Papyrological section of the Nordrhein-Westfälische Akademie der Wissenschaften und der Künste at Cologne, 1974-90; he became lecturer at the Philipps University of Marburg, 1989-90; Professor 16 March 1990; Professor at the University of Cologne, 1 May 1992-31 March 2005; he was an editor of the periodical *Enchoria*, 1971-2014; a volume of studies in his honour was published by H. Knuf and others, *Honi soit qui mal y pense. Studien zum pharaonischen, griechisch-römischen und spätantiken Ägypten zu Ehren von Heinz-Josef Thissen*, 2010; he edited with Zauzich, *Grammatika Demotika* in honour of Lüddeckens (q.v.), 1984 and *Res severa verum gaudium*, 2004 in honour of Zauzich; apart from articles, his publications include *Studien zum Raphiadekret*, 1966; with others, *Die ägyptischen Personennamen* III, 1977; *Die Lehre des Anchscheschonqi*, 1984; *Die Graffiti von Medinet Habu*, 1989; *Der verkommene Harfenspieler*, 1992; *Vom Bild zum Buchstaben*, 1998; *Des Niloten Horapollon Hieroglyphenbuch* I, 2001; with G. Burkard, *Einführung in die altägyptische Literaturgeschichte*, I, 2003; II, 2009; he died in Erfstadt, 25 July 2014.

H. Knuf and others, *Honi soit qui mal y pense*, XI-XVII (bibl.); *ZÄS* 142 (2015), 97-103 (G. Burkard (portr.), (bibl.)); *Enchoria* 34 (2014/5), XI-XVI (K.T. Zauzich) (portr.).

THOMAS, (Mary) Elizabeth (1907-1986)
American Egyptologist; she was born in Memphis, Tenn., 29 March 1907, daughter of John Talbert T. and Ruth Archer; she was educated at Hollins College, Virginia and the University of Mississippi where she received her BA in 1937; inspired by a trip to Egypt in 1935, she began to study Egyptology at the Oriental Institute, University of Chicago in 1938, but her studies were interrupted by World War II during which she served as a cryptographer, 1942-6; she resumed her research at Chicago and obtained her MA, 1948; she worked on the tomb of Ramesses VI with Piankoff (q.v.) and Rambova (q.v.), 1949-50, and returned again in 1953 concentrating her research on the Theban royal tombs; her last season in 1959-60 was sponsored by the American Research Center; apart from several articles on this topic, she produced the authoritative *The Royal Necropoleis of Thebes*, 1966; her papers and library were presented to the Institute of Egyptian Art and Archaeology at the University of Memphis; she died in Jackson, Miss., 28 Nov. 1986.

Varia Aegyptiaca 3 (1987), 3 (C. Van Siclen); *JARCE* XXIV (1987), 1-2 (R. Freed); *NARCE* 136-7 (1987), 33-4 (C. Roehrig); inf. J. Larson.

THOMPSON, (*Sir*) Henry Francis Herbert *2nd Bart.* (1859-1944)
British Coptologist and Demotic scholar; he was born in London, 2 April 1859, son of Sir Henry T., 1st Bart., FRCS, and Kate Fanny Loder; he was educated at Marlborough College and Trinity College, Cambridge; he studied Law and was called to the Bar, but finding it uncongenial, he turned to medicine; biological work in the laboratories at University College London, and especially the use of the microscope brought on eye trouble, and his second career was thus ended; he took up Egyptology at he age of 40 under the influence of Petrie (q.v.), and studied under Griffith (q.v.) and Crum (q.v.) at University Coll.; he succeeded as 2nd Bart. in 1904; after a general grounding in Egyptology he specialized in Coptic and Demotic becoming one of the foremost scholars of his generation; he lectured at University College London, 1915-16; Fellow of University College; Hon. DLitt Oxford; FBA; he published many independent works as well as making substantial contributions to those of others, and edited many texts; he also gave great assistance to Crum in the completion of his Coptic Dictionary; he was a generous supporter of archaeology as well, and presented his library to the EEF in 1919, retaining only a few books, mainly Coptic and Demotic, for his own use; he published *The Demotic Magical Papyrus of London and Leiden*, 3 vols., with F.

Ll. Griffith, 1904-9; *The Coptic, Sahidic, version of certain books of the Old Testament, from a papyrus in the British Museum*, 1908; *A Coptic Palimpsest containing Joshua, Judges, Ruth, Judith and Esther, in the Sahidic dialect*, 1911; *The New Biblical Papyrus; a Sahidic Version of Deuteronomy, Jonah and the Acts of the Apostles, from MS. Or. 7594 of the British Museum: notes and a collation by Sir H. T.*, 1913; *Theban Ostraca*, pt. 2, 'Demotic Texts', pt. 4, 'Coptic Texts' in Gardiner's publ., 1913; *The Gospel of St John, according to the earliest Coptic manuscript*, 1924; *The Coptic Version of the Acts of the Apostles, and the Pauline Epistles in the Sahidic dialect*, 1932; *A Family Archive from Siut, from papyri in the British Museum, including an account of a trial before the Laocritae in year B.C. 170*, 2 vols. 1934; he also wrote chapters in Petrie's *Gizeh and Rifeh* and Quibell's *Monastery of Apa Jeremias*; by his will he founded a chair of Egyptology in Cambridge; he died in Bath, 25 May 1944.

S. R. K. Glanville, *The Growth and Nature of Egyptology* (1947), 12-14; *JEA* 30 (1944) 67-8 (portr.) (S. R. K. Glanville); *WWW* iv, 1145-6; *DNB* 1941-50, 880-1 (S. Glanville); *ODNB* 54, 443-5; R. Janssen, *The First Hundred Years*, 1992, 13; *The Coptic Encyclopedia* 7, 2257 (A. S. Atiya).

THORVALDSEN, Bertel (1770-1844)
Danish sculptor and collector; he was probably born in Copenhagen, 19 Nov. 1770, son of Gotskálk Thorvaldsen and Karen Dagnes, but may have been born 13 Nov. 1768, the illegitimate child of a householder and servant; he studied at the Copenhagen Academy of Fine Art, and was awarded a scholarship to travel to Italy in 1795; he lived in Rome from 1797 to 1838, where he became a leading Neo-classical sculptor after the death of Canova in 1822; there he formed a large collection of antiquities, including over 400 Egyptian objects; he was described by Kestner (q.v.) as his main rival for Egyptian antiquities in Rome; he returned to Copenhagen, 1838; he donated his collections and money to Copenhagen to found the Thorvaldsen Museum, which opened in 1848; he died in Copenhagen, 24 March 1844.

Dansk Biografisk Leksikon 14, 538-46; *Grove Dictionary of Art* 30, 763-6; L. Muller, *Description des Antiquités du Musée Thorvaldsen*, 1847; T. Melander, *Thorvaldsens Antikker*, 1993; M.-L. Buhl, *L'art statuaire égyptien au Musée Thorvaldsen*, 2000.

THURBURN, Robert (1784-1860)
British official; he was born at Keith, Scotland, 18 July 1784, son of James T. and Barbara Anderson; he was secretary to E. Missett (q.v.), British Consul-General in Egypt, and afterwards a partner in the house of Briggs & Co., Alexandria; British Consul in Alexandria 1833-8; he was very helpful to British travellers and explorers in Egypt; he died at Lyons, 24 April 1860.

Travels of Lady H. Stanhope, i, 134, 138; Hogg, Visit to Alexandria, 123, 127, 139; Light, 23; Madden, *Travels*, i, 214, 269; Madox, i, 25; Richardson, i, 25; Salt, ii, 276-80; Westcar Diary, 6, 8, 13.

TIELE, Cornelis Petrus (1830-1902)
Dutch scholar; he was born in Leiden, 16 Dec. 1830, son of Cornelis T. and Maria Johanna van Kampen; he specialized in the history of religions, first Professor for the History of Religions at Leiden University and published *Vergelijkende Geschiedenis van de Egyptische en Mesopotamische Godsdiensten*, 1872, which was translated into English, 1882, as were other works of a similar nature; his largest work was on the ancient religions from the time of Alexander the Great; he died in Leiden, 11 Jan. 1902.

Hilmy, ii, 287; *OLZ* 5, 77; *NBW* 4, 1332-5.

TIGRANE (*Pasha*) (*d.*1904)
Egyptian statesman and collector; he was of Armenian origin; Foreign Minister and member of the Comité d'Archéologie, Cairo; he was son-in-law of the celebrated Nubar Pasha, and visited England in 1885; he formed a collection of Egyptian antiquities, some of the stelae and larger stone monuments being displayed in the garden of his house; he presented a fine bas-relief from Heliopolis to the Museum of Alexandria; some years after his death a catalogue of his collection was published in Paris by Daninos Pasha (q.v.), *Collection d'Antiquités ég. de Tigrane Pacha d'Abro*, 1911; he died in 1904.

Lord Cromer, *Modern Eg.* ii, 221-5; and *Abbas II*, 44, 46, 58; Maspero, *Rapports sur ... le Serv. des Antiq.* vi; Wilbour, 174.

TILL, Walter Curt Franz Theodor Karl Alois (1894-1963)
Austrian Coptologist; born at Stockerau, 22 Feb. 1894; he studied at the University of Vienna, 1917-20, under Junker (q.v.); became lecturer in Egyptology there, 1928; visited Egypt for study, 1930-1; he was also in charge of the papyri in the National Library, 1931-51; he was appointed Professor at Vienna, 1939-45; acted as guest Professor in the University of Cairo and at Manchester, 1950; senior lecturer in Coptic at Manchester,

1951-59; he was a specialist in Coptic and an authority on grammar; he was also associated with the journals *Biblica* and *Orientalia*; Till wrote an excellent Sahidic grammar and a number of studies relating to the Biblical prophets and stories of the saints; *Die Achmîmische Version der zwölf kleinen Propheten ...*, 1927; *Achmîmisch-koptische Grammatik, mit Chrestomathie und Wörterbuch*, 1928; *Koptische Chrestomathie für den fayumischen Dialekt, mit grammatischer Skizze und Anmerkungen*, 1930; *Koptische Dialektgrammatik, mit Lesestücken und Wörterbuch*, 1931; *Koptische Pergamente theologischen Inhalts*, 1934; *Koptische Heiligen- und Martyrerlegenden*, 1935-6; *Die Arzneikunde der Kopten*, 1951; *Koptische Grammatik, Saïdischer Dialekt mit Bibliographie, Lesestücken und Wörterverzeichnissen*, 1955; he died in Herzogenburg, Lower Austria, near Vienna, 3 Sept. 1963.

BSAC 17 (1963-4), 1964, 1-12 (portr.) (Mirrit Boutros Ghali); *FuF* 38 (1964), 28 (J. Leipoldt); *Orientalia* 33 (1964), 169 (anon.); *ZÄS* 91 (1964), xi-xv (E. Lüddeckens); R. Teichl, *Österreicher der Gegenwart*, 1951, 310.

TILL, William (1782-1844)
British dealer; he was baptized in Upton cum Chalvey, Buckinghamshire, 27 June 1782, son of William T. and Mary Fry; he dealt in coins and antiquities at 17 Gt. Russell St., London; he supplied many Egyptian antiquities to John Lee (q.v.) and other collectors, and was agent for Belzoni (q.v.) who left in his charge a number of mummies and other antiquities for disposal; his coins were sold at Sotheby's 6-11 Jan. 1845, 28 July-4 Aug. 1845, 20-27 April 1846, and 12-14 May 1846; he died at Windsor, 8 April 1844.

Hartwell Registers; Lugt 17574, 17869, 18153, and 18198.

TIMSAH (*c*.1788-*c*.1865)
Arabic 'Crocodile', the sobriquet given to a native of Luxor who rendered great services to Champollion (q.v.) and acted as his *reis* in 1829, having previously so acted for Drovetti (q.v.); on the recommendation of Mimaut (q.v.), the French Consul-General, Timsah and his family were made French protégés, and exempted from corvées, etc.; Timsah held a certificate from Champollion of which he was very proud, and when Brugsch (q.v.) met him at Thebes in 1854 he provided many reminiscences of Champollion; he was still living in 1863; his sons and grandsons were employed by Mariette (q.v.) and for many years after by the Antiquities Service; two of them, Dieb and Aguil, had more than thirty years service.

Champollion, ii, 248; Brugsch, *Mein Leben*, 183; *Rec. Trav.* 12. 218; Wilbour, 498.

TIRARD, (*Lady*) **Helen Mary** (*née* **Beloe**) (1852-1943)
British translator; she was born in Kings Lynn, 10 May 1852, daughter of the Revd R. Albert Seppings Beloe and Elizabeth Mary Ware; she married in 1885 Dr. (later Sir) Nestor Tirard, FRCP (1853-1928); she was an early member and zealous supporter of the EEF and served on the Committee for many years; she translated Erman's *Aegypten und aegyptisches Leben* under the title *Life in Ancient Egypt*, 1893, which was for many years one of the most popular general works on Egypt and which still contains much of interest; although in her last years she became blind, she maintained her interest to the end, at nearly 90 years of age; she died in Newbury, 21 May 1943.

Private inf.; C. Lewis, *EA* 53 (2018), 42-5.

TODA Y GÜELL, Eduardo (1855-1941)
Spanish historian and diplomat; he was born in Reus, Tarragona, 1855; he studied law and in 1873 he entered the Spanish diplomatic service; Consul-General in Egypt 1884-6; he undertook numerous trips throughout the country and in Jan-March 1886 acccompanied Maspero (q.v.) to Upper Egypt; and afterwards published a number of works relating to ancient Egypt; *Estudios egiptológicos. Sesostris,* 1886; *Estudios egiptológicos. La muerte en el Antiguo Egipto,* 1887; *Inventario y textos de un sepulcro egipcio de la XX dinastia,* 1887; trans. *Historia del Antiguo Egipto par Jorge Rawlinson,* 1894; also *A través del Egipto,* 1889; and an account of the discovery of the tomb of Sennedjem at Deir el-Medina in *Boletin de la Real Academia de la Historia* X (1887), 91-148 partly trans. in *ASAE* 20 (1920), 145-158; he donated objects to the Museo Balaguer in Vilanova i la Geltru (catalogue, 1887) while others have been acquired by the Museo Arqueologico Nacional, Madrid; he died in Poblet, 26 April 1941.

Espasa-calpe Enciclopedia Universal Illustrada europeo-americana, 62 (1928), 334-5; id., Apendice, 10 (1933), 507; id., Suplemento anual, 1940-1 (1948), 374; G. Fort, *Eduard Toda* 1975; J. Padro, *BSFE* 113 (1988), 32-45; È. Gran-Aymerich, *Dictionnaire biographique d'archéologie 1798-1945*, 2001, incorporated in *Les Chercheurs de passé 1798-1945*, 2007, 1195-6.

TODROUS BOULOS (*d.* 1898)
Egyptian antiquities dealer; he was a Copt and Consular Agent in Luxor for Prussia (later Germany); he was active as a dealer from 1856; according to Rhind (q.v.), he had been trained as a silversmith and used his knowledge of metal-working in the fabrication of forged antiquities; many genuine antiquities passed through his hands, however, some of which were bought by Maspero (q.v.) for the Bulaq Museum; he was succeeded in his business and as consular agent by his son Mohareb Todrous (*c.*1847-1937) who was educated in English and German and became the most prominent dealer in Luxor; he was associated with Aslanian (q.v.); he died 22 Nov. 1937 and his business was taken over by his son Zaki (1901-1978).

Inf. obtained by G. R. Hughes, Chicago House, Luxor; letter from R. Moss 12 Aug. 1953; Lady Duff-Gordon, *Letters*, 221; Myers Diary, 1897; Rhind, *Thebes, its Tombs*, etc., 248, 253; Wilbour, 48 and often; F. Hagen and K. Ryholt, *The Antiquities Trade in Egypt 1880-1930*, 2017, 248-50.

TOIVARI-VIITALA, Jaana (1964-2017)
Finnish Egyptologist; she was born in Loviisa 1964; she studied at the University of Helsinki, BA; MA; and then at the University of Leiden, PhD; she was a postdoctoral researcher for the Deir el-Medina Database, 2001-4; she was supervisor of Egyptological studies in the Dept. of World Cultures at the University of Helsinki and curator at the Loviisa Museum 2014-7; she was chairman of the Finnish Egyptological Society, 2005-15; she undertook excavations at Wad ben Naga, 2009 and the Valley of the Kings; she published *Women at Deir el-Medina*, 2001; *Ancient Egyptian Book of the Dead*, 2001; *Letters in Ancient Egypt*, 2004; she died in Helsinki, 12 May 2017.

TOMKINS, (*Revd*) **Henry George** (1826-1907)
British Biblical archaeologist; he was born in Abingdon, Berks., 13 May 1826, son of Charles T. and Maria Hobbs; he was educated at Cambridge and entered the Church; he lived at Weston-super-Mare and was a friend of Amelia Edwards (q.v.) and an early member of the EEF which he joined in 1883, serving on the Committee until 1902; he was very interested in Biblical archaeology and published many papers thereon in *PSBA, JAI*, and other journals; he translated Maspero's (q.v.) communication to the Victoria Institute on the names relating to Judea in the lists of Thutmose III; he died in Weston-super-Mare, 21 Feb. 1907.

Hilmy, ii, 290; *JEA* 33 (1947), 88; *Al. Cantab.*

TOMLINSON, (*Rt Revd*) **George** (1801-1863)
British divine; he was born in 1801; educated at St. John's College, Cambridge, BA, 1823; MA, 1826; DD, 1842; he was consecrated Bishop of Gibraltar, 1842; he contributed articles to the *Trans. of the R. Soc. Literature* on subjects relating to Egyptology, such as the astronomical ceiling of the Memnonium (Ramesseum) at Thebes, etc.; he died in Gibraltar, 9 Feb. 1863.

Al. Cantab; Hilmy, ii, 291.

TORR, Cecil (1857-1928)
British landowner and writer; he was born in London, 11 Oct. 1857, son of John Smale T. and Augusta Elizabeth King; he was educated at Harrow, 1872-6 and Trinity College, Cambridge, 1876-80; BA, 1880, MA, 1883; he was admitted to the Inner Temple, 1879 and called to the Bar, 1882; he was greatly interested in the relations between Egypt and Greece; apart from several articles, he was the author of *Ancient Ships,* 1895 and *Memphis and Mycenae,* 1896 as well as books on his home estate at Wreyland; he died at Yonder Wreyland, Lustleigh, Devon, 17 Dec. 1928.

Al. Cantab; WWW 2, 1047; *The Times*, 20 Dec. 1928, 16.

TOSI, Mario (1926-2014)
Italian Egyptologist; he published, with A. Roccati, *Stele e altre epigrafi di Deir el Medina*, 1972; *A Theban Private Tomb: tomb 295*, with El-Sayed Aly Hegazy, 1983; *Nelle sede della verità. Deir el-Medina e l'ipogeo di Thutmosi III*, with A. Fornari, 1987; *La capella di Maia*, 1994; *Vivere nell'antico Egitto. Deir el-Medina, il villagio degli artefici delle tombe dei re*, with E. Leospo, 1998; *The Tomb of Nefertari*, with Mohamed Nasr, 1997; *The Tomb of Pashed and the Valley of the Artisans*, with Mohamed Nasr, 2001; *Vita quotidiana nel villagio operaio di Deir el-Medina da ostraca inscritti e figurati (circa 1540-1070 a.C.)*, with M. T. Nicola, 2003; *Dizionario enciclopedico della divinità dell'antico Egitto*, 2004; *Vita quotidiana al tempo dei faraoni*, with G. Magi, 2005; English version, *Daily Life in the Egypt of the Pharaohs*, 2007; *Tausert, l'ultima regina*, 2007; *Dizionario della divinità dell'antico Egitto*, 2011; he also edited Lanzone's (q.v.) *Dizionario mitologi Egizia*, 4 vols., 1974-5; he died in Mondovi, 21 May 2014.

Private inf.

TOTT, (*Baron*), **François de** (1733-1793)
French-Hungarian diplomat and soldier; he was born at Chamigny, 18 Aug. 1733, son of Andras Toth, a Hungarian exile in the French army and diplomatic agent; he accompanied the French ambassador to Constantinople in 1755 and later entered Turkish service; he returned to France in 1776 and suggested the possible French occupation of Egypt; he was sent to Egypt and the Levant in 1776 ostensibly as an inspector-general of French trading stations but also to examine the feasibility of French intervention; he reached Alexandria on 3 July 1777, proceeded to Cairo, and eventually left from Damietta on 26 Aug. 1777; he was accompanied by several experts including Savary (q.v.) and Sonnini (q.v.); he then toured Palestine, Asia Minor, and Greece, returning to France in 1778; he produced his secret report in 1779 which was later to form the basis for Napoleon's invasion; he then served in the French army at Douai but was forced by the French Revolution to emigrate to Hungary in 1790; he published *Mémoires sur les Turcs et les Tartares*, 1784; he died at Tarcs, 24 Sept. 1793.

Biographie universelle 42, 6-8*; NBG* 45, 521-2; F. Toth, *Etudes sur la région méditerrannée* 7 (1997), 51-68; F. Toth, *Africa* 47 (2003), 147-78.

TOUSSOUN, (*Prince*) **Omar** (1872-1944)
Egyptian geographer; he was born at Alexandria, 8 Sept. 1872, son of Prince Toussan, son of Said Pasha and Bachachat-nur; he was educated in Egypt, Switzerland, France and England; he closely managed his estates and became President of the Société royale d'agriculture, 1932; he was also Honorary President of the Société royale d'archéologie d'Alexandrie and the Société d'archéologie copte; in 1905 he undertook excavations on his estate near Aboukir and presented the finds to the Graeco-Roman Museum in Alexandria; in 1929 he encouraged excavation at the Mosque of Nebi Mend in Alexandria and in 1933 underwater explorations at Aboukir; his great interest was Egyptian geography and his works include *Mémoires sur les anciennes branches du Nil*, 1923; *Mémoire sur les finances de l'Égypte depuis les Pharaons jusqu'à nos jours*, 1924; *Mémoire sur l'histoire du Nil*, 1925; *La géographie de l'Égypte à l'époque arabe*, 1926-36; *Étude sur le Wadi Natroun, ses moines et ses couvents*, 1931; he died at Alexandria, 26 Jan. 1944.

BIE 26 (1942-4), 2-19 (bibl.) (G. Wiet and M. Ratib); *BSAC* 10 (1944), v-viii (portr.) (M. B. Ghali); *Bulletin de la Société royale d'archéologie d'Alexandrie* 36 (1943-4), 98-103 (E. Combe); S. Hamouda, *Omar Toussoun, Prince of Alexandria*, 2005.

TRAD, May (1930-2016)
Egyptian curator; she was born in Cairo, 1930 of Lebanese origin; she studied Egyptology at Cairo University, graduating 1968; she was librarian and general assistant at Chicago House, Luxor, 1976-81 and at ARCE in Cairo, 1976-85; she worked at the Cairo Museum from 1982 until retirement; she organized exhibitions such as the EES Centenary Exhibition in 1982 and was extremely knowlegeable on the records and objects in the Cairo collection; she also taught at the American University in Cairo, 1982-9 and the faculties of Tourism at Helwan University and Alexandria; Hon. Life Member of ARCE, 1987; she died in Lebanon, 12 Dec. 2016.

Inf. H. Bassir; *Al-Ahram* 10 Jan 2017 (H. Bassir).

TRAILL, James (*d.*1853)
British botanist and gardener; he was gardener to the Royal Hortic. Soc. at Chiswick; ALS, 1827; he became superintendent of the gardens of Ibrahim Pasha, 1834-53; he died in Cairo, 11 Feb. 1853.

BIBIB 304; Lindsay, 31; Vyse, ii, 75; Yates, ii, 363; St. John, ii, 446.

TRESSON, (*Abbé*) **Paul Louis Joseph** (1876-1959)
French Egyptologist; he was born at Reméreville, 25 Aug. 1876, son of Émile T. and Anne Marie Sauveur; he was Professor at Lunéville; he entered Egyptology in 1919, when he translated the inscription of Weni; in 1922 he translated the Quban stala in Grenoble Museum; he was an active reviewer in *Kêmi, BIFAO, Revue Biblique*, and the *Mélanges Maspero*; he organized the Bibl. Saint-Ferréol at Grenoble; he died in Saint Robert, 25 March 1959.

BSFE 30 (Nov. 1959), 39-40 (É. Drioton); *Bulletin de la Faculté Catholique de Lyon*, July-Dec. 1964 *Compte Rendu mensuel de l'Académie Delphinale* May 1950, CCXXIII-CCXXV (L. Bassette). 15-22 (A. Barucq).

TRIANTAPHYLLOS, Georgios *alias* **Wardi** (*d.*1852)
Greek merchant; he was the son of Georgios T.; he apparently came to Luxor, about 1824; he shared a house with G. d'Athanasi (q.v.) at Qurna and superintended his operations in his absence; he is often mentioned by contemporary travellers and diarists with his name spelled in a variety of ways.

Inf. Dr. Mosconas, Librarian of the Patriarchal Library, Alexandria; Hay Diary, 1826; Hoskins, *Oasis*, 2, 28; Lane Corresp. 56; Letter from Lieder, Cairo, 19 Oct. 1852; Westcar Diary, 221; M. Dewachter, *Rev. d'Ég.* 36 (1985), 49-52; M. Dewachter in *Entre Égypte et Grèce*, 1995, 119-29; J. Thompson, *Edward William Lane*, 2010, 161.

TRIGGER, Bruce Graham (1937-2006)

Canadian anthropologist; he was born in Preston, Ontario, 18 June 1937, son of John Wesley T., a hydroelectric operator, and Gertrude Graham; he studied anthropology at the University of Toronto; BA 1959; he did his postgraduate work at Yale University; PhD, 1963; he first taught at Northwestern University in Illinois and then at McGill University in Montreal, becoming Professor of Anthropology and in 2006 James McGill Professor Emeritus; he specialized in archaeological theory, Huron and other eastern North American Indian archaeology, and Nubian archaeology; he excavated in Nubia notably at Arminna West during the Nubian Rescue campaign of 1960s; he was a Fellow of the Royal Society of Canada, 1976, National Order of Quebec, 2001, and the Order of Canada, 2005; in the field of Egyptology; he received hon. doctorates from the Universities of McMaster, New Brunswick, Toronto, Waterloo and Western Ontario; a volume of studies in his honour *The Archaeology of Bruce Trigger: Theoretical Empiricism* was published in 2006; he published *History and Settlement in Lower Nubia*, 1965; *The Late Nubian Settlement at Arminna West*, 1967; *The Meroitic Funerary Inscriptions from Arminna West*, 1970; *Nubia under the Pharaohs*, 1976; *Ancient Egypt. A Social History*, with others, 1983; *Early Civilizations: Ancient Egypt in Context*, 1993; apart from his studies on North American archaeology, other works included *Beyond History: The Methods of Prehistory*, 1968; *Archaeology as Historical Science*, 1985; *History of Archaeological Thought*, 1989, 2nd ed. 2006; *Socio-cultural Evolution: Calculation and Contingency*, 1998; and *Understanding Early Civilizations: A Comparative Study*, 2003; he died in Montreal, 1 Dec. 2006.

The Times 7 Dec. 2006; *SSEA Newsletter* (Winter 2007), 5-6 (K. Goebs); *Die Antiken Sudan* 18 (2007), 219-226 (portr.) (bibl.), (J. Phillips).

TRIST, John William (1847-1913)

British antiquary, collector and numismatist; he was born London, 3 Aug. 1847, son of George T. and Ellen Smith; FSA, 1887; FRNS; his collections which included many Egyptian antiquities, were sold at Sotheby's, 19-20 July 1895; he died in Westcliff, Essex, 24 Oct. 1913.

Lugt 53720.

TSUBOI, Shogoro (1863-1913)

Japanese anthropologist and archaeologist; he was born at Ryogoku, the eastern section of Tokyo, 5 June 1863, son of Shinryo T., a doctor, and his wife Makiko; he studied at the Faculty of Science of the University of Tokyo, specialising in Zoology and Anthropology, and later in England, 1889-92; Professor of Anthropology at the University of Tokyo; President of the Association of Anthropology in Japan, 1896; he was interested in Egyptology and gave lectures on the subject at the High Normal School in Tokyo and at various public meetings; he visited Cairo in 1911 and brought back a collection of Egyptian antiquities for the University of Tokyo; he died suddenly while attending the International Congress of Royal Academies in St Petersburg, 26 May 1913.

AE (1914), 59 (K. Hamada and T. Chiba); T. Saitoh, *Dictionary of the Archaeological History of Japan* (1984) in Japanese; inf. D. Sakai.

TUAN-FANG (1861-1911)

Chinese collector and administrator; he was born 20 April 1861, son of Kuei-ho, a magistrate; he was awarded his degree in 1882; he became successively inspector of customs at Kalgan, 1896; intendant of Pa-chang Circuit, 1898, superintendant of the Bureau of Agriculture, Industry and Commerce, 1898, judicial commissioner of Shensi, 1898, and then Acting-Gov., financial commissioner of Honan, 1900; Gov. of Hopeh, 1901-4; Acting-Gov. of Kiangsu, 1904; and Gov. of Hunan, 1904-5; he was part of a Chinese delegation which visited the USA, Japan, and then Europe to study administration, 1905-6; on his return, he became Gov.-Gen. of Liang-Kiang, Aug. 1906; Gov. of Chihli, 1909; and Acting-Gov. of Szechwan, 1911; he was an avid collector of antiquities and a student of calligraphy; he evidently stopped in Cairo on his return journey in 1906, where he acquired a large number of Egyptian antiquities including more than 50 stelae and at least one wooden coffin; a few of the original stelae are now in Peking University Museum, while around 50 cement copies are in the Museum of the Forbidden City; rubbings from the Egyptian antiquities are in the National Library, Peking; he was killed at Tzu-chou during the Chinese Revolution, 27 Nov. 1911.

W. H. Hummel, *Eminent Chinese of the Ching Period* 2, 1944, 780-2; H. Yan and W. Clarysse, 'Aegypten in der verbotenen Stadt', *Antike Welt* 37 (2006), 45-51.

TUFNELL, Olga (1905-1985)

British archaeologist; she was born at Babergh Hall, Great Waldingfield, Suffolk, 26 Jan. 1905 daughter of Beauchamp T. and Blanche Olivia Davidson; her mother was a friend of Lady Petrie (q.v.) and in 1922 she became secretary and assistant to Lady Petrie in the management of the British School in Egypt; in 1927 she went out to Qau with Myrtle Broome (q.v.) to copy tombs and then on to Palestine to excavate with Starkey (q.v.) and Petrie (q.v.) at Tell Fara, 1927-30, Tell el-Ajjul, 1930-2, and Lachish, 1932-8; following her publication of the last site, she devoted her energies to the study of Egyptian scarabs culminating in her publication *Studies on Scarab Seals*, Vol. 2, 1984; she was elected FSA, 1951; she died in London, 11 April 1985.

Levant 18 (1986), 1-2 (R. Henry and V. Hankey); *AfO* 33 (1986), 313-4 (R. D. Barnett).

TURAEV, Boris Alexandrovitch (1868-1920)

Russian Egyptologist; he was born in Novogrudok, 24 July/5 Aug. 1868, son of Alexander T.; he studied first in St. Petersburg under Golenischeff (q.v.), graduating 1891, and later under Erman (q.v.) in Berlin, 1893-5 and Maspero (q.v.) in Paris; on returning to Russia, he was appointed private lecturer in Ancient History in the University of St. Petersburg, 1896, Associate Professor, 1904, Professor, 1911; he was made Keeper of Egyptian Antiquities in the Museum of Moscow when it acquired the Golenischeff Collection, 1912; in 1918 he was elected a member of the Russian Acad. of Sciences; he had assembled a large private collection of antiquities which it was his intention to bequeath to Moscow Museum; he published *Bog Tot*, 1898; *Istoriya Drevnego Vostoka*, 1911; *Opisanie Egipetskago sobraniya I. Statui i statuétki golenishchevskago sobraniya*, 4° 1917; *Drevnei egipetskaya literatura*, 1920; posth. *Papyrus Prachov, sobraniya B.A. Turaeva*, fol., 1927; also articles in *JEA, ZÄS*, and other journals; he died in Petrograd, 23 July 1920.

Erman, 283; *JEA* 7 (1921), 109; *VDI* 2 (128), (1974), 111-14 (M. Korostovtsev); *Great Soviet Encyclopedia* 26, 441; *Drevnii Vostok*, Sbornik 2, 1980, 3-55; E. Endesfelder, *Die Ägyptologie an der Berliner Universität. Zur Geschichte eines Fachgebietes*, 1988, 27.

TURNER, (*Sir*) Eric Gardner (1911-1983)

British papyrologist; he was born at Sheffield, 26 Feb. 1911, son of William Ernest Stephen Turner, Professor of Glass Technology at Sheffield University, and Mary Isobel Marshall; he was educated at King Edward VII School, Sheffield and Magdalen College, Oxford; he was appointed Assistant in Humanity, University of Aberdeen, 1936; Lecturer in Classics, 1938-48; Reader in Papyrology, University of London, 1948-50, Professor, 1950-78; Director of the Institute of Classical Studies, 1953-63; President of the International Association of Papyrologists, 1965-74; Chairman of the Committee of the Egypt Exploration Society, 1956-78, Joint Editor of its Graeco-Roman publications, and Vice-President, 1978-83; Fellow of the British Academy, 1956 and Hon. and Corr. Member of various European academies; Hon. Dr Phil. et Lettres, Brussels, 1956; Hon Dès, Geneva, 1976; Hon. DLitt, Liverpool, 1978; CBE, 1975, Knighted, 1981; his scholarly work centred on the publication of Greek and Latin papyri from Egypt, both documentary and literary; he published *Catalogue of Greek and Latin Papyri and Ostraca in the possession of the University of Aberdeen*, 1939; *Athenian Books in the fifth and fourth centuries BC.*, 1952, (2nd ed. 1977); *Catalogue of the Greek and Latin Papyri in the John Rylands Library* IV, with C H Roberts, 1952; *The Hibeh Papyri* II, with M. Th. Lenger, 1955; *The Oxyrhynchus Papyri*, Parts XXIV, XXV, XXVII, XXXI, XXIII, XXXVIII, XLI, XLVIII, L, with others, 1957-83; *The Abbinnaeus Archive*, with H. Bell, V. Martin, and D. van Berchem, 1962; *New Fragments of the Misoumenos of Menander*, 1965; *Greek Papyri. An Introduction*, 1968 2nd ed. 1980; *Greek Manuscripts of the Ancient World*, 1971, 2nd ed. 1987; *The Girl from Samos or The In-Laws*, 1972; *The Papyrologist at Work*, 1973; *The Written Word on Papyrus*, with T. Pattie, 1974; *The Typology of the Early Codex*, 1977; *The terms recto and verso: the anatomy of the papyrus roll*, 1978; fifty colleagues from ten countries produced a volume *Papyri Greek and Egyptian edited in Honour of E. G. Turner*, 1981; he died at Inverness, 20 April 1983.

JEA 70 (1984), 128-9 (portr.) (P. J. Parsons); *WW* 1983; *Papyri Greek and Egyptian*, XII-XX (bibl.); *ODNB* 55, 611-2; M. Capasso (ed.), *Hermae*, 2007, 317-25 (portr.).

TURNER, (*Sir*) (Tomkyns) Hilgrove (1764-1843)

British army officer; he was born at Uxbridge, Middlesex, 12 Jan. 1764, son of Richard T., surgeon-major, and Magdalen Hilgrove; he entered the Army, 1782 as ensign in the 3rd Regiment of Foot Guards; Lt., 1789;

he served in Belgium and Holland, 1793-4; Capt. and Lt.-Col., 194; Col., 1801; he took part in the Egyptian campaign, 1801; he was entrusted with the difficult task of recovering and transporting to England the Rosetta Stone and other antiquities ceded to the British on the capitulation of Alexandria; Brig.-Gen., 1804, Major-Gen., 1808, General, 1830; Lt.-Gov. of Jersey, 1814-6; Gov. of Bermuda, 1826-32; KCH; Hon. DCL; he died at Gouray Lodge, Grouville, Jersey 6 May 1843.

ODNB 55, 670-1; *DNB* 57, 361-3; Budge, *The Rosetta Stone* (1913), 1-2; Edwards, *Lives of the Founders of the B. M.*, 364; A. Loveday, *Sir Hilgrove Turner*, 1964.

TURNER, William (1792-1867)
British diplomat and author; he was born at Great Yarmouth, 5 Sept. 1792, son of Richard T. and Elizabeth Rede; he was on the staff of the Embassy at Constantinople 1811-16; he married Mary Anne Mansfield, 1824; later envoy to Colombia, 1829-30; he travelled extensively in Greece, Egypt, etc. and in 1820 published *Journals of a Tour of the Levant*, 3 vols., in the second of which is a long description of the Eastern Desert; he died in Leamington, 10 Jan. 1867.

DNB 57, 368-9; Hilmy, ii, 297.

TYCHSEN, Olaus (Olaf) Gerhard (1734-1815)
German Hebraist and Rabbinic scholar; he was born in Tondern, Schleswig-Holstein 14 Dec. 1734, son of Jaern Tukason, a Norwegian tailor and soldier in Danish service; he studied at the University of Halle; he became Professor of Oriental Languages at the University of Bützow in Mecklenburg, 1760-89 and then Chief Librarian and Museum Director at Rostock; he attempted the decipherment of hieroglyphic and cuneiform writing, and published his results in two works; *Ueber die Buchstabenschrift der alten Aegypter*, Göttingen, 1790, and *De Cuneatis Inscriptionibus Persepolitanis Lucubratio*, 1793; he died in Rostock, 30 Dec. 1815.

Budge, *R & P*, 39-40; *The Jewish Encyclopedia* 12, 291.

TYLOR, Joseph John (1851-1901)
British engineer and archaeologist; he was born 6 Aug. 1851, son of Alfred T., FGS, AMICE, and Isabella Harris; he retired from business in 1891 on account of ill health contracted while professionally engaged in Mexico; in association with Somers Clarke (q.v.) and others he undertook much work at Elkab, and financed the publication of a fine series of memoirs on the wall-paintings and monuments there; he bequeathed his library to University College London, with duplicates to Oxford; he died at Villa La Guérite, La Turbie, 5 April 1901.

ODNB 55, 775; EEF *Arch. Rep.* (1900-1), 52, 53; EEF *Annual Report* 1900-1, 16

TYSZKIEWICZ, (*Count*) Michael (1828-1897)
Polish collector; he was born in 1828, son of Count Joseph T. and Anna Zabiello; he inherited the estate of Birze from his uncle Jan T.; he spent the winter season of 1861-2 in Egypt and Nubia visiting ancient monuments; in Cairo he became acquainted with Mariette (q.v.) and obtained from the Viceroy Said Pasha permission to conduct excavations in Egypt; from Dec. 1861 to Jan. 1862 he undertook excavations at Luxor behind the temple of Karnak and on the West Bank; he also obtained a coffin with a mummy from Mustapha Aga (q.v.); he made further soundings at Esna, Wadi es-Sebua, and Saqqara; he purchased two private collections in Cairo, the most important belonging to Dr. Meymar; he presented one statue to the Museum at Boulaq, 194 objects to the Louvre in 1862, and a further 228 objects to Museum of Antiquities in Vilnius; the remaining objects, about 400, were deposited in various family residences; from 1862 he resided in France and in Italy where his successive collections were formed; they were sold or offered to private persons or to great European museums; he visited Egypt again in 1867-8; he also conducted excavations in South Italy and in Rome; his last collection was sold after his death at an auction in Paris, 8-10 June 1898; W. Froehner, *Catalogue de vente de la collection T.*, Paris, 1898; many objects from the T. collection are now in Paris, London, Copenhagen, Berlin, Boston and Rome; in Poland only a small amount of antiquities from the T. collection, which passed to the Tyszkiewicz Palace at Lohojsk, White Ruthenia, can be identified; in 1901 this collection was transferred to Warsaw as a property of the Society for the Promotion of Fine Arts, and in 1919 to the National Museum in Warsaw; there are about 100 Egyptian items, mostly small bronzes,

amulets, ushabtis and scarabs; his Egyptian travels and his archaeological activity there were described in his *Diary of a Journey to Egypt and Nubia*, Vol. I, Paris, 1863, published in Polish; the second part remained unpublished until a complete edition was prepared *Dziennik Podrózy do Egiptu i Nubii 1861-1862*, 1994; he died at Rome, 18 Nov. 1897.

W. Froehner, *La Collection T. Choix de monuments antiques avec texte explicatif*, Part 1: Munich 1891, Parts 2 and 3: Munich 1897; F. Bruckmann, *La collection T.*, about 1890-1898; *Antiquary remembrances from Italy* by Joseph T. (in Polish), *Przeglad Polski* 104, no. 312, XII, 1892; reprinted in French in *Rev. arch.* 3rd ser, 27 (1895), 273-285; 28 (1896), 6-16, 129-37, 289-95; 29 (1896), 198-203; 30 (1897), 1-7, 129-33, 358-372; 31 (1897), 166-71, 305-12; and in English as *Memoirs of an Old Collector*, London 1898; *Rev. de l'Art* 43, 168, 284; Lugt 56420; Józef T., *Tyszkiewiciana*, Poznan, 1903; *Archeologia* 17 (1966) 223-30 (R. W. Rybicki); *Rocznik Muzeum Narodowego w Warszawie* 14 (1970) 461-7 (J. Lipinska); *VDI* 1990, 174-91 (A. Snitkuviené); A. Niwinski in *Egipt zapomniany czyli Michala he. Tyszkiewicza Dziennik Podrózy do Egiptu i Nubii 1861-1862*, 1994; inf. J. Śliwa and A. Niwinski.

TYTUS, Robb de Peyster (1878-1913)
American archaeologist and writer; he was born in Asheville, N. Carolina, 2 Feb. 1876, son of Edward Jefferson T. and Charlotte Mathilde Davies; educated at St. Mark's School, Southboro, Mass., and Yale University; BA, 1897; MA, 1903; he studied art in London, Paris, and Munich; he went to Egypt in 1899-1900 and again 1901-2, when he worked with Newberry (q.v.) on the site of the Palace of Amenhotep III at Thebes, publishing a preliminary report in 1903; in 1904-6 he published a collection of poems and stories relating to Egypt, some of them in collaboration with his wife; after his death, his mother, Charlotte Mathilde de Tytus (née Davies), financed the publication of a fine series of volumes on the Theban Tombs, five of which have appeared; these known as the 'Robb de Peyster Tytus Memorial Series' form a splendid monument to his memory; he died at Saranac Lake, NY, 14 Aug. 1913.

N. de G. Davies, *Tomb of Nakht*, pref. x; inf. Dr Ludlow Bull; Newberry Corr; *National Cyclopedia of American Biography* 47, 541.

UHLEMANN, Maximilian Adolf (1829-1862)
German philologist; he was born in Berlin, 13 May 1829, son of Friedrich Gottlob U., Professor of Theology, and Auguste Therese von Wolfersdorf; he was a disciple of Seyffarth (q.v.) whose system of hieroglyphic decipherment he defended and expounded in a number of lengthy works; lecturer at Göttingen, 1854-62; he died in 1862.

Hilmy ii, 298; Renouf, *Life-Work* i, 1-31; *Gött. Misz.* 28 (1978), 11, 14.

ULANOV, Pavel Vasilevitch (1794-1846)
Pioneer of Russian interest in Egyptian art; he was born in Saratov, 25 May 1794; he studied at Moscow University, 1816-18, preparing a Magister's thesis *Considerations about characteristic traits of Egyptian monuments and about the question why the illustrious of modern artists do not follow this example,* printed in Moscow in 1818, being the first study in Russian concerning ancient Egyptian art; after a successful clerical career, he died in St. Petersburg, 10 Oct. 1846.

Palestinskiy Sbornik 4 (67), 1959, 182-185 (I. S. Katznelson); inf. J. Śliwa

ULFELDT, Jacob (1567-1630)
Danish traveller; he was born in Bavelse, 25 June 1567, son of Jacob U. and Anne Flemming; he was educated at Jena, Geneva, Padua and Siena; he then embarked on a tour of the Levant with Christian Barnekow meeting Keichel (q.v.) in Constantinople in 1588; he visited Cairo, Giza and Saqqara, entering the Great Pyramid and drawing the Step Pyramid; a manuscript account of his travels is in the Royal Library in Copenhagen; he returned to Denmark in 1591 and later became active in politics under Christian IV; he died at Nyborg, 25 June 1630.

Dansk Biografisk Leksikon 15, 147-9; M.-L. Buhl, *Les dessins archéologiques et topographiques de l'Égypte ancienne faits par F. L. Norden 1737-1738*, 1993, 21-2.

UNGARELLI, (*Padre*) **Luigi Maria** (1779-1845)
Italian Egyptologist and orientalist; he was born in Bologna, 15 Feb. 1779; he first arranged the Egyptian Museum in the Vatican galleries founded by Pope Gregory XVI; his best known Egyptological work is *Interpretatio obeliscorum*, 2 folio vols. Rome, 1842; he died 21 Aug. 1845.

Garollo, *Diz. Biogr. Univ.*; Hilmy, ii, 299.

UPHAM, Edward (1777-1834)
British bookseller; he was born at Exeter in 1777 and baptized at St. Petrock, Exeter 13 June 1777, son of Charles U., FSA, Mayor of Exeter, and his wife Elizabeth; Mayor of Exeter 1839; after a business career he retired early to Bath and devoted himself to writing, especially oriental history; he published many works, mostly anonymously; these included *Remarks on Mummies, and Observations on the Process of Embalming,* 1822; *Memoranda, Illustrative of the Tombs and Sepulchral Decorations of the Egyptians,* 1822, *Ramesses,* an Egyptian tale in 3 vols., 1824; and other works; he died in Bath, 24 Jan. 1834.

GM 1834, 336; *ODNB* 55, 925.

UPHILL, Eric Parrington (1929-2018)
British Egyptologist; he was born in South Croydon, 15 Sept. 1929, son of Walter Eric U., a schoolmaster, and Ada Elizabeth Prest; after national service, 1948-50, he studied history, archaeology and Egyptology at Emmanuel, Cambridge, 1951-6 under Glanville (q.v.); BA, 1954; MA, 1957; he later studied at University College London with Emery (q.v.), Arkell (q.v.), and Faulkner (q.v.); he became lecturer in Egyptology and archaeology in the Dept. of Extra-mural Studies, University of London and later lecturer in Egyptian archaeology at the Faculty of Continuing Education, Birkbeck College, giving lectures and courses in London and elsewhere from 1960-94, examiner since 1995; Hon. Research Fellow in the Dept. of Egyptology, University College London; he excavated at Saqqara, 1954-5, and Buhen, 1959-60 under Emery; he served on the committee of the EES, 1965-85; he was the editor of *Who Was Who in Egyptology,* 1968-84; he published *Who Was Who in Egyptology,* 2nd ed., 1972; *The Temples of Per Ramesses,* 1984; *Egyptian Towns and Cities,* 1988; and *Pharaoh's Gateway to Eternity,* 2000; he died in Redhill, Surrey, 11 March 2018.

S. Quirke and J. Picton, *Archaeology International* 21 (2018), 17-18 (portr.).

ÜXKÜLL, (*Baron*) **Alexander von** (1800-1853)
Russian traveller and artist; he was born in St. Petersburg, 29 March 1800, son of Berend Johann Baron von Ü., army officer and official, and Elisabeth Countess von Sievers; he studied at Göttingen and Prague and served in the army; Member of the Art Academy of St. Petersburg; in 1820-3 he travelled in the Levant and was in Egypt in 1822-3 going as far as the Third Cataract with Medem (q.v.) and Théodore de Lesseps; he made copies of many

inscriptions including objects in the Salt (q.v.) collection, which he communicated to Letronne (q.v.) and Lanci (q.v.); he met Champollion (q.v.) in Italy in 1825; he later concentrated on his artistic work; his travel diary is unpublished; he died in Vienna, 2 Aug. 1853.

Inf. S. Stadnikov; M. Dewachter, *Cahiers du Musée Champollion* 2 (1993), 34-35, 38; W. Lenz, *Deutsch-baltisches Biographisches Lexikon 1710-1960,* 1970, 816; S. Stadnikov, *Gött. Misz.* 146 (1995), 71-92.

VÁHALA, František (1911-1974)
Czech Egyptologist; he was born in Jičina near Nový Jičin, 29 Jan. 1911; he was educated at Brno University studying Czech and German; he became a teacher of these languages and, after World War II, was attached to the Institute for the Study of the Czech Language, Czechoslovak Academy of Sciences, Prague; at the same time he attended lectures in Egyptology by Lexa (q.v.), Černý (q.v.), and Žába (q.v.); in 1960 he began to teach Egyptian at the Faculty of Philosophy, Charles University, and in 1962 joined the Czechoslovak Institute of Egyptology; he took part in the epigraphic work in Nubia 1964-5 and at Abusir; on the death of Žába, he was in charge of the Institute 1971-4; he died in a hospital near Nový Jičin, 29 Dec. 1974.

Novy Orient 30 no. 3(1975), 87 (M. Verner).

VALENTIA *see* **ANNESLEY.**

VALERIANI, Domenico (*fl.* 1823-37)
Italian writer; he was from Florence and violently attacked Champollion's system of decipherment in *Antologia* (no. 33, Sept. 1823) to which C. rejoined in the *Rev. Encyc.* 21 (1823), 225; he also published *Nuova Illustrazione istorico-monumentale del Basso e dell'Alto Egitto*, 2 vols. with 2 vols. of plates, mostly copied from the works of Denon, Gailliaud, Rosellini, and others, Florence, 1835-7.

Champollion, i, 2227, 245; Hilmy, ii, 301; *Rec. Champ.* 768, no. 25.

VALLE, Pietro della (1586-1652)
Italian nobleman and traveller; he was born in Rome, 11 April 1586, son of Pompeo della V. and Giovanna Alberni; he is said to have travelled to the East after an unsuccessful love-affair; he visited Turkey, 1614-5, Egypt, Sept. 1615-March 1616, and afterwards Palestine, Baghdad, Persia and India, 1616-24, returning to Rome in 1626; his *Viaggi* was published in three parts, 1650-63; in Egypt he described the Giza pyramids accepting the not very accurate figures of Belon (q.v.), and gave an account of most of the interior of the Great Pyramid with measurements for the King's Chamber, also examining the smaller monuments and Sphinx; he was a keen collector of Egyptiana and acquired two mummies of the Roman Period, now in Dresden, and Coptic MSS including grammars and two Bohairic vocabularies, which were to be of great use to Kircher (q.v.) in his work on the Coptic language later in the century; he died in Rome, 21 April 1652.

Iversen, 91; Vyse, ii, 202-3; C. Bertacchi, *Pietro della Valle*, 1892; R. G. Bietenholz, *Pietro della Valle 1586-1652*, 1962; P. M. Holt in P. and J. Starkey (eds.), *Travellers in Egypt*, 1998, 15-23; J. Speake (ed.), *Literature of Travel and Exploration*, 2003, 326-8; Lamy, 106-8.

VANDEKERCKHOVE, Hans (1959-1989)
Belgian Egyptologist; he was born at Port-Francqui (Congo), 16 April 1959, son of Adelin V. and Andrea Beernaert; he studied Egyptology at the University of Ghent under Herman De Meulenaere and at the Eberhard-Karls-Universität Tübingen under Wolfgang Schenkel, 1979-89; he participated as an epigrapher in four field campaigns of the Belgian archaeological mission to Elkab, 1981-7; he obtained his PhD at the University of Ghent, 29 June 1989 with a thesis on the Old Kingdom rock inscriptions at Elkab; he died from a cardiac arrest during a research stay in Tübingen, 10 Nov. 1989; his thesis, edited in German by Renate Müller-Wollermann and supplemented by her with rock inscriptions from later periods, was published posthumously, *Elkab* VI. *Die Felsinschriften des Wadi Hilâl*, 2001.

Inf. D. Huyge.

VANDIER, Jacques Victor Edmond Raymond (1904-1973)
French Egyptologist; he was born in Haubourdin, 28 Oct. 1904, son of Jacques V. and Marie Mouzé; he studied classics at the École Pratique des Hautes Études, but he was attracted to Egyptology taught by Lefebvre (q.v.); diploma, 1933; he also attended the lectures of Boreux (q.v.) at the École du Louvre; he married 5 Nov. 1931 Jeanne d'Abbadie (see next) who ably supported him in his career; he was attached to the French Institute in Cairo, 1932-6 when he worked at Deir el-Medina and Tod; he was entrusted with the publication of the tomb of Ankhtifi at Moalla and became an authority on the First Intermediate Period; he joined the Louvre in 1935, assistant keeper, 1937, acting Keeper, 1940, Keeper, 1946-73; Inspecteur genéral des Musées de France, 1972;

he lectured at the Institut Catholique, Paris, 1936-1951 and was Professor of Egyptian archaeology at the École du Louvre, 1940-55; Member of the Académie des Inscriptions et Belles-Lettres, 1965; Corresponding Member of the Bavarian Academy and the British Academy; he organized the installation of the Egyptian antiquities in the Louvre following World War II and pursued an active policy of acquisition; in 1955 he was incapacitated by an attack of polio which paralyzed his lower limbs, but he continued in his duties and academic work; he was the author of standard reference works on Egyptian history, religion, and archaeology; apart from his articles and reviews, he was the author of *La tombe de Nefer-Abou*, 1935; his thesis *La famine dans l'Egypte ancienne*, 1936, 2nd ed. 1948; *L'Égypte*, with É. Drioton, 1938 and subsequent eds,; *La religion égyptienne*, 1944, 2nd ed. 1949; *Musée du Louvre. Le Département des antiquités égyptiennes. Guide sommaire*, 1948 and subsequent eds.; *Textes de la Première Période Intermédiaire et de la XIe dynastie*, with J. J. Clère, 1948; *Moalla. La tombe d'Ankhtifi et la tombe de Sebekhotep*, 1950; *Les premières civilisations*, with P. Jouguet et al, 1950; *La sculpture égyptienne*, 1951, English ed. 1951; *La sculpture égyptienne au Musée du Louvre*, 1952; *Manuel d'archéologie égyptienne*, 1952-1978; *Le papyrus Jumilhac*, 1961; *Les bateaux égyptiens*, 1965; his copies of the texts at the temple of Tod were published by J. Grenier *Tôd* I, 1980; he died in Paris, 15 Oct. 1973.

Rev. d'Eg. 27 (1975), 6-13 (portr) (G. Posener), 14-20 (bibl.) (F. Le Corsu); *Journal Asiatique* 262 (1974), 11-18 (J. Leclant); *BSFE* 68 (1973), 3-5 (portr.) (G. Posener); *Chron d'Ég.* 49(1974), 113-4 (B. van de Walle); *JEA* 60 (1974), 4 (I.E.S. Edwards); *Syria* 51 (1975), 220-1; È. Gran-Aymerich, *Dictionnaire biographique d'archéologie 1798-1945*, 2001, incorporated in *Les Chercheurs de passé 1798-1945*, 2007, 1206-8.

VANDIER d'ABBADIE, Jeanne Marie Thérèse (1899-1977)
French Egyptologist; née d'Abbadie d'Arrast; she was born at Nuremberg, 26 Sept. 1899 and married Jacques Vandier (q.v.) on 5 Nov. 1931; she was with her husband in Egypt 1932-6 and was involved in the publication of the work of the French Institute at Thebes; she published *La tombe de Nefer-abou*, with J. Vandier, 1935; *Catalogue des ostraca figurés de Deir el-Médineh*, fasc. 1-4, 1936-59; *Deux tombes ramessides à Gournet-Mourraï*, 1954; *Nestor l'Hôte (1804-1842)*, she died at Neuilly-sur-Seine, 25 April 1977.

AfO 25 (1974/77), 357 (H. Brunner)

VARILLE, Alexandre (1909-1951)
French Egyptologist; he was born in Lyons, 12 March 1909, son of Mathieu René Augustin Louis V. and Jeanne Paule Marthe Rougier; he studied under Victor Loret (q.v.) at Lyons University, 1925-9 and visited Egypt for the first time in 1931, joining the Institut Français the following year; he excavated at Medamud, 1934-9 and with R. Weill (q.v.) at Zawyet el-Maiyitin, 1933-4; he then began to collaborate with Robichon (q.v.) and excavated the temple of Amenhotep, son of Hapu, 1934-5; Varille worked on the Montu temple-enclosure at North Karnak from 1940-43 and after the war was asked to prepare the scientific publication of the Saqqara monuments,1944-48; in 1948 he was made Assistant Egyptologist to the Director of Works for the Antiquities Service at Karnak, H. Chevrier (q.v.) and again worked with Robichon; he was interested in the New Kingdom and particularly in the reign of Amenhotep III; an excellent and most thorough archaeologist and researcher he was later to become associated with theories which had not a scientific backing and which were derived from unusual not to say unorthodox conceptions based on the design of temples; he wrote five books and over 40 articles among which may be cited, *Le Temple du scribe royal Amenhotep fils de Hapou*, 1936; *Description sommaire du temple primitif de Medamoud*, 1940, both in conjunction with Robichon; *En Égypte*, 1937; *Karnak*, 1943; and posthumusly *Inscriptions concernant l'architecte Amenhotep fils de Hapou*, 1968; he obtained from the Egyptian Government in 1938 as a gift two large Ptolemaic doorways from the temple of Medamud which were taken to the Palais Saint-Pierre (Musée des Beaux Arts) at Lyons; his library and archives were acquired by the Egyptological Archives of the Università degli Studi di Milano in 2001-2; he died accidentally at Joigny, 1 Nov. 1951.

ASAE 53 (1956), 69-78 (portr.) (bibl.) (L. A. Christophe) *BSFE*, no. 10 (June 1952), 37-8 (P. Montet); *Chron. d'Ég.* 27 (1952), 143-4 (A. Mekhitarian); *CHE,* serie iv, fasc. 2 (Feb. 1952), 161 (anon.); *Kémi* 12 (1952), 97-8 (M. Malinine); *Mercure de France,* Paris, 313 (1951), no. 1060, 745-6 (A. Rousseaux); *Rev. Arch.* 41 (1953), 194-6 (P. Montet); *Rev.d'Eg.* 9 (1952), i-vii, 7, (portr.) (bibl.) (M. Alliot); *BSAC* 146 1956-7), 253-5 (L. Christophe); *Inscriptions, op. cit.,* 153-6 (bibl.); È. Gran-Aymerich, *Dictionnaire biographique d'archéologie 1798-1945*, 2001, incorporated in *Les Chercheurs de passé 1798-1945*, 2007, 1208-9; P. Piacentini, *Egypt and the Pharaohs from the Sand to the Library*, 2010, 648. Photograph courtesy of the Università degli Studi di Milano.

VASSALLI, *(Bey)* **Luigi** (1812-1887)
Italian Egyptologist; he was born in Milan, 8 Jan. 1812, son of Giuseppe V. and Maddalena Brutpacher; he studied painting but was later involved in a political plot, and was condemned to death, although afterwards the sentence was commuted and he was released; he took refuge in Switzerland, France and England where he earned a living by teaching Italian and selling pictures; he went to Egypt about 1841 where he lived as a portrait-painter and dealer; he returned to Milan, 1848, but again went into exile in Egypt in 1849; he travelled to Constantinople and Smyrna, where he married; his wife died a few months later, and he returned to Egypt; as a dealer he had become acquainted with Mariette (q.v.) by 1853 when he sold him the coffin of King Intef; in 1856 he sold some important papyri to the British Museum (EA 100068, 100083, 10403); in 1859 he became assistant to Mariette and conducted many of his excavations; he served in Garibaldi's army, 1860, and was named curator of Egyptian antiquities at the Naples Museum, 1860; he was Keeper of the Bulaq Museum, 1865-83; temporary Director, 18 Jan.-7 Feb. 1881; he retired to Milan in 1883 and then Rome in 1884; he published *Opuscules Divers*, 2 vols. 1864-7; *I Monumenti istorici egizi, il Musueo e gli scavi d'antichità eseguiti per ordine di S. A. Vicerè Ismail Pascia; notizia sommaria*, 1869; *I Musei Egizi d'Italia*, 1873; there is a marble bust of him in the Cairo Museum; a collection of his Egyptian antiquities and books was acquired in the 1930s by the American collector Horace L. Mayer, who were donated many to the Boston Museum; his papers are in the Griffith Institute, Oxford, and at Milan; he died in Rome, 13 June 1887.

Bibl. Ég, 18, cxi; Brugsch, *Mein Leben*, 207; Hilmy, ii, 306; *ZÄS* 25 (1887), iii (H. Brugsch); Wilbour, 613; R. Almagia, *L'Opera degli Italiani per la cognoscenza dell'Egitto*, 7-8, 20 (bibl.); *L'egittologo Luigi Vassalli (1812-1887), Disegni e documente nei Civici Instituti Culturali Milanesi*, 1994; E. David, *Mariette Pacha 1812-1831*, 1994, 110; *Des dieux, des tombeaux, un savant. En Égypte, sur les pas de Mariette Pacha*, 2004, 20.

VATTIER DE BOURVILLE, Charles Joseph Auguste Désiré (*d.*1883)
French diplomat; he was the son of Charles Hyacinthe Salvator V. de B., French consul at Chios and Marie Joséphine Jouvin; he was vice-consul in Tunis, 1829-33, consul in Tripoli, Syria, 1834-8, consul in Cairo, 1839-46, and consul in Damascus, 1847.

Carré, i, 358; ii, 28.

VAUCELLES, Alexandre Louis Henry de (1798-1851)
French traveller; he was born at Argenton, 14 Nov. 1798, son of Emmanuel Alexandre de V. and Marie Henriette Elisabeth Le Forestier; he visited Egypt and Nubia Feb.-Sep. 1826 going as far as the Second Cataract; he later published *Chronologie des monuments de la Nubie*, Paris, 1829; his antiquities are still with his family; he died Paris, 12 Aug. 1851.

Champollion, i, 272; Hilmy, ii, 306 *Rev. d'Eg.* 14 (1962), 7-20; *Mélanges Maspero* I/4 (1961), 11-16; du Bourguet, *BSFE* 27 (1958), 57-63.

VAUDEY, Alexandre (1818-1854)
Savoyard explorer and trader; he was born Saint- Michel-de-Maurienne 1818 and became secretary to Clot Bey (q.v.) in Cairo, 1837-49; he afterwards travelled, explored and traded in the Sudan, first with Petherick (q.v.) and later on his own; he was made Sardinian Vice-Consul in Khartoum, returning to France, 1851; with his two nephews Ambroise and Jules Poncet he returned to Khartoum and established the firm of Poncet Frères, dealing chiefly in ivory; Vaudey was killed in a clash with the Bari people while on an expedition to Gondokoro, 5 April 1854.

Hill, 372.

VERCOUTTER, Jean (1911-2000)
French Egyptologist; he was born at Lambersart, 20 Jan. 1911, son of Georges V. and Aline Bertin; he studied history and geography at the Sorbonne and Egyptology at the École Pratique des hautes études; Diploma 1939; he was sent on a mission to Tunisia in 1937 where he studied Egyptian objects; he served in World War II, being taken prisoner and released in 1940; he was attached to the Louvre, 1942-5 and IFAO, 1945-50 where he took part in excavations at Karnak and Tod, 1947-9; he then joined CNRS and was director of excavations at Dara, 1950-1 for the University of Paris; Docteur ès lettres from the Sorbonne, 1953; Head of the French archaeological mission to the Sudan 1953-5, excavating at Kor, 1953 and Sai, 1954; director of the Sudan Archaeological Service, 1955-60; Professor at Lille and Director of the French mission in the Sudan, 1960-76 where he undertook work at Aksha, 1960-2, and Mirgissa, 1963-7 for the Nubian rescue campaign; Director of IFAO, Jan. 1977-May 81; he became a member of the Académie des Inscriptions 11 May 1984; President of the Société français d'égyptologie,

1982-97; Hon President of the Nubian Society 1982; member of the Institut d'Égypte 1976; he was awarded the légion d'honneur; a festschrift *Mélanges offerts à Jean Vercoutter* was compiled in his honour in 1985; he published *Les objets égyptiens et égyptisants du mobilier funéraire carthininois*, 1945; *L'Égypte ancienne*, 1947, 14th ed 1992; *Essai sur les Relations entre Égyptiens et Préhéllènes*, 1954; *L'Egypte et le monde égéen préhellenique*, 1956; *Textes biographiques du Sérapéum de Memphis*, 1962; *La Nubie soudanaise et la nouveau barrage d'Assouan*, 1963 *Aksha* I, 1966; *Catalogue des stèles du Sérapéum de Memphis* I (with G. Posener and M. Malinine), 1968; *Mirgissa* I-III, 1970-6; *Études sur l'Égypte et le Soudain anciens*, 1973; *A la recherche de l'Égypte oubliée*, 1986; Eng. trans. 1992; *L'Égypte et la vallée du Nil*, 1993; he died in Paris, 16 July 2000.

F. Geus and F. Thill, *Mélanges offerts à Jean Vercotter*, 1985, 3-6 (portr.) (H. S. Smith); *WWF* 2000, 1711; *Le Monde* 29 July 2000 (J.-P. Corteggiani); *BSFE* 149 (2000), 5-6 (portr.); *BIFAO* 100 (2000), VIII-X (J.-P. Corteggiani), XI-XVIII (bibl.) (A. Minault-Gout); *CRIPEL* 22 (2001), 17-19 (F. Geus); *Rev d'Ég* 52 (2001), 5 (portr.).

VERGOTE, Jozef Antoon Leo Maria (1910-1992)

Belgian Egyptologist and Coptologist; he was born in Ghent, 16 March 1910, son of Antoon V. and Georgina van Lanuker; he studied at St. Joseph's College in Tielt and from 1928 at the University of Louvain where he studied classical philology and oriental languages under Lefort (q.v.); PhD, 1932; licentiate in philology and oriental history, 1933; he continued his studies on scholarships at Paris, 1934; Berlin, 1934-7 under Sethe (q.v.), Grapow (q.v.) and Anthes (q.v.); and Rome, 1937-8; he taught Coptic and Ancient Egyptian at Louvain from 1938; lecturer, 1939; and reader 1941; Professor, 1943; President of the Institut orientaliste, 1962-8; Head of the Oriental Dept. in the University of Leuven, 1974-8 when he retired; editor of *Orientalia Lovaniensia Periodica*; member of the Koninklijke Vlaamse Academie voor Wetenschappen, Letteren en Schone Kunsten of Belgium; a Festschrift in his honour was published in *Orientalia Lovaniensia Periodica* 6/7 (1975/1976); he published over 140 articles and books, mainly on philology; his principal publications were *Joseph en Egypte*, 1959; *Toutankhamon dans les archives hittites*, 1961; and *Grammaire Copte*, 1973, 1983; he died at Heverlee, 8 Jan. 1992.

Orientalia Lovaniensia Periodica 6/7 (1975/76), 5-9 (portr.) (P. Naster), 11-20 (bibl.) (J. Quaegebeur); 23 (1992), 5-13 (portr.,) (bibl.) (J. Quaegebeur); *Koninklijke Academie voor Wetenschappen,Letteren en Schone Kunsten van Belgie*, 1992 (E. van't Dack); *Phoenix* 38 (1992), 2-3 (M. Heerma van Voss) (portr.); *Orbis* 35 (1988-90), 354-7 (P. Swiggers); *Acta Orientalia Beligica* XI (1998), x-xiii.

VERNIER, Émile Séraphin (1852-1927)

French medallist; he was born in Paris, 16 Oct. 1852, son of ...Vernier and Victoire Gervaise; he was apprenticed to an engraver in 1865 and worked for various firms; he developed a technique for applying engraving to jewellery; he had a great interest in Egyptian jewellery and was asked by Maspero (q.v.) to catalogue the jewellery in the Cairo Museum; he was a member of IFAO and president of the Société des Artistes Décorateurs, 1905-10; his main publications on Egyptian jewellery were *La bijouterie et la joaillerie égyptiennes*, 1907 and the Cairo catalogue, *Bijoux et orfèvreries*, 1907-27; he died in Paris, 7 Sept. 1927.

L. Forrer, *Biographical Dictionary of Medallists* 6 (1916), 225-35 (portr.); E. Bénézit, *Dictionnaire des Peintres, Sculpteurs, Dessinateurs et Graveurs*, new ed. 10 (1976), 469.

VIDAL, Robert Studley (1770-1841)

British antiquary and collector; he was born 1770, son of Robert Studley V. of Exeter and Elizabeth Blinch; he was a barrister, Middle Temple 1795, but practised little, spending most of his time on his estate in Devon; FSA, 1804; he contributed two papers to *Archaeologia,* vol 15; he had an extensive library and a large collection of coins, medals, and antiquities, including Egyptian; the former was sold at Sotheby's, 11-12 July 1842, the latter 27-30 July 1842; he was a benefactor of St. John's College, Cambridge; he died in Cornborough House, near Bideford, Devon, 21 Nov. 1841.

ODNB 56, 462-3; *DNB* 58, 303; *Jackson's Oxford Journal* 4 Dec. 1841; Lugt 16665, 16673.

VIDUA di Conzano, (*Count*) Carlo (1785-1830)

Italian traveller; he was born in Casele Monferrato, 28 Feb. 1785, son of Count Pio Gerolamo V. and Marianna Gambera; he studied law in Turin; he visited Greece and Syria, 1816-22, and Egypt in 1819-20,

proceeding as far as the Second Cataract; his name is carved on the rock of Abu Sir and the Temple of Abu Simbel; he was involved in the negotiations over the sale of Drovetti's (q.v.) collection to Turin; he met Champollion (q.v.) in Italy and offered to join his expedition to Egypt, but eventually withdrew; he travelled in Mexico, 1826-7 and afterwards in the Dutch East Indies where he died at Amboyna, 25 Dec 1830; his books are in the library of the Academy of Sciences, Turin.

Champollion, i, 393, ii, v; *Enc. It.*; Westcar Diary, 134; M. Dewachter, *BIFAO* 69 (1971) 171-189; S. Curto, 'Carlo Vidua e il Museo Egizio di Torino', *Studi Piemontesi*, 1986, 327; A. Roccati in M. Betrò and G. Miniaci, *Talking along the Nile*, 2013, 211-14.

VIKENTIEV, Vladimir Michaelovitch (1882-1960)
Russian Egyptologist; he was born in he was born in Kostroma, Russia, 6 July 1882, son of Michael V.; he studied Egyptian philology with A. Erman (q.v.) and B. Turaev (q.v.) at the the University of Moscow, 1908-1913; his greatest interest lay in Egyptian literary tales and his imagination led him to look for parallels in these tales with folklore, as is shown in his first work, *Le Conte des Deux Frères*, 1917; he was appointed Keeper of the Oriental Collections in the Historical Museum, Moscow, 1915 and then became Keeper of Near Eastern antiquities at the Beaux-Arts Museum and Director of the Museum-Institute of the Classical Orient; he later settled in Egypt, 1923, and began teaching Egyptian philology and ancient Near Eastern history in Cairo the following year; as an author his output was considerable especially in the form of articles in journals, but his later work is often characterized by eccentric theories and concepts which mar its value; see also *La haute crue du Nil et l'averse de l'an 6 du Roi Taharqa*: *Le dieu 'Hemen' et son chef-lieu 'Hefat'*, 1930; *Collections of antiquities purchased in Syria and Egypt,* with P. Bobrovsky, 1937; *Voyage vers l'île lointaine: les nouveaux aspects du Conte du Naufragé*, 1941; *L'énigme d'un papyrus*, 1941, dealing with the Tale of Two Brothers; he died in Cairo, 8 Feb. 1960.

Chron. d'Ég. 35, 69-70 (1960), 197 (R. Marquebreucq); *La Revue du Caire,* 23rd year, vol. xliv, no. 236 (April 1960), 306-13 (A. Papadopoulo) (bibl.); inf. Dia' Abou Ghazi.

VILA, André (1923-2011)
French archaeologist; he was born in Revel, 25 March 1923, son of Marie Emmanuel V. and Juliette Lydia Ruffel; he worked as a dental assistant, 1940-55; he was a keen photographer and also a member of the Société des Explorateurs; as a result of these interests, he was invited to join an expedition to West Africa as a photographer, 1955; he then served on an expedition to Tassili in the Sahara to record rock paintings; he was also involved in archaeological work in France; he took part in the Nubian rescue campaign at Aksha from 1961-2 and Mirgissa, 1962-8 under Vercoutter (q.v.) and at Ukma, 1968; he then became director of the French survey team in the Sudan, 1970-5, investigating among other sites Amara West; he published *Aksha* II, 1967; *Le Cimetière Kermaique d'Ukma Ouest*, 1987; in 15 volumes, *La prospection archéologique de la vallée du Nil au sud de la cataracte de Dal*, 1975-85; and he contributed to *Mirgissa* I, 1971; *Mirgissa* II, 1975; he died in Castres, 13 March 2011.

Sudan and Nubia 16 (2012), 162-3 (portr.), (W. Y. Adams).

VILÍMKOVÁ, Milada (1921-1991)
Czech Egyptologist; she was born in Vizovice, 26 Dec. 1921; she studied art at the School of Applied Arts in Zlín, also working with the restorer F. Petr, 1945-8; she then studied classical archaeology and art history at Charles University, Prague, 1945-8, and Egyptology under Lexa (q.v.), 1950-3; she was an assistant in the Institute of Classical Archaeology and from 1955 she worked in the State Institute for Reconstruction in the architectural history section; she wrote *Ägyptische Kunst* (English ed. *Egyptian Art*), with W. and B. Forman, 1962; *Egyptian Ornament*, with the designs of Pavla Fořtová-Šámalová, 1963; *Altägyptische Goldschmiedekunst*, 1969; English ed. *Egyptian Jewellery*, 1969; *Starověký Egypt*, 1977; she died in Prague, 5 Oct. 199.

J. Ruzková in *Gött. Misz.* 152 (1996), 100; inf. J. Ruzková and W. Oerter.

VILLAMONT, Jacques (*Seigneur*) **de** (*c.*1558-1628)
French traveller; he was born in Britanny *c.*1558; he left France in 1588 to visit Italy and the Levant staying in Egypt from 10 Oct. 1589 to 23 March 1590; he visited Alexandria and Cairo where he saw the pyramids and Sphinx at Giza and entered and climbed the Great Pyramids; he went to the ruins of Memphis which he was one of the first to identify in print and also explored the underground tomb shafts at Saqqara; he published his *Voyages* in 1595; he died *c.*1628.

C. Burri and S. Sauneron, *Voyages en Egypte des années 1589, 1590 & 1591,* 1971, 157-259; Lamy, 94-8.

VILLIERS DU TERRAGE, (René) Édouard de (1780-1855)
French civil engineer; he was born in Versailles, 27 Aug. 1780, son of Marc Étienne de V., a financial officer, and Suzanne Rose de Villantroyes; he was educated at the École Polytechnique from 1796; he was a member of Napoleon's Commission, and took a prominent part in its archaeological activities, entering the tomb of Amenhotep III, and contributing to the *Description de l'Égypte*; he later joined the department of bridges and roads, becoming inspector-general and retiring in 1850; his journal was published in 1899; his son gave Egyptian objects to the Louvre in 1873 and 1906, including a number of shabtis of Amenhotep III; he died in Paris, 21 April 1855.

Carré, i, 148; *CRAIBL* 1900, 31; Hilmy, i, 186; *Biographie Universelle* 43, 523; Vapareau; *Les Donateurs du Louvre*, 1989, 339.

VINCENT, Alexandre Joseph Hidulphe (1797-1868)
French Mathematician; he was born at Hesdin, Pas de Calais, 20 Nov, 1797; he served as Professor at Rennes, 1820; at Collège Rollin, 1826; at Collège Bourbon 1830, and the Collège St-Louis, 1831; he was elected a member of the Institut de France, 10 May 1850; he was a friend of Letronne (q.v.) and de Rougé (q.v.); he wrote many works on the Egyptian calendar and chronology; he died in Paris, 26 Nov. 1868.

E. Havet, *Notice sur A. J. H. Vincent,* Paris, 1869; Hilmy, ii, 310; *Larousse* 15,1077; A. C. E. Franquet de Franqueville, *Le Premier Siècle de l'Institut de France*, 1895, I, 287.

VIREY, Philippe (1853-1920)
French Egyptologist; he was born in Paris, 14 June 1853, son of Jean Baptiste V. and Leontine Déjardin, he studied Egyptology first under Chabas (q.v.) and then under Maspero (q.v.) in Paris; he joined the French Arch. Mission in Cairo in 1884 and was employed chiefly in copying Theban tombs many of which were then published in the *Mémoires* of the Mission, but his standard of epigraphic accuracy was poor; he published, *Études sur le Papyrus Prisse; le livre de Kagimna et les leçons de Ptah-Hotep, 1887; Le tombeau de Rekhmara, préfet de Thèbes sous la XVIIIe dynastie,* 1889; *Sept tombeaux thébains de la XVIIIe dynastie,*1891; *La Religion de l'ancienne Egypte,* 1910; also articles in journals and the biographies of Chabas, Lefébure (q.v.), and Horrack (q.v.) for the collected edition of their works in the *Bibl. Ég.*; after his return from Egypt he was appointed lecturer in Egyptology at the Institut Catholique, Paris; he died at the Chateau de Montceau-Lamartine, Prissé, 5 May 1920.

JEA 33 (1947), 81; *Annales de l'Académie de Maçon,* 3e serie, 22 (1920-1), 165-183*; Les Collections égyptiennes dans les musées de Saône-et-Loire*, 1998, 21-2.

VITELLI, Girolamo (1849-1935)
Italian papyrologist; he was born at Sanat Croce del Sannio, 27 July 1849, son of Serafino V. and Maria Vittoria Cassella; he studied classics at Naples and Pisa; he obtained teaching posts at Catania, Naples and finally the University of Florence, 1874; he was inspired by the papyri finds from the excavations of Grenfell (q.v.) and Hunt (q.v.) and raised funds in 1902 to obtain papyri through purchase and excavation; he visited Egypt in 1902 with Breccia (q.v.), 1904, 1906/7, and 1909; he was the founder and director of Società Italiana per la ricerca dei papyri greci e latini in Egitto in 1908 (from 1928 Istituto Papyrologico); he published several editions of papyri; he died in Florence, 2 Sept. 1935.

In Memoria di Girolamo Vitelli, 1936 (bibl.), 87-125; M. Capasso (ed.), *Hermae*, 2007, 45-52 (portr.) (M. Manfredi); *Aegyptus* 15 (1935), 253-62 (E. Breccia); *Chron. d'Ég.* 15 (1936), 210-17 (E. Breccia).

VIVENEL, Antoine (1799-1862)
French collector; he was born in Compiègne, 17 March 1799; he became a successful entrepreneur and architect in Paris; he formed a collection of works of art, which he gave to his hometown from 1839 onwards, to become the Musée Vivenel; this included over 200 Egyptian objects, and books in Egyptian topics including a copy of the *Description de l'Égypte*; he died in Paris, 19 Feb. 1862.

Journal of the History of Collections, 2/1 (1990), 21-39; L. Camino and C. Papier-Lecostey, *Collections égyptiennes du Musée Antoine Vivenel de Compiègne*, 2007.

VIVIAN, (*Lord*) Hussey Crespigny, 3rd Baron (1834-1893)
British Diplomat; he was born in London, 19 June 1834, eldest son of Charles, 2nd Baron V. and Arabella Scott; clerk in the Foreign Office, 1851-72; Agent at Alexandria, 1873; Agent at Bucharest, 1874-6; Consul-General in Egypt, 10 May 1876-79; Ambassador at European Courts, 1879-93; Plenipotentiary to the Slave-trade Conference at Brussels, 1889, GCMG, 1889; succeeded as 3rd Baron, 1886; he died in Rome, 21 Oct. 1893.

Burke's Peerage; Lord Cromer, *Mod. Eg.* i, passim; *Khedives and Pashas,* 217-20; *ODNB* 56, 575-6.

VOGLIANO, Achille (1881-1953)
Italian papyrologist; he was born in Florence, 17 Oct. 1881, son of Germano V. and Giulia Bonini; he taught at Cagliari from 1927; Palermo from 1927; Bologna from 1929; Milan from 1932; and later Professor of papyrology at Berlin from 1950; he took part in the excavations at Tebtunis, 1934 and at Medinet Madi organised by the University of Milan, 1935-9; he published five reports on these excavations 1936-9; he died in Berlin, 26 June 1953.

Chron. d`Eg. 29 (1954), 102 (anon.); *Prolegomena*, 2 (1953) (S. Donadoni); inf. E. Hornung; *Acme* VIII (1955), 3-10 (bibl.); *Atene e Roma* 11-12 (1953), 177-86; *Gnomon* 26 (1954), 287-8 (R. Keydell); *Enciclopedia Italiana* Appendice III (M-Z),1113-4; *Chi è?* 1931, 781-2; Rina La Guardia, *Achille Vogliano e I Civici Musei di Milano*, 1996; M. Capasso (ed.), *Hermae*, 2007, 247-61 (C. Gallazzi).

VOLKOV, Ivan Mikhailovitch (1882-1919)
Russian orientalist, especially interested in Hebrew, Assyrian and Egyptian; he was born on 25 May 1882; he studied Egyptology under Turaev (q.v.); from 1914 lecturer at the University of St. Petersburg; Volkov translated into Russian for the first time the Code of Hammurabi, 1914 and the Aramaic documents found on Elephantine *Arameyskie dokumenty iudeyskoy kolonii n Elefantine V v. do r. Chr.*, 1915; he wrote also a study on the Egyptian god Sobek *Drevneegipetskiy bog Sebek*, 1917; he died on 16 Oct. 1919.

Inf. J. Śliwa

VOLNEY, (*Comte*) **Constantin François Chasseboeuf** (1757-1820)
French savant and traveller; he was born in Craon (Maine-et-Loire) 3 Feb. 1757, son of Jaques René C. and Jeanne Gigault de la Giraudais; he journeyed in Egypt and Syria, 1785-85 studying their history and political and social institutions, afterwards publishing a descriptive work *Voyage en Égypte et en Syrie,* 1787 (new ed., 1799 and 1959); he was member of the States-General and of the Constituent Assembly; in 1792 he bought an estate in Corsica where he attempted to put into practice his social and economic theories; he was imprisoned by the Jacobins, but escaped the guillotine; after being for some time Professor of History at the École Normale, he visited America, 1795, but was accused of being a spy and had to return to France in 1798; although not a partisan of Napoleon, he was pressed into his service and made a Senator, 24 Dec. 1799-1814 and a Comte, 26 April 1808, and under the Restoration, a Peer of France; elected a Member of the Institut, 20 Nov. 1795; he died in Paris, 26 April 1820.

Carré, i, 79-116; *EB*; Hilmy, i, 186; J. Gaulmier, *L'idéologue Volney 1757-1820*, 1951; *Les Savants en Égypte*, 1998, 47-8; Lamy, 225-30.); A. C. E. Franquet de Franqueville, *Le Premier Siècle de l'Institut de France*, 1895, I, 77; E. Hindie Lemay, *Dictionnaire des Constituants 1789-91*, 1991, 942-3; È. Gran-Aymerich, *Dictionnaire biographique d'archéologie 1798-1945*, 2001, incorporated in *Les Chercheurs de passé 1798-1945*, 2007, 1226-7; J. Speake (ed.), *Literature of Travel and Exploration*, 2003, 3, 1254-5.

VOLTEN, Aksel Peter Fritz (1896-1963)
Danish Egyptologist and Demotist; he was born Asa, 7 Jan. 1896, son of Peter Rasmussen V. and Fritze Marie Christiane Hasselbach; he studied in Copenhagen under H. O. Lange (q.v.); PhD, 1941; he was attached to the University of Copenhagen, 1943; he specialized in Demotic studies and papyri, and published a number of important documents in the Ny Carlsberg Glyptotek; among these were wisdom books such as Papyrus Insinger, and dream books; he also worked on Middle Kingdom texts; his publications included, *Statuen und Statuetten*, pt. v of Borchardt's great Cairo Cat. vols., 1936; *Studien zum Weisheitsbuch des Anii*, 1937; *Kopenhagener Texte zum demotischen Weisheitsbuch. Pap. Carlsberg II, III verso, IV verso und V*, 1940; *Das demotische Weisheitsbuch, Studien und Bearbeitung*, 1941; *Demotische Traumdeutung. Pap. Carlsberg XIII und XIV verso*, 1942; *Zwei altägyptische politische, Schriften. Die Lehre für Konig Merikare. Pap. Carlsberg VI, und die Lehre des Königs Amenemhet*, 1945; *Ägypter und Amazonen: eine demotische Erzählung des Inaros-Petubastis-Kreises,* 1962; he died in Gentofte, 12 Jan. 1963.

AfO 21 (1966), 275 (H. Brunner); *Acta Orientalia* 27 (1963), 79-82 (W. Erichsen); *Chron. d'Eg.* 38(110-12) (B. van de Walle); *Dansk Biografisk Leksikon* 16, 36.

VYCICHL, Werner (1909-1999)
Swiss linguist and Egyptologist; he was born at Prague, 20 Jan. 1909, son of an Austrian army officer; he studied at the Institut für Ägyptologie und Afrikanistik, University of Vienna under Czermak (q.v.) and Till (q.v.), obtaining his doctorate, 1932; he was sent on a mission to Luxor, 1934-9; he specialized in the linguistic history of ancient Egyptian and its Hamitic and Semitic affinities; he settled in Paris, 1948-60 and then Geneva from 1960 where he worked as a translator and teacher of Latin; he became a lecturer and later Professor at the University of Fribourg,

1968-80, teaching Egyptian language and history; 1980; he helped to found the Société d'Égyptologie Genève, 1978 and became its vice-president and later president, 1987-9; a volume of *BSEG* 4 (1980) was dedicated to him; apart from articles and works on African languages, he published with W. Worrell, *Coptic Texts in the University of Michigan Collection*, 1942; *Dictionaire étymologique de la langue copte*, 1983 and *Vocalisation de la langue égyptienne. I, La phonétique*, 1990 as well as works on the Berber language; his papers have been deposited at the University of Frankfurt; he died at Geneva, 23 Sept. 1999.

BSEG 23 (1999), 5-10 (portr.) (P. Germond, J.-L. Chappaz, R. Kasser); *BSEG* 4 (1980), 9-17 (bibl.); *BSFE* 146 (1999), 3; *WZKM* 91 (2001), 9-14 (portr.) (E. Lucchesi); *DIE* 54 (2002), 5-33 (portr.) (bibl.) (A. Vycichl); *Aegyptus* 81 (2001), 341-43 (E. Lucchesi); *Voyages en Égypte de l'Antiquité au début du XXe siècle*, 2003, 326.

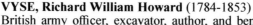

VYSE, Richard William Howard (1784-1853)
British army officer, excavator, author, and benefactor; he was born on 25 July 1784, son of General Richard V. and his wife Anne, daughter of Field-Marshal Sir George Howard; in 1812 by royal licence, he assumed the additional name and arms of Howard; he entered the Army, 1800; Lieut., 1801; Capt., 1802; Major, 1813; Colonel, 1837; Major-General, 1846, in 2nd Life Guards; he married Frances Hesketh, 1810; Hon. DCL, Oxford, 1810; MP, 1807, 1812-18; he visited Egypt in 1835, and carried out excavations at the Pyramids of Giza with Caviglia (q.v.); having secured the assistance of John Shea Perring (q.v.) in Jan. 1837, he returned to England leaving Perring to complete the work at his expense; he published a very full account of it, *Operations carried on at the pyramids of Gizeh in 1837: with an account of a voyage into Upper Egypt, and an appendix (containing a survey by J. S. Perring Esq., of the pyramids at Abu Roash, and those to the southward, including those in the Faiyoum)*, 3 vols. 1840, 1842; this survey and the consequent excavations formed much the most important work undertaken on the pyramid fields during the nineteenth century and the published account remained a standard work until modern times; Vyse presented some antiquities, including a statue of Senwosret I (EA 44), the later wooden coffin of Menkaure (EA 6647) and a number of papyri to the British Museum, 1838; he died at his seat, Stoke Poges, Bucks., 8 June 1853, and was buried at Great Bookham, Surrey; monument and hatchment at Stoke Poges Church.

ODNB 56, 621-2; *DNB* 58, 398; Hilmy, ii, 313; Lindsay 39, 78, 85, 97, 155; Edwards, *Pyramids of Egypt*, frequently; Lauer, *Le Problème des Pyramides d'Égypte*, 1948, 15, 28, 36, 51, 55-65, 128.

WACE, Alan John Bayard (1879-1957)

British archaeologist; he was born in Cambridge, 13 July 1879, second son of Frederick Charles W., mathematics don of St John's College and one time Mayor of Cambridge, and Fanny Bayard; he studied classics at Pembroke College, Cambridge, 1898-1901, with a fourth year of classical archaeology, 1901-2; he became a student of the British School at Athens in 1902 where he was attached throughout his career; he joined the British School at Rome in 1903 and became its librarian while working in Greece; he was a fellow at Pembroke College, 1904-13; he was appointed Director of the British School at Athens 1914-23, Curator of Textiles, Victoria and Albert Museum 1924-34, and Laurence Professor of Classical Archaeology in the University of Cambridge 1934-44; Fellow of Pembroke College, 1934-44; Hon. Fellow, 1951; in Greece he excavated in Laconia (including Sparta itself), in Thessaly and notably at Mycenae (1920-23, 1939, 1950-55); he was evacuated from Greece to Cairo in 1941 and worked in vetting the preparation of documents for those being sent back into Greece; he was urged by the British Council to accept the new post of Professor of Classics and Archaeology at the Farouk I University Alexandria, 1944-52 where he renewed his interests in Hellenistic and Roman archaeology; he excavated for the University at the Government Hospital site and on the fort of Kom el- Dikka in the city and at Ashmunein (Hermopolis Magna) in Middle Egypt; he served on the Commission for the Preservation of Monuments in Egypt under Drioton (q.v.) and went with the War Damage Commission to assess the situation in Cyrenaica at the end of the war; he was a frequent lecturer for the Archaeological Society of Alexandria and served both as librarian and as Secretary for the Society; he accomplished much, with the assistance of colleagues in the UK and elsewhere, toward improving the library resources of both the University and the Society; through his instigation a number of senior colleagues were invited to Alexandria to lecture during his time there; he organized with Drioton an exhibition of Coptic art in Cairo (1944) and was elected an officer of the patriarchal order of St Mark the Evangelist in Alexandria (1952); FBA, 1947; apart from his publications dealing with his work in Greece and articles on work in Egypt, he published *Cyrenaica, Handbook Part III*, 1947; with others, *Hermopolis Magna, Ashmunein: The Ptolemaic Sanctuary and the Basilica*, 1959; all notebooks and plans of excavations in Egypt are held in the Archives of the British School at Athens and MSS of the report on the excavations of Kom el-Dikka together with an account of the Islamic Pottery by Arthur Lane is held by SOAS; publications concerned with Cyrene are with the Libyan Society; he died in Athens, 9 Nov. 1957.

ODNB 56, 632-5; Private inf. from E. B. French (daughter); H. Waterhouse, 'Bibliography 1903-1950', *Annual of the British School at Athens* XLVI (1951), 232-243; H. Waterhouse, 'A.J.B.Wace: Supplementary Bibliography', *Annual of the British School at Athens* 63 (1968), 327-329; *PBA* 44 (1958), 263-80 (F. Stubbings); *American Philosophical Society Yearbook* 1958, 162-71 (C. Blegen); *Gnomon* 30 (1958), 158-9 (S. Hood).

WADDELL, William Gillan (1884-1945)

British Classical scholar; he was born at Neilston, Renfrewshire, 21 April 1884, son of Robert Gillan W., an accountant, and June Lyle Jeffrey; he was educated at the University of Glasgow; MA; Prizeman in Latin and Greek; he held various teaching and lecturing appointments; Professor of Classics in Cairo University, 1929-32 and 1937-44; he contributed articles on Greek papyri, etc. to journals; he also published an edition of *Herodotus, Book II*, and the text and translation of *Manetho* in the Loeb Classical Library; he died 25 Jan. 1945.

WWW iv, 1187; *Bulletin de la Société Archéologique d'Alexandrie* 36 (1943-4), 146-7.

WADDINGTON (*Very Revd*), **George** (1793-1869)

British traveller; he was born in Tuxford, Notts., 7 Sept. 1793, son of George W. and Anne Dollond; educated at Charterhouse, 1808-11, and Trinity College, Cambridge; Fellow, 1817; MA, 1818; DD, 1840; he visited Nubia with the Revd Barnard Hanbury (q.v.) in 1821, and Greece, 1823-4; he published a narrative of his Nubian journey, 1822, trans. into German, 1823; he was the first to attempt to describe the Egyptian occupation of the Sudan; Vicar of Masham, 1833-40; Dean of Durham, 1840-69; he died in Durham, 20 July 1869.

ODNB 56, 653-4; *DNB* 58, 410; Cailliaud, *Voyage à Méroé*, i, 395; Budge, *Eg. Sudan* i, 34-8; Hilmy, ii, 314; Moorehead, 152-78.

WADDINGTON, (James) Hilary Sheffield (1903-1989)

British architect and archaeologist; he was born in London, 21 Sept. 1903, son of Quintin W., assistant curator at the Guildhall Museum, and Maude Mary Hewitt; he was educated at Westminster School, 1918-21 and then trained as an architect in an Architectural Association school; he worked with Pendlebury (q.v.) at Amarna, 1930-33; he became an inspector in the Palestine Antiquities Service, 1932-36; he served as assistant superintendent in the Archaeological Survey of India from 1937; superintendent, 1946-55; he was appointed lecturer in the Extramural Dept., Bristol University, 1955; he excavated at Nimrud and Balawat in Iraq, 1956; FSA, 1947; MBE, 1947; he died at Painswick, Stroud, 25 July 1989.

The Antiquaries Journal 70 (1990), 526-7; The Record of Old Westminsters 3 (1963), 388; C. Naunton, KMT 21, 3 (2010), 45-53.

WAINWRIGHT, Gerald Avery (1879-1964)

British Egyptologist and archaeologist; he was born at Clifton, 4 March 1879, son of William Frederick W., brewer, and Emily Helen Jones; educated Clifton College, but he was unable to go on to University afterwards; his interest in Egyptology was awakened by reading Rawlinson's *Ancient Egypt* at 15, but he was unable to follow it up and had to work in a timber office when he was 17; in 1900 he attended evening classes in Egyptian and Coptic at the University College, Bristol, Mackay (q.v.) being also a student; he first visited Egypt in 1904, and on meeting Petrie (q.v.), 1907, asked to be taken on as an assistant on his digs; he went to Sohag and remained excavating with Petrie until 1912, contributing to no fewer than six of Petrie's archaeological vols., *Meydum and Memphis* III, 1910; *The Labyrinth and Gerzeh*, 1911; *Tarkhan* I *and Memphis* V, 1913; *Heliopolis, Kafr Ammar and Shurafa*, 1915; and pls. in *Memphis* I *and* II; during the summers he studied with Petrie and Margaret Murray (q.v.) at University College London, and received some instruction in language from Griffith (q.v.) in Oxford, in return for help with the Nubian finds; he next joined Wellcome (q.v.) in the Sudan, and having saved enough money was able to study and take his BLitt Oxon, 1913, the subject being *The Foreign Relations of the New Kingdom* which dealt with the Keftiu and which was published later in *Liverpool Annals*; Wainwright dug for the EES at Abydos, 1913-14, and at Es-Sawama, and in 1915 at El-Balabish for the American branch; in 1914 he also joined Woolley (q.v.) and Lawrence (q.v.) at Carchemish; to support himself he taught at Christ's Hospital School and the Tewfikia School in Cairo, 1916-21; he was appointed Chief Inspector of Middle Egypt by the Antiquities Service, 1921-4; in 1926 he retired to Bournemouth with sufficient money saved plus the compensation given by the Egyptian Government to retiring officers, to enable him to devote the rest of his life to research and publication; to this end he regularly visited Oxford, and the list of his publications is thus very long, reaching hundreds of items; only two books came out under his own name, *Balabish*, 1920; *The Sky Religion of Egypt*, 1937; his interests were very wide and his articles and reviews embraced archaeology and anthropology in areas far beyond Egypt; in all he contributed to at least 15 journals and also reviewed for the *Times Literary Supplement*; his main studies were technical, e.g. iron, bronze, tin, obsidian; religious and anthropological, e.g. the origins of the gods Amun and Min; and ethnic, e.g. the Sea Peoples; he did much to encourage young people and students, founding a prize of £50 for an essay written on Egyptian Archaeology by a boy or girl at school; he left the bulk of his estate to the University of Oxford to endow two Research Fellowships in the study of Near Eastern Archaeology; he also donated a generous sum for books for the library of the EES; he died in Bournemouth, 28 May 1964.

Private inf.; EES *Report,* 1964/1965, 4-5 (I. E. S. Edwards); *JEA* 50 (1964), 173-6 (G. A. D. Tait).

WAKELING, Thomas George (1864-1942)

British doctor and author; he was born at Southend-on-Sea, 6 July 1864, son of George Lionel W., waterman, and Emma Ingram; he studied medicine at St Bartholemew's Hospital, London; he was practising in Egypt by 1910, when he wrote a paper on fever caused by the sandfly; he achieved the rank of temporary Captain in the Army Medical Service during World War I, and was president of a recruiting medical board; OBE, 1918; he wrote *Forged Egyptian Antiquities*, 1912, an anecdotal but important presentation of this field; he lived in Jamaica in the 1920s; he died in Bourne End, Bucks., 24 Feb. 1942.

Inf. T. Hardwick.

WAŁEK-CZERNECKI, Tadeusz Bronisław (1889-1949)

Polish historian, born in Wadowice, 27 Nov. 1889, son of Bronisław W., a lawyer, and Mary Simon; he studied history and archaeology at the Jagellonian University, Cracow 1907-10, as a pupil of Peter Bieńkowski (q.v.); in 1910 he went abroad and studied in Berlin under Ed. Meyer (q.v.) and A. Erman (q.v.) and in Paris under A. Moret (q.v.); PhD, 1911; in the winter of 1913-14 he took part in the Austrian excavations at Giza conducted by Junker (q.v.); habilitation at the Jagellonian University, Cracow in 1921; he presented a paper "La population de l'Égypte ancienne" at the International Congress of Population, Paris 1937; Professor of Ancient History at the Warsaw University, 1922-39; during the years 1939-41 he stayed at IFAO, Cairo; 1941-45 in Rhodesia, and after 1945 again in Cairo; from1947 he resided in England, author of an exhaustive *History of Greece* (Polish), Warsaw, 1934 and of the *Economic History of Ancient World* (Polish) Vol. 1-2, Warsaw, 1948, where ancient Egypt is covered in Vol.1, 7-96; he died in Brighton, 25 Dec. 1949.

Filomate 361, Cracow, 1984 151-164 (portr.) (R. Gansiniec); *W Kregu wielkich humanistow,* Warsaw, 1991, 124-142 (portr.) (bibl.) (W. Lengauer); inf. J. Śliwa.

WALKER, James Herbert (1858-1914)

British medical practioner and Egyptologist; he was born at Corwen, 16 March 1858, son of James Richards W., surgeon, and Anne Roberts; he was educated at Oxford, 1876-80; BA, 1880; MA; MRCS; LRCP; he retired early from medical practice and studied Egyptology, attending the classes of Griffith (q.v.) at University College London, from 1893; he became Petrie's assistant as library supervisor from 1893, as lecturer in Egyptian in 1904 and Coptic in 1905; he translated the inscriptions in many of Petrie's excavation memoirs and was in charge of the Egyptian Dept. at the College during Petrie's absence; he contributed chapters to Petrie's *Memphis* I, 1909; *The Palace of Apries*, 1909; *Qurneh*, 1909, etc., and also wrote articles in *PSBA*; he died at London, 21 July 1914.

AE A (1914), 190; *JEA* 1 (1914), 295; M. A. Murray, *My First Hundred Years*; R. Janssen *The First Hundred Years,* 1992, 11.

WALLE, Baudoin van de (1901-1988)

Belgian Egyptologist; he was born at Bruges, 21 Oct. 1901, son of Maurice van de Walle, a judge, and Valentine Visart de Bocarmé; he was educated at the Collège Saint Louis in Bruges 1911-9 when his interest in Egyptology was aroused; advised by Capart (q.v.) he studied for two years at the Institute Saint-Louis in Brussels as well as taking courses in Egyptology at the Musée du Cinquantenaire and in art at the Institut Supérieur d'Histoire de l'Art et d'Archéologie from 1919 and then continued his studies at the Université de Liège, obtaining his doctorate in 1924; from 1922-3 he taught a course at the École des Hautes Études in Ghent; in 1925 he visited Egypt and took part in excavations at Abydos in 1925 and at the Bucheum at Armant in 1930; he succeeded Capart in his teaching posts at the University of Liège, at the Institut Supérieur d'Histoire de l'Art et d'Archéologie at Brussels, the Institut des Hautes Études de Belgique, and the École Supérieure de Jeunes Filles, 1929-72; Member of the Conseil d'Administration of the Fondation Égyptologique Reine Élisabeth, 1947-88; Corr. Member of the Académie royale d'Archéologie de Belgique, 1926, full member 1929; Associate member of the Institut d'Egypte, 1953; Corr. member of the Deutsches Institut 1965; he published nearly 150 monographs and articles notably *La Tombe de Nakht*, with M. Werbrouck, 1929; *Le mastaba de Neferirtenef aux Musées Royaux d'Art et d'Histoire à Bruxelles*, 1930; *La transmission des textes littéraires égyptiens*, 1948; *L'humour dans la littérature et dans l'art de l'ancienne Égypte*, 1969; *La mastaba de Neferirtenef*, 1973; *La chapelle funéraire de Neferirtenef,* 1978; *La collection égyptienne. Les étapes marquantes de son développement*, with L. Limme, 1980; *Champollion, le père de l'Égyptologie*, 1983; he also edited *Voyage en Égypte. Vincent Stochove. Gilles Fermanel. Robert Fauvel 1631,* 1975; he died in Brussels, 26 Dec. 1988.

Chron. d'Ég. 64 (1989), 3-15 (portr.) (A. Mekhitarian), 16-23 (bibl.) (M. Malaise); *BSFE* 114 (1989), 7-12 (A. Mekhitarian).

WALLIN, George August (1811-1852)

Finnish traveller; he was born in Sund in the Aland archipelago in Finland, 24 Oct. 1811, son of Israel Wallin, a royal tax-collector, and Johanna Maria Ahrenberg; he studied Arabic under Muhammad Aijad el-Tantawi and Senkowski (q.v.) at the University of St. Petersburg; he visited Egypt in 1843-4 and 1847-9 travelling up to the Second Cataract; he obtained a large collection of manuscripts, zoological specimens, and some antiquities of which one coffin is now in the National Museum of Finland; his letters and diaries were later published in Swedish, *Georg August Wallins reseanteckningar från Orienten åren 1843-1849*, ed. S. Elmgren, 1864-6 and further documents, *Brief ach dagboksanteckningar af Georg August Walline*, ed. K. Tallqvist, 1905; *Skrifter 1. Studieåren och resan till Alexandria*, 2010; *Skrifter 2. Det första året I Egypten 1843-1844,* 2011; *Skrifter 3. Kairo och resan till Övre Egypten 1844-1845*, 2012; and some of his English articles in *Travels in Arabia (1845 and 1847)*, 1979; he died in Helsinki, 23 Oct. 1852.

Inf. Prof. R Holthoer; H. Holma, *Georg August Wallin, 1811-1852*, 1952, 3-12, 13-16 (bibl.); M. Trautz in *Travels in Arabia (1845 and 1847),* 1979 xxii-xli; K. Öhrnberg in J. Speake (ed.), *Literature of Travel and Exploration*, 2003, 3, 1265-7; J. Thompson, *Edward William Lane 1810-1867*, 2010, 536-7; K. Öhrnberg and P. Berg, *G. A. Wallin. Skrifter* 1, 2010; P. Berg in M. Betrò and G. Miniaci, *Talking along the Nile*, 2013, 35-41; P. Berg in N. Cooke and V. Daubney, *Every Traveller Needs a Compass*, 2015, 23-32; P. Berg and others, *Dolce far niente in Arabia: Georg August Wallin and his Travels in the 1840s*, 2014.

WALLIS, Henry (1830-1916)

British artist and writer; he was born in London, 21 Feb. 1830, son of Mary Ann Thomas and adopted by his step-father Andrew Wallis; his best-known picture, 'The Death of Chatterton", was exhibited at the

Royal Academy, 1856, and is now in the Tate Gallery; for some years he visited Egypt annually and bought antiquities there which he sold to museums and collectors to pay his expenses; he sold a collection of Coptic textiles to the South Kensington (Victoria and Albert) Museum, 1886; in the 1880s he was a prime mover in the foundation of the Society for the Preservation of the Monuments of Ancient Egypt;he was an authority on Near Eastern ceramics, and published *Egyptian Ceramic Art: the Macgregor Collection*, 1898; his drawings of the tombs of Aswan were published in monochrome, *PSBA* 10, plates facing pp. 26, 30, 34; he had a collection of oriental ceramics, embroideries, and antiquities which was dispersed after his death, some passing to the Victoria and Albert Museum, others being sold at Sotheby's, 8-9 Aug. 1917, Christie's, 5 March 1919, and Sotheby's, 9 June 1937; other Egyptian material was sold at Keys Auctioneers in Norfolk, 9-10 May 2007; his papers are in the Bodleian Library; he died at Croydon, 20 Dec 1916 and was buried in Highgate Cemetery.

DNB Missing Persons, 697-8; *ODNB* 57, 13-4; inf. P E. Newberry; Budge, N & T, i, 82, 109, 132; Petrie, 120, 121; T. Wilson, 'A Victorian artist as ceramic-collector: the letters of Henry Wallis' I and II, *Journal of the History of Collections* 14.1 and 14.2 (2002), 139-59, 231-69. Lugt 77078, 78573.

WALLON, Henri Alexandre (1812-1904)
French historian; he was born in Valenciennes, 23 Dec. 1812, son of Martin Alexandre Joseph W., secretary to the local army commissioner, and Fébronie Josèphe Caffiaux; he taught at various schools until he became Professor of Modern History at the Faculté des Lettres in Paris in Nov. 1849; dean 1876-81; he served as a deputy 1848, 1849-50, and 1871-5 and senator from 1875; he was Minister of Public Instruction, 1875-6; he was elected to the Académie des Inscriptions 22 Nov. 1850; Secrétaire perpétual, 1873; he published *Hist. de l'Esclavage dans l'antiquité*, Paris, 1847; also a long biography of Mariette (q.v.) in *CRAIBL* sér.iv, vol. xi (1883), 481-584; he died in Paris, 13 Nov. 1904.

A. C. E. Franquet de Franqueville, *Le Premier Siècle de l'Institut de France*, 1895, I, 287; A. Robert et al, *Dictionnaire des Parlementaires Français*, 1891, 5, 555-6; C. Charle, *Les Professeurs de la Faculté des Lettres de Paris*, I, 1985, 174-6.

WALMAS, Francis (*fl.*1810-1840)
Egyptian banker under British protection; he was partner in the house of Samuel Briggs (q.v.) at Alexandria, and very helpful to European travellers in Egypt.

Athanasi, 17; Belzoni, i, 401; Madden, i, 217; Richardson, i, 52, 115; ii, 174; Salt, ii, 144; St John, i, 57; Westcar Diary, 40.

WALNE, Alfred Septimus (1805-1881)
British surgeon and diplomat; he was born at Market Weston, Suffolk 22 Feb. 1805, son of Thomas W., later of Brockdish, Norfolk, and Elizabeth Cole; MRCS, 1828; LSA, 1828; he practised in London, at Chancery Lane, 1829-34, and at Bloomsbury Square, 1834-6; he went to Egypt before 1834 and presented the head of a mummy to St. Bartholomew's Hospital early that year when he is described as a traveller; he was appointed British Vice-Consul in Cairo 1836-41, and Consul from 1841 to 1868 when he was succeeded by Rogers Bey (q.v.); he also practised as a surgeon in Cairo; whilst there, he established a library and museum; he died in London, 17 June 1881.

RCS Records; G. Melley, *Khartoum*, 78; ii, 89, 267; Romer, i, 79; Vyse, i, 198, 264; ii, 34, 75; *The Ipswich Journal* 18 Jan. 1834, 1 Feb 1834 and 28 June 1881.

WALPOLE, (*Revd*) **Robert** (1781-1856)
British traveller and author; he was born at Lisbon, 8 Aug. 1781, son of Robert W., clerk of Privy Council and envoy to Portugal, and Diana Grosset; educated at Trinity College, Cambridge; MA, 1809; BD, 1828; Rector of Mannington, Norfolk, 1809-56; he visited Greece and various countries in the Near East, and published his *Memoirs relating to European and Asiatic Turkey and other Countries of the East, edited from Manuscript Journals*, 1817 (2nd ed. 1818); this contains much valuable matter including the journal of Nathaniel Davison (q.v.); he died in London, 16 April 1856.

ODNB 57, 92; *DNB* 59, 207; Light, pref, xi.

WALTERS, Henry (1848-1931)
American railroad executive, art collector and benefactor; he was born at Baltimore, Maryland, 26 Sept. 1848, son of William Thompson W. (1820-97), and Ellen Harper; he was educated at Loyala Coll. Baltimore, Georgetown University and Paris; MA, 1871; Lawrence Scientific School Harvard, 1869-73; BS, 1873; as chairman and chief stockholder of the Atlantic Coast Line Railroad of Virginia, he had control of 10,000 miles of railway track, with other lines added; later he is said at the height of his career to have become the richest

man in the southern USA; he married Mrs Sarah Wharton (Green) Jones, 1922; yachtsman and owner of the *Narada*; a notable benefactor, he was the builder of public baths in Baltimore, Trustee of the Metropolitan Museum, New York, and the New York Public Library; Officer Légion d'honneur; he expanded the extensive art collection begun by his father and although neither father nor son apparently ever visited Egypt, Henry bought from many of the important dealers of his time, especially from Kelekian (q.v.); his growing collections were housed in specially built galleries, opened in 1909, and in his will he left them to the city of Baltimore, together with one quarter of his estate as endowment; among them were a large number of Egyptian objects forming one of the finest collections in America; a catalogue of the sculpture being published in 1946 by Steindorff (q.v.), and including 745 items among them pieces added later; he died in New York, 30 Nov. 1931, and was buried in Baltimore.

Inf. Craig S. Korr and Mrs E. Reifstahl; *DAB* 19, 399-400; *Webster Biogr. Dict.,* 1540;*WWWA* 1, 1295; W. R. Johnston, *William and Henry Walters: the reticent collectors,* 1999; R. Schulz, *Egyptian Art: the Walters Art Museum,* 2009, 9-13.

WÅNGSTEDT, Sten Valter (1904-1986)
Swedish Demotist; he was born in Kinnarum, 13 Dec. 1904, son of Alfred W.and his wife Ida; he began his studies at the University of Uppsala in 1926 and concentrated on Demotic under the influence of Erichsen (q.v.) and Volten (q.v.); he travelled extensively in Europe visiting museum collections to examine Demotic ostraca; he became secretary at the Victoria Museum of the University of Uppsala; in 1954 he obtained his doctorate; from 1955-70 he was director of the Egyptian section of the Medelhavsmuseet, Stockholm; Reader in Egyptology at the University of Uppsala, 1955-86; by his will he established the Margrethe-und-Sten-Wangstedt-Stipendium at Uppsala for students of Demotic; apart from his numerous articles in *Bibliotheca Ekmaniana, Orientalia Suecana,* and *Medelhavsmuseet Bulletin* mostly on Demotic ostraca, he published his thesis *Ausgewahlte demotische Ostraka aus der Sammlung des Victoria-Museums zu Uppsala und der Staalichen Papyrussammlung zu Berlin,* 1954; and *Die demotischen Ostraka der Universität zu Zurich,* 1965; he died at Uppsala, 23 April 1986.

Enchoria 14 (1986), VII-VIII (portr). (R. Holthoer).

WANSLEBEN, Johann Michael (1635-1679)
German traveller and collector; he was born at Sommerda, near Erfurt, 1 Nov. 1635, son of Johann W., a Lutheran pastor; he was educated at Königsberg and later became a teacher, soldier, and protégé of the orientalist Job Ludolf; in 1663 he was sent on a mission to Ethiopia by the Duke of Saxe-Gotha but only reached Egypt where he remained until 1664; as his mission had been a failure, he did not return to Germany but went to Rome where in 1666 he converted to Catholicism and became a Dominican; his talents were brought to the notice of the French government and in 1671 he was sent back to the East to collect manuscripts and antiquities for the royal collection; he travelled extensively in Egypt in 1672-3 to the Wadi Natrun and as far south as Girga; he forwarded over three hundred manuscripts to Paris before he left in 1673; he was disgraced on his return in 1676 for not carrying out all his instructions; his accounts of his journeys were published as *Relazione delle Stato Presente (1663) dell'Egitto,* 1671 and *Nouvelle relation en forme de journal d'un voyage fait en Egypte par le P. Vansleb religieux dominicain en 1672 et 1673,* 1677; he died at Bourron near Fontainbleau, 12 June 1679.

Biog. Univ. 44, 319-20; *ADB* 41,159-162; Carré, i, 24-36; Keimer, *BIÉ* 31 (1949), 165-170. A. Pougeois, *Vie et voyages de Vansleb,* 1869; Lamy, 132-5.

WARBURTON, (Bartholomew) Elliott George (1810-1852)
Irish lawyer, traveller and novelist; he was born near Tullamore, King's Co., 1810, son of George W and Anna Acton; called to the Bar, 1837; in 1843 he made an extensive tour in Syria, Palestine, and Egypt, and published *The Crescent and the Cross,* 1845; he also wrote historical novels and memoirs of Prince Rupert; he died at sea while on a mission to Darien, 4 Jan. 1852.

Alum. Cantab; *DNB* 59, 294-6; Lindsay, 134; *ODNB* 57, 257.

WARBURTON, (Rt Revd) William (1698-1779)
British ecclesiastic and writer; he was born in Newark, 24 Dec. 1698, son of George W. and Elizabeth Holman; he was one of the most prominent scholars of his time; he trained in an attorney's office, but was ordained 1723; he held various benefices, and was made Bishop of Gloucester, 1759; he was the author of numerous literary and ecclesiastical works; his connection with Egyptology is his *The Divine Legation of Moses,* 2 vols, 1738-41, and several later eds.; this contains an essay on the decipherment of hieroglyphs, which according to Gauthier (q.v.)

was the only work of its kind in the period before Champollion (q.v.) that showed the correct method of approach to bring results, although the author did not of course attempt actual readings of inscriptions; it was translated into French, 1744; Warburton died in his palace at Gloucester, 7 June 1779.

ODNB 57, 268-74 (portr.); *DNB* 59, 301-11; *BIFAO* 5 (1906), 82; Hilmy, ii, 319; Nichols, *Lit. Anecd.* ii, 144, 165; Lamy, 288-90; P. Lurbe in C. Grell, *L'Égypte imaginaire*, 2001, 49-57.

WARD, John (1832-1912)
British artist and traveller; JP; FSA; he was born in Belfast, 7 Aug. 1832, son of Marcus Ward, printer and publisher, by his second wife Ellen Veacock; his intention to become an architect was changed by his father's death, and he entered the family firm, becoming a director and retiring in 1876; he published many works on art and travelled extensively in Greece and the Near East; member of the EEF Committee, he published *Pyramids and Progress,* 1900; *The Sacred Beetle,* 1901; *Greek Coins,* 1902; *Our Sudan,* 1905; he died Farningham, Kent, 20 Feb. 1912.

Andrews Diary; *Sayce,* 315; *WWW* i, 741; inf. T. Snoddy.

WARD, William Ayres (1928-1996)
American Egyptologist; he was born in Chicago, 10 June 1928, son of William M. W. and Wilma Hite; he was educated at Butler University in Indianapolis majoring in the History of Religion, BA, 1951; he then studied Egyptology at the University of Chicago, MA, 1955; and Semitic Languages at Brandeis University, PhD, 1958; he first taught at the Beirut College for Women and then at the American University of Beirut, 1963-86; he served as chairman of the Departments of Religious History, History and Archaeology, and as Associate Dean of the Faculty of Arts and Sciences; he became Visiting Professor at Brown University, 1986-96; he also taught at the University of Arizona, 1987-8; he was co-editor of the journal *Berytus* and editorial assistant for the *Anchor Bible Dictionary*; he was especially interested in the relations between Egypt and the Levant, Egyptian-Semitic etymological studies and lexicography, and the study of scarabs and titles from the Old and Middle Kingdoms; a volume of studies *Ancient Egyptian and Mediterranean Studies in memory of William A. Ward* was published in 1998; apart from over sixty articles, his principal publications in the field of Egyptology were *Egypt and the East Mediterranean World 2200-1900 B.C.,* 1971; *Studies on Scarab Seals* I, 1978; *The Four Egyptian Homographic Roots B-3,* 1978; *Index of Egyptian Administrative and Religious Titles of the Middle Kingdom,* 1982; and *Essays on Feminine Titles of the Middle Kingdom,* 1986; he died at Providence, 13 Sept. 1996.

JARCE 34 (1997), ix-x (L. Lesko); *Ancient Egyptian and Mediterranean Studies,* ix-x (B. and L. Lesko); International Association of Egyptologists online obituary (L. Lesko).

WARDI, Antoun (*c.*1800-*c.*1877)
Egyptian dragoman; the correct form of the name is uncertain, and he is stated by Maspero (q.v.) and T. D. Mosconas, to have been a Syrian; Archibald Campbell (q.v.) bought the papyrus of Pinodjem from him which came from the cache of Royal Mummies, and in 1875 when he was at Beirut he had in his possession the Queen Nodjmet papyrus (part of which is now in the British Museum and part in the Louvre), from the same source; it is therefore evident that he was an accomplice of the Abderrassul family (q.v.); and helped to dispose of the papyri before the whereabouts of the cache was made known; he is not be confused with Triantaphyllos (q.v.)

Letter from Dr. Mosconas, 15 June 1951; Chabas, 147; Maspero, *Momies Royales,* 512; Tresson, 32.

WARNER, Charles Dudley (1829-1899)
American author; he was born at Planfield, Mass., 12 Sept. 1829, son of Justus W., a farmer, and Sylvia Hitchcock; he was educated at Hamilton College, BA, 1851 and Univ. of Pa. LLB, 1858; he became editor of the Hartford Press and a contributor to *Harper's New Monthly Magazine*; he visited Egypt in 1876 and published an account *Mummies and Moslems,* 1876; he was a friend of W Fiske (q.v.); he helped to promote the EEF and encouraged Amelia Edwards' (q.v.) lecture tour in America; Honorary Vice-President of EEF; he died at Hartford, Conn., 20 Oct 1899.

WWA I, 1300-1; *DAB* 19,462-3; EEF *Annual Report 1899-1900,* 26.

WAROCQUÉ, Raoul (1870-1917)
Belgian industrialist and collector; he was born at Brussels, 4 Feb. 1870, son of Arthur Hippolyte W. and Mary Orville; he came from a wealthy family of industrialists whose seat was the Château of Mariemont; he was an avid collector and visited Egypt in 1911-12 when he acquired various antiquities; he financed the excavation of Daninos (q.v.) at Heliopolis in 1912; he left his chateau and collection to the nation, now the Musée Royal de Mariemont; he died in Brussels, 28 May 1917.

Biog. Nat. de Belgique 27,96-9; *Rev. Arch.* 1917,312-3; *Actes du XXIe Congrès orientale*, 44-6; A. Verbanck-Pierard, *Archeologia* 241 (Dec. 1988) 76; M-C Bruwier, *Chron.d'Ég* 64 (1989), 33-36; A. Verbanck-Pierard in A.-F. Laurens and K. Pomian, *L'Anticomanie*, 1988, 169-204; M. C. Bruwier, *L'Egypte dans la bibliothèque de Raoul Warocqué*, 1992; Jean-Michel Bruffaerts, 'Capart-Warocqué: une amitié manquée', in C. Derriks et L. Delvaux (eds), *Antiquités égyptiennes au Musée royal de Mariemont, Morlanwelz, Musée royal de Mariemont*, 2009, 39-48.

WARREN, John Collins (1778-1856)

American surgeon; he was born at Boston, 1 Aug. 1778, son of John W., a surgeon, and Abigail Collins, he was first Professor of Anatomy and Surgery at Harvard; when surgeon of Massachusetts General Hospital, he unrolled and described a Ptolemaic mummy in 1821, which had been presented to the museum of the hospital by A. O. van Lennep, a Smyrna merchant; he died in Boston, 4 May 1856.

Hilmy, ii, 321; *Mem.* I. E. 13. 47; *N.Y. Hist. Soc. Bull.* 4. 4; *DAB* 19, 480-1.

WATANABE, Yasutada (1922-2000)

Japanese architectural historian; he was born in Tokyo, 1922, and studied architecture at Waseda University, PhD, 1951; he was appointed Professor at Waseda University in 1955; he joined the Waseda University expedition to Egypt at Malkata near Thebes from 1973 and contributed to the final report in Japanese and a summarized English version *The Architecture of Kom el-Samak at Malkata-South*, 1986; he retired in 1993 and died, 11 May 2000.

Gott. Misz. 181 (2001), 5-8 (portr.) (S. Nishimoto)

WATTIER DE BOURVILLE *see* **VATTIER de BOURVILLE.**

WEBSTER, James (1802-1828)

Scottish traveller; he was born at Inverarity, 7 Nov. 1802, son of the Revd John W., minister of Inverarity, Forfar, and Mary Bryce; following his father's early death his mother resided with her father Patrick Bryce, minister of Carmylie; he was educated at Carmylie, Montrose, and University of St. Andrews, 1816-20; MA 1823; he studied law in Edinburgh 1820-22 and joined the Inner Temple; he set off on a tour of Europe and the Levant in 1825 reaching Egypt with W. H. Newham in Jan. 1828; he journeyed as far south as Philae visiting the main sites and meeting Hay and his associates and other English travellers; he was taken ill following a trip to Sinai and died at Cairo, 26 Aug. 1828; his journal was later published as *Travels through the Crimea, Turkey and Egypt*, 1830.

Webster, *Travels,* i, v-xxiii, xcix-cxx.

WEEKS, Susan Lisabeth (*née* HOWE) (1943-2009)

American artist and archaeologist; she was born in Chicago, 11 Feb. 1943, daughter of Harold M. Howe, a businessman, and Ilse Nickel; she was educated at the University of Washington; BA, 1964; she married Kent R. Weeks, an Egyptologist, 19 Aug. 1966; she worked as an artist on the Gebal Adda expeditions of the American Research Center in Egypt, 1964-66, the Hierakonpolis expedition of the American Museum of Natural History, 1966-68, various Giza expeditions of the Museum of Fine Arts, Boston, and the American University in Cairo; and on the Egyptian collections of the Peabody Museum of Yale University; she acquired and organized the Ahmed Fakhry Collection of Egyptian Oases Ethnographic Art at the University of California, Berkeley; she was residence manager of the Epigraphic Survey headquarters at Chicago House,1971-75; she was co-director of the Theban Mapping Project's rediscovery and clearing of KV5, the Valley of the Kings tomb of sons of Rameses II; she also worked on objects from Giza, Saqqara, Thebes, and Kharga and Dakhla oases; her art work appears in many publications, including K.-C. Chang, *The Archaeology of Ancient Chica*, 1964; K. Weeks, *The Classic Christian Townsite at Arminna West*, 1967; B. Trigger, *Beyond History,* 1968; B. Trigger, *Meroitic Funerary Inscriptions from Arminna West*, 1970; K. Weeks*, Mastabas of Giza Cemetery G6000, Including Neferbauptah, Iymery, Ity, and Shepseskafankh*, 1994, K. Weeks, *The Lost Tomb*, 1998, K. Weeks, *KV5: A Preliminary Report*, 2000, and others; her detailed notes and drawings on Egyptian folk art, Bedouin jewellery, Upper Egyptian village life, Qurna house painting, 19th century Nile boats, and Nile Valley natural history, are preserved in the Special Collection Library of the American University in Cairo; she drowned in the Nile at Luxor, 12 Dec. 2009, and is buried in Luxor, Egypt.

Inf. K. Weeks.

WEIDENBACH, (Theodor) Ernst (1818-1882)

German artist and draughtsman; he was born in Naumburg an der Saale, 4 Dec. 1818, son of Friedrich August W., drawing master, and Christiane Friedericke Vollmer; he accompanied the expedition of Lepsius (q.v.) to Egypt,

1842-4, and executed the drawings for many of the plates of the *Denkmäler*; on his return he joined the staff of Berlin Museum until 1878 when he resigned on account of ill health; he also accompanied Lepsius to Egypt in 1866; he executed many drawings for the illustrations of other works by Lepsius, and by Ebers (q.v.), Mariette (q.v.), and others; he decorated the walls of the Egyptian rooms in the Kunsthistorisches Museum in Vienna; he died in Merseburg, 14 Sept. 1882.

Inf. Prof. Weidenbach of Giessen (grandson); *Bibl. Ég.* 18, pp. clii, clxxiii; Chabas, 70, 72, 74; Lepsius, 12 and often; S. Binder, *The Bulletin of the Australian Centre for Egyptology* 25 (2014), 9-29; S. Binder and B. Ockinga in N. Cooke and V. Daubney (eds.), *Lost and Now Found*, 2017, 1-24.

WEIDENBACH, Maximilian Ferdinand (1823-1890)
German artist and draughtsman; he was born in Naumburg, 6 March 1823, the younger brother of the previous, with whom he worked during Lepsius's (q.v.) expedition, 1842-5 and drew the plates for Lepsius *Das Totenbuch*, 1847; in 1848 he emigrated to Australia; Acting Prussian Consul for South Australia; some of his Egyptological books including the diary of his travels with Lepsius as well as antiquities, were donated to the South Australian Museum in 1944; he died in Glen Osmond, Adelaide, 24 Aug. 1890.

Inf. Prof. Weidenbach of Giessen, and Mr. F. Thrupp; R. S. Merrillees, *Living with Egypt's Past in Australia*, 1990, 8-10; C. Illert, *Commemorative Biography of Maximilian Ferdinand Weidenbach*, 1981; S. Binder and B. Ockinga in N. Cooke and V. Daubney (eds.), *Lost and Now Found*, 2017, 1-24.

WEIGALL, Arthur Edward Pearse Brome (1880-1934)
British Egyptologist and author; born St Helier, Jersey, 20 Nov. 1880, son of Major Arthur Archibald Denny W. and Alice Cowan; he was educated at Hillside School, Malvern, and Wellington College; he entered New College, Oxford, 1900, but left after a short residence to become assistant to Flinders Petrie on the staff of the EEF, 1901; he married twice, first Hortense Schleiter of Chicago, second Muriel Frances Lillie of Hillsborough, Co. Down; he was Inspector-General of Antiquities for the Egyptian Government, 1905-14; he was closely associated with excavations in the Theban Necropolis carried out by Sir Robert Mond (q.v.), and also with those of Theodore Davis (q.v.) in the Valley of Kings; he was an efficient and energetic official and for the first time probably since Pharaonic times the tombs and temples of Western Thebes became well ordered and properly conserved; he initiated the numbering of the Tombs of the Nobles now in general use, and assisted in their opening up and restoration; with A. H. Gardiner (q.v.) he produced the *Topographical Catalogue of the Private Tombs of Thebes* later supplemented by Engelbach (q.v.); his later popular works are better known but were often written in haste; his later life was that of a writer and journalist, and a scene designer, and shows a very individualistic stamp; for his archaeological work Weigall was awarded the Cross 4th Class Red Eagle, Germany, Officer's Cross of Franz Joseph, Austria, 3rd Class Medjidieh, Egypt; he published many works serious and popular, see *Abydos* I, in part, 1902; *Abydos* III, 1904; *A Report on the Antiquities of Lower Nubia*, 1907; *A Catalogue of the Weights and Balances in the Cairo Museum*, 1908; *Travels in the Upper Egyptian Deserts*, 1909; *A Guide to the Antiquities of Upper Egypt*, 1910, like Baikie's a very useful book for the tourist; *The Life of Akhenaten, Pharaoh of Egypt*, 1910, rev. 1922; *The Treasury of Ancient Egypt*, 1911; *A Topographical Catalogue of the Tombs of Thebes*, with A. H. Gardiner, 1913; *The Life of Cleopatra, Queen of Egypt*, 1914, rev. 1924; *Egypt from 1798 to 1914*, 1915; *The Glory of the Pharaohs*, 1923; *Tutankhamen and other Essays*, 1923; *Ancient Egyptian Works of Art*, 1924; *A History of the Pharaohs*, vol.i, 1925, vol. ii, 1926, never completed, a work of great originality and very well written, but marred by the author's individual approach to certain philological and historical matters, and displaying considerable arrogance towards other contemporary Egyptologists; at this stage of his career Weigall's writing became more general with works such as *Flights into Antiquity*, 1928, *Sappho*, 1932, and *Laura Was My Camel*, 1933; but he produced a final Egyptological book *A Short History of Ancient Egypt*, 1934; he died in London, 2 Jan. 1934.

Egyptian Religion, ii, 75; *JEA* 20 (1934), 107 (A. H. Gardiner); *WWW* iii, 1431; J. Hankey, *Minerva* 5 no. 4 (1994), 16-23; *KMT* 9/2 (1998), 41-45; J. Hankey, *A Passion for Egypt*, 2001; *KMT* 27 (2016), 70-2.

WEILL, Raymond Charles Isaac (1874-1950)
French Egyptologist; he was born in Elbeuf-sur-Seine, 28 Jan. 1874, son of Hippolite W. and Matilda Cohen; he at first went in for a military career; he did not turn to Egyptology until he was 30, when he studied under Maspero (q.v.) at the École des Hautes Études; he accompanied Petrie (q.v.) on his Sinai expedition, and shortly after this the future President of the United States, H. Hoover, then prospecting in this desert, used his work as the base for his own researches; Weill next excavated at Coptos with A. Reinach and discovered the famous series of royal decrees of the Old Kingdom; he excavated at Gezer and Jerusalem in Palestine before and after World War I; between the wars he dug at Zawiyet el-Maietin, Kom el-Ahmar, and Tuna; after the Second World War in which he again served his country, he carried out three further excavation seasons at Dara in Upper Egypt; he was appointed Director of the École des Hautes Études (History and Egyptian Archaeology), 1928-45 and was

President of the Soc. Franç. d'Egyptologie; he specialized in the Second Intermediate Period and the Hyksos question, and was also interested in submerged harbours and port installations; he amassed a large collection of Egyptian antiquities which was acquired by the Louvre between 1911-48, to be followed by more after his death; he published many important works and articles in journals; *Recueil des inscriptions égyptiennes du Sinai: bibliographie, texte, traduction et commentaire, précédé de la géographie, de l'histoire et de la bibliographie des établissements égyptiens de la péninsule,* 1904, a work used by Gardiner in his preparation of the Sinai texts; *Des monuments et de l'histoire des 2e et 3e dynasties égyptiennes. . .,* thesis, 1908; *La Presqu'île du Sinai: étude de géographie et d'histoire,* 1908; *Les Décrets royaux de l'ancien empire égyptien...étude sur les décrets royaux trouvés à Koptos... 1910 et 1911...,* 1912; *La fin du Moyen Empire égyptien: étude sur les monuments et l'histoire de la période comprise entre la 12e et la 18e dynastie,* 2 vols., 1918; *Bases, méthodes et resultats de la chronologie égyptiénne,* 2 Pts., 1926-8; *Le Champ des roseaux et le champ des offrandes dans la religion funéraire et la religion générale,* 1936; posth. *Douzième Dynastie, royauté de Haute-Égypte et domination Hyksos dans le nord,* 1953; *Dara: campagnes de 1946-1948,* with Madame Tony-Revillon and M. Pillet, 1958; he died in Paris, 13 July 1950.

AfO 15 (1945-51), 200; *BSFE,* 4 (1950), 29-31 (portr.), 5 (1950), 63-5; *Chron. d'Ég.* 26 (1951), 115-19 (M. Stracmans); EES *Report* 1950, 5; *JEA* 36 (1950), 1; *Les Donateurs du Louvre,* 189, 343; È. Gran-Aymerich, *Dictionnaire biographique d'archéologie 1798-1945,* 2001, incorporated in *Les Chercheurs de passé 1798-1945,* 2007, 1236-7; G. Miniaci and P. Rigault, *EA* 54 (2019), 32-5.

WELLCOME, (*Sir*) **Henry Solomon** (1853-1936)
British manufacturing chemist of American origin; patron of science and amateur archaeologist; he was born in a log cabin at Almond, Wisconsin, 21 Aug. 1835, son of the Revd Solomon Cummings W., farmer and missionary, and Mary Curtis; he was educated at frontier schools, and then qualified at the Philadelphia College of Pharmacy; he was apprenticed to several American firms, and at this period explored the cinchona forests of Peru and Ecuador; in 1885 he was awarded the Royal Humane Soc. Medal for life-saving; Wellcome came to England in 1880 and with the American S. M. Burroughs founded the firm of Burroughs, Wellcome Co., chemical and pharmaceutical manufacturers; he became sole owner after 1895; he founded the Physiological Research Laboratories, 1894, and chemical research laboratories, 1896; also the tropical research laboratories at Khartoum, 1901, and the Wellcome Historical Medical Museum, 1913; he left nearly all his great wealth to these and other institutions through the Wellcome Foundation; FRS, 1932; knighted 1932; LLD Edinburgh; DSc; Hon. FRCS Eng.; Officer of the Légion d'honneur, 1936; in 1901 he married Gwendoline Maude Syrie, daughter of Thomas Barnardo; he divorced her in 1916 and she married the novelist Somerset Maugham; he was naturalized British, 1910; his interest in exploration seems to have been encouraged by his friendship with H. M. Stanley, and he conducted Archaeological and Ethnological expeditions in the Upper Nile regions of the Sudan, 1901, himself directing excavations at a late neolithic site at Gebel Moya, and employing others to dig for him elsewhere; in all he excavated four sites in the Fung area, Gebel Moya, Abu Geili, Sequadi and Dar el-Melik, 1910-14; the enormous labour force, 500 men rising to 3,000 at times, made for staff difficulties in supervision, and a huge amount of archaeological material was brought back to England and stored in depots and warehouses at Dartford, Marylebone, Stanmore and Willesden; to this material must be added further collections that he acquired by purchase which related to areas outside the Nile valley; he was a pioneer of aerial photography both for exploration and surveying archaeological sites, and used kites with aerial cameras attached in his work; between the 1890s and his death in 1936 he formed an enormous collection of objects, books, and manuscripts on medical, anthropological, and social topics, which formed the Wellcome Historical Medical Museum, partly dispersed after his death; this contained a very valuable and large collection of Egyptian antiquities, much material deriving from excavations supported by Wellcome and includes a substantial number of objects from the EES excavations at El-Amarna and Armant, and from Garstang's work at Meroe; he also purchased a considerable number of items at the sale of the MacGregor (q.v.) Collection in 1922 and other sales of this period such as those of the Rustafjaell (q.v.), Meux (q.v.), and Hilton Price (q.v.) collections; much of this was presented by his Trustees to University College London in Nov. 1964, to be incorporated in the Petrie Collection; other portions of his Egyptological collections were distributed to the British Museum and other British museums, including Durham, Swansea, Birmingham and Bolton; some papers are in the Griffith Institute, Oxford; he died in London, 25 July 1936.

ODNB 57, 99-1001 (portr.); *DNB,* 1931-1940, 894-5, *PEQ* 1936, 171-2; *Sudan Notes and Records* xxxvii(1956), R. Kirk, 'Sir Henry Wellcome and the Sudan'; *WWW* iii, 1434; R. R. James, *Henry Wellcome,* 1994; K. Arnold and D. Olsen (eds), *Medicine Man: The Forgotten Museum of Henry Wellcome,* 2003; F. Larson, *An Infinity of Things,* 2009.

WELLSTED, James Raymond (1805-1842)
British Naval officer and surveyor; Lieut. in the East India Co.'s surveying-ship in the Red Sea, 1830-3; he visited Upper Egypt and made measurements of the Theban temples and Dendera, 1834; he surveyed Socotra island, 1834, and visited Oman, 1835-7; he retired through ill health, 1839; he published *Travels in Arabia*, 2 vols. 1828 (Province of Oman; Peninsula of Sinai: Red Sea Coast); *Travels in the City of the Caliphs*, 1840; he died in London, 25 Oct. 1842.

ODNB 58, 79-80; *DNB* 60, 236; Hilmy, ii, 324; St. John, *Eg. and Moh. Ali,* i, 318; ii, 38, 133, 135.

WENDORF, (Denver) Fred (1924-2015)
American prehistorian and archaeologist; he was born in Terrell,Texas, 31 July 1924, son of Denver Fred Wendorf, dealer in autoparts, and Margaret Hall; he studied anthropology at the University of Arizona 1942-3 when he joined the armed forces and served in World War II, being wounded in action in Italy; he resumed his studies after the war, 1947; BA in anthropology, 1948; he then studied at the University of Harvard, 1948-53; PhD, 1953; Hon. D of Science from SMU, 2003; he undertook archaeological work in New Mexico and Texas; he worked as research archaeologist for the Museum of New Mexico and then joined Texas Technological University in the anthropological faculty, 1956-8 and served also as director of the Fort Burgwin Research Center, 1956-76; he became associate director of the Museum of New Mexico, 1958-64; he was appointed professor at the Southern Methodist University, 1964-2002 founding its anthropology department; he formed the Combined Prehistoric Expedition to take part in the Nubian rescue campaign, 1962-7 concentrating on palaeolithic sites; he continued its work in Egypt near Edfu and Esna, 1967, at Maskhatma and Dishna near Luxor, 1968; in the Faiyum, 1969; at Dakhla, 1972; Wadi Kubbaniya, 1978 and 1981-4; Bir Sahara and Bir Tarwafi in the Western Desert, 1973-4 and 1985-8; Bir Kiseiba, 1979-80; Dag Dag Safsaf, 1985, Bir Misaha, 1985, Nabta Playa 1974-7, 1990-4, 1996-9, 2001; Gebel Nabta, 1977, 1994, 1997; and near Esna, 1995; he retired as director of the Combined Prehistoric Expedition, 1999; he donated his collection of antiquities to the British Museum, 2001; he became a member of the National Academy of Sciences, 1987; he was treasurer of the Society for American Archaeology, 1974 and president, 1978; he served as president of the Society of Professional Archaeologists, 1995-7; he was awarded the Egyptian Geological Survey Award by the Supreme Council of Antiquities in Egypt, 1974, the Distinguished Service Medal for Conservation Service by the US Min. of the Interior, 1988, the Lucy Wharton Drexel Medal for Archaeological Achievement by the University of Pennsylvania, 1996, and the Egyptian Geological Survey Award, 1997; apart from numerous articles, he edited *The Prehistory of Nubia*, 1968 and published, with R. Schild, *A Middle Stone Age Sequence from the Central Rift Valley*, 1974; with R. Schild, *Prehistory of the Nile Valley*, 1976; with R. Schild, *Prehistory of the Eastern Sahara*, 1980; with others, *Cattle-Keepers of the Eastern Sahara*, 1984; *The Prehistory of the Wadi Kubbaniya* I-III, 1986-9; with others, *Egypt during the Last Interglacial*, 1993; with others, *Holocene Settlement of the Egyptian Sahara* I, 2001; *Desert Days: My Life as a Field Archaeologist*, 2008; he died in Dallas, 15 July 2015.

Sudan and Nubia 19 (2015), 181-4 (R. Schild); Internet obit.

WERBROUCK, Marcelle (1889-1959)
Belgian Egyptologist; she was born at Antwerp, 23 May 1889, daughter of General Auguste W.; after having been introduced to J. Capart (q.v.); she became interested in Egyptology; she studied at the École du Louvre and gained the degree of Doctor of the Institut Supérieur d'Histoire de l'Art et d'Archéologie; she was sent several times to Egypt by the Fondation Égyptologique Reine Élisabeth, and helped Capart to produce his two large books on Thebes and Memphis; she also worked in both the Foundation and at the Cinquantenaire Museum, Brussels; assistant director under Capart; Keeper of Egyptian Antiquities and Director after Capart; she wrote 159 books, articles, and reviews between 1922 and 1959; *Thebes, The Glory of a Great Past*, 1926; *La tombe de Nakht*, with B. van de Walle, 1929; *Musées royaux d'Art et d'Histoire, Bruxelles; Département ég. Album*, 1934; *Les pleureuses dans l'Égypte ancienne*, 1938; *Iconographie de Nekhabit* in *Fouilles de El-Kab*, 1940; *Le temple d'Hatshepsout à Deir el Bahari*, 1949; *Ostraca à figures*, 1953; she died at Issoire, 1 Aug. 1959.

AfO 19 (1959-60), 260 (H. Brunner); *Chron. d'Ég.* 34 (1959), 187-91 (P. Gilbert) (bibl.), 192-202 (R. Marquebreucq); 35 (1960), 5-9; inf. J.-M. Bruffaerts.

WESSELY, Carl Franz Josef (1860-1931)
Austrian papyrologist; he was born in Vienna, 27 June 1860, son of Anton W., an engineer, and Karoline Moranetz; he studied at Vienna University, PhD, 1883; he was a schoolmaster in Vienna until 1889, but between 1883 and 1888 he visited Paris, Leipzig, Dresden and Berlin to study Greek papyri; from 1883 he was a voluntary unpaid

assistant in the Archduke Rainer's collection which in 1899 was incorporated in the Hofbibliothek, Vienna; Privatdocent in Palaeography and Papyrology, Vienna University, 1919; Corr. Member of the Bologna Acad.; Member of the Vienna Acad., 1893; he made many contributions to papyrological literature, his two memoirs on the magical papyri (1888, 1893) being perhaps the best-known; he died at Vienna, 21 Nov. 1931.

Aegyptus 12 (1932), 250; *Archiv f. Papyruskunde*, 10, 314; *JEA* 18 (1932), 104; Kürschner 1931; C.R. Gregory, *Die Schriften von K. Wessely zu seinem 50. Geburtstag,* Leipzig, 1910; *Rev. Arch.* 5e serie 135 (1932), 137; M. Capasso (ed.), *Hermae*, 2007, 71-5 (portr.).

WESSETZKY, Vilmos (1909-1997)
Hungarian Egyptologist; he was born in Budapest, 2 Feb. 1909, son of Márton W. and Albina Ilona Rezek; he studied at the Pázmany Péter University in Budapest under Mahler (q.v.); PhD, 1934 with a thesis on heart scarabs; he then worked in the Museum of Fine Arts and the Budapest Library; he studied in Vienna under Czermak (q.v.), 1940-3; he then returned to work in the library; he obtained a post in the Museum of Fine Arts in 1953; head of the Egyptian Department, 1957-75; he also taught at Eötvös University, 1949-97; hon. Professor of the University and Doctor of Sciences from the Hungarian Academy of Sciences; he was honoured with a Festschrift in *Studia Aegyptiaca* I (1974) and one in Hungarian in 1983; his principal publications were *Egytomi Kiallitas*, with E. Varga, 1955 rev, ed. 1964 illustrating the Egyptian collection of the Museum of Fine Arts, Budapest; *Die ägyptischen Kulte zur Römerzeit in Ungarn*, 1961; and a selection of his articles in *Studia Aegyptiaca* VII (1981); he died in Budapest, 6 Feb. 1997.

ZÄS 125 (1998), v-vii (portr.) (U. Luft), xiv-xx (bibl.) (L. Fóti); IAE Internet obituary (L. Kákosy); inf. G. Vörös.

WESTCAR, Henry (1798-1868)
British traveller and collector; he was born on 26 June 1798, son of Henry W. and Elizabeth Weatherstone; he was educated at Exeter College, Oxford, 1817; BWWA, 1820; MA, 1826; he visited Egypt, 1823-4, going as far south as Wadi Halfa in company with F. Catherwood (q.v.), J. J. Scoles (q.v.) and H. Parke (q.v.); he kept a full journal of the tour, the MS formerly in the possession of L. Keimer (q.v.) of Cairo is now in the German Institute, Cairo, a transcript by W. R. Dawson (q.v.) being in the British Library (Add. MS. 52283); while in Egypt, he bought horses and some antiquities; although it is not specifically mentioned, it is probable that he acquired the famous papyrus, afterwards in the possession of Lepsius (q.v.), and now known by his name; the journal is of great value for the information it supplies on the movements of other travellers, collectors, and dealers; he died at Brenchley, Kent 18 Oct. 1868. See next entry.

Inf. G. Rowland (descendant); *Al. Oxon.*; MS Journal; Madox, i, 404; R. Herzog, *MDAIK* 24 (1969), 201-11; H. Schmidt, *Westcar on the Nile*, 2012.

WESTCAR, Mary (1781-1844)
Cousin of above; she was baptized at Whitchurch, Bucks., 27 Feb. 1781, only child of John W. of Creslow Manor, Bucks. and Mary Hedges, her mother dying soon after, 14 March; her father (*d.*1833) was a large landowner and breeder of pedigree cattle and a friend and neighbour of Dr. Lee (q.v.) of Hartwell; she married Edmund Turberville, RN, 3 June 1819; Lepsius (q.v.) alleged that the Westcar Papyrus was given to him in 1838 by Miss Mary W. which is impossible as she had ceased to be this on her marriage nearly 20 years before and was in any case living in Italy at the time of his visit to England; it is thus much more likely that the papyrus was brought to England in 1824 by her cousin Henry (q.v.), the only member of the family who visited Egypt, and that he gave it to Dr. Lee; Lepsius visited Lee at Hartwell in 1838, and probably borrowed the papyrus from him and did not return it; this would account for the fact that he never published it nor deposited in the Berlin Museum, but kept it in his private possession all his life; it was found amongst his papers and presented to the museum by his son after his death; the statements contained in the preface to Erman's edition of the text are therefore erroneous, and the papyrus cannot in any way be associated with Mary Westcar (Turberville); she died in Cheltenham, 12 March 1844.

Inf. G Rowland (descendant); Erman, *Die Märchen des Papyrus Westcar*, preface; G. Lipscomb, *Hist. Bucks.*, iii. 520; O'Byrne, *Naval Biogr.*, 1214; Whitchurch Parish Register.

WESTENDORF, Wolfhart (1924-2018)
German Egyptologist; he was born in Schwiebus (Swiebodzin), Poland, 18 Sept. 1924, son of Otto W., a banker, and Charlotte Mechler; he was educated at Humboldt University in Berlin; PhD, 1951; Habilitation, 1961; he worked as an assistant on the *Wörterbuch* project in Berlin under Grapow (q.v.) and was attached to the Berlin Academy, 1951-62; he served as lecturer at the University of Munich, 1962-5, professor 1965-7, and professor at Göttingen, 1967-89; he was the co-editor of *Lexikon der Ägyptologie* and *Göttinger Orientforschungen.*Three volumes were published in his honour, *Studien zu Sprache und Religions Ägyptens*, 1984; H. Behlmer, ... *Quaerentes Scientiam*, 1994; and C. Peust (ed.), *Miscellanea in honorem Wolfhart Westendorf*, 2008; apart from munerous articles, he

published *Der Gebrauch des Passivs in der klassichen Literatur der Ägypter*, 1953; with H. Grapow and H. Deines, *Grundriss der Medizin der alten Ägypter* 4, 1958; 7/1, 1961;7/2, 1962; 8: *Grammatik der medizinischen Texte*, 1962; 9, 1973; *Altägyptische Darstellungen des Sonnenlaufs auf der abschüssigen Himmelsbahn*, 1966; *Papyrus Edwin Smith*, 1966; *Das alte Ägypten*, 1968; *Koptisches Handwörterbuch*, 1977; *Das Aufkommen der Gottesvorsellung*, 1985; *Bemerkungen und Korrekturen zum Lexikon der Ägyptologie*, 1989; *Bemerkungen und Korrekturen zum Lexikon der Ägyptologie. Index*, 1990; *Erwachen der Heilkunst*, 1992, and *Handbuch der altägyptischen Medizin*, 1998; he died in Berlin, 23 Feb. 2018

Wer ist Wer 2015/6, 1071; *Studien zu Sprache und Religions Ägyptens*, 1984, 13-21 (bibl.); H. Behlmer (ed.), *...Quaerentes Scientiam*, 1984, 9-12 (C. Müller).

WESTREENEN VAN TIELLANDT (*Baron*) **William Hendrik Jacob van** (1783-1848)
Dutch collector; he was born at The Hague, 2 Oct. 1783, son of Johann Adriaan van W. and Maria Catherina Dierkens; as a result of his historical studies, he was appointed assistant keeper in the royal archives in 1807 but later resigned on the annexation of Holland by France; he supported the restoration of the House of Orange and was created a baron in 1821; in 1842 he was appointed Keeper of the Royal Library at the Hague; he wrote a number of studies on Dutch printing and archaeology; he formed a collection of antiquities including Egyptian objects, some of which were purchased from the De Lescluze (q.v.) collection; he left his collection and library to the State, now the Meermanno-Westreenianum Museum in the Hague; he died at The Hague, 22 Nov. 1848.

Nieu Nederlandsch Biografisch Woordenboek iv, 447; *Biog. Univ.* 44,517; F. J. E. Boddens Hosang, *De Egyptische Verzameling van Baron van Westreenen*, 1989.

WEYNANTS-RONDAY, Marie Claire (1895-1951)
Belgian Egyptologist; born 1895; a student of Capart (q.v.), in 1922 she wrote a study on *Monuments égyptiens périptères*, in 1926 her thesis *Les statues vivantes* was published; she contributed a number of articles to *Chronique d'Égypte*, and also published some of the unedited letters of Mariette (q.v.); she died 13 Nov. 1951.

Chron. d'Ég. 27 (1952), 145-7 (M. Werbrouck).

WHITE, (*Revd*) **Joseph** (1746-1814)
British orientalist and theologian; he was born in Ruscombe, Gloucs. and baptized at Stroud 19 Feb. 1746, son of Thomas W., a weaver, and Elizabeth Harmer; he was educated at Wadham College, Oxford; BA, 1769; MA, 1773; DD, 1787; he married Mary Turner 1790; he was appointed Laudian Professor of Arabic, 1775-1814, in which position he corresponded with Silvestre de Sacy (q.v.); he edited biblical and other oriental texts; he published *Aegyptiaca*, 1801, and also edited Abdullatif's *Description of Egypt*; he died at Oxford, 23 May 1814.

ODNB 58, 600-1 (portr.); *DNB* 61, 62-3; Hilmy, ii, 326; *GM* 84 (1814), 626-8.

WHITE, Rachel Evelyn (1867-1943)
British classical scholar; she was born at Aberdeen, 13 April 1867, daughter of John Forbes W. and Ina Johnston; she was educated at Newnham College, Cambridge, 1891-5; 1st Class Classical Tripos, 1894; Associate of Newnham and College lecturer, 1897-1919; she studied Egyptology under Renouf (q.v.); she married Nathaniel Webb, MA, Fellow of King's College, Cambridge, 1906; she died 1943.

Inf. Newnham College; Renouf Corr. 291;

WHITEHOUSE, Frederic Cope (1842-1911)
American lawyer and writer; he was born in Rochester, NY, 9 Nov. 1842, son of Rt Revd Henry John W., Bishop of Illinois, and Eveline Harriet Bruen; he was educated at Columbia University; BA, 1861; MA, 1863 and later studied in France, Germany, and Italy; called to the Bar, 1871; he made a prolonged stay in Egypt and discovered in 1882 the Wadi Raiyan in the Fayum, a vast depression which he connected with the ancient Lake Moeris; he made a special study of this little-explored region and published many articles on it; he also wrote on ethnology and geology; he died in New York, 16 Nov. 1911.

Hilmy, ii, 326, 457; *WWWA* i, 1337; Wilbour, 373; 20, 132-3; *New York Times* 17 Nov. 1911 (courtesy of R. Ansell and P. Spencer).

WHITTEMORE, Thomas (1871-1950)

American educator, philanthropist, and supporter of archaeology; he was born in Cambridgeport, Mass., 2 Jan. 1871, son of Joseph W. and Elizabeth St Clair; he received his BA in English Literature from Tufts College; he lectured at Tufts College, Columbia University, and New York University on English and Byzantine and Coptic art; his connection with Egyptology began while serving as American representative for the EES and assisting in excavations at Abydos, Sawama, Balabish, and El-Amarna; he contributed archaeological preliminary reports to *JEA*; Keeper of Byzantine Coins and Seals in the Fogg Museum, Harvard University; Founder and Director of the Byzantine Institute; he is perhaps best remembered for his work on the conservation and restoration of the mosaics in Hagia Sophia carried out with the permission of the Turkish Govt., 1931; he died in Washington, D.C., 8 June 1950.

Numismatic Circular, 58, col. 378; The Times, 9 June 1950; WWWA 3, 913. Photograph © Dumbarton Oaks, Image Collections and Fieldwork Archives, Washington, DC.

WHYTE, Edward Towry (1847-1932)

British antiquary, architect and traveller; he was born at Stanwix, Cumberland, 19 June 1847, son of Admiral Henry Towry White and Matilda Jameson; he was educated at Pembroke College, Cambridge; FSA, 1894; he travelled in Egypt and published articles on Egyptian antiquities in *PSBA* and other journals; his collection is largely in the Fitzwilliam Museum, Cambridge, he died at Fittleworth, Sussex, 20 April 1932.

Al. Cantab. vi, pt. 2; *Ant. Journ.* 12. 352; Griffith Corr. 376.

WIEDEMANN, Karl Alfred (1856-1936)

German Egyptologist; he was born in Berlin, 18 July 1856, younger son of Gustav Heinrich W. (1826-99) a well-known physicist, and Laura Mitscherlich; he studied under Ebers (q.v.), then Maspero (q.v.) and Lepsius (q.v.), taking his doctorate at Leipzig 1878 and his habilitation at the University of Bonn, 1883; he was appointed Professor of Egyptology at Bonn, 1891; Hon. Professor, 1908; Ordinarius Professor, 1920; retiring in 1924 although he continued to teach until 1928; he wrote many books and articles on every branch of Egyptology, and published the latter in all the oriental journals of his day; his history and study of the religion of ancient Egypt were translated into English; see *Sammlung altägyptischer Wörter welche von klassischen Autoren umschrieben oder übersetzt worden sind*, 1883; *Ägyptische Geschichte*, 2 vols., 1884; *The Ancient Egyptian doctrine of the immortality of the soul*, 1895; *Religion of the ancient Egyptians*, 1897; *Popular literature in ancient Egypt*, trans. J. Hutchinson, 1902; *The Realms of the Egyptian dead, according to the belief of the ancient Egyptians*, trans. J. Hutchinson, 1902; *Das Alte Ägypten*, 1920; he also made an index of gods and demon names for the Lepsius, *Denkmäler* text and contributed a chapter to Petrie's *Medum*; he died in Bonn, 7 Dec. 1936.

Chron. d'Ég. 12 (1937), 232-3 (J. Capart); *Nature*, 139 (July 1937), 1045 (F.W. Freih. v Bissing); *ZÄS* 73 (1937), unnumbered page at front (H. Bonnet); Hilmy, ii, 328; O. Wenig, *Verzeichnis der Professoren und Dozenten der Rheinischen, Friedrich-Williams-University zu Bonn 1818-1968*, 1970.

WIJNGAARDEN, Willem Dirk van (1893-1980)

Dutch Egyptologist; he was born in Nieu Amsterdam, 26 June 1893, son of Corstiaan v. W. and Cornelia Amarantha van Doorn; he was educated at the Leiden Gymnasium, 1906-12 and then the University of Leiden, 1912-19 where he studied Egyptology under Boeser (q.v.) and Semitic literature; Dr theol. 1919; 1919-20 he studied at the University of Berlin; he was appointed a research assistant at the Rijksmuseum van Oudheden 1 Aug. 1922; Keeper of Egyptian Antiquities, 1 Jan. 1925 in succession to Boeser; Director of the Museum 1 Aug. 1939-29 April 1959; his publications include *Beschrijving van de Egypt. verzam. in het Rs. Mus. van oudh. te Leiden*, dl. XIII *Lijkvazen en lijkvazenkisten*, 1926; dl. XIV *Grafborden en papyruskokers*, 1932; *Het book der wijsheid van Amen-em-ope, de zoon van Kanecht*, 1930; *Van Hernius tot Boeser*, 1935; *Messterwerken der Egyptische Kunst te Leiden*, 1938; *De Grieks-Egyptische terracottas in het Rijksmuseum van Oudeheden*, 1958; he died at Leiden, 3 Oct. 1980.

Phoenix 27 (1981), 3-4 (Heerma van Voss); *Wie is dat*, 1948, 573; inf M. Raven.

WILBOUR, Charles Edwin (1833-1896)
American businessman and traveller; he was born Little Compton, RI, 17 March 1833, son of Charles W. and Sarah Soule; he attended Brown University, 1850-2, leaving due to ill-health; he moved to New York, 1854, and became a court reporter at the New York *Tribune*; he was admitted to the New York Bar in 1859, but never practised; he was a gifted linguist, and his translations of Victor Hugo's *Les Miserables*, and *The Life of Christ* by Renan (q.v.) enjoyed great popularity; in the 1860s and 70s he became wealthy through his association with the 'ring' of Democratic Party official William M. Tweed; upon its exposure in the 1870s, Wilbour left the United States for Europe in 1874; there he studied Egyptology under Maspero (q.v.) in Paris and also in Berlin and in Heidelberg under Eisenlohr (q.v.); he first visited Egypt in 1880, and thereafter; his life was spent alternately in Egypt and in France; whilst he had considerable knowledge of Egyptian language and archaeology, he published almost nothing, and was a spectator rather than a worker in the field; he was an accurate copyist of texts and supplied many of his colleagues with material; for several winters he was Maspero's guest on the Antiquities Service steamer, before buying his own dahabiya, *The Seven Hathors*; his acute observations, fully detailed in his letters, were published by the Brooklyn Museum in 1936; he formed a valuable collection of antiquities which, with his fine library and MSS, are now in the Brooklyn Museum, where his son Victor later established an endowment to maintain the Egyptological collections and library, now known as the Wilbour Library of Egyptology; the Wilbour Professorship of Egyptology was later established in his memory at Brown University, Providence, RI; his name is particularly associated with the great papyrus of the reign of Ramesses V, edited by Sir Alan Gardiner, which was purchased as a memorial to him; a catalogue of his library was published by the Brooklyn Museum as *Catalogue of the Egyptological Library and Other Books*, 1924; he died in Paris, 17 Dec. 1896.

J. Capart, *Travels in Egypt* (Wilbour Letters) 1936 (portr.); Maspero, *L'Égyptologie*, 1915; *Sphinx* i, 254; inf. J. Adams and T. Hardwick.

WILCKEN, Ulrich Emil Elias Friedrich Wilhelm (1862-1944)
German papyrologist; he was born in Stettin, 18 Dec. 1862, son of Heinrich W., a merchant, and Pauline Krüger; he studied at Leipzig under Ebers (q.v.) and Meyer (q.v.), at Tübingen and at Berlin under Mommsen and Erman (q.v.), 1881-3; PhD, 1885; Privatdocent, Berlin, 1888; he held lectureships or professorships at Breslau, Würzburg, Halle, Leipzig, Bonn, and Munich, 1889-1915; Professor at Berlin, 1917-31, and on his retirement Professor Emeritus; PhD; DJur; Hon. DLitt, Oxford; Member of Berlin Acad., and Foreign or Corr. Member of the Acads. of Saxony, Bavaria, Göttingen, Vienna, Turin (Lincei), Oslo, Leningrad, Cracow, Amsterdam, Athens and London (Brit. Acad.); he excavated with Schäfer (q.v.) at Herakleopolis Magna (Ihnasya), 3 Jan.-21 March 1899; his report was published in of *Archiv für Papyrusforschung* 2 (1902), 294-336; he was the founder and editor of *Archiv für Papyrusforschung*, 1901-41; he was the foremost papyrologist of his generation and his publications are both numerous and important; he died in Baden-Baden, 10 Dec. 1944.

Bildnisse berühmter Mitgleider der Deutschen Akad. der Wiss. zu Berlin, 1950, 105 (potr); *Chron.d'Ég.* 23 (1948), 250-6 (C. Préaux); Erman, 194, 201, 220, 283; *Gnomon* 21 (1949). 88 (W. Schubart); *JEA* 31 (1945), 2 (H. I. Bell); Kürschner, 1931; E. Endesfelder, *Die Ägyptologie an der Berliner Universität-zur Geschichte eines Fachgebietes,* 1988, 26; M. Capasso (ed.), *Hermae,* 2007, 82-96 (portr.).

WILD, Henri (1902-1983)
Swiss Egyptologist; he was born at St. Imier, 27 Aug. 1902; he was educated at the Collège de Genève, graduating in 1925; he obtained a position as a French teacher at an American college in Asyut, Egypt where his interest in Egyptology was aroused; he went to Paris to acquire a degree to teach French but in 1933 decided to follow a career in Egyptology; he attended classes at the École du Louvre, at the École Pratique, at the Institut Catholique, and at the Collège de France; he obtained his diploma from the Louvre in 1938 with a thesis *La Danse dans l'Égypte ancienne*; in 1938 he joined the French Institute in Cairo but passed World War II in Switzerland where he compiled an inventory of Egyptian antiquities in Swiss collections; he was attached to the French Institute in Cairo from 1945-72 apart from a period in 1950-2 when he was in Europe for hospital treatment as the result of an accident; he took part in the excavations at Qasr Qarun in 1948 and acted as epigraphist at Saqqara and Deir el-Medina; his publications included *Qasr-Qarun/Dionysias 1948,* with J. Schwartz, 1950; *Le Tombeau de Ti* fasc. 2-3, 1953-66; *Antiquités égyptiennes de la collection du Dr. Widmer,* 1956; *Qasr-Qarun/Dionysias 1950,* with J. Schwartz, 1969; and *La Tombe de Néfer.hotep (I) et Néb.nefer à Deir el Medina (No. 6) et autres documents les concernant* II, 1979; he died at St. Imier, 21 Sept. 1983.

BSEG 9-10 (1984-5), 7-14 (portr.) (bibl.) (C. Maystre); *BSFE* 99(1984), 6; *Voyages en Égypte de l'Antiquité au début du XXe siècle*, 2003, 226-7 (M. Vallogia).

WILD, James William (1814-1892)

British architect; he was born in Lincoln, 9 March 1814, son of Charles W., a painter, and Margaret Gelling; a pupil of George Basevi, he accompanied as a volunteer the expedition of Lepsius (q.v.) to Egypt in 1842 and remained during the exploration of Lower Egypt, but then stayed in Cairo to study Arabic architecture; he returned to England in 1848, where he designed many buildings and was decorative architect to the Great Exhibition of 1851; he was curator of Sir John Soane's Museum in London, 1878-92 in succession to Bonomi (q.v.); his note-books and drawings are in the Griffith Inst., Oxford; he was the last survivor of Lepsius's expedition at his death in London, 7 Nov. 1892.

ODNB 58, 895-7; *DNB* 61, 221; EEF *Arch. Report,* 1892-3, 27; Lepsius, 12, 35, 56.

WILD, Johann (1585-1611+)

German traveller; he was baptized at Sebald Nuremberg, 19 Oct, 1585, son of Hans W. and his wife Catherine; in early life Wild may have received a classical education as he later refers to a number of classical authors in his account of his travels; he seems to have left his own country and gone to Hungary as a professional soldier, and while fighting with the imperial forces of Rudolf II he was made prisoner by the Hungarians at St. Andra on 27 or 28 Dec. 1604, and sold ten days later to a Turk who ceded him to a colonel; when his master died, he was next sold to an officer of Janissaries and after other adventures he reached Constantinople where his second master was poisoned, and he was sold for sixty ducats to a slave merchant; he was next taken to Egypt and sold to a Persian, with whom he made the pilgrimage to Mecca; he returned by boat to Suez and Cairo, where his master left with a caravan for Jerusalem and Damascus; finally on returning to Cairo, Wild was sold to a Turk who at the end of a year freed him, 1609; his boat was shipwrecked, but eventually he returned to Germany via Poland, 1611; his published account of his adventures, *Reysbeschreibung eines Gefangenen Christen Anno 1604,* is of interest to the Egyptologist but does not give the detail or information of some of the other travellers of this period; he briefly describes some of the antiquities of Alexandria in Book II, Chapter 3, but in general does not give much description of Egyptian monuments; Book III, Chapter 31 is best and has an account of the Giza pyramids here called 'the Egyptian columns', and states that many bizarre figures of men and animals were carved on them; he also noted the entrance in the middle one but says that no one was allowed inside; another reference is to the obelisk of Senusret I at Mataria and to its being near the ancient wall, he observed the hieroglyphs on it and tried to guess their purpose if not meaning; his subsequent life and the date of his death are still not established.

Voyages en Egypte. Johann Wild, 1606-1610, trans. and annotated by Oleg V. Volkoff, 1973.

WILKINSON, Alexandra (Alix) Helen (*née* Macfarlane) (1932-2011)

British Egyptologist; she was born in Cheltenham, 8 Feb. 1932, daughter of Henry Macfarlane and Bertha Stevens; she studied Ancient History at University College London and later worked in the Dept. of Egyptian Antiquities, British Museum under Edwards (q.v.) as research assistant 1958-69; she also excavated in Serbia and Jericho; in 1966 she married John Wilkinson (born Wimbledon, 28 March 1929, died London, 13 Jan. 2018), Dean of St George's College, Jerusalem, 1969-75 and Director of the British School of Archaeology, 1979-84, son of Revd Donald W. and Hilda Smyth; she obtained a PhD in Linguistics at Georgetown University in Washington; she was secretary of the Association for the Study of Travel in Egypt and the Near East, 2004-6; she published *Ancient Egyptian Jewellery,* 1971; and *The Garden in Ancient Egypt,* 1998; she died in London, 28 Jan. 2011.

Inf. J. Wilkinson and Y. Neville-Rolfe; *ASTENE Bulletin* 47 (2011), 2-3.

WILKINSON, Charles Kyrle (1897-1986)

British artist and museum curator; he was born in London, 13 Oct. 1897, son of Horace W., a stained-glass-window maker, and Frances Adkins; he was educated at the Slade School of Art after serving in World War I; in 1920 he joined the Metropolitan Museum of Art's excavation team at Thebes as a graphic artist and worked with Davies (q.v.) in Egypt until 1931; he took part in excavations in Iran; he was appointed Curator of Ancient Near Eastern Art at the Metropolitan Museum in 1956; he retired in 1963 as curator emeritus; he held the position of Hagop Kevorkian Curator of Middle Eastern Art and Archaeology at The Brooklyn Museum 1970-74; he was responsible for copying many Theban tomb paintings which he published in *Egyptian Wall Paintings. The Metropolitan Museum of Art's Collection of Facsimiles,* 1983; he died in Sharon, Connecticut, 18 April 1986.

Inf. C. Lilyquist.

WILKINSON, (*Sir*) John Gardner (1797-1875)

British Egyptologist and traveller; he was probably born in Little Missenden, Bucks, 5 Oct 1797, son of the Revd John W. and Mary Anne Gardner; Wilkinson may be regarded as the real founder of Egyptology in Great Britain; he was educated at Harrow, 1813-16, where he came under the influence of the head master, George Butler (q.v.) who

was a friend of Thomas Young (q.v.) and an erstwhile student of his in the decipherment of Egyptian hieroglyphs; he entered Exeter College, Oxford, 1816, but left in 1818 without taking a degree; he embarked on a tour of Europe and Egypt in 1819 prior to joining the army, visiting Italy in 1820 where he met Sir William Gell (q.v.) who first persuaded him to abandon his intended army career and devote his life to the study of Egyptian and other archaeology; possessed of a small income, Wilkinson was able to take up the study of Egyptian hieroglyphic writing as yet incompletely deciphered and not properly understood, and went to Egypt in 1821, where he remained for no fewer than 12 years continuously, except for visits to Nubia and the surrounding deserts; he journeyed as far south as the Second Cataract twice, and carried out excavations at Thebes in 1824, 1827-8; he worked mainly among the tombs as he did not have the resources to engage in greater works; while in Egypt he also studied Arabic and Coptic, learning the latter like Champollion (q.v.) so that it might help him in his work of deciphering inscriptions which he accomplished by dint of hard work and the study of all the material available but also by using and at times correcting his results; there was at this date probably nobody else capable of doing this; after gathering an immense amount of material Wilkinson returned to England, 1833; he was made FRS, 1834; knighted, 1839; DCL, Oxford University, 1852; he revisited Egypt in 1841-2 and surveyed the Natron lakes, publishing an account of his travels, 1843; in 1843-4 he made a great survey of Montenegro, Herzegovina, and Bosnia and published an account of this expedition in two vols.; he visited Egypt again in 1843 and 1848-9, and spent the following winter in Italy, 1849-50; here he studied the Turin Canon of Kings more thoroughly than it had ever been done before, and published a new facsimile; he visited Egypt for the last time, 1855-6; in 1856 he married Caroline Catherine Lucas, a botanist and authoress; he was the first to recognize correctly many royal names and to sort out and put into a reasonable chronological order the dynasties and kings of Egypt; the first to make an adequate working survey of all the main sites in Egypt and Nubia from an archaeological and historical point of view, which he did single-handed unlike the teams who made the French general survey or who assisted Champollion and Lepsius (q.v.) afterwards; the first to draw up a *comprehensive* plan of ancient Thebes; he preceded both Champollion and Rosellini (q.v.) at Beni Hasan where he made very exact drawings of paintings in the tombs, and where, as at El-Amarna and many other sites throughout Egypt, he noted important archaeological and historical material before other Egyptologists; he was also among the first to identify the site of the Labyrinth at Hawara and many other similar sites; most of his material has never been made available to scholars in adequate form unlike that gathered by Lepsius and other officially sponsored expeditions; he took a prominent part in all archaeological movements in his day and occupied a position in Egyptology analogous to Rawlinson in Assyrian archaeology; he collected natural history specimens, on which he made many important contributions to zoological and geological journals; he was a considerable benefactor to the British Museum, to which he presented many antiquities including articles of furniture and smaller objects connected with daily life such as bread and tools in 1834; these were from tombs and were acquired or excavated by him during his early years in Egypt; he also gave two large collections of papyri (mostly Demotic) in 1834 and 1835; in order to interest young people in the subject he gave his own large collection of classical and Egyptian antiquities to Harrow School, a catalogue of which was published by Budge, 1887; unlike other great Egyptologists such as Champollion and Lepsius, Wilkinson received no government aid for his researches and had to accomplish his vast work on his own; his range of interests far exceeded that of most other Egyptologists before or since; in his monumental account of Egyptian manners and customs he covered, and, although not an expert in all of them, adequately dealt with, over fifty basic subjects, ranging from daily life to chronology, and from botany, astronomy, and geology to funerary beliefs; this work with his survey of modern Egypt and Thebes comprehended in about 2,700 pages the greatest review of ancient Egyptian civilization ever undertaken; during his lifetime Wilkinson was loaded with more honours than any other Egyptologist, he was Vice-Pres. of the British Archaeological Assoc.; Hon. MRIBA; Corresp. Member of Entomological Soc.; Memb. of the Ethnological Soc. of London; Hon. Corr. MRSL; Hon Memb. of the Egyptian Inst. of Alexandria; Hon. Memb. of the Ethnological and Oriental Societies of America; Corr. Member of the Bombay Branch the Roy. Asiatic Soc.; Hon. Memb. of the Egyptian Soc. of Cairo; Vice-Pres. of the Cambrian Arch Soc.; Corr. Memb. of the Arch. Soc. of Edinburgh; Vice-Pres. of the Lincoln Diocesan Soc.; Hon. Memb. of the Ethnological and Oriental Socs. of New York; Hon. Member. of the Archit. Soc. of Oxford; Hon. Member of the Oriental Soc. of Paris; Memb. of the Institute of Arch. Corr. of Rome; Corr. Memb. of the Roy. Acad. of Turin; Corr. Member of the Roy. & Imp. Acad. of Vienna; etc.; his principal publications were, *Materia Hieroglyphica. Containing the Egyptian pantheon and the succession of the Pharaohs, from the earliest Times to the Conquest by Alexander, and other Hieroglyphical Subjects*, 2 vols., 1828-30; *Extracts from several Hieroglyphical subjects found at Thebes and other parts of Egypt. With remarks on the same*, 1830; *Topographical survey of Thebes, Tape, Thaba or Diospolis Magna*, fol. includes Pyramids of Giza, 1830; *Topography of Thebes, and general view of Egypt. Being a short account of the principal objects worthy of notice in the Valley of the Nile, to the Second Cataract and Wadee Samneh, with the Fayoom, Oases, and Eastern Desert, from Sooez to Berenice: with remarks on the Manners and Customs of the ancient Egyptians and the productions of* the country etc., 1835; *Manners and Customs of the Ancient Egyptians. Including their Private Life, Government, Laws, Arts, Manufactures, Religion, Agriculture, and Early History, derived from a comparison of the painting, sculptures, and monuments still existing, with the accounts of ancient authors*, 3 vols., 1837, a number of subsequent eds., of which that revised and corrected by Samuel Birch, 3 vols. 1878 is the most popular; *Modern Egypt and Thebes. Being a* description of Egypt, including the information required for travellers in that Country, 2 vols., 1843; *A Handbook for Egypt. Including descriptions of the course of the Nile to the Second Cataract, Alexandria, Cairo, The Pyramids, and Thebes, the overland transit to India, the Peninsula of Mount Sinai, the Oases, etc.*, a new and shorter ed. of the previous work, and one which became Murray's standard guide for travellers, 1847; *The Architecture of Ancient Egypt: in which the columns are arranged in orders, and the temples classified, with remarks on the early progress of Architecture, etc.*, 2 vols., one of fol. plates, 1850; *The Fragments of the hieratic papyrus at Turin, containing the names of Egyptian Kings, with the hieratic inscription at the back*, 2 vols., fol. plates, 1851; *A popular account of the Ancient Egyptians, revised and abridged from his larger work*, 2 vols. 1854; *The Egyptians in the time of the Pharaohs. Being a Companion to the Crystal Palace Egyptian Collections. To which is added an Introduction to the Study of the Egyptian Hieroglyphs by Samuel Birch*, 1857; posth. *Desert plants of Egypt. Illustrations with descriptions, by Wm Carruthers F.R.S.*, 1887; in addition to these and articles in journals he contributed notes to Rawlinson's translation of Herodotus; Wilkinson continued his Egyptological studies to the last, and left a large mass of MSS and drawings, most of which are now deposited in the Bodleian Library, Oxford; these consist of 56 bound volumes, folders, and note-books, containing rough sketches and beautifully coloured drawings, done in great detail, and with the hieroglyphic texts very accurately copied; other pages are in the Griffith Institute, Oxford, and his squeezes are in the Department of Egyptian Antiquities, British Museum; they cover a very wide area of Egypt; he died at Llandovery in Wales, 29 Oct. 1875, and was buried there.

J. Thompson, *Sir Gardner Wilkinson and his Circle*, 1992; *ODNB* 58, 1013-5 (portr.); *DNB* 61. 274-6 (D.S. Margoliouth); Budge, *N. & T* i. 14, 25-6, 41, 71 (biased); Gardiner, *Egypt of the Pharaohs*, 15; Budge, *A Guide to the Fourth, Fifth and Sixth Egyptian Rooms, and the Coptic Room*, 1922, 28, 49, 83, 114, 136, 200, 206; *JEA* 2 (1915), 141-64 (H. R. H. Hall); 35 (1949), 13-20; *La Grande Enc.* 31. 1219; he is frequently mentioned in contemporary diaries, e.g. Hay, Bonomi, Westcar; Hilmy, ii, 330; *Griffith Studies*, 474-6 (Seymour de Ricci); R. Moss, *JEA* 62 (1976), 108-9; J. Thompson in *JEA* 78 (1992), 273-4; J. Thompson and R. Lucas in *Journal of the Gower Society* 46 (1995), 6-14; J. Thompson in *KMT* 7 (1996), 52-9; S. J. A. Flynn, *Sir John Gardner Wilkinson, Traveller and Egyptologist 1797-1875*, 1997; È. Gran-Aymerich, *Dictionnaire biographique d'archéologie 1798-1945*, 2001, incorporated in *Les Chercheurs de passé 1798-1945*, 2007, 1247-8.

WILLIAMS, Caroline Louise (*née* Ransom) (1872-1952)
American Egyptologist; she was born in Toledo, 24 Feb. 1872, daughter of John W. and Ella Randolph; she was educated at Lake Erie College and Mount Holyoke; BA, 1896; Hon. PhD, 1912; she visited Egypt and also studied under Erman (q.v.) in Berlin, 1900-3; she was a student of Breasted (q.v.); PhD Chicago University, 1905; assistant Professor, Bryn Mawr College, 1905-10; appointed assistant curator in the Metropolitan Museum, New York, 1910; she catalogued the Egyptian collection of the Cleveland Museum; she served with the Chicago Expedition in Egypt 1926-7, 1935-6; also curator of Egyptian Antiquities NY Historical Society, 1917-24; Hon. PhD, Toledo, 1937; in 1920 she brought the Edwin Smith Papyrus to Breasted's notice after it had been left unpublished for fifty years; she herself published articles in *JEA* and other journals; her main works were, *The New York Historical Society Catalogue of Egyptian Antiquities, Numbers 1-160. Gold and Silver Jewellery and Related Objects*, 1924; *The Decoration of the Tomb of Per-neb: he Technique and the Color Conventions*, 1932; her correspondence with Breasted (q.v.) was edited by K. L. Sheppard, *My dear Miss Ransom*, 2018; she died in Toledo, 1 Feb. 1952.

Toledo Blade, 2 Feb. 1952; Erman, 283; inf. B. Lesko; L. Berman, *The Cleveland Museum of Art. Catalogue of Egyptian Art*, 1999, 9-11.

WILLIAMS, John (1797-1874)
British antiquarian and astronomer; he was born in London, 19 Oct. 1797; in early life he was very interested in Egyptology, and he invented a process of taking rubbings of inscriptions and a method of taking impressions of seals, scarabs, etc.; he published an *Essay on the Hieroglyphics of the Ancient Egyptians*, 1836; much associated with John Lee (q.v.) in Egyptology and astronomy; FSA; FRAS, but resigned fellowship on joining the staff of the Royal Asiatic Society as Assistant Secretary, 1848-74; member of the Chronological Inst.; he also studied Chinese, and published many papers in this subject; his collection of Egyptian rubbings was presented to the Griffith Institute, Oxford by his grandson in 1941; he died in London, 3 Dec. 1874.

P. W. Clayden, *Life of Samuel Sharpe*, 70; Hartwell Reg.; *JEA* 27 (1941), 7-11 (R Moss); *Proc. Soc. Ant.* 2nd ser. 6. 354; *RAS Monthly Notices*, 35. 181; Boase 3, 1368.

WILLIAMS, Morgan Stuart de Aven (1846-1909)
British antiquary of Aberpergwm, Neath, and St. Donat's Castle, Llantwit Major; he was born at Aberpergwn, 25 Jan. 1846, son of William W., landowner, and Matilda Susannah Smith; he was educated at Eton and Peterhouse, Cambridge; DL; JP; High Sheriff of Glamorganshire, 1875; he had a large collection of ancient armour, on which

he was an authority, as well as other antiquities; in 1898 he presented to the British Museum Middle Kingdom and one New Kingdom stelae (EA 1244, 1246-8); he died at St. Donat's Castle, Llantwit, which was later purchased by W. R. Hearst (q.v.), 13 Dec. 1909.

WWW i, 767; *Proc. Soc. Ant.* 2nd ser. 23, 174.

WILLIAMS, Ronald James (1917-1993)
Canadian Egyptologist and Biblical scholar; he was born in Dublin, 9 May 1917, son of James W.; his family emigrated to Toronto, and he was educated at Jarvis Collegiate and Victoria College, University of Toronto, 1936-40; BA, 1940 specializing in Biblical Studies and Hebrew; Governor-General's Silver Medal, 1940; Regent's Gold Medal in Oriental Languages, 1940; he was awarded the Thayer Fellowship at the American School in Jerusalem but was unable to take it up due to the war; he then studied Egyptology at the Oriental Institute, University of Chicago and at the Divinity School there, 1940-2, and again at Toronto, 1942-3; MA, 1943; BD, Victoria University, 1943; he was ordained a minister in 1943 and briefly held a post at Snowflake, Manitoba, 1943-4; he was appointed as a lecturer and later Associate Professor in Oriental languages at the University of Toronto, 1944-57; he taught the first course in Egyptian, 1948; on leave of absence from Toronto, he served as research associate with the rank of Assistant Professor at The Oriental Institute, University of Chicago, 1 Oct. 1947-30 Sept. 1948; PhD from Chicago, 18 June 1948 with a thesis *The Morphology and Syntax of Papyrus Insinger*; Professor of Near Eastern Studies, University of Toronto, 1957-82; Chairman of the Department of Near Eastern Studies, 1967-72; Keeper of the Near Eastern Department, Royal Ontario Museum, 1947-51; Hon. Curator, 1951-4; Special Lecturer in the Department of Art and Archaeology, 1948-51; Nuffield Fellow, Oxford, 1953-4; he began the teaching of Egyptian language in Toronto in 1946; he took part in the Nubian rescue campaign at Serra East, 1961-2, and Semna South, 1966; Canada Medal, 1967; Fellow of the Royal Society of Canada, 1968; Trustee of the American School of Oriental Research, 1969-73; Governor of the American Research Center in Egypt, 1969-86; Trustee of the Society for the Study of Egyptian Antiquities, 1969-93; Hon. DD, 1991; his main interest lay in Egyptian philology and literature and Egyptian links with ancient Israel; two volumes were published in his honour *Studies in Philology in Honour of Ronald James Williams*, 1982 and *The Ancient World* VI (1983); his energies principally were directed to teaching but, in addition to *Hebrew Syntax*, 1967, 2nd ed. 1976, he wrote over fifty articles and reviews, notably a discussion of Amenemope in *JEA* 47 (1961), 100-6 and the section *Egypt and Israel* in *The Legacy of Egypt*, 2nd ed., 1971; he died in Toronto, 19 Nov. 1993.

Studies in Philology in Honour of Ronald James Williams, ed. by G. Kadish and G. Freeman, 1982, iii-iv, vii-xi (portr.), 155-160 (bibl.); *The Ancient World* VI (1983), 126-8 (bibl.); *Canadian Mediterranean Institute Bulletin* 10 (1990), 2; *Directory of American Scholars* III, 530; *SSEA Newsletter* Jan. 1994, 3 (R. Sweet); *JARCE* 31 (1994), ii-iii (R. Leprohon); inf. J. Larson.

WILSON, Edward Livingston (1838-1903)
American photographer; he was born in Flemington, NJ, 4 March 1838, son of Hart D. L. W. and Amelia C. Hart; he took a large series of photographs of Philae and other temples in Egypt, many of which were published; he went with Maspero (q.v.) and Emile Brugsch (q.v.) to make a final exploration of the tomb in which the Royal Mummies were found, in Jan. 1882; he published an account of this in an illustrated American magazine *The Century* 34, 1 (May 1887); also 'The Temples of Egypt' in *Scribner's Mag.* 4 Oct. 1888, 387; he died at Vineland, New Jersey, 23 June 1903.

Maspero, Les Momies Royales, 520; Wilbour, 125; *WWWA* 1, 1360; *KMT* 20/4 (2009-10), 60-8.

WILSON, John Albert (1899-1976)
American Egyptologist; he was born at Pawling, New York, 12 Sept. 1899, son of Warren H. W. and Pauline E. Lane; he was educated at Princeton, B.A. 1920, the American University of Beirut, 1920-3, MA 1923, during which time he taught English there, and on a fellowship, at the Oriental Institute, Chicago, 1923-6 where he studied under Breasted (q.v.), PhD 1926; in 1925 he was appointed secretary of the Haskell Oriental Museum, Chicago and from 1926-31 he was an epigraphist with the Chicago Epigraphic Survey in Luxor; Assistant Professor at Chicago, 1931-5, Associate Professor, 1935-6, Professor, 1936-68, Andrew MacLeish Distinguished Service Professor of Egyptology, 1952-68; Director of the Oriental Institute Chicago, 1936-46 (except 1942-4 when he undertook war work in Washington) and 1960-1; Fulbright scholar in Egypt, 1952-3; Director of Chicago House, Luxor, 1958-9; DLitt from Princeton, 1961; Professor Emeritus, 1968-76; from 1960-72 he served on the UNESCO Committee to save the Nubian monuments; founder member of ARCE and President 1971-4;

in 1968 the John A Wilson Professorship of Oriental Studies was established at Chicago in his honour; he was primarily responsible for the survival of the Oriental Institute following the death of Breasted and the cessation of funds during the depression and World War II; although he considered himself a grammarian and a teacher, his publications covered the wider area of Egyptian culture; he contributed to *Medinet Habu Studies 1928/9*, 1930 and the final report *Medinet Habu* Vols. I-VII, 1930-1964; his other publications include *Historical Records of Ramses III* with W. Edgerton, 1936; *The Intellectual Adventure of Ancient Man* with H. Frankfort, T. Jacobsen and W. Irwin, 1946, later published as *Before Philosophy*, 1949; *The Burden of Egypt*, 1951, later published as *The Culture of Ancient Egypt*, 1956; the Egyptian section of *Ancient Near Eastern Texts relating to the Old Testament* edited by J. B. Pritchard, 1950 and 1955; *Most Ancient Verse* with T. Jacobsen, 1963; *Signs and Wonders upon Pharaoh: A History of American Egyptology*, 1964; and his autobiography *Thousands of years*, 1972; he died at Hightstown, New Jersey, 30 Aug. 1976.

WWA 7, 619; *Studies in Honor of John A Wilson*, ed. G. Kadish,1969, (portr.) (bibl.), 115-124. *Report of the Oriental Institute* 1973/4 (portr.) (G. Hughes); *ARCE Newsletter* 97/8 (1976), 1-2 (J. Dorman); *ARCE* 13 (1976), 3 (anon.); *JEA* 63 (1977), 4 (E. Wente); *BSFE* 77-8 (1976-7), 5; D. Schmandt-Besserat, *Immortal Egypt* (Malibu, 1978), 3-4 (G. Hughes).

WILSON Robert (1787-1871)
British surgeon and traveller; he was born in Banff, 25 April 1787, son of Andrew W. of Banffshire and Mary Reid; he was educated at Marischal College, Aberdeen from 1802 studying medicine; he served as a surgeon on East India Company ships from 1805; member of the Royal College of Surgeons, 1810; MD, King's College, Aberdeen, 1815; he undertook journeys in Europe, the Levant, and Persia, visiting Egypt and Nubia in 1820 (MS notebook 415); later secretary to Lord Hastings, the Governor-General of Malta (*d.*1825); he retired to Forres in Scotland; his papers are in the University of Aberdeen and his antiquities are in the Marischal Museum, Aberdeen; he also established a travelling fellowship for medical graduates; he died at Glenairne Cottage, Ardlach, near Forres, 24 Sept. 1871.

ODNB 59, 628-9; H. Hargreaves, *Aberdeen University Review* 43 (1969-70), 374-384.

WILSON, (*Sir*) (William James) Erasmus (1809-1884)
British surgeon and benefactor; he was born in High St., Marylebone, London, 25 Nov. 1809, son of William W., a naval surgeon, and his wife, née Bransdorph; educated at Dartford Grammar School; he studied medicine at St. Bartholemew's Hospital, and was Demonstrator of Anatomy at University College London; he founded a Chair of Dermatology, R.Coll. Surg.; MRCS, 1831; FRCS, 1843; FRS, 1845; President, RCS, 1881; knighted, 1881; President SBA; he married Miss Doherty, 1881; he was very interested in ancient Egypt and in 1877 defrayed the cost of bringing Cleopatra's Needle from Egypt to London, i.e. about £10,000; he published *Cleopatra's Needle. With brief notes on Egypt and Egyptian obelisks*, 1878; *Egypt of the Past*, 1881, and other works; he took a leading part with Amelia Edwards (q.v.) in founding the EEF in 1882, gave much financial assistance and was its first president, 1882-4; he died in Westgate-on-Sea, 8 Aug. 1884.

ODNB 59, 526-8 (portr.); *DNB* 62, 148; Hilmy, ii, 337; *JEA* 33 (1947), 71.

WILSON, William Rae (1772-1849)
British lawyer and traveller; he was born in Paisley, 7 June 1772, son of Peter Rae and his wife née Wilson and was adopted by his maternal uncle; Hon. LLD Glasgow; FSA; he visited Egypt and Palestine and published *Travels in Europe, Egypt and the Holy Land*, 2 vols. 1823 (4th ed. 1847); he died in London, 2 June 1849.

ODNB 59, 666; *DNB* 62, 150; Hilmy, ii, 338.

WINCKELMANN, Johann Joachim (1717-1768)
German scholar; he was born in Stendahl, Brandenberg, 9 Dec. 1717, son of Martin W., cobbler, and Anna Maria Meyer; he was educated at Halle and Jena Universities; he moved to the Court of Augustus III, Elector of Saxony at Dresden, 1754; he converted to Catholicism, 1754, and moved to Rome, 1755; there he became librarian for the collector Cardinal Alessandro Albani, 1758, and Commissioner of Antiquities for the Vatican, 1763; his writings effectively created the concept of stylistic and developmental analysis of ancient material culture, and contributed to the popularity of neo-Classical style; *Geschichte der Kunst des Alterthums*, 1764 (widely reprinted

and translated), concentrated on the sculpture of Classical Greece (a country he never visited), but also contained the earliest significant articulation of Egyptian style, of derived mostly from objects then in Roman collections; he recognized that some pieces were Roman copies of Egyptian originals, and also ventured to date some pieces as relatively later or earlier than others; his *Monumenti Antichi Inediti*, 1767, also illustrated a number of Egyptian objects; he was murdered in Trieste, 8 June 1768.

Grove Dictionary of Art 33, 241-2; A. Grimm and S. Schoske, *Winckelmann und Ägypten*, 2005.

WINKLER, Hans Alexander (1900-1945)
German ethnographer; he was born at Bremerhaven 14 Feb. 1900, son of Erwin A. W., director of a technical school at Göttingen, and Margarethe Traenckner; he was educated at Göttingen and then served in World War I from 1917; he studied at the University of Göttingen, 1919-21 when he left for economic reasons and briefly became a miner and a radical; he returned to his studies at the University of Tübingen, 1923-25 specializing in religious history and Semitic philology; PhD 1925, Habilitation 1928; lecturer at Tübingen, 1928-33 when he was dismissed for his previous radical views; he visited Egypt in 1932 and 1933-4 when he became interested in Egyptian folk history; he returned to Egypt in 1935 teaching Semitic philology at Cairo University from Oct.-Dec.; he visited Upper Egypt in early 1936 and copied rock drawings; he then joined the expedition of Sir Robert Mond (q.v.) at Armant and copied further drawings in the Libyan Desert, 1936-7 and 1937-8; apart from his publications on ethnography, he produced *Ägyptische Volkskunde*, 1936; *Völker und Völkerbewegungen im vorgeschichtlichen Oberägypten im Lichte neuer Felsbilderfunde*, 1937; and *Rock-Drawings of Southern Upper Egypt*, 2 vols., 1938-9; he was killed in action at Schlusau, Poland, 20 Jan. 1945.

Inf. EES archives and P. Červíček.

WINLOCK, Herbert Eustis (1884-1950)
American Egyptologist; he was born in Washington DC, 1 Feb. 1884, son of William Crawford W., assistant secretary of the Smithsonian Institution, and Alice Broom; BA Harvard, 1906; Hon. Litt.D. Yale, 1933; Princeton University, 1934; University of Michigan, 1936; Art.D. Harvard, 1938; he married Helen Chandler, 1912; Winlock excavated extensively for the Metropolitan Museum, New York, digging at sites throughout Egypt in the years 1906-31, apart from 1914-17 when he was in New York, and 1917-9 when he was in service as a major in World War I; he worked at Lisht, Kharga Oasis, Thebes, etc., and was Director of the Egyptian Expedition, 1928-32; he was appointed Curator of the Egyptian Department of the Metropolitan Museum, 1929-39, and was Director MMA, 18 Jan. 1932-9, retiring due to ill health; Director emeritus, 1939-50; he acquired membership of many learned societies, Hon. Fellow Amer. Numismatic Soc.; Member of the Amer. Oriental Soc.; of the Amer. Museums Assn., and President, 1936-8; of the Amer. Philos. Soc., of American Acad. of Arts and Sciences; Hon. Member Roy. Asiatic Soc., etc.; awarded rank of Chevalier of the Légion d'honneur and the Orders of Leopold and the Crown (Belgium); it is as an archaeologist and writer of historical books that he is best remembered, his standard of work being high, and his field technique being praised by Petrie (q.v.) and other excavators; Weigall (q.v.) indeed called him the most brilliant of his generation; his work at Deir el-Bahri, where he continued Naville's work on the clearance of the Hatshepsut and Mentuhotep temples, was a classic in the story of Egyptian archaeology; here he also found and recorded many notable tombs - their contents as well as many other objects found in the work now enrich the museums of Cairo and New York; unique and of outstanding importance among these finds were the models of the house and craft workshops found in the tomb of the Eleventh Dynasty chancellor Meket-Re, and the equally illuminating letters of Hekanakhte which throw much light on life at this period; an immense amount of material was also brought to light which helped in the study of the two Intermediate Periods particularly at Thebes, and Winlock contributed valuable discussions of these in his works; unfortunately the equally important excavations on the Malkata palace of Amenhotep III at Thebes have never been published except for some articles on specific subjects; his list of publications is long and the following may be cited, *The Tomb of Senebtisi at Lisht*, with A. C. Mace, 1916; *Bas-reliefs from the temple of Ramesses I at Abydos*, 1921; *The Monastery of Epiphanius at Thebes* I, with W. E. Crum, 1926; *The Tomb of Queen Meryet-Amun at Thebes*, fol. 1932; *The Treasure of El Lahun*, sm. fol. 1934; *Ed Dakkleh Oasis: Journal of a camel trip made in 1908, with appendix by Ludlow Bull*, 1936; *The Temple of Rameses I at Abydos*, 1937; *The Temple of Hibis in El Khargeh oasis* I. *The Excavations*, fol. 1941; *Materials used in the embalming of Tutankhamen*, 1941; *Excavations of Deir el Bahari, 1911-1931*, 1942; *The Slain Soldiers of Neb-hepet-Re Mentu-hotep*, 1945; *The Rise and Fall of the Middle Kingdom at Thebes*, 1947; *The Treasure of three Egyptian Princesses*, sm. fol. 1948; posth. *Models of Daily Life in Ancient Egypt from the tomb of Meket-Re at Thebes*, 1955; he also wrote many important articles in *BMMA, JEA,* and other journals; he died in Venice, Florida, 26 Jan. 1950.

BMMA 9 (1950-1), 7-9; *JEA* 36 (1950), I; Newberry Corr.; *The Times,* 30 Jan. and 7 Feb. 1950; *WWWA* 2, 586; Wilson; *The New Yorker* 29 July, 1933, 16-19; *DAB* Suppl. 4, 901-2; *KMT* 9/1 (1998), 82-84.

WINNICKI, (Jan) Krzysztof (1942-2009)
Polish demotist and papyrologist; he was born in Warsaw in 1942; he studied Egyptology at the University of Warsaw to 1965, 1969-74; BA, 1965; PhD, 1974; Habilitation, 1992; he studied at the University of Leiden under Pestman (q.v.), 1976-7; he became assistant professor, Department of Papyrology, University of Warsaw, teaching demotic and classical studies; Professor, 1992; he published his thesis *Ptolemäerarmee in Thebais*, 1978; *Late Egypt and Her Neighbours; Foreign Population in the Egypt in the First Millennium BC*, 2009; he also contributed to *A Guide to the Zenon Archive*, 1981; he died in Warsaw, 27 Feb. 2009

The Journal of Juristic Papyrology 39 (2009), 9-14 (portr.) (T. Derda).

WINSLOW, (Revd) William Copley (1840-1925)
American clergyman; he was born in Boston, 13 Jan. 1840, son of Revd Hubbard W. and Susan Ward Cutler; he was educated at Hamilton College, Clinton, New York, and the General Seminary, New York 1862-5; he was ordained in 1867; rector of St. George's Church, Lee, Mass. 1867-70 and chaplain of St. Luke's Home, Boston 1877-82; in 1880 he visited Egypt and developed a great interest in Egyptian archaeology; he entered into correspondence with Amelia Edwards (q.v.) and in 1883 founded the American branch of the Egypt Exploration Fund of which he was Hon. Treasurer, 1883, Vice-President, 1885, and Hon. Secretary, 1889; he helped to popularize Egyptology in America and organized the lecture tour of Miss Edwards; he was awarded a number of honorary degrees notably LLD from St Andrews; differences with the Committee of the EEF led to his removal from his posts in 1902, an action he denounced in his pamphlet *The Truth about the Egypt Exploration Fund*, 1903; he later became Hon. Treasurer and Hon. Vice-President of the American Branch of Petrie's British School of Archaeology; he died in Boston, 2 Feb. 1925.

DAB 20, 402-3; *WWWA* 1, 1367.

WISŁOCKI, Nicholas (1821-1886)
Polish collector and traveller, and amateur archaeologist; he was born in Hrymiacze near Grodno in 1821, son of Clement W. and Lucy Stecka; he attended school at Brest Litovsk, and later studied at the Kiev University; in 1843 he started on a journey to Asia Minor, which widened to include Palestine where he visited the Holy Sepulchre in Jerusalem, and later also Egypt; while in Jerusalem he met the Prussian Prince Waldemar who gave him, on hearing about his plans to go later to Egypt, the order of the Black Eagle destined for Lepsius (q.v.); he stayed in Egypt in 1844-45 sailing along the Nile from Delta up to the cataracts; he met Lepsius at Thebes and began a close friendship; he took part in Lepsius' activities at Karnak and in his other undertakings in Upper Egypt; he spent the winter of 1845 in Cairo; part of his collection including objects obtained on his voyage to Egypt was exhibited in Warsaw, 1856; later some items were transferred by the owner to the Archaeological Cabinet of the Cracow University, (probably the limestone stela of Amennakht from Deir el-Medina, Inv. No. 10.598, and an uninscribed statuette of kneeling man in black granite from the XXVIth Dynasty, Inv. No. 10.562) and to the Czartoryski Collection in Cracow (not yet identified), his notes and a diary of his stay in Egypt are now lost, but may be in the possession of the family; he died in 1886.

Tygodnik Lustrowany (Illustrated Weekly), No. 159 (1886), 38 (L. Jenike); J. Śliwa, *Meander* 9 (1993), 471-481.

WITT, Constant Henri Emmanuel Arthur de (1907-1989)
Belgian Egyptologist; he was born in Antwerp, 15 May 1907, son of Léon de W., painter and restorer, and Henrietta Verbuecken; he studied Egyptology at the Université Libre in Brussels under Gilbert (q.v.) and Stracmans (q.v.) and at Leiden under de Buck (q.v.) and Janssen (q.v.) 1951-2; he also studied Demotic with Glanville (q.v.) at Cambridge and Ptolemaic with Fairman (q.v.) at Liverpool; he was attached to the Musée Royal in Brussels, 1954-72 and was lecturer in Egyptian Art at the University of Leuven, 1969-75; after his retirement, he emigrated to Egypt where he worked for Thomas Cook; he was the author of *La Statuaire de Tell el Amarna*, 1950 *Le Rôle et le Sens du Lion dans l'Égypte ancienne*, 1951; and *Les Inscriptions du Temple d'Opet à Karnak*, 1958-68; he died in Luxor, 20 Nov. 1989

JEA 76 (1990), xii (K. A. Kitchen); inf. H. De Meulenaere and E. Warmenbol; inf. E. Serdiuk.

WITTE, (Baron) Jean Joseph Antoine Marie de (1808-1889)
Belgian archaeologist and numismatist; he was born in Antwerp, 24 Feb. 1808, son of Jean Joseph de W. and Marie Thérèse Antonie Josèphe Herry; he edited with Longpérier (q.v.) the *Bulletin archéologique de l'Athènaeum français*, which contained works by Chabas, Brugsch, de Rougé, Mariette (qq.v.), and other Egyptologists; he died in Paris, 29 July 1889.

Larousse; Lepsius, 85; *Biographie nationale de Belgique* 27, 374-5; È. Gran-Aymerich, *Dictionnaire biographique d'archéologie 1798-1945*, 2001, incorporated in *Les Chercheurs de passé 1798-1945*, 2007, 1252-4.

WOIDE, Carl Gottfried (1725-1790)
Polish orientalist; he was born in Liassa, Poland, 4 July 1725, son of Martin Gottleib W., postmaster; he studied at Frankfurt-an-der-Oder under Jablonski (q.v.) and at Leiden; he was appointed a minister at Lissa, Poland and in 1770 at the German Chapel Royal, London and later the Savoy; he specialized in the study of Coptic editing La Croze's *Lexicon Aegyptiaco-Latinum*, 1775 and C. Scholtz, *Grammatica Aegyptiaca*, 1778 as well as the Greek New Testament; he was appointed assistant librarian at the British Museum in 1782; DD (University of Copenhagen); DCL (Oxford), 1786; FSA 1778; FRS 1785; he died in London, 9 May 1790.

ODNB 59, 948-9; *DNB* 62, 289-90; *Al. Oxon.*; *GM* 22 (1970), 7; *The Coptic Encyclopedia* 7, 2324; W. Bickerirch, *Zeitschrift der Historischen Gesellschaft für die Provinz Posen* 20 (1905), 193-211.

WOLDERING, Irmgard Elisabeth (1919-1969)
German Egyptologist; she was born in Osnabrück, 26 Feb. 1919, daughter of Josef W., a banker and Carla Hugo, a noted political figure; she studied at the University of Munich; PhD, 1950; she was associated with the Kestner Museum, Hanover from 1950 onwards; assistant, 1952; Director, 1955; Corr. Member of German Archaeological Institute; it is as an art historian that she is best remembered, having published a highly successful study on Egyptian art with editions in seven languages; publications include *Führer durch das Kestner-Museum* with C. Mosel, 1952, 2nd ed. 1961; *Ausgewählte Werke der aegyptischen Sammlung* in *Bildkatalogue des Kestner-Museums Hannover* I, 1955, 2nd ed. 1958; *Meisterwerke das Kestner-Museum zu Hannover*, 1961; *Ägypten, Die Kunst der Pharaonen*, *Kunst der Welt* series, 1962, (English, French, Italian, Spanish, Dutch and Swedish eds) see also *Egypt, the art of the Pharaohs*, trans. Ann E. Keep, 1963; *Götter und Pharaonen: die Kultur Ägyptens im Wandel der Geschichte*, 1967; contributed also to *Jber.d. Kestner-Mus.*; she died after a long illness in Hanover, 24 April 1969.

Inf. C. Mosel; *AfO* 23 (1970), 226 (H. Brunner); Kürschner llth ed. (1970), 3331.

WOLF, Walther August (1900-1973)
German Egyptologist; he was born in Hildesheim, 24 Nov. 1900, son of Peter W., a teacher, and his wife, née Stinde; his interest in Egyptology was aroused by the monuments in the Pelizaeus Museum; he studied under Ranke (q.v.) at Heidelberg, 1919-21 and under Sethe (q.v.) at Göttingen and Berlin, 1922-3; from 1922 he was an assistant in the Egyptian Museum in Berlin; in 1923 he obtained his PhD from Heidelberg; 1926-7 he worked in Cairo with Borchardt (q.v.), 1926-7, before returning to Berlin; on 1 July 1928 he took up the post as assistant to Steindorff (q.v.) in Leipzig and obtained his habilitation there in 1928; he was named Associate Professor at Leipzig, 1 Oct. 1934 and Professor, 1 Aug. 1939; he succeeded Steindorff as editor of *ZÄS* in 1937; he served in World War II; as a supporter of the Nazi government, he was unable to return to Leipzig after the conflict; he was guest Professor at Münster from 1949 and Professor, 1959-69; his published works include *Die Bewaffnung des altägyptischen Heeres*, 1929; *Das Schöne Fest von Opet*, 1931; *Wesen und Wert der Ägyptologie,* 1937; *Die Stellung der ägyptischen Kunst zur antiken und abendländischen und Das Problem des Kunstlers in der ägyptischen Kunst*, 1951; *Die Welt der Ägypter*, 1955; *Die Kunst Ägyptens*, 1957; *Kulturgeschichte des Alten Ägypten*, 1962; *Funde in Ägypten. Geschichte ihrer Entdeckung*, 1966; *Frühe Hochkulturen*, 1969, Eng. trans. *The origins of Western Art*, 1971; he died in Hamburg, 11 Jan. 1973.

ZÄS 101 (1974), V-VI (M. Krause); E. Blumenthal, *Altes Ägypten in Leipzig,* 1981, 29, 32-3; *BSFE* 67 (1973), *Wer ist Wer 1969/70*, 1465; inf. T. Schneider.

WOLFF, (*Rt. Hon. Sir***) Henry Drummond** (1830-1908)
British diplomat; he was born in Malta 12 Oct. 1830; son of Joseph Wolff, a missionary, and Lady Georgina Walpole; he was educated at Rugby; he entered the Foreign Office, 1846, and was employed in many diplomatic missions including Egypt; PC, 1885; GCB, 1889; GCMG, 1878; he was present at the unwrapping of some of the Royal Mummies; he died in Brighton, 11 Oct. 1908.

Maspero, *Momies Royales,* 525, 765; *WWW* i, 776; *ODNB* 59, 974-7 (portr.); *DNB* 1901-1911, 699-702.

WOOD, Robert (*c*.1717-1771)
British traveller; he was born at Riverstown Castle, near Trim, County Meath, Ireland, *c*.1717, son of Revd Alexander James Wood of Summmerhill; he was educated at the universities of Glasgow and Padua; he travelled in the East, 1742-3, visiting Egypt from Feb. 1743; in 1750-1 he again visited the East with John Bouverie (died Guzel Hissar 19 Sept. 1750), James Dawkins, and an Italian artist Giovanni or Torquilino Borra to make accurate drawings of the monuments; they were in Egypt from 4 Nov. 1750 and toured Alexandria and the pyramids at Giza, Saqqara and Dahshur, where measurements and drawings were made; on his return to London, he became involved in a political

career holding various government offices; only two volumes concerning his travels, *The Ruins of Palmyra*, 1753 and *The Ruins of Balbeck*, 1757 were published; his diaries are now with the Society for the Promotion of Hellenic Studies and the drawings are in the Mellon Centre of British Art, Yale University; he died in Putney, 9 Sept. 1771.

ODNB 60, 135-6; *DNB* 62, 373-5; inf. I.E.S. Edwards; È. Gran-Aymerich, *Dictionnaire biographique d'archéologie 1798-1945*, 2001, incorporated in *Les Chercheurs de passé 1798-1945*, 2007, 1254-5; *Dictionary of Irish Biography*, 2009, 9, 1025-6.

WOOD-JONES, Frederic (1879-1954)

British anatomist; born Shacklewell, London, 23 Jan. 1879, son of Charles Henry Jones, an architect, and Lucy Allin; he was educated at Enfield Grammar School and the Medical School of the London Hospital, 1897, graduated 1903, MB, 1904; in 1907 he joined Elliot Smith (q.v.) in Egypt to assist in the study of anthropological material from the archaeological survey of Nubia; he later became Lecturer in Anatomy at Manchester, 1908; served in the First World War, afterwards Professor of Anat. at University of Adelaide 1919-26; FRS, 1925; Professor, Hawaii, 1927-30; Melbourne, 1930-7; and at University of Manchester, 1938; he was the first Professor of Human and Comparative Anat., Roy. Coll. Surgeons, 1945; he published many works, see *Arch. Survey of Nubia. Report on the human remains*, vol. 2, G. E. Smith and F. W.-J., 1910; he died in London, 29 Sept. 1954.

Man 56 (1956), 79 (portr.) (J. Dobson); *The Times,* 30 Sept. 1954.

WOOLLEY, (*Sir*) (Charles) Leonard (1880-1960)

British archaeologist; he was born in London, 17 April 1880, son of the Revd George Herbert W. and Sarah Cathcart; he was educated New College, Oxford where he took a degree in Theology; MA, Oxon; Hon. DLitt Dublin; Hon. LLD St Andrews; Hon. Fellow of New College, Oxford and of Türk Tarih Kurumu; Hon. ARIBA; FSA, OBE, MC; he married Katharine Keeling, 1926, who accompanied him on his excavations until her death in 1945; Assistant Keeper in the Ashmolean Museum, Oxford, 1905-7 under Sir Arthur Evans (q.v.); he excavated in Nubia for the Eckley B. Coxe Jnr. Expedition, 1907-11; also for the Oxford Univ. Expedition to Nubia in 1912; at Karanog Woolley dug the first big Meroitic cemetery on record; he then left Egypt for Sinai where he carried out archaeological work for the PEF in 1914; during the First World War he was a Capt. RFA and did intelligence work while on the Staff in Egypt, 1914-16, dispatches, Croix de Guerre; he was a prisoner in Turkey, 1916-18, and only released at the end of the war; after excavating at Carchemish he again returned to Egypt, this time working for the EES at El-Amarna, 1921-2; he then returned to Mesopotamia to carry out his most famous excavations of all, i.e. his 12 seasons at Ur, 1922-34; one of his architects on this expedition was F. G. Newton (q.v.), 1922-4, who had done work at El-Amarna, and it is interesting to note that he had trained his foreman Shaikh Hamoudi ibn Ibrahim from 1912 onwards at Carchemish, the latter teaching Lawrence (q.v.) Arabic and initiating him in the ways of Arab life; in the Second World War he was promoted Lt.-Col. GS Archaeological Adviser to Civil Affairs Directorate 1943-6, a position in which he had to act as full-time archaeological adviser; on his advice the Allied Supreme Commander Gen. Eisenhower issued an order preventing the looting and damaging of buildings which also included art treasures such as those of the Uffizi; Woolley was Univ. of London Petrie Medallist 1957; he published a vast output among which may be cited: *Areika*, 1909; *Karanog,* 1910; *Karanog: the town*, 1911; *Buhen,* 1911 with D Randall-MacIver relating to excavations in Nubia on behalf of the University Museum, Philadelphia; the *Wilderness of Zin,* 1936, in conjunction with T.E. Lawrence; *The City of Akhenaten,* vol. i, 1923, with T. E. Peet, relating to excavations carried out or the EES in the Southern City and Workmen's Village at El-Amarna; he died in London, 20 Feb. 1960.

As I seem to remember, 1962 (posth.); *AfO* 19 (1959-60), 265-6 (portr.) (E. W.); *Iraq* 22 (1960), 1-19 (portr.) (M. E. L. Mallowan) a memorial vol.; *JRAS* (1960), 204-5; *Sumer* 16 (1960), 86-7 (portr.) (anon.) (bibl.); *Syria* 37 (1960), 384-6 (portr.) (A. P.); *The Times,* 22 Feb. 1960; *WWW* v, 1192; *ODNB* 60, 275-7 (portr.); *DNB* 1951-60; 1082-4; H.F.V. Winstone, *Woolley of Ur,* 1990.); È. Gran-Aymerich, *Dictionnaire biographique d'archéologie 1798-1945*, 2001, incorporated in *Les Chercheurs de passé 1798-1945*, 2007, 1255-6.

WORRELL, William Hoyt (1879-1952)

American Semiticist; he was born Toledo, Ohio, 20 April 1879, son of William Clifford W. and Alta Hoyt; he was Professor Emeritus of Semitics at the University of Michigan; Director of the American Oriental Society from 1928; he published *The Coptic Manuscripts in the Freer Collection*, 1923; and an edition of *The Proverbs of Solomon in Sahidic Coptic*, 1931; he died in Haverhill, Massachusetts, 3 Dec. 1952.

JAOS 73 (1953), 183 (F. J. Stephens); *WWWA* 3, 941.

WRESZINSKI, Walter (1880-1935)
German Egyptologist; he was born in Mogilno, Poland, then East Prussia, 18 March 1880, son of Joseph W.; he studied at the University of Königsberg and in Berlin under Erman (q.v.); PhD, 1904; he was appointed lecturer at the University of Königsberg, 1909; Hon Professor, 1920; Professor, 1927, ; he visited Egypt several times and made an important photographic survey, the results of which are embodied in his *Atlas*; his other main interest was in medical papyri and he published texts in this field; he was also the editor of *OLZ* 1921-31; his principal works were, *Die Hohenpriester des Amon...*, inaug. dissertation, 1904; *Aegyptische Inschriften aus dem K.K. Hofmuseum in Wien*, 1906; *Die Medizin der alten Ägypter. I. Der Grosse Medizinische Papyrus des Berliner Museums, Pap. Berl. 3038....mit Übersetzung, Kommentar und Glossar. II. Der Londoner Medizinische Papyrus, Brit. Mus. Nr. 10059 und der Papyrus Hearst, in Transkription, Übersetzung und Kommentar. III. Der Papyrus Ebers, Umschrift, Übersetzung und Kommentar*, 3 vols. 1909-13; *Atlas zur altaegyptischen Kulturgeschichte*, 3 pts., in 5 vols., 1913-36, this is his most important and largest work; *Bericht über die photographische Expedition von Kairo bis Wadi Halfa, zwecks Abschluss der Materialsammlung für meinen Atlas zur altägyptischen Kulturgeschichte*, 1927; he also assisted Naville (q.v.) in bringing out the vols. of the text of Lepsius *Denk.*, he died at Königsberg, 9 April 1935.

Kürschner, 1931; *OLZ* 38 (1935), cols. 273-6 (R. Hartmann); *ZÄS* 71 (1935), iv (G. Steindorff); E. Endesfelder, *Die Ägyptologie an der Berliner Universität-Zur Geschichte eines Fachgebietes*, 1988, 27; inf. T. Schneider.

WRIGHT, John Bowes (1779-1836)
British traveller and collector; he was baptized in Newcastle-upon-Tyne 16 Dec. 1779, son of John W., attorney-at-law; educated at Witton-le-Wear, Newcastle, and Edinburgh; Jesus College, Cambridge, 1802; BA, 1806; MA, 1809; and Fellow; admitted at Lincoln's Inn, 1801; a man of great linguistic attainments he travelled extensively in Europe, Asia, and Africa; he visited Egypt 1818-9 and left graffiti at Debod and Kertassi; he presented to the Newcastle Literary and Philosophical Society a mummy in two coffins he had bought at the Denon (q.v.) Sale (Lots 242-3) which was of exceptional interest, and is now in the Hancock Museum, Newcastle; he died 26 Jan 1836.

Alum. Cantab. pt.2; Pettigrew, *Autobiogr.* 31; *Hist. Newcastle Lit. & Phil. Soc.*, 304.

WUNDERLICH, Ernest Julius (1859-1945)
Australian merchant and collector; he was born in London, 16 May 1859, son of Charles Frederick W., an indigo merchant, and Caroline Schmedes; he studied architectural and mechanical drawing in Paris and Lausanne; after working as a salesman, he emigrated to Australia in 1885 and began a company with his brothers making stamped metal ceilings, later Wunderlich Patent Ceiling and Roofing Co. Ltd, 1904 and Wunderlich Ltd., 1908; he became chairman but devoted his time to cultural pursuits; he visited Egypt at least as early as 1900 and met Petrie (q.v.) through whom he became interested in archaeology; he donated to the Australian Museum in Sydney in 1913 a large collection of antiquities from Petrie's work and a further donation of purchased objects, and made further donations in 1921 and 1935; he was a trustee from 1914 and president in 1926 of the Australian Museum, Sydney but resigned in 1927 in frustration at the conservatism of other trustees; he wrote his autobiography, *All My Yesterdays*, 1945; his archaeological library was donated to the School of History, Philosophy and Politics at Macquarie University; he died at Bondi Junction, 11 April 1945.

Australian Dictionary of Biography, 12, 587-9; R. S. Merrillees, *Living with Egypt's Past in Australia*, 1990, 17-20.

WUTTMANN, Michel (1955-2013)
French conservator; he was born in Strasbourg, 6 July 1955; he was educated as a chemist in Nancy; his interest in archaeology led to his work as a restorer of archaeological materials for the Centre d'étude franco-égyptien in Karnak and IFAO; he formally joined IFAO as a researcher, 1992; he created a laboratory for conservation and in 2006 a laboratory for radiocarbon dating; he took part in the excavations at Douch from 1996, carrying out a survey in the area of Baris; he contributed to the following publications, *Balat* III, 1990; *Balat* II, 1992; *Balat* VI, 2002; *Le gisement épipaléolithique de ML1 à 'Ayn-Manâwir*, 2008; he was killed in Cairo, 10 Feb 2013.

BSFE 185 (2013), 4 (portr.); internet obit.

XIA *see* **HSIA**

YAHUDA, Abraham Shalom Ezekiel (1877-1951)
Jewish orientalist and Hebraist; born Jerusalem, 18 June 1877, son of Benjamin Ezekiel Yahuda and Bochora Bergman; married 1921, Ethel Rachel Judes, Johannesburg; he was educated at the Universities of Heidelberg and Strassburg; PhD Strassburg; he was appointed Professor of Biblical Exegesis and Semitic Philology at the High School of Hebrew Learning, Berlin, 1905 and remained there until 1914; he became Professsor of Hebrew Literature and Language of the Jewish Spanish period in Madrid Univ., 1915-22; also Professor of Semitic Philology at the Centro de Estudios Históricos, Madrid, 1914-20; he was much interested in the relationship of the Egyptian language to Semitic languages and published *The Language of the Pentateuch in its Relations to Egyptian*, 1933; *Sigmund Freud and his Moses* (in Hebrew); *Les Récits bibliques de Joseph et l'exode; confirmés à la lumière des monuments égyptiens*, 1940; *Joseph's Rule in Egypt* (in Hebrew), 1941; *The Osiris cult in the Bible*, 1944; *Hebrew words of Egyptian origin*, 1947; *Medical and anatomical terms in the Pentateuch in the light of Egyptian medical papyri*, 1948; he died at New Haven, Connecticut, 13 Aug. 1951.

Sefarad II (1951), 489-90 (J. M. Millás); *WWW* v, 1199-1200.

YATES, William Holt (1802-1874)
British physician and traveller; he was born in London in 1802 and baptized in St. Mary's Kensington, 19 Dec. 1802, son of William Y. and Elizabeth Titcomb; MD Edinb., 1825; Senior Physician of the General Dispensary, London; Pres. Royal Med. and Phys. Soc., Edinburgh; he visited Egypt and Nubia, 1829-30; he published medical works, and *Modern History and Condition of Egypt*, 2 vols. 1843; he was a member of the Syro-Egyptian Soc. for which he published a memoir on obelisks, 1845; he died in London, 26 Jan. 1874.

Hilmy, ii, 345; *Lancet,* 1832-3; ii, 477, 790, 821; 1833-4, i, 76.

YEATES, Thomas (1768-1839)
British orientalist; he was born in London, 9 Oct. 1768, son of John Y., wood turner, and Jane Boult; at All Souls College, Oxford, 1802; he was employed by Claudius Buchanan to catalogue and describe the oriental MSS brought by him from India, *c.*1808-15; Assistant in Dept. of Printed Books, British Museum, 1823-39; he published *A Dissertation on the Antiquity of the Pyramids,*1833; *Remarks on the History of Ancient Egypt*, 1835, an antiquated work; he died in London, 7 Oct. 1839.

ODNB 60, 763; *DNB* 63, 311-12; *GM* 12 n.s. (1839), 658-60; Hilmy, ii, 347.

YEIVIN, Shemuel (1896-1982)
Israeli archaeologist; he was born at Odessa, 2 Sept. 1896, son of Nissan Y. and Esther Yonis; he emigrated to Palestine at the age of nine and was educated at the Herzliya Gymnasium, Tel Aviv, Jaffa; he served in the Turkish army in World War I; he studied archaeology under Petrie (q.v.) at University College London, 1920-23, BA, 1923, MA, 1928; he excavated with Petrie and Brunton (q.v.) at Badari in 1923-4 and then took part in the Mond excavations at Luxor, 1924; he also excavated at Karanis with Starkey (q.v.), 1924-6; his interest then shifted to the Near East excavating at Beth-Shean, 1924-8, Seleucia in Iraq, 1929-37 and Ali, 1933; he became Chairman of the Jewish Palestine Exploration Society, 1944-6, chief Hebrew translator for the British Mandatory Government, 1944-8, first Director of the Department of Antiquities in Israel, 1948-61, and founder and Professor of the Institute of Archaeology, Tel Aviv University; he died at Kfar Sava, Israel, 28 Feb. 1982.

IEJ 32 (1982), 167-8; 35 (1985), 288; *Qadmoniot* 15 (1982), 40 (portr.) (B. Mazar); *Atiqot* (D. Ussishkin); (Hebrew series) 8 (1982) (portr.); *Tel Aviv* 9 (1982), 1-2; Y. Aharoni, *Excavations and Studies: Essays in Honour of Professor Shemuel Yeivin*, 1973, 9-11 (bibl.); *Encyclopedia Judaica* (1971), 16, 734; inf. from University College London and R. S. Merrillees.

YORKE, (*Rt. Hon***) Charles Philip** (1764-1834)
British statesman and antiquary; he was born 24 March 1764, son of Lord Chancellor Charles Yorke and Agneta Johnson; he was educated at Harrow and St. John's College, Cambridge; MA, 1783; barrister, Middle Temple, 1787; FRS, 1801; FSA; PC, 1801; he married Harriett Manningham; Secretary at War, 1801-3; Home Secretary, 1803-4; First Lord of the Admiralty, 1810-11; he was the friend and patron of Henry Salt (q.v.) and strongly advocated the purchase of Salt's Egyptian collection by the British Museum; he published with William Martin Leake (q.v.), *Remarks on some Egyptian monuments in England*, 1826, French edition *Les principaux monumens égyptiens du Musée Britannique et quelques autres qui se trouvent en Angleterre, expliqués d'après le système phonétique*, 1827, an account of the Egyptian antiquities in the British Museum and other collections; he died in London, 13 March 1834.

ODNB 60, 834-6; *DNB* 63, 341-2; Salt, i, 390; ii, 142, 168, 171, 317; Hilmy, ii, 347.

YOUNG, Thomas (1773-1829)
British physician, physicist, and pioneer in Egyptology; he was born at Milverton, Somerset, 13 June 1773, son of Thomas Y., a Quaker mercer and banker, and Sarah Davis; the eldest of ten children he was a genius and most precocious in his studies; said to have learnt to read fluently at the age of two, at 14 he had some knowledge of Greek, Latin, French, Italian, Hebrew, Chaldee, Syriac, Samaritan, Arabic, Persian, Turkish and Ethiopic; this interest in linguistics he always retained as a scientist and later reviewed *four hundred* languages for the *EB*; he studied medicine in London and Edinburgh, 1792-4, and at this time wrote a paper on the eye, 1793, which gained him FRS; further study at Göttingen, 1795-7, where he started his work in physics and gained a doctorate, and Cambridge, 1797-9; entered Emmanuel College as Fellow Commoner, 1797, and at this time made friends with Sir Wm. Gell (q.v.); he practised as a physician in London, and married Eliza daughter of James Primrose Maxwell, 1804; MD of Cambridge, 1808; Fellow of the Roy. Coll. of Physicians, 1809; elected to the staff of St. George's Hospital, 1811; his most important research was in the field of physiological optics, being the first to recognize astigmatism in the human eye, and according to Clerk Maxwell the first to establish a consistent theory of light, 1802 (published 1807), in which he anticipated Fresnel; to mark these discoveries he was elected one of the eight foreign associates of the Paris Acad. 1827; in 1801 he was made Professor of Natural Philosophy at the Royal Institution; Young first became interested in Egyptology and the Rosetta Stone through reading an article *Mithridates* by Adelung, but his first work was done on a damaged papyrus brought back from Luxor by Sir W. Rouse Boughton (q.v.); from this he turned to the Rosetta decree; his discoveries although partial were far from being insignificant, and while they cannot be compared with those of Champollion (q.v.) were systematic and far ahead of everything that had been achieved up to that time; Young detected at once a relationship with Coptic because three month names in the Greek version agreed with known Coptic names; he rightly abandoned Åkerblad's (q.v.) alphabet for Demotic as a working tool, and de Sacy (q.v.) agreed with him in this, and was the first to state that the Egyptians employed both alphabetic and non-alphabetic signs in texts; he noted that Demotic characters in certain cases derived from hieroglyphs and that linear hieroglyphs and hieratic did the same; he divided the Demotic text of the Rosetta Stone into eighty-six word groups, most of them correct; he noted that the funerary papyri had different characters with the same powers, i.e. homophony, and that many examples of the New Kingdom had sections in common, derived from a master text; he guessed that the cartouches contained royal names without knowing that others had already suggested this, and was able to read the name Ptolemy and that of queen Berenike recognizing the feminine oval ending and letter *t* used in the latter; out of thirteen signs in his list he had six correct, three partly correct, and four wrong, but he later added the horned snake *f* and some other signs; from this beginning he later correctly suggested another cartouche was Thutmose, and in the longer cartouches of Ptolemy read the titles 'Beloved of Ptah' and Living for Ever'; Young also claimed to have discovered the numerals and method of representing plurality; his MSS papers for the years 1814-18 with his works on hieroglyphs are now in the British Library (Add. MSS. 27281-5); in 1819 he formed an Egyptian Society to publish hieroglyphic inscriptions, plates of which were issued in parts and appeared later under the auspices of the Royal Soc. of Literature; he had great difficulty in getting adequate support for his Egyptological schemes and in raising sufficient funds for the work to continue; in 1827 he decided to abandon work on hieroglyphs and concentrate on Demotic, but was again hampered by his many other duties and illness; in all he produced 16 Egyptological works, the principal ones being, *Remarks on Egyptian papyri and on the inscription of Rosetta*, 1815; *Account of some Thebaic manuscripts written on leather. Legh's narrative*, 1816; 'Egypt', article in the *Supplement* to the *Encyclopaedia Brittanica*, 1819; Appendix to the second edition of Belzoni's *Travels*, 1821; *An Account of some recent discoveries in hieroglyphical literature and Egyptian antiquities, including the author's original alphabet as extended by M. Champollion*, 1823; *Hieroglyphics, collected by the Egyptian Society*, 1823; *Hieroglyphics, continued by the Royal Society of Literature*. II, 1828; *Rudiments of an Egyptian Dictionary in the ancient enchorial character; containing all the words of which the sense has been ascertained*, Appendix to Tattam's *Coptic Grammar*, 1831; he died in London 10 May 1829, and was buried in Farnborough, Kent with a memorial in Westminster Abbey.

Wood, Alexander, and Oldham, Frank, *Thomas Young,* 1954, (definitive and his bibl. of all his works); *Life,* by Dean G. Peacock, in vol. i, of *Collected Works,* 1855 (biased); *Life,* by Frank Oldham, 1933 (portr.); *ODNB* 60, 945-9 (portr.); *DNB* 63, 393; EB; Hilmy, ii, 348; A. Robinson, *Thomas Young: The Last Man who Knew Everything,* 2006; Lamy, 307-11; É. Gran-Aymerich, *Dictionnaire biographique d'archéologie 1798-1945,* 2001, incorporated in *Les Chercheurs de passé 1798-1945,* 2007, 1262-3.

YOUSSEF, Abd al-Baqi (1904-1961)
Egyptian archaeologist; he was born at Mit Ghamr, 1904, and educated at Cairo University; he joined the Egyptian Antiquities Service and worked as an inspector with Emery (q.v.) during the Second Archaeological Survey in Nubia 1929-35; he later held posts at Edfu, Sohag and Luxor, and finally was Chief Inspector of Upper Egypt; in 1944 he became Librarian of the Egyptian Museum, Cairo until 1946; he was then

appointed a curator at the Coptic Museum when he carried out excavations at Abu Mina and Tell Basta; he was first curator at the Egyptian Museum, Cairo 1960-1; he died in 1961.

D. Abou-Ghazi, *The Library of Egyptian Museum,* 1988, 19.

YOYOTTE, Jean (1927-2009)
French Egyptologist; he was born in Lyon, 4 Aug. 1927, son of a chemical engineer from Martinique; he was educated at lycée Henri IV with Sauneron (q.v.) and Godron (q.v.) where he developed an interest in Egyptology, 1937-42; he studied at the École du Louvre, 1942-44 under Vandier (q.v.) and the École Pratique des Hautes Études under Posener (q.v.), Garnot (q.v.), Clère (q.v.), and Malinine (q.v.), 1942-5; he gained his baccalauréat, 1945 and diploma, 1951; he joined CNRS, 1948 and undertook research at IFAO in Egypt, 1952-6; he continued at CNRS, becoming maître de recherches, 1963; he was served as Director d'études at the École Pratique and director of Centre Wladimir Golénischeff, 1 Nov. 1964-91; he succeeded Montet (q.v.) as director of the excavations at Tanis, 1965-84; he was appointed Professor at the Collège de France, 5 Oct. 1991-7; he organized the exhibition, 'Tanis: L'or des pharaons', in Paris, Marseilles, Edinburgh, and several Australian cities, 1987-8; he later served as scientific adviser to the underwater excavations at Alexandria; Pres of the Société française d'Égyptologie 1979-80; *Rev. Ég.* 61 (2010) was dedicated to his memory; apart from numerous articles, he published *Objets pharaoniques à inscription carienne,* with O. Masson, 1956; *Dictionnaire de la civilisation égyptienne,* with Posener and Sauneron, 1959, English ed. 1962; *Le jugement des morts dans l'Égypte ancienne,* with others, 1962; *Les trésors des pharaons,* 1968; *Grenoble Musée des Beaux-Arts. Collections égyptiennes,* with G. Kueny, 1979; *Tanis: L'Or des pharaons,* with others, 1987, English ed., *Gold of the Pharaohs,* 1987; *L'Égypte des millénaires obscurs,* with others, 1990; *Leçon inaugurale,* 1992; *Dictionnaire des pharaons,* with P. Vernus, 1996 and later editions, English ed. 2003; *Le voyage en Égypte: Un regard romain,* with others, 1997; *Les statuettes funéraires de la deuxième cachette à Deir el Bahari,* with L. Aubert, 1998; *L'Égypte ancienne,* with others, 1998; *Alexandria: The Submerged Royal Quarters,* with others, 1998; *Calendrier égyptien,* English ed., *The Egyptian Calendar,* with A. S. von Bomhard, 1999; *Bestiaire des pharaons,* 2005; *Alexandria II. Portus Magnus,* with others, 2005; *Heracleion: The Submerged Western Canopic Region,* with others, 2007; *Histoire, géographie et religion de l'Égypte ancienne: Opera selecta,* edited I. Guermeur, 2013. he also edited, with C. Montet-Beaucour, *P. Montet. Lettres de Tanis 1939-40,* 1998; he died in Paris, 1 July 2009. His archives are in the Centre W. Golénischeff, at the Ecole Pratique des Hautes Etudes, in Paris.

Le Monde 5/6 July 2009; *Rev. d'Ég.* 61 (2010), iv-xiv (portr.) (O. Perdu); *Égypte, Afrique & Orient* 56 (2009/10), 3-8 (O. Perdu).

YURCO, Frank(lin) Joseph (1944-2004)
American Egyptologist; he was born in New York, 31 July 1944; he studied at New York University, and at the Oriental Institute, University of Chicago; he served as epigrapher at Chicago House, Luxor in the Luxor and Karnak temples; he taught adult education courses on Egyptology at the Oriental Institute, Field Museum, Oakton Community College, and the University of Chicago Continuing Education Program; he acted as curriculum evaluator for Chicago and Washington DC public schools; he was also lecturer for the Chicago Academic alliance Teacher Enrichment Program; he helped to organize the special exhibition, Inside Egypt, at the Field Museum and Egypt in Africa, at the Indianapolis Museum of Art; he was specialist in the war reliefs of Merenptah at Karnak and the reign of Amenmesse; he was latterly librarian at the Regenstein Library, University of Chicago; he died in Chicago, 6 Feb, 2004.

KMT 15/2 (2004), 19 (portr.) (Janet Johnson).

YUSUFIAN, *(Bey)* **Boghos** (1775-1844)
Egyptian official of Armenian descent; he was born in Smyrna in 1775, son of Hovsep (Yusuf), a merchant and Marta Abroyan; he succeeded his maternal uncle as interpreter to the British consulate at Smyrna and later went to Egypt where he became interpreter for the British and by 1816 acted as interpreter and private secretary to Muhammad Ali; in 1823 he became First Secretary, in 1826 Minister of Commerce, and in 1837 Minister of Commerce and Foreign Affairs; he was the most trusted servant of Muhammad Ali; applications for firmans to excavate and export antiquities had to go through his office, and Boghos often showed partiality in recommending them; he had a country house at Heliopolis in the garden of which stood the famous obelisk of Sesostris I, marking the site of the ancient sun temple; he encouraged the public careers of other Armenians in Egypt; he died at Alexandria, 10 Jan. 1844 and was buried near the Church of Sourp Boghos-Bedros.

R. Adalian, *The Armenian Review* 33 (1980), 134, 137-140; Champollion, ii, 45; Forbin, 22,67; Salt, i, 468; Lelorrain, 9; Minutoli, 1720 Pueckler-Muskau, 1,9, 10; Yates, i, 97 ff.; Madden, i, 216, 336; Hogg, i, 242-7; Esdale, 128; Vyse, i, xviii; ii, 98; Lepsius 40, 46, 189; Stanhope i, 159; St John, i, 50, 58, ii, 363, 531; *Khedives & Pashas*, 146; Carré, i, 280, 290.

ŽÁBA, Zbynek (1917-1971)
Czech Egyptologist; he was born at Doubravice near Dvur Králové, 19 July 1917, son of František Z. and his wife Anna; he was educated at Hradec Králové where he acquired a knowledge of classical languages, and enrolled at Charles University, Prague to study classical philology; his studies were interrupted by World War II; when he returned to University at the end of the war, he decided to study Egyptology under Lexa (q.v.) and Černý (q.v.); PhD, 1949; he became an assistant to Lexa and was appointed reader at Prague in 1954; he taught the Czech language at the High School of Languages in Cairo, 1955-7; in 1956 he visited Egypt as part of a Czechoslavak cultural mission and was involved in negotiations which resulted in the formation of the Czechoslovak Institute of Egyptology in Prague in 1958 and in Cairo in 1959; he was appointed Professor of Egyptology at Charles University in 1959 and Director of the Institute in 1960 in succession to Lexa; in 1960 he initiated the Czechoslovak excavations at Abusir at the Mastaba of Ptahshepses and from 1961-5 worked in the Nubian rescue campaign at Taphis, Qertasi and Wadi Qitna and also recorded rock inscriptions; he published *L'Orientation astronomique dans l'ancienne Égypte et la précession de l'axe du monde*, 1953; *Les Maximes de Ptahhotep*, 1956; and posth. *The Rock Inscriptions of Lower Nubia*, 1974; he died in Prague, 15 Aug. 1971.

ZÄS 100 (1973), I-III (F. Váhala); *Archiv Orientalní* 40 (1972), 1-5 (bibl.) (M. Verner); *BSFE* 62 (1971), 4; *Novy Orient* 26 (1971), 257-61 (F. Váhala).

ZABKAR, Louis Vico (1914-1994)
American Egyptologist; he was born at Lagosta, Italy 7 Dec. 1914, son of Aloysius Z. and Maria Carminatti; he was educated at Split, the University of Zagreb, the Pontifical Biblical Institute in Rome, and the University of Chicago; PhD,1958; he taught in the Department of History, Loyola University, Chicago, 1955-69 and Brandeis University, 1969-85 where he served as Director of Graduate Studies and Joseph and Esther Foster Professor of Classical and Oriental Studies; Research Associate of the Oriental Institute Chicago, 1962-77; he took part in the Nubian rescue campaign at Khor-Dehmit to Beit el-Wali, 1960-1; Serra East, 1962-3; Qustul-Ballana and Adindan, 1962-3; and Semna South, 1966-8 where he was director; he undertook a study of the history and inscriptions of Philae during its dismantling; he published *A Study of the BA Concept in Ancient Egyptian Texts*, 1968; *Apedemak, Lion God of Meroe*, 1975; *Hymns to Isis in Her Temple at Philae*, 1988; he died in Rockport, Mass., 15 Sept. 1994.

JARCE 32 (1995), iv-v (L. Lesko and F. Friedman); inf. Mrs. J. Zabkar.

ZALOSCER, Hilde (1903-1999)
Austrian art historian and Coptologist; she was born in Tuzla, Bosnia, 15 June 1903, daughter of Dr Jacob Z., a lawyer and judge, and Bertha Kallach; the family emigrated to Austria in 1919; she studied art history in Vienna under Strzgowski (q.v.), 1921-6; PhD, 1926; she worked as a guide at the Vienna Museum and editor of the art magazine *Belvedere*; due to increasing anti-semitism, she emigrated to Alexandria in 1936 and became an Egyptian citizen in 1939; she also worked at the Alexandria Museum; unable to find a position in Vienna after the war, she became a lecturer at the University of Alexandria from 1946 until 1967 when she was forced to leave Egypt; she became guest professor at Carleton University in Ottawa, 1969-72; she returned to Austria in 1974 to become a lecturer at the Institute of Arts at the University of Vienna, 1974-8; apart from works on modern art, she published *Une collection de pierres sculptées au Musée Copte du Vieux-Caire*, 1948; *Ägyptische Wirkereien*, 1952; *Porträts aus dem Wüstenstand*, 1961 on mummy portraits; *Tissus Coptes*, 1963; *Vom Mumienbildnis zur Ikone*, 1969; *Die Kunst im christlichen Ägypten*, 1974; *Zur Genese der koptischen Kunst*, 1991; and her autobiography, *Eine Heimkehr gibt es nicht*, 1988; she died in Vienna, 20 Dec. 1999; her estate is partly kept in the Wiener Literaturhaus.

Inf. M. Eaton-Krauss and P. Janosi; Edith Prost, 'Emigration und Exil österreichischer Wissenschaftlerinnen' in F. Stadler (ed.), *Vertriebene Vernunft* I: *Emigration und Exil österreichischer Wissenschaft 1930-1940*, 1987, 444-70; Hilde Zaloscer, 'Das dreimalige Exil' in F. Stadler (ed.): *Vertriebene Vernunf* I: *Emigration und Exil österreichischer Wissenschaft 1930-1940*, 1987, pp. 544-72; U. Wendland, *Biographisches Handbuch deutschsprachiger Kunsthistoriker im Exil*, 1999, 2, 804-6 (bibl.).

ZANDEE, Jan (1914-1991)
Dutch Egyptologist; he was born in Leiden, 9 Sept. 1914, son of Pieter Cornelis Z. and Gertruida van Polanen; he studied theology and oriental languages at the University of Leiden under Kristensen (q.v.), de Buck (q.v.), and Janssen (q.v.); he obtained his degree of doctor of theology in 1948 with a thesis on the hymn to Amun in Pap. Leiden I 350 and a further doctor's degree in the faculty of arts in 1960 with his study on death; from

1939 he was a minister of the Dutch Reformed Church in various places and later taught Hebrew; in 1957 he was appointed a lecturer in Coptic at the University of Utrecht; 1969-82 Professor of the History of Ancient Religions and their Phenomena and the Egyptian Language and Literature at Utrecht; he was also Professor of Egyptology at the University of Amsterdam 1965-79; he specialized in the study of the Egyptian religion in all its phases; his principal publications were *De hymnen aan Amon van Papyrus Leiden I 350*, 1948; *Death as an Enemy according to Ancient Egyptian Conceptions*, 1960, reprint 1977; *The Terminology of Plotinus and of some Gnostic Writings, mainly the Fourth Treatise of the Jung Codex*, 1961; *An Ancient Egyptian Crossword Puzzle*, 1966; '*The Teachings of Silvanus' and Clement of Alexandria*, 1977; and posthumously *The Teachings of Silvanus (Nag Hammadi Codex VII, 4*, 1991; and *Der Amunhymnus des Papyrus Leiden I 344, verso*, 1992; a Festschrift *Studies in Egyptian Religion*, edited by M. Heerma van Voss and others was dedicated to him in 1982; he died in Utrecht, 23 Jan. 1991.

Phoenix 37 (1991), 4-5 (M. Heerma van Voss); *Mededelinggenblad Vereniging van Vrienden Allard Pierson Museum* 50 (1991), 34; inf. M. Heerma van Voss; M. Heerma van Voss and others, *Studies in Egyptian Religion*, 1982, 1-10 (bibl.); *Nederlands Theologisch Tijdschrift* 46 (1992), 51 (D. van der Plas); *BiOr* 48 (1991), 697-9 (J. Helderman) (portr.); D. Nauta (ed.), *Biografisch Lexikon voor de Geschiedenis van het nederlandse protestantisme* 5, 581-3; inf. M.Raven.

ZANNONI, Giovanni Battista (1774-1832)
Italian archaeologist, Etruscan historian, and littérateur; born Florence, 29 March 1774; he was secretary of the Accademia della Crusca; he was helpful to Champollion (q.v.) and gave him facilities for studying the Egyptian collection at Florence which was in the care of G. Alessandri (q.v.) and himself; he died at Florence, 13 Aug. 1832.

Garollo, *Diz. Biogr. Univ.; Enc. It.;* Champollion, i, 234, 236, 238, 392.

ZAYED, Abd el-Hamid (1915-c.2004/17)
Egyptian archaeologist; he was born 5 Oct. 1915; he was educated at the Faculty of Arts, Geography Dept., University of Cairo; BA, 1939; he later studied at the Institute of Egyptology; Dipl., 1944; he served as assistant curator at the Cairo Museum, 1945-9; he then went to Paris to study museology at the Louvre, 1949-53 and Egyptology at the Sorbonne under Clère (q.v.) and Posener (q.v.); he was awarded a PhD from Ain Shams University, 1954; he became a full curator at the Egyptian Museum, 1954-8 and then Chief Inspector of Middle Egypt, 1958-63; he served as assistant professor at Cairo University, 1963-6 and at the Faculty of Arts, Kuwait University, 1966-80; he taught at the Universities of Cairo and Alexandria, 1984-98; he was a member of several committees, notably of the Egyptian Antiquities Organization, 1982-7 and later the Supreme Council of Antiquities; he married a sister of Moktar (q.v) and was a cousin of el-Sawi (q.v.); apart from articles in English and Arabic, he published *Trois études d'égyptologie*, 1956; *Égyptian Antiquities*, 1962; *The Antiquities of El-Minia*, 1962; and *Abydos*, 1963; he died between 2004-17.

ASAE 78 (2004), 15-17 (portr.), 17-9 (bibl.) (Z. Hawass)

ZINCKE, (*Revd*) Foster Barham (1817-1893)
British antiquary; he was born in Jamaica, 5 Jan. 1817 son of Frederick Burt Z. and Emily Lawrence; he was educated Wadham College, Oxford; BA, 1839; Vicar of Wherstead, Suffolk, 1847; one of Queen Victoria's chaplains; he travelled extensively and published works on the countries he visited; his *Egypt of the Pharaohs and of the Khedive*,1871, 2nd ed. 1873, enjoyed great popularity; he died in Wherstead, 23 Aug. 1893.

ODNB 60, 998-9; *DNB* 63, 409-10; Hilmy, ii, 367.

ZIZINIA, (*Count*) Stephan (1794-1868)
Greek-Egyptian businessman and collector; he was born at Chios, 9 Oct. 1794, son of Menandre Z., who was hanged by the Turks during the troubles at Chios in 1822, and Angerou Ralli; he went into business at Marseilles and became a naturalized Frenchman, but commercial contacts with Egypt and personal relations with Muhammad Ali led him to settle in Egypt; he was named Belgian Consul at Alexandria in 1840 and Consul-General 1847; he was ennobled by the Duke of Lucca in 1847; he was head of the Greek community in Alexandria, 1854-7; he formed a large collection of Egyptian antiquities, the best known piece being the Zizinia fragment from the tomb of Horemheb; he died at Alexandria, 15 May 1868.

P. Argenti, *Libro d'oro de la noblesse de Chios*,1955, I, 136; II, 281; A.G. Politis, *L'héllenisme et l'Egypte moderne* I, 1929, 186-7 note 2, 273-4, 280; B. Stacquez, *L'Egypte, la Basse Nubia, et le Sinai*, 1865, 16-17; E. Driault, *L'Égypte et l'Europe*,1930, II, 112; J. Malek, *Chron. d'Ég.* 58 (1983), 66 note 1.

ZOEGA, Georg (Jorgen) (1755-1809)
Danish antiquarian and scholar; he was born in Daler, Schleswig, 20 Dec. 1755, son of Christian Z., a Lutheran minister, and Henriette Emilie Clausen; he was educated at the University of Göttingen, 1773, and developed a

bent for archaeology which arose out of the study of the works of Winckelmann (q.v.); he visited Rome, Venice, Dresden and Leipzig, returning home in 1777; he then became tutor to a family in Fuhnen, 1778; he visited Italy again, 1780, but his work was suddenly stopped by the death of his father and he again returned home; he was next employed on classifying the coins in the national collection at Copenhagen; in 1782 he was sent on a mission in connection with numismatics, but the journey became a prolonged residence in Italy which lasted for the rest of his life; in 1783 he came to the notice of Cardinal Stefano Borgia (q.v.) in Rome and secured his patronage; thus began his archaeological work, and his interest in Egyptian coins grew while working on those in the Borgia collection; he married Maria Elisabetta Geltrude daughter of the painter Petrucioli, 1783, and was received into the Roman Catholic Church; he published a catalogue of the Borgia Egyptian coins and spent seven years preparing his great work on the obelisks; he was interested in the decipherment of hieroglyphs and learned Coptic to assist his studies; Zoëga's interest in antiquity seems to have been inspired by Heyne; he was a careful observer of his material and noted that the direction in which the hieroglyphs faced in an inscription was important, also making a corpus of all the signs that he could find; another discovery, following on from Barthélemy (q.v.), was that cartouche rings contained royal names, 1797, but while he did much to correct misconceptions of the period and to formulate a systematic approach to the subject, he did not try to decipher the signs himself; he published *Numi Aegyptii Imperatorii prostantes in Museo Borgiano Velitris*, et., 1787; *De Origine usu Obeliscorum*, Rome fol., 1797; *Catalogus Codicum Copticorum Manuscriptorum (in Museo Borgiano)*, 1810; these works influenced Champollion (q.v.); his personal papers were published as *Briefe und Dokumente*, I-VI, 1967-2013; he died in Rome, 10 Feb. 1809.

F. G. Welcker, *Zoega's Leben*, 1819; A. D. Jorgensen, *George Zoega*, 1881; *Bricka Dansk Biogr. Leksikon,* 26, 486-92; Budge, *Mummy*, 1925 ed., 139, 155; Hartleben (see index); Iversen, 117-21, 128; Hilmy ii, 368; Lamy, 291.); È. Gran-Aymerich, *Dictionnaire biographique d'archéologie 1798-1945*, 2001, incorporated in *Les Chercheurs de passé 1798-1945*, 2007, 1270-1; K. Ascani, P. Buzi, and D. Picchi, *The Forgotten Scholar: Georg Zoega (1755-1809)*, 2015.

ZOUCHE, Baron *see* CURZON.

ZUCKER, Friedrich (1881-1973)
German classical philologist; he was born in Fürth, 30 June 1881, son of Adolf Z., a teacher; he studied at Munich; PhD, 1904; he took part in German excavations at Elephantine from 1906-8 and succeeded Rubensohn (q.v.) as director of German papyrological excavations, 1907-10, notably at Elephantine, 1907-8, Darb Gerze (Philadelphia), Dime (Soknopaiu Nesos) and Medinet Madi (Narmuthis), 1909-10 with Schubart (q.v.); their dig diary was published in *Archiv für Papyrusforschung* 21 (1971), 5-55; he completed his habilitation in 1911; he was appointed Professor at at Münster 1917-8, at Tübingen, 1918-9 and at Jena (later renamed Friedrich-Schiller University in 1934), 1919-61; he was rector of the University, 1945-8; he was editor of *Archiv für Papyrusforschung*, 1953-69, and co-editor of *Philologus*, 1954-63; among his publications was *Ägypten im römischen Reich*, 1958; he died at Wedel, 4 April 1973.

DBE 10, 891; H. G. Walther, *Erinnerungen an einen Rektor*, 2001.

ZUENDEL, Johannes (1813-1871)
Swiss Egyptologist; he was born in Schaffhausen, 30 Aug. 1813, son of Johann Konrad Z. (1789-1853), banker and President of the Tribunal de la Ville, Berne; Professor of Greek and Literature, Acad. of Lausanne; master of Greek and Latin, École Réale, Berne; he studied Egyptology and published a few independent works and some articles in *ZÄS* and *Rev. Arch.*; he was a correspondent of Chabas (q.v.), to whom he introduced Naville (q.v.); he died 9 June 1871.

Chabas, 45, 49, 71, 73, 110; *Dict. Hist. et Biogr. de la Suisse*; Hilmy, ii, 370, 459.

ZYHLARZ, Ernest Josef (1890-1964)
Austrian orientalist; he was born in Königliche Weinberge (Král. Vinohrady) near Prague, Czechoslovakia, son of Johann Z. and Franziska Josefa Marie Loescher; he was educated at the Karl-Ludwigs-Gymnasium in Vienna and showed an early aptitude for the study of languages; his family intended him to study law, but these studies were interrupted by service in World War I; he then studied Egyptology and Semitic Languages under Junker (q.v.) at Vienna, PhD in 1921 with the dissertation *Die ägyptishe Kultsprache in den domotischen Totenpapyri Rhind*; his interest then broadened to African philology and he completed a second dissertation in 1930, *Grundzüge der nubischen Grammatik im christlichen Frühmittelalter*; lecturer at Vienna 1930-1; he then joined the African seminar at Hamburg where he was appointed Professor 1937; he published numerous articles on Nubian and Meroitic philology; he died at Hamburg, 12 July 1964.

ZDMG 135, 21-5* (bibl.) (K. Post-Zyhlarz).